D0868411

FAR-AIM
1989

**FEDERAL AVIATION REGULATIONS
CUSTOMS GUIDE FOR PRIVATE FLYERS
AIRMAN'S INFORMATION MANUAL**

INCLUDES
FREE UPDATE SERVICE

PUBLISHED BY

asa Publications, Inc.
6001 SIXTH AVENUE SO.
SEATTLE, WA 98108-3307

COPYRIGHT© 1989 by ASA, INC.

FAR
1989

FEDERAL
AVIATION
REGULATIONS

INCLUDES
FREE UPDATE SERVICE

PUBLISHED BY

asa Publications, Inc.
6001 SIXTH AVENUE SO.
SEATTLE, WA 98108-3307

COPYRIGHT© 1989 by ASA, INC.

TABLE OF CONTENTS

FEDERAL AVIATION REGULATIONS (FAR)

AIRMAN'S INFORMATION MANUAL (AIM)

EXAM CROSS-REFERENCE INDEX

Applicants preparing for written exams should have full knowledge of the following applicable FARs.

PRIVATE / COMMERCIAL

Part #	Sec. #	Part #	Sec. #	Part #	Sec. #	Part #	Sec. #	Part #	Sec. #
Part 1	All	Part 91	91.3	Part 91	91.40	Part 91	91.85	Part 91	91.169
Part 61	61.3		91.4		91.51		91.87		91.171
	61.5		91.5		91.52		91.89		91.172
	61.19		91.11		91.65		91.90		91.173
	61.23		91.14		91.67		91.91		91.174
	61.31		91.19		91.70		91.95		91.175
	61.51		91.22		91.71		91.97	Part 135	135.1
	61.55		91.27		91.73		91.105	NTSB	830.1
	61.57		91.29		91.75		91.107		830.2
	61.58		91.31		91.77		91.109		830.5
	61.60		91.32		91.79		91.163		830.15
	61.118		91.33		91.81		91.165		
	61.139		91.39		91.83		91.167		

FLIGHT INSTRUCTOR-AIRPLANE
FLIGHT INSTRUCTOR-INSTRUMENT

Part #	Sec. #	Part #	Sec. #	Part #	Sec. #	Part #	Sec. #	Part #	Sec. #
Part 1	All	Part 91	91.3	Part 91	91.33	Part 91	91.83	Part 91	91.124
Part 61	61.3		91.4		91.38		91.84		91.125
	61.5		91.5		91.39		91.85		91.127
	61.11		91.7		91.40		91.87		91.129
	61.13		91.8		91.42		91.89		91.163
	61.15		91.9		91.43		91.90		91.165
	61.19		91.11		91.45		91.91		91.167
	61.23		91.12		91.47		91.93		91.169
	61.31		91.13		91.49		91.95		91.171
	61.51		91.14		91.51		91.97		91.172
	61.53		91.15		91.52		91.101		91.173
	61.55		91.17		91.53		91.102		91.174
	61.57		91.19		91.63		91.103		91.175
	61.59		91.21		91.65		91.104	NTSB	830.1
	61.60		91.23		91.67		91.105		830.2
	61.65		91.24		91.70		91.107		830.5
	61.69		91.25		91.71		91.109		830.6
	61.89		91.27		91.73		91.115		830.10
	61.118		91.28		91.75		91.116		830.15
	61.139		91.29		91.77		91.119		
	61.189		91.31		91.79		91.121		
	61.197		91.32		91.81		91.123		

INSTRUMENT-AIRPLANE

ATP Airplane (FAR 135)

iv

SUBCHAPTER A—DEFINITIONS

PART 1—DEFINITIONS AND ABBREVIATIONS

Sec.
1.1 General definitions.
1.2 Abbreviations and symbols.
1.3 Rules of construction.

AUTHORITY: 49 U.S.C. 1347, 1348, 1354(a), 1357(d)(2), 1372, 1421 through 1430, 1432, 1442, 1443, 1472, 1510, 1522, 1652(e), 1655(c), 1657(f), 49 U.S.C. 106(g) (Revised Pub. L. 97–449, Jan. 12, 1983).

§ 1.1 General definitions.

As used in Subchapters A through K of this chapter, unless the context requires otherwise:

"Administrator" means the Federal Aviation Administrator or any person to whom he has delegated his authority in the matter concerned.

"Aerodynamic coefficients" means non-dimensional coefficients for aerodynamic forces and moments.

"Air carrier" means a person who undertakes directly by lease, or other arrangement, to engage in air transportation.

"Air commerce" means interstate, overseas, or foreign air commerce or the transportation of mail by aircraft or any operation or navigation of aircraft within the limits of any Federal airway or any operation or navigation of aircraft which directly affects, or which may endanger safety in, interstate, overseas, or foreign air commerce.

"Aircraft" means a device that is used or intended to be used for flight in the air.

"Aircraft engine" means an engine that is used or intended to be used for propelling aircraft. It includes turbosuperchargers, appurtenances, and accessories necessary for its functioning, but does not include propellers.

"Airframe" means the fuselage, booms, nacelles, cowlings, fairings, airfoil surfaces (including rotors but excluding propellers and rotating airfoils of engines), and landing gear of an aircraft and their accessories and controls.

"Airplane" means an engine-driven fixed-wing aircraft heavier than air, that is supported in flight by the dynamic reaction of the air against its wings.

"Airport" means an area of land or water that is used or intended to be used for the landing and takeoff of aircraft, and includes its buildings and facilities, if any.

"Airport traffic area" means, unless otherwise specifically designated in Part 93, that airspace within a horizontal radius of 5 statute miles from the geographical center of any airport at which a control tower is operating, extending from the surface up to, but not including, an altitude of 3,000 feet above the elevation of the airport.

"Airship" means an engine-driven lighter-than-air aircraft that can be steered.

"Air traffic" means aircraft operating in the air or on an airport surface, exclusive of loading ramps and parking areas.

"Air traffic clearance" means an authorization by air traffic control, for the purpose of preventing collision between known aircraft, for an aircraft to proceed under specified traffic conditions within controlled airspace.

"Air traffic control" means a service operated by appropriate authority to promote the safe, orderly, and expeditious flow of air traffic.

"Air transportation" means interstate, overseas, or foreign air transportation or the transportation of mail by aircraft.

"Alternate airport" means an airport at which an aircraft may land if a landing at the intended airport becomes inadvisable.

"Altitude engine" means a reciprocating aircraft engine having a rated takeoff power that is producible from sea level to an established higher altitude.

"Appliance" means any instrument, mechanism, equipment, part, apparatus, appurtenance, or accessory, including communications equipment, that is used or intended to be used in operating or controlling an aircraft in flight, is installed in or attached to the aircraft, and is not part of an airframe, engine, or propeller.

"Approved", unless used with reference to another person, means approved by the Administrator.

"Area navigation (RNAV)" means a method of navigation that permits aircraft operations on any desired course within the coverage of station-referenced navigation signals or within the limits of self-contained system capability.

"Area navigation low route" means an area navigation route within the airspace extending upward from 1,200 feet above the surface of the earth to, but not including, 18,000 feet MSL.

"Area navigation high route" means an area navigation route within the airspace extending upward from, and including, 18,000 feet MSL to flight level 450.

"Armed Forces" means the Army, Navy, Air Force, Marine Corps, and Coast Guard, including their regular and reserve components and members serving without component status.

"Autorotation" means a rotorcraft flight condition in which the lifting rotor is driven entirely by action of the air when the rotorcraft is in motion.

"Auxiliary rotor" means a rotor that serves either to counteract the effect of the main rotor torque on a rotorcraft or to maneuver the rotorcraft about one or more of its three principal axes.

"Balloon" means a lighter-than-air aircraft that is not engine driven.

"Brake horsepower" means the power delivered at the propeller shaft (main drive or main output) of an aircraft engine.

"Calibrated airspeed" means the indicated airspeed of an aircraft, corrected for position and instrument error. Calibrated airspeed is equal to true airspeed in standard atmosphere at sea level.

"Category":

(1) As used with respect to the certification, ratings, privileges, and limitations of airmen, means a broad classification of aircraft. Examples include: airplane; rotorcraft; glider; and lighter-than-air; and

(2) As used with respect to the certification of aircraft, means a grouping of aircraft based upon intended use or operating limitations. Examples include: transport, normal, utility, acrobatic, limited, restricted, and provisional.

"Category A," with respect to transport category rotorcraft, means multiengine rotorcraft designed with engine and system isolation features specified in Part 29 and utilizing scheduled takeoff and landing operations under a critical engine failure concept which assures adequate designated surface area and adequate performance capability for continued safe flight in the event of engine failure.

"Category B," with respect to transport category rotorcraft, means single-engine or multiengine rotorcraft which do not fully meet all Category A standards. Category B rotorcraft have no guaranteed stay-up ability in the event of engine failure and unscheduled landing is assumed.

"Category II operations", with respect to the operation of aircraft, means a straight-in ILS approach to the runway of an airport under a Category II ILS instrument approach procedure issued by the Administrator or other appropriate authority.

"Category III operations," with respect to the operation of aircraft, means an ILS approach to, and landing on, the runway of an airport using a Category III ILS instrument approach procedure issued by the Administrator or other appropriate authority.

"Ceiling" means the height above the earth's surface of the lowest layer of clouds or obscuring phenomena that is reported as "broken", "overcast", or "obscuration", and not classified as "thin" or "partial".

"Civil aircraft" means aircraft other than public aircraft.

"Class":

(1) As used with respect to the certification, ratings, privileges, and limitations of airmen, means a classification of aircraft within a category having similar operating characteristics. Examples include: single engine; multiengine; land; water; gyroplane; helicopter; airship; and free balloon; and

(2) As used with respect to the certification of aircraft, means a broad grouping of aircraft having similar characteristics of propulsion, flight, or landing. Examples include: airplane;

rotorcraft; glider; balloon; landplane; and seaplane.

"Clearway" means:

(1) For turbine engine powered airplanes certificated after August 29, 1959, an area beyond the runway, not less than 500 feet wide, centrally located about the extended centerline of the runway, and under the control of the airport authorities. The clearway is expressed in terms of a clearway plane, extending from the end of the runway with an upward slope not exceeding 1.25 percent, above which no object nor any terrain protrudes. However, threshold lights may protrude above the plane if their height above the end of the runway is 26 inches or less and if they are located to each side of the runway.

(2) For turbine engine powered airplanes certificated after September 30, 1958, but before August 30, 1959, an area beyond the takeoff runway extending no less than 300 feet on either side of the extended centerline of the runway, at an elevation no higher than the elevation of the end of the runway, clear of all fixed obstacles, and under the control of the airport authorities.

"Climbout speed," with respect to rotorcraft, means a referenced airspeed which results in a flight path clear of the height-velocity envelope during initial climbout.

"Commercial operator" means a person who, for compensation or hire, engages in the carriage by aircraft in air commerce of persons or property, other than as an air carrier or foreign air carrier or under the authority of Part 375 of this title. Where it is doubtful that an operation is for "compensation or hire", the test applied is whether the carriage by air is merely incidental to the person's other business or is, in itself, a major enterprise for profit.

"Controlled airspace" means airspace designated as a continental control area, control area, control zone, terminal control area, or transition area, within which some or all aircraft may be subject to air traffic control.

"Crewmember" means a person assigned to perform duty in an aircraft during flight time.

"Critical altitude" means the maximum altitude at which, in standard atmosphere, it is possible to maintain, at a specified rotational speed, a specified power or a specified manifold pressure. Unless otherwise stated, the critical altitude is the maximum altitude at which it is possible to maintain, at the maximum continuous rotational speed, one of the following:

(1) The maximum continuous power, in the case of engines for which this power rating is the same at sea level and at the rated altitude.

(2) The maximum continuous rated manifold pressure, in the case of engines, the maximum continuous power of which is governed by a constant manifold pressure.

"Critical engine" means the engine whose failure would most adversely affect the performance or handling qualities of an aircraft.

"Decision height," with respect to the operation of aircraft, means the height at which a decision must be made, during an ILS or PAR instrument approach, to either continue the approach or to execute a missed approach.

"Equivalent airspeed" means the calibrated airspeed of an aircraft corrected for adiabatic compressible flow for the particular altitude. Equivalent airspeed is equal to calibrated airspeed in standard atmosphere at sea level.

"Extended over-water operation" means—

(1) With respect to aircraft other than helicopters, an operation over water at a horizontal distance of more than 50 nautical miles from the nearest shoreline; and

(2) With respect to helicopters, an operation over water at a horizontal distance of more than 50 nautical miles from the nearest shoreline and more than 50 nautical miles from an off-shore heliport structure.

"External load" means a load that is carried, or extends, outside of the aircraft fuselage.

"External-load attaching means" means the structural components used to attach an external load to an aircraft, including external-load containers, the backup structure at the attachment points, and any quick-release device used to jettison the external load.

"Fireproof"—

(1) With respect to materials and parts used to confine fire in a designated fire zone, means the capacity to withstand at least as well as steel in dimensions appropriate for the purpose for which they are used, the heat produced when there is a severe fire of extended duration in that zone; and

(2) With respect to other materials and parts, means the capacity to withstand the heat associated with fire at least as well as steel in dimensions appropriate for the purpose for which they are used.

"Fire resistant"—

(1) With respect to sheet or structural members means the capacity to withstand the heat associated with fire at least as well as aluminum alloy in dimensions appropriate for the purpose for which they are used; and

(2) With respect to fluid-carrying lines, fluid system parts, wiring, air ducts, fittings, and powerplant controls, means the capacity to perform the intended functions under the heat and other conditions likely to occur when there is a fire at the place concerned.

"Flame resistant" means not susceptible to combustion to the point of propagating a flame, beyond safe limits, after the ignition source is removed.

"Flammable", with respect to a fluid or gas, means susceptible to igniting readily or to exploding.

"Flap extended speed" means the highest speed permissible with wing flaps in a prescribed extended position.

"Flash resistant" means not susceptible to burning violently when ignited.

"Flightcrew member" means a pilot, flight engineer, or flight navigator assigned to duty in an aircraft during flight time.

"Flight level" means a level of constant atmospheric pressure related to a reference datum of 29.92 inches of mercury. Each is stated in three digits that represent hundreds of feet. For example, flight level 250 represents a barometric altimeter indication of 25,000 feet; flight level 255, an indication of 25,500 feet.

"Flight plan" means specified information, relating to the intended flight of an aircraft, that is filed orally or in writing with air traffic control.

"Flight time" means the time from the moment the aircraft first moves under its own power for the purpose of flight until the moment it comes to rest at the next point of landing. ("Block-to-block" time.)

"Flight visibility" means the average forward horizontal distance, from the cockpit of an aircraft in flight, at which prominent unlighted objects may be seen and identified by day and prominent lighted objects may be seen and identified by night.

"Foreign air carrier" means any person other than a citizen of the United States, who undertakes directly, by lease or other arrangement, to engage in air transportation.

"Foreign air commerce" means the carriage by aircraft of persons or property for compensation or hire, or the carriage of mail by aircraft, or the operation or navigation of aircraft in the conduct or furtherance of a business or vocation, in commerce between a place in the United States and any place outside thereof; whether such commerce moves wholly by aircraft or partly by aircraft and partly by other forms of transportation.

"Foreign air transportation" means the carriage by aircraft of persons or property as a common carrier for compensation or hire, or the carriage of mail by aircraft, in commerce between a place in the United States and any place outside of the United States, whether that commerce moves wholly by aircraft or partly by aircraft and partly by other forms of transportation.

"Glider" means a heavier-than-air aircraft, that is supported in flight by the dynamic reaction of the air against its lifting surfaces and whose free flight does not depend principally on an engine.

"Ground visibility" means prevailing horizontal visibility near the earth's surface as reported by the United States National Weather Service or an accredited observer.

"Gyrodyne" means a rotorcraft whose rotors are normally engine-driven for takeoff, hovering, and landing, and for forward flight through part of its speed range, and whose means of propulsion, consisting usually of conventional propellers, is independent of the rotor system.

"Gyroplane" means a rotorcraft whose rotors are not engine-driven, except for initial starting, but are made to rotate by action of the air when the rotorcraft is moving; and whose means of propulsion, consisting usually of conventional propellers, is independent of the rotor system.

"Helicopter" means a rotorcraft that, for its horizontal motion, depends principally on its engine-driven rotors.

"Heliport" means an area of land, water, or structure used or intended to be used for the landing and takeoff of helicopters.

"Idle thrust" means the jet thrust obtained with the engine power control level set at the stop for the least thrust position at which it can be placed.

"IFR conditions" means weather conditions below the minimum for flight under visual flight rules.

"IFR over-the-top", with respect to the operation of aircraft, means the operation of an aircraft over-the-top on an IFR flight plan when cleared by air traffic control to maintain "VFR conditions" or "VFR conditions on top".

"Indicated airspeed" means the speed of an aircraft as shown on its pitot static airspeed indicator calibrated to reflect standard atmosphere adiabatic compressible flow at sea level uncorrected for airspeed system errors.

"Instrument" means a device using an internal mechanism to show visually or aurally the attitude, altitude, or operation of an aircraft or aircraft part. It includes electronic devices for automatically controlling an aircraft in flight.

"Interstate air commerce" means the carriage by aircraft of persons or property for compensation or hire, or the carriage of mail by aircraft, or the operation or navigation of aircraft in the conduct or furtherance of a business or vocation, in commerce between a place in any State of the United States, or the District of Columbia, and a place in any other State of the United States, or the District of Columbia; or between places in the same State of the United States through the airspace over any place outside thereof; or between places in the same territory or possession of the United States, or the District of Columbia.

"Interstate air transportation" means the carriage by aircraft of persons or property as a common carrier for compensation or hire, or the carriage of mail by aircraft in commerce:

(1) Between a place in a State or the District of Columbia and another place in another State or the District of Columbia;

(2) Between places in the same State through the airspace over any place outside that State; or

(3) Between places in the same possession of the United States;

Whether that commerce moves wholly by aircraft of partly by aircraft and partly by other forms of transportation.

"Intrastate air transportation" means the carriage of persons or property as a common carrier for compensation or hire, by turbojet-powered aircraft capable of carrying thirty or more persons, wholly within the same State of the United States.

"Kite" means a framework, covered with paper, cloth, metal, or other material, intended to be flown at the end of a rope or cable, and having as its only support the force of the wind moving past its surfaces.

"Landing gear extended speed" means the maximum speed at which an aircraft can be safely flown with the landing gear extended.

"Landing gear operating speed" means the maximum speed at which the landing gear can be safely extended or retracted.

"Large aircraft" means aircraft of more than 12,500 pounds, maximum certificated takeoff weight.

"Lighter-than-air aircraft" means aircraft that can rise and remain suspended by using contained gas weighing less than the air that is displaced by the gas.

"Load factor" means the ratio of a specified load to the total weight of the aircraft. The specified load is expressed in terms of any of the following: aerodynamic forces, inertia forces, or ground or water reactions.

"Mach number" means the ratio of true airspeed to the speed of sound.

"Main rotor" means the rotor that supplies the principal lift to a rotorcraft.

"Maintenance" means inspection, overhaul, repair, preservation, and the replacement of parts, but excludes preventive maintenance.

"Major ·alteration" means an alteration not listed in the aircraft, aircraft engine, or propeller specifications—

(1) That might appreciably affect weight, balance, structural strength, performance, powerplant operation, flight characteristics, or other qualities affecting airworthiness; or

(2) That is not done according to accepted practices or cannot be done by elementary operations.

"Major repair" means a repair:

(1) That, if improperly done, might appreciably affect weight, balance, structural strength, performance, powerplant operation, flight characteristics, or other qualities affecting airworthiness; or

(2) That is not done according to accepted practices or cannot be done by elementary operations.

"Manifold pressure" means absolute pressure as measured at the appropriate point in the induction system and usually expressed in inches of mercury.

"Medical certificate" means acceptable evidence of physical fitness on a form prescribed by the Administrator.

"Minimum descent altitude" means the lowest altitude, expressed in feet above mean sea level, to which descent is authorized on final approach or during circle-to-land maneuvering in execution of a standard instrument approach procedure, where no electronic glide slope is provided.

"Minor alteration" means an alteration other than a major alteration.

"Minor repair" means a repair other than a major repair.

"Navigable airspace" means airspace at and above the minimum flight altitudes prescribed by or under this chapter, including airspace needed for safe takeoff and landing.

"Night" means the time between the end of evening civil twilight and the beginning of morning civil twilight, as published in the American Air Almanac, converted to local time.

"Nonprecision approach procedure" means a standard instrument approach procedure in which no electronic glide slope is provided.

"Operate," with respect to aircraft, means use, cause to use or authorize to use aircraft, for the purpose (except as provided in § 91.10 of this chapter) of air navigation including the piloting of aircraft, with or without the right of legal control (as owner, lessee, or otherwise).

"Operational control", with respect to a flight, means the exercise of authority over initiating, conducting or terminating a flight.

"Overseas air commerce" means the carriage by aircraft of persons or property for compensation or hire, or the carriage of mail by aircraft, or the operation or navigation of aircraft in the conduct or furtherance of a business or vocation, in commerce between a place in any State of the United States, or the District of Columbia, and any place in a territory or possession of the United States; or between a place in a territory or possession of the United States, and a place in any other territory or possession of the United States.

"Overseas air transportation" means the carriage by aircraft of persons or property as a common carrier for compensation or hire, or the carriage of mail by aircraft, in commerce:

(1) Between a place in a State or the District of Columbia and a place ·in a possession of the United States; or

(2) Between a place in a possession of the United States and a place in another possession of the United States; whether that commerce moves wholly by aircraft or partly by aircraft and partly by other forms of transportation.

"Over-the-top" means above the layer of clouds or other obscuring phenomena forming the ceiling.

"Parachute" means a device used or intended to be used to retard the fall of a body or object through the air.

"Person" means an individual, firm, partnership, corporation, company, association, joint-stock association, or governmental entity. It includes a trustee, receiver, assignee, or similar representative of any of them.

"Pilotage" means navigation by visual reference to landmarks.

"Pilot in command" means the pilot responsible for the operation and safety of an aircraft during flight time.

"Pitch setting" means the propeller blade setting as determined by the blade angle measured in a manner, and at a radius, specified by the instructional manual for the propeller.

"Positive control" means control of all air traffic, within designated airspace, by air traffic control.

"Precision approach procedure" means a standard instrument approach procedure in which an electronic glide slope is provided, such as ILS and PAR.

"Preventive maintenance" means simple or minor preservation operations and the replacement of small standard parts not involving complex assembly operations.

"Prohibited area" means designated airspace within which the flight of the aircraft is prohibited.

"Propeller" means a device for propelling an aircraft that has blades on an engine-driven shaft and that, when rotated, produces by its action on the air, a thrust approximately perpendicular to its plane of rotation. It includes control components normally supplied by its manufacturer, but does not include main and auxilliary rotors or rotating airfoils of engines.

"Public aircraft" means aircraft used only in the service of a government or a political subdivision. It does not include any government-owned aircraft engaged in carrying persons or property for commercial purposes.

"Rated continuous OEI power," with respect to rotorcraft turbine engines, means the approved brake horsepower developed under static conditions at specified altitudes and temperatures within the operating limitations established for the engine under Part 33 of this chapter, and limited in use to the time required to complete the flight after the failure of one engine of a multiengine rotorcraft.

"Rated maximum continuous augmented thrust", with respect to turbojet engine type certification, means the approved jet thrust that is developed statically or in flight, in standard atmosphere at a specified altitude, with fluid injection or with the burning of fuel in a separate combustion chamber, within the engine operating limitations established under Part 33 of this chapter, and approved for unrestricted periods of use.

of this chapter, and approved for unrestricted periods of use.

"Rated maximum continuous power," with respect to reciprocating, turbopropeller, and turboshaft engines, means the approved brake horsepower that is developed statically or in flight, in standard atmosphere at a specified altitude, within the engine operating limitations established under Part 33, and approved for unrestricted periods of use.

"Rated maximum continuous thrust", with respect to turbojet engine type certification, means the approved jet thrust that is developed statically or in flight, in standard atmosphere at a specified altitude, without fluid injection and without the burning of fuel in a separate combustion chamber, within the engine operating limitations established under Part 33 of this chapter, and approved for unrestricted periods of use.

"Rated takeoff augmented thrust", with respect to turbojet engine type certification, means the approved jet thrust that is developed statically under standard sea level conditions, with fluid injection or with the burning of fuel in a separate combustion chamber, within the engine operating limitations established under Part 33 of this chapter, and limited in use to periods of not over 5 minutes for takeoff operation.

"Rated takeoff power", with respect to reciprocating, turbopropeller, and turboshaft engine type certification, means the approved brake horsepower that is developed statically under standard sea level conditions, within the engine operating limitations established under Part 33, and limited in use to periods of not over 5 minutes for takeoff operation.

"Rated takeoff thrust", with respect to turbojet engine type certification, means the approved jet thrust that is developed statically under standard sea level conditions, without fluid injection and without the burning of fuel in a separate combustion chamber, within the engine operating limitations established under Part 33 of this chapter, and limited in use to periods of not over 5 minutes for takeoff operation.

"Rated 30 minute OEI power," with respect to rotorcraft turbine engines, means the approved brake horsepower develped under static conditions at specified altitudes and temperatures within the operating limitations established for the engine under Part 33 of this chapter, and limited in use to a period of not more than 30 minutes after the failure of one engine of a multiengine rotorcraft.

"Rated 2½-minute OEI power," with respect to rotorcraft turbine engines, means the approved brake horsepower developed under static conditons at specified altitudes and temperatures within the operating limitations established for the engine under part 33 of this chapter, and limited in use to a period of not more than 2½ minutes after the failure of one engine of a multiengine rotorcraft.

"Rating" means a statement that, as a part of a certitificate, sets forth special conditons, privileges, or limitations.

"Reporting point" means a geographical location in relation to which the position of an aircaft is reported.

"Restricted area" means airspace designated under Part 73 of this chapter within which the flight of aircraft while not wholly prohibited, is subject to restriction.

"RNAV way point (W/P)" means a predetermined geographical position used for route or instrument approach definition or progress reporting purposes that is defined relative to a VORTAC station position.

"Rocket" means an aircraft propelled by ejected expanding gases generated in the engine from self-contained propellants and not dependent on the intake of outside substances. It includes any part which becomes separated during the operation.

"Rotorcraft" means a heavier-than-air aircraft that depends principally for its support in flight on the lift generated by one or more rotors.

"Rotorcraft-load combination means the combination of a rotorcraft and an external load, including the external-load attaching means. Rotorcraft-load combinations are designated as Class A, Class B, Class C, and Class D, as follows:

(1) "Class A rotorcraft-load combination" means one in which the external load cannot move freely, cannot be jettisoned, and does not extend below the landing gear.

(2) "Class B rotorcraft-load combination" means one in which the external load is jettisonable and is lifted free of land or water during the rotorcraft operation.

(3) "Class C rotorcraft-load combination" means one in which the external load is jettisonable and remains in contact with land or water during the rotorcraft operation.

(4) "Class D rotorcraft-load combination" means one in which the external-load is other than a Class A, B, or C and has been specifically approved by the Administrator for that operation.

"Route segment" means a part of a route. Each end of that part is identified by:

(1) A continental or insular geographical location; or

(2) A point at which a definite radio fix can be established.

"Sea level engine" means a reciprocating aircraft engine having a rated takeoff power that is producible only at sea level.

"Second in command" means a pilot who is designated to be second in command of an aircraft during flight time.

"Show", unless the context otherwise requires, means to show to the satisfaction of the Administrator.

"Small aircraft" means aircraft of 12,500 pounds or less, maximum certificated takeoff weight.

"Standard atmosphere" means the atmosphere defined in U.S. Standard Atmosphere, 1962 (Geopotential altitude tables).

"Stopway" means an area beyond the takeoff runway, no less wide than the runway and centered upon the extended centerline of the runway, able to support the airplane during an aborted takeoff, without causing structural damage to the airplane, and designated by the airport authorities for use in decelerating the airplane during an aborted takeoff.

"Takeoff power":

(1) With respect to reciprocating engines, means the brake horsepower that is developed under standard sea level conditions, and under the maximum conditions of crankshaft rota-

tional speed and engine manifold pressure approved for the normal takeoff, and limited in continuous use to the period of time shown in the approved engine specification; and

(2) With respect to turbine engines, means the brake horsepower that is developed under static conditions at a specified altitude and atmospheric temperature, and under the maximum conditions of rotor shaft rotational speed and gas temperature approved for the normal takeoff, and limited in continuous use to the period of time shown in the approved engine specification.

"Takeoff safety speed" means a referenced airspeed obtained after lift-off at which the required one-engine-inoperative climb performance can be achieved.

"Takeoff thrust", with respect to turbine engines, means the jet thrust that is developed under static conditions at a specific altitude and atmospheric temperature under the maximum conditions of rotorshaft rotational speed and gas temperature approved for the normal takeoff, and limited in continuous use to the period of time shown in the approved engine specification.

"Time in service", with respect to maintenance time records, means the time from the moment an aircraft leaves the surface of the earth until it touches it at the next point of landing.

"True airspeed" means the airspeed of an aircraft relative to undisturbed air. True airspeed is equal to equivalent airspeed multiplied by $(\rho 0/\rho)^{1/2}$.

"Traffic pattern" means the traffic flow that is prescribed for aircraft landing at, taxiing on, or taking off from, an airport.

"Type":

(1) As used with respect to the certification, ratings, privileges, and limitations of airmen, means a specific make and basic model of aircraft, including modifications thereto that do not change its handling or flight characteristics. Examples include: DC-7, 1049, and F-27; and

(2) As used with respect to the certification of aircraft, means those aircraft which are similar in design. Examples include: DC-7 and DC-7C;

1049G and 1049H; and F-27 and F-27F.

(3) As used with respect to the certification of aircraft engines means those engines which are similar in design. For example, JT8D and JT8D-7 are engines of the same type, and JT9D-3A and JT9D-7 are engines of the same type.

"United States", in a geographical sense, means (1) the States, the District of Columbia, Puerto Rico, and the possessions, including the territorial waters, and (2) the airspace of those areas.

"United States air carrier" means a citizen of the United States who undertakes directly by lease, or other arrangement, to engage in air transportation.

"VFR over-the-top", with respect to the operation of aircraft, means the operation of an aircraft over-the-top under VFR when it is not being operated on an IFR flight plan.

[Doc. No. 1150, 27 FR 4588, May 15, 1962]

EDITORIAL NOTE: For Federal Register citations affecting §1.1, see the List of CFR Sections Affected appearing in the Finding Aids section of this volume.

§1.2   Abbreviations and symbols.

In Subchapters A through K of this chapter:

"AGL" means above ground level.

"ALS" means approach light system.

"ASR" means airport surveillance radar.

"ATC" means air traffic control.

"CAS" means calibrated airspeed.

"CAT II" means Category II.

"CONSOL or CONSOLAN" means a kind of low or medium frequency long range navigational aid.

"DH" means decision height.

"DME" means distance measuring equipment compatible with TACAN.

"EAS" means equivalent airspeed.

"FAA" means Federal Aviation Administration.

"FM" means fan marker.

"GS" means glide slope.

"HIRL" means high-intensity runway light system.

"IAS" means indicated airspeed.

"ICAO" means International Civil Aviation Organization.

"IFR" means instrument flight rules.

"ILS" means instrument landing system.

"IM" means ILS inner marker.

"INT" means intersection.

"LDA" means localizer-type directional aid.

"LFR" means low-frequency radio range.

"LMM" means compass locator at middle marker.

"LOC" means ILS localizer.

"LOM" means compass locator at outer marker.

"*M*" means mach number.

"MAA" means maximum authorized IFR altitude.

"MALS" means medium intensity approach light system.

"MALSR" means medium intensity approach light system with runway alignment indicator lights.

"MCA" means minimum crossing altitude.

"MDA" means minimum descent altitude.

"MEA" means minimum en route IFR altitude.

"MM" means ILS middle marker.

"MOCA" means minimum obstruction clearance altitude.

"MRA" means minimum reception altitude.

"MSL" means mean sea level.

"NDB(ADF)" means nondirectional beacon (automatic direction finder).

"NOPT" means no procedure turn required.

"OEI" means one engine inoperative.

"OM" means ILS outer marker.

"PAR" means precision approach radar.

"RAIL" means runway alignment indicator light system.

"RBN" means radio beacon.

"RCLM" means runway centerline marking.

"RCLS" means runway centerline light system.

"REIL" means runway end identification lights.

"RR" means low or medium frequency radio range station.

"RVR" means runway visual range as measured in the touchdown zone area.

"SALS" means short approach light system.

"SSALS" means simplified short approach light system.

"SSALSR" means simplified short approach light system with runway alignment indicator lights.

"TACAN" means ultra-high frequency tactical air navigational aid.

"TAS" means true airspeed.

"TDZL" means touchdown zone lights.

"TVOR" means very high frequency terminal omnirange station.

V_A means design maneuvering speed.

V_B means design speed for maximum gust intensity.

V_C means design cruising speed.

V_D means design diving speed.

V_{DF}/M_{DF} means demonstrated flight diving speed.

V_F means design flap speed.

V_{FC}/M_{FC} means maximum speed for stability characteristics.

V_{FE} means maximum flap extended speed.

V_H means maximum speed in level flight with maximum continuous power.

V_{LE} means maximum landing gear extended speed.

V_{LO} means maximum landing gear operating speed.

V_{LOF} means lift-off speed.

V_{MC} means minimum control speed with the critical engine inoperative.

V_{MO}/M_{MO} means maximum operating limit speed.

V_{MU} means minimum unstick speed.

V_{NE} means never-exceed speed.

V_{NO} means maximum structural cruising speed.

V_R means rotation speed.

V_S means the stalling speed or the minimum steady flight speed at which the airplane is controllable.

V_{So} means the stalling speed or the minimum steady flight speed in the landing configuration.

V_{S1} means the stalling speed or the minimum steady flight speed obtained in a specific configuration.

V_{TOSS} means takeoff safety speed for Category A rotorcraft.

V_X means speed for best angle of climb.

V_Y means speed for best rate of climb.

V_1 means takeoff decision speed (formerly denoted as critical engine failure speed).

V_2 means takeoff safety speed.

V_2 min means minimum takeoff safety speed.

"VFR" means visual flight rules.

"VHF" means very high frequency.

"VOR" means very high frequency omnirange station.

"VORTAC" means collocated VOR and TACAN.

[Doc. No. 1150, 27 FR 4590, May 15, 1962]

EDITORIAL NOTE: For FEDERAL REGISTER citations affecting § 1.2, see the List of CFR Sections Affected appearing in the Finding Aids, section of this volume.

§ 1.3 Rules of construction.

(a) In Subchapters A through K of this chapter, unless the context requires otherwise:

(1) Words importing the singular include the plural;

(2) Words importing the plural include the singular; and

(3) Words importing the masculine gender include the feminine.

(b) In Subchapters A through K of this chapter, the word:

(1) "Shall" is used in an imperative sense;

(2) "May" is used in a permissive sense to state authority or permission to do the act prescribed, and the words "no person may * * *" or "a person may not * * *" mean that no person is required, authorized, or permitted to do the act prescribed; and

(3) "Includes" means "includes but is not limited to".

[Doc. No. 1150, 27 FR 4590, May 15, 1962, as amended by Amdt. 1-10, 31 FR 5055, Mar. 29, 1966]

SUBCHAPTER D—AIRMEN

PART 60—[RESERVED]

PART 61—CERTIFICATION: PILOTS AND FLIGHT INSTRUCTORS

AUTHORITY: 49 U.S.C. 1354(a), 1355, 1421, 1422, and 1427; 49 U.S.C. 106(g) (Revised, Pub. L. 97–449; Jan. 12, 1983).

SOURCE: Docket No. 11802, Amdt. 61–60, 38 FR 3161, Feb. 1, 1973, unless otherwise noted.

Subpart A—General

§ 61.1 Applicability.

(a) This part prescribes the requirements for issuing pilot and flight instructor certificates and ratings, the conditions under which those certificates and ratings are necessary, and the privileges and limitations of those certificates and ratings.

(b) Except as provided in § 61.71 of this part, an applicant for a certificate or rating may, until November 1, 1974, meet either the requirements of this part, or the requirements in effect immediately before November 1, 1973. However, the applicant for a private pilot certificate with a free balloon class rating must meet the requirements of this part.

[Doc. No. 11802, Amdt. 61–60, 38 FR 3161, Feb. 1, 1973, as amended by Amdt. 61–63, 39 FR 20057, June 6, 1974]

§ 61.2 Certification of foreign pilots and flight instructors.

A person who is neither a United States citizen nor a resident alien is issued a certificate under this part (other than under § 61.75 or § 61.77), outside the United States, only when the Administrator finds that the pilot certificate is needed for the operation of a U.S.-registered civil aircraft or finds that the flight instructor certificate is needed for the training of students who are citizens of the United States.

[Amdt. 61–72, 47 FR 35693, Aug. 16, 1982]

§ 61.3 Requirement for certificates, rating, and authorizations.

(a) *Pilot certificate.* No person may act as pilot in command or in any other capacity as a required pilot flight crewmember of a civil aircraft of United States registry unless he has in his personal possession a current pilot certificate issued to him under this part. However, when the aircraft is operated within a foreign country a current pilot license issued by the country in which the aircraft is operated may be used.

(b) *Pilot certificate: foreign aircraft.* No person may, within the United States, act as pilot in command or in any other capacity as a required pilot flight crewmember of a civil aircraft of foreign registry unless he has in his personal possession a current pilot certificate issued to him under this part, or a pilot license issued to him or validated for him by the country in which the aircraft is registered.

(c) *Medical certificate.* Except for free balloon pilots piloting balloons and glider pilots piloting gliders, no person may act as pilot in command or in any other capacity as a required pilot flight crewmember of an aircraft under a certificate issued to him under this part, unless he has in his personal possession an appropriate current medical certificate issued under Part 67 of this chapter. However, when the aircraft is operated within a foreign country with a current pilot license issued by that country, evidence of current medical qualification for that license, issued by that country, may be used. In the case of a pilot certificate issued on the basis of a foreign pilot license under § 61.75, evidence of current medical qualification accepted for the issue of that license is used in place of a medical certificate.

(d) *Flight instructor certificate.* Except for lighter-than-air flight instruction in lighter-than-air aircraft, and for instruction in air transportation service given by the holder of an Airline Transport Pilot Certificate under § 61.169, no person other than the holder of a flight instructor certificate issued by the Administrator with an appropriate rating on that certificate may—

(1) Give any of the flight instruction required to qualify for a solo flight, solo cross-country flight, or for the issue of a pilot or flight instructor certificate or rating;

(2) Endorse a pilot logbook to show that he has given any flight instruction; or

(3) Endorse a student pilot certificate or logbook for solo operating privileges.

(e) *Instrument rating.* No person may act as pilot in command of a civil aircraft under instrument flight rules, or in weather conditions less than the minimums prescribed for VFR flight unless—

(1) In the case of an airplane, he holds an instrument rating or an airline transport pilot certificate with an airplane category rating on it;

(2) In the case of a helicopter, he holds a helicopter instrument rating or an airline transport pilot certificate with a rotorcraft category and helicopter class rating not limited to VFR;

(3) In the case of a glider, he holds an instrument rating (airplane) or an airline transport pilot certificate with an airplane category rating; or

(4) In the case of an airship, he holds a commercial pilot certificate with lighter-than-air category and airship class ratings.

(f) *Category II pilot authorization.* (1) No person may act as pilot in command of a civil aircraft in a Category II operation unless he holds a current Category II pilot authorization for that type aircraft or, in the case of a civil aircraft of foreign registry, he is authorized by the country of registry to act as pilot in command of that aircraft in Category II operations.

(2) No person may act as second in command of a civil aircraft in a Category II operation unless he holds a current appropriate instrument rating or an appropriate airline transport pilot certificate or, in the case of a civil aircraft of foreign registry, he is authorized by the country of registry to act as second in command of that aircraft in Category II operations.

This paragraph does not apply to operations conducted by the holder of a certificate issued under Parts 121 and 135 of this chapter.

(g) *Category A aircraft pilot authorization.* The Administrator may issue a certificate of authorization to the pilot of a small aircraft identified as a Category A aircraft in § 97.3(b)(1) of this chapter to use that aircraft in a Category II operation, if he finds that the proposed operation can be safely conducted under the terms of the certificate. Such authorization does not permit operation of the aircraft carrying persons or property for compensation or hire.

(h) *Inspection of certificate.* Each person who holds a pilot certificate, flight instructor certificate, medical certificate, authorization, or license required by this part shall present it for inspection upon the request of the Administrator, an authorized representative of the National Transportation Safety Board,.or any Federal, State, or local law enforcement officer.

[Doc. No. 11802, Amdt. No. 61-60, 38 FR 3161, Feb. 1, 1973, as amended by Amdt. 61-77, 51 FR 40703, Nov. 7, 1986]

§ 61.5 **Certificates and ratings issued under this part.**

(a) The following certificates are issued under this part:
(1) Pilot certificates:
(i) Student pilot.
(ii) Private pilot.
(iii) Commercial pilot.
(iv) Airline transport pilot.
(2) Flight instructor certificates.

(b) The following ratings are placed on pilot certificates (other than student pilot) where applicable:
(1) Aircraft category ratings:
(i) Airplane.
(ii) Rotorcraft.
(iii) Glider.
(iv) Lighter-than-air.
(2) Airplane class ratings:
(i) Single-engine land.
(ii) Multiengine land.
(iii) Single-engine sea.
(iv) Multiengine sea.
(3) Rotorcraft class ratings:
(i) Helicopter.
(ii) Gyroplane.
(4) Lighter-than-air class ratings:
(i) Airship.
(ii) Free balloon.
(5) Aircraft type ratings are listed in Advisory Circular 61-1 entitled "Aircraft Type Ratings." This list includes ratings for the following:
(i) Large aircraft, other than lighter-than-air.
(ii) Small turbojet-powered airplanes.
(iii) Small helicopters for operations requiring an airline transport pilot certificate.
(iv) Other aircraft type ratings specified by the Administrator through aircraft type certificate procedures.

(6) Instrument ratings (on private and commercial pilot certificates only):
(i) Instrument—airplanes.
(ii) Instrument—helicopter.
(c) The following ratings are placed on flight instructor certificates where applicable:
(1) Aircraft category ratings:
(i) Airplane.
(ii) Rotorcraft.
(iii) Glider.
(2) Airplane class ratings:
(i) Single-engine.
(ii) Multiengine.
(3) Rotorcraft class ratings:
(i) Helicopter.
(ii) Gyroplane.
(4) Instrument ratings:
(i) Instrument—airplane.
(ii) Instrument—helicopter.

[Doc. No. 11802, Amdt. 61-60, 38 FR 3161, Feb. 1, 1973, as amended by Amdt. 61-64, 41 FR 51392, Nov. 22, 1976]

§ 61.7 **Obsolete certificates and ratings.**

(a) The holder of a free balloon pilot certificate issued before November 1, 1973, may not exercise the privileges of that certificate.

(b) The holder of a pilot certificate that bears any of the following category ratings without an associated class rating, may not exercise the privileges of that category rating:
(1) Rotorcraft.
(2) Lighter-than-air.
(3) Helicopter.
(4) Autogiro.

§ 61.9 **Exchange of obsolete certificates and ratings for current certificates and ratings.**

(a) The holder of an unexpired free balloon pilot certificate, or an unexpired pilot certificate with an obsolete category rating listed in § 61.7(b) may exchange that certificate for a certificate with the following applicable category and class rating, without a further showing of competency, until October 31, 1975. After that date, a free balloon pilot certificate or certificate with an obsolete rating expires.

(b) *Private or commercial pilot certificate with rotorcraft category rating.* The holder of a private or commercial pilot certificate with a rotorcraft category rating is issued that certificate with a rotorcraft category rating, and a helicopter or gyroplane class rating, depending upon whether a helicopter or a gyroplane is used to qualify for the rotorcraft category rating.

(c) *Private or commercial pilot certificate with helicopter or autogiro category rating.* The holder of a private or commercial pilot certificate with a helicopter or autogiro category rating is issued that certificate with a rotorcraft category rating and a helicopter class rating (in the case of a helicopter category rating), or a gyroplane class rating (in the case of an autogiro rating).

(d) *Airline transport pilot certificate with helicopter or autogiro category rating.* The holder of an airline transport pilot certificate with a helicopter or autogiro category rating is issued that certificate with a rotorcraft category rating (limited to VFR) and a helicopter class and type rating (in the case of a helicopter category rating), or a gyroplane class rating (in the case of an autogiro category rating).

(e) *Airline transport pilot certificate with a rotorcraft category rating (without a class rating).* The holder of an airline transport pilot certificate with a rotorcraft category rating (without a class rating) is issued that certificate with a rotorcraft category rating limited to VFR, and a helicopter and type rating or a gyroplane class rating, depending upon whether a helicopter or gyroplane is used to qualify for the rotorcraft category rating.

(f) *Free balloon pilot certificate.* The holder of a free balloon pilot certificate is issued a commercial pilot certificate with a lighter-than-air category rating and a free balloon class rating. However, a free balloon class rating may be issued with the limitations provided in § 61.141.

(g) *Lighter-than-air pilot certificate or pilot certificate with lighter-than-air category (without a class rating).*
(1) In the case of an application made before November 1, 1975, the holder of a lighter-than-air pilot certificate or a pilot certificate with a lighter-than-air category rating (without a class rating) is issued a private or commer-

cial pilot certificate, as appropriate, with a lighter-than-air category rating and airship and free balloon class ratings.

(2) In the case of an application made after October 31, 1975, the holder of a lighter-than-air pilot certificate with an airship rating issued prior to November 1, 1973, may be issued a free balloon class rating upon passing the appropriate flight test in a free balloon.

[Doc. No. 11802, Amdt. 61-60, 38 FR 3161, Feb. 1, 1973, as amended by Amdt. 61-64, 41 FR 51392, Nov. 22, 1976]

§ 61.11 Expired pilot certificates and reissuance.

(a) No person who holds an expired pilot certificate or rating may exercise the privileges of that pilot certificate, or rating.

(b) Except as provided, the following certificates and ratings have expired and are not reissued:

(1) An airline transport pilot certificate issued before May 1, 1949, or containing a horsepower rating. However, an airline transport pilot certificate bearing an expiration date and issued after April 30, 1949, may be reissued without an expiration date if it does not contain a horsepower rating.

(2) A private or commercial pilot certificate, or a lighter-than-air or free balloon pilot certificate, issued before July 1, 1945. However, each of those certificates issued after June 30, 1945, and bearing an expiration date, may be reissued without an expiration date.

(c) A private or commercial pilot certificate or a special purpose pilot certificate, issued on the basis of a foreign pilot license, expires on the expiration date stated thereon. A certificate without an expiration date is issued to the holder of the expired certificate only if he meets the requirements of § 61.75 for the issue of a pilot certificate based on a foreign pilot license.

§ 61.13 Application and qualification.

(a) An application for a certificate and rating or for an additional rating under this part is made on a form and in a manner prescribed by the Administrator. Each person who is neither a United States citizen nor a resident alien must show evidence that the fee prescribed by Appendix A of Part 187 of this chapter has been paid if that person—

(1) Applies for a student pilot certificate to be issued outside the United States; or

(2) Applies for a written or practical test to be administered outside the United States for any certificate or rating issued under this part.

(b) An applicant who meets the requirements of this part is entitled to an appropriate pilot certificate with aircraft ratings. Additional aircraft category, class, type and other ratings, for which the applicant is qualified, are added to his certificate. However, the Administrator may refuse to issue certificates to persons who are not citizens of the United States and who do not reside in the United States.

(c) An applicant who cannot comply with all of the flight proficiency requirements prescribed by this part because the aircraft used by him for his flight training or flight test is characteristically incapable of performing a required pilot operation, but who meets all other requirements for the certificate or rating sought, is issued the certificate or rating with appropriate limitations.

(d) An applicant for a pilot certificate who holds a medical certificate under § 67.19 of this chapter with special limitations on it, but who meets all other requirements for that pilot certificate, is issued a pilot certificate containing such operating limitations as the Administrator determines are necessary because of the applicant's medical deficiency.

(e) A Category II pilot authorization is issued as a part of the applicant's instrument rating or airline transport pilot certificate. Upon original issue the authorization contains a limitation for Category II operations of 1,600 feet RVR and a 150 foot decision height. This limitation is removed when the holder shows that since the beginning of the sixth preceding month he has made three Category II ILS approaches to a landing under actual or simulated instrument conditions with a 150 foot decision height.

(f) Unless authorized by the Administrator—

(1) A person whose pilot certificate is suspended may not apply for any pilot or flight instructor certificate or rating during the period of suspension; and

(2) A person whose flight instructor certificate only is suspended may not apply for any rating to be added to that certificate during the period of suspension.

(g) Unless the order of revocation provides otherwise—

(1) A person whose pilot certificate is revoked may not apply for any pilot or flight instructor certificate or rating for 1 year after the date of revocation; and

(2) A person whose flight instructor certificate only is revoked may not apply for any flight instructor certificate for 1 year after the date of revocation.

[Doc. No. 11802, Amdt. 61-60, 38 FR 3161, Feb. 1, 1973, as amended by Amdt. 61-72, 47 FR 35693, Aug. 16, 1982]

§ 61.15 Offenses involving alcohol or drugs.

(a) A conviction for the violation of any Federal or state statute relating to the growing, processing, manufacture, sale, disposition, possession, transportation, or importation of narcotic drugs, marihuana, or depressant or stimulant drugs or substances is grounds for—

(1) Denial of an application for any certificate or rating issued under this Part for a period of up to 1 year after the date of final conviction; or

(2) Suspension or revocation of any certificate or rating issued under this part.

(b) The commission of an act prohibited by § 91.11(a) or § 91.12(a) of this chapter is grounds for—

(1) Denial of an application for a certificate or rating issued under this part for a period of up to 1 year after the date of that act; or

(2) Suspension or revocation of any certificate or rating issued under this part.

[Doc. No. 21956, Amdt. 61-74, 50 FR 15379, Apr. 17, 1985]

§ 61.16 Refusal to submit to an alcohol test or to furnish test results.

A refusal to submit to a test to indicate the percentage by weight of alcohol in the blood, when requested by a law enforcement officer in accordance with § 91.11(c) of this chapter, or a refusal to furnish or authorize the release of the test results requested by the Administrator in accordance with § 91.11 (c) or (d) of this chapter, is grounds for—

(a) Denial of an application for any certificate or rating issued under this part for a period of up to 1 year after the date of that refusal; or

(b) Suspension or revocation of any certificate or rating issued under this part.

[Doc. No. 21956, Amdt. 61-76, 51 FR 1229, Jan. 9, 1986]

§ 61.17 Temporary certificate.

(a) A temporary pilot or flight instructor certificate, or a rating, effective for a period of not more than 120 days, is issued to a qualified applicant pending a review of his qualifications and the issuance of a permanent certificate or rating by the Administrator. The permanent certificate or rating is issued to an applicant found qualified and a denial thereof is issued to an applicant found not qualified.

(b) A temporary certificate issued under paragraph (a) of this section expires—

(1) At the end of the expiration date stated thereon; or

(2) Upon receipt by the applicant, of—

(i) The certificate or rating sought; or

(ii) Notice that the certificate or rating sought is denied.

[Doc. No. 11802, Amdt. 61-60, 38 FR 3161, Feb. 1, 1973, as amended by Amdt. 61-66, 43 FR 22639, May 25, 1978]

§ 61.19 Duration of pilot and flight instructor certificates.

(a) *General.* The holder of a certificate with an expiration date may not, after that date, exercise the privileges of that certificate.

(b) *Student pilot certificate.* A student pilot certificate expires at the end of the 24th month after the month in which it is issued.

(c) *Other pilot certificates.* Any pilot certificate (other than a student pilot certificate) issued under this part is issued without a specific expiration date. However, the holder of a pilot certificate issued on the basis of a foreign pilot license may exercise the privileges of that certificate only while the foreign pilot license on which that certificate is based is effective.

(d) *Flight instructor certificate.* A flight instructor certificate—

(1) Is effective only while the holder has a current pilot certificate and a medical certificate appropriate to the pilot privileges being exercised; and

(2) Expires at the end of the 24th month after the month in which it was last issued or renewed.

(e) *Surrender, suspension, or revocation.* Any pilot certificate or flight instructor certificate issued under this part ceases to be effective if it is surrendered, suspended, or revoked.

(f) *Return of certificate.* The holder of any certificate issued under this part that is suspended or revoked shall, upon the Administrator's request, return it to the Administrator.

§ 61.21 Duration of Category II pilot authorization.

A Category II pilot authorization expires at the end of the sixth month after it was last issued or renewed. Upon passing a practical test it is renewed for each type aircraft for which an authorization is held. However, an authorization for any particular type aircraft for which an authorization is held will not be renewed to extend beyond the end of the 12th month after the practical test was passed in that type aircraft. If the holder of the authorization passes the practical test for a renewal in the month before the authorization expires, he is considered to have passed it during the month the authorization expired.

[Doc. No. 11802, Amdt. 61-60, 38 FR 3161, Feb. 1, 1973, as amended by Amdt. 61-77, 51 FR 40703, Nov. 7, 1986]

§ 61.23 Duration of medical certificates.

(a) A first-class medical certificate expires at the end of the last day of—

(1) The sixth month after the month of the date of examination shown on the certificate, for operations requiring an airline transport pilot certificate;

(2) The 12th month after the month of the date of examination shown on the certificate, for operations requiring only a commercial pilot certificate; and

(3) The 24th month after the month of the date of examination shown on the certificate, for operations requiring only a private or student pilot certificate.

(b) A second-class medical certificate expires at the end of the last day of—

(1) The 12th month after the month of the date of examination shown on the certificate, for operations requiring a commercial pilot certificate or an air traffic control tower operator certificate; and

(2) The 24th month after the month of the date of examination shown on the certificate, for operations requiring only a private or student pilot certificate.

(c) A third-class medical certificate expires at the end of the last day of the 24th month after the month of the date of examination shown on the certificate, for operations requiring a private or student pilot certificate.

[Doc. No. 11802, Amdt. 61-60, 38 FR 3161, Feb. 1, 1973, as amended by Amdt. 61-68, 45 FR 18911, Mar. 24, 1980]

§ 61.25 Change of name.

An application for the change of a name on a certificate issued under this part must be accompanied by the applicant's current certificate and a copy of the marriage license, court order, or other document verifying the change. The documents are returned to the applicant after inspection.

§ 61.27 Voluntary surrender or exchange of certificate.

The holder of a certificate issued under this part may voluntarily surrender it for cancellation, or for the issue of a certificate of lower grade, or another certificate with specific ratings deleted. If he so requests, he must include the following signed statement or its equivalent:

This request is made for my own reasons, with full knowledge that my (insert name of certificate or rating, as appropriate) may not be reissued to me unless I again pass the tests prescribed for its issue.

§ 61.29 Replacement of lost or destroyed certificate.

(a) An application for the replacement of a lost or destroyed airman certificate issued under this part is made by letter to the Department of Transportation, Federal Aviation Administration, Airman Certification Branch, Post Office Box 25082, Oklahoma City, OK 73125. The letter must—

(1) State the name of the person to whom the certificate was issued, the permanent mailing address (including zip code), social security number (if any), date and place of birth of the certificate holder, and any available information regarding the grade, number, and date of issue of the certificate, and the ratings on it; and

(2) Be accompanied by a check or money order for $2, payable to the Federal Aviation Administration.

(b) An application for the replacement of a lost or destroyed medical certificate is made by letter to the Department of Transportation, Federal Aviation Administration, Aeromedical Certification Branch, Post Office Box 25082, Oklahoma City, OK 73125, accompanied by a check or money order for $2.

(c) A person who has lost a certificate issued under this part, or a medical certificate issued under Part 67 of this chapter, or both, may obtain a telegram from the FAA confirming that it was issued. The telegram may be carried as a certificate for a period not to exceed 60 days pending his receipt of a duplicate certificate under paragraph (a) or (b) of this section, unless he has been notified that the certificate has been suspended or revoked. The request for such a telegram may be made by letter or prepaid telegram, including the date upon which a duplicate certificate was previously requested, if a request had been made, and a money order for the cost of the duplicate certificate. The request for a telegraphic certificate is sent to the office listed in paragraph (a) or (b) of this section, as appropriate. However, a request for both airman and medical certificates at the same time must be sent to the office prescribed in paragraph (a) of this section.

§ 61.31 General limitations.

(a) *Type ratings required.* A person may not act as pilot in command of any of the following aircraft unless he holds a type rating for that aircraft:

(1) A large aircraft (except lighter-than-air).

(2) A helicopter, for operations requiring an airline transport pilot certificate.

(3) A turbojet powered airplane.

(4) Other aircraft specified by the Administrator through aircraft type certificate procedures.

(b) *Authorization in lieu of a type rating.* (1) In lieu of a type rating required under paragraphs (a) (1), (3), and (4) of this section, an aircraft may be operated under an authorization issued by the Administrator, for a flight or series of flights within the United States, if—

(i) The particular operation for which the authorization is requested involves a ferry flight, a practice or training flight, a flight test for a pilot type rating, or a test flight of an aircraft, for a period that does not exceed 60 days;

(ii) The applicant shows that compliance with paragraph (a) of this section is impracticable for the particular operation; and

(iii) The Administrator finds that an equivalent level of safety may be achieved through operating limitations on the authorization.

(2) Aircraft operated under an authorization issued under this paragraph—

(i) May not be operated for compensation or hire; and

(ii) May carry only flight crewmembers necessary for the flight.

(3) An authorization issued under this paragraph may be reissued for an additional 60-day period for the same operation if the applicant shows that he was prevented from carrying out the purpose of the particular operation before his authorization expired.

The prohibition of paragraph (b)(2)(i) of this section does not prohibit compensation for the use of an aircraft by a pilot solely to prepare for or take a flight test for a type rating.

(c) *Category and class rating: Carrying another person or operating for compensation or hire.* Unless he holds a category and class rating for that aircraft, a person may not act as pilot in command of an aircraft that is carrying another person or is operated for compensation or hire. In addition, he may not act as pilot in command of that aircraft for compensation or hire.

(d) *Category and class rating: Other operations.* No person may act as pilot in command of an aircraft in solo flight in operations not subject to paragraph (c) of this section, unless he meets at least one of the following:

(1) He holds a category and class rating appropriate to that aircraft.

(2) He has received flight instruction in the pilot operations required by this part, appropriate to the category and class of aircraft for first solo, given to him by a certificated flight instructor who found him competent to solo that category and class of aircraft and has so endorsed his pilot logbook.

(3) He has soloed and logged pilot-in-command time in that category and class of aircraft before November 1, 1973.

(e) *High performance airplanes.* A person holding a private or commercial pilot certificate may not act as pilot in command of an airplane that has more than 200 horsepower, or that has a retractable landing gear, flaps, and a controllable propeller, unless he has received flight instruction from an authorized flight instructor who has certified in his logbook that he is competent to pilot an airplane that has more than 200 horsepower, or that has a retractable landing gear, flaps, and a controllable propeller, as the case may be. However, this instruction is not required if he has logged flight time as pilot in command in high performance airplanes before November 1, 1973.

(f) *Exception.* This section does not require a class rating for gliders, or category and class ratings for aircraft that are not type certificated as airplanes, rotorcraft, or lighter-than-air aircraft. In addition, the rating limitations of this section do not apply to—

(1) The holder of a student pilot certificate;

(2) The holder of a pilot certificate when operating an aircraft under the authority of an experimental or provisional type certificate;

(3) An applicant when taking a flight test given by the Administrator; or

(4) The holder of a pilot certificate with a lighter-than-air category rating when operating a hot air balloon without an airborne heater.

§ 61.33 Tests: General procedure.

Tests prescribed by or under this part are given at times and places, and by persons, designated by the Administrator.

§ 61.35 Written test: Prerequisites and passing grades.

(a) An applicant for a written test must—

(1) Show that he has satisfactorily completed the ground instruction or home study course required by this part for the certificate or rating sought;

(2) Present as personal identification an airman certificate, driver's license, or other official document; and

(3) Present a birth certificate or other official document showing that he meets the age requirement prescribed in this part for the certificate sought not later than 2 years from the date of application for the test.

(b) The minimum passing grade is specified by the Administrator on each written test sheet or booklet furnished to the applicant.

This section does not apply to the written test for an airline transport pilot certificate or a rating associated with that certificate.

§ 61.37 Written tests: Cheating or other unauthorized conduct.

(a) Except as authorized by the Administrator, no person may—

(1) Copy, or intentionally remove, a written test under this part;

(2) Give to another, or receive from another, any part or copy of that test;

(3) Give help on that test to, or receive help on that test from, any person during the period that test is being given;

(4) Take any part of that test in behalf of another person;

(5) Use any material or aid during the period that test is being given: or

(6) Intentionally cause, assist, or participate in any act prohibited by this paragraph.

(b) No person whom the Administrator finds to have committed an act prohibited by paragraph (a) of this section is eligible for any airman or ground instructor certificate or rating, or to take any test therefor, under this chapter for a period of 1 year after the date of that act. In addition, the commission of that act is a basis for suspending or revoking any airman or ground instructor certificate or rating held by that person.

§ 61.39 Prerequisites for flight tests.

(a) To be eligible for a flight test for a certificate, or an aircraft or instrument rating issued under this part, the applicant must—

(1) Have passed any required written test since the beginning of the 24th month before the month in which he takes the flight test;

(2) Have the applicable instruction and aeronautical experience prescribed in this part;

(3) Hold a current medical certificate appropriate to the certificate he seeks or, in the case of a rating to be added to his pilot certificate, at least a third-class medical certificate issued since the beginning of the 24th month before the month in which he takes the flight test;

(4) Except for a flight test for an airline transport pilot certificate, meet the age requirement for the issuance of the certificate or rating he seeks; and

(5) Have a written statement from an appropriately certificated flight instructor certifying that he has given the applicant flight instruction in preparation for the flight test within 60 days preceding the date of application, and finds him competent to pass the test and to have satisfactory knowledge of the subject areas in which he is shown to be deficient by his FAA airman written test report. However, an applicant need not have this written statement if he—

(i) Holds a foreign pilot license issued by a contracting State to the Convention on International Civil Aviation that authorizes at least the pilot privileges of the airman certificate sought by him;

(ii) Is applying for a type rating only, or a class rating with an associated type rating; or

(iii) Is applying for an airline transport pilot certificate or an additional aircraft rating on that certificate.

(b) Notwithstanding the provisions of paragraph (a)(1) of this section, an applicant for an airline transport pilot certificate or rating may take the flight test for that certificate or rating if—

(1) The applicant—

(i) Within the period ending 24 calendar months after the month in which the applicant passed the first of any required written tests, was employed as a flight crewmember by a U.S. air carrier or commercial operator operating either under Part 121 or as a commuter air carrier under Part 135 (as defined in Part 298 of this title) and is employed by such a certificate holder at the time of the flight test;

(ii) Has completed initial training, and, if appropriate, transition or upgrade training; and

(iii) Meets the recurrent training requirements of the applicable part; or

(2) Within the period ending 24 calendar months after the month in which the applicant passed the first of any required written tests, the applicant participated as a pilot in a pilot training program of a U.S. scheduled military air transportation service and is currently participating in that program.

[Doc. No. 11802, Amdt. 61–60, 38 FR 3161, Feb. 1, 1973, as amended by Amdt. 61–71, 47 FR 13312, Mar. 29, 1982]

§ 61.41 Flight instruction received from flight instructors not certificated by FAA.

Flight instruction may be credited toward the requirements for a pilot certificate or rating issued under this part if it is received from—

(a) An Armed Force of either the United States or a foreign contracting State to the Convention on International Civil Aviation in a program for training military pilots; or

(b) A flight instructor who is authorized to give that flight instruction by the licensing authority of a foreign contracting State to the Convention on International Civil Aviation and the flight instruction is given outside the United States.

§ 61.43 Flight tests: General procedures.

(a) The ability of an applicant for a private or commercial pilot certificate, or for an aircraft or instrument rating on that certificate to perform the required pilot operations is based on the following:

(1) Executing procedures and maneuvers within the aircraft's performance capabilities and limitations, including use of the aircraft's systems.

(2) Executing emergency procedures and maneuvers appropriate to the aircraft.

(3) Piloting the aircraft with smoothness and accuracy.

(4) Exercising judgment.

(5) Applying his aeronautical knowledge.

(6) Showing that he is the master of the aircraft, with the successful outcome of a procedure or maneuver never seriously in doubt.

(b) If the applicant fails any of the required pilot operations in accordance with the applicable provisions of paragraph (a) of this section, the applicant fails the flight test. The applicant is not eligible for the certificate or rating sought until he passes any pilot operations he has failed.

(c) The examiner or the applicant may discontinue the test at any time when the failure of a required pilot operation makes the applicant ineligible for the certificate or rating sought. If the test is discontinued the applicant is entitled to credit for only those entire pilot operations that he has successfully performed.

§ 61.45 Flight tests: Required aircraft and equipment.

(a) *General.* An applicant for a certificate or rating under this part must furnish, for each flight test that he is required to take, an appropriate aircraft of United States registry that has a current standard or limited airworthiness certificate. However, the applicant may, at the discretion of the inspector or examiner conducting the test, furnish an aircraft of U.S. registry that has a current airworthiness certificate other than standard or limited, an aircraft of foreign registry that is properly certificated by the country of registry, or a military aircraft in an operational status if its use is allowed by an appropriate military authority.

(b) *Required equipment (other than controls)*. Aircraft furnished for a flight test must have—

(1) The equipment for each pilot operation required for the flight test;

(2) No prescribed operating limitations that prohibit its use in any pilot operation required on the test;

(3) Pilot seats with adequate visibility for each pilot to operate the aircraft safely, except as provided in paragraph (d) of this section; and

(4) Cockpit and outside visibility adequate to evaluate the performance of the applicant, where an additional jump seat is provided for the examiner.

(c) *Required controls*. An aircraft (other than lighter-than-air) furnished under paragraph (a) of this section for any pilot flight test must have engine power controls and flight controls that are easily reached and operable in a normal manner by both pilots, unless after considering all the factors, the examiner determines that the flight test can be conducted safely without them. However, an aircraft having other controls such as nosewheel steering, brakes, switches, fuel selectors, and engine air flow controls that are not easily reached and operable in a normal manner by both pilots may be used, if more than one pilot is required under its airworthiness certificate, or if the examiner determines that the flight can be conducted safely.

(d) *Simulated instrument flight equipment*. An applicant for any flight test involving flight maneuvers solely by reference to instruments must furnish equipment satisfactory to the examiner that excludes the visual reference of the applicant outside of the aircraft.

(e) *Aircraft with single controls*. At the discretion of the examiner, an aircraft furnished under paragraph (a) of this section for a flight test may, in the cases listed herein, have a single set of controls. In such case, the examiner determines the competence of the applicant by observation from the ground or from another aircraft.

(1) A flight test for addition of a class or type rating, not involving demonstration of instrument skills, to a private or commercial pilot certificate.

(2) A flight test in a single-place gyroplane for—

(i) A private pilot certificate with a rotorcraft category rating and gyroplane class rating, in which case the certificate bears the limitation "rotorcraft single-place gyroplane only"; or

(ii) Addition of a rotorcraft category rating and gyroplane class rating to a pilot certificate, in which case a certificate higher than a private pilot certificate bears the limitation "rotorcraft single-place gyroplane, private pilot privileges, only".

The limitations prescribed by this subparagraph may be removed if the holder of the certificate passes the appropriate flight test in a gyroplane with two pilot stations or otherwise passes the appropriate flight test for a rotorcraft category rating.

§ 61.47   Flight tests: Status of FAA inspectors and other authorized flight examiners.

An FAA inspector or other authorized flight examiner conducts the flight test of an applicant for a pilot certificate or rating for the purpose of observing the applicant's ability to perform satisfactorily the procedures and maneuvers on the flight test. The inspector or other examiner is not pilot in command of the aircraft during the flight test unless he acts in that capacity for the flight, or portion of the flight, by prior arrangement with the applicant or other person who would otherwise act as pilot in command of the flight, or portion of the flight. Notwithstanding the type of aircraft used during a flight test, the applicant and the inspector or other examiner are not, with respect to each other (or other occupants authorized by the inspector or other examiner), subject to the requirements or limitations for the carriage of passengers specified in this chapter.

§61.49 Retesting after failure.

An applicant for a written or flight test who fails that test may not apply for retesting until after 30 days after the date he failed the test. However, in the case of his first failure he may apply for retesting before the 30 days have expired upon presenting a written statement from an authorized instructor certifying that he has given flight or ground instruction as appropriate to the applicant and finds him competent to pass the test.

§61.51 Pilot logbooks.

(a) The aeronautical training and experience used to meet the requirements for a certificate or rating, or the recent flight experience requirements of this part must be shown by a reliable record. The logging of other flight time is not required.

(b) *Logbook entries.* Each pilot shall enter the following information for each flight or lesson logged:

(1) *General.* (i) Date.

(ii) Total time of flight.

(iii) Place, or points of departure and arrival.

(iv) Type and identification of aircraft.

(2) *Type of pilot experience or training.* (i) Pilot in command or solo.

(ii) Second in command.

(iii) Flight instruction received from an authorized flight instructor.

(iv) Instrument flight instruction from an authorized flight instructor.

(v) Pilot ground trainer instruction.

(vi) Participating crew (lighter-than-air).

(vii) Other pilot time.

(3) *Conditions of flight.* (i) Day or night.

(ii) Actual instrument.

(iii) Simulated instrument conditions.

(c) *Logging of pilot time*—(1) *Solo-flight time.* A pilot may log as solo flight time only that flight time when he is the sole occupant of the aircraft. However, a student pilot may also log as solo flight time that time during which he acts as the pilot in command

of an airship requiring more than one flight crewmember.

(2) *Pilot-in-command flight time.* (i) A private or commercial pilot may log as pilot in command time only that flight time during which he is the sole manipulator of the controls of an aircraft for which he is rated, or when he is the sole occupant of the aircraft, or when he acts as pilot in command of an aircraft on which more than one pilot is required under the type certification of the aircraft, or the regulations under which the flight is conducted.

(ii) An airline transport pilot may log as pilot in command time all of the flight time during which he acts as pilot in command.

(iii) A certificated flight instructor may log as pilot in command time all flight time during which he acts as a flight instructor.

(3) *Second-in-command flight time.* A pilot may log as second in command time all flight time during which he acts as second in command of an aircraft on which more than one pilot is required under the type certification of the aircraft, or the regulations under which the flight is conducted.

(4) *Instrument flight time.* A pilot may log as instrument flight time only that time during which he operates the aircraft solely by reference to instruments, under actual or simulated instrument flight conditions. Each entry must include the place and type of each instrument approach completed, and the name of the safety pilot for each simulated instrument flight. An instrument flight instructor may log as instrument time that time during which he acts as instrument flight instructor in actual instrument weather conditions.

(5) *Instruction time.* All time logged as flight instruction, instrument flight instruction, pilot ground trainer instruction, or ground instruction time must be certified by the appropriately rated and certificated instructor from whom it was received.

(d) *Presentation of logbook.* (1) A pilot must present his logbook (or other record required by this section) for inspection upon reasonable request by the Administrator, an authorized representative of the National Transportation Safety Board, or any State or local law enforcement officer.

(2) A student pilot must carry his logbook (or other record required by this section) with him on all solo cross-country flights, as evidence of the required instructor clearances and endorsements.

§ 61.53 Operations during medical deficiency.

No person may act as pilot in command, or in any other capacity as a required pilot flight crewmember while he has a known medical deficiency, or increase of a known medical deficiency, that would make him unable to meet the requirements for his current medical certificate.

§ 61.55 Second-in-command qualifications.

(a) Except as provided in paragraph (d) of this section, no person may serve as second in command of an aircraft type certificated for more than one required pilot flight crewmember unless that person holds—

(1) At least a current private pilot certificate with appropriate category and class ratings; and

(2) An appropriate instrument rating in the case of flight under IFR.

(b) Except as provided in paragraph (d) of this section, no person may serve as second in command of an aircraft type certificated for more than one required pilot flight crewmember unless, since the beginning of the 12th calendar month before the month in which the pilot serves, the pilot has, with respect to that type of aircraft—

(1) Become familiar with all information concerning the aircraft's powerplant, major components and systems, major appliances, performance and limitations, standard and emergency operating procedures, and the contents of the approved aircraft flight manual or approved flight manual material, placards, and markings.

(2) Except as provided in paragraph (e) of this section, performed and logged—

(i) Three takeoffs and three landings to a full stop in the aircraft as the sole manipulator of the flight controls; and

(ii) Engine-out procedures and maneuvering with an engine out while executing the duties of a pilot in command. For airplanes, this requirement may be satisfied in a simulator acceptable to the Administrator.

For the purpose of meeting the requirements of paragraph (b)(2) of this section, a person may act as second in command of a flight under day VFR or day IFR, if no persons or property, other than as necessary for the operation, are carried.

(c) If a pilot complies with the requirements in paragraph (b) of this section in the calendar month before, or the calendar month after, the month in which compliance with those requirements is due, he is considered to have complied with them in the month they are due.

(d) This section does not apply to a pilot who—

(1) Meets the pilot in command proficiency check requirements of Part 121, 125, 127, or 135 of this chapter;

(2) Is designated as the second in command of an aircraft operated under the provisions of Part 121, 125, 127, or 135 of this chapter; or

(3) Is designated as the second in command of an aircraft for the purpose of receiving flight training required by this section and no passengers or cargo are carried on that aircraft.

(e) The holder of a commercial or airline transport pilot certificate with appropriate category and class ratings need not meet the requirements of paragraph (b)(2) of this section for the conduct of ferry flights, aircraft flight tests, or airborne equipment evaluation, if no persons or property other than as necessary for the operation are carried.

[Doc. No. 11802, Amdt. 61-60, 38 FR 3161, Feb. 1, 1973, as amended by Amdt. 61-64, 41 FR 51392, Nov. 22, 1976; Amdt. 61-65, 42 FR 18391, Apr. 7, 1977; Amdt. 61-77, 51 FR 40703, Nov. 7, 1986]

§ 61.57 Recent flight experience: Pilot in command.

(a) *Flight review.* No person may act as pilot in command of an aircraft unless, within the preceding 24 calendar months, that person has—

(1) Accomplished a flight review given to him, in an aircraft for which

he is rated, by an appropriately certificated instructor or other person designated by the Administrator; and

(2) Had his log book endorsed by the person who gave him the review certifying that he has satisfactorily accomplished the flight review.

However, a person who has, within the preceding 24 calendar months, satisfactorily completed a pilot proficiency check conducted by the FAA, an approved pilot check airman or a U.S. armed force for a pilot certificate, rating or operating privilege, need not accomplish the flight review required by this section.

(b) *Meaning of flight review.* As used in this section, a flight review consists of—

(1) A review of the current general operating and flight rules of Part 91 of this chapter; and

(2) A review of those maneuvers and procedures which in the discretion of the person giving the review are necessary for the pilot to demonstrate that he can safely exercise the privileges of his pilot certificate.

(c) *General experience.* No person may act as pilot in command of an aircraft carrying passengers, nor of an aircraft certificated for more than one required pilot flight crewmember, unless within the preceding 90 days, he has made three takeoffs and three landings as the sole manipulator of the flight controls in an aircraft of the same category and class and, if a type rating is required, of the same type. If the aircraft is a tailwheel airplane, the landings must have been made to a full stop in a tailwheel airplane. For the purpose of meeting the requirements of the paragraph a person may act as pilot-in-command of a flight under day VFR or day IFR if no persons or property other than as necessary for his compliance thereunder, are carried. This paragraph does not apply to operations requiring an airline transport pilot certificate, or to operations conducted under Part 135 of this chapter.

(d) *Night experience.* No person may act as pilot in command of an aircraft carrying passengers during the period beginning 1 hour after sunset and ending 1 hour before sunrise (as published in the American Air Almanac) unless, within the preceding 90 days, he has made at least three takeoffs and three landings to a full stop during that period in the category and class of aircraft to be used. This paragraph does not apply to operations requiring an airline transport pilot certificate.

(e) *Instrument*—(1) *Recent IFR experience.* No pilot may act as pilot in command under IFR, nor in weather conditions less than the minimums prescribed for VFR, unless he has, within the past 6 calendar months—

(i) In the case of an aircraft other than a glider, logged at least 6 hours of instrument time under actual or simulated IFR conditions, at least 3 of which were in flight in the category of aircraft involved, including at least six instrument approaches, or passed an instrument competency check in the category of aircraft involved.

(ii) In the case of a glider, logged at least 3 hours of instrument time, at least half of which were in a glider or an airplane. If a passenger is carried in the glider, at least 3 hours of instrument flight time must have been in gliders.

(2) *Instrument competency check.* A pilot who does not meet the recent instrument experience requirements of paragraph (e)(1) of this section during the prescribed time or 6 calendar months thereafter may not serve as pilot in command under IFR, nor in weather conditions less than the minimums prescribed for VFR, until he passes an instrument competency check in the category of aircraft involved, given by an FAA inspector, a member of an armed force of the United States authorized to conduct flight tests, an FAA-approved check pilot, or a certificated instrument flight instructor. The Administrator may authorize the conduct of part or all of this check in a pilot ground trainer equipped for instruments or an aircraft simulator.

[Doc. No. 11802, Amdt. 61-60, 38 FR 3161, Feb. 1, 1973, as amended by Amdt. 61-77, 51 FR 40703, Nov. 7, 1986]

§ 61.58 Pilot-in-command proficiency check: Operation of aircraft requiring more than one required pilot.

(a) Except as provided in paragraph (e) of this section, after November 1, 1974, no person may act as pilot in command of an aircraft that is type certificated for more than one required pilot crewmember unless he has satisfactorily completed the proficiency checks or flight checks prescribed in paragraphs (b) and (c) of this section.

(b) Since the beginning of the 12th calendar month before the month in which a person acts as pilot in command of an aircraft that is type certificated for more than one required pilot crewmember he must have completed one of the following:

(1) For an airplane—a proficiency or flight check in either an airplane that is type certificated for more than one required pilot crewmember, or in an approved simulator or other training device, given to him by an FAA inspector or designated pilot examiner and consisting of those maneuvers and procedures set forth in Appendix F of Part 121 of this chapter which may be performed in a simulator or training device.

(2) For other aircraft—a proficiency or flight check in an aircraft that is type certificated for more than one required pilot crewmember given to him by an FAA inspector or designated pilot examiner which includes those maneuvers and procedures required for the original issuance of a type rating for the aircraft used in the check.

(3) A pilot in command proficiency check given to him in accordance with the provisions for that check under Parts 121, 123, or 135 of this chapter. However, in the case of a person acting as pilot in command of a helicopter he may complete a proficiency check given to him in accordance with Part 127 of this chapter.

(4) A flight test required for an aircraft type rating.

(5) An initial or periodic flight check for the purpose of the issuance of a pilot examiner or check airman designation.

(6) A military proficiency check required for pilot in command and instrument privileges in an aircraft which the military requires to be operated by more than one pilot.

(c) Except as provided in paragraph (d) of this section, since the beginning of the 24th calendar month before the month in which a person acts as pilot in command of an aircraft that is type certificated for more than one required pilot crewmember he must have completed one of the following proficiency or flight checks in the particular type aircraft in which he is to serve as pilot in command:

(1) A proficiency check or flight check given to him by an FAA inspector or a designated pilot examiner which includes the maneuvers, procedures, and standards required for the original issuance of a type rating for the aircraft used in the check.

(2) A pilot in command proficiency check given to him in accordance with the provisions for that check under Parts 121, 123, or 135 of this chapter. However, in the case of a person acting as pilot in command of a helicopter he may complete a proficiency check given to him in accordance with Part 127 of this chapter.

(3) A flight test required for an aircraft type rating.

(4) An initial or periodic flight check for the purpose of the issuance of a pilot examiner or check airman designation.

(5) A military proficiency check required for pilot in command and instrument privileges in an aircraft which the military requires to be operated by more than one pilot.

(d) For airplanes, the maneuvers and procedures required for the checks and test prescribed in paragraphs (c) (1), (2), (4), and (5) of this section, and paragraph (c)(3) of this section in the case of type ratings obtained in conjunction with a Part 121 of this chapter training program may be performed in a simulator or training device if—

(1) The maneuver or procedure can be performed in a simulator or training device as set forth in Appendix F to Part 121 of this chapter; and

(2) The simulator or training device is one that is approved for the particular maneuver or procedure.

(e) This section does not apply to persons conducting operations subject to Parts 121, 123, 127, 133, 135, and 137 of this chapter.

(f) For the purpose of meeting the proficiency check requirements of paragraphs (b) and (c) of this section, a person may act as pilot in command of a flight under day VFR or day IFR if no persons or property, other than as necessary for his compliance thereunder, are carried.

(g) If a pilot takes the proficiency check required by paragraph (a) of this section in the calendar month before, or the calendar month after, the month in which it is due, he is considered to have taken it in the month it is due.

§ 61.59 Falsification, reproduction, or alteration of applications, certificates, logbooks, reports, or records.

(a) No person may make or cause to be made—

(1) Any fraudulent or intentionally false statement on any application for a certificate, rating, or duplicate thereof, issued under this part;

(2) Any fraudulent or intentionally false entry in any logbook, record, or report that is required to be kept, made, or used, to show compliance with any requirement for the issuance, or exercise of the privileges, or any certificate or rating under this part;

(3) Any reproduction, for fraudulent purpose, of any certificate or rating under this part; or

(4) Any alteration of any certificate or rating under this part.

(b) The commission by any person of an act prohibited under paragraph (a) of this section is a basis for suspending or revoking any airman or ground instructor certificate or rating held by that person.

§ 61.60 Change of address.

The holder of a pilot or flight instructor certificate who has made a change in his permanent mailing address may not after 30 days from the date he moved, exercise the privileges of his certificate unless he has notified in writing the Department of Transportation, Federal Aviation Administration, Airman Certification Branch,

Box 25082, Oklahoma City, OK 73125, of his new address.

Subpart B—Aircraft Ratings and Special Certificates

§ 61.61 Applicability.

This subpart prescribes the requirements for the issuance of additional aircraft ratings after a pilot or instructor certificate is issued, and the requirements and limitations for special pilot certificates and ratings issued by the Administrator.

§ 61.63 Additional aircraft ratings (other than airline transport pilot).

(a) *General.* To be eligible for an aircraft rating after his certificate is issued to him an applicant must meet the requirements of paragraphs (b) through (d) of this section, as appropriate to the rating sought.

(b) *Category rating.* An applicant for a category rating to be added on his pilot certificate must meet the requirements of this part for the issue of the pilot certificate appropriate to the privileges for which the category rating is sought. However, the holder of a category rating for powered aircraft is not required to take a written test for the addition of a category rating on his pilot certificate.

(c) *Class rating.* An applicant for an aircraft class rating to be added on his pilot certificate must—

(1) Present a logbook record certified by an authorized flight instructor showing that the applicant has received flight instruction in the class of aircraft for which a rating is sought and has been found competent in the pilot operations appropriate to the pilot certificate to which his category rating applies; and

(2) Pass a flight test appropriate to his pilot certificate and applicable to the aircraft category and class rating sought.

A person who holds a lighter-than-air category rating with a free balloon class rating, who seeks an airship class rating, must meet the requirements of paragraph (b) of this section as though seeking a lighter-than-air category rating.

(d) *Type rating.* An applicant for a type rating to be added on his pilot certificate must meet the following requirements:

(1) He must hold, or concurrently obtain, an instrument rating appropriate to the aircraft for which a type rating is sought.

(2) He must pass a flight test showing competence in pilot operations appropriate to the pilot certificate he holds and to the type rating sought.

(3) He must pass a flight test showing competence in pilot operations under instrument flight rules in an aircraft of the type for which the type rating is sought or, in the case of a single pilot station airplane, meet the requirements of paragraph (d)(3) (i) or (ii) of this section, whichever is applicable.

(i) The applicant must have met the requirements of this paragraph in a multiengine airplane for which the type rating is required.

(ii) If he does not meet the requirements of paragraph (d)(3)(i) of this section and he seeks a type rating for a single-engine airplane, he must meet the requirements of this subparagraph in either a single or multiengine airplane, and have the recent instrument experience set forth in § 61.57(e), when he applies for the flight test under paragraph (d)(2) of this section.

(4) An applicant who does not meet the requirements of paragraphs (d) (1) and (3) of this section may obtain a type rating limited to "VFR only." Upon meeting these instrument requirements or the requirements of § 61.73(e)(2), the "VFR only" limitation may be removed for the particular type of aircraft in which competence is shown.

(5) When an instrument rating is issued to the holder of one or more type ratings, the type ratings on the amended certificate bear the limitation described in paragraph (d)(4) of this section for each airplane type rating for which he has not shown his instrument competency under this paragraph.

§ 61.65 Instrument rating requirements.

(a) *General.* To be eligible for an instrument rating (airplane) or an instrument rating (helicopter), an applicant must—

(1) Hold at least a current private pilot certificate with an aircraft rating appropriate to the instrument rating sought;

(2) Be able to read, speak, and understand the English language; and

(3) Comply with the applicable requirements of this section.

(b) *Ground instruction.* An applicant for the written test for an instrument rating must have received ground instruction, or have logged home study in at least the following areas of aeronautical knowledge appropriate to the rating sought.

(1) The regulations of this chapter that apply to flight under IFR conditions, the Airman's Information Manual, and the IFR air traffic system and procedures;

(2) Dead reckoning appropriate to IFR navigation, IFR navigation by radio aids using the VOR, ADF, and ILS systems, and the use of IFR charts and instrument approach plates;

(3) The procurement and use of aviation weather reports and forecasts, and the elements of forecasting weather trends on the basis of that information and personal observation of weather conditions; and

(4) The safe and efficient operation of airplanes or helicopters, as appropriate, under instrument weather conditions.

(c) *Flight instruction and skill—airplanes.* An applicant for the flight test for an instrument rating (airplane) must present a logbook record certified by an authorized flight instructor showing that he has received instrument flight instruction in an airplane in the following pilot operations, and has been found competent in each of them:

(1) Control and accurate maneuvering of an airplane solely by reference to instruments.

(2) IFR navigation by the use of the VOR and ADF systems, including compliance with air traffic control instructions and procedures.

(3) Instrument approaches to published minimums using the VOR, ADF, and ILS systems (instruction in the use of the ADF and ILS may be re-

ceived in an instrument ground trainer and instruction in the use of the ILS glide slope may be received in an airborne ILS simulator).

(4) Cross-country flying in simulated or actual IFR conditions, on Federal airways or as routed by ATC, including one such trip of at least 250 nautical miles, including VOR, ADF, and ILS approaches at different airports.

(5) Simulated emergencies, including the recovery from unusual attitudes, equipment or instrument malfunctions, loss of communications, and engine-out emergencies if a multiengine airplane is used, and missed approach procedure.

(d) *Instrument instruction and skill—(helicopter).* An applicant for the flight test for an instrument rating (helicopter) must present a logbook record certified to by an authorized flight instructor showing that he has received instrument flight instruction in a helicopter in the following pilot operations, and has been found competent in each of them:

(1) The control and accurate maneuvering of a helicopter solely by reference to instruments.

(2) IFR navigation by the use of the VOR and ADF systems, including compliance with air traffic instructions and procedures.

(3) Instrument approaches to published minimums using the VOR, ADF, and ILS systems (instruction in the use of the ADF and ILS may be received in an instrument ground trainer, and instruction in the use of the ILS glide slope may be received in an airborne ILS simulator).

(4) Cross-country flying under simulated or actual IFR conditions, on Federal airways or as routed by ATC, including one flight of at least 100 nautical miles, including VOR, ADF, and ILS approaches at different airports.

(5) Simulated IFR emergencies, including equipment malfunctions, missed approach procedures, and deviations to unplanned alternates.

(e) *Flight experience.* An applicant for an instrument rating must have at least the following flight time as a pilot:

(1) A total of 125 hours of pilot flight time, of which 50 hours are as pilot in command in cross-country

flight in a powered aircraft with other than a student pilot certificate. Each cross-country flight must have a landing at a point more than 50 nautical miles from the original departure point.

(2) 40 hours of simulated or actual instrument time, of which not more than 20 hours may be instrument instruction by an authorized instructor in an instrument ground trainer acceptable to the Administrator.

(3) 15 hours of instrument flight instruction by an authorized flight instructor, including at least 5 hours in an airplane or a helicopter, as appropriate.

(f) *Written test.* An applicant for an instrument rating must pass a written test appropriate to the instrument rating sought on the subjects in which ground instruction is required by paragraph (b) of this section.

(g) *Practical test.* An applicant for an instrument rating must pass a flight test in an airplane or a helicopter, as appropriate. The test must include instrument flight procedures selected by the inspector or examiner conducting the test to determine the applicant's ability to perform competently the IFR operations on which instruction is required by paragraph (c) or (d) of this section.

[Doc. No. 11802, Amdt. 61-60, 38 FR 3161, Feb. 1, 1973, as amended by Amdt. 61-70, 47 FR 3486, Jan. 25, 1982; Amdt. 61-75, 50 FR 19294, May 7, 1985]

§ 61.67 **Category II pilot authorization requirements.**

(a) *General.* An applicant for a Category II pilot authorization must hold—

(1) A pilot certificate with an instrument rating or an airline transport pilot certificate; and

(2) A type rating for the aircraft type if the authorization is requested for a large aircraft or a small turbojet aircraft.

(b) *Experience requirements.* Except for the holder of an airline transport pilot certificate, an applicant for a Category II authorization must have at least—

(1) 50 hours of night flight time under VFR conditions as pilot in command;

(2) 75 hours of instrument time under actual or simulated conditions that may include 25 hours in a synthetic trainer; and

(3) 250 hours of cross-country flight time as pilot in command.

Night flight and instrument flight time used to meet the requirements of paragraphs (b) (1) and (2) of this section may also be used to meet the requirements of paragraph (b)(3) of this section.

(c) *Practical test required.* (1) The practical test must be passed by—

(i) An applicant for issue or renewal of an authorization; and

(ii) An applicant for the addition of another type aircraft to his authorization.

(2) To be eligible for the practical test an applicant must meet the requirements of paragraph (a) of this section and, if he has not passed a practical test since the beginning of the twelfth month before the test, he must meet the following recent experience requirements:

(i) The requirements of § 61.57(e).

(ii) At least six ILS approaches since the beginning of the sixth month before the test. These approaches must be under actual or simulated instrument flight conditions down to the minimum landing altitude for the ILS approach in the type aircraft in which the flight test is to be conducted. However, the approaches need not be conducted down to the decision heights authorized for Category II operations. At least three of these approaches must have been conducted manually, without the use of an approach coupler.

The flight time acquired in meeting the requirements of paragraph (c)(2)(ii) of this section may be used to meet the requirements of paragraph (c)(2)(i) of this section.

(d) *Practical test procedures.* The practical test consists of two phases:

(1) *Phase I—oral operational test.* The applicant must demonstrate his knowledge of the following:

(i) Required landing distance.

(ii) Recognition of the decision height.

(iii) Missed approach procedures and techniques utilizing computed or fixed attitude guidance displays.

(iv) RVR, its use and limitations.

(v) Use of visual clues, their availability or limitations, and altitude at which they are normally discernible at reduced RVR readings.

(vi) Procedures and techniques related to transition from nonvisual to visual flight during a final approach under reduced RVR.

(vii) Effects of vertical and horizontal wind shear.

(viii) Characteristics and limitations of the ILS and runway lighting system.

(ix) Characteristics and limitations of the flight director system, auto approach coupler (including split axis type if equipped), auto throttle system (if equipped), and other required Category II equipment.

(x) Assigned duties of the second in command during Category II approaches.

(xi) Instrument and equipment failure warning systems.

(2) *Phase II—flight test.* The flight test must be taken in an aircraft that meets the requirements of Part 91 of this chapter for Category II operations. The test consists of at least two ILS approaches to 100 feet including at least one landing and one missed approach. All approaches must be made with the approved flight control guidance system. However, if an approved automatic approach coupler is installed, at least one approach must be made manually. In the case of a multiengine aircraft that has performance capability to execute a missed approach with an engine out, the missed approach must be executed with one engine set in idle or zero thrust position before reaching the middle marker. The required flight maneuvers must be performed solely by reference to instruments and in coordination with a second in command who holds a class rating and, in the case of a large aircraft or a small turbojet aircraft, a type rating for that aircraft.

[Doc. No. 11802, Amdt. 61–60, 38 FR 3161, Feb. 1, 1973, as amended by Amdt. 61–77, 51 FR 40703, Nov. 7, 1986]

§61.69 Glider towing: Experience and instruction requirements.

No person may act as pilot in command of an aircraft towing a glider unless he meets the following requirements:

(a) He holds a current pilot certificate (other than a student pilot certificate) issued under this part.

(b) He has an endorsement in his pilot logbook from a person authorized to give flight instruction in gliders, certifying that he has received ground and flight instruction in gliders and is familiar with the techniques and procedures essential to the safe towing of gliders, including airspeed limitations, emergency procedures, signals used, and maximum angles of bank.

(c) He has made and entered in his pilot logbook—

(1) At least three flights as sole manipulator of the controls of an aircraft towing a glider while accompanied by a pilot who has met the requirements of this section and made and logged at least 10 flights as pilot-in-command of an aircraft towing a glider; or

(2) At least three flights as sole manipulator of the controls of an aircraft simulating glider towing flight procedures (while accompanied by a pilot who meets the requirements of this section), and at least three flights as pilot or observer in a glider being towed by an aircraft.

However, any person who, before May 17, 1967, made, and entered in his pilot logbook, 10 or more flights as pilot in command of an aircraft towing a glider in accordance with a certificate of waiver need not comply with paragraphs (c)(1) and (2) of this section.

(d) If he holds only a private pilot certificate he must have had, and entered in his pilot logbook at least—

(1) 100 hours of pilot flight time in powered aircraft; or

(2) 200 total hours of pilot flight time in powered or other aircraft.

(e) Within the preceding 12 months he has—

(1) Made at least three actual or simulated glider tows while accompanied by a qualified pilot who meets the requirements of this section; or

(2) Made at least three flights as pilot in command of a glider towed by an aircraft.

[Doc. No. 11802, Amdt. 61–60, 38 FR 3161, Feb. 1, 1973, as amended by Amdt. 61–64, 41 FR 51392, Nov. 22, 1976]

§61.71 Graduates of certificated flying schools: Special rules.

(a) A graduate of a flying school that is certificated under Part 141 of this chapter is considered to meet the applicable aeronautical experience requirements of this part if he presents an appropriate graduation certificate within 60 days after the date he is graduated. However, if he applies for a flight test for an instrument rating he must hold a commercial pilot certificate, or hold a private pilot certificate and meet the requirements of §§ 61.65(e)(1) and 61.123 (except paragraphs (d) and (e) thereof). In addition, if he applies for a flight instructor certificate he must hold a commercial pilot certificate.

(b) An applicant for a certificate or rating under this part is considered to meet the aeronautical knowledge and skill requirements, or both, applicable to that certificate or rating, if he applies within 90 days after graduation from an appropriate course given by a flying school that is certificated under Part 141 of this chapter and is authorized to test applicants on aeronautical knowledge or skill, or both.

However, until January 1, 1977, a graduate of a flying school certificated and operated under the provisions of § 141.29 of this chapter, is considered to meet the aeronautical experience requirements of this part, and may be tested under the requirements of Part 61 that were in effect prior to November 1, 1973.

[Doc. No. 11802, Amdt. 61–60, 38 FR 3161, Feb. 1, 1973, as amended by Amdt. 61–63, 39 FR 20057, June 6, 1974]

§61.73 Military pilots or former military pilots: Special rules.

(a) *General.* A rated military pilot or former rated military pilot who applies for a private or commercial pilot certificate, or an aircraft or instrument rating, is entitled to that certificate with appropriate ratings or to the addition of a rating on the pilot certificate he holds, if he meets the applicable requirements of this section. This section does not apply to a military pilot or former military pilot who has been removed from flying status for lack of proficiency or because of disciplinary action involving aircraft operations.

(b) *Military pilots on active flying status within 12 months.* A rated military pilot or former rated military pilot who has been on active flying status within the 12 months before he applies must pass a written test on the parts of this chapter relating to pilot privileges and limitations, air traffic and general operating rules, and accident reporting rules. In addition, he must present documents showing that he meets the requirements of paragraph (d) of this section for at least one aircraft rating, and that he is, or was at any time since the beginning of the twelfth month before the month in which he applies—

(1) A rated military pilot on active flying status in an armed force of the United States; or

(2) A rated military pilot of an armed force of a foreign contracting State to the Convention on International Civil Aviation, assigned to pilot duties (other than flight training) with an armed force of the United States who holds, at the time he applies, a current civil pilot license issued by that foreign State authorizing at least the privileges of the pilot certificate he seeks.

(c) *Military pilots not on active flying status within previous 12 months.* A rated military pilot or former military pilot who has not been on active flying status within the 12 months before he applies must pass the appropriate written and flight tests prescribed in this part for the certificate or rating he seeks. In addition, he must show that he holds an FAA medical certificate appropriate to the pilot certificate he seeks and present documents showing that he was, before the beginning of the twelfth month before the month in which he applies, a rated military pilot

as prescribed by either paragraph (b) (1) or (2) of this section.

(d) *Aircraft ratings: Other than airplane category and type.* An applicant for a category, class, or type rating (other than airplane category and type rating) to be added on the pilot certificate he holds, or for which he has applied, is issued that rating if he presents documentary evidence showing one of the following:

(1) That he has passed an official United States military checkout as pilot in command of aircraft of the category, class, or type for which he seeks a rating since the beginning of the twelfth month before the month in which he applies.

(2) That he has had at least 10 hours of flight time serving as pilot in command of aircraft of the category, class, or type for which he seeks a rating since the beginning of the twelfth month before the month in which he applies and previously has had an official United States military checkout as pilot in command of that aircraft.

(3) That he has met the requirements of paragraph (b) (1) or (2) of this section, has had an official United States military checkout in the category of aircraft for which he seeks a rating, and that he passes an FAA flight test appropriate to that category and the class or type rating he seeks. To be eligible for that flight test, he must have a written statement from an authorized flight instructor, made not more than 60 days before he applies for the flight test, certifying that he is competent to pass the test. A type rating is issued only for aircraft types that the Administrator has certificated for civil operations. Any rating placed on an airline transport pilot certificate is limited to commercial pilot privileges.

(e) *Airplane category and type ratings.* (1) An applicant for a commercial pilot certificate with an airplane category rating, or an applicant for the addition of an airplane category rating on his commercial pilot certificate, must hold an airplane instrument rating, or his certificate is endorsed with the following limitation: "Not valid for the carriage of passengers or property for hire in airplanes on cross-country flights of more than 50 nautical miles, or at night."

(2) An applicant for a private or commercial pilot certificate with an airplane type rating, or for the addition of an airplane type rating on his private or commercial pilot certificate who holds an instrument rating (airplane), must present documentary evidence showing that he has demonstrated instrument competency in the type of airplane for which the type rating is sought, or his certificate is endorsed with the following limitation: "VFR only."

(f) *Instrument rating.* An applicant for an airplane instrument rating or a helicopter instrument rating to be added on the pilot certificate he holds, or for which he has applied, is entitled to that rating if he has, within the 12 months preceding the month in which he applies, satisfactorily accomplished an instrument flight check of a U.S. Armed Force in an aircraft of the category for which he seeks the instrument rating and is authorized to conduct IFR flights on Federal airways. A helicopter instrument rating added on an airline transport pilot certificate is limited to commercial pilot privileges.

(g) *Evidentiary documents.* The following documents are satisfactory evidence for the purposes indicated:

(1) To show that the applicant is a member of the armed forces, an official identification card issued to the applicant by an armed force may be used.

(2) To show the applicant's discharge or release from an armed force, or his former membership therein, an original or a copy of a certificate of discharge or release may be used.

(3) To show current or previous status as a rated military pilot on flying status with a U.S. Armed Force, one of the following may be used:

(i) An official U.S. Armed Force order to flight duty as a military pilot.

(ii) An official U.S. Armed Force form or logbook showing military pilot status.

(iii) An official order showing that the applicant graduated from a U.S. military pilot school and is rated as a military pilot.

(4) To show flight time in military aircraft as a member of a U.S. Armed

Force, an appropriate U.S. Armed Force form or summary of it, or a certified United States military logbook may be used.

(5) To show pilot-in-command status, an official U.S. Armed Force record of a military checkout as pilot in command, may be used.

(6) To show instrument pilot qualification, a current instrument card issued by a U.S. Armed Force, or an official record of the satisfactory completion of an instrument flight check within the 12 months preceding the month of the application may be used. However, a Tactical (Pink) instrument card issued by the U.S. Army is not acceptable.

§ 61.75 Pilot certificate issued on basis of a foreign pilot license.

(a) *Purpose.* The holder of a current private, commercial, senior commercial, or airline transport pilot license issued by a foreign contracting State to the Convention on International Civil Aviation may apply for a pilot certificate under this section authorizing him to act as a pilot of a civil aircraft of U.S. registry.

(b) *Certificate issued.* A pilot certificate is issued to an applicant under this section, specifying the number and State of issuance of the foreign pilot license on which it is based. An applicant who holds a foreign private pilot license is issued a private pilot certificate, and an applicant who holds a foreign commercial, senior commercial, or airline transport pilot license is issued a commercial pilot certificate, if—

(1) He meets the requirements of this section;

(2) His foreign pilot license does not contain an endorsement that he has not met all of the standards of ICAO for that license; and

(3) He does not hold a U.S. pilot certificate of private pilot grade or higher.

(c) *Limitation on licenses used as basis for U.S. certificate.* Only one foreign pilot license may be used as a basis for issuing a pilot certificate under this section.

(d) *Aircraft ratings issued.* Aircraft ratings listed on the applicant's foreign pilot license, in addition to any issued after testing under the provisions of this part, are placed on the applicant's pilot certificate.

(e) *Instrument rating issued.* An instrument rating is issued to an applicant if—

(1) His foreign pilot license authorizes instrument privileges; and

(2) Within 24 months preceding the month in which he makes application for a certificate, he passed a test on the instrument flight rules in Subpart B of Part 91 of this chapter, including the related procedures for the operation of the aircraft under instrument flight rules.

(f) *Medical standards and certification.* An applicant must submit evidence that he currently meets the medical standards for the foreign pilot license on which the application for a certificate under this section is based. A current medical certificate issued under Part 67 of this chapter is accepted as evidence that the applicant meets those standards. However, a medical certificate issued under Part 67 of this chapter is not evidence that the applicant meets those standards outside the United States, unless the State that issued the applicant's foreign pilot license also accepts that medical certificate as evidence of meeting the medical standards for his foreign pilot license.

(g) *Limitations placed on pilot certificate.* (1) If the applicant cannot read, speak, and understand the English language, the Administrator places any limitation on the certificate that he considers necessary for safety.

(2) A certificate issued under this section is not valid for agricultural aircraft operations, or the operation of an aircraft in which persons or property are carried for compensation or hire. This limitation is also placed on the certificate.

(h) *Operating privileges and limitations.* The holder of a pilot certificate issued under this section may act as a pilot of a civil aircraft of U.S. registry in accordance with the pilot privileges authorized by the foreign pilot license on which that certificate is based, subject to the limitations of this part and any additional limitations placed on his certificate by the Administrator.

He is subject to these limitations while he is acting as a pilot of the aircraft within or outside the United States. However, he may not act as pilot in command, or in any other capacity as a required pilot flight crewmember, of a civil aircraft of U.S. registry that is carrying persons or property for compensation or hire.

(i) *Flight instructor certificate.* A pilot certificate issued under this section does not satisfy any of the requirements of this part for the issuance of a flight instructor certificate.

§ 61.77 Special purpose pilot certificate: Operation of U.S.-registered civil airplanes leased by a person not a U.S. citizen.

(a) *General.* The holder of a current foreign pilot certificate or license issued by a foreign contracting State to the Convention on International Civil Aviation, who meets the requirements of this section, may hold a special purpose pilot certificate authorizing the holder to perform pilot duties on a civil airplane of U.S. registry, leased to a person not a citizen of the United States, carrying persons or property for compensation or hire. Special purpose pilot certificates are issued under this section only for airplane types that can have a maximum passenger seating configuration, excluding any flight crewmember seat, of more than 30 seats or a maximum payload capacity (as defined, in § 135.2(e) of this chapter) of more than 7,500 pounds.

(b) *Eligibility.* To be eligible for the issuance or renewal of a certificate under this section, an applicant or a representative of the applicant must present the following to the Administrator:

(1) A current foreign pilot certificate or license, issued by the aeronautical authority of a foreign contracting State to the Convention on International Civil Aviation, or a facsimile acceptable to the Administrator. The certificate or license must authorize the applicant to perform the pilot duties to be authorized by a certificate issued under this section on the same airplane type as the leased airplane.

(2) A current certification by the lessee of the airplane—

(i) Stating that the applicant is employed by the lessee;

(ii) Specifying the airplane type on which the applicant will perform pilot duties; and

(iii) Stating that the applicant has received ground and flight instruction which qualifies the applicant to perform the duties to be assigned on the airplane.

(3) Documentation showing that the applicant has not reached the age of 60 and that the applicant currently meets the medical standards for the foreign pilot certificate or license required by paragraph (b)(1) of this section, except that a U.S. medical certificate issued under Part 67 of this chapter is not evidence that the applicant meets those standards unless the State which issued the applicant's foreign pilot certificate or license accepts a U.S. medical certificate as evidence of medical fitness for a pilot certificate or license.

(c) *Privileges.* The holder of a special purpose pilot certificate issued under this section may exercise the same privileges as those shown on the certificate or license specified in paragraph (b)(1) of this section, subject to the limitations specified in this section. The certificate holder is not subject to the requirements of §§ 61.55, 61.57, and 61.58 of this part.

(d) *Limitations.* Each certificate issued under this section is subject to the following limitations:

(1) It is valid only—

(i) For flights between foreign countries or for flights in foreign air commerce;

(ii) While it and the foreign pilot certificate or license required by paragraph (b)(1) of this section are in the certificate holder's personal possession and are current;

(iii) While the certificate holder is employed by the person to whom the airplane described in the certification required by paragraph (b)(2) of this section is leased;

(iv) While the certificate holder is performing pilot duties on the U.S.-registered civil airplane described in the certification required by paragraph (b)(2) of this section;

(v) While the medical documentation required by paragraph (b)(3) of this section is in the certificate holder's personal possession and is currently valid; and

(vi) While the certificate holder is under 60 years of age.

(2) Each certificate issued under this section contains the following:

(i) The name of the person to whom the U.S.-registered civil aircraft is leased.

(ii) The type of aircraft.

(iii) The limitation: "Issued under, and subject to, § 61.77 of the Federal Aviation Regulations."

(iv) The limitation: "Subject to the privileges and limitations shown on the holder's foreign pilot certificate or license."

(3) Any additional limitations placed on the certificate which the Administrator considers necessary.

(e) *Termination.* Each special purpose pilot certificate issued under this section terminates—

(1) When the lease agreement for the airplane described in the certification required by paragraph (b)(2) of this section terminates;

(2) When the foreign pilot certificate or license, or the medical documentation, required by paragraph (b) of this section is suspended, revoked, or no longer valid;

(3) When the certificate holder reaches the age of 60; or

(4) After 24 months after the month in which the special purpose pilot certificate was issued.

(f) *Surrender of certificate.* The certificate holder shall surrender the special purpose pilot certificate to the Administrator within 7 days after the date it terminates.

(g) *Renewal.* The certificate holder may have the certificate renewed by complying with the requirements of paragraph (b) of this section at the time of application for renewal.

[Doc. No. 19300, Amdt. 61–67, 45 FR 5671, Jan. 24, 1980]

Subpart C—Student Pilots

§ 61.81 Applicability.

This subpart prescribes the requirements for the issuance of student pilot certificates, the conditions under which those certificates are necessary, and the general operating rules for the holders of those certificates.

§ 61.83 Eligibility requirements: General.

To be eligible for a student pilot certificate, a person must—

(a) Be at least 16 years of age, or at least 14 years of age for a student pilot certificate limited to the operation of a glider or free balloon;

(b) Be able to read, speak, and understand the English language, or have such operating limitations placed on his pilot certificate as are necessary for the safe operation of aircraft, to be removed when he shows that he can read, speak, and understand the English language; and

(c) Hold at least a current third-class medical certificate issued under Part 67 of this chapter, or, in the case of glider or free balloon operations, certify that he has no known medical defect that makes him unable to pilot a glider or a free balloon.

[Doc. No. 11802, Amdt. 61-60, 38 FR 3161, Feb. 1, 1973, as amended by Amdt. 61-64, 41 FR 51392, Nov. 22, 1976]

§ 61.85 Application.

An application for a student pilot certificate is made on a form and in a manner provided by the Administrator and is submitted to—

(a) A designated aviation medical examiner when applying for an FAA medical certificate in the United States; or

(b) An FAA operations inspector or designated pilot examiner, accompanied by a current FAA medical certificate, or in the case of an application for a glider or free balloon pilot certificate it may be accompanied by a certification by the applicant that he has no known medical defect that makes him unable to pilot a glider or free balloon.

[Doc. No. 11802, Amdt. 61-60, 38 FR 3161, Feb. 1, 1973, as amended by Amdt. 61-72, 47 FR 35693, Aug. 16, 1982]

§ 61.87 Requirements for solo flight.

(a) *General.* A student pilot may not operate an aircraft in solo flight until he has complied with the require-

ments of this section. As used in this subpart the term solo flight means that flight time during which a student pilot is the sole occupant of the aircraft, or that flight time during which he acts as pilot in command of an airship requiring more than one flight crewmember.

(b) *Aeronautical knowledge.* He must have demonstrated to an authorized instructor that he is familiar with the flight rules of Part 91 of this chapter which are pertinent to student solo flights.

(c) *Flight proficiency training.* He must have received ground and flight instruction in at least the following procedures and operations:

(1) *In airplanes.* (i) Flight preparation procedures, including preflight inspection and powerplant operation;

(ii) Ground maneuvering and runups;

(iii) Straight and level flight, climbs, turns, and descents;

(iv) Flight at minimum controllable airspeeds, and stall recognition and recovery;

(v) Normal takeoffs and landings;

(vi) Airport traffic patterns, including collision avoidance precautions and wake turbulence; and

(vii) Emergencies, including elementary emergency landings.

Instruction must be given by a flight instructor who is authorized to give instruction in airplanes.

(2) *In rotorcraft other than single-place gyroplanes.* (i) Flight preparation procedures, including preflight inspections and powerplant operation;

(ii) Ground maneuvering and runups;

(iii) Hovering turns and air taxi (helicopter only);

(iv) Straight and level flight, turns, climbs, and descents;

(v) Rapid decelerations (helicopters only);

(vi) Maneuvering by ground references, airport traffic patterns including collision avoidance precautions;

(vii) Normal takeoffs and landings; and

(viii) Simulated emergency procedures, including autorotational descents with a power recovery or running landing in gyroplanes, a power recovery to a hover in single-engine helicopters, or approaches to a hover or landing with one engine inoperative in multiengine helicopters.

Instruction must be given by a flight instructor who is authorized to give instruction in helicopters or gyroplanes, as appropriate.

(3) *In single-place gyroplanes.* (i) Flight preparation procedures, including preflight inspection and powerplant operation;

(ii) Ground maneuvering and runups;

(iii) Straight and level flight, turns, climbs, and descents;

(iv) Navigation by ground references, airport traffic patterns, and collision avoidance procedures;

(v) Normal takeoffs and landings;

(vi) Simulated emergency procedures, including autorotational descents with a power recovery or a running landing; and

(vii) At least three successful flights in a gyroplane under the observation of a qualified instructor. Items in paragraphs (c)(3) (iii) and (iv) of this section may be accomplished in a dual-control helicopter or gyroplane. Instruction must be given by a flight instructor who is authorized to give instruction in helicopters or gyroplanes, as appropriate.

Instruction must be given by a flight instructor who is authorized to give instruction in airplanes, or rotorcraft.

(4) *In gliders.* (i) Flight preparation procedures, including preflight inspections, towline rigging, signals, and release procedures;

(ii) Aero tows or ground tows;

(iii) Straight glides, turns, and spirals;

(iv) Flight at minimum controllable airspeeds, and stall recognition and recoveries;

(v) Traffic patterns, including collision avoidance precautions; and

(vi) Normal landings.

Instruction must be given by a flight instructor who is authorized to give instruction in gliders.

(5) *In airships.* (i) Flight preparation procedures, including preflight inspection and powerplant operation;

(ii) Rigging, ballasting, controlling pressure in the ballonets, and superheating;

(iii) Takeoffs and ascents;

(iv) Straight and level flight, climbs, turns, and descents; and

(v) Landings with positive and with negative static balance.

Instruction must be given by an authorized flight instructor or the holder of a commercial pilot certificate with a lighter-than-air category and airship class rating.

(6) *In free balloons.* (i) Flight preparation procedures, including preflight operations;

(ii) Operation of hot air or gas source, ballast, valves, and rip panels, as appropriate;

(iii) Liftoffs and climbs; and

(iv) Descents, landings, and emergency use of rip panel (may be simulated).

Instruction must be given by an authorized flight instructor or the holder of a commercial pilot certificate with a lighter-than-air category and free balloon class rating.

(d) *Flight instructor endorsements.* A student pilot may not operate an aircraft in solo flight unless his student pilot certificate is endorsed, and unless within the preceding 90 days his pilot logbook has been endorsed, by an authorized flight instructor who—

(1) Has given him instruction in the make and model of aircraft in which the solo flight is made;

(2) Finds that he has met the requirements of this section; and

(3) Finds that he is competent to make a safe solo flight in that aircraft.

[Doc. No. 11802, Amdt. 61-60, 38 FR 3161, Feb. 1, 1973, as amended at 38 FR 6276, Mar. 8, 1973; Amdt. 61-64, 41 FR 51392, Nov. 22, 1976; Amdt. 61-77, 51 FR 40703, Nov. 7, 1986]

§ 61.89   General limitations.

(a) A student pilot may not act as pilot in command of an aircraft—

(1) That is carrying a passenger;

(2) That is carrying property for compensation or hire;

(3) For compensation or hire;

(4) In furtherance of a business; or

(5) On an international flight, except that a student pilot may make

solo training flights from Haines, Gustavus, or Juneau, Alaska, to White Horse, Yukon, Canada, and return, over the province of British Columbia.

(b) A student pilot may not act as a required pilot flight crewmember on any aircraft for which more than one pilot is required, except when receiving flight instruction from an authorized flight instructor on board an airship and no person other than a required flight crewmember is carried on the aircraft.

§ 61.91   Aircraft limitations: Pilot in command.

A student pilot may not serve as pilot in command of any airship requiring more than one flight crewmember unless he has met the pertinent requirements prescribed in § 61.87.

§ 61.93   Cross-country flight requirements.

(a) *General.* A student pilot may not operate an aircraft in a solo cross-country flight, nor may he, except in an emergency, make a solo flight landing at any point other than the airport of takeoff, until he meets the requirements prescribed in this section. However, an authorized flight instructor may allow a student pilot to practice solo landings and takeoffs at another airport within 25 nautical miles from the airport at which the student pilot receives instruction if he finds that the student pilot is competent to make those landings and takeoffs. As used in this section the term cross-country flight means a flight beyond a radius of 25 nautical miles from the point of takeoff.

(b) *Flight training.* A student pilot must receive instruction from an authorized instructor in at least the following pilot operations pertinent to the aircraft to be operated in a solo cross-country flight:

(1) For solo cross-country in airplanes—

(i) The use of aeronautical charts, pilotage, and elementary dead reckoning using the magnetic compass;

(ii) The use of radio for VFR navigation, and for two-way communication;

(iii) Control of an airplane by reference to flight instruments;

(iv) Short field and soft field procedures, and crosswind takeoffs and landings;

(v) Recognition of critical weather situations, estimating visibility while in flight, and the procurement and use of aeronautical weather reports and forecasts; and

(vi) Cross-country emergency procedures.

(2) For solo cross-country in rotorcraft—

(i) The use of aeronautical charts and the magnetic compass for pilotage and for elementary dead reckoning;

(ii) The recognition of critical weather situations, estimating visibility while in flight, and the procurement and use of aeronautical weather reports and forecasts; and

(iii) Radio communications; and

(iv) Cross-country emergencies.

(3) For solo cross-country in gliders—

(i) The recognition of critical weather situations and conditions favorable for soaring flight, and the procurement and use of aeronautical weather reports and forecasts;

(ii) The use of aeronautical charts and the magnetic compass for pilotage; and

(iii) Cross-country emergency procedures.

(4) For student cross-country in airships—

(i) The use of aeronautical charts and the magnetic compass for pilotage and dead reckoning, and the use of radio for navigation and two-way communications;

(ii) The control of an airship solely by reference to flight instruments;

(iii) The control of gas pressures, with regard to superheating and altitude changes;

(iv) The recognition of critical weather situations, and the procurement and use of aeronautical weather reports and forecasts; and

(v) Cross-country emergency procedures.

(5) For solo cross-country in free balloons—

(i) The use of aeronautical charts and the magnetic compass for pilotage;

(ii) The recognition of critical weather situations, and the procurement and use of aeronautical weather reports and forecasts; and

(iii) Cross-country emergency procedures.

(c) *Flight instructor endorsements.* A student pilot must have the following endorsements from an authorized flight instructor:

(1) An endorsement on his student pilot certificate stating that he has received instruction in solo cross-country flying and the applicable training requirements of this section, and is competent to make cross-country solo flights in the category of aircraft involved.

(2) An endorsement in his pilot logbook that the instructor has reviewed the preflight planning and preparation for each solo cross-country flight, and he is prepared to make the flight safely under the known circumstances and the conditions listed by the instructor in the logbook. The instructor may also endorse the logbook for repeated solo cross-country flights under stipulated conditions over a course not more than 50 nautical miles from the point of departure if he has given the student flight instruction in both directions over the route, including takeoffs and landings at the airports to be used.

§61.95 Operations in a terminal control area and at airports located within a terminal control area.

(a) **A student pilot may not operate an aircraft on a solo flight in the airspace of a terminal control area unless—**

(1) **The student pilot has received both ground and flight instruction from an authorized instructor on that terminal control area and the flight instruction was received in the specific terminal control area for which solo flight is authorized;**

(2) **The logbook of that student pilot has been endorsed within the preceding 90 days for conducting solo flight in that specific terminal control area by the instructor who gave the flight training; and**

(3) **The logbook endorsement specifies that the student pilot has received the required ground and flight instruction and has been found competent to conduct solo flight in that specific terminal control area.**

(b) **Pursuant to §91.90(b), a student pilot may not operate an aircraft on a solo flight to, from, or at an airport located within a terminal control area unless—**

(1) **That student pilot has received both ground and flight instruction from an authorized instructor to operate at that airport and the flight and ground instruction has been received at the specific airport for which the solo flight is authorized;**

(2) **The logbook of that student pilot has been endorsed within the preceding 90 days for conducting solo flight at that specific airport by the instructor who gave the flight training; and**

(3) **The logbook endorsement specifies that the student pilot has received the required ground and flight instruction and has been found competent to conduct solo flight operations at that specific airport.**

Subpart D—Private Pilots

§61.101 Applicability.

This subpart prescribes the requirements for the issuance of private pilot certificates and ratings, the conditions under which those certificates and ratings are necessary, and the general operating rules for the holders of those certificates and ratings.

§61.103 Eligibility requirements: General.

To be eligible for a private pilot certificate, a person must—

(a) Be at least 17 years of age, except that a private pilot certificate with a free balloon or a glider rating only may be issued to a qualified applicant who is at least 16 years of age;

(b) Be able to read, speak and understand the English language, or have such operating limitations placed on his pilot certificate as are necessary for the safe operation of aircraft, to be removed when he shows that he can read, speak, and understand the English language;

(c) Hold at least a current third-class medical certificate issued under Part 67 of this chapter, or, in the case of a glider or free balloon rating, certify that he has no known medical defect that makes him unable to pilot a glider or free balloon, as appropriate;

(d) Pass a written test on the subject areas on which instruction or home study is required by §61.105;

(e) Pass an oral and flight test on procedures and maneuvers selected by an FAA inspector or examiner to determine the applicant's competency in the flight operations on which instruction is required by the flight proficiency provisions of §61.107; and

(f) Comply with the sections of this part that apply to the rating he seeks.

§61.105 Aeronautical knowledge.

An applicant for a private pilot certificate must have logged ground instruction from an authorized instructor or must present evidence showing that he has satisfactorily completed a course of instruction or home study in at least the following areas of aeronautical knowledge appropriate to the category of aircraft for which a rating is sought.

(a) *Airplanes and rotorcraft.* (1) The accident reporting requirements of the National Transportation Safety Board and the Federal Aviation Regulations applicable to private pilot privileges, limitations, and flight operations for airplanes or rotorcraft, as appropriate, the use of the "Airman's Information Manual," and FAA advisory circulars;

(2) VFR navigation using pilotage, dead reckoning, and radio aids;

(3) The recognition of critical weather situations from the ground and in flight, the procurement and use of aeronautical weather reports and forecasts;

(4) The safe and efficient operation of airplanes or rotorcraft, as appropriate, including high-density airport operations, collision avoidance precautions, and radio communication procedures; and

(5) Basic aerodynamics and the principles of flight which apply to airplanes or rotorcraft, as appropriate.

(b) *Gliders.* (1) The accident reporting requirements of the National Transportation Safety Board and the Federal Aviation Regulations applicable to glider pilot privileges, limitations, and flight operations;

(2) Glider navigation, including the use of aeronautical charts and the magnetic compass;

(3) Recognition of weather situations of concern to the glider pilot, and the procurement and use of aeronautical weather reports and forecasts; and

(4) The safe and efficient operation of gliders, including ground and aero tow procedures, signals, and safety precautions.

(c) *Airships.* (1) The Federal Aviation Regulations applicable to private lighter-than-air pilot privileges, limitations, and airship flight operations;

(2) Airship navigation, including pilotage, dead reckoning, and the use of radio aids;

(3) The recognition of weather conditions of concern to the airship pilot, and the procurement and use of aeronautical weather reports and forecasts; and

(4) Airship operations, including free ballooning, the effects of superheating, and positive and negative lift.

(d) *Free balloons.* (1) The Federal Aviation Regulations applicable to private free balloon pilot privileges, limitations, and flight operations;

(2) The use of aeronautical charts and the magnetic compass for free balloon navigation;

(3) The recognition of weather conditions of concern to the free balloon pilot, and the procurement and use of aeronautical weather reports and forecasts appropriate to free balloon operations; and

(4) Operating principles and procedures of free balloons, including gas and hot air inflation systems.

[Doc. No. 11802, Amdt. 61-60, 38 FR 3161, Feb. 1, 1973, as amended by Amdt. 61-77, 51 FR 40703, Nov. 7, 1986]

§ 61.107   Flight proficiency.

The applicant for a private pilot certificate must have logged instruction from an authorized flight instructor in at least the following pilot operations. In addition, his logbook must contain an endorsement by an authorized flight instructor who has found him competent to perform each of those operations safely as a private pilot.

(a) *In airplanes.* (1) Preflight operations, including weight and balance determination, line inspection, and airplane servicing;

(2) Airport and traffic pattern operations, including operations at controlled airports, radio communications, and collision avoidance precautions;

(3) Flight maneuvering by reference to ground objects;

(4) Flight at critically slow airspeeds, and the recognition of and recovery from imminent and full stalls entered from straight flight and from turns;

(5) Normal and crosswind takeoffs and landings;

(6) Control and maneuvering an airplane solely by reference to instruments, including descents and climbs using radio aids or radar directives;

(7) Cross-country flying, using pilotage, dead reckoning, and radio aids, including one 2-hour flight;

(8) Maximum performance takeoffs and landings;

(9) Night flying, including takeoffs, landings, and VFR navigation; and

(10) Emergency operations, including simulated aircraft and equipment malfunctions.

(b) *In helicopters.* (1) Preflight operations, including the line inspection and servicing of helicopters;

(2) Hovering, air taxiing, and maneuvering by ground references;

(3) Airport and traffic pattern operations, including collision avoidance precautions;

(4) Cross-country flying, using pilotage, dead reckoning, and radio aids, including one 1-hour flight;

(5) Operations in confined areas and on pinnacles, rapid decelerations, landings on slopes, high-altitude takeoffs, and run-on landings;

(6) Night flying, including takeoffs, landings, and VFR navigation; and

(7) Simulated emergency procedures, including aircraft and equipment malfunctions, approaches to a hover or landing with an engine inoperative in a multiengine helicopter, or autorotational descents with a power recovery to a hover in single-engine helicopters.

(c) *In gyroplanes.* (1) Preflight operations, including the line inspection and servicing of gyroplanes;

(2) Flight maneuvering by ground references;

(3) Maneuvering at critically slow airspeeds, and the recognition of and recovery from high rates of descent at low airspeeds;

(4) Airport and traffic pattern operations, including collision avoidance precautions and radio communication procedures;

(5) Cross-country flying by pilotage, dead reckoning, and the use of radio aids; and

(6) Emergency procedures, including maximum performance takeoffs and landings.

(d) *In gliders.* (1) Preflight operations, including the installation of wings and tail surfaces specifically designed for quick removal and installation by pilots, and line inspection;

(2) Ground (auto or winch) tow or aero tow (the applicant's certificate is limited to the kind of tow selected);

(3) Precision maneuvering, including steep turns and spirals in both directions;

(4) The correct use of critical sailplane performance speeds;

(5) Flight at critically slow airspeeds, and the recognition of and recovery from imminent and full stalls entered from straight and from turning flight; and

(6) Accuracy approaches and landings with the nose of the glider stopping short of and within 200 feet of a line or mark.

(e) *In airships.* (1) Ground handling, mooring, rigging, and preflight operations;

(2) Takeoffs and landing with static lift, and with negative and positive lift, and the use of two-way radio;

(3) Straight and level flight, climbs, turns, and descents;

(4) Precision flight maneuvering;

(5) Navigation, using pilotage, dead reckoning, and radio aids; and

(6) Simulated emergencies, including equipment malfunction, the valving of gas, and the loss of power on one engine.

(f) *In free balloons.* (1) Rigging and tethering, including the installation of baskets and burners specifically designed for quick removal or installation by a pilot and the interchange of baskets or burners, when provided for in the type certificate data, classified as preventive maintenance, and subject to the recording requirements of §43.9 of this chapter;

(2) Operation of burner, if airborne heater used;

(3) Ascents and descents;

(4) Landing; and

(5) Emergencies, including the use of the ripcord (may be simulated).

[Doc. No. 11802, Amdt. 61-60, 38 FR 3161, Feb. 1, 1973, as amended by Amdt. 61-77, 51 FR 40704, Nov. 7, 1986; Amdt. 61-79, 52 FR 17277, May 6, 1987]

§61.109 Airplane rating: Aeronautical experience.

An applicant for a private pilot certificate with an airplane rating must have had at least a total of 40 hours of flight instruction and solo flight time which must include the following:

(a) Twenty hours of flight instruction from an authorized flight instructor, including at least—

(1) Three hours of cross country;

(2) Three hours at night, including 10 takeoffs and landings for applicants seeking night flying privileges; and

(3) Three hours in airplanes in preparation for the private pilot flight test within 60 days prior to that test.

An applicant who does not meet the night flying requirement in paragraph (a)(2) of this section is issued a private pilot certificate bearing the limitation "Night flying prohibited." This limitation may be removed if the holder of the certificate shows that he has met the requirements of paragraph (a)(2) of this section.

(b) Twenty hours of solo flight time, including at least:

(1) Ten hours in airplanes.

(2) Ten hours of cross-country flights, each flight with a landing at a point more than 50 nautical miles from the original departure point. One flight must be of at least 300 nautical miles with landings at a minimum of three points, one of which is at least 100 nautical miles from the original departure point.

(3) Three solo takeoffs and landings to a full stop at an airport with an operating control tower.

[Doc. No. 11802, Amdt. 61-60, 38 FR 3161, Feb. 1, 1973, as amended by Amdt. 61-73, 47 FR 46065, Oct. 14, 1982]

§ 61.111   Cross-country   flights: Pilots based on small islands.

(a) An applicant who shows that he is located on an island from which the required flights cannot be accomplished without flying over water more than 10 nautical miles from the nearest shoreline need not comply with paragraph (b)(2) of § 61.109. However, if other airports that permit civil operations are available to which a flight may be made without flying over water more than 10 nautical miles from the nearest shoreline, he must show that he has completed two round trip solo flights between those two airports that are farthest apart, including a landing at each airport on both flights.

(b) The pilot certificate issued to a person under paragraph (a) of this section contains an endorsement with the following limitation which may be subsequently amended to include another island if the applicant complies with paragraph (a) of this section with respect to that island:

Passenger carrying prohibited on flights more than 10 nautical miles from (appropriate island).

(c) If an applicant for a private pilot certificate under paragraph (a) of this section does not have at least 3 hours of solo cross-country flight time, including a round trip flight to an airport at least 50 nautical miles from the place of departure with at least two full stop landings at different points along the route, his pilot certificate is also endorsed as follows:

Holder does not meet the cross-country flight requirements of ICAO.

(d) The holder of a private pilot certificate with an endorsement described in paragraph (b) or (c) of this section, is entitled to a removal of the endorsement, if he presents satisfactory evidence to an FAA inspector or designated pilot examiner that he has complied with the applicable solo cross-country flight requirements and has passed a practical test on cross-country flying.

§ 61.113   Rotorcraft   rating: Aeronautical experience.

An applicant for a private pilot certificate with a rotorcraft category rating must have at least the following aeronautical experience:

(a) After April 30, 1987, *for a helicopter class rating*, 40 hours of flight instruction and solo flight time in aircraft, including at least—

(1) 20 hours of flight instruction from an authorized flight instructor, 15 hours of which must be in a helicopter, including—

(i) 3 hours of cross-country flying in helicopters;

(ii) 3 hours of night flying in helicopters, including 10 takeoffs and landings, each of which must be separated by an en route phase of flight;

(iii) 3 hours in helicopters in preparation for the private pilot flight test within 60 days before that test; and

(iv) A flight in a helicopter with a landing at a point other than an airport; and

(2) 20 hours of solo flight time, 15 hours of which must be in a helicopter, including at least—

(i) 3 hours of cross-country flying in helicopters, including one flight with a landing at three or more points, each of which must be more than 25 nautical miles from each of the other two points; and

(ii) Three takeoffs and landings in helicopters at an airport with an operating control tower, each of which must be separated by an en route phase of flight.

(b) After April 30, 1987, *for a gyroplane class rating*, 40 hours of flight instruction and solo flight time in aircraft, including at least—

(1) 20 hours of flight instruction from an authorized flight instructor, 15 hours of which must be in a gyroplane, including—

(i) 3 hours of cross-country flying in gyroplanes;

(ii) 3 hours of night flying in gyroplanes, including 10 takeoffs and landings; and

(iii) 3 hours in gyroplanes in preparation for the private pilot flight test within 60 days before that test; and

(2) 20 hours of solo flight time, 10 hours of which must be in a gyroplane, including—

(i) 3 hours of cross-country flying in gyroplanes, including one flight with a landing at three or more points, each of which must be more than 25 nautical miles from each of the other two points; and

(ii) Three takeoffs and landings in gyroplanes at an airport with an operating control tower.

(c) An applicant who does not meet the night flying requirement in paragraphs (a)(1)(ii) or (b)(1)(ii) of this section is issued a private pilot certificate bearing the limitation "night flying prohibited." This limitation may be removed if the holder of the certificate demonstrates compliance with the requirements of paragraphs (a)(1)(ii) or (b)(1)(ii) of this section, as appropriate. This limitation is not placed on the certificate of an applicant who qualifies under paragraph (d) or (e) of this section.

(d) Until May 1, 1987, for a helicopter rating an applicant must have at least a total of 40 hours of flight instruction and solo flight time in aircraft with at least 15 hours of solo flight time in helicopters, which must include—

(1) A takeoff and landing at an airport that serves both airplanes and helicopters;

(2) A flight with a landing at a point other than an airport; and

(3) Three hours of cross-country flying, including one flight with landings at three or more points, each of which must be more than 25 nautical miles from each of the other two points.

(e) Until May 1, 1987, for a gyroplane rating an applicant must have at least a total of 40 hours of flight instruction and solo flight time in aircraft with at least 10 hours of solo flight time in a gyroplane, which must include—

(1) Flights with takeoffs and landings at paved and unpaved airports; and

(2) Three hours of cross-country flying, including a flight with landings at three or more points, each of which must be more than 25 nautical miles from each of the other two points.

[Doc. No. 24550, Amdt. 61-77, 51 FR 40704, Nov. 7, 1986, as amended by Amdt. 61-78, 52 FR 4846, Feb. 17, 1987]

§ 61.115 Glider rating: Aeronautical experience.

An applicant for a private pilot certificate with a glider rating must have logged at least one of the following:

(a) Seventy solo glider flights, including 20 flights during which 360° turns were made.

(b) Seven hours of solo flight in gliders, including 35 glider flights launched by ground tows, or 20 glider flights launched by aero tows.

(c) Forty hours of flight time in gliders and single-engine airplanes, including 10 solo glider flights during which 360° turns were made.

§ 61.117 Lighter-than-air rating: Aeronautical experience.

An applicant for a private pilot certificate with a lighter-than-air category rating must have at least the aeronautical experience prescribed in paragraph (a) or (b) of this section, appropriate to the rating sought.

(a) *Airships.* A total of 50 hours of flight time as pilot with at least 25 hours in airships, which must include 5 hours of solo flight time in airships, or time performing the functions of pilot in command of an airship for which more than one pilot is required.

(b) *Free balloons.* (1) If a gas balloon or a hot air balloon with an airborne heater is used, a total of 10 hours in free balloons with at least six flights under the supervision of a person holding a commercial pilot certificate with a free balloon rating. These flights must include—

(i) Two flights, each of at least 1 hour's duration, if a gas balloon is used, or of 30 minutes' duration, if a hot air balloon with an airborne heater is used;

(ii) One ascent under control to 5,000 feet above the point of takeoff, if a gas balloon is used, or 3,000 feet above the point of takeoff, if a hot air balloon with an airborne heater is used; and

(iii) One solo flight in a free balloon.

(2) If a hot air balloon without an airborne heater is used, six flights in a free balloon under the supervision of a commercial balloon pilot, including at least one solo flight.

[Doc. No. 11802, Amdt. 61-60, 38 FR 3161, Feb. 1, 1973, as amended at 38 FR 9292, Apr. 13, 1973]

§ 61.118   Private pilot privileges and limitations: Pilot in command.

Except as provided in paragraphs (a) through (d) of this section, a private pilot may not act as pilot in command of an aircraft that is carrying passengers or property for compensation or hire; nor may he, for compensation or hire, act as pilot in command of an aircraft.

(a) A private pilot may, for compensation or hire, act as pilot in command of an aircraft in connection with any business or employment if the flight is only incidental to that business or employment and the aircraft does not carry passengers or property for compensation or hire.

(b) A private pilot may share the operating expenses of a flight with his passengers.

(c) A private pilot who is an aircraft salesman and who has at least 200 hours of logged flight time may demonstrate an aircraft in flight to a prospective buyer.

(d) A private pilot may act as pilot in command of an aircraft used in a passenger-carrying airlift sponsored by a charitable organization, and for which the passengers make a donation to the organization, if—

(1) The sponsor of the airlift notifies the FAA General Aviation District Office having jurisdiction over the area concerned, at least 7 days before the flight, and furnishes any essential information that the office requests;

(2) The flight is conducted from a public airport adequate for the aircraft used, or from another airport that has been approved for the operation by an FAA inspector;

(3) He has logged at least 200 hours of flight time;

(4) No acrobatic or formation flights are conducted;

(5) Each aircraft used is certificated in the standard category and complies with the 100-hour inspection requirement of § 91.169 of this chapter; and

(6) The flight is made under VFR during the day.

For the purpose of paragraph (d) of this section, a "charitable organization" means an organization listed in Publication No. 78 of the Department of the Treasury called the "Cumulative List of Organizations described in section 170(c) of the Internal Revenue Code of 1954," as amended from time to time by published supplemental lists.

§ 61.119   Free balloon rating: Limitations.

(a) If the applicant for a free balloon rating takes his flight test in a hot air balloon with an airborne heater, his pilot certificate contains an endorsement restricting the exercise of the privilege of that rating to hot air balloons with airborne heaters. The restriction may be deleted when the holder of the certificate obtains the pilot experience required for a rating on a gas balloon.

(b) If the applicant for a free balloon rating takes his flight test in a hot air balloon without an airborne heater, his pilot certificate contains an endorsement restricting the exercise of the privileges of that rating to hot air balloons without airborne heaters. The restriction may be deleted when the holder of the certificate obtains the pilot experience and passes the tests required for a rating on a free balloon with an airborne heater or a gas balloon.

§ 61.120   Private pilot privileges and limitations: Second in command of aircraft requiring more than one required pilot.

Except as provided in paragraphs (a) through (d) of § 61.118 a private pilot may not, for compensation or hire, act as second in command of an aircraft that is type certificated for more than one required pilot, nor may he act as second in command of such an aircraft that is carrying passengers or property for compensation or hire.

Subpart E—Commercial Pilots

§ 61.121 Applicability.

This subpart prescribes the requirements for the issuance of commercial pilot certificates and ratings, the conditions under which those certificates and ratings are necessary, and the limitations upon those certificates and ratings.

§ 61.123 Eligibility requirements: General.

To be eligible for a commercial pilot certificate, a person must—

(a) Be at least 18 years of age;

(b) Be able to read, speak, and understand the English language, or have such operating limitations placed on his pilot certificate as are necessary for safety, to be removed when he shows that he can read, speak, and understand the English language;

(c) Hold at least a valid second-class medical certificate issued under Part 67 of this chapter, or, in the case of a glider or free balloon rating, certify that he has no known medical deficiency that makes him unable to pilot a glider or a free balloon, as appropriate;

(d) Pass a written examination appropriate to the aircraft rating sought on the subjects in which ground instruction is required by § 61.125;

(e) Pass an oral and flight test appropriate to the rating he seeks, covering items selected by the inspector or examiner from those on which training is required by § 61.127; and

(f) Comply with the provisions of this subpart which apply to the rating he seeks.

[Doc. No. 11802, Amdt. 61-60, 38 FR 3161, Feb. 1, 1973, as amended by Amdt. 61-64, 41 FR 51392, Nov. 22, 1976]

§ 61.125 Aeronautical knowledge.

An applicant for a commercial pilot certificate must have logged ground instruction from an authorized instructor, or must present evidence showing that he has satisfactorily completed a course of instruction or home study, in at least the following areas of aeronautical knowledge appropriate to the category of aircraft for which a rating is sought.

(a) *Airplanes.* (1) The regulations of this chapter governing the operations, privileges, and limitations of a commercial pilot, and the accident reporting requirements of the National Transportation Safety Board;

(2) Basic aerodynamics and the principles of flight which apply to airplanes; and

(3) Airplane operations, including the use of flaps, retractable landing gears, controllable propellers, high altitude operation with and without pressurization, loading and balance computations, and the significance and use of airplane performance speeds.

(b) *Rotorcraft.* (1) The regulations of this chapter which apply to the operations, privileges, and limitations of a commercial rotorcraft pilot, and the accident reporting requirements of the National Transportation Safety Board;

(2) Meteorology, including the characteristics of air masses and fronts, elements of weather forecasting, and the procurement and use of aeronautical weather reports and forecasts;

(3) The use of aeronautical charts and the magnetic compass for pilotage and dead reckoning, and the use of radio aids for VFR navigation;

(4) The safe and efficient operation of helicopters or gyroplanes, as appropriate to the rating sought; and

(5) Basic aerodynamics and principles of flight which apply to rotorcraft and the significance and use of performance charts.

(c) *Gliders.* (1) The regulations of this chapter pertinent to commercial glider pilot operations, privileges, and limitations, and the accident reporting requirements of the National Transportation Safety Board;

(2) Glider navigation, including the use of aeronautical charts and the magnetic compass, and radio orientation;

(3) The recognition of weather situations of concern to the glider pilot from the ground and in flight, and the procurement and use of aeronautical weather reports and forecasts; and

(4) The safe and efficient operation of gliders, including ground and aero tow procedures, signals, critical sailplane performance speeds, and safety precautions.

(d) *Airships.* (1) The regulations of this chapter pertinent to airship operations, VFR and IFR, including the privileges and limitations of a commercial airship pilot;

(2) Airship navigation, including pilotage, dead reckoning, and the use of radio aids for VFR and IFR navigation, and IFR approaches;

(3) The use and limitations of the required flight instruments;

(4) ATC procedures for VFR and IFR operations, and the use of IFR charts and approach plates;

(5) Meteorology, including the characteristics of air masses and fronts, and the procurement and use of aeronautical weather reports and forecasts;

(6) Airship ground and flight instruction procedures; and

(7) Airship operating procedures and emergency operations, including free ballooning procedures.

(e) *Free balloons.* (1) The regulations of this chapter pertinent to commercial free balloon piloting privileges, limitations, and flight operations;

(2) The use of aeronautical charts and the magnetic compass for free balloon navigation;

(3) The recognition of weather conditions significant to free balloon flight operations, and the procurement and use of aeronautical weather reports and forecasts appropriate to free ballooning;

(4) Free balloon flight and ground instruction procedures; and

(5) Operating principles and procedures for free balloons, including emergency procedures such as crowd control and protection, high wind and water landings, and operations in proximity to buildings and power lines.

[Doc. No. 11802, Amdt. 61-60, 38 FR 3161, Feb. 1, 1973, as amended by Amdt. 61-77, 51 FR 40704, Nov. 7, 1986]

§ 61.127   Flight proficiency.

The applicant for a commercial pilot certificate must have logged instruction from an authorized flight instructor in at least the following pilot operations. In addition, his logbook must contain an endorsement by an authorized flight instructor who has given him the instruction certifying that he has found the applicant prepared to perform each of those operations competently as a commercial pilot.

(a) *Airplanes.* (1) Preflight duties, including load and balance determination, line inspection, and aircraft servicing;

(2) Flight at critically slow airspeeds, recognition of imminent stalls, and recovery from stalls with and without power;

(3) Normal and crosswind takeoffs and landings, using precision approaches, flaps, power as appropriate, and specified approach speeds;

(4) Maximum performance takeoffs and landings, climbs, and descents;

(5) Operation of an airplane equipped with a retractable landing gear, flaps, and controllable propeller(s), including normal and emergency operations; and

(6) Emergency procedures, such as coping with power loss or equipment malfunctions, fire in flight, collision avoidance precautions, and engine-out procedures if a multiengine airplane is used.

(b) *Helicopters.* (1) Preflight duties, including line inspection and helicopter servicing;

(2) Straight and level flight, climbs, turns, and descents;

(3) Air taxiing, hovering, and maneuvering by ground references;

(4) Normal and crosswind takeoffs and landings;

(5) Recognition of and recovery from imminent flight at critical/rapid descent with power (settling with power);

(6) Airport and traffic pattern operations, including collision avoidance precautions and radio communications;

(7) Cross-country flight operations;

(8) Operations in confined areas and on pinnacles, rapid decelerations, landing on slopes, high-altitude takeoffs, and run-on landings; and

(9) Simulated emergency procedures, including failure of an engine or other component or system, and approaches to a hover or landing with one engine inoperative in multiengine helicopters, or autorotational descents with a power recovery to a hover in single-engine helicopters.

(c) *Gyroplanes.* (1) Preflight operations, including line inspection and gyroplane servicing;

(2) Straight and level flight, turns, climbs, and descents;

(3) Flight maneuvering by ground references;

(4) Maneuvering at critically slow airspeeds, and the recognition of and recovery from high rates of descent at slow airspeeds;

(5) Normal and crosswind takeoffs and landings;

(6) Airport and traffic pattern operations, including collision avoidance precautions and radio communications;

(7) Cross-country flight operations; and

(8) Emergency procedures, such as power failures, equipment malfunctions, maximum performance takeoffs and landings and simulated liftoffs at low airspeed and high angles of attack.

(d) *Gliders.* (1) Preflight duties, including glider assembly and preflight inspection;

(2) Glider launches by ground (auto or winch) or by aero tows (the applicant's certificate is limited to the kind of tow selected);

(3) Precision maneuvering, including straight glides, turns to headings, steep turns, and spirals in both directions;

(4) The correct use of sailplane performance speeds, flight at critically slow airspeeds, and the recognition of and recovery from stalls entered from straight flight and from turns; and

(5) Accuracy approaches and landings, with the nose of the glider coming to rest short of and within 100 feet of a line or mark.

(e) *Airships.* (1) Ground handling, mooring, and preflight operations;

(2) Straight and level flight, turns, climbs, and descents, under VFR and simulated IFR conditions;

(3) Takeoffs and landings with positive and with negative static lift;

(4) Turns and figure eights;

(5) Precision turns to headings under simulated IFR conditions;

(6) Preparing and filing IFR flight plans, and complying with IFR clearances;

(7) IFR radio navigation and instrument approach procedures;

(8) Cross-country flight operations, using pilotage, dead reckoning, and radio aids; and

(9) Emergency operations, including engine-out operations, free ballooning an airship, and ripcord procedures (may be simulated).

(f) *Free balloons.* (1) Assembly of basket and burner to the envelope, and rigging, inflating, and tethering of a free balloon;

(2) Ground and flight crew briefing;

(3) Ascents;

(4) Descents;

(5) Landings;

(6) Operation of airborne heater, if balloon is so equipped; and

(7) Emergency operations, including the use of the ripcord (may be simulated), and recovery from a terminal velocity descent if a balloon with an airborne heater is used.

[Doc. No. 11802, Amdt. 61-60, 38 FR 3161, Feb. 1, 1973, as amended by Amdt. 61-77, 51 FR 40704, Nov. 7, 1986; Amdt. 61-79, 52 FR 17277, May 6, 1987]

§ 61.129 **Airplane rating: Aeronautical experience.**

(a) *General.* An applicant for a commercial pilot certificate with an airplane rating must hold a private pilot certificate with an airplane rating. If he does not hold that certificate and rating he must meet the flight experience requirements for a private pilot certificate and airplane rating and pass the applicable written and practical test prescribed in Subpart D of this part. In addition, the applicant must hold an instrument rating (airplane), or the commercial pilot certificate that is issued is endorsed with a limitation prohibiting the carriage of passengers for hire in airplanes on cross-country flights of more than 50 nautical miles, or at night.

(b) *Flight time as pilot.* An applicant for a commercial pilot certificate with an airplane rating must have a total of at least 250 hours of flight time as pilot, which may include not more than 50 hours of instruction from an authorized instructor in a ground trainer acceptable to the Administrator. The total flight time as pilot must include—

(1) 100 hours in powered aircraft, including at least—

(i) 50 hours in airplanes, and

(ii) 10 hours of flight instruction and practice given by an authorized flight instructor in an airplane having a retractable landing gear, flaps, and a controllable pitch propeller; and

(2) 50 hours of flight instruction given by an authorized flight instructor, including—

(i) 10 hours of instrument instruction, of which at least 5 hours must be in flight in airplanes, and

(ii) 10 hours of instruction in preparation for the commercial pilot flight test; and

(3) 100 hours of pilot in command time, including at least:

(i) 50 hours in airplanes.

(ii) 50 hours of cross-country flights, each flight with a landing at a point more than 50 nautical miles from the original departure point. One flight must have landings at a minimum of three points, one of which is at least 150 nautical miles from the original departure point if the flight is conducted in Hawaii, or at least 250 nautical miles from the original departure point if it is conducted elsewhere.

(iii) 5 hours of night flying including at least 10 takeoffs and landings as sole manipulator of the controls.

[Doc. No. 11802, Amdt. 61-60, 38 FR 3161, Feb. 1, 1973, as amended by Amdt. 61-73, 47 FR 46066, Oct. 14, 1982]

§ 61.131 Rotorcraft ratings: Aeronautical experience.

An applicant for a commercial pilot certificate with a rotorcraft category rating must have at least the following aeronautical experience as a pilot:

(a) After April 30, 1987, *for a helicopter class rating*, 150 hours of flight time, including at least 100 hours in powered aircraft, 50 hours of which must be in a helicopter, including at least—

(1) 40 hours of flight instruction from an authorized flight instructor, 15 hours of which must be in a helicopter, including—

(i) 3 hours of cross-country flying in helicopters;

(ii) 3 hours of night flying in helicopters, including 10 takeoffs and landings, each of which must be separated by an en route phase of flight;

(iii) 3 hours in helicopters preparing for the commercial pilot flight test within 60 days before that test; and

(iv) Takeoffs and landings at three points other than airports; and

(2) 100 hours of pilot-in-command flight time, 35 hours of which must be in a helicopter, including at least—

(i) 10 hours of cross-country flying in helicopters, including one flight with a landing at three or more points, each of which must be more than 50 nautical miles from each of the other two points; and

(ii) Three takeoffs and landings in helicopters, each of which must be separated by an en route phase of flight, at an airport with an operating control tower.

(b) After April 30, 1987, *for a gyroplane class rating*, 150 hours of flight time in aircraft, including at least 100 hours in powered aircraft, 25 hours of which must be in a gyroplane, including at least—

(1) 40 hours of flight instruction from an authorized flight instructor, 10 hours of which must be in a gyroplane, including at least—

(i) 3 hours of cross-country flying in gyroplanes;

(ii) 3 hours of night flying in gyroplanes, including 10 takeoffs and landings; and

(iii) 3 hours in gyroplanes preparing for the commercial pilot flight test within 60 days before that test; and

(2) 100 hours of pilot-in-command flight time, 15 hours of which must be in a gyroplane, including at least—

(i) 10 hours of cross-country flying in gyroplanes, including one flight with a landing at three or more points, each of which is more than 50 nautical miles from each of the other two points; and

(ii) Three takeoffs and landings in gyroplanes at an airport with an operating control tower.

(c) Until May 1, 1987, for a helicopter rating at least 150 hours of flight time as pilot, including at least—

(1) 100 hours in powered aircraft and at least 50 hours in helicopters;

(2) 100 hours of pilot in command time, including a cross-country flight with landings at three points, each of

which is more than 50 nautical miles from each of the other points;

(3) 40 hours of flight instruction from an authorized flight instructor, including 15 hours in helicopters; and

(4) 10 hours as pilot in command in helicopters, including—

(i) Five takeoffs and landings at night;

(ii) Takeoffs and landings at three different airports that serve both airplanes and helicopters; and

(iii) Takeoffs and landings at three points other than airports.

(d) Until May 1, 1987, for a gyroplane rating at least 200 hours of flight time as pilot, including—

(1) 100 hours in powered aircraft;

(2) 100 hours as pilot in command, including a cross-country flight with landings at three points, each of which is more than 50 nautical miles from each of the other two points;

(3) 75 hours as pilot in command in gyroplanes, including—

(i) Flights with takeoffs and landings at three different paved airports and three unpaved airports; and

(ii) Three flights with takeoffs and landings at an airport with an operating control tower; and

(4) Twenty hours of flight instruction in gyroplanes, including 5 hours in preparation for the commercial pilot flight test.

[Doc. No. 24550, Amdt. No. 61–77, 51 FR 40704, Nov. 7, 1986, as amended by Amdt. 61–78, 52 FR 4847, Feb. 17, 1987]

§61.133 Glider rating: Aeronautical experience.

An applicant for a commercial pilot certificate with a glider rating must meet either of the following aeronautical experience requirements:

(a) A total of at least 25 hours of pilot time in aircraft, including 20 hours in gliders, and a total of 100 glider flights as pilot in command, including 25 flights during which 360° turns were made; or

(b) A total of 200 hours of pilot time in heavier-than-air aircraft, including, 20 glider flights as pilot in command during which 360° turns were made.

§61.135 Airship rating: Aeronautical experience.

An applicant for a commercial pilot certificate with an airship rating must have a total of at least 200 hours of flight time as pilot, including—

(a) Fifty hours of flight time as pilot in airships;

(b) 30 hours of flight time performing the duties of pilot in command in airships, including—

(1) 10 hours of cross-country flight; and

(2) 10 hours of night flight; and

(c) 40 hours of instrument time, of which at least 20 hours must be in flight with 10 hours of that flight time in airships.

§61.137 Free balloon rating: Aeronautical experience.

An applicant for a commercial pilot certificate with a free balloon rating must have the following flight time as pilot:

(a) If a gas balloon or a hot air balloon with an airborne heater is used, a total of at least 35 hours of flight time as pilot including—

(1) 20 hours in free balloons; and

(2) 10 flights in free balloons, including—

(i) Six flights under the supervision of a commercial free balloon pilot;

(ii) Two solo flights;

(iii) Two flights of at least 2 hours duration if a gas balloon is used, or at least 1 hour duration if a hot air balloon with an airborne heater is used; and

(iv) One ascent under control to more than 10,000 feet above the takeoff point if a gas balloon is used or 5,000 feet above the take off point if a hot air balloon with an airborne heater is used.

(b) If a hot air balloon without an airborne heater is used, 10 flights in free balloons including—

(1) Six flights under the supervision of a commercial free balloon pilot; and

(2) Two solo flights.

§61.139 Commercial pilot privileges and limitations: General.

The holder of a commercial pilot certificate may:

(a) Act as pilot in command of an aircraft carrying persons or property for compensation or hire;

(b) Act as pilot in command of an aircraft for compensation or hire; and

(c) Give flight instruction in an airship if he holds a lighter-than-air category and an airship class rating, or in a free balloon if he holds a free balloon class rating.

§ 61.141 Airship and free balloon ratings: Limitations.

(a) If the applicant for a free balloon class rating takes his flight test in a hot air balloon without an airborne heater, his pilot certificate contains an endorsement restricting the exercise of the privileges of that rating to hot air balloons without airborne heaters. The restriction may be deleted when the holder of the certificate obtains the pilot experience and passes the test required for a rating on a free balloon with an airborne heater or a gas balloon.

(b) If the applicant for a free balloon class rating takes his flight test in a hot air balloon with an airborne heater, his pilot certificate contains an endorsement restricting the exercise of the privileges of that rating to hot air balloons with airborne heaters. The restriction may be deleted when the holder of the certificate obtains the pilot experience required for a rating on a gas balloon.

Subpart F—Airline Transport Pilots

AUTHORITY: Secs. 313(a), 314, 601, and 607; 49 U.S.C. 1354(a), 1355, 1421, and 1427.

§ 61.151 Eligibility requirements: General.

To be eligible for an airline transport pilot certificate, a person must—

(a) Be at least 23 years of age;

(b) Be of good moral character;

(c) Be able to read, write, and understand the English language and speak it without accent or impediment of speech that would interfere with two-way radio conversation;

(d) Be a high school graduate, or its equivalent in the Administrator's opinion, based on the applicant's general experience and aeronautical experience, knowledge, and skill;

(e) Have a first-class medical certificate issued under Part 67 of this chapter within the 6 months before the date he applies; and

(f) Comply with the sections of this part that apply to the rating he seeks

[Doc. No. 1179, 27 FR 7965, Aug. 10, 1962. Redesignated by Doc. No. 11802, Amdt. 61-60, 38 FR 3161, Feb. 1, 1973]

§ 61.153 Airplane rating: Aeronautical knowledge.

An applicant for an airline transport pilot certificate with an airplane rating must, after meeting the requirements of §§ 61.151 (except paragraph (a) thereof) and 61.155, pass a written test on—

(a) The sections of this part relating to airline transport pilots and Part 121, Subpart C of Part 65, and §§ 91.1 through 91.9 and Subpart B of Part 91 of this chapter, and so much of Parts 21 and 25 of this chapter as relate to the operations of air carrier aircraft;

(b) The fundamentals of air navigation and use of formulas, instruments, and other navigational aids, both in aircraft and on the ground, that are necessary for navigating aircraft by instruments;

(c) The general system of weather collection and dissemination;

(d) Weather maps, weather forecasting, and weather sequence abbreviations symbols, and nomenclature;

(e) Elementary meteorology, including knowledge of cyclones as associated with fronts;

(f) Cloud forms;

(g) National Weather Service Federal Meteorological Handbook No. 1, as amended;

(h) Weather conditions, including icing conditions and upper-air winds, that affect aeronautical activities;

(i) Air navigation facilities used on Federal airways, including rotating beacons, course lights, radio ranges, and radio marker beacons;

(j) Information from airplane weather observations and meteorological data reported from observations made by pilots on air carrier flights;

(k) The influence of terrain on meteorological conditions and developments, and their relation to air carrier flight operations;

(l) Radio communication procedure in aircraft operations; and

(m) Basic principles of loading and weight distribution and their effect on flight characteristics.

[Doc. No. 1179, 27 FR 7965, Aug. 10, 1962, as amended by Amdt. 61–11, 29 FR 14916, Nov. 4, 1964; Amdt. 61–30, 32 FR 5770, Apr. 11, 1967; Amdt. 61–64, 36 FR 13911, July 28, 1971. Redesignated by Doc. No. 11802, Amdt. 61–60, 38 FR 3161, Feb. 1, 1973, as amended by Amdt. 61–64, 41 FR 51392, Nov. 22, 1976]

§ 61.155 Airplane rating: Aeronautical experience.

(a) An application for an airline transport pilot certificate with an airplane rating must hold a commercial pilot certificate or a foreign airline transport pilot or commercial pilot license without limitations, issued by a member state of ICAO, or he must be a pilot in an Armed Force of the United States whose military experience qualifies him for a commercial pilot certificate under § 61.73.

(b) An applicant must have had—

(1) At least 250 hours of flight time as pilot in command of an airplane, or as copilot of an airplane performing the duties and functions of a pilot in command under the supervision of a pilot in command, or any combination thereof, at least 100 hours of which were cross-country time and 25 hours of which were night flight time; and

(2) At least 1,500 hours of flight time as a pilot, including at least—

(i) 500 hours of cross-country flight time;

(ii) 100 hours of night flight time; and

(iii) 75 hours of actual or simulated instrument time, at least 50 hours of which were in actual flight.

Flight time used to meet the requirements of paragraph (b)(1) of this section may also be used to meet the requirements of paragraph (b)(2) of this section. Also, an applicant who has made at least 20 night takeoffs and landings to a full stop may substitute one additional night takeoff and landing to a full stop for each hour of night flight time required by paragraph (b)(2)(ii) of this section. However, not more than 25 hours of night

flight time may be credited in this manner.

(c) If an applicant with less than 150 hours of pilot-in-command time otherwise meets the requirements of paragraph (b)(1) of this section, his certificate will be endorsed "Holder does not meet the pilot-in-command flight experience requirement of ICAO", as prescribed by article 39 of the "Convention on International Civil Aviation." Whenever he presents satisfactory written evidence that he has accumulated the 150 hours of pilot-in-command time, he is entitled to a new certificate without the endorsement.

(d) A commercial pilot may credit the following flight time toward the 1,500 hours total flight time requirement of paragraph (b)(2) of this section:

(1) All second-in-command time acquired in airplanes required to have more than one pilot by their approved Aircraft Flight Manuals or airworthiness certificates; and

(2) Flight engineer time acquired in airplanes required to have a flight engineer by their approved Aircraft Flight Manuals, while participating at the same time in an approved pilot training program approved under Part 121 of this chapter.

However, the applicant may not credit under paragraph (d)(2) of this section more than 1 hour for each 3 hours of flight engineer flight time so acquired, nor more than a total of 500 hours.

(e) If an applicant who credits second-in-command or flight engineer time under paragraph (d) of this section toward the 1,500 hours total flight time requirement of paragraph (b)(2) of this section—

(1) Does not have at least 1,200 hours of flight time as a pilot including no more than 50 percent of his second-in-command time and none of his flight engineer time; but

(2) Otherwise meets the requirements of paragraph (b)(2) of this section,

his certificate will be endorsed "Holder does not meet the pilot flight experience requirements of ICAO," as prescribed by Article 39 of the "Convention on International Civil Aviation." Whenever he presents satisfactory evidence that he has accumulated 1,200 hours of flight time as a pilot including no more than 50 percent of his second-in-command time and none of his flight engineer time, he is entitled to a new certificate without the endorsement.

[Doc. No. 1179, 27 FR 7965, Aug. 10, 1962, as amended by Amdt. 61-44, 34 FR 17164, Oct. 23, 1969. Redesignated by Doc. No. 11802, Amdt. 61-60, 38 FR 3161, Feb. 1, 1973, as amended by Amdt. 61-64, 41 FR 51392, Nov. 22, 1976; Amdt. 61-71, 47 FR 13316, Mar. 29, 1982]

§ 61.157 Airplane rating: Aeronautical skill.

(a) An applicant for an airline transport pilot certificate with a single-engine or multiengine class rating or an additional type rating must pass a practical test that includes the items set forth in Appendix A of this part. The FAA inspector or designated examiner may modify any required maneuver where necessary for the reasonable and safe operation of the airplane being used and, unless specifically prohibited in Appendix A, may combine any required maneuvers and may permit their performance in any convenient sequence.

(b) Whenever an applicant for an airline transport pilot certificate does not already have an instrument rating he shall, as part of the oral part of the practical test, comply with § 61.65(g), and, as part of the flight part, perform each additional maneuver required by § 61.65(g) that is appropriate to the airplane type and not required in Appendix A of this part.

(c) Unless the Administrator requires certain or all maneuvers to be performed, the person giving a flight test for an airline transport pilot certificate or additional airplane class or type rating may, in his discretion, waive any of the maneuvers for which a specific waiver authority is contained in Appendix A of this part if a pilot being checked—

(1) Is employed as a pilot by a Part 121 certificate holder; and

(2) Within the preceding 6 calendar months, has successfully completed that certificate holder's approved training program for the airplane type involved.

(d) The items specified in paragraph (a) of this section may be performed in the airplane simulator or other training device specified in Appendix A to this part for the particular item if—

(1) The airplane simulator or other training device meets the requirements of § 121.407 of this chapter; and

(2) In the case of the items preceded by an asterisk (*) in Appendix A, the applicant has successfully completed the training set forth in § 121.424(d) of this chapter.

However, the FAA inspector or designated examiner may require Items II(d), V(f), or V(g) of Appendix A to this part to be performed in the airplane if he determines that action is necessary to determine the applicant's competence with respect to that maneuver.

(e) An approved simulator may be used instead of the airplane to satisfy the in-flight requirements of Appendix A of this part, if the simulator—

(1) Is approved under § 121.407 of this chapter and meets the appropriate simulator requirements of Appendix H of Part 121; and

(2) Is used as part of an approved program that meets the training requirements of § 121.424 (a) and (c) and Appendix H of Part 121 of this chapter.

[Amdt. 61-27, 32 FR 262, Jan. 11, 1967, as amended by Amdt. 61-31, 32 FR 5987, Apr. 14, 1967; Amdt. 61-45, 35 FR 88, Jan. 3, 1970. Redesignated by Doc. No. 11802, Amdt. 61-60, 38 FR 3161, Feb. 1, 1973, as amended by Amdt. 61-64, 41 FR 51392, Nov. 22, 1976; Amdt. 61-69, 45 FR 44183, June 30, 1980]

§ 61.159 Rotorcraft rating: Aeronautical knowledge.

An applicant for an airline transport pilot certificate with a rotorcraft category and a helicopter class rating must pass a written test on—

(a) So much of this chapter as relates to air carrier rotorcraft operations;

(b) Rotorcraft design, components, systems, and performance limitations;

(c) Basic principles of loading and weight distribution and their effect on rotorcraft flight characteristics;

(d) Air traffic control systems and procedures relating to rotorcraft;

(e) Procedures for operating rotorcraft in potentially hazardous meteorological conditions;

(f) Flight theory as applicable to rotorcraft; and

(g) The items listed under paragraphs (b) through (m) of § 61.153.

[Doc. No. 24550, Amdt. 61-7, 51 FR 40705, Nov. 7, 1986]

§ 61.161 Rotorcraft rating: Aeronautical experience.

(a) An applicant for an airline transport pilot certificate with a rotorcraft category and helicopter class rating must hold a commercial pilot certificate, or a foreign airline transport pilot or commercial pilot certificate with a rotorcraft category and helicopter class rating issued by a member of ICAO, or be a pilot in an armed force of the United States whose military experience qualifies that pilot for the issuance of a commercial pilot certificate under § 61.73.

(b) An applicant must have had at least 1,200 hours of flight time as a pilot, including at least—

(1) 500 hours of cross-country flight time;

(2) 100 hours of night flight time, of which at least 15 hours are in helicopters;

(3) 200 hours in helicopters, including at least 75 hours as pilot in command, or as second in command performing the duties and functions of a pilot in command under the supervision of a pilot in command, or any combination thereof; and

(4) 75 hours of instrument time under actual or simulated instrument conditions of which at least 50 hours were completed in flight with at least 25 hours in helicopters as pilot in command, or as second in command performing the duties of a pilot in command under the supervision of a pilot in command, or any combination thereof.

[Doc. No. 24550, Amdt. No. 61-77, 51 FR 40705, Nov. 7, 1986]

§ 61.163 Rotorcraft rating: Aeronautical skill.

(a) An applicant for an airline transport pilot certificate with a rotorcraft category and helicopter class rating, or

additional aircraft rating, must pass a practical test on those maneuvers set forth in Appendix B of this part in a helicopter. The FAA inspector or designated examiner may modify or waive any maneuver where necessary for the reasonable and safe operation of the rotorcraft being used and may combine any maneuvers and permit their performance in any convenient sequence to determine the applicant's competency.

(b) Whenever an applicant for an airline transport pilot certificate with a rotorcraft category and helicopter class rating does not already have an instrument rating, the applicant shall, as part of the practical test, comply with § 61.65(g).

[Doc. No. 24550, Amdt. No. 61-77, 51 FR 40704, Nov. 7, 1986]

§ 61.165 Additional category ratings.

(a) *Rotorcraft category with a helicopter class rating.* The holder of an airline transport pilot certificate (airplane category) who applies for a rotorcraft category with a helicopter class rating must meet the applicable requirements of §§ 61.159, 61.161, and 61.163 and—

(1) Have at least 100 hours, including at least 15 hours at night, of rotorcraft flight time as pilot in command or as second in command performing the duties and functions of a pilot in command under the supervision of a pilot in command who holds an airline transport pilot certificate with an appropriate rotorcraft rating, or any combination thereof; or

(2) Complete a training program conducted by a certificated air carrier or other approved agency requiring at least 75 hours of rotorcraft flight time as pilot in command, second in command, or as flight instruction from an appropriately rated FAA certificated flight instructor or an airline transport pilot, or any combination thereof, including at least 15 hours of night flight time.

(b) *Airplane rating.* The holder of an airline transport pilot certificate (rotorcraft category) who applies for an airplane category must comply with §§ 61.153, 61.155 (except § 61.155(b)(1)), and 61.157 and—

(1) Have at least 100 hours, including at least 15 hours at night, of airplane flight time as pilot in command or as second in command performing the duties and functions of a pilot in command under the supervision of a pilot in command who holds an airline transport pilot certificate with an appropriate airplane rating, or any combination thereof; or

(2) Complete a training program conducted by a certificated air carrier or other approved agency requiring at least 75 hours of airplane flight time as pilot in command, second in command, or as flight instruction from an appropriately rated FAA certificated flight instructor or an airline transport pilot, or any combination thereof, including at least 15 hours of night flight time.

[Doc. No. 1179, 27 FR 7965, Aug. 10, 1962, as amended by Amdt. 61-29, 32 FR 4493, Mar. 24, 1967. Redesignated by Doc. No. 11802, Amdt. 61-60, 38 FR 3161, Feb. 1, 1973, as amended by Amdt. 61-64, 41 FR 51392, Nov. 22, 1976]

§ 61.167   Tests.

(a) Each applicant for an airline transport pilot certificate must pass each practical and theoretical test to the satisfaction of the Administrator. The minimum passing grade in each subject is 70 percent. Each flight maneuver is graded separately. Other tests are graded as a whole.

(b) Information collected incidentally to such a test shall be treated as a confidential matter by the persons giving the test and by employees of the FAA.

[Doc. No. 1179, 27 FR 7965, Aug. 10, 1962. Redesignated by Doc. No. 11802, Amdt. 61-60, 38 FR 3161, Feb. 1, 1973]

§ 61.169   Instruction in air transportation service.

An airline transport pilot may instruct other pilots in air transportation service in aircraft of the category, class, and type for which he is rated. However, he may not instruct for more than 8 hours in one day nor more than 36 hours in any 7-day period. He may instruct under this section only in aircraft with functioning dual controls. Unless he has a flight instructor certificate, an airline transport pilot may instruct only as provided in this section.

[Doc. No. 1179, 27 FR 7965, Aug. 10, 1962. Redesignated by Doc. No. 11802, Amdt. 61-60, 38 FR 3161, Feb. 1, 1973]

§ 61.171   General privileges and limitations.

An airline transport pilot has the privileges of a commercial pilot with an instrument rating. The holder of a commercial pilot certificate who qualifies for an airline transport pilot certificate retains the ratings on his commercial pilot certificate, but he may exercise only the privileges of a commercial pilot with respect to them.

[Doc. No. 1179, 27 FR 7965, Aug. 10, 1962, as amended by Amdt. 61-20, 30 FR 11905, Sept. 17, 1965]

Subpart G—Flight Instructors

§ 61.181   Applicability.

This subpart prescribes the requirements for the issuance of flight instructor certificates and ratings, the conditions under which those certificates and ratings are necessary, and the limitations upon these certificates and ratings.

§ 61.183   Eligibility requirements: General.

To be eligible for a flight instructor certificate a person must—

(a) Be at least 18 years of age;

(b) Read, write, and converse fluently in English;

(c) Hold—

(1) A commercial or airline transport pilot certificate with an aircraft rating appropriate to the flight instructor rating sought, and

(2) An instrument rating, if the person is applying for an airplane or an instrument instructor rating:

(d) Pass a written test on the subjects in which ground instruction is required by § 61.185; and

(e) Pass an oral and flight test on those items in which instruction is required by § 61.187.

§ 61.185   Aeronautical knowledge.

(a) Present evidence showing that he has satisfactorily completed a course of instruction in at least the following subjects:

(1) The learning process.

(2) Elements of effective teaching.

(3) Student evaluation, quizzing, and testing.

(4) Course development.

(5) Lesson planning.

(6) Classroom instructing techniques.

(b) Have logged ground instruction from an authorized ground or flight instructor in all of the subjects in which ground instruction is required for a private and commercial pilot certificate, and for an instrument rating, if an airplane or instrument instructor rating is sought.

§ **61.187 Flight proficiency.**

(a) An applicant for a flight instructor certificate must have received flight instruction, appropriate to the instructor rating sought in the subjects listed in this paragraph by a person authorized in paragraph (b) of this section. In addition, his logbook must contain an endorsement by the person who has given him the instruction certifying that he has found the applicant competent to pass a practical test on the following subjects:

(1) Preparation and conduct of lesson plans for students with varying backgrounds and levels of experience and ability.

(2) The evaluation of student flight performance.

(3) Effective preflight and postflight instruction.

(4) Flight instructor responsibilities and certifying procedures.

(5) Effective analysis and correction of common student pilot flight errors.

(6) Performance and analysis of standard flight training procedures and maneuvers appropriate to the flight instructor rating sought.

(b) The flight instruction required by paragraph (a) of this section must be given by a person who has held a flight instructor certificate during the 24 months immediately preceding the date the instruction is given, who meets the general requirements for a flight instructor certificate prescribed in § 61.183, and who has given at least 200 hours of flight instruction, or 80 hours in the case of glider instruction, as a certificated flight instructor.

§ **61.189 Flight instructor records.**

(a) Each certificated flight instructor shall sign the logbook of each person to whom he has given flight or ground instruction and specify in that book the amount of the time and the date on which it was given. In addition, he shall maintain a record in his flight instructor logbook, or in a separate document containing the following:

(1) The name of each person whose logbook or student pilot certificate he has endorsed for solo flight privileges. The record must include the type and date of each endorsement.

(2) The name of each person for whom he has signed a certification for a written, flight, or practical test, including the kind of test, date of his certification, and the result of the test.

(b) The record required by this section shall be retained by the flight instructor separately or in his logbook for at least 3 years.

§ **61.191 Additional flight instructor ratings.**

The holder of a flight instructor certificate who applies for an additional rating on that certificate must—

(a) Hold an effective pilot certificate with ratings appropriate to the flight instructor rating sought.

(b) Have had at least 15 hours as pilot in command in the category and class of aircraft appropriate to the rating sought; and

(c) Pass the written and practical test prescribed in this subpart for the issuance of a flight instructor certificate with the rating sought.

§ **61.193 Flight instructor authorizations.**

(a) The holder of a flight instructor certificate is authorized, within the limitations of his instructor certificate and ratings, to give—

(1) In accordance with his pilot ratings, the flight instruction required by this part for a pilot certificate or rating;

(2) Ground instruction or a home study course required by this part for a pilot certificate and rating;

(3) Ground and flight instruction required by this subpart for a flight instructor certificate and rating, if he meets the requirements prescribed in § 61.187 for the issuance of a flight instructor certificate;

(4) The flight instruction required for an initial solo or cross-country flight; and

(5) The flight review required in § 61.57(a).

(b) The holder of a flight instructor certificate is authorized within the limitations of his instructor certificate to endorse—

(1) In accordance with § §61.87(d)(1) and 61.93 (c) (1), the pilot certificate of a student pilot he has instructed authorizing the student to conduct solo or solo cross-country flights, or act as pilot-in-command of an airship requiring more than one flight crewmember;

(2) In accordance with § 61.87 (d) (1), the logbook of a student pilot he has instructed authorizing single or repeated solo flights;

(3) In accordance with § 61.93 (c)(2), the logbook of a student pilot whose preparation and preflight planning for a solo cross-country flight he has reviewed and found adequate for a safe flight under the conditions he has listed in the logbook;

(4) In accordance with §61.95, the logbook of a student pilot he has instructed authorizing solo flights in a terminal control area or at an airport within a terminal control area.

(5) The logbook of a pilot or flight instructor he has examined certifying that the pilot or flight instructor is prepared for a written or flight test required by this part; and

(6) In accordance with § 61.187, the logbook of an applicant for a flight instructor certificate certifying that he has examined the applicant and found him competent to pass the practical test required by this part.

(c) A flight instructor with a rotorcraft and helicopter rating or an airplane single-engine rating may also endorse the pilot certificate and logbook of a student pilot he has instructed authorizing the student to conduct solo and cross-country flights in a single-place gyroplane.

§ 61.195 Flight instructor limitations.

The holder of a flight instructor certificate is subject to the following limitations:

(a) *Hours of instruction.* He may not conduct more than eight hours of flight instruction in any period of 24 consecutive hours.

(b) *Ratings.* He may not conduct flight instruction in any aircraft for which he does not hold a category, class, and type rating, if appropriate on his pilot and flight instructor certificate. However, the holder of a flight instructor certificate effective on November 1, 1973, may continue to exercise the privileges of that certificate until it expires, but not later than November 1, 1975.

(c) *Endorsement of student pilot certificate.* He may not endorse a student pilot certificate for initial solo or solo cross-country flight privileges, unless he has given that student pilot flight instruction required by this part for the endorsement, and considers that the student is prepared to conduct the flight safely with the aircraft involved.

(d) *Logbook endorsement.* He may not endorse a student pilot's logbook—

(1) For solo flight unless he has given that student flight instruction and found that student pilot prepared for solo flight in the type of aircraft involved;

(2) For a cross-country flight, unless he has reviewed the student's flight preparation, planning, equipment, and proposed procedures and found them to be adequate for the flight proposed under existing circumstances; or

(3) For solo flights in a terminal control area or at an airport within the surface area of a terminal control area unless he has given that student ground and flight instruction and has found that student prepared and competent to conduct the operations authorized.

(e) *Solo Flights.* He may not authorize any student pilot to make a solo flight unless he possesses a valid student pilot certificate endorsed for solo in the make and model aircraft to be flown. In addition, he may not authorize any student pilot to make a solo cross-country flight unless he possesses a valid student pilot certificate endorsed for solo cross-country flight in the category of aircraft to be flown.

(f) *Instruction in multiengine airplane or helicopter.* He may not give flight instruction required for the issuance of a certificate or a category, or class rating, in a multiengine airplane or a helicopter, unless he has at least 5 hours of experience as a pilot in command in the make and model of that airplane or helicopter, as the case may be.

§ 61.197 Renewal of flight instructor certificates.

The holder of a flight instructor certificate may have his certificate renewed for an additional period of 24 months if he passes the practical test for a flight instructor certificate and the rating involved, or those portions of that test that the Administrator considers necessary to determine his competency as a flight instructor. His certificate may be renewed without taking the practical test if—

(a) His record of instruction shows that he is a competent flight instructor;

(b) He has a satisfactory record as a company check pilot, chief flight instructor, pilot in command of an aircraft operated under Part 121 of this chapter, or other activity involving the regular evaluation of pilots, and passes any oral test that may be necessary to determine that instructor's knowledge of current pilot training and certification requirements and standards; or

(c) He has successfully completed, within 90 days before the application for the renewal of his certificate, an approved flight instructor refresher course consisting of not less than 24 hours of ground or flight instruction, or both.

§ 61.199 Expired flight instructor certificates and ratings.

(a) *Flight instructor certificates.* The holder of an expired flight instructor certificate may exchange that certificate for a new certificate by passing the practical test prescribed in § 61.187.

(b) *Flight instructor ratings.* A flight instructor rating or a limited flight instructor rating on a pilot certificate is no longer valid and may not be exchanged for a similar rating or a flight instructor certificate. The holder of either of those ratings is issued a flight instructor certificate only if he passes the written and practical test prescribed in this subpart for the issue of that certificate.

§ 61.201 Conversion to new system of instructor ratings.

(a) *General.* The holder of a flight instructor certificate that does not bear any of the new class or instrument ratings listed in § 61.5(c) (2), (3), or (4) for an instructor certificate, may not exercise the privileges of that certificate after November 1, 1975. Before that date he may exchange a certificate which has not expired for a flight instructor certificate with the appropriate new ratings in accordance with the provisions of this section. The holder of a flight instructor certificate with a glider rating need not convert that rating to a new class rating to exercise the privileges of that certificate and rating.

(b) *Airplane—single-engine.* An airplane—single-engine rating may be issued to the holder of an effective flight instructor certificate with an airplane rating who has passed the flight instructor practical test in a single-engine airplane, or who has given at least 20 hours of flight instruction in single-engine airplanes as a certificated flight instructor.

(c) *Airplane—multiengine.* An airplane—multiengine class rating may be issued to the holder of an effective flight instructor certificate with an airplane rating who has passed the flight instructor practical test in a multiengine airplane, or who has given at least 20 hours of flight instruction in multiengine airplane as a certificated flight instructor.

(d) *Rotorcraft—helicopter.* A rotorcraft—helicopter class rating may be issued to the holder of an effective flight instructor certificate with a rotorcraft rating who has passed the flight instructor practical test in a helicopter, or who has given at least 20 hours of flight instruction in helicopters as a certificated flight instructor.

(e) *Rotorcraft—gyroplane.* A rotorcraft—gyroplane class rating may be issued to the holder of an effective flight instructor certificate with a rotorcraft rating who has passed the flight instructor practical test in a gyroplane, or who has given at least 20 hours of flight instruction in gyroplanes as a certificated flight instructor.

(f) *Instrument—airplane.* An instrument—airplane instructor rating may be issued to the holder of an effective flight instructor certificate with an instrument rating who has passed the instrument instructor practical test in an airplane, or who has given at least 20 hours of instrument instruction in an airplane as a certificated flight instructor.

(g) *Instrument—helicopter.* An instrument—helicopter rating may be issued to the holder of an effective flight instructor certificate with an instrument rating who has passed the instrument instructor practical test in a helicopter, or who has given at least 20 hours of instrument flight instruction in helicopters as a certificated flight instructor.

APPENDIX A—PRACTICAL TEST REQUIRE-
MENTS FOR AIRPLANE AIRLINE
TRANSPORT PILOT CERTIFICATES AND
ASSOCIATED CLASS AND TYPE RAT-
INGS

Throughout the maneuvers prescribed in this appendix, good judgment commensurate with a high level of safety must be demonstrated. In determining whether such judgment has been shown, the FAA inspector or designated examiner who conducts the check considers adherence to approved procedures, actions based on analysis of situations for which there is no prescribed procedure or recommended practice, and qualities of prudence and care in selecting a course of action.

Each maneuver or procedure must be performed inflight except to the extent that certain maneuvers or procedures may be performed in an airplane simulator with a visual system (visual simulator) or an airplane simulator without a visual system (nonvisual simulator) or may be waived as indicated by an X in the appropriate columns. A maneuver authorized to be performed in a nonvisual simulator may be performed in a visual simulator, and a maneuver authorized to be performed in a training device may be performed in a nonvisual or a visual simulator.

An asterisk (*) preceding a maneuver or procedure indicates that the maneuver or procedure may be performed in an airplane simulator or other training device as indicated, provided the applicant has successfully completed the training set forth in § 121.424(d) of this chapter.

When a maneuver or procedure is preceded by this symbol (#), it indicates that the FAA inspector or designated examiner may require the maneuver or procedure to be performed in the airplane if he determines such action is necessary to determine the applicant's competence with respect to that maneuver.

An X and asterisk (X*) indicates that a particular condition is specified in connection with the maneuver, procedure, or waiver provisions.

Maneuvers/Procedures	Required		Permitted			
	Simulated instrument conditions	Inflight	Visual simulator	Nonvisual simulator	Training device	Waiver provisions of § 61.157(c)
The procedures and maneuvers set forth in this appendix must be performed in a manner that satisfactorily demonstrates knowledge and skill with respect to—						
(1) The airplane, its systems and components;						
(2) Proper control of airspeed, configuration, direction, altitude, and attitude in accordance with procedures and limitations contained in the approved Airplane Flight Manual, check lists, or other approved material appropriate to the airplane type; and						
(3) Compliance with approved en route, instrument approach, missed approach, ATC, or other applicable procedures						

Maneuvers/Procedures	Required		Permitted			
	Simulated instrument conditions	Inflight	Visual simulator	Nonvisual simulator	Training device	Waiver provisions of § 61.157(c)
I. Preflight:						
(a) Equipment examination (oral). As part of the practical test the equipment examination must be closely coordinated with and related to, the flight maneuvers portion but may not be given during the flight maneuvers portion. Notwithstanding § 61.21 the equipment examination may be given to an applicant who has completed a ground school that is part of an approved training program under Federal Aviation Regulations Part 121 for the airplane type involved and who is recommended by his instructor. The equipment examination must be repeated if the flight maneuvers portion is not satisfactorily completed within 60 days. The equipment examination must cover—					X	
(1) Subjects requiring a practical knowledge of the airplane, its powerplants, systems, components, operational, and performance factors;						
(2) Normal, abnormal, and emergency procedures, and the operations and limitations relating thereto; and						
(3) The appropriate provisions of the approved Airplane Flight Manual						
(b) Preflight Inspection. The pilot must—						
(1) Conduct an actual visual inspection of the exterior and interior of the airplane, locating each item and explaining briefly the purpose of inspecting it; and					X	X*
(2) Demonstrate the use of the prestart check list, appropriate control system checks, starting procedures, radio and electronic equipment checks, and the selection of proper navigation and communications radio facilities and frequencies prior to flight				X		
If a flight engineer is a required crewmember for the particular type airplane, the actual visual inspection may either be waived or it may be replaced by using an approved pictorial means that realistically portrays the location and detail of inspection items						
(c) Taxiing. This maneuver includes taxiing, sailing, or docking procedures in compliance with instructions issued by the appropriate traffic control authority or by the FAA inspector or designated examiner		/X				
(d) Powerplant checks. As appropriate to the airplane type				X		
II. Takeoffs:						
(a) Normal. One normal takeoff which, for the purpose of this maneuver begins when the airplane is taxied into position on the runway to be used		X				
*(b) Instrument. One takeoff with instrument conditions simulated at or before reaching an altitude of 100 feet above the airport elevation	X		X			
(c) Cross wind. One cross wind takeoff, if practical under the existing meteorological, airport, and traffic conditions		X*				
#*(d) Powerplant failure. One takeoff with a simulated failure of the most critical powerplant—			X			
(1) At a point after V_1 and before V_2 that in the judgment of the person conducting the check is appropriate to the airplane type under the prevailing conditions;						
(2) At a point as close as possible after V_1 when V_1 and V_2 or V_1 and V_R are identical; or						
(3) At the appropriate speed for nontransport category airplanes						

Maneuvers/Procedures	Required		Permitted			
	Simulated instrument conditions	Inflight	Visual simulator	Nonvisual simulator	Training device	Waiver provisions of § 61.157(c)
For additional type rating in an airplane group with engines mounted in similar positions or from wing-mounted engines to aft fuselage-mounted engines this maneuver may be performed in a nonvisual simulator						
(e) Rejected. A rejected takeoff performed in an airplane during a normal takeoff run after reaching a reasonable speed determined by giving due consideration to aircraft characteristics, runway length, surface conditions, wind direction and velocity, brake heat energy, and any other pertinent factors that may adversely affect safety or the airplane				X		X°
III. Instrument Procedures:						
°(a) Area departure and area arrival. During each of these maneuvers the applicant must—	X			X		X°
(1) Adhere to actual or simulated ATC clearances (including assigned radials); and						
(2) Properly use available navigation facilities						
Either area arrival or area departure, but not both, may be waived under § 61.157(c)						
(b) Holding. This maneuver includes entering, maintaining, and leaving holding patterns. It may be performed under either area departure or area arrival	X			X		X°
(c) ILS and other instrument approaches. There must be the following:						
°(1) At least one normal ILS approach	X		X			
#(2) At least one manually controlled ILS approach with a simulated failure of one powerplant. The simulated failure should occur before initiating the final approach course and must continue to touchdown or through the missed approach procedure	X		X			
However, either the normal ILS approach or the manually controlled ILS approach must be performed in flight						
(3) At least one nonprecision approach procedure that is representative of the nonprecision approach procedures that the applicant is likely to use	X		X			
(4) Demonstration of at least one nonprecision approach procedure on a letdown aid other than the approach procedure performed under subparagraph (3) of this paragraph that the applicant is likely to use. If performed in a synthetic instrument trainer, the procedures must be observed by the FAA inspector or designated examiner, or if the applicant has completed an approved training course under Part 121 of this chapter for the airplane type involved, the procedures may be observed by a person qualified to act as an instructor or check airman under that approved training program	X				X	
Each instrument approach must be performed according to any procedures and limitations approved for the approach facility used. The instrument approach begins when the airplane is over the initial approach fix for the approach procedure being used (or turned over to the final approach controller in the case of GCA approach) and ends when the airplane touches down on the runway or when transition to a missed approach configuration is completed. Instrument conditions need not be simulated below 100′ above touchdown zone elevation						
(d) Circling approaches. At least one circling approach must be made under the following conditions:			X			X°
(1) The portion of the circling approach to the authorized minimum circling approach altitude must be made under simulated instrument conditions	X					
(2) The approach must be made to the authorized minimum circling approach altitude followed by a change in heading and the necessary maneuvering (by visual reference) to maintain a flight path that permits a normal landing on a runway at least 90° from the final approach course of the simulated instrument portion of the approach						

Maneuvers/Procedures	Required		Permitted			
	Simulated instrument conditions	Inflight	Visual simulator	Nonvisual simulator	Training device	Waiver provisions of § 61.157(c)
(3) The circling approach must be performed without excessive maneuvering, and without exceeding the normal operating limits of the airplane. The angle of bank should not exceed 30°..........						
When the maneuver is performed in an airplane, it may be waived as provided in § 61.157(c) if local conditions beyond the control of the pilot prohibit the maneuver or prevent it from being performed as required						
The circling approach maneuver is not required for a pilot employed by a certificate holder subject to the operating rules of Part 121 of this chapter, if the certificate holder's manual prohibits a circling approach in weather conditions below 1000–3 (ceiling and visibility)						
*(e) Missed approaches. Each applicant must perform at least two missed approaches, with at least one missed approach from an ILS approach. A complete approved missed approach procedure must be accomplished at least once and, at the discretion of the FAA inspector or designated examiner, a simulated powerplant failure may be required during any of the missed approaches. These maneuvers may be performed either independently or in conjunction with maneuvers required under sections III or V or this appendix. At least one must be performed inflight	X	X*	X*			
IV. Inflight Maneuvers:						
*(a) Steep turns. At least one steep turn in each direction must be performed. Each steep turn must involve a bank angle of 45° with a heading change of at least 180° but not more than 360°..........	X			X		X
*(b) Approaches to stalls. For the purpose of this maneuver the required approach to a stall is reached when there is a perceptible buffet or other response to the initial stall entry. Except as provided below, there must be at least three approaches to stalls as follows:	X			X		X*
(1) One must be in the takeoff configuration (except where the airplane uses only a zero-flap takeoff configuration)..........						
(2) One in a clean configuration						
(3) One in a landing configuration						
At the discretion of the FAA inspector or designated examiner, one approach to a stall must be performed in one of the above configurations while in a turn with a bank angle between 15° and 30°. Two out of the three approaches required by this paragraph may be waived as provided in § 61.157(c)						
*(c) Specific flight characteristics. Recovery from specific flight characteristics that are peculiar to the airplane type				X		X
(d) Powerplant failures. In addition to the specific requirements for maneuvers with simulated powerplant failures, the FAA inspector or designated examiner may require a simulated powerplant failure at any time during the check..........		X				
V. Landings and Approaches to Landings:						
Notwithstanding the authorizations for combining of maneuvers and for waiver of maneuvers, at least three actual landings (one to a full stop), must be made. These landings must include the types listed below but more than one type can be combined where appropriate:						
(a) Normal landing		X				

Maneuvers/Procedures	Required		Permitted			
	Simulated instrument conditions	Inflight	Visual simulator	Nonvisual simulator	Training device	Waiver provisions of § 61.157(c)
#(b) Landing in sequence from an ILS instrument approach except that if circumstances beyond the control of the pilot prevent an actual landing, the person conducting the check may accept an approach to a point where in his judgment a landing to a full stop could have been made. In addition, where a simulator approved for the landing maneuver out of an ILS approach is used, the approach may be continued through the landing and credit given for 1 of the 3 landings required by this section			X*			
(c) Cross wind landing, if practical under existing meteorological, airport, and traffic conditions		X*				
#(d) Maneuvering to a landing with simulated powerplant failure, as follows:			X*			
(1) In the case of 3–engine airplanes, maneuvering to a landing with an approved procedure that approximates the loss of 2 powerplants (center and 1 outboard engine); or						
(2) In the case of other multiengine airplanes, maneuvering to a landing with a simulated failure of 50 percent of available powerplants, with the simulated loss of power on one side of the airplane. However, before Jan. 1, 1975, in the case of a 4–engine turbojet-powered airplane, maneuvering to a landing with a simulated failure of the most critical powerplant may be substituted therefor, if a flight instructor in an approved training program under pt. 121 of this chapter certifies to the Administrator that he has observed the applicant satisfactorily perform a landing in that type airplane with a simulated failure of 50 percent of the available powerplants. The substitute maneuver may not be used if the Administrator determines that training in the 2–engine out landing maneuver provided in the training program is unsatisfactory						
If an applicant performs this maneuver in a visual simulator, he must, in addition, maneuver in flight to a landing with a simulated failure of the most critical powerplant						
*(e) Except as provided in par. (f), landing under simulated circling approach conditions except that if circumstances beyond the control of the pilot prevent a landing, the person conducting the check may accept an approach to a point where, in his judgment, a landing to a fuel stop could have been made			X			
The circling approach maneuver is not required for a pilot employed by a certificate holder subject to the operating rules of pt. 121 of this chapter, if the certificate holder's manual prohibits a circling approach in weather conditions below 1000–3 (ceiling and visibility)						
*#(f) A rejected landing, including a normal missed approach procedure, that is rejected approximately 50' over the runway and approximately over the runway threshold. This maneuver may be combined with instrument, circling, or missed approach procedures, but instrument conditions need not be simulated below 100' above the runway	X*		X*			
#(g) A zero-flap visual approach to a point where, in the judgment of the person conducting the check, a landing to a full stop on the appropriate runway could be made. This maneuver is not required for a particular airplane type if the Administrator has determined that the probability of flap extension failure on that type is extremely remote due to system design. In making this determination, the Administrator determines whether checking on slats only and partial flap approaches is necessary			X*			

Maneuvers/Procedures	Required		Permitted			
	Simulated instrument conditions	Inflight	Visual simulator	Nonvisual simulator	Training device	Waiver provisions of § 61.157(c)
(h) For a single powerplant rating only, unless the applicant holds a commercial pilot certificate, he must accomplish accuracy approaches and spot landings that include a series of three landings from an altitude of 1,000′ or less, with the engine throttled and 180° change in direction. The airplane must touch the ground in a normal landing attitude beyond and within 200′ from a designated line. At least one landing must be from a forward slip. One hundred eighty degree approaches using two 90° turns with a straight base leg are preferred although circular approaches are acceptable		X				
VI. Normal and Abnormal Procedures. Each applicant must demonstrate the proper use of as many of the systems and devices listed below as the FAA inspector or designated examiner finds are necessary to determine that the person being checked has a practical knowledge of the use of the systems and devices appropriate to the aircraft type:						
(a) Anti-icing and deicing systems				X		
(b) Auto-pilot systems				X		
(c) Automatic or other approach aid systems				X		
(d) Stall warning devices, stall avoidance devices, and stability augmentation devices				X		
(e) Airborne radar devices				X		
(f) Any other systems, devices, or aids available				X		
(g) Hydraulic and electrical system failures and malfunctions					X	
(h) Landing gear and flap systems failures or malfunctions					X	
(i) Failure of navigation or communications equipment				X		
VII. Emergency Procedures. Each applicant must demonstrate the proper emergency procedures for as many of the emergency situations listed below as the FAA inspector or designated examiner finds are necessary to determine that the person being checked has an adequate knowledge of, and ability to perform, such procedures:						
(a) Fire inflight				X		
(b) Smoke control				X		
(c) Rapid decompression				X		
(d) Emergency descent				X		
(e) Any other emergency procedures outlined in the appropriate approved airplane flight manual				X		

[Amdt. 61–45, 35 FR 88, Jan. 3, 1970; 35 FR 2819, Feb. 11, 1970, as amended by Amdt. 61–56, 37 FR 10729, May 27, 1972; Amdt. 61–57, 37 FR 12716, June 28, 1972; Amdt. 61–62, 38 FR 35445, Dec. 28, 1973; Amdt. 61–77, 51 FR 40705, Nov. 7, 1986]

APPENDIX B—PRACTICAL TEST REQUIREMENTS FOR ROTORCRAFT AIRLINE TRANSPORT PILOT CERTIFICATES WITH A HELICOPTER CLASS RATING AND ASSOCIATED TYPE RATINGS

Throughout the maneuvers prescribed in this appendix, good judgment commensurate with a high level of safety must be demonstrated. In determining whether such judgment has been shown, the FAA inspector or designated pilot examiner who conducts the check considers adherence to approved procedures, actions based on analysis of situations for which there is no prescribed procedure or recommended practice, and qualities of prudence and care in selecting a course of action. The successful outcome of a procedure or maneuver will never be in doubt.

Maneuvers/Procedures

The maneuvers and procedures in this appendix must be performed in a manner that satisfactorily demonstrates knowledge and skill with respect to—

(1) The helicopter, its systems, and components;

(2) Proper control of airspeed, direction, altitude, and attitude in accordance with procedures and limitations contained in the approved Rotorcraft Flight Manual, check-

lists, or other approved material appropriate to the rotorcraft type; and

(3) Compliance with approved en route, instrument approach, missed approach, ATC, and other applicable procedures.

I. Preflight

(a) *Equipment examination* (*oral*). The equipment examination must be repeated if the flight maneuvers portion is not satisfactorily completed within 60 days. The equipment examination must cover—

(1) Subjects requiring a practical knowledge of the helicopter, its powerplants, systems, components, and operational and performance factors;

(2) Normal, abnormal, and emergency procedures and related operations and limitations; and

(3) The appropriate provisions of the approved helicopter Flight Manual or manual material.

(b) *Preflight inspection.* The pilot must—

(1) Conduct an actual visual inspection of the exterior and interior of the helicopter, locating each item and explaining briefly the purpose of inspecting it; and

(2) Demonstrate the use of the prestart checklist, appropriate control system checks, starting procedures, radio and electronic equipment checks, and the selection of proper navigation and communications radio facilities and frequencies before flight.

(c) *Taxiing.* The maneuver includes ground taxiing, hover taxiing (including performance checks),,and docking procedures, as appropriate, in compliance with instructions issued by ATC, the FAA inspector, or the designated pilot examiner.

(d) *Powerplant checks.* As appropriate to the helicopter type in accordance with the Rotorcraft Flight Manual procedures.

II. Takeoffs

(a) *Normal.* One normal takeoff from a stabilized hover which begins when the helicopter is taxied into position for takeoff.

(b) *Instrument.* One takeoff with instrument conditions simulated at or before reaching 100 feet above airport elevation.

(c) *Crosswind.* One crosswind takeoff from a stabilized hover, if practical under the existing meteorological, airport, and traffic conditions.

(d) *Powerplant failure.* (1) For single-engine rotorcraft, one normal takeoff with simulated powerplant failure.

(2) For multiengine rotorcraft, one normal takeoff with simulated failure of one engine—

(i) At an appropriate airspeed that would allow continued climb performance in forward flight; or

(ii) At an appropriate airspeed that is 50 percent of normal cruise speed, if there is no published single-engine climb airspeed for that type of helicopter.

(e) *Rejected.* One normal takeoff that is rejected after simulated engine failure at a reasonable airspeed, determined by giving due consideration to the helicopter's characteristics, length of landing area, surface conditions, wind direction and velocity, and any other pertinent factors that may adversely affect safety.

III. Instrument Procedures

(a) *Area departure and arrival.* During each of these maneuvers, the applicant must—

(1) Adhere to actual or simulated ATC clearances (including assigned bearings or radials); and

(2) Properly use available navigation facilities.

(b) *Holding.* This maneuver includes entering, maintaining, and leaving holding patterns.

(c) *ILS and other instrument approaches.* The instrument approach begins when the helicopter is over the initial approach fix for the approach procedure being used (or turned over to the final controller in case of a surveillance or precision radar approach) and ends when the helicopter terminates at a hover or touches down or where transition to a missed approach is completed. The following approaches must be performed:

(1) At least one normal ILS approach.

(2) For multiengine rotorcraft, at least one manually controlled ILS approach with a simulated failure of one powerplant. The simulated engine failure should occur before initiating the final approach course and continue to a hover to touchdown or through the missed approach procedure.

(3) At least one nonprecision approach procedure that is representative of the nonprecision approach procedure that the applicant is likely to use.

(4) At least one nonprecision approach procedure on a letdown aid other than the approach procedure performed under subparagraph (3) of this paragraph that the applicant is likely to use.

(d) *Circling approaches.* At least one circling approach must be made under the following conditions:

(1) The portion of the circling approach to the authorized minimum circling approach altitude must be made under simulated instrument conditions.

(2) The approach must be made to the authorized minimum circling approach altitude followed by a change in heading and the necessary maneuvering (by visual reference) to maintain a flight path that permits a normal landing on a runway at least 90 degrees from the final approach course of the simulated instrument portion of the approach.

(3) The circling approach must be performed without excessive maneuvering and without exceeding the normal operating limits of the rotorcraft. The angle of bank should not exceed 30 degrees.

(e) *Missed approaches.* Each applicant must perform at least two missed approaches with at least one missed approach from an ILS approach. At the discretion of the FAA inspector or designated examiner, a simulated powerplant failure may be required during any of the missed approaches. The maneuvers may be performed either independently or in conjunction with maneuvers required under section III or V of this appendix. At least one must be performed in flight.

IV. In-flight Maneuvers

(a) *Steep turns.* At least one steep turn in each direction must be performed. Each steep turn must involve a bank angle of 30 degrees with a heading change of at least 180 degrees but not more than 360 degrees.

(b) *Settling with power.* Demonstrate recognition of and recovery from imminent flight at critical/rapid descent with power. For the purpose of this maneuver, settling with power is reached when a perceptive buffet or other indications of imminent settling with power have been induced.

(c) *Powerplant failure.* In addition to the specific requirements for maneuvers with simulated powerplant failures, the FAA inspector or designated examiner may require a simulated powerplant failure at any time during the check.

(d) Recovery from unusual attitudes.

V. Approaches and Landings

(a) *Normal.* One normal approach to a stabilized hover or to the ground must be performed.

(b) *Instrument.* One approach to a hover or to a landing in sequence from an ILS instrument approach.

(c) *Crosswind.* One crosswind approach to a hover or to the ground, if practical under the existing meteorological, airport, or traffic conditions.

(d) *Powerplant failure.* For a multiengine rotorcraft, maneuvering to a landing with simulated powerplant failure of one engine.

(e) *Rejected.* Rejected landing, including a normal missed approach procedure at approximately 50 feet above the runway. This maneuver may be combined with instrument or missed approach procedures, but instrument conditions need not be simulated below 100 feet above the runway or landing area.

(f) *Autorotative landings.* Autorotative landings in a single-engine helicopter. The applicant may be required to accomplish at least one autorotative approach and landing

from any phase of flight as specified by the FAA inspector or designated examiner.

VI. Normal and Abnormal Procedures

Each applicant must demonstrate the proper use of as many systems and devices listed below as the FAA inspector or designated examiner finds are necessary to determine that the applicant has a practical knowledge of the use of the systems and devices appropriate to the helicopter type:

(a) Anti-icing or deicing systems.

(b) Autopilot or other stability augmentation devices.

(c) Airborne radar devices.

(d) Hydraulic and electrical systems failures or malfunctions.

(e) Landing gear failures or malfunctions.

(f) Failure of navigation or communications equipment.

(g) Any other system appropriate to the helicopter as outlined in the approved Rotorcraft Flight Manual.

II. Emergency Procedures

Each applicant must demonstrate the proper emergency procedures for as many of the emergency situations listed below as the FAA inspector or designated examiner finds are necessary to determine that the applicant has adequate knowledge of, and ability to perform, such procedures:

(a) Fire or smoke control in flight.

(b) Ditching.

(c) Evacuation.

(d) Operation of emergency equipment.

(e) Emergency descent.

(f) Any other emergency procedure outline in the approved Rotorcraft Flight Manual.

[Doc. No. 24550, Amdt. No. 61-77, 51 FR 40705, Nov. 7, 1986]

PART 67—MEDICAL STANDARDS AND CERTIFICATION

AUTHORITY: Secs. 313(a), 314, 601, 607, 72 Stat. 752; 49 U.S.C. 1354(a), 1355, 1421, and 1427.

SOURCE: Docket No. 1179, 27 FR 7980, Aug. 10, 1962, unless otherwise noted.

EDITORIAL NOTE: For nomenclature changes to Part 67, see 30 FR 12025, Sept. 21, 1965.

Subpart A—General

§ 67.1 Applicability.

This subpart prescribes the medical standards for issuing medical certificates for airmen.

§ 67.11 Issue.

Except as provided in § 67.12, an applicant who meets the medical standards prescribed in this part, based on medical examination and evaluation of his history and condition, is entitled to an appropriate medical certificate.

(Secs. 313, 601, 602, Federal Aviation Act of 1958, as amended (49 U.S.C. 1354, 1421, and 1422); sec. 6(c), Department of Transportation Act (49 U.S.C. 1655(c)); Title V, Independent Offices Appropriations Act of 1952 (31 U.S.C. 483(a)); sec. 28, International Air Transportation Competition Act of 1979 (49 U.S.C. 1159(b)))

[Amdt. 67-12, 47 FR 35693, Aug. 16, 1982]

§ 67.12 Certification of foreign airmen.

A person who is neither a United States citizen nor a resident alien is issued a certificate under this part, outside the United States, only when the Administrator finds that the certificate is needed for operation of a U.S.-registered civil aircraft.

(Secs. 313, 601, 602, Federal Aviation Act of 1958, as amended (49 U.S.C. 1354, 1421, and 1422); sec. 6(c), Department of Transportation Act (49 U.S.C. 1655(c)); Title V, Independent Offices Appropriations Act of 1952 (31 U.S.C. 483(a)); sec. 28, International Air Transportation Competition Act of 1979 (49 U.S.C. 1159(b)))

[Amdt. 67-12, 47 FR 35694, Aug. 16, 1982]

§ 67.13 First-class medical certificate.

(a) To be eligible for a first-class medical certificate, an applicant must meet the requirements of paragraphs (b) through (f) of this section.

(b) Eye: (1) Distant visual acuity of 20/20 or better in each eye separately, without correction; or of at least 20/100 in each eye separately corrected to 20/20 or better with corrective lenses (glasses or contact lenses) in which case the applicant may be qualified only on the condition that he wears those corrective lenses while exercising the privileges of his airman certificate.

(2) Near vision of at least $v = 1.00$ at 18 inches with each eye separately, with or without corrective glasses.

(3) Normal color vision.

(4) Normal fields of vision.

(5) No acute or chronic pathological condition of either eye or adenexae that might interfere with its proper function, might progress to that degree, or might be aggravated by flying.

(6) Bifoveal fixation and vergence-phoria relationship sufficient to prevent a break in fusion under conditions that may reasonably occur in performing airman duties.

Tests for the factors named in paragraph (b)(6) of this section are not required except for applicants found to have more than one prism diopter of hyperphoria, six prism diopters of esophoria, or six prism diopters of exophoria. If these values are exceeded, the Federal Air Surgeon may require the applicant to be examined by a qualified eye specialist to determine if there is bifoveal fixation and adequate vergencephoria relationship. However, if the applicant is otherwise qualified, he is entitled to a medical certificate pending the results of the examination.

(c) Ear, nose, throat, and equilibrium:

(1) Ability to—

(i) Hear the whispered voice at a distance of at least 20 feet with each ear separately; or

(ii) Demonstrate a hearing acuity of at least 50 percent of normal in each ear throughout the effective speech and radio range as shown by a standard audiometer.

(2) No acute or chronic disease of the middle or internal ear.

(3) No disease of the mastoid.

(4) No unhealed (unclosed) perforation of the eardrum.

(5) No disease or malformation of the nose or throat that might interfere with, or be aggravated by, flying.

(6) No disturbance in equilibrium.

(d) *Mental and neurologic*—(1) *Mental.* (i) No established medical history or clinical diagnosis of any of the following:

(*a*) A personality disorder that is severe enough to have repeatedly manifested itself by overt acts.

(*b*) A psychosis.

(*c*) Alcoholism, unless there is established clinical evidence, satisfactory to the Federal Air Surgeon, of recovery, including sustained total abstinence from alcohol for not less than the preceding 2 years. As used in this section, "alcoholism" means a condition in which a person's intake of alcohol is great enough to damage physical health or personal or social functioning, or when alcohol has become a prerequisite to normal functioning.

(*d*) *Drug dependence.* As used in this section, "drug dependence" means a condition in which a person is addicted to or dependent on drugs other than alcohol, tobacco, or ordinary caffeine-containing beverages, as evidenced by habitual use or a clear sense of need for the drug.

(ii) No other personality disorder, neurosis, or mental condition that the Federal Air Surgeon finds—

(*a*) Makes the applicant unable to safely perform the duties or exercise the privileges of the airman certificate that he holds or for which he is applying; or

(*b*) May reasonably be expected, within 2 years after the finding, to make him unable to perform those duties or exercise those privileges;

and the findings are based on the case history and appropriate, qualified, medical judgment relating to the condition involved.

(2) *Neurologic.* (i) No established medical history or clinical diagnosis of either of the following:

(*a*) Epilepsy.

(*b*) A disturbance of consciousness without satisfactory medical explanation of the cause.

(ii) No other convulsive disorder, disturbance of consciousness, or neurologic condition that the Federal Air Surgeon finds—

(*a*) Makes the applicant unable to safely perform the duties or exercise the privileges of the airman certificate that he holds or for which he is applying; or

(*b*) May reasonably be expected, within 2 years after the finding, to make him unable to perform those duties or exercise those privileges;

and the findings are based on the case history and appropriate, qualified, medical judgment relating to the condition involved.

(e) *Cardiovascular.* (1) No established medical history or clinical diagnosis of—

(i) Myocardial infarction;

(ii) Angina pectoris; or

(iii) Coronary heart disease that has required treatment or, if untreated, that has been symptomatic or clinically significant.

(2) If the applicant has passed his thirty-fifth birthday but not his fortieth, he must, on the first examination after his thirty-fifth birthday, show an absence of myocardial infarction on electrocardiographic examination.

(3) If the applicant has passed his fortieth birthday, he must annually show an absence of myocardial infarction on electrocardiographic examination.

(4) Unless the adjusted maximum readings apply, the applicant's reclining blood pressure may not be more than the maximum reading for his age group in the following table:

Age group	Maximum readings (reclining blood pressure in mm)		Adjusted maximum readings (reclining blood pressure in mm)[1]	
	Systolic	Diastolic	Systolic	Diastolic
20–29	140	88	....	
30–39	145	92	155	98
40–49	155	96	165	100
50 and over..	160	98	170	100

[1] For an applicant at least 30 years of age whose reclining blood pressure is more than the maximum reading for his age group and whose cardiac and kidney conditions, after complete cardiovascular examination, are found to be normal.

(5) If the applicant is at least 40 years of age, he must show a degree of circulatory efficiency that is compatible with the safe operation of aircraft at high altitudes.

An electrocardiogram, made according to acceptable standards and techniques within the 90 days before an examination for a first-class certificate, is accepted at the time of the physical examination as meeting the requirements of paragraphs (e)(2) and (3) of this section.

(f) *General medical condition:*

(1) No established medical history or clinical diagnosis of diabetes mellitus that requires insulin or any other hypoglycemic drug for control.

(2) No other organic, functional, or structural disease, defect, or limitation that the Federal Air Surgeon finds—

(i) Makes the applicant unable to safely perform the duties or exercise the privileges of the airman certificate that he holds or for which he is applying; or

(ii) May reasonably be expected, within two years after the finding, to make him unable to perform those duties or exercise those privileges;

and the findings are based on the case history and appropriate, qualified medical judgment relating to the condition involved.

(g) An applicant who does not meet the provisions of paragraphs (b) through (f) of this section may apply for the discretionary issuance of a certificate under § 67.19.

(Secs. 313(a), 601, and 602, Federal Aviation Act of 1958, as amended (49 U.S.C. 1354(a), 1421, and 1422); sec. 6(c), Department of Transportation Act (49 U.S.C. 1655(c)))

[Doc. No. 1179, 27 FR 7980, Aug. 10, 1962, as amended by Amdt. 67-9, 37 FR 4071, Feb. 26, 1972; Amdt. 67-10, 41 FR 46433, Oct. 21, 1976; Amdt. 67-11, 47 FR 16308, Apr. 15, 1982]

§ 67.15 **Second-class medical certificate.**

(a) To be eligible for a second-class medical certificate, an applicant must meet the requirements of paragraphs (b) through (f) of this section.

(b) Eye:

(1) Distant visual acuity of 20/20 or better in each eye separately, without correction; or of at least 20/100 in each eye separately corrected to 20/20

or better with corrective lenses (glasses or contact lenses), in which case the applicant may be qualified only on the condition that he wears those corrective lenses while exercising the privileges of his airman certificate.

(2) Enough accommodation to pass a test prescribed by the Administrator based primarily on ability to read official aeronautical maps.

(3) Normal fields of vision.

(4) No pathology of the eye.

(5) Ability to distinguish aviation signal red, aviation signal green, and white.

(6) Bifoveal fixation and vergence-phoria relationship sufficient to prevent a break in fusion under conditions that may reasonably occur in performing airman duties.

Tests for the factors named in paragraph (b)(6) of this section are not required except for applicants found to have more than one prism diopter of hyperphoria, six prism diopters of esophoria, or six prism diopters of exophoria. If these values are exceeded, the Federal Air Surgeon may require the applicant to be examined by a qualified eye specialist to determine if there is bifoveal fixation and adequate vergencephoria relationship. However, if the applicant is otherwise qualified, he is entitled to a medical certificate pending the results of the examination.

(c) Ear, nose, throat, and equilibrium:

(1) Ability to hear the whispered voice at 8 feet with each ear separately.

(2) No acute or chronic disease of the middle or internal ear.

(3) No disease of the mastoid.

(4) No unhealed (unclosed) perforation of the eardrum.

(5) No disease or malformation of the nose or throat that might interfere with or be aggravated by, flying.

(6) No disturbance in equilibrium.

(d) *Mental and neurologic*—(1) *Mental.* (i) No established medical history or clinical diagnosis of any of the following:

(*a*) A personality disorder that is severe enough to have repeatedly manifested itself by overt acts.

(*b*) *A psychosis.*

(*c*) Alcoholism, unless there is established clinical evidence, satisfactory to the Federal Air Surgeon, of recovery, including sustained total abstinence from alcohol for not less than the preceding 2 years. As used in this section, "alcoholism" means a condition in which a person's intake of alcohol is great enough to damage physical health or personal or social functioning, or when alcohol has become a prerequisite to normal functioning.

(*d*) *Drug dependence.* As used in this section, "drug dependence" means a condition in which a person is addicted to or dependent on drugs other than alcohol, tobacco, or ordinary caffeine-containing beverages, as evidenced by habitual use or a clear sense of need for the drug.

(ii) No other personality disorder, neurosis, or mental condition that the Federal Air Surgeon finds—

(*a*) Makes the applicant unable to safely perform the duties or exercise the privileges of the airman certificate that he holds or for which he is applying; or

(*b*) May reasonably be expected, within two years after the finding, to make him unable to perform those duties or exercise those privileges;

and the findings are based on the case history and appropriate, qualified, medical judgment relating to the condition involved.

(2) *Neurologic.* (i) No established medical history or clinical diagnosis of either of the following:

(*a*) Epilepsy.

(*b*) A disturbance of consciousness without satisfactory medical explanation of the cause.

(ii) No other convulsive disorder, disturbance of consciousness, or neurologic condition that the Federal Air Surgeon finds—

(*a*) Makes the applicant unable to safely perform the duties or exercise the privileges of the airman certificate that he holds or for which he is applying; or

(*b*) May reasonably be expected, within two years after the finding, to make him unable to perform those duties or exercise those privileges;

and the findings are based on the case history and appropriate, qualified, medical judgment relating to the condition involved.

(e) *Cardiovascular.* (1) No established medical history or clinical diagnosis of—

(i) Myocardial infarction;

(ii) Angina pectoris; or

(iii) Coronary heart disease that has required treatment or, if untreated, that has been symptomatic or clinically significant.

(f) *General medical condition:*

(1) No established medical history or clinical diagnosis of diabetes mellitus that requires insulin or any other hypoglycemic drug for control.

(2) No other organic, functional, or structural disease, defect, or limitation that the Federal Air Surgeon finds—

(i) Makes the applicant unable to safely perform the duties or exercise the privileges of the airman certificate that he holds or for which he is applying; or

(ii) May reasonably be expected, within two years after the finding to make him unable to perform those duties or exercise those privileges;

and the findings are based on the case history and appropriate, qualified, medical judgment relating to the condition involved.

(g) An applicant who does not meet the provisions of paragraphs (b) through (f) of this section may apply for the discretionary issuance of a certificate under §67.19.

(Secs. 313(a), 601, and 602, Federal Aviation Act of 1958, as amended (49 U.S.C. 1354(a), 1421, and 1422); sec. 6(c), Department of Transportation Act (49 U.S.C. 1655(c)))

[Doc. No. 1179, 27 FR 7980, Aug. 10, 1962, as amended by Amdt. 67-9, 37 FR 4071, Feb. 26, 1972; Amdt. 67-10, 41 FR 46433, Oct. 21, 1976; Amdt. 67-11, 47 FR 16308, Apr. 15, 1982]

§ 67.17 **Third-class medical certificate.**

(a) To be eligible for a third-class medical certificate, an applicant must meet the requirements of paragraphs (b) through (f) of this section.

(b) Eye:

(1) Distant visual acuity of 20/50 or better in each eye separately, without correction; or if the vision in either or both eyes is poorer than 20/50 and is corrected to 20/30 or better in each eye with corrective lenses (glasses or contact lenses), the applicant may be qualified on the condition that he wears those corrective lenses while exercising the priviledges of his airman certificate.

(2) No serious pathology of the eye.

(3) Ability to distinguish aviation signal red, aviation signal green, and white.

(c) Ears, nose, throat, and equilibrium:

(1) Ability to hear the whispered voice at 3 feet.

(2) No acute or chronic disease of the internal ear.

(3) No disease or malformation of the nose or throat that might interfere with, or be aggravated by, flying.

(4) No disturbance in equilibrium.

(d) *Mental and neurologic*—(1) *Mental.* (i) No established medical history or clinical diagnosis of any of the following:

(a) A personality disorder that is severe enough to have repeatedly manifested itself by overt acts.

(b) A psychosis.

(c) Alcoholism, unless there is established clinical evidence, satisfactory to the Federal Air Surgeon, of recovery, including sustained total abstinence from alcohol for not less than the preceding 2 years. As used in this section, "alcoholism" means a condition in which a person's intake of alcohol is great enough to damage physical health or personal or social functioning, or when alcohol has become a prerequisite to normal functioning.

(d) *Drug dependence.* As used in this section, "drug dependence" means a condition in which a person is addicted to or dependent on drugs other than alcohol, tobacco, or ordinary caffeine-containing beverages, as evidenced by habitual use or a clear sense of need for the drug.

(ii) No other personality disorder, neurosis, or mental condition that the Federal Air Surgeon finds—

(a) Makes the applicant unable to safely perform the duties or exercise the privileges of the airman certificate that he holds or for which he is applying; or

(b) May reasonably be expected, within 2 years after the finding, to make him unable to perform those duties or exercise those privileges;

and the findings are based on the case history and appropriate, qualified, medical judgment relating to the condition involved.

(2) *Neurologic.* (i) No established medical history or clinical diagnosis of either of the following:

(a) Epilepsy.

(b) A disturbance of consciousness without satisfactory medical explanation of the cause.

(ii) No other convulsive disorder, disturbance of consciousness, or neurologic condition that the Federal Air Surgeon finds—

(a) Makes the applicant unable to safely perform the duties or exercise the privileges of the airman certificate that he holds or for which he is applying; or

(b) May reasonably be expected, within 2 years after the finding, to make him unable to perform those duties or exercise those privileges; and the findings are based on the case history and appropriate, qualified, medical judgment relating to the condition involved.

(e) *Cardiovascular.* (1) No established medical history or clinical diagnosis of—

(i) Myocardial infarction;

(ii) Angina pectoris; or

(iii) Coronary heart disease that has required treatment or, if untreated, that has been symptomatic or clinically significant.

(f) *General medical condition:*

(1) No established medical history or clinical diagnosis of diabetes mellitus that requires insulin or any other hypoglycemic drug for control;

(2) No other organic, functional or structural disease, defect, or limitation that the Federal Air Surgeon finds—

(i) Makes the applicant unable to safely perform the duties or exercise the privileges of the airman certificate that he holds or for which he is applying; or

(ii) May reasonably be expected, within two years after the finding, to make him unable to perform those duties or exercise those privileges;

and the findings are based on the case history and appropriate, qualified,

medical judgment relating to the condition involved.

(g) An applicant who does not meet the provisions of paragraphs (b) through (f) of this section may apply for the discretionary issuance of a certificate under § 67.19.

(Secs. 313(a), 601, and 602, Federal Aviation Act of 1958, as amended (49 U.S.C. 1354(a), 1421, and 1422); sec. 6(c), Department of Transportation Act (49 U.S.C. 1655(c)))

[Doc. No. 1179, 27 FR 7980, Aug. 10, 1962, as amended by Amdt. 67-9, 37 FR 4072, Feb. 26, 1972; Amdt. 67-10, 41 FR 46433, Oct. 21, 1976; Amdt. 67-11, 47 FR 16308, Apr. 15, 1982]

§ 67.19 Special issue of medical certificates.

(a) At the discretion of the Federal Air Surgeon, a medical certificate may be issued to an applicant who does not meet the applicable provisions of § 67.13, § 67.15, or § 67.17 if the applicant shows to the satisfaction of the Federal Air Surgeon that the duties authorized by the class of medical certificate applied for can be performed without endangering air commerce during the period in which the certificate would be in force. The Federal Air Surgeon may authorize a special medical flight test, practical test, or medical evaluation for this purpose.

(b) The Federal Air Surgeon may consider the applicant's operational experience and any medical facts that may affect the ability of the applicant to perform airman duties including:

(1) The combined effect on the applicant of failure to meet more than one requirement of this part; and

(2) The prognosis derived from professional consideration of all available information regarding the airman.

(c) In determining whether the special issuance of a third-class medical certificate should be made to an applicant, the Federal Air Surgeon considers the freedom of an airman, exercising the privileges of a private pilot certificate, to accept reasonable risks to his or her person and property that are not acceptable in the exercise of commercial or airline transport privileges, and, at the same time, considers the need to protect the public safety of persons and property in other aircraft and on the ground.

(d) In issuing a medical certificate under this section, the Federal Air Surgeon may do any or all of the following:

(1) Limit the duration of the certificate.

(2) Condition the continued effect of the certificate on the results of subsequent medical tests, examinations, or evaluations.

(3) Impose any operational limitation on the certificate needed for safety.

(4) Condition the continued effect of a second- or third-class medical certificate on compliance with a statement of functional limitations issued to the applicant in coordination with the Director of Flight Operations or the Director's designee.

(e) An applicant who has been issued a medical certificate under this section based on a special medical flight or practical test need not take the test again during later physical examinations unless the Federal Air Surgeon determines that the physical deficiency has become enough more pronounced to require another special medical flight or practical test.

(f) The authority of the Federal Air Surgeon under this section is also exercised by the Chief, Aeromedical Certification Branch, Civil Aeromedical Institute, and each Regional Flight Surgeon.

(Secs. 313(a), 601, and 602, Federal Aviation Act of 1958, as amended (49 U.S.C. 1354(a), 1421, and 1422); sec. 6(c), Department of Transportation Act (49 U.S.C. 1655(c)))
[Amdt. 67-11, 47 FR 16308, Apr. 15, 1982]

§ 67.20 Applications, certificates, logbooks, reports, and records: Falsification, reproduction, or alteration.

(a) No person may make or cause to be made—

(1) Any fraudulent or intentionally false statement on any application for a medical certificate under this part;

(2) Any fraudulent or intentionally false entry in any logbook, record, or report that is required to be kept, made, or used, to show compliance with any requirement for any medical certificate under this part;

(3) Any reproduction, for fraudulent purpose, of any medical certificate under this part;

(4) Any alteration of any medical certificate under this part.

(b) The commission by any person of an act prohibited under paragraph (a) of this section is a basis for suspending or revoking any airman, ground instructor, or medical certificate or rating held by that person.

[Amdt. 67-1, 30 FR 2197, Feb. 18, 1965]

Subpart B—Certification Procedures

§ 67.21 Applicability.

This subpart prescribes the general procedures that apply to the issue of medical certificates for airmen.

§ 67.23 Medical examinations: Who may give.

(a) *First class.* Any aviation medical examiner who is specifically designated for the purpose may give the examination for the first class certificate. Any interested person may obtain a list of these aviation medical examiners, in any area, from the FAA Regional Director of the region in which the areas is located.

(b) *Second class and third class.* Any aviation medical examiner may give the examination for the second or third class certificate. Any interested person may obtain a list of aviation medical examiners, in any area, from the FAA regional Director of the region in which the area is located.

[Doc. No. 1179, 27 FR 7980, Aug. 10, 1962, as amended by Amdt. 67-8, 35 FR 14075, Sept. 4, 1970]

§ 67.25 Delegation of authority.

(a) The authority of the Administrator, under section 602 of the Federal Aviation Act of 1958 (49 U.S.C. 1422), to issue or deny medical certificates is delegated to the Federal Air Surgeon, to the extent necessary to—

(1) Examine applicants for and holders of medical certificates for compliance with applicable medical standards; and

(2) Issue, renew, or deny medical certificates to applicants and holders based upon compliance or noncompli-

ance with applicable medical standards.

Subject to limitations in this chapter, the authority delegated in paragraphs (a)(1) and (2) of this section is also delegated to aviation medical examiners and to authorized representatives of the Federal Air Surgeon within the FAA.

(b) The authority of the Administrator, under subsection 314(b) of the Federal Aviation Act of 1958 (49 U.S.C. 1355(b)), to reconsider the action of an aviation medical examiner is delegated to the Federal Air Surgeon, the Chief, Aeromedical Certification Branch, Civil Aeromedical Institute, and each Regional Flight Surgeon. Where the applicant does not meet the standards of § 67.13(d)(1)(ii), (d)(2)(ii), or (f)(2), § 67.15(d)(1)(ii), (d)(2)(ii), or (f)(2), or § 67.17(d)(1)(ii), (d)(2)(ii), or (f)(2), any action taken under this paragraph other than by the Federal Air Surgeon is subject to reconsideration by the Federal Air Surgeon. A certificate issued by an aviation medical examiner is considered to be affirmed as issued unless an FAA official named in this paragraph on his own initiative reverses that issuance within 60 days after the date of issuance. However, if within 60 days after the date of issuance that official requests the certificate holder to submit additional medical information, he may on his own initiative reverse the issuance within 60 days after he receives the requested information.

(c) The authority of the Administrator, under section 609 of the Federal Aviation Act of 1958 (49 U.S.C. 1429), to re-examine any civil airman, to the extent necessary to determine an airman's qualification to continue to hold an airman medical certificate, is delegated to the Federal Air Surgeon and his authorized representatives within the FAA.

(Sec. 303, 72 Stat. 747, 49 U.S.C. 1344; sec. 602, 72 Stat. 776, 49 U.S.C. 1422; secs. 313(a), 601, and 602, Federal Aviation Act of 1958, as amended (49 U.S.C. 1354(a), 1421, and 1422); sec. 6(c), Department of Transportation Act (49 U.S.C. 1655(c)))

[Doc. No. 1179, 27 FR 7980, Aug. 10, 1962, as amended by Amdt. 67-5, 31 FR 8356, June 15, 1966; Amdt. 67-7, 34 FR 248, Jan. 8, 1969;

34 FR 550, Jan. 15, 1969; Amdt. 67-9, 37 FR 4072, Feb. 26, 1972; Amdt. 67-11, 47 FR 16309, Apr. 15, 1982]

§ 67.27 Denial of medical certificate.

(a) Any person who is denied a medical certificate by an aviation medical examiner may, within 30 days after the date of the denial, apply in writing and in duplicate to the Federal Air Surgeon, Attention: Chief, Aeromedical Certification Branch, Civil Aeromedical Institute, Federal Aviation Administration, Post Office Box 25082, Oklahoma City, Okla. 73125, for reconsideration of that denial. If he does not apply for reconsideration during the 30-day period after the date of the denial, he is considered to have withdrawn his application for a medical certificate.

(b) The denial of a medical certificate—

(1) By an aviation medical examiner is not a denial by the Administrator under section 602 of the Federal Aviation Act of 1958 (49 U.S.C. 1422);

(2) By the Federal Air Surgeon is considered to be a denial by the Administrator under that section of the Act; and

(3) By the Chief, Aeromedical Certification Branch, Civil Aeromedical Institute, or a Regional Flight Surgeon is considered to be a denial by the Administrator under the Act except where the applicant does not meet the standards of § 67.13(d)(1)(ii), (d)(2)(ii), or (f)(2), § 67.15(d)(1)(ii), (d)(2)(ii), or (f)(2), or § 67.17(d)(1)(ii), (d)(2)(ii), or (f)(2).

(c) Any action taken under § 67.25(b) that wholly or partly reverses the issue of a medical certificate by an aviation medical examiner is the denial of a medical certificate under paragraph (b) of this section.

(d) If the issue of a medical certificate is wholly or partly reversed upon reconsideration by the Federal Air Surgeon, the Chief, Aeromedical Certification Branch, Civil Aeromedical Institute, or a Regional Flight Surgeon, the person holding that certificate shall surrender it, upon request of the FAA.

(Secs. 313(a), 601, and 602, Federal Aviation Act of 1958, as amended (49 U.S.C. 1354(a),

1421, and 1422); sec. 6(c), Department of Transportation Act (49 U.S.C. 1655(c)))

[Doc. No. 7077, Amdt. 67–5, 31 FR 8357, June 15, 1966, as amended by Doc. No. 8084, 32 FR 5769, Apr. 11, 1967; Amdt. 67–9, 37 FR 4072, Feb. 26, 1972; Amdt. 67–11, 47 FR 16309, Apr. 15, 1982]

§ 67.29 Medical certificates by senior flight surgeons of armed forces.

(a) The FAA has designated senior flight surgeons of the armed forces on specified military posts, stations, and facilities, as aviation medical examiners.

(b) An aviation medical examiner described in paragraph (a) of this section may give physical examinations to applicants for FAA medical certificates who are on active duty or who are, under Department of Defense medical programs, eligible for FAA medical certification as civil airmen. In addition, such an examiner may issue or deny an appropriate FAA medical certificate in accordance with the regulations of this chapter and the policies of the FAA.

(c) Any interested person may obtain a list of the military posts, stations, and facilities at which a senior flight surgeon has been designated as an aviation medical examiner, from the Surgeon General of the armed force concerned or from the Chief, Aeromedical Certification Branch, AC–130, Department of Transporta-tion, Federal Aviation Administration, Civil Aeromedical Institute, Post Office Box 25082, Oklahoma City, Okla. 73125.

[Doc. No. 1179, 27 FR 7980, Aug. 10, 1962, as amended by Doc. No. 8084, 32 FR 5769, Apr. 11, 1967; Amdt. 67–8, 35 FR 14076, Sept. 4, 1970]

§ 67.31 Medical records.

Whenever the Administrator finds that additional medical information or history is necessary to determine whether an applicant for or the holder of a medical certificate meets the medical standards for it, he requests that person to furnish that information or authorize any clinic, hospital, doctor, or other person to release to the Administrator any available information or records concerning that history. If the applicant, or holder, refuses to provide the requested medical information or history or to authorize the release so requested, the Administrator may suspend, modify, or revoke any medical certificate that he holds or may, in the case of an applicant, refuse to issue a medical certificate to him.

(Secs. 303(d), 313(a), 314(b), 601, 602, 609, Federal Aviation Act of 1958 (49 U.S.C. 1344, 1354, 1355(b), 1421, 1422, 1429))

[Amdt. 67–5, 31 FR 8357, June 15, 1966]

SUBCHAPTER E—AIRSPACE

PART 71—DESIGNATION OF FEDERAL AIRWAYS, AREA LOW ROUTES, CONTROLLED AIRSPACE, AND REPORTING POINTS

SPECIAL FEDERAL AVIATION REGULATION No. 45-1

Subpart A—General

Sec.
71.1 Applicability.
71.3 Classification of Federal airways.
71.5 Extent of Federal airways.
71.6 Extent of area low routes.
71.7 Control areas.
71.9 Continental Control Area.
71.11 Control zones.
71.12 Terminal control areas.
71.13 Transition areas.
71.14 Airport radar service areas.
71.15 Positive control areas.
71.17 Reporting points.
71.19 Bearings; radials; miles.

Subparts B–K [Note]

Subpart L—Airport Radar Service

71.501 Designation.

SPECIAL FEDERAL AVIATION REGULATION No. 45-1

Contrary provisions of the Federal Aviation Regulations notwithstanding,

1. The Robert Mueller Municipal Airport, Austin, TX, and the Port Columbus International Airport, Columbus, OH, are designated Airport Radar Service Areas (ARSA) airports at which, unless otherwise provided for in a Notice to Airmen issued by the ARSA facility, radar services will be provided continuously.

2. For purposes of this Special Federal Aviation Regulation:

(a) The Austin, TX, ARSA is that airspace extending upward from the surface to and including 4,600 feet MSL within a 5 nautical mile radius of the Robert Mueller Municipal Airport and that airspace extending upward from 2,000 feet MSL to 4,600 feet MSL, within a 10 nautical mile radius of Robert Mueller Municipal Airport from the 027° true bearing from the airport clockwise to the 207° true bearing from the airport and that airspace extending upward from 2,300 feet MSL to 4,600 feet MSL within a 10 nautical mile radius of the airport from the 207° true bearing from the airport clockwise to the 027° true bearing from the airport.

(b) The Columbus, OH, ARSA is that airspace extending upward from the surface to and including 4,800 feet MSL within a 5 nautical mile radius of the Port Columbus International Airport and that airspace extending upward from 2,500 feet MSL to 4,800 feet MSL within a 10 nautical mile radius of Port Columbus International Airport from the 008° true bearing from the airport clockwise to the 127° true bearing from the airport and that airspace extending upward from 2,200 feet MSL to 4,800 feet MSL within a 10 nautical mile radius of the airport from the 127° true bearing from the airport clockwise to the 008° true bearing from the airport.

(c) The primary airport is the airport for which the ARSA is designated; a satellite airport is any other airport, heliport, helipad, etc., within that ARSA.

3. Unless otherwise authorized or required by ATC—

(a) Arrivals and Overflights—no person may operate an aircraft in an ARSA unless two-way radio communication is established with ATC prior to entering that ARSA and is thereafter maintained with ATC while within that ARSA.

(b) Departures—no person may operate an aircraft within an ARSA unless two-way radio communication is maintained with ATC while within that ARSA, except that for aircraft departing a satellite airport, two-way radio communication is established as soon as practicable and thereafter maintained with ATC while within that ARSA;

(c) ATC Instructions and Clearances—except in an emergency, no person may, while within an ARSA, operate an aircraft contrary to an ATC clearance or instruction;

(d) Traffic Patterns—no person may takeoff or land an aircraft within an ARSA except in compliance with FAA arrival and departure traffic patterns; and

(e) Ultralight Vehicle and Parachute Jump Operations—no person may operate an ultralight vehicle within, or make a parachute jump within or into, an ARSA except under the terms of an ATC authorization issued by the ATC facility having jurisdiction over that ARSA.

4. In addition to the required preflight actions of FAR Section 91.5, each pilot in command shall review NOTAM's pertaining to flight within an ARSA prior to conducting flight in an ARSA.

This SFAR terminates at 12:01 a.m. local time on June 21, 1985, unless sooner superseded or rescinded.

(Secs. 307 and 313(a), Federal Aviation Act of 1985, as amended (49 U.S.C. 1348, 1354(a)); 49 U.S.C. 106(g) (Revised, Pub. L.

97–449, January 12, 1983); 14 CFR 11.45; and 14 CFR 11.65)

[Doc. No. 23708, 49 FR 47177, Nov. 30, 1984; 49 FR 49089, Dec. 18, 1984]

Subpart A—General

AUTHORITY: 49 U.S.C. 1348(a) and 1354(a); 49 U.S.C. 106(g) (Revised, Pub. L. 97–449, January 12, 1983); 14 CFR 11.69.

SOURCE: 46 FR 403, Jan. 2, 1981, unless otherwise noted.

§ 71.1 Applicability.

(a) The airspace assignments described in Subparts B and C are designated as Federal airways.

(b) The airspace assignments described in Subparts B through I are designated as control areas, the continental control area, control zones, transition areas, positive control areas, and reporting points, as described in the appropriate subpart.

(c) The airspace assignments described in Subpart K of this part are designated as terminal control areas.

(d) The airspace assignments described in Subpart J are designated as area low routes.

(e) The airspace assignments described in Subpart L of this part are designated as airport radar service areas.

[46 FR 403, Jan. 2, 1981, as amended at 50 FR 9258, Mar. 6, 1985]

§ 71.3 Classification of Federal airways.

Federal airways are classified as follows:

(a) Colored Federal airways:
(1) Green Federal airways.
(2) Amber Federal airways.
(3) Red Federal airways.
(4) Blue Federal airways.
(b) VOR Federal airways.

§ 71.5 Extent of Federal airways.

(a) Each Federal airway is based on a centerline that extends from one navigational aid or intersection to another navigational aid (or through several navigational aids or intersections) specified for that airway.

(b) Unless otherwise specified in Subpart B or C—

(1) Each Federal airway includes the airspace within parallel boundary lines 4 miles each side of the centerline.

Where an airway changes direction, it includes that airspace enclosed by extending the boundary lines of the airway segments until they meet.

(2) Where the changeover point for an airway segment is more than 51 miles from either of the navigational aids defining that segment, and—

(i) The changeover point is midway between the navigational aids, the airway includes the airspace between lines diverging at angles of 4.5° from the centerline at each navigational aid and extending until they intersect opposite the changeover point; or

(ii) The changeover point is not midway between the navigational aids, the airway includes the airspace between lines diverging at angles of 4.5° from the centerline at the navigational aid more distant from the changeover point, and extending until they intersect with the bisector of the angle of the centerlines at the changeover point; and between lines connecting these points of intersection and the navigational aid nearer to the changeover point.

(3) Where an airway terminates at a point or intersection more than 51 miles from the closest associated navigational aid it includes the additional airspace within lines diverging at angles of 4.5° from the centerline extending from the associated navigational aid to a line perpendicular to the centerline at the termination point.

(4) Where an airway terminates, it includes the airspace within a circle centered at the specified navigational aid or intersection having a diameter equal to the airway width at that point. However, an airway does not extend beyond the domestic/oceanic control area boundary.

(c) Unless otherwise specified in Subpart B or C—

(1) Each Federal airway includes that airspace extending upward from 1,200 feet above the surface of the earth to, but not including, 18,000 feet MSL, except that Federal airways for Hawaii have no upper limits. Variations of the lower limits of an airway are expressed in digits representing hundreds of feet above the surface (AGL) or mean sea level (MSL) and, unless otherwise specified, apply to

the segment of an airway between adjoining navigational aids or intersections; and

(2) The airspace of a Federal airway within the lateral limits of a transition area has a floor coincident with the floor of the transition area.

(d) One or more alternate airways may be designated between specified navigational aids or intersections along each VOR Federal airway described in Subpart C. Unless otherwise specified, the centerline of an alternate VOR Federal airway and the centerline of the corresponding segment of the main VOR Federal airway are separated by 15°.

(e) A Federal airway does not include the airspace of a prohibited area.

§ 71.6   Extent of area low routes.

(a) Each area low route is based on a centerline that extends from one waypoint to another waypoint (or through several waypoints) specified for that area low route. An area low route does not include the airspace of a prohibited area. All mileages specified in connection with area low routes are nautical miles.

(b) Unless otherwise specified in Subpart J, the following apply:

(1) Except as provided in paragraph (b)(2) of this section, each area low route includes, and is limited to, that airspace within parallel boundary lines 4 or more miles on each side of the route centerline as described in the middle column of the following table, plus that additional airspace outside of those parallel lines and within lines drawn outward from those parallel lines at angles of 3.25°, beginning at the distance from the tangent point specified in the right-hand column of the following table:

Miles from reference facility to tangent point	Miles from centerline to parallel lines	Miles from tangent point along parallel lines to vortices of 3.25° angles
Less than 17	4	51.
17 to, but not including 27	4	50.
27 to, but not including 33	4	49.
33 to, but not including 38	4	48.
38 to, but not including 43	4	47.
43 to, but not including 47	4	46.
47 to, but not including 51	4	45.
51 to, but not including 55	4	44.
55 to, but not including 58	4	43.
58 to, but not including 61	4	42.
61 to, but not including 63	4	41.
63 to, but not including 66	4	40.
66 to, but not including 68	4	39.
68 to, but not including 70	4	38.
70 to, but not including 72	4	37.
72 to, but not including 74	4	36.
74 to, but not including 76	4	35.
76 to, but not including 78	4	34.
78 to, but not including 79	4	33.
79 to, but not including 81	4	32.
81 to, but not including 83	4	31.
83 to, but not including 84	4	30.
84 to, but not including 86	4	29.
86 to, but not including 87	4	28.
87 to, but not including 88	4	27.
88 to, but not including 89	4	26.
89 to, but not including 91	4	25.
91 to, but not including 92	4	24.
92 to, but not including 93	4	23.
93 to, but not including 94	4	22.
94 to, but not including 95	4	21.
95 to, but not including 96	4	19.
96 to, but not including 97	4	18.
97 to, but not including 98	4	17.
98 to, but not including 99	4	15.
99 to, but not including 100	4	13.
100 to, but not including 101	4	11.
101 to, but not including 102	4	8.
102 to, but not including 105	4	0 (i.e., at tangent point).

Miles from reference facility to tangent point	Miles from centerline to parallel lines	Miles from tangent point along parallel lines to vortices of 3.25° angles
105 to, but not including 115	4.25	0 (i.e., at tangent point).
115 to, but not including 125	4.50	0 (i.e., at tangent point).
125 to, but not including 135	4.75	0 (i.e., at tangent point).
135 to, but not including 145	5.00	0 (i.e., at tangent point).
145 to, but not including 150	5.25	0 (i.e., at tangent point).

(2) Each area low route, whose centerline is at least 2 miles, and not more than 3 miles from the reference facility, includes, in addition to the airspace specified in paragraph (b)(1) of this section, that airspace on the reference facility side of the centerline that is within lines connecting the point that is 4.9 miles from the tangent point on a perpendicular line from the centerline through the reference facility, thence to the edges of the boundary lines described in paragraph (b)(1) of this section, intersecting those boundary lines at angles of 5.15°.

(3) Where an area low route changes direction, it includes that airspace enclosed by extending the boundary lines of the route segments until they meet.

(4) Where the widths of adjoining route segments are unequal, the following apply:

(i) If the tangent point of the narrower segment is on the route centerline, the width of the narrower segment includes that additional airspace within lines from the lateral extremity of the wider segment where the route segments join, thence toward the tangent point of the narrower route segment, until intersecting the boundary of the narrower segment.

(ii) If the tangent point of the narrower segment is on the route centerline extended, the width of the narrower segment includes that additional airspace within lines from the lateral extremity of the wider segment where the route segments join, thence toward the tangent point until reaching the point where the narrower segment terminates or changes direction, or until intersecting the boundary of the narrower segment.

(5) Where an area low route terminates, it includes that airspace within a circle whose center is the terminating waypoint, and whose diameter is equal to the route segment width at that waypoint, except that an area low route does not extend beyond the domestic/oceanic control area boundary.

(6) Each area low route includes that airspace extending upward from 1,200 feet above the surface of the earth to, but not including, 18,000 feet MSL, except that area low routes for Hawaii have no upper limits. Variations of the lower limits of an area low route are expressed in digits representing hundreds of feet above the surface (AGL) or mean sea level (MSL) and, unless otherwise specified, apply to the route segment between adjoining waypoints used in the description of the route.

(7) The airspace of an area low route within the lateral limits of a transition area has a floor coincident with the floor of the transition area.

§ 71.7   Control areas.

Control areas consist of the airspace designated in Subparts B, C, E, and J, but do not include the continental control area. Unless otherwise designated, control areas include the airspace between a segment of a main VOR Federal airway and its associated alternate segments with the vertical extent of the area corresponding to the vertical extent of the related segment of the main airway.

§ 71.9   Continental Control Area.

The Continental Control Area consists of the airspace of the 48 contiguous States, the District of Columbia and Alaska, excluding the Alaska peninsula west of longitude 160°00′00″ W., at and above 14,500 feet M.S.L., but does not include—

(a) The airspace less than 1,500 feet above the surface of the earth; or

(b) Prohibited and restricted areas, other than restricted areas listed in Subpart D of this part.

§ 71.11   Control zones.

The control zones listed in Subpart F of this part consist of controlled airspace which extends upward from the surface of the earth and terminates at the base of the continental control area. Control zones that do not underlie the continental control area have no upper limit. A control zone may include one or more airports and is normally a circular area with a radius of 5 miles and any extensions necessary to include instrument approach and departure paths.

§ 71.12   Terminal control areas.

The terminal control areas listed in Subpart K of this part consist of controlled airspace extending upward from the surface or higher to specified altitudes, within which all aircraft are subject to operating rules and pilot and equipment requirements specified in Part 91 of this chapter. Each such location includes at least one primary airport around which the terminal control area is located.

§ 71.13   Transition areas.

The transition areas listed in Subpart G consist of controlled airspace extending upward from 700 feet or more above the surface of the earth when designated in conjunction with an airport for which an approved instrument approach procedure has been prescribed; or from 1,200 feet or more above the surface of the earth when designated in conjunction with airway route structures or segments. Unless otherwise specified, transition areas terminate at the base of the overlying controlled airspace.

§ 71.14   Airport radar service areas.

The airport radar service areas listed in Subpart L of this part consist of controlled airspace extending upward from the surface or higher to specified altitudes, within which all aircraft are subject to operating rules and equipment requirements specified in Part 91 of this chapter. Each location listed includes at least one primary airport around which the airport radar service area is located.

[50 FR 9258, Mar. 6, 1985]

§ 71.15   Positive control areas.

The positive control areas listed in Subpart H consist of controlled airspace within which there is positive control of aircraft.

§ 71.17   Reporting points.

(a) The reporting points listed in Subpart I consist of geographic locations, in relation to which the position of an aircraft must be reported in accordance with § 91.125 of this chapter.

(b) Unless otherwise designated, each reporting point applies to all directions of flight. In any case where a geographic location is designated as a reporting point for less than all airways passing through that point, or for a particular direction of flight along an airway only, it is so indicated by including the airways or direction of flight in the designation of geographical location.

(c) Unless otherwise specified, place names appearing in the reporting point descriptions indicate VOR or VORTAC facilities identified by those names.

§ 71.19   Bearings; radials; miles.

(a) All bearings and radials in this part are true, and are applied from point of origin.

(b) Except as otherwise specified and except that mileages for Federal airways are stated as nautical miles, all mileages in this part are stated as statute miles.

Subparts B–K

EDITORIAL NOTE: The full text of Subparts B–K was published in the FEDERAL REGISTER but is not carried in the Code of Federal Regulations. For Federal Register citations affecting these subparts, see the List of CFR Sections Affected in the Finding Aids section of this volume.

Subpart L—Airport Radar Service Areas

§ 71.501   Designation.

The airspace descriptions listed below are designated as airport radar service areas. The primary airport for each airport radar service area is also designated. Except as otherwise specified, all mileages are nautical miles and all altitudes are above mean sea level.

[50 FR 9258, Mar. 6, 1985]

PART 73—SPECIAL USE AIRSPACE

AUTHORITY: 49 U.S.C. 1348(a), 1354(a), 1510, 1522; Executive Order 10854; 49 U.S.C. 106(g) (Revised Pub. L. 97–449, January 12, 1983); 14 CFR 11.69.

SOURCE: 46 FR 779, Jan. 2, 1981, unless otherwise noted.

Subpart A—General

§ 73.1 Applicability.

The airspace that is described in Subpart B and Subpart C of this part is designated as special use airspace. These parts prescribe the requirements for the use of that airspace.

§ 73.3 Special use airspace.

(a) Special use airspace consists of airspace of defined dimensions identified by an area on the surface of the earth wherein activities must be confined because of their nature, or wherein limitations are imposed upon aircraft operations that are not a part of those activities, or both.

(b) The vertical limits of special use airspace are measured by designated altitude floors and ceilings expressed as flight levels or as feet above mean sea level. Unless otherwise specified, the word "to" (an altitude or flight level) means "to and including" (that altitude or flight level).

(c) The horizontal limits of special use airspace are measured by boundaries described by geographic coordi-

nates or other appropriate references that clearly define their perimeter.

(d) The period of time during which a designation of special use airspace is in effect is stated in the designation.

§ 73.5 Bearings; radials; miles.

(a) All bearings and radials in this part are true from point of origin.

(b) Unless otherwise specified, all mileages in this part are stated as statute miles.

Subpart B—Restricted Areas

§ 73.11 Applicability.

This subpart designates restricted areas and prescribes limitations on the operation of aircraft within them.

§ 73.13 Restrictions.

No person may operate an aircraft within a restricted area between the designated altitudes and during the time of designation, unless he has the advance permission of

(a) The using agency described in § 73.15; or

(b) The controlling agency described in § 73.17.

§ 73.15 Using agency.

(a) For the purposes of this subpart, the following are using agencies;

(1) The agency, organization, or military command whose activity within a restricted area necessitated the area being so designated.

(b) Upon the request of the FAA, the using agency shall execute a letter establishing procedures for joint use of a restricted area by the using agency and the controlling agency, under which the using agency would notify the controlling agency whenever the controlling agency may grant permission for transit through the restricted area in accordance with the terms of the letter.

(c) The using agency shall—

(1) Schedule activities within the restricted area;

(2) Authorize transit through, or flight within, the restricted area as feasible; and

(3) Contain within the restricted area all activities conducted therein in accordance with the purpose for which it was designated.

§ 73.17   Controlling agency.

For the purposes of this part, the controlling agency is the FAA facility that may authorize transit through or flight within a restricted area in accordance with a joint-use letter issued under § 73.15.

§ 73.19   Reports by using agency.

(a) Each using agency shall prepare a report on the use of each restricted area assigned thereto during any part of the preceding 12-month period ended September 30, and transmit it by the following January 31 of each year to the Chief, Air Traffic Division in the regional office of the Federal Aviation Administration having jurisdiction over the area in which the restricted area is located, with a copy to the Director, Air Traffic Service, Federal Aviation Administration, Washington, D.C. 20591.

(b) In the report under this section the using agency shall:

(1) State the name and number of the restricted area as published in this part, and the period covered by the report.

(2) State the activities (including average daily number of operations if appropriate) conducted in the area, and any other pertinent information concerning current and future electronic-monitoring devices.

(3) State the number of hours daily, the days of the week, and the number of weeks during the year that the area was used.

(4) For restricted areas having a joint-use designation, also state the number of hours daily, the days of the week, and the number of weeks during the year that the restricted area was released to the controlling agency for public use.

(5) State the mean sea level altitudes or flight levels (whichever is appropriate) used in aircraft operations and the maximum and average ordinate of surface firing (expressed in feet, mean sea level altitude) used on a daily, weekly, and yearly basis.

(6) Include a chart of the area (of optional scale and design) depicting, if used, aircraft operating areas, flight patterns, ordnance delivery areas, surface firing points, and target, fan, and impact areas. After once submitting an appropriate chart, subsequent annual charts are not required unless there is a change in the area, activity or altitude (or flight levels) used, which might alter the depiction of the activities originally reported. If no change is to be submitted, a statement indicating "no change" shall be included in the report.

(7) Include any other information not otherwise required under this part which is considered pertinent to activities carried on in the restricted area.

(c) If it is determined that the information submitted under paragraph (b) of this section is not sufficient to evaluate the nature and extent of the use of a restricted area, the FAA may request the using agency to submit supplementary reports. Within 60 days after receiving a request for additional information, the using agency shall submit such information as the Director of the Air Traffic Service considers appropriate. Supplementary reports must be sent to the FAA officials designated in paragraph (a) of this section.

(Secs. 307 and 313(a), Federal Aviation Act of 1958 (49 U.S.C. 1348 and 1354(a)))

[Doc. No. 15379, Amdt. 73-4, 42 FR 54798, Oct. 11, 1977]

EDITORIAL NOTE: The restricted areas formerly carried as §§ 608.21 to 608.72 of this title were transferred to Part 73 as §§ 73.21 to 73.72 under Subpart B but are not carried in the Code of Federal Regulations. For Federal Register citations affecting these restricted areas, see the List of CFR Sections Affected in the Finding Aids section of this volume.

Subpart C—Prohibited Areas

§ 73.81   Applicability.

This subpart designates prohibited areas and prescribes limitations on the operation of aircraft therein.

§ 73.83   Restrictions.

No person may operate an aircraft within a prohibited area unless authorization has been granted by the using agency.

§ 73.85 Using agency.

For the purpose of this subpart, the using agency is the agency, organization or military command that established the requirements for the prohibited area.

EDITORIAL NOTE: Sections 73.87 through 73.99 are reserved for descriptions of designated prohibited areas. For Federal Register citations affecting these prohibited areas, see the List of CFR Sections Affected in the Finding Aids section of this volume.

SUBCHAPTER F—AIR TRAFFIC AND GENERAL OPERATING RULES

PART 91—GENERAL OPERATING AND FLIGHT RULES

Sec.

Subpart A—General

§ 91.1 Applicability.

(a) Except as provided in paragraph (b) of this section, this part describes rules governing the operation of aircraft (other than moored balloons, kites, unmanned rockets, and unmanned free balloons) within the United States.

(b) Each person operating a civil aircraft of U.S. registry outside of the United States shall—

(1) When over the high seas, comply with Annex 2 (Rules of the Air) to the Convention on International Civil Aviation and with §§ 91.70(c), 91.88, and 91.90 of Subpart B;

(2) When within a foreign country, comply with the regulations relating to the flight and maneuver of aircraft there in force;

(3) Except for §§ 91.15(b), 91.17, 91.38 and 91.43, comply with Subparts A, C, and D of this part so far as they are not inconsistent with applicable regulations of the foreign country where the aircraft is operated or Annex 2 to the Convention on International Civil Aviation; and

(4) When over the North Atlantic within airspace designated as Minimum Navigation Performance Specifications airspace, comply with § 91.20.

(c) Annex 2 to the Convention on International Civil Aviation, Sixth Edition—September 1970, with amendments through Amendment 20 effective August 1976, to which reference is made in this part is incorporated into this part and made a part hereof as provided in 5 U.S.C. 552 and pursuant to 1 CFR Part 51, Annex 2 (including a complete historic file of changes thereto) is available for public inspection at the Rules Docket, AGC–24, Federal Aviation Administration, 800 Independence Avenue, SW., Washington, D.C. 20591. In addition, Annex 2 may be purchased from the International Civil Aviation Organization (Attention: Distribution Officer), P.O. Box 400, Succursale; Place de L'Aviation Internationale, 1000 Sherbrooke Street West, Montreal, Quebec, Canada H3A 2R2.

[Amdt. 61–22, 31 FR 8355, June 15, 1966, as amended by Amdt. 91–78, 35 FR 7784, May 21, 1970; Amdt. 91–112, 38 FR 8054, Mar. 28, 1973; Amdt. 91–137, 42 FR 22139, May 2, 1977; Amdt. 91–144, 42 FR 64881, Dec. 29, 1977; Amdt. 91–153, 43 FR 28420, June 29, 1978; Amdt. 91–187, 50 FR 9258, Mar. 6, 1985]

§ 91.2 Certificate of authorization for certain Category II operations.

The Admistrator may issue a certificate of authorization authorizing deviations from the requirements of §§ 91.6, 91.33(f), and 91.34 for the operation of small aircrafts identified as Category A aircraft in § 97.3 of this chapter in Category II operations, if he finds that the proposed operation can be safely conducted under the terms of the certificate. Such authorization does not permit operation of the aircraft carrying persons or property for compensation or hire.

[Amdt. 91–88, 36 FR 4592, Mar. 10, 1971, as amended by Amdt. 91–196, 51 FR 40707, Nov. 7, 1986]

§ 91.3 Responsibility and authority of the pilot in command.

(a) The pilot in command of an aircraft is directly responsible for, and is the final authority as to, the operation of that aircraft.

(b) In an emergency requiring immediate action, the pilot in command may deviate from any rule of this subpart or of Subpart B to the extent required to meet that emergency.

(c) Each pilot in command who deviates from a rule under paragraph (b) of this section shall, upon the request of the Administrator, send a written report of that deviation to the Administrator.

§ 91.4 Pilot in command of aircraft requiring more than one required pilot.

No person may operate an aircraft that is type certificated for more than one required pilot flight crewmember unless the pilot flight crew consists of a pilot in command who meets the requirements of § 61.58 of this chapter.

[Doc. No. 10916, Amdt. 91–111, 38 FR 3179, Feb. 1, 1973, as amended by Amdt. 91–133, 41 FR 47228, Oct. 28, 1976]

§ 91.5 Preflight action.

Each pilot in command shall, before beginning a flight, familiarize himself with all available information concerning that flight. This information must include:

(a) For a flight under IFR or a flight not in the vicinity of an airport, weather reports and forecasts, fuel requirements, alternatives available if the planned flight cannot be completed, and any known traffic delays of which he has been advised by ATC.

(b) For any flight, runway lengths at airports of intended use, and the following takeoff and landing distance information:

(1) For civil aircraft for which an approved airplane or rotorcraft flight manual containing takeoff and landing distance data is required, the takeoff and landing distance data contained therein; and

(2) For civil aircraft other than those specified in paragraph (b)(1) of this section, other reliable information appropriate to the aircraft, relating to aircraft performance under expected values of airport elevation and runway slope, aircraft gross weight, and wind and temperature.

[Amdt. 91–87, 36 FR 2482, Feb. 5, 1971]

§ 91.6 Category II and III operations: General operating rules.

(a) No person may operate a civil aircraft in a Category II or Category III operation unless:

(1) The flightcrew of the aircraft consists of a pilot in command and a second in command who hold the appropriate authorizations and ratings prescribed in § 61.3 of this chapter;

(2) Each flight crewmember has adequate knowledge of, and familiarity

with, the aircraft and the procedures to be used; and

(3) The instrument panel in front of the pilot who is controlling the aircraft has appropriate instrumentation for the type of flight control guidance system that is being used.

(b) Unless otherwise authorized by the Administrator, no person may operate a civil aircraft in a Category II or Category III operation unless each ground component required for that operation and the related airborne equipment is installed and operating.

(c) For the purpose of this section, when the approach procedure being used provides for and requires use of a DH, the authorized decision height is the DH prescribed by the approach procedure, the DH prescribed for the pilot in command, or the DH for which the aircraft is equipped, whichever is higher.

(d) Unless otherwise authorized by the Administrator, no pilot operating an aircraft in a Category II or Category III approach that provides and requires use of a DH may continue the approach below the authorized decision height unless the following conditions are met:

(1) The aircraft is in a position from which a descent to a landing on the intended runway can be made at a normal rate of descent using normal maneuvers, and where that descent rate will allow touchdown to occur within the touchdown zone of the runway of intended landing.

(2) At least one of the following visual references for the intended runway is distinctly visible and identifiable to the pilot:

(i) The approach light system, except that the pilot may not descend below 100 feet above the touchdown zone elevation using the approach lights as a reference unless the red terminating bars or the red side row bars are also distinctly visible and identifiable.

(ii) The threshold.

(iii) The threshold markings.

(iv) The threshold lights.

(v) The touchdown zone or touchdown zone markings.

(vi) The touchdown zone lights.

(e) Unless otherwise authorized by the Administrator, each pilot operating an aircraft shall immediately execute an appropriate missed approach whenever prior to touchdown the requirements of paragraph (d) of this section are not met.

(f) No person operating an aircraft using a Category III approach without decision height may land that aircraft except in accordance with the provisions of the letter of authorization issued by the Administrator.

(g) Paragraphs (a) through (f) of this section do not apply to operations conducted by the holders of certificates issued under Part 121, 123, 125, 129, or 135 of this chapter. No person may operate a civil aircraft in a Category II or Category III operation conducted by the holder of a certificate issued under Part 121, 123, 125, 129, or 135 of this chapter unless the operation is conducted in accordance with that certificate holder's operations specifications.

[Amdt. 91-173, 46 FR 2289, Jan. 8, 1981]

§ 91.7   Flight crewmembers at stations.

(a) During takeoff and landing, and while en route, each required flight crewmember shall—

(1) Be at his station unless his absence is necessary in the performance of his duties in connection with the operation of the aircraft or in connection with his physiological needs; and

(2) Keep his seat belt fastened while at his station.

(b) After July 18, 1978, each required flight crewmember of a U.S. registered civil airplane shall, during takeoff and landing, keep the shoulder harness fastened while at his station. This paragraph does not apply if—

(1) The seat at the crewmember's station is not equipped with a shoulder harness; or

(2) The crewmember would be unable to perform his required duties with the shoulder harness fastened.

[Doc. No. 1580, Amdt. 1-1, 28 FR 6704, June 29, 1963, as amended by Amdt. 91-24, 30 FR 13120, Oct. 15, 1965; Amdt. 91-139, 42 FR 30603, June 16, 1977]

§ 91.8   Prohibition against interference with crewmembers.

(a) No person may assault, threaten, intimidate, or interfere with a crewmember in the performance of the crewmember's duties aboard an aircraft being operated.

[Amdt. 91-152, 43 FR 22640, May 25, 1978]

§91.9   Careless or reckless operation.

No person may operate an aircraft in a careless or reckless manner so as to endanger the life or property of another.

§91.10   Careless or reckless operation other than for the purpose of air navigation.

No person may operate an aircraft other than for the purpose of air navigation, on any part of the surface of an airport used by aircraft for air commerce (including areas used by those aircraft for receiving or discharging persons or cargo), in a careless or reckless manner so as to endanger the life or property of another.

[Amdt. 91-43, 32 FR 9641, July 4, 1967]

§91.11   Alcohol or drugs.

(a) No person may act or attempt to act as a crewmember of a civil aircraft—

(1) Within 8 hours after the consumption of any alcoholic beverage;

(2) While under the influence of alcohol;

(3) While using any drug that affects the person's faculties in any way contrary to safety; or

(4) While having .04 percent by weight or more alcohol in the blood.

(b) Except in an emergency, no pilot of a civil aircraft may allow a person who appears to be intoxicated or who demonstrates by manner or physical indications that the individual is under the influence of drugs (except a medical patient under proper care) to be carried in that aircraft.

(c) A crewmember shall do the following:

(1) On request of a law enforcement officer, submit to a test to indicate the percentage by weight of alcohol in the blood, when—

(i) The law enforcement officer is authorized under State or local law to conduct the test or to have the test conducted; and

(ii) The law enforcement officer is requesting submission to the test to investigate a suspected violation of State or local law governing the same or substantially similar conduct prohibited by paragraph (a)(1), (a)(2), or (a)(4) of this section.

(2) Whenever the Administrator has a reasonable basis to believe that a person may have violated paragraph (a)(1), (a)(2), or (a)(4) of this section, that person shall, upon request by the Administrator, furnish the Administrator, or authorize any clinic, hospital, doctor, or other person to release to the Administrator, the results of each test taken within 4 hours after acting or attempting to act as a crewmember that indicates percentage by weight of alcohol in the blood.

(d) Whenever the Administrator has a reasonable basis to believe that a person may have violated paragraph (a)(3) of this section, that person shall, upon request by the Administrator, furnish the Administrator, or authorize any clinic, hospital, doctor, or other person to release to the Administrator, the results of each test taken within 4 hours after acting or attempting to act as a crewmember that indicates the presence of any drugs in the body.

(e) Any test information obtained by the Administrator under paragraph (c) or (d) of this section may be evaluated in determining a person's qualifications for any airman certificate or possible violations of this chapter and may be used as evidence in any legal proceeding under section 602, 609, or 901 of the Federal Aviation Act of 1958.

[Doc. No. 21956, Amdt. 91-188, 50 FR 15380, Apr. 17 1985, as amended by Amdt. 91-194, 51 FR 1229, Jan. 9, 1986]

§91.12   Carriage of narcotic drugs, marihuana, and depressant or stimulant drugs or substances.

(a) Except as provided in paragraph (b) of this section, no person may operate a civil aircraft within the United States with knowledge that narcotic drugs, marihuana, and depressant or stimulant drugs or substances as defined in Federal or State statutes are carried in the aircraft.

(b) Paragraph (a) of this section does not apply to any carriage of narcotic drugs, marihuana, and depressant or stimulant drugs or substances authorized by or under any Federal or State statute or by any Federal or State agency.

[Doc. No. 12035, Amdt. 91-117, 38 FR 17493, July 2, 1973]

§ 91.13 Dropping objects.

No pilot in command of a civil aircraft may allow any object to be dropped from that aircraft in flight that creates a hazard to persons or property. However, this section does not prohibit the dropping of any object if reasonable precautions are taken to avoid injury or damage to persons or property.

§ 91.14 Use of safety belts and shoulder harnesses.

(a) Unless otherwise authorized by the Administrator—

(1) No pilot may take off a U.S. registered civil aircraft (except a free balloon that incorporates a basket or gondola and an airship) unless the pilot in command of that aircraft ensures that each person on board is briefed on how to fasten and unfasten that person's safety belt and shoulder harness, if installed.

(2) No pilot may take off or land a U.S. registered civil aircraft (except free balloons that incorporate baskets or gondolas and airships) unless the pilot in command of that aircraft ensures that each person on board has been notified to fasten his safety belt and shoulder harness, if installed.

(3) During the takeoff and landing of U.S. registered civil aircraft (except free balloons that incorporate baskets or gondolas and airships), each person on board that aircraft must occupy a seat or berth with a safety belt and shoulder harness, if installed, properly secured about him. However, a person who has not reached his second birthday may be held by an adult who is occupying a seat or berth, and a person on board for the purpose of engaging in sport parachuting may use the floor of the aircraft as a seat.

(b) This section does not apply to operations conducted under Part 121, 123, or 127 of this chapter. Paragraph (a)(3) of this section does not apply to persons subject to § 91.7.

[Amdt. 91-89, 36 FR 12571, July 1, 1971; 36 FR 14128, July 30, 1971, as amended by Amdt. 91-135, 41 FR 55475, Dec. 20, 1976; Amdt. 91-154, 43 FR 46233, Oct. 5, 1978; Amdt. 91-191, 50 FR 46877, Nov. 13, 1985]

§ 91.15 Parachutes and parachuting.

(a) No pilot of a civil aircraft may allow a parachute that is available for emergency use to be carried in that aircraft unless it is an approved type and—

(1) If a chair type (canopy in back), it has been packed by a certificated and appropriately rated parachute rigger within the preceding 120 days; or

(2) If any other type, it has been packed by a certificated and appropriately rated parachute rigger—

(i) Within the preceding 120 days, if its canopy, shrouds, and harness are composed exclusively of nylon, rayon, or other similar synthetic fiber or materials that are substantial resistant to damage from mold, mildew, or other fungi and other rotting agents propagated in a moist environment; or

(ii) Within the preceding 60 days, if any part of the parachute is composed of silk, pongee, or other natural fiber, or materials not specified in paragraph (a)(2)(i) of this section.

(b) Except in an emergency, no pilot in command may allow, and no person may make, a parachute jump from an aircraft within the United States except in accordance with Part 105 of this chapter.

(c) Unless each occupant of the aircraft is wearing an approved parachute, no pilot of a civil aircraft, carrying any person (other than a crewmember) may execute any intentional maneuver that exceeds—

(1) A bank of 60° relative to the horizon; or

(2) A nose-up or nose-down attitude of 30° relative to the horizon.

(d) Paragraph (c) of this section does not apply to—

(1) Flight tests for pilot certification or rating; or

(2) Spins and other flight maneuvers required by the regulations for any certificate or rating when given by—

(i) A certificated flight instructor; or

(ii) An airline transport pilot instructing in accordance with § 61.169 of this chapter.

(e) For the purposes of this section, "approved parachute" means—

(1) A parachute manufactured under a type certificate or a technical standard order (C–23 series); or

(2) A personnel-carrying military parachute identified by an NAF, AAF, or AN drawing number, an AAF order number, or any other military designation or specification number.

[Doc. No. 1580, Amdt. 1–1, 28 FR 6704, June 29, 1963, as amended by Amdt. 91–29, 31 FR 8355, June 15, 1966; Amdt. 91–65, 34 FR 12883, Aug. 8, 1969; Amdt. 91–100, 37 FR 13252, July 6, 1972; Amdt. 91–114, 38 FR 12203, May 10, 1973; Amdt. 91–152, 43 FR 22640, May 25, 1978]

§ 91.17 Towing: Gliders.

(a) No person may operate a civil aircraft towing a glider unless:

(1) The pilot in command of the towing aircraft is qualified under § 61.69 of this chapter.

(2) The towing aircraft is equipped with a towhitch of a kind, and installed in a manner, approved by the Administrator.

(3) The towline used has a breaking strength not less than 80 percent of the maximum certificated operating weight of the glider, and not more than twice this operating weight. However, the towline used may have a breaking strength more than twice the maximum certificated operating weight of the glider if—

(i) A safety link is installed at the point of attachment of the towline to the glider, with a breaking strength not less than 80 percent of the maximum certificated operating weight of the glider, and not greater than twice this operating weight; and

(ii) A safety link is installed at the point of attachment of the towline to the towing aircraft with a breaking strength greater, but not more than 25 percent greater, than that of the safety link at the towed glider end of the towline, and not greater than twice the maximum certificated operating weight of the glider.

(4) Before conducting any towing operations within a control zone, or before making each towing flight within a control zone if required by ATC, the pilot in command notifies the control tower if one is in operation in that control zone. If such a control tower is not in operation, he must notify the FAA flight service station serving the control zone before conducting any towing operations in that control zone.

(5) The pilots of the towing aircraft and the glider have agreed upon a general course of action including takeoff and release signals, airspeeds, and emergency procedures for each pilot.

(b) No pilot of a civil aircraft may intentionally release a towline, after release of a glider, in a manner so as to endanger the life or property of another.

[Amdt. 91–38, 32 FR 3000, Feb. 17, 1967, as amended by Amdt. 91–133, 41 FR 47228, Oct. 28, 1976; Amdt. 91–152, 43 FR 22640, May 25, 1978]

§ 91.18 Towing: Other than under § 91.17.

(a) No pilot of a civil aircraft may tow anything with that aircraft (other than under § 91.17) except in accordance with the terms of a certificate of waiver issued by the Administrator.

(b) An application for a certificate of waiver under this section is made on a form and in a manner prescribed by the Administrator and must be submitted to the nearest Flight Standards District Office.

[Amdt. 91–38, 32 FR 3001, Feb. 17, 1967, as amended by Amdt. 91–114, 38 FR 12203, May 10, 1973; Amdt. 91–152, 43 FR 22640, May 25, 1978]

§ 91.19 Portable electronic devices.

(a) Except as provided in paragraph (b) of this section, no person may operate, nor may any operator or pilot in command of an aircraft allow the operation of, any portable electronic device on any of the following U.S. registered civil aircraft:

(1) Aircraft operated by an air carrier or commercial operator; or

(2) Any other aircraft while it is operated under IFR.

(b) Paragraph (a) of this section does not apply to:

(1) Portable voice recorders;

(2) Hearing aids;

(3) Heart pacemakers;

(4) Electric shavers; or

(5) Any other portable electronic device that the operator of the aircraft has determined will not cause interference with the navigation or communication system of the aircraft on which it is to be used.

(c) In the case of an aircraft operated by an air carrier or commercial operator, the determination required by paragraph (b)(5) of this section shall be made by the air carrier or commercial operator of the aircraft on which the particular device is to be used. In the case of other aircraft, the determination may be made by the pilot in command or other operator of the aircraft.

[Amdt. 91-35, 31 FR 15318, Dec. 7, 1966]

§ 91.20 Operations Within the North Atlantic Minimum Navigation Performance Specifications Airspace.

Unless otherwise authorized by the Administrator, no person may operate a civil aircraft of U.S. registry in North Atlantic (NAT) airspace designated as Minimum Navigation Performance Specifications (MNPS) airspace unless that aircraft has approved navigation performance capability which complies with the requirements of Appendix C to this part. The Administrator authorizes deviations from the requirements of this section in accordance with section 3 of Appendix C to this part.

[Amdt. 91-144, 42 FR 64881, Dec. 29, 1977]

§ 91.21 Flight instruction; simulated instrument flight and certain flight tests.'

(a) No person may operate a civil aircraft (except a manned free balloon) that is being used for flight instruction unless that aircraft has fully functioning dual controls. However, instrument flight instruction may be given in a single-engine airplane equipped with a single, functioning, throwover control wheel, in place of fixed, dual controls of the elevator and ailerons, when:

(1) The instructor has determined that the flight can be conducted safely; and

(2) The person manipulating the controls has at least a private pilot

certificate with appropriate category and class ratings.

(b) No person may operate a civil aircraft in simulated instrument flight unless—

(1) An appropriately rated pilot occupies the other control seat as safety pilot;

(2) The safety pilot has adequate vision forward and to each side of the aircraft, or a competent observer in the aircraft adequately supplements the vision of the safety pilot; and

(3) Except in the case of lighter-than-air aircraft, that aircraft is equipped with fully functioning dual controls. However, simulated instrument flight may be conducted in a single-engine airplane, equipped with a single, functioning, throwover control wheel, in place of fixed, dual controls of the elevator and ailerons, when—

(i) The safety pilot has determined that the flight can be conducted safely; and

(ii) The person manipulating the control has at least a private pilot certificate with appropriate category and clas ratings.

(c) No person may operate a civil aircraft that is being used for a flight test for an airline transport pilot certificate or a class or type rating on that certificate, or for a Federal Aviation Regulation Part 121 proficiency flight test, unless the pilot seated at the controls, other than the pilot being checked, is fully qualified to act as pilot in command of the aircraft.

[Doc. No. 1580, Amdt. 1-1, 28 FR 6704, June 29, 1963, as amended by Amdt. 91-36, 32 FR 262, Jan. 11, 1967; Amdt. 91-135, 41 FR 54475, Dec. 20, 1976; Amdt 91-154, 43 FR 46233, Oct. 5, 1978]

§ 91.22 Fuel requirements for flight under VFR.

(a) No person may begin a flight in an airplane under VFR unless (considering wind and forecast weather conditions) there is enough fuel to fly to the first point of intended landing and, assuming normal cruising speed—

(1) During the day, to fly after that for at least 30 minutes; or

(2) At night, to fly after that for at least 45 minutes.

Federal Aviation Administration, DOT

§ 91.24

(b) No person may begin a flight in a rotorcraft under VFR unless (considering wind and forecast weather conditions) there is enough fuel to fly to the first point of intended landing and, assuming normal cruising speed, to fly after that for at least 20 minutes.

§ 91.23 Fuel requirements for flight in IFR conditions.

(a) Except as provided in paragraph (b) of this section, no person may operate a civil aircraft in IFR conditions unless it carries enough fuel (considering weather reports and forecasts, and weather conditions) to—

(1) Complete the flight to the first airport of intended landing;

(2) Fly from that airport to the alternate airport; and

(3) Fly after that for 45 minutes at normal crusing speed or, for helicopters, fly after that for 30 minutes at normal crusing speed.

(b) Paragraph (a)(2) of this section does not apply if—

(1) Part 97 of this subchapter prescribes a standard instrument approach procedure for the first airport of intended landing; and

(2) For at least 1 hour before and 1 hour after the estimated time of arrival at the airport, the weather reports or forecasts or any combination of them, indicate—

(i) The ceiling will be at least 2,000 feet above airport elevation; and

(ii) Visibility will be at least 3 miles.

§ 91.24 ATC transponder and altitude reporting equipment and use.

(a) *All airspace: U.S.-registered civil aircraft.* For operations not conducted under parts 121, 127, or 135 of this chapter, ATC transponder equipment installed within the time periods indicated below must meet the performance and environmental requirements of the following TSO's:.

(1) *Through January 1, 1992:* (i) Any class of TSO-C74b or any class of TSO-C74c as appropriate, provided that the equiment was manufactured before January 1, 1990; or

(ii) The appropriate class of TSO-C112 (Mode S).

(2) *After January 1, 1992:* The appropriate class of TSO-C112 (Mode S). For purposes of paragraph (a)(2) of this section "installation" does not include—

(i) Temporary installation of TSO-C74b or TSO-C74c substitute equipment, as appropriate, during maintenance of the permanent equipment;

(ii) Reinstallation of equipment after temporary removal for maintenance; or

(iii) For fleet operations, installation of equipment in a fleet aircraft after removal of the equipment for maintenance from another aircraft in the same operator's fleet.

(b) *All airspace.* No person may operate an aircraft in the airspace described in paragraphs (b)(1) through (b)(5) of this section, unless that aircraft is equipped with an operable coded radar beacon transponder having either Mode 3/A 4096 code capability, replying to Mode 3/A interrogations with the code specified by ATC or a Mode S capability, replying to Mode 3/A interrogations with the code specified by ATC and intermode and Mode S interrogations in accordance with the applicable provisions specified in TSO C-112, and that aircraft is equipped with automatic pressure altitude reporting equipment having a Mode C capability that automatically replies to Mode C interrogations by transmitting pressure altitude information in 100-foot increments. This requirement applies—

(1) *All aircraft.* In terminal control areas and positive control areas;

(2) *Effective July 1 1989. All aircraft.* In all airspace within 30 nautical miles of a terminal control area primary airport, from the surface upward to 10,000 feet MSL;

(3) *Effective July 1, 1989.* Notwithstanding paragraph (b)(2) of this section, any aircraft which was not originally certificated with an engine-driven electrical system or which has not subsequently been certified with such a system installed, balloon, or glider may conduct operations in the airspace within 30 nautical miles of a terminal control area primary airport provided such operations are conducted—

(i) Outside any terminal control area and positive control area; and

(ii) Below the altitude of the terminal control area ceiling or 10,000 feet MSL, whichever is lower; and

(4) *Effective December 30, 1990— All aircraft.*

(i) In the airspace of an airport radar service area, and

(ii) In all airspace above the ceiling and within the lateral boundaries of an airport radar service area upward to 10,000 feet MSL; and

(5) *All aircraft except any aircraft which was not originally certificated with an engine-driven electrical system or which has not subsequently been certified with such a system installed, balloon, or glider.*

(i) In all airspace of the 48 contiguous states and the District of Columbia.

(A) *Through June 30, 1989.* Above 12,500 feet MSL and below the floor of a positive control area, excluding the airspace at and below 2,500 feet AGL.

(B) *Effective July 1, 1989.* At and above 10,000 feet MSL and below the floor of a positive control area, excluding the airspace at and below 2,500 feet AGL; and

(ii) *Effective December 30, 1990.* In the airspace from the surface to 10,000 feet MSL within a 10-nautical-mile radius of any airport listed in Appendix D of this part excluding the airspace below 1,200 feet AGL outside of the airport traffic area for that airport.

(c) *Transponder-on operation.* While in the airspace as specified in (b) of this section or in all controlled airspace, each person operating an aircraft equipped with an operable ATC transponder maintained in accordance with §91.172 of this part shall operate the transponder, including Mode C equipment if installed, and shall reply on the appropriate code or as assigned by ATC.

(c) *Controlled Airspace, all aircraft, transponder-on operation.* While in controlled airspace, each person operating an aircraft equipped with an operable ATC transponder maintained in accordance with § 91.172 of this Part shall operate the transponder, including Mode C equipment if installed, and shall reply on the appropriate code or as assigned by ATC.

(d) *ATC authorized deviations.* ATC may authorize deviations from paragraph (b) of this section—

(1) Immediately, to allow an aircraft with an inoperative transponder to continue to the airport of ultimate destination, including any intermediate stops, or to proceed to a place where suitable repairs can be made, or both;

(2) Immediately, for operations of aircraft with an operating transponder but without operating automatic pressure altitude reporting equipment having a Model C capability; and

(3) On a continuing basis, or for individual flights, for operations of aircraft without a transponder, in which case the request for a deviation must be submitted to the ATC facility having jurisdiction over the airspace concerned at least one hour before the proposed operation.

§ 91.25   VOR equipment check for IFR operations.

(a) No person may operate a civil aircraft under IFR using the VOR system of radio navigation unless the VOR equipment of that aircraft—

(1) Is maintained, checked, and inspected under an approved procedure; or

(2) Has been operationally checked within the preceding 30 days and was found to be within the limits of the permissible indicated bearing error set forth in paragraph (b) or (c) of this section.

(b) Except as provided in paragraph (c) of this section, each person conducting a VOR check under paragraph (a) (2) of this section shall—

(1) Use, at the airport of intended departure, an FAA operated or approved test signal or a test signal radiated by a certificated and appropriately rated radio repair station or, outside the United States, a test signal operated or approved by appropriate authority, to check the VOR equipment (the maximum permissible indicated bearing error is plus or minus 4 degrees).

(2) If a test signal is not available at the airport of intended departure, use a point on an airport surface designated as a VOR system checkpoint by the Administrator or, outside the United States, by appropriate authority (the maximum permissible bearing error is plus or minus 4 degrees);

(3) If neither a test signal nor a designated checkpoint on the surface is available, use an airborne checkpoint designated by the Administrator or, outside the United States, by appropriate authority (the maximum permissible bearing error is plus or minus 6 degrees) or

(4) If no check signal or point is available, while in flight—

(i) Select a VOR radial that lies along the centerline of an established VOR airway;

(ii) Select a prominent ground point along the selected radial preferably more than 20 miles from the VOR ground facility and maneuver the aircraft directly over the point at a reasonably low altitude; and

(iii) Note the VOR bearing indicated by the receiver when over the ground point (the maximum permissible variation between the published radial and the indicated bearing is 6 degrees).

(c) If dual system VOR (units independent of each other except for the antenna) is installed in the aircraft, the person checking the equipment may check one system against the other in place of the check procedures specified in paragraph (b) of this section. He shall tune both systems to the same VOR ground facility and note the indicated bearings to that station. The maximum permissible variation between the two indicated bearings is 4 degrees.

152

(d) Each person making the VOR operational check as specified in paragraph (b) or (c) of this section shall enter the date, place, bearing error, and sign the aircraft log or other record. In addition, if a test signal radiated by a repair station, as specified in paragraph (b)(1) of this section, is used, an entry must be made in the aircraft log or other record by the repair station certificate holder or the certificate holder's representative certifying to the bearing transmitted by the repair station for the check and the date of transmission.

[Doc. No. 1580, Amdt. 1–1, 28 FR 6704, June 29, 1963, as amended by Doc. No. 8254, 32 FR 16483, Dec. 1, 1967; Amdt. 91–122, 39 FR 19204, May 31, 1974; Amdt. 91–154, 43 FR 46234, Oct. 5, 1978]

§ **91.27 Civil aircraft: Certifications required.**

(a) Except as provided in § 91.28, no person may operate a civil aircraft unless it has within it the following:

(1) An appropriate and current airworthiness certificate. Each U.S. airworthiness certificate used to comply with this paragraph (except a special flight permit, a copy of the applicable operations specifications issued under § 21.197(c) of this chapter, appropriate sections of the air carrier manual required by Parts 121 and 127 of this chapter containing that portion of the operations specifications issued under § 21.197(c), or an authorization under § 91.45), must have on it the registration number assigned to the aircraft under Part 47 of this chapter. However, the airworthiness certificate need not have on it an assigned special identification number before 10 days after that number is first affixed to the aircraft. A revised airworthiness certificate having on it an assigned special identification number, that has been affixed to an aircraft, may only be obtained upon application to an FAA Flight Standards District Office.

(2) A registration certificate issued to its owner.

(b) No person may operate a civil aircraft unless the airworthiness certificate required by paragraph (a) of this section or a special flight authorization issued under § 91.28 is displayed at the cabin or cockpit entrance so that it is legible to passengers or crew.

(c) No person may operate an aircraft with a fuel tank installed within the passenger compartment or a baggage compartment unless the installation was accomplished pursuant to Part 43 of this chapter, and a copy of FAA Form 337 authorizing that installation is on board the aircraft.

[Amdt. 91–9, 29 FR 14563, Oct. 24, 1964, as amended by Amdt. 91–15, 30 FR 3638, Mar. 19, 1965; Amdt. 91–54, 33 FR 7623, May 23, 1968; Amdt. 91–56, 33 FR 11901, Aug. 22, 1968; Amdt. 91–20, 39 FR 1353, Jan. 8, 1974; Amdt. 91–206, 52 FR 34102, Sept. 9, 1987]

§ **91.28 Special flight authorizations for foreign civil aircraft.**

(a) Foreign civil aircraft may be operated without airworthiness certificates required under § 91.27 if a special flight authorization for that operation is issued under this section. Application for a special flight authorization must be made to the Regional Director of the FAA region in which the applicant is located, or to the region within which the U.S. point of entry is located. However, in the case of an aircraft to be operated in the U.S. for the purpose of demonstration at an air show, the application may be made to the Regional Director of the FAA region in which the air show is located.

(b) The Administrator may issue a special flight authorization for a foreign civil aircraft subject to any conditions and limitations that the Administrator considers necessary for safe operation in the U.S. airspace.

(c) No person may operate a foreign civil aircraft under a special flight authorization unless that operation also complies with Part 375 of the Special Regulations of the Civil Aeronautics Board (14 CFR Part 375).

[Amdt. 91–178, 47 FR 13316, Mar. 29, 1982]

§ **91.29 Civil aircraft airworthiness.**

(a) No person may operate a civil aircraft unless it is in an airworthy condition.

(b) The pilot in command of a civil aircraft is responsible for determining whether that aircraft is in condition for safe flight. He shall discontinue the flight when unairworthy mechanical or structural conditions occur.

§ 91.30   Inoperable instruments and equipment for multiengine aircraft.

(a) No person may take off a multiengine civil aircraft with inoperable instruments or equipment installed unless the following conditions are met:

(1) An approved Minimum Equipment List exists for that aircraft.

(2) The aircraft has within it a letter of authorization, issued by the FAA Flight Standards Office having jurisdiction over the area in which the operator is located, authorizing operation of the aircraft under the Minimum Equipment List. The letter of authorization may be obtained by written request of the airworthiness certificate holder. The Minimum Equipment List and the letter of authorization constitute a supplemental type certificate for the aircraft.

(3) The approved Minimum Equipment List must:

(i) Be prepared in accordance with the limitations specified in paragraph (b) of this section.

(ii) Provide for the operation of the aircraft with the instruments and equipment in an inoperable condition.

(4) The aircraft records available to the pilot must include an entry describing the inoperable instruments and equipment.

(5) The aircraft is operated under all applicable conditions and limitations contained in the Minimum Equipment List and the letter authorizing the use of the list.

(b) The following instruments and equipment may not be included in a Minimum Equipment List:

(1) Instruments and equipment that are either specifically or otherwise required by the airworthiness requirements under which the aircraft is type certificated and which are essential for safe operations under all operating conditions.

(2) Instruments and equipment required by an airworthiness directive to be in operable condition unless the airworthiness directive provides otherwise.

(3) Instruments and equipment required for specific operations by this part.

(c) A person authorized to use an approved Minimum Equipment List issued under Part 121 or 135 for a specific aircraft may use that Minimum Equipment List in connection with operations conducted with that aircraft under this part.

(d) Notwithstanding any other provision of this section, an aircraft with inoperable instruments or equipment may be operated under a special flight permit issued in accordance with §§ 21.197 and 21.199 of this chapter.

[Amdt. 91-157, 44 FR 43716, July 26, 1979]

§ 91.31   Civil aircraft flight manual, marking, and placard requirements.

(a) Except as provided in paragraph (d) of this section, no person may operate a civil aircraft without complying with the operating limitations specified in the approved Airplane or Rotorcraft Flight Manual, markings, and placards, or as otherwise prescribed by the certificating authority of the country of registry.

(b) No person may operate a U.S. registered civil aircraft—

(1) For which an Airplane or Rotorcraft Flight Manual is required by § 21.5 unless there is available in the aircraft a current approved Airplane of Rotorcraft Flight Manual or the manual provided for in § 121.141(b); and

(2) For which an Airplane or Rotorcraft Flight Manual is not required by § 21.5, unless there is available in the aircraft a current approved Airplane or Rotorcraft Flight Manual, approved manual material, markings, and placards, or any combination thereof.

(c) No person may operate a U.S. registered civil aircraft unless that aircraft is identified in accordance with Part 45.

(d) Any person taking off or landing a helicopter certificated under Part 29 of this chapter at a heliport constructed over water may make such momentary flight as is necessary for takeoff or landing through the prohibited range of the limiting height-speed envelope established for that helicopter if that flight through the prohibited range takes place over water on which a safe ditching can be accomplished, and if the helicopter is amphibious or is equipped with floats or other emergency flotation gear adequate to accomplish a safe emergency ditching on open water.

[Doc. No. 1580, Amdt. 1-1, 28 FR 6704, June 29, 1963, as amended by Amdt. 91-30, 31 FR 9211, July 6, 1966, as amended by Amdt. 91-103, 37 FR 20024, Sept. 23, 1972; Amdt. 91-115, 38 FR 12905, May 17, 1973; Amdt. 91-145, 43 FR 2328, Jan. 16, 1978; Amdt. 91-185, 49 FR 44440, Nov. 6, 1984]

§ **91.32** **Supplemental oxygen.**

(a) *General.* No person may operate a civil aircraft of U.S. registry—

(1) At cabin pressure altitudes above 12,500 feet (MSL) up to and including 14,000 feet (MSL), unless the required minimum flight crew is provided with and uses supplemental oxygen for that part of the flight at those altitudes that is of more than 30 minutes duration;

(2) At cabin pressure altitudes above 14,000 feet (MSL), unless the required minimum flight crew is provided with and uses supplemental oxygen during the entire flight time at those altitudes; and

(3) At cabin pressure altitudes above 15,000 feet (MSL), unless each occupant of the aircraft is provided with supplemental oxygen.

(b) *Pressurized cabin aircraft.* (1) No person may operate a civil aircraft of U.S. registry with a pressurized cabin—

(i) At flight altitudes above flight level 250, unless at least a 10-minute supply of supplemental oxygen in addition to any oxygen required to satisfy paragraph (a) of this section, is available for each occupant of the aircraft for use in the event that a descent is necessitated by loss of cabin pressurization; and

(ii) At flight altitudes above flight level 350, unless one pilot at the controls of the airplane is wearing and using an oxygen mask that is secured and sealed, and that either supplies oxygen at all times or automatically supplies oxygen whenever the cabin pressure altitude of the airplane exceeds 14,000 feet (MSL), except that the one pilot need not wear and use an

oxygen mask while at or below flight level 410 if there are two pilots at the controls and each pilot has a quick-donning type of oxygen mask that can be placed on the face with one hand from the ready position within five seconds, supplying oxygen and properly secured and sealed.

(2) Notwithstanding paragraph (b)(1)(ii) of this section, if for any reason at any time it is necessary for one pilot to leave his station at the controls of the aircraft when operating at flight altitudes above flight level 350, the remaining pilot at the controls shall put on and use his oxygen mask until the other pilot has returned to his station.

[Amdt. 91-75, 35 FR 6387, Apr. 21, 1970]

§ **91.33** **Powered civil aircraft with standard category U.S. airworthiness certificates; instrument and equipment requirements.**

(a) *General.* Except as provided in paragraphs (c)(3) and (e) of this section, no person may operate a powered civil aircraft with a standard category U.S. airworthiness certificate in any operation described in paragraphs (b) through (f) of this section unless that aircraft contains the instruments and equipment specified in those paragraphs for FAA-approved equivalents for that type of operation, and those instruments and items of equipment are in operable condition.

(b) *Visual flight rules (day).* For VFR flight during the day the following instruments and equipment are required.

(1) Airspeed indicator.

(2) Altimeter.

(3) Magnetic direction indicator.

(4) Tachometer for each engine.

(5) Oil pressure gauge for each engine using pressure system.

(6) Temperature gauge for each liquid-cooled engine.

(7) Oil temperature gauge for each air-cooled engine.

(8) Manifold pressure gauge for each altitude engine.

(9) Fuel gauge indicating the quantity of fuel in each tank.

(10) Landing gear position indicator, if the aircraft has a retractable landing gear.

(11) If the aircraft is operated for hire over water and beyond power-off gliding distance from shore, approved flotation gear readily available to each occupant, and at least one pyrotechnic signaling device.

(12) Except as to airships, an approved safety belt for all occupants who have reached their second birthday. After December 4, 1981, each safety belt must be equipped with an approved metal to metal latching device. The rated strength of each safety belt shall not be less than that corresponding with the ultimate load factors specified in the current applicable aircraft airworthiness requirements considering the dimensional characteristics of the safety belt installation for the specific seat or berth arrangement. The webbing of each safety belt shall be replaced as required by the Administrator.

(13) For small civil airplanes manufactured after July 18, 1978, an approved shoulder harness for each front seat. The shoulder harness must be designed to protect the occupant from serious head injury when the occupant experiences the ultimate intertia forces specified in § 23.561(b)(2) of this chapter. Each shoulder harness installed at a flight crewmember station must permit the crewmember, when seated and with his safety belt and shoulder harness fastened, to perform all functions necessary for flight operations. For purposes of this paragraph—

(i) The date of manufacture of an airplane is the date the inspection acceptance records reflect that the airplane is complete and meets the FAA Approved Type Design Data; and

(ii) A front seat is a seat located at a flight crewmember station or any seat located alongside such a seat.

(14) For normal, utility, and acrobatic category airplanes with a seating configuration, excluding pilot seats, of nine or less, manufactured after December 12, 1986, a shoulder harness for—

(i) Each front seat that meets the requirements of § 23.785 (g) and (h) of this chapter in effect on December 12, 1985;

(ii) Each additional seat that meets the requirements of § 23.785(g) of this chapter in effect on December 12, 1985.

(c) *Visual flight rules (night).* For VFR flight at night the following instruments and equipment are required:

(1) Instruments and equipment specified in paragraph (b) of this section.

(2) Approved position lights.

(3) An approved aviation red or aviation white anticollision light system on all U.S. registered civil aircraft. Anticollision light systems initially installed after August 11, 1971, on aircraft for which a type certificate was issued or applied for before August 11, 1971, must at least meet the anticollision light standards of Part 23, 25, 27, or 29, as applicable, that were in effect on August 10, 1971, except that the color may be either aviation red or aviation white. In the event of failure of any light of the anticollision light system, operations with the aircraft may be continued to a stop where repairs or replacement can be made.

(4) If the aircraft is operated for hire, one electric landing light.

(5) An adequate source of electrical energy for all installed electrical and radio equipment.

(6) One spare set of fuses, or three spare fuses of each kind required.

(d) *Instrument flight rules.* For IFR flight the following instruments and equipment are required:

(1) Instruments and equipment specified in paragraph (b) of this section and for night flight, instruments and equipment specified in paragraph (c) of this section.

(2) Two-way radio communications system and navigational equipment appropriate to the ground facilities to be used.

(3) Gyroscopic rate-of-turn indicator, except on the following aircraft:

(i) Large airplanes with a third attitude instrument system useable through flight attitudes of 360 degrees of pitch and roll and installed in accordance with § 121.305(j) of this chapter; and

(ii) Rotorcraft, type certificated under Part 29 of this chapter, with a third attitude instrument system useable through flight attitudes of ±80 degrees of pitch and ±120 degrees of roll and installed in accordance with § 29.1303(g) of this chapter.

(4) Slip-skid indicator.

(5) Sensitive altimeter adjustable for barometric pressure.

(6) A clock displaying hours, minutes, and seconds with a sweep-second pointer or digital presentation.

(7) Generator of adequate capacity.

(8) Gyroscopic bank and pitch indicator (artificial horizon).

(9) Gyroscopic direction indicator (directional gyro or equivalent).

(e) *Flight at and above 24,000 feet MSL.* If VOR navigational equipment is required under paragraph (d)(2) of this section, no person may operate a U.S. registered civil aircraft within the 50 states, and the District of Columbia, at or above 24,000 feet MSL unless that aircraft is equipped with approved distance measuring equipment (DME). When DME required by this paragraph fails at and above 24,000 feet MSL, the pilot in command of the aircraft shall notify ATC immediatley, and may then continue operations at and above 24,000 feet MSL to the next airport of intended landing at which repairs or replacement of the equipment can be made.

(f) *Category II operations.* For Category II operations the instruments and equipment specified in paragraph (d) of this section and Appendix A to this part are required. This paragraph does not apply to operations conducted by the holder of a certificate issued under Part 121 of this chapter.

§ 91.34 Category II manual.

(a) No person may operate a civil aircraft of U.S. registry in a Category II operation unless—

(1) There is available in the aircraft a current approved Category II manual for that aircraft;

(2) The operation is conducted in accordance with the procedures, instructions, and limitations in that manual; and

(3) The instruments and equipment listed in the manual that are required for a particular Category II operation have been inspected and maintained in accordance with the maintenance program contained in that manual.

(b) Each operator shall keep a current copy of the approved manual at its principal base of operations and shall make it available for inspection upon request of the Administrator.

(c) This section does not apply to operations conducted by the holder of a certificate issued under Part 121 of this chapter.

§ 91.35 Flight recorders and cockpit voice recorders.

(a) No holder of an air carrier or commercial operator certificate may conduct any operation under this part with an aircraft listed in his operations specifications or current list of aircraft used in air transportation unless that aircraft complies with any applicable flight recorder and cockpit voice recorder requirements of the part under which its certificate is issued; except that it may—

(1) Ferry an aircraft with an inoperative flight recorder or cockpit voice recorder from a place where repair or replacement cannot be made to a place where they can be made;

(2) Continue a flight as originally planned, if the flight recorder or cockpit voice recorder becomes inoperative after the aircraft has taken off;

(3) Conduct an airworthiness flight test , during whiich the flight recorder or cockpit voice recorder is turned off to test it or to test any communications or electrical equipment installed in the aircraft; or

(4) Ferry a newly acquired aircraft from the place where possession of it was taken to a place where the flight recorder or cockpit voice recorder is to be installed.

(b) No person may operate a U.S. civil registered, multiengine, turbine-powered airplane or rotorcraft having a passenger seating configuration, excluding any pilot seats of 10 or more that has been manufactured after October 11, 1991, unless it is equipped with one or more approved flight recorders that utilize a digital method of recording and storing data and a method of readily retrieving that data from the storage medium, that are capable of recording the data specified in Appendix E, for an airplane, or Appendix F, for a rotorcraft, of this part within the range, accuracy, and recording interval specified, and that are capable of retaining no less than 8 hours of aircraft operation.

(c) Whenever a flight recorder, required by this section, is isntalled, it must be operated continuously from the instant the airplane begins the takeoff roll or the rotorcraft begins lift-off until the airpane has completed the landing roll or the rotorcraft has landed at its destination.

(d) Unless otherwise authorized by the Administrator, after October 11, 1991, no person may operate a U.S. civil registered, multiengine, turbine-powered airplane or rotorcraft having a passenger seating configuration of six passengers or more and for which two pilots are required by type certification or operating rule unless it is equipped with an approved cockpit voice recorder that:

(1) Is installed in compliance with §23.1457 (a)(1) and (2), (b), (c), (d), (e), (f), and (g); §25.1457 (a) (1) and (2), (b), (c),(d),(e), (f), and (g); §27.1457(a) (1) and (2), (b), (c), (d), (e), 16 Takeoff and landing under IFR.

(2) Is operated continuously from the use of the check list before the flight to completion of the final check list at the end of the flight.

(e) In complying with this section, an approved cockpit voice recorder having an erasure feature may be used, so that at any time during the operation of the recorder, information recorded more than 15 minutes earlier may be erased or otherwise obliterated.

(f) In the event of an accident or occurrence requiring immediate notification to the National Transportation Safety Board under Part 830 of its regulations that results in the termination of the flight, any operator who has installed approved flight recorders and approved cockpit voice recorders shall keep the recorded information for at least 60 days, or if requested by the Administrator or the Board, for a longer period. Information obtained from the record is used to assist in determining the cause of accidents or occurrences in connection with investigation under Part 830. The Administrator does not use the cockpit voice recorder record in any civil penalty or certificate action.

§ 91.36 Data correspondence between automatically reported pressure altitude data and the pilot's altitude reference.

No person may operate any automatic pressure altitude reporting equipment associated with a radar beacon transponder—

(a) When deactivation of that equipment is directed by ATC;

(b) Unless, as installed, that equipment was tested and calibrated to transmit altitude data corresponding within 125 feet (on a 95-percent probability basis) of the indicated or calibrated datum of the altimeter normally used to maintain flight altitude, with that altimeter referenced to 29.92 inches of mercury for altitudes from sea level to the maximum operating altitude of the aircraft; or

(c) After September 1, 1979, unless the altimeters and digitizers in that equipment meet the standards in TSO-C10b and TSO-C88, respectively.

§ 91.37 Transport category civil airplane weight limitations

(a) No person may take off any transport category airplane (other than a turbine engine powered airplane certificated after September 30, 1958) unless—

(1) The takeoff weight does not exceed the authorized maximum takeoff weight for the elevation of the airport of takeoff;

(2) The elevation of the airport of takeoff is within the altitude range for which maximum takeoff weights have been determined;

(3) Normal consumption of fuel and oil in flight to the airport of intended landing will leave a weight on arrival not in excess of the authorized maximum landing weight for the elevation of that airport; and

(4) The elevations of the airport of intended landing and of all specified alternate airports are within the altitude range for which maximum landing weights have been determined.

(b) No person may operate a turbine engine powered transport category airplane certificated after September 30, 1958 contrary to the Airplane Flight Manual, nor take off that airplane unless—

(1) The takeoff weight does not exceed the takeoff weight specified in the Airplane Flight Manual for the elevation of the airport and for the ambient temperature existing at the time of takeoff;

(2) Normal consumption of fuel and oil in flight to the airport of intended landing and to the alternate airports will leave a weight on arrival not in excess of the landing weight specified in the Airplane Flight Manual for the elevation of each of the airports involved and for the ambient temperatures expected at the time of landing;

(3) The takeoff weight does not exceed the weight shown in the Airplane Flight Manual to correspond with the minimum distances required for takeoff considering the elevation of the airport, the runway to be used, the effective runway gradient, and the ambient temperature and wind component existing at the time of takeoff; and

(4) Where the takeoff distance includes a clearway, the clearway distance is not greater than one-half of—

(i) The takeoff run, in the case of airplanes certificated after September 30, 1958 and before August 30, 1959; or

(ii) The runway length, in the case of airplanes certificated after August 29, 1959.

(c) No person may take off a turbine engine powered transport category airplane certificated after August 29, 1959 unless, in addition to the requirements of paragraph (b) of this section—

(1) The accelerate-stop distance is no greater than the length of the runway plus the length of the stopway (if present);

(2) The takeoff distance is no greater than the length of the runway plus the length of the clearway (if present); and

(3) The takeoff run is no greater than the length of the runway.

[Amdt. 91-10, 29 FR 18290, Dec. 24, 1964]

§91.38 Increased maximum certificated weights for certain airplanes operated in Alaska.

(a) Notwithstanding any other provision of the Federal Aviation Regulations, the Administrator will, as provided in this section, approve an increase in the maximum certificated weight of any airplane type certificated under Aeronautics Bulletin No. 7-A of the U.S. Department of Commerce dated January 1, 1931, as amended, or under the normal category of Part 4a of the former Civil Air Regulations (Part 4a of this chapter, 1964 ed.), if that airplane is operated in the State of Alaska by—

(1) An air taxi operator or other air carrier; or

(2) The U.S. Department of Interior in conducting its game and fish law enforcement activities or its management, fire detection, and fire suppression activities concerning public lands.

(b) The maximum certificated weight approved under this section may not exceed—

(1) 12,500 pounds;

(2) 115 percent of the maximum weight listed in the FAA Aircraft Specifications;

(3) The weight at which the airplane meets the positive maneuvering load factor requirement for the normal category specified in §23.337 of this chapter; or

(4) The weight at which the airplane meets the climb performance requirements under which it was type certificated.

(c) In determining the maximum certificated weight the Administrator considers the structural soundness of the airplane and the terrain to be traversed.

(d) The maximum certificated weight determined under this section is added to the airplane's operation limitations and is identified as the maximum weight authorized for operations within the State of Alaska.

[Amdt. 91-27, 31 FR 5250, Apr. 1, 1966, as amended by Amdt. 91-41, 32 FR 8406, June 13, 1967]

§91.39 Restricted category civil aircraft; operating limitations.

(a) No person may operate a restricted category civil aircraft:

(1) For other than the special purpose for which it is certificated; or

(2) In an operation other than one necessary for the accomplishment of the work activity directly associated with that special purpose.

For the purposes of this paragraph, the operation of a restricted category civil aircraft to provide flight crewmember training in a special purpose operation for which the aircraft is certificated is considered to be an operation for that special purpose.

(b) No person may operate a restricted category civil aircraft carrying persons or property for compensation or hire. For the purposes of this paragraph, a special purpose operation involving the carriage of persons or materials necessary for the accomplishment of that operation such as crop dusting, seeding, spraying, and banner towing (including the carrying of required persons or materials to the location of that operation), and an operation for the purpose of providing flight crew-member training in a special purpose operation, are not considered to be the carrying of persons or property for compensation or hire.

(c) No person may be carried on a restricted category civil aircraft unless:

(1) He is a flight crewmember;

(2) He is a flight crewmember trainee;

(3) He performs an essential function in connection with a special purpose operation for which the aircraft is certificated; or

(4) He is necessary for the accomplishment of the work activity directly associated with that special purpose.

(d) Except when operating in accordance with the terms and conditions of a certificate of waiver or special operating limitations issued by the Admin-

§ 91.40   14 CFR Ch. I (1-1-88 Edition)

istrator, no person may operate a restricted category civil aircraft within
the United States—
(1) Over a densely populated area;
(2) In a congested airway; or
(3) Near a busy airport where passenger transport operations are conducted.
(e) An application for a certificate of
waiver under paragraph (d) of this section is made on a form and in a
manner prescribed by the Administrator and must be submitted to the
Flight Standards District Office
having jurisdiction over the area in
which the applicant is located.
(f) After December 9, 1977, this section does not apply to nonpassenger-
carrying civil rotorcraft external-load
operations conducted under Part 133
of this chapter.
(g) No person may operate a small
restricted category civil airplane, manufactured after July 18, 1978, unless
an approved shoulder harness is installed for each front seat. The shoulder harness must be designed to protect each occupant from serious head
injury when the occupant experiences
the ultimate inertia forces specified in
§ 23.561(b)(2) of this chapter. The
shoulder harness installation at each
flight crewmember station must
permit the crewmember, when seated
and with his safety belt and shoulder
harness fastened, to perform all functions necessary for flight operations.
For purposes of this paragraph—
(1) The date of manufacture of an
airplane is the date the inspection acceptance records reflect that the airplane is complete and meets the FAA
Approved Type Design Data; and
(2) A front seat is a seat located at a
flight crewmember station or any seat
located alongside such a seat.

[Doc. No. 1580, Amdt. 1-1, 28 FR 6704, June
29, 1963, as amended by Amdt. 91-12, 30 FR
2532, Feb. 26, 1965; Amdt. 91-29, 21 FR 8355,
June 15, 1966; Amdt. 91-58, 33 FR 12826,
Sept. 11, 1968; Amdt. 91-138, 42 FR 24197,
May 12, 1977; Amdt. 91-139, 42 FR 30603,
June 16, 1977]

§ 91.40 Limited category civil aircraft; operating limitations.

No person may operate a limited category civil aircraft carrying persons or
property for compensation or hire.

[Amdt. 91-9, 29 FR 14563, Oct. 24, 1964]

§ 91.41 Provisionally certificated civil aircraft; operating limitations.

(a) No person may operate a provisionally certificated civil aircraft
unless he is eligible for a provisional
airworthiness certificate under
§ 21.213 of this chapter.
(b) No person may operate a provisionally certificated civil aircraft outside the United States unless he has
specific authority to do so from the
Administrator and each foreign country involved.
(c) Unless otherwise authorized by
the Director of Airworthiness, no
person may operate a provisionally
certificated civil aircraft in air transportation.
(d) Unless otherwise authorized by
the Administrator, no person may operate a provisionally certificated civil
aircraft except—
(1) In direct conjunction with the
type or supplemental type certification of that aircraft;
(2) For training flight crews, including simulated air carrier operations;
(3) Demonstration flights by the
manufacturer for prospective purchas-
ers;
(4) Market surveys by the manufacturer;
(5) Flight checking of instruments,
accessories, and equipment, that do
not affect the basic airworthiness of
the aircraft; or
(6) Service testing of the aircraft.
(e) Each person operating a provisionally certificated civil aircraft shall
operate within the prescribed limitations displayed in the aircraft or set
forth in the provisional aircraft flight
manual or other appropriate document. However, when operating in
direct conjunction with the type or
supplemental type certification of the
aircraft, he shall operate under the experimental aircraft limitations of
§ 21.191 of this chapter and when
flight testing, shall operate under the
requirements of § 91.93 of this chapter.
(f) Each person operating a provisionally certificated civil aircraft shall
establish approved procedures for—

(1) The use and guidance of flight and ground personnel in operating under this section; and

(2) Operating in and out of airports where takeoffs or approaches over populated areas are necessary.

No person may operate that aircraft except in compliance with the approved procedures.

(g) Each person operating a provisionally certificated civil aircraft shall ensure that each flight crewmember is properly certificated and has adequate knowledge of, and familiarity with, the aircraft and procedures to be used by that crewmember.

(h) Each person operating a provisionally certificated civil aircraft shall maintain it as required by applicable regulations and as may be specially prescribed by the Administrator.

(i) Whenever the manufacturer, or the Administrator, determines that a change in design, construction or operation is necessary to ensure safe operation, no person may operate a provisionally certificated civil aircraft until that change has been made and approved. Section 21.99 of this chapter applies to operations under this section.

(j) Each person operating a provisionally certificated civil aircraft—

(1) May carry in that aircraft only persons who have a proper interest in the operations allowed by this section or who are specifically authorized by both the manufacturer and the Administrator; and

(2) Shall advise each person carried that the aircraft is provisionally certificated.

(k) The Administrator may prescribe additional limitations or procedures that he considers necessary, including limitations on the number of persons who may be carried in the aircraft.

[Doc. No. 1580, Amdt. 1-1, 28 FR 6704, June 29, 1963, as amended by Amdt. 91-30, 31 FR 9211, July 6, 1966; Amdt. 91-166, 45 FR 47838, July 17, 1980]

§ 91.42 Aircraft having experimental certificates; operating limitations.

(a) No person may operate an aircraft that has an experimental certificate:

(1) For other than the purpose for which the certificate was issued; or

(2) Carrying persons or property for compensation or hire.

(b) No person may operate an aircraft that has an experimental certificate outside of an area assigned by the Administrator until it is shown that:

(1) The aircraft is controllable throughout its normal range of speeds and throughout all the maneuvers to be executed; and

(2) The aircraft has no hazardous operating characteristics or design features.

(c) Unless otherwise authorized by the Administrator in special operating limitations, no person may operate an aircraft that has an experimental certificate over a densely populated area or in a congested airway. The Administrator may issue special operating limitations for particular aircraft to permit takeoffs and landings to be conducted over a densely populated area or in a congested airway, in accordance with terms and conditions specified in the authorization in the interest of safety in air commerce.

(d) Each person operating an aircraft that has an experimental certificate shall:

(1) Advise each person carried of the experimental nature of the aircraft;

(2) Operate under VFR, day only, unless otherwise specifically authorized by the Administrator; and

(3) Notify the control tower of the experimental nature of the aircraft when operating the aircraft into or out of airports with operating control towers.

(e) The Administrator may prescribe additional limitations that he considers necessary, including limitations on the persons that may be carried in the aircraft.

[Amdt. 91-53, 33 FR 6859, May 7, 1968, as amended by Amdt. 91-109, 38 FR 1176, Jan. 10, 1973]

§ 91.43 Special rules for foreign civil aircraft.

(a) *General.* In addition to the other applicable regulations of this part, each person operating a foreign civil aircraft within the United States shall comply with this section.

(b) *VFR.* No person may conduct VFR operations which require two-way radio communications under this part, unless at least one crewmember of that aircraft is able to conduct two-way radio communications in the English language and is on duty during that operation.

(c) *IFR.* No person may operate a foreign civil aircraft under IFR unless—

(1) That aircraft is equipped with—

(i) Radio equipment allowing two-way radio communication with ATC when it is operated in a control zone or control area; and

(ii) Radio navigational equipment appropriate to the navigational facilities to be used.

(2) Each person piloting the aircraft—

(i) Holds a current United States instrument rating or is authorized by his foreign airman certificate to pilot under IFR; and

(ii) Is thoroughly familiar with the United States en route, holding, and letdown procedures; and

(3) At least one crewmember of that aircraft is able to conduct two-way radiotelephone communications in the English language and that crewmember is on duty while the aircraft is approaching, operating within, or leaving the United States.

(d) *Overwater.* Each person operating a foreign civil aircraft overwater off the shores of the United States shall give flight notification or file a flight plan, in accordance with the Supplementary Procedures for the ICAO region concerned.

(e) *Flight at and above 24,000 feet MSL.* If VOR navigation equipment is required under paragraph (c)(1)(ii) of this section, no person may operate a foreign civil aircraft within the 50 states and the District of Columbia at or above 24,000 feet MSL, unless the aircraft is equipped with distance measuring equipment (DME) capable of receiving and indicating distance information from the VORTAC facilities to be used. When DME required by this paragraph fails at and above 24,000 feet MSL the pilot in command of the aircraft shall notify ATC immediately, and may then continue operations at and above 24,000 feet MSL to the next airport of intended landing at

which repairs or replacement of the equipment can be made.

However, paragraph (e) of this section does not apply to foreign civil aircraft that are not equipped with DME when operated for the following purposes, and if ATC is notified prior to each takeoff:

(1) Ferry flights to and from a place in the United States where repairs or alterations are to be made.

(2) Ferry flights to a new country of registry.

(3) Flight of a new aircraft of U.S. manufacture for the purpose of—

(i) Flight testing the aircraft;

(ii) Training foreign flight crews in the operation of the aircraft; or

(iii) Ferrying the aircraft for export delivery outside the United States.

(4) Ferry, demonstration, and test flights of an aircraft brought to the United States for the purpose of demonstration or testing the whole or any part thereof.

[Doc. No. 1580, Amdt. 1-1, 28 FR 6704, June 29, 1963, as amended by Amdt. 91-23, 30 FR 10288, Aug. 19, 1965; Amdt. 91-28, 31 FR 6265, Apr. 23, 1966; Amdt. 91-48, 32 FR 16392, Nov. 30, 1967; Amdt. 91-59, 33 FR 12825, Sept. 11, 1968; Amdt. 91-133, 41 FR 47228, Oct. 28, 1976; Amdt. 91-152, 43 FR 22640, May 25, 1978]

§ 91.45 Authorization for ferry flights with one engine inoperative.

(a) *General.* The holder of an air carrier operating certificate, an operating certificate issued under Part 125, or until January 1, 1983, an operating certificate issued under Part 121, may conduct a ferry flight of a four-engine airplane or a turbine-engine-powered airplane equipped with three engines, with one engine inoperative, to a base for the purpose of repairing that engine subject to the following:

(1) The airplane model has been test flown and found satisfactory for safe flight in accordance with paragraph (b) or (c) of this section, as appropriate. However, each operator who before November 19, 1966, has shown that a model of airplane with an engine inoperative is satisfactory for safe flight by a test flight conducted in accordance with performance data contained in the applicable Airplane

Flight Manual under paragraph (a)(2) of this section need not repeat the test flight for that model.

(2) The approved Airplane Flight Manual contains the following performance data and the flight is conducted in accordance with that data:

(i) Maximum weight.

(ii) Center of gravity limits.

(iii) Configuration of the inoperative propeller (if applicable).

(iv) Runway length for takeoff (including temperature accountability).

(v) Altitude range.

(vi) Certificate limitations.

(vii) Ranges of operational limits.

(viii) Performance information.

(ix) Operating procedures.

(3) The operator's manual contains operating procedures for the safe operation of the airplane, including specific requirements for—

(i) A limitation that the operating weight on any ferry flight must be the minimum necessary therefor with the necessary reserve fuel load;

(ii) A limitation that takeoffs must be made from dry runways unless, based on a showing of actual operating takeoff techniques on wet runways with one engine inoperative, takeoffs with full controllability from wet runways have been approved for the specific model aircraft and included in the Airplane Flight Manual;

(iii) Operations from airports where the runways may require a takeoff or approach over populated areas; and

(iv) Inspection procedures for determining the operating condition of the operative engines.

(4) No person may take off an airplane under this section if—

(i) The initial climb is over thickly populated areas; or

(ii) Weather conditions at the takeoff or destination airport are less than those required for VFR flight.

(5) Persons other than required flight crewmembers shall not be carried during the flight.

(6) No person may use a flight crewmember for flight under this section unless that crewmember is thoroughly familiar with the operating procedures for one-engine inoperative ferry flight contained in the certificate holder's manual, and the limitations and performance information in the Airplane Flight Manual.

(b) *Flight tests: Reciprocating engine powered airplanes.* The airplane performance of a reciprocating engine powered airplane with one engine inoperative must be determined by flight test as follows:

(1) A speed not less than $1.3V_{s1}$ must be chosen at which the airplane may be controlled satisfactorily in a climb with the critical engine inoperative (with its propeller removed or in a configuration desired by the operator) and with all other engines operating at the maximum power determined in paragraph (b)(3) of this section.

(2) The distance required to accelerate to the speed listed in paragraph (b)(1) of this section and to climb to 50 feet must be determined with—

(i) The landing gear extended;

(ii) The critical engine inoperative and its propeller removed or in a configuration desired by the operator; and

(iii) The other engines operating at not more than the maximum power established under paragraph (b)(3) of this section.

(3) The takeoff, flight, and landing procedures such as the approximate trim settings, method of power application, maximum power, and speed, must be established.

(4) The performance must be determined at a maximum weight not greater than the weight that allows a rate of climb of at least 400 feet a minute in the en route configuration set forth in §25.67(d) of this chapter at an altitude of 5,000 feet.

(5) The performance must be determined using temperature accountability for the takeoff field length, computed in accordance with §25.61 of this chapter.

(c) *Flight tests: Turbine engine powered airplanes.* The airplane performance of a turbine engine powered airplane with one engine inoperative must be determined in accordance with the following, by flight tests including at least three takeoff tests:

(1) Takeoff speeds V_R and V_2, not less than the corresponding speeds under which the airplane was type certificated under §25.107 of this chapter, must be chosen at which the airplane may be controlled satisfactorily

with the critical engine inoperative (with its propeller removed or in a configuration desired by the operator, if applicable) and with all other engines operating at not more than the power selected for type certification, as set forth in § 25.101 of this chapter.

(2) The minimum takeoff field length must be the horizontal distance required to accelerate, and climb to the 35-foot height at V₂ speed (including any additional speed increment obtained in the tests), multiplied by 115 percent, and determined with—

(i) The landing gear extended;

(ii) The critical engine inoperative and its propeller removed or in a configuration desired by the operator (if applicable); and

(iii) The other engines operating at not more than the power selected for type certification, as set forth in § 25.101 of this chapter.

(3) The takeoff, flight, and landing procedures such as the approximate trim settings, method of power application, maximum power, and speed, must be established. The airplane must be satisfactorily controllable during the entire takeoff run when operated according to these procedures.

(4) The performance must be determined at a maximum weight not greater than the weight determined under § 25.121(c) of this chapter, but with—

(i) The actual steady gradient of the final takeoff climb requirement not less than 1.2 percent at the end of the takeoff path with two critical engines inoperative; and

(ii) The climb speed not less than the two-engine inoperative trim speed for the actual steady gradient of the final takeoff climb prescribed by paragraph (c)(4)(i) of this section.

(5) The airplane must be satisfactorily controllable in a climb with two critical engines inoperative. Climb performance may be ·shown by calculations based on, and equal in accuracy to, the results of testing.

(6) The performance must be determined using temperature accountability for takeoff distance and final takeoff climb, computed in accordance with § 25.101 of this chapter.

For the purposes of paragraphs (c) (4) and (5) of this section, "two critical engines" means two adjacent engines on one side of an airplane with four engines, and the center engine and one outboard engine on an airplane with three engines.

[Amdt. 91-33, 31 FR 13526, Oct. 20, 1966, as amended by Amdt. 91-34, 31 FR 14929, Nov. 26, 1966; Amdt. 91-133, 41 FR 47228, Oct. 28, 1976; Amdt. 91-179, 47 FR 25117, June 10, 1982]

§ 91.47 Emergency exits for airplanes carrying passengers for hire.

(a) Notwithstanding any other provision of this chapter, no person may operate a large airplane (type certificated under the Civil Air Regulations effective before April 9, 1957) in passenger-carrying operations for hire, with more than the number of occupants:

(1) Allowed under Civil Air Regulation § 4b.362 (a), (b), and (c) of this chapter, as in effect on December 20 1951; or

(2) Approved under Special Civil Air Regulations SR-387, SR-389, SR-389A or SR-389B, or under this section as in effect.

However, an airplane type listed in the following table may be operated with up to the listed number of occupants (including crewmembers) and the corresponding number of exits (including emergency exits and doors) approved for the emergency exit of passengers or with an occupant-exit configuration approved under paragraph (b) or (c) of this section:

Airplane type	Maximum number of occupants including all crewmembers	Corresponding number of exits authorized for passenger use
B-307	61	4
B-377	96	9
C-46	67	4
CV-240	53	6
CV-340 and CV-440	53	6
DC-3	35	4
DC-3(Super)	39	5
DC-4	86	5
DC-6	87	7
DC-6B	112	11
L-18	17	3
L-049, L-649, L-749	87	7
L-1049 series	96	9
M-202	53	6
M-404	53	7

Airplane type	Maximum number of occupants including all crewmembers	Corresponding number of exits authorized for passenger use
Viscount 700 series.....................	53	7

(b) Occupants in addition to those authorized under paragraph (a) of this section may be carried as follows:

(1) For each additional floor-level exit at least 24 inches wide by 48 inches high, with an unobstructed 20-inch wide access aisleway between the exit and the main passenger aisle: 12 additional occupants.

(2) For each additional window exit located over a wing that meets the requirements of the airworthiness standards under which the airplane was type certificated or that is large enough to inscribe an ellipse 19 x 26 inches: Eight additional occupants.

(3) For each additional window exit that is not located over a wing but that otherwise complies with paragraph (b)(2) of this section: Five additional occupants.

(4) For each airplane having a ratio (as computed from the table in paragraph (a) of this section) of maximum number of occupants to number of exits greater than 14:1, and for each airplane that does not have at least one full-size door-type exit in the side of the fuselage in the rear part of the cabin, the first additional exit must be a floor-level exit that complies with paragraph (b)(1) of this section and must be located in the rear part of the cabin on the opposite side of the fuselage from the main entrance door. However, no person may operate an airplane under this section carrying more than 115 occupants unless there is such an exit on each side of the fuselage in the rear part of the cabin.

(c) No person may eliminate any approved exit except in accordance with the following:

(1) The previously authorized maximum number of occupants must be reduced by the same number of additional occupants authorized for that exit under this section.

(2) Exits must be eliminated in accordance with the following priority schedule: First, non-over-wing window exits; second, over-wing-window exits; third, floor-level exits located in the forward part of the cabin; fourth, floor-level exits located in the rear of the cabin.

(3) At least one exit must be retained on each side of the fuselage regardless of the number of occupants.

(4) No person may remove any exit that would result in a ratio of maximum number of occupants to approved exits greater than 14:1.

(d) This section does not relieve any person operating under Part 121 of this chapter from complying with § 121.291 of this chapter.

[Amdt. 91–22, 30 FR 8516, July 3, 1965]

§ 91.49 Aural speed warning device.

No person may operate a transport category airplane in air commerce unless that airplane is equipped with an aural speed warning device that complies with § 25.1303(c)(1).

[Amdt. 91–15, 30, FR 3638, Mar. 19, 1965, as amended by Amdt. 91–97, 37 FR 4327, Mar. 2, 1972]

§ 91.50 [Reserved]

§ 91.51 Altitude alerting system or device; turbojet powered civil airplanes.

(a) Except as provided in paragraph (d) of this section, no person may operate a turbojet powered U.S. registered civil airplane unless that airplane is equipped with an approved altitude alerting system or device that is in operable condition and meets the requirements of paragraph (b) of this section.

(b) Each altitude alerting system or device required by paragraph (a) of this section must be able to—

(1) Alert the pilot: (i) Upon approaching a preselected altitude in either ascent or descent, by a sequence of both aural and visual signals in sufficient time to establish level flight at that preselected altitude; or

(ii) Upon approaching a preselected altitude in either ascent or descent, by a sequence of visual signals in sufficient time to establish level flight at that preselected altitude, and when deviating above and below that preselected altitude, by an aural signal;

(2) Provide the required signals from sea level to the highest operating altitude approved for the airplane in which it is installed;

(3) Preselect altitudes in increments that are commensurate with the altitudes at which the aircraft is operated;

(4) Be tested without special equipment to determine proper operation of the alerting signals; and

(5) Accept necessary barometric pressure settings if the system or device operates on barometric pressure.

However, for operations below 3,000 feet AGL, the system or device need only provide one signal, either visual or aural, to comply with this paragraph. A radio altimeter may be included to provide the signal, if the operator has an approved procedure for its use to determine DH or MDA, as appropriate.

(c) Each operator to which this section applies must establish and assign procedures for the use of the altitude alerting system or device and each flight crewmember must comply with those procedures assigned to him.

(d) Paragraph (a) of this section does not apply to any operation of an airplane that has an experimental certificate or to the operation of an airplane for the following purposes:

(1) Ferrying a newly acquired airplane from the place where possession of it was taken to a place where the altitude alerting system or device is to be installed.

(2) Continuing a flight as originally planned, if the altitude alerting system or device becomes inoperative after the airplane has taken off; however, the flight may not depart from a place where repair or replacement can be made.

(3) Ferrying an airplane with an inoperative altitude alerting system or device from a place where repair or replacement cannot be made to a place where they can be made.

(4) Conducting an airworthiness flight test of the airplane.

(5) Ferrying an airplane to a place outside the United States for the purpose of registering it in a foreign country.

(6) Conducting a sales demonstration of the operation of the airplane.

(7) Training foreign flight crews in the operation of the airplane prior to ferrying it to a place outside the United States for the purpose of registering it in a foreign country.

[Amdt. 91-57, 33 FR 12180, Aug. 29, 1968, as amended by Amdt. 91-97, 37 FR 4327, Mar. 2, 1972; Amdt. 91-133, 41 FR 47228, Oct. 28, 1976; Amdt. No. 91-142, 42 FR 42187, Aug. 22, 1977]

§ 91.52 Emergency locator transmitters.

(a) Except as provided in paragraphs (e) and (f) of this section, no person may operate a U.S. registered civil airplane unless it meets the applicable requirements of paragraphs (b), (c), and (d) of this section.

(b) To comply with paragraph (a) of this section, each U.S. registered civil airplane must be equipped as follows:

(1) For operations governed by the supplemental air carrier and commercial operator rules of Part 121 of this chapter, or the air travel club rules of Part 123 of this chapter, there must be attached to the airplane an automatic type emergency locator transmitter that is in operable condition and meets the applicable requirements of TSO-C91;

(2) For charter flights governed by the domestic and flag air carrier rules of Part 121 of this chapter, there must be attached to the airplane an automatic type emergency locator transmitter that is in operable condition and meets the applicable requirements of TSO-C91;

(3) For operations governed by Part 135 of this chapter, there must be attached to the airplane an automatic type emergency locator transmitter that is in operable condition and meets the applicable requirements of TSO-C91; and

(4) For operations other than those specified in paragraphs (b) (1), (2), and (3) of this section, there must be attached to the airplane a personal type or an automatic type emergency locator transmitter that is in operable condition and meets the applicable requirements of TSO-C91.

(c) Each emergency locator transmitter required by paragraphs (a) and

(b) of this section must be attached to the airplane in such a manner that the probability of damage to the transmitter, in the event of crash impact, is minimized. Fixed and deployable automatic type transmitters must be attached to the airplane as far aft as practicable.

(d) Batteries used in the emergency locator transmitters required by paragraphs (a) and (b) of this section must be replaced (or recharged, if the battery is rechargeable)—

(1) When the transmitter has been in use for more than one cumulative hour; or

(2) When 50 percent of their useful life (or, for rechargeable batteries, 50 percent of their useful life of charge), as established by the transmitter manufacturer under TSO–C91, paragraph (g)(2) has expired.

The new expiration date for the replacement (or recharge) of the battery must be legibly marked on the outside of the transmitter and entered in the aircraft maintenance record. Paragraph (d)(2) of this section does not apply to batteries (such as water-activated batteries) that are essentially unaffected during probable storage intervals.

(e) Notwithstanding paragraphs (a) and (b) of this section, a person may—

(1) Ferry a newly acquired airplane from the place where possession of it was taken to a place where the emergency locator transmitter is to be installed; and

(2) Ferry an airplane with an inoperative emergency locator transmitter from a place where repairs or replacement cannot be made to a place where they can be made.

No persons other than required crewmembers may be carried aboard an airplane being ferried pursuant to this paragraph (e).

(f) Paragraphs (a) and (b) of this section do not apply to—

(1) Turbojet-powered aircraft;

(2) Aircraft while engaged in scheduled flights by scheduled air carriers certificated by the Civil Aeronautics Board;

(3) Aircraft while engaged in training operations conducted entirely within a 50-mile radius of the airport from which such local flight operations began;

(4) Aircraft while engaged in flight operations incident to design and testing;

(5) New aircraft while engaged in flight operations incident to their manufacture, preparation, and delivery;

(6) Aircraft while engaged in flight operations incident to the aerial application of chemicals and other substances for agricultural purposes;

(7) Aircraft certificated by the Administrator for research and development purposes;

(8) Aircraft while used for showing compliance with regulations, crew training, exhibition, air racing, or market surveys;

(9) Aircraft equipped to carry not more than one person; and

(10) An aircraft during any period for which the transmitter has been temporarily removed for inspection, repair, modification or replacement, subject to the following:

(i) No person may operate the aircraft unless the aircraft records contain an entry which includes the date of initial removal, the make, model, serial number and reason for removal of the transmitter, and a placard is located in view of the pilot to show "ELT not installed."

(ii) No person may operate the aircraft more than 90 days after the ELT is initially removed from the aircraft.

[Doc. No. 10915, Amdt. 91–95, 36 FR 18723, Sept. 21, 1971, as amended by Amdt. 91–121, 39 FR 6516, Feb. 20, 1974; Amdt. 91–123, 39 FR 25315, July 10, 1974; Amdt. 91–133, 41 FR 47228, Oct. 28, 1976; Amdt. 91–151, 43 FR 10905, Mar. 16, 1978; Amdt. 91–152, 43 FR 22640, May 25, 1978; Amdt. 91–163, 45 FR 38348, June 9, 1980]

§ 91.53 [Reserved]

§ 91.54 Truth in leasing clause requirement in leases and conditional sales contracts.

(a) Except as provided in paragraph (b) of this section, the parties to a lease or contract of conditional sale involving a United States registered large civil aircraft and entered into after January 2, 1973, shall execute a written lease or contract and include therein a written truth in leasing clause as a concluding paragraph in large print, immediately preceding the space for the signature of the parties, which contains the following with respect to each such aircraft:

(1) Identification of the Federal Aviation Regulations under which the aircraft has been maintained and inspected during the 12 months preceding the execution of the lease or contract of conditional sale; and certification by the parties thereto regarding the aircraft's status of compliance with applicable maintenance and inspection requirements in this part for the operation to be conducted under the lease or contract of conditional sale.

(2) The name and address (printed or typed) and the signature of the person responsible for operational control of the aircraft under the lease or contract of conditional sale, and certification that each person understands that person's responsibilities for compliance with applicable Federal Aviation Regulations.

(3) A statement that an explanation of factors bearing on operational control and pertinent Federal Aviation Regulations can be obtained from the nearest FAA Flight Standards District Office, General Aviation District Office, or Air Carrier District Office.

(b) The requirements of paragraph (a) of this section do not apply—

(1) To a lease or contract of conditional sale when:

(i) The party to whom the aircraft is furnished is a foreign air carrier or certificate holder under Part 121, 123, 125, 127, 135, or 141 of this chapter; or

(ii) The party furnishing the aircraft is a foreign air carrier, certificate holder under Part 121, 123, 125, 127, or 141 of this chapter, or a certificate holder under Part 135 of this chapter having appropriate authority to engage in air taxi operations with large aircraft.

(2) To a contract of conditional sale, when the aircraft involved has not been registered anywhere prior to the execution of the contract, except as a new aircraft under a dealer's aircraft registration certificate issued in accordance with § 47.61 of this chapter.

(c) No person may operate a large civil aircraft of U.S. registry that is subject to a lease or contract of conditional sale to which paragraph (a) of this section applies, unless—

(1) The lessee or conditional buyer, or the registered owner if the lessee is not a citizen of the United States, has mailed a copy of the lease or contract that complies with the requirements of paragraph (a) of this section, within 24 hours of its execution, to the Flight Standards Technical Division, Post Office Box 25724, Oklahoma City, OK 73125;

(2) A copy of the lease or contract that complies with the requirements of paragraph (a) of this section is carried in the aircraft. The copy of the lease or contract shall be made available for review upon request by the Administrator; and

(3) The lessee or conditional buyer, or the registered owner if the lessee is not a citizen of the United States, has notified by telephone or in person, the FAA Flight Standards District Office, General Aviation District Office, Air Carrier District Office, or International Field Office nearest the airport where the flight will originate. Unless otherwise authorized by that office, the notification shall be given at least 48 hours prior to takeoff in the case of the first flight of that aircraft under that lease or contract and inform the FAA of—

(i) The location of the airport of departure;

(ii) The departure time; and

(iii) The registration number of the aircraft involved.

(d) The copy of the lease or contract furnished to the FAA under paragraph (c) of this section is commercial or financial information obtained from a person. It is, therefore, privileged and confidential, and will not be made available by the FAA for public inspection or copying under 5 U.S.C. 552(b)(4), unless recorded with the FAA under Part 49 of this chapter.

(e) For the purpose of this section, a lease means any agreement by a person to furnish an aircraft to another person for compensation or hire, whether with or without flight crewmembers, other than an agreement for the sale of an aircraft and a contract of conditional sale under section 101 of the Federal Aviation Act of 1958. The person furnishing the aircraft is referred to as the lessor and the person to whom it is furnished the lessee.

[Amdt. 91-104, 37 FR 20935, Oct. 5, 1972, as amended by Amdt. 91-108, 38 FR 852, Jan. 5, 1973; Amdt. 91-143, 42 FR 57448, Nov. 3, 1977; Amdt. 91-154, 43 FR 46234, Oct. 5, 1978; Amdt. 91-169, 45 FR 67234, Oct. 9, 1980]

§ 91.55   Civil aircraft sonic boom.

(a) No person may operate a civil aircraft in the United States at a true flight Mach number greater than 1 except in compliance with conditions and limitations in an authorization to exceed Mach 1 issued to the operator under Appendix B of this part.

(b) In addition, no person may operate a civil aircraft, for which the maximum operating limit speed M_{mo} exceeds a Mach number of 1, to or from an airport in the United States unless—

(1) Information available to the flight crew includes flight limitations that insure that flights entering or leaving the United States will not cause a sonic boom to reach the surface within the United States; and

(2) The operator complies with the flight limitations prescribed in paragraph (b)(1) of this section or complies with conditions and limitations in an authorization to exceed Mach 1 issued under Appendix B of this part.

[Doc. No. 10261, Amdt. 91-112, 38 FR 8054, Mar. 28, 1973; Amdt. 91-153, 43 FR 28421, June 29, 1978]

§ 91.56   Agricultural and fire fighting airplanes; noise operating limitations.

(a) This section applies to propeller-driven, small airplanes having standard airworthiness certificates, that are designed for "agricultural aircraft operations" (as defined in § 137.3 of this chapter, as efective on January 1, 1966) or for dispensing fire fighting materials.

(b) If the Airplane Flight Manual, or other approved manual material, information, markings, or placards for the airplane indicate that the airplane has not been shown to comply with the noise limits under Part 36 of this chapter, no person may operate that airplane, except—

(1) To the extent necessary to accomplish the work activity directly associated with the purpose for which it is designed;

(2) To provide flight crewmember training in the special purpose operation for which the airplane is designed; and

(3) To conduct "nondispensing aerial work operations" in accordance with the requirements under § 137.29(c) of this chapter.

[Doc. No. 16382, Amdt. 91-168, 45 FR 67066, Oct. 9, 1980]

§ 91.57   Aviation Safety Reporting Program; prohibition against use of reports for enforcement purposes.

The Administrator of the FAA will not use reports submitted to the National Aeronautics and Space Administration under the Aviation Safety Reporting Program (or information derived therefrom) in any enforcement action, except information concerning criminal offenses or accidents which are wholly excluded from the Program.

[Doc. No. 19301, Amdt. 91-156, 44 FR 37625, June 28, 1979]

§ 91.58   Materials for compartment interiors.

No person may operate an airplane that conforms to an amended or supplemental type certificate issued in accordance with SFAR No. 41 for a maximum certificated takeoff weight in excess of 12,500 pounds, unless within one year after issuance of the initial airworthiness certificate under that SFAR, the airplane meets the compartment interior requirements set forth in § 25.853 (a), (b), (b-1), (b-2), and (b-3) of this chapter in effect on September 26, 1978.

[Doc. No. 18315, Amdt. 91-159, 44 FR 53731, Sept. 17, 1979]

§ 91.59   Carriage of candidates in Federal elections.

(a) An aircraft operator, other than one operating an aircraft under the rules of Part 121, 127, or 135 of this chapter, may receive payment for the carriage of a candidate in a Federal election, an agent of the candidate, or a person traveling on behalf of the candidate, if—

(1) That operator's primary business is not as an air carrier or commercial operator;

(2) The carriage is conducted under the rules of Part 91; and

(3) The payment for the carriage is required, and does not exceed the amount required to be paid, by regulations of the Federal Election Commission (11 CFR et seq.).

(b) For the purposes of this section, the terms "candidate" and "election" have the same meaning as that set forth in the regulations of the Federal Election Commission.

[Doc. No. 18313, Amdt. 91-164, 45 FR 43162, June 26, 1980]

Subpart B—Flight Rules

GENERAL

§ 91.61 Applicability.

This subpart prescribes flight rules governing the operation of aircraft within the United States.

§ 91.63 Waivers.

(a) The Administrator may issue a certificate of waiver authorizing the operation of aircraft in deviation of any rule of this subpart if he finds that the proposed operation can be safely conducted under the terms of that certificate of waiver.

(b) An application for a certificate of waiver under this section is made on a form and in a manner prescribed by the Administrator and may be submitted to any FAA office.

(c) A certificate of waiver is effective as specified in that certificate.

§ 91.65 Operating near other aircraft.

(a) No person may operate an aircraft so close to another aircraft as to create a collision hazard.

(b) No person may operate an aircraft in formation flight except by arrangement with the pilot in command of each aircraft in the formation.

(c) No person may operate an aircraft, carrying passengers for hire, in formation flight.

(d) Unless otherwise authorized by ATC, no person operating an aircraft may operate his aircraft in accordance with any clearance or instruction that has been issued to the pilot of another aircraft for radar Air Traffic Control purposes.

[Doc. No. 1580, Amdt. 1-1, 28 FR 6704, June 29, 1963, as amended by Amdt. 91-8, 29 FR 14404, Oct. 20, 1964]

§ 91.67 Right-of-way rules; except water operations.

(a) *General.* When weather conditions permit, regardless of whether an operation is conducted under Instrument Flight Rules or Visual Flight Rules, vigilance shall be maintained by each person operating an aircraft so as to see and avoid other aircraft in compliance with this section. When a rule of this section gives another aircraft the right of way, he shall give way to that aircraft and may not pass over, under, or ahead of it, unless well clear.

(b) *In distress.* An aircraft in distress has the right of way over all other air traffic.

(c) *Converging.* When aircraft of the same category are converging at approximately the same altitude (except head-on, or nearly so) the aircraft to the other's right has the right of way. If the aircraft are of different categories—

(1) A balloon has the right of way over any other category of aircraft;

(2) A glider has the right of way over an airship, airplane or rotorcraft; and

(3) An airship has the right of way over an airplane or rotorcraft.

However, an aircraft towing or refueling other aircraft has the right of way over all other engine-driven aircraft.

(d) *Approaching head-on.* When aircraft are approaching each other head-on, or nearly so, each pilot of each aircraft shall alter course to the right.

(e) *Overtaking.* Each aircraft that is being overtaken has the right of way and each pilot of an overtaking aircraft shall alter course to the right to pass well clear.

(f) *Landing.* Aircraft, while on final approach to land, or while landing, have the right of way over other aircraft in flight or operating on the surface. When two or more aircraft are approaching an airport for the purpose of landing, the aircraft at the lower altitude has the right of way, but it shall not take advantage of this rule to cut in front of another which is on final approach to land, or to overtake that aircraft.

(g) *Inapplicability.* This section does not apply to the operation of an aircraft on water.

[Doc. No. 1580, Amdt. 1-1, 28 FR 6704, June 29, 1963, as amended by Amdt. 91-55, 33 FR 10505, July 24, 1968]

§91.69 Right-of-way rules; water operations.

(a) *General.* Each person operating an aircraft on the water shall, insofar as possible, keep clear of all vessels and avoid impeding their navigation, and shall give way to any vessel or other aircraft that is given the right of way by any rule of this section.

(b) *Crossing.* When aircraft, or an aircraft and a vessel are on crossing courses, the aircraft or vessel to the others right has the right of way.

(c) *Approaching head-on.* When aircraft, or an aircraft and a vessel, are approaching head-on or nearly so, each shall alter its course to the right to keep well clear.

(d) *Overtaking.* Each aircraft or vessel that is being overtaken has the right of way, and the one overtaking shall alter course to keep well clear.

(e) *Special circumstances.* When aircraft, or an aircraft and a vessel, approach so as to involve risk of collision, each aircraft or vessel shall proceed with careful regard to existing circumstances, including the limitations of the respective craft.

§91.70 Aircraft speed.

(a) Unless otherwise authorized by the Administrator, no person may operate an aircraft below 10,000 feet MSL at an indicated airspeed of more than 250 knots (288 m.p.h.).

(b) Unless otherwise authorized or required by ATC, no person may operate an aircraft within an airport traffic area at an indicated airspeed of more than—

(1) In the case of a reciprocating engine aircraft, 156 knots (180 m.p.h.); or

(2) In the case of a turbine-powered aircraft, 200 knots (230 m.p.h.).

Paragraph (b) of this section does not apply to any operations within a Terminal Control Area. Such operations shall comply with paragraph (a) of this section.

(c) No person may operate an aircraft in the airspace underlying a terminal control area, or in a VFR corridor designated through a terminal control area, at an indicated airspeed of more than 200 knots (230 m.p.h.).

However, if the minimum safe airspeed for any particular operation is greater than the maximum speed prescribed in this section, the aircraft may be operated at that minimum speed.

[Doc. No. 13543, Amdt. 91-47, 32 FR 15709, Nov. 15, 1967, as amended by Amdt. 91-78, 35 FR 7784, May 21, 1970; Amdt. 91-113, 38 FR 8135, Mar. 29, 1973; Amdt. 91-125, 39 FR 26888, July 24, 1974]

§91.71 Acrobatic flight.

No person may operate an aircraft in acrobatic flight—

(a) Over any congested area of a city, town, or settlement;

(b) Over an open air assembly of persons;

(c) Within a control zone or Federal Airway;

(d) Below an altitude of 1,500 feet above the surface; or

(e) When flight visibility is less than three miles.

For the purposes of this section, acrobatic flight means an intentional maneuver involving an abrupt change in an aircraft's attitude, an abnormal attitude, or abnormal acceleration, not necessary for normal flight.

[Doc. No. 1580, Amdt. 1-1, 28 FR 6704, June 29, 1963, as amended by Amdt. 91-6, 29 FR 9823, July 22, 1964, Amdt. 91-65, 34 FR 12883, Aug. 8, 1969; Amdt. 91-65, 34 FR 13467, Aug. 21, 1969]

§91.73 Aircraft lights.

No person may, during the period from sunset to sunrise (or, in Alaska, during the period a prominent unlighted object cannot be seen from a distance of three statute miles or the sun is more than six degrees below the horizon)—

(a) Operate an aircraft unless it has lighted position lights;

(b) Park or move an aircraft in, or in dangerous proximity to, a night flight operations area of an airport unless the aircraft—

(1) Is clearly illuminated;

(2) Has lighted position lights; or

(3) Is in an area which is marked by obstruction lights.

(c) Anchor an aircraft unless the aircraft—

(1) Has lighted anchor lights; or

(2) Is in an area where anchor lights are not required on vessels; or

(d) Operate an aircraft, required by § 91.33(c)(3) to be equipped with an anticollision light system, unless it has approved and lighted aviation red or aviation white anticollision lights. However, the anticollision lights need not be lighted when the pilot in command determines that, because of operating conditions, it would be in the interest of safety to turn the lights off.

[Doc. No. 1580, Amdt. 1-1, 28 FR 6704, June 29, 1963, as amended by Amdt. 91-152, 43 FR 22640, May 25, 1978]

§ 91.75 Compliance with ATC clearances and instructions.

(a) When an ATC clearance has been obtained, no pilot in command may deviate from that clearance, except in an emergency, unless he obtains an amended clearance. However, except in positive controlled airspace, this paragraph does not prohibit him from cancelling an IFR flight plan if he is operating in VFR weather conditions. If a pilot is uncertain of the meaning of an ATC clearance, he shall immediately request clarification from ATC.

(b) Except in an emergency, no person may, in an area in which air traffic control is exercised, operate an aircraft contrary to an ATC instruction.

(c) Each pilot in command who deviates, in an emergency, from an ATC clearance or instruction shall notify ATC of that deviation as soon as possible.

(d) Each pilot in command who (though not deviating from a rule of this subpart) is given priority by ATC in an emergency, shall, if requested by ATC, submit a detailed report of that emergency within 48 hours to the chief of that ATC facility.

[Doc. No. 1580, Amdt. 1-1, 28 FR 6704, June 29, 1963, as amended by Amdt. 91-50, 33 FR 452, Jan. 12, 1968; Amdt. 91-126, 40 FR 10451, Mar. 6, 1975]

§ 91.77 ATC light signals.

ATC light signals have the meaning shown in the following table:

Color and type of signal	Meaning with respect to aircraft on the surface	Meaning with respect to aircraft in flight
Steady green......	Cleared for take-off....	Cleared to land.
Flashing green ..	Cleared to taxi	Return for landing (to be followed by steady green at proper time).
Steady red.........	Stop...............................	Give way to other aircraft and continue circling.
Flashing red	Taxi clear of runway in use.	Airport unsafe—do not land.
Flashing white...	Return to starting point on airport.	Not applicable.
Alternating red and green.	Exercise extreme caution.	Exercise extreme caution.

§ 91.79 Minimum safe altitudes; general.

Except when necessary for takeoff or landing, no person may operate an aircraft below the following altitudes:

(a) *Anywhere.* An altitude allowing, if a power unit fails, an emergency landing without undue hazard to persons or property on the surface.

(b) *Over congested areas.* Over any congested area of a city, town, or settlement, or over any open air assembly of persons, an altitude of 1,000 feet above the highest obstacle within a horizontal radius of 2,000 feet of the aircraft.

(c) *Over other than congested areas.* An altitude of 500 feet above the surface except over open water or sparsely populated areas. In that case, the aircraft may not be operated closer than 500 feet to any person, vessel, vehicle, or structure.

(d) *Helicopters.* Helicopters may be operated at less than the minimums prescribed in paragraph (b) or (c) of this section if the operation is conducted without hazard to persons or property on the surface. In addition, each person operating a helicopter shall comply with routes or altitudes specifically prescribed for helicopters by the Administrator.

§ 91.81   Altimeter settings.

(a) Each person operating an aircraft shall maintain the cruising altitude or flight level of that aircraft, as the case may be, by reference to an altimeter that is set, when operating—

(1) Below 18,000 feet MSL, to—

(i) The current reported altimeter setting of a station along the route and within 100 nautical miles of the aircraft;

(ii) If there is no station within the area prescribed in paragraph (a)(1)(i) of this section, the current reported altimeter setting of an appropriate available station; or

(iii) In the case of an aircraft not equipped with a radio, the elevation of the departure airport or an appropriate altimeter setting available before departure; or

(2) At or above 18,000 feet MSL, to 29.92″ Hg.

(b) The lowest usable flight level is determined by the atmospheric pressure in the area of operation, as shown in the following table:

Current altimeter setting	Lowest usable flight level
29.92 or higher	180
29.91 through 29.42	185
29.41 through 28.92	190
28.91 through 28.42	195
28.41 through 27.92	200
27.91 through 27.42	205
27.41 through 26.92	210

(c) To convert minimum altitude prescribed under §§ 91.79 and 91.119 to the minimum flight level, the pilot shall take the flight-level equivalent of the minimum altitude in feet and add the appropriate number of feet specified below, according to the current reported altimeter setting:

Current altimeter setting	Adjustment factor
29.92 or higher	None.
29.91 through 29.42	500 feet.
29.41 through 28.92	1,000 feet.
28.91 through 28.42	1,500 feet.
28.41 through 27.92	2,000 feet.
27.91 through 27.42	2,500 feet.
27.41 through 26.92	3,000 feet.

[Amdt. 91-7, 29 FR 9894, July 23, 1964]

§ 91.83   Flight plan; information required.

(a) Unless otherwise authorized by ATC, each person filing an IFR or VFR flight plan shall include in it the following information:

(1) The aircraft identification number and, if necessary, its radio call sign.

(2) The type of the aircraft or, in the case of a formation flight, the type of each aircraft and the number of aircraft in the formation.

(3) The full name and address of the pilot in command or, in the case of a formation flight, the formation commander.

(4) The point and proposed time of departure.

(5) The proposed route, cruising altitude (or flight level), and true air speed at that altitude.

(6) The point of first intended landing and the estimated elapsed time until over that point.

(7) The radio frequencies to be used.

(8) The amount of fuel on board (in hours).

(9) In the case of an IFR flight plan, an alternate airport, except as provided in paragraph (b) of this section.

(10) The number of persons in the aircraft, except where that information is otherwise readily available to the FAA.

(11) Any other information the pilot in command or ATC believes is necessary for ATC purposes.

(b) *Exceptions to applicability of paragraph (a)(9) of this section.* Paragraph (a)(9) of this section does not apply if Part 97 of this subchapter prescribes a standard instrument approach procedure for the first airport of intended landing and, for at least one hour before and one hour after the estimated time of arrival, the weather reports or forecasts or any combination of them, indicate—

(1) The ceiling will be at least 2,000 feet above the airport elevation; and

(2) Visibility will be at least 3 miles.

(c) *IFR alternate airport weather minimums.* Unless otherwise authorized by the Administrator, no person may include an alternate airport in an IFR flight plan unless current weather forecasts indicate that, at the estimated time of arrival at the alternate airport, the ceiling and visibility at that airport will be at or above the following alternate airport weather minimums:

(1) If an instrument approach procedure has been published in Part 97 of this chapter for that airport, the alternate airport minimums specified in that procedure or, if none are so specified, the following minimums:

(i) Precision approach procedure: Ceiling 600 feet and visibility 2 statute miles.

(ii) Nonprecision approach procedure: Ceiling 800 feet and visibility 2 statute miles.

(2) If no instrument approach procedure has been published in Part 97 of this chapter for that airport, the ceiling and visibility minimums are those allowing descent from the MEA, approach, and landing, under basic VFR.

(d) *Cancellation.* When a flight plan has been activated, the pilot in command, upon cancelling or completing the flight under the flight plan, shall notify an FAA Flight Service Station or ATC facility.

[Doc. No. 1580, Amdt. 1-1, 28 FR 6704, June 29, 1963, as amended by Amdt. 91-18, 30 FR 6070, Apr. 29, 1965; Amdt. 91-44, 32 FR 13910, Oct. 6, 1967; Amdt. 91-152, 43 FR 22640, May 25, 1978; Amdt. 91-154, 43 FR 46234, Oct. 5, 1978; Amdt. 91-155, 44 FR 15656, Mar. 15, 1979]

§ 91.84 Flights between Mexico or Canada and the United States.

Unless otherwise authorized by ATC, no person may operate a civil aircraft between Mexico or Canada and the United States without filing an IFR or VFR flight plan, as appropriate.

[Doc. No. 12035, Amdt. 91-117, 38 FR 17493, July 2, 1973]

§ 91.85 Operating on or in the vicinity of an airport; general rules.

(a) Unless otherwise required by Part 93 of this chapter, each person operating an aircraft on or in the vicinity of an airport shall comply with the requirements of this section and of §§ 91.87 and 91.89.

(b) Unless otherwise authorized or required by ATC, no person may operate an aircraft within an airport traffic area except for the purpose of landing at, or taking off from, an airport within that area. ATC authorizations may be given as individual approval of specific operations or may be contained in written agreements between airport users and the tower concerned.

(c) After March 28, 1977, except when necessary for training or certification, the pilot in command of a civil turbojet-powered airplane shall use, as a final landing flap setting, the minimum certificated landing flap setting set forth in the approved performance information in the Airplane Flight Manual for the applicable conditions. However, each pilot in command has the final authority and responsibility for the safe operation of his airplane, and he may use a different flap setting approved for that airplane if he determines that it is necessary in the interest of safety.

[Doc. No. 1580, Amdt. 1-1, 28 FR 6704, June 29, 1963, as amended by Amdt. 91-47, 32 FR 15709, Nov. 15, 1967; Amdt. 91-134, 41 FR 52392, Nov. 29, 1976]

§ 91.87 Operation at airports with operating control towers.

(a) *General.* Unless otherwise authorized or required by ATC, each person operating an aircraft to, from, or on an airport with an operating control tower shall comply with the applicable provisions of this section.

(b) *Communications with control towers operated by the United States.* No person may, within an airport traffic area, operate an aircraft to, from, or on an airport having a control tower operated by the United States unless two-way radio communications are maintained between that aircraft and the control tower. However, if the aircraft radio fails in flight, he may operate that aircraft and land if weather conditions are at or above basic VFR weather minimums, he maintains visual contact with the tower, and he receives a clearance to land. If the aircraft radio fails while in flight under IFR, he must comply with § 91.127.

(c) *Communications with other control towers.* No person may, within an airport traffic area, operate an aircraft to, from, or on an airport having a control tower that is operated by any person other than the United States unless—

(1) If that aircraft's radio equipment so allows, two-way radio communications are maintained between the aircraft and the tower; or

(2) If that aircraft's radio equipment allows only reception from the tower, the pilot has the tower's frequency monitored.

(d) *Minimum altitudes.* When operating to an airport with an operating control tower, each pilot of—

(1) A turbine-powered airplane or a large airplane shall, unless otherwise required by the applicable distance from cloud criteria, enter the airport traffic area at an altitude of at least 1,500 feet above the surface of the airport and maintain at least 1,500 feet within the airport traffic area, including the traffic pattern, until further descent is required for a safe landing;

(2) A turbine-powered airplane or a large airplane approaching to land on a runway being served by an ILS, shall, if the airplane is ILS equipped, fly that airplane at an altitude at or above the glide slope between the outer marker (or the point of interception with the glide slope, if compliance with the applicable distance from clouds criteria requires interception closer in) and the middle marker; and

(3) An airplane approaching to land on a runway served by a visual approach slope indicator, shall maintain an altitude at or above the glide slope until a lower altitude is necessary for a safe landing.

However, paragraphs (d) (2) and (3) of this section do not prohibit normal bracketing maneuvers above or below the glide slope that are conducted for the purpose of remaining on the glide slope.

(e) *Approaches.* When approaching to land at an airport with an operating control tower, each pilot of—

(1) An airplane, shall circle the airport to the left; and

(2) A helicopter, shall avoid the flow of fixed-wing aircraft.

(f) *Departures.* No person may operate an aircraft taking off from an airport with an operating control tower except in compliance with the following:

(1) Each pilot shall comply with any departure procedures established for that airport by the FAA.

(2) Unless otherwise required by the departure procedure or the applicable distance from clouds criteria, each pilot of a turbine-powered airplane and each pilot of a large airplane shall climb to an altitude of 1,500 feet above the surface as rapidly as practicable.

(g) *Noise abatement runway system.* When landing or taking off from an airport with an operating control tower, and for which a formal runway use program has been established by the FAA, each pilot of a turbine-powered airplane and each pilot of a large airplane assigned a noise abatement runway by ATC, shall use that runway. However, consistent with the final authority of the pilot in command concerning the safe operation of the aircraft as prescribed in § 91.3(a), ATC may assign a different runway if requested by the pilot in the interest of safety.

(h) *Clearances required.* No person may, at any airport with an operating control tower, operate an aircraft on a runway or taxiway, or takeoff or land an aircraft, unless an appropriate clearance is received from ATC. A clearance to "taxi to" the takeoff runway assigned to the aircraft is not a clearance to cross that assigned takeoff runway, or to taxi on that runway at any point, but is a clearance to cross other runways that intersect the taxi route to that assigned takeoff runway. A clearance to "taxi to" any point other than an assigned takeoff runway is a clearance to cross all runways that intersect the taxi route to that point.

[Doc. No. 1580, Amdt. 1-1, 28 FR 6704, June 29, 1963, as amended by Amdt. 91-46. 32 FR 15422, Nov. 4, 1967; Amdt. 91-129, 40 FR

§ 91.88   Airport radar service areas.

(a) *General.* For the purposes of this section, the primary airport is the airport designated in Part 71, Subpart L, for which the airport radar service area is designated. A satellite airport is any other airport within the airport radar service area.

(b) *Deviations.* An operator may deviate from any provision of this section under the provisions of an ATC authorization issued by the ATC facility having jurisdiction of the airport radar service area. ATC may authorize a deviation on a continuing basis or for an individual flight, as appropriate.

(c) *Arrivals and Overflights.* No person may operate an aircraft in an airport radar service area unless two-way radio communication is established with ATC prior to entering that area and is thereafter maintained with ATC while within that area.

(d) *Departures.* No person may operate an aircraft within an airport radar service area unless two-way radio communication is maintained with ATC while within that area, except that for aircraft departing a satellite airport, two-way radio communication is established as soon as practicable and thereafter maintained with ATC while within that area.

(e) *Traffic Patterns.* No person may take off or land an aircraft at a satellite airport within an airport radar service area except in compliance with FAA arrival and departure traffic patterns.

(f) *Equipment requirement.* Unless otherwise authorized by ATC, no person may operate an aircraft within an airport radar service area unless that aircraft is equipped with the applicable equipment specified in § 91.24

§ 91.89   Operation at airports without control towers.

(a) Each person operating an aircraft to or from an airport without an operating control tower shall—

(1) In the case of an airplane approaching to land, make all turns of that airplane to the left unless the airport displays approved light signals or visual markings indicating that turns should be made to the right, in which case the pilot shall make all turns to the right;

(2) In the case of a helicopter approaching to land, avoid the flow of fixed-wing aircraft; and

(3) In the case of an aircraft departing the airport, comply with any FAA traffic pattern for that airport.

[Amdt. 91-17, 30 FR 5507, Apr. 17, 1965]

§ 91.90   Terminal control areas.

(a) *Operating rules.* No person may operate an aircraft within a terminal control area designated in Part 71 of this chapter except in compliance with the following rules:.

(1) No person may operate an aircraft within a terminal control area unless that person has received an appropriate authorization from ATC prior to operation of that aircraft in that area.

(2) Unless otherwise authorized by ATC, each person operating a large turbine engine-powered airplane to or from a primary airport shall operate at or above the designated floors while within the lateral limits of the terminal control area.

(3) Any person conducting pilot training operations at an airport within a terminal control area shall comply with any procedures established by ATC for such operations in terminal control area.

(b) *Pilot requirements.* (1) No person may takeoff or land a civil aircraft at an airport within a terminal control area or operate a civil aircraft within a terminal control area unless:

(i) The pilot-in-command holds at least a private pilot certificate; or

(ii) The aircraft is operated by a student pilot who has met the requirements of § 61.95.

(2) Notwithstanding the provisions of (b)(1)(ii) of this section, at the following TCA primary airports, no person may takeoff or land a civil aircraft unless the pilot-in-command holds at least a private pilot certificate:

(i)   Atlanta Hartsfield Airport, GA.

(ii)   Boston Logan Airport, MA.

(iii) Chicago O'Hare International Airport, IL.

(iv) Dallas/Forth Worth International Airport, TX.

(v) Los Angeles International Airport, CA.

(vi) Miami International Airport, FL.

(vii) Newark International Airport, NJ.

(viii) New York Kennedy Airport, NY.

(ix) New York LaGuardia Airport, NY.

(x) San Francisco International Airport, CA.

(xi) Washington National Airport, DC.

(xii) Andrews Air Force Base, MD.

(c) *Communications and navigation equipment requirements.* Unless otherwise authorized by ATC, no person may operate an aircraft within a terminal control area unless that aircraft is equipped with—

(1) An operable VOR or TACAN receiver (except for helicopter operations prior to July 1, 1989); and

(2) An operable two-way radio capable of communications with ATC on appropriate frequencies for that terminal control area.

(d) *Transponder requirement.* No person may operate an aircraft in a terminal control area unless the aircraft is equipped with the applicable operating transponder and automatic altitude reporting equipment specified in paragraph (a) of § 91.24 except as provided in paragraph (d) of that section.

§ 91.91 Temporary flight restrictions.

(a) The Administrator will issue a Notice to Airmen (NOTAM) designating an area within which temporary flight restrictions apply and specifying the hazard or condition requiring their imposition, whenever he determines it is necessary in order to—

(1) protect persons and property on the surface or in the air from a hazard associated with an incident on the surface;

(2) provide a safe environment for the operation of disaster relief aircraft; or

(3) prevent an unsafe congestion of sightseeing and other aircraft above an incident or event which may generate a high degree of public interest.

The Notice to Airmen will specify the hazard or condition that requires the imposition of temporary flight restrictions.

(b) When a NOTAM has been issued under paragraph (a)(1) of this section, no person may operate an aircraft within the designated area unless that aircraft is participating in the hazard relief activities and is being operated under the direction of the official in charge of on scene emergency response activities.

(c) When a NOTAM has been issued under paragraph (a)(2) of this section, no person may operate an aircraft within the designated area unless at least one of the following conditions are met:

(1) The aircraft is participating in hazard relief activities and is being operated under the direction of the official in charge of on scene emergency response activities.

(2) The aircraft is carrying law enforcement officials.

(3) The aircraft is operating under an ATC approved IFR flight plan.

(4) The operation is conducted directly to or from an airport within the area, or is necessitated by the impracticability of VFR flight above or around the area due to weather, or terrain; notification is given to the Flight Service Station (FSS) or ATC facility specified in the NOTAM to receive advisories concerning disaster relief aircraft operations; and the operation does not hamper or endanger relief activities and is not conducted for the purpose of observing the disaster.

(5) The aircraft is carrying properly accredited news representatives, and, prior to entering the area, a flight plan is filed with the appropriate FAA or ATC facility specified in the Notice to Airmen and the operation is conducted above the altitude used by the disaster relief aircraft, unless otherwise authorized by the official in charge of on scene emergency response activities.

(d) When a NOTAM has been issued under paragraph (a)(3) of this section, no person may operate an aircraft within the designated area unless at least one of the following conditions is met:

(1) The operation is conducted directly to or from an airport within the area, or is necessitated by the impracticability of VFR flight above or around the area due to weather or terrain, and the operation is not conducted for the purpose of observing the incident or event.

(2) The aircraft is operating under an ATC approved IFR flight plan.

(3) The aircraft is carrying incident or event personnel, or law enforcement officials.

(4) The aircraft is carrying properly accredited news representatives and, prior to entering that area, a flight plan is filed with the appropriate FSS or ATC facility specified in the NOTAM.

(e) Flight plans filed and notifications made with an FSS or ATC facility under this section shall include the following information:

(1) Aircraft identification, type and color.

(2) Radio communications frequencies to be used.

(3) Proposed times of entry of, and exit from, the designated area.

(4) Name of news media or organization and purpose of flight.

(5) Any other information requested by ATC.

[Doc. No. 22961, Amdt. 91-186, 49 FR 48032, Dec. 10, 1984]

§ 91.93   Flight test areas.

No person may flight test an aircraft except over open water, or sparsely populated areas, having light air traffic.

[Amdt. 91-21, 30 FR 8473, July 2, 1965]

§ 91.95   Restricted and prohibited areas.

(a) No person may operate an aircraft within a restricted area (designated in Part 73 contrary to the restrictions imposed, or within a prohibited area, unless he has the permission of the using or controlling agency, as appropriate.

(b) Each person conducting, within a restricted area, an aircraft operation (approved by the using agency) that creates the same hazards as the operations for which the restricted area was designated, may deviate from the rules of this subpart that are not compatible with his operation of the aircraft.

§ 91.97   Positive control areas and route segments.

(a) Except as provided in paragraph (b) of this section, no person may operate an aircraft within a positive control area, or positive control route segment designated in Part 71 of this chapter, unless that aircraft is—

(1) Operated under IFR at a specific flight level assigned by ATC;

(2) Equipped with instruments and equipment required for IFR operations;

(3) Flown by a pilot rated for instrument flight; and

(4) Equipped, when in a positive control area, with—

(i) The applicable equipment specified in § 91.24; and

(ii) A radio providing direct pilot/controller communication on the frequency specified by ATC for the area concerned.

(b) ATC may authorize deviations from the requirements of paragraph (a) of this section. In the case of an inoperative transponder, ATC may immediately approve an operation within a positive control area allowing flight to continue, if desired, to the airport of ultimate destination, including any intermediate stops, or to proceed to a place where suitable repairs can be made, or both. A request for authorization to deviate from a requirement of paragraph (a) of this section, other than for operation with an inoperative transponder as outlined above, must be submitted at least 4 days before the proposed operation, in writing, to the ATC center having jurisdiction over the positive control area concerned. ATC may authorize a deviation on a continuing basis or for an individual flight, as appropriate.

[Amdt. No. 91-32, 31 FR 10517, Aug. 5, 1966, as amended at 31 FR 11641, Sept. 3, 1966; Amdt. 91-116, 38 FR 14677, June 4, 1973; Amdt. 91-147, 43 FR 7205, Feb. 21, 1978]

§ 91.100   Emergency air traffic rules.

(a) This section prescribes a process for utilizing Notices to Airmen (NOTAM) to advise of the issuance and operations under emergency air traffic rules and regulations and designates the official who is authorized to issue NOTAMs on behalf of the Administrator in certain matters under this section.

(b) Whenever the Administrator determines that an emergency condition exists, or will exist, relating to the FAA's ability to operate the Air Traffic Control System and during which normal flight operations under this chapter cannot be conducted consistent with the required levels of safety and efficiency—

(1) The Administrator issues an immediately effective Air Traffic rule or regulation in response to that emergency condition, and

(2) The Administrator, or the Director, Air Traffic Service, may utilize the Notice to Airmen (NOTAMs) system to provide notification of the issuance of the rule or regulation.

Those NOTAMs communicate information concerning the rules and regulations that govern flight operations, the use of navigation facilities, and

designation of that airspace in which the rules and regulations apply.

(c) When a NOTAM has been issued under this section, no person may operate an aircraft, or other device governed by the regulation concerned, within the designated airspace, except in accordance with the authorizations, terms, and conditions prescribed in the regulation covered by the NOTAM.

[Amdt. 91-175, 46 FR 16891, Mar. 16, 1981]

§ 91.101   Operations to Cuba.

No person may operate a civil aircraft from the United States to Cuba unless—

(a) Departure is from an international airport of entry designated in § 6.13 of the Air Commerce Regulations of the Bureau of Customs (19 CFR 6.13); and

(b) In the case of departure from any of the 48 contiguous States or the District of Columbia, the pilot in command of the aircraft has filed—

(1) A DVFR or IFR flight plan as prescribed in § 99.11 or § 99.13 of this chapter; and

(2) A written statement, within one hour before departure, with the office of Immigration and Naturalization Service at the airport of departure, containing—

(i) All information in the flight plan;

(ii) The name of each occupant of the aircraft;

(iii) The number of occupants of the aircraft; and

(iv) A description of the cargo, if any.

This section does not apply to the operation of aircraft by a scheduled air carrier over routes authorized in operations specifications issued by the Administrator.

[Doc. No. 1580, Amdt. 1-1, 28 FR 6704, June 29, 1966, as amended by Amdt. 91-30, 31 FR 9211, July 6, 1966; Amdt. 91-105, 37 FR 21990, Oct. 18, 1972]

§ 91.102   Flight limitation in the proximity of space flight operations.

No person may operate any aircraft of U.S. registry, or pilot any aircraft under the authority of an airman certificate issued by the Federal Aviation Administration within areas designated in a NOTAM for space flight operations except when authorized by ATC, or operated under the control of the Department of Defense Manager for Space Transportation System Contingency Support Operations.

[Doc. No. 25069, Amdt. 91-195, 51 FR 31098, Sept. 2, 1986]

§ 91.103 Operation of civil aircraft of Cuban registry.

No person may operate a civil aircraft of Cuban registry except in controlled airspace and in accordance with air traffic clearances or air traffic control instructions that may require use of specific airways or routes and landings at specific airports.

[Amdt. 91-15, 30 FR 3638, Mar. 19, 1965]

§ 91.104 Flight restrictions in the proximity of the Presidential and other parties.

No person may operate an aircraft over or in the vicinity of any area to be visited or traveled by the President, the Vice President, or other public figures contrary to the restrictions established by the Administrator and published in a Notice to Airmen (NOTAM).

[Amdt. 91-64, 34 FR 2551, Feb. 25, 1969]

VISUAL FLIGHT RULES

§ 91.105 Basic VFR weather minimums.

(a) Except as provided in § 91.107, no person may operate an aircraft under VFR when the flight visibility is less, or at a distance from clouds that is less, than that prescribed for the corresponding altitude in the following table:

Altitude	Flight visibility	Distance from clouds
1,200 feet or less above the surface (regardless of MSL altitude)—		
Within controlled airspace	3 statute miles	500 feet below. 1,000 feet above. 2,000 feet horizontal.
Outside controlled airspace	1 statute mile except as provided in § 91.105(b).	Clear of clouds.
More than 1,200 feet above the surface but less than 10,000 feet MSL—		
Within controlled airspace	3 statute miles	500 feet below. 1,000 feet above. 2,000 feet horizontal.
Outside controlled airspace	1 statute mile	500 feet below. 1,000 feet above. 2,000 feet horizontal.
More than 1,200 feet above the surface and at or above 10,000 feet MSL.	5 statute miles	1,000 feet below. 1,000 feet above. 1 mile horizontal.

(b) When the visibility is less than one mile, a helicopter may be operated outside controlled airspace at 1,200 feet or less above the surface if operated at a speed that allows the pilot adequate opportunity to see any air traffic or other obstruction in time to avoid a collision.

(c) Except as provided in § 91.107, no person may operate an aircraft, under VFR, within a control zone beneath the ceiling when the ceiling is less than 1,000 feet.

(d) Except as provided in § 91.107, no person may take off or land an aircraft, or enter the traffic pattern of an airport, under VFR, within a control zone—

(1) Unless ground visibility at that airport is at least 3 statute miles; or

(2) If ground visibility is not reported at that airport, unless flight visibility during landing or takeoff, or while operating in the traffic pattern, is at least 3 statute miles.

(e) For the purposes of this section, an aircraft operating at the base altitude of a transition area or control area is considered to be within the airspace directly below that area.

[Amdt. 91-51, 33 FR 2992, Feb. 15, 1968]

§ 91.107 Special VFR weather minimums.

(a) Except as provided in § 93.113 of this chapter, when a person has received an appropriate ATC clearance, the special weather minimums of this section instead of those contained in § 91.105 apply to the operation of an aircraft by that person in a control zone under VFR.

(b) No person may operate an aircraft in a control zone under VFR except clear of clouds.

(c) No person may operate an aircraft (other than a helicopter) in a control zone under VFR unless flight visibility is at least one statute mile.

(d) No person may takeoff or land an aircraft (other than a helicopter) at any airport in a control zone under VFR—

(1) Unless ground visibility at that airport is at least 1 statute mile; or

(2) If ground visibility is not reported at that airport, unless flight visibility during landing or takeoff is at least 1 statute mile.

(e) No person may operate an aircraft (other than a helicopter) in a control zone under the special weather minimums of this section, between sunset and sunrise (or in Alaska, when the sun is more than 6 degrees below the horizon) unless:

(1) That person meets the applicable requirements for instrument flight under Part 61 of this chapter; and

(2) The aircraft is equipped as required in § 91.33(d).

[Doc No. 1580, Amdt. 1-1, 28 FR 6704, June 29, 1963, as amended by Amdt. 91-37, 32 FR 2940, Feb. 16, 1967; Amdt. 91-52, 33 FR 4096, Mar. 2, 1968; Amdt. 91-99, 37 FR 10435, May 23, 1972]

§ 91.109 VFR cruising altitude or flight level.

Except while holding in a holding pattern of 2 minutes or less, or while turning, each person operating an aircraft under VFR in level cruising flight more than 3,000 feet above the surface shall maintain the appropriate altitude or flight level prescribed below, unless otherwise authorized by ATC:

(a) When operating below 18,000 feet MSL and—

(1) On a magnetic course of zero degrees through 179 degrees, any odd thousand foot MSL altitude plus 500 feet (such as 3,500, 5,500, or 7,500); or

(2) On a magnetic course of 180 degrees through 359 degrees, any even thousand foot MSL altitude plus 500 feet (such as 4,500, 6,500, or 8,500).

(b) When operating above 18,000 feet MSL to flight level 290 (inclusive), and—

(1) On a magnetic course of zero degrees through 179 degrees, any odd flight level plus 500 feet (such as 195, 215, or 235); or

(2) On a magnetic course of 180 degrees through 359 degrees, any even flight level plus 500 feet (such as 185, 205, or 225).

(c) When operating above flight level 290 and—

(1) On a magnetic course of zero degrees through 179 degrees, any flight level, at 4,000 foot intervals, beginning at and including flight level 300 (such as flight level 300, 340, or 380); or

(2) On a magnetic course of 180 degrees through 359 degrees, any flight level, at 4,000 foot intervals, beginning at and including flight level 320 (such as flight level 320, 360, or 400).

[Amdt. 91-7, 29 FR 9894, July 23, 1964, as amended by Amdt. 91-84, 36 FR 43, Jan. 5, 1971; Amdt. 91-149, 43 FR 10904, Mar. 16, 1978]

INSTRUMENT FLIGHT RULES

§ 91.115 ATC clearance and flight plan required.

No person may operate an aircraft in controlled airspace under IFR unless—

(a) He has filed an IFR flight plan; and

(b) He has received an appropriate ATC clearance.

§ 91.116 Takeoff and landing under IFR: General.

(a) *Instrument approaches to civil airports.* Unless otherwise authorized by the Administrator for paragraphs (a) through (k) of this section, when an instrument letdown to a civil airport is necessary, each person operating an aircraft, except a military aircraft of the United States, shall use a standard instrument approach procedure prescribed for the airport in Part 97 of this chapter.

(b) *Authorized DH or MDA.* For the purpose of this section, when the approach procedure being used provides for and requires use of a DH or MDA, the authorized decision height or authorized minimum descent altitude is the DH or MDA prescribed by the approach procedure, the DH or MDA prescribed for the pilot in command, or the DH or MDA for which the aircraft is equipped, whichever is higher.

(c) *Operation below DH or MDA.* Where a DH or MDA is applicable, no pilot may operate an aircraft, except a military aircraft of the United States, at any airport below the authorized MDA or continue an approach below the authorized DH unless—

(1) The aircraft is continuously in a position from which a descent to a landing on the intended runway can be made at a normal rate of descent using normal maneuvers, and for operations conducted under Part 121 or Part 135 unless that descent rate will allow touchdown to occur within the touchdown zone of the runway of intended landing;

(2) The flight visibility is not less than the visibility prescribed in the standard instrument approach procedure being used;

(3) Except for a Category II or Category III approach where any necessary visual reference requirements are specified by the Administrator, at least one of the following visual references for the intended runway is distinctly visible and identifiable to the pilot:

(i) The approach light system, except that the pilot may not descend below 100 feet above the touchdown zone elevation using the approach lights as a reference unless the red terminating bars or the red side row bars are also distinctly visible and identifiable.

(ii) The threshold.

(iii) The threshold markings.

(iv) The threshold lights.

(v) The runway end identifier lights.

(vi) The visual approach slope indicator.

(vii) The touchdown zone or touchdown zone markings.

(viii) The touchdown zone lights.

(ix) The runway or runway markings.

(x) The runway lights; and

(4) When the aircraft is on a straight-in nonprecision approach procedure which incorporates a visual descent point, the aircraft has reached the visual descent point, except where the aircraft is not equipped for or capable of establishing that point or a descent to the runway cannot be made using normal procedures or rates of descent if descent is delayed until reaching that point.

(d) *Landing.* No pilot operating an aircraft, except a military aircraft of the United States, may land that aircraft when the flight visibility is less than the visibility prescribed in the standard instrument approach procedure being used.

(e) *Missed approach procedures.* Each pilot operating an aircraft, except a military aircraft of the United States, shall immediately execute an appropriate missed approach procedure when either of the following conditions exist:

(1) Whenever the requirements of paragraph (c) of this section are not met at either of the following times:

(i) When the aircraft is being operated below MDA; or

(ii) Upon arrival at the missed approach point, including a DH where a DH is specified and its use is required, and at any time after that until touchdown.

(2) Whenever an identifiable part of the airport is not distinctly visible to the pilot during a circling maneuver at or above MDA, unless the inability to see an identifiable part of the airport results only from a normal bank of the aircraft during the circling approach.

(f) *Civil airport takeoff minimums.* Unless otherwise authorized by the Administrator, no person operating an aircraft under Part 121, 125, 127, 129, or 135 of this chapter may take off from a civil airport under IFR unless weather conditions are at or above the weather minimums for IFR takeoff prescribed for that airport under Part 97 of this chapter. If takeoff minimums are not prescribed under Part 97 of this chapter for a particular airport, the following minimums apply to takeoffs under IFR for aircraft operating under those parts:

(1) For aircraft, other than helicopters, having two engines or less—1 statute mile visibility.

(2) For aircraft having more than two engines—½ statute mile visibility.

(3) For helicopters—1/2 statute mile visibility.

(g) *Military airports.* Unless otherwise prescribed by the Administrator, each person operating a civil aircraft under IFR into or out of a military airport shall comply with the instrument approach procedures and the takeoff and landing minimums prescribed by the military authority having jurisdiction of that airport.

(h) *Comparable values of RVR and ground visibility.* (1) Except for Category II or Category III minimums, if RVR minimums for takeoff or landing are prescribed in an instrument approach procedure, but RVR is not reported for the runway of intended operation, the RVR minimum shall be converted to ground visibility in accordance with the table in paragraph (h)(2) of this section and shall be the visibility minimum for takeoff or landing on that runway.

(2)

RVR (feet)	Visibility (statute miles)
1,600	¼
2,400	½
3,200	⅝
4,000	¾
4,500	⅞
5,000	1
6,000	1¼

(i) *Operations on unpublished routes and use of radar in instrument approach procedures.* When radar is approved at certain locations for ATC purposes, it may be used not only for surveillance and precision radar approaches, as applicable, but also may be used in conjunction with instrument approach procedures predicated on other types of radio navigational aids. Radar vectors may be authorized to provide course guidance through the segments of an approach procedure to the final approach course or fix. When operating on an unpublished route or while being radar vectored, the pilot, when an approach clearance is received, shall, in addition to complying with §91.119, maintain the last altitude assigned to that pilot until the aircraft is established on a segment of a published route or instrument approach procedure unless a different altitude is assigned by ATC. After the aircraft is so established, published altitudes apply to descent within each succeeding route or approach segment unless a different altitude is assigned by ATC. Upon reaching the final approach course or fix, the pilot may either complete the instrument approach in accordance with a procedure approved for the facility or continue a surveillance or precision radar approach to a landing.

(j) *Limitation on procedure turns.* In the case of a radar vector to a final approach course or fix, a timed approach from a holding fix, or an approach for which the procedure specifies "No PT", no pilot may make a procedure turn unless cleared to do so by ATC.

(k) *ILS components.* The basic ground components of an ILS are the localizer, glide slope, outer marker, middle marker, and, when installed for use with Category II or Category III instrument approach procedures, an inner marker. A compass locator or precision radar may be substituted for the outer or middle marker. DME, VOR, or nondirectional beacon fixes authorized in the standard instrument approach procedure or surveillance radar may be substituted for the outer marker. Applicability of, and substitution for, the inner marker for Category II or III approaches is determined by the appropriate Part 97 approach procedure, letter of authorization, or operations specification pertinent to the operation.

[Amdt. 91-173, 46 FR 2290, Jan. 8, 1981, as amended by Amdt. 91-196, 51 FR 40707, Nov. 7, 1986]

§91.117 [Reserved]

§91.119 Minimum altitudes for IFR operations.

(a) Except when necessary for takeoff or landing, or unless otherwise authorized by the Administrator, no person may operate an aircraft under IFR below—

(1) The applicable minimum altitudes prescribed in Parts 95 and 97 of this chapter; or

(2) If no applicable minimum altitude is prescribed in those parts—

(i) In the case of operations over an area designated as a mountainous area in Part 95 an altitude of 2,000 feet above the highest obstacle within a horizontal distance of five statute miles from the course to be flown; or

(ii) In any other case, an altitude of 1,000 feet above the highest obstacle within a horizontal distance of five statute miles from the course to be flown.

However, if both a MEA and a MOCA are prescribed for a particular route or route segment, a person may operate an aircraft below the MEA down to, but not below, the MOCA, when within 25 statute miles of the VOR concerned (based on the pilot's reasonable estimate of that distance).

(b) *Climb.* Climb to a higher minimum IFR altitude shall begin immediately after passing the point beyond which that minimum altitude applies, except that, when ground obstructions intervene, the point beyond which the higher minimum altitude applies shall be crossed at or above the applicable MCA.

§ 91.121 IFR cruising altitude or flight level.

(a) *In controlled airspace.* Each person operating an aircraft under IFR in level cruising flight in controlled airspace shall maintain the altitude or flight level assigned that aircraft by ATC. However, if the ATC clearance assigns "VFR conditions on-top," he shall maintain an altitude or flight level as prescribed by § 91.109.

(b) *In uncontrolled airspace.* Except while holding in a holding pattern of two minutes or less, or while turning, each person operating an aircraft under IFR in level cruising flight, in uncontrolled airspace, shall maintain an appropriate altitude as follows:

(1) When operating below 18,000 feet MSL and—

(i) On a magnetic course of zero degrees through 179 degrees, any odd thousand foot MSL altitude (such as 3,000, 5,000, or 7,000); or

(ii) On a magnetic course of 180 degrees through 359 degrees, any even thousand foot MSL altitude (such as 2,000, 4,000, or 6,000).

(2) When operating at or above 18,000 feet MSL but below flight level 290, and—

(i) On a magnetic course of zero degrees through 179 degrees, any odd flight level (such as 190, 210, or 230); or

(ii) On a magnetic course of 180 degrees through 359 degrees, any even flight level (such as 180, 200, or 220).

(3) When operating at flight level 290 and above, and—

(i) On a magnetic course of zero degrees through 179 degrees, any flight level, at 4,000 foot intervals, beginning at and including flight level 290 (such as flight level 290, 330, or 370); or

(ii) On a magnetic course of 180 degrees through 359 degrees, any flight level, at 4,000 foot intervals, beginning at and including flight level 310 (such as flight level 310, 350, or 390).

[Amdt. 91-7, 29 FR 9894, July 23, 1964]

§ 91.123 Course to be flown.

Unless otherwise authorized by ATC, no person may operate an aircraft within controlled airspace, under IFR, except as follows:

(a) On a Federal airway, along the centerline of that airway. .

(b) On any other route, along the direct course between the navigational aids or fixes defining that route.

However, this section does not prohibit maneuvering the aircraft to pass well clear of other air traffic or the maneuvering of the aircraft, in VFR conditions to clear the intended flight path both before and during climb or descent.

§ 91.125 IFR radio communications.

The pilot in command of each aircraft operated under IFR in controlled airspace shall have a continuous watch maintained on the appropriate frequency and shall report by radio as soon as possible—

(a) The time and altitude of passing each designated reporting point, or the reporting points specified by ATC, except that while the aircraft is under radar control, only the passing of those reporting points specifically requested by ATC need be reported;

(b) Any unforecast weather conditions encountered; and

(c) Any other information relating to the safety of flight.

[Doc. No. 1580, Amdt. 1–1, 28 FR 6704, June 29, 1963, as amended by Amdt. 91–5, 30 FR 15322, Dec. 11, 1965]

§91.127 IFR operations; two-way radio communications failure.

(a) *General.* Unless otherwise authorized by ATC, each pilot who has two-way radio communications failure when operating under IFR shall comply with the rules of this section.

(b) *VFR conditions.* If the failure occurs in VFR conditions, or if VFR conditions are encountered after the failure, each pilot shall continue the flight under VFR and land as soon as practicable.

(c) *IFR conditions.* If the failure occurs in IFR conditions, or if paragraph (b) of this section cannot be complied with, each pilot shall continue the flight according to the following:

(1) *Route.* (i) By the route assigned in the last ATC clearance received;

(ii) If being radar vectored, by the direct route from the point of radio failure to the fix, route, or airway specified in the vector clearance;

(iii) In the absence of an assigned route, by the route that ATC has advised may be expected in a further clearance; or

(iv) In the absence of an assigned route or a route that ATC has advised may be expected in a further clearance, by the route filed in the flight plan.

(2) *Altitude.* At the highest of the following altitudes or flight levels for the route segment being flown:

(i) The altitude or flight level assigned in the last ATC clearance received;

(ii) The minimum altitude (converted, if appropriate, to minimum flight level as prescribed in §91.81(c)) for IFR operations; or

(iii) The altitude or flight level ATC has advised may be expected in a further clearance.

(3) *Leave clearance limit.* (i) When the clearance limit is a fix from which an approach begins, commence descent or descent and approach as close as possible to the expect further clearance time if one has been received, or if one has not been received, as close as possible to the estimated time of arrival as calculated from the filed or amended (with ATC) estimated time en route.

(ii) If the clearance limit is not a fix from which an approach begins, leave the clearance limit at the expect further clearance time if one has been received, or if none has been received, upon arrival over the clearance limit, and proceed to a fix from which an approach begins and commence descent or descent and approach as close as possible to the estimated time of arrival as calculated from the filed or amended (with ATC) estimated time en route.

[Doc. No. 1580, Amdt. 1–1, 28 FR 6704, June 29, 1963, as amended by Amdt. 91–14, 30 FR 3706, Mar. 20, 1965; Amdt. 91–86, 36 FR 2481, Feb. 5, 1971; Amdt. 91–189, 50 FR 31588, Aug. 5, 1985]

§91.129 Operation under IFR in controlled airspace; malfunction reports.

(a) The pilot in command of each aircraft operated in controlled airspace under IFR, shall report immediately to ATC any of the following malfunctions of equipment occurring in flight:

(1) Loss of VOR, TACAN, ADF, or low frequency navigation receiver capability.

(2) Complete or partial loss of ILS receiver capability.

(3) Impairment of air/ground communications capability.

(b) In each report required by paragraph (a) of this section, the pilot in command shall include the—

(1) Aircraft identification;

(2) Equipment affected;

(3) Degree to which the capability of the pilot to operate under IFR in the ATC system is impaired; and

(4) Nature and extent of assistance he desires from ATC.

Subpart C—Maintenance, Preventive Maintenance, and Alterations

§ 91.161 Applicability.

(a) This subpart prescribes rules governing the maintenance, preventative maintenance, and alteration of U.S. registered civil aircraft operating within or without the United States.

(b) Sections 91.165, 91.169, 91.171, 91.173, and 91.174 of this subpart do not apply to an aircraft maintained in accordance with a continuous airworthiness maintenance program as provided in Part 121, 127, 129, or § 135.411(a)(2) of this chapter.

(c) Sections 91.165, 91.169, 91.171, and Subpart D of this part do not apply to an airplane inspected in accordance with Part 125 of this chapter.

[Amdt. 91–29, 31 FR 8355, June 15, 1966; as amended by Amdt. 91–169, 45 FR 67234, Oct. 9, 1980; Amdt. 91–181, 47 FR 41086, Sept. 16, 1982; Amdt. 91–201, 52 FR 20028, May 28, 1987]

§ 91.163 General.

(a) The owner or operator of an aircraft is primarily responsible for maintaining that aircraft in an airworthy condition, including compliance with Part 39 of this chapter.

(b) No person may perform maintenance, preventive maintenance, or alterations on an aircraft other than as prescribed in this subpart and other applicable regulations, including Part 43 of this chapter.

(c) No person may operate an aircraft for which a manufacturer's maintenance manual or Instructions for Continued Airworthiness has been issued that contains an Airworthiness Limitations section unless the mandatory replacement times, inspection intervals, and related procedures specified in that section or alternative inspection intervals and related procedures set forth in an operations specification approved by the Administrator under Parts 121, 123, 127, or 135, or in accordance with an inspection program approved under § 91.217(e), have been complied with.

[Amdt. 91–19, 30 FR 8033, June 23, 1965, as amended by Amdt. 91–29, 31 FR 8355, June 15, 1966; Amdt. 91–167, 45 FR 60183, Sept. 11, 1980]

§ 91.165 Maintenance required.

Each owner or operator of an aircraft shall have that aircraft inspected as prescribed in §§ 91.169, 91.171, and 91.172 and shall, between required inspections, have discrepancies repaired as prescribed in Part 43 of this chapter. In addition, each owner or operator shall ensure that maintenance personnel make appropriate entries in the aircraft maintenance records indicating that the aircraft has been approved for return to service.

[Doc. No. 21071, Amdt. 91–181, 47 FR 41086, Sept. 16, 1982]

§ 91.167 Operation after maintenance, preventive maintenance, rebuilding, or alteration.

(a) No person may operate any aircraft that has undergone maintenance, preventive maintenance, rebuilding, or alteration unless—

(1) It has been approved for return to service by a person authorized under § 43.7 of this chapter; and

(2) The maintenance record entry required by §43.9 or §43.11, as applicable, of this chapter has been made.

(b) No person may carry any person (other than crewmembers) in an aircraft that has been maintained, rebuilt, or altered in a manner that may have appreciably changed its flight characteristics or substantially affected its operation in flight until an appropriately rated pilot with at least a private pilot certificate flies the aircraft, makes an operational check of the maintenance performed or alteration made, and logs the flight in the aircraft records.

(c) The aircraft does not have to be flown as required by paragraph (b) of this section if, prior to flight, ground tests, inspections, or both show conclusively that the maintenance, preventive maintenance, rebuilding, or alteration has not appreciably changed the flight characteristics or substantially affected the flight operation of the aircraft.

(Approved by the Office of Management and Budget under OMB control number 2120–0005)

[Doc. No. 21071, Amdt. 91–181, 47 FR 41086, Sept. 16, 1982]

§ 91.169 Inspections.

(a) Except as provided in paragraph (c) of this section, no person may operate an aircraft unless, within the preceding 12 calendar months, it has had—

(1) An annual inspection in accordance with Part 43 of this chapter and has been approved for return to service by a person authorized by § 43.7 of this chapter; or

(2) An inspection for the issue of an airworthiness certificate.

No inspection performed under paragraph (b) of this section may be substituted for any inspection required by this paragraph unless it is performed by a person authorized to perform annual inspections, and is entered as an "annual" inspection in the required maintenance records.

(b) Except as provided in paragraph (c) of this section, no person may operate an aircraft carrying any person (other than a crewmember) for hire, and no person may give flight instruction for hire in an aircraft which that person provides, unless within the preceding 100 hours of time in service it has received an annual or 100-hour inspection and been approved for return to service in accordance with Part 43 of this chapter, or received an inspection for the issuance of an airworthiness certificate in accordance with Part 21 of this chapter. The 100-hour limitation may be exceeded by not more than 10 hours if necessary to reach a place at which the inspection can be done. The excess time, however, is included in computing the next 100 hours of time in service.

(c) Paragraphs (a) and (b) of this section do not apply to—

(1) An aircraft that carries a special flight permit, a current experimental certificate, or a provisional airworthiness certificate;

(2) An aircraft inspected in accordance with an approved aircraft inspection program under Part 123, 125, or 135 of this chapter and so identified by the registration number in the operations specifications of the certificate holder having the approved inspection program; or

(3) An aircraft subject to the requirements of paragraph (d) or (e) of this section.

(d) *Progressive inspection.* Each registered owner or operator of an aircraft desiring to use a progressive inspection program must submit a written request to the FAA Flight Standards district office having jurisdiction over the area in which the applicant is located, and shall provide—

(1) A certificated mechanic holding an inspection authorization, a certificated airframe repair station, or the manufacturer of the aircraft to supervise or conduct the progressive inspection;

(2) A current inspection procedures manual available and readily understandable to pilot and maintenance personnel containing, in detail—

(i) An explanation of the progressive inspection, including the continuity of inspection responsibility, the making of reports, and the keeping of records and technical reference material;

(ii) An inspection schedule, specifying the intervals in hours or days when routine and detailed inspections will be performed and including instructions for exceeding an inspection interval by not more than 10 hours while en route and for changing an inspection interval because of service experience;

(iii) Sample routine and detailed inspection forms and instructions for their use; and

(iv) Sample reports and records and instructions for their use;

(3) Enough housing and equipment for necessary disassembly and proper inspection of the aircraft; and

(4) Appropriate current technical information for the aircraft.

The frequency and detail of the progressive inspection shall provide for the complete inspection of the aircraft within each 12-calendar months and be consistent with the manufacturer's recommendations, field service experience, and the kind of operation in which the aircraft is engaged. The progressive inspection schedule must ensure that the aircraft, at all times, will be airworthy and will conform to all applicable FAA aircraft specifications, type certificate data sheets, airworthiness directives, and other approved data. If the progressive inspection is discontinued, the owner or operator shall immediately notify the local FAA Flight Standards district office, in writing, of the discontinuance. After the discontinuance, the first annual inspection under § 91.169(a) is due within 12-calendar months after the last complete inspection of the aircraft under the progressive inspection. The 100-hour inspection under § 91.169(b) is due within 100 hours after that complete inspection. A complete inspection of the aircraft, for the purpose of determining when the annual and 100-hour inspections are due, requires a detailed inspection of the aircraft and all its components in accordance with the progressive inspection. A routine inspection of the aircraft and a detailed inspection of several components is not considered to be a complete inspection.

(e) *Large airplanes (to which Part 125 is not applicable), turbojet multiengine airplanes, and turbopropeller-powered multiengine airplanes.* No person may operate a large airplane, turbojet multiengine airplane, or turbopropeller-powered multiengine airplane unless the replacement times for life-limited parts specified in the aircraft specifications, type data sheets, or other documents approved by the Administrator are complied with and the airplane, including the airframe, engines, propellers, appliances, survival equipment, and emergency equipment, is inspected in accordance with an inspection program selected under the provisions of paragraph (f) of this section.

(f) *Selection of inspection programs under paragraph (e) of this section.* The registered owner or operator of each airplane described in paragraph (e) of this section must select, identify in the aircraft maintenance records, and use one of the following programs for the inspection of that airplane:

(1) A continuous airworthiness inspection program that is part of a continuous airworthiness maintenance program currently in use by a person holding an air carrier operating certificate or an operating certificate issued under Part 121, 127, or 135 of this chapter and operating that make and model airplane under Part 121 or 127 or operating that make and model under Part 135 and maintaining it under § 135.411(a)(2).

(2) An approved aircraft inspection program approved under § 135.419 of this chapter and currently in use by a person holding an operating certificate issued under Part 135.

(3) An approved continuous inspection program currently in use by a person certificated under Part 123 of this chapter.

(4) A current inspection program recommended by the manufacturer.

(5) Any other inspection program established by the registered owner or operator of that airplane and approved by the Administrator under paragraph (g) of this section. However, the Administrator may require revision to this inspection program in accordance with the provisions of § 91.170.

Each operator shall include in the selected program the name and address of the person responsible for scheduling the inspections required by the program and make a copy of that program available to the person performing inspections on the airplane and, upon request, to the Administrator.

(g) *Inspection program approval under paragraph (e) of this section.* Each operator of an airplane desiring to establish or change an approved inspection program under paragraph (f)(5) of this section must submit the program for approval to the local FAA Flight Standards district office having jurisdiction over the area in which the airplane is based. The program must be in writing and include at least the following information:

(1) Instruction and procedures for the conduct of inspections for the particular make and model airplane, including necessary tests and checks. The instructions and procedures must set forth in detail the parts and areas of the airframe, engines, propellers, and appliances, including survival and emergency equipment required to be inspected.

(2) A schedule for performing the inspections that must be performed under the program expressed in terms

of the time in service, calendar time, number of system operations, or any combination of these.

(h) *Changes from one inspection program to another.* When an operator changes from one inspection program under paragraph (f) of this section to another, the time in service, calendar times, or cycles of operation accumulated under the previous program must be applied in determining inspection due times under the new program.

(Approved by the Office of Management and Budget under OMB control number 2120–0005)

[Doc. No. 1580, Amdt. 1–1, 28 FR 6704, June 29, 1963, as amended by Amdt. 91–26, 31 FR 3337, Mar. 3, 1966; Amdt. 91–30, 31 FR 9211, July 6, 1966; Amdt. 91–74, 35 FR 4116, Mar. 5, 1970; Amdt. 91–181, 47 FR 41086, Sept. 16, 1982]

§ 91.170 Changes to aircraft inspection programs.

(a) Whenever the Administrator finds that revisions to an approved aircraft inspection program under § 91.169(f)(5) are necessary for the continued adequacy of the program, the owner or operator shall, after notification by the Administrator, make any changes in the program found to be necessary by the Administrator.

(b) The owner or operator may petition the Administrator to reconsider the notice to make any changes in a program in accordance with paragraph (a) of this section.

(c) The petition must be filed with the FAA Flight Standards district office which requested the change to the program within 30 days after the certificate holder receives the notice.

(d) Except in the case of an emergency requiring immediate action in the interest of safety, the filing of the petition stays the notice pending a decision by the Administrator.

[Doc. No. 21071, Amdt. 91–181, 47 FR 41087, Sept. 16, 1982]

§ 91.171 Altimeter system and altitude reporting equipment tests and inspections.

(a) No person may operate an airplane or helicopter in controlled airspace under IFR unless—

(1) Within the preceding 24 calendar months, each static pressure system, each altimeter instrument, and each automatic pressure altitude reporting system has been tested and inspected and found to comply with Appendices E and F of Part 43 of this chapter;

(2) Except for the use of system drain and alternate static pressure valves, following any opening and closing of the static pressure system, that system has been tested and inspected and found to comply with paragraph (a), Appendix E, of Part 43 of this chapter; and

(3) Following installation or maintenance on the automatic pressure altitude reporting system or the ATC transponder where data correspondence error could be introduced, the integrated system has been tested, inspected, and found to comply with paragraph (c), Appendix E, of Part 43 of this chapter.

(b) The tests required by paragraph (a) of this section must be conducted by—

(1) The manufacturer of the airplane or helicopter on which the tests and inspections are to be performed;

(2) A certificated repair station properly equipped to perform those functions and holding—

(i) An instrument rating, Class I;

(ii) A limited instrument rating appropriate to the make and model of appliance to be tested;

(iii) A limited rating appropriate to the test to be performed;

(iv) An airframe rating appropriate to the airplane or helicopter to be tested; or

(v) A limited rating for a manufacturer issued for the appliance in accordance with § 145.101(b)(4) of this chapter; or

(3) A certificated mechanic with an airframe rating (static pressure system tests and inspections only).

(c) Altimeter and altitude reporting equipment approved under Technical Standard Orders are considered to be tested and inspected as of the date of their manufacture.

(d) No person may operate an airplane or helicopter in controlled airspace under IFR at an altitude above the maximum altitude at which all altimeters and the automatic altitude reporting system of that airplane have been tested.

[Doc. No. 21071, Amdt. 91-181, 47 FR 41088, Sept. 16, 1982, as amended by Amdt. 91-196, 51 FR 40707, Nov. 7, 1986]

§ 91.172 ATC transponder tests and inspections.

(a) No person may use an ATC transponder that is specified in Part 125, § 91.24(a), § 121.345(c), § 127.123(b) or § 135.143(c) of this chapter unless, within the preceding 24 calendar months, that ATC transponder has been tested and inspected and found to comply with Appendix F of Part 43 of this chapter; and

(b) Following any installation or maintenance on an ATC transponder where data correspondence error could be introduced, the integrated system has been tested, inspected, and found to comply with paragraph (c), Appendix E, of Part 43 of this chapter.

(c) The tests and inspections specified in this section must be conducted by—

(1) A certificated repair station properly equipped to perform those functions and holding—

(i) A radio rating, Class III;

(ii) A limited radio rating appropriate to the make and model transponder to be tested;

(iii) A limited rating appropriate to the test to be performed;

(iv) A limited rating for a manufacturer issued for the transponder in accordance with § 145.101(b)(4) of this chapter; or

(2) A holder of a continuous airworthiness maintenance program as provided in Part 121, 127, or § 135.411(a)(2) of this chapter; or

(3) The manufacturer of the aircraft on which the transponder to be tested is installed, if the transponder was installed by that manufacturer.

[Doc. No. 21071, Amdt. 91-181, 47 FR 41088, Sept. 16, 1982; 47 FR 44246, Oct. 7, 1982]

§ 91.173 Maintenance records.

(a) Except for work performed in accordance with § 91.171, each registered owner or operator shall keep the following records for the periods specified in paragraph (b) of this section:

(1) Records of the maintenance, preventive maintenance, and alteration, and records of the 100-hour, annual, progressive, and other required or approved inspections, as appropriate, for each aircraft (including the airframe) and each engine, propeller, rotor, and appliance of an aircraft. The records must include—

(i) A description (or reference to data acceptable to the Administrator) of the work performed;

(ii) The date of completion of the work performed; and

(iii) The signature and certificate number of the person approving the aircraft for return to service.

(2) Records containing the following information:

(i) The total time in service of the airframe, each engine and each propeller.

(ii) The current status of life-limited parts of each airframe, engine, propeller, rotor, and appliance.

(iii) The time since last overhaul of all items installed on the aircraft which are required to be overhauled on a specified time basis.

(iv) The identification of the current inspection status of the aircraft, including the times since the last inspections required by the inspection program under which the aircraft and its appliances are maintained.

(v) The current status of applicable airworthiness directives (AD) including, for each, the method of compliance, the AD number, and revision date. If the AD involves recurring action, the time and date when the next action is required.

(vi) Copies of the forms prescribed by § 43.9(a) of this chapter for each major alteration to the airframe and currently installed engines, rotors, propellers, and appliances.

(b) The owner or operator shall retain the following records for the periods prescribed:

(1) The records specified in paragraph (a)(1) of this section shall be retained until the work is repeated or superseded by other work or for 1 year after the work is performed.

(2) The records specified in paragraph (a)(2) of this section shall be retained and transferred with the aircraft at the time the aircraft is sold.

(3) A list of defects furnished to a registered owner or operator under § 43.11 of this chapter, shall be retained until the defects are repaired

and the aircraft is approved for return to service.

(c) The owner or operator shall make all maintenance records required to be kept by this section available for inspection by the Administrator or any authorized representative of the National Transportation Safety Board (NTSB). In addition, the owner or operator shall present the Form 337 described in paragraph (d) of this section for inspection upon request of any law enforcement officer.

(d) When a fuel tank is installed within the passenger compartment or a baggage compartment pursuant to Part 43, a copy of the FAA Form 337 shall be kept on board the modified aircraft by the owner or operator.

(Approved by the Office of Management and Budget under OMB control number 2120-0005)

[Doc. No. 10658, Amdt. 91-102, 37 FR 15983, Aug. 9, 1972, as amended by Amdt. 91-152, 43 FR 22640, May 25, 1978; Amdt. 91-167, 45 FR 60183, Sept. 11, 1980; Amdt. 91-181, 47 FR 41088, Sept. 16, 1982; Amdt. 91-200, 52 FR 17277, May 6, 1987; Amdt. 91-206, 52 FR 34102, Sept. 9, 1987]

§ **91.174 Transfer of maintenance records.**

Any owner or operator who sells a U.S. registered aircraft shall transfer to the purchaser, at the time of sale, the following records of that aircraft, in plain language form or in coded form at the election of the purchaser, if the coded form provides for the preservation and retrieval of information in a manner acceptable to the Administrator:

(a) The records specified in § 91.173(a)(2).

(b) The records specified in § 91.173(a)(1) which are not included in the records covered by paragraph (a) of this section, except that the purchaser may permit the seller to keep physical custody of such records. However, custody of records in the seller does not relieve the purchaser of his responsibility under § 91.173(c), to make the records available for inspection by the Administrator or any authorized representative of the National Transportation Safety Board (NTSB).

[Doc. No. 10658, Amdt. 91-102, 37 FR 15983, Aug. 9, 1972]

§ **91.175 Rebuilt engine maintenance records.**

(a) The owner or operator may use a new maintenance record, without previous operating history, for an aircraft engine rebuilt by the manufacturer or by an agency approved by the manufacturer.

(b) Each manufacturer or agency that grants zero time to an engine rebuilt by it shall enter, in the new record—

(1) A signed statement of the date the engine was rebuilt;

(2) Each change made as required by Airworthiness Directives; and

(3) Each change made in compliance with manufacturer's service bulletins, if the entry is specifically requested in that bulletin.

(c) For the purposes of this section, a rebuilt engine is a used engine that has been completely disassembled, inspected, repaired as necessary, reassembled, tested, and approved in the same manner and to the same tolerances and limits as a new engine with either new or used parts. However, all parts used in it must conform to the production drawing tolerances and limits for new parts or be of approved oversize or undersize dimensions for a new engine.

Subpart D—Large and Turbine-Powered Multiengine Airplanes

SOURCE: Docket No. 11437, Amdt. 91-101, 37 FR 14763, July 25, 1972, unless otherwise noted.

§ **91.181 Applicability.**

(a) Sections 91.181 through 91.215 prescribe operating rules, in addition to those prescribed in other subparts of this part, governing the operation of large and of turbojet-powered multiengine civil airplanes of U.S. registry. The operating rules in this subpart do not apply to those airplanes when they are required to be operated under Parts 121, 123, 125, 129, 135, and 137 of this chapter. Section 91.169 prescribes an inspection program for large and for turbine-powered (turbojet and turboprop) multiengine airplanes of U.S. registry when they are operated under this part or Part 129 or 137.

(b) Operations that may be conducted under the rules in this subpart instead of those in Parts 121, 123, 129, 135, and 137 of this chapter, when common carriage is not involved, include—

(1) Ferry or training flights;

(2) Aerial work operations such as aerial photography or survey, or pipeline patrol, but not including firefighting operations;

(3) Flights for the demonstration of an airplane to prospective customers when no charge is made except for those specified in paragraph (d) of this section;

(4) Flights conducted by the operator of an airplane for his personal transportation, or the transportation of his guests when no charge, assessment, or fee is made for the transportation;

(5) The carriage of officials, employees, guests, and property of a company on an airplane operated by that company, or the parent or a subsidiary of that company or a subsidiary of the parent, when the carriage is within the scope of, and incidental to, the business of the company (other than transportation by air) and no charge, assessment or fee is made for the carriage in excess of the cost of owning, operating, and maintaining the airplane, except that no charge of any kind may be made for the carriage of a guest of a company, when the carriage is not within the scope of, and incidental to, the business of that company;

(6) The carriage of company officials, employees, and guests of the company on an airplane operated under a time sharing, interchange, or joint ownership agreement as defined in paragraph (c) of this section;

(7) The carriage of property (other than mail) on an airplane operated by a person in the furtherance of a business or employment (other than transportation by air) when the carriage is within the scope of, and incidental to, that business or employment and no charge, assessment, or fee is made for the carriage other than those specified in paragraph (d) of this section;

(8) The carriage on an airplane of an athletic team, sports group, choral group, or similar group having a common purpose or objective when there is no charge, assessment, or fee of any kind made by any person for that carriage; and

(9) The carriage of persons on an airplane operated by a person in the furtherance of a business (other than transportation by air) for the purpose of selling to them land, goods, or property, including franchises or distributorships, when the carriage is within the scope of, and incidental to, that business and no charge, assessment, or fee is made for that carriage.

(c) As used in this section:

(1) A "time sharing agreement" means an arrangement whereby a person leases his airplane with flight crew to another person, and no charge is made for the flights conducted under that arrangement other than those specified in paragraph (d) of this section;

(2) An "interchange agreement" means an arrangement whereby a person leases his airplane to another person in exchange for equal time, when needed, on the other person's airplane, and no charge, assessment, or fee is made, except that a charge may be made not to exceed the difference between the cost of owning, operating, and maintaining the two airplanes;

(3) A "joint ownership agreement" means an arrangement whereby one of the registered joint owners of an airplane employs and furnishes the flight crew for that airplane and each of the registered joint owners pays a share of the charges specified in the agreement.

(d) The following may be charged, as expenses of a specific flight, for transportation as authorized by paragraphs (b)(3) and (7) and (c)(1) of this section:

(1) Fuel, oil, lubricants, and other additives.

(2) Travel expenses of the crew, including food, lodging, and ground transportation.

(3) Hangar and tie-down costs away from the aircraft's base of operations.

(4) Insurance obtained for the specific flight.

(5) Landing fees, airport taxes, and similar assessments.

(6) Customs, foreign permit, and similar fees directly related to the flight.

(7) In flight food and beverages.

(8) Passenger ground transportation.

(9) Flight planning and weather contract services.

(10) An additional charge equal to 100 percent of the expenses listed in paragraph (d)(1) of this section.

[Doc. No. 11437, Amdt. 91–101, 37 FR 14763, July 25, 1972, as amended by Amdt. 91–118, 38 FR 19025, July 17, 1973; Amdt. 91–133, 41 FR 47229, Oct. 28, 1976; Amdt. 91–164, 45 FR 67234, Oct. 9, 1980; Amdt. 91–181, 47 FR 41088, Sept. 16, 1982]

§ 91.183   Flying equipment and operating information.

(a) The pilot in command of an airplane shall insure that the following flying equipment and aeronautical charts and data, in current and appropriate form, are accessible for each flight at the pilot station of the airplane:

(1) A flashlight having at least two size D cells, or the equivalent, that is in good working order.

(2) A cockpit checklist containing the procedures required by paragraph (b) of this section.

(3) Pertinent aeronautical charts.

(4) For IFR, VFR over-the-top, or night operations, each pertinent navigational en route, terminal area, and approach and letdown chart.

(5) In the case of multiengine airplanes, one-engine inoperative climb performance data.

(b) Each cockpit checklist must contain the following procedures and shall be used by the flight crewmembers when operating the airplane:

(1) Before starting engines.

(2) Before takeoff.

(3) Cruise.

(4) Before landing.

(5) After landing.

(6) Stopping engines.

(7) Emergencies.

(c) Each emergency cockpit checklist procedure required by paragraph (b)(7) of this section must contain the following procedures, as appropriate:

(1) Emergency operation of fuel, hydraulic, electrical, and mechanical systems.

(2) Emergency operation of instruments and controls.

(3) Engine inoperative procedures.

(4) Any other procedures necessary for safety.

(d) The equipment, charts, and data prescribed in this section shall be used by the pilot in command and other members of the flight crew, when pertinent.

§ 91.185   Familiarity with operating limitations and emergency equipment.

(a) Each pilot in command of an airplane shall, before beginning a flight, familiarize himself with the airplane flight manual for that airplane, if one is required, and with any placards, listings, instrument markings, or any combination thereof, containing each operating limitation prescribed for that airplane by the Administrator, including those specified in § 91.31(b).

(b) Each required member of the crew shall, before beginning a flight, familiarize himself with the emergency equipment installed on the airplane to which he is assigned and with the procedures to be followed for the use of that equipment in an emergency situation.

§ 91.187   Equipment requirements: Over-the-top, or night VFR operations.

No person may operate an airplane over-the-top, or at night under VFR unless that airplane is equipped with the instruments and equipment required for IFR operations under § 91.33(d) and one electric landing light for night operations. Each required instrument and item of equipment must be in operable condition.

§ 91.189   Survival equipment for overwater operations.

(a) No person may take off an airplane for a flight over water more than 50 nautical miles from the nearest shoreline, unless that airplane is equipped with a life preserver or an approved flotation means for each occupant of the airplane.

(b) No person may take off an airplane for a flight over water more than 30 minutes flying time or 100 nautical miles from the nearest shoreline, unless it has on board the following survival equipment:

(1) A life preserver equipped with an approved survivor locator light, for each occupant of the airplane.

(2) Enough liferafts (each equipped with an approved survivor locator light) of a rated capacity and buoyancy to accommodate the occupants of the airplane.

(3) At least one pyrotechnic signaling device for each raft.

(4) One self-buoyant, water-resistant, portable emergency radio signaling device, that is capable of transmission on the appropriate emergency frequency or frequencies, and not dependent upon the airplane power supply.

(5) After June 26, 1979, a lifeline stored in accordance with § 25.1411(g) of this chapter.

(c) The required liferafts, life preservers, and signaling devices must be installed in conspicuously marked locations and easily accessible in the event of a ditching without appreciable time for preparatory procedures.

(d) A survival kit, appropriately equipped for the route to be flown, must be attached to each required liferaft.

[Doc. No. 1580, Amdt. 1-1, 28 FR 6704, June 29, 1963, as amended by Amdt. 91-152, 43 FR 22641, May 25, 1978]

§ 91.191 Radio equipment for overwater operations.

(a) Except as provided in paragraphs (c) and (d) of this section, no person may takeoff an airplane for a flight over water more than 30 minutes flying time or 100 nautical miles from the nearest shoreline, unless it has at least the following operable radio communication and navigational equipment appropriate to the facilities to be used and able to transmit to, and receive from, at any place on the route, at least one surface facility:

(1) Two transmitters.

(2) Two microphones.

(3) Two headsets or one headset and one speaker.

(4) Two independent receivers for navigation.

(5) Two independent receivers for communications.

However, a receiver that can receive both communications and navigational signals may be used in place of a separate communications receiver and a separate navigational signal receiver.

(b) For the purposes of paragraphs (a) (4) and (5) of this section, a receiver is independent if the function of any part of it does not depend on the functioning of any part of another receiver.

(c) Notwithstanding the provisions of paragraph (a) of this section, a person may operate an airplane on which no passengers are carried from a place where repairs or replacement cannot be made to a place where they can be made, if not more than one of each of the dual items of radio communication and navigation equipment specified in paragraphs (a) (1) through (5) of this section malfunctions or becomes inoperative.

(d) Notwithstanding the provisions of paragraph (a) of this section, when both VHF and HF communications equipment are required for the route and the airplane has two VHF transmitters and two VHF receivers for communications, only one HF transmitter and one HF receiver is required for communications.

[Doc. No. 11437, Amdt. 91-101, 37 FR 14763, July 25, 1972, as amended by Amdt. 91-132, 41 FR 16795, Apr. 22, 1976]

§ 91.193 Emergency equipment.

(a) No person may operate an airplane unless it is equipped with the emergency equipment listed in this section:

(b) Each item of equipment—

(1) Must be inspected in accordance with § 91.217 to insure its continued serviceability and immediate readiness for its intended purposes;

(2) Must be readily accessible to the crew;

(3) Must clearly indicate its method of operation; and

(4) When carried in a compartment or container, must have that compartment or container marked as to contents and date of last inspection.

(c) Hand fire extinguishers must be provided for use in crew, passenger, and cargo compartments in accordance with the following:

(1) The type and quantity of extinguishing agent must be suitable for the kinds of fires likely to occur in the

compartment where the extinguisher is intended to be used.

(2) At least one hand fire extinguisher must be provided and located on or near the flight deck in a place that is readily accessible to the flight crew.

(3) At least one hand fire extinguisher must be conveniently located in the passenger compartment of each airplane accommodating more than six but less than 31 passengers, and at least two hand fire extinguishers must be conveniently located in the passenger compartment of each airplane accommodating more than 30 passengers.

(4) Hand fire extinguishers must be installed and secured in such a manner that they will not interfere with the safe operation of the airplane or adversely affect the safety of the crew and passengers. They must be readily accessible, and unless the locations of the fire extinguishers are obvious, their stowage provisions must be properly identified.

(d) First aid kits for treatment of injuries likely to occur in flight or in minor accidents must be provided.

(e) Each airplane accommodating more than 19 passengers must be equipped with a crash ax.

(f) Each passenger-carrying airplane must have a portable battery-powered megaphone or megaphones readily accessible to the crewmembers assigned to direct emergency evacuation, installed as follows:

(1) One megaphone on each airplane with a seating capacity of more than 60 but less than 100 passengers, at the most rearward location in the passenger cabin where it would be readily accessible to a normal flight attendant seat. However, the Administrator may grant a deviation from the requirements of this paragraph if he finds that a different location would be more useful for evacuation of persons during an emergency.

(2) Two megaphones in the passenger cabin on each airplane with a seating capacity of more than 99 passengers, one installed at the forward end and the other at the most rearward location where it would be readily accessible to a normal flight attendant seat.

[Doc. No. 11437, Amdt. 91–101, 37 FR 14763, July 25, 1972, as amended by Amdt. 91–167, 45 FR 60183, Sept. 11, 1980]

§ 91.195   Flight altitude rules.

(a) Notwithstanding § 91.79, and except as provided in paragraph (b) of this section, no person may operate an airplane under VFR at less than—

(1) One thousand feet above the surface, or 1,000 feet from any mountain, hill, or other obstruction to flight, for day operations; and

(2) The altitudes prescribed in § 91.119, for night operations.

(b) This section does not apply—

(1) During takeoff or landing;

(2) When a different altitude is authorized by a waiver to this section under § 91.63; or

(3) When a flight is conducted under the special VFR weather minimums of § 91.107 with an appropriate clearance from ATC.

§ 91.197   Smoking and safety belt signs.

(a) Except as provided in paragraph (b) of this section, no person may operate an airplane carrying passengers unless it is equipped with signs that are visible to passengers and cabin attendants to notify them when smoking is prohibited and when safety belts should be fastened. The signs must be so constructed that the crew can turn them on and off. They must be turned on for each takeoff and each landing and when otherwise considered to be necessary by the pilot in command.

(b) The pilot in command of an airplane that is not equipped as provided in paragraph (a) of this section shall insure that the passengers are orally notified each time that it is necessary to fasten their safety belts and when smoking is prohibited.

§ 91.199   Passenger briefing.

(a) Before each takeoff the pilot in command of an airplane carrying passengers shall ensure that all passengers have been orally briefed on:

(1) Smoking;

(2) Use of safety belts;

(3) Location and means for opening the passenger entry door and emergency exits;

(4) Location of survival equipment;

(5) Ditching procedures and the use of flotation equipment required under § 91.189 for a flight over water; and

(6) The normal and emergency use of oxygen equipment installed on the airplane.

(b) The oral briefing required by paragraph (a) of this section shall be given by the pilot in command or a member of the crew, but need not be given when the pilot in command determines that the passengers are familiar with the contents of the briefing. It may be supplemented by printed cards for the use of each passenger containing—

(1) A diagram of, and methods of operating, the emergency exits; and

(2) Other instructions necessary for use of emergency equipment.

Each card used under this paragraph must be carried in convenient locations on the airplane for use of each passenger and must contain information that is pertinent only to the type and model airplane on which it is used.

§ 91.200   Shoulder harness.

(a) No person may operate a transport category airplane that was type certificated after January 1, 1958, unless it is equipped at each seat at a flight-deck station with a combined safety belt and shoulder harness that meets the applicable requirements specified in § 25.785 of this chapter, except that—

(1) Shoulder harnesses and combined safety belt and shoulder harnesses that were approved and installed before March 6, 1980, may continue to be used; and

(2) Safety belt and shoulder harness restraint systems may be designed to the inertia load factors established under the certification basis of the airplane.

(b) No person may operate a transport category airplane unless it is equipped at each required flight attendant seat in the passenger compartment with a combined safety belt and shoulder harness that meets the applicable requirements specified in § 25.785 of this chapter, except that—

(1) Shoulder harnesses and combined safety belt and shoulder harnesses that were approved and in-

stalled before March 6, 1980, may continue to be used; and

(2) Safety belt and shoulder harness restraint systems may be designed to the inertia load factors established under the certification basis of the airplane.

[Doc. No. 23584, Amdt. 91-183, 48 FR 13663, Mar. 31, 1983]

§ 91.201   Carry-on-baggage.

No pilot in command of an airplane having a seating capacity of more than 19 passengers may permit a passenger to stow his baggage aboard that airplane except—

(a) In a suitable baggage or cargo storage compartment, or as provided in § 91.203; or

(b) Under a passenger seat in such a way that it will not slide forward under crash impacts severe enough to induce the ultimate inertia forces specified in § 25.561(b)(3) of this chapter, or the requirements of the regulations under which the airplane was type certificated. After December 4, 1979, restraining devices must also limit sideward motion of under-seat baggage and be designed to withstand crash impacts severe enough to induce sideward forces specified in § 25.561(b)(3) of this chapter.

[Doc. No. 1580, Amdt. 91-1, 28 FR 6704, June 29, 1963, as amended by Amdt. 91-154, 43 FR 46234, Oct. 5, 1978]

§ 91.203   Carriage of cargo.

(a) No pilot in command may permit cargo to be carried in any airplane unless—

(1) It is carried in an approved cargo rack, bin, or compartment installed in the airplane;

(2) It is secured by means approved by the Administrator; or

(3) It is carried in accordance with each of the following:

(i) It is properly secured by a safety belt or other tiedown having enough strength to eliminate the possibility of shifting under all normally anticipated flight and ground conditions.

(ii) It is packaged or covered to avoid possible injury to passengers.

(iii) It does not impose any load on seats or on the floor structure that exceeds the load limitation for those components.

(iv) It is not located in a position that restricts the access to or use of any required emergency or regular exit, or the use of the aisle between the crew and the passenger compartment.

(v) It is not carried directly above seated passengers.

(b) When cargo is carried in cargo compartments that are designed to require the physical entry of a crewmember to extinguish any fire that may occur during flight, the cargo must be loaded so as to allow a crewmember to effectively reach all parts of the compartment with the contents of a hand fire extinguisher.

§91.205 Transport category airplane weight limitations.

No person may take off a transport category airplane, except in accordance with the weight limitations prescribed for that airplane in §91.37.

§91.209 Operating in icing conditions.

(a) No pilot may take off an airplane that has—

(1) Frost, snow, or ice adhering to any propeller, windshield, or powerplant installation, or to an airspeed, altimeter, rate of climb, or flight attitude instrument system;

(2) Snow or ice adhering to the wings, or stabilizing or control surfaces; or

(3) Any frost adhering to the wings, or stabilizing or control surfaces, unless that frost has been polished to make it smooth.

(b) Except for an airplane that has ice protection provisions that meet the requirements in section 34 of Special Federal Aviation Regulation No. 23, or those for transport category airplane type certification, no pilot may fly—

(1) Under IFR into known or forecast moderate icing conditions; or

(2) Under VFR into known light or moderate icing conditions; unless the aircraft has functioning de-icing or anti-icing equipment protecting each propeller, windshield, wing, stabilizing or control surface, and each airspeed, altimeter, rate of climb, or flight attitude instrument system.

(c) Except for an airplane that has ice protection provisions that meet the requirements in section 34 of Special Federal Aviation Regulation No. 23, or those for transport category airplane type certification, no pilot may fly an airplane into known or forecast severe icing conditions.

(d) If current weather reports and briefing information relied upon by the pilot in command indicate that the forecast icing conditions that would otherwise prohibit the flight will not be encountered during the flight because of changed weather conditions since the forecast, the restrictions in paragraphs (b) and (c) of this section based on forecast conditions do not apply.

§91.211 Flight engineer requirements.

(a) No person may operate the following airplanes without a flight crewmember holding a current flight engineer certificate:

(1) An airplane for which a type certificate was issued before January 2, 1964, having a maximum certificated takeoff weight of more than 80,000 pounds.

(2) An airplane type certificated after January 1, 1964, for which a flight engineer is required by the type certification requirements.

(b) No person may serve as a required flight engineer on an airplane unless, within the preceding 6 calendar months, he has had at least 50 hours of flight time as a flight engineer on that type airplane, or the Administrator has checked him on that type airplane and determined that he is familiar and competent with all essential current information and operating procedures.

§91.213 Second in command requirements.

(a) Except as provided in paragraph (b) of this section, no person may operate the following airplanes without a pilot who is designated as second in command of that airplane:

(1) A large airplane, except that a person may operate an airplane certificated under SFAR 41 without a pilot who is designated as second in com-

mand if that airplane is certificated for operation with one pilot.

(2) A turbojet-powered multiengine airplane for which two pilots are required under the type certification requirements for that airplane.

(3) A commuter category airplane, except that a person may operate a commuter category airplane notwithstanding paragraph (a)(1) of this section, that has a passenger seating configuration, excluding pilot seats, of nine or less without a pilot who is designated as second in command if that airplane is type certificated for operations with one pilot.

(b) The Administrator may issue a letter of authorization for the operation of an airplane without compliance with the requirements of paragraph (a) of this section if that airplane is designed for and type certificated with only one pilot station. The authorization contains any conditions that the Administrator finds necessary for safe operation.

(c) No person may designate a pilot to serve as second in command nor may any pilot serve as second in command of an airplane required under this section to have two pilots, unless that pilot meets the qualifications for second in command prescribed in § 61.55 of this chapter.

[Doc. No. 11437, Amdt. 91-101, 37 FR 14763, July 25, 1972, as amended by Amdt. 91-133, 41 FR 47229, Oct. 28, 1976; Amdt. 91-154, 43 FR 46234, Oct. 5, 1978; Amdt. 91-180, 47 FR 30947, July 15, 1982; Amdt. 91-197, 52 FR 1836, Jan. 15, 1987]

§ 91.215 Flight-attendant requirements.

(a) No person may operate an airplane unless at least the following number of flight attendants are on board the airplane:

(1) For airplanes having more than 19 but less than 51 passengers on board—one flight attendant.

(2) For airplanes having more than 50 but less than 101 passengers on board—two flight attendants.

(3) For airplanes having more than 100 passengers on board—two flight attendants plus one additional flight attendant for each unit (or part of a unit) of 50 passengers above 100.

(b) No person may serve as a flight attendant on an airplane when re-quired by paragraph (a) of this section, unless that person has demonstrated to the pilot in command that he is familiar with the necessary functions to be performed in an emergency or a situation requiring emergency evacuation and is capable of using the emergency equipment installed on that airplane for the performance of those functions.

Subpart E—Operating Noise Limits

AUTHORITY: Secs. 307, 313(a), 601, 603, 604, and 611, Federal Aviation Act of 1958 (49 U.S.C. 1348, 1354(a), 1421, 1423, 1424 and 1431 as amended by the Noise Control Act of 1972 (Pub. L. 92-574)); sec. 6(c), Dept. of Transportation Act.

§ 91.301 Applicability; relation to Part 36.

(a) This subpart prescribes operating noise limits and related requirements that apply, as follows, to the operation of civil aircraft in the United States:

(1) Sections 91.303, 91.305, 91.306, and 91.307 apply to civil subsonic turbojet airplanes with maximum weights of more than 75,000 pounds and—

(i) If U.S. registered, that have standard airworthiness certificates; or

(ii) If foreign registered, that would be required by this chapter to have a U.S. standard airworthiness certificate in order to conduct the operations intended for the airplane were it registered in the United States.

Those sections apply to operations to or from airports in the United States under this part and Parts 121, 123, 129, and 135 of this chapter.

(2) Section 91.308 applies to U.S. operators of civil subsonic turbojet airplanes covered by this subpart. That section applies to operators operating to or from airports in the United States under this part and Parts 121, 123, 125, and 135 but not to those operating under Part 129 of this chapter.

(3) Sections 91.302, 91.309 and 91.311 apply to U.S. registered civil supersonic airplanes having standard airworthiness certificates, and to foreign registered civil supersonic airplanes that, if registered in the United States, would be required by this chapter to have a U.S. standard airworthiness certificate in order to conduct the operations intended for the airplane. Those sec-

tions apply to operations under this part and under Parts 121, 123, 125, 129, and 135 of this chapter.

(b) Unless otherwise specified, as used in this subpart "Part 36" refers to 14 CFR Part 36, including the noise levels under Appendix C of that part, notwithstanding the provisions of that part excepting certain airplanes from the specified noise requirements. For purposes of this subpart, the various stages of noise levels, the terms used to describe airplanes with respect to those levels, and the terms "subsonic airplane" and "supersonic airplane" have the meanings specified under Part 36 of this chapter. For purposes of this subpart, for subsonic airplanes operated in foreign air commerce in the United States, the Administrator may accept compliance with the noise requirements under Annex 16 of the International Civil Aviation Organization when those requirements have been shown to be substantially compatible with, and achieve results equivalent to those achievable under, Part 36 for that airplane. Determinations made under these provisions are subject to the limitations of § 36.5 of this chapter as if those noise levels were Part 36 noise levels.

[Docs. 13582 and 14317, Amdt. 91-136, 41 FR 56055, Dec. 23, 1976, as amended by Amdt. 91-153, 43 FR 28421, June 29, 1978; Amdt. 91-161, 44 FR 75562, Dec. 20, 1979; Amdt. 91-170, 45 FR 67259, Oct. 9, 1980; Amdt. 91-171, 45 FR 79315, Nov. 28, 1980]

§ 91.302 Part 125 operators: Designation of applicable regulations.

For airplanes covered by this subpart and operated under Part 125, the following regulations apply as specified:

(a) For each airplane operation to which requirements prescribed under this subpart applied before November 29, 1980, those requirements of this subpart continue to apply.

(b) For each subsonic airplane operation to which requirements prescribed under this subpart did not apply before November 29, 1980, because the airplane was not operated in the United States under this part or Part 121, 123, 129 or 135, the requirements prescribed under §§ 91.303, 91.306, 91.307, and 91.308 of this subpart apply.

(c) For each supersonic airplane operation to which requirements prescribed under this subpart did not apply before November 29, 1980, because the airplane was not operated in the United States under this part or Part 121, 123, 129, or 135, the requirements of §§ 91.309 and 91.311 of this subpart apply.

(d) For each airplane required to operate under Part 125 for which a deviation under that part is approved to operate, in whole or in part, under this part or Part 121, 123, 129, or 135, notwithstanding the approval, the requirements prescribed under paragraphs (a), (b), and (c) of this section continue to apply.

[Doc. No. 20813, Amdt. 91-170, 45 FR 67259, Oct. 9, 1980, as amended by Amdt. 91-170A, 45 FR 79302, Nov. 28, 1980]

§ 91.303 Final compliance: Subsonic airplanes.

Except as provided in §§ 91.306 and 91.307, on and after January 1, 1985, no person may operate to or from an airport in the United States any subsonic airplane covered by this subpart, unless that airplane has been shown to comply with Stage 2 or Stage 3 noise levels under Part 36 of this chapter.

[Doc. No. 20251, Amdt. 91-171, 45 FR 79315, Nov. 28, 1980]

§ 91.305 Phased compliance under Parts 121, and 135: Subsonic airplanes.

(a) *General.* Each person operating airplanes under Parts 121 or 135 of this chapter, regardless of the State of registry of the airplane, shall comply with this section with respect to subsonic airplanes covered by this subpart.

(b) *Compliance schedule.* Except for airplanes shown to be operated in foreign air commerce under paragraph (c) of this section or covered by an exemption (including those issued under § 91.307), airplanes operated by U.S. operators in air commerce in the United States must be shown to comply with Stage 2 or Stage 3 noise levels under Part 36, in accordance with the following schedule, or they may not be operated to or from airports in the United States:

(1) By January 1, 1981:

(i) At least one quarter of the airplanes that have four engines with no bypass ratio or with a bypass ratio less that two.

(ii) At least half of the airplanes powered by engines with any other bypass ratio or by another number of engines.

(2) By January 1, 1983:

(i) At least one half of the airplanes that have four engines with no bypass ratio or with a bypass ratio less than two.

(ii) All airplanes powered by engines with any other bypass ratio or by another number of engines.

(c) *Apportionment of airplanes.* For purposes of paragraph (b) of this section, a person operating airplanes engaged in domestic and foreign air commerce in the United States may elect not to comply with the phased schedule with respect to that portion of the airplanes operated by that person shown, under an approved method of apportionment, to be engaged in foreign air commerce in the United States.

[Doc. No. 20251, Amdt. 91-171, 45 FR 79315, Nov. 28, 1980]

§ 91.306 Replacement airplanes.

A Stage 1 airplane may be operated after the otherwise applicable compliance dates prescribed under §§ 91.303 and 91.305 if, under an approved plan, a replacement airplane has been ordered by the operator under a binding contract as follows:

(a) For replacement of an airplane powered by two engines, until January 1, 1986, but not after the date specified in the plan, if the contract is entered into by January 1, 1983, and specifies delivery before January 1, 1986, of a replacement airplane which has been shown to comply with Stage 3 noise levels under Part 36 of this chapter.

(b) For replacement of an airplane powered by three engines, until January 1, 1985, but not after the date specified in the plan, if the contract is entered into by January 1, 1983, and specifies delivery before January 1, 1985, of a replacement airplane which

has been shown to comply with Stage 3 noise levels under Part 36 of this chapter.

(c) For replacement of any other airplane, until January 1, 1985, but not after the date specified in the plan, if the contract specifies delivery before January 1, 1985, of a replacement airplane which—

(1) Has been shown to comply with Stage 2 or Stage 3 noise levels under Part 36 of this chapter prior to issuance of an original standard airworthiness certificate; or

(2) Has been shown to comply with Stage 3 noise levels under Part 36 of this chapter prior to issuance of a standard airworthiness certificate other than original issue.

(d) Each operator of a Stage 1 airplane for which approval of a replacement plan is requested under this section shall submit to the FAA Director of the Office of Environment and Energy an application constituting the proposed replacement plan (or revised Plan) that contains the information specified under this paragraph and which is certified (under penalty of 18 U.S.C. 1001) as true and correct. Each application for approval must provide information corresponding to that specified in the contract, upon which the FAA may rely in considering its approval, as follows:

(1) Name and address of the applicant.

(2) Aircraft type and model and registration number for each airplane to be replaced under the plan.

(3) Aircraft type and model of each replacement airplane.

(4) Scheduled dates of delivery and introduction into service of each replacement airplane.

(5) Name and addresses of the parties to the contract and any other persons who may effectively cancel the contract or otherwise control the performance of any party.

(6) Information specifying the anticipated disposition of the airplanes to be replaced.

(7) A statement that the contract represents a legally enforceable, mutual agreement for delivery of an eligible replacement airplane.

(8) Any other information or documentation requested by the Director,

Office of Environment and Energy reasonably necessary to determine whether the plan should be approved.

[Doc. No. 20251, Amdt. 91-171, 45 FR 79315, Nov. 28, 1980]

§ 91.307 Service to small communities exemption: Two-engine, subsonic airplanes.

(a) A Stage 1 airplane powered by two engines may be operated after the compliance dates prescribed under §§ 91.303, 92.305, and 91.306, when, with respect to that airplane, the Administrator issues an exemption to the operator from the noise level requirements under this subpart. Each exemption issued under this section terminates on the earlier of the following dates—

(1) For an exempted airplane sold, or otherwise disposed of, to another person on or after January 1, 1983—on the date of delivery to that person;

(2) For an exempted airplane with a seating configuration of 100 passenger seats or less—on January 1, 1988; or

(3) For an exempted airplane with a seating configuration of more than 100 passenger seats—on January 1, 1985.

(b) For purposes of this section, the seating configuration of an airplane is governed by that shown to exist on December 1, 1979, or an earlier date established for that airplane by the Administrator.

[Doc. No. 20251, Amdt. 91-171, 45 FR 79316, Nov. 28, 1980]

§ 91.308 Compliance plans and status: U.S. operators of subsonic airplanes.

(a) Each U.S. operator of a civil subsonic airplane covered by this subpart (regardless of the State of registry) shall submit to the FAA, Director of the Office of Environment and Energy, in accordance with this section, the operator's current compliance status and plan for achieving and maintaining compliance with the applicable noise level requirements of this subpart. If appropriate, an operator may substitute for the required plan a notice, certified as true (under penalty of 18 U.S.C. 1001) by that operator, that no change in the plan or status of any airplane affected by the plan has occurred since the date of the plan most recently submitted under this section.

(b) Each compliance plan, including any revised plans, must contain the information specified under paragraph (c) of this section for each airplane covered by this section that is operated by the operator. Unless otherwise approved by the Administrator, compliance plans must provide the required plan and status information as it exists on the date 30 days before the date specified for submission of the plan. Plans must be certified by the operator as true and complete (under penalty of 18 U.S.C. 1001) and be submitted for each airplane covered by this section on or before the following dates—

(1) May 1, 1980 or 90 days after initially commencing operation of airplanes covered by this section, whichever is later, and thereafter;

(2) Thirty days after any change in the operator's fleet or compliance planning decisions that has a separate or cumulative effect on 10 percent or more of the airplanes in either class of airplanes covered by § 91.305(b); and

(3) Thirty days after each compliance date applicable to that airplane under this subpart and annually thereafter through 1985 or until any later compliance date for that airplane prescribed under this subpart, on the anniversary of that submission date, to show continuous compliance with this subpart.

(c) Each compliance plan submitted under this section must identify the operator and include information regarding the compliance plan and status for each airplane covered by the plan as follows:

(1) Name and address of the airplane operator.

(2) Name and telephone number of the person designated by the operator to be responsible for the preparation of the compliance plan and its submission.

(3) The total number of airplanes covered by this section and in each of the following classes and subclasses:

(i) Airplanes engaged in domestic air commerce.

(A) Airplanes powered by four turbojet engines with no bypass ratio or with a bypass ratio less than two.

(B) Airplanes powered by engines with any other bypass ratio or by another number of engines.

(C) Airplanes covered by an exemption issued under § 91.307 of this subpart.

(ii) Airplanes engaged in foreign air commerce under an approved apportionment plan.

(A) Airplanes powered by four turbojet engines with no bypass ratio or with a bypass ratio less than two.

(B) Airplanes powered by engines with any other bypass ratio or by another number of engines.

(C) Airplanes covered by an exemption issued under § 91.307 of this subpart.

(4) For each airplane covered by this section—

(i) Aircraft type and model;

(ii) Aircraft registration number;

(iii) Aircraft manufacturer serial number;

(iv) Aircraft power plant make and model;

(v) Aircraft year of manufacture;

(vi) Whether Part 36 noise level compliance has been shown: Yes/No;

(vii) [Reserved]

(viii) The appropriate code prescribed under paragraph (c)(5) of this section which indicates the acoustical technology installed, or to be installed, on the airplane;

(ix) For airplanes on which acoustical technology has been or will be applied, following the appropriate code entry, the actual or scheduled month and year of installation on the airplane;

(x) For DC-8 and B-707 airplanes operated in domestic U.S. air commerce which have been or will be retired from service in the United States without replacement between January 24, 1977, and January 1, 1985, the appropriate code prescribed under paragraph (c)(5) of this section followed by the actual or scheduled month and year of retirement of the airplane from service;

(xi) For DC-8 and B-707 airplanes operated in foreign air commerce in the United States, which have been or will be retired from service in the United States without replacement between April 14, 1980, and January 1, 1985, the appropriate code prescribed

under paragraph (c)(5) of this section followed by the actual or scheduled month and year of retirement of the airplane from service;

(xii) For airplanes covered by an approved replacement plan under § 91.305(c) of this subpart, the appropriate code prescribed under paragraph (c)(5) of this section followed by the scheduled month and year for replacement of the airplane;

(xiii) For airplanes designated as "engaged in foreign commerce" in accordance with an approved method of apportionment under § 91.305(c) of this subpart, the appropriate code prescribed under paragraph (c)(5) of this section;

(xiv) For airplanes covered by an exemption issued to the operator granting relief from noise level requirements of this subpart, the appropriate code prescribed under paragraph (c)(5) of this section followed by the actual or scheduled month and year of expiration of the exemption and the appropriate code and applicable dates which indicate the compliance strategy planned or implemented for the airplane;

(xv) For all airplanes covered by this section, the number of spare shipsets of acoustical components needed for continuous compliance and the number available on demand to the operator in support of those airplanes; and

(xvi) For airplanes for which none of the other codes prescribed under paragraph (c)(5) of this section describes either the technology applied, or to be applied to the airplane in accordance with the certification requirements under Parts 21 and 36 of this chapter, or the compliance strategy or methodology, following the code "OTH" enter the date of any certificate action and attach an addendum to the plan explaining the nature and extent of the certificated technology, strategy, or methodology employed, together with reference to the type certificate documentation.

(5) TABLE OF ACOUSTICAL TECHNOLOGY/
STRATEGY CODES

Code	Airplane type/model	Certificated technology
A	B-707-120B B-707-320B/C B-720B	Quiet nacelles + 1-ring.
B	B-727-100	Double wall fan duct treatment.
C	B-727-200	Double wall fan duct treatment (pre-January 1977 installations and amended type certificate).
D	B-727-200 B-737-100 B-737-200	Quiet nacelles + double wall fan duct treatement.
E	B-747-100 [1] B-747-200 [1]	Fixed lip inlets + sound absorbing material treatment.
F	DC-8	New extended inlet and bullet with treatment + fan duct treatment areas.
G	DC-9	P-36 sound absorbing material treatment kit.
H	BAC-111-200	Silencer kit (BAC acoustic report 522).
I	BAC-111-400	(To be identified later if certificated.)
J	B-707 DC-8	Reengined with high bypass ratio turbojet engines + quiet nacelles (if certificated under stage 3 noise level requirements).

[1] Pre-December 1971.

REP—For airplanes covered by an approved replacement plan under § 91.305(c) of this subpart.

EFC—For airplanes designated as "engated in foreign commerce" in accordance with an approved method of apportionment under § 91.307 of this subpart.

RET—For DC-8 and B-707 airplanes operated in domestic U.S. air commerce and retired from service in the United States without replacement between January 24, 1977, and January 1, 1985.

RFC—For DC-8 and B-707 airplanes operated by U.S. operators in foreign air commerce in the United States and retired from service in the United States without replacement between April 14, 1980, and January 1, 1985.

EXD—For airplanes exempted from showing compliance with the noise level requirements of this subpart.

OTH—For airplanes for which no other prescribed code describes either the certificated technology applied, or to be applied to the airplane, or the compliance strategy or methodology. (An addendum must explain the nature and extent of technology, strategy or methodology and reference the type certificate documentation.

[Doc. Nos. 18955 and 18924, Amdt. 91-161, 44 FR 75563, Dec. 20, 1979; Amdt. 91-161A,

45 FR 6923, Jan. 31, 1980; Amdt. 91-171, 45 FR 79316, Nov. 28, 1980]

§ 91.309   Civil supersonic airplanes that do not comply with Part 36.

(a) *Applicability.* This section applies to civil supersonic airplanes that have not been shown to comply with the stage 2 noise limits of Part 36 in effect on October 13, 1977, using applicable tradeoff provisions, and that are operated in the United States after July 31, 1978.

(b) *Airport use.* Except in an emergency, the following apply to each person who operates a civil supersonic airplane to or from an airport in the United States:

(1) Regardless of whether a type design change approval is applied for under Part 21 of this chapter, no person may land or take off an airplane, covered by this section, for which the type design is changed, after July 31, 1978, in a manner constituting an "acoustical change" under § 21.93, unless the acoustical change requirements of Part 36 are complied with.

(2) No flight may be scheduled, or otherwise planned, for takeoff or landing after 10 p.m. and before 7 a.m. local time.

[Amdt. 91-153, 43 FR 28421, June 29, 1978]

§ 91.311   Civil supersonic airplanes: Noise limits.

Except for Concorde airplanes having flight time before January 1, 1980, no person may, after July 31, 1978, operate, in the United States, a civil supersonic airplane that does not comply with the stage 2 noise limits of Part 36 in effect on October 13, 1977, using applicable trade-off provisions.

[Amdt. 91-153, 43 FR 28421, June 29, 1978]

APPENDIX A—CATEGORY II OPERATIONS: MANUAL, INSTRUMENTS, EQUIPMENT AND MAINTENANCE

1. *Category II Manual*—(a) *Application for approval.* An applicant for approval of a Category II manual or an amendment to an approved Category II manual must submit the proposed manual or amendment to the Flight Standards District Office having jurisdiction of the area in which the applicant

is located. If the application requests an evaluation program, it must include the following:

(1) The location of the aircraft and the place where the demonstrations are to be conducted; and

(2) The date the demonstrations are to commence (at least 10 days after filing the application).

(b) *Contents.* Each Category II manual must contain—

(1) the registration number, make, and model of the aircraft to which it applies;

(2) A maintenance program as specified in section 4 of this appendix; and

(3) The procedures and instructions related to recognition of decision height, use of runway visual range information, approach monitoring, the decision region (the region between the middle marker and the decision height), the maximum permissible deviations of the basic ILS indicator within the decision region, a missed approach, use of airborne low approach equipment, minimum altitude for the use of the autopilot, instrument and equipment failure warning systems, instrument failure, and other procedures, instructions, and limitations that may be found necessary by the Administrator.

2. *Required instruments and equipment.* The instruments and equipment listed in this section must be installed in each aircraft operated in a Category II operation. This section does not require duplication of instruments and equipment required by § 91.33 or any other provisions of this chapter.

(a) *Group I.* (1) Two localizer and glide slope receiving systems. Each system must provide a basic ILS display and each side of the instrument panel must have a basic ILS display. However, a single localizer antenna and a single glide slope antenna may be used.

(2) A communications system that does not affect the operation of at least one of the ILS systems.

(3) A marker beacon receiver that provides distinctive aural and visual indications of the outer and the middle marker.

(4) Two gyroscopic pitch and bank indicating systems.

(5) Two gyroscopic direction indicating systems.

(6) Two airspeed indicators.

(7) Two sensitive altimeters adjustable for barometric pressure, each having a placarded correction for altimeter scale error and for the wheel height of the aircraft. After June 26, 1979, two sensitive altimeters adjustable for barometric pressure, having markings at 20-foot intervals and each having a placarded correction for altimeter scale error and for the wheel height of the aircraft.

(8) Two vertical speed indicators.

(9) A flight control guidance system that consists of either an automatic approach coupler or a flight director system. A flight director system must display computed information as steering command in relation to an ILS localizer and, on the same instrument, either computed information as pitch command in relation to an ILS glide slope or basic ILS glide slope information. An automatic approach coupler must provide at least automatic steering in relation to an ILS localizer. The flight control guidance system may be operated from one of the receiving systems required by paragraph (1) of this paragraph (a).

(10) For Category II operations with decision heights below 150 feet, either a marker beacon receiver providing aural and visual indications of the inner marker or a radio altimeter.

(b) *Group II.* (1) Warning systems for immediate detection by the pilot of system faults in items (1), (4), (5), and (9) of Group I and, if installed, for use in Category II operations, the radio altimeter and auto throttle system.

(2) Dual controls.

(3) An externally vented static pressure system with an alternate static pressure source.

(4) A windshield wiper or equivalent means of providing adequate cockpit visibility for a safe visual transition by either pilot to touch down and roll out.

(5) A heat source for each airspeed system pitot tube installed or an equivalent means of preventing malfunctioning due to icing of the pitot system.

3. *Instruments and equipment approval*—(a) *General.* The instruments and equipment required by section 2 of this appendix must be approved as provided in this section before being used in Category II operations. Before presenting an aircraft for approval of the instruments and equipment, it must be shown that, since the beginning of the 12th calendar month before the date of submission—

(1) The ILS localizer and glide slope equipment were bench checked according to the manufacturer's instructions and found to meet those standards specified in RTCA Paper 23-63/DO-117, dated March 14, 1963. "Standard Adjustment Criteria for Airborne Localizer and Glide Slope Receivers," which may be obtained from the RTCA Secretariat, 2000 K Street NW., Washington, D.C. 20006, at cost of 50 cents per copy, payment in cash or by check or money order payable to the Radio Technical Commission for Aeronautics;

(2) The altimeters and the static pressure systems were tested and inspected in accordance with Appendix E to Part 43 of this chapter; and

(3) All other instruments and items of equipment specified in section 2(a) of this appendix that are listed in the proposed maintenance program were bench checked and found to meet the manufacturer's specifications.

(b) *Flight control guidance system.* All components of the flight control guidance system must be approved as installed by the evaluation program specified in paragraph (e) of this section if they have not been approved for Category II operations under applicable type or supplemental type certification procedures. In addition, subsequent changes to make, model or design of these components must be approved under this paragraph. Related systems or devices such as the auto throttle and computed missed approach guidance system must be approved in the same manner if they are to be used for Category II operations.

(c) *Radio altimeter.* A radio altimeter must meet the performance criteria of this paragraph for original approval and after each subsequent alteration.

(1) It must display to the flight crew clearly and positively the wheel height of the main landing gear above the terrain.

(2) It must display wheel height above the terrain to an accuracy of plus or minus 5 feet or 5 percent, whichever is greater, under the following conditions:

(i) Pitch angles of zero to plus or minus 5 degrees about the mean approach altitude.

(ii) Roll angles of zero to 20 degrees in either direction.

(iii) Forward velocities from minimum approach speed up to 200 knots.

(iv) Sink rates from zero to 15 feet per second at altitudes from 100 to 200 feet.

(3) Over level ground, it must track the actual altitude of the aircraft without significant lag or oscillation.

(4) With the aircraft at an altitude of 200 feet or less, any abrupt change in terrain representing no more than 10 percent of the aircraft's altitude must not cause the altimeter to unlock, and indicator response to such changes must not exceed 0.1 second and in addition, if the system unlocks for greater changes, it must reacquire the signal in less than 1 second.

(5) Systems that contain a push-to-test feature must test the entire system (with or without an antenna) at a simulated altitude of less than 500 feet.

(6) The system must provide to the flight crew a positive failure warning display any time there is a loss of power or an absence of ground return signals within the designed range of operating altitudes.

(d) *Other instruments and equipment.* All other instruments and items of equipment required by section 2 of this appendix must be capable of performing as necessary for Category II operations. Approval is also re-

quired after each subsequent alteration to these instruments and items of equipment.

(e) *Evaluation program*—(1) *Application.* Approval by evaluation is requested as a part of the application for approval of the Category II manual.

(2) *Demonstrations.* Unless otherwise authorized by the Administrator, the evaluation program for each aircraft requires the demonstrations specified in this paragraph. At least 50 ILS approaches must be flown with at least five approaches on each of three different ILS facilities and no more than one-half of the total approaches on any one ILS facility. All approaches shall be flown under simulated instrument conditions to a 100-foot decision height and 90 percent of the total approaches made must be successful. A successful approach is one in which—

(i) At the 100-foot decision height, the indicated airspeed and heading are satisfactory for a normal flare and landing (speed must be plus or minus 5 knots of programed airspeed but may not be less than computed threshold speed, if auto throttles are used);

(ii) The aircraft, at the 100-foot decision height, is positioned so that the cockpit is within, and tracking so as to remain within, the lateral confines of the runway extended;

(iii) Deviation from glide slope after leaving the outer marker does not exceed 50 percent of full scale deflection as displayed on the ILS indicator;

(iv) No unusual roughness or excessive attitude changes occur after leaving the middle marker; and

(v) In the case of an aircraft equipped with an approach coupler, the aircraft is sufficiently in trim when the approach coupler is disconnected at the decision height to allow for the continuation of a normal approach and landing.

(3) *Records.* During the evaluation program the following information must be maintained by the applicant for the aircraft with respect to each approach and made available to the Administrator upon request:

(i) Each deficiency in airborne instruments and equipment that prevented the initiation of an approach.

(ii) The reasons for discontinuing an approach including the altitude above the runway at which it was discontinued.

(iii) Speed control at the 100-foot decision height if auto throttles are used.

(iv) Trim condition of the aircraft upon disconnecting the auto coupler with respect to continuation to flare and landing.

(v) Position of the aircraft at the middle marker and at the decision height indicated both on a diagram of the basic ILS display and a diagram of the runway extended to the middle marker. Estimated touch down point must be indicated on the runway diagram.

(vi) Compatibility of flight director with the auto coupler, if applicable.

(vii) Quality of overall system performance.

(4) *Evaluation.* A final evaluation of the flight control guidance system is made upon successful completion of the demonstrations. If no hazardous tendencies have been displayed or are otherwise known to exist, the system is approved as installed.

4. *Maintenance program.* (a) Each maintenance program must contain the following:

(1) A list of each instrument and item of equipment specified in section 2 of this ppendix that is installed in the aircraft and approved for Category II operations, including the make and model of those specified in section 2(a).

(2) A schedule that provides for the performance of inspections under subparagraph (5) of this paragraph within 3 calendar months after the date of the previous inspection. The inspection must be performed by a person authorized by Part 43 of this chapter, except that each alternate inspection may be replaced by a functional flight check. This functional flight check must be performed by a pilot holding a Category II pilot authorization for the type aircraft checked.

(3) A schedule that provides for the performance of bench checks for each listed instrument and item of equipment that is specified in section 2(a) within 12 calendar months after the date of the previous bench check.

(4) A schedule that provides for the performance of a test and inspection of each static pressure system in accordance with Appendix E to Part 43 of this chapter within 12 calendar months after the date of the previous test and inspection.

(5) The procedures for the performance of the periodic inspections and functional flight checks to determine the ability of each listed instrument and item of equipment specified in section 2(a) of this Appendix to perform as approved for Category II operations including a procedure for recording functional flight checks.

(6) A procedure for assuring that the pilot is informed of all defects in listed instruments and items of equipment.

(7) A procedure for assuring that the condition of each listed instrument and item of equipment upon which maintenance is performed is at least equal to its Category II approval condition before it is returned to service for Category II operations.

(8) A procedure for an entry in the maintenance records required by § 43.9 of this chapter that shows the date, airport, and reasons for each discontinued Category II operation because of a malfunction of a listed instrument or item of equipment.

(b) *Bench check.* A bench check required by this section must comply with this paragraph.

(1) It must be performed by a certificated repair station holding one of the following ratings as appropriate to the equipment checked:

(i) An instrument rating.

(ii) A radio rating.

(iii) A rating issued under Subpart D of Part 145.

(2) It must consist of removal of an instrument or item of equipment and performance of the following:

(i) A visual inspection for cleanliness, impending failure, and the need for lubrication, repair, or replacement of parts;

(ii) Correction of items found by that visual inspection; and

(iii) Calibration to at least the manufacturer's specifications unless otherwise specified in the approved Category II manual for the aircraft in which the instrument or item of equipment is installed.

(c) *Extensions.* After the completion of one maintenance cycle of 12 calendar months a request to extend the period for checks, tests, and inspections is approved if it is shown that the performance of particular equipment justifies the requested extension.

[Amdt. 91-39, 32 FR 6906, May 5, 1967; 32 FR 8127, June 7, 1967; Amdt. 91-63, 33 FR 17291, Nov. 22, 1968; Amdt. 91-152, 43 FR 22641, May 25, 1978; Amdt. 91-196, 51 FR 40707, Nov. 7, 1986]

APPENDIX B—AUTHORIZATIONS TO EXCEED MACH 1 (§ 91.55)

SECTION 1. *Application.* (a) An applicant for an authorization to exceed mach 1 must apply in a form and manner prescribed by the Administrator and must comply with this appendix.

(b) In addition, each application for an authorization to exceed mach 1 covered by section 2(a) of this appendix must contain all information, requested by the Administrator, that he deems necessary to assist him in determining whether the designation of a particular test area, or issuance of a particular authorization, is a "major Federal action significantly affecting the quality of the human environment" within the meaning of the National Environmental Policy Act of 1969 (42 U.S.C. 4321 et seq.), and to assist him in complying with that Act, and with related Executive orders, guidelines, and orders, prior to such action.

(c) In addition, each application for an authorization to exceed mach 1 covered by section 2(a) of this appendix must contain—

(1) Information showing that operation at a speed greater than mach 1 is necessary to

accomplish one or more of the purposes specified in section 2(a) of this appendix, including a showing that the purpose of the test cannot be safely or properly accomplished by overocean testing;

(2) A description of the test area proposed by the applicant, including an environmental analysis of that area meeting the requirements of paragraph (b) of this section; and

(3) Conditions and limitations that will insure that no measurable sonic boom overpressure will reach the surface outside of the designated test area.

(d) An application is denied if the Administrator finds that such action is necessary to protect or enhance the environment.

SEC. 2. *Issuance.* (a) For a flight in a designated test area, an authorization to exceed mach 1 may be issued when the Administrator has taken the environmental protective actions specified in section 1(b) of this appendix, and the applicant shows one or more of the following:

(1) The flight is necessary to show compliance with airworthiness requirements.

(2) The flight is necessary to determine the sonic boom characteristics of the airplane, or is necessary to establish means of reducing or eliminating the effects of sonic boom.

(3) The flight is necessary to demonstrate the conditions and limitations under which speeds greater than a true flight mach number of 1 will not cause a measurable sonic boom overpressure to reach the surface.

(b) For a flight outside of a designated test area, an authorization to exceed mach 1 may be issued if the applicant shows conservatively under paragraph (a)(3) of this section that—

(1) The flight will not cause a measurable sonic boom overpressure to reach the surface when the aircraft is operated under conditions and limitations demonstrated under paragraph (a)(3) of this section; and

(2) Those conditions and limitations represent all foreseeable operating conditions.

SEC. 3. *Duration.* (a) An authorization to exceed mach 1 is effective until it expires or is surrendered, or until it is suspended or terminated by the Administrator. Such an authorization may be amended or suspended by the Administrator at any time if he finds that such action is necessary to protect the environment. Within 30 days of notification of amendment, the holder of the authorization must request reconsideration or the amendment becomes final. Within 30 days of notification of suspension, the holder of the authorization must request reconsideration or the authorization is automatically terminated. If reconsideration is requested within the 30-day period, the amendment or suspension continues until the holder shows why, in his opinion, the

authorization should not be amended or terminated. Upon such showing, the Administrator may terminate or amend the authorization if he finds that such action is necessary to protect the environment, or he may reinstate the authorization without amendment if he finds that termination or amendment is not necessary to protect the environment.

(b) Findings and actions by the Administrator under this section do not affect any certificate issued under title VI of the Federal Aviation Act of 1958.

(Sec. 307(c), 313(a), 611, Federal Aviation Act of 1958, 49 U.S.C. 1348(c), 1354(a), 1431; sec. 2(b)(2), 6(c), Department of Transportation Act, 49 U.S.C. 1651(b)(2), 1655(c), Title I of the National Environmental Policy Act of 1969, 42 U.S.C. 4321 et seq., E. O. 11514, Protection and Enhancement of Environmental Quality, Mar. 5, 1970)

[Doc. No. 10261, Amdt. 91-112, 38 FR 8055, Mar. 28, 1973]

APPENDIX C—OPERATIONS IN THE NORTH ATLANTIC (NAT) MINIMUM NAVIGATION PERFORMANCE SPECIFICATIONS (MNPS) AIRSPACE

Section 1. NAT MNPS airspace is that volume of airspace between FL 275 and FL 400 extending between latitude 27 degrees north and the North Pole, bounded in the east by the eastern boundaries of control areas Santa Maria Oceanic, Shanwick Oceanic, and Reykjavik Oceanic and in the west by the western boundary of Reykjavik Oceanic Control Area, the western boundary of Gander Oceanic Control Area, and the western boundary of New York Oceanic Control Area, excluding the areas west of 60 degrees west and south of 38 degrees 30 minutes north.

Section 2. The navigation performance capability required for aircraft to be operated in the airspace defined in Sec. 1 of this appendix is as follows:

(a) The standard deviation of lateral track errors shall be less than 6.3 NM (11.7 Km). Standard deviation is a statistical measure of data about a mean value. The mean is zero nautical miles. The overall form of data is such that the plus and minus one standard deviation about the mean encompasses approximately 68 percent of the data and plus or minus two deviations encompasses approximately 95 percent.

(b) The proportion of the total flight time spent by aircraft 30 NM (55.6 Km) or more off the cleared track shall be less than 5.3 x 10^{-4} (less than one hour in 1,887 flight hours).

(c) The proportion of the total flight time spent by aircraft between 50 NM and 70 NM

(92.6 Km and 129.6 Km) off the cleared track shall be less than 13×10^{-5} (less than one hour in 7,693 hours).

Section 3. Air traffic control (ATC) may authorize an aircraft operator to deviate from the requirements of § 91.20 for a speicific flight if, at the time of flight plan filing for that flight, ATC determines that the aircraft may be provided appropriate separation and that the flight will not interfere with, or impose a burden upon, the operations of other aircraft which meet the requirements of § 91.20.

APPENDIX D — AIRPORTS/LOCATIONS WHERE THE TRANSPONDER REQUIRE-MENTS OF SECTION 91.24(b)(5)(ii) APPLY

Section 1. The requirements of §91.24(b)(5)(ii) apply to operation in the vicinity of each of the following airports.

Logan International Airport, Billings, MT

Hector International Airport, Fargo ND

APPENDIX E—AIRPLANE FLIGHT RECORDER SPECIFICATIONS

Parameters	Range	Installed system [1] minimum accuracy (to recovered data)	Sampling interval (per second)	Resolution [4] read out
Relative Time (From Recorded on Prior to Takeoff).	8 hr minimum	±0.125% per hour	1	1 sec.
Indicated Airspeed	V_{so} to V_D (KIAS)	±5% or ±10 kts., whichever is greater. Resolution 2 kts. below 175 KIAS.	1	1% [3]
Altitude	−1,000 ft. to max cert. alt. of A/C	±100 to ±700 ft. (see Table 1, TSO C51-a).	1	25 to 150 ft.
Magnetic Heading	360°	±5°	1	1°
Vertical Acceleration	−3g to +6g	±0.2g in addition to ±0.3g maximum datum.	4 (or 1 per second where peaks, ref. to 1g are recorded).	0.03g.
Longitudinal Acceleration	±1.0g	±1.5% max. range excluding datum error of ±5%.	2	0.01g.
Pitch Altitude	100% of useable	±2°	1	0.8°.
Roll Altitude	±60° or 100% of usale range, whichever is greater.	±2°	1	0.8°
Stabilizer Trim Position, or	Full Range	±3% unless higher uniquely required	1	1% [3]
Pitch Control Position	Full Range	±3% unless higher uniquely required	1	1% [3]
Engine Power, Each Engine: Fan or N_1 Speed or EPR or Cockpit indications Used for Aircraft Certification OR	Maximum Range	±5%	1	1% [3]
Prop. speed and Torque (Sample Once/Sec as Close together as Practicable).			1 (prop Speed) 1 (torque)	1% [3] 1% [3]
Altitude Rate [2] (need depends on altitude resolution).	±8,000 fpm.	±10%. Resolution 250 fpm below 12,000 ft. indicated.	1	250 fpm. below 12,000
Angle of Attack [2] (need depends on altitude resolution).	−20° to 40° or of usuable range	±2°	1	0.8° [3]
Radio Transmitter Keying (Discrete)	On/Off		1	
TE Flaps (Discrete or Analog)	Each discrete position (U, D, T/O, AAP) OR		1	
	Analog 0-100% range	±3°	1	1% [3]
LE Flaps (Discrete or Analog)	Each discrete position (U, D, T/O, AAP) OR		1	
	Analog 0-100% range	±3°	1	1% [3]
Thrust Reverser, Each Engine (Discrete)	Stowed or full reverse		1	
Spoiler/Speedbrake (Discrete)	Stowed or out		1	
Autopilot Engaged (Discrete)	Engaged or Disengaged		1	

[1] When data sources are aircraft instruments (except altimeters) of acceptable quality to fly the aircraft the recording system excluding these sensors (but including all other characteristics of the recording system) shall contribute no more than half of the values in this column.
[2] If data from the altitude encoding altimeter (100 ft. resolution) is used, then either one of these parameters should also be recorded. If however, altitude is recorded at a minimum resolution of 25 feet, then these two parameters can be omitted.
[3] Per cent of full range.
[4] This column applies to aircraft manufactured after October 11, 1991

APPENDIX F—HELICOPTER FLIGHT RECORDER SPECIFICATION

Parameters	Range	Installed system [1] minimum accuracy (to recovered data)	Sampling interval (per second)	Resolution [3] read out
Relative Time (From Recorded on Prior to Takeoff).	4 hr minimum	±0.125% per hour	1	1 sec
Indicated Airspeed	V_{so} in to V_D (KIAS) (minimum airspeed signal attainable with installed pilot-static system).	±5% or ±10 kts., whichever is greater.	1	1 kt
Altitude	−1,000 ft. to 20,000 ft. pressure altitude	±100 to ±700 ft. (see Table 1, TSO C51-a).	1	25 to 150 ft
Magnetic Heading	360°	±5°	1	1°
Vertical Acceleration	−3g to +6g	±0.2g in addition to ±0.3g maximum datum.	4 (or 1 per second where peaks, ref. to 1g are recorded).	0.05g.
Longitudinal Acceleration	±1.0g	±1.5% max. range excluding datum error of ±5%.	2	0.03g.
Pitch Attitude	100% of usable range	±2°	1	0.8°
Roll Attitude	±60° or 100% of usable range, whichever is greater.	±2°	1	0.8°
Altitude Rate	±8,000 fpm.	±10% Resolution 250 fpm below 12,000 ft. indicated.	1	250 fpm below 12,000.
Engine Power, Each Engine Main Rotor Speed	Maximum Range	±5%	1	1% [2]
Free or Power Turbine	Maximum Range	+5%	1	1% [2]
Engine Torque	Maximum Range	±5%	1	1% [2]

PART 97—STANDARD INSTRUMENT
APPROACH PROCEDURES

AUTHORITY: 49 U.S.C. 1348, 1354(a), 1421,
and 1510; 49 U.S.C. 106(g) (Revised, Pub. L.
97-449, January 12, 1983; and 14 CFR
11.49(b)(2)).

SOURCE: Docket No. 1580, Amdt. 1-1, 28
FR 6719, June 29, 1963, unless otherwise
noted.

CROSS REFERENCE: For changes in isogenic
values based on the U.S. Coast and Geodetic
Survey for Epoch 1965, which minutely
affect the Standard Instrument Approach
Procedures of this part, see 30 FR 7598,
June 11, 1965.

Subpart A—General

§ 97.1 Applicability.

This part prescribes standard instrument approach procedures for instrument letdown to airports in the United
States and the weather minimums
that apply to takeoffs and landings
under IFR at those airports.

§ 97.3 Symbols and terms used in proce-
dures.

As used in the standard terminal instrument procedures prescribed in this
part—

(a) "A" means alternate airport
weather minimum.

(b) "Aircraft approach category"
means a grouping of aircraft based on
a speed of 1.3 V_{so} (at maximum certificated landing weight). V_{so} and the
maximum certificated landing weight
are those values as established for the
aircraft by the certificating authority
of the country of registry. The categories are as follows:

(1) Category A: Speed less than 91
knots.

(2) Category B: Speed 91 knots or
more but less than 121 knots.

(3) Category C: Speed 121 knots or
more but less than 141 knots.

(4) Category D: Speed 141 knots or
more but less than 166 knots.

(5) Category E: Speed 166 knots or
more.

(c) Approach procedure segments for
which altitudes (all altitudes prescribed are minimum altitudes unless
otherwise specified) or courses, or
both, are prescribed in procedures, are
as follows:

(1) "Initial approach" is the segment
between the intial approach fix and
the intermediate fix or the point
where the aircraft is established on
the intermediate course or final approach course.

(2) "Initial approach altitude" means the altitude (or altitudes, in High Altitude Procedures) prescribed for the initial approach segment of an instrument approach.

(3) "Intermediate approach" is the segment between the intermediate fix or point and the final approach fix.

(4) "Final approach" is the segment between the final approach fix or point and the runway, airport, or missed-approach point.

(5) "Missed approach" is the segment between the missed-approach point, or point of arrival at decision height, and the missed-approach fix at the prescribed altitude.

(d) "C" means circling landing minimum, a statement of ceiling and visibility values, or minimum descent altitude and visibility, required for the circle-to-land maneuver.

(d-1) "Copter procedures" means helicopter procedures, with applicable minimums as prescribed in § 97.35 of this part. Helicopters may also use other procedures prescribed in Subpart C of this part and may use the Category A minimum descent altitude (MDA) or decision height (DH). The required visibility minimum may be reduced to one-half the published visibility minimum for Category A aircraft, but in no case may it be reduced to less than one-quarter mile or 1,200 feet RVR.

(e) "Ceiling minimum" means the minimum ceiling, expressed in feet above the surface of the airport, required for takeoff or required for designating an airport as an alternate airport.

(f) "D" means day.

(g) "FAF" means final approach fix.

(h) "HAA" means height above airport.

(h-1) "HAL" means height above a designated helicopter landing area used for helicopter instrument approach procedures.

(i) "HAT" means height above touchdown.

(j) "MAP" means missed approach point.

(k) "More than 65 knots" means an aircraft that has a stalling speed of more than 65 knots (as established in an approved flight manual) at maximum certificated landing weight with

full flaps, landing gear extended, and power off.

(l) "MSA" means minimum safe altitude, an emergency altitude expressed in feet above mean sea level, which provides 1,000 feet clearance over all obstructions in that sector within 25 miles of the facility on which the procedure is based (LOM in ILS procedures).

(m) "N" means night.

(n) "NA" means not authorized.

(o) "NOPT" means no procedure turn required (altitude prescribed applies only if procedure turn is not executed).

(o-1) "Point in space approach" means a helicopter instrument approach procedure to a missed approach point that is more than 2,600 feet from an associated helicopter landing area.

(p) "Procedure turn" means the maneuver prescribed when it is necessary to reverse direction to establish the aircraft on an intermediate or final approach course. The outbound course, direction of turn, distance within which the turn must be completed, and minimum altitude are specified in the procedure. However, the point at which the turn may be commenced, and the type and rate of turn, is left to the discretion of the pilot.

(q) "RA" means radio altimeter setting height.

(r) "RVV" means runway visibility value.

(s) "S" means straight-in landing minimum, a statement of ceiling and visibility, minimum descent altitude and visibility, or decision height and visibility, required for a straight-in landing on a specified runway. The number appearing with the "S" indicates the runway to which the minimum applies. If a straight-in minimum is not prescribed in the procedure, the circling minimum specified applies to a straight-in landing.

(t) "Shuttle" means a shuttle, or race-track-type, pattern with 2-minute legs prescribed in lieu of a procedure turn.

(u) "65 knots or less" means an aircraft that has a stalling speed of 65 knots or less (as established in an approved flight manual) at maximum certificated landing weight with full flaps, landing gear extended, and power off.

(v) "T" means takeoff minimum.

(w) "TDZ" means touchdown zone.

(x) "Visibility minimum" means the minimum visibility specified for approach, or landing, or takeoff, expressed in statute miles, or in feet where RVR is reported.

(Secs. 307(c), 313(a), 601, Federal Aviation Act of 1958, as amended (49 U.S.C. 1348(c), 1354(a), 1421); sec. 6(c), Department of Transportation Act (49 U.S.C. 1655(c)))

[Amdt. 97-561, 32 FR 13911, Oct. 6, 1967, as amended by Amdt. 97-803, 37 FR 6287, Mar. 28, 1972; Amdt. 97-1133, 44 FR 15659, Mar. 15, 1979]

§ 97.5 Bearings; courses; headings; radials; miles.

(a) All bearings, courses, headings, and radials in this part are magnetic.

(b) RVR values are stated in feet. Other visibility values are stated in statute miles. All other mileages are stated in nautical miles.

[Amdt. 97-561, 32 FR 13912, Oct. 6, 1967]

Subpart B—Procedures

EDITORIAL NOTE: The procedures set forth in this subpart were formerly carried as §§ 609.100 through 609.500 of this title and were transferred to Part 97 as §§ 97.11 through 97.19, respectively, but are not carried in the Code of Federal Regulations. For Federal Register citations affecting these procedures, see the List of CFR Sections Affected in the Finding Aids section of this volume.

§ 97.10 General.

This subpart prescribes standard instrument approach procedures other than those based on the criteria contained in the U.S. Standard for Terminal Instrument Approach Procedures (TERPs). Standard instrument approach procedures adopted by the FAA and described on FAA Form 3139 are incorporated into this part and made a part hereof as provided in 5 U.S.C. 552(a)(1) and pursuant to 1 CFR Part 20. The incorporated standard instrument approach procedures are available for examination at the Rules Docket and at the National Flight Data Center, Federal Aviation Administration, 800 Independence Avenue SW., Washington, D.C. 20590.

Copies of SIAPs adopted in a particular FAA Region are also available for examination at the headquarters of that region. Moreover, copies of SIAPs originating in a particular Flight Inspection District Office are available for examination at that office. Based on the information contained on FAA Form 3139, standard instrument approach procedures are portrayed on charts prepared for the use of pilots by the U.S. Coast and Geodetic Survey and other publishers of aeronautical charts.

[Amdt. 97-969, 35 FR 5609, Apr. 7, 1970]

Subpart C—TERPS Procedures

SOURCE: Docket No. 8130, Amdt. 97-561, 32 FR 13912, Oct. 6, 1967, unless otherwise noted.

EDITORIAL NOTE: The procedures for §§ 97.21 through 97.35, respectively, are not carried in the Code of Federal Regulations. For FEDERAL REGISTER citations affecting these procedures, see the List of CFR Sections Affected in the Finding Aids section of this volume.

§ 97.20 General.

This subpart prescribes standard instrument approach procedures based on the criteria contained in the U.S. Standard for Terminal Instrument Approach Procedures (TERPs). The standard instrument approach procedures adopted by the FAA and described on FAA Form 8260-3, 8260-4, or 8260-5 are incorporated into this part and made a part hereof as provided in 5 U.S.C. 552(a)(1) and pursuant to 1 CFR Part 20. The incorporated standard instrument approach procedures are available for examination at the Rules Docket and at the National Flight Data Center, Federal Aviation Administration, 800 Independence Avenue SW., Washington, D.C. 20590. Copies of SIAPs adopted in a particular FAA Region are also available for examination at the headquarters of that Region. Moreover, copies of SIAPs originating in a particular Flight Inspection District Office are available for examination at that Office. Based on the information contained on FAA Form 8260-3, 8260-4, and 8260-5, standard instrument approach procedures are portrayed on charts prepared for the use of pilots by the U.S. Coast and Geodetic Survey and other publishers of aeronautical charts.

(Sec. 6(c) Department of Transportation Act. 49 U.S.C. 1655(c) and 5 U.S.C. 552(a)(1))

[Amdt. 97-969, 35 FR 5609, Apr. 7, 1970]

PART 103—ULTRALIGHT VEHICLES

SPECIAL FEDERAL AVIATION REGULATION No.
45–1 [NOTE]

Subpart A—General

Subpart B—Operating Rules

AUTHORITY: Secs. 307, 313(a), 601(a), 602, and 603, Federal Aviation Act of 1958 (49 U.S.C. 1348, 1354(a), 1421(a), 1422, and 1423); sec. 6(c), Department of Transportation Act (49 U.S.C. 1655(c).

SOURCE: Docket No. 21631, 47 FR 38776, Sept. 2, 1982, unless otherwise noted.

Subpart A—General

§ 103.1   Applicability.

This part prescribes rules governing the operation of ultralight vehicles in the United States. For the purposes of this part, an ultralight vehicle is a vehicle that:

(a) Is used or intended to be used for manned operation in the air by a single occupant;

(b) Is used or intended to be used for recreation or sport purposes only;

(c) Does not have any U.S. or foreign airworthiness certificate; and

(d) If unpowered, weighs less than 155 pounds; or

(e) If powered:

(1) Weighs less than 254 pounds empty weight, excluding floats and safety devices which are intended for deployment in a potentially catastrophic situation;

(2) Has a fuel capacity not exceeding 5 U.S. gallons;

(3) Is not capable of more than 55 knots calibrated airspeed at full power in level flight; and

(4) Has a power-off stall speed which does not exceed 24 knots calibrated airspeed.

§ 103.3   Inspection requirements.

(a) Any person operating an ultralight vehicle under this part shall, upon request, allow the Administrator, or his designee, to inspect the vehicle to determine the applicability of this part.

(b) The pilot or operator of an ultralight vehicle must, upon request of the Administrator, furnish satisfactory evidence that the vehicle is subject only to the provisions of this part.

§ 103.5   Waivers.

No person may conduct operations that require a deviation from this part except under a written waiver issued by the Administrator.

§ 103.7   Certification and registration.

(a) Notwithstanding any other section pertaining to certification of aircraft or their parts or equipment, ultralight vehicles and their component parts and equipment are not required to meet the airworthiness certification standards specified for aircraft or to have certificates of airworthiness.

(b) Notwithstanding any other section pertaining to airman certification, operators of ultralight vehicles are not required to meet any aeronautical knowledge, age, or experience requirements to operate those vehicles or to have airman or medical certificates.

(c) Notwithstanding any other section pertaining to registration and marking of aircraft, ultralight vehicles are not required to be registered or to bear markings of any type.

Subpart B—Operating Rules

§ 103.9 Hazardous operations.

(a) No person may operate any ultralight vehicle in a manner that creates a hazard to other persons or property.

(b) No person may allow an object to be dropped from an ultralight vehicle if such action creates a hazard to other persons or property.

§ 103.11 Daylight operations.

(a) No person may operate an ultralight vehicle except between the hours of sunrise and sunset.

(b) Notwithstanding paragraph (a) of this section, ultralight vehicles may be operated during the twilight periods 30 minutes before official sunrise and 30 minutes after official sunset or, in Alaska, during the period of civil twilight as defined in the Air Almanac, if:

(1) The vehicle is equipped with an operating anticollision light visible for at least 3 statute miles; and

(2) All operations are conducted in uncontrolled airspace.

§ 103.13 Operation near aircraft; right-of-way rules.

(a) Each person operating an ultralight vehicle shall maintain vigilance so as to see and avoid aircraft and shall yield the right-of-way to all aircraft.

(b) No person may operate an ultralight vehicle in a manner that creates a collision hazard with respect to any aircraft.

(c) Powered ultralights shall yield the right-of-way to unpowered ultralights.

§ 103.15 Operations over congested areas.

No person may operate an ultralight vehicle over any congested area of a city, town, or settlement, or over any open air assembly of persons.

§ 103.17 Operations in certain airspace.

No person may operate an ultralight vehicle within an airport traffic area, control zone, airport radar service area, terminal control area, or positive control area unless that person has prior authorization from the air traffic control facility having jurisdiction over that airspace.

[Doc. No. 23708, 50 FR 9259, Mar. 6, 1985]

§ 103.19 Operations in prohibited or restricted areas.

No person may operate an ultralight vehicle in prohibited or restricted areas unless that person has permission from the using or controlling agency, as appropriate.

§ 103.20 Flight restrictions in the proximity of certain areas designated by notice to airmen.

No person may operate an ultralight vehicle in areas designated in a Notice to Airmen under § 91.102 or § 91.104 of this chapter, unless authorized by ATC.

[Doc. No. 24454, 50 FR 4969, Feb. 5, 1985]

§ 103.21 Visual reference with the surface.

No person may operate an ultralight vehicle except by visual reference with the surface.

§ 103.23 Flight visibility and cloud clearance requirements.

No person may operate an ultralight vehicle when the flight visibility or distance from clouds is less than that in the following table, as appropriate:

Flight altitudes	Minimum flight visibility [1]	Minimum distance from clouds
1,200 feet or less above the surface regardless of MSL altitude:		
(1) Within controlled airspace	3	500 feet below, 1,000 feet above, 2,000 feet horizontal.
(2) Outside controlled airspace	1	Clear of clouds.
More than 1,200 feet above the surface but less than 10,000 feet MSL:		
(1) Within controlled airspace	3	500 feet below, 1,000 feet above, 2,000 feet horizontal.
(2) Outside controlled airspace	1	500 feet below, 1,000 feet above, 2,000 feet horizontal.
More than 1,200 feet above the surface and at or above 10,000 feet MSL.	5	1,000 feet below, 1,000 feet above, 1 statute mile horizontal.

[1] Statute miles.

PART 135—AIR TAXI OPERATORS
AND COMMERCIAL OPERATORS

Subpart A—General

§ 135.1 **Applicability.**

(a) Except as provided in paragraph (b) of this section, this part prescribes rules governing—

(1) Air taxi operations conducted under the exemption authority of Part 298 of this title;

(2) The transportation of mail by aircraft conducted under a postal service contract awarded under section 5402c of Title 39, United States Code;

(3) The carriage in air commerce of persons or property for compensation or hire as a commercial operator (not an air carrier) in aircraft having a maximum seating capacity of less than 20 passengers or a maximum payload capacity of less than 6,000 pounds, or the carriage in air commerce of persons or property in common carriage operations solely between points entirely within any state of the United States in aircraft having a maximum seating capacity of 30 seats or less or a maximum payload capacity of 7,500 pounds or less; and

(4) Each person who is on board an aircraft being operated under this part.

(b) This part does not apply to—

(1) Student instruction;

(2) Nonstop sightseeing flights that begin and end at the same airport, and are conducted within a 25 statute mile radius of that airport;

(3) Ferry or training flights;

(4) Aerial work operations, including—

(i) Crop dusting, seeding, spraying, and bird chasing;

(ii) Banner towing;

(iii) Aerial photography or survey;

(iv) Fire fighting;

(v) Helicopter operations in construction or repair work (but not including transportation to and from the site of operations); and

(vi) Powerline or pipeline patrol, or similar types of patrol approved by the Administrator;

(5) Sightseeing flights conducted in hot air balloons;

(6) Nonstop flights conducted within a 25 statute mile radius of the airport of takeoff carrying persons for the purpose of intentional parachute jumps;

(7) Helicopter flights conducted within a 25 statute mile radius of the airport of takeoff, if—

(i) Not more than two passengers are carried in the helicopter in addition to the required flight crew;

(ii) Each flight is made under VFR during the day;

(iii) The helicopter used is certificated in the standard category and complies with the 100-hour inspection requirements of Part 91 of this chapter;

(iv) The operator notifies the FAA Flight Standards District Office responsible for the geographic area concerned at least 72 hours before each flight and furnishes any essential information that the office requests;

(v) The number of flights does not exceed a total of six in any calendar year;

(vi) Each flight has been approved by the Administrator; and

(vii) Cargo is not carried in or on the helicopter;

(8) Operations conducted under Part 133 or 375 of this title;

(9) Emergency mail service conducted under section 405(h) of the Federal Aviation Act of 1958; or

(10) This part does not apply to operations conducted under the provisions of § 91.59.

[Doc. No. 16097, 43 FR 46783, Oct. 10, 1978, as amended by Amdt. 135-5, 45 FR 43162, June 26, 1980; Amdt. 135-7, 45 FR 67235, Oct. 9, 1980; Amdt. 135-20, 51 FR 40709, Nov. 7, 1986]

§ 135.2 Air taxi operations with large aircraft.

(a) Except as provided in paragraph (d) of this section, no person may conduct air taxi operations in large aircraft under an individual exemption and authorization issued by the Civil Aeronautics Board or under the exemption authority of Part 298 of this title, unless that person—

(1) Complies with the certification requirements for supplemental air carriers in Part 121 of this chapter, except that the person need not obtain, and that person is not eligible for, a certificate under that part; and

(2) Conducts those operations under the rules of Part 121 of this chapter that apply to supplemental air carriers.

However, the Administrator may issue operations specifications which require an operator to comply with the rules of Part 121 of this chapter that apply to domestic or flag air carriers, as appropriate, in place of the rules required by paragraph (a)(2) of this section, if the Administrator determines compliance with those rules is necessary to provide an appropriate level of safety for the operation.

(b) The holder of an operating certificate issued under this part who is required to comply with Subpart L of Part 121 of this chapter, under paragraph (a) of this section, may perform and approve maintenance, preventive maintenance, and alterations on aircraft having a maximum passenger seating configuration, excluding any pilot seat, of 30 seats or less and a maximum payload capacity of 7,500 pounds or less as provided in that subpart. The aircraft so maintained shall be identified by registration number in the operations specifications of the certificate holder using the aircraft.

(c) Operations that are subject to paragraph (a) of this section are not subject to §§ 135.21 through 135.43 of Subpart A and Subparts B through J of this part. Seaplanes used in operations that are subject to paragraph (a) of this section are not subject to § 121.291(a) of this chapter.

(d) Operations conducted with aircraft having a maximum passenger seating configuration, excluding any pilot seat, of 30 seats or less, and a maximum payload capacity of 7,500 pounds or less shall be conducted under the rules of this part. However, a certificate holder who is conducting operations on December 1, 1978, in aircraft described in this paragraph may continue to operate under paragraph (a) of this section.

(e) For the purposes of this part—

(1) "Maximum payload capacity" means:

(i) For an aircraft for which a maximum zero fuel weight is prescribed in FAA technical specifications, the maximum zero fuel weight, less empty weight, less all justifiable aircraft equipment, and less the operating load (consisting of minimum flight crew, foods and beverages and supplies and equipment related to foods and beverages, but not including disposable fuel or oil);

(ii) For all other aircraft, the maximum certificated takeoff weight of an aircraft, less the empty weight, less all justifiable aircraft equipment, and less the operating load (consisting of minimum fuel load, oil, and flight crew). The allowance for the weight of the crew, oil, and fuel is as follows:

(A) Crew—200 pounds for each crewmember required under this chapter.

(B) Oil—350 pounds.

(C) Fuel—the minimum weight of fuel required under this chapter for a flight between domestic points 174 nautical miles apart under VFR weather conditions that does not involve extended overwater operations.

(2) "Empty weight" means the weight of the airframe, engines, propellers, rotors, and fixed equipment. Empty weight excludes the weight of the crew and payload, but includes the weight of all fixed ballast, unusable fuel supply, undrainable oil, total quantity of engine coolant, and total quantity of hydraulic fluid.

(3) "Maximum zero fuel weight" means the maximum permissible weight of an aircraft with no disposable fuel or oil. The zero fuel weight figure may be found in either the aircraft type certificate data sheet or the approved Aircraft Flight Manual, or both.

(4) For the purposes of this paragraph, "justifiable aircraft equipment"

means any equipment necessary for the operation of the aircraft. It does not include equipment or ballast specifically installed, permanently or otherwise, for the purpose of altering the empty weight of an aircraft to meet the maximum payload capacity specified in paragraph (d) of this section.

§ 135.3 Rules applicable to operations subject to this part.

Each person operating an aircraft in operations under this part shall—

(a) While operating inside the United States, comply with the applicable rules of this chapter; and

(b) While operating outside the United States, comply with Annex 2, Rules of the Air, to the Convention on International Civil Aviation or the regulations of any foreign country, whichever applies, and with any rules of Parts 61 and 91 of this chapter and this part that are more restrictive than that Annex or those regulations and that can be complied with without violating that Annex or those regulations. Annex 2 is incorporated by reference in § 91.1(c) of this chapter.

§ 135.5 Certificate and operations specifications required.

No person may operate an aircraft under this part without, or in violation of, an air taxi/commercial operator (ATCO) operating certificate and appropriate operations specifications issued under this part, or, for operations with large aircraft having a maximum passenger seating configuration, excluding any pilot seat, of more than 30 seats, or a maximum payload capacity of more than 7,500 pounds, without, or in violation of, appropriate operations specifications issued under Part 121 of this chapter.

§ 135.7 Applicability of rules to unauthorized operators.

The rules in this part which apply to a person certificated under § 135.5 also apply to a person who engages in any operation governed by this part without an appropriate certificate and operations specifications required by § 135.5.

§ 135.9 Duration of certificate.

(a) An ATCO operating certificate is effective until surrendered, suspended or revoked. The holder of an ATCO operating certificate that is suspended or revoked shall return it to the Administrator.

(b) Except as provided in paragraphs (c) and (d) of this section, an ATCO operating certificate in effect on December 1, 1978, expires on February 1, 1979. The certificate holder must continue to conduct operations under Part 135 and the operations specifications in effect on November 30, 1978, until the certificate expires.

(c) If the certificate holder applies before February 1, 1979, for new operations specifications under this part, the operating certificate held continues in effect and the certificate holder must continue operations under Part 135 and operations specifications in effect on November 30, 1978, until the earliest of the following—

(1) The date on which new operations specifications are issued; or

(2) The date on which the Administrator notifies the certificate holder that the application is denied; or

(3) August 1, 1979.

If new operations specifications are issued under paragraph (c)(1) of this section, the ATCO operating certificate continues in effect until surrendered, suspended or revoked under paragraph (a) of this section.

(d) A certificate holder may obtain an extension of the expiration date in paragraph (c) of this section, but not beyond December 1, 1979, from the Director, Flight Standards Service, if before July 1, 1979, the certificate holder—

(1) Shows that due to the circumstances beyond its control it cannot comply by the expiration date; and

(2) Submits a schedule for compliance, acceptable to the Director, indicating that compliance will be achieved at the earliest practicable date.

(e) The holder of an ATCO operating certificate that expires, under paragraph (b), (c), or (d) of this section, shall return it to the Administrator.

§ 135.10 Compliance dates for certain rules.

After January 2, 1991, no certificate holder may use a person as a flight crewmember unless that person has completed the windshear ground training required by §§ 135.345(b)(6) and 135.351(b)(2) of this part.

(a) A certificate holder or pilot is allowed until June 1, 1979, to comply with the following sections:

(1) A third bank and pitch indicator (artificial horizon) (§ 135.149(c)).

(2) Shoulder harness at flight crewmember stations (§ 135.171(a)).

(3) Airline transport pilot certificate (§ 135.243(a)).

(b) A certificate holder is allowed until December 1, 1979, to comply with the following sections:

(1) Cockpit voice recorder (§ 135.151).

(2) Ground proximity warning system or other approved system (§ 135.153).

(3) Airborne thunderstorm detection equipment (§ 135.173).

(c) A certificate holder or pilot is allowed until August 1, 1981, to comply with the instrument rating requirements of § 135.243(b)(3).

(d) A certificate holder or pilot may obtain an extension of the compliance date in paragraph (a) or (b) of this section, but not beyond December 1, 1980, from the Director, of Flight Operations, if before the compliance date in paragraph (a) or (b) of this section—

(1) The certificate holder or pilot shows that due to the circumstances beyond its control they cannot comply by that date; and

(2) The certificate holder or pilot has submitted before that date a schedule for compliance, acceptable to the Director, indicating that compliance will be achieved at the earliest practicable date.

§ 135.11 Application and issue of certificate and operations specifications.

(a) An application for an ATCO operating certificate and appropriate operations specifications is made on a form and in a manner prescribed by the Administrator and filed with the FAA Flight Standards District Office that has jurisdiction over the area in which the applicant's principal business office is located.

(b) An applicant who meets the requirements of this part is entitled to—

(1) An ATCO operating certificate containing all business names under which the certificate holder may conduct operations and the address of each business office used by the certificate holder; and

(2) Separate operations specifications, issued to the certificate holder, containing:

(i) The type and area of operations authorized.

(ii) The category and class of aircraft that may be used in those operations.

(iii) Registration numbers and types of aircraft that are subject to an airworthiness maintenance program required by § 135.411(a)(2), including time limitations or standards for determining time limitations, for overhauls, inspections, and checks for airframes, aircraft engines, propellers, rotors, appliances, and emergency equipment.

(iv) Registration numbers of aircraft that are to be inspected under an approved aircraft inspection program under § 135.419.

(v) Additional maintenance items required by the Administrator under § 135.421.

(vi) Any authorized deviation from this part.

(vii) Any other items the Administrator may require or allow to meet any particular situation.

(c) No person holding operations specifications issued under this part may list on its operations specifications or on the current list of aircraft required by § 135.63(a)(3) any airplane listed on operations specifications issued under Part 125.

[Doc. No. 16097, 43 FR 467883, Oct. 10, 1978, as amended by Amdt. 135–24, 52 FR 20029, May 28, 1987]

§ 135.13 **Eligibility for certificate and operations specifications.**

(a) To be eligible for an ATCO operating certificate and appropriate operations specifications, a person must—

(1) Be a citizen of the United States, a partnership of which each member is a citizen of the United States, or a corporation or association created or organized under the laws of the United States or any state, territory, or possession of the United States, of which the president and two-thirds or more of the board of directors and other managing officers are citizens of the United States and in which at least 75 percent of the voting interest is owned or controlled by citizens of the United States or one of its possessions; and

(2) Show, to the satisfaction of the Administrator, that the person is able to conduct each kind of operation for which the person seeks authorization in compliance with applicable regulations; and

(3) Hold any economic authority that may be required by the Civil Aeronautics Board.

However, no person holding a commercial operator operating certificate issued under Part 121 of this chapter is eligible for an ATCO operating certificate unless the person shows to the satisfaction of the Administrator that the person's contract carriage business in large aircraft, having a maximum passenger seating configuration, excluding any pilot seat, of more than 30 seats or a maximum payload capacity of more than 7,500 pounds, will not result directly or indirectly from the person's air taxi business.

(b) The Administrator may deny any applicant a certificate under this part if the Administrator finds—

(1) That an air carrier or commercial operator operating certificate under Part 121 or an ATCO operating certificate previously issued to the applicant was revoked; or

(2) That a person who was employed in a position similar to general manager, director of operations, director of maintenance, chief pilot, or chief inspector, or who has exercised control with respect to any ATCO operating certificate holder, air carrier, or commercial operator whose operating certificate has been revoked, will be employed in any of those positions or a similar position, or will be in control of or have a substantial ownership interest in the applicant, and that the person's employment or control contributed materially to the reasons for revoking that certificate.

§ 135.15 Amendment of certificate.

(a) The Administrator may amend an ATCO operating certificate—

(1) On the Administrator's own initiative, under section 609 of the Federal Aviation Act of 1958 (49 U.S.C. 1429) and Part 13 of this chapter; or

(2) Upon application by the holder of that certificate.

(b) The certificate holder must file an application to amend an ATCO operating certificate at least 15 days before the date proposed by the applicant for the amendment to become effective, unless a shorter filing period is approved. The application must be on a form and in a manner prescribed by the Administrator and must be submitted to the FAA Flight Standards District Office charged with the overall inspection of the certificate holder.

(c) The FAA Flight Standards District Office charged with the overall inspection of the certificate holder grants an amendment to the ATCO operating certificate if it is determined that safety in air commerce and the public interest allow that amendment.

(d) Within 30 days after receiving a refusal to amend the operating certificate, the certificate holder may petition the Director, Flight Standards Service, to reconsider the request.

§ 135.17 Amendment of operations specifications.

(a) The FAA Flight Standards District Office charged with the overall inspection of the certificate holder may amend any operations specifications issued under this part if—

(1) It determines that safety in air commerce requires that amendment; or

(2) Upon application by the holder, that District Office determines that safety in air commerce allows that amendment.

(b) The certificate holder must file an application to amend operations specifications at least 15 days before the date proposed by the applicant for the amendment to become effective, unless a shorter filing period is approved. The application must be on a form and in a manner prescribed by the Administrator and be submitted to the FAA Flight Standards District Office charged with the overall inspection of the certificate holder.

(c) Within 30 days after a notice of refusal to approve a holder's application for amendment is received, the holder may petition the Director of Airworthiness, for amendments pertaining to airworthiness or the Director of Flight Operations for amendments pertaining to flight operations to reconsider the refusal to amend.

(d) When the FAA Flight Standards District Office charged with the overall inspection of the certificate holder amends operations specifications, that District Office gives notice in writing to the holder of a proposed amendment to the operations specifications, fixing a period of not less than 7 days within which the holder may submit written information, views, and arguments concerning the proposed amendment. After consideration of all relevant matter presented, that District Office notifies the holder of any amendment adopted, or a rescission of the notice. The amendment becomes effective not less than 30 days after the holder receives notice of the adoption of the amendment, unless the holder petitions the Director of Airworthiness for amendments pertaining to airworthiness or the Director of Flight Operations for amendments pertaining to flight operations for reconsideration of the amendment. In that case, the effective date of the amendment is stayed pending a decision by the Director. If the Director finds there is an emergency requiring immediate action as to safety in air commerce that makes the provisions of this paragraph impracticable or contrary to the public interest, the Director notifies the certificate holder that the amendment is effective on the date of receipt, without previous notice.

[Doc. No 16097, 43 FR 46783, Oct. 10, 1978, as amended by Amdt. 135-6, 45 FR 47838, July 17, 1980]

§ 135.19 Emergency operations.

(a) In an emergency involving the safety of persons or property, the certificate holder may deviate from the rules of this part relating to aircraft and equipment and weather minimums to the extent required to meet that emergency.

(b) In an emergency involving the safety of persons or property, the pilot in command may deviate from the rules of this part to the extent required to meet that emergency.

(c) Each person who, under the authority of this section, deviates from a rule of this part shall, within 10 days, excluding Saturdays, Sundays, and Federal holidays, after the deviation, send to the FAA Flight Standards District Office charged with the overall inspection of the certificate holder a complete report of the aircraft operation involved, including a description of the deviation and reasons for it.

§ **135.21 Manual requirements.**

(a) Each certificate holder, other than one who uses only one pilot in the certificate holder's operations, shall prepare and keep current a manual setting forth the certificate holder's procedures and policies acceptable to the Administrator. This manual must be used by the certificate holder's flight, ground, and maintenance personnel in conducting its operations. However, the Administrator may authorize a deviation from this paragraph if the Administrator finds that, because of the limited size of the operation, all or part of the manual is not necessary for guidance of flight, ground, or maintenance personnel.

(b) Each certificate holder shall maintain at least one copy of the manual at its principal operations base.

(c) The manual must not be contrary to any applicable Federal regulations, foreign regulation applicable to the certificate holder's operations in foreign countries, or the certificate holder's operating certificate or operations specifications.

(d) A copy of the manual, or appropriate portions of the manual (and changes and additions) shall be made available to maintenance and ground operations personnel by the certificate holder and furnished to—

(1) Its flight crewmembers; and

(2) Representatives of the Administrator assigned to the certificate holder.

(e) Each employee of the certificate holder to whom a manual or appropriate portions of it are furnished under paragraph (d)(1) of this section shall keep it up to date with the changes and additions furnished to them.

(f) Except as provided in paragraph (g) of this section, each certificate holder shall carry appropriate parts of the manual on each aircraft when away from the principal operations base. The appropriate parts must be available for use by ground or flight personnel.

(g) If a certificate holder conducts aircraft inspections or maintenance at specified stations where it keeps the approved inspection program manual, it is not required to carry the manual aboard the aircraft en route to those stations.

[Doc. No. 16097, 43 FR 46783, Oct. 10, 1978, as amended by Amdt. 135-18, 47 FR 33396, Aug. 2, 1982]

§ **135.23 Manual contents.**

Each manual shall have the date of the last revision on each revised page. The manual must include—

(a) The name of each management person required under § 135.37(a) who is authorized to act for the certificate holder, the person's assigned area of responsibility, the person's duties, responsibilities, and authority, and the name and title of each person authorized to exercise operational control under § 135.77;

(b) Procedures for ensuring compliance with aircraft weight and balance limitations and, for multiengine aircraft, for determining compliance with § 135.185;

(c) Copies of the certificate holder's operations specifications or appropriate extracted information, including area of operations authorized, category and class of aircraft authorized, crew complements, and types of operations authorized;

(d) Procedures for complying with accident notification requirements;

(e) Procedures for ensuring that the pilot in command knows that required airworthiness inspections have been made and that the aircraft has been approved for return to service in compliance with applicable maintenance requirements;

(f) Procedures for reporting and recording mechanical irregularities that come to the attention of the pilot in command before, during, and after completion of a flight;

(g) Procedures to be followed by the pilot in command for determining that mechanical irregularities or defects reported for previous flights have been corrected or that correction has been deferred;

(h) Procedures to be followed by the pilot in command to obtain maintenance, preventive maintenance, and servicing of the aircraft at a place where previous arrangements have not been made by the operator, when the pilot is authorized to so act for the operator;

(i) Procedures under § 135.179 for the release for, or continuation of, flight if any item of equipment required for the particular type of operation becomes inoperative or unserviceable en route;

(j) Procedures for refueling aircraft, eliminating fuel contamination, protecting from fire (including electrostatic protection), and supervising and protecting passengers during refueling;

(k) Procedures to be followed by the pilot in command in the briefing under § 135.117;

(l) Flight locating procedures, when applicable;

(m) Procedures for ensuring compliance with emergency procedures, including a list of the functions assigned each category of required crewmembers in connection with an emergency and emergency evacuation duties under § 135.123;

(n) En route qualification procedures for pilots, when applicable;

(o) The approved aircraft inspection program, when applicable;

(p) Procedures and instructions to enable personnel to recognize hazardous materials, as defined in Title 49 CFR, and if these materials are to be carried, stored, or handled, procedures and instructions for—

(1) Accepting shipment of hazardous material required by Title 49 CFR, to assure proper packaging, marking, labeling, shipping documents, compat-

ibility of articles, and instructions on their loading, storage, and handling;

(2) Notification and reporting hazardous material incidents as required by Title 49 CFR; and

(3) Notification of the pilot in command when there are hazardous materials aboard, as required by Title 49 CFR;

(q) Procedures for the evacuation of persons who may need the assistance of another person to move expeditiously to an exit if an emergency occurs; and

(r) Other procedures and policy instructions regarding the certificate holder's operations, that are issued by the certificate holder.

[Doc. No. 16097, 43 FR 46783, Oct. 10, 1978, as amended by Amdt. 135-20, 51 FR 40709, Nov. 7, 1986]

§ 135.25   Aircraft requirements.

(a) Except as provided in paragraph (d) of this section, no certificate holder may operate an aircraft under this part unless that aircraft—

(1) Is registered as a civil aircraft of the United States and carries an appropriate and current airworthiness certificate issued under this chapter; and

(2) Is in an airworthy condition and meets the applicable airworthiness requirements of this chapter, including those relating to identification and equipment.

(b) Each certificate holder must have the exclusive use of at least one aircraft that meets the requirements for at least one kind of operation authorized in the certificate holder's operations specifications. In addition, for each kind of operation for which the certificate holder does not have the exclusive use of an aircraft, the certificate holder must have available for use under a written agreement (including arrangements for performing required maintenance) at least one aircraft that meets the requirements for that kind of operation. However, this paragraph does not prohibit the operator from using or authorizing the use of the aircraft for other than air taxi or commercial operations and does not require the certificate holder to have exclusive use of all aircraft that the certificate holder uses.

(c) For the purposes of paragraph (b) of this section, a person has exclusive use of an aircraft if that person has the sole possession, control, and use of it for flight, as owner, or has a written agreement (including arrangements for performing required maintenance), in effect when the aircraft is operated, giving the person that possession, control, and use for at least 6 consecutive months.

(d) A certificate holder may operate in common carriage, and for the carriage of mail, a civil aircraft which is leased or chartered to it without crew and is registered in a country which is a party to the Convention on International Civil Aviation if—

(1) The aircraft carries an appropriate airworthiness certificate issued by the country of registration and meets the registration and identification requirements of that country;

(2) The aircraft is of a type design which is approved under a U.S. type certificate and complies with all of the requirements of this chapter (14 CFR Chapter I) that would be applicable to that aircraft were it registered in the United States, including the requirements which must be met for issuance of a U.S. standard airworthiness certificate (including type design conformity, condition for safe operation, and the noise, fuel venting, and engine emission requirements of this chapter), except that a U.S. registration certificate and a U.S. standard airworthiness certificate will not be issued for the aircraft;

(3) The aircraft is operated by U.S.-certificated airmen employed by the certificate holder; and

(4) The certificate holder files a copy of the aircraft lease or charter agreement with the FAA Aircraft Registry, Department of Transportation, 6400 South MacArthur Boulevard, Oklahoma City, Oklahoma (Mailing address: P.O. Box 25504, Oklahoma City, Oklahoma 73125).

[Doc. No. 16097, 43 FR 46783, Oct. 10, 1978, as amended by Amdt. 135-8, 45 FR 68649, Oct. 16, 1980]

§ 135.27 Business office and operations base.

(a) Each certificate holder shall maintain a principal business office.

(b) Each certificate holder shall, before establishing or changing the location of any business office or operations base, except a temporary operations base, notify in writing the FAA Flight Standards District Office charged with the overall inspection of the certificate holder.

(c) No certificate holder who establishes or changes the location of any business office or operations base, except a temporary operations base, may operate an aircraft under this part unless the certificate holder complies with paragraph (b) of this section.

§ 135.29 Use of business names.

No certificate holder may operate an aircraft under this part under a business name that is not on the certificate holder's operating certificate.

§ 135.31 Advertising.

No certificate holder may advertise or otherwise offer to perform operations subject to this part that are not authorized by the certificate holder's operating certificate and operations specifications.

§ 135.33 Area limitations on operations.

(a) No person may operate an aircraft in a geographical area that is not specifically authorized by appropriate operations specifications issued under this part.

(b) No person may operate an aircraft in a foreign country unless that person is authorized to do so by that country.

§ 135.35 Termination of operations.

Within 30 days after a certificate holder terminates operations under this part, the operating certificate and operations specifications must be surrendered by the certificate holder to the FAA Flight Standards District Office charged with the overall inspection of the certificate holder.

§ 135.37 Management personnel required.

(a) Each certificate holder, other than one who uses only one pilot in the certificate holder's operations, must have enough qualified management personnel in the following or equivalent positions to ensure safety in its operations:

(1) Director of operations.

(2) Chief pilot.

(3) Director of maintenance.

(b) Upon application by the certificate holder, the Administrator may approve different positions or numbers of positions than those listed in paragraph (a) of this section for a particular operation if the certificate holder shows that it can perform its operations safely under the direction of fewer or different categories of management personnel.

(c) Each certificate holder shall—

(1) Set forth the duties, responsibilities, and authority of the personnel required by this section in the manual required by § 135.21;

(2) List in the manual required by § 135.21 the name of the person or persons assigned to those positions; and

(3) Within 10 working days, notify the FAA Flight Standards District Office charged with the overall inspection of the certificate holder of any change made in the assignment of persons to the listed positions.

[Doc. No. 16097, 43 FR 46783, Oct. 10, 1978, as amended by Amdt. 135-18, 47 FR 33396, Aug. 2, 1982]

§ 135.39 Management personnel qualifications.

(a) *Director of operations.* No person may serve as director of operations under § 135.37(a) unless that person knows the contents of the manual required by § 135.21, the operations specifications, the provisions of this part and other applicable regulations necessary for the proper performance of the person's duties and responsibilities and:

(1) The director of operations for a certificate holder conducting any operations for which the pilot in command is required to hold an airline transport pilot certificate must—

(i) Hold or have held an airline transport pilot certificate; and

(ii) Have at least 3 years of experience as pilot in command of an aircraft operated under this part, Part 121 or Part 127 of this chapter; or

(iii) Have at least 3 years of experience as director of operations with a certificate holder operating under this part, Part 121 or Part 127 of this chapter.

(2) The director of operations for a certificate holder who is not conducting any operation for which the pilot in command is required to hold an airline transport pilot certificate must—

(i) Hold or have held a commercial pilot certificate; and

(ii) Have at least 3 years of experience as a pilot in command of an aircraft operated under this part, Part 121 or Part 127 of this chapter; or

(iii) Have at least 3 years of experience as director of operations with a certificate holder operating under this part, Part 121 or Part 127 of this chapter.

(b) *Chief pilot.* No person may serve as chief pilot under § 135.37(a) unless that person knows the contents of the manual required by § 135.21, the operations specifications, the provisions of this part and other applicable regulations necessary for the proper performance of the person's duties, and:

(1) The chief pilot of a certificate holder conducting any operation for which the pilot in command is required to hold an airline transport pilot certificate must—

(i) Hold a current airline transport pilot certificate with appropriate ratings for at least one of the types of aircraft used; and

(ii) Have at least 3 years of experience as a pilot in command of an aircraft under this part, Part 121 or Part 127 of this chapter.

(2) The chief pilot of a certificate holder who is not conducting any operation for which the pilot in command is required to hold an airline transport pilot certificate must—

(i) Hold a current, commercial pilot certificate with an instrument rating. If an instrument rating is not required for the pilot in command under this part, the chief pilot must hold a current, commercial pilot certificate; and

(ii) Have at least 3 years of experience as a pilot in command of an aircraft under this part, Part 121 or Part 127 of this chapter.

(c) *Director of maintenance.* No person may serve as a director of maintenance under § 135.37(a) unless that person knows the maintenance sections of the certificate holder's manual, the operations specifications, the provisions of this part and other applicable regulations necessary for the proper performance of the person's duties, and—

(1) Holds a mechanic certificate with both airframe and powerplant ratings; and

(2) Has at least 3 years of maintenance experience as a certificated mechanic on aircraft, including, at the time of appointment as director of maintenance, the recent experience requirements of § 65.83 of this chapter in the same category and class of aircraft as used by the certificate holder, or at least 3 years of experience with a certificated airframe repair station, including 1 year in the capacity of approving aircraft for return to service.

(d) Deviation from this section may be authorized if the person has had equivalent aeronautical experience. The Chief of the Flight Standards Division in the region of the certificate holding district office may authorize a deviation for the director of operations, chief pilot, and the director of maintenance.

[Doc. No. 16097, 43 FR 46783, Oct. 10, 1978, as amended by Amdt. 135-18, 47 FR 33396, Aug. 2, 1982; Amdt. 133-20, 51 FR 40709, Nov. 7, 1986]

§ 135.41 **Carriage of narcotic drugs, marihuana, and depressant or stimulant drugs or substances.**

If the holder of a certificate issued under this part allows any aircraft owned or leased by that holder to be engaged in any operation that the certificate holder knows to be in violation of § 91.12(a) of this chapter, that operation is a basis for suspending or revoking the certificate.

§ 135.43 **Crewmember certificate: International operations: Application and issue.**

(a) This section provides for the issuance of a crewmember certificate to United States citizens who are employed by certificate holders as crewmembers on United States registered aircraft engaged in international air commerce. The purpose of the certificate is to facilitate the entry and clearance of those crewmembers into ICAO contracting states. They are issued under Annex 9, as amended, to the Convention on International Civil Aviation.

(b) An application for a crewmember certificate is made on FAA Form 8060-6, "Application for Crewmember Certificate," to the FAA Flight Standards District Office charged with the overall inspection of the certificate holder by whom the applicant is employed. The certificate is issued on FAA Form 8060-42, "Crewmember Certificate."

(c) The holder of a certificate issued under this section, or the certificate holder by whom the holder is employed, shall surrender the certificate for cancellation at the nearest FAA Flight Standards District Office or submit it for cancellation to the Airmen Certification Branch, AAC-260, P.O. Box 25082, Oklahoma City, Oklahoma 73125, at the termination of the holder's employment with that certificate holder.

Subpart B—Flight Operations

§ 135.61 **General.**

This subpart prescribes rules, in addition to those in Part 91 of this chapter, that apply to operations under this part.

§ 135.63 **Recordkeeping requirements.**

(a) Each certificate holder shall keep at its principal business office or at other places approved by the Administrator, and shall make available for inspection by the Administrator the following—

(1) The certificate holder's operating certificate;

(2) The certificate holder's operations specifications;

(3) A current list of the aircraft used or available for use in operations under this part and the operations for which each is equipped; and

(4) An individual record of each pilot used in operations under this part, including the following information:

(i) The full name of the pilot.

(ii) The pilot certificate (by type and number) and ratings that the pilot holds.

(iii) The pilot's aeronautical experience in sufficient detail to determine the pilot's qualifications to pilot aircraft in operations under this part.

(iv) The pilot's current duties and the date of the pilot's assignment to those duties.

(v) The effective date and class of the medical certificate that the pilot holds.

(vi) The date and result of each of the initial and recurrent competency tests and proficiency and route checks required by this part and the type of aircraft flown during that test or check.

(vii) The pilot's flight time in sufficient detail to determine compliance with the flight time limitations of this part.

(viii) The pilot's check pilot authorization, if any.

(ix) Any action taken concerning the pilot's release from employment for physical or professional disqualification.

(x) The date of the completion of the initial phase and each recurrent phase of the training required by this part.

(b) Each certificate holder shall keep each record required by paragraph (a)(3) of this section for at least 6 months, and each record required by paragraph (a)(4) of this section for at least 12 months, after it is made.

(c) For multiengine aircraft, each certificate holder is responsible for the preparation and accuracy of a load manifest in duplicate containing information concerning the loading of the aircraft. The manifest must be prepared before each takeoff and must include:

(1) The number of passengers;

(2) The total weight of the loaded aircraft;

(3) The maximum allowable takeoff weight for that flight;

(4) The center of gravity limits;

(5) The center of gravity of the loaded aircraft, except that the actual center of gravity need not be computed if the aircraft is loaded according to a loading schedule or other approved method that ensures that the center of gravity of the loaded aircraft is within approved limits. In those cases, an entry shall be made on the manifest indicating that the center of gravity is within limits according to a loading schedule or other approved method;

(6) The registration number of the aircraft or flight number;

(7) The origin and destination; and

(8) Identification of crew members and their crew position assignments.

(d) The pilot in command of an aircraft for which a load manifest must be prepared shall carry a copy of the completed load manifest in the aircraft to its destination. The certificate holder shall keep copies of completed load manifests for at least 30 days at its principal operations base, or at another location used by it and approved by the Administrator.

§ 135.65 Reporting mechanical irregularities.

(a) Each certificate holder shall provide an aircraft maintenance log to be carried on board each aircraft for recording or deferring mechanical irregularities and their correction.

(b) The pilot in command shall enter or have entered in the aircraft maintenance log each mechanical irregularity that comes to the pilot's attention during flight time. Before each flight, the pilot in command shall, if the pilot does not already know, determine the status of each irregularity entered in the maintenance log at the end of the preceding flight.

(c) Each person who takes corrective action or defers action concerning a reported or observed failure or malfunction of an airframe, powerplant, propeller, rotor, or applicance, shall record the action taken in the aircraft maintenance log under the applicable maintenance requirements of this chapter.

(d) Each certificate holder shall establish a procedure for keeping copies of the aircraft maintenance log required by this section in the aircraft for access by appropriate personnel and shall include that procedure in the manual required by § 135.21.

§ 135.67 Reporting potentially hazardous meteorological conditions and irregularities of communications or navigation facilities.

Whenever a pilot encounters a potentially hazardous meteorological condition or an irregularity in a ground communications or navigational facility in flight, the knowledge of which the pilot considers essential to the safety of other flights, the pilot shall notify an appropriate ground radio station as soon as practicable.

[Doc. No. 16097, 43 FR 46783, Oct. 1, 1978, as amended at 44 FR 26737, May 7, 1979]

§ 135.69 Restriction or suspension of operations: Continuation of flight in an emergency.

(a) During operations under this part, if a certificate holder or pilot in command knows of conditions, including airport and runway conditions, that are a hazard to safe operations, the certificate holder or pilot in command, as the case may be, shall restrict or suspend operations as necessary until those conditions are corrected.

(b) No pilot in command may allow a flight to continue toward any airport of intended landing under the conditions set forth in paragraph (a) of this section, unless, in the opinion of the pilot in command, the conditions that are a hazard to safe operations may reasonably be expected to be corrected by the estimated time of arrival or, unless there is no safer procedure. In the latter event, the continuation toward that airport is an emergency situation under § 135.19.

§ 135.71 Airworthiness check.

The pilot in command may not begin a flight unless the pilot determines that the airworthiness inspections required by § 91.169 of this chapter, or § 135.419, whichever is applicable, have been made.

§ 135.73 Inspections and tests.

Each certificate holder and each person employed by the certificate holder shall allow the Administrator, at any time or place, to make inspections or tests (including en route inspections) to determine the holder's compliance with the Federal Aviation Act of 1958, applicable regulations, and the certificate holder's operating certificate, and operations specifications.

§ 135.75 Inspectors credentials: admission to pilots' compartment: Forward observer's seat.

(a) Whenever, in performing the duties of conducting an inspection, an FAA inspector presents an Aviation Safety Inspector credential, FAA Form 110A, to the pilot in command of an aircraft operated by the certificate holder, the inspector must be given free and uninterrupted access to the pilot compartment of that aircraft. However, this paragraph does not limit the emergency authority of the pilot in command to exclude any person from the pilot compartment in the interest of safety.

(b) A forward observer's seat on the flight deck, or forward passenger seat with headset or speaker must be provided for use by the Administrator while conducting en route inspections. The suitability of the location of the seat and the headset or speaker for use in conducting en route inspections is determined by the Administrator.

§ 135.77 Responsibility for operational control.

Each certificate holder is responsible for operational control and shall list, in the manual required by § 135.21, the name and title of each person authorized by it to exercise operational control.

§ 135.79 Flight locating requirements.

(a) Each certificate holder must have procedures established for locating each flight, for which an FAA flight plan is not filed, that—

(1) Provide the certificate holder with at least the information required to be included in a VFR flight plan;

(2) Provide for timely notification of an FAA facility or search and rescue facility, if an aircraft is overdue or missing; and

(3) Provide the certificate holder with the location, date, and estimated time for reestablishing radio or telephone communications, if the flight

will operate in an area where communications cannot be maintained.

(b) Flight locating information shall be retained at the certificate holder's principal place of business, or at other places designated by the certificate holder in the flight locating procedures, until the completion of the flight.

(c) Each certificate holder shall furnish the representative of the Administrator assigned to it with a copy of its flight locating procedures and any changes or additions, unless those procedures are included in a manual required under this part.

§ 135.81 Informing personnel of operational information and appropriate changes.

Each certificate holder shall inform each person in its employment of the operations specifications that apply to that person's duties and responsibilities and shall make available to each pilot in the certificate holder's employ the following materials in current form:

(a) Airman's Information Manual (Alaska Supplement in Alaska and Pacific Chart Supplement in Pacific-Asia Regions) or a commercial publication that contains the same information.

(b) This part and Part 91 of this chapter.

(c) Aircraft Equipment Manuals, and Aircraft Flight Manual or equivalent.

(d) For foreign operations, the International Flight Information Manual or a commercial publication that contains the same information concerning the pertinent operational and entry requirements of the foreign country or countries involved.

§ 135.83 Operating information required.

(a) The operator of an aircraft must provide the following materials, in current and appropriate form, accessible to the pilot at the pilot station, and the pilot shall use them:

(1) A cockpit checklist.

(2) For multiengine aircraft or for aircraft with retractable landing gear, an emergency cockpit checklist containing the procedures required by paragraph (c) of this section, as appropriate.

(3) Pertinent aeronautical charts.

(4) For IFR operations, each pertinent navigational en route, terminal area, and approach and letdown chart.

(5) For multiengine aircraft, one-engine-inoperative climb performance data and if the aircraft is approved for use in IFR or over-the-top operations, that data must be sufficient to enable the pilot to determine compliance with § 135.181(a)(2).

(b) Each cockpit checklist required by paragraph (a)(1) of this section must contain the following procedures:

(1) Before starting engines;

(2) Before takeoff;

(3) Cruise;

(4) Before landing;

(5) After landing;

(6) Stopping engines.

(c) Each emergency cockpit checklist required by paragraph (a)(2) of this section must contain the following procedures, as appropriate:

(1) Emergency operation of fuel, hydraulic, electrical, and mechanical systems.

(2) Emergency operation of instruments and controls.

(3) Engine inoperative procedures.

(4) Any other emergency procedures necessary for safety.

§ 135.85 Carriage of persons without compliance with the passenger-carrying provisions of this part.

The following persons may be carried aboard an aircraft without complying with the passenger-carrying requirements of this part:

(a) A crewmember or other employee of the certificate holder.

(b) A person necessary for the safe handling of animals on the aircraft.

(c) A person necessary for the safe handling of hazardous materials (as defined in Subchapter C of Title 49 CFR).

(d) A person performing duty as a security or honor guard accompanying a shipment made by or under the authority of the U.S. Government.

(e) A military courier or a military route supervisor carried by a military cargo contract air carrier or commercial operator in operations under a military cargo contract, if that carriage is specifically authorized by the appropriate military service.

(f) An authorized representative of the Administrator conducting an en route inspection.

(g) A person, authorized by the Administrator, who is performing a duty connected with a cargo operation of the certificate holder.

§ 135.87 Carriage of cargo including carry-on baggage.

No person may carry cargo, including carry-on baggage, in or on any aircraft unless—

(a) It is carried in an approved cargo rack, bin, or compartment installed in or on the aircraft;

(b) It is secured by an approved means; or

(c) It is carried in accordance with each of the following:

(1) For cargo, it is properly secured by a safety belt or other tie-down having enough strength to eliminate the possibility of shifting under all normally anticipated flight and ground conditions, or for carry-on baggage, it is restrained so as to prevent its movement during air turbulence.

(2) It is packaged or covered to avoid possible injury to occupants.

(3) It does not impose any load on seats or on the floor structure that exceeds the load limitation for those components.

(4) It is not located in a position that obstructs the access to, or use of, any required emergency or regular exit, or the use of the aisle between the crew and the passenger compartment, or located in a position that obscures any passenger's view of the "seat belt" sign, "no smoking" sign, or any required exit sign, unless an auxiliary sign or other approved means for proper notification of the passengers is provided.

(5) It is not carried directly above seated occupants.

(6) It is stowed in compliance with this section for takeoff and landing.

(7) For cargo only operations, paragraph (c)(4) of this section does not apply if the cargo is loaded so that at least one emergency or regular exit is available to provide all occupants of the aircraft a means of unobstructed

exit from the aircraft if an emergency occurs.

(d) Each passenger seat under which baggage is stowed shall be fitted with a means to prevent articles of baggage stowed under it from sliding under crash impacts severe enough to induce the ultimate inertia forces specified in the emergency landing condition regulations under which the aircraft was type certificated.

(e) When cargo is carried in cargo compartments that are designed to require the physical entry of a crewmember to extinguish any fire that may occur during flight, the cargo must be loaded so as to allow a crewmember to effectively reach all parts of the compartment with the contents of a hand fire extinguisher.

§ 135.89 Pilot requirements: Use of oxygen.

(a) *Unpressurized aircraft.* Each pilot of an unpressurized aircraft shall use oxygen continuously when flying—

(1) At altitudes above 10,000 feet through 12,000 feet MSL for that part of the flight at those altitudes that is of more than 30 minutes duration; and

(2) Above 12,000 feet MSL.

(b) *Pressurized aircraft.* (1) Whenever a pressurized aircraft is operated with the cabin pressure altitude more than 10,000 feet MSL, each pilot shall comply with paragraph (a) of this section.

(2) Whenever a pressurized aircraft is operated at altitudes above 25,000 feet through 35,000 feet MSL, unless each pilot has an approved quick-donning type oxygen mask—

(i) At least one pilot at the controls shall wear, secured and sealed, an oxygen mask that either supplies oxygen at all times or automatically supplies oxygen whenever the cabin pressure altitude exceeds 12,000 feet MSL; and

(ii) During that flight, each other pilot on flight deck duty shall have an oxygen mask, connected to an oxygen supply, located so as to allow immediate placing of the mask on the pilot's face sealed and secured for use.

(3) Whenever a pressurized aircraft is operated at altitudes above 35,000 feet MSL, at least one pilot at the con-

trols shall wear, secured and sealed, an oxygen mask required by paragraph (b)(2)(i) of this section.

(4) If one pilot leaves a pilot duty station of an aircraft when operating at altitudes above 25,000 feet MSL, the remaining pilot at the controls shall put on and use an approved oxygen mask until the other pilot returns to the pilot duty station of the aircraft.

§ 135.91 Oxygen for medical use by passengers.

(a) Except as provided in paragraphs (d) and (e) of this section, no certificate holder may allow the carriage or operation of equipment for the storage, generation or dispensing of medical oxygen unless the unit to be carried is constructed so that all valves, fittings, and gauges are protected from damage during that carriage or operation and unless the following conditions are met—

(1) The equipment must be—

(i) Of an approved type or in conformity with the manufacturing, packaging, marking, labeling, and maintenance requirements of Title 49 CFR Parts 171, 172, and 173, except § 173.24(a)(1);

(ii) When owned by the certificate holder, maintained under the certificate holder's approved maintenance program;

(iii) Free of flammable contaminants on all exterior surfaces; and

(iv) Appropriately secured.

(2) When the oxygen is stored in the form of a liquid, the equipment must have been under the certificate holder's approved maintenance program since its purchase new or since the storage container was last purged.

(3) When the oxygen is stored in the form of a compressed gas as defined in Title 49 CFR 173.300(a)—

(i) When owned by the certificate holder, it must be maintained under its approved maintenance program; and

(ii) The pressure in any oxygen cylinder must not exceed the rated cylinder pressure.

(4) The pilot in command must be advised when the equipment is on board, and when it is intended to be used.

(5) The equipment must be stowed, and each person using the equipment must be seated, so as not to restrict access to or use of any required emergency or regular exit, or of the aisle in the passenger compartment.

(b) No person may smoke and no certificate holder may allow any person to smoke within 10 feet of oxygen storage and dispensing equipment carried under paragraph (a) of this section.

(c) No certificate holder may allow any person other than a person trained in the use of medical oxygen equipment to connect or disconnect oxygen bottles or any other ancillary component while any passenger is aboard the aircraft.

(d) Paragraph (a)(1)(i) of this section does not apply when that equipment is furnished by a professional or medical emergency service for use on board an aircraft in a medical emergency when no other practical means of transportation (including any other properly equipped certificate holder) is reasonably available and the person carried under the medical emergency is accompanied by a person trained in the use of medical oxygen.

(e) Each certificate holder who, under the authority of paragraph (d) of this section, deviates from paragraph (a)(1)(i) of this section under a medical emergency shall, within 10 days, excluding Saturdays, Sundays, and Federal holidays, after the deviation, send to the FAA Flight Standards District Office charged with the overall inspection of the certificate holder a complete report of the operation involved, including a description of the deviation and the reasons for it.

§ 135.93 Autopilot: Minimum altitudes for use.

(a) Except as provided in paragraphs (b), (c), and (d) of this section, no person may use an autopilot at an altitude above the terrain which is less than 500 feet or less than twice the maximum altitude loss specified in the approved Aircraft Flight Manual or equivalent for a malfunction of the autopilot, whichever is higher.

(b) When using an instrument approach facility other than ILS, no person may use an autopilot at an altitude above the terrain that is less than 50 feet below the approved minimum descent altitude for that procedure, or less than twice the maximum loss specified in the approved Airplane Flight Manual or equivalent for a malfunction of the autopilot under approach conditions, whichever is higher.

(c) For ILS approaches, when reported weather conditions are less than the basic weather conditions in §91.105 of this chapter, no person may use an autopilot with an approach coupler at an altitude above the terrain that is less than 50 feet above the terrain, or the maximum altitude loss specified in the approved Airplane Flight Manual or equivalent for the malfunction of the autopilot with approach coupler, whichever is higher.

(d) Without regard to paragraph (a), (b), or (c) of this section, the Administrator may issue operations specifications to allow the use, to touchdown, of an approved flight control guidance system with automatic capability, if—

(1) The system does not contain any altitude loss (above zero) specified in the approved Aircraft Flight Manual or equivalent for malfunction of the autopilot with approach coupler; and

(2) The Administrator finds that the use of the system to touchdown will not otherwise adversely affect the safety standards of this section.

(e) This section does not apply to operations conducted in rotorcraft.

§135.95 Airmen: Limitations on use of services.

No certificate holder may use the services of any person as an airman unless the person performing those services—

(a) Holds an appropriate and current airman certificate; and

(b) Is qualified, under this chapter, for the operation for which the person is to be used.

§135.97 Aircraft and facilities for recent flight experience.

Each certificate holder shall provide aircraft and facilities to enable each of its pilots to maintain and demonstrate the pilot's ability to conduct all operations for which the pilot is authorized.

§135.99 Composition of flight crew.

(a) No certificate holder may operate an aircraft with less than the minimum flight crew specified in the aircraft operating limitations or the Aircraft Flight Manual for that aircraft and required by this part for the kind of operation being conducted.

(b) No certificate holder may operate an aircraft without a second in command if that aircraft has a passenger seating configuration, excluding any pilot seat, of ten seats or more.

§135.100 Flight crewmember duties.

(a) No certificate holder shall require, nor may any flight crewmember perform, any duties during a critical phase of flight except those duties required for the safe operation of the aircraft. Duties such as company required calls made for such nonsafety related purposes as ordering galley supplies and confirming passenger connections, announcements made to passengers promoting the air carrier or pointing out sights of interest, and filling out company payroll and related records are not required for the safe operation of the aircraft.

(b) No flight crewmember may engage in, nor may any pilot in command permit, any activity during a critical phase of flight which could distract any flight crewmember from the performance of his or her duties or which could interfere in any way with the proper conduct of those duties. Activities such as eating meals, engaging in nonessential conversations within the cockpit and nonessential communications between the cabin and cockpit crews, and reading publications not related to the proper conduct of the flight are not required for the safe operation of the aircraft.

(c) For the purposes of this section, critical phases of flight includes all ground operations involving taxi, takeoff and landing, and all other flight operations conducted below 10,000 feet, except cruise flight.

NOTE: Taxi is defined as "movement of an airplane under its own power on the surface of an airport."

[Amdt. 135–11, 46 FR 5502, Jan. 19, 1981]

§ 135.101 Second in command required in IFR conditions.

Except as provided in §§ 135.103 and 135.105, no person may operate an aircraft carrying passengers in IFR conditions, unless there is a second in command in the aircraft.

§ 135.103 Exception to second in command requirement: IFR operations.

The pilot in command of an aircraft carrying passengers may conduct IFR operations without a second in command under the following conditions:

(a) A takeoff may be conducted under IFR conditions if the weather reports or forecasts, or any combination of them, indicate that the weather along the planned route of flight allows flight under VFR within 15 minutes flying time, at normal cruise speed, from the takeoff airport.

(b) En route IFR may be conducted if unforecast weather conditions below the VFR minimums of this chapter are encountered on a flight that was planned to be conducted under VFR.

(c) An IFR approach may be conducted if, upon arrival at the destination airport, unforecast weather conditions do not allow an approach to be completed under VFR.

(d) When IFR operations are conducted under this section:

(1) The aircraft must be properly equipped for IFR operations under this part.

(2) The pilot must be authorized to conduct IFR operations under this part.

(3) The flight must be conducted in accordance with an ATC IFR clearance.

IFR operations without a second in command may not be conducted under this section in an aircraft requiring a second in command under § 135.99.

§ 135.105 Exception to second in command requirement: Approval for use of autopilot system.

(a) Except as provided in §§ 135.99 and 135.111, unless two pilots are required by this chapter for operations under VFR, a person may operate an aircraft without a second in command, if it is equipped with an operative approved autopilot system and the use of that system is authorized by appropriate operations specifications. No certificate holder may use any person, nor may any person serve, as a pilot in command under this section of an aircraft operated by a Commuter Air Carrier (as defined in § 298.2 of this title) in passenger-carrying operations unless that person has at least 100 hours pilot in command flight time in the make and model of aircraft to be flown and has met all other applicable requirements of this part.

(b) The certificate holder may apply for an amendment of its operations specifications to authorize the use of an autopilot system in place of a second in command.

(c) The Administrator issues an amendment to the operations specifications authorizing the use of an autopilot system, in place of a second in command, if—

(1) The autopilot is capable of operating the aircraft controls to maintain flight and maneuver it about the three axes; and

(2) The certificate holder shows, to the satisfaction of the Administrator, that operations using the autopilot system can be conducted safely and in compliance with this part.

The amendment contains any conditions or limitations on the use of the autopilot system that the Administrator determines are needed in the interest of safety.

[Doc. No. 16097, 43 FR 46783, Oct. 10, 1978, as amended by Amdt. 135–3, 45 FR 7542, Feb. 4, 1980]

§ 135.107 Flight attendant crewmember requirement.

No certificate holder may operate an aircraft that has a passenger seating configuration, excluding any pilot seat, of more than 19 unless there is a flight attendant crewmember on board the aircraft.

§ 135.109 Pilot in command or second in command: Designation required.

(a) Each certificate holder shall designate a—

(1) Pilot in command for each flight; and

(2) Second in command for each flight requiring two pilots.

(b) The pilot in command, as designated by the certificate holder, shall remain the pilot in command at all times during that flight.

§ 135.111 Second in command required in Category II operations.

No person may operate an aircraft in a Category II operation unless there is a second in command of the aircraft.

§ 135.113 Passenger occupancy of pilot seat.

No certificate holder may operate an aircraft type certificated after October 15, 1971, that has a passenger seating configuration, excluding any pilot seat, of more than eight seats if any person other than the pilot in command, a second in command, a company check airman, or an authorized representative of the Administrator, the National Transportation Safety Board, or the United States Postal Service occupies a pilot seat.

§ 135.115 Manipulation of controls.

No pilot in command may allow any person to manipulate the flight controls of an aircraft during flight conducted under this part, nor may any person manipulate the controls during such flight unless that person is—

(a) A pilot employed by the certificate holder and qualified in the aircraft; or

(b) An authorized safety representative of the Administrator who has the permission of the pilot in command, is qualified in the aircraft, and is checking flight operations.

§ 135.117 Briefing of passengers before flight.

(a) Before each takeoff each pilot in command of an aircraft carrying passengers shall ensure that all passengers have been orally briefed on—

(1) Smoking. Each passenger shall be briefed on when, where, and under what conditions smoking is prohibited (including, but not limited to, the pertinent requirements of Part 252 of this title). This briefing shall include a statement that the Federal Aviation Regulations require passenger compliance with the lighted passenger information signs (if such signs are required) and posted placards. The briefing shall also include a statement (if the aircraft is equipped with a lavatory) that Federal law prohibits tampering with, disabling, or destroying any smoke detector installed in an aircraft lavatory.

(2) Use of seat belts;

(3) The placement of seat backs in an upright position before takeoff and landing;

(4) Location and means for opening the passenger entry door and emergency exits;

(5) Location of survival equipment;

(6) If the flight involves extended overwater operation, ditching procedures and the use of required flotation equipment;

(7) If the flight involves operations above 12,000 feet MSL, the normal and emergency use of oxygen; and

(8) Location and operation of fire extinguishers.

(b) Before each takeoff the pilot in command shall ensure that each person who may need the assistance of another person to move expeditiously to an exit if an emergency occurs and that person's attendant, if any, has received a briefing as to the procedures to be followed if an evacuation occurs. This paragraph does not apply to a person who has been given a briefing before a previous leg of a flight in the same aircraft.

(c) The oral briefing required by paragraph (a) of this section shall be given by the pilot in command or a crewmember.

(d) Notwithstanding the provisions of paragraph (c) of this section, for aircraft certificated to carry 19 passengers or less, the oral briefing required by paragraph (a) of this section shall be given by the pilot in command, a crewmember, or other qualified person designated by the certificate holder and approved by the Administrator.

(e) The oral briefing required by paragraph (a) shall be supplemented by printed cards which must be carried in the aircraft in locations convenient for the use of each passenger. The cards must—

(1) Be appropriate for the aircraft on which they are to be used;

(2) Contain a diagram of, and method of operating, the emergency exits; and

(3) Contain other instructions necessary for the use of emergency equipment on board the aircraft.

(f) The briefing required by paragraph (a) may be delivered by means of an approved recording playback device that is audible to each passenger under normal noise levels.

[Doc. No. 16097, 43 FR 46783, Oct. 10, 1978, as amended by Amdt. 135-9, 51 FR 40709, Nov. 7, 1986]

§ 135.119 Prohibition against carriage of weapons.

No person may, while on board an aircraft being operated by a certificate holder, carry on or about that person a deadly or dangerous weapon, either concealed or unconcealed. This section does not apply to—

(a) Officials or employees of a municipality or a State, or of the United States, who are authorized to carry arms; or

(b) Crewmembers and other persons authorized by the certificate holder to carry arms.

§ 135.121 Alcoholic beverages.

(a) No person may drink any alcoholic beverage aboard an aircraft unless the certificate holder operating the aircraft has served that beverage.

(b) No certificate holder may serve any alcoholic beverage to any person aboard its aircraft if that person appears to be intoxicated.

(c) No certificate holder may allow any person to board any of its aircraft if that person appears to be intoxicated.

§ 135.123 Emergency and emergency evacuation duties.

(a) Each certificate holder shall assign to each required crewmember for each type of aircraft as appropriate, the necessary functions to be performed in an emergency or in a situation requiring emergency evacuation. The certificate holder shall ensure that those functions can be practicably accomplished, and will meet any reasonably anticipated emergency including incapacitation of individual crewmembers or their inability to reach the passenger cabin because of shifting cargo in combination cargo-passenger aircraft.

(b) The certificate holder shall describe in the manual required under § 135.21 the functions of each category of required crewmembers assigned under paragraph (a) of this section.

§ 135.125 Airplane security.

Certificate holders conducting operations under this part shall comply with the applicable security requirements in Part 108 of this chapter.

§ 135.127 Passenger information.

(a) The no smoking signs required by § 135.177(a)(3) of this part must be turned on:

(1) During flight time on flight segments which are scheduled in the current North American Edition of the Official Airline Guide to be 2 hours or less in duration, except those flight segments between a point in the United States and point in another country; or

(2) On flight segments other than those described in paragraph (a)(1) of this section, for each takeoff and landing, and at any other time considered necessary by the pilot in command.

(b) No person may smoke while a no smoking sign is lighted, except that the pilot in command may authorize smoking on the flight deck (if it is physically separated from the passenger cabin) except during takeoff and landing.

(c) No person may smoke in any aircraft lavatory.

(d) After December 31, 1988, no person may operate an aircraft with a lavatory equipped with a smoke detector unless there is in that lavatory a sign or placard which reads: "Federal law provides for a penalty of up to $2,000 for tampering with the smoke detector installed in this lavatory."

(e) The provisions of paragraph (a)(1) of this section shall cease to be effective on April 24, 1990.

Subpart C—Aircraft and Equipment

§ 135.141 Applicability.

This subpart prescribes aircraft and equipment requirements for operations under this part. The requirements of this subpart are in addition to the aircraft and equipment requirements of Part 91 of this chapter. However, this part does not require the duplication of any equipment required by this chapter.

§ 135.143 General requirements.

(a) No person may operate an aircraft under this part unless that aircraft and its equipment meet the applicable regulations of this chapter.

(b) Except as provided in § 135.179, no person may operate an aircraft under the part unless the required instruments and equipment in it have been approved and are in an operable condition.

(c) ATC transponder equipment installed within the time periods indicated below must meet the performance and environmental requirements of the following TSO's:

(1) *Through January 1, 1992:* (i) Any class of TSO-C74b or any class of TSO-C74c as appropriate , provided that the equipment was manufactured before January 1, 1990; or

(ii) The appropriate class of TSO-C112 (Mode S).

(2) *After January 1, 1992:* The appropriate class of TSO-C112 (Mode S). For purposes of paragraph (c)(2) of this section, "installation" does not include—

(i) Temporary installation of TSO-C74b or TSO-C74c substitute equipment, as appropriate, during maintenance of the permanent equipment;

(ii) Reinstallation of equipment after temporary removal for maintenance; or

(iii) For fleet operations, installation of equipment in a fleet aircraft after removal of the equipment for maintenance from another aircraft in the same operator's fleet.

§ 135.145 Aircraft proving tests.

(a) No certificate holder may operate a turbojet airplane, or an aircraft for which two pilots are required by this chapter for operations under VFR, if it has not previously proved that aircraft or an aircraft of the same make and similar design in any operation under this part unless, in addition to the aircraft certification tests, at least 25 hours of proving tests acceptable to the Administrator have been flown by that certificate holder including—

(1) Five hours of night time, if night flights are to be authorized;

(2) Five instrument approach procedures under simulated or actual instrument weather conditions, if IFR flights are to be authorized; and

(3) Entry into a representative number of en route airports as determined by the Administrator.

(b) No certificate holder may carry passengers in an aircraft during proving tests, except those needed to make the tests and those designated by the Administrator to observe the tests. However, pilot flight training may be conducted during the proving tests.

(c) For the purposes of paragraph (a) of this section an aircraft is not considered to be of similar design if an altenation includes—

(1) The installation of powerplants other than those of a type similar to those with which it is certificated; or

(2) Alterations to the aircraft or its components that materially affect flight characteristics.

(d) The Administrator may authorize deviations from this section if the Administrator finds that special circumstances make full compliance with this section unnecessary.

§ 135.147 Dual controls required.

No person may operate an aircraft in operations requiring two pilots unless it is equipped with functioning dual controls. However, if the aircraft type certification operating limitations do not require two pilots, a throwover control wheel may be used in place two control wheels.

§ 135.149 Equipment requirements: General.

No person may operate an aircraft unless it is equipped with—

(a) A sensitive altimeter that is adjustable for barometric pressure;

(b) Heating or deicing equipment for each carburetor or, for a pressure carburetor, an alternate air source;

(c) For turbojet airplanes, in addition to two gyroscopic bank-and-pitch indicators (artificial horizons) for use at the pilot stations, a third indicator that—

(1) Is powered from a source independent of the aircraft's electrical generating system;

(2) Continues reliable operation for at least 30 minutes after total failure of the aircraft's electrical generating system;

(3) Operates independently of any other attitude indicating system;

(4) Is operative without selection after total failure of the aircraft's electrical generating system;

(5) Is located on the instrument panel in a position that will make it plainly visible to, and useable by, any pilot at the pilot's station; and

(6) Is appropriately lighted during all phases of operation;

(d) For aircraft having a passenger seating configuration, excluding any pilot seat, of more than 19, a public address system and a crewmember interphone system approved under § 21.305 of this chapter, which meet §§ 121.318 and 121.319, respectively, of this chapter; and

(e) For turbine powered aircraft, any other equipment as the Administrator may require.

§ 135.151 Cockpit voice recorders.

(a) After October 11, 1991, no person may operate a multiengine, turbine-powered airplane or rotorcraft having a passenger seating configuration of six or more and for which two pilots are required by certification or operating rules unless it is equipped with an approved cockpit voice recorder that:

(1) Is installed in compliance with § 23.1457(a) (1) and (2), (b), (c), (d), (e), (f), and (g); § 25.1457(a) (1) and (2), (b), (c), (d), (e), (f), and (g); § 27.1457(a) (1) and (2), (b), (c), (d), (e), (f), and (g) or § 29.1457(a) (1) and 2, (b), (c), (d), (e), (f), and (g) of this chapter, as applicable; and

(2) Is operated continuously from the use of the check list before the flight to completion of the final check list at the end of the flight.

(b) After October 11, 1991, no person may operate a multiengine, turbine-powered airplane or rotorcraft having a passenger seating configuration of 20 or more seats unless it is equipped with an approved cockpit recorder that—

(1) Is installed in compliance with § 23.1457, § 25.1457, § 27.1457 or § 29.1457 of this chapter, as applicable; and

(2) Is operated continuously from the use of the check list before the flight to completion of the final check list at the end of the flight.

(c) In the event of an accident, or occurrence requiring immediate notification of the National Transportation Safety Board which results in termination of the flight, the certificate holder shall keep the recorded information for at least 60 days or, if requested by the Administrator or the Board, for a longer period. Information obtained from the record may be used to assist in determining the cause of accidents or occurrences in connection with investigations. The Administrator does not use the record in any civil penalty or certificate action.

(d) For those aircraft equipped to record the uninterrupted audio signals received by a boom or mask microphone the flight crewmembers are required to use the boom microphone below 18,000 feet mean sea level. No person may operate a large turbine engine powered airplane manufactured after October 11, 1991, or on which a cockpit voice recorder has been installed after October 11, 1991, unless it is equipped to record the uninterrupted audio signal received by a boom or mask microphone in accordance with § 25.1457(c)(5) of this chapter.

(e) In complying with this section, an approved cockpit voice recorder having an erasure feature may be used, so that during the operation of the recorder, information:

(1) Recorded in accordance with paragraph (a) of this section and recorded more than 15 minutes earlier; or

(2) Recorded in accordance with paragraph (b) of this section and recorded more than 30 minutes earlier; may be erased or otherwise obliterated.

§ 135.152 Flight recorders.

(a) No person may operate a multiengine turbine-powered airplane or rotorcraft having a passenger seating configuration, excluding any pilot seat, of 10 to 19 seats, that is brought onto the U.S. register after October 11, 1991, unless it is equipped with one or more approved flight recorders that utilize a digital method of recording and storing data, and a method of readily retrieving that data from the storage medium. The parameters specified in Appendix B or C, as applicable, of this part must be recorded within the range accuracy, resolution, and recording intervals as specified. The recorder shall retain no less than 8 hours of aircraft operation.

(b) After October 11, 1991, no person may operate a multiengine, turbine-powered airplane having a passenger seating configuration of 20 to 30 seats or a multiengine, turbine-powered rotorcraft having a passenger seating configuration of 20 or more seats unless it is equipped with one or more approved flight recorders that utilize a digital method of recording and storing data, and a method of readily retrieving that data from the storage medium. The parameters in Appendix D or E of this part, as applicable, that are set forth below, must be recorded within the ranges, accuracies, resolutions, and sampling intervals as specified.

(1) Except as provided in paragraph (b)(3) of this section for aircraft type certificated before October 1, 1969, the following parameters must be recorded:

(i)   Time;
(i)   Altitude;
(iii) Airspeed;
(iv)   Vertical acceleration;
(v)   Heading;
(vi)   Time of each radio transmission to or from air traffic control;
(vii) Pitch attitude;
(viii) Roll attitude;
(ix)   Longitudinal acceleration;
(x)   Control column or pitch control surface position; and
(xi)   Thrust of each engine.

(2) Except as provided in paragraph (b)(3) of this section for aircraft type certificated after September 30, 1969, the following parameters must be recorded:

(i)   Time;
(ii)   Altitude;
(iii) Airspeed;
(iv)   Vertical acceleration;
(v)   Heading;
(vi)   Time of each radio transmission either to or from air traffic control;
(vii) Pitch attitude;

(viii) Roll attitude;
(ix)   Longitudinal acceleration;
(x)   Pitch trim position;
(xi)   Control column or pitch control surface position; and
(xii) Control wheel or lateral control surface position;
(xiii) Rudder pedal or yaw control surface position;
(xiv) Thrust of each engine;
(xv)   Position of each thrust reverser;
(xvi) Trailing edge flap or cockpit flap control position; and
(xvii) Leading edge flap or cockpit flap control position.

(3) For aircraft manufactured after October 11, 1991, all of the parameters listed in Appendix D or E of this part, as applicable, must be recorded.

(c) Whenever a flight recorder required by this section is installed, it must be operated continuously from the instant the airplane begins the takeoff roll or the rotorcraft begins the lift-off until the airplane has completed the landing roll or the rotorcraft has landed at its destination.

(d) Except as provided in paragraph (c) of this section, and except for recorded data erased as authorized in this paragraph, each certificate holder shall keep the recorded data prescribed in paragraph (a) of this section until the aircraft has been operating for at least 8 hours of the operating time specified in paragraph (c) of this section. In addition, each certificate holder shall keep the recorded data prescribed in paragraph (b) of this section for an airplane until the airplane has been operating for at least 25 hours, and for a rotorcraft until the rotorcraft has been operating for at least 10 hours, of the operating time specified in paragraph (c) of this section. A total of 1 hour of recorded data may be erased for the purpose of testing the flight recorder or the flight recorder system. Any erasure made in accordance with this paragraph must be of the oldest recorded data accumulated at the time of testing. Except as provided in paragraph (c) of this section, no record need be kept more than 60 days.

(e) In the event of an accident or occurrence that requires the immediate notification of the National Transportation Safety Board under 49 CFR Part 830 of its regulations and that results in termination of the flight, the certificate holder shall remove the recording media from the aircraft and keep the recorded data required by paragraphs (a) and (b) of this section for at least 60 days or for a longer period upon request of the Board or the Administrator.

(f) Each flight recorder required by this section must be installed in accordance with the requirements of §§ 23.1459, 25.1459, 27.1459 or 29.1459, as appropriate, of this chapter. The correlation required by paragraph (c) of §§ 23.1459, 25.1459, 27.1459, or 29.1459, as appropriate, of this chapter need be established only on one aircraft of a group of aircraft:

(1) That are of the same type;

(2) On which the flight recorder models and their installations are the same; and

(3) On which there are no differences in the type design with respect to the installation of the first pilot's instruments associated with the flight recorder. The most recent instrument calibration, including the recording medium from which this calibration is derived, and the recorder correlation must be retained by the certificate holder.

(g) Each flight recorder required by this section that records the data specified in paragraphs (a) and (b) this section must have an approved device to assist in locating that recorder under water.

§ 135.153 Ground proximity warning system.

No person may operate a turbojet airplane having a passenger seating configuration, excluding any pilot seat, of 10 seats or more, unless it is equipped with—

(a) A ground proximity warning system that meets § 37.201 of this chapter; or

(b) A system that conveys warnings of excessive closure rates with the terrain and any deviations below glide slope by visual and audible means. This system must—

(1) Be approved by the Director of Flight Operations; and

(2) Have a means of alerting the pilot when a malfunction occurs in the system.

(c) For the system required by this section,

the Airplane Flight Manual shall contain—

(1) Appropriate procedures for—

(i) The use of the equipment;

(ii) Proper flight crew action with respect to the equipment; and

(iii) Deactiviation for planned abnormal and emergency conditions; and

(2) An outline of all input sources that must be operating.

(d) No person may deactivate a system required by this section except under procedures in the Airplane Flight Manual.

(e) Whenever a system required by this section is deactivated, an entry shall be made in the airplane maintenance record that includes the date and time of deactivation.

(f) For a system required by paragraph (b) of this section, procedures acceptable to the FAA Flight Standards District Office charged with the overall inspection of the certificate holder shall be established by the certificate holder to ensure that the performance of the system can be appropriately monitored.

§ 135.155 Fire extinguishers: passenger-carrying aircraft.

No person may operate an aircraft carrying passengers unless it is equipped with hand fire extinguishers of an approved type for use in crew and passenger compartments as follows—

(a) The type and quantity of extinguishing agents must be suitable for the kinds of fires likely to occur.

(b) At least one hand fire extinguisher must be provided and conveniently located on the flight deck for use by the flight crew; and

(c) At least one hand fire extinguisher must be conveniently located in the passenger compartment of each aircraft having a passenger seating configuration, excluding any pilot seat, of at least 10 seats but less than 31 seats.

§ 135.157 Oxygen equipment requirements.

(a) *Unpressurized aircraft*. No person may operate an unpressurized aircraft at altitudes prescribed in this section unless it is equipped with enough oxygen dispensers and oxygen to supply the pilots under § 135.89(a) and to supply, when flying—

(1) At altitudes above 10,000 feet through 15,000 feet MSL, oxygen to at least 10 percent of the occupants of the aircraft, other than the pilots, for that part of the flight at those altitudes that is of more than 30 minutes duration; and

(2) Above 15,000 feet MSL, oxygen to each occupant of the aircraft other than the pilots.

(b) *Pressurized aircraft.* No person may operate a pressurized aircraft—

(1) At altitudes above 25,000 feet MSL, unless at least a 10-minute supply of supplemental oxygen is available for each occupant of the aircraft, other than the pilots, for use when a descent is necessary due to loss of cabin pressurization; and

(2) Unless it is equipped with enough oxygen dispensers and oxygen to comply with paragraph (a) of this section whenever the cabin pressure altitude exceeds 10,000 feet MSL and, if the cabin pressurization fails, to comply with § 135.89 (a) or to provide a 2-hour supply for each pilot, whichever is greater, and to supply when flying—

(i) At altitudes above 10,000 feet through 15,000 feet MSL, oxygen to at least 10 percent of the occupants of the aircraft, other than the pilots, for that part of the flight at those altitudes that is of more than 30 minutes duration; and

(ii) Above 15,000 feet MSL, oxygen to each occupant of the aircraft, other than the pilots, for one hour unless, at all times during flight above that altitude, the aircraft can safely descend to 15,000 feet MSL within four minutes, in which case only a 30-minute supply is required.

(c) The equipment required by this section must have a means—

(1) To enable the pilots to readily determine, in flight, the amount of oxygen available in each source of supply and whether the oxygen is being delivered to the dispensing units; or

(2) In the case of individual dispensing units, to enable each user to make

those determinations with respect to that person's oxygen supply and delivery; and

(3) To allow the pilots to use undiluted oxygen at their discretion at altitudes above 25,000 feet MSL.

§ 135.158 Pitot heat indication systems.

(a) Except as provided in paragraph (b) of this section, after April 12, 1981, no person may operate a transport category airplane equipped with a flight instrument pitot heating system unless the airplane is also equipped with an operable pitot heat indication system that complies with § 25.1326 of this chapter in effect on April 12, 1978.

(b) A certificate holder may obtain an extension of the April 12, 1981, compliance date specified in paragraph (a) of this section, but not beyond April 12, 1983, from the Director of Flight Operations if the certificate holder—

(1) Shows that due to circumstances beyond its control it cannot comply by the specified compliance date; and

(2) Submits by the specified compliance date a schedule for compliance, acceptable to the Director, indicating that compliance will be achieved at the earliest practicable date.

[Amdt. 135–17, 46 FR 48306, Aug. 31, 1981]

§ 135.159 Equipment requirements: Carrying passengers under VFR at night or under VFR over-the-top conditions.

No person may operate an aircraft carrying passengers under VFR at night or under VFR over-the-top, unless it is equipped with—

(a) A gyroscopic rate-of-turn indicator except on the following aircraft:

(1) Helicopters with a third attitude instrument system usable through flight attitudes of ±80 degrees of pitch and ±120 degrees of roll and installed in accordance with § 29.1303(g) of this chapter.

(2) Helicopters with a maximum certificated takeoff weight of 6,000 pounds or less.

(b) A slip skid indicator.

(c) A gyroscopic bank-and-pitch indicator.

(d) A gyroscopic direction indicator.

(e) A generator or generators able to supply all probable combinations of continuous in-flight electrical loads for required equipment and for recharging the battery.

(f) For night flights—

(1) An anticollision light system;

(2) Instrument lights to make all instruments, switches, and gauges easily readable, the direct rays of which are shielded from the pilots' eyes; and

(3) A flashlight having at least two size "D" cells or equivalent.

(g) For the purpose of paragraph (e) of this section, a continuous in-flight electrical load includes one that draws current continuously during flight, such as radio equipment and electrically driven instruments and lights, but does not include occasional intermittent loads.

(h) Notwithstanding provisions of paragraphs (b), (c), and (d), helicopters having a maximum certificated takeoff weight of 6,000 pounds or less may be operated until January 6, 1988, under visual flight rules at night without a slip skid indicator, a gyroscopic bank-and-pitch indicator, or a gyroscopic direction indicator.

[Doc. No. 24550, Amdt. No. 135–20, 51 FR 40709, Nov. 7, 1986]

§135.161 Radio and navigational equipment: Carrying passengers under VFR at night or under VFR over-the-top.

(a) No person may operate an aircraft carrying passengers under VFR at night, or under VFR over-the-top, unless it has two-way radio communications equipment able, at least in flight, to transmit to, and receive from, ground facilities 25 miles away.

(b) No person may operate an aircraft carrying passengers under VFR over-the-top unless it has radio navigational equipment able to receive radio signals from the ground facilities to be used.

(c) No person may operate an airplane carrying passengers under VFR at night unless it has radio navigational equipment able to receive radio signals from the ground facilities to be used.

§135.163 Equipment requirements: Aircraft carrying passengers under IFR.

No person may operate an aircraft under IFR, carrying passengers, unless it has—

(a) A vertical speed indicator;

(b) A free-air temperature indicator;

(c) A heated pitot tube for each airspeed indicator;

(d) A power failure warning device or vacuum indicator to show the power available for gyroscopic instruments from each power source;

(e) An alternate source of static pressure for the altimeter and the airspeed and vertical speed indicators;

(f) For a single-engine aircraft, a generator or generators able to supply all probable combinations of continuous inflight electrical loads for required equipment and for recharging the battery;

(g) For multiengine aircraft, at least two generators each of which is on a separate engine, of which any combination of one-half of the total number are rated sufficiently to supply the electrical loads of all required instruments and equipment necessary for safe emergency operation of the aircraft except that for multiengine helicopters, the two required generators may be mounted on the main rotor drive train; and

(h) Two independent sources of energy (with means of selecting either), of which at least one is an engine-driven pump or generator, each of which is able to drive all gyroscopic instruments and installed so that failure of one instrument or source does not interfere with the energy supply to the remaining instruments or the other energy source, unless, for single-engine aircraft, the rate-of-turn indicator has a source of energy separate from the bank and pitch and direction indicators. For the purpose of this paragraph, for multiengine aircraft, each engine-driven source of energy must be on a different engine.

(i) For the purpose of paragraph (f) of this section, a continuous inflight electrical load includes one that draws current continuously during flight, such as radio equipment, electrically driven instruments, and lights, but does not include occasional intermittent loads.

§ 135.165 Radio and navigational equipment: Extended overwater or IFR operations.

(a) No person may operate a turbojet airplane having a passenger seating configuration, excluding any pilot seat, of 10 seats or more, or a multiengine airplane carrying passengers as a "Commuter Air Carrier" as defined in Part 298 of this title, under IFR or in extended overwater operations unless it has at least the following radio communication and navigational equipment appropriate to the facilities to be used which are capable of transmitting to, and receiving from, at any place on the route to be flown, at least one ground facility:

(1) Two transmitters, (2) two microphones, (3) two headsets or one headset and one speaker, (4) a marker beacon receiver, (5) two independent receivers for navigation, and (6) two independent receivers for communications.

(b) No person may operate an aircraft other than that specified in paragraph (a) of this section, under IFR or in extended overwater operations unless it has at least the following radio communication and navigational equipment appropriate to the facilities to be used and which are capable of transmitting to, and receiving from, at any place on the route, at least one ground facility:

(1) A transmitter, (2) two microphones, (3) two headsets or one headset and one speaker, (4) a marker beacon receiver, (5) two independent receivers for navigation, (6) two independent receivers for communications, and (7) for extended overwater operations only, an additional transmitter.

(c) For the purpose of paragraphs (a)(5), (a)(6), (b)(5), and (b)(6) of this section, a receiver is independent if the function of any part of it does not depend on the functioning of any part of another receiver. However, a receiver that can receive both communications and navigational signals may be used in place of a separate communications receiver and a separate navigational signal receiver.

§ 135.167 Emergency equipment: Extended overwater operations.

(a) No person may operate an aircraft in extended overwater operations unless it carries, installed in conspicuously marked locations easily accessible to the occupants if a ditching occurs, the following equipment:

(1) An approved life preserver equipped with an approved survivor locator light for each occupant of the aircraft. The life preserver must be easily accessible to each seated occupant.

(2) Enough approved liferafts of a rated capacity and buoyancy to accommodate the occupants of the aircraft.

(b) Each liferaft required by paragraph (a) of this section must be equipped with or contain at least the following:

(1) One approved survivor locator light.

(2) One approved pyrotechnic signaling device.

(3) Either—

(i) One survival kit, appropriately equipped for the route to be flown; or

(ii) One canopy (for sail, sunshade, or rain catcher);

(iii) One radar reflector;

(iv) One liferaft repair kit;

(v) One bailing bucket;

(vi) One signaling mirror;

(vii) One police whistle;

(viii) One raft knife;

(ix) One CO_2 bottle for emergency inflation;

(x) One inflation pump;

(xi) Two oars;

(xii) One 75-foot retaining line;

(xiii) One magnetic compass;

(xiv) One dye marker;

(xv) One flashlight having at least two size "D" cells or equivalent;

(xvi) A 2-day supply of emergency food rations supplying at least 1,000 calories per day for each person;

(xvii) For each two persons the raft is rated to carry, two pints of water or one sea water desalting kit;

(xviii) One fishing kit; and

(xix) One book on survival appropriate for the area in which the aircraft is operated.

(c) No person may operate an aircraft in extended overwater operations unless there is attached to one of the life rafts required by paragraph (a) of this section, a survival type emergency locator transmitter that meets the applicable requirements of TSO–C91. Batteries used in this transmitter must be replaced (or recharged, if the battery is rechargeable) when the transmitter has been in use for more than 1 cumulative hour, and also when 50 percent of their useful life (or for rechargeable batteries, 50 percent of their useful life of charge), as established by the transmitter manufacturer under TSO–C91, paragraph (g)(2) of this section has expired. The new expiration date for the replacement or recharged battery must be legibly marked on the outside of the transmitter. The battery useful life or useful life of charge requirements of this paragraph do not apply to batteries (such as water-activated batteries) that are essentially unaffected during probable storage intervals.

[Doc. No. 16097, 43 FR 46783, Oct. 10, 1978, as amended by Amdt. 135–4, 45 FR 38348, June 30, 1980; Amdt. 135–20, 51 FR 40710, Nov. 7, 1986]

§ 135.169 Additional   airworthiness   requirements.

(a) Except for commuter category airplanes, no person may operate a large airplane unless it meets the additional airworthiness requirements of §§ 121.213 through 121.283, 121.307, and 121.312 of this chapter.

(b) No person may operate a reciprocating-engine or turbopropeller-powered small airplane that has a passenger seating configuration, excluding pilot seats, of 10 seats or more unless it is type certificated—

(1) In the transport category;

(2) Before July 1, 1970, in the normal category and meets special conditions issued by the Administrator for airplanes intended for use in operations under this part;

(3) Before July 19, 1970, in the normal category and meets the additional airworthiness standards in Special Federal Aviation Regulation No. 23;

(4) In the normal category and meets the additional airworthiness standards in Appendix A;

(5) In the normal category and complies with section 1.(a) of Special Federal Aviation Regulation No. 41;

(6) In the normal category and complies with section 1.(b) of Special Federal Aviation Regulation No. 41; or

(7) In the commuter category.

(c) No person may operate a small airplane with a passenger seating configuration, excluding any pilot seat, of 10 seats or more, with a seating configuration greater than the maximum seating configuration used in that type airplane in operations under this part before August 19, 1977. This paragraph does not apply to—

(1) An airplane that is type certificated in the transport category; or

(2) An airplane that complies with—

(i) Appendix A of this part provided that its passenger seating configuration, excluding pilot seats, does not exceed 19 seats; or

(ii) Special Federal Aviation Regulation No. 41.

[Doc. No. 16097, 43 FR 46783, Oct. 10, 1978, as amended at 44 FR 53731, Sept. 17, 1979; Amdt. 135–21, 52 FR 1836, Jan. 15, 1987; 52 FR 34745, Sept. 14, 1987]

§ 135.170 Materials for compartment interiors.

No person may operate an airplane that conforms to an amended or supplemental type certificate issued in accordance with SFAR No. 41 for a maximum certificated takeoff weight in excess of 12,500 pounds, unless within one year after issuance of the initial airworthiness certificate under that SFAR, the airplane meets the compartment interior requirements set forth in § 25.853 (a), (b), (b–1), (b–2), and (b–3) of this chapter in effect on September 26, 1978.

[44 FR 53731, Sept. 17, 1979]

§ 135.171 Shoulder harness installation at flight crewmember stations.

(a) No person may operate a turbojet aircraft or an aircraft having a passenger seating configuration, excluding any pilot seat, of 10 seats or more unless it is equipped with an approved shoulder harness installed for each flight crewmember station.

(b) Each flight crewmember occupying a station equipped with a shoulder harness must fasten the shoulder harness during takeoff and landing, except that the shoulder harness may be unfastened if the crewmember cannot perform the required duties with the shoulder harness fastened.

§ 135.173 Airborne thunderstorm detection equipment requirements.

(a) No person may operate an aircraft that has a passenger seating configuration, excluding any pilot seat, of 10 seats or more in passenger-carrying operations, except a helicopter operating under day VFR conditions, unless the aircraft is equipped with either approved thunderstorm detection equipment or approved airborne weather radar equipment.

(b) After January 6, 1988, no person may operate a helicopter that has a passenger seating configuration, excluding any pilot seat, of 10 seats or more in passenger-carrying operations, under night VFR when current weather reports indicate that thunderstorms or other potentially hazardous weather conditions that can be detected with airborne thunderstorm detection equipment may reasonably be expected along the route to be flown, unless the helicopter is equipped with either approved thunderstorm detection equipment or approved airborne weather radar equipment.

(c) No person may begin a flight under IFR or night VFR conditions when current weather reports indicate that thunderstorms or other potentially hazardous weather conditions that can be detected with airborne thunderstorm detection equipment, required by paragraph (a) or (b) of this section, may reasonably be expected along the route to be flown, unless the airborne thunderstorm detection equipment is in satisfactory operating condition.

(d) If the airborne thunderstorm detection equipment becomes inoperative en route, the aircraft must be operated under the instructions and procedures specified for that event in the manual required by § 135.21.

(e) This section does not apply to aircraft used solely within the State of Hawaii, within the State of Alaska,

within that part of Canada west of longitude 130 degrees W, between latitude 70 degrees N, and latitude 53 degrees N, or during any training, test, or ferry flight.

(f) Without regard to any other provision of this part, an alternate electrical power supply is not required for airborne thunderstorm detection equipment.

[Doc. No. 16097, 43 FR 46783, Oct. 10, 1978, as amended by Amdt. 135-20, 51 FR 40710, Nov. 7, 1986]

§ 135.175 Airborne weather radar equipment requirements.

(a) No person may operate a large, transport category aircraft in passenger-carrying operations unless approved airborne weather radar equipment is installed in the aircraft.

(b) No person may begin a flight under IFR or night VFR conditions when current weather reports indicate that thunderstorms, or other potentially hazardous weather conditions that can be detected with airborne weather radar equipment, may reasonably be expected along the route to be flown, unless the airborne weather radar equipment required by paragraph (a) of this section is in satisfactory operating condition.

(c) If the airborne weather radar equipment becomes inoperative en route, the aircraft must be operated under the instructions and procedures specified for that event in the manual required by § 135.21.

(d) This section does not apply to aircraft used solely within the State of Hawaii, within the State of Alaska, within that part of Canada west of longitude 130 degrees W, between latitude 70 degrees N, and latitude 53 degrees N, or during any training, test, or ferry flight.

(e) Without regard to any other provision of this part, an alternate electrical power supply is not required for airborne weather radar equipment.

§ 135.177 Emergency equipment requirements for aircraft having a passenger seating configuration of more than 19 passengers.

(a) No person may operate an aircraft having a passenger seating configuration, excluding any pilot seat, of more than 19 seats unless it is equipped with the following emergency equipment:

(1) One approved first aid kit for treatment of injuries likely to occur in flight or in a minor accident, which meets the following specifications and requirements:

(i) Each first aid kit must be dust and moisture proof, and contain only materials that either meet Federal Specifications GGK-319a, as revised, or as approved by the Administrator.

(ii) Required first aid kits must be readily accessible to the cabin flight attendants.

(iii) At time of takeoff, each first aid kit must contain at least the following or other contents approved by the Administrator:

Contents	Quantity
Adhesive bandage compressors, 1 in	16
Antiseptic swabs	20
Ammonia inhalants	10
Bandage compressors, 4 in	8
Triangular bandage compressors, 40 in	5
Burn compound, ⅛ oz or an equivalent of other burn remedy	6
Arm splint, noninflatable	1
Leg splint, noninflatable	1
Roller bandage, 4 in	4
Adhesive tape, 1-in standard roll	2
Bandage scissors	1

(2) A crash axe carried so as to be accessible to the crew but inaccessible to passengers during normal operations.

(3) Signs that are visible to all occupants to notify them when smoking is prohibited and when safety belts should be fastened. The signs must be constructed so that they can be turned on and off by a crewmember. Seat belt signs must be turnnd on for each takeoff and landing, and at other times considered necessary by the pilot in command. No smoking signs shall be turned on when required by § 135.127 of this part.

(4) For airplanes has the additional emergency equipment specified in § 121.310 of this chapter.

(b) Each item of equipment must be inspected regularly under inspection periods established in the operations specifications to ensure its condition for continued serviceability and immediate readiness to perform its intended emergency purposes.

§ 135.179 Inoperable instruments and equipment for multiengine aircraft.

(a) No person may take off a multiengine aircraft unless the following instruments and equipment are in an operable condition:

(1) Instruments and equipment that are either specifically or otherwise required by the airworthiness requirements under which the aircraft is type certificated and which are essential for safe operations under all operating conditions.

(2) Instruments and equipment required by an airworthiness directive to be in operable condition unless the airworthiness directive provides otherwise.

(b) No person may take off any multiengine aircraft with inoperable instruments or equipment installed, other than those described in paragraph (a) of this section, unless the following conditions are met:

(1) An approved Minimum Equipment List exists for the aircraft type.

(2) The aircraft has within it a letter of authorization, issued by the FAA Flight Standards District Office having certification responsibility for the certificate holder, authorizing operation of the aircraft under the Minimum Equipment List. The letter of authorization may be obtained by written request of the certificate holder. The Minimum Equipment List and the letter of authorization constitute a supplemental type certificate for the aircraft.

(3) The approved Minimum Equipment List must provide for the operation of the aircraft with the instruments and equipment in an inoperable condition.

(4) The aircraft records available to the pilot must include an entry describing the inoperable instruments and equipment.

(5) The aircraft is operated under all applicable conditions and limitations contained in the Minimum Equipment List and the letter authorizing the use of the list.

(c) Without regard to the requirements of paragraph (a)(1) of this section, an aircraft with inoperable instruments or equipment may be operated under a special flight permit under §§ 21.197 and 21.199 of this chapter.

§ 135.181   Performance requirements: Aircraft operated over-the-top or in IFR conditions.

(a) Except as provided in paragraphs (b) and (c) of this section, no person may—

(1) Operate a single-engine aircraft carrying passengers over-the-top or in IFR conditions; or

(2) Operate a multiengine aircraft carrying passengers over-the-top or in IFR conditions at a weight that will not allow it to climb, with the critical engine inoperative, at least 50 feet a minute when operating at the MEAs of the route to be flown or 5,000 feet MSL, whichever is higher.

(b) Notwithstanding the restrictions in paragraph (a)(2) of this section, multiengine helicopters carrying passengers offshore may conduct such operations in over-the-top or in IFR conditions at a weight that will allow the helicopter to climb at least 50 feet per minute with the critical engine inoperative when operating at the MEA of the route to be flown or 1,500 feet MSL, whichever is higher.

(c) Without regard to paragraph (a) of this section—

(1) If the latest weather reports or forecasts, or any combination of them, indicate that the weather along the planned route (including takeoff and landing) allows flight under VFR under the ceiling (if a ceiling exists) and that the weather is forecast to remain so until at least 1 hour after the estimated time of arrival at the destination, a person may operate an aircraft over-the-top; or

(2) If the latest weather reports or forecasts, or any combination of them, indicate that the weather along the planned route allows flight under VFR under the ceiling (if a ceiling exists) beginning at a point no more than 15 minutes flying time at normal cruise speed from the departure airport, a person may—

(i) Take off from the departure airport in IFR conditions and fly in IFR conditions to a point no more than 15 minutes flying time at normal cruise speed from that airport;

(ii) Operate an aircraft in IFR conditions if unforecast weather conditions are encountered while en route on a flight planned to be conducted under VFR; and

(iii) Make an IFR approach at the destination airport if unforecast weather conditions are encountered at the airport that do not allow an approach to be completed under VFR.

(d) Without regard to paragraph (a) of this section, a person may operate an aircraft over-the-top under conditions allowing—

(1) For multiengine aircraft, descent or continuance of the flight under VFR if its critical engine fails; or

(2) For single-engine aircraft, descent under VFR if its engine fails.

[Doc. No. 16097, 43 FR 46783, Oct. 10, 1978, as amended by Amdt. 135-20, 51 FR 40710, Nov. 7, 1986]

§ 135.183   Performance requirements: Land aircraft operated over water.

No person may operate a land aircraft carrying passengers over water unless—

(a) It is operated at an altitude that allows it to reach land in the case of engine failure;

(b) It is necessary for takeoff or landing;

(c) It is a multiengine aircraft operated at a weight that will allow it to climb, with the critical engine inoperative, at least 50 feet a minute, at an altitude of 1,000 feet above the surface; or

(d) It is a helicopter equipped with helicopter flotation devices.

§ 135.185   Empty weight and center of gravity: Currency requirement.

(a) No person may operate a multiengine aircraft unless the current empty weight and center of gravity are calculated from values established by actual weighing of the aircraft within the preceding 36 calendar months.

(b) Paragraph (a) of this section does not apply to—

(1) Aircraft issued an original airworthiness certificate within the preceding 36 calendar months; and

(2) Aircraft operated under a weight and balance system approved in the

operations specifications of the certificate holder.

Subpart D—VFR/IFR Operating Limitations and Weather Requirements

§ 135.201 Applicability.

This subpart prescribes the operating limitations for VFR/IFR flight operations and associated weather requirements for operations under this part.

§ 135.203 VFR: Minimum altitudes.

Except when necessary for takeoff and landing, no person may operate under VFR—

(a) An airplane—

(1) During the day, below 500 feet above the surface or less than 500 feet horizontally from any obstacle; or

(2) At night, at an altitude less than 1,000 feet above the highest obstacle within a horizontal distance of 5 miles from the course intended to be flown or, in designated mountainous terrain, less than 2,000 feet above the highest obstacle within a horizontal distance of 5 miles from the course intended to be flown; or

(b) A helicopter over a congested area at an altitude less than 300 feet above the surface.

§ 135.205 VFR: Visibility requirements.

(a) No person may operate an airplane under VFR in uncontrolled airspace when the ceiling is less than 1,000 feet unless flight visibility is at least 2 miles.

(b) No person may operate a helicopter under VFR in uncontrolled airspace at an altitude of 1,200 feet or less above the surface or in control zones unless the visibility is at least—

(1) During the day—½ mile; or

(2) At night—1 mile.

§ 135.207 VFR: Helicopter surface reference requirements.

No person may operate a helicopter under VFR unless that person has visual surface reference or, at night, visual surface light reference, sufficient to safely control the helicopter.

§ 135.209 VFR: Fuel supply.

(a) No person may begin a flight operation in an airplane under VFR unless, considering wind and forecast weather conditions, it has enough fuel to fly to the first point of intended landing and, assuming normal cruising fuel consumption—

(1) During the day, to fly after that for at least 30 minutes; or

(2) At night, to fly after that for at least 45 minutes.

(b) No person may begin a flight operation in a helicopter under VFR unless, considering wind and forecast weather conditions, it has enough fuel to fly to the first point of intended landing and, assuming normal cruising fuel consumption, to fly after that for at least 20 minutes.

§ 135.211 VFR: Over-the-top carrying passengers: Operating limitations.

Subject to any additional limitations in § 135.181, no person may operate an aircraft under VFR over-the-top carrying passengers, unless—

(a) Weather reports or forecasts, or any combination of them, indicate that the weather at the intended point of termination of over-the-top flight—

(1) Allows descent to beneath the ceiling under VFR and is forecast to remain so until at least 1 hour after the estimated time of arrival at that point; or

(2) Allows an IFR approach and landing with flight clear of the clouds until reaching the prescribed initial approach altitude over the final approach facility, unless the approach is made with the use of radar under § 91.116(f) of this chapter; or

(b) It is operated under conditions allowing—

(1) For multiengine aircraft, descent or continuation of the flight under VFR if its critical engine fails; or

(2) For single-engine aircraft, descent under VFR if its engine fails.

§ 135.213 Weather reports and forecasts.

(a) Whenever a person operating an aircraft under this part is required to use a weather report or forecast, that person shall use that of the U.S. National Weather Service, a source approved by the U.S. National Weather

Service, or a source approved by the Administrator. However, for operations under VFR, the pilot in command may, if such a report is not available, use weather information based on that pilot's own observations or on those of other persons competent to supply appropriate observations.

(b) For the purposes of paragraph (a) of this section, weather observations made and furnished to pilots to conduct IFR operations at an airport must be taken at the airport where those IFR operations are conducted, unless the Administrator issues operations specifications allowing the use of weather observations taken at a location not at the airport where the IFR operations are conducted. The Administrator issues such operations specifications when, after investigation by the U.S. National Weather Service and the FAA Flight Standards District Office charged with the overall inspection of the certificate holder, it is found that the standards of safety for that operation would allow the deviation from this paragraph for a particular operation for which an ATCO operating certificate has been issued.

§ 135.215   IFR: Operating limitations.

(a) Except as provided in paragraphs (b), (c) and (d) of this section, no person may operate an aircraft under IFR outside of controlled airspace or at any airport that does not have an approved standard instrument approach procedure.

(b) The Administrator may issue operations specifications to the certificate holder to allow it to operate under IFR over routes outside controlled airspace if—

(1) The certificate holder shows the Administrator that the flight crew is able to navigate, without visual reference to the ground, over an intended track without deviating more than 5 degrees or 5 miles, whichever is less, from that track; and

(2) The Administrator determines that the proposed operations can be conducted safely.

(c) A person may operate an aircraft under IFR outside of controlled airspace if the certificate holder has been

approved for the operations and that operation is necessary to—

(1) Conduct an instrument approach to an airport for which there is in use a current approved standard or special instrument approach procedure; or

(2) Climb into controlled airspace during an approved missed approach procedure; or

(3) Make an IFR departure from an airport having an approved instrument approach procedure.

(d) The Administrator may issue operations specifications to the certificate holder to allow it to depart at an airport that does not have an approved standard instrument approach procedure when the Administrator determines that it is necessary to make an IFR departure from that airport and that the proposed operations can be conducted safely. The approval to operate at that airport does not include an approval to make an IFR approach to that airport.

§ 135.217   IFR: Takeoff limitations.

No person may takeoff an aircraft under IFR from an airport where weather conditions are at or above takeoff minimums but are below authorized IFR landing minimums unless there is an alternate airport within 1 hour's flying time (at normal cruising speed, in still air) of the airport of departure.

§ 135.219   IFR: Destination airport weather minimums.

No person may take off an aircraft under IFR or begin an IFR or over-the-top operation unless the latest weather reports or forecasts, or any combination of them, indicate that weather conditions at the estimated time of arrival at the next airport of intended landing will be at or above authorized IFR landing minimums.

§ 135.221   IFR: Alternate airport weather minimums.

No person may designate an alternate airport unless the weather reports or forecasts, or any combination of them, indicate that the weather conditions will be at or above authorized alternate airport landing minimums for that airport at the estimated time of arrival.

§ 135.223 IFR: Alternate airport requirements.

(a) Except as provided in paragraph (b) of this section, no person may operate an aircraft in IFR conditions unless it carries enough fuel (considering weather reports or forecasts or any combination of them) to—

(1) Complete the flight to the first airport of intended landing;

(2) Fly from that airport to the alternate airport; and

(3) Fly after that for 45 minutes at normal cruising speed or, for helicopters, fly after that for 30 minutes at normal cruising speed.

(b) Paragraph (a)(2) of this section does not apply if Part 97 of this chapter prescribes a standard instrument approach procedure for the first airport of intended landing and, for at least one hour before and after the estimated time of arrival, the appropriate weather reports or forecasts, or any combination of them, indicate that—

(1) The ceiling will be at least 1,500 feet above the lowest circling approach MDA; or

(2) If a circling instrument approach is not authorized for the airport, the ceiling will be at least 1,500 feet above the lowest published minimum or 2,000 feet above the airport elevation, whichever is higher; and

(3) Visibility for that airport is forecast to be at least three miles, or two miles more than the lowest applicable visibility minimums, whichever is the greater, for the instrument approach procedure to be used at the destination airport.

[Doc. No. 16097, 43 FR 46783, Oct. 10, 1978, as amended by Amdt. 135-20, 51 FR 40710, Nov. 7, 1986]

§ 135.225 IFR: Takeoff, approach and landing minimums.

(a) No pilot may begin an instrument approach procedure to an airport unless—

(1) That airport has a weather reporting facility operated by the U.S. National Weather Service, a source approved by U.S. National Weather Service, or a source approved by the Administrator; and

(2) The latest weather report issued by that weather reporting facility indicates that weather conditions are at or above the authorized IFR landing minimums for that airport.

(b) No pilot may begin the final approach segment of an instrument approach procedure to an airport unless the latest weather reported by the facility described in paragraph (a)(1) of this section indicates that weather conditions are at or above the authorized IFR landing minimums for that procedure.

(c) If a pilot has begun the final approach segment of an instrument approach to an airport under paragraph (b) of this section and a later weather report indicating below minimum conditions is received after the aircraft is—

(1) On an ILS final approach and has passed the final approach fix; or

(2) On an ASR or PAR final approach and has been turned over to the final approach controller; or

(3) On a final approach using a VOR, NDB, or comparable approach procedure; and the aircraft—

(i) Has passed the appropriate facility or final approach fix; or

(ii) Where a final approach fix is not specified, has completed the procedure turn and is established inbound toward the airport on the final approach course within the distance prescribed in the procedure; the approach may be continued and a landing made if the pilot finds, upon reaching the authorized MDA or DH, that actual weather conditions are at least equal to the minimums prescribed for the procedure.

(d) The MDA or DH and visibility landing minimums prescribed in Part 97 of this chapter or in the operator's operations specifications are increased by 100 feet and ½ mile respectively, but not to exceed the ceiling and visibility minimums for that airport when used as an alternate airport, for each pilot in command of a turbine-powered airplane who has not served at least 100 hours as pilot in command in that type of airplane.

(e) Each pilot making an IFR takeoff or approach and landing at a military or foreign airport shall comply with applicable instrument approach procedures and weather minimums prescribed by the authority having jurisdiction over that airport. In addition, no pilot may, at that airport—

(1) Take off under IFR when the visibility is less than 1 mile; or

(2) Make an instrument approach when the visibility is less than ½ mile.

(f) If takeoff minimums are specified in Part 97 of this chapter for the takeoff airport, no pilot may take off an aircraft under IFR when the weather conditions reported by the facility described in paragraph (a)(1) of this section are less than the takeoff minimums specified for the takeoff airport in Part 97 or in the certificate holder's operations specifications.

(g) Except as provided in paragraph (h) of this section, if takeoff minimums are not prescribed in Part 97 of this chapter for the takeoff airport, no pilot may take off an aircraft under IFR when the weather conditions reported by the facility described in paragraph (a)(1) of this section are less than that prescribed in Part 91 of this chapter or in the certificate holder's operations specifications.

(h) At airports where straight-in instrument approach procedures are authorized, a pilot may take off an aircraft under IFR when the weather conditions reported by the facility described in paragraph (a)(1) of this section are equal to or better than the lowest straight-in landing minimums, unless otherwise restricted, if—

(1) The wind direction and velocity at the time of takeoff are such that a straight-in instrument approach can be made to the runway served by the instrument approach;

(2) The associated ground facilities upon which the landing minimums are predicated and the related airborne equipment are in normal operation; and

(3) The certificate holder has been approved for such operations.

§ 135.227   Icing conditions: Operating limitations.

(a) No pilot may take off an aircraft that has—

(1) Frost, snow, or ice adhering to any rotor blade, propeller, windshield, or powerplant installation, or to an airspeed, altimeter, rate of climb, or flight attitude instrument system;

(2) Snow or ice adhering to the wings or stabilizing or control surfaces; or

(3) Any frost adhering to the wings, or stabilizing or control surfaces, unless that frost has been polished to make it smooth.

(b) Except for an airplane that has ice protection provisions that meet section 34 of Appendix A, or those for transport category airplane type certification, no pilot may fly—

(1) Under IFR into known or forecast light or moderate icing conditions; or

(2) Under VFR into known light or moderate icing conditions; unless the aircraft has functioning deicing or anti-icing equipment protecting each rotor blade, propeller, windshield, wing, stabilizing or control surface, and each airspeed, altimeter, rate of climb, or flight attitude instrument system.

(c) No pilot may fly a helicopter under IFR into known or forecast icing conditions or under VFR into known icing conditions unless it has been type certificated and appropriately equipped for operations in icing conditions.

(d) Except for an airplane that has ice protection provisions that meet section 34 of Appendix A, or those for transport category airplane type certification, no pilot may fly an aircraft into known or forecast severe icing conditions.

(e) If current weather reports and briefing information relied upon by the pilot in command indicate that the forecast icing condition that would otherwise prohibit the flight will not be encountered during the flight because of changed weather conditions since the forecast, the restrictions in paragraphs (b), (c), and (d) of this section based on forecast conditions do not apply.

[Doc. No. 16097, 43 FR 46783, Oct. 10, 1978, as amended by Amdt. 133–20, 51 FR 40710, Nov. 7, 1986]

§ 135.229   Airport requirements.

(a) No certificate holder may use any airport unless it is adequate for the proposed operation, considering such items as size, surface, obstructions, and lighting.

(b) No pilot of an aircraft carrying passengers at night may take off from, or land on, an airport unless—

(1) That pilot has determined the wind direction from an illuminated wind direction indicator or local ground communications or, in the case of takeoff, that pilot's personal observations; and

(2) The limits of the area to be used for landing or takeoff are clearly shown—

(i) For airplanes, by boundary or runway marker lights;

(ii) For helicopters, by boundary or runway marker lights or reflective material.

(c) For the purpose of paragraph (b) of this section, if the area to be used for takeoff or landing is marked by flare pots or lanterns, their use must be approved by the Administrator.

Subpart E—Flight Crewmember Requirements

§ 135.241   Applicability.

This subpart prescribes the flight crewmember requirements for operations under this part.

§ 135.243   Pilot in command qualifications.

(a) No certificate holder may use a person, nor may any person serve, as pilot in command in passenger-carrying operations of a turbojet airplane, of an airplane having a passenger seating configuration, excluding any pilot seat, of 10 seats or more, or a multiengine airplane being operated by the "Commuter Air Carrier" (as defined in Part 298 of this title), unless that person holds an airline transport pilot certificate with appropriate category and class ratings and, if required, an appropriate type rating for that airplane.

(b) Except as provided in paragraph (a) of this section, no certificate holder may use a person, nor may any person serve, as pilot in command of an aircraft under VFR unless that person—

(1) Holds at least a commercial pilot certificate with appropriate category and class ratings and, if required, an appropriate type rating for that aircraft; and

(2) Has had at least 500 hours time as a pilot, including at least 100 hours of cross-country flight time, at least 25 hours of which were at night; and

(3) For an airplane, holds an instrument rating or an airline transport pilot certificate with an airplane category rating; or

(4) For helicopter operations conducted VFR over-the-top, holds a helicopter instrument rating, or an airline transport pilot certificate with a category and class rating for that aircraft, not limited to VFR.

(c) Except as provided in paragraph (a) of this section, no certificate holder may use a person, nor may any person serve, as pilot in command of an aircraft under IFR unless that person—

(1) Holds at least a commercial pilot certificate with appropriate category and class ratings and, if required, an appropriate type rating for that aircraft; and

(2) Has had at least 1,200 hours of flight time as a pilot, including 500 hours of cross country flight time, 100 hours of night flight time, and 75 hours of actual or simulated instrument time at least 50 hours of which were in actual flight; and

(3) For an airplane, holds an instrument rating or an airline transport pilot certificate with an airplane category rating; or

(4) For a helicopter, holds a helicopter instrument rating, or an airline transport pilot certificate with a category and class rating for that aircraft, not limited to VFR.

(d) Paragraph (b)(3) of this section does not apply when—

(1) The aircraft used is a single reciprocating-engine-powered airplane;

(2) The certificate holder does not conduct any operation pursuant to a published flight schedule which specifies five or more round trips a week between two or more points and places between which the round trips are performed, and does not transport

mail by air under a contract or contracts with the United States Postal Service having total amount estimated at the beginning of any semiannual reporting period (January 1–June 30; July 1–December 31) to be in excess of $20,000 over the 12 months commencing with the beginning of the reporting period;

(3) The area, as specified in the certificate holder's operations specifications, is an isolated area, as determined by the Flight Standards district office, if it is shown that—

(i) The primary means of navigation in the area is by pilotage, since radio navigational aids are largely ineffective; and

(ii) The primary means of transportation in the area is by air;

(4) Each flight is conducted under day VFR with a ceiling of not less than 1,000 feet and visibility not less than 3 statute miles;

(5) Weather reports or forecasts, or any combination of them, indicate that for the period commencing with the planned departure and ending 30 minutes after the planned arrival at the destination the flight may be conducted under VFR with a ceiling of not less than 1,000 feet and visibility of not less than 3 statute miles, except that if weather reports and forecasts are not available, the pilot in command may use that pilot's observations or those of other persons competent to supply weather observations if those observations indicate the flight may be conducted under VFR with the ceiling and visibility required in this paragraph;

(6) The distance of each flight from the certificate holder's base of operation to destination does not exceed 250 nautical miles for a pilot who holds a commercial pilot certificate with an airplane rating without an instrument rating, provided the pilot's certificate does not contain any limitation to the contrary; and

(7) The areas to be flown are approved by the certificate-holding FAA Flight Standards district office and are listed in the certificate holder's operations specifications.

[Doc. No. 16097, 43 FR 46783, Oct. 10, 1978; 43 FR 49975, Oct 26, 1978, as amended by Amdt. 135-15, 46 FR 30971, June 11, 1981]

§ 135.244   Operating experience.

(a) No certificate holder may use any person, nor may any person serve, as a pilot in command of an aircraft operated by a Commuter Air Carrier (as defined in § 298.2 of this title) in passenger-carrying operations, unless that person has completed, prior to designation as pilot in command, on that make and basic model aircraft and in that crewmember position, the following operating experience in each make and basic model of aircraft to be flown:

(1) Aircraft, single engine—10 hours.

(2) Aircraft multiengine, reciprocating engine-powered—15 hours.

(3) Aircraft multiengine, turbine engine-powered—20 hours.

(4) Airplane, turbojet-powered—25 hours.

(b) In acquiring the operating experience, each person must comply with the following:

(1) The operating experience must be acquired after satisfactory completion of the appropriate ground and flight training for the aircraft and crewmember position. Approved provisions for the operating experience must be included in the certificate holder's training program.

(2) The experience must be acquired in flight during commuter passenger-carrying operations under this part. However, in the case of an aircraft not previously used by the certificate holder in operations under this part, operating experience acquired in the aircraft during proving flights or ferry flights may be used to meet this requirement.

(3) Each person must acquire the operating experience while performing the duties of a pilot in command under the supervision of a qualified check pilot.

(4) The hours of operating experience may be reduced to not less than 50 percent of the hours required by this section by the substitution of one additional takeoff and landing for each hour of flight.

[Doc. No. 20011, 45 FR 7541, Feb. 4, 1980, as amended by Amdt. 135-9, 45 FR 80461, Dec. 14, 1980]

§ 135.245 Second in command qualifications.

(a) Except as provided in paragraph (b), no certificate holder may use any person, nor may any person serve, as second in command of an aircraft unless that person holds at least a commercial pilot certificate with appropriate category and class ratings and an instrument rating. For flight under IFR, that person must meet the recent instrument experience requirements of Part 61 of this chapter.

(b) A second in command of a helicopter operated under VFR, other than over-the-top, must have at least a commercial pilot certificate with an appropriate aircraft category and class rating.

[44 FR 26738, May 7, 1979]

§ 135.247 Pilot qualifications: Recent experience.

(a) No certificate holder may use any person, nor may any person serve, as pilot in command of an aircraft carrying passengers unless, within the preceding 90 days, that person has—

(1) Made three takeoffs and three landings as the sole manipulator of the flight controls in an aircraft of the same category and class and, if a type rating is required, of the same type in which that person is to serve; or

(2) For operation during the period beginning 1 hour after sunset and ending 1 hour before sunrise (as published in the Air Almanac), made three takeoffs and three landings during that period as the sole manipulator of the flight controls in an aircraft of the same category and class and, if a type rating is required, of the same type in which that person is to serve.

A person who complies with paragraph (a)(2) of this section need not comply with paragraph (a)(1) of this section.

(b) For the purpose of paragraph (a) of this section, if the aircraft is a tailwheel airplane, each takeoff must be made in a tailwheel airplane and each landing must be made to a full stop in a tailwheel airplane.

Subpart F—Flight Crewmember Flight Time Limitations and Rest Requirements

Source: Docket No. 23634, 50 FR 29320, July 18, 1985.

§ 135.261 Applicability.

Sections 135.263 through 135.271 prescribe flight time limitations and rest requirements for operations conducted under this part as follows:

(a) Section 135.263 applies to all operations under this subpart.

(b) Section 135.265 applies to:

(1) Scheduled passenger-carrying operations except those conducted solely within the state of Alaska. "Scheduled passenger-carrying operations" means passenger-carrying operations that are conducted in accordance with a published schedule which covers at least five round trips per week on at least one route between two or more points, includes dates or times (or both), and is openly advertised or otherwise made readily available to the general public, and

(2) Any other operation under this part, if the operator elects to comply with § 135.265 and obtains an appropriate operations specification amendment.

(c) Sections 135.267 and 135.269 apply to any operation that is not a scheduled passenger-carrying operation and to any operation conducted solely within the State of Alaska, unless the operator elects to comply with § 135.265 as authorized under paragraph (b)(2) of this section.

(d) Section 135.271 contains special daily flight time limits for operations conducted under the helicopter emergency medical evacuation service (HEMES).

§ 135.263 Flight time limitations and rest requirements: All certificate holders.

(a) A certificate holder may assign a flight crewmember and a flight crewmember may accept an assignment for flight time only when the applicable requirements of §§ 135.263 through 135.271 are met.

(b) No certificate holder may assign any flight crewmember to any duty with the certificate holder during any required rest period.

(c) Time spent in transportation, not local in character, that a certificate holder requires of a flight crewmember and provides to transport the crewmember to an airport at which he is to serve on a flight as a crewmember, or from an airport at which he was relieved from duty to return to his home station, is not considered part of a rest period.

(d) A flight crewmember is not considered to be assigned flight time in excess of flight time limitations if the flights to which he is assigned normally terminate within the limitations, but due to circumstances beyond the control of the certificate holder or flight crewmember (such as adverse weather conditions), are not at the time of departure expected to reach their destination within the planned flight time.

§ 135.265 Flight time limitations and rest requirements: Scheduled operations.

(a) No certificate holder may schedule any flight crewmember, and no flight crewmember may accept an assignment, for flight time in scheduled operations or in other commercial flying if that crewmember's total flight time in all commercial flying will exceed—

(1) 1,200 hours in any calendar year.

(2) 120 hours in any calendar month.

(3) 34 hours in any 7 consecutive days.

(4) 8 hours during any 24 consecutive hours for a flight crew consisting of one pilot.

(5) 8 hours between required rest periods for a flight crew consisting of two pilots qualified under this part for the operation being conducted.

(b) Except as provided in paragraph (c) of this section, no certificate holder may schedule a flight crewmember, and no flight crewmember may accept an assignment, for flight time during the 24 consecutive hours preceding the scheduled completion of any flight segment without a scheduled rest period during that 24 hours of at least the following:

(1) 9 consecutive hours of rest for less than 8 hours of scheduled flight time.

(2) 10 consecutive hours of rest for 8 or more but less than 9 hours of scheduled flight time.

(3) 11 consecutive hours of rest for 9 or more hours of scheduled flight time.

(c) A certificate holder may schedule a flight crewmember for less than the rest required in paragraph (b) of this section or may reduce a scheduled rest under the following conditions:

(1) A rest required under paragraph (b)(1) of this section may be scheduled for or reduced to a minimum of 8 hours if the flight crewmember is given a rest period of at least 10 hours that must begin no later than 24 hours after the commencement of the reduced rest period.

(2) A rest required under paragraph (b)(2) of this section may be scheduled for or reduced to a minimum of 8 hours if the flight crewmember is given a rest period of at least 11 hours that must begin no later than 24 hours after the commencement of the reduced rest period.

(3) A rest required under paragraph (b)(3) of this section may be scheduled for or reduced to a minimum of 9 hours if the flight crewmember is given a rest period of at least 12 hours that must begin no later than 24 hours after the commencement of the reduced rest period.

(d) Each certificate holder shall relieve each flight crewmember engaged in scheduled air transportation from all further duty for at least 24 consecutive hours during any 7 consecutive days.

§ 135.267 Flight time limitations and rest requirements: Unscheduled one- and two-pilot crews.

(a) No certificate holder may assign any flight crewmember, and no flight crewmember may accept an assignment, for flight time as a member of a one- or two-pilot crew if that crewmember's total flight time in all commercial flying will exceed—

(1) 500 hours in any calendar quarter.

(2) 800 hours in any two consecutive calendar quarters.

(3) 1,400 hours in any calendar year.

(b) Except as provided in paragraph (c) of this section, during any 24 consecutive hours the total flight time of the assigned flight when added to any other commercial flying by that flight crewmember may not exceed—

(1) 8 hours for a flight crew consisting of one pilot; or

(2) 10 hours for a flight crew consisting of two pilots qualified under this Part for the operation being conducted.

(c) A flight crewmember's flight time may exceed the flight time limits of paragraph (b) of this section if the assigned flight time occurs during a regularly assigned duty period of no more than 14 hours and—

(1) If this duty period is immediately preceded by and followed by a required rest period of at least 10 consecutive hours of rest;

(2) If flight time is assigned during this period, that total flight time when added to any other commercial flying by the flight crewmember may not exceed—

(i) 8 hours for a flight crew consisting of one pilot; or

(ii) 10 hours for a flight crew consisting of two pilots; and

(3) If the combined duty and rest periods equal 24 hours.

(d) Each assignment under paragraph (b) of this section must provide for at least 10 consecutive hours of rest during the 24-hour period that precedes the planned completion time of the assignment.

(e) When a flight crewmember has exceeded the daily flight time limitations in this section, because of circumstances beyond the control of the certificate holder or flight crewmember (such as adverse weather conditions), that flight crewmember must have a rest period before being assigned or accepting an assignment for flight time of at least—

(1) 11 consecutive hours of rest if the flight time limitation is exceeded by not more than 30 minutes;

(2) 12 consecutive hours of rest if the flight time limitation is exceeded by more than 30 minutes, but not more than 60 minutes; and

(3) 16 consecutive hours of rest if the flight time limitation is exceeded by more than 60 minutes.

(f) The certificate holder must provide each flight crewmember at least 13 rest periods of at least 24 consecutive hours each in each calendar quarter.

(g) The Director of Flight Operations may issue operations specifications authorizing a deviation from any specific requirement of this section if he finds that the deviation is justified to allow a certificate holder additional time, but in no case beyond October 1, 1987, to bring its operations into full compliance with the requirements of this section. Each application for a deviation must be submitted to the Director of Flight Operations before October 1, 1986. Each applicant for a deviation may continue to operate under the requirements of Subpart F of this part as in effect on September 30, 1985 until the Director of Flight Operations has responded to the deviation request.

§ 135.269   Flight time limitations and rest requirements: Unscheduled three- and four-pilot crews.

(a) No certificate holder may assign any flight crewmember, and no flight crewmember may accept an assignment, for flight time as a member of a three- or four-pilot crew if that crewmember's total flight time in all commercial flying will exceed—

(1) 500 hours in any calendar quarter.

(2) 800 hours in any two consecutive calendar quarters.

(3) 1,400 hours in any calendar year.

(b) No certificate holder may assign any pilot to a crew of three or four pilots, unless that assignment provides—

(1) At least 10 consecutive hours of rest immediately preceding the assignment;

(2) No more than 8 hours of flight deck duty in any 24 consecutive hours;

(3) No more than 18 duty hours for a three-pilot crew or 20 duty hours for a four-pilot crew in any 24 consecutive hours;

(4) No more than 12 hours aloft for a three-pilot crew or 16 hours aloft for a four-pilot crew during the maximum duty hours specified in paragraph (b)(3) of this section;

(5) Adequate sleeping facilities on the aircraft for the relief pilot;

(6) Upon completion of the assignment, a rest period of at least 12 hours;

(7) For a three-pilot crew, a crew which consists of at least the following:

(i) A pilot in command (PIC) who meets the applicable flight crewmember requirements of Subpart E of Part 135;

(ii) A PIC who meets the applicable flight crewmember requirements of Subpart E of Part 135, except those prescribed in §§ 135.244 and 135.247; and

(iii) A second in command (SIC) who meets the SIC qualifications of § 135.245.

(8) For a four-pilot crew, at least three pilots who meet the conditions of paragraph (b)(7) of this section, plus a fourth pilot who meets the SIC qualifications of § 135.245.

(c) When a flight crewmember has exceeded the daily flight deck duty limitation in this section by more than 60 minutes, because of circumstances beyond the control of the certificate holder or flight crewmember, that flight crewmember must have a rest period before the next duty period of at least 16 consecutive hours.

(d) A certificate holder must provide each flight crewmember at least 13 rest periods of at least 24 consecutive hours each in each calendar quarter.

§ 135.271 Helicopter hospital emergency medical evacuation service (HEMES).

(a) No certificate holder may assign any flight crewmember, and no flight crewmember may accept an assignment for flight time if that crewmember's total flight time in all commercial flight will exceed—

(1) 500 hours in any calendar quarter.

(2) 800 hours in any two consecutive calendar quarters.

(3) 1,400 hours in any calendar year.

(b) No certificate holder may assign a helicopter flight crewmember, and no flight crewmember may accept an assignment, for hospital emergency medical evacuation service helicopter operations unless that assignment provides for at least 10 consecutive hours of rest immediately preceding reporting to the hospital for availability for flight time.

(c) No flight crewmember may accrue more than 8 hours of flight time during any 24-consecutive hour period of a HEMES assignment, unless an emergency medical evacuation operation is prolonged. Each flight crewmember who exceeds the daily 8 hour flight time limitation in this paragraph must be relieved of the HEMES assignment immediately upon the completion of that emergency medical evacuation operation and must be given a rest period in compliance with paragraph (h) of this section.

(d) Each flight crewmember must receive at least 8 consecutive hours of rest during any 24 consecutive hour period of a HEMES assignment. A flight crewmember must be relieved of the HEMES assignment if he or she has not or cannot receive at least 8 consecutive hours of rest during any 24 consecutive hour period of a HEMES assignment.

(e) A HEMES assignment may not exceed 72 consecutive hours at the hospital.

(f) An adequate place of rest must be provided at, or in close proximity to, the hospital at which the HEMES assignment is being performed.

(g) No certificate holder may assign any other duties to a flight crewmember during a HEMES assignment.

(h) Each pilot must be given a rest period upon completion of the HEMES assignment and prior to being assigned any further duty with the certificate holder of—

(1) At least 12 consecutive hours for an assignment of less than 48 hours.

(2) At least 16 consecutive hours for an assignment of more than 48 hours.

(i) The certificate holder must provide each flight crewmember at least 13 rest periods of at least 24 consecutive hours each in each calendar quarter.

Subpart G—Crewmember Testing Requirements

§ 135.291   Applicability.

This subpart prescribes the tests and checks required for pilot and flight attendant crewmembers and for the approval of check pilots in operations under this part.

§ 135.293 Initial and recurrent pilot testing requirements.

(a) No certificate holder may use a pilot, nor may any person serve as a pilot, unless, since the beginning of the 12th calendar month before that service, that pilot has passed a written or oral test, given by the Administrator or an authorized check pilot, on that pilot's knowledge in the following areas—

(1) The appropriate provisions of Parts 61, 91, and 135 of this chapter and the operations specifications and the manual of the certificate holder;

(2) For each type of aircraft to be flown by the pilot, the aircraft powerplant, major components and systems, major appliances, performance and operating limitations, standard and emergency operating procedures, and the contents of the approved Aircraft Flight Manual or equivalent, as applicable;

(3) For each type of aircraft to be flown by the pilot, the method of determining compliance with weight and balance limitations for takeoff, landing and en route operations;

(4) Navigation and use of air navigation aids appropriate to the operation or pilot authorization, including, when applicable, instrument approach facilities and procedures;

(5) Air traffic control procedures, including IFR procedures when applicable;

(6) Meteorology in general, including the principles of frontal systems, icing, fog, thunderstorms, and windshear, and, if appropriate for the operation of the certificate holder, high altitude weather;

(7) Procedures for—

(i) Recognizing and avoiding severe weather situations;

(ii) Escaping from severe weather situations, in case of inadvertent encounters, including low-altitude windshear (except that rotorcraft pilots are not required to be trained in escaping from low-altitude windshear); and

(iii) Operating in or near thunderstorms (including best penetrating altitudes),turbulent air (including clear air turbulence), icing, hail, and other potentially hazardous meteorological conditions; and

(8) New equipment, procedures, or techniques, as appropriate.

(b) No certificate holder may use a pilot, nor may any person serve as a pilot, in any aircraft unless, since the beginning of the 12th calendar month before that service, that pilot has passed a competency check given by the Administrator or an authorized check pilot in that class of aircraft, if single-engine airplane other than turbojet, or that type of aircraft, if helicopter, multiengine airplane, or turbojet airplane, to determine the pilot's competence in practical skills and techniques in that aircraft or class of aircraft. The extent of the competency check shall be determined by the Administrator or authorized check pilot conducting the competency check. The competency check may include any of the maneuvers and procedures currently required for the original issuance of the particular pilot certificate required for the operations authorized and appropriate to the category, class and type of aircraft involved. For the purposes of this paragraph, type, as to an airplane, means any one of a group of airplanes determined by the Administrator to have a similar means of propulsion, the same manufacturer, and no significantly different handling or flight characteristics. For the purposes of this paragraph, type, as to a helicopter, means a basic make and model.

(c) The instrument proficiency check required by § 135.297 may be substituted for the competency check required by this section for the type of aircraft used in the check.

(d) For the purpose of this part, competent performance of a procedure or maneuver by a person to be used as a pilot requires that the pilot be the obvious master of the aircraft, with the successful outcome of the maneuver never in doubt.

(e) The Administrator or authorized check pilot certifies the competency of each pilot who passes the knowledge or flight check in the certificate holder's pilot records.

(f) Portions of a required competency check may be given in an aircraft simulator or other appropriate training device, if approved by the Administrator.

§ 135.295 Initial and recurrent flight attendant crewmember testing requirements.

No certificate holder may use a flight attendant crewmember, nor may any person serve as a flight attendant crewmember unless, since the beginning of the 12th calendar month before that service, the certificate holder has determined by appropriate initial and recurrent testing that the person is knowledgeable and competent in the following areas as appropriate to assigned duties and responsibilities—

(a) Authority of the pilot in command;

(b) Passenger handling, including procedures to be followed in handling deranged persons or other persons whose conduct might jeopardize safety;

(c) Crewmember assignments, functions, and responsibilities during ditching and evacuation of persons who may need the assistance of another person to move expeditiously to an exit in an emergency;

(d) Briefing of passengers;

(e) Location and operation of portable fire extinguishers and other items of emergency equipment;

(f) Proper use of cabin equipment and controls;

(g) Location and operation of passenger oxygen equipment;

(h) Location and operation of all normal and emergency exits, including evacuation chutes and escape ropes; and

(i) Seating of persons who may need assistance of another person to move rapidly to an exit in an emergency as prescribed by the certificate holder's operations manual.

§ 135.297 Pilot in command: Instrument proficiency check requirements.

(a) No certificate holder may use a pilot, nor may any person serve, as a pilot in command of an aircraft under IFR unless, since the beginning of the 6th calendar month before that service, that pilot has passed an instrument proficiency check under this section administered by the Administrator or an authorized check pilot.

(b) No pilot may use any type of precision instrument approach procedure under IFR unless, since the beginning of the 6th calendar month before that use, the pilot satisfactorily demonstrated that type of approach procedure. No pilot may use any type of nonprecision approach procedure under IFR unless, since the beginning of the 6th calendar month before that use, the pilot has satisfactorily demonstrated either that type of approach procedure or any other two different types of nonprecision approach procedures. The instrument approach procedure or procedures must include at least one straight-in approach, one circling approach, and one missed approach. Each type of approach procedure demonstrated must be conducted to published minimums for that procedure.

(c) The instrument proficiency check required by paragraph (a) of this section consists of an oral or written equipment test and a flight check under simulated or actual IFR conditions. The equipment test includes questions on emergency procedures, engine operation, fuel and lubrication systems, power settings, stall speeds, best engine-out speed, propeller and supercharger operations, and hydraulic, mechanical, and electrical systems, as appropriate. The flight check includes navigation by instruments, recovery from simulated emergencies, and standard instrument approaches involving navigational facilities which that pilot is to be authorized to use. Each pilot taking the instrument proficiency check must show that standard of competence required by § 135.293(d).

(1) The instrument proficiency check must—

(i) For a pilot in command of an airplane under § 135.243(a), include the procedures and maneuvers for an airline transport pilot certificate in the particular type of airplane, if appropriate; and

(ii) For a pilot in command of an airplane or helicopter under § 135.243(c), include the procedures and maneuvers for a commercial pilot certificate with an instrument rating and, if required, for the appropriate type rating.

(2) The instrument proficiency check must be given by an authorized check airman or by the Administrator.

(d) If the pilot in command is assigned to pilot only one type of aircraft, that pilot must take the instrument proficiency check required by paragraph (a) of this section in that type of aircraft.

(e) If the pilot in command is assigned to pilot more than one type of aircraft, that pilot must take the instrument proficiency check required by paragraph (a) of this section in each type of aircraft to which that pilot is assigned, in rotation, but not more than one flight check during each period described in paragraph (a) of this section.

(f) If the pilot in command is assigned to pilot both single-engine and multiengine aircraft, that pilot must initially take the instrument proficiency check required by paragraph (a) of this section in a multiengine aircraft, and each succeeding check alternately in single-engine and multiengine aircraft, but not more than one flight check during each period described in paragraph (a) of this section. Portions of a required flight check may be given in an aircraft simulator or other appropriate training device, if approved by the Administrator.

(g) If the pilot in command is authorized to use an autopilot system in place of a second in command, that pilot must show, during the required instrument proficiency check, that the pilot is able (without a second in command) both with and without using the autopilot to—

(1) Conduct instrument operations competently; and

(2) Properly conduct air-ground communications and comply with complex air traffic control instructions.

(3) Each pilot taking the autopilot check must show that, while using the autopilot, the airplane can be operated as proficiently as it would be if a second in command were present to handle air-ground communications and air traffic control instructions. The autopilot check need only be demonstrated once every 12 calendar months during the instrument proficiency check required under paragraph (a) of this section.

§ 135.299 Pilot in command: Line checks: Routes and airports.

(a) No certificate holder may use a pilot, nor may any person serve, as a pilot in command of a flight unless,

since the beginning of the 12th calendar month before that service, that pilot has passed a flight check in one of the types of aircraft which that pilot is to fly. The flight check shall—

(1) Be given by an approved check pilot or by the Administrator;

(2) Consist of at least one flight over one route segment; and

(3) Include takeoffs and landings at one or more representative airports. In addition to the requirements of this paragraph, for a pilot authorized to conduct IFR operations, at least one flight shall be flown over a civil airway, an approved off-airway route, or a portion of either of them.

(b) The pilot who conducts the check shall determine whether the pilot being checked satisfactorily performs the duties and responsibilities of a pilot in command in operations under this part, and shall so certify in the pilot training record.

(c) Each certificate holder shall establish in the manual required by § 135.21 a procedure which will ensure that each pilot who has not flown over a route and into an airport within the preceding 90 days will, before beginning the flight, become familiar with all available information required for the safe operation of that flight.

§ 135.301 Crewmember: Tests and checks, grace provisions, training to accepted standards.

(a) If a crewmember who is required to take a test or a flight check under this part, completes the test or flight check in the calendar month before or after the calendar month in which it is required, that crewmember is considered to have completed the test or check in the calendar month in which it is required.

(b) If a pilot being checked under this subpart fails any of the required maneuvers, the person giving the check may give additional training to the pilot during the course of the check. In addition to repeating the maneuvers failed, the person giving the check may require the pilot being checked to repeat any other maneuvers that are necessary to determine the pilot's proficiency. If the pilot being checked is unable to demonstrate satisfactory performance to the person conducting the check, the certificate holder may not use the pilot, nor may the pilot serve, as a flight crewmember in operations under this part until the pilot has satisfactorily completed the check.

§ 135.303   Check pilot authorization: Application and issue.

Each certificate holder desiring FAA approval of a check pilot shall submit a request in writing to the FAA Flight Standards District Office charged with the overall inspection of the certificate holder. The Administrator may issue a letter of authority to each check pilot if that pilot passes the appropriate oral and flight test. The letter of authority lists the tests and checks in this part that the check pilot is qualified to give, and the category, class and type aircraft, where appropriate, for which the check pilot is qualified.

Subpart H—Training

§ 135.321   Applicability and terms used.

(a) This subpart prescribes requirements for establishing and maintaining an approved training program for crewmembers, check airmen and instructors, and other operations personnel, and for the approval and use of aircraft simulators and other training devices in the conduct of that program.

(b) For the purposes of this subpart, the following terms and definitions apply:

(1) *Initial training.* The training required for crewmembers who have not qualified and served in the same capacity on an aircraft.

(2) *Transition training.* The training required for crewmembers who have qualified and served in the same capacity on another aircraft.

(3) *Upgrade training.* The training required for crewmembers who have qualified and served as second in command on a particular aircraft type, before they serve as pilot in command on that aircraft.

(4) *Differences training.* The training required for crewmembers who have qualified and served on a particular type aircraft, when the Adminis-

trator finds differences training is necessary before a crewmember serves in the same capacity on a particular variation of that aircraft.

(5) *Recurrent training.* The training required for crewmembers to remain adequately trained and currently proficient for each aircraft, crewmember position, and type of operation in which the crewmember serves.

(6) *In flight.* The maneuvers, procedures, or functions that must be conducted in the aircraft.

§ 135.323   Training program: General.

(a) Each certificate holder required to have a training program under § 135.341 shall:

(1) Establish, obtain the appropriate initial and final approval of, and provide a training program that meets this subpart and that ensures that each crewmember, flight instructor, check airman, and each person assigned duties for the carriage and handling of hazardous materials (as defined in 49 CFR 171.8) is adequately trained to perform their assigned duties.

(2) Provide adequate ground and flight training facilities and properly qualified ground instructors for the training required by this subpart.

(3) Provide and keep current for each aircraft type used and, if applicable, the particular variations within the aircraft type, appropriate training material, examinations, forms, instructions, and procedures for use in conducting the training and checks required by this subpart.

(4) Provide enough flight instructors, check airmen, and simulator instructors to conduct required flight training and flight checks, and simulator training courses allowed under this subpart.

(b) Whenever a crewmember who is required to take recurrent training under this subpart completes the training in the calendar month before, or the calendar month after, the month in which that training is required, the crewmember is considered to have completed it in the calendar month in which it was required.

(c) Each instructor, supervisor, or check airman who is responsible for a particular ground training subject, segment of flight training, course of training, flight check, or competence check under this part shall certify as to the proficiency and knowledge of the crewmember, flight instructor, or check airman concerned upon completion of that training or check. That certification shall be made a part of the crewmember's record. When the certification required by this paragraph is made by an entry in a computerized recordkeeping system, the certifying instructor, supervisor, or check airman, must be identified with that entry. However, the signature of the certifying instructor, supervisor, or check airman, is not required for computerized entries.

(d) Training subjects that apply to more than one aircraft or crewmember position and that have been satisfactorily completed during previous training while employed by the certificate holder for another aircraft or another crewmember position, need not be repeated during subsequent training other than recurrent training.

(e) Aircraft simulators and other training devices may be used in the certificate holder's training program if approved by the Administrator.

§ 135.325 Training program and revision: Initial and final approval.

(a) To obtain initial and final approval of a training program, or a revision to an approved training program, each certificate holder must submit to the Administrator—

(1) An outline of the proposed or revised curriculum, that provides enough information for a preliminary evaluation of the proposed training program or revision; and

(2) Additional relevant information that may be requested by the Administrator.

(b) If the proposed training program or revision complies with this subpart, the Administrator grants initial approval in writing after which the certificate holder may conduct the training under that program. The Administrator then evaluates the effectiveness of the training program and advises the certificate holder of deficiencies, if any, that must be corrected.

(c) The Administrator grants final approval of the proposed training program or revision if the certificate holder shows that the training conducted under the initial approval in paragraph (b) of this section ensures that each person who successfully completes the training is adequately trained to perform that person's assigned duties.

(d) Whenever the Administrator finds that revisions are necessary for the continued adequacy of a training program that has been granted final approval, the certificate holder shall, after notification by the Administrator, make any changes in the program that are found necessary by the Administrator. Within 30 days after the certificate holder receives the notice, it may file a petition to reconsider the notice with the Administrator. The filing of a petition to reconsider stays the notice pending a decision by the Administrator. However, if the Administrator finds that there is an emergency that requires immediate action in the interest of safety, the Administrator may, upon a statement of the reasons, require a change effective without stay.

§ 135.327 Training program: Curriculum.

(a) Each certificate holder must prepare and keep current a written training program curriculum for each type of aircraft for each crewmember required for that type aircraft. The curriculum must include ground and flight training required by this subpart.

(b) Each training program curriculum must include the following:

(1) A list of principal ground training subjects, including emergency training subjects, that are provided.

(2) A list of all the training devices, mockups, systems trainers, procedures trainers, or other training aids that the certificate holder will use.

(3) Detailed descriptions or pictorial displays of the approved normal, abnormal, and emergency maneuvers, procedures and functions that will be performed during each flight training phase or flight check, indicating those maneuvers, procedures and functions that are to be performed during the

inflight portions of flight training and flight checks.

§ 135.329 Crewmember training requirements.

(a) Each certificate holder must include in its training program the following initial and transition ground training as appropriate to the particular assignment of the crewmember:

(1) Basic indoctrination ground training for newly hired crewmembers including instruction in at least the—

(i) Duties and responsibilities of crewmembers as applicable;

(ii) Appropriate provisions of this chapter;

(iii) Contents of the certificate holder's operating certificate and operations specifications (not required for flight attendants); and

(iv) Appropriate portions of the certificate holder's operating manual.

(2) The initial and transition ground training in §§ 135.345 and 135.349, as applicable.

(3) Emergency training in § 135.331.

(b) Each training program must provide the initial and transition flight training in § 135.347, as applicable.

(c) Each training program must provide recurrent ground and flight training in § 135.351.

(d) Upgrade training in §§ 135.345 and 135.347 for a particular type aircraft may be included in the training program for crewmembers who have qualified and served as second in command on that aircraft.

(e) In addition to initial, transition, upgrade and recurrent training, each training program must provide ground and flight training, instruction, and practice necessary to ensure that each crewmember—

(1) Remains adequately trained and currently proficient for each aircraft, crewmember position, and type of operation in which the crewmember serves; and

(2) Qualifies in new equipment, facilities, procedures, and techniques, including modifications to aircraft.

§ 135.331 Crewmember emergency training.

(a) Each training program must provide emergency training under this section for each aircraft type, model, and configuration, each crewmember, and each kind of operation conducted, as appropriate for each crewmember and the certificate holder.

(b) Emergency training must provide the following:

(1) Instruction in emergency assignments and procedures, including coordination among crewmembers.

(2) Individual instruction in the location, function, and operation of emergency equipment including—

(i) Equipment used in ditching and evacuation;

(ii) First aid equipment and its proper use; and

(iii) Portable fire extinguishers, with emphasis on the type of extinguisher to be used on different classes of fires.

(3) Instruction in the handling of emergency situations including—

(i) Rapid decompression;

(ii) Fire in flight or on the surface and smoke control procedures with emphasis on electrical equipment and related circuit breakers found in cabin areas;

(iii) Ditching and evacuation;

(iv) Illness, injury, or other abnormal situations involving passengers or crewmembers; and

(v) Hijacking and other unusual situations.

(4) Review of the certificate holder's previous aircraft accidents and incidents involving actual emergency situations.

(c) Each crewmember must perform at least the following emergency drills, using the proper emergency equipment and procedures, unless the Administrator finds that, for a particular drill, the crewmember can be adequately trained by demonstration:

(1) Ditching, if applicable.

(2) Emergency evacuation.

(3) Fire extinguishing and smoke control.

(4) Operation and use of emergency exits, including deployment and use of evacuation chutes, if applicable.

(5) Use of crew and passenger oxygen.

(6) Removal of life rafts from the aircraft, inflation of the life rafts, use of life lines, and boarding of passengers and crew, if applicable.

(7) Donning and inflation of life vests and the use of other individual flotation devices, if applicable.

(d) Crewmembers who serve in operations above 25,000 feet must receive instruction in the following:

(1) Respiration.

(2) Hypoxia.

(3) Duration of consciousness without supplemental oxygen at altitude.

(4) Gas expansion.

(5) Gas bubble formation.

(6) Physical phenomena and incidents of decompression.

§ 135.333   Training requirements: Handling and carriage of hazardous materials.

(a) Except as provided in paragraph (d) of this section, no certificate holder may use any person to perform, and no person may perform, any assigned duties and responsibilities for the handling or carriage of hazardous materials (as defined in 49 CFR 171.8), unless within the preceding 12 calendar months that person has satisfactorily completed initial or recurrent training in an appropriate training program established by the certificate holder, which includes instruction regarding—

(1) The proper shipper certification, packaging, marking, labeling, and documentation for hazardous materials; and

(2) The compatibility, loading, storage, and handling characteristics of hazardous materials.

(b) Each certificate holder shall maintain a record of the satisfactory completion of the initial and recurrent training given to crewmembers and ground personnel who perform assigned duties and responsibilities for the handling and carriage of hazardous materials.

(c) Each certificate holder that elects not to accept hazardous materials shall ensure that each crewmember is adequately trained to recognize those items classified as hazardous materials.

(d) If a certificate holder operates into or out of airports at which trained employees or contract personnel are not available, it may use persons not meeting the requirements of paragraphs (a) and (b) of this section to load, offload, or otherwise handle hazardous materials if these persons are supervised by a crewmember who is qualified under paragraphs (a) and (b) of this section.

§ 135.335   Approval of aircraft simulators and other training devices.

(a) Training courses using aircraft simulators and other training devices may be included in the certificate holder's training program if approved by the Administrator.

(b) Each aircraft simulator and other training device that is used in a training course or in checks required under this subpart must meet the following requirements:

(1) It must be specifically approved for—

(i) The certificate holder; and

(ii) The particular maneuver, procedure, or crewmember function involved.

(2) It must maintain the performance, functional, and other characteristics that are required for approval.

(3) Additionally, for aircraft simulators, it must be—

(i) Approved for the type aircraft and, if applicable, the particular variation within type for which the training or check is being conducted; and

(ii) Modified to conform with any modification to the aircraft being simulated that changes the performance, functional, or other characteristics required for approval.

(c) A particular aircraft simulator or other training device may be used by more than one certificate holder.

(d) In granting initial and final approval of training programs or revisions to them, the Administrator considers the training devices, methods and procedures listed in the certificate holder's curriculum under § 135.327.

[Doc. No. 16907, 43 FR 46783, Oct. 10, 1978, as amended at 44 FR 26738, May 7, 1979]

§ 135.337   Training program: Check airmen and instructor qualifications.

(a) No certificate holder may use a person, nor may any person serve, as a flight instructor or check airman in a training program established under this subpart unless, for the particular aircraft type involved, that person—

(1) Holds the airman certificate and ratings that must be held to serve as a pilot in command in operations under this part;

(2) Has satisfactorily completed the appropriate training phases for the aircraft, including recurrent training, required to serve as a pilot in command in operations under this part;

(3) Has satisfactorily completed the appropriate proficiency or competency checks required to serve as a pilot in command in operations under this part;

(4) Has satisfactorily completed the applicable training requirements of § 135.339;

(5) Holds a Class I or Class II medical certificate required to serve as a pilot in command in operations under this part;

(6) In the case of a check airman, has been approved by the Administrator for the airman duties involved; and

(7) In the case of a check airman used in an aircraft simulator only, holds a Class III medical certificate.

(b) No certificate holder may use a person, nor may any person serve, as a simulator instructor for a course of training given in an aircraft simulator under this subpart unless that person—

(1) Holds at least a commercial pilot certificate; and

(2) Has satisfactorily completed the following as evidenced by the approval of a check airman—

(i) Appropriate initial pilot and flight instructor ground training under this subpart; and

(ii) A simulator flight training course in the type simulator in which that person instructs under this subpart.

§ 135.339   Check airmen and flight instructors: Initial and transition training.

(a) The initial and transition ground training for pilot check airmen must include the following:

(1) Pilot check airman duties, functions, and responsibilities.

(2) The applicable provisions of this chapter and certificate holder's policies and procedures.

(3) The appropriate methods, procedures, and techniques for conducting the required checks.

(4) Proper evaluation of pilot performance including the detection of—

(i) Improper and insufficient training; and

(ii) Personal characteristics that could adversely affect safety.

(5) The appropriate corrective action for unsatisfactory checks.

(6) The approved methods, procedures, and limitations for performing the required normal, abnormal, and emergency procedures in the aircraft.

(b) The initial and transition ground training for pilot flight instructors, except for the holder of a valid flight instructor certificate, must include the following:

(1) The fundamental principles of the teaching-learning process.

(2) Teaching methods and procedures.

(3) The instructor-student relationship.

(c) The initial and transition flight training for pilot check airmen and pilot flight instructors must include the following:

(1) Enough inflight training and practice in conducting flight checks from the left and right pilot seats in the required normal, abnormal, and emergency maneuvers to ensure that person's competence to conduct the pilot flight checks and flight training under this subpart.

(2) The appropriate safety measures to be taken from either pilot seat for emergency situations that are likely to develop in training.

(3) The potential results of improper or untimely safety measures during training.

The requirements of paragraphs (c)(2) and (3) of this section may be accomplished in flight or in an approved simulator.

§ 135.341   Pilot and flight attendant crewmember training programs.

(a) Each certificate holder, other than one who uses only one pilot in the certificate holder's operations, shall establish and maintain an approved pilot training program, and each certificate holder who uses a flight attendant crewmember shall establish and maintain an approved flight attendant training program, that is appropriate to the operations to which each pilot and flight attendant is to be assigned, and will ensure that they are adequately trained to meet the applicable knowledge and practical testing requirements of §§ 135.293 through 135.301. However, the Administrator may authorize a deviation from this section if the Administrator finds that, because of the limited size and scope of the operation, safety will allow a deviation from these requirements.

(b) Each certificate holder required to have a training program by paragraph (a) of this section shall include in that program ground and flight training curriculums for—

(1) Initial training;

(2) Transition training;

(3) Upgrade training;

(4) Differences training; and

(5) Recurrent training.

(c) Each certificate holder required to have a training program by paragraph (a) of this section shall provide current and appropriate study materials for use by each required pilot and flight attendant.

(d) The certificate holder shall furnish copies of the pilot and flight attendant crewmember training program, and all changes and additions, to the assigned representative of the Administrator. If the certificate holder uses training facilities of other persons, a copy of those training programs or appropriate portions used for those facilities shall also be furnished. Curricula that follow FAA published curricula may be cited by reference in the copy of the training program furnished to the representative of the Administrator and need not be furnished with the program.

§ 135.343 Crewmember initial and recurrent training requirements.

No certificate holder may use a person, nor may any person serve, as a crewmember in operations under this part unless that crewmember has completed the appropriate initial or recurrent training phase of the training program appropriate to the type of operation in which the crewmember is to

serve since the beginning of the 12th calendar month before that service. This section does not apply to a certificate holder that uses only one pilot in the certificate holder's operations.

§ 135.345 Pilots: Initial, transition, and upgrade ground training.

Initial, transition, and upgrade ground training for pilots must include instruction in at least the following, as applicable to their duties:

(a) General subjects—

(1) The certificate holder's flight locating procedures;

(2) Principles and methods for determining weight and balance, and runway limitations for takeoff and landing;

(3) Enough meteorology to ensure a practical knowledge of weather phenomena, including the principles of frontal systems, icing, fog, thunderstorms, windshear and, if appropriate, high altitude weather situations;

(4) Air traffic control systems, procedures, and phraseology;

(5) Navigation and the use of navigational aids, including instrument approach procedures;

(6) Normal and emergency communication procedures;

(7) Visual cues before and during descent below DH or MDA; and

(8) Other instructions necessary to ensure the pilot's competence.

(b) For each aircraft type—

(1) A general description;

(2) Performance characteristics;

(3) Engines and propellers;

(4) Major components;

(5) Major aircraft systems (i.e., flight controls, electrical, and hydraulic), other systems, as appropriate, principles of normal, abnormal, and emergency operations, appropriate procedures and limitations;

(6) Procedures for—

(i) Recognizing and avoiding severe weather situations;

(ii) Escaping from severe weather situations, in case of inadvertent encounters, including low-altitude windshear (except that rotorcraft pilots are not required to be trained in escaping from low altitude windshear); and

(iii) Operating in or near thunderstorms (including best penetrating altitudes), turbulent air (including clear air turbulence), icing, hail, and other potentially hazardous meteorological conditions;

(7) Operating limitations;

(8) Fuel consumption and cruise control;

(9) Flight planning;

(10) Each normal and emergency procedure; and

(11) The approved Aircraft Flight Manual, or equivalent.

§ 135.347 Pilots: Initial, transition, upgrade, and differences flight training.

(a) Initial, transition, upgrade, and differences training for pilots must include flight and practice in each of the maneuvers and procedures in the approved training program curriculum.

(b) The maneuvers and procedures required by paragraph (a) of this section must be performed in flight, except to the extent that certain maneuvers and procedures may be performed in an aircraft simulator, or an appropriate training device, as allowed by this subpart.

(c) If the certificate holder's approved training program includes a course of training using an aircraft simulator or other training device, each pilot must successfully complete—

(1) Training and practice in the simulator or training device in at least the maneuvers and procedures in this subpart that are capable of being performed in the aircraft simulator or training device; and

(2) A flight check in the aircraft or a check in the simulator or training device to the level of proficiency of a pilot in command or second in command, as applicable, in at least the maneuvers and procedures that are capable of being performed in an aircraft simulator or training device.

§ 135.349 Flight attendants: Initial and transition ground training.

Initial and transition ground training for flight attendants must include instruction in at least the following—

(a) General subjects—

(1) The authority of the pilot in command; and

(2) Passenger handling, including procedures to be followed in handling deranged persons or other persons whose conduct might jeopardize safety.

(b) For each aircraft type—

(1) A general description of the aircraft emphasizing physical characteristics that may have a bearing on ditching, evacuation, and inflight emergency procedures and on other related duties;

(2) The use of both the public address system and the means of communicating with other flight crewmembers, including emergency means in the case of attempted hijacking or other unusual situations; and

(3) Proper use of electrical galley equipment and the controls for cabin heat and ventilation.

§ 135.351 Recurrent training.

(a) Each certificate holder must ensure that each crewmember receives recurrent training and is adequately trained and currently proficient for the type aircraft and crewmember position involved.

(b) Recurrent ground training for crewmembers must include at least the following:

(1) A quiz or other review to determine the crewmember's knowledge of the aircraft and crewmember position involved.

(2) Instruction as necessary in the subjects required for initial ground training by this subpart, as appropriate, including low-altitude windshear training as prescribed in § 135.345 of this part and emergency training.

(c) Recurrent flight training for pilots must include, at least, flight training in the maneuvers or procedures in this subpart, except that satisfactory completion of the check required by § 135.293 within the preceding 12 calendar months may be substituted for recurrent flight training.

Subpart I—Airplane Performance Operating Limitations

§ 135.361 Applicability.

(a) This subpart prescribes airplane performance operating limitations applicable to the operation of the categories of airplanes listed in § 135.363 when operated under this part.

(b) For the purpose of this subpart, "effective length of the runway," for landing means the distance from the point at which the obstruction clearance plane associated with the approach end of the runway intersects the centerline of the runway to the far end of the runway.

(c) For the purpose of this subpart, "obstruction clearance plane" means a plane sloping upward from the runway at a slope of 1:20 to the horizontal, and tangent to or clearing all obstructions within a specified area surrounding the runway as shown in a profile view of that area. In the plan view, the centerline of the specified area coincides with the centerline of the runway, beginning at the point where the obstruction clearance plane intersects the centerline of the runway and proceeding to a point at least 1,500 feet from the beginning point. After that the centerline coincides with the takeoff path over the ground for the runway (in the case of takeoffs) or with the instrument approach counterpart (for landings), or, where the applicable one of these paths has not been established, it proceeds consistent with turns of at least 4,000-foot radius until a point is reached beyond which the obstruction clearance plane clears all obstructions. This area extends laterally 200 feet on each side of the centerline at the point where the obstruction clearance plane intersects the runway and continues at this width to the end of the runway; then it increases uniformly to 500 feet on each side of the centerline at a point 1,500 feet from the intersection of the obstruction clearance plane with the runway; after that it extends laterally 500 feet on each side of the centerline.

§135.363 General.

(a) Each certificate holder operating a reciprocating engine powered large transport category airplane shall comply with §§135.365 through 135.377.

(b) Each certificate holder operating a turbine engine powered large transport category airplane shall comply with §§135.379 through 135.387, except that when it operates a turbopropeller-powered large transport category airplane certificated after August 29, 1959, but previously type certificated with the same number of reciprocating engines, it may comply with §§135.365 through 135.377.

(c) Each certificate holder operating a large nontransport category airplane shall comply with §§135.389 through 135.395 and any determination of compliance must be based only on approved performance data. For the purpose of this subpart, a large nontransport category airplane is an airplane that was type certificated before July 1, 1942.

(d) Each certificate holder operating a small transport category airplane shall comply with §135.397.

(e) Each certificate holder operating a small nontransport category airplane shall comply with §135.399.

(f) The performance data in the Airplane Flight Manual applies in determining compliance with §§135.365 through 135.387. Where conditions are different from those on which the performance data is based, compliance is determined by interpolation or by computing the effects of change in the specific variables, if the results of the interpolation or computations are substantially as accurate as the results of direct tests.

(g) No person may take off a reciprocating engine powered large transport category airplane at a weight that is more than the allowable weight for the runway being used (determined under the runway takeoff limitations of the transport category operating rules of this subpart) after taking into account the temperature operating correction factors in section 4a.749a-T or section 4b.117 of the Civil Air Regulations in effect on January 31, 1965, and in the applicable Airplane Flight Manual.

(h) The Administrator may authorize in the operations specifications deviations from this subpart if special circumstances make a literal observance of a requirement unnecessary for safety.

(i) The 10-mile width specified in §§135.369 through 135.373 may be reduced to 5 miles, for not more than 20 miles, when operating under VFR or where navigation facilities furnish reliable and accurate identification of high ground and obstructions located outside of 5 miles, but within 10 miles, on each side of the intended track.

(j) Each certificate holder operating a commuter category airplane shall comply with §135.398.

[Doc. No. 16097, 43 FR 46783, Oct. 10, 1978, as amended by Amdt. 135–21, 52 FR 1836, Jan. 15, 1987]

§ 135.365 Large transport category airplanes: Reciprocating engine powered: Weight limitations.

(a) No person may take off a reciprocating engine powered large transport category airplane from an airport located at an elevation outside of the range for which maximum takeoff weights have been determined for that airplane.

(b) No person may take off a reciprocating engine powered large transport category airplane for an airport of intended destination that is located at an elevation outside of the range for which maximum landing weights have been determined for that airplane.

(c) No person may specify, or have specified, an alternate airport that is located at an elevation outside of the range for which maximum landing weights have been determined for the reciprocating engine powered large transport category airplane concerned.

(d) No person may take off a reciprocating engine powered large transport category airplane at a weight more than the maximum authorized takeoff weight for the elevation of the airport.

(e) No person may take off a reciprocating engine powered large transport category airplane if its weight on arrival at the airport of destination will be more than the maximum authorized landing weight for the elevation of that airport, allowing for normal consumption of fuel and oil en route.

§ 135.367 Large transport category airplanes: Reciprocating engine powered: Takeoff limitations.

(a) No person operating a reciprocating engine powered large transport category airplane may take off that airplane unless it is possible—

(1) To stop the airplane safely on the runway, as shown by the accelerate-stop distance data, at any time during takeoff until reaching critical-engine failure speed;

(2) If the critical engine fails at any time after the airplane reaches critical-engine failure speed V_1, to continue the takeoff and reach a height of 50 feet, as indicated by the takeoff path data, before passing over the end of the runway; and

(3) To clear all obstacles either by at least 50 feet vertically (as shown by the takeoff path data) or 200 feet horizontally within the airport boundaries and 300 feet horizontally beyond the boundaries, without banking before reaching a height of 50 feet (as shown by the takeoff path data) and after that without banking more than 15 degrees.

(b) In applying this section, corrections must be made for any runway gradient. To allow for wind effect, takeoff data based on still air may be corrected by taking into account not more than 50 percent of any reported headwind component and not less than 150 percent of any reported tailwind component.

§ 135.369 Large transport category airplanes: Reciprocating engine powered: En route limitations: All engines operating.

(a) No person operating a reciprocating engine powered large transport category airplane may take off that airplane at a weight, allowing for normal consumption of fuel and oil, that does not allow a rate of climb (in feet per minute), with all engines operating, of at least 6.90 V_{s_0} (that is, the number of feet per minute obtained by multiplying the number of knots by 6.90) at an altitude of a least 1,000 feet above the highest ground or obstruction within ten miles of each side of the intended track.

(b) This section does not apply to large transport category airplanes certificated under Part 4a of the Civil Air Regulations.

§ 135.371 Large transport category airplanes: Reciprocating engine powered: En route limitations: One engine inoperative.

(a) Except as provided in paragraph (b) of this section, no person operating a reciprocating engine powered large transport category airplane may take off that airplane at a weight, allowing for normal consumption of fuel and oil, that does not allow a rate of climb (in feet per minute), with one engine inoperative, of at least $(0.079 - 0.106/$

N) Vs_o^2 (where N is the number of engines installed and Vs_o is expressed in knots) at an altitude of least 1,000 feet above the highest ground or obstruction within 10 miles of each side of the intended track. However, for the purposes of this paragraph the rate of climb for transport category airplanes certificated under Part 4a of the Civil Air Regulations is $0.026\ Vs_o^2$.

(b) In place of the requirements of paragraph (a) of this section, a person may, under an approved procedure, operate a reciprocating engine powered large transport category airplane at an all-engines-operating altitude that allows the airplane to continue, after an engine failure, to an alternate airport where a landing can be made under § 135.377, allowing for normal consumption of fuel and oil. After the assumed failure, the flight path must clear the ground and any obstruction within five miles on each side of the intended track by at least 2,000 feet.

(c) If an approved procedure under paragraph (b) of this section is used, the certificate holder shall comply with the following:

(1) The rate of climb (as prescribed in the Airplane Flight Manual for the appropriate weight and altitude) used in calculating the airplane's flight path shall be diminished by an amount in feet per minute, equal to $(0.079-0.106/N)\ Vs_o^2$ (when N is the number of engines installed and Vs_o is expressed in knots) for airplanes certificated under Part 25 of this chapter and by $0.026\ Vs_o^2$ for airplanes certificated under Part 4a of the Civil Air Regulations.

(2) The all-engines-operating altitude shall be sufficient so that in the event the critical engine becomes inoperative at any point along the route, the flight will be able to proceed to a predetermined alternate airport by use of this procedure. In determining the takeoff weight, the airplane is assumed to pass over the critical obstruction following engine failure at a point no closer to the critical obstruction than the nearest approved radio navigational fix, unless the Administrator approves a procedure established on a different basis upon finding that adequate operational safeguards exist.

(3) The airplane must meet the provisions of paragraph (a) of this section at 1,000 feet above the airport used as an alternate in this procedure.

(4) The procedure must include an approved method of accounting for winds and temperatures that would otherwise adversely affect the flight path.

(5) In complying with this procedure, fuel jettisoning is allowed if the certificate holder shows that it has an adequate training program, that proper instructions are given to the flight crew, and all other precautions are taken to ensure a safe procedure.

(6) The certificate holder and the pilot in command shall jointly elect an alternate airport for which the appropriate weather reports or forecasts, or any combination of them, indicate that weather conditions will be at or above the alternate weather minimum specified in the certificate holder's operations specifications for that airport when the flight arrives.

§ 135.373   Part 25 transport category airplanes with four or more engines: Reciprocating engine powered: En route limitations: Two engines inoperative.

(a) No person may operate an airplane certificated under Part 25 and having four or more engines unless—

(1) There is no place along the intended track that is more than 90 minutes (with all engines operating at cruising power) from an airport that meets § 135.377; or

(2) It is operated at a weight allowing the airplane, with the two critical engines inoperative, to climb at $0.013\ Vs_o^2$ feet per minute (that is, the number of feet per minute obtained by multiplying the number of knots squared by 0.013) at an altitude of 1,000 feet above the highest ground or obstruction within 10 miles on each side of the intended track, or at an altitude of 5,000 feet, whichever is higher.

(b) For the purposes of paragraph (a)(2) of this section, it is assumed that—

(1) The two engines fail at the point that is most critical with respect to the takeoff weight;

(2) Consumption of fuel and oil is normal with all engines operating up to the point where the two engines fail with two engines operating beyond that point;

(3) Where the engines are assumed to fail at an altitude above the prescribed minimum altitude, compliance with the prescribed rate of climb at the prescribed minimum altitude need not be shown during the descent from the cruising altitude to the prescribed minimum altitude, if those requirements can be met once the prescribed minimum altitude is reached, and assuming descent to be along a net flight path and the rate of descent to be 0.013 $Vs_o{}^2$ greater than the rate in the approved performance data; and

(4) If fuel jettisoning is provided, the airplane's weight at the point where the two engines fail is considered to be not less than that which would include enough fuel to proceed to an airport meeting § 135.377 and to arrive at an altitude of at least 1,000 feet directly over that airport.

§ 135.375 Large transport category airplanes: Reciprocating engine powered: Landing limitations: Destination airports.

(a) Except as provided in paragraph (b) of this section, no person operating a reciprocating engine powered large transport category airplane may take off that airplane, unless its weight on arrival, allowing for normal consumption of fuel and oil in flight, would allow a full stop landing at the intended destination within 60 percent of the effective length of each runway described below from a point 50 feet directly above the intersection of the obstruction clearance plane and the runway. For the purposes of determining the allowable landing weight at the destination airport the following is assumed:

(1) The airplane is landed on the most favorable runway and in the most favorable direction in still air.

(2) The airplane is landed on the most suitable runway considering the probable wind velocity and direction (forecast for the expected time of arrival), the ground handling characteristics of the type of airplane, and other conditions such as landing aids and terrain, and allowing for the effect of the landing path and roll of not more than 50 percent of the headwind component or not less than 150 percent of the tailwind component.

(b) An airplane that would be prohibited from being taken off because it could not meet paragraph (a)(2) of this section may be taken off if an alternate airport is selected that meets all of this section except that the airplane can accomplish a full stop landing within 70 percent of the effective length of the runway.

§ 135.377 Large transport category airplanes: Reciprocating engine powered: Landing limitations: Alternate airports.

No person may list an airport as an alternate airport in a flight plan unless the airplane (at the weight anticipated at the time of arrival at the airport), based on the assumptions in § 135.375(a) (1) and (2), can be brought to a full stop landing within 70 percent of the effective length of the runway.

§ 135.379 Large transport category airplanes: Turbine engine powered: Takeoff limitations.

(a) No person operating a turbine engine powered large transport category airplane may take off that airplane at a weight greater than that listed in the Airplane Flight Manual for the elevation of the airport and for the ambient temperature existing at takeoff.

(b) No person operating a turbine engine powered large transport category airplane certificated after August 26, 1957, but before August 30, 1959 (SR422, 422A), may take off that airplane at a weight greater than that listed in the Airplane Flight Manual for the minumum distance required for takeoff. In the case of an airplane certificated after September 30, 1958 (SR422A, 422B), the takeoff distance may include a clearway distance but the clearway distance included may not be greater than one-half of the takeoff run.

(c) No person operating a turbine engine powered large transport category airplane certificated after August 29, 1959 (SR422B), may take off that airplane at a weight greater than that listed in the Airplane Flight Manual at which compliance with the following may be shown:

(1) The accelerate-stop distance, as defined in § 25.109 of this chapter, must not exceed the length of the runway plus the length of any stopway.

(2) The takeoff distance must not exceed the length of the runway plus the length of any clearway except that the length of any clearway included must not be greater than one-half the length of the runway.

(3) The takeoff run must not be greater than the length of the runway.

(d) No person operating a turbine engine powered large transport category airplane may take off that airplane at a weight greater than that listed in the Airplane Flight Manual—

(1) For an airplane certificated after August 26, 1957, but before October 1, 1958 (SR422), that allows a takeoff path that clears all obstacles either by at least (35+0.01 D) feet vertically (D is the distance along the intended flight path from the end of the runway in feet), or by at least 200 feet horizontally within the airport boundaries and by at least 300 feet horizontally after passing the boundaries; or

(2) For an airplane certificated after September 30, 1958 (SR422A, 422B), that allows a net takeoff flight path that clears all obstacles either by a height of at least 35 feet vertically, or by at least 200 feet horizontally within the airport boundaries and by at least 300 feet horizontally after passing the boundaries.

(e) In determining maximum weights, minimum distances and flight paths under paragraphs (a) through (d) of this section, correction must be made for the runway to be used, the elevation of the airport, the effective runway gradient, and the ambient temperature and wind component at the time of takeoff.

(f) For the purposes of this section, it is assumed that the airplane is not banked before reaching a height of 50 feet, as shown by the takeoff path or net takeoff flight path data (as appropriate) in the Airplane Flight Manual,

and after that the maximum bank is not more than 15 degrees.

(g) For the purposes of this section, the terms, "takeoff distance," "takeoff run," "net takeoff flight path," have the same meanings as set forth in the rules under which the airplane was certificated.

§ 135.381 Large transport category airplanes: Turbine engine powered: En route limitations: One engine inoperative.

(a) No person operating a turbine engine powered large transport category airplane may take off that airplane at a weight, allowing for normal consumption of fuel and oil, that is greater than that which (under the approved, one engine inoperative, en route net flight path data in the Airplane Flight Manual for that airplane) will allow compliance with paragraph (a) (1) or (2) of this section, based on the ambient temperatures expected en route.

(1) There is a positive slope at an altitude of at least 1,000 feet above all terrain and obstructions within five statute miles on each side of the intended track, and, in addition, if that airplane was certificated after August 29, 1958 (SR422B), there is a positive slope at 1,500 feet above the airport where the airplane is assumed to land after an engine fails.

(2) The net flight path allows the airplane to continue flight from the cruising altitude to an airport where a landing can be made under § 135.387 clearing all terrain and obstructions within five statute miles of the intended track by at least 2,000 feet vertically and with a positive slope at 1,000 feet above the airport where the airplane lands after an engine fails, or, if that airplane was certificated after September 30, 1958 (SR422A, 422B), with a positive slope at 1,500 feet above the airport where the airplane lands after an engine fails.

(b) For the purpose of paragraph (a)(2) of this section, it is assumed that—

(1) The engine fails at the most critical point en route;

(2) The airplane passes over the critical obstruction, after engine failure at

a point that is no closer to the obstruction than the approved radio navigation fix, unless the Administrator authorizes a different procedure based on adequate operational safeguards;

(3) An approved method is used to allow for adverse winds;

(4) Fuel jettisoning will be allowed if the certificate holder shows that the crew is properly instructed, that the training program is adequate, and that all other precautions are taken to ensure a safe procedure;

(5) The alternate airport is selected and meets the prescribed weather minimums; and

(6) The consumption of fuel and oil after engine failure is the same as the consumption that is allowed for in the approved net flight path data in the Airplane Flight Manual.

§ 135.383 Large transport category airplanes: Turbine engine powered: En route limitations: Two engines inoperative.

(a) Airplanes certificated after August 26, 1957, but before October 1, 1958 (SR422). No person may operate a turbine engine powered large transport category airplane along an intended route unless that person complies with either of the following:

(1) There is no place along the intended track that is more than 90 minutes (with all engines operating at cruising power) from an airport that meets § 135.387.

(2) Its weight, according to the two-engine-inoperative, en route, net flight path data in the Airplane Flight Manual, allows the airplane to fly from the point where the two engines are assumed to fail simultaneously to an airport that meets § 135.387, with a net flight path (considering the ambient temperature anticipated along the track) having a positive slope at an altitude of at least 1,000 feet above all terrain and obstructions within five statute miles on each side of the intended track, or at an altitude of 5,000 feet, whichever is higher.

For the purposes of paragraph (a)(2) of this section, it is assumed that the two engines fail at the most critical point en route, that if fuel jettisoning is provided, the airplane's weight at the point where the engines fail includes enough fuel to continue to the airport and to arrive at an altitude of at least 1,000 feet directly over the airport, and that the fuel and oil consumption after engine failure is the same as the consumption allowed for in the net flight path data in the Airplane Flight Manual.

(b) Airplanes certificated after September 30, 1958, but before August 30, 1959 (SR422A). No person may operate a turbine engine powered large transport category airplane along an intended route unless that person complies with either of the following:

(1) There is no place along the intended track that is more than 90 minutes (with all engines operating at cruising power) from an airport that meets § 135.387.

(2) Its weight, according to the two-engine-inoperative, en route, net flight path data in the Airplane Flight Manual allows the airplane to fly from the point where the two engines are assumed to fail simultaneously to an airport that meets § 135.387 with a net flight path (considering the ambient temperatures anticipated along the track) having a positive slope at an altitude of at least 1,000 feet above all terrain and obstructions within five statute miles on each side of the intended track, or at an altitude of 2,000 feet, whichever is higher.

For the purpose of paragraph (b)(2) of this section, it is assumed that the two engines fail at the most critical point en route, that the airplane's weight at the point where the engines fail includes enough fuel to continue to the airport, to arrive at an altitude of at least 1,500 feet directly over the airport, and after that to fly for 15 minutes at cruise power or thrust, or both, and that the consumption of fuel and oil after engine failure is the same as the consumption allowed for in the net flight path data in the Airplane Flight Manual.

(c) Aircraft certificated after August 29, 1959 (SR422B). No person may operate a turbine engine powered large transport category airplane along an intended route unless that person complies with either of the following:

(1) There is no place along the intended track that is more than 90 min-

utes (with all engines operating at cruising power) from an airport that meets § 135.387.

(2) Its weight, according to the two-engine-inoperative, en route, net flight path data in the Airplane Flight Manual, allows the airplane to fly from the point where the two engines are assumed to fail simultaneously to an airport that meets § 135.387, with the net flight path (considering the ambient temperatures anticipated along the track) clearing vertically by at least 2,000 feet all terrain and obstructions within five statute miles on each side of the intended track. For the purposes of this paragraph, it is assumed that—

(i) The two engines fail at the most critical point en route;

(ii) The net flight path has a positive slope at 1,500 feet above the airport where the landing is assumed to be made after the engines fail;

(iii) Fuel jettisoning will be approved if the certificate holder shows that the crew is properly instructed, that the training program is adequate, and that all other precautions are taken to ensure a safe procedure;

(iv) The airplane's weight at the point where the two engines are assumed to fail provides enough fuel to continue to the airport, to arrive at an altitude of at least 1,500 feet directly over the airport, and after that to fly for 15 minutes at cruise power or thrust, or both; and

(v) The consumption of fuel and oil after the engines fail is the same as the consumption that is allowed for in the net flight path data in the Airplane Flight Manual.

§ 135.385 Large transport category airplanes: Turbine engine powered: Landing limitations: Destination airports.

(a) No person operating a turbine engine powered large transport category airplane may take off that airplane at a weight that (allowing for normal consumption of fuel and oil in flight to the destination or alternate airport) the weight of the airplane on arrival would exceed the landing weight in the Airplane Flight Manual for the elevation of the destination or alternate airport and the ambient tempera-

ture anticipated at the time of landing.

(b) Except as provided in paragraph (c), (d), or (e) of this section, no person operating a turbine engine powered large transport category airplane may take off that airplane unless its weight on arrival, allowing for normal consumption of fuel and oil in flight (in accordance with the landing distance in the Airplane Flight Manual for the elevation of the destination airport and the wind conditions anticipated there at the time of landing), would allow a full stop landing at the intended destination airport within 60 percent of the effective length of each runway described below from a point 50 feet above the intersection of the obstruction clearance plane and the runway. For the purpose of determining the allowable landing weight at the destination airport the following is assumed:

(1) The airplane is landed on the most favorable runway and in the most favorable direction, in still air.

(2) The airplane is landed on the most suitable runway considering the probable wind velocity and direction and the ground handling characteristics of the airplane, and considering other conditions such as landing aids and terrain.

(c) A turbopropeller powered airplane that would be prohibited from being taken off because it could not meet paragraph (b)(2) of this section, may be taken off if an alternate airport is selected that meets all of this section except that the airplane can accomplish a full stop landing within 70 percent of the effective length of the runway.

(d) Unless, based on a showing of actual operating landing techniques on wet runways, a shorter landing distance (but never less than that required by paragraph (b) of this section) has been approved for a specific type and model airplane and included in the Airplane Flight Manual, no person may take off a turbojet airplane when the appropriate weather reports or forecasts, or any combination of them, indicate that the runways at the destination airport may be wet or slippery at the estimated time of arrival unless the effective runway length at the destination airport is at least 115 percent of the runway length required under paragraph (b) of this section.

(e) A turbojet airplane that would be prohibited from being taken off because it could not meet paragraph (b)(2) of this section may be taken off if an alternate airport is selected that meets all of paragraph (b) of this section.

§ 135.387 Large transport category airplanes: Turbine engine powered: Landing limitations: Alternate airports.

No person may select an airport as an alternate airport for a turbine engine powered large transport category airplane unless (based on the assumptions in § 135.385(b)) that airplane, at the weight anticipated at the time of arrival, can be brought to a full stop landing within 70 percent of the effective length of the runway for turbopropeller-powered airplanes and 60 percent of the effective length of the runway for turbojet airplanes, from a point 50 feet above the intersection of the obstruction clearance plane and the runway.

§ 135.389 Large nontransport category airplanes: Takeoff limitations.

(a) No person operating a large nontransport category airplane may take off that airplane at a weight greater than the weight that would allow the airplane to be brought to a safe stop within the effective length of the runway, from any point during the takeoff before reaching 105 percent of minimum control speed (the minimum speed at which an airplane can be safely controlled in flight after an engine becomes inoperative) or 115 percent of the power off stalling speed in the takeoff configuration, whichever is greater.

(b) For the purposes of this section—

(1) It may be assumed that takeoff power is used on all engines during the acceleration;

(2) Not more than 50 percent of the reported headwind component, or not less than 150 percent of the reported tailwind component, may be taken into account;

(3) The average runway gradient (the difference between the elevations of the endpoints of the runway divided by the total length) must be considered if it is more than one-half of one percent;

(4) It is assumed that the airplane is operating in standard atmosphere; and

(5) For takeoff, "effective length of the runway" means the distance from the end of the runway at which the takeoff is started to a point at which the obstruction clearance plane associated with the other end of the runway intersects the runway centerline.

§ 135.391 Large nontransport category airplanes: En route limitations: One engine inoperative.

(a) Except as provided in paragraph (b) of this section, no person operating a large nontransport category airplane may take off that airplane at a weight that does not allow a rate of climb of at least 50 feet a minute, with the critical engine inoperative, at an altitude of at least 1,000 feet above the highest obstruction within five miles on each side of the intended track, or 5,000 feet, whichever is higher.

(b) Without regard to paragraph (a) of this section, if the Administrator finds that safe operations are not impaired, a person may operate the airplane at an altitude that allows the airplane, in case of engine failure, to clear all obstructions within five miles on each side of the intended track by 1,000 feet. If this procedure is used, the rate of descent for the appropriate weight and altitude is assumed to be 50 feet a minute greater than the rate in the approved performance data. Before approving such a procedure, the Administrator considers the following for the route, route segment, or area concerned:

(1) The reliability of wind and weather forecasting.

(2) The location and kinds of navigation aids.

(3) The prevailing weather conditions, particularly the frequency and amount of turbulence normally encountered.

(4) Terrain features.

(5) Air traffic problems.

(6) Any other operational factors that affect the operations.

(c) For the purposes of this section, it is assumed that—

(1) The critical engine is inoperative;

(2) The propeller of the inoperative engine is in the minimum drag position;

(3) The wing flaps and landing gear are in the most favorable position;

(4) The operating engines are operating at the maximum continuous power available;

(5) The airplane is operating in standard atmosphere; and

(6) The weight of the airplane is progressively reduced by the anticipated consumption of fuel and oil.

§ 135.393 Large nontransport category airplanes: Landing limitations: Destination airports.

(a) No person operating a large nontransport category airplane may take off that airplane at a weight that—

(1) Allowing for anticipated consumption of fuel and oil, is greater than the weight that would allow a full stop landing within 60 percent of the effective length of the most suitable runway at the destination airport; and

(2) Is greater than the weight allowable if the landing is to be made on the runway—

(i) With the greatest effective length in still air; and

(ii) Required by the probable wind, taking into account not more than 50 percent of the headwind component or not less than 150 percent of the tailwind component.

(b) For the purpose of this section, it is assumed that—

(1) The airplane passes directly over the intersection of the obstruction clearance plane and the runway at a height of 50 feet in a steady gliding approach at a true indicated airspeed of at least 1.3 V_{so};

(2) The landing does not require exceptional pilot skill; and

(3) The airplane is operating in standard atmosphere.

§ 135.395 Large nontransport category airplanes: Landing limitations: Alternate airports.

No person may select an airport as an alternate airport for a large nontransport category airplane unless that airplane (at the weight anticipated at the time of arrival), based on the assumptions in § 135.393(b), can be brought to a full stop landing within 70 percent of the effective length of the runway.

§ 135.397 Small transport category airplane performance operating limitations.

(a) No person may operate a reciprocating engine powered small transport category airplane unless that person complies with the weight limitations in § 135.365, the takeoff limitations in § 135.367 (except paragraph (a)(3)), and the landing limitations in §§ 135.375 and 135.377.

(b) No person may operate a turbine engine powered small transport category airplane unless that person complies with the takeoff limitations in § 135.379 (except paragraphs (d) and (f)) and the landing limitations in §§ 135.385 and 135.387.

§ 135.398 Commuter category airplanes performance operating limitations.

(a) No person may operate a commuter category airplane unless that person complies with the takeoff weight limitations in the approved Airplane Flight Manual.

(b) No person may take off an airplane type certificated in the commuter category at a weight greater than that listed in the Airplane Flight Manual that allows a net takeoff flight path that clears all obstacles either by a height of at least 35 feet vertically, or at least 200 feet horizontally within the airport boundaries and by at least 300 feet horizontally after passing the boundaries.

(c) No person may operate a commuter category airplane unless that person complies with the landing limitations prescribed in §§ 135.385 and 135.387 of this Part. For purposes of this paragraph, §§ 135.385 and 135.387 are applicable to all commuter category airplanes notwithstanding their stated applicability to turbine-engine-powered large transport category airplanes.

(d) In determining maximum weights, minimum distances and flight paths under paragraphs (a) through

(c) of this section, correction must be made for the runway to be used, the elevation of the airport, the effective runway gradient, and ambient temperature, and wind component at the time of takeoff.

(e) For the purposes of this section, the assumption is that the airplane is not banked before reaching a height of 50 feet as shown by the net takeoff flight path data in the Airplane Flight Manual and thereafter the maximum bank is not more than 15 degrees.

[Doc. No. 23516, Amdt. 135-21, 52 FR 1836, Jan. 15, 1987]

§ 135.399 Small nontransport category airplane performance operating limitations.

(a) No person may operate a reciprocating engine or turbopropeller-powered small airplane that is certificated under § 135.169(b) (2), (3), (4), (5), or (6) unless that person complies with the takeoff weight limitations in the approved Airplane Flight Manual or equivalent for operations under this part, and, if the airplane is certificated under § 135.169(b) (4) or (5) with the landing weight limitations in the Approved Airplane Flight Manual or equivalent for operations under this part.

(b) No person may operate an airplane that is certificated under § 135.169(b)(6) unless that person complies with the landing limitations prescribed in §§ 135.385 and 135.387 of this part. For purposes of this paragraph, §§ 135.385 and 135.387 are applicable to reciprocating and turbopropeller-powered small airplanes notwithstanding their stated applicability to turbine engine powered large transport category airplanes.

[44 FR 53731, Sept. 17, 1979]

Subpart J—Maintenance, Preventive Maintenance, and Alterations

§ 135.411 Applicability.

(a) This subpart prescribes rules in addition to those in other parts of this chapter for the maintenance, preventive maintenance, and alterations for each certificate holder as follows:

(1) Aircraft that are type certificated for a passenger seating configuration, excluding any pilot seat, of nine seats or less, shall be maintained under Parts 91 and 43 of this chapter and §§ 135.415, 135.417, and 135.421. An approved aircraft inspection program may be used under § 135.419.

(2) Aircraft that are type certificated for a passenger seating configuration, excluding any pilot seat, of ten seats or more, shall be maintained under a maintenance program in §§ 135.415, 135.417, and 135.423 through 135.443.

(b) A certificate holder who is not otherwise required, may elect to maintain its aircraft under paragraph (a)(2) of this section.

§ 135.413 Responsibility for airworthiness.

(a) Each certificate holder is primarily responsible for the airworthiness of its aircraft, including airframes, aircraft engines, propellers, rotors, appliances, and parts, and shall have its aircraft maintained under this chapter, and shall have defects repaired between required maintenance under Part 43 of this chapter.

(b) Each certificate holder who maintains its aircraft under § 135.411(a)(2) shall—

(1) Perform the maintenance, preventive maintenance, and alteration of its aircraft, including airframe, aircraft engines, propellers, rotors, appliances, emergency equipment and parts, under its manual and this chapter; or

(2) Make arrangements with another person for the performance of maintenance, preventive maintenance, or alteration. However, the certificate holder shall ensure that any maintenance, preventive maintenance, or alteration that is performed by another person is performed under the certificate holder's manual and this chapter.

§ 135.415 Mechanical reliability reports.

(a) Each certificate holder shall report the occurrence or detection of each failure, malfunction, or defect in an aircraft concerning—

(1) Fires during flight and whether the related fire-warning system functioned properly;

(2) Fires during flight not protected by related fire-warning system;

(3) False fire-warning during flight;

(4) An exhaust system that causes damage during flight to the engine, adjacent structure, equipment, or components;

(5) An aircraft component that causes accumulation or circulation of smoke, vapor, or toxic or noxious fumes in the crew compartment or passenger cabin during flight;

(6) Engine shutdown during flight because of flameout;

(7) Engine shutdown during flight when external damage to the engine or aircraft structure occurs;

(8) Engine shutdown during flight due to foreign object ingestion or icing;

(9) Shutdown of more than one engine during flight;

(10) A propeller feathering system or ability of the system to control overspeed during flight;

(11) A fuel or fuel-dumping system that affects fuel flow or causes hazardous leakage during flight;

(12) An unwanted landing gear extension or retraction or opening or closing of landing gear doors during flight;

(13) Brake system components that result in loss of brake actuating force when the aircraft is in motion on the ground;

(14) Aircraft structure that requires major repair;

(15) Cracks, permanent deformation, or corrosion of aircraft structures, if more than the maximum acceptable to the manufacturer or the FAA; and

(16) Aircraft components or systems that result in taking emergency actions during flight (except action to shut-down an engine).

(b) For the purpose of this section, "during flight" means the period from the moment the aircraft leaves the surface of the earth on takeoff until it touches down on landing.

(c) In addition to the reports required by paragraph (a) of this section, each certificate holder shall report any other failure, malfunction, or defect in an aircraft that occurs or is detected at any time if, in its opinion, the failure, malfunction, or defect has endangered or may endanger the safe operation of the aircraft.

(d) Each certificate holder shall send each report required by this section, in writing, covering each 24-hour period beginning at 0900 hours local time of each day and ending at 0900 hours local time on the next day to the FAA Flight Standards District Office charged with the overall inspection of the certificate holder. Each report of occurrences during a 24-hour period must be mailed or delivered to that office within the next 72 hours. However, a report that is due on Saturday or Sunday may be mailed or delivered on the following Monday and one that is due on a holiday may be mailed or delivered on the next work day. For aircraft operated in areas where mail is not collected, reports may be mailed or delivered within 72 hours after the aircraft returns to a point where the mail is collected.

(e) The certificate holder shall transmit the reports required by this section on a form and in a manner prescribed by the Administrator, and shall include as much of the following as is available:

(1) The type and identification number of the aircraft.

(2) The name of the operator.

(3) The date.

(4) The nature of the failure, malfunction, or defect.

(5) Identification of the part and system involved, including available information pertaining to type designation of the major component and time since last overhaul, if known.

(6) Apparent cause of the failure, malfunction or defect (e.g., wear, crack, design deficiency, or personnel error).

(7) Other pertinent information necessary for more complete identification, determination of seriousness, or corrective action.

(f) A certificate holder that is also the holder of a type certificate (including a supplemental type certificate), a Parts Manufacturer Approval, or a Technical Standard Order Authorization, or that is the licensee of a type certificate need not report a failure, malfunction, or defect under this section if the failure, malfunction, or defect has been reported by it under § 21.3 or § 37.17 of this chapter or under the accident reporting provisions of Part 830 of the regulations of the National Transportation Safety Board.

(g) No person may withhold a report required by this section even though all information required by this section is not available.

(h) When the certificate holder gets additional information, including information from the manufacturer or other agency, concerning a report required by this section, it shall expeditiously submit it as a supplement to the first report and reference the date and place of submission of the first report.

§ 135.417   Mechanical interruption summary report.

Each certificate holder shall mail or deliver, before the end of the 10th day of the following month, a summary report of the following occurrences in multiengine aircraft for the preceding month to the FAA Flight Standards District Office charged with the overall inspection of the certificate holder:

(a) Each interruption to a flight, unscheduled change of aircraft en route, or unscheduled stop or diversion from a route, caused by known or suspected mechanical difficulties or malfunctions that are not required to be reported under § 135.415.

(b) The number of propeller featherings in flight, listed by type of propeller and engine and aircraft on which it was installed. Propeller featherings for training, demonstration, or flight check purposes need not be reported.

§ 135.419   Approved aircraft inspection program.

(a) Whenever the Administrator finds that the aircraft inspections required or allowed under Part 91 of this chapter are not adequate to meet this part, or upon application by a certificate holder, the Administrator may amend the certificate holder's operations specifications under § 135.17, to require or allow an approved aircraft inspection program for any make and model aircraft of which the certificate holder has the exclusive use of at least one aircraft (as defined in § 135.25(b)).

(b) A certificate holder who applies for an amendment of its operations specifications to allow an approved aircraft inspection program must submit that program with its application for approval by the Administrator.

(c) Each certificate holder who is required by its operations specifications to have an approved aircraft inspection program shall submit a program for approval by the Administrator within 30 days of the amendment of its operations specifications or within any other period that the Administrator may prescribe in the operations specifications.

(d) The aircraft inspection program submitted for approval by the Administrator must contain the following:

(1) Instructions and procedures for the conduct of aircraft inspections (which must include necessary tests and checks), setting forth in detail the parts and areas of the airframe, engines, propellers, rotors, and appliances, including emergency equipment, that must be inspected.

(2) A schedule for the performance of the aircraft inspections under paragraph (d)(1) of this section expressed in terms of the time in service, calendar time, number of system operations, or any combination of these.

(3) Instructions and procedures for recording discrepancies found during inspections and correction or deferral of discrepancies including form and disposition of records.

(e) After approval, the certificate holder shall include the approved aircraft inspection program in the manual required by § 135.21.

(f) Whenever the Administrator finds that revisions to an approved aircraft inspection program are necessary for the continued adequacy of the program, the certificate holder shall, after notification by the Administrator, make any changes in the program found by the Administrator to be necessary. The certificate holder may petition the Administrator to reconsider the notice to make any changes in a program. The petition must be filed with the representatives of the Administrator assigned to it within 30 days after the certificate holder receives the notice. Except in the case of an emergency requiring immediate action in the interest of safety, the filing of the petition stays the notice pending a decision by the Administrator.

(g) Each certificate holder who has an approved aircraft inspection program shall have each aircraft that is subject to the program inspected in accordance with the program.

(h) The registration number of each aircraft that is subject to an approved aircraft inspection program must be included in the operations specifications of the certificate holder.

§135.421 Additional maintenance requirements.

(a) Each certificate holder who operates an aircraft type certificated for a passenger seating configuration, excluding any pilot seat, of nine seats or less, must comply with the manufacturer's recommended maintenance programs, or a program approved by the Administrator, for each aircraft engine, propeller, rotor, and each item of emergency equipment required by this chapter.

(b) For the purpose of this section, a manufacturer's maintenance program is one which is contained in the maintenance manual or maintenance instructions set forth by the manufacturer as required by this chapter for the aircraft, aircraft engine, propeller, rotor or item of emergency equipment.

§135.423 Maintenance, preventive maintenance, and alteration organization.

(a) Each certificate holder that performs any of its maintenance (other than required inspections), preventive maintenance, or alterations, and each person with whom it arranges for the performance of that work, must have an organization adequate to perform the work.

(b) Each certificate holder that performs any inspections required by its manual under § 135.427(b) (2) or (3), (in this subpart referred to as "required inspections"), and each person with whom it arranges for the performance of that work, must have an organization adequate to perform that work.

(c) Each person performing required inspections in addition to other maintenance, preventive maintenance, or alterations, shall organize the performance of those functions so as to separate the required inspection functions from the other maintenance, preventive maintenance, and alteration functions. The separation shall be below the level of administrative control at which overall responsibility for the required inspection functions and other maintenance, preventive maintenance, and alteration functions is exercised.

§135.425 Maintenance, preventive maintenance, and alteration programs.

Each certificate holder shall have an inspection program and a program covering other maintenance, preventive maintenance, and alterations, that ensures that—

(a) Maintenance, preventive maintenance, and alterations performed by it, or by other persons, are performed under the certificate holder's manual;

(b) Competent personnel and adequate facilities and equipment are provided for the proper performance of maintenance, preventive maintenance, and alterations; and

(c) Each aircraft released to service is airworthy and has been properly maintained for operation under this part.

§135.427 Manual requirements.

(a) Each certificate holder shall put in its manual the chart or description of the certificate holder's organization required by § 135.423 and a list of persons with whom it has arranged for the performance of any of its required inspections, other maintenance, preventive maintenance, or alterations, including a general description of that work.

(b) Each certificate holder shall put in its manual the programs required by § 135.425 that must be followed in performing maintenance, preventive maintenance, and alterations of that certificate holder's aircraft, including airframes, aircraft engines, propellers, rotors, appliances, emergency equipment, and parts, and must include at least the following:

(1) The method of performing routine and nonroutine maintenance (other than required inspections), preventive maintenance, and alterations.

(2) A designation of the items of maintenance and alteration that must be inspected (required inspections) in-

cluding at least those that could result in a failure, malfunction, or defect endangering the safe operation of the aircraft, if not performed properly or if improper parts or materials are used.

(3) The method of performing required inspections and a designation by occupational title of personnel authorized to perform each required inspection.

(4) Procedures for the reinspection of work performed under previous required inspection findings ("buy-back procedures").

(5) Procedures, standards, and limits necessary for required inspections and acceptance or rejection of the items required to be inspected and for periodic inspection and calibration of precision tools, measuring devices, and test equipment.

(6) Procedures to ensure that all required inspections are performed.

(7) Instructions to prevent any person who performs any item of work from performing any required inspection of that work.

(8) Instructions and procedures to prevent any decision of an inspector regarding any required inspection from being countermanded by persons other than supervisory personnel of the inspection unit, or a person at the level of administrative control that has overall responsibility for the management of both the required inspection functions and the other maintenance, preventive maintenance, and alterations functions.

(9) Procedures to ensure that required inspections, other maintenance, preventive maintenance, and alterations that are not completed as a result of work interruptions are properly completed before the aircraft is released to service.

(c) Each certificate holder shall put in its manual a suitable system (which may include a coded system) that provides for the retention of the following information—

(1) A description (or reference to data acceptable to the Administrator) of the work performed;

(2) The name of the person performing the work if the work is performed by a person outside the organization of the certificate holder; and

(3) The name or other positive identification of the individual approving the work.

§ 135.429   Required inspection personnel.

(a) No person may use any person to perform required inspections unless the person performing the inspection is appropriately certificated, properly trained, qualified, and authorized to do so.

(b) No person may allow any person to perform a required inspection unless, at the time, the person performing that inspection is under the supervision and control of an inspection unit.

(c) No person may perform a required inspection if that person performed the item of work required to be inspected.

(d) In the case of rotorcraft that operate in remote areas or sites, the Administrator may approve procedures for the performance of required inspection items by a pilot when no other qualified person is available, provided—

(1) The pilot is employed by the certificate holder;

(2) It can be shown to the satisfaction of the Administrator that each pilot authorized to perform required inspections is properly trained and qualified;

(3) The required inspection is a result of a mechanical interruption and is not a part of a certificate holder's continuous airworthiness maintenance program;

(4) Each item is inspected after each flight until the item has been inspected by an appropriately certificated mechanic other than the one who originally performed the item of work; and

(5) Each item of work that is a required inspection item that is part of the flight control system shall be flight tested and reinspected before the aircraft is approved for return to service.

(e) Each certificate holder shall maintain, or shall determine that each person with whom it arranges to perform its required inspections maintains, a current listing of persons who have been trained, qualified, and authorized to conduct required inspections. The persons must be identified by name, occupational title and the inspections that they are authorized to perform. The certificate holder (or person with whom it arranges to perform its required inspections) shall give written information to each person so authorized, describing the extent of that person's responsibilities, authorities, and inspectional limitations. The list shall be made available for inspection by the Administrator upon request.

[Doc. No. 16097, 43 FR 46783, Oct. 10, 1978, as amended by Amdt. No. 135-20, 51 FR 40710, Nov. 7, 1986]

§ 135.431 Continuing analysis and surveillance.

(a) Each certificate holder shall establish and maintain a system for the continuing analysis and surveillance of the performance and effectiveness of its inspection program and the program covering other maintenance, preventive maintenance, and alterations and for the correction of any deficiency in those programs, regardless of whether those programs are carried out by the certificate holder or by another person.

(b) Whenever the Administrator finds that either or both of the programs described in paragraph (a) of this section does not contain adequate procedures and standards to meet this part, the certificate holder shall, after notification by the Administrator, make changes in those programs requested by the Administrator.

(c) A certificate holder may petition the Administrator to reconsider the notice to make a change in a program. The petition must be filed with the FAA Flight Standards District Office charged with the overall inspection of the certificate holder within 30 days after the certificate holder receives the notice. Except in the case of an emergency requiring immediate action in the interest of safety, the filing of the petition stays the notice pending a decision by the Administrator.

§ 135.433 Maintenance and preventive maintenance training program.

Each certificate holder or a person performing maintenance or preventive maintenance functions for it shall have a training program to ensure that each person (including inspection personnel) who determines the adequacy of work done is fully informed about procedures and techniques and new equipment in use and is competent to perform that person's duties.

§ 135.435 Certificate requirements.

(a) Except for maintenance, preventive maintenance, alterations, and required inspections performed by repair stations certificated under the provisions of Subpart C of Part 145 of this chapter, each person who is directly in charge of maintenance, preventive maintenance, or alterations, and each person performing required inspections must hold an appropriate airman certificate.

(b) For the purpose of this section, a person "directly in charge" is each person assigned to a position in which that person is responsible for the work of a shop or station that performs maintenance, preventive maintenance, alterations, or other functions affecting airworthiness. A person who is "directly in charge" need not physically observe and direct each worker constantly but must be available for consultation and decision on matters requiring instruction or decision from higher authority than that of the person performing the work.

§ 135.437 Authority to perform and approve maintenance, preventive maintenance, and alterations.

(a) A certificate holder may perform or make arrangements with other persons to perform maintenance, preventive maintenance, and alterations as provided in its maintenance manual. In addition, a certificate holder may perform these functions for another certificate holder as provided in the maintenance manual of the other certificate holder.

(b) A certificate holder may approve any airframe, aircraft engine, propeller, rotor, or appliance for return to service after maintenance, preventive maintenance, or alterations that are performed under paragraph (a) of this section. However, in the case of a major repair or alteration, the work must have been done in accordance with technical data approved by the Administrator.

§ 135.439 Maintenance recording requirements.

(a) Each certificate holder shall keep (using the system specified in the manual required in § 135.427) the following records for the periods specified in paragraph (b) of this section:

(1) All the records necessary to show that all requirements for the issuance of an airworthiness release under § 135.443 have been met.

(2) Records containing the following information:

(i) The total time in service of the airframe, engine, propeller, and rotor.

(ii) The current status of life-limited parts of each airframe, engine, propeller, rotor, and appliance.

(iii) The time since last overhaul of each item installed on the aircraft which are required to be overhauled on a specified time basis.

(iv) The identification of the current inspection status of the aircraft, including the time since the last inspections required by the inspection program under which the aircraft and its appliances are maintained.

(v) The current status of applicable airworthiness directives, including the date and methods of compliance, and, if the airworthiness directive involves recurring action, the time and date when the next action is required.

(vi) A list of current major alterations and repairs to each airframe, engine, propeller, rotor, and appliance.

(b) Each certificate holder shall retain the records required to be kept by this section for the following periods:

(1) Except for the records of the last complete overhaul of each airframe, engine, propeller, rotor, and appliance the records specified in paragraph (a)(1) of this section shall be retained until the work is repeated or superseded by other work or for one year after the work is performed.

(2) The records of the last complete overhaul of each airframe, engine, propeller, rotor, and appliance shall be retained until the work is superseded by work of equivalent scope and detail.

(3) The records specified in paragraph (a)(2) of this section shall be retained and transferred with the aircraft at the time the aircraft is sold.

(c) The certificate holder shall make all maintenance records required to be kept by this section available for inspection by the Administrator or any representative of the National Transportation Safety Board.

[Doc. No. 16097, 43 FR 46783, Oct. 10, 1978; 43 FR 49975, Oct. 26, 1978]

§ 135.441 Transfer of maintenance records.

Each certificate holder who sells a United States registered aircraft shall transfer to the purchaser, at the time of the sale, the following records of that aircraft, in plain language form or in coded form which provides for the preservation and retrieval of information in a manner acceptable to the Administrator:

(a) The records specified in § 135.439(a)(2).

(b) The records specified in § 135.439(a)(1) which are not included in the records covered by paragraph (a) of this section, except that the purchaser may allow the seller to keep physical custody of such records. However, custody of records by the seller does not relieve the purchaser of its responsibility under § 135.439(c) to make the records available for inspection by the Administrator or any representative of the National Transportation Safety Board.

§ 135.443 Airworthiness release or aircraft maintenance log entry.

(a) No certificate holder may operate an aircraft after maintenance, preventive maintenance, or alterations are performed on the aircraft unless the certificate holder prepares, or causes the person with whom the certificate holder arranges for the performance of the maintenance, preventive maintenance, or alterations, to prepare—

(1) An airworthiness release; or

(2) An appropriate entry in the aircraft maintenance log.

(b) The airworthiness release or log entry required by paragraph (a) of this section must—

(1) Be prepared in accordance with the procedure in the certificate holder's manual;

(2) Include a certification that—

(i) The work was performed in accordance with the requirements of the certificate holder's manual;

(ii) All items required to be inspected were inspected by an authorized person who determined that the work was satisfactorily completed;

(iii) No known condition exists that would make the aircraft unairworthy;

(iv) So far as the work performed is concerned, the aircraft is in condition for safe operation; and

(3) Be signed by an authorized certificated mechanic or repairman, except that a certificated repairman may sign the release or entry only for the work for which that person is employed and for which that person is certificated.

(c) Instead of restating each of the conditions of the certification required by paragraph (b) of this section, the certificate holder may state in its manual that the signature of an authorized certificated mechanic or repairman constitutes that certification.

APPENDIX A—ADDITIONAL AIRWORTHINESS STANDARDS FOR 10 OR MORE PASSENGER AIRPLANES

Applicability

1. *Applicability.* This appendix prescribes the additional airworthiness standards required by § 135.169.

2. *References.* Unless otherwise provided, references in this appendix to specific sections of Part 23 of the Federal Aviation Regulations (FAR Part 23) are to those sections of Part 23 in effect on March 30, 1967.

Flight Requirements

3. *General.* Compliance must be shown with the applicable requirements of Subpart B of FAR Part 23, as supplemented or modified in §§ 4 through 10.

Performance

4. *General.* (a) Unless otherwise prescribed in this appendix, compliance with each applicable performance requirement in sections 4 through 7 must be shown for ambient atmospheric conditions and still air.

(b) The performance must correspond to the propulsive thrust available under the particular ambient atmospheric conditions and the particular flight condition. The available propulsive thrust must correspond to engine power or thrust, not exceeding the approved power or thrust less—

(1) Installation losses; and

(2) The power or equivalent thrust absorbed by the accessories and services appropriate to the particular ambient atmospheric conditions and the particular flight condition.

(c) Unless otherwise prescribed in this appendix, the applicant must select the takeoff, en route, and landing configurations for the airplane.

(d) The airplane configuration may vary with weight, altitude, and temperature, to the extent they are compatible with the operating procedures required by paragraph (e) of this section.

(e) Unless otherwise prescribed in this appendix, in determining the critical engine inoperative takeoff performance, the accelerate-stop distance, takeoff distance, changes in the airplane's configuration, speed, power, and thrust must be made under procedures established by the applicant for operation in service.

(f) Procedures for the execution of balked landings must be established by the applicant and included in the Airplane Flight Manual.

(g) The procedures established under paragraphs (e) and (f) of this section must—

(1) Be able to be consistently executed in service by a crew of average skill;

(2) Use methods or devices that are safe and reliable; and

(3) Include allowance for any time delays, in the execution of the procedures, that may reasonably be expected in service.

5. *Takeoff*—(a) *General.* Takeoff speeds, the accelerate-stop distance, the takeoff distance, and the one-engine-inoperative takeoff flight path data (described in paragraphs (b), (c), (d), and (f) of this section), must be determined for—

(1) Each weight, altitude, and ambient temperature within the operational limits selected by the applicant;

(2) The selected configuration for takeoff;

(3) The center of gravity in the most unfavorable position;

(4) The operating engine within approved operating limitations; and

(5) Takeoff data based on smooth, dry, hard-surface runway.

(b) *Takeoff speeds.* (1) The decision speed V_1 is the calibrated airspeed on the ground at which, as a result of engine failure or other reasons, the pilot is assumed to have made a decision to continue or discontinue the takeoff. The speed V_1 must be selected by the applicant but may not be less than—

(i) $1.10 V_{S1}$;

(ii) $1.10 V_{MC}$;

(iii) A speed that allows acceleration to V_1 and stop under paragraph (c) of this section; or

(iv) A speed at which the airplane can be rotated for takeoff and shown to be adequate to safely continue the takeoff, using normal piloting skill, when the critical engine is suddenly made inoperative.

(2) The initial climb out speed V_2, in terms of calibrated airspeed, must be selected by the applicant so as to allow the gradient of climb required in section 6(b)(2), but it must not be less than V_1 or less than $1.2 V_{S1}$.

(3) Other essential take off speeds necessary for safe operation of the airplane.

(c) *Accelerate-stop distance.* (1) The accelerate-stop distance is the sum of the distances necessary to—

(i) Accelerate the airplane from a standing start to V_1; and

(ii) Come to a full stop from the point at which V_1 is reached assuming that in the case of engine failure, failure of the critical engine is recognized by the pilot at the speed V_1.

(2) Means other than wheel brakes may be used to determine the accelerate-stop distance if that means is available with the critical engine inoperative and—

(i) Is safe and reliable;

(ii) Is used so that consistent results can be expected under normal operating conditions; and

(iii) Is such that exceptional skill is not required to control the airplane.

(d) *All engines operating takeoff distance.* The all engine operating takeoff distance is the horizontal distance required to takeoff and climb to a height of 50 feet above the takeoff surface under the procedures in FAR 23.51(a).

(e) *One-engine-inoperative takeoff.* Determine the weight for each altitude and temperature within the operational limits established for the airplane, at which the airplane has the capability, after failure of the critical engine at V_1 determined under paragraph (b) of this section, to take off and climb at not less than V_2, to a height 1,000 feet above the takeoff surface and attain the speed and configuration at which compliance is shown with the en route one-engine-inoperative gradient of climb specified in section 6(c).

(f) *One-engine-inoperative takeoff flight path data.* The one-engine-inoperative takeoff flight path data consist of takeoff flight paths extending from a standing start to a point in the takeoff at which the airplane reaches a height 1,000 feet above the takeoff surface under paragraph (e) of this section.

6. *Climb*—(a) *Landing climb: All-engines-operating.* The maximum weight must be determined with the airplane in the landing configuration, for each altitude, and ambient temperature within the operational limits established for the airplane, with the most unfavorable center of gravity, and out-of-ground effect in free air, at which the steady gradient of climb will not be less than 3.3 percent, with:

(1) The engines at the power that is available 8 seconds after initiation of movement of the power or thrust controls from the minimum flight idle to the takeoff position.

(2) A climb speed not greater than the approach speed established under section 7 and not less than the greater of $1.05 V_{MC}$ or $1.10 V_{S1}$.

(b) *Takeoff climb: one-engine-inoperative.* The maximum weight at which the airplane meets the minimum climb performance specified in paragraphs (1) and (2) of this paragraph must be determined for each altitude and ambient temperature within the operational limits established for the airplane, out of ground effect in free air, with the airplane in the takeoff configuration, with the most unfavorable center of gravity, the critical engine inoperative, the remaining engines at the maximum takeoff power or thrust, and the propeller of the inoperative engine windmilling with the propeller controls in the normal position except that, if an approved automatic feathering system is installed, the propellers may be in the feathered position:

(1) *Takeoff: landing gear extended.* The minimum steady gradient of climb must be measurably positive at the speed V_1.

(2) *Takeoff: landing gear retracted.* The minimum steady gradient of climb may not be less than 2 percent at speed V_2. For airplanes with fixed landing gear this requirement must be met with the landing gear extended.

(c) *En route climb: one-engine-inoperative.* The maximum weight must be determined for each altitude and ambient temperature within the operational limits established for the airplane, at which the steady gradient of climb is not less 1.2 percent at an altitude 1,000 feet above the takeoff surface, with the airplane in the en route configuration, the critical engine inoperative, the remaining engine at the maximum continuous power or thrust, and the most unfavorable center of gravity.

7. *Landing.* (a) The landing field length described in paragraph (b) of this section must be determined for standard atmosphere at each weight and altitude within the operational limits established by the applicant.

(b) The landing field length is equal to the landing distance determined under FAR 23.75(a) divided by a factor of 0.6 for the destination airport and 0.7 for the alternate airport. Instead of the gliding approach specified in FAR 23.75(a)(1), the landing may be preceded by a steady approach down to the 50-foot height at a gradient of descent not greater than 5.2 percent (3°) at a calibrated airspeed not less than $1.3V_{S1}$.

Trim

8—*Trim* (a) *Lateral and directional trim.* The airplane must maintain lateral and directional trim in level flight at a speed of V_H or V_{MO}/M_{MO}, whichever is lower, with landing gear and wing flaps retracted.

(b) *Longitudinal trim.* The airplane must maintain longitudinal trim during the following conditions, except that it need not maintain trim at a speed greater than V_{MO}/M_{MO}:

(1) In the approach conditons specified in FAR 23.161(c) (3) through (5), except that instead of the speeds specified in those paragraphs, trim must be maintained with a stick force of not more than 10 pounds down to a speed used in showing compliance with section 7 or $1.4V_{S1}$ whichever is lower.

(2) In level flight at any speed from V_H or V_{MO}/M_{MO}, whichever is lower, to either V_z or $1.4V_{S1}$, with the landing gear and wing flaps retracted.

Stability

9. *Static longitudinal stability.* (a) In showing compliance with FAR 23.175(b) and with paragraph (b) of this section, the airspeed must return to within ±7½ percent of the trim speed.

(b) *Cruise stability.* The stick force curve must have a stable slope for a speed range of ±50 knots from the trim speed except that the speeds need not exceed V_{FC}/M_{FC} or be less than $1.4V_{S1}$. This speed range will be considered to begin at the outer extremes of the friction band and the stick force may not exceed 50 pounds with—

(1) Landing gear retracted;

(2) Wing flaps retracted;

(3) The maximum cruising power as selected by the applicant as an operating limitation for turbine engines or 75 percent of maximum continuous power for reciprocating engines except that the power need not exceed that required at V_{MO}/M_{MO};

(4) Maximum takeoff weight; and

(5) The airplane trimmed for level flight with the power specified in paragraph (3) of this paragraph.

V_{FC}/M_{FC} may not be less than a speed midway between V_{MO}/M_{MO} and V_{DF}/M_{DF}, except that, for altitudes where Mach number is the limiting factor, M_{FC} need not exceed the Mach number at which effective speed warning occurs.

(c) *Climb stability (turbopropeller powered airplanes only).* In showing compliance with FAR 23.175(a), an applicant must, instead of the power specified in FAR 23.175(a)(4), use the maximum power or thrust selected by the applicant as an operating limitation for use during climb at the best rate of climb speed, except that the speed need not be less than $1.4V_{S1}$.

Stalls

10. *Stall warning.* If artificial stall warning is required to comply with FAR 23.207, the warning device must give clearly distinguishable indications under expected conditions of flight. The use of a visual warning device that requires the attention of the crew within the cockpit is not acceptable by itself.

Control Systems

11. *Electric trim tabs.* The airplane must meet FAR 23.677 and in addition it must be shown that the airplane is safely controllable and that a pilot can perform all the maneuvers and operations necessary to effect a safe landing following any probable electric trim tab runaway which might be reasonably expected in service allowing for appropriate time delay after pilot recognition of the runaway. This demonstration must be conducted at the critical airplane weights and center of gravity positions.

Instruments: Installation

12. *Arrangement and visibility.* Each instrument must meet FAR 23.1321 and in addition:

(a) Each flight, navigation, and powerplant instrument for use by any pilot must be plainly visible to the pilot from the pilot's station with the minimum practicable deviation from the pilot's normal position and line of vision when the pilot is looking forward along the flight path.

(b) The flight instruments required by FAR 23.1303 and by the applicable operating rules must be grouped on the instrument panel and centered as nearly as practicable about the vertical plane of each pilot's forward vision. In addition—

(1) The instrument that most effectively indicates the attitude must be in the panel in the top center position;

(2) The instrument that most effectively indicates the airspeed must be on the panel directly to the left of the instrument in the top center position;

(3) The instrument that most effectively indicates altitude must be adjacent to and directly to the right of the instrument in the top center position; and

(4) The instrument that most effectively indicates direction of flight must be adjacent to and directly below the instrument in the top center position.

13. *Airspeed indicating system.* Each airspeed indicating system must meet FAR 23.1323 and in addition:

(a) Airspeed indicating instruments must be of an approved type and must be calibrated to indicate true airspeed at sea level in the standard atmosphere with a minimum practicable instrument calibration error when the corresponding pitot and static pressures are supplied to the instruments.

(b) The airspeed indicating system must be calibrated to determine the system error, i.e., the relation between IAS and CAS, in flight and during the accelerate-takeoff ground run. The ground run calibration must be obtained between 0.8 of the minimum value of V_1 and 1.2 times the maximum value of V_1, considering the approved ranges of altitude and weight. The ground run calibration is determined assuming an engine failure at the minimum value of V_1.

(c) The airspeed error of the installation excluding the instrument calibration error, must not exceed 3 percent or 5 knots whichever is greater, throughout the speed range from V_{MO} to $1.3V_{S1}$ with flaps retracted and from $1.3V_{SO}$ to V_{FE} with flaps in the landing position.

(d) Information showing the relationship between IAS and CAS must be shown in the Airplane Flight manual.

14. *Static air vent system.* The static air vent system must meet FAR 23.1325. The altimeter system calibration must be determined and shown in the Airplane Flight Manual.

Operating Limitations and Information

15. *Maximum operating limit speed V_{MO}/M_{MO}.* Instead of establishing operating limitations based on V_{NE} and V_{NO}, the applicant must establish a maximum operating limit speed V_{MO}/M_{MO} as follows:

(a) The maximum operating limit speed must not exceed the design cruising speed V_C and must be sufficiently below V_D/M_D or V_{DF}/M_{DF} to make it highly improbable that the latter speeds will be inadvertently exceeded in flight.

(b) The speed V_{MO} must not exceed $0.8V_D/M_D$ or $0.8V_{DF}/M_{DF}$ unless flight demonstrations involving upsets as specified by the Administrator indicates a lower speed margin will not result in speeds exceeding V_D/M_D or V^{DF}. Atmospheric variations, horizontal gusts, system and equipment errors, and airframe production variations are taken into account.

16. *Minimum flight crew.* In addition to meeting FAR 23.1523, the applicant must establish the minimum number and type of qualified flight crew personnel sufficient for safe operation of the airplane considering—

(a) Each kind of operation for which the applicant desires approval;

(b) The workload on each crewmember considering the following:

(1) Flight path control.
(2) Collision avoidance.
(3) Navigation.
(4) Communications.

(5) Operation and monitoring of all essential aircraft systems.

(6) Command decisions; and

(c) The accessibility and ease of operation of necessary controls by the appropriate crewmember during all normal and emergency operations when at the crewmember flight station.

17. *Airspeed indicator.* The airspeed indicator must meet FAR 23.1545 except that, the airspeed notations and markings in terms of V_{NO} and V_{NH} must be replaced by the V_{MO}/M_{MO} notations. The airspeed indicator markings must be easily read and understood by the pilot. A placard adjacent to the airspeed indicator is an acceptable means of showing compliance with FAR 23.1545(c).

Airplane Flight Manual

18. *General.* The Airplane Flight Manual must be prepared under FARs 23.1583 and 23.1587, and in addition the operating limitations and performance information in sections 19 and 20 must be included.

19. *Operating limitations.* The Airplane Flight Manual must include the following limitations—

(a) *Airspeed limitations.* (1) The maximum operating limit speed V_{MO}/M_{MO} and a statement that this speed limit may not be deliberately exceeded in any regime of flight (climb, cruise, or descent) unless a higher speed is authorized for flight test or pilot training;

(2) If an airspeed limitation is based upon compressibility effects, a statement to this effect and informaton as to any symptoms, the probable behavior of the airplane, and the recommended recovery procedures; and

(3) The airspeed limits, shown in terms of V_{MO}/M_{MO} instead of V_{NO} and V_{NE}.

(b) *Takeoff weight limitations.* The maximum takeoff weight for each airport elevation, ambient temperature, and available takeoff runway length within the range selected by the applicant may not exceed the weight at which—

(1) The all-engine-operating takeoff distance determined under section 5(b) or the accelerate-stop distance determined under section 5(c), whichever is greater, is equal to the available runway length;

(2) The airplane complies with the one-engine-inoperative takeoff requirements specified in section 5(e); and

(3) The airplane complies with the one-engine-inoperative takeoff and en route climb requirements specified in sections 6(b) and (c).

(c) *Landing weight limitations.* The maximum landing weight for each airport elevation (standard temperature) and available landing runway length, within the range selected by the applicant. This weight may not exceed the weight at which the landing field length determined under section 7(b) is equal to the available runway length. In showing compliance with this operating limitation, it is acceptable to assume that the landing weight at the destination will be equal to the takeoff weight reduced by the normal consumption of fuel and oil en route.

20. *Performance information.* The Airplane Flight Manual must contain the performance information determined under the performance requirements of this appendix. The information must include the following:

(a) Sufficient information so that the takeoff weight limits specified in section 19(b) can be determined for all temperatures and altitudes within the operation limitations selected by the applicant.

(b) The conditions under which the performance information was obtained, including the airspeed at the 50-foot height used to determine landing distances.

(c) The performance information (determined by extrapolation and computed for the range of weights between the maximum landing and takeoff weights) for—

(1) Climb in the landing configuration; and

(2) Landing distance.

(d) Procedure established under section 4 related to the limitations and information required by this section in the form of guidance material including any relevant limitations or information.

(e) An explanation of significant or unusual flight or ground handling characteristics of the airplane.

(f) Airspeeds, as indicated airspeeds, corresponding to those determined for takeoff under section 5(b).

21. *Maximum operating altitudes.* The maximum operating altitude to which operation is allowed, as limited by flight, structural, powerplant, functional, or equipment characteristics, must be specified in the Airplane Flight Manual.

22. *Stowage provision for airplane flight manual.* Provision must be made for stowing the Airplane Flight Manual in a suitable fixed container which is readily accessible to the pilot.

23. *Operating procedures.* Procedures for restarting turbine engines in flight (including the effects of altitude) must be set forth in the Airplane Flight Manual.

Airframe Requirements

Flight Loads

24. *Engine torque.* (a) Each turbopropeller engine mount and its supporting structure must be designed for the torque effects of:

(1) The conditions in FAR 23.361(a).

(2) The limit engine torque corresponding to takeoff power and propeller speed multiplied by a factor accounting for propeller control system malfunction, including quick feathering action, simultaneously with 1g

level flight loads. In the absence of a rational analysis, a factor of 1.6 must be used.

(b) The limit torque is obtained by multiplying the mean torque by a factor of 1.25.

25. *Turbine engine gyroscopic loads.* Each turbopropeller engine mount and its supporting structure must be designed for the gyroscopic loads that result, with the engines at maximum continuous r.p.m., under either—

(a) The conditions in FARs 23.351 and 23.423; or

(b) All possible combinations of the following:

(1) A yaw velocity of 2.5 radians per second.

(2) A pitch velocity of 1.0 radians per second.

(3) A normal load factor of 2.5.

(4) Maximum continuous thrust.

26. *Unsymmetrical loads due to engine failure.* (a) Turbopropeller powered airplanes must be designed for the unsymmetrical loads resulting from the failure of the critical engine including the following conditions in combination with a single malfunction of the propeller drag limiting system, considering the probable pilot corrective action on the flight controls:

(1) At speeds between V_{mo} and V_D, the loads resulting from power failure because of fuel flow interruption are considered to be limit loads.

(2) At speeds between V_{mo} and V_c, the loads resulting from the disconnection of the engine compressor from the turbine or from loss of the turbine blades are considered to be ultimate loads.

(3) The time history of the thrust decay and drag buildup occurring as a result of the prescribed engine failures must be substantiated by test or other data applicable to the particular engine-propeller combination.

(4) The timing and magnitude of the probable pilot corrective action must be conservatively estimated, considering the characteristics of the particular engine-propeller-airplane combination.

(b) Pilot corrective action may be assumed to be initiated at the time maximum yawing velocity is reached, but not earlier than 2 seconds after the engine failure. The magnitude of the corrective action may be based on the control forces in FAR 23.397 except that lower forces may be assumed where it is shown by analysis or test that these forces can control the yaw and roll resulting from the prescribed engine failure conditions.

Ground Loads

27. *Dual wheel landing gear units.* Each dual wheel landing gear unit and its supporting structure must be shown to comply with the following:

(a) *Pivoting.* The airplane must be assumed to pivot about one side of the main gear with the brakes on that side locked. The limit vertical load factor must be 1.0 and the coefficient of friction 0.8. This condition need apply only to the main gear and its supporting structure.

(b) *Unequal tire inflation.* A 60-40 percent distribution of the loads established under FAR 23.471 through FAR 23.483 must be applied to the dual wheels.

(c) *Flat tire.* (1) Sixty percent of the loads in FAR 23.471 through FAR 23.483 must be applied to either wheel in a unit.

(2) Sixty percent of the limit drag and side loads and 100 percent of the limit vertical load established under FARs 23.493 and 23.485 must be applied to either wheel in a unit except that the vertical load need not exceed the maximum vertical load in paragraph (c)(1) of this section.

Fatigue Evaluation

28. *Fatigue evaluation of wing and associated structure.* Unless it is shown that the structure, operating stress levels, materials and expected use are comparable from a fatigue standpoint to a similar design which has had substantial satisfactory service experience, the strength, detail design, and the fabrication of those parts of the wing, wing carrythrough, and attaching structure whose failure would be catastrophic must be evaluated under either—

(a) A fatigue strength investigation in which the structure is shown by analysis, tests, or both to be able to withstand the repeated loads of variable magnitude expected in service; or

(b) A fail-safe strength investigation in which it is shown by analysis, tests, or both that catastrophic failure of the structure is not probable after fatigue, or obvious partial failure, of a principal structural element, and that the remaining structure is able to withstand a static ultimate load factor of 75 percent of the critical limit load factor at V_c. These loads must be multiplied by a factor of 1.15 unless the dynamic effects of failure under static load are otherwise considered.

Design and Construction

29. *Flutter.* For multiengine turbopropeller powered airplanes, a dynamic evaluation must be made and must include—

(a) The significant elastic, inertia, and aerodynamic forces associated with the rotations and displacements of the plane of the propeller; and

(b) Engine-propeller-nacelle stiffness and damping variations appropriate to the particular configuration.

Landing Gear

30. *Flap operated landing gear warning device.* Airplanes having retractable landing gear and wing flaps must be equipped with a warning device that functions continuously when the wing flaps are extended to a flap position that activates the warning device to give adequate warning before landing, using normal landing procedures, if the landing gear is not fully extended and locked. There may not be a manual shut off for this warning device. The flap position sensing unit may be installed at any suitable location. The system for this device may use any part of the system (including the aural warning device) provided for other landing gear warning devices.

Personnel and Cargo Accommodations

31. *Cargo and baggage compartments.* Cargo and baggage compartments must be designed to meet FAR 23.787 (a) and (b), and in addition means must be provided to protect passengers from injury by the contents of any cargo or baggage compartment when the ultimate forward inertia force is $9g$.

32. *Doors and exits.* The airplane must meet FAR 23.783 and FAR 23.807 (a)(3), (b), and (c), and in addition:

(a) There must be a means to lock and safeguard each external door and exit against opening in flight either inadvertently by persons, or as a result of mechanical failure. Each external door must be operable from both the inside and the outside.

(b) There must be means for direct visual inspection of the locking mechanism by crewmembers to determine whether external doors and exits, for which the initial opening movement is outward, are fully locked. In addition, there must be a visual means to signal to crewmembers when normally used external doors are closed and fully locked.

(c) The passenger entrance door must qualify as a floor level emergency exit. Each additional required emergency exit except floor level exits must be located over the wing or must be provided with acceptable means to assist the occupants in descending to the ground. In addition to the passenger entrance door:

(1) For a total seating capacity of 15 or less, an emergency exit as defined in FAR 23.807(b) is required on each side of the cabin.

(2) For a total seating capacity of 16 through 23, three emergency exits as defined in FAR 23.807(b) are required with one on the same side as the door and two on the side opposite the door.

(d) An evacuation demonstration must be conducted utilizing the maximum number of occupants for which certification is desired. It must be conducted under simulated night conditions utilizing only the emergency exits on the most critical side of the aircraft. The participants must be representative of average airline passengers with no previous practice or rehearsal for the demonstration. Evacuation must be completed within 90 seconds.

(e) Each emergency exit must be marked with the word "Exit" by a sign which has white letters 1 inch high on a red background 2 inches high, be self-illuminated or independently internally electrically illuminated, and have a minimum luminescence (brightness) of at least 160 microlamberts. The colors may be reversed if the passenger compartment illumination is essentially the same.

(f) Access to window type emergency exits must not be obstructed by seats or seat backs.

(g) The width of the main passenger aisle at any point between seats must equal or exceed the values in the following table:

Total seating capacity	Minimum main passenger aisle width	
	Less than 25 inches from floor	25 inches and more from floor
10 through 23.............................	9 inches..........	15 inches.

Miscellaneous

33. *Lightning strike protection.* Parts that are electrically insulated from the basic airframe must be connected to it through lightning arrestors unless a lightning strike on the insulated part—

(a) Is improbable because of shielding by other parts; or

(b) Is not hazardous.

34. *Ice protection.* If certification with ice protection provisions is desired, compliance with the following must be shown:

(a) The recommended procedures for the use of the ice protection equipment must be set forth in the Airplane Flight Manual.

(b) An analysis must be performed to establish, on the basis of the airplane's operational needs, the adequacy of the ice protection system for the various components of the airplane. In addition, tests of the ice protection system must be conducted to demonstrate that the airplane is capable of operating safely in continuous maximum and intermittent maximum icing conditions as described in Appendix C of Part 25 of this chapter.

(c) Compliance with all or portions of this section may be accomplished by reference, where applicable because of similarity of the designs, to analysis and tests performed by the applicant for a type certificated model.

35. *Maintenance information.* The applicant must make available to the owner at the time of delivery of the airplane the information the applicant considers essential for the proper maintenance of the airplane. That information must include the following:

(a) Description of systems, including electrical, hydraulic, and fuel controls.

(b) Lubrication instructions setting forth the frequency and the lubricants and fluids which are to be used in the various systems.

(c) Pressures and electrical loads applicable to the various systems.

(d) Tolerances and adjustments necessary for proper functioning.

(e) Methods of leveling, raising, and towing.

(f) Methods of balancing control surfaces.

(g) Identification of primary and secondary structures.

(h) Frequency and extent of inspections necessary to the proper operation of the airplane.

(i) Special repair methods applicable to the airplane.

(j) Special inspection techniques, such as X-ray, ultrasonic, and magnetic particle inspection.

(k) List of special tools.

Propulsion

General

36. *Vibration characteristics.* For turbopropeller powered airplanes, the engine installation must not result in vibration characteristics of the engine exceeding those established during the type certification of the engine.

37. *In flight restarting of engine.* If the engine on turbopropeller powered airplanes cannot be restarted at the maximum cruise altitude, a determination must be made of the altitude below which restarts can be consistently accomplished. Restart information must be provided in the Airplane Flight Manual.

38. *Engines.* (a) *For turbopropeller powered airplanes.* The engine installation must comply with the following:

(1) *Engine isolation.* The powerplants must be arranged and isolated from each other to allow operation, in at least one configuration, so that the failure or malfunction of any engine, or of any system that can affect the engine, will not—

(i) Prevent the continued safe operation of the remaining engines; or

(ii) Require immediate action by any crewmember for continued safe operation.

(2) *Control of engine rotation.* There must be a means to individually stop and restart the rotation of any engine in flight except that engine rotation need not be stopped if continued rotation could not jeopardize the

safety of the airplane. Each component of the stopping and restarting system on the engine side of the firewall, and that might be exposed to fire, must be at least fire resistant. If hydraulic propeller feathering systems are used for this purpose, the feathering lines must be at least fire resistant under the operating conditions that may be expected to exist during feathering.

(3) *Engine speed and gas temperature control devices.* The powerplant systems associated with engine control devices, systems, and instrumentation must provide reasonable assurance that those engine operating limitations that adversely affect turbine rotor structural integrity will not be exceeded in service.

(b) *For reciprocating engine powered airplanes.* To provide engine isolation, the powerplants must be arranged and isolated from each other to allow operation, in at least one configuration, so that the failure or malfunction of any engine, or of any system that can affect that engine, will not—

(1) Prevent the continued safe operation of the remaining engines; or

(2) Require immediate action by any crewmember for continued safe operation.

39. *Turbopropeller reversing systems.* (a) Turbopropeller reversing systems intended for ground operation must be designed so that no single failure or malfunction of the system will result in unwanted reverse thrust under any expected operating condition. Failure of structural elements need not be considered if the probability of this kind of failure is extremely remote.

(b) Turbopropeller reversing systems intended for in flight use must be designed so that no unsafe condition will result during normal operation of the system, or from any failure (or reasonably likely combination of failures) of the reversing system, under any anticipated condition of operation of the airplane. Failure of structural elements need not be considered if the probability of this kind of failure is extremely remote.

(c) Compliance with this section may be shown by failure analysis, testing, or both for propeller systems that allow propeller blades to move from the flight low-pitch position to a position that is substantially less than that at the normal flight low-pitch stop position. The analysis may include or be supported by the analysis made to show compliance with the type certification of the propeller and associated installation components. Credit will be given for pertinent analysis and testing completed by the engine and propeller manufacturers.

40. *Turbopropeller drag-limiting systems.* Turbopropeller drag-limiting systems must be designed so that no single failure or malfunction of any of the systems during normal or emergency operation results in propeller drag in excess of that for which the airplane was designed. Failure of structural elements of the drag-limiting systems need not be considered if the probability of this kind of failure is extremely remote.

41. *Turbine engine powerplant operating characteristics.* For turbopropeller powered airplanes, the turbine engine powerplant operating characteristics must be investigated in flight to determine that no adverse characteristics (such as stall, surge, or flameout) are present to a hazardous degree, during normal and emergency operation within the range of operating limitations of the airplane and of the engine.

42. *Fuel flow.* (a) For turbopropeller powered airplanes—

(1) The fuel system must provide for continuous supply of fuel to the engines for normal operation without interruption due to depletion of fuel in any tank other than the main tank; and

(2) The fuel flow rate for turbopropeller engine fuel pump systems must not be less than 125 percent of the fuel flow required to develop the standard sea level atmospheric conditions takeoff power selected and included as an operating limitation in the Airplane Flight Manual.

(b) For reciprocating engine powered airplanes, it is acceptable for the fuel flow rate for each pump system (main and reserve supply) to be 125 percent of the takeoff fuel consumption of the engine.

Fuel System Components

43. *Fuel pumps.* For turbopropeller powered airplanes, a reliable and independent power source must be provided for each pump used with turbine engines which do not have provisions for mechanically driving the main pumps. It must be demonstrated that the pump installations provide a reliability and durability equivalent to that in FAR 23.991(a).

44. *Fuel strainer or filter.* For turbopropeller powered airplanes, the following apply:

(a) There must be a fuel strainer or filter between the tank outlet and the fuel metering device of the engine. In addition, the fuel strainer or filter must be—

(1) Between the tank outlet and the engine-driven positive displacement pump inlet, if there is an engine-driven positive displacement pump;

(2) Accessible for drainage and cleaning and, for the strainer screen, easily removable; and

(3) Mounted so that its weight is not supported by the connecting lines or by the inlet or outlet connections of the strainer or filter itself.

(b) Unless there are means in the fuel system to prevent the accumulation of ice on the filter, there must be means to automatically maintain the fuel-flow if ice-clogging of the filter occurs; and

(c) The fuel strainer or filter must be of adequate capacity (for operating limitations established to ensure proper service) and of appropriate mesh to insure proper engine operation, with the fuel contaminated to a degree (for particle size and density) that can be reasonably expected in service. The degree of fuel filtering may not be less than that established for the engine type certification.

45. *Lightning strike protection.* Protection must be provided against the ignition of flammable vapors in the fuel vent system due to lightning strikes.

Cooling

46. *Cooling test procedures for turbopropeller powered airplanes.* (a) Turbopropeller powered airplanes must be shown to comply with FAR 23.1041 during takeoff, climb, en route, and landing stages of flight that correspond to the applicable performance requirements. The cooling tests must be conducted with the airplane in the configuration, and operating under the conditions that are critical relative to cooling during each stage of flight. For the cooling tests a temperature is "stabilized" when its rate of change is less than 2° F. per minute.

(b) Temperatures must be stabilized under the conditions from which entry is made into each stage of flight being investigated unless the entry condition is not one during which component and engine fluid temperatures would stabilize, in which case, operation through the full entry condition must be conducted before entry into the stage of flight being investigated to allow temperatures to reach their natural levels at the time of entry. The takeoff cooling test must be preceded by a period during which the powerplant component and engine fluid temperatures are stabilized with the engines at ground idle.

(c) Cooling tests for each stage of flight must be continued until—

(1) The component and engine fluid temperatures stabilize;

(2) The stage of flight is completed; or

(3) An operating limitation is reached.

Induction System

47. *Air induction.* For turbopropeller powered airplanes—

(a) There must be means to prevent hazardous quantities of fuel leakage or overflow from drains, vents, or other components of flammable fluid systems from entering the engine intake systems; and

(b) The air inlet ducts must be located or protected so as to minimize the ingestion of foreign matter during takeoff, landing, and taxiing.

48. *Induction system icing protection.* For turbopropeller powered airplanes, each turbine engine must be able to operate throughout its flight power range without adverse effect on engine operation or serious loss of power or thrust, under the icing conditions specified in Appendix C of Part 25 of this chapter. In addition, there must be means to indicate to appropriate flight crewmembers the functioning of the powerplant ice protection system.

49. *Turbine engine bleed air systems.* Turbine engine bleed air systems of turbopropeller powered airplanes must be investigated to determine—

(a) That no hazard to the airplane will result if a duct rupture occurs. This condition must consider that a failure of the duct can occur anywhere between the engine port and the airplane bleed air service; and

(b) That, if the bleed air system is used for direct cabin pressurization, it is not possible for hazardous contamination of the cabin air system to occur in event of lubrication system failure.

Exhaust System

50. *Exhaust system drains.* Turbopropeller engine exhaust systems having low spots or pockets must incorporate drains at those locations. These drains must discharge clear of the airplane in normal and ground attitudes to prevent the accumulation of fuel after the failure of an attempted engine start.

Powerplant Controls and Accessories

51. *Engine controls.* If throttles or power levers for turbopropeller powered airplanes are such that any position of these controls will reduce the fuel flow to the engine(s) below that necessary for satisfactory and safe idle operation of the engine while the airplane is in flight, a means must be provided to prevent inadvertent movement of the control into this position. The means provided must incorporate a positive lock or stop at this idle position and must require a separate and distinct operation by the crew to displace the control from the normal engine operating range.

52. *Reverse thrust controls.* For turbopropeller powered airplanes, the propeller reverse thrust controls must have a means to prevent their inadvertent operation. The means must have a positive lock or stop at the idle position and must require a separate and distinct operation by the crew to displace the control from the flight regime.

53. *Engine ignition systems.* Each turbopropeller airplane ignition system must be considered an essential electrical load.

54. *Powerplant accessories.* The powerplant accessories must meet FAR 23.1163, and if the continued rotation of any accessory remotely driven by the engine is hazardous when malfunctioning occurs, there must be means to prevent rotation without inter-

fering with the continued operation of the engine.

Powerplant Fire Protection

55. Fire detector system. For turbopropeller powered airplanes, the following apply:

(a) There must be a means that ensures prompt detection of fire in the engine compartment. An overtemperature switch in each engine cooling air exit is an acceptable method of meeting this requirement.

(b) Each fire detector must be constructed and installed to withstand the vibration, inertia, and other loads to which it may be subjected in operation.

(c) No fire detector may be affected by any oil, water, other fluids, or fumes that might be present.

(d) There must be means to allow the flight crew to check, in flight, the functioning of each fire detector electric circuit.

(e) Wiring and other components of each fire detector system in a fire zone must be at least fire resistant.

56. Fire protection, cowling and nacelle skin. For reciprocating engine powered airplanes, the engine cowling must be designed and constructed so that no fire originating in the engine compartment can enter either through openings or by burn through, any other region where it would create additional hazards.

57. Flammable fluid fire protection. If flammable fluids or vapors might be liberated by the leakage of fluid systems in areas other than engine compartments, there must be means to—

(a) Prevent the ignition of those fluids or vapors by any other equipment; or

(b) Control any fire resulting from that ignition.

Equipment

58. Powerplant instruments. (a) The following are required for turbopropeller airplanes:

(1) The instruments required by FAR 23.1305 (a) (1) through (4), (b) (2) and (4).

(2) A gas temperature indicator for each engine.

(3) Free air temperature indicator.

(4) A fuel flowmeter indicator for each engine.

(5) Oil pressure warning means for each engine.

(6) A torque indicator or adequate means for indicating power output for each engine.

(7) Fire warning indicator for each engine.

(8) A means to indicate when the propeller blade angle is below the low-pitch position corresponding to idle operation in flight.

(9) A means to indicate the functioning of the ice protection system for each engine.

(b) For turbopropeller powered airplanes, the turbopropeller blade position indicator must begin indicating when the blade has moved below the flight low-pitch position.

(c) The following instruments are required for reciprocating engine powered airplanes:

(1) The instruments required by FAR 23.1305.

(2) A cylinder head temperature indicator for each engine.

(3) A manifold pressure indicator for each engine.

Systems and Equipments

General

59. Function and installation. The systems and equipment of the airplane must meet FAR 23.1301, and the following:

(a) Each item of additional installed equipment must—

(1) Be of a kind and design appropriate to its intended function;

(2) Be labeled as to its identification, function, or operating limitations, or any applicable combination of these factors, unless misuse or inadvertent actuation cannot create a hazard;

(3) Be installed according to limitations specified for that equipment; and

(4) Function properly when installed.

(b) Systems and installations must be designed to safeguard against hazards to the aircraft in the event of their malfunction or failure.

(c) Where an installation, the functioning of which is necessary in showing compliance with the applicable requirements, requires a power supply, that installation must be considered an essential load on the power supply, and the power sources and the distribution system must be capable of supplying the following power loads in probable operation combinations and for probable durations:

(1) All essential loads after failure of any prime mover, power converter, or energy storage device.

(2) All essential loads after failure of any one engine on two-engine airplanes.

(3) In determining the probable operating combinations and durations of essential loads for the power failure conditions described in paragraphs (1) and (2) of this paragraph, it is permissible to assume that the power loads are reduced in accordance with a monitoring procedure which is consistent with safety in the types of operations authorized.

60. Ventilation. The ventilation system of the airplane must meet FAR 23.831, and in addition, for pressurized aircraft, the ventilating air in flight crew and passenger compartments must be free of harmful or hazardous concentrations of gases and vapors in normal operation and in the event of reasonably probable failures or malfunctioning of the ventilating, heating, pressurization, or other systems, and equipment. If accumulation of hazardous quantities of smoke in the cockpit area is reasonably probable, smoke evacuation must be readily accomplished.

Electrical Systems and Equipment

61. *General.* The electrical systems and equipment of the airplane must meet FAR 23.1351, and the following:

(a) *Electrical system capacity.* The required generating capacity, and number and kinds of power sources must—

(1) Be determined by an electrical load analysis; and

(2) Meet FAR 23.1301.

(b) *Generating system.* The generating system includes electrical power sources, main power busses, transmission cables, and associated control, regulation and protective devices. It must be designed so that—

(1) The system voltage and frequency (as applicable) at the terminals of all essential load equipment can be maintained within the limits for which the equipment is designed, during any probable operating conditions;

(2) System transients due to switching, fault clearing, or other causes do not make essential loads inoperative, and do not cause a smoke or fire hazard;

(3) There are means, accessible in flight to appropriate crewmembers, for the individual and collective disconnection of the electrical power sources from the system; and

(4) There are means to indicate to appropriate crewmembers the generating system quantities essential for the safe operation of the system, including the voltage and current supplied by each generator.

62. *Electrical equipment and installation.* Electrical equipment, controls, and wiring must be installed so that operation of any one unit or system of units will not adversely affect the simultaneous operation of any other electrical unit or system essential to the safe operation.

63. *Distribution system.* (a) For the purpose of complying with this section, the distribution system includes the distribution busses, their associated feeders, and each control and protective device.

(b) Each system must be designed so that essential load circuits can be supplied in the event of reasonably probable faults or open circuits, including faults in heavy current carrying cables.

(c) If two independent sources of electrical power for particular equipment or systems are required under this appendix, their electrical energy supply must be ensured by means such as duplicate electrical equipment, throwover switching, or multichannel or loop circuits separately routed.

64. *Circuit protective devices.* The circuit protective devices for the electrical circuits of the airplane must meet FAR 23.1357, and

in addition circuits for loads which are essential to safe operation must have individual and exclusive circuit protection.

APPENDIX B—AIRPLANE FLIGHT RECORDER SPECIFICATIONS

Parameters	Range	Installed system [1] minimum accuracy (to recovered data)	Sampling interval (per second)	Resolution [4] read out
Relative time (from recorded on prior to takeoff).	8 hr minimum	±0.125% per hour	1	1 sec.
Indicated airspeed	V_{so} to V_D (KIAS)	±5% or ±10 kts., whichever is greater. Resolution 2 kts below 175 KIAS.	1	1% [3]
Altitude	−1,000 ft. to max cert. alt. of A/C	±100 to ±700 ft. (see Table 1, TSO C51-a).	1	25 to 150
Magnetic heading	360°	±5°.	1	1°
Vertical acceleration	−3g to +6g	±0.2g in addition to ±0.3g maximum datum.	4 (or 1 per second where peaks, ref. to 1g are recorded).	0.03g.
Longitudinal acceleration	±1.0g	±1.5% max. range excluding datum error of ±5%.	2	0.01g.
Pitch attitude	100% of usable	±2°	1	0.8°
Roll attitude	±60° or 100% of usable range, whichever is greater.	±2°	1	0.8°
Stabilizer trim position	Full range	±3% unless higher uniquely required	1	1% [3]
Or				
Pitch control position	Full range	±3% unless higher uniquely required	1	1% [3]
Engine Power, Each Engine				
Fan or N_1 speed or EPR or cockpit indications used for aircraft certification.	Maximum range	±5%	1	1% [3]
Or				
Prop. speed and torque (sample once/sec as close together as practicable).			1 (prop speed), 1 (torque).	
Altitude rate [3] (need depends on altitude resolution).	±8,000 fpm	±10%. Resolution 250 fpm below 12,000 ft. indicated.	1	250 fpm Below 12,000.
Angle of attack [3] (need depends on altitude resolution).	−20° to 40° or of usable range	±2°	1	0.8% [3]
Radio transmitter keying (discrete)	On/off		1	
TE flaps (discrete or analog)	Each discrete position (U, D, T/O, AAP)		1	
	Or			
	Analog 0-100% range	±3°	1	1% [3]
LE flaps (discrete or analog)	Each discrete position (U, D, T/O, AAP)		1	
	Or			
	Analog 0-100% range	±3°	1	1% [3]
Thrust reverser, each engine (Discrete)	Stowed or full reverse		1	
Spoiler/speedbrake (discrete)	Stowed or out		1	
Autopilot engaged (discrete)	Engaged or disengaged		1	

[1] When data sources are aircraft instruments (except altimeters) of acceptable quality to fly the aircraft the recording system excluding these sensors (but including all other characteristics of the recording system) shall contribute no more than half of the values in this column.
[2] If data from the altitude encoding altimeter (100 ft. resolution) is used, then either one of these parameters should also be recorded. If however, altitude is recorded at a minimum resolution of 25 feet, then these two parameters can be omitted.
[3] Per cent of full range.
[4] This column applies to aircraft manufacturing after October 11, 1991

APPENDIX C—HELICOPTER FLIGHT RECORDER SPECIFICATIONS

Parameters	Range	Installed system [1] minimum accuracy (to recovered data)	Sampling interval (per second)	Resolution [3] read out
Relative time (from recorded on prior to takeoff)	8 hr minimum	±0.125% per hour	1	1 sec
Indicated airspeed	V_{min} to V_D (KIAS) (minimum airspeed signal attainable with installed pilot-static system)	±5% or ±10 kts., whichever is greater	1	1 kt
Altitude	−1,000 ft to 20,000 ft pressure altitude	±100 to ±700 ft. (see Table 1, TSO C51–a).	1	25 to 150 ft.
Magnetic heading	360°	±5°	1	1°
Vertical acceleration	−3g to +6g	±0.2g in addition to ±0.3g maximum datum.	4 (or 1 per second where peaks, ref. to 1g are recorded)	0.05g
Longitudinal acceleration	±1.0g	±1.5% max range excluding datum error of ±5%.	2	0.03g.
Pitch attitude	100% of usable range	±2°	1	0.8°
Roll attitude	±60° or 100% of usable range, whichever is greater	±2°	1	0.8°
Altitude rate	±8,000 fpm	±10% Resolution 250 fpm below 12,000 ft indicated	1	250 fpm below 12,000
Engine Power, Each Engine				
Main rotor speed	Maximum range	±5%	1	1% [2]
Free or power turbine	Maximum range	±5%	1	1% [2]
Engine torque	Maximum range	±5%	1	1% [2]
Flight Control—Hydraulic Pressure				
Primary (discrete)	High/low		1	
Secondary—if applicable (discrete)	High/low		1	
Radio transmitter keying (discrete)	On/off		1	
Autopilot engaged (discrete)	Engaged or disengaged		1	
SAS status—engaged (discrete)	Engaged/disengaged		1	
SAS fault status (discrete)	Fault/OK		1	
Flight Controls				
Collective	Full range	±3%	2	1% [2]
Pedal position	Full range	±3%	2	1% [2]
Lat. cyclic	Full range	±3%	2	1% [2]
Long. cyclic	Full range	±3%	2	1% [2]
Controllable stabilator position	Full range	±3%	2	1% [2]

[1] When data sources are aircraft instruments (except altimeters) of acceptable quality to fly the aircraft the recording system excluding these sensors (but including all other characteristics of the recording system) shall contribute no more than half of the values in this column

[2] Per cent of full range.

[3] This column applies to aircraft manufactured after October 11, 1991

APPENDIX D—AIRPLANE FLIGHT RECORDER SPECIFICATION

Parameters	Range	Accuracy sensor input to DFDR readout	Sampling interval (per second)	resolution [4] read out
Time (GMT or Frame Counter) (range 0 to 4095, sampled 1 per frame).	24 Hrs	±0.125% Per Hour	0.25 (1 per 4 seconds).	1 sec.
Altitude	−1,000 ft to max certificated altitude of aircraft.	±100 to ±700 ft (See Table 1, TSO-C51a).	1	5' to 35' [1]
Airspeed	50 KIAS to V_{so} and V_{so} to 1.2 V_D	±5%, ±3%	1	1kt.
Heading	360°	±2°	1	0.5°
Normal Acceleration (Vertical)	−3g to +6g	±1% of max range excluding datum error of ±5%.	8	0.01g
Pitch Attitude	±75°	±2°	1	0.5°
Roll Attitude	±180°	±2°	1	0.5°
Radio Transmitter Keying	On-Off (Discrete)		1	
Thrust/Power on Each Engine	Full range forward	±2%	1 (per engine)	0.2% [2]
Trailing Edge Flap or Cockpit Control Selection.	Full range or each discrete position.	±3° or as pilot's indicator	0.5	0.5% [2]
Leading Edge Flap on or Cockpit Control Selection.	Full range or each discrete position.	±3° or as pilot's indicator	0.5	0.5% [2]
Thrust Reverser Position	Stowed, in transit, and reverse discrete		1 (per 4 seconds per engine).	
Ground Spoiler Position/Speed Brake Selection.	Full range or each discrete position.	±2% unless higher accuracy uniquely required.	1	0.22 [2]
Marker Beacon Passage	Discrete		1	
Autopilot Engagement	Discrete		1	
Longitudinal Acceleration	±1g	±1.5% max range excluding datum error of ±5%.	4	0.01g
Pilot Input And/or Surface Position-Primary Controls (Pitch, Roll, Yaw) [3].	Full range	±2° unless higher accuracy uniquely required.	1	0.2% [2]
Lateral Acceleration	±1g	±1.5% max range excluding datum error of ±5%.	4	0.01g
Pitch Trim Position	Full range	±3% unless higher accuracy uniquely required.	1	0.3% [2]
Glideslope Deviation	±400 Microamps	±3%	1	0.3% [2]
Localizer Deviation	±400 Microamps	±3%	1	0.3% [2]
AFCS Mode And Engagement Status	Discrete		1	
Radio Altitude	−20 ft to 2,500 ft	±2 Ft or ±3% whichever is greater below 500 ft and ±5% above 500 ft.	1	1 ft + 5% [2] above 500'
Master Warning	Discrete		1	
Main Gear Squat Switch Status	Discrete		1	
Angle of Attack (if recorded directly)	As installed	As installed	2	0.3% [2]
Outside Air Temperature or Total Air Temperature.	−50°C to +90°c	±2°c	0.5	0.3 c
Hydraulics, Each System Low Pressure	Discrete		0.5	or 0.5% [2]
Groundspeed	As installed	Most accurate systems installed (IMS equipped aircraft only).	1	0.2% [3]

If additional recording capacity is available, recording of the following parameters is recommended. The parameters are listed in order of significance:

Parameters	Range	Accuracy sensor input to DFDR readout	Sampling interval (per second)	resolution read out
Drift Angle	When available. As installed	As installed	4	
Wind Speed and Direction	When available. As installed	As installed	4	
Latitude and Longitude	When available. As installed	As installed	4	
Brake pressure/Brake pedal position	As installed	As installed	4	
Additional engine parameters:				
EPR	As installed	As installed	1 (per engine)	
N1	As installed	As installed	1 (per engine)	
N2	As installed	As installed	1 (per engine)	
EGT	As installed	As installed	1 (per engine)	
Throttle Lever Position	As installed	As installed	1 (per engine)	
Fuel Flow	As installed	As installed	1 (per engine)	
TCAS:				
TA	As installed	As installed	1	
RA	As installed	As installed	1	
Sensitivity level (as selected by crew).	As installed	As installed	2	
GPWS (ground proximity warning system)	Discrete		1	
Landing gear or gear selector position	Discrete		0.25 (1 per 4 seconds)	
DME 1 and 2 Distance	0-200 NM;	As installed	0.25	1mi
Nav 1 and 2 Frequency Selection	Full range	As installed	0.25	

[1] When altitude rate is recorded. Altitude rate must have sufficient resolution and sampling to permit the derivation of altitude to 5 feet.

[2] Per cent of full range.

[3] For airplanes that can demonstrate the capability of deriving either the control input on control movement (one from the other) for all modes of operation and flight regimes, the "or" applies. For airplanes with non-mechanical control systems (fly-by-wire) the "and" applies. In airplanes with split surfaces, suitable combination of inputs is acceptable in lieu of recording each surface separately.

[4] This column applies to aircraft manufactured after October 11, 1991

APPENDIX E—HELICOPTER FLIGHT RECORDER SPECIFICATIONS

Parameters	Range	Accuracy sensor input to DFDR readout	Sampling interval (per second)	Resolution [2] read out
Time (GMT)	24 Hrs	±0 125% Per Hour	0 25 (1 per 4 seconds)	1 sec
Altitude	−1,000 ft to max certificated altitude of aircraft.	±100 to ±700 ft (See Table 1, TSO–C51a).	1	5' to 30'
Airspeed	As the installed measuring system	±3%	1	1 kt.
Heading	360°	±2°	1	0.5°
Normal Acceleration (Vertical)	−3g to +6g	±1% of max range excluding datum error of ±5%.	8	0.01g
Pitch Attitude	±75°	±2°	2	0.5°
Roll Attitude	±180°	±2°	2	0.5°
Radio Transmitter Keying	On-Off (Discrete)		1	0.25 sec.
Power in Each Engine: Free Power Turbine Speed and Engine Torque.	0–130% (power Turbine Speed) Full range (Torque).	±2%	1 speed 1 torque (per engine).	0.2% [1] to 0.4% [1]
Main Rotor Speed	0–130%	±2%	2	0.3% [1]
Altitude Rate	±6,000 ft/min	As installed	2	0.2% [1]
Pilot Input—Primary Controls (Collective, Longitudinal Cyclic, Lateral Cyclic, Pedal).	Full range	±3%	2	0.5% [1]
Flight Control Hydraulic Pressure Low	Discrete, each circuit		1	
Flight Control Hydraulic Pressure Selector Switch Position, 1st and 2nd stage.	Discrete		1	
AFCS Mode and Engagement Status	Discrete (5 bits necessary)		1	
Stability Augmentation System Engage	Discrete		1	
SAS Fault Status	Discrete		0.25	
Main Gearbox Temperature Low	As installed	As installed	0.25	0.5% [1]
Main Gearbox Temperature High	As installed	As installed	0.5	0.5% [1]
Controllable Stabilator Position	Full Range	±3%	2	0.4% [1]
Longitudinal Acceleration	±1g	±1.5% max range excluding datum error of ±5%.	4	0.01g.
Lateral Acceleration	±1g	±1.5% max range excluding datum of ±5%.	4	0.01g.
Master Warning	Discrete		1	
Nav 1 and 2 Frequency Selection	Full range	As installed	0 25	
Outside Air Temperature	−50°C to +90°C	±2°c	0 5	0.3°c

[1] Per cent of full range.
[2] This column applies to aircraft manufactured after October 11, 1991.

SUBCHAPTER H—SCHOOLS AND OTHER CERTIFICATED AGENCIES

PART 141—PILOT SCHOOLS

Subpart A—General

AUTHORITY: Secs. 313(a), 314, 601, 602, and 607 of the Federal Aviation Act of 1958 (49 U.S.C. 1354(a), 1355, 1421, 1422, and 1427), and sec. 6(c) of the Dept. of Transportation Act (49 U.S.C. 1655(c)).

SOURCE: Docket No. 12547, 39 FR 20152, June 6, 1974, unless otherwise noted.

Subpart A—General

§ 141.1 Applicability.

This part prescribes the requirements for issuing pilot school certificates, provisional pilot school certificates, and associated ratings and the general operating rules for the holders of those certificates and ratings.

§ 141.3 Certificate required.

No person may operate as a certificated pilot school without, or in violation of, a pilot school certificate or provisional pilot school certificate issued under this part.

§ 141.5 Pilot school certificate.

An applicant is issued a pilot school certificate with associated ratings for that certificate if—

(a) It meets the pertinent requirements of Subparts A through C of this part; and

(b) Within the 24 months before the date of application, it has trained and recommended for pilot certification and rating tests, at least 10 applicants for pilot certificates and ratings and at least 8 of the 10 most recent graduates tested by an FAA inspector or designated pilot examiner, passed that test the first time.

§ 141.7 Provisional pilot school certificate.

An applicant is issued a provisional pilot school certificate with associated ratings if it meets the pertinent requirements of Subparts A through C of this part, but does not meet the recent training activity requirement specified in § 141.5(b).

§ 141.9 Examining authority.

An applicant is issued an examining authority for its pilot school certificate if it meets the requirements of Subpart D of this part.

§ 141.11 Pilot school ratings.

Associated ratings are issued with a pilot school certificate or a provisional pilot school certificate, specifying each of the following courses that the school is authorized to conduct:

(a) *Certification courses.*
(1) Private pilot.
(2) Private test course.
(3) Instrument rating.
(4) Commercial pilot.
(5) Commercial test course.
(6) Additional aircraft rating.
(b) *Pilot ground school course.*
(1) Pilot ground school.
(c) *Test preparation courses.*
(1) Flight instructor certification.
(2) Additional flight instructor rating.
(3) Additional instrument rating.
(4) Airline transport pilot certification.
(5) Pilot refresher course.
(6) Agricultural aircraft operations course.
(7) Rotorcraft external load operations course.

[Doc. No. 12547, 39 FR 20152, June 6, 1974; 39 FR 25473, July 11, 1974]

§ 141.13 Application for issuance, amendment, or renewal.

(a) Application for an original certificate and rating, for an additional rating, or for the renewal of a certificate under this part is made on a form and in a manner prescribed by the Administrator.

(b) An application for the issuance or amendment of a certificate or rating must be accompanied by three copies of the proposed training course outline for each course for which approval is sought.

§ 141.15 Location of facilities.

Neither a pilot school certificate nor a provisional pilot school certificate is issued for a school having a base or other facilities located outside the United States unless the Administrator finds that the location of the base or facilities at that place is needed for the training of students who are citizens of the United States.

§ 141.17 Duration of certificates.

(a) Unless sooner surrendered, suspended, or revoked, a pilot school certificate or a provisional pilot school certificate expires—

(1) At the end of the twenty-fourth month after the month in which it was issued or renewed; or

(2) Except as provided in paragraph (b) of this section, on the date that any change in ownership of the school or the facilities upon which its certification is based occurs; or

(3) Upon notice by the Administrator that the school has failed for more than 60 days to maintain the facilities, aircraft, and personnel required for at least one of its approved courses.

(b) A change in the ownership of a certificated pilot school or provisional pilot school does not terminate that certificate if within 30 days after the date that any change in ownership of the school occurs, application is made for an appropriate amendment to the certificate and no change in the facilities, instructor, personnel or training course is involved.

(c) An examining authority issued to the holder of a pilot school certificate expires on the date that the pilot school certificate expires, or is surrendered, suspended, or revoked.

§ 141.18 **Carriage of narcotic drugs, marihuana, and depressant or stimulant drugs or substances.**

If the holder of a certificate issued under this part permits any aircraft owned or leased by that holder to be engaged in any operation that the certificate holder knows to be in violation of § 91.12(a) of this chapter, that operation is a basis for suspending or revoking the certificate.

§ 141.19 **Display of certificate.**

(a) Each holder of a pilot school certificate or a provisional pilot school certificate shall display that certificate at a place in the school that is normally accessible to the public and is not obscured.

(b) A certificate shall be made available for inspection upon request by the Administrator, or an authorized representative of the National Transportation Safety Board, or of any Federal, State, or local law enforcement officer.

§ 141.21 **Inspections.**

Each holder of a certificate issued under this part shall allow the Administrator to inspect its personnel, facilities, equipment, and records to determine its compliance with the Federal Aviation Act of 1958, and the Federal Aviation Regulations, and its eligibility to hold its certificate.

§ 141.23 **Advertising limitations.**

(a) The holder of a pilot school certificate or a provisional pilot school certificate may not make any statement relating to its certification and ratings which is false or designed to mislead any person contemplating enrollment in that school.

(b) The holder of a pilot school certificate or a provisional pilot school certificate may not advertise that the school is certificated unless it clearly differentiates between courses that have been approved and those that have not.

(c) The holder of a pilot school certificate or a provisional pilot school certificate—

(1) That has relocated its school shall promptly remove from the premises it has vacated all signs indicating that the school was certificated by the Administrator; or

(2) Whose certificate has expired, or has been surrendered, suspended, or revoked shall promptly remove all indications (including signs), wherever located, that the school is certificated by the Administrator.

§ 141.25 **Business office and operations base.**

(a) Each holder of a pilot school or a provisional pilot school certificate shall maintain a principal business office with a mailing address in the name shown on its certificate. The business office shall have facilities and equipment that are adequate to maintain the required school files and records and to operate the business of the school. The office may not be shared with, or used by, another pilot school.

(b) Each certificate holder shall, before changing the location of its business office or base of operations, notify the FAA District Office having jurisdiction over the area of the new location. The notice shall be submitted in writing at least 30 days before the change. For a change in the holder's base of operations, the notice shall be accompanied by any amendments needed for the holder's approved training course outline.

(c) No certificate holder may conduct training at an operations base other than the one specified in its certificate, until—

(1) The base has been inspected and approved by the FAA District Office having jurisdiction over the school for use by the certificate holder; and

(2) The course of training and any needed amendments thereto have been approved for training at that base.

§ 141.27 **Renewal of certificates and ratings.**

(a) *Pilot school certificates.* The holder of a pilot school certificate may apply for a renewal of the certificate not less than 30 days before the certificate expires. If the school meets the requirements of this part for the issuance of the certificate, its certificate is renewed for 24 months.

(b) *Pilot school ratings.* Each pilot school rating on a pilot school certificate may be renewed with that certificate for another 24 months if the Administrator finds that the school meets the requirements prescribed in this part for the issuance of the rating.

(c) *Provisional pilot school certificates.* (1) A provisional pilot school certificate and any ratings on that certificate may not be renewed. However, the holder of that certificate may apply for a pilot school certificate with appropriate ratings not less than 30 days before the provisional certificate expires. The school is issued a pilot school certificate with appropriate ratings, if it meets the appropriate requirements of this part.

(2) The holder of a provisional pilot school certificate may not reapply for a provisional pilot school certificate for at least 180 days after the date of its expiration.

§ 141.29   Existing pilot school certificates; validity.

(a) A pilot school certificate issued before November 1, 1974 remains in effect until the expiration date on that certificate, unless it is sooner surrendered, suspended, or revoked.

(b) A pilot school certificate issued before November 1, 1974, may be renewed under the requirements of Part 141 in effect before November 1, 1974, to allow those students enrolled in a school's approved course of training prior to November 1, 1974, to complete that training. The renewal is issued for a period long enough for the students to complete their training in the enrolled course, but not for more than 24 months after November 1, 1974.

Subpart B—Personnel, Aircraft, and Facilities Requirements

§ 141.31   Applicability.

This subpart prescribes the personnel and aircraft requirements for a pilot school or a provisional pilot school certificate. It also prescribes the facilities an applicant must have

available to him on a continuous use basis to hold a pilot school or provisional pilot school certificate. As used in this subpart, a person has the continuous use of a facility, including an airport, if it has the use of the facility when needed as the owner, or under a written agreement giving it that use for at least 6 calendar months from the date of the application for the initial certificate or a renewal of that certificate.

§ 141.33   Personnel.

(a) An applicant for a pilot school or provisional pilot school certificate must show that—

(1) It has adequate personnel and authorized instructors, including a chief instructor for each course of training, who are qualified and competent to perform the duties to which they are assigned;

(2) Each dispatcher, aircraft handler, line crewman, and serviceman to be used has been instructed in the procedures and responsibilities of his employment. (Qualified operations personnel may serve in more than one capacity with a pilot school or provisional pilot school); and

(3) Each instructor to be used for ground or flight instruction holds a flight or ground instructor certificate, as appropriate, with ratings for the course of instruction and any aircraft used in that course.

(b) An applicant for a pilot school or a provisional pilot school certificate shall designate a chief instructor for each course of training who meets the requirements of a § 141.35 of this part. Where necessary, the applicant shall also designate at least one instructor to assist the chief instructor and serve for the chief instructor in his absence. A chief instructor or his assistant may be designated to serve in that capacity for more than one approved course but not for more than one school.

§ 141.35   Chief instructor qualifications.

(a) To be eligible for a designation as a chief flight instructor or an assistant chief flight instructor for a course of training, a person must meet the following requirements:

(1) He must pass—

(i) An oral test on this part and on Parts 61 and 91 of this chapter and on the training standards and objectives of the course for which he is designated; and

(ii) A flight test on the flight procedures and maneuvers appropriate to that course.

(2) He must meet the applicable requirements of paragraphs (b), (c), and (d) of this section. However, a chief flight instructor or an assistant chief flight instructor for a course of training for gliders, free balloons or airships is only required to have 40 percent of the hours required in paragraphs (b) and (c) of this section.

(b) For a course of training leading to the issuance of a private pilot certificate or rating, a chief flight instructor or an assistant chief flight instructor must have—

(1) At least a commercial pilot certificate and a flight instructor certificate, each with a rating for the category and class of aircraft used in the course;

(2) At least 1,000 hours as pilot in command;

(3) Primary flight instruction experience, acquired as either a certificated flight instructor or an instructor in a military pilot primary flight training program, or a combination thereof, consisting of at least—

(i) Two years and a total of 500 flight hours; or

(ii) 1,000 flight hours; and

(4) Within the year preceding designation, at least 100 hours of flight instruction as a certificated flight instructor in the category of aircraft used in the course.

(c) For a course of training leading to the issuance of an instrument rating or a rating with instrument privileges, a chief flight instructor or an assistant chief flight instructor must have—

(1) At least a commercial pilot certificate and a flight instructor certificate, each with an appropriate instrument rating;

(2) At least 100 hours of flight time under actual or simulated instrument conditions;

(3) At least 1,000 hours as pilot in command;

(4) Instrument flight instructor experience, acquired as either a certificated instrument flight instructor or an instructor in a military pilot basic or instrument flight training program, or a combination thereof; consisting of at least—

(i) Two years and a total of 250 flight hours; or

(ii) 400 flight hours; and

(5) Within the year preceding designation, at least—

(i) 100 hours of instrument flight instruction as a certificated instrument flight instructor; or

(ii) One year of active service as an FAA designated instrument rating examiner.

(d) For a course of training other than those that lead to the issuance of a private pilot certificate or rating, or an instrument rating or a rating with instrument privileges, a chief flight instructor or an assistant chief flight instructor must have—

(1) At least a commercial pilot certificate and a flight instructor certificate, each with a rating for the category and class of aircraft used in the course of training and, for a course of training using airplanes or airships, an instrument rating on his commercial pilot certificate;

(2) At least 2,000 hours as pilot in command;

(3) Flight instruction experience, acquired as either a certificated flight instructor or an instructor in a military pilot primary or basic flight training program or a combination thereof, consisting of at least—

(i) Three years and a total of 1,000 flight hours; or

(ii) 1,500 flight hours; and

(4) Within the year preceding designation, at least—

(i) 100 hours of pilot instruction as a certificated flight instructor in the category of aircraft use in the course;

(ii) One year of active service as chief flight instructor of an approved course of training; or

(iii) One year of active service as an FAA designated pilot examiner.

(e) To be eligible for designation as a chief instructor or an assistant chief instructor for a ground school course, a person must have one year of experience as a ground school instructor in a certificated pilot school.

§ 141.37   Airports.

(a) An applicant for a pilot school certificate or a provisional pilot school certificate must show that it has continuous use of each airport at which training flights originate.

(b) Each airport used for airplanes and gliders must have at least one runway or takeoff area that allows training aircraft to make a normal takeoff or landing at full gross weight—

(1) Under calm wind (not more than five miles per hour) conditions and temperatures equal to the mean high temperature for the hottest month of the year in the operating area;

(2) Clearing all obstacles in the takeoff flight path by at least 50 feet;

(3) With the powerplant operation and landing gear and flap operation, if applicable recommended by the manufacturer; and

(4) With smooth transition from liftoff to the best rate of climb speed without exceptional piloting skills or techniques.

(c) Each airport must have a wind direction indicator that is visible from the ends of each runway at ground level.

(d) Each airport must have a traffic direction indicator when the airport has not operating control tower and UNICOM advisories are not available.

(e) Each airport used for night training flights must have permanent runway lights.

§ 141.39   Aircraft.

An applicant for a pilot school or provisional pilot school certificate must show that each aircraft used by that school for flight instruction and solo flights meets the following requirements:

(a) It must be registered as a civil aircraft of the United States.

(b) Except for aircraft used for flight instruction and solo flights in a course of training for agricultural aircraft operations, external load operations and similar aerial work operations, it must be certificated in the standard airworthiness category.

(c) It must be maintained and inspected in accordance with the requirements of Part 91 of this chapter that apply to aircraft used to give flight instruction for hire.

(d) For use in flight instruction, it must be at least a two place aircraft having engine power controls and flight controls that are easily reached and that operate in a normal manner from both pilot stations.

(e) For use in IFR en route operations and instrument approaches, it must be equipped and maintained for IFR operations. However, for instruction in the control and precision maneuvering of an aircraft by reference to instruments, the aircraft may be equipped as provided in the approved course of training.

§ 141.41   Ground trainers and training aids.

An applicant for a pilot school or a provisional pilot school certificate must show that its ground trainers, and training aids and equipment meet the following requirements:

(a) *Pilot ground trainers.* (1) Each pilot ground trainer used to obtain the maximum flight training credit allowed for ground trainers in an approved pilot training course curriculum must have—

(i) An enclosed pilot's station or cockpit which accommodates one or more flight crewmembers;

(ii) Controls to simulate the rotation of the trainer about three axes;

(iii) The minimum instrumentation and equipment required for powered aircraft in § 91.33 of this chapter, for the type of flight operations simulated;

(iv) For VFR instruction, a means for simulating visual flight conditions, including motion of the trainer, or projections, or models operated by the flight controls; and

(v) For IFR instruction, a means for recording the flight path simulated by the trainer.

(2) Pilot ground trainers other than those covered under paragraph (a)(1) of this section must have—

(i) An enclosed pilot's station or cockpit, which accommodates one or more flight crewmembers;

(ii) Controls to simulate the rotation of the trainer about three axes; and

(iii) The minimum instrumentation and equipment required for powered aircraft in § 91.33 of this chapter, for the type of flight operations simulated.

(b) *Training aids and equipment.* Each training aid, including any audio-visuals, mockup, chart, or aircraft component listed in the approved training course outline must be accurate and appropriate to the course for which it is used.

§ 141.43 Pilot briefing areas.

(a) An applicant for a pilot school or provisional pilot school certificate must show that it has the continuous use of a briefing area located at each airport at which training flights originate, that is—

(1) Adequate to shelter students waiting to engage in their training flights;

(2) Arranged and equipped for the conduct of pilot briefings; and

(3) For a school with an instrument or commercial pilot course rating, equipped with private landline or telephone communication to the nearest FAA Flight Service Station, except that this communication equipment is not required if the briefing area and the flight service station are located on the same airport and are readily accessible to each other.

(b) A briefing area required by paragraph (a) of this section may not be used by the applicant if it is available for use by any other pilot school during the period it is required for use by the applicant.

§ 141.45 Ground training facilities.

An applicant for a pilot school or provisional pilot school certificate must show that each room, training booth, or other space used for instructional purposes is heated, lighted, and ventilated to conform to local building, sanitation, and health codes. In addition, the training facility must be so located that the students in that facility are not distracted by the instruction conducted in other rooms, or by flight and maintenance operations on the airport.

Subpart C—Training Course Outline and Curriculum

§ 141.51 Applicability.

This subpart prescribes the curriculum and course outline requirements for the issuance of a pilot school or provisional pilot school certificate and ratings.

§ 141.53 Training course outline: General.

(a) *General.* An applicant for a pilot school or provisional pilot school certificate must obtain the Administrator's approval of the outline of each training course for which certification and rating is sought.

(b) *Application.* An application for the approval of an initial or amended training course outline is made in triplicate to the FAA District Office having jurisdiction over the area in which the operations base of the applicant is located. It must be made at least 30 days before any training under that course, or any amendment thereto, is scheduled to begin. An application for an amendment to an approved training course must be accompanied by three copies of the pages in the course outline for which an amendment is requested.

§ 141.55 Training course outline: Contents.

(a) *General.* The outline for each course of training for which approval is requested must meet the minimum curriculum for that course prescribed in the appropriate appendix of this part, and contain the following information:

(1) A description of each room used for ground training, including its size and the maximum number of students that may be instructed in the room at one time.

(2) A description of each type of audio-visual aid, projector, tape recorder, mockup, aircraft component and other special training aid used for ground training.

(3) A description of each pilot ground trainer used for instruction.

(4) A listing of the airports at which training flights originate and a description of the facilities, including pilot briefing areas that are available

for use by the students and operating personnel at each of those airports.

(5) A description of the type of aircraft including any special equipment, used for each phase of instruction.

(6) The minimum qualifications and ratings for each instructor used for ground or flight training.

(b) *Training syllabus.* In addition to the items specified in paragraph (a) of this section, the course outline must include a training syllabus for each course of training that includes at least the following information:

(1) The pilot certificate and ratings, if any; the medical certificate, if necessary; and the training, pilot experience and knowledge, required for enrollment in the course.

(2) A description of each lesson, including its objectives and standards and the measurable unit of student accomplishment or learning to be derived from the lesson or course.

(3) The stage of training (including the standards therefor) normally accomplished within each training period of not more than 90 days.

(4) A description of the tests and checks used to measure a student's accomplishment for each stage of training.

§ 141.57   Special curricula.

An applicant for a pilot school or provisional pilot school certificate may apply for approval to conduct a special course of pilot training for which a curriculum is not prescribed in the appendixes to this part, if it shows that the special course of pilot training contains features which can be expected to achieve a level of pilot competency equivalent to that achieved by the curriculum prescribed in the appendixes to this part or the requirements of Part 61 of this chapter.

Subpart D—Examining Authority

§ 141.61   Applicability.

This subpart prescribes the requirements for the issuance of an examining authority to the holder of a pilot school certificate and the privileges and limitations of that authority.

§ 141.63   Application and qualification.

(a) Application for an examining authority is made on a form and in a manner prescribed by the Administrator.

(b) To be eligible for an examining authority an applicant must hold a pilot school certificate. In addition, the applicant must show that—

(1) It has actively conducted a certificated pilot school for at least 24 months before the date of application; and

(2) Within the 24 months before the date of application for the examining authority, at least 10 students were graduated from the course for which the authority is requested, and at least 9 of the most recent 10 graduates of that course, who were given an interim or final test by an FAA inspector or a designated pilot examiner, passed that test the first time.

§ 141.65   Privileges.

The holder of an examining authority may recommend graduates of the school's approved certification courses for pilot certificates and ratings except flight instructor certificates, airline transport pilot certificates and ratings, and turbojet type ratings, without taking the FAA flight or written test, or both, in accordance with the provisions of this subpart.

§ 141.67   Limitations and reports.

(a) The holder of an examining authority may not recommend any person for the issuance of a pilot certificate or rating without taking the FAA written or flight test unless that person has—

(1) Been enrolled by the holder of the examining authority in its approved course of training for the particular pilot certificate or rating recommended; and

(2) Satisfactorily completed all of that course of training at its school.

(b) Each final written or flight test given by the holder of an examining authority to a person who has completed the approved course of training must be at least equal in scope, depth, and difficulty to the comparable written or flight test prescribed by the Administrator under Part 61 of this chapter.

(c) A final ground school written test may not be given by the holder of an examining authority to a student enrolled in its approved course of training unless the test has been approved by the FAA District Office having jurisdiction over the area in which the holder of the examining authority is located. In addition, an approved test may not be given by the holder of an examining authority when—

(1) It knows or has reason to believe that the test has been compromised; or

(2) It has been notified that the District Office knows or has reason to believe that the test has been compromised.

(d) The holder of an examining authority shall submit to the FAA District Office a copy of the appropriate training record for each person recommended by it for a pilot certificate or rating.

Subpart E—Operating Rules

§ 141.71 Applicability.

This subpart prescribes the operating rules that are applicable to a pilot school or provisional pilot school certificated under the provisions of this part.

§ 141.73 Privileges.

(a) The holder of a pilot school or a provisional pilot school certificate may advertise and conduct approved pilot training courses in accordance with the certificate and ratings that it holds.

(b) A certificate pilot school holding an examining authority for a certification course may recommend each graduate of that course for the issuance of a pilot certificate and rating appropriate to that course without the necessity of taking an FAA written or flight test from an FAA inspector or designated pilot examiner.

§ 141.75 Aircraft requirements.

(a) A pretakeoff and prelanding checklist, and the operator's handbook for the aircraft (if one is furnished by the manufacturer) or copies of the handbook if furnished to each student using the aircraft, must be carried on each aircraft used for flight instruction and solo flights.

(b) Each aircraft used for flight instruction and solo flight must have a standard airworthiness certificate, except that an aircraft certificated in the restricted category may be used for flight training and solo flights conducted under special courses for agricultural aircraft operation, external load operations, and similar aerial work operations if its use for training is not prohibited by the operating limitations for the aircraft.

§ 141.77 Limitations.

(a) The holder of a pilot school or a provisional pilot school certificate may not issue a graduation certificate to a student, nor may a certificated pilot school recommend a student for a pilot certificate or rating, unless the student has completed the training therefor specified in the school's course of training and passed the required final tests.

(b) The holder of a pilot school or a provisional pilot school certificate may not graduate a student from a course of training unless he has completed all of the curriculum requirements of that course. A student may be credited, but not for more than one-half of the curriculum requirements, with previous pilot experience and knowledge, based upon an appropriate flight check or test by the school. Course credits may be transferred from one certificated school to another. The receiving school shall determine the amount to be transferred, based on a flight check or written test, or both, of the student. Credit for training and instruction received in another school may not be given unless—

(1) The other school holds a certificate issued under this part and certifies to the kind and amount of training and to the result of each stage and final test given to that student;

(2) The training and instruction was conducted by the other school in accordance with that school's approved training course; and

(3) The student was enrolled in the other school's approved training

course before he received the instruction and training.

§ 141.79 Flight instruction.

(a) No person other than a flight instructor who has the ratings and the minimum qualifications specified in the approved training course outline may give a student flight instruction under an approved course of training.

(b) No student pilot may be authorized to start a solo practice flight from an airport until the flight has been approved by an authorized flight instructor who is present at that airport.

(c) Each chief flight instructor must complete at least once each 12 months, a flight instructor refresher course consisting of not less than 24 hours of ground or flight instruction, or both.

(d) Each flight instructor for an approved course of training must satisfactorily accomplish a flight check given to him by the designated chief flight instructor for the school by whom he is employed. He must also satisfactorily accomplish this flight check each 12 months from the month in which the initial check is given. In addition, he must satisfactorily accomplish a flight check in each type of aircraft in which he gives instruction.

(e) An instructor may not be used in an approved course of training until he has been briefed in regard to the objectives and standards of the course by the designated chief instructor or his assistant.

§ 141.81 Ground training.

(a) Except as provided in paragraph (b) of this section, each instructor used for ground training in an approved course of training must hold a flight or ground instructor certificate with an appropriate rating for the course of training.

(b) A person who does not meet the requirements of paragraph (a) of this section may be used for ground training in an approved course of training if—

(1) The chief instructor for that course of training finds him qualified to give that instruction; and

(2) The instruction is given under the direct supervision of the chief instructor or the assistant chief instructor who is present at the base when the instruction is given.

(c) An instructor may not be used in an approved course of training until he has been briefed in regard to the objectives and standards of that course by the designated chief instructor or his assistant.

§ 141.83 Quality of instruction.

(a) Each holder of a pilot school or provisional pilot school certificate must comply with the approved course of training and must provide training and instruction of such quality that at least 8 out of the 10 students or graduates of that school most recently tested by an FAA inspector or designated pilot examiner, passed on their first attempt either of the following tests:

(1) A test for a pilot certificate or rating, or for an operating privilege appropriate to the course from which the student graduated; or

(2) A test given to a student to determine his competence and knowledge of a completed stage of the training course in which he is enrolled.

(b) The failure of a certificated pilot school or provisional pilot school to maintain the quality of instruction specified in paragraph (a) of this section is considered to be the basis for the suspension or revocation of the certificate held by that school.

(c) The holder of a pilot school or provisional pilot school certificate shall allow the Administrator to make any test, flight check, or examination of its students to determine compliance with its approved course of training and the quality of its instruction and training. A flight check conducted under the provisions of this paragraph is based upon the standards prescribed in the school's approved course of training. However, if the student has completed a course of training for a pilot certificate or rating, the flight test is based upon the standards prescribed in Part 61 of this chapter.

§ 141.85 Chief instructor responsibilities.

(a) Each person designated as a chief instructor for a certificated pilot school or provisional pilot school shall be responsible for—

(1) Certifying training records, graduation certificates, stage and final test reports, and student recommendations;

(2) Conducting an initial proficiency check of each instructor before he is used in an approved course of instruction and, thereafter, at least once each 12 months from the month in which the initial check was conducted;

(3) Conducting each stage or final test given to a student enrolled in an approved course of instruction; and

(4) Maintaining training techniques, procedures, and standards for the school that are acceptable to the Administrator.

(b) The chief instructor or his designated assistant shall be available at the school's base of operations during the time that instruction is given for an approved course of training.

§ 141.87   Change of chief instructor.

(a) The holder of a pilot school or provisional pilot school certificate shall immediately notify in writing the FAA District Office having jurisdiction over the area in which the school is located, of any change in its designation of a chief instructor of an approved training course.

(b) The holder of a pilot school or provisional pilot school certificate may, after providing the notification required in paragraph (a) of this section and pending the designation and approval of another chief instructor, conduct training or instruction without a chief instructor for that course of training for a period of not more than 60 days. However, during that time each stage or final test of a student enrolled in that approved course of training must be given by an FAA inspector, or a designated pilot examiner.

§ 141.89   Maintenance of personnel, facilities, and equipment.

The holder of a pilot school or provisional pilot school certificate may not give instruction or training to a student who is enrolled in an approved course of training unless—

(a) Each airport, aircraft, and facility necessary for that instruction or training meets the standards specified in the holder's approved training

course outline and the appropriate requirements of this part; and

(b) Except as provided in § 141.87, each instructor or chief instructor meets the qualifications specified in the holder's approved course of training and the appropriate requirements of this part.

§ 141.91   Satellite bases.

The holder of a pilot school or provisional pilot school certificate may conduct ground or flight training and instruction in an approved course of training at a base other than its main operations base if—

(a) The satellite base is located not more than 25 nautical miles from its main operations base;

(b) The airport, facilities, and personnel used at the satellite base meet the appropriate requirements of Subpart B of this part and its approved training course outline;

(c) The instructors are under the direct supervision of the chief instructor for the appropriate training course, who is readily available for consultation; and

(d) The FAA District Office having juridiction over the area in which the school is located is notified in writing if training or instruction is conducted there for more than seven consecutive days.

§ 141.93   Enrollment.

(a) The holder of a pilot school or a provisional pilot school certificate shall furnish each student, at the time he is enrolled in each approved training course, with the following:

(1) A certificate of enrollment containing—

(i) The name of the course in which he is enrolled; and

(ii) The date of that enrollment.

(2) A copy of the training syllabus required under § 141.55(b).

(3) A copy of the safety procedures and practices developed by the school covering the use of its facilities and the operation of its aircraft, including instructions on the following:

(i) The weather minimums required by the school for dual and solo flights.

(ii) The procedures for starting and taxiing aircraft on the ramp.

(iii) Fire precautions and procedures.

(iv) Redispatch procedures after unprogrammed landings, on and off airports.

(v) Aircraft discrepancies and write offs.

(vi) Securing of aircraft when not in use.

(vii) Fuel reserves necessary for local and cross-country flights.

(viii) Avoidance of other aircraft in flight and on the ground.

(ix) Minimum altitude limitations and simulated emergency landing instructions.

(x) Description and use of assigned practice areas.

(b) The holder of a pilot school or provisional pilot school certificate shall, within 5 days after the date of enrollment, forward a copy of each certificate of enrollment required by paragraph (a)(1) of this section to the FAA District Office having jurisdiction over the area in which the school is located.

§ 141.95   Graduation certificate.

(a) The holder of a pilot school or provisional pilot school certificate shall issue a graduation certificate to each student who completes its approved course of training.

(b) The certificate shall be issued to the student upon his completion of the course of training and contain at least the following information:

(1) The name of the school and the number of the school certificate.

(2) The name of the graduate to whom it was issued.

(3) The course of training for which it was issued.

(4) The date of graduation.

(5) A statement that the student has satisfactorily completed each required stage of the approved course of training including the tests for those stages.

(6) A certification of the information contained in the certificate by the chief instructor for that course of training.

(7) A statement showing the cross-country training the student received in the course of training.

Subpart F—Records

§ 141.101   Training records.

(a) Each holder of a pilot school or provisional pilot school certificate shall establish and maintain a current and accurate record of the participation and accomplishment of each student enrolled in an approved course of training conducted by the school (the student's logbook is not acceptable for this record). The record shall include—

(1) The date the student was enrolled;

(2) A chronological log of the student's attendance, subjects, and flight operations covered in his training and instruction, and the names and grades of any tests taken by the student; and

(3) The date the student graduated, terminated his training, or transferred to another school.

(b) Whenever a student graduates, terminates his training, or transfers to another school, his record shall be certified to that effect by the chief instructor.

(c) The holder of a certificate for a pilot school or a provisional pilot school shall retain each student record required by this section for at least 1 year from the date that the student graduates from the course to which the record pertains, terminates his enrollment in that course, or transfers to another school.

(d) The holder of a certificate for a pilot school or a provisional pilot school shall, upon request of a student, make a copy of his record available to him.

APPENDIX A—PRIVATE PILOT
CERTIFICATION COURSE (AIRPLANES)

1. *Applicability.* This Appendix prescribes the minimum curriculum for a private pilot certification course (airplanes) required by § 141.55.

2. *Ground training.* The course must consist of at least 35 hours of ground training in the following subjects:

(a) The Federal Aviation Regulations applicable to private pilot privileges, limitations, and flight operations; the rules of the National Transportation Safety Board pertaining to accident reporting; the use of the

Airman's Information Manual; and the FAA Advisory Circular System.

(b) VFR navigation using pilotage, dead reckoning, and radio aids.

(c) The recognition of critical weather situations from the ground and in flight and the procurement and use of aeronautical weather reports and forecasts.

(d) The safe and efficient operation of airplanes, including high density airport operations, collision avoidance precautions, and radio communication procedures.

3. *Flight training.*

(a) The course must consist of at least 35 hours of the flight training listed in this section and section 4 of this Appendix. Instruction in a pilot ground trainer that meets the requirements of § 141.41(a)(1) may be credited for not more than 5 of the required 35 hours of flight time. Instruction in a pilot ground trainer that meets the requirement of § 141.41(a)(2) may be credited for not more than 2.5 hours of the required 35 hours of flight time.

(b) Each training flight must include a preflight briefing and a postflight critique of the student by the instructor assigned to that flight.

(c) Flight training must consist of at least 20 hours of instruction in the following subjects:

(1) Preflight operations, including weight and balance determination, line inspection, starting and runups, and airplane servicing.

(2) Airport and traffic pattern operations, including operations at controlled airports, radio communications, and collision avoidance precautions.

(3) Flight maneuvering by reference to ground objects.

(4) Flight at critically slow airspeeds, recognition of imminent stalls, and recovery from imminent and full stalls.

(5) Normal and crosswind takeoffs and landings.

(6) Control and maneuvering an airplane solely by reference to instruments, including emergency descents and climbs using radio aids or radar directives.

(7) Cross-country flying using pilotage, dead reckoning, and radio aids, including a two-hour dual flight at least part of which must be on Federal airways.

(8) Maximum performance takeoffs and landings.

(9) Night flying, including 5 takeoffs and landings as sole manipulator of the controls, and VFR navigation.

(10) Emergency operations, including simulated aircraft and equipment malfunctions, lost procedures, and emergency go-arounds.

4. *Solo flights.* The course must provide at least 15 hours of solo flights, including:

(a) *Solo practice.* Directed solo practice on all VFR flight operations for which flight instruction is required (except simulated

emergencies) to develop proficiency, resourcefulness, and self-reliance.

(b) *Cross-country flights.* (1) Ten hours of cross-country flights, each flight with a landing at a point more than 50 nautical miles from the original departure point. One flight must be of at least 300 nautical miles with landings at a minimum of three points, one of which is at least 100 nautical miles from the original departure point.

(2) If a pilot school or a provisional pilot school shows that it is located on an island from which cross-country flights cannot be accomplished without flying over water more than 10 nautical miles from the nearest shoreline, it need not include cross-country flights under paragraph (1) of this paragraph. However, if other airports that permit civil operations are available to which a flight may be made without flying over water more than 10 nautical miles from the nearest shoreline, the school must include in its course, two round trip solo flights between those airports that are farthest apart, including a landing at each airport on both flights.

5. *Stage and final tests.* (a) Each student enrolled in a private pilot certification course must satisfactorily accomplish the stage and final tests prescribed in this section. The written tests may not be credited for more than 3 hours of the 35 hours of required ground training, and the flight tests may not be credited for more than 4 hours of the 35 hours of required flight training.

(b) Each student must satisfactorily accomplish a written examination at the completion of each stage of training specified in the approved training syllabus for the private pilot certification course and a final test at the conclusion of that course.

(c) Each student must satisfactorily accomplish a flight test at the completion of the first solo flight and at the completion of the first solo cross-country flight and at the conclusion of that course.

[Doc. No. 12547, 39 FR 20152, June 6, 1974; 39 FR 25473, July 11, 1974, as amended by Amdt. 141-1, 47 FR 46066, Oct. 14, 1982]

APPENDIX B—PRIVATE TEST COURSE (AIRPLANES)

1. *Applicability.* This Appendix prescribes the minimum curriculum for a private test course (airplanes) required by § 141.55.

2. *Experience.* For enrollment as a student in a private test course (airplanes) an applicant must—

(a) Have logged at least 30 hours of flight time as a pilot; and

(b) Have such experience and flight training that upon completion of his approved private test course (airplanes) he will meet the aeronautical experience requirements prescribed in Part 61 of this chapter for a private pilot certificate.

3. *Ground training.* The course must consist of at least 35 hours of ground training in the subjects listed in section 2 of Appendix A of this part.

4. *Flight training.* (a) The course must consist of a total of at least 10 hours of flight instruction in the subjects listed in section 3(c) of Appendix A of this part.

(b) Each training flight must include a preflight briefing and a postflight critique of the student by the instructor assigned to that flight.

5. *Stage and final tests.* Each student enrolled in the course must satisfactorily accomplish the final tests prescribed in § 5 of Appendix A of this part. Written tests may not be credited for more than 3 hours of the required 35 hours of ground training, and the flight tests may not be credited for more than 2 hours of the required 10 hours of flight training.

APPENDIX C—INSTRUMENT RATING COURSE (AIRPLANES)

1. *Applicability.* This Appendix prescribes the minimum curriculum for a training course for an Instrument Rating Course (airplanes) required by § 141.55.

2. *Ground training.* The course must consist of at least 30 hours of ground training instruction in the following subjects:

(a) The Federal Aviation Regulations that apply to flight under IFR conditions, the IFR air traffic system and procedures, and the provisions of the Airman's Information Manual pertinent to IFR flights.

(b) Dead reckoning appropriate to IFR navigation, IFR navigation by radio aids using the VOR, ADF, and ILS systems, and the use of IFR charts and instrument approach procedure charts.

(c) The procurement and use of aviation weather reports and forecasts, and the elements of forecasting weather trends on the basis of that information and personal observation of weather conditions.

(d) The function, use, and limitations of flight instruments required for IFR flight, including transponders, radar and radio aids to navigation.

3. *Flight training.* The course must consist of at least 35 hours of instrument flight instruction given by an appropriately rated flight instructor, covering the operations listed in paragraphs (a) through (d) of this section. Instruction given by an authorized instructor in a pilot ground trainer which meets the requirements of § 141.41(a)(1) may be credited for not more than 15 hours of the required flight instruction. Instruction in a pilot ground trainer that meets the requirements of § 141.41(a)(2) may be cred-

ited for not more than 7.5 of the required 35 hours of flight time.

(a) Control and accurate maneuvering of an airplane solely by reference to flight instruments.

(b) IFR navigation by the use of VOR and ADF systems, including time, speed and distance computations and compliance with air traffic control instructions and procedures.

(c) Instrument approaches to published minimums using the VOR, ADF, and ILS systems (instruction in the use of the ILS glide slope may be given in an instrument ground trainer or with an airborne ILS simulator).

(d) Cross-country flying in simulated or actual IFR conditions, on Federal airways or as routed by ATC, including one such trip of at least 250 nautical miles including VOR, ADF, and ILS approaches at different airports.

(e) Emergency procedures appropriate to the maneuvering of an airplane solely by reference to flight instruments.

4. *Stage and final tests.*

(a) Each student must satisfactorily accomplish a written test at the completion of each stage of training specified in the approved training syllabus for the instrument rating course. In addition, he must satisfactorily accomplish a final written test at the conclusion of that course. The written tests may not be credited for more than 5 hours of the 30 hours of required ground training.

(b) Each student must satisfactorily accomplish a flight stage test at the completion of each operation listed in paragraphs (a), (b), and (c) of section 3 of this Appendix. In addition, he must satisfactorily accomplish a final flight test at the completion of the course. The stage and final tests may not be credited for more than 5 hours of the required 35 hours of flight training.

APPENDIX D—COMMERCIAL PILOT CERTIFICATION COURSE (AIRPLANES)

1. *Applicability.* This Appendix prescribes the minimum curriculum for a commercial pilot certification course (airplanes) required by § 141.55.

2. *Ground training.* The course must consist of at least 100 hours of ground training instruction in the following subjects:

(a) The ground training subjects prescribed in section 2 of Appendix A of this part for a private pilot certification course, except the private pilot privileges and limitations of paragraph (a) of that section.

(b) The ground training subjects prescribed in section 2 of Appendix C of this Part 141 for an Instrument Rating Course.

(c) The Federal Aviation Regulations covering the privileges, limitations, and operations of a commercial pilot, and the operations for which an air taxi/commercial operator, agricultural aircraft operator, and external load operator certificate, waiver, or exemption is required.

(d) Basic aerodynamics, and the principles of flight which apply to airplanes.

(e) The safe and efficient operation of airplanes, including inspection and certification requirements, operating limitations, high altitude operations and physiological considerations, loading computations, the significance of the use of airplane performance speeds, the computations involved in runway and obstacle clearance and crosswind component considerations, and cruise control.

3. *Flight training*—(a) *General.* The course must consist of at least 190 hours of the flight training and instruction prescribed in this section. Instruction in a pilot ground trainer that meets the requirements of § 141.41(a)(1) may be credited for not more than 40 hours of the required 190 hours of flight time. Instruction in a pilot ground trainer that meets the requirements of § 141.41(a)(2) may be credited for not more than 20 hours of the required 190 hours of flight time.

(b) *Flight instruction.* The course must consist of at least 75 hours of instruction in the operations listed in subparagraphs (1) through (6) of this paragraph. Instruction in a pilot ground trainer that meets the requirements of § 141.41(a)(1) may be credited for not more than 20 hours of the required 75 hours. Instruction in a pilot ground trainer that meets the requirements of § 141.41(a)(2) may be credited for not more than 10 hours of the required 75 hours.

(1) The pilot operations for the Private Pilot Course prescribed in section 3 of Appendix A of this part.

(2) The IFR operations for the Instrument Rating Course prescribed in section 3 of Appendix C of this part.

(3) Ten hours of flight instruction in an airplane with retractable gear, flaps, a controllable propeller, and powered by at least 180 hp. engine.

(4) Night flying, including a cross-country night flight with a landing at a point more than 100 miles from the point of departure.

(5) Normal and maximum performance takeoffs and landings using precision approaches and prescribed airplane performance speeds, including operations at maximum authorized takeoff weight.

(6) Emergency procedures appropriate to VFR and IFR flight and to the operation of complex airplane systems.

(c) *Solo practice.* The course must consist of at least 100 hours of the flights listed in paragraphs (1) through (4) of this paragraph. Flight time as pilot in command of an airplane carrying only those persons who are pilots assigned by the school to specific flight crew duties on the flight may be cred-

ited for not more than 50 hours of that requirement.

(1) Directed solo practice on each VFR operation for which flight instruction is required (except simulated emergencies).

(2) At least 40 hours of solo cross-country flights, each flight with a landing at a point more than 50 nautical miles from the original departure point. One flight must have landings at a minimum of three points, one of which is at least 150 nautical miles from the original departure point if the flight is conducted in Hawaii, or at least 250 nautical miles from the original departure point if it is conducted elsewhere.

(3) At least 5 hours of pilot in command time in an airplane described in paragraph (b)(3) of this section, including not less than 10 takeoffs and 10 landings to a full stop.

(4) At least 5 hours of night flight, including at least 10 takeoffs and 10 landings to a full stop.

4. *Stage and final tests*—(a) *Written examinations.* Each student enrolled in the course must satisfactorily accomplish a written test upon the completion of each stage of training specified in the approved training syllabus for the commercial pilot certification course. In addition, he must satisfactorily accomplish a final stage test at the completion of all of that course. The stage and final tests may be credited for not more than 6 hours of the required 100 hours of ground training.

(b) *Flight tests.* Each student enrolled in a commercial pilot certification course (airplanes) must satisfactorily accomplish a stage flight test at the completion of each of the stages listed in paragraphs (1), (2), (3), (4), and (5), of this paragraph. In addition, he must satisfactorily accomplish a final test at the completion of all of those stages. The stage and final tests may not be credited for more than 10 hours of the required 190 hours of flight training.

(1) Solo.

(2) Cross-country.

(3) High performance airplane operations.

(4) IFR operations.

(5) Commercial Pilot Course test, VFR and IFR.

[Doc. No. 12547, 39 FR 20152, June 6, 1974, as amended by Amdt. 141-1, 47 FR 46066, Oct. 14, 1982]

APPENDIX E—COMMERCIAL TEST COURSE (AIRPLANES)

1. *Applicability.* This Appendix prescribes the minimum curriculum for a commercial test course (airplanes) required by § 141.55.

2. *Experience.* For enrollment as a student in a commercial test course (airplanes) an applicant must—

(a) Hold a valid private pilot certificate;

(b) Hold a valid instrument rating, or be enrolled in an approved instrument rating course; and

(c) Have such experience and flight training that upon completion of his approved commercial test course he will meet the aeronautical experience requirements prescribed in Part 61 of this chapter for a commercial pilot certificate.

3. *Ground training.* The course must consist of at least 50 hours of ground training instruction in the following subjects:

(a) A review of the ground training subjects prescribed in section 2 of Appendix A of this Part 141 for a private pilot certification.

(b) A review of the ground training subjects prescribed in section 2 of Appendix C of this Part 141 for an instrument rating course.

(c) The Federal Aviation Regulations covering the privileges, limitations, and operations of a commercial pilot, and the operations for which an air taxi/commercial operator, agricultural aircraft operator, and external load operator certificate, waiver or exemption is required.

(d) Basic aerodynamics, and the principles of flight that apply to airplanes.

(e) The safe and efficient operation of airplanes, including inspection and certification requirements, operating limitations, high altitude operations and psysiological considerations, loading computations, the significance and use of airplane performance speeds, and computations involved in runway and obstacle clearance and crosswind component considerations.

4. *Flight training*—(a) *General.* The course must consist of at least 25 hours of flight training prescribed in this section. Instruction in a pilot ground trainer that meets the requirements of § 141.41(a)(1) may be credited for not more than 20 per cent of the total number of hours of flight time. Instruction in a pilot ground trainer that meets the requirements of § 141.41(a)(2) may be credited for not more than 10 per cent of the total number of hours of flight time.

(b) *Flight instruction.* The course must consist of at least 20 hours of flight instruction in the subjects listed in subparagraphs (1) through (3) of this paragraph. Instruction in a ground trainer that meets the requirements of § 141.41(a)(1) may be credited for not more than 4 hours of the required 20 hours. Instruction in a ground trainer that meets the requirements of § 141.41(a)(2) may be credited for not more than 2 hours of the required 20 hours.

(1) A review of the VFR operations prescribed in section 3 of Appendix A of this part for a private course.

(2) A review of the IFR operations prescribed in section 3 of Appendix C of this part for an instrument rating course.

(3) A review of the VFR operations prescribed in section 3(b)(3) through (6) of Appendix D of this part for a commercial pilot certification course.

(c) *Directed solo practice.* If the course includes directed solo practice necessary to develop the flight proficiency of each student, the practice may not exceed a ratio of 3 hours of directed solo practice for each hour of the flight instruction required by the school's approved course outline.

5. *Stage and final tests*—(a) *Written tests.* Each student enrolled in the course must satisfactorily accomplish a stage test upon the completion of each stage of training specified in the approved training syllabus for the commercial test course. In addition, he must satisfactorily accomplish a final test at the conclusion of that course. The stage and final tests may not be credited for more than 4 hours of the required 50 hours of ground training.

(b) *Flight tests.* Each student enrolled in the course must satisfactorily accomplish a final test at the completion of the course. However, if the approved course of training exceeds 35 hours he must be given a test at an appropriate stage prior to completon of 35 hours of flight training. The flight tests may not be credited for more than 3 of the required hours of flight training.

(c) *Total flight experience.* The approved training course outline must specify the minimum number of hours of flight instruction and directed solo practice (if any) that is provided for each student under the requirements of paragraphs (b) and (c) of section 4 of this appendix. The total number of hours of all flight training given to a student under this section and the minimum experience required for enrollment under section 2 of this appendix must meet the minimum aeronautical experience requirements of § 61.129 of this chapter for the issuance of a commercial pilot certificate.

APPENDIX F—ROTORCRAFT, GLIDERS, LIGHTER-THAN-AIR AIRCRAFT AND AIRCRAFT RATING COURSES

A. *Applicability.* This appendix prescribes the minimum curriculum for a pilot certification course for a rotorcraft, glider, lighter-than-air aircraft, or aircraft rating, required by § 141.55.

B. *General Requirements.* The course must be comparable in scope, depth, and detail with the curriculum prescribed in Appendices A through D of this part for a pilot certification course (airplanes) with the same rating. Each course must provide ground and flight training covering the aeronautical knowledge and skill items required by Part 61 of this chapter for the certificate or rating concerned. In addition, each course must meet the appropriate requirements of this appendix.

C. *Rotorcraft*—I. *Kinds of rotorcraft pilot certification courses.* An approved rotorcraft pilot certification course includes—

(a) A helicopter or gyroplane course—private pilots;

(b) A helicopter or gyroplane course—commercial pilots; and

(c) An instrument rating—helicopter.

II. *Helicopter or gyroplane course: Private pilots.*

(a) A private pilot certification course for helicopters or gyroplanes must consist of at least the following:

(1) Ground training—35 hours.

(2) Flight training—35 hours, including the following:

(i) Flight instruction—20 hours.

(ii) Solo practice—10 hours, including a flight with landings at three points, each of which is more than 25 nautical miles from the other two points.

(b) Stage and final tests may be credited for not more than 3 hours of the 35 hours of ground training, and for not more than 4 hours of the 35 hours of flight training required by paragraphs (a)(1) and (a)(2) of this section.

III. *Helicopter or gyroplane course—commercial pilots.* (a) A commercial pilot certification course of training for helicopters or gyroplanes must consist of at least the following:

(1) Ground training—65 hours.

(2) Flight training—150 hours of flight training at least 50 hours of which must be in helicopters or gyroplanes.

The flight training must include the following:

(i) Flight instruction—50 hours.

(ii) Directed solo—100 hours (including a cross-country flight with landings at three points, each of which is more than 50 nautical miles from the other two points).

(b) Stage and final tests may be credited for not more than 5 hours of the required 65 hours of ground training, and for not more than 7 hours of the required 150 hours of flight training prescribed in paragraphs (a)(1) and (a)(2) of this section.

IV. *Instrument rating—helicopter course.* (a) An instrument rating—helicopter course of training must consist of at least the following:

(1) Ground training—35 hours.

(2) Instrument flight training—35 hours. Instrument instruction in a pilot ground trainer that meets the requirements of § 141.41(a)(1) may be credited for not more than 10 hours of the required 35 hours of flight training. Instruction in a ground trainer that meets the requirements of § 141.41(a)(2) may be credited for not more than 5 hours of the required 35 hours. The instrument flight instruction must include a

100-mile simulated or actual IFR cross-country flight, and 25 hours of flight instruction.

(3) Stage and final tests may be credited for not more than 5 hours of the 35 hours of required ground training, and not more than 5 hours of the 35 hours of instrument training.

D. *Gliders*—I. *Kinds of glider pilot certification courses.* An approved glider certification course includes—

(a) A glider course—private pilots; and

(b) A glider course—commercial pilots.

II. *Glider course: Private pilot.* A private pilot certification course for gliders must consist of at least the following:

(a) Ground training—15 hours.

(b) Flight training—8 hours (including 35 flights if ground tows are used, or 20 flights if aero tows are used). The flight training must include the following:

(1) Flight instruction—2 hours (including 20 flights if ground tows are used or 15 flights if aero tows are used).

(2) Directed solo—5 hours (including at least 15 flights if ground tows are used or 5 flights if aero tows are used).

(c) Stage and flight tests may be credited for not more than one hour of the 15 hours of ground training, and for not more than one-half hour of the 2 hours of flight instruction required by paragraphs (a)(1) and (a)(2) of this section.

III. *Glider course: Commercial pilot.* (a) An approved commercial pilot certification course for gliders must consist of at least the following:

(1) Ground training—25 hours.

(2) Flight training—20 hours of flight time in gliders (consisting of at least 50 flights), including the following:

(i) Flight instruction—8 hours.

(ii) Directed solo—10 hours.

(b) Stage and final tests may be credited for not more than 2 hours of the 25 hours of ground training, and for not more than 2 hours of the 20 hours of flight training required by paragraphs (a)(1) and (a)(2) of this section.

E. *Lighter-than-air aircraft*—I. *Kinds of lighter-than-air pilot certification courses.* An approved lighter-than-air pilot certification course includes—

(a) An airship course—private pilot;

(b) A free balloon course—private pilot;

(c) An airship course—commercial pilot; and

(d) A free balloon course—commercial pilot.

II. *Airship—private pilot.* (a) A private pilot certification course for an airship must consist of at least the following:

(1) Ground training—35 hours.

(2) Flight training—50 hours (45 hours must be in airships), including the following:

(i) Flight instruction—20 hours in airships.

(ii) Directed solo, or performing the functions of a pilot in command of an airship for which more than one pilot is required—10 hours.

(b) Stage and final tests may be credited for not more than 5 hours of the 35 hours of ground training, and not more than 5 hours of the 50 hours of flight training required by paragraphs (a)(1) and (a)(2) of this section.

III. *Free balloon course; private pilot.* (a) A private pilot course for a free balloon must consist of at least the following:

(1) Ground training—10 hours.

(2) Flight training—6 free flights, including—

(i) Two flights of one hour duration each if a gas balloon is used, or of 30 minutes duration if a hot air balloon is used;

(ii) At least one solo flight; and

(iii) One ascent under control to 5,000 feet above the point of takeoff if a gas balloon is used, or 3,000 feet above the point of takeoff if a hot air balloon is used.

(b) The written and stage checks may be credited for not more than one hour of the ground training, and not more than one of the 6 flights required by paragraph (a)(1) and (a)(2) of this section.

IV. *Airship course—commercial pilot.* (a) A commercial pilot course for an airship must consist of at least the following:

(1) Ground training—100 hours.

(2) Flight training—190 hours in airships as follows:

(i) Flight instruction—80 hours, including 30 hours instrument time.

(ii) 100 hours of solo time, or flight time performing the functions of a pilot in command in an airship that requires more than one pilot, including 10 hours of cross-country flying and 10 hours of night flying.

(b) Stage and final tests may be credited for not more than 6 hours of the 100 hours of ground training, and not more than 10 hours of the 190 hours of flight training required by paragraphs (a)(1) and (a)(2), respectively, of this section.

V. *Free balloon course; commercial pilot.* (a) A commercial pilot certification course for free balloons must consist of at least the following:

(1) Ground training—20 hours.

(2) Flight training—8 free flights, including—

(i) 2 flights of more than 2 hours duration if a gas balloon is used, or 2 flights of more than 1 hour duration if a hot air balloon is used;

(ii) 1 ascent under control to more than 10,000 feet above the takeoff point if a gas balloon is used, or to more than 5,000 feet above the takeoff point if a hot air balloon is used; and

(iii) 2 solo flights.

(b) Stage and final tests may be credited for not more than 2 hours of the 20 hours of ground training, and not more than one of the flights required by paragraphs (a)(1) and (a)(2), respectively, of this section.

F. *Aircraft rating course*—I. *Kinds of aircraft rating courses.* An approved aircraft rating course includes—

(a) An aircraft category rating;

(b) An aircraft class rating; and

(c) An aircraft type rating.

II. *Aircraft category rating.* An aircraft category rating course must include at least the ground training and flight instruction required by Part 61 of this chapter for the issuance of a pilot certificate with a category rating appropriate to the course. However, the Administrator may approve a lesser number of hours of ground training, or flight instruction, or both, if the course provides for the use of special training aids, such as ground procedures, trainers, systems mockups, and audio-visual training materials, or requires appropriate aeronautical experience of the students as a prerequisite for enrollment in the course.

III. *Aircraft class rating.* An aircraft class rating course must include at least the flight instruction required by Part 61 of this chapter for the issuance of a pilot certificate with a class rating appropriate to the course.

IV. *Aircraft type rating.* An aircraft type rating course must include at least 10 hours of ground training on the aircraft systems, performance, operation, and loading. In addition, it must include at least 10 hours of flight instruction. Instruction in a pilot ground trainer that meets the requirements of § 141.41(a)(1) may be credited for not more than 5 of the 10 hours of required flight instruction. Instruction in a pilot ground trainer that meets the requirements of § 141.41(a)(2) may be credited for not more than 2.5 of the 10 hours of required flight instruction.

APPENDIX G—PILOT GROUND SCHOOL COURSE

1. *Applicability.* This appendix prescribes the minimum curriculum for a pilot ground school course required by § 141.55.

2. *General requirements.* An approved course of training for a pilot ground school course must contain the instruction necessary to provide each student with adequate knowledge of those subjects needed to safely exercise the privileges of the pilot certificate sought.

3. *Ground training instruction.* A pilot ground school course must include at least the subjects and the number of hours of ground training specified in the ground training section of the curriculum pre-

scribed in the appendixes to this part for the certification or test preparation course to which the ground school course is directed.

4. *Stage and final tests.* Each student must pass a written test at the completion of each stage of training specified in the approved training syllabus for each ground training course in which he is enrolled. In addition, he must pass a final written test at the completion of the course. The stage and final tests may be credited towards the total ground training time required for each certification and test preparation course as provided in the curriculum prescribed in the appendixes to this part for that course.

APPENDIX H—TEST PREPARATION COURSES

1. *Applicability.* This appendix prescribes the minimum curriculum required under § 141.55 of this Part 141 for each test preparation course listed in § 141.11.

2. *General requirements.*

(a) A test preparation course is eligible for approval if the Administrator determines that it is adequate for a student enrolled in that course, upon graduation, to safely exercise the privileges of the certificate, rating, or authority for which the course is conducted.

(b) Each course for a test preparation must be equivalent in scope, depth, and detail with the curriculum for the corresponding test course prescribed in Appendices A, B, C, and D of this Part 141. However, the number of hours of ground training and flight training included in the course must meet the curriculum prescribed in this appendix. (The minimums prescribed in this appendix for each test preparation course are based upon the amount of training that is required for students who meet the total flight experience requirements prescribed in Part 61 of this chapter at the time of enrollment.)

(c) Minimum experience, knowledge, or skill, requirements necessary as a prerequisite for enrollment are prescribed in the appropriate test preparation courses contained in this appendix.

3. *Flight instructor certification course.*

(a) An approved course of training for a flight instructor certification course must contain at least the following:

(1) *Ground training*—40 hours.

(2) *Instructor training*—25 hours, including—

(i) 10 hours of flight instruction in the analysis and performance of flight training maneuvers;

(ii) 5 hours of practice ground instruction; and

(iii) 10 hours of practice flight instruction (with the instructor in the aircraft).

(b) *Credit for previous training of experience:* A student may be credited with the following training and experience acquired before his enrollment in the course.

(1) Satisfactory completion of two years of study on the principles of education in a college or university may be credited for 20 hours of the required 40 hours of ground training prescribed in paragraph (a)(1) of this section.

(2) One year of experience as a full-time instructor in an institution of secondary or advanced education may be credited for 5 hours of the required practice ground instruction prescribed in paragraph (a)(2) of this section.

(c) *Prerequisite for enrollment.* To be eligible for enrollment each student must hold—

(1) A commercial pilot certificate;

(2) A rating for the aircraft used in the course; and

(3) An instrument rating for enrollment in an airplane instructor rating course.

4. *Additional flight instructor rating courses.*

(a) An approved course of training for an additional flight instructor rating course must consist of at least the following:

(1) *Ground training*—20 hours.

(2) *Instructor training* (with an instructor in the aircraft). 20 hours, including—

(i) 10 hours of analysis of flight training maneuvers, or, in the case of a glider instructor rating course, 10 flights in a glider; and

(ii) 10 hours of practice flight instruction, or, in the case of glider instructor rating course, 10 flights in a glider.

5. *Additional instrument rating course* (airplane or helicopter).

(a) An approved training course for an additional instrument rating course must include at least the following:

(1) *Ground training*—15 hours.

(2) *Flight instruction*—15 hours.

(b) *Prerequisites for enrollment.* To be eligible for enrollment each student must hold a valid pilot certificate with an instrument rating, and an aircraft rating for the aircraft used in the course.

6. *Airline transport pilot test course.*

(a) An approved training course for an airline transport pilot test course must include at least the following:

(1) *Ground training*—40 hours.

(2) *Flight instruction*—25 hours, including at least 15 hours of instrument flight instruction.

(b) *Prerequisites for enrollment.* To be eligible for enrollment each student must—

(1) Hold a commercial pilot certificate with an instrument rating and a rating for the aircraft used in the course; and

(2) Meet the experience requirements of Part 61 of this chapter for the issuance of an airline transport pilot certificate.

7. *Pilot certificate, aircraft or instrument rating refresher course.*

(a) An approved refresher training course for a pilot certificate, aircraft rating, or an instrument rating must contain at least the following:

(1) *Ground training*—4 hours.

(2) *Flight instruction*—6 hours, which may include not more than 2 hours of directed solo or pilot in command practice.

(b) *Prerequisites for enrollment.* To be eligible for enrollment each student must hold a valid pilot certificate with ratings appropriate to the refresher course.

8. *Agricultural aircraft operations course.*

(a) An approved training course for pilots of agricultural aircraft must include at least the following:

(1) *Ground training*—25 hours, including at least 15 hours on the handling of agricultural and industrial chemicals.

(2) *Flight instruction*—15 hours, which may include not more than 5 hours of directed solo practice.

(b) *Prerequisite for enrollment.* To be eligible for enrollment each student must hold a valid commercial pilot certificate with a rating for the aircraft used in the course.

9. *Rotorcraft external-load operations course.*

(a) An approved training course for pilots of a rotorcraft with an external-load must contain at least the following:

(1) *Ground training*—10 hours.

(2) *Flight instruction*—15 hours.

(b) *Prerequisite for enrollment.* To be eligible for enrollment each student must hold a valid commercial pilot certificate with a rating for the rotorcraft used in the course.

PART 830-NOTIFICATION AND REPORTING OF AIRCRAFT ACCIDENTS OR INCIDENTS AND OVERDUE AIRCRAFT, AND PRESERVATION OF AIRCRAFT WRECKAGE, MAIL, CARGO, AND RECORDS

   Authority: 49 U.S.C. 1441 and 1901 et seq.

Subpart A-General

§830.1 Applicability.

   This part contains rules pertaining to:
   (a) Notification and reporting aircraft accidents and incidents and certain other occurrences in the operation of aircraft when they involve civil aircraft of the United States wherever they occur, or foreign civil aircraft when such events occur in the United States, its territories or possessions.
   (b) Reporting aircraft accidents and listed incidents in the operation of aircraft when they involve certain public aircraft.
   (c) Preservation of aircraft wreckage, mail, cargo, and records involving all civil aircraft in the United States, its territories or possessions.

§830.2 Definitions.

   As used in this part the following words or phrases are defined as follows:
   "Aircraft accident" means an occurrence associated with the operation of an aircraft which takes place between the time any person boards the aircraft with the intention of flight and all such persons have disembarked, and in which any person suffers death or serious injury, or in which the aircraft receives substantial damage.
   "Civil aircraft" means any aircraft other than a public aircraft.
   "Fatal injury" means any injury which results in death within 30 days of the accident.
   "Incident" means an occurrence other than an accident, associated with the operation of an aircraft, which affects or could affect the safety of operations.
   "Operator" means any person who causes or authorizes the operation of an aircraft, such as the owner, lessee, or bailee of an aircraft.
   "Public aircraft" means an aircraft used exclusively in the service of any government or of any political subdivision thereof, including the government of any State, Territory, or possession of the United States, or the District of Columbia, but not including any government-owned aircraft engaged in carrying persons or property for commercial purposes. For purposes of this section "used exclusively in the service of" means, for other than the Federal Government, an aircraft which is owned and operated by a governmental entity for other than commercial purposes or which is exclusively leased by such governmental entity for not less than 90 continuous days.
   "Serious injury" means an injury which: (1) Requires hospitalization for more than 48 hours, commencing within 7 days from the date of the injury was received; (2) results in a fracture of any bone (except simple fractures of fingers, toes, or nose); (3) causes severe hemorrhages, nerve, muscle, or tendon damage; (4) involves any internal organ; or (5) involves second-or-third degree burns, or any burns affecting more than 5 percent of the body surface.
   "Substantial damage" means damage or failure which adversely affects the structural strength, performance, or flight characteristics of the aircraft, and which would normally require major repair or replacement of the affected component. Engine failure or damage limited to an engine if only one engine fails or is damaged, bent fairings or cowling, dented skin, small punctured holes in the skin or fabric, ground damage to rotor or propeller blades, and damage to landing gear, wheels, tires, flaps, engine accessories, brakes, or wingtips are not considered "substantial damage" for the purpose of this part.

Subpart B-Initial Notification of Aircraft Accidents, Incidents, and Overdue Aircraft

§830.5 Immediate notification.

The operator of an aircraft shall immediately, and by the most expeditious means available, notify the nearest National Transportation Safety Board (Board), field office when:

(a) An aircraft accident or any of the following listed incidents occur:

(1) Flight control system malfunction or failure;

(2) Inability of any required flight crewmember to perform normal flight duties as a result of injury or illness;

(3) Failure of structural components of a turbine engine excluding compressor and turbine blades and vanes;

(4) In-flight fire; or

(5) Aircraft collide in flight.

(6) Damage to property, other than the aircraft, estimated to exceed $25,000 for repair (including materials and labor) or fair market value in the event of total loss, whichever is less.

(7) For large multiengine aircraft (more than 12,500 pounds maximum certificated takeoff weight):

(i) In-flight failure of electrical systems which requires the sustained use of an emergency bus powered by a back-up source such as a battery, auxiliary power unit, or air-driven generator to retain flight control or essential instruments;

(ii) In-flight failure of hydraulic systems that results in sustained reliance on the sole remaining hydraulic or mechanical system for movement of flight control surfaces;

(iii) Sustained loss of the power or thrust produced by two or more engines; and

(iv) An evacuation of an aircraft in which an emergency egress system is utilized.

(b) An aircraft is overdue and is believed to have been involved in an accident.

§830.6 Information to be given in notification.

The notification required in §830.5 shall contain the following information, if available:

(a) Type, nationality, and registration marks of the aircraft;

(b) Name of owner, and operator of the aircraft;

(c) Name of the pilot-in-command;

(d) Date and time of the accident;

(e) Last point of departure and point of intended landing of the aircraft;

(f) Position of the aircraft with reference to some easily defined geographical point;

(g) Number of persons aboard, number killed, and number seriously injured;

(h) Nature of the accident, the weather and the extent of damage to the aircraft, so far as is known; and

(i) A description of any explosives, radioactive materials, or other dangerous articles carried.

Subpart C-Preservation of Aircraft Wreckage, Mail, Cargo and Records

§830.10 Preservation of aircraft wreckage, mail, cargo, and records.

(a) The operator of an aircraft involved in an accident or incident for which notification must be given is responsible for preserving to the extent possible any aircraft wreckage, cargo, and mail aboard the aircraft, and all records, including all recording mediums of flight, maintenance, and voice recorders, pertaining to the operation and maintenance of the aircraft and to the airmen until the Board takes custody thereof or a release is granted pursuant to §831.12(b) of this chapter.

(b) Prior to the time the Board or its authorized representative takes custody of aircraft wreckage, mail or cargo, such wreckage, mail, or cargo may not be disturbed or moved except to the extent necessary:

(1) To remove persons injured or trapped;

(2) To protect the wreckage from further damage; or

(3) To protect the public from injury.

(c) Where it is necessary to move aircraft wreckage, mail or cargo, sketches, descriptive notes, and photographs shall be made, if possible, of the original positions and condition of the wreckage and any significant impact marks.

(d) The operator of an aircraft involved in an accident or incident shall retain all records, reports, internal documents, and memoranda dealing with the accident or incident, until authorized by the Board to the contrary.

Subpart D-Reporting of Aircraft Accidents, Incidents, and Overdue Aircraft

§830.15 Reports and statements to be filed.

(a) *Reports.* The operator of an aircraft shall file a report on Board Form 6120.1(OMB No. 3147-005) or Board Form 7120.2 (OMB No. 3147-0001) within 10 days after an accident, or after 7 days if an overdue aircraft is still missing. A report on an incident for which notification is required by §830.5(a) shall be filed only as requested by an authorized representative of the Board.

(b) *Crewmember statement.* Each crewmember, if physically able at the time the report is submitted, shall attach a statement setting forth the facts, conditions, and circumstances relating to the accident or incident as they appear to him. If the crewmember is incapacitated, he shall submit the statement as soon as he is physically able.

(c) *Where to file the reports.* The operator of an aircraft shall file any report with the field office of the Board nearest the accident or incident.

Subpart E-Reporting of Public Aircraft Accidents and Incidents

§830.20 Reports to be filed.

The operator of a public aircraft other than an aircraft of the Armed Forces or Intelligence Agencies shall file a report on NTSB Form 6120.1 (OMB No. 3147-001) within 10 days after an accident or incident listed in §830.5(a). The operator shall file the report with the field office of the Board nearest the accident or incident.

AIM
1989

AIRMAN'S INFORMATION MANUAL
PILOT/CONTROLLER GLOSSARY
CUSTOMS GUIDE FOR PRIVATE FLYERS

INCLUDES
FREE UPDATE SERVICE
(See form in back of publication.)

PUBLISHED BY

asa Publications, Inc.
6001 SIXTH AVENUE SO.
SEATTLE, WA 98108-3307

COPYRIGHT© 1989 by ASA, INC.

EXAM CROSS-REFERENCE INDEX

Applicants preparing for written exams should have full knowledge of the following applicable AIMs.

PRIVATE / COMMERCIAL / CFI

AIM #	AIM #	AIM #	AIM #	AIM #
2	90	152	225	471
3	91	156	226	505
4	92	157	233	513
5	93	158	235	514
6	94	160	237	515
7	95	161	241	527
16	96	162	243	531
22	97	164	247	540
30	99	170	260	541
31	100	190	264	542
41	101	191	270	543
42	110	192	290	544
46	111	193	294	545
47	112	195	295	551
50	113	204	302	552
52	114	205	304	600
60	115	206	440	601
70	116	220	441	602
71	117	221	450	603
80	130	222	451	604
81	131	223	452	605
83	150	224	454	607
84	151			

135 / ATP

AIM #	AIM #	AIM #	AIM #	AIM #
1	95	226	324	383
2	96	230	325	384
4	97	245	340	385
10	111	262	341	430
11	112	263	343	431
12	113	264	344	Ch.5,Sec.1
13	114	266	345	452
16	115	271	346	461
22	130	272	347	462
30	131	273	360	463
32	133	274	362	464
33	151	290(d)	363	470
40	152	295	365	501
41	156	296	370	505
44	158	297	373	506
45	160	298	375	507
60	161	300	380	520
83	162	302	381	Ch.6,Sec.3
92	164	303	382	Ch.7
93	165	320		
94	170	322		

INSTRUMENT-AIRPLANE / FLIGHT INSTRUCTOR-INSTRUMENT

Introduction

Customs Guide for Private Flyers is for you—the private, corporate, and charter pilot—on business or pleasure flights to and from foreign countries. It sets forth the basic Customs requirements, provides a list of airports at which Customs clearance may be obtained and explains overtime charges.

You can facilitate your air travel if you know Customs regulations and follow them. Additional valuable information on regulations concerning international flights is available in the International Flight Information Manual published by the Federal Aviation Administration (FAA) and sold by the Superintendent of Documents, U.S. Government Printing Office, Washington, D.C. 20402.

If you are in doubt, don't guess. Ask your local Customs officers or the Customs officers at the airport of your intended return to the United States.

Happy landing!

The Narcotics Smuggling Threat

The United States Customs Service is requesting the assistance of Fixed Base Operators, Fuel Service Facilities, Aircraft Brokers, Aircraft Charter Services, Airport Security, pilots, crew, airport personnel and others associated with general aviation activities.

Over the past several years, Puerto Rico, Florida, Louisiana, Texas, Arizona, New Mexico and California have been inundated by persons and/or organizations that are responsible for smuggling large amounts of narcotics into the United States by airplane. In an attempt to identify these individuals and/or groups, we are asking for your assistance. Through the use of the following indicators, it is believed that you can assist us in deterring the smuggling of narcotics into the United States.

Remember these smugglers endanger you as the general aviation community and your family as the public community. They tarnish the highly thought of general aviation community name.

The basic indicators that you should be cognizant of are as follows (it should be noted these are only guidelines and may vary with individuals. The presence of one or more of these indicators does not necessarily mean that there is an air smuggler):

1. Passenger seats removed from the aircraft.

2. Carrying gas cans inside the aircraft or persons without an aircraft buying large amounts of aviation gas in gas cans.

3. Carrying numerous cardboard boxes, duffle bags, plastic bags, etc., inside the aircraft, or seeds, green vegetable matter, fragments of various colored butcher or cellophane paper indicating possible marijuana debris visible inside the aircraft; tape marking or residue around aircraft number.

4. Maps or other evidence of flights to Mexico, the Caribbean, Central, or South America present in aircraft when the pilot avoids reference to such flights, or a pilot requesting maps or information pertaining to areas in Mexico, the Caribbean, Central or South America when it appears he is not going to follow official procedures for such trips.

5. Strong odors from the aircraft (perfumes and deodorizers are often used to disguise the odor of marijuana and cocaine).

6. FAA registration numbers on the aircraft which appear to be incomplete, crooked or to have otherwise been altered or concealed.

7. Muddy wheels, dirty or dusty aircraft, beat-up props or other evidence of having landed on unpaved strips or fields or in sand, etc.

8. Vans, panel trucks or campers meeting the aircraft at an isolated location on the field.

9. Pilot or passengers reluctant to leave the immediate area of the aircraft or to allow others close to the aircraft during refueling or servicing.

10. Payment of cash for fuel or services or display of large amounts of cash by the pilot or passengers.

11. Persons who on aircraft rental applications list themselves as being self employed operating out of their residences.

12. Persons who rent hangars for one month or similarly short term bases, particularly when paying cash in advance and giving minimal information.

13. Pilots with no visible means of support who own or operate expensive aircraft, or any other factors that might lead you to believe the individual might be trafficking in narcotics.

14. Pilots reluctant to discuss destination or point of origin, or reluctant to discuss any of the above listed conditions.

Any of the aforementioned points, when coupled with other suspicious behavior by the aircraft operator or occupants, could possibly indicate the aircraft is being used in an illegal activity.

When the above conditions are observed and you feel there is a possibility these individuals might be engaged in smuggling, please note any information regarding the identity of the pilot(s), other occupants, aircraft, description and license numbers of vehicles. Under no circumstances should you take any direct action on your own. Immediately, or as soon as it can be done safely, notify U.S. Customs. Use the national 1-800-BE ALERT number or contact the nearest Customs Office of Enforcement. All information received will be held in confidence.

If, as a result of your information, the United States Customs Service seizes and forfeits currency or monetary instruments, a reward of up to $150,000 can by paid. In the case of vessel, aircraft, vehicle or other property, a reward of up to $250,000 can be paid for the information.

Scope and Definitions

1. The information in this pamphlet applies to private aircraft of both United States and foreign registry.

2. Customs requirements vary according to whether an aircraft is operating as a commercial or private flight. It is the nature of each particular flight that determines whether an aircraft is operating in a private or commercial capacity. The owners, aircraft type or predominant usage of the aircraft has little bearing on this determination. In fact, **many corporate and business aircraft typically operate as "private aircraft" for Customs purposes.**

Aircraft not qualifying as private aircraft must comply with the applicable entry and clearance requirements for commercial aircraft as specified in Part 6, Customs Regulations (19 CFR Part 6). For additional information on these requirements, please contact the nearest U.S. Customs office.

3. For Customs purposes, a "private" aircraft is any civilian aircraft not being used to transport persons or property for compensation or hire. A "*commercial*" aircraft is any civilian aircraft being used in the transportation of persons or property for compensation or hire.

    The term "person transported for compensation or hire" means a person who would not be transported unless there was some payment or other consideration, including monetary or services rendered, by or for the person and who is not connected with the operation of the aircraft or its navigation, ownership or business. The major criterion for determining whether an aircraft is private or commercial will be the use of the aircraft on a particular flight, and this determination would be the same if the owner or lessee is a corporation, partnership, sole proprietorship or an individual.

    An aircraft will be presumed not to be carrying persons or merchandise for hire, and thus will be a private aircraft for Customs purposes, when the aircraft is transporting only the aircraft owner's employees, invited guests or the aircraft owner's own property. This presumption may be overcome by evidence that the employees, "guests", or property are being transported for compensation or other consideration. If an aircraft is used by a group of individuals, one of whom is the pilot making the flight for his own convenience, and all persons aboard the aircraft including the pilot contribute equally toward payment of the expense of operating the aircraft owned or rented by them, the aircraft would be considered private.

    Usually those aircraft arriving in the United States which have raised the question as to whether they are private or commercial are operated by the owner or lessee. For purposes of determining if an aircraft is private or commercial, the lessee of an aircraft will be considered as its owner if the pilot is a regular employee of the lessee and the lessee has complete control of the aircraft and its itinerary. Accordingly, aircraft operated by the owner or by a lessee as described in the preceding sentence will be classified as private or commercial depending on the use of the aircraft on a particular flight; that is, whether the aircraft is being used in the transportation of persons or property for compensation or hire. On the other hand, a leased aircraft will be considered commercial for Customs purposes if the pilot and/or crew are part of the leasing arrangement of the aircraft.

    An amendment to Part 6.14 of the Customs Regulations, effective December 31, 1984, redefined certain air taxi and air charter flights as "private" *for Customs reporting purposes only*. Air charter or air taxi flights are now subject to Customs reporting requirements for private aircraft if they have a passenger seating capacity of 30 or less and they have a payload of 7,500 pounds or less. Therefore, the affected aircraft now must land at one of the 27 Customs-designated southern border airports when arriving in the United States by crossing our southern borders. For additional information on this subject see "Special Reporting Requirements" in the "Inward Flights" section of this booklet.
    It must be emphasized that although considered "private" for Customs reporting purposes, these smaller air taxi and air charter flights are still commercial for other than reporting purposes. This means that these aircraft may be subject to

Customs processing fees for commercial flights rather than the fees for private aircraft ($25 limit). The air taxi and air charter flights must also provide Customs, upon arrival into the United States, with the normal commercial entry documents (e.g., the General Manifest). Further, Federal Aviation Administration designations, as part 91 (private) or part 135 (commercial) aircraft, need not necessarily coincide with Customs designations. Thus a given flight might be considered private under FAA regulations, commercial for Customs entrance and clearance purposes, and private for Customs reporting purposes.

4. The term "international airport" means any airport designated by the Secretary of the Treasury or the Commissioner of Customs as a port of entry for civil aircraft arriving in the United States from any place outside thereof and for cargo carried on such aircraft. It is also designated by the Attorney General as a port of entry for certain classes of aliens arriving on such aircraft, and by the Secretary of Health and Human Services as a place for quarantine inspection. This pamphlet lists all such airports that have been officially designated to date.

   (Note: Frequently the word "International" is included in the name of an airport for other than Customs purposes, in which case it has no special Customs meaning.)

5. The term "landing rights airport" means an airport at which permission to land may be granted by the appropriate Customs officer with acknowledgement of the Immigration and Naturalization Service, the Public Health Service and the Animal and Plant Health Inspection Service of the Department of Agriculture. Such landing rights are required before an aircraft may land at an airport which has not been designated for Customs purposes as an international airport.

6. The term "United States" for Customs purposes includes the States, the District of Columbia and Puerto Rico. In some circumstances aircraft from Puerto Rico will have to provide Customs with an advance notice of penetration of U.S. airspace. See "Special Reporting Requirements" in the "Inward Flight" section of this booklet for further details. For information regarding U.S. possesions refer to the FAA International Flight Information Manual.

Outward Flights

advance notice of arrival in Canada and Mexico

Many countries, including Canada and Mexico, require advance notice of the intent of pilots to arrive in those countries.

Under agreements between the United States, Canada and Mexico, operators of private planes may, in most cases, include this advance notice in a flight plan to be filed prior to departure from the United States at the nearest FAA Flight Service Station. That station will then cause the message to be transmitted to the proper authorities in the country of destination. Contact the nearest FAA Flight Service Station regarding this procedure.

Aircraft carrying passengers or cargo for hire or compensation on either the outbound or inbound portions of a flight are not considered to be "private aircraft" for Customs purposes and must comply with the clearance requirements specified for commercial aircraft as set forth in Part 6, Customs Regulations. Aircraft leaving the U.S. for a foreign destination may be subjected to a search by Customs Officers.

Inward Flights

providing notification to Customs

In order to have an officer present to provide Customs service for you and your aircraft, Customs must be notified of your intention to land and time of arrival.

This notification may be provided through FAA; however, this entails the relaying of information and is not as timely or reliable as direct communication. It is recommended that if possible, pilots attempt to communicate directly with Customs by telephone or other means to insure that an officer will be available at the time requested. It is the ultimate responsibility of the pilot to insure Customs is properly notified, and the failure to do so may subject the pilot to penalty action (see "Penalties for Violations"). The last section of this guide lists telephone numbers to facilitate this notification process.

special reporting requirements—southern border, Pacific, Gulf of Mexico and Atlantic Coastlines)

The U.S. Customs Service has identified general aviation aircraft as the highest-risk vehicles for narcotics smuggling. This is especially true for aircraft flying from areas south of the U.S. Therefore the following special reporting procedures have been instituted.

All private aircraft arriving in the United States via the United States/Mexican border or the Pacific Coast from a foreign place in the Western Hemisphere south of 33 degrees north latitude shall furnish a notice of intended arrival to the Customs Service at the *nearest* designated airport to the point of first border crossing listed below. All private aircraft arriving in the United States via the Gulf of Mexico and Atlantic Coast from a foreign place in the Western Hemisphere south of 30 degrees north latitude, from any place in Mexico or from the U.S. Virgin Islands, shall furnish a notice of intended arrival to the Customs Service at the *nearest* designated airport to the point of crossing listed below. They then must land at this airport for inspection, unless they have an overflight exemption. Landing rights must be obtained from Customs to land at designated airports that are *not* also approved as international airports. See the individual airport listings in this booklet for further information on this subject. The requirement to furnish a notice of intended arrival shall not apply to private aircraft departing from Puerto Rico and conducting their flights under instrument flight rules (IFR) until crossing the United States coastline or proceeding north of 30 degrees north latitude. The notice must be furnished at least 1 hour before crossing the United States coastline or border. The notice may be furnished directly to Customs by telephone, radio or other means, or may be furnished by means of a flight plan through the Federal Aviation Administration to Customs. This notice will be valid as long as actual arrival is within 15 minutes of the original ETA. If you cannot land within 15 minutes of the original ETA, you must give Customs a new notice. Customs and the FAA will accept these notices up to 23 hours in advance.

A penetration notice (but not landing) requirement also exists for private aircraft arriving in the contintental United States from Puerto Rico which are *not* conducting their flights in accordance with Instrument Flight Rules, and those private aircraft which have flown beyond the inner boundary of the Air Defense Identification Zone south of 30° north latitude on the Atlantic Coast, beyond the inner boundary of the Gulf Coast ADIZ, south of the United States/Mexican border, or beyond the inner boundary of the Pacific Coast ADIZ south of 33° north latitude and *have not landed in a foreign place*. This notice requirement may be satisfied either by filing a flight plan with the FAA or contacting Customs directly at least 1 hour prior to the inbound crossing of the U.S. border or coastline. Customs may be contacted by telephone at (305) 536-6591 in Miami, Florida, and at (714) 351-6674 in Riverside, California. If you cannot cross within 15 minutes of the original estimated time, you must give Customs a new notice. Customs and the FAA will accept these notices up to 23 hours in advance.

Any time you wish to communicate to Customs through the FAA you should have the notation "ADCUS" on your flight plan.

The notice to Customs required by this section shall include the following:

(1) Aircraft registration number;
(2) Name of aircraft commander;
(3) Number of United States citizen passengers;
(4) Number of alien passengers;
(5) Place of last departure;
(6) Estimated time and location of crossing United States border/coastline;
(7) Name of United States airport of first landing.
(8) Estimated time of arrival.

Private aircraft that are coming from a foreign place are required to furnish a notice of intended arrival in compliance with these special reporting requirements and must land for Customs processing at the nearest designated airport to the border or coastline crossing point as listed below, *unless* exempted (see below) from this requirement. In addition to the requirements of this paragraph, private aircraft commanders must comply with all other landing and notice of arrival requirements. This landing requirement shall not apply to private aircraft which have *not landed in foreign places* or are arriving directly from Puerto Rico or if inspected (precleared) by Customs Officers in the U.S. Virgin Islands.

Location	Name
Beaumont, TX	Jefferson County Airport
Brownsville, TX	*Brownsville International Airport
Calexico, CA	*Calexico International Airport
Corpus Christi, TX	Corpus Christi Int'l Airport
Del Rio, TX	*Del Rio International Airport
Douglas, AZ	*Bisbee-Douglas Int'l Airport
Eagle Pass, TX	*Eagle Pass Municipal Airport
El Paso, TX	*El Paso International Airport
Fort Lauderdale, FL	Fort Lauderdale Executive Airport
Fort Lauderdale, FL	Fort Lauderdale-Hollywood Airport
Fort Pierce, FL	St. Lucie County Airport
Houston, TX	William P. Hobby Airport
Key West, FL	Key West International Airport
Las Cruces, NM	Crawford International Airport
Laredo, TX	*Laredo International Airport
McAllen, TX	*Miller International Airport
Miami, FL	Miami International Airport
Miami, FL	Opa-Locka Airport
New Orleans, LA	New Orleans Int'l AP (Moisant Field)
New Orleans, LA	New Orleans Lakefront Airport
Nogales, AZ	*Nogales International Airport
Presidio, TX	*Presidio-Lely International Airport
San Diego, CA	*Brown Field
Tampa, FL	Tampa International Airport
Tucson, AZ	Tucson International Airport
West Palm Beach, FL	Palm Beach International Airport
Yuma, AZ	Yuma International Airport

The asterisk (*) designates 24-hour free service is provided Monday through Saturday.

This map is for use only to locate airports designated for landing when entering the U.S. from the southern border.

exemption from special landing requirements

Applicants for overflight exemption request the privilege of being-exempt from one specific provision of the U.S. Customs Regulations. If approved, the applicant is bound to comply with all other requirements, including advance notice of penetration, to U.S. Customs at least one hour in advance of crossing the border or coastline, furnishing advance notice of arrival at the intended airport of landing, etc.

The U.S. Customs Service district offices have been instructed to review carefully all requests for overflight exemptions. The two main concerns are completeness and accuracy of the specific required information and the demonstration by the applicant of genuine need for this privilege. Control of aircraft arrivals in the United States is of paramount importance if the Customs Service is to successfully combat the flow of illegal drugs and contraband. In order for an exemption to be granted to an individual or corporation, the deciding official must be reasonably assured that the party requesting exemption will not compromise the mission of the U.S. Customs Service.

The information contained in your application is reviewed and background checks are performed in conjunction with law enforcement agencies. Some elements of the application are required by law, others are strictly voluntary. Processing of background checks may be a lengthy and prolonged procedure. By providing information which is voluntary, e.g. social security numbers, you will substantially reduce the time required to act on your application. A limited number of "identifiers" for people or corporations can not only create a cloud of uncertainty but delay background reports forwarded to the deciding official.

Your application should be addressed to the District Director of U.S. Customs having jurisdiction over the airport you will utilize most frequently when arriving from points South of the U.S. You should request exemption for either a single specific flight or term (one year) approval. Applications for a single overflight exemption must be received at least fifteen days in advance; for term exemption at least thirty days in advance.

Air charters or taxi service cannot be granted an unqualified term exemption since they cannot reasonably comply with the requirements of a term application, namely, comprehensive details of the passengers they will transport in the course of one year. By submitting all other details, air charters/taxis will accrue the benefit of "conditional" approval. This approval is "conditional" because the operator must receive the concurrence of the District Director prior to each trip. Concurrence will be based upon factors such as the foreign point of departure to the U.S. and the passengers being transported. The benefit realized by the charter/taxi operator is that the time constraints listed above for timely submission of single overflight exemptions can be drastically reduced. The local districts will establish minimum time frames in accordance with their own requirements.

Required elements of any overflight exemption include the following:

— Aircraft registration number.

— Identity of the aircraft (make, model, color scheme and type, such as turboprop, etc.)

— A statement that the aircraft is equipped with a functioning transponder which will be in use during overflight.

— A statement that Instrument Flight Rules will be utilized for the entire duration of an overflight.

— Names, home addresses and dates of birth of owners of the aircraft (if the aircraft is being operated under a lease, the name and address of the lessee, in addition to that of the owner).

— Names, home addresses, and dates of birth of all crewmembers.

— Name, home addresses and dates of birth of usual and potential passengers to the greatest extent possible.

— Description of usual or anticipated cargo or baggage.

— Description of the company's usual business activity, if the aircraft is company owned.

— Name of intended airport of first landing in the U.S.

— Foreign place(s) from which the flight(s) will originate.

— Reason for the request of overflight exemption.

Your information should be as complete and accurate as possible, but it should be specific rather than generalized. The following points will assist you in preparing an acceptable application:

— Include all potential crewmembers who might be present on the aircraft during the term of the desired exemption. In order for overflight exemptions to remain valid, at least one crewmember listed on your application must be present on every flight. It is to your advantage to make your listing as comprehensive as possible.

— Include details on all of the passengers you expect to be aboard your aircraft for the tenure of the exemption. U.S. Customs will monitor your arrival records and compare those records with your application. The deciding official may deny your application or renewal based upon the suspicion that you are deliberately withholding information.

— Provide as many "identifiers" as possible for all crew and passengers. Social security numbers, passport numbers, aircraft pilot license numbers, etc. will contribute greatly to expediting background investigations.

— Describe the type of business your corporation is engaged in. If the corporation which owns the aircraft is merely an air transportation service for the benefit of an affiliated company, please provide details.

— List the foreign cities and countries your aircraft will visit. It is to your advantage to describe the nature of your business in each, or to indicate that certain destinations are vacation/entertainment locations.

— The reason for overflight exemption requests should be as tangible and concretely stated as possible. Estimate the costs incurred by making an extra landing at a "designated airport" (fuel, wear on aircraft components, landing fees, additional time/distance). Your flight crew or aviation references can advise you of the above and others, e.g. safety factors.

Applicants should be aware that the processing of term applications requires time for all background reports to be prepared for the deciding official. Incomplete applications will not be processed and the applicant will be notified of additional information which must be supplied.

Should your application for overflight be denied at the district level, an appeal process is available. Letters of denial will include the name and address of the

Regional Commissioner of Customs responsible for the district in which your application was denied. You may petition the Regional Commissioner for reconsideration of your request.

PRECLEARANCE FROM THE VIRGIN ISLANDS

Private aircraft departing the U.S. Virgin Islands destined for the mainland or Puerto Rico may request preclearance service at St. Croix and St. Thomas. This service will be provided 0800 to 1700 hours, Monday through Sunday, workload permitting. Preclearance outside of these hours may be authorized at the discretion of the District Director on a case-by-case basis. All private aircraft pilots desiring preclearance to the U.S. are required to make advance arrangements for clearance directly with Customs or through the Federal Aviation Administration by radio or other means. FAA will notify Customs of all preclearance requests.

At time of preclearance, you will complete a General Declaration (CF-7507) which will be authenticated by the inspecting officer as evidence of your having been precleared.

If for any reason you find that you cannot come directly to the U.S (must stop for refueling or any other reason), your preclearance becomes invalid and you must report to Customs on your arrival in the U.S. or Puerto Rico.

Use of the General Declaration, although not required for general aviation aircraft unless carrying persons or cargo for hire, will serve as evidence of your having been precleared if challenged upon your arrival in the Customs territory. However, this does not preclude reinspection by Customs, although such reinspection would be rare.

entry and clearance—Cuba

Aircraft arriving from or departing for Cuba must land at or depart from Fort Lauderdale-Hollywood Airport as provided by section 6.3 a, Customs Regulations.

Upon arrival the pilot will present a manifest of all passengers on board to an officer of the United States Immigration Service or to a Customs officer acting as an Immigration officer. No passenger arriving from Cuba by aircraft will be released by Customs, nor will the aircraft be cleared or permitted to depart, before the passenger is released by an Immigration officer or a Customs officer acting on behalf of that agency.

Aircraft proceeding to Cuba are required to have a validated license issued by the Department of Commerce or a license issued by the Department of State.

These special requirements do not apply to aircraft arriving from or departing to the U.S. Naval Base at Guantanamo Bay. Aircraft from this base must meet the same requirements as aircraft arriving from other Caribbean nations.

"International Airports"

It is unnecessary for aircraft arriving at these airports to request permission to land or "landing rights" from Customs. However, an advance notice of the estimated time of arrival (in local time) is required to be transmitted to U.S. Customs for each flight. In general 1-hour advance notice is sufficient, although you will note in the "Special Arrangements or Restrictions" column that a longer time is required at certain airports. Aircraft operators must bear in mind that this advance notice is predicated on the time that the Customs Officer receives the notification, and not on the time that the flight plan or message is filed.

Except in the case of "Short Flight" (see below), requests to transmit such notices may be included in flight plans to be filed at certain airports in Canada and Mexico under agreements with those countries. Information concerning the availability of this service at United States airports has been included in the column "FAA Flight Plan Notification Available." If "Advise Customs" or "ADCUS" is not included on the flight plan, FAA will not advise Customs of intended arrival. The pilot is ultimately responsible for insuring that Customs is properly notified.

At those airports where the flight plan notification service is not available, notices of arrival must be transmitted directly to U.S. Customs.

For private aircraft arriving in the United States from certain foreign areas south of the United States, refer to "Special Reporting Requirements" under Inward Flights.

landing rights airports

In addition to advance notice of arrival as described under "International Airports," specific permission to land at a "Landing Rights" airport must be obtained in advance of contemplated use. Except in the case of "Short Flights" advance notice of arrival may be transmitted to Customs in flight plans where flight notification service is rendered. Such notices will be treated as applications for permission to land although the pilot is still ultimately responsible for insuring that Customs is properly notified, and pilots should be aware that "landing rights" can be denied if inspection service cannot be provided. If the notification service is not available, pilots must submit applications for landing rights and provide arrival notices directly to U.S. Customs.

Customs officers may at their discretion grant blanket "Landing Rights" to persons to land at certain airports for a specified period of time, in which event advance notices of arrival will be the only requirement.

to other airports

Permission to land at airports other than those listed in this booklet may be obtained in some limited cases; however, advance arrangements (preferably in writing) must be made with the Customs office nearest the airport of intended arrival. Advance notice of arrivals is required as usual. Pilots should be aware that mileage and per diem costs may be accrued in addition to any overtime charges if applicable.

what to report

Except at airports where the flight plan notification service is rendered, applications for landing rights and arrival notices shall specify:

    Type of aircraft
    Registration marks
    Name of commander
    Place of last departure
    Other countries visited
    Airport of arrival and code designation
    Number of alien passengers
    Number of citizen passengers
    Estimated time of arrival

The above requirements do not apply to private aircraft arriving in the United States from certain foreign areas south of the United States. (See "Special Reporting Requirements" under Inward Flights.)

short flights

If flying time from the foreign airport to the U.S. airport is less than 1 hour the pilot should request his application for landing rights when required and transmit his arrival notice directly to the U.S. Customs office before departure from the foreign airport (unless prior arrangements were made). This is necessary to allow inspectional personnel to be assigned and at the airport prior to arrival of the aircraft. FAA cannot guarantee delivery of a message (under the flight plan notification arrangement) in sufficient time on such short notice. It is still the pilot's responsibility to give timely notice even though a flight plan has been filed.

For private aircraft arriving in the United States from certain foreign areas south of the United States, refer to "Special Reporting Requirements" under Inward Flights.

changing destination en route

Pilots may find it necessary or convenient to change the intended airport of destination en route; however, definite confirmation *from Customs* permitting a change must be received. Failure to obtain permission in advance to alter the airport of destination may result in Customs initiated penalty action.

documentation and examination on arrival

Private aircraft are required to report directly to Customs for inspection immediately upon arrival. Normally a Customs officer (or an officer from the Immigration and Naturalization Service or Department of Agriculture) will be present if a pilot has given proper advance notice of arrival. Should no inspecting officer be present, the pilot should report his arrival to Customs by telephone or most convenient means. He should keep the aircraft, passengers, crewmembers, baggage, food and cargo intact in a segregated place until the officer arrives or until he has received special instructions from a Customs officer.

The pilot should provide the necessary information to assist the inspecting officer in the preparation of the required documentation unless the pilot has prepared the necessary documents in advance. Customs form 178 must be filled out for all private aircraft arrivals. This form is obtainable from Customs.

The pilot may also be requested to produce for inspection a valid airman's certificate, medical certificate (14 CFR 61.3) and the aircraft registration certificate.

Crew and passenger baggage will be examined in the same manner as that of other international travelers. A verbal declaration of articles acquired abroad will suffice, except that a written declaration, Customs Form 6059-B (or appropriate substitute), shall be presented when duty is to be collected or when the inspecting officer deems a written declaration necessary. Noncommercial cargo and unaccompanied baggage carried on board private aircraft shall be accounted for on a baggage declaration (CF 6059-B) prepared by the pilot in command, and appropriate entry for same shall be required. Customs officers will furnish the necessary forms. In addition the inspecting officer may require that baggage and cargo be removed from the aircraft for inspection, and he may physically inspect the aircraft. It is the responsibility of the pilot to assist in opening baggage and compartments. Commercial aircraft operators may have to employ the service of a certified mechanic in the event of intensive examination.

personal exemptions

Persons engaged in the operation of a private aircraft are not considered crewmembers for tariff purposes, and they are to be treated as returning residents for exemption purposes (19 CFR 148.61). Charter aircraft crews may be considered crewmembers for exemption purposes. For additional information about exemptions and the importation of typical tourist items, refer to the Customs pamphlets *Know Before You Go*, and *Customs Hints for Visitors (Nonresident)*.

Immigration Requirements for Private Aircraft

Persons arriving from a foreign place (including Canada) must report for immigration inspection immediately upon arrival in the United States.

With few exceptions, all persons who are not U.S. citizens or permanent resident aliens are required to present a visa upon entering the U.S. Visas can be obtained only at a U.S. Consulate or Embassy abroad. Canadian citizens are exempt from visa requirements in most cases.

U.S. and Canadian citizens are advised to carry proof of citizenship which may include a passport, birth certificate, naturalization papers, or other documents that support your claimed citizenship. A driver's license alone is not proof of citizenship. Most aliens are required to present a valid unexpired passport. If you are in doubt as to what documents you require for entry, call the nearest U.S. Consulate, Embassy, or U.S. Immigration Office.

Most alien passengers must execute and present Form I-94, Arrival/Departure Record. INS has revised form I-94, effective March 1, 1986, and prior editions may not be used. Form I-94 must be completed by all persons except U.S. citizens, returning resident aliens, aliens with immigrant visas and Canadians visiting or in transit. Mexican nationals in possession of Immigration Form I-86 or Form I-586, are exempted from Form I-94 reporting requirements when their itinerary is limited to California, Arizona, New Mexico or Texas, and will not exceed 72 hours in duration. This exemption does not apply when travel will exceed 25 miles from the international border between Mexico and the U.S. Travel to Nevada by Mexican nationals is exempted for periods of time less than 30 days. Mexican nationals proceeding to destinations more than 25 miles from the border in these states will have to obtain a visitors permit I-444 when arriving in the U.S. Mexican nationals presenting official or diplomatic passports and destined to the U.S. for purposes other than permanent assignment are exempted from Form I-94 reporting requirement.

The form is available for sale by the Superintendent of Documents, Government Printing Office, Washington, D.C. 20402. Forms and printing specifications are also available through the INS Form I-94 Support Desk, Appalachian Computer Services, Inc., Highway 21 South, London, Kentucky 40241 (606-878-7900). The forms are available in English and in 13 foreign languages.

Individuals entering the U.S. by private aircraft should indicate PRIVATE in block #7 — Airline and Flight Number. Individuals entering by private aircraft do not need to complete block #9 — City Where You Boarded. All other items on the form are self-explanatory and should be completed prior to actual arrival in the U.S. The completed forms must be presented to either a U.S. Immmigration or U.S. Customs inspector upon arrival.

Aircraft owners are responsible for the proper completion and submission of Form I-94 for all crew and passengers affected by the reporting requirement. Departure documents should be annotated on the reverse of the document to indicate Port of Departure and Date of Departure. Following Carrier, print the word PRIVATE. In the space provided for Flight Number/Ship Name, print the tail number of the aircraft. Departure documents should be submitted to a U.S. Immigration or U.S. Customs Inspector, at the time of departure from the U.S., or mailed to the Appalachian Computer Service address in London, Kentucky. Aircraft owners are responsible for the submission of all I-94 Departure Records upon departure to a foreign destination.

plant and animal quarantines of the U.S. department of agriculture

To prevent the entry of dangerous agricultural pests the following are restricted: fruits, vegetables, plants, plant products, soil, meats, meat products, birds, snails and other live animals or animal products. Failure to declare all such items to a Customs/Agriculture officer can result in fines or other penalties. Agricultural items, whether in baggage, stores, lunches or garbage must be called to the attention of the inspecting officer. Prohibited items on board will be confiscated. Agricultural items should not be brought to the United States unless you are informed in advance by Agriculture inspectors of the Animal and Plant Health Inspection Service (APHIS) or Customs inspectors that such items are admissible. An APHIS officer must be present when you return from an area where there has been a outbreak of destructive pests or diseases. Customs will advise APHIS of flights arriving from, or stopping in such an area. For further information on this subject, refer to the FAA International Flight Information Manual or contact your local USDA APHIS Office.

Endangered species of plant and animal wildlife and products thereof may be prohibited or require permits or certification by the U.S. Fish and Wildlife Service.

repairs to private aircraft

Aircraft belonging to a resident of the U.S. and taken abroad for noncommercial purposes and returned by the resident shall be admitted free of duty upon being satisfactorily identified. Repairs made abroad to such aircraft, must be reported to Customs but are not subject to duty. The reimportation of U.S. made parts may require entry. It is advisable that the nearest U.S. Customs office be contacted for clarification of this matter in each particular instance.

in case of emergency

If an emergency landing is made in the United States, the pilot should report as promptly as possible by telephone or most convenient means to the nearest Customs office. He should keep all merchandise or baggage in a segregated place and should not permit any passenger or crewmember to depart the place of arrival or come in contact with the public without official permission, unless other action is necessary for preservation of life, health, or property.

hours of service

Generally speaking, free service is provided at airports during regular business hours (usually 8 AM to 5 PM), Monday through Saturday. However, tours of duty at airports are based on the need for services and are altered at some ports to coincide with schedule changes and peak workloads. The normal hours of service are listed in this booklet, however to be positive that processing fees and/or overtime changes will not accrue, private aircraft operators may contact, prior to departure, the Customs officer in charge at the U.S airport of intended arrival in order to ascertain those hours during which free service can normally be expected. Phone numbers which may be used for this purpose are listed herein.

A private aircraft will be charged a processing fee of $25 once every calendar year. This will be charged the first time the aircraft arrives from a foreign place in the calendar year or may be paid in advance. A fee of $12.50 will be charged once in calendar year 1986 on or after the legal implementation date of July 7th, 1986. This fee is charged to the aircraft, not the pilot, and the receipt should be kept with the aircraft.

DEPARTMENT OF THE TREASURY
UNITED STATES CUSTOMS SERVICE

**PRIVATE AIRCRAFT
INSPECTION REPORT**
6.2, 6.14, C.R.

PARTIAL LIST OF COUNTRY CODES

AC	ANTIGUA	DR	DOMINICAN	MX	MEXICO	ST	ST LUCIA
BB	BARBADOS		REPUBLIC	NA	NETHER-	TD	TRINIDAD &
BD	BERMUDA	EL	EL SALVADOR		LANDS		TOBAGO
BF	BAHAMAS	GJ	GRENADA		ANTILLES	TK	TURKS &
BH	BRITISH	GP	GUADELOUPE	NU	NICARAGUA		CAICOS IS
	HONDURAS	GT	GUATEMALA	PN	PANAMA	VC	ST VINCENT
CA	CANADA	GY	GUYANA	PQ	CANAL ZONE	VE	VENEZUELA
CJ	CAYMAN IS	HA	HAITI	SC	ST CHRISTO-	VI	BRITISH V I
CK	COCOS IS.	HO	HONDURAS		PHER NEVIS	VQ	V I (U.S)
CO	COLOMBIA	JM	JAMAICA		ANGUILLA		
CS	COSTA RICA	MB	MARTINIQUE	SQ	SWAN IS		

1. AIRCRAFT NUMBER `3 1 :` ▢▢▢▢▢▢▢ ● 2. SYSDINO `2 0 : A` ▢▢▢▢ ●

3. PILOT NAME `3 8 :` Last Name ▢▢▢ / First Name ▢ M.I.

4. FOREIGN DEPARTURE Last Foreign City ▢▢▢ / Country Code ▢

5. ARRIVAL IN U.S. U.S. Airport Code ▢ / Time of Arrival ▢ / Arrival Date (MMDDYY) ●

6. AIRCRAFT `6 1 :` Make ▢▢▢ Model ▢ /
Color(s) ▢ ●

7. PILOT DATA `6 6 :` Pilot's name as in Item no. 3 above / Date of Birth (MMDDYY) / License No. / Nationality ●

8. PILOT ADDRESS

9. OWNER NAME AND ADDRESS

10. FOREIGN ITINERARY

11. DATE/TIME OF DEPARTURE FOR U.S.

12. U.S.-BASED AIRCRAFT ONLY ▶ | a. U.S. Airport of Departure | b. Date/Time of U.S. Departure

13. PASSENGERS

a. Last Name	b. First Name	c. M.I.	d. Nationality	Date of Birth

INSPECTOR SIGNATURE & BADGE NO.

Agriculture Data
☐ Fruits ☐ Plants
☐ Meats ☐ Veget.
Country of Origin

PAIRS Entry
Sta. Code:
Date:
Time:

Inspection Data
Travel Time:
Waiting Time:
Inspection Time:

☐ INS ☐ USDA ☐ OTHER: _____

(PAIRS ENTRY—New Record: Items 1, 3, 4, 5, 6, & 7, Modify: Items 1, 2, 3, 4, 5, & 7 if new.)

GPO 946-690

Customs Form 178 (10-30-81)

Commercial aircraft operators will be charged a processing fee of $5 per paying passenger for each arrival from foreign to the U.S. This fee will not be charged for passengers arriving from Canada, Mexico, and certain nearby Caribbean countries.

overtime charges

Private aircraft will be processed free of overtime charge during regular hours of duty. Overtime charges will accrue after regular hours of duty on weekdays, and on Sundays and holidays. However, at the specially designated airports along the southwest border (see "Special Reporting Requirements"), Customs overtime charges will accrue only on Sundays and holidays (except for Las Cruces, New Mexico). If an officer from an inspecting agency other than Customs is providing the service, overtime charges after regular working hours during weekdays may be incurred.

A maximum charge of $25 has been established as a private aircraft pilot's liability for the cost of all overtime services performed by Federal inspection service employees in connection with each arrival or departure. Overtime charges are prorated if services are performed for more than one operator or owner by the same inspector during an overtime assignment. Depending on the overtime charge and the number of inspections performed, the cost can be less that the $25 maximum. However, private aircraft operators should expect to pay $25 for overtime services. Refunds, if applicable, will usually be made at a later date by Customs' central accounting office.

For information about requirements of other federal inspectional agencies and the manner in which overtime services are performed by them, operators should contact the respective services listed below:

APHIS Port Operations Staff
U.S. Department of Agriculture
Federal Building
Hyattsville, MD 20782

Chief, Quarantine Branch
Epidemiology Program
Center for Disease Control
Atlanta, Georgia 30333

Associate Commissioner, Management
U.S. Immigration and Naturalization Service
425 Eye Street, N.W.
Washington, D.C. 20136

A Customs bond on form 301 could be of particular advantage to aircraft owners and operators who frequently travel abroad. It is recommended that a copy of the bond be carried aboard the aircraft to simplify verification. For further information, contact the nearest Customs office.

penalties for violations

Since the law provides for substantial penalties for violations of the Customs Regulations, aircraft operators and pilots should make every effort to comply with them. Examples of the more common violations and resulting penalties include:

- Failure to report arrival [19 CFR 6.2(a)—$500].

- Failure to obtain landing rights [19 CFR 6.2(a)—$500].
- Failure to provide advance notice of arrival [19 CFR 6.2(b)—$500].
- Failure to provide penetration report on southern border [19 CFR 6.14(a)—$500].
- Departing without permission or discharging passengers or cargo without permission [19 CFR 6.2(c)—$500].
- Importation of contraband, including agriculture materials, or undeclared merchandise can result in penalty action and seizure of aircraft which varies according to the nature of the violation and pertinent provision of law. In some instances Customs utilizes a notice of violation or warning instead of a penalty. Repeat violators, however, can normally expect to be penalized.

If a penalty is incurred, application may be made to the Customs officer in charge for reduction in amount or cancellation) giving the grounds upon which relief is believed to be justified. If the operator or pilot desires to further petition for relief of the penalty, he may appeal to the appropriate District Director of Customs. If still further review of the penalty is desired, written appeal may be made to the proper Regional Commissioner of Customs and, in some cases, to Customs Headquarters.

Narcotics Smuggling

Aircraft used to smuggle narcotics are subject to seizure. Title 19. Sec. 1595(a) of the U.S. code provides that such an aircraft may be forfeited. It makes no difference whether the narcotics are being smuggled by a crewmember or a passenger. Individuals involved in these activities are also subject to criminal prosecution.

customs districts

All correspondence should be sent to the District Director of Customs at the following locations (designations preceding addresses indicate the region in which the district is located):

Pac.	Anchorage, Alaska 99501/620 E. Tenth Ave.
N.E.	Baltimore, Maryland, 21202/40 S. Gay St.
N.E.	Boston, Massachusetts 02109/2 India St.
N.E.	Buffalo, New York 14202/111 W. Huron St.
S.E.	Charleston, South Carolina 29402/200 E. Bay St.
S.E.	Charlotte Amalie, St Thomas-Virgin Islands 00801/Main P.O. Sugar Estate
N.Cen.	Chicago, Illinois 60607/610 S. Canal St.
N.Cen.	Cleveland, Ohio 44114/55 Erieview Plaza
S.W.	Dallas/Fort Worth, Texas 75261/P.O. Box 61050
N.Cen.	Detroit, Michigan 48226/477 Michigan Ave.
N.Cen.	Duluth, Minnesota 55802/515 W. First St., 209 Fed. Bld.
S.W.	El Paso, Texas 79985/Bldg. B, Room 134 Bridge of the Americas (PO Box 9516)
N.Cen.	Great Falls, Montana 59401/215 1st Ave., N.
Pac.	Honolulu, Hawaii 96813/335 Merchant St.
S.W.	Houston/Galveston, Texas 77052/701 San Jacinto St.
S.W.	Laredo Texas 78040/Mann Rd. & Santa Maria/(POB 3130)
Pac.	Los Angeles/Long Beach, California/300 S. Ferry St. Terminal Island, San Pedro 90731
S.E.	Miami, Florida 33131/77 S.E. 5th St.

N.Cen. Milwaukee, Wisconsin 53202/628 E. Michigan St.
N.Cen. Minneapolis, Minnesota 11401/110 S. Fourth St.
S.Cen. Mobile, Alabama 36602/210 N. Water St.
S.Cen. New Orleans, Louisiana 70130/423 Canal St.
N.Y.   New York, New York
        New York Seaport Area), New York, New York 10048
            Customhouse, 6 World Trade Center
        Kennedy Airport Area, Jamaica, New York 11430
            Cargo Bldg. 80, Room 2E
        Newark Area, Newark, New Jersey 07114
            Airport International Plaza
S.W.   Nogales, Arizona 85621/International & Terrace Sts.
S.E.   Norfolk, Virginia 23510/101 E. Main St.
N.E.   Ogdensburg, New York, 13669/127 N. Water St.
N.Cen. Pembina, North Dakota 18271/Post Office Bldg.
N.E.   Philadelphia, Pennsylvania 19106/2nd & Chestnut Sts.
S.W.   Port Arthur, Texas 77640/5th & Austin Ave.
N.E.   Portland, Maine 04111/312 Fore St.
Pac.   Portland, Oregon 97209/N.W. Broadway & Glisan Sts.
N.E.   Providence, Rhode Island 02903/24 Weybosset St.
N.E.   St. Albans, Vermont 01478/Main & Stebbins St., (POB 2450)
N.Cen. St. Louis, Missouri 63105/120 S. Central Ave.
S.E.   St. Thomas Virgin Islands 00801/P.O. Box 510
Pac.   San Diego, California 92188/880 Front St.
Pac.   San Francisco, California 94126/55 Battery St., (POB 2450)
S.E.   San Juan, Puerto Rico 00903/POB 2112
S.E.   Savannah, Georgia 31401/1 East Bay St.
Pac.   Seattle, Washington 98174/909 First Ave.
S.E.   Tampa, Florida 33602/301 S. Ashley Dr.
S.E.   Washington, D.C. 20041/POB 17423
        Gateway 1 Bldg., Dulles Int'l Apt., Chantilly, Va. 22021
S.E.   Wilmington, North Carolina 28401/2094 Polk St.
(Note: New York has Area Directors instead of District Director)

customs regions

Address all correspondence to the Regional Commissioner of Customs at the following location:
N.E.   Boston, Massachusetts 02110/100 Summer St.
N.Y.   New York, New York 10048/6 World Trade Center
S.E.   Miami, Florida 33131/99 S.E. 5th St.
S.Cen. New Orleans, Louisiana 70112/423 Canal St.
S.W.   Houston, Texas 77057/5850 San Felipe St.
Pac.   Los Angeles, California 90053/300 N. Los Angeles St./P.O. Box 2071
N.Cen. Chicago, Illinois 60603/55 E. Monroe St.

customs headquarters

Address all correspondence to the Commissioner of Customs, 1301 Constitution Avenue N.W., Washington, D.C. 20229.

(Operations questions) Attn: Office of Inspection & Control
(Legal questions) Attn: Office of Regulations & Rulings

Airports at Which Customs Service Is Normally Available

Information in this section is provided in the following order:
1st line:
Location/Name of Airport/Code/FAA Flight Plan Notification /Customs (USCS) Phone Number (2nd line used if more than one phone number:).
Remaining lines:
Special Arrangements or Restrictions.

- indicates USCS 24-hour numbers; F.S. indicates FAA Flight Service Station number.

The term "advance arrangement must be made" means that inspection services cannot be provided on a timely basis if only advance notice of arrival is given. Arrangements in writing or by telephone must be made prior to the flight by the pilot.

The term "regular business hours" means 0800 to 1700 hours, Monday through Saturday, except where otherwise indicated and these are the hours that the Customs office is normally staffed to make arrangements for service.

The notation "MP/F: 10," or other number, indicates maximum number of passengers which may be cleared per flight.

ALABAMA

Birmingham/Birmingham Municipal/BHM/FAA: Yes/USCS 205-254-1464.
   On-call basis. 2 hours advance notice required. MP/F: 20

Huntsville/Huntsville Madison County Jetplex/HSV/FAA: Yes/USCS 205-772-3404.
   On-call basis. 2 hours advance notice required.

Mobile/Bates Field/FAA: Yes/USCS 205-690-2111.
   On-call basis. 2 hours advance notice required during regular business hours, 0800-1700, Monday through Saturday. 3 hours advance notice after regular business hours.

Montgomery/Dannelly/MGM/FAA: Yes/USCS 205-254-1464 (Birmingham).
   Not staffed by Customs. Advance arrangements must be made for inspection by Customs through Birmingham.

ALASKA
   Note: to assure timely inspection in Alaska, Customs requests that all calls (notice of advance arrival), regardless of when service is required, be made during regular business hours, 0800-1700, Monday through Friday, unless other hours are indicated.

Anchorage/Anchorage Int'l/FAA: Yes/USCS 907-243-4312.
   1 hour advance notice required.

Cold Bay/Cold Bay/CDB/FAA: Yes/USCS 907-532-2482.
   Prior written permission required to land for refueling. MP/F: 15. Customs inspection cannot be effected at Cold Bay. The written request must be sent to the District Director in Anchorage. The aircraft will be issued a "permit to

proceed" at Cold Bay for presentation at the airport where Customs inspection is to be made. Landing rights must be requested if that airport is not designated an international airport. It is recommended that written confirmation from all Customs offices be obtained prior to initiation of flight.

Eagle/Eagle Municipal/EEA/FAA: No./USCS none. Phone 907-547-2211
Report on arrival. (Contact U.S. Postmaster, Eagle.) MP/F: 15.

Fairbanks/Fairbanks Int'l/FAI/FAA: Yes/USCS 907-766-2374.
1 hour advance notice required. Regular business hours, 0800-2400, Monday through Sunday.

Hyder/Hyder Seaplane Base/4Z7/FAA: No/USCS 907-225-2254.
Advance arrangements must be made for inspection by Customs through Ketchikan.

Juneau/•Juneau Municipal/JNU/FAA: Yes/USCS 907-586-7211.
On-call basis. 2 hours advance notice required. Regular business hours, 0800-1700, Monday through Saturday.

Juneau/•Juneau Harbor Seaplane Base/JSE/FAA: Yes/USCS 907-586-7211.
On-call basis. 2 hours advance notice required. Regular business hours 0800-1700, Monday through Saturday MP/F: 15.

Ketchikan/•Ketchikan Int'l/KTN/FAA: No./USCS 907-778-6223.
1 hour advance notice required. On-call basis only during 0630-2130. Regular business hours, 0800-1700, Monday through Saturday.

Ketchikan/•Ketchikan Harbor Seaplane Base/ECH/FAA: Yes/USCS 907-225-2254.
On-call basis 2 hours advance notice required. Regular business hours, 0800-1700, Monday through Saturday.

Northway/Northway/ORT/FAA: Yes/USCS 907-778-6223.
1 hour advance notice required. Regular business hours, 0800-1700, Monday through Friday, MP/F: 15. Service May-September; October through April; Contact Customs at 907-774-2252, or UNICOM 122.8 MHZ for Information.

Sitka/Sitka/SIT/FAA: Yes/USCS 907-747-3374.
1 hour advance notice required. Regular business hours, 0800-1700, Monday through Friday. MP/F: 15.

Skagway/Skagway Municipal/SGY/FAA: Yes/USCS 907-983-2325.
1 hour advance notice required. Regular business hours, 0800-2400, Monday through Sunday. MP/F: 15.

Wrangell/•Wrangell Seaplane Base/WRG/FAA: No/USCS 907-874-3415.
On-call basis. 2 hours advance notice required. Regular business hours, 0800-1700, Monday through Friday. MP/F: 15.

Wrangell/Wrangell/RGL/FAA: No./USCS 907-874-3415.
On-call basis. 2 hours advance notice required. Regular business hours, 0800-1700, Monday through Friday. MP/F: 15.

Yukon/Ft. Yukon/FYU/FAA: No/USCS 907-452-3307 (Fairbanks).
Advance arrangements must be made through Fairbanks. MP/F: 15.

ARIZONA

Douglas/•Bisbee Douglas Int'l/DUG/FAA: Yes/USCS 602-364-8486.
F.S. 602-364-8458.
Comunicate direct via radio or telephone to Customs or FAA intention to land and advise intended point and time of border penetration not later than 1 hour prior to entering U.S. airspace.

Nogales/•Nogales Int'l/OLS/FAA: Yes/USCS †602-364-2562.
F.S. 602-287-5161.
Communicate direct via radio or telephone to Customs or FAA intention to land and advise intended point and time of border penetration not later than 1 hour prior to entering U.S. airspace.

Phoenix/Sky Harbor Int'l/PHX/FAA: Yes, if radio contact with tower/
USCS 602-261-3514. F.S. 1-800-228-4160 (Landing Rights Airport)
Private aircraft entering U.S. from south of the border not designated to land at Sky Harbor Int'l. Advance arrangements must be made. Regular business hours, 0830-1630, Monday through Friday. Saturday and Sunday requests for service must be made prior to 1630 hours on Friday. MP/F. 20 (including crew). Private aircraft entering U.S. from south of the border not designated to land at Sky Harbor Int'l.

Tucson/•Tucson Int'l/TUS/FAA: Yes/USCS 602-287-2562.
F.S. 602-889-9689.
Communicate direct via radio or telephone to Customs or FAA intention to land and advise intended point and time of border penetration not later than 1 hour prior to entering U.S. airspace. Free Customs service varies. During one 2-week period, service is free 0800-1700 hours, Monday through Sunday. The following 2-week period, service is free 0800-2000 hours, Monday through Saturday and 0800-1700 hours on Sundays and holidays. All other times on an overtime basis.

Yuma/•Yuma Int'l/YUM/FAA: Yes/USCS 602627-8326, 602-726-2550
(San Luis). F.S. 602-762-2550, 1000 to 1800 hours only.
Communicate direct via radio or telephone to Customs or FAA intention to land and advise intended point and time of border penetration not later than 1 hour prior to entering U.S. alrspace. Free Customs service provided 0900-1700 hours, Monday through Sunday; overtime basis all other times.

ARKANSAS

Little Rock/Adams Field/LIT/FAA: Yes/USCS 501-378-5289.
On-call basis. 2 hours advance notice required.

CALIFORNIA

Calexico/•Calexico Int'l/CXL/FAA: Yes/USCS 619-357-1195, 619-357-4841.
F.S. 619-352-8740.
Communicate direct via radio or telephone to Customs or FAA intention to land and advise intended point and time of border penetration not later than 1 hour prior to entering U.S. airspace.

Eureka/Eureka/EKA/FAA: Yes/USCS 707-442-4822.
On-call basis. 2 hours advance notice required.

Fresno/Fresno Municipal/FAT/FAA: Yes/USCS 209-487-5460.
On-call basis. 2 hours advance notice required during regular business hours, 0800-1700, Monday through Friday. Advance notice by 1630 Friday on all flights requesting service on Saturdays and Sundays. MP/F: 10.

Los Angeles/Los Angeles Int'l/LAX/FAA: Yes/USCS 213-215-2418, 213-215-2240, 213-646-0356.
1 hour advance notice required. Regular business hours, 0800-1700, Monday through Friday. Advance arrangements must be made during other times. Int'l Arrivals Bldg. usually not available for private aircraft. MP/F: 10.

Oakland/Metropolitan Oakland Int'l/OAK/FAA: Yes/USCS 415-876-2812 (San Francisco).
On-call basis. 4 hours advance notice required. Regular business hours, 0800-1700, Monday through Friday. Advance arrangements must be made for service during other times, in writing or by telephone, prior to flight by pilot.

Sacramento/Sacramento Metropolitan/SMF/FAA: Yes/USCS 415-876-2812 (San Francisco).
On-call basis. 4 hours advance notice required during regular business hours, 0800-1700 Monday through Friday. Pilot must make advance arrangements in writing or by telephone prior to flight.

San Diego/•San Diego Int'l (Lindbergh)/SAN/FAA: Yes/USCS 619-428-7201
F.S. 619-291-6381 or 800-532-3815.
No longer a designated airport. Private aircraft arriving from areas south of the U.S. (as defined in Special Reporting Requirements in the Inwards Flight section of this book) cannot proceed directly to this airport unless they have an overflight exemption to do so. Communicate direct via radio to Customs or FAA intention to land and advise (if applicable) intended point and time of border penetration not later than 1 hour prior to entering U.S. airspace.

San Diego/Brown Field/SDM/FAA: Yes/USCS •619-428-7201.
F.S. 619-291-6381 or 800-532-3815.
Communicate direct via radio or telephone to Customs or FAA intention to land and advise intended point and time of border penetration not later the 1 hour prior to entering U.S. airspace.

San Francisco/San Francisco Int'l/SFO/FAA: Yes/USCS 415-876-2812.
2 hours advance notice required during regular business hours, 0800-1700, Monday through Saturday; 4 hours advance notice required during regular business hours, 1700-2400 hours, Monday through Saturday. Advance arrangements must be made during other times, in writing or by telephone, prior to flight by pilot.

San Jose/San Jose Municipal/SJC/FAA: Yes/USCS 415-876-2812 (San Francisco)
4 hours advance permission required. MP/F: 6.

COLORADO
Denver/Stapleton Int'l/DEN/FAA:. Yes/USCS 303-398-0852; FSS 303-799-7016.
2 hours advance notice required during regular business hours. Regular business hours are 0830-1700 hours. At least 3 hours otherwise.

COLORADO SPRINGS
Colorado/COS/FAA: No/USCS 303-574-6607
2 hours advance notice required during regular business hours. Regular business hours are 0830-1700 hours.

CONNECTICUT
Bridgeport/Igor I. Sikorsky Memorial/BDR/FAA: Yes/USCS 203-579-5606.
Not staffed by Customs. Advance arrangements must be made for Customs

inspection prior to departure. Regular business hours, 0800-1700, Monday through Friday. Requests for Saturday and Sunday service must be made prior to 1700 hours on Friday.

Groton/Groton-New London/GON/FAA: Yes/USCS 203-442-7123, 203-773-2040/2041.
Not staffed by Customs. Advance arrangements must be made for Customs inspection prior to departure. Regular business hours, 0800-1700, Monday through Friday. Requests for Saturday and Sunday service must be made prior to 1700 hours on Friday.

New Haven/Tweed-New Haven Muncipal/HVN/FAA: Yes/USC 203-432-2040/2041.
Not staffed by Customs. Advance arrangement must be made for Customs inspection prior to departure. Regular business hours, 0800-1700, Monday through Friday. Request for Saturday and Sunday service must be made prior to 1700 hours on Friday.

Windsor Locks/Bradley Int'l/BDL/FAA: Yes/USCS 203-722-2680, after hours 203-722-3189 Sector Communications 1-800-343-2840.
2 hours advance notice required during regular business hours, 0800-1700, Monday through Friday. Requests for Saturday and Sunday service must be made prior to 1700 hours on Friday.

DELAWARE

Wilmington/Greater Wilmington/ILG/FAA: No/USCS 302-573-6191.
Not staffed by Customs personnel. Advance arrangements must be made for Customs inspection by party of interest prior to departure. Regular business hours 0800-1700, Monday through Friday. Saturday and Sunday requests for service must be made prior to 1700 hours Friday. Requests for holiday service must be made prior to 1700 hours on the preceding work day.

DISTRICT OF COLUMBIA

Washington/Dulles Int'l/IAD/FAA: Yes/USCS 703-471-5885, 202-566-8213/14.
2 hours advance notice required after regular business hours, 0800-1700, Monday through Saturday. For flights with over 10 persons, including crew, persons and baggage must be transported to inspection area for clearance.

FLORIDA

Fort Lauderdale/•Fort Lauderdale-Hollywood Int'l/FLL/FAA: Yes/USCS 305-522-3218.
Regular business hours, 0900-1700, Monday through Saturday.

Fort Lauderdale/Executive/FXE/FAA: Yes/USCS 305-771-8095.
Regular business hours, 0900-1700, Monday through Saturday. Tower will direct flyers to Customs ramp. MP/F: 20.

Fort Pierce/St. Lucie County/FPR/FAA: Yes/USCS 305-461-1200.
1 hour advance notice required. Regular business hours 0800-1900, Monday through Saturday.

Jacksonville/Jacksonville Int'l/JAX/FAA: Yes/USCS 904-791-2775.
Not staffed by Customs. Advance arrangements must be made for Customs inspection by-party of interest prior to departure. Regular business hours, 0800-1700, Monday through Friday. Saturday and Sunday requests for service must be made prior to 1700 hours Friday.

Key West/•Key West Int'l/EYW/FAA: Yes/305-296-5411.
Regular business hours 0800-1700, Monday through Saturday.

Marathon/Marathon/MTH/FAA: Yes at Key West/USCS 305-743-6054
On-call basis. 2 hours advance notice required at all times. MP/F: 20.

Miami/Chalk's Seaplane Base/X44 FAA: No/USCS 305-350-5281.
After regular business hours, 0800-1700, Monday through Sunday call
305-526-2875.

Miami/Miami Int'l/MIA/FAA: Yes/USCS 305-526-2875.
24-hour service provided. Landing rights granted after 2100 hours with concurrence of FAA.

Orlando/Orlando Int'l/MCO/FAA: Yes/USCS 305-420-6308
Regular business hours, 0800-1700, Monday through Saturday. Tower will direct
to Customs ramp. One hour advance notice required.

Panama City/Panama City-Bay County (Fannin Field)/PFN/FAA: Yes/
USCS 904-785-4688.
Advance arrangements must be made during regular business hours, 0800-1700,
Monday through Friday. MP/F: 20.

Pensacola/Pensacola Municipal/PNS/FAA: Yes/USCS 904-432-6811.
On-call basis. 3 hours advance notice required. MP/F: 20.

St. Petersburg/Clearwater/St. Petersburg-Clearwater/PIE/FAA: Yes/USCS 813-536-7311.
1 hour advance notice required. Regular business hours 0830-1700, Monday
through Saturday.

Tampa/•Tampa Int'l/TPA/FAA: Yes/USCS 813-228-2395.
Nights: 813-228-2385
1 hour advance notice required. Communicated direct via radio or telephone to
Customs or FAA intention to land and advise of ETA not later than one hour prior
to entering U.S. airspace. Regular business hours, 0830-1700, Monday through
Saturday. MP/F: 18. With 19 or more passengers and crew, report to gate 31, Air-
side C, main passenger terminal.

West Palm Beach/•Palm Beach Int'/PBL/FAA: Yes/USCS 305-683-1806.
Regular business hours, 0800-1900, Monday through Sunday. 1 hour advance
notice required.

GEORGIA
Atlanta/Charlie Brown County/FTY/FAA: Yes/USCS 404-763-7125.
On-call basis. 2 hours or more advance notice required.

Atlanta/DeKalb-Peachtree/PDK/FAA: Yes/USCS 404-763-7125.
On-call basis. 2 hours or more advance notice required.

Atlanta/William B. Hartsfield Int'l (Atlanta)/ATL/FAA: Yes/USCS 404-763-7125/7126.
On-call basis. 2 hours or more advance notice required.

Brunswick/Glynco Jetport/BQK/FAA: Yes/USCS 912-267-2803.
Limited personnel available. Daylight hours only. Advance arrangements must
be made for inspection by Customs. MP/F: 10.

Brunswick/Malcolm-McKinnon/SSI/FAA: Yes/USCS 912-267-2803.
> Limited personnel available. Advance arrangements must be made for inspection by Customs. MP/F: 10.

Savannah/Savannah Municipal/SAV/FAA: Yes/USCS 912-232-7507.
> On-call basis. 2 hours or more advance notice required during regular business hours, 0800-1700, Monday through Friday.

HAWAII

Hilo/Gen. Lyman Field (Hilo)/ITO/FAA: No./USCS 808-935-6976.
> On-call basis. Advance arrangements must be made during regular business hours, 0800-1700, Monday through Friday.

Honolulu/Honolulu Int'l/HNL/FAA: Limited basis, pilot must specify that Government inspection agencies must be given prior notice. /USCS 808-836-3613. Advance arrangements must be made for landing rights. 1 hour advance notice required during regular business hours, 0800-1600, Monday through Saturday; at least 2 hours during other hours.

Kahului/Kahului/OGG/FAA: Yes/USCS 808-877-6013.
> On-call basis. Advance arrangements must be made during regular business hours, 0800-1700, Monday through Friday. MP/G: 15.

Lihue Airport/Nawiliwili (Hanapepe)/Nawiliwili/Port Allen/PAK/FAA: No/
USCS 808-822-5521.
> Advance arrangements must be made during business hours, 0800-1700, Monday through Friday. On-call basis. MP/F: 15.

IDAHO

Porthill/Eckhart Int'l/1S1/FAA: No/USCS 208-267-5309.
> Grass airstrip does not have landing lights. Float plane landing also. Radio communications. 1 hour advance notice required which must be made during regular business hours, 0800-1700, Monday through Friday. MP/F: 15.

Boise/Boise Air Terminal (Gowenfield)/BOI/FAA: Yes/USCS 208-334-9062;
FSS 208-343-2525.
> 1 hour advance notice required. Regular business hours 0800-1700, Monday through Friday, for weekend service, prior arrangements must be made no later than Thursday, MP/F: 15.

ILLINOIS

Chicago/•Chicago Midway/MDW/FAA: Yes/USCS 312-767-2266.
> 1 hour advance notice required. Regular business hours, 0830-1700, Monday through Friday. MP/F: 15.

Chicago/Chicago-O'Hare Int'l/ORD/FAA: Yes/USCS 312-686-2133.
Nights: 312-626-8266.
> 1 hour advance notice required during regular business hours, 0800-2130, Monday through Friday; 1200-2130 on Saturdays. 2 hours advance notice required at other times.

Chicago/Merrill C. Meigs field/CGX/FAA: Yes/USCS 312-686-2133.
Nights: 312-626-8266.
> 1 hour advance notice required during regular business hours 0830-1700, Monday through Friday. MP/F: 10.

Peoria/Greater Peoria/PIA/FAA: No/USCS 309-671-7047. Nights: 309-673-0195.
    On-call basis. 2 hours advance notice required during regular business hours,
    0830-1700, Monday through Friday, 3 hours advance notice required after regular
    business hours, Saturdays, Sundays, and holidays. MP/F: 10.

INDIANA
Indianapolis/Indianapolis Int'l/IND/FAA: Yes/USCS 317-248-4060.
    Advance arrangements for the granting of landing rights must be made. Regular
    business hours, 0830-1700, Monday through Friday. Saturday and Sunday requests
    for service must be made prior to 1700 hours on Friday.

IOWA
Des Moines/Des Moines Municipal/DSM/FAA: Yes/USCS 515-284-4403.
    Nights: 515-285-4640.
    On-call basis. 2 hours advance notice required during regular business hours,
    0830-1700, Monday through Friday. 3 hours advance notice required after regular
    business hours, Saturdays, Sundays, and holidays. MP/F: 10.

KANSAS
Kansas City/Fairfax/KCK/FAA: Yes/USCS 816-374-3958.
    Nights: 816-374-3068.
    Advance arrangements for the granting of landing rights must be made. Regular
    business hours, 0800-1630, Monday through Friday. Saturday and Sunday requests
    for service must be made prior to 1630 hours on Friday.

Wichita/Mid-Continent/ICT/FAA: Yes/USCS 316-269-7040.
    Nights: 316-942-4131.
    Advance arrangements for the granting of landing rights must be made. Regular
    business hours, 0830-1700, Monday through Friday. Saturday and Sunday requests
    for service must be made prior to 1700 hours on Friday. MP/F: 15.

KENTUCKY
Louisville/Bowman Field/LOU/FAA: Yes/USCS 502-582-5183.
    Advance arrangements for the granting of landing rights must be made at least
    2 hours in advance of arrival. Regular business hours 0800-1700, Monday through
    Friday. Saturday and Sunday requests for service must be made prior to 1700
    hours on Friday.

Louisville/Standiford Field/SDF/FAA: Yes/USCS 502-582-5183.
    Advance arrangements for the granting of landing rights must be made at least
    2 hours in advance of arrival. Regular business hours 0800-1700, Monday through
    Friday. Saturday and Sunday requests for service must be made prior to 1700
    hours on Friday.

Owensboro/Davies County Airport/OWB/FAA: No/USCS 502-683-5133.
    24 hours notice of arrival required. Regular business hours 0800-1630 Monday
    through Friday. Saturday and Sunday request for service must be made prior
    to 1630 hours on Friday.

LOUISIANA
Baton Rouge/Ryan/BTR/FAA: Yes/USCS 504-389-0261.
    On-call basis. 2 hours advance notice required.

Lake Charles/Lake Charles Municipal/LCH/FAA: Yes/USCS 318-439-5512.
    2 hours advance notice required.

New Orleans/New Orleans Int'l (Moisant Field)/MSY/FAA: Yes/USCS 504-589-2510. Nights: 504-589-6804.
2 hours advance notice required. Regular business hours, 0800-1700 Monday through Saturday.

New Orleans/New Orleans Lakefront Airport/NEW/FAA: Yes/USCS 504-589-2510. Nights: 504-589-6804.
On-call basis. 2 hours advance notice required. Regular business hours, 0800-1700, Monday through Saturday. MP/F: 20.

MAINE

Bangor/Bangor Int'l/BGR/FAA: Yes/USCS †207-947-7861.
1 hour advance notice required. Regular business hours, 0800-2400, Monday through Saturday. Due to limited staffing, aircraft arrivals after 1700 may be subject to inspectional overtime charge.

Bar Harbor/Bar Harbor/BHB/FAA: Yes/USCS †207-947-7861.
On-call basis. 1 hour advance notice required. Pilots are requested to telephone Customs prior to takeoff from Canada. However, due to limited Customs staffing at Bangor and a round trip of 100 miles (Bangor/Bar Harbor), availability of Customs service to this airport may be restricted. Pilots are advised to use Bangor as an alternate landing site. MP/F: 12.

Baring/St. Croix/FAA: No/USCS 207-454-3621 (Calais).
On-call basis. To insure timely service, pilots are requested to telephone Customs prior to takeoff from Canada. 1 hour advance notice required. Regular business hours, 0800-1700 (daylight hours only), 7 days per week. MP/F: 10.

Caribou/•Caribou Muncipal/CAR/FAA: Yes/USCS 207-473-7474 (Fort Fairfield); if no answer, call 207-473-7396 (Fort Fairfield).
On-call basis. To insure timely service, pilots are requested to telephone Customs prior to takeoff from Canada. 1 hour advance notice required. Charge is made for mileage. Inspectional overtime charges may be applicable after 1700 depending upon manpower availability at the port of Fort Fairfield, Maine. MP/F: 10.

Eastport/Eastport Municipal/47B/FAA: No/USCS 207-853-4313.
On-call basis. To insure timely service, pilots are requested to telephone Customs prior to takeoff from Canada. 1 hour advance notice required. Regular business hours, 0800-1700 (daylight hours only), Monday through Saturday MP/F: 10.

Fort Fairfield/Fairfied Municipal/1B4/FAA: No/USCS 207-853-4313.
On-call basis. To insure timely service, pilots are requested to telephone Customs prior to takeoff from Canada. 1 hour advance notice required. Regular business hours, 0800-1700 (daylight hours only), Monday through Saturday. MP/F: 10.

Frenchville/Northern Aroostook Regional Airport/FVE/FAA: Yes/USCS 207-728-4376 (Madawaska).
On-call basis. 1 hour advance notice during regular business hours, 0800-1700, Monday through Saturday. 2 hours advance notice required after 1700, and on Sundays and holidays. Charge is made for mileage. Inspectional overtime charge may be applicable after 1700 depending upon the availability of manpower at the Port of Madawaska. MP/F: 10.

Houlton/•Houlton Int'l/HUL/FAA: Yes/USCS †207-532-2131, F.S. 207-532-2475.
1 hour advance notice required. Regular business hours: 24-hour service, Monday through Saturday, except holidays.

Jackman/Moose River Seaplane Base/60B/FAA: No/USCS 207-668-3711.
1 hour advance notice required.

Jackman/Newton Field/59B/FAA: No/USCS 207-668-3711.
On-call basis to insure timely service, pilots are requested to telephone Customs prior to takeoff from Canada. 1 hour advance notice required. MP/F: 20.

Lubec/Lubec Municipal/65B/FAA: No/USCS 207-733-4331.
On-call basis. To insure timely service, pilots are requested to telephone Customs prior to takeoff from Canada. 1 hour advance notice required. Regular business hours, 0800-1700 (daylight hours only), Monday through Saturday. MP/F: 10.

Old Town/Old Town Municipal (DeWitt Field)/OLD/FAA: Yes/USCS 207-947-7861 (Bangor), †207-945-6320.
On-call basis. To insure timely service, pilots are requested to telephone Customs prior to takeoff from Canada. Charge is made for mileage. 1 hour advance notice required. MP/F: 20.

Portland/Portland Int'l Jetport/PWM/FAA: Yes/USCS 207-780-3328, 0800-1700 hours. F.S. 207-833-0602, 0700-2300 hours.
To insure timely service, pilots are requested to telephone Customs prior to takeoff from Canada. 1 hour advance notice required. Due to limited staffing aircraft arrivals after 1700 maybe subject to inspectional overtime charge.

Presque Isle/Presque Isle Municipal/PQI/FAA: Yes/USCS †207-473-7474, †207-473-7396 (Fort Fairfield).
On-call basis. To insure timely service, pilots are requested to telephone Customs prior to takeoff from Canada. 1 hour advance notice required for permission to land. Charge is made for mileage. Inspectional overtime charge may be applicable after 1700 depending upon manpower availability at the port of Fort Fairfield, Maine. MP/F: 10.

Princeton/Princeton Municipal/PNN/FAA: No/USCS 207-454-3621 (Calais).
On-call basis. To insure timely service, pilots are requested to telephone Customs prior to takeoff from Canada. 1 hour advance notice required. Charge is made for mileage. MP/F: 10.

Van Buren/St. John River Sea Plane Base/FAA: No/USCS 207-868-3391.
One hour advance notice required. MP/F: 10.

MARYLAND

Baltimore/Baltimore-Washington Int'l/BAL/FAA: Yes/USCS 301-962-3170, 301-962-3843. 617-223-0981 (24 hrs.)
1 hour advance notice required during regular business hours. 2 hours advance notice required after 1700 hours and on Sundays and holidays. With 10 or more passengers report to International Arrivals Building. MP/F: 12.

MASSACHUSETTS

Bedford/Laurence G. Hanscom Field/BED/FAA: Yes/USCS 617-686-1363 (Methuen), 617-223-0981.
2 hours advance notice required. Regular business hours, 0830-1700, Monday through Friday. Charge is made for mileage.

Beverly/Beverly Municipal/BVY/FAA: Yes/USCS 617-283-0425.
 1 hour advance notice required. Regular business hours, 0800-1700, Monday through Friday. MP/F: 15.

Boston/General Edward Lawrence Logan Int'l/BOS/FAA: Yes/USCS 617-223-5531, †617-223-1341, †617-223-5260.
 Regular business hours, 0800-2400, Monday through Saturday.

Chicopee/Westover Air Park/CEF/FAA: Yes/USCS 413-785-0365.
 1 hour advance notice required. Regular business hours, 0800-1700, Monday through Friday.

Lawrence/Lawrence Municipal/LWM/FAA: Yes/USCS 617-686-1363, 617-223-0981.
 1 hour advance notice required. Regular business hours, 0800-1700, Monday through Friday. MP/F: 10.

New Bedford/New Bedford Municipal/EWB/FAA: Yes/USCS 617-997-0721, ext. 257, 617-223-6530.
 1 hour advance notice required. Regular business hours, 0800-1700, Monday through Friday. MP/F: 5.

Westfield/Barnes Municipal/BAF/FAA: Yes/USCS 413-785-0365.
 1 hour advance notice required. Regular business hours, 0800-1700, Monday through Friday.

Worcester/Worcester Municipal/ORH/FAA: Yes/USCS 617-793-0293.
 On-call basis. To insure timely service, pilots are requested to telephone Customs prior to takeoff from Canada. 2 hours advance notice required for permission to land.

MICHIGAN

Alpena/Phelps Collins/APN/FAA: No/USCS 517-356-0910.
 Telephone call from pilot requesting service before takeoff from Canada. Charge is made for mileage. MP/F: 5.

Battle Creek/Kellogg Regional/BTL/FAA: No/USCS 616-965-3349.
 Nights: 616-964-8991, 616-657-5872.
 Telephone call from pilot requesting service before takeoff from Canada. Regular business hours, 0800-1630, Monday through Friday. MP/F: 10.

Bay City/James Clements Municipal/3CM/FAA: No/USCS 517-892-4222.
 Nights: 517-686-3720.
 Telephone call from pilot requesting service before takeoff from Canada. 1 hour advance notice required MP/F: 5.

Detroit/•Detroit City/DET/FAA: Yes/USCS 313-226-3140.
 Telephone call from pilot requesting service before takeoff from Canada. 1 hour advance notice required. MP/F: 15.

Detroit/•Detroit Metropolitan-Wayne County/DTW/FAA: Yes/USCS 313-226-3140.
 Telephone call from pilot requesting service before takeoff from Canada during hours of 2400-0800. At other times flight service notification is sufficient.

Flint/Bishop Int'l/FNT/FAA: No/USCS 517-892-4222.
Nights: 517-686-3720.
Telephone call from pilot requesting service before takeoff from Canada. 1 hour advance notice required MP/F: 5.

Grand Rapids/Kent County Int'l/GRR/FAA: No/USCS 616-456-2515.
Nights: 616-949-6309.
Telephone call from pilot requesting service before takeoff from Canada. Regular business hours, 0800-1630, Monday through Friday. MP/F: 20.

Kalamazoo/Kalamazoo Municipal/AZO/FAA: No/USCS 616-965-3349.
Nights: 616-964-8991, 616-657-5872.
Telephone call from pilot requesting service before takeoff from Canada. Regular business hours, 0800-1630, Monday through Friday. MP/F: 10.

Marquette/Marquette County/MQT/USCS 906-475-7282.
Nights: 906-475-4082.
Telephone call from pilot requesting service before takeoff from Canada. Charge is made for mileage. MP/F: 5.

Muskegon/Muskegon County/MKG/FAA: No/USCS 616-722-2913.
Nights: 616-894-2201.
Telephone call from pilot requesting service before takeoff from Canada. Regular business hours, 0800-1630, Monday through Friday.

Port Huron/Baker's Field/90G/FAA: Yes/Direct radio contact not available./
USCS 313-985-9541.
1 hour notice required. Seaplane use only. On-call from Blue Water Bridge. MP/F: 5.

Port Huron/•St. Clair County/PHN/FAA: Yes/USCS 313-985-9541.
Telephone call from pilot requesting service before takeoff from Canada with at least 1 hour advance notice. MP/F: 10.

Saginaw/Tri-City/MBS/FAA: No/USCS 517-892-4222.
1 hour advance notice required. Telephone call from pilot requesting service before takeoff from Canada. MP/F: 10.

Sault Ste. Marie/Chippewa County Int'l/CIU/FAA: Yes/
USCS 906-632-7222, 906-632-2631.
Telephone call from pilot requesting service before takeoff from Canada. 1 hour advance notice required. On-call from International Bridge. MP/F: 10.

MINNESOTA

Baudette/•Baudette Int'l/BDE/FAA: No/USCS 218-634-2661.
On-call from border station. 1 hour advance notice required. MP/F: 4.

Crane Lake/Scott's Seaplane Base/8Y8/FAA: No/USCS 218-993-2321.
1 hour advance notice required.

Duluth/•Duluth Int'l/DLH/FAA: Yes/USCS 218-720-5203.
On-call basis. 1 hour advance notice required. Service furnished on request.

Duluth/•Sky Harbor/D36/FAA: Yes/USCS 218-720-5203.
On-call basis. 1 hour advance notice required. Service furnished on request.

Ely/Ely Municipal/ELO/FAA: No/USCS 218-365-3262.
  Advance notice required. Communicate direct to airport base via radio or telephone to Customs. Open on a seasonal basis May 15 through October 14.

Ely/Northern Lakes Aviation Seaplane Base/9Y3/FAA: No/USCS 218-365-3262.
  Advance notice required. Communicate direct to seaplane base via radio or telephone to Customs. Open on a seasonal basis May 15 through October 14.

Grand Marais/Devil's Track/GRM/FAA: No/USCS 218-387-1750.
  Nights: 218-475-2244.
  Open on a seasonal basis from May 15 through October 14. Advance arrangements must be made.

International Falls/•Falls Int'l/INL/FAA: Yes/USCS 218-283-2541.
  On-call basis. 1 hour advance notice required.

Minneapolis/Minneapolis-St. Paul Int'l/MSP/FAA: Yes/USCS 612-725-3689.
  *Sunday and Holidays: 612-725-3690.
  1 hour advance notice required.

Oak Island/Oak Island/FAA: No/USCS none.
  On-call basis. Advance arrangements must be made.
  Radio phone 218-386-2935.

Pinecreek/Pinecreek/48Y/FAA: No/USCS 218-463-1952.
  Serviced from border station 0900-2200.

Ranier/•Int'l Seaplane base/50Y/FAA: Yes/USCS 218-286-5211, 218-283-2541.
  On-call basis. 1 hour advance notice required.

St. Paul/St. Paul Downtown (Holman Field)/STP/FAA: Yes/INS 612-725-7103.
  F.S. Day or Nights: 612-726-1130.
  1 hour advance notice required. Regular business hours, 0800-1630, Monday through Friday. Saturday and Sunday on-call basis.

Warroad/Warroad Int'l Seaplane Base/75Y/FAA: No/USCS 218-386-1676.
  On-call basis. 1 hour advance notice required. MP/F: 4.

Warroad/Warroad Municipal/D45/FAA: No/USCS 218-386-1676.
  On-call basis. 1 hour advance notice required. MP/F: 4.

MISSISSIPPI

Gulfport/Gulfport Biloxi Regional/GPT/FAA: Yes/USCS 601-864-6794.
  On-call basis. 2 hours advance notice required during regular business hours, 0800-1700, Monday through Friday. MP/F: 10.

Pascagoula/Jackson County/PGL/FAA: No/USCS 601-762-7311.
  On-call basis. 2 hours advance notice required during regular business hours, 0800-1700, Monday through Friday.

Vicksburg/Vicksburg Municipal Airport/FAA: No/USCS 601-634-7186.
  On-call basis. 2 hours advance notice required during regular business hours, 0800-1700, Monday through Friday.

MISSOURI

Kansas City/Kansas City Int'l/MCI/FAA: Yes/USCS 816-374-3958.
  Nights: 816-374-3068.
  Advance arrangements for the granting of landing rights must be made. Regular business hours, 0800-1630, Monday through Friday. Saturday and Sunday requests for service must be made prior to 1630 hours on Friday.

Kansas City/Downtown Airport/MKC/FAA: Yes/USCS 816-374-3958.
  Nights: 816-374-3068.
  Advance arrangements for the granting of landing rights must be made. Regular business hours 0800-1630, Monday through Friday. Saturday and Sunday requests for service must be made prior to 1630 hours on Friday.

Springfield/Springfield Regional/SGF/FAA: Yes/USCS 417-831-4035.
  Nights: 417-865-9992.
  Advance arrangements must be made. Regular business hours, 0830-1700, Monday through Friday. Saturday and Sunday requests for service must be made prior to 1700 on Friday. MP/F: 15.

St. Louis/Lambert-St. Louis Municipal/STL/FAA: Yes/USCS 314-425-3142.
  Nights and weekends: 314-532-1011.
  On-call basis. 2 hours advance notice required. Regular business hours, 0800-1700, Monday through Friday.

St. Louis/Spirit of St. Louis/SUS/FAA: Yes/USCS 314-425-3142.
  Nights and weekends: 314-532-1011.
  Advance arrangements must be made with Customs for the granting of landing rights during regular business hours, 0830-1700, Monday through Friday. Nights and weekends, two hours advance notice through FAA.

MONTANA

Note: To assure timely inspection of locations in Montana, Customs requests that all calls (notice of advance arrival), regardless of when service is required, be made during regular business hours, unless other hours are specified.

Billings/Logan Int'l/BIL/FAA: Yes/USCS 406-457-8495; FSS 406-259-4545.
  1 hour advance notice required. Commercial cargo cannot be entered at this airport. On-call basis. MP/F: 15.

Butte/Bert Mooney/BTM/FAA: Yes/USCS 406-494-3492.
  1 hour advance notice required. Regular business hours, 0800-1700, Monday through Friday.

Cut Bank/•Cut Bank/CTB/FAA: Yes/USCS 406-873-2711.
  1 hour advance notice required. On-call basis. Commercial cargo cannot be entered at this airport. MP/F: 15.

Del Bonita/Del Bonita/FAA: No/USCS 406-336-2130.
  Airstrip does not have landing lights. 1 hour advance not required during regular business hours, 0800-1700, Monday through Friday.

Glasgow/Glasgow Int'l/GGW/FAA: Yes/USCS 1-800-824-7706.
  2 hours advance notice required. On-call basis. Commercial cargo cannot be entered at this airport. MP/F: 15.

Great Falls/•Great Falls Int'l/GTF/FAA: Yes/USCS 406-453-0861; FSS 406-761-7110.
1 hour advance notice required. Regular business hours, 0800-1700, Monday
through Friday.

Havre/•Havre City-County/HVR/FAA: Yes/USCS 406-265-4361.
On-call basis. Commercial cargo cannot be entered at this airport. MP/F: 15.

Kalispell/Glacier Park Int'l/FCA/FAA: Yes/USCS 406-257-7034; FSS 406-761-7110.
On-call basis. 2 hours advance notice required. Commercial cargo cannot be
entered at this airport.

Morgan-Loring/Morgan/7U4/FAA: No/USCS 406-674-5248.
1 hour advance notice required. Regular business hours, 0900-1700, Monday
through Friday. MP/F: 15.

Scobey/E. Poplar Int'l/8U3/FAA: No/USCS 406-783-5372.
1 hour advance notice required. Regular business hours, 0900-1700, Monday
through Friday. MP/F: 15.

Sweetgrass/Ross Int'l/7S8/FAA: No/USCS 406-335-2434.
Airstrip does not have landing lights. 1 hour advance notice required. Regular
business hours, 0800-1700, Monday through Friday.

NEBRASKA

Omaha/Eppley Airfield/OMA/FAA: Yes/USCS 402-221-4661.
Nights: 402-344-8304.
On-call basis. 2 hours advance notice required during regular business hours
0800-1630, Monday through Friday; 3 hours advance notice required after regular
business hours, Saturdays, Sundays, and holidays. MP/F: 10.

NEVADA

Las Vegas/McCarran Int'l/LAS/FAA: Yes/USCS †702-385-6480.
On-call basis. 2 hour advance notice required during regular business hours,
0800-1700, Monday through Friday; for all flights MP/F: 20.

Reno/Reno Int'l/RNO/FAA: Yes/USCS 702-784-5585.
On-call basis. 2 hours advance notice required. Arrangements should be made
during regular business hours, 0800-1700, Monday through Friday, for all flights.
MP/F: 25.

NEW HAMPSHIRE

Manchester/Manchester Municipal/MHT/FAA: No/USCS 617-686-1363, 617-223-0981.
On-call basis. 2 hours advance notice required. Regular business hours, 0800-1700,
Monday through Friday. Charge is made for mileage. MP/F: 10.

NEW JERSEY

Newark/Newark Int'l/EWR/FAA: Yes/USCS 201-645-3409, 201-645-2236.
F.S. †800-932-0835, Butler Aviation †201-961-2600.
2 hours advance notice required after regular business hours and on Sundays
and holidays. MP/F: 20.

Teterboro/Teterboro/TEB/FAA: Yes/USCS 201-288-8799, 201-288-1740, Saturdays
201-645-3409. F.S. †201-288-9521.
On-call basis. 1 hour advance notice required during regular business hours. 2
hours after 1700 hours and on Sundays and holidays. MP/F: 20.

NEW MEXICO

Albuquerque/Albuquerque Int'l/ABQ/FAA: Yes/USCS 505-766-2621.
2 hours advance notice required during regular business hours, 0800-1700, Monday through Friday. At least 3 hours otherwise.

NEW YORK

Albany/•Albany County/ALB/FAA: Yes/USCS 518-472-3457.
2 hours advance notice required at all times. After 1700 hours, Sundays and holidays, call 518-869-9225 (Albany Flight Service)

Buffalo/Greater Buffalo Int'l/BUF/FAA: Yes/USCS 716-632-4727; if no answer, call 716-846-4316.
Advance arrangements for Customs inspection must be made at all times 2 hours prior to arrival. Regular business hours, 0800-1700, Monday through Saturday.

Farmingdale/Republic Aviation/FRG/FAA: No/USCS 718-626-2250/2251, 800-522-5270 (N.Y.), 800-221-4265 (Outside N.Y.)
On call basis. 24 hour advance notice required. No service 0800-1700 Saturdays, Sundays, and holidays. Charge may be made for mileage. MP/F: 20.

Islip/MacArthur/ISP/FAA: No/USCS 718-626-2250/1, 800-522-5270 (N.Y.), 800-221-4265 (outside N.Y.)
On-call basis. 24 hour advance notice required. No service 0800-1700 hours on Saturday, Sundays, and holidays. Charge may be made for mileage. MP/F: 20.

Massena/•Richards Field/MSS/FAA: Yes/USCS 315-769-3091.
On-call basis. 1 hour advance notice required.

New York/John F. Kennedy/JFK/FAA: Yes/USCS 718-917-1648 (24 hour number), 718-917-1649.
Private aircraft handled only on an emergency basis.

New York/La Guardia/LGA/FAA: Yes/USCS 718-476-4378, 718-917-1648, (24 hour number) 1 hour advance notice required. MP/F: 15.

Newburgh/Stewart/SWF/FAA: Yes/USCS 914-564-7490, 800-522-5270 (N.Y.), 800-221-4265 (Outside N.Y.)
1 hour advance notice during regular business hours (Mon.-Fr. 0800-1700) 2 hours advance notice after hours, on weekends and holidays. Charge may be made for mileage. MP/F: 20.

Niagara Falls/Niagara Falls Int'l/IAG/FAA: Yes/USCS 716-694-6617 for service 0800-1700 hours Monday through Saturday. For service after 1700 hours and before 1800 hours weekdays, and all Sundays and U.S. holidays, call 716-846-4311. On-call basis. 2 hours advance notice required.

Ogdensburg/•Ogdensburg Harbor/FAA: No/USCS 315-393-1390.
On-call basis. 1 hour advance notice required.

Ogdensburg/•Ogdensburg Int'l/OGS/FAA: Yes/USCS 315-393-1390.
On-call basis. 1 hour advance notice required.

Rochester/Mayers Marina/FAA: Yes/USCS 716-263-6295.
On-call basis. 1 hour advance notice required.

Rochester/•Rochester Monroe County/ROC/FAA: Yes/USCS 716-263-6295.
On-call basis. 1 hour advance notice required.

Rouses Point/•Rouses Point Seaplane Base/NY47/FAA: No/USCS 518-298-8321,
†518-298-8341.
On-call basis. 1 hour advance notice required.

Schenectady/Schenectady County/SCH/FAA: Yes/USCS 518-472-3457 (Albany),
Albany Flight Service 518-869-9225.
24 hours advance notice required. Prior permission to land must be obtained
during regular business hours. (Mon.-Fri. 0800-1700) Charge may be made for
mileage.

Syracuse/Syracuse Hancock Int'l/SYR/FAA: Yes/USCS 315-482-9904.
1 hour advance notice required. Use Gate 6 (Flying Tigers).

Watertown/Watertown New York Int'l/ART/FAA: Yes/USCS 315-482-2261.
(Alexandria Bay), F.S. 315-639-6228.
On-call basis. 2 hours advance notice required.

White Plains/Westchester County/HPN/FAA: Yes/USCS 914-428-7858, 800-522-5270
(N.Y.) 800-221-4265 (outside N.Y.) 1 hour advance notice during regular business
hours (Mon.-Fri. 0800-1700) 2 hours advance notice after hours, on weekends and
holidays MP/F: 20.

NORTH CAROLINA
Charlotte/Douglas Municipal/CLT/FAA: Yes/USCS 704-392-9328.
On-call basis. 1 hour advance notice required during regular business hours
0830-1700, Monday through Friday. 3 hours notice required after 1700 hours and
on Saturdays, Sundays, and holidays.

Greensboro/Greensboro/Highpoint/Winston-Salem Regional/GSO/FAA: Yes/USCS
919-761-3001 (Winston-Salem).
On-call basis. 2 hours advance notice required during regular business hours,
0830-1700, Monday through Friday. 3 hours notice required after 1700 hours and
on Saturdays, Sundays and holidays. Charge is made for mileage.

Raleigh-Durham/Raleigh-Durham/RDU/FAA Yes, but not satisfactory due to prior
assignment of Customs personnel./USCS 919-541-5211.
Advance arrangements must be made for Customs inspection by party of interest prior to departure. Regular business hours, 0800-1700, Monday through
Friday. Saturday and Sunday request for service must be made prior to 1700 hours
Friday. Requests for holidays service must be made prior to 1700 hours on the
preceding work day. Charge is made for mileage.

Wilmington/New Hanover County/ILM/FAA: Yes/USCS 919-343-4616.
On-call basis. 2 hours advance notice required during regular business hours,
0800-1700. 3 hours notice required after 1700 hours and on Sundays and holidays.

Winston-Salem/Smith Reynolds/INT/FAA: Yes/USCS 919-761-3001.
On-call basis. 1 hour advance notice required during regular business hours,
0830-1700, Monday through Friday. 2 hours notice required after 1700 hours and
on Saturdays, Sundays, and holidays.

NORTH DAKOTA

Dunseith/Int'l Peace Garden/S28/FAA: No/USCS 701-263-4513.
Nights: 701-825-6551 (Pembina).
Serviced from border station. Border station open 24 hours year-round. Radio communication available. Airport not lighted. Hard surface MP/F: 4.

Grand Forks/•Grand Forks Int'l/GFK/FAA: Yes/USCS 701-772-3301.
Nights: 701-825-6551 (Pembina).
1 hour advance notice required during regular business hours. Regular business hours 0900-1700. On-call basis during other hours and on Sundays and holidays.

Minot/•Minot Int'l/MCT/FAA: Yes/USCS 701-838-6704.
Nights: 701-926-4411 (Portal).
1 hour advance notice required during regular business hours. Regular business hours 0800-1700. On-call basis at other times. MP/F: 20.

Noonan/Border Int'l/ND48/FAA: No/USCS 701-925-5615.
Nights: 701-926-4411 (Portal).
1 hour advance notice required. Radio communication available. Serviced from border station. Border station hours, 0900-2200. Airport not lighted. Sod runway. MP/F: 4.

Pembina/•Pembina Municipal/PMB/FAA: Yes, through Grand Forks, N.D./USCS 701-825-6551, 701-825-6421.
1 hour advance notice required. Contact airport manager to request lighted border.

Williston/•Sloulin Field Int'l/ISN/FAA: Yes/USCS 701-572-6552, 701-572-2107.
On-call basis. 1 hour advance notice required, MP/F: 10.

OHIO

Akron/Akron-Canton/CAK/FAA: Yes/USCS 216-375-5496.
On-call basis. 2 hours advance notice required. Regular business hours, 0830-1700, Monday through Friday. Requests for service on Saturday, Sunday, and holidays must be made prior to 1700 hours on Friday. MP/F: 15.

Akron/•Akron-Municipal/AKR/FAA: Yes/USCS 216-375-5496.
On-call basis. 2 hours advance notice required. Regular business hours, 0830-1700, Monday through Friday. Requests for service on Saturday, Sunday, and holidays must be made prior to 1700 hours on Friday. MP/F: 15.

Cincinnati/Cincinnati Municipal Airport-Lunken Field/LUK/FAA: Yes/
USCS 513-684-3528.
2 hour advance arrangements for granting of landing rights must be made. Regular business hours 0830-1700, Monday through Friday. Saturday and Sunday request for service must be made prior to 1700 hours on Friday. MP/F: 10.

Cincinnati (Covington, Ky.)/Greater Cincinnati/CVG/FAA: Yes/USCS 513-684-3528.
2 hour advance arrangements for granting of landing rights must be made. Regular business hours 0830-1700, Monday through Friday. Saturday and Sunday requests for service must be made prior to 1700 hours on Friday.

Cleveland/Cleveland Hopkins Int'l/CLE/FAA: Yes/USCS 216-522-7030.
1 hour advance notice required. Regular business hours, 0800-2100, Monday through Friday; 0830-1900 Saturday.

Cleveland/Burke Lakefront/BKL/FAA: Yes/USCS 216-267-3700.
Advance arrangements for the granting of landing rights must be made. Service provided Monday-Friday, from 9 AM-3 PM. No service provided at other times. 2 hours advance notice required. MP/F:8.

Columbus/Port Columbus Int'l/CMH/FAA: Yes/USCS 614-469-6670.
Advance arrangements for the granting of landing rights must be made. Regular business hours 0830-1700, Monday through Friday. Saturday and Sunday requests for service must be made prior to 1700 hours on Friday.

Dayton/Cox International/DAY/FAA: Yes/USCS 513-225-2876 or 2877.
Advance arrangements for granting of landing rights must be made. Regular business hours 0830-1700, Monday through Friday. Saturday and Sunday requests for service must be made prior to 1700 hours on Friday.

Sandusky/•Friffing-Sandusky/SKY/FAA: Yes/USCS 419-625-2194.
1 hour advance notice required. Regular business hours, 0830-1700, Monday through Friday.

Toledo/Toledo Express/TOL/FAA: No/USCS 419-259-6424.
Advance arrangements must be made during regular business hours. Regular business hours, 0830-1700, Monday through Friday. Saturday and Sunday requests for service must be made prior to 1700 hours on Friday. MP/F: 15.

OKLAHOMA

Oklahoma City/Will Rogers World/OKC/FAA: Yes/USCS 405-231-4347.
Advance arrangements must be made. Regular business hours, 0830-1700, Monday through Friday. Saturday and Sunday requests for service must be made prior to 1700 hours on Friday. MP/F: 8 (including crew).

Tulsa/Tulsa Int'l/TUL/FAA: Yes/USCS 918-835-7631.
Advance arrangements must be made. Regular business hours, 0830-1700, Monday through Friday. Saturday and Sunday requests for service must be made prior to 1700 hours on Friday. MP/F: 8 (including crew).

OREGON

Portland/Portable Int'l/PDX/FAA: Yes/USCS 503-221-3515.
For service 0800-1700 Monday through Saturday. 503-222-1699 for service 1700-0800 and on Sundays and Holidays. 1 hour advance notice required.

PENNSYLVANIA

Erie/Erie Int'l/ERI/FAA: Yes/USCS 814-838-3742, 814-452-2905, ERI FSS 814-833-1345.
On-call basis. 2 hour advance notice required during regular business hours 0830-1700, Monday through Friday. Requests for service on Saturday, Sunday, and holidays must be made before 1700 hours on the preceding workday.

Harrisburg/Harrisburg Int'l/MDT/FAA: Yes/USCS 717-782-4510.
2 hours advance notice required. Regular business hours 0830-1700, Monday through Friday. Saturday, Sunday, and holidays requests for service must be made prior to 1700 hours on the preceding work day. Notification can be made through Flight Service 717-782-3777.

Philadelphia/Philadelphia Int'l/PHL/FAA: Yes/USCS 215-596-1973.
Inspectional personnel are frequently available from 0600-2100 hours. Regular business hours, 0800-1700, Sunday through Saturday. Advance arrangements with Customs required during other than regular hours.

Pittsburgh/Allegheny County/AGC/FAA: No/USCS 412-644-3592, 412-644-3587.
On-call basis. Advance arrangements must be made for Customs inspection.

Pittsburgh/Greater Pittsburgh Int'l/PIT/FAA: No/USCS 412-644-3587, 412-644-3588.
Two hours advance notice required during regular business hours, 0800-1700 Monday through Friday. Requests for service outside these hours must be made directly with Customs during regular business hours.

Wilkes-Barre/Scranton/Wilkes-Barre/Scranton/AVP/FAA: Yes/USCS 717-654-3674.
Regular business hours 0800-1700, Monday through Friday. 2 hours advance notice required. Notify FAA Flight Service 717-346-4512.

PUERTO RICO

Culebra/Culebra/CPX/FAA: No/USCS 809-742-3531.
1 hour advance notice required during regular business hours, 0800-1700, Monday through Saturday. Arrivals from U.S. Virgin Islands only.

Fajardo/Fajardo/FAA: No/USCS 809-863-0950.
1 hour advance notice required during regular business hours, 0800-1700, Monday through Saturday. Arrivals from U.S. Virgin Islands only.

Isla de Vieques/Vieques/VQS/FAA: No/USCS 809-741-8366.
1 hour advance notice required during regular business hours, 0800-1700, Monday through Saturday. Arrivals from U.S. Virgin Islands only.

Mayaguez/El Mani Airport/MAZ/FAA: No/USCS 809-832-0042, 809-832-8308, 809-834-2440.
On-call basis. 1 hour advance notice required.

Ponce/Mercedita/PSE/FAA: No/USCS 809-842-3195, 809-842-3195, 809-843-5998.
On-call basis. 1 hour advance notice required.

San Juan/Puerto Rico Int'l/SJU/FAA: Yes/USCS 809-791-5245, 809-791-0222/5927.
Regular business hours, 0800-2300, Monday through Saturday.

San Juan/San Juan/Isla Grande/SIG/FAA: Yes/USCS 809-725-6911.
Regular business hours, 0800-1900, Monday through Saturday.

RHODE ISLAND

North Kingston/Quonset Point State/OQU/FAA: Yes/USCS 401-528-4384.
†617-223-0981.
3 hours advance notice required.

Providence/Theodore Francis Green State/PVD/FAA: Yes/USCS 401-528-4384.
617-223-0981.
1 hour advance notice required during regular business hours. 3 hours otherwise.

SOUTH CAROLINA

Charleston/Charleston International/CHS/FAA: Yes/USCS 803-744-0712.
†803-723-1272.
1 hour advance notice required.

Columbia/Columbia Metropolitan/CAE/FAA: No/USCS 803-794-0782.
1 hour advance notice required during regular business hours, 0800-1700, Monday through Friday.

Greer/Greenville-Spartanburg/GSP/FAA: No/USCS 803-877-8006.
1 hour advance notice required, during regular business hours, 0800-1700 Monday through Friday.

TENNESSEE

Chattanooga/Lovell Field/CHA/FAA: Yes/USCS 615-267-1327.
On-call basis. 2 hours advance notice required.

Knoxville/McGhee Tyson/TYS/FAA: Yes/USCS 615-970-4158.
On-call basis. 2 hours advance notice required.

Memphis/Memphis Int'l/MEM/FAA: Yes/USCS 901-521-3558.
On-call basis. 2 hours advance notice required.

Nashville/Nashville Metropolitan/BNA/FAA: Yes/USCS 615-936-5861.
On-call basis. 2 hours advance notice required.

TEXAS

Amarillo/Amarillo Int'l/AMA/FAA: Yes/USCS 806-376-2347.
Advance arrangements must be made. Regular business hours, 0830-1700, Monday through Friday. Saturday and Sunday requests for service must be made prior to 1700 hours on Friday. MP/F: 8 (including crew).

Austin/Robert Mueller Municipal/AUS/FAA: Yes/USCS 512-482-5309.
Advance arrangements must be made. Regular business hours, 0830-1700, Monday through Friday. Saturday and Sunday requests for service must be made prior to 1700 hours on Friday. MP/F: 10 (including crew).

Beaumont/Jefferson County/BPT/FAA: Yes/USCS 409-727-0285 (Port Arthur).
On-call basis. 2 hours advance notice required. Regular business hours, 0800-1700, Monday through Friday.

Brownsville/•Brownsville Int'l/BRO/FAA: No/USCS 512-542-4232.
Communicate direct via radio or telephone to Customs or FAA intention to land and advise intended point and time of border penetration not later than 1 hour prior to entering U.S. airspace.

Corpus Christi/Corpus Christi Int'l/CRP/FAA: Yes/USCS 512-888-3352.
2 hours advance notice required. Regular business hours, 0830-1700, Monday through Friday. Saturday 8 to 5; 512-884-7019. All other times 512-853-5859.

Dallas/DFW Regional/DFW/FAA: Yes/USCS 214-574-2131, 0830-1700 hours.
F.S. 214-350-7340 after 1700 hours.
1 hour advance notice required prior to 1700 hours. 2 hours notice after 1700 hours.

Dallas/Dallas Love Field/DAL/FAA: Yes/USCS 214-574-2131.
2 hours advance notice required. After 1700 hours call FAA 214-350-7340 MP/F: 10 (including crew).

Del Rio/•Del Rio Int'l/DRT/FAA: Yes/USCS 512-775-8502.
Communicate direct via radio or telephone to Customs or FAA intention to land

and advise intended point and time of border penetration not later than 1 hour prior to entering U.S airspace.

Eagle Pass/•Eagle Pass Municipal/EGP/FAA: No/USCS 512-733-9468.
Communicate direct via radio or telephone to Customs or FAA intention to land and advise intended point and time of border penetration not later than 1 hour prior to entering U.S. airspace.

El Paso/•El Paso Int'l/ELP/FAA: Yes/USCS 915-543-7430.
Communicate direct via radio to FAA or telephone to Customs intention to land and advise intended point and time of border penetration not later than 1 hour prior to entering U.S. airspace.

Ft. Worth/Meachem Field/FTW/FAA: Yes/USCS 214-574-2131.
2 hours advance notice required. After 1700 hours call FAA. MP/F: 10 (including crew).

Galveston/Scholes Field/GLS/FAA: Yes/USCS 409-766-3787.
Landing rights granted in case of emergency with concurrence of the other interested agencies.

Houston/Houston Intercontinental/IAH/FAA: Yes/USCS 713-443-5938 M-F, 443-5910 other times.
1 hour advance notice required during business hours, 0800-1700, Monday through Saturday, 2 hours otherwise.

Houston/William P. Hobby/HOU/FAA: Yes/USCS 713-644-1174 Mon.-Fri. other times 713-644-2681
1 hour advance notice required during regular business hours; 2 hours otherwise. MP/F: 20 (including crew) with concurrence of other interested agencies.

Laredo/•Laredo Int'l/LOI/FAA: Yes/USCS 512-722-1113.
Communicate direct via radio or telephone to Customs or FAA intention to land and advise intended point and time of border penetration not later than 1 hour prior to entering U.S. airspace.

Lubbock/Lubbock Int'l/LBB/FAA: Yes/USCS 806-743-7458.
Advance arrangements must be made. Regular business hours, 0830-1700, Monday through Friday. Saturday and Sunday requests for service must be made prior to 1630 hours on Friday. MP/F: 8 (including crew).

McAllen/•Miller Int'l/MFE/FAA: Yes/USCS 512-843-2231.
Communicate direct via radio or telephone to Customs or FAA intention to land and advise intended point and time of border penetration not later than 1 hour prior to entering U.S. airspace.

Presidio/•Presidio-Lely Int'l/TXO7/FAA: Yes/USCS 915-229-3349.
On-call basis. 1 hour advance notice required during regular business hours, 0830-1700, Monday through Friday. 2 hours advance notice required after 1700 hours Monday through Friday or any time on Saturday, Sunday, and holidays.

San Antonio/San Antonio Int'l/SAT/FAA: Yes/USCS 512-822-0471, 512-229-5137.
1 hour advance notice required during regular business hours. 2 hours otherwise.

UTAH

Salt Lake City/Salt Lake City Int'l/SLC/FAA: Yes/USCS 801-524-5093.
   On-call basis. 1 hour advance notice required. MP/F: 40.

VERMONT

Burlington/•Burlington Int'l/BTV/FAA: Yes/USCS 802-864-5181. F.S. †802-878-3393.
   On-call basis. 1 hour advance notice required.

Highgate/Franklin County/1B7/FAA: No/USCS 802-868-3341.
   1 hour advance notice required. MP/F: 12.

Newport/Newport State/EFK/FAA: No/USCS 802-873-3219.
   1 hour advance notice required. MP/F: 8.

VIRGIN ISLANDS

St. Thomas/Harry S. Truman/STT/FAA: Yes/USCS 809-774-1719 (Charlotte Amalie).
   1 hour advance notice required during regular business hours, Sundays, and
   holidays.

St. Croix/Alexander Hamilton/STX/FAA: Yes/USCS 809-778-0216 (Christiansted).
   1 hour advance notice required during regular business hours, 0800-1700, Monday through Saturday. 2 hours advance notice required at other times and on
   Sundays or holidays.

VIRGINIA

Chantilly/Dulles Int'l (See District of Columbia)

Newport News/Patrick Henry Int'l/PHF/FAA: Yes/USCS 804-247-5837, 804-247-5836,
   301-962-0870.
   2 hours advance notice required. MP/F: 10.

Norfolk/Norfolk Int'l/ORF/FAA: Yes/USCS 804-441-6741, 804-441-6778, 804-441-6731.
   2 hours advance notice required during other than regular business hours,
   0800-1700. Nights, Sundays, and holidays, call 441-6741 only. MP/F: 10.

Richmond/Richard E. Byrd Int'l/RIC/FAA: Yes/USCS 804-771-2071.
   2 hours advance notice required during regular business hours, 0800-1700, Monday through Fridays. Requests for service on Saturdays and Sundays must be
   made prior to 1700 on the previous regular business day. MP/F: 10.

WASHINGTON

Note: To assure timely inspection at locations in Washington, Customs requests
at all airports a phone call (notice of arrival), regardless of when service is required, be made during regular business hours, unless other hours are indicated.

Anacortes/Anacortes/74S/FAA: No/USCS 206-293-2331.
   On-call basis. 1 hour advance notice required. Regular business hours, 0800-1700,
   Monday through Friday. MP/F: 15.

Anacortes/Skyline Seaplane Base/WAO3/FAA: No/USCS 206-293-2331.
   On-call basis. 1 hour advance notice required. Regular business hours, 0800-1700,
   Monday through Friday. MP/F: 15.

Bellingham/•Bellingham Int'l/BLI/FAA: Yes/USCS 206-734-5463.
On-call basis. I hour advance notice required. Regular business hours, 0800-1700, Monday through Friday. MP/F: 15.

Blaine/Blaine Municipal/WA-09/FAA: No/USCS 206-332-5771.
On-call basis. 1 hour advance notice required. Regular business hours, 0000-2400, Monday through Sunday. MP/F: 15.

Everette/Paine Field Snohomish County/PAE/FAA: No./USCS 206-259-0246.
On-call basis. 2 hours advance notice required. Regular business hours, 0800-1700, Monday through Friday. Permission granted only if workload permits. MP/F: 15.

Friday Harbor/•Friday Harbor Seaplane Base/WA24/FAA: Yes/USCS 206-378-2080.
On-call basis. Requests for landing rights must be made at least one hour in advance during regular business hours, Monday through Friday, 0800-1700 hours. Permission granted only if workload permits. MP/F: 15.

Friday Harbor/Friday Harbor/S19/FAA: No/USCS 206-378-2080.
On-call basis. 1 hour advance notice required. Regular business hours, 0800-1700, Monday through Friday. MP/F: 15.

Hoquaim/Bowerman/HQM/FAA: No/USCS 206-532-2030.
1 hour advance notice required. Regular business hours, 0800-1700, Monday through Friday. Permission granted only if workload permits. MP/F: 15.

Kelso/Kelso-Longview/KLS/FAA: Yes/USCS 206-425-3710.
1 hour advance notice required. Regular business hours, 0800-1700, Monday through Friday. Runway and facilities are not maintained. MP/F: 15.

Laurier/Avey Field State Airport/69F/FAA: No/USCS 509-684-2100.
On-call basis. Request for landing rights must be made at least one hour in advance during normal business hours, Monday through Sunday, 0800 to 2400 hours. Airstrip does not have landing lights.

Northport/James A. Lowry Municipal/WA42/FAA: No/USCS 509-732-4418.
1 hour advance notice required. Regular business hours, 0800-2400, Monday through Sunday. Permission granted only if workload permits. Airstrip does not have landing lights. MP/F: 15.

Olympia/Olympia Municipal/OLM/FAA: No/USCS 206-246-8805 (Tacoma).
2 hours advance notice required. Regular business hours, 0800-1700, Monday through Friday. Permission granted only if workload permits. MP/F: 15.

Oroville/•Dorothy Scott/OS7/FAA: No/USCS 206-246-8805 (Tacoma).
2 hours advance notice required. Regular business hours, 0800-1700, Monday through Friday. Permission granted only if workload permits. MP/F: 15.

Oroville/•Dorothy Scott Seaplane Base/FAA: Yes/USCS 509-476-3514.
On-call basis. 1 hour advance notice required. Regular business hours, 0800-1700. Monday through Friday. Airstrip does not have landing lights. MP/F: 15.

Port Angeles/William R. Fairchild Int'l/CLM/FAA: No/USCS 206-457-4311.
1 hour advance notice required. Regular business hours, 0800-1700, Monday through Friday. Permission granted only if workload permits. MP/F: 15.

Port Angeles/Port Angeles Marine Dock/NOW/FAA: No/USCS 206-457-4311.
   1 hour advance notice required. Regular business hours, 0800-1700, Monday through Friday. Permission granted only it workload permits. MP/F: 15.

Port Townsend/•Jefferson County Int'l/OS9/FAA: No/USCS 206-385-3777.
   On-call basis. 1 hour advance notice required. Regular business hours, 0800-1700, Monday through Friday. Recommend advance arrangement for all flights be made during regular business hours. Permission granted only if workload permits. MP/F: 15.

Seattle/•Boeing Field/King County Int'l/BFI/FAA: Yes/USCS 206-442-4674.
   1 hour advance notice required. Regular business hours, 0800-1700, Monday through Saturday MP/F: 30.

Seattle/Kenmore Air Harbor/S60/FAA: Yes/USCS 206-442-4674.
   2 hours advance notice required. Regular business hours, 0800-1700, Monday through Saturday MP/F: 15.

Seattle/Kurtzer's Flying Service/WA56/FAA: Yes/USCS 206-442-4674.
   2 hours advance notice required. Regular business hours, 0800-1700, Monday through Saturday. MP/F: 15.

Seattle/•Lake Union Air Service/WA57/FAA: Yes/USCS 206-442-4674.
   2 hours advance notice required. Regular business hours, 0800-1700, Monday through Saturday. MP/F: 15.

Seattle/Seattle-Tacoma Int'l/SEA/FAA: Yes/USCS 206-442-7960.
   2 hours advance notice required. Regular business hours, 0600-2200, Monday through Saturday.

Seattle/Renton Municipal/RNT/FAA: Yes/USCS 206-442-4674.
   2 hours advance notice required. Regular business hours, 0800-1700, Monday through Saturday.

Seattle/Renton Seaplane Base/WA47/FAA: Yes/USCS 206-442-4674.
   2 hours advance notice required. Regular business hours, 0800-1700, Monday through Saturday.

Spokane/Felts Field/SFF/FAA: Yes/USCS 509-456-4661.
   On-call basis. 2 hours advance notice required. Regular busness hours, 0800-1700, Monday through Friday. MP/F: 15.

Spokane/Spokane Int'l/GEG/FAA: Yes/USCS 509-456-4661.
   On-call basis. 1 hour advance notice required. Regular business hours, 0800-1700, Monday through Friday. MP/F: 15.

Tacoma/Tacoma Industrial/TIW/FAA: Yes/USCS 206-593-6338.
   On-call basis. 1 hour advance notice required. Regular business hours, 0800-1700, Monday through Friday. MP/F: 15.

WEST VIRGINIA

Charleston/Kanawha/CRW/FAA: Yes/USCS 304-343-6181 ext. 423 or 424.
   1 hour advance notice required. Regular business hours, 0800-1700, Monday through Friday. Prior arrangements must be made for Saturday and Sunday arrivals.

Huntington/Tri-State/HTS/FAA: Yes/USCS 304-343-6181 ext 423 or 424.
On-call basis. Advance arrangements must be made.

WISCONSIN

Green Bay/Austin Straubel/GRB/FAA: Yes/USCS 414-433-3923.
Nights: 414-494-7417.
1 hour advance notice required during regular business hours, 0800-1700, Monday through Friday. 2 hours at other times.

Milwaukee/General Mitchell Field/MKE/FAA: Yes/USCS 414-291-3932.
Nights: 414-481-1060.
1 hour advance notice required during regular business hours, 0800-1700, Monday through Friday. 2 hours at other times.

Racine/Horlick-Racine/RAC/FAA: Yes/USCS 414-633-0286.
Nights: 414-481-1060.
1 hour advance notice required. Regular business hours, 0830-1700, Monday through Friday. MP/F: 8.

WYOMING

Casper/Natrona County Int'l/CPR/FAA: Yes/F.S. 307-235-1555.
On-call basis. MP/F: 15.

PRECLEARANCE FROM THE VIRGIN ISLANDS

Private aircraft departing the U.S. Virgin Islands destined for the mainland or Puerto Rico may request preclearance service at St. Croix and St. Thomas. This service will be provided 0800 to 1700 hours, Monday through Sunday. Preclearance outside of these hours may be authorized at the discretion of the District Director on a case-by-case basis. All private aircraft pilots desiring preclearance to the U.S. are required to make advance arrangements for clearance directly with Customs or through the Federal Aviation Administration by radio or other means. FAA will notify Customs of all preclearance requests.

At time of preclearance, you will complete a General Declaration (CF-7507) which will be authenticated by the inspecting officer as evidence of your having been precleared.

If for any reason you find that you cannot come directly to the U.S. (must stop for refueling or any other reason), your preclearance becomes invalid and you must report to Customs on your arrival in the U.S. or Puerto Rico.

Use of the General Declaration, although not required for general aviation aircraft unless carrying persons or cargo for hire, will serve as evidence of your having been precleared if challenged upon your arrival in the Customs territory. However, this does not preclude reinspection by Customs, although such reinspection would be rare.

AIRMAN'S INFORMATION MANUAL (AIM)

FOREWORD

This manual is designed to provide airmen with basic flight information and ATC procedures for use in the National Airspace System (NAS) of the United States. The information contained parallels the U.S. Aeronautical Information Publication (AIP) distributed internationally.

This manual contains the fundamentals required in order to fly in the U.S. NAS. It also contains items of interest to pilots concerning health and medical facts, factors affecting flight safety, a pilot/controller glossary of terms used in the Air Traffic Control System, and information on safety, accident and hazard reporting.

This manual is complemented by other operational publications which are available upon separate subscription. These publications are:

Notices to Airmen (Class-II)— A publication containing current Notices to Airmen (NOTAMs) which are considered essential to the safety of flight as well as supplemental data affecting the other operational publications listed here. It also includes current FDC NOTAMs, which are regulatory in nature, issued to establish restrictions to flight or amend charts or published Instrument Approach Procedures. This publication is issued every 14 days and is available through subscription from the Superintendent of Documents.

Airport/Facility Directory, Alaska Supplement, Pacific Chart Supplement— These publications contain information on airports, communications, navigation aids, instrument landing systems, VOR receiver check points, preferred routes, FSS/Weather Service telephone numbers, Air Route Traffic Control Center (ARTCC) frequencies, part-time control zones, and various other pertinent special notices essential to air navigation. These publications are available upon subscription from the NOAA Distribution Branch N/CG33, National Ocean Service, Riverdale, Maryland 20737.

TABLE OF CONTENTS

JUNE 30, 1988

Chapter 1. NAVIGATION AIDS

Section 1. AIR NAVIGATION RADIO AIDS

Section 2. RADAR SERVICES AND PROCEDURES

Chapter 2. AERONAUTICAL LIGHTING AND AIRPORT MARKING AIDS

Section 1. AIRPORT LIGHTING AIDS

Section 2. AIR NAVIGATION AND OBSTRUCTION LIGHTING

Chapter 4. AIR TRAFFIC CONTROL

Section 1. SERVICES AVAILABLE TO PILOTS

Section 2. RADIO COMMUNICATIONS PHRASEOLOGY AND TECHNIQUES

Section 3. AIRPORT OPERATIONS

TABLE OF CONTENTS—Continued

Chapter 8. AERONAUTICAL CHARTS AND RELATED PUBLICATIONS

Section 1. TYPES OF CHARTS AVAILABLE

APPENDIX 1 (Figures)

APPENDIX 2 (Tables)

APPENDIX 3 (Aeronautical Charts)

SUPPLEMENT

Chapter 1. NAVIGATION AIDS

Section 1. AIR NAVIGATION RADIO AIDS

1. GENERAL

Various types of air navigation aids are in use today, each serving a special purpose. These aids have varied owners and operators, namely: the Federal Aviation Administration (FAA), the military services, private organizations, individual states and foreign governments. The FAA has the statutory authority to establish, operate, maintain air navigation facilities and to prescribe standards for the operation of any of these aids which are used for instrument flight in federally controlled airspace. These aids are tabulated in the Airport/Facility Directory.

2. NONDIRECTIONAL RADIO BEACON (NDB)

a. A low or medium frequency radio beacon transmits nondirectional signals whereby the pilot of an aircraft properly equipped can determine his bearing and "home" on the station. These facilities normally operate in the frequency band of 190 to 535 kHz and transmit a continuous carrier with either 400 or 1020 Hz modulation. All radio beacons except the compass locators transmit a continuous three-letter identification in code except during voice transmissions.

b. When a radio beacon is used in conjunction with the Instrument Landing System markers, it is called a Compass Locator.

c. Voice transmissions are made on radio beacons unless the letter "W" (without voice) is included in the class designator (HW).

d. Radio beacons are subject to disturbances that may result in erroneous bearing information. Such disturbances result from such factors as lightning, precipitation static, etc. At night radio beacons are vulnerable to interference from distant stations. Nearly all disturbances which affect the ADF bearing also affect the facility's identification. Noisy identification usually occurs when the ADF needle is erratic. Voice, music or erroneous identification may be heard when a steady false bearing is being displayed. Since ADF receivers do not have a "FLAG" to warn the pilot when erroneous bearing information is being displayed, the pilot should continuously monitor the NDB's identification.

3. VHF OMNI-DIRECTIONAL RANGE (VOR)

a. VORs operate within the 108.0 to 117.95 MHz frequency band and have a power output necessary to provide coverage within their assigned operational service volume. They are subject to line-of-sight restrictions, and the range varies proportionally to the altitude of the receiving equipment. The normal service ranges for the various classes of VORs are given in PARA. 10.d.

b. Most VORs are equipped for voice transmission on the VOR frequency. VORs without voice capability are indicated by the letter "W" (without voice) included in the class designator (VORW).

c. The only positive method of identifying a VOR is by its Morse Code identification or by the recorded automatic voice identification which is always indicated by use of the word "VOR"

following the range's name. Reliance on determining the identification of an omnirange should never be placed on listening to voice transmissions by the Flight Service Station (FSS) (or approach control facility) involved. Many FSSs remotely operate several omniranges with different names. In some cases, none of the VORs have the name of the "parent" FSS. During periods of maintenance, the facility may radiate a T-E-S-T code (— • ••• —) or the code may be removed.

d. Voice identification has been added to numerous VORs. The transmission consists of a voice announcement, "AIRVILLE VOR" alternating with the usual Morse Code identification.

e. The effectiveness of the VOR depends upon proper use and adjustment of both ground and airborne equipment.

(1) Accuracy: The accuracy of course alignment of the VOR is excellent, being generally plus or minus 1 degree.

(2) Roughness: On some VORs, minor course roughness may be observed, evidenced by course needle or brief flag alarm activity (some receivers are more susceptible to these irregularities than others). At a few stations, usually in mountainous terrain, the pilot may occasionally observe a brief course needle oscillation, similar to the indication of "approaching station." Pilots flying over unfamiliar routes are cautioned to be on the alert for these vagaries, and in particular, to use the "to/from" indicator to determine positive station passage.

(a) Certain propeller RPM settings or helicopter rotor speeds can cause the VOR Course Deviation Indicator to fluctuate as much as plus or minus six degrees. Slight changes to the RPM setting will normally smooth out this roughness. Pilots are urged to check for this modulation phenomenon prior to reporting a VOR station or aircraft equipment for unsatisfactory operation.

4. VOR RECEIVER CHECK

a. The FAA VOR test facility (VOT) transmits a test signal which provides users a convenient means to determine the operational status and accuracy of a VOR receiver while on the ground where a VOT is located. The airborne use of VOT is permitted; however, its use is strictly limited to those areas/altitudes specifically authorized in the Airport/Facility Directory or appropriate supplement.

b. To use the VOT service, tune in the VOT frequency on your VOR receiver. With the Course Deviation Indicator (CDI) centered, the omni-bearing selector should read 0 degrees with the to/from indication showing "from" or the omni-bearing selector should read 180 degrees with the to/from indication showing "to". Should the VOR receiver operate an RMI (Radio Magnetic Indicator), it will indicate 180 degrees on any OBS setting. Two means of identification are used. One is a series of dots and the other is a continuous tone. Information concerning an individual test signal can be obtained from the local FSS.

c. Periodic VOR receiver calibration is most important. If a receiver's Automatic Gain Control or modulation circuit deteriorates, it is possible for it to display acceptable accuracy and sensitivity close into the VOR or VOT and display out-of-tolerance readings when located at greater distances where weaker signal areas exist. The likelihood of this deterioration varies between receivers, and is generally considered a function of time. The best assurance of having an accurate receiver is periodic calibration. Yearly intervals are recommended at which time an authorized repair facility should recalibrate the receiver to the manufacturer's specifications.

d. Federal Aviation Regulations (FAR 91.25) provides for certain VOR equipment accuracy checks prior to flight under instrument flight rules. To comply with this requirement and to ensure satisfactory operation of the airborne system, the FAA has provided pilots with the following means of checking VOR receiver accuracy:

(1) VOT or a radiated test signal from an appropriately rated radio repair station.

(2) Certified airborne check points.

(3) Certified check points on the airport surface.

e. A radiated VOR test signal from an appropriately rated radio repair station serves the same purpose as an FAA VOR signal and the check is made in much the same manner as a VOT with the following differences:

(1) The frequency normally approved by the FCC is 108.0 MHz.

(2) Repair stations are not permitted to radiate the VOR test signal continuously; consequently, the owner or operator must make arrangements with the repair station to have the test signal transmitted. This service is not provided by all radio repair stations. The aircraft owner or operator must determine which repair station in his local area provides this service. A representative of the repair station must make an entry into the aircraft logbook or other permanent record certifying to the radial accuracy and the date of transmission. The owner, operator or representative of the repair station may accomplish the necessary checks in the aircraft and make a logbook entry stating the results. It is necessary to verify which test radial is being transmitted and whether you should get a "to" or "from" indication.

f. Airborne and ground check points consist of certified radials that should be received at specific points on the airport surface or over specific landmarks while airborne in the immediate vicinity of the airport.

(1) Should an error in excess of plus or minus 4 degrees be indicated through use of a ground check, or plus or minus 6 degrees using the airborne check, IFR flight shall not be attempted without first correcting the source of the error.

CAUTION: No correction other than the correction card figures supplied by the manufacturer should be applied in making these VOR receiver checks.

(2) Locations of airborne check points, ground check points and VOTs are published in the Airport/Facility Directory.

(3) If a dual system VOR (units independent of each other except for the antenna) is installed in the aircraft one system may be checked against the other. Turn both systems to the same VOR ground facility and note the indicated bearing to that station. The maximum permissible variations between the two indicated bearings is 4 degrees.

5. TACTICAL AIR NAVIGATION (TACAN)

a. For reasons peculiar to military or naval operations (unusual siting conditions, the pitching and rolling of a naval vessel, etc.) the civil VOR/DME system of air navigation was considered unsuitable for military or naval use. A new navigational system, TACAN, was therefore developed by the military and naval forces to more readily lend itself to military and naval requirements. As a result, the FAA has been in the process of integrating TACAN facilities with the civil VOR/DME program. Although the theoretical, or technical principles of operation of TACAN equipment are quite different from those of VOR/DME facilities, the end result, as far as the navigating pilot is concerned, is the same. These integrated facilities are called VORTAC's.

b. TACAN ground equipment consists of either a fixed or mobile transmitting unit. The airborne unit in conjunction with the ground unit reduces the transmitted signal to a visual presentation of both azimuth and distance information. TACAN is a pulse system and operates in the UHF band of frequencies. Its use requires TACAN airborne equipment and does not operate through conventional VOR equipment.

6. VHF OMNI-DIRECTIONAL RANGE/TACTICAL AIR NAVIGATION (VORTAC)

a. A VORTAC is a facility consisting of two components, VOR and TACAN, which provides three individual services: VOR azimuth, TACAN azimuth and TACAN distance (DME) at one site. Although consisting of more than one component, incorporating more than one operating frequency, and using more than one antenna system, a VORTAC is considered to be a unified navigational aid. Both components of a VORTAC are envisioned as operating simultaneously and providing the three services at all times.

b. Transmitted signals of VOR and TACAN are each identified by three-letter code transmission and are interlocked so that pilots using VOR azimuth with TACAN distance can be assured that both signals being received are definitely from the same ground station. The frequency channels of the VOR and the TACAN at each VORTAC facility are "paired" in accordance with a national plan to simplify airborne operation.

7. DISTANCE MEASURING EQUIPMENT (DME)

a. In the operation of DME, paired pulses at a specific spacing are sent out from the aircraft (this is the interrogation) and are received at the ground station. The ground station (transponder) then transmits paired pulses back to the aircraft at the same pulse spacing but on a different frequency. The time required for the round trip of this signal exchange is measured in the airborne DME unit and is translated into distance (Nautical Miles) from the aircraft to the ground station.

b. Operating on the line-of-sight principle, DME furnishes distance information with a very high degree of accuracy. Reliable signals may be received at distances up to 199 NM at line-of-sight altitude with an accuracy of better than 1/2 mile or 3 percent of the distance, whichever is greater. Distance information received from DME equipment is SLANT RANGE distance and not actual horizontal distance.

c. DME operates on frequencies in the UHF spectrum between 962 MHz and 1213 MHz. Aircraft equipped with TACAN equipment will receive distance information from a VORTAC automatically, while aircraft equipped with VOR must have a separate DME airborne unit.

d. VOR/DME, VORTAC, ILS/DME, and LOC/DME navigation facilities established by the FAA provide course and distance information from collocated components under a frequency pairing plan. Aircraft receiving equipment which provides for automatic DME selection assures reception of azimuth and distance information from a common source when designated VOR/DME, VORTAC, ILS/DME, and LOC/DME are selected.

e. Due to the limited number of available frequencies, assignment of paired frequencies is required for certain military noncollocated VOR and TACAN facilities which serve the same area but which may be separated by distances up to a few miles. The military is presently undergoing a program to collocate VOR and TACAN facilities or to assign nonpaired frequencies to those that cannot be collocated.

f. VOR/DME, VORTAC, ILS/DME, and LOC/DME facilities are identified by synchronized identifications which are transmitted on a time share basis. The VOR or localizer portion of the facility is identified by a coded tone modulated at 1020 Hz or a combination of code and voice. The TACAN or DME is identified by a coded tone modulated at 1350 Hz. The DME or TACAN coded identification is transmitted one time for each three or four times that the VOR or localizer coded identification is transmitted. When either the VOR or the DME is inoperative, it is important to recognize which identifier is retained for the operative facility. A single coded identification with a repetition interval of approximately 30 seconds indicates that the DME is operative.

g. Aircraft equipment which provides for automatic DME selection assures reception of azimuth and distance information from a common source when designated VOR/DME, VORTAC and ILS/DME navigation facilities are selected. Pilots are cautioned to disregard any distance displays from automatically selected DME equipment when VOR or ILS facilities, which do not have the DME feature installed, are being used for position determination.

8—9. RESERVED

10. NAVAID SERVICE VOLUMES

a. Most air navigation radio aids which provide positive course guidance have a designated standard service volume (SSV). The SSV defines the reception limits of unrestricted NAVAIDS which are usable for random/unpublished route navigation.

b. A NAVAID will be classified as restricted if it does not conform to flight inspection signal strength and course quality standards throughout the published SSV. However, the NAVAID should not be considered usable at altitudes below that which could be flown while operating under random route IFR conditions (FAR 91.119), even though these altitudes may lie within the designated SSV. Service volume restrictions are first published in the Notices to Airman (NOTAM) and then with the alphabetical listing of the NAVAID's in the Airport/Facility Directory.

c. Standard Service Volume limitations do not apply to published IFR routes or procedures.

d. VOR/DME/TACAN STANDARD SERVICE VOLUMES (SSV)

Standard service volumes (SSVs) are graphically shown in Figures 1-1 through 1-5. The SSV of a station is indicated by using the class designator as a prefix to the station type designation.

EXAMPLE:

TVOR, LDME, and HVORTAC.

Within 25 NM, the bottom of the T service volume is defined by the curve in Figure 1-4. Within 40 NM, the bottoms of the L and H service volumes are defined by the curve in Figure 1-5. *(See Table 1-1).*

e. NONDIRECTIONAL RADIO BEACON (NDB)

NDBs are classified according to their intended use. The ranges of NDB service volumes are shown in Table 1-2. The distances (radius) are the same at all altitudes. *(See Table 1-2)*

11. MARKER BEACON

a. Marker beacons serve to identify a particular location in space along an airway or on the approach to an instrument runway. This is done by means of a 75 MHz transmitter which transmits a directional signal to be received by aircraft flying overhead. These markers are generally used in conjunction with en route NAVAIDs and ILS as point designators.

b. There are three classes of en route marker beacons: Fan Marker (FM), Low Powered Fan Markers (LFM) and Z Markers. They transmit the letter "R" (dot dash dot) identification, or (if additional markers are in the same area) the letter "K," "P," "X," or "Z."

(1) Class FMs are used to provide a positive identification of positions at definite points along the airways. The transmitters have a power output of approximately 100 watts. Two types of antenna array are used with class FMs.

(a) The first type used, and generally referred to as the standard type, produces an elliptical shaped pattern, which, at an elevation of 1,000 feet above the station, is about 4 NM wide and 12 NM long. At 10,000 feet the pattern widens to about 12 NM wide and 35 NM long.

(b) The second array produces a dumbbell or boneshaped pattern, which, at the "handle", is about three miles wide at 1,000 feet. The boneshaped marker is preferred at approach control locations where "timed" approaches are used.

(2) The class LFM or low powered FMs have a rated power output of 5 watts. The antenna array produces a circular pattern which appears elongated at right angles to the airway due to the directional characteristics of the aircraft receiving antenna.

(3) The Station Location, or Z-Marker, was developed to meet the need for a positive position indicator for aircraft operating under instrument flight conditions to show the pilot when he was passing directly over a low frequency navigational aid. This marker consists of a 5 watt transmitter and a directional antenna array which is located on the range plot between the towers or the loop antennas.

NOTE—ILS marker beacon information is included in PARA. 12 - INSTRUMENT LANDING SYSTEMS (ILS).

12. INSTRUMENT LANDING SYSTEM (ILS)

a. GENERAL

(1) The ILS is designed to provide an approach path for exact alignment and descent of an aircraft on final approach to a runway.

(2) The ground equipment consists of two highly directional transmitting systems and, along the approach, three (or fewer) marker beacons. The directional transmitters are known as the localizer and glide slope transmitters.

(3) The system may be divided functionally into three parts:

(a) **Guidance information** —localizer, glide slope

(b) **Range information** —marker beacon, DME

(c) **Visual information** —approach lights, touchdown and centerline lights, runway lights

(4) Compass locators located at the Outer Marker (OM) or Middle Marker (MM) may be substituted for marker beacons. DME, when specified in the procedure, may be substituted for the OM.

(5) Where a complete ILS system is installed on each end of a runway; (i.e. the approach end of Runway 4 and the approach end of Runway 22) the ILS systems are not in service simultaneously.

b. LOCALIZER

(1) The localizer transmitter operates on one of 40 ILS channels within the frequency range of 108.10 to 111.95 MHz. Signals provide the pilot with course guidance to the runway centerline.

(2) The approach course of the localizer is called the front course and is used with other functional parts, e.g., glide slope, marker beacons, etc. The localizer signal is transmitted at the far end of the runway. It is adjusted for a course width of (full scale fly-left to a full scale fly-right) of 700 feet at the runway threshold.

(3) The course line along the extended centerline of a runway, in the opposite direction to the front course is called the back course.

CAUTION: Unless the aircraft's ILS equipment includes reverse sensing capability, when flying inbound on the back course it is necessary to steer the aircraft in the direction opposite the needle deflection when making corrections from off-course to on-course. This "flying away from the needle" is also required when flying outbound on the front course of the localizer. DO NOT USE BACK COURSE SIGNALS for approach unless a BACK COURSE APPROACH PROCEDURE is published for that particular runway and the approach is authorized by ATC.

(4) Identification is in International Morse Code and consists of a three-letter identifier preceded by the letter I (..) transmitted on the localizer frequency.

EXAMPLE:

I-DIA

(5) The localizer provides course guidance throughout the descent path to the runway threshold from a distance of 18 NM from the antenna between an altitude of 1,000 feet above the highest terrain along the course line and 4,500 feet above the elevation of the antenna site. Proper off-course indications are provided throughout the following angular areas of the operational service volume:

(a) To 10 degrees either side of the course along a radius of 18 NM from the antenna, and

(b) From 10 to 35 degrees either side of the course along a radius of 10 NM. *(See Figure 1-6)*

(6) Unreliable signals may be received outside these areas.

c. LOCALIZER—TYPE DIRECTIONAL AID

(1) The Localizer-type Directional Aid (LDA) is of comparable use and accuracy to a localizer but is not part of a complete ILS. The LDA course usually provides a more precise approach course than the similar Simplified Directional Facility (SDF) installation, which may have a course width of 6 or 12 degrees. The LDA is not aligned with the runway. Straight-in minimums may be published where alignment does not exceed 30 degrees between the course and runway. Circling minimums only are published where this alignment exceeds 30 degrees.

d. GLIDE SLOPE/GLIDE PATH

(1) The UHF glide slope transmitter, operating on one of the 40 ILS channels within the frequency range 329.15 MHz, to 335.00 MHz radiates its signals in the direction of the localizer front course. The term "glide path" means that portion of the glide slope that intersects the localizer.

CAUTION: False glide slope signals may exist in the area of the localizer back course approach which can cause the glide slope flag alarm to disappear and present unreliable glide slope information. Disregard all glide slope signal indications when making a localizer back course approach unless a glide slope is specified on the approach and landing chart.

(2) The glide slope transmitter is located between 750 feet and 1,250 feet from the approach end of the runway (down the runway) and offset 250 to 650 feet from the runway centerline. It transmits a glide path beam 1.4 degrees wide. The signal provides descent information for navigation down to the lowest authorized decision height (DH) specified in the approved ILS approach procedure. The glidepath may not be suitable for navigation below the lowest authorized DH and any reference to glidepath indications below that height must be supplemented by visual reference to the runway environment. Glidepaths with no published DH are usable to runway threshold.

(3) The glide path projection angle is normally adjusted to 3 degrees above horizontal so that it intersects the MM at about 200 feet and the OM at about 1,400 feet above the runway elevation. The glide slope is normally usable to the distance of 10 NM. However, at some locations, the glide slope has been certified for an extended service volume which exceeds 10 NM.

(4) Pilots must be alert when approaching the glidepath interception. False courses and reverse sensing will occur at angles considerably greater than the published path.

(5) Make every effort to remain on the indicated glide path (reference: FAR 91.87(d)(2)). Exercise caution: avoid flying below the glide path to assure obstacle/terrain clearance is maintained.

(6) The published glide slope threshold crossing height (TCH) *DOES NOT* represent the height of the actual glide path on course indication above the runway threshold. It is used as a reference for planning purposes which represents the height above the runway threshold that an aircraft's glide slope antenna should be, if that aircraft remains on a trajectory formed by the four-mile-to-middle marker glidepath segment.

(7) Pilots must be aware of the vertical height between the aircraft's glide slope antenna and the main gear in the landing configuration and, at the DH, plan to adjust the descent angle accordingly if the published TCH indicates the wheel crossing height over the runway threshold may not be satisfactory. Tests indicate a comfortable wheel crossing height is approximately 20 to 30 feet, depending on the type of aircraft.

e. DISTANCE MEASURING EQUIPMENT (DME)

(1) When installed with the ILS and specified in the approach procedure, DME may be used:

(a) In lieu of the OM.

(b) As a back course (BC) final approach fix (FAF).

(c) To establish other fixes on the localizer course.

(2) In some cases, DME from a separate facility may be used within Terminal Instrument Procedures (TERPS) limitations:

(a) To provide ARC initial approach segments.

(b) As a FAF for BC approaches.

(c) As a substitute for the OM.

f. MARKER BEACON

(1) ILS marker beacons have a rated power output of 3 watts or less and an antenna)array designed to produce a elliptical pattern with dimensions, at 1,000 feet above the antenna, of approximately 2,400 feet in width and 4,200 feet in length. Airborne marker beacon receivers with a selective sensitivity feature should always be operated in the "low" sensitivity position for proper reception of ILS marker beacons.

(2) Ordinarily, there are two marker beacons associated with an ILS, the OM and MM. Locations with a Category II and III ILS also have an inner marker (IM). When an aircraft passes over a marker, the pilot will receive the following indications:

MARKER	CODE	LIGHT
OM	− − −	BLUE
MM	○ − ○ −	AMBER
IM	○○○○	WHITE
BC	○○ ○○	WHITE

(a) The OM normally indicates a position at which an aircraft at the appropriate altitude on the localizer course will intercept the ILS glide path.

(b) The MM indicates a position approximately 3,500 feet from the landing threshold. This is also the position where an aircraft on the glide path will be at an altitude of approximately 200 feet above the elevation of the touchdown zone.

(c) The inner marker (IM) will indicate a point at which an aircraft is at a designated decision height (DH) on the glide path between the MM and landing threshold.

(3) A back course marker normally indicates the ILS back course final approach fix where approach descent is commenced.

g. COMPASS LOCATOR

(1) Compass locator transmitters are often situated at the MM and OM sites. The transmitters have a power of less than 25 watts, a range of at least 15 miles and operate between 190 and 535 kHz. At some locations, higher powered radio beacons, up to 400 watts, are used as OM compass locators. These generally carry Transcribed Weather Broadcast (TWEB) information.

(2) Compass locators transmit two letter identification groups. The outer locator transmits the first two letters of the localizer identification group, and the middle locator transmits the last two letters of the localizer identification group.

h. ILS FREQUENCY

(1) See Table 1-3 for frequency pairs allocated for ILS.

i. ILS MINIMUMS

(1) The lowest authorized ILS minimums, with all required ground and airborne systems components operative, are

(a) Category I - Decision Height (DH) 200 feet and Runway Visual Range (RVR) 2,400 feet (with touchdown zone and centerline lighting, RVR 1800 Category A, B, C; RVR 2000 Category D).

(b) Category II - DH 100 feet and RVR 1,200 feet.

(c) Category IIIA - RVR 700 feet.

NOTE—Special authorization and equipment are required for Category II and IIIA.

j. INOPERATIVE ILS COMPONENTS

(1) Inoperative localizer: When the localizer fails, an ILS approach is not authorized.

(2) Inoperative glide slope: When the glide slope fails, the ILS reverts to a nonprecision localizer approach.

NOTE—Refer to the Inoperative Component Table in the U.S. Government IAPs publications, Supplementary Information Section, for adjustments to minimums due to inoperative airborne or ground system equipment.

k. ILS COURSE DISTORTION

(1) All pilots should be aware that disturbances to ILS localizer and glide slope courses may occur when surface vehicles or aircraft are operated near the localizer or glide slope antennas. Most ILS installations are subject to signal interference by either surface vehicles, aircraft or both. ILS CRITICAL AREAS are established near each localizer and glide slope antenna.

(2) ATC issues control instructions to avoid interfering operations within ILS critical areas at controlled airports during the hours the Airport Traffic Control Tower (ATCT) is in operations as follows:

(a) Weather Conditions - Less than ceiling 800 feet and/or visibility 2 miles.

(I) LOCALIZER CRITICAL AREA - Except for aircraft that land, exit a runway, depart or miss approach, vehicles and aircraft are not authorized in or over the critical area when an arriving aircraft is between the ILS final approach fix and the airport. Additionally, when the ceiling is less than 200 feet and/or the visibility is RVR 2,000 or less, vehicle and aircraft operations in or over the area are not authorized when an arriving aircraft is inside the ILS MM.

(II) GLIDE SLOPE CRITICAL AREA - Vehicles and aircraft are not authorized in the area when an arriving aircraft is between the ILS final approach fix and the airport unless the aircraft has reported the airport in sight and is circling or side stepping to land on a runway other than the ILS runway.

(b) Weather Conditions - At or above ceiling 800 feet and/or visibility 2 miles.

(I) No critical area protective action is provided under these conditions

(II) If an aircraft advises the TOWER that an AUTOLAND or COUPLED approach will be conducted, an advisory will be promptly issued if a vehicle or aircraft will be in or over a critical area when the arriving aircraft is inside the ILS MM.

EXAMPLE:

GLIDE SLOPE SIGNAL NOT PROTECTED.

(3) Aircraft holding below 5000 feet between the outer marker and the airport may cause localizer signal variations for aircraft conducting the ILS Approach. Accordingly, such holding is not authorized when weather or visibility conditions are less than ceiling 800 feet and/or visibility 2 miles.

(4) Pilots are cautioned that vehicular traffic not subject to ATC may cause momentary deviation to ILS course or glide slope signals. Also, critical areas are not protected at uncontrolled airports or at airports with an operating control tower when weather or visibility conditions are above those requiring protective measures. Aircraft conducting coupled or autoland operations should be especially alert in monitoring automatic flight control systems. (See Figure 1-7.)

13. SIMPLIFIED DIRECTIONAL FACILITY (SDF)

a. The SDF provides a final approach course similar to that of the ILS localizer. It does not provide glide slope information. A clear understanding of the ILS localizer and the additional factors listed below completely describe the operational characteristics and use of the SDF.

b. The SDF transmits signals within the range of 108.10 to 111.95 MHz.

c. The approach techniques and procedures used in an SDF instrument approach are essentially the same as those employed in executing a standard localizer approach except the SDF course may not be aligned with the runway and the course may be wider, resulting in less precision.

d. Usable off-course indications are limited to 35 degrees either side of the course centerline. Instrument indications received beyond 35 degrees should be disregarded.

e. The SDF antenna may be offset from the runway centerline. Because of this, the angle of convergence between the final approach course and the runway bearing should be determined by reference to the instrument approach procedure chart. This angle is generally not more than 3 degrees. However, it should be noted that inasmuch as the approach course originates at the antenna site, an approach which is continued beyond the runway threshold will lead the aircraft to the SDF offset position rather than along the runway centerline.

f. The SDF signal is fixed at either 6 degrees or 12 degrees as necessary to provide maximum flyability and optimum course quality.

g. Identification consists of a three-letter identifier transmitted in Morse Code on the SDF frequency. The appropriate instrument approach chart will indicate the identifier used at a particular airport.

14. MICROWAVE LANDING SYSTEM (MLS)

a. GENERAL

(1) The MLS provides precision navigation guidance for exact alignment and descent of aircraft on approach to a runway. It provides azimuth, elevation, and distance.

(2) Both lateral and vertical guidance may be displayed on conventional course deviation indicators or incorporated into multipurpose cockpit displays. Range information can be displayed by conventional DME indicators and also incorporated into multipurpose displays.

(3) The MLS initially supplements and will eventually replace ILS as the standard landing system in the United States for civil, military and international civil aviation. The transition plan assures duplicate ILS and MLS facilities where needed to protect current users of ILS. At international airports ILS service is protected to the year 1995.

(4) The system may be divided into five functions:

(a) Approach azimuth.

(b) Back azimuth.

(c) Approach elevation.

(d) Range.

(e) Data communications.

(5) The *standard configuration* of MLS ground equipment includes:

(a) An azimuth station to perform functions (a) and (e) above. In addition to providing azimuth navigation guidance, the station transmits basic data which consists of information associated directly with the operation of the landing system, as well as advisory data on the performance of the ground equipment.

(b) An elevation station to perform function (c).

(c) Precision Distance Measuring Equipment (DME/P) to perform function (d). The DME/P provides continuous range information that is compatible with standard navigation DME but has improved accuracy and additional channel capabilities.

(6) MLS Expansion Capabilities — The standard configuration can be expanded by adding one or more of the following functions or characteristics.

(a) Back azimuth — Provides lateral guidance for missed approach and departure navigation.

(b) Auxiliary data transmissions — Provides *additional* data, including refined airborne positioning, meteorological information, runway status, and other supplementary information.

(c) Larger proportional guidance.

(7) MLS identification is a four-letter designation starting with the letter M. It is transmitted in International Morse Code at least six times per minute by the approach azimuth (and back azimuth) ground equipment.

b. APPROACH AZIMUTH GUIDANCE

(1) The azimuth station transmits MLS angle and data on one of 200 channels within the frequency range of 5031 to 5091 MHz. *(See Table 1-4)* for MLS angle and data channeling, and *(See Table 1-5.)* for the DME.

(2) The equipment is normally located about 1,000 feet beyond the stop end of the runway, but there is considerable flexibility in selecting sites. For example, for heliport operations the azimuth transmitter can be collocated with the elevation transmitter.

(3) The azimuth coverage *(See Figure 1-8.)* extends:

(a) Laterally, at least 40 degrees on either side of the runway.

(b) In elevation, up to an angle of 15 degrees — and to at least 20,000 feet.

(c) In range, to at least 20 NM.

c. BACK AZIMUTH GUIDANCE.

(1) The back azimuth transmitter is essentially the same as the approach azimuth transmitter. However, the equipment transmits at a somewhat lower data rate because the guidance accuracy requirements are not as stringent as for the landing approach. The equipment operates on the same frequency as the approach azimuth but at a different time in the transmission sequence. *(See Figure 1-8.)*

(2) The equipment is normally located about 1,000 feet in front of the approach end of the runway. On runways that have MLS service on both ends (e.g., Runway 9 and 27), the azimuth equipment can be switched in their operation from the approach azimuth to the back azimuth and vice versa, and thereby reduce the amount of equipment required.

(3) The back azimuth provides coverage as follows:

(a) Laterally, at least 40 degrees on either side of the runway centerline.

(b) In elevation, up to an angle of 15 degrees.

(c) In range, to at least 7 NM from the runway stop end.

NOTE—The actual coverage is normally the same as for the approach azimuth.

d. ELEVATION GUIDANCE

(1) The elevation station transmits signals on the same frequency as the azimuth station. A single frequency is time-shared between angle and data functions.

(2) The elevation transmitter is normally located about 400 feet from the side of the runway between runway threshold and the touchdown zone.

(3) Elevation coverage is provided in the same airspace as the azimuth guidance signals:

(a) In elevation, to at least+15 degrees.

(b) Laterally, 40 degrees on either side of the runway centerline.

(c) In range, to at least 20 NM.

e. RANGE GUIDANCE

(1) The MLS Precision Distance Measuring Equipment (DME/P) functions the same as the navigation DME described in PARA. 7, but there are some technical differences. The beacon transponder operates in the frequency band 962 to 1105 MHz and responds to an aircraft interrogator. The MLS DME/P accuracy is improved to be consistent with the accuracy provided by the MLS azimuth and elevation stations.

(2) A DME/P channel is paired with the azimuth and elevation channel. A complete listing of the 200 paired channels of the DME/P with the angle functions is contained in FAA Standard 022 (MLS Interoperability and Performance Requirements).

(3) The DME/P is an integral part of the MLS and is installed at all MLS facilities unless a waiver is obtained. This occurs infrequently — and only at outlying, low density airports where marker beacons or compass locators are already in place.

f. DATA COMMUNICATIONS

(1) The data transmission can include both basic and auxiliary data words. All MLS facilities transmit basic data. In the future facilities at some airports, including most high density airports, will also transmit auxiliary data.

(2) Coverage limits — MLS data are transmitted throughout the azimuth (and back azimuth when provided) coverage sectors.

(3) Basic data content — Representative data include:

(a) Station identification.

(b) Exact locations of azimuth, elevation and DME/P stations (for MLS receiver processing functions).

(c) Ground equipment performance level.

(d) DME/P channel and status.

(4) Auxiliary data content — Representative data include:

(a) 3-D locations of MLS equipment.

(b) Waypoint coordinates.

(c) Runway conditions.

(d) Weather (e.g., RVR, ceiling, altimeter setting, wind, wake vortex, wind shear).

g. Operational flexibility. The MLS has the capability to fulfill a variety of needs in the transition, approach, landing, missed approach and departure phases of flight. For example: Curved and segmented approaches; selectable glide path angles; accurate 3-D positioning of the aircraft in space; and the establishment of boundaries to ensure clearance from obstructions in the terminal area. While many of these capabilities are available to any MLS-equipped aircraft, the more sophisticated capabilities (such as curved and segmented approaches) are dependent upon the particular capabilities of the airborne equipment.

h. SUMMARY

(1) Accuracy. The MLS provides precision three-dimensional navigation guidance accurate enough for all approach and landing maneuvers.

(2) Coverage. Accuracy is consistent throughout the coverage volumes. (See Figure 1-8.)

(3) Environment. The system has low susceptibility to interference from weather conditions and airport ground traffic.

(4) Channels. MLS has 200 channels — enough for any foreseeable need.

(5) Data. The MLS transmits ground-air data messages associated with the systems operation.

(6) Range information. Continuous range information is provided with an accuracy of about 100 feet.

15. INTERIM STANDARD MICROWAVE LANDING SYSTEM (ISMLS)

a. The ISMLS is designed to provide approach information similar to the ILS for an aircraft on final approach to a runway. The system provides both lateral and vertical guidance which is displayed on a conventional course deviation indicator or approach horizon. Operational performance and coverage areas are similar to the ILS system.

b. ISMLS operates in the C-band microwave frequency range (about 5000 MHz). ISMLS signals will not be received by unmodified VHF/UHF ILS receivers. Aircraft with ISMLS must be equipped with a C-band receiving antenna in addition to other special equipment mentioned below. The C-band antenna limits reception of the signal to an angle of about 50 degrees from the inbound course. An aircraft so equipped will not receive the ISMLS signal until flying a magnetic heading within 50 degrees either side of the inbound course. Because of this, ISMLS procedures are designed to restrict the use of the ISMLS signal until the aircraft is in position for the final approach. Transition to the ISMLS, holding and procedure turns at the ISMLS facility must be predicated on other navigation aids such as NDB, VOR, etc. Once established on the approach course inbound, the system can be flown the same as an ILS. No back course is provided.

c. The ISMLS consists of the following basic components:

(1) C-Band (5000 MHz-5030 MHz) localizer.

(2) C-Band (5220 MHz-5250 MHz) glide path.

(3) VHF marker beacons (75 MHz).

(4) A VHF/UHF ILS receiver modified to receive ISMLS signals.

(5) C-Band antenna.

(6) Converter unit.

(7) A Microwave/ILS Mode Control.

d. Identification consists of a three letter Morse Code identifier preceded by the Morse Code for "M" (- -) (e.g., M—STP). The "M" distinguishes this system from ILS which is preceded by the Morse Code for "I" (..) (e.g., I-STP).

e. Approaches published in conjunction with the ISMLS are identified as "MLS Rwy—(Interim)." The frequency displayed on the ISMLS approach chart is a VHF frequency. ISMLS frequencies are tuned by setting the receiver to the listed VHF frequencies. When the ISMLS mode is selected, receivers modified to accept ISMLS signals receive a paired C-band frequency that is processed by the receiver.

CAUTION: Pilots should not attempt to fly ISMLS procedures unless the aircraft is so equipped.

16. NAVAID IDENTIFIER REMOVAL DURING MAINTENANCE

During periods of routine or emergency maintenance, coded identification (or code and voice, where applicable) is removed from certain FAA NAVAIDs. Removal of identification serves as a warning to pilots that the facility is officially off the air for tune-up or repair and may be unreliable even though intermittent or constant signals are received.

NOTE-During periods of maintenance VHF ranges may radiate a T-E-S-T code (— • ••• —).

17. NAVAIDS WITH VOICE

a. Voice equipped en route radio navigational aids are under the operational control of either an FAA FSS or an approach control facility. Most NAVAIDs are remotely operated.

b. Unless otherwise noted on the chart, all radio navigation aids operate continuously except during interruptions for voice transmissions on the same frequencies where simultaneous transmission is not available, and during shutdowns for maintenance. Hours of operation of facilities not operating continuously are annotated on charts and in the Airport/Facility Directory.

18. RESERVED

19. USER REPORTS ON NAVAID PERFORMANCE

a. Users of the National Airspace System (NAS) can render valuable assistance in the early correction of NAVAID malfunctions by reporting their observations of undesirable NAVAID performance. Although NAVAID's are monitored by electronic detectors, adverse effects of electronic interference, new obstructions or changes in terrain near the NAVAID can exist without detection by the ground monitors. Some of the characteristics of malfunction or deteriorating performance which should be reported are: erratic course or bearing indications; intermittent, or full, flag alarm; garbled, missing or obviously improper coded identification; poor quality communications reception; or, in the case of frequency interference, an audible hum or tone accompanying radio communications or NAVAID identification.

b. Reporters should identify the NAVAID, location of the aircraft, time of the observation, type of aircraft and describe the condition observed; the type of receivers in use is also useful information. Reports can be made in any of the following ways:

(1) Immediate report by direct radio communication to the controlling Air Route Traffic Control Center (ARTCC), Control Tower, or FSS. This method provides the quickest result.

(2) By telephone to the nearest FAA facility.

(3) By FAA Form 8000-7, Safety Improvement Report, a postage-paid card designed for this purpose. These cards may be obtained at FAA FSSs, General Aviation District Offices, Flight Standards District Offices, and General Aviation Fixed Base Operations.

c. In aircraft that have more than one receiver, there are many combinations of possible interference between units. This can cause either erroneous navigation indications or, complete or partial blanking out of the communications. Pilots should be familiar enough with the radio installation of the particular airplanes they fly to recognize this type of interference.

20. LORAN

a. LORAN-A service has been terminated in the U.S. coastal confluence region.

b. LORAN-C was developed to provide the Department of Defense with a radio navigation capability having longer range and much greater accuracy than its predecessor, LORAN-A. It was subsequently selected as the U.S. Government provided radio navigation system for civil marine use in the U.S. coastal areas.

c. Operation

LORAN-C is a pulsed, hyperbolic system, operating in the 90-110 kHz frequency band. The system is based upon measurement of the difference in time of arrival of pulses of radio-frequency energy radiated by a group, or chain of transmitters which are separated by hundreds of miles. Within a chain, one station is designated as the Master station (M), and the other stations are designated as Secondary stations, Whiskey (W), X-ray (X), Yankee (Y), and Zulu (Z). Signals transmitted from the Secondary stations are synchronized with those from the Master station. The measurement of a time-difference (TD) is made by a receiver that achieves accuracy by comparing a zero crossing of a specified radio-frequency cycle within the pulses received from the Master and Secondary stations of a chain. Only groundwave signals are used for air navigation in the National Airspace System. Within the groundwave range, LORAN-C will provide the user, who uses an adequate receiver, with predictable accuracy of 0.25 nautical miles (2 drms) or better. All accuracy is dependent on the user's location within the signal coverage area of the chain of stations.

d. Signal coverage

Expansion of the LORAN-C system to meet the requirement for the U.S. coastal waters of the conterminous 48 states and southern Alaska was completed in late 1979. Stations have been built to provide service to the U.S. east and west coasts, the Gulf of Mexico, the Gulf of Alaska and Aleutians, and the Great Lakes. The coastal transmitters also provide inland coverage over about two-thirds of the area of the 48 states and over the southwestern portion of Alaska. Missing, from an aviation view point, is signal coverage over the mid-continent area.

e. Aviation uses

LORAN-C has been approved as an en route IFR navigation aid under provisions of Advisory Circular 20-121, "Airworthiness Approval of Airborne LORAN-C Systems for Use in the U.S. National Airspace System," August 23, 1984. The first LORAN-C guided nonprecision approach was made at Bedford, Massachusetts, on November 4, 1985, as part of an early implementation project established by the FAA in close cooperation with the National Association of State Aviation Officials. Until operational signal monitor receivers, similar in function to those used in the limited implementation project, are installed in existing coverage areas, the number of approved nonprecision approach procedures will be limited.

f. Planned expansion

Current plans are to procure and install signal monitors in existing signal coverage areas with completion expected by mid-1988. The monitors will serve two functions: (1) they will provide immediate advisories on signal status to air traffic for use in granting approach clearances, and (2) they will be the source of calibration values that will be published on approach charts. The calibration values will remove most of the seasonal error that could cause LORAN-C accuracy to be worse than approach accuracy requirements. The mid-continent area will be provided with signal coverage after the planned installation of additional transmitters; completion of the installation is expected in 1989. In addition to the transmitters, signal monitors will be installed in the mid-continent to support nonprecision approaches.

g. Notices to Airmen (NOTAMs) are issued for LORAN-C chain or station outages. Domestic NOTAM (D)'s are issued under the identifier "LRN." International NOTAMs are issued under the KNMH series. Pilots may obtain these NOTAMs from FSS briefers upon request.

h. LORAN-C status information

Prerecorded telephone answering service messages pertaining to LORAN-C are available in *Tables 1-6 and 1-7*.

21. OMEGA AND OMEGA/VLF NAVIGATION SYSTEMS

a. OMEGA

(1) OMEGA is a network of eight transmitting stations located throughout the world to provide worldwide signal coverage. These stations transmit in the Very Low Frequency (VLF) band. Because of the low frequency, the signals are receivable to ranges of thousands of miles. The stations are located in Norway, Liberia, Hawaii, North Dakota (USA), La Reunion, Argentina, Australia, and Japan.

(2) Presently each station transmits on four basic navigational frequencies: 10.2 kHz, 11.05 kHz, 11.3 kHz, and 13.6 kHz, in sequenced format. This time sequenced format prevents interstation signal interference. With eight stations and a silent .2-second interval between each transmission, the entire cycle repeats every 10 seconds.

(3) In addition to the four basic navigational frequencies, each station transmits a unique navigation frequency. An OMEGA station is said to be operating in full format when the station transmits on the basic frequencies plus the unique frequency. Unique frequencies are presently assigned as follows:

STATION	LOCATION	FREQUENCY
Station A	Norway	12.1 kHz
Station B	Liberia	12.0 kHz
Station C	Hawaii	11.8 kHz
Station D	North Dakota	13.1 kHz
Station E	La Reunion	12.3 kHz
Station F	Argentina	12.9 kHz
Station G	Australia	13.0 kHz
Station H	Japan	12.8 kHz

b. VLF

(1) The U.S. Navy operates a communications system in the VLF band. The stations are located worldwide and transmit at powers of 500-1000 kW. Some airborne OMEGA receivers have the capability to receive and process these VLF signals for navigation in addition to OMEGA signals. The VLF stations generally used for navigation are located in Australia, Japan, England, Hawaii and in the U.S. in Maine, Washington and Maryland.

(2) Although the Navy does not object to the use of VLF communications signals for navigation, the system is not dedicated to navigation. Signal format, transmission, and other parameters of the VLF system are subject to change at the Navy's discretion. The VLF communications stations are individually shut down for scheduled maintenance for a few hours each week. Regular NOTAM service regarding the VLF system or station status is not available. However, the Naval Observatory provides a taped message concerning phase differences, phase values, and shutdown information for both the VLF communications network and the OMEGA system (phone 202-653-1757).

c. Operational Use of OMEGA and OMEGA/VLF

(1) The OMEGA navigation network is capable of providing consistent fixing information to an accuracy of plus or minus 2 NM depending upon the level of sophistication of the receiver/process-

ing system. OMEGA signals are affected by propagation variables which may degrade fix accuracy. These variables include daily variation of phase velocity, polar cap absorption, and sudden solar activity. Daily compensation for variation within the receiver/processor, or occasional excessive solar activity and its effect on OMEGA, cannot be accurately forecast or anticipated. If an unusual amount of solar activity disturbs the OMEGA signal enlargement paths to any extent, the U.S. Coast Guard advises the FAA and an appropriate NOTAM is sent.

(2) At 16 minutes past each hour, WWV (Fort Collins, Colorado) broadcasts a message concerning the status of each OMEGA station, signal irregularities, and other information concerning OMEGA. At 47 minutes past each hour, WWVH (Hawaii) broadcasts similar information. The U.S. Coast Guard provides a taped OMEGA status report (703-866-3801). NOTAMS concerning OMEGA are available through any FSS. OMEGA NOTAMs should be requested by OMEGA station name.

(3) The FAA has recognized OMEGA and OMEGA/VLF systems as an additional means of en route IFR navigation in the conterminous United States and Alaska when approved in accordance with FAA guidance information. Use of OMEGA or OMEGA/VLF requires that all navigation equipment otherwise required by the Federal Aviation Regulations be installed and operating. When flying RNAV routes, VOR and DME equipment is required.

(4) The FAA recognizes the use of the Naval VLF communications system as a supplement to OMEGA, but not the sole means of navigation.

22. VHF DIRECTION FINDER

a. The VHF Direction Finder (VHF/DF) is one of the common systems that helps pilots without their being aware of its operation. It is a ground based radio receiver used by the operator of the ground station. FAA facilities that provide VHF/DF service are identified in the Airport/Facility Directory.

b. The equipment consists of a directional antenna system and a VHF radio receiver.

c. The VHF/DF receiver display indicates the magnetic direction of the aircraft from the ground station each time the aircraft transmits.

d. DF equipment is of particular value in locating lost aircraft and in helping to identify aircraft on radar. (See PARA. 452 - DIRECTION FINDING INSTRUMENT APPROACH PROCEDURE.)

23. INERTIAL NAVIGATION SYSTEM (INS)

A totally self-contained navigation system, comprised of gyros, accelerometers, and a navigation computer, which provides aircraft position and navigation information in response to signals resulting from inertial effects on system components, and does not require information from external references. INS is aligned with accurate position information prior to departure, and thereafter calculates its position as it progresses to the destination. By programming a series of waypoints, the system will navigate along a predetermined track. New waypoints can be inserted at any time if a revised routing is desired. INS accuracy is very high initially following alignment, and decays with time at the rate of about 1-2 nautical miles per hour. Position update alignment can be accomplished inflight using ground based references, and many INS systems now have sophisticated automatic update using dual DME and or VOR inputs. INS may be approved as the sole means of navigation or may be used in combination with other systems.

24. DOPPLER RADAR

A semiautomatic self-contained dead reckoning navigation system (radar sensor plus computer) which is not continuously dependent on information derived from ground based or external aids. The system employs radar signals to detect and measure ground speed and drift angle, using the aircraft compass system as its directional reference. Doppler is less accurate than INS or OMEGA however, and the use of an external reference is required for periodic updates if acceptable position accuracy is to be achieved on long range flights.

25. FLIGHT MANAGEMENT SYSTEM (FMS)

A computer system that uses a large data base to allow routes to be preprogrammed and fed into the system by means of a data loader. The system is constantly updated with respect to position accuracy by reference to conventional navigation aids. The sophisticated program and its associated data base insures that the most appropriate aids are automatically selected during the information update cycle.

26. GLOBAL POSITIONING SYSTEM (GPS)

A space-base radio positioning, navigation, and time-transfer system being developed by Department of Defense. When fully deployed, the system is intended to provide highly accurate position and velocity information, and precise time, on a continuous global basis, to an unlimited number of properly equipped users. The system will be unaffected by weather, and will provide a worldwide common grid reference system. The GPS concept is predicated upon accurate and continuous knowledge of the spatial position of each satellite in the system with respect to time and distance from a transmitting satellite to the user. The GPS receiver automatically selects appropriate signals from the satellites in view and translates these into a three-dimensional position, velocity, and time. Predictable system accuracy for civil users is projected to be 100 meters horizontally. Performance standards and certification criteria have not yet been established.

27—29. RESERVED

Section 2. RADAR SERVICES AND PROCEDURES

30. RADAR

a. Capabilities

(1) Radar is a method whereby radio waves are transmitted into the air and are then received when they have been reflected by an object in the path of the beam. *Range* is determined by measuring the time it takes (at the speed of light) for the radio wave to go out to the object and then return to the receiving antenna. The *direction* of a detected object from a radar site is determined by the position of the rotating antenna when the reflected portion of the radio wave is received.

(2) More reliable maintenance and improved equipment have reduced radar system failures to a negligible factor. Most facilities actually have some components duplicated-one operating and another which immediately takes over when a malfunction occurs to the primary component.

b. Limitations

(1) It is very important for the aviation community to recognize the fact that there are limitations to radar service and that ATC controllers may not always be able to issue traffic advisories concerning aircraft which are not under ATC control and cannot be seen on radar. *(See Figure 1-9.)*

(a) The characteristics of radio waves are such that they normally travel in a continuous straight line unless they are:

1. "Bent" by abnormal atmospheric phenomena such as temperature inversions;

2. Reflected or attenuated by dense objects such as heavy clouds, precipitation, ground obstacles, mountains, etc.; or

3. Screened by high terrain features.

(b) The bending of radar pulses, often called anomalous propagation or ducting, may cause many extraneous blips to appear on the radar operator's display if the beam has been bent toward the ground or may decrease the detection range if the wave is bent upward. It is difficult to solve the effects of anomalous propagation, but using beacon radar and electronically eliminating stationary and slow moving targets by a method called moving target indicator (MTI) usually negate the problem.

(c) Radar energy that strikes dense objects will be reflected and displayed on the operator's scope thereby blocking out aircraft at the same range and greatly weakening or completely eliminating the display of targets at a greater range. Again, radar beacon and MTI are very effectively used to combat ground clutter and weather phenomena, and a method of circularly polarizing the radar beam will eliminate some weather returns. A negative characteristic of MTI is that an aircraft flying a speed that coincides with the canceling signal of the MTI (tangential or "blind" speed) may not be displayed to the radar controller.

(d) Relatively low altitude aircraft will not be seen if they are screened by mountains or are below the radar beam due to earth curvature. The only solution to screening is the installation of strategically placed multiple radars which has been done in some areas.

(e) There are several other factors which affect radar control. The amount of reflective surface of an aircraft will determine the size of the radar return. Therefore, a small light airplane or a sleek jet fighter will be more difficult to see on radar than a large commercial jet or military bomber. Here again, the use of radar beacon is invaluable if the aircraft is equipped with an airborne transponder. All ARTCC radars in the conterminous U.S. and many airport surveillance radars have the capability to interrogate MODE C and display altitude information to the controller from appropriately equipped aircraft. However, there are a number of airport surveillance radars that are still two dimensional (range and azimuth) only and altitude information must be obtained from the pilot.

(f) At some locations within the ATC en route environment, secondary-radar-only (no primary radar) gap filler radar systems are used to give lower altitude radar coverage between two larger radar systems, each of which provides both primary and secondary radar coverage. In those geographical areas served by secondary-radar only, aircraft without transponders cannot be provided with radar service. Additionally, transponder equipped aircraft cannot be provided with radar advisories concerning primary targets and weather. (See RADAR/RADIO DETECTION AND RANGING in the Pilot/Controller Glossary.)

(g) The controllers' ability to advise a pilot flying on instruments or in visual conditions of his proximity to another aircraft will be limited if the unknown aircraft is not observed on radar, if no flight plan information is available, or if the volume of traffic and workload prevent his issuing traffic information. The controller's first priority is given to establishing vertical, lateral, or longitudinal separation between aircraft flying IFR under the control of ATC.

c. FAA radar units operate continuously at the locations shown in the Airport/Facility Directory, and their services are available to all pilots, both civil and military. Contact the associated FAA control tower or ARTCC on any frequency guarded for initial instructions, or in an emergency, any FAA facility for information on the nearest radar service.

31. AIR TRAFFIC CONTROL RADAR BEACON SYSTEM (ATCRBS)

a. The ATCRBS, sometimes referred to as secondary surveillance radar, consists of three main components:

(1) **Interrogator.** Primary radar relies on a signal being transmitted from the radar antenna site and for this signal to be reflected or "bounced back" from an object (such as an aircraft). This reflected signal is then displayed as a "target" on the controller's radarscope. In the ATCRBS, the *Interrogator*, a ground based radar beacon transmitter-receiver, scans in synchronism with the primary radar and transmits discrete radio signals which repetitiously requests all transponders, on the mode being used, to reply. The replies received are then mixed with the primary returns and both are displayed on the same radarscope.

(2) **Transponder.** This airborne radar beacon transmitter-receiver automatically receives the signals from the interrogator and selectively replies with a specific pulse group (code) only to those interrogations being received on the mode to which it is set. These replies are independent of, and much stronger than a primary radar return.

(3) **Radarscope.** The radarscope used by the controller displays returns from both the primary radar system and the ATCRBS.

These returns, called targets, are what the controller refers to in the control and separation of traffic.

b. The job of identifying and maintaining identification of primary radar targets is a long and tedious task for the controller. Some of the advantages of ATCRBS over primary radar are:

(1) **Reinforcement of radar targets.**

(2) **Rapid target identification.**

(3) **Unique display of selected codes.**

c. A part of the ATCRBS ground equipment is the decoder. This equipment enables the controller to assign discrete transponder codes to each aircraft under his control. Normally only one code will be assigned for the entire flight. Assignments are made by the ARTCC computer on the basis of the National Beacon Code Allocation Plan. The equipment is also designed to receive MODE C altitude information from the aircraft.

NOTE.—Refer to figures with explanatory legends for an illustration of the target symbology depicted on radar scopes in the NAS Stage A (en route), the ARTS III (terminal) systems, and other nonautomated (broadband) radar systems. *(See Figures 1-10 and 1-11.)*

d. It should be emphasized that aircraft transponders greatly improve the effectiveness of radar systems. (See PARA—170 - TRANSPONDER OPERATION.)

32. SURVEILLANCE RADAR

a. Surveillance radars are divided into two general categories: Airport Surveillance Radar (ASR) and Air Route Surveillance Radar (ARSR).

(1) ASR is designed to provide relatively short-range coverage in the general vicinity of an airport and to serve as an expeditious means of handling terminal area traffic through observation of precise aircraft locations on a radarscope. The ASR can also be used as an instrument approach aid.

(2) ARSR is a long-range radar system designed primarily to provide a display of aircraft locations over large areas.

b. Surveillance radars scan through 360 degrees of azimuth and present target information on a radar display located in a tower or center. This information is used independently or in conjunction with other navigational aids in the control of air traffic.

33. PRECISION APPROACH RADAR (PAR)

a. PAR is designed to be used as a *landing aid,* rather than an aid for sequencing and spacing aircraft. PAR equipment may be used as a primary landing aid, or it may be used to monitor other types of approaches. It is designed to display *range, azimuth* and *elevation* information.

b. Two antennas are used in the PAR array, one scanning a vertical plane, and the other scanning horizontally. Since the range is limited to 10 miles, azimuth to 20 degrees, and elevation to 7 degrees, only the final approach area is covered. Each scope is divided into two parts. The upper half presents altitude and distance information, and the lower half presents azimuth and distance.

34—39. RESERVED

Chapter 2.   AERONAUTICAL LIGHTING AND AIRPORT MARKING AIDS

Section 1.   AIRPORT LIGHTING AIDS

40. APPROACH LIGHT SYSTEMS (ALS)

a. Approach light systems provide the basic means to transition from instrument flight to visual flight for landing. Operational requirements dictate the sophistication and configuration of the approach light system for a particular runway.

b. Approach light systems are a configuration of signal lights starting at the landing threshold and extending into the approach area a distance of 2400-3000 feet for precision instrument runways and 1400-1500 feet for nonprecision instrument runways. Some systems include sequenced flashing lights which appear to the pilot as a ball of light traveling towards the runway at high speed (twice a second). *(See Figure 2-1.)*

41. VISUAL GLIDESLOPE INDICATORS

a.   Visual Approach Slope Indicator (VASI)

(1) The VASI is a system of lights so arranged to provide visual descent guidance information during the approach to a runway. These lights are visible from 3-5 miles during the day and up to 20 miles or more at night. The visual glide path of the VASI provides safe obstruction clearance within plus or minus 10 degrees of the extended runway centerline and to 4 NM from the runway threshold. Descent, using the VASI, should not be initiated until the aircraft is visually aligned with the runway. Lateral course guidance is provided by the runway or runway lights.

(2) VASI installations may consist of either 2, 4, 6, 12, or 16 lights units arranged in bars referred to as near, middle, and far bars. Most VASI installations consist of 2 bars, near and far, and may consist of 2, 4, or 12 light units. Some VASIs consist of three bars, near, middle, and far, which provide an additional visual glide path to accommodate high cockpit aircraft. This installation may consist of either 6 or 16 light units. VASI installations consisting of 2, 4, or 6 light units are located on one side of the runway, usually the left. Where the installation consists of 12 or 16 light units, the units are located on both sides of the runway.

(3) Two-bar VASI installations provide one visual glide path which is normally set at 3 degrees. Three-bar VASI installations provide two visual glide paths. The lower glide path is provided by the near and middle bars and is normally set at 3 degrees while the upper glide path, provided by the middle and far bars, is normally 1/4 degree higher. This higher glide path is intended for use only by high cockpit aircraft to provide a sufficient threshold crossing height. Although normal glide path angles are three degrees, angles at some locations may be as high as 4.5 degrees to give proper obstacle clearance. Pilots of high performance aircraft are cautioned that use of VASI angles in excess of 3.5 degrees may cause an increase in runway length required for landing and rollout.

(4) The basic principle of the VASI is that of color differentiation between red and white. Each light unit projects a beam of light having a white segment in the upper part of the beam and red segment in the lower part of the beam. The light units are arranged so that the pilot using the VASIs during an approach will see the combination of lights shown below.

(5) For 2-bar VASI (4 light units) *See Figure 2-2.*

(6) For 3-bar VASI (6 light units) *See Figure 2-3.*

(7) For other VASI configurations *See Figure 2-4.*

b.   Precision Approach Path Indicator (PAPI)

(1) The precision approach path indicator (PAPI) uses light units similar to the VASI but are installed in a single row of either two or four light units. These systems have an effective visual range of about 5 miles during the day and up to 20 miles at night. The row of light units is normally installed on the left side of the runway and the glide path indications are as depicted. *(See Figure 2-5.)*

c.   Tri-color Systems

(1) Tri-color visual approach slope indicators normally consist of a single light unit projecting a three-color visual approach path into the final approach area of the runway upon which the indicator is installed. The below glide path indication is red, the above glide path indication is amber, and the on glide path indication is green. These types of indicators have a useful range of approximately one-half to one mile during the day and up to five miles at night depending upon the visibility conditions. *(See Figure 2-6.)*

d.   Pulsating Systems

(1) Pulsating visual approach slope indicators normally consist of a single light unit projecting a two-color visual approach path into the final approach area of the runway upon which the indicator is installed. The below glide path indication is normally pulsating red and the above glide path indication is normally pulsating white. On the glide path indication for one type of system is a steady white light while for another type system the on glide path indication consists of an alternating red and white light. The useful range of these systems is about four miles during the day and up to ten miles at night. *(See Figure 2-7.)*

e.   Alignment of Elements Systems

(1) Alignment of elements systems are installed on some small general aviation airports and are a low-cost system consisting of painted plywood panels, normally black and white or fluorescent orange. Some of these systems are lighted for night use. The useful range of these systems is approximately three-quarter miles. To use the system the pilot positions his aircraft so the elements are in alignment. The glide path indications are as follows. *(See Figure 2-8.)*

42. RESERVED

43. RUNWAY END IDENTIFIER LIGHTS (REIL)

REILs are installed at many airfields to provide rapid and positive identification of the approach end of a particular runway. The system consists of a pair of synchronized flashing lights located laterally on each side of the runway threshold. REILs may be either omnidirectional or unidirectional facing the approach area. REILs may be located longitudinally 200 feet either upwind or downwind from the runway threshold. They are effective for:

(1) Identification of a runway surrounded by a preponderance of other lighting.

(2) Identification of a runway which lacks contrast with surrounding terrain.

(3) Identification of a runway during reduced visibility.

44. RUNWAY EDGE LIGHT SYSTEMS

a. Runway edge lights are used to outline the edges of runways during periods of darkness or restricted visibility conditions. These light systems are classified according to the intensity or brightness they are capable of producing: they are the High Intensity Runway Lights (HIRL), Medium Intensity Runway Lights (MIRL), and the Low Intensity Runway Lights (LIRL). The HIRL and MIRL systems have variable intensity controls, whereas the LIRLs normally have one intensity setting.

b. The runway edge lights are white, except on instrument runways amber replaces white on the last 2,000 feet or half the runway length, whichever is less, to form a caution zone for landings.

c. The lights marking the ends of the runway emit red light toward the runway to indicate the end of runway to a departing aircraft and emit green outward from the runway end to indicate the threshold to landing aircraft.

45. IN-RUNWAY LIGHTING

a. Touchdown zone lights and runway centerline lights are installed on some precision approach runways to facilitate landing under adverse visibility conditions. Taxiway turnoff lights may be added to expedite movement of aircraft from the runway.

(1) Touchdown Zone Lighting (TDZL) —two rows of transverse light bars disposed symmetrically about the runway centerline in the runway touchdown zone. The system starts 100 feet from the landing threshold and extends to 3000 feet from the threshold or the midpoint of the runway, whichever is the lesser.

(2) Runway Centerline Lighting (RCLS) —flush centerline lights spaced at 50-foot intervals beginning 75 feet from the landing threshold and extending to within 75 feet of opposite end of the runway.

(3) Runway Remaining Lighting —centerline lighting systems in the final 3,000 feet as viewed from the takeoff or approach position. Alternate red and white lights are seen from the 3,000 foot points to the 1,000 foot points, and all red lights are seen for the last 1,000 feet of the runway. From the opposite direction, these lights are seen as white lights.

(4) Taxiway turnoff lights —flush lights spaced at 50 foot intervals defining the curved path of aircraft travel from the runway centerline to a point on the taxiway.

46. CONTROL OF LIGHTING SYSTEMS

a. Operation of approach light systems and runway lighting is controlled by the control tower (ATCT). At some locations the FSS may control the lights where there is no control tower in operation.

b. Pilots may request that lights be turned on or off. Runway edge lights, in-pavement lights and approach lights also have intensity controls which may be varied to meet the pilots request. Sequenced flashing lights (SFL) may be turned on and off. Some sequenced flashing light systems also have intensity control.

c. The Medium Intensity Approach Lighting System with Runway Alignment Indicators (MALSR) is installed at many airports. The control is by ATCTs or radio from approaching aircraft when the tower is closed (See PARA—47 - PILOT CONTROL OF AIRPORT LIGHTING.)

47. PILOT CONTROL OF AIRPORT LIGHTING

a. Radio control of lighting is available at selected airports to provide airborne control of lights by keying the aircraft's microphone. Control of lighting systems is often available at locations without specified hours for lighting and where there is no control tower or FSS or when the tower or FSS is closed (locations with a part-time tower or FSS) or specified hours. All lighting systems which are radio controlled at an airport, whether on a single runway or multiple runways, operate on the same radio frequency. *(See Tables 2-1 and 2-2.)*

b. With FAA approved systems, various combinations of medium intensity approach lights, runway lights, taxiway lights, VASI and/or REIL may be activated by radio control. On runways with both approach lighting and runway lighting (runway edge lights, taxiway lights, etc.) systems, the approach lighting system takes precedence for air-to-ground radio control over the runway lighting system which is set at a predetermined intensity step, based on expected visibility conditions. Runways without approach lighting may provide radio controlled intensity adjustments of runway edge lights. Other lighting systems, including VASI, REIL, and taxiway lights may be either controlled with the runway edge lights or controlled independently of the runway edge lights.

c. The control system consists of a 3-step control responsive to 7, 5, and/or 3 microphone clicks. This 3-step control will turn on lighting facilities capable of either 3-step, 2-step or 1-step operation. The 3-step and 2-step lighting facilities can be altered in intensity, while the 1-step cannot. All lighting is illuminated for a period of 15 minutes from the most recent time of activation and may not be extinguished prior to end of the 15 minute period (except for 1-step and 2-step REILs which may be turned off when desired by keying the mike 5 or 3 times respectively).

d. Suggested use is to always initially key the mike 7 times; this assures that all controlled lights are turned on to the maximum available intensity. If desired, adjustment can then be made, where the capability is provided, to a lower intensity (or the REIL turned off) by keying 5 and/or 3 times. Due to the close proximity of airports using the same frequency, radio controlled lighting receivers may be set at a low sensitivity requiring the aircraft to be relatively close to activate the system. Consequently, even when lights are on, always key mike as directed when overflying an airport of intended landing or just prior to entering the final segment of an approach. This will assure the aircraft is close enough to activate the system and a full 15 minutes lighting duration is available. Approved lighting systems may be activated by keying the mike (within 5 seconds) as indicated below:

RADIO CONTROL SYSTEM

Key Mike	Function
7 times within 5 seconds	Highest intensity available
5 times within 5 seconds	Medium or lower intensity (Lower REIL or REIL-off)
3 times within 5 seconds	Lowest intensity available (Lower REIL or REIL-off)

e. For all public use airports with FAA standard systems the Airport/Facility Directory contains the types of lighting, runway and the frequency that is used to activate the system. Airports with IAPs include data on the approach chart identifying the light system, the runway on which they are installed, and the frequency that is used to activate the system.

f. Where the airport is not served by an IAP, it may have either the standard FAA approved control system or an independent type system of different specification installed by the airport sponsor. The Airport/Facility Directory contains descriptions of pilot controlled lighting systems for each airport having other than FAA approved systems, and explains the type lights, method of control, and operating frequency in clear text.

48. AIRPORT (ROTATING) BEACONS

a. The airport beacon has a vertical light distribution to make it most effective from one to 10 degrees above the horizon; however, it can be seen well above and below this peak spread. The beacon may be an omnidirectional capacitor-discharge device, or it may rotate at a constant speed which produces the visual effect of flashes at regular intervals. Flashes may be one or two colors alternately. The total number of flashes are:

(1) 12 to 30 per minute for beacons marking airports, landmarks, and points on Federal airways.

(2) 30 to 60 per minute for beacons marking heliports.

b. The colors and color combinations of beacons are:

(1) White and Green — Lighted land airport

(2) *Green alone — Lighted land airport

(3) White and Yellow — Lighted water airport

(4) *Yellow alone — Lighted water airport

(5) White and Red — Landmark or navigational point (rare installation)

(6) White alone — Unlighted land airport (rare installation)

(7) Green, Yellow, and White — Lighted heliport

NOTE.—*Green alone or amber alone is used only in connection with a white-and-green or white-and-amber beacon display, respectively.

c. Military airport beacons flash alternately white and green, but are differentiated from civil beacons by dualpeaked (two quick) white flashes between the green flashes.

d. In control zones, operation of the airport beacon during the hours of daylight often indicates that the ground visibility is less than 3 miles and/or the ceiling is less than 1,000 feet. ATC clearance in accordance with FAR—91 is required for landing, takeoff and flight in the traffic pattern. Pilots should not rely solely on the operation of the airport beacon to indicate if weather conditions are IFR or VFR. At some locations with operating control towers, ATC personnel turn the beacon on or off when controls are in the tower. At many airports the airport beacon is turned on by a photoelectric cell or time clocks and ATC personnel can not control them. There is no regulatory requirement for daylight operation and it is the pilot's responsibility to comply with proper preflight planning as required by FAR—91.5.

49. RUNWAY DISTANCE REMAINING MARKERS

Runway distance remaining markers are signs located along the sides of a runway to indicate the remaining runway distance in increments of 1,000 feet. The signs may be located on both sides, or only one side. The signs have white numbers on a black background and are lighted for nighttime and low visibility operations. Since runways rarely exist in exact multiples of 1,000 feet, the excess distance is added to the runway ends. Therefore, the last sign on each runway end may be located more, but never less, then 1,000 feet from the runway end. For this reason, the runway distance remaining markers may not exactly coincide with distance remaining information from other lighting systems.

Section 2.   AIR NAVIGATION AND OBSTRUCTION LIGHTING

50. AERONAUTICAL LIGHT BEACONS

a. An aeronautical light beacon is a visual NAVAID displaying flashes of white and/or colored light to indicate the location of an airport, a heliport, a landmark, a certain point of a Federal airway in mountainous terrain, or an obstruction. The light used may be a rotating beacon or one or more flashing lights. The flashing lights may be supplemented by steady burning lights of lesser intensity.

b. The color or color combination displayed by a particular beacon and/or its auxiliary lights tell whether the beacon is indicating a landing place, landmark, point of the Federal airways, or an obstruction. Coded flashes of the auxiliary lights, if employed, further identify the beacon site.

51. CODE BEACONS AND COURSE LIGHTS

a. CODE BEACONS

(1) The code beacon, which can be seen from all directions, is used to identify airports and landmarks and to mark obstructions. The number of code beacon flashes are:

(a) **Green coded flashes** not exceeding 40 flashes or character elements per minute, or constant flashes 12 to 15 per minute, for identifying land airports.

(b) **Yellow coded flashes** not exceeding 40 flashes or character elements per minute, or constant flashes 12 to 15 per minute, for identifying water airports.

(c) **Red flashes,** constant rate, 12 to 40 flashes per minute for marking hazards.

b. COURSE LIGHTS

(1) The course light, which can be seen clearly from only one direction, is used only with rotating beacons of the Federal Airway System: two course lights, back to back, direct coded flashing beams of light in either direction along the course of airway.

NOTE.—Airway beacons are remnants of the "lighted" airways which antedated the present electronically equipped Federal Airways System. Only a few of these beacons exist today to mark airway segments in remote mountain areas. Flashes in Morse Code identify the beacon site.

52. OBSTRUCTION LIGHTS

a. Obstructions are marked/lighted to warn airmen of its presence during daytime and nighttime conditions. They may be marked/lighted in any of the following combinations:

(1) **Aviation Red Obstruction Lights.** Flashing aviation red beacons and steady burning aviation red lights during nighttime operation. Aviation orange and white paint is used for daytime marking.

(2) **High Intensity White Obstruction Lights.** Flashing high intensity white lights during daytime with reduced intensity for twilight and nighttime operation. When this type system is used, the marking of structures with red obstruction lights and aviation orange and white paint may be omitted.

(3) **Dual Lighting.** A combination of flashing aviation red beacons and steady burning aviation red lights for nighttime operation and flashing high intensity white lights for daytime operation. Aviation orange and white paint may be omitted.

b. High intensity flashing white lights are being used to identify some supporting structures of overhead transmission lines located across rivers, chasms, gorges, etc. These lights flash in a middle, top, lower light sequence at approximately 60 flashes per minute. The top light is normally installed near the top of the supporting structure, while the lower light indicates the approximate lower portion of the wire span. The lights are beamed towards the companion structure and identify the area of the wire span.

c. High intensity, flashing white lights are also employed to identify tall structures, such as chimneys and towers, as obstructions to air navigation. The lights provide a 360 degree coverage about the structure at 40 flashes per minute and consist of from one to seven levels of lights depending upon the height of the structure. Where more than one level is used the vertical banks flash simultaneously.

53—59. RESERVED

Section 3. AIRPORT MARKING AIDS

60. AIRPORT MARKING AIDS

a. In the interest of safety, regularity, or efficiency of aircraft operations, the FAA has recommended, for the guidance of the public, the following airport marking.

NOTE.—Refer to ADVISORY CIRCULAR—150/5340-1 Marking of Paved Areas on Airports for detailed airport marking information.

b. Runway designators —Runway numbers and letters are determined from the approach direction. The runway number is the whole number nearest one-tenth the magnetic azimuth of the centerline of the runway, measured clockwise from the magnetic north. The letter, or letters, differentiate between left (L), right (R), or center (C) parallel runways, as applicable:

    (1) For two parallel runways "L" "R"

    (2) For three parallel runways "L" "C" "R"

c. Visual Runway Marking —Used for operations under Visual Flight Rules: *(See Figure 2-9.)*

    (1) Centerline marking.

    (2) Designation marking.

    (3) Threshold marking (on runways used or intended to be used by international commercial air transport.)

    (4) Fixed distance marking (on runways 4,000 feet (1200 m) or longer used by jet aircraft.)

    (5) Holding position markings (for taxiway/runway intersections.)

d. NonPrecision Instrument Runway Marking —Used on runways served by a nonvisual navigation aid and intended for landings under instrument weather conditions: *(See Figure 2-10.)*

    (1) Centerline marking.

    (2) Designation marking.

    (3) Threshold marking.

    (4) Fixed distance marking (on runways 4,000 feet (1200 m) or longer used by jet aircraft.

    (5) Holding position markings (for taxiway/runway intersections and instrument landing system (ILS) critical areas.)

e. Precision Instrument Runway Marking —Used on runways served by nonvisual precision approach aids and on runways having special operational requirements: *(See Figure 2-11.)*

    (1) Centerline marking.

    (2) Designation marking.

    (3) Threshold marking.

    (4) Fixed distance marking.

    (5) Touchdown zone marking.

    (6) Side stripes.

    (7) Holding position markings (for taxiway/runway intersections and ILS critical areas.)

f. Threshold —The designated beginning of the runway that is available and suitable for the landing of aircraft.

g. Displaced Threshold —A threshold that is not at the beginning of the full strength runway pavement. The paved area behind the displaced runway threshold is available for taxiing, the landing rollout, and the takeoff of aircraft. *(See Figure 2-12.)*

h. Stopway Areas —Any surface or area extending beyond the usable runway which appears usable but which, due to the nature of its structure, is unusable. *(See Figure 2-13.)*

i. Closed Runway —A runway which is unusable and may be hazardous even though it may appear usable. *(See Figure 2-14.)*

j. Fixed Distance Marker —To provide a fixed distance marker for landing of turbojet aircraft on other than a precision instrument runway. This marking is similar to the fixed distance marking on a precision instrument runway and located 1,000 feet from the threshold.

k. STOL (Short Take Off and Landing) Runway —In addition to the normal runway number marking, the letters STOL are painted on the approach end of the runway and a touchdown aim point is shown. *(See Figure 2-15.)*

l. Taxiway Marking —The taxiway centerline is marked with a continuous yellow line. The taxiway edge may be marked with two continuous yellow lines 6 inches apart. Taxiway HOLDING LINES consist of two continuous and two dashed lines, spaced 6 inches between lines, perpendicular to the taxiway centerline; more recently, HOLD LINES also consist of one or more signs at the edge of the taxiway, with white characters on a red sign face.

NOTE.—When instructed by ATC "HOLD SHORT OF (runway, ILS critical area, etc.)," the pilot should stop so no part of the aircraft extends beyond the holding line. When approaching the holding line from the side with the continuous lines, a pilot should not cross the holding line without ATC clearance at a controlled airport or without making sure of adequate separation from other aircraft at uncontrolled airports. An aircraft exiting the runway is not clear until all parts of the aircraft have crossed the holding line.

m. Helicopter Landing Areas —Details on heliport markings can be found in ADVISORY CIRCULAR—150/5390-1, Heliport Design Guide. *(See Figure 2-16.)*

61. AIRCRAFT ARRESTING DEVICES

a. Certain airports are equipped with a means of rapidly stopping military aircraft on a runway. This equipment, normally referred to as EMERGENCY ARRESTING GEAR, generally consists of pendant cables supported over the runway surface by rubber "donuts". Although most devices are located in the overrun areas, a few of these arresting systems have cables stretched over the operational areas near the ends of a runway.

b. Arresting cables which cross over a runway require special markings on the runway to identify the cable location. These markings consist of 10 feet diameter solid circles painted "identification yellow", 30 feet on center, perpendicular to the runway centerline across the entire runway width. Additional details are contained in ADVISORY CIRCULAR—150/5220-9, Aircraft Arresting Systems for Joint/Civil Military Airports.

NOTE.—Aircraft operations on the runway are NOT restricted by the installation of aircraft arresting devices.

62—69. RESERVED

Chapter 3.   AIRSPACE

Section 1.   GENERAL

70. GENERAL

Because of the nature of some operations, restrictions are required for safety reasons. The complexity or density of aircraft movements in other airspace areas may result in additional aircraft and pilot requirements for operation within such airspace. It is important that pilots be familiar with the operational requirements for the various airspace segments.

71. GENERAL DIMENSIONS OF AIRSPACE SEGMENTS

Refer to Federal Aviation Regulations (FARs) for specific dimensions, exceptions, geographical areas covered, exclusions, specific transponder or equipment requirements, and flight operations. In the following illustration, arrows ending near but not touching reference lines mean up to or down to, but not including, the referenced altitude. *(See Figure 3-1.)*

72—79. RESERVED

Section 2. UNCONTROLLED AIRSPACE

80. GENERAL

Uncontrolled airspace is that portion of the airspace that has not been designated as Continental Control Area, Control Area, Control Zone, Terminal Control Area, or Transition Area.

81. VFR REQUIREMENTS

Rules governing VFR flight have been adopted to assist the pilot in meeting his responsibility to see and avoid other aircraft. Minimum weather conditions and distance from clouds required for VFR flight are contained in these rules. (FAR—91.105.)

82. IFR REQUIREMENTS

FARs specify the pilot and aircraft equipment requirements for IFR flight. Pilots are reminded that in addition to altitude or flight level requirements, FAR—91.119 includes a requirement to remain at least 1,000 feet (2,000 feet in designated mountainous terrain) above the highest obstacle within a horizontal distance of 5 statute miles from the course to be flown.

83. MINIMUM VFR VISIBILITY AND DISTANCE FROM CLOUDS

(See Table 3-1.)

84. ALTITUDES AND FLIGHT LEVELS

(See Tables 3-2 and 3-3.)

85—89. RESERVED

Section 3. CONTROLLED AIRSPACE

90. GENERAL

Controlled airspace consists of those areas designated as Continental Control Area, Control Area, Control Zones, Terminal Control Areas, Airport Radar Service Area and Transition Areas, within which some or all aircraft may be subject to ATC. Safety, users' needs, and volume of flight operations are some of the factors considered in the designation of controlled airspace. When so designated, the airspace is supported by ground to air communications, navigation aids, and air traffic services.

91. CONTINENTAL CONTROL AREA

a. The Continental Control Area consists of the airspace of the 48 contiguous States, the District of Columbia and Alaska, excluding the Alaska peninsula west of longitude 160 degrees 00 minutes 00 seconds W, at and above 14,500 feet MSL, but does not include:

(1) The airspace less than 1,500 feet above the surface of the earth; or

(2) Prohibited and Restricted areas, other than the Restricted areas listed in FAR—71 Subpart D.

92. CONTROL AREAS

Control Areas consist of the airspace designated as Colored Federal airways, VOR Federal airways, Additional Control Areas, and Control Area Extensions, but do not include the Continental Control Area. Unless otherwise designated, Control Areas also include the airspace between a segment of a main VOR airway and its associated alternate segments. The vertical extent of the various categories of airspace contained in Control Areas is defined in FAR—71.

93. POSITIVE CONTROL AREA

Positive Control Area is airspace so designated as positive control area in FAR—71.193. This area includes specified airspace within the conterminous U.S. from 18,000 feet to and including FL 600, excluding Santa Barbara Island, Farallon Island, and that portion south of latitude 25 degrees 04 minutes north. In Alaska, it includes the airspace over the State of Alaska from 18,000 feet to and including FL 600, but not including the airspace less than 1,500 feet above the surface of the earth and the Alaskan Peninsula west of longitude 160 degrees 00 minutes west. Rules for operating in Positive Control Area are found in FAR—91.97 and FAR—91.24.

94. TRANSITION AREAS

a. Transition Areas are designated to contain IFR operations in controlled airspace during portions of the terminal operation and while transitioning between the terminal and en route environments.

b. Transition Areas are controlled airspace extending upward from 700 feet or more above the surface when designated in conjunction with an airport for which an instrument approach procedure has been prescribed; or from 1,200 feet or more above the surface when designated in conjunction with airway route structures or segments. Unless specified otherwise, Transition Areas terminate at the base of overlying controlled airspace.

95. CONTROL ZONES

a. Control Zones are regulatory in nature and established as controlled airspace. They extend upward from the surface and terminate at the base of the Continental Control Area. Control Zones that do not underlie the Continental Control Area have no upper limit. A Control Zone is based on a primary airport but may include one or more airports and is normally a circular area within a radius of 5 statute miles around the primary airport, except that it may include extensions necessary to include instrument departure and arrival paths.

b. Some basic requirements for designating a control zone are communications and weather observation reporting:

(1) Communications capability with aircraft which normally operate within the control zone must exist down to the runway surface of the primary airport. Communications may be either direct from the ATC facility having jurisdiction over the control zone or by rapid relay through other communications facilities which are acceptable to that ATC facility.

(2) Federally certificated weather observers take hourly and special weather observations at the primary airport in the control zone during the times and dates a control zone is designated. The required weather observations must be forwarded expeditiously to the ATC facility having jurisdiction over the control zones.

c. Control Zones are depicted on charts (for example, on the Sectional Charts the Control Zone is outlined by a broken blue line). If a Control Zone is effective only during certain hours of the day (a part-time Control Zone as prescribed in the regulation) it will be reflected on the charts. A typical Control Zone is depicted in PARA—71. (See PARA—264 - SPECIAL VFR CLEARANCES.)

96. TERMINAL CONTROL AREA

a. A Terminal Control Area (TCA) consists of controlled airspace extending upward from the surface or higher to specified altitudes, within which **all aircraft** are subject to the operating rules and pilot and equipment requirements specified in FAR—91. TCAs are described in FAR—71. Each TCA location is designated as either a Group I or Group II TCA, and includes at least one primary airport around which the TCA is located. (See FAR—71.12.)

(1) Group I TCAs represent some of the busiest locations in terms of aircraft operations and passengers carried. For reasons of safety it is necessary to have strict requirements for operation within Group I TCAs. (See FAR—91.70(c) and FAR—91.90.)

(2) Group II TCAs represent less busy locations, and though safety dictates some pilot and equipment requirements, requirements are not as stringent as those for Group I locations. (See FAR—91.70(c) and FAR—91.90.)

b. TCAs are charted on Sectional, World Aeronautical, En route Low Altitude, DOD FLIP and TCA Charts. *(See Tables 3-4 and 3-5.)*

97. TERMINAL CONTROL AREA (TCA) OPERATION

a. Operating Rules and Equipment Requirements. RE-GARDLESS OF WEATHER CONDITIONS, AN ATC AUTHORIZATION IS REQUIRED PRIOR TO OPERATING WITHIN A TCA. Pilots should not request an authorization to operate within a TCA unless the requirements of FAR—91.24 and FAR—91.90 are met. Included among these requirements are:

(1) Group I TCAs

(a) A two-way radio capable of communicating with ATC on appropriate frequencies.

(b) A VOR or TACAN receiver, except for helicopters.

(c) A 4096 code transponder with MODE C automatic altitude reporting equipment, except for helicopters operating at or below 1,000 feet AGL under a Letter of Agreement.

NOTE.—ATC may, upon notification, immediately authorize a deviation from the altitude reporting equipment requirement; however, request for a deviation from the 4096 transponder equipment requirement must be submitted to the controlling ATC facility at least 1 hour before the proposed operation.

(d) A private pilot certificate or better in order to land or takeoff from an airport within the TCA.

(e) Unless otherwise authorized by ATC, each person operating a large turbine engine powered airplane to or from a primary airport shall operate at or above the designated floors while within the lateral limits of the TCA.

(f) ′ No person may operate an aircraft in the airspace underlying a TCA, at an indicated airspeed of more than 200 knots (230 mph) (FAR—91.70).

(2) Group II TCAs.

(a) A two-way radio capable of communicating with ATC on appropriate frequencies.

(b) A VOR or TACAN receiver, except for helicopters.

(c) A 4096 code transponder with MODE C automatic altitude reporting equipment, except for helicopters operating at or below 1,000 feet under a Letter of Agreement, or for IFR flights operating to or from an airport outside of but in close proximity to the TCA when the commonly used transition, approach, or departure procedures to such airport require flight within the TCA.

NOTE.—ATC may authorize deviations from the transponder requirements. Requests for deviation must be submitted to the controlling ATC facility at least 1 hour before the proposed operation.

(d) Unless otherwise authorized by ATC, each person operating a large turbine engine powered airplane to or from a primary airport shall operate at or above the designated floors while within the lateral limits of the TCA.

(e) No person may operate an aircraft in the airspace underlying a TCA, at an indicated airspeed of more than 200 knots (230 mph) (FAR—91.70).

b. Flight Procedures.

(1) *IFR Flights.* Aircraft within the TCA are required to operate in accordance with current IFR procedures. A clearance for a visual approach to a primary airport is not authorization for turbine powered airplanes to operate below the designated floors of the TCA.

(2) *VFR Flights.*

(a) ARRIVING AIRCRAFT MUST OBTAIN AUTHORIZATION PRIOR TO ENTERING A TCA AND MUST CONTACT ATC ON THE APPROPRIATE FREQUENCY, and in relation to geographical fixes shown on local charts. Although a pilot may be operating beneath the floor of the TCA on initial contact, communications with ATC should be established in relation to the points indicated for spacing and sequencing purposes.

(b) Departing aircraft require a clearance to depart the TCA and should advise the clearance delivery position of their intended altitude and route of flight. ATC will normally advise VFR aircraft when leaving the geographical limits of the TCA. Radar service is not automatically terminated with this advisory unless specifically stated by the controller.

(c) Aircraft not landing or departing the primary airport may obtain ATC clearance to transit the TCA when traffic conditions permit and provided the requirements of FAR—91.90 are met. Such VFR aircraft are encouraged, to the extent possible, to operate at altitudes above or below the TCA or transit through established VFR corridors. Pilots operating in VFR corridors are urged to use frequency 122.750 MHZ for the exchange of aircraft position information.

(d) VFR non-TCA aircraft are cautioned against operating too closely to TCA boundaries, especially where the floor of the TCA is 3,000 feet or less or where VFR cruise altitudes are at or near the floor of higher levels. Observance of this precaution will reduce the potential for encountering a TCA aircraft operating at TCA floor altitudes. Additionally, VFR non-TCA aircraft are encouraged to utilize the VFR Planning Chart as a tool for planning flight in proximity to a TCA. Charted VFR Flyway Planning charts are published on the back of the existing VFR Terminal Area Charts.

c. ATC Clearances and Separation. AN ATC AUTHORIZATION IS REQUIRED TO ENTER AND OPERATE WITHIN A TCA. While operating within a TCA, pilots are provided the service and separation as in Stage III. (See PARA—165 - TERMINAL RADAR PROGRAM FOR VFR AIRCRAFT.) In the event of a radar outage, separation and sequencing of VFR aircraft will be suspended as this service is dependent on radar. The pilot will be advised that the service is not available and issued wind, runway information and the time or place to contact the tower. Traffic information will be provided on a workload permitting basis.

(1) This program is not to be interpreted as relieving pilots of their responsibilities to see and avoid other traffic operating in basic VFR weather conditions, to adjust their operations and flight path as necessary to preclude serious wake encounters, to maintain appropriate terrain and obstruction clearance, or to remain in weather conditions equal to or better than the minimums required by FAR—91.105. Whenever compliance with an assigned route, heading and/or altitude is likely to compromise pilot responsibility respecting terrain and obstruction clearance, vortex exposure, and weather minimums, approach control should be so advised and a revised clearance or instruction obtained.

(2) ATC may assign altitudes to VFR aircraft that do not conform to FAR—91.109. When the altitude assignment is no longer needed for separation or when leaving the TCA, the instruction will be broadcast. "Resume Appropriate VFR Altitudes." Pilots must return to an altitude that conforms to FAR—91.109 as soon as practicable.

98. IFR ALTITUDES AND FLIGHT LEVELS

Pilots operating IFR within controlled airspace will fly at an altitude or flight level assigned by ATC. When operating IFR within controlled airspace with an altitude assignment of **VFR ON TOP**, flight is to be conducted at an appropriate VFR altitude which is not below the minimum IFR altitude for the route. (See PARA—84.) **VFR ON TOP** is not permitted in certain airspace areas, such as positive control airspace, certain Restricted Areas, etc. Consequently, IFR flights operating **VFR ON TOP** will avoid such airspace.

99. RESERVED

100. AIRPORT RADAR SERVICE AREA (ARSA)

a. An Airport Radar Service Area (ARSA) consists of controlled airspace extending upward from the surface or higher to specified altitudes, within which all aircraft are subject to the operating rules and pilot and equipment requirements specified in FAR—91. ARSAs are described in FAR—71. (See FAR—71.14.)

b. Dimensions

(1) *ARSA* (A basic standard design with minor site specific variations.) The ARSA airspace consists of two circles, both centered on the primary/ARSA airport. The inner circle has a radius of 5NM. The outer circle has a radius of 10NM. The airspace of the inner circle extends from the surface of the ARSA airport up to 4,000 feet above that airport. The airspace area between the 5 and 10NM rings begins at a height 1,200 feet AGL and extends to the same altitude cap as the inner circle.

(2) *OUTER AREA* The normal radius will be 20NM, with some variations based on site specific requirements. The outer area extends outward from the primary/ARSA airport and extends from the lower limits of radar/radio coverage up to the ceiling of the approach control's delegated airspace, excluding the ARSA and other airspace as appropriate.

c. ARSAs are charted on Sectional Charts, and some Terminal Control Area Charts. *(See Table 3-6.)*

101. AIRPORT RADAR SERVICE AREA (ARSA) OPERATION

a. Operating Rules and Pilot/Equipment Requirements

(1) Pilot Certification: No specific certification required.

(2) Equipment: Two-Way Radio.

(3) Arrivals and Overflights: No person may operate an aircraft in an airport radar service area unless two-way radio communication is established with ATC prior to entering that ARSA and is thereafter maintained with ATC, while within that area.

(4) Departures:

(a) Primary Airport: No person may operate an aircraft within the ARSA unless two-way radio communication is maintained with ATC while within that ARSA.

(b) Satellite Airports: Aircraft departing satellite airports/heliports within the ARSA surface area shall establish two-way communication with ATC as soon as possible. Pilots must comply with approved FAA traffic patterns when departing these airports.

(5) ULTRALIGHT VEHICLES: No person may operate an ultralight vehicle within an airport radar service area unless that

person has prior authorization from the air traffic control facility having jurisdiction over that airspace. (FAR—103)

(6) Parachute Jumps: No person may make a parachute jump and no pilot in command may allow a parachute jump to be made from that aircraft in or into an airport radar service area without, or in violation of, the terms of an ATC authorization. (FAR—105)

b. ATC Services

(See Figure 3-2.)

(1) Within The ARSA:

(a) Sequencing of all arriving aircraft to the primary/ARSA airport.

(b) Standard IFR separation between IFR aircraft.

(c) Between IFR and VFR aircraft - traffic advisories and conflict resolution so that radar targets do not touch, or 500 feet vertical separation.

(d) Between VFR aircraft - traffic advisories and as appropriate, safety alerts.

(2) Within The Outer Area:

(a) The same services are provided for aircraft operating within the outer area, as within the ARSA, *when two-way communication and radar contact is established.*

(b) While pilot participation in this area is strongly encouraged, it is not a VFR requirement.

(3) Beyond The Outer Area:

(a) Standard IFR separation.

(b) Basic Radar Service.

(c) Stage II/Stage III Service, where appropriate.

(d) Safety Alert, as appropriate.

c. Since this is a radar program ARSA services will only be provided within radar/radio coverage. In the event of a radar outage, separation and sequencing of VFR aircraft will be suspended. The pilot will be advised that the service is not available and issued wind, runway information and the time to contact the tower.

d. While pilot participation is required within the ARSA, it is voluntary within the outer area and can be discontinued, within the outer area, at the pilots request.

e. ARSA services will be provided in the outer area unless the pilot requests termination of the service.

f. Service provided beyond the outer area will be on a workload permitting basis and can be terminated by the controller if workload dictates.

g. In some locations an ARSA may overlap the airport traffic area of a secondary airport. In order to allow that control tower to provide service to aircraft, portions of the overlapping ARSA may be procedurally excluded when the secondary airport tower is in operation. Aircraft operating in these procedurally excluded areas will only be provided airport traffic control services when in communication with the secondary airport tower. ARSA service to aircraft inbound to these airports will be discontinued when the aircraft is instructed to contact the tower.

h. Aircraft departing secondary controlled airports will not receive ARSA service until they have been radar identified and two-way communication has been established with the ARSA facility.

i. ARSA service to aircraft proceeding to a satellite airport will be terminated at a sufficient distance to allow time to change to the appropriate tower or advisory frequency.

j. Some ARSA facilities shut down for portions of the night. When this occurs, the effective hours of the ARSA will be the same as the operating hours of the serving facility.

k. This program is not to be interpreted as relieving pilots of their responsibilities to see and avoid other traffic operating in basic VFR weather conditions, to adjust their operations and flight path as necessary to preclude serious wake encounters, to maintain appropriate terrain and obstruction clearance, or to remain in weather conditions equal to or better than the minimums required by FAR—91.105. Whenever compliance with an assigned route, heading and/or altitude is likely to compromise pilot responsibility respecting terrain and obstruction clearance, vortex exposure, and weather minimums, approach control should be so advised and a revised clearance or instruction obtained.

l. Pilots of arriving aircraft should contact the ARSA facility on the publicized frequency and give their position, altitude, radar beacon code (if transponder equipped), destination, and request ARSA service. Radio contact should be initiated far enough from the ARSA boundary to preclude entering the ARSA before radio communication is established.

102—109. RESERVED

Section 4. SPECIAL USE AIRSPACE

110. GENERAL

Special use airspace consists of that airspace wherein activities must be confined because of their nature, or wherein limitations are imposed upon aircraft operations that are not a part of those activities, or both. Except for Controlled Firing Areas, special use airspace areas are depicted on aeronautical charts.

111. PROHIBITED AREA

Prohibited Areas contain airspace of defined dimensions identified by an area on the surface of the earth within which the flight of aircraft is prohibited. Such areas are established for security or other reasons associated with the national welfare. These areas are published in the Federal Register and are depicted on aeronautical charts.

112. RESTRICTED AREA

a. Restricted Areas contain airspace identified by an area on the surface of the earth within which the flight of aircraft, while not wholly prohibited, is subject to restrictions. Activities within these areas must be confined because of their nature or limitations imposed upon aircraft operations that are not a part of those activities or both. Restricted areas denote the existence of unusual, often invisible, hazards to aircraft such as artillery firing, aerial gunnery, or guided missiles. Penetration of Restricted Areas without authorization from the using or controlling agency may be extremely hazardous to the aircraft and its occupants. Restricted Areas are published in the Federal Register and constitute FAR—73.

b. ATC facilities apply the following procedures when aircraft are operating on an IFR clearance (including those cleared by ATC to maintain VFR ON TOP) via a route which lies within joint-use restricted airspace.

(1) If the restricted area is not active and has been released to the controlling agency (FAA), the ATC facility will allow the aircraft to operate in the restricted airspace without issuing specific clearance for it to do so.

(2) If the restricted area is active and has not been released to the controlling agency (FAA), the ATC facility will issue a clearance which will ensure the aircraft avoids the restricted airspace unless it is on an approved altitude reservation mission or has obtained its own permission to operate in the airspace and so informs the controlling facility.

NOTE.—The above apply only to joint-use restricted airspace and not to prohibited and nonjoint-use airspace. For the latter categories, the ATC facility will issue a clearance so the aircraft will avoid the restricted airspace unless it is on an approved altitude reservation mission or has obtained its own permission to operate in the airspace and so informs the controlling facility.

c. Restricted airspace is depicted on the En Route Chart appropriate for use at the altitude or flight level being flown. For joint-use restricted areas, the name of the controlling agency is shown on these charts. For all prohibited areas and nonjoint-use restricted areas, unless otherwise requested by the using agency, the phrase "NO A/G" is shown.

113. WARNING AREA

Warning Areas are airspace which may contain hazards to non-participating aircraft in international airspace. Warning Areas are established beyond the 3 mile limit. Though the activities conducted within Warning Areas may be as hazardous as those in Restricted Areas, Warning Areas cannot be legally designated as Restricted Areas because they are over international waters. Penetration of Warning Areas during periods of activity may be hazardous to the aircraft and its occupants. Official descriptions of Warning Areas may be obtained on request to the FAA, Washington, D.C.

114. MILITARY OPERATIONS AREAS (MOA)

a. MOAs consist of airspace of defined vertical and lateral limits established for the purpose of separating certain military training activities from IFR traffic. Whenever a MOA is being used, nonparticipating IFR traffic may be cleared through a MOA if IFR separation can be provided by ATC. Otherwise, ATC will reroute or restrict nonparticipating IFR traffic.

b. Most training activities necessitate acrobatic or abrupt flight maneuvers. Military pilots conducting flight in Department of Defense aircraft within a designated and active military operations area (MOA) are exempted from the provisions of FAR 91.71(c) and (d) which prohibit acrobatic flight within Federal airways and control zones.

c. Pilots operating under VFR should exercise extreme caution while flying within a MOA when military activity is being conducted. The activity status (active/inactive) of MOA's may change frequently. Therefore, pilots should contact any FSS within 100 miles of the area to obtain accurate real-time information concerning the MOA hours of operation. Prior to entering an active MOA, pilots should contact the controlling agency for traffic advisories.

d. MOA's are depicted on Sectional, VFR Terminal, Area and Low Altitude En Route Charts.

115. ALERT AREA

Alert Areas are depicted on aeronautical charts to inform nonparticipating pilots of areas that may contain a high volume of pilot training or an unusual type of aerial activity. Pilots should be particularly alert when flying in these areas. All activity within an Alert Area shall be conducted in accordance with FARs, without waiver, and pilots of participating aircraft as well as pilots transiting the area shall be equally responsible for collision avoidance. Information concerning these areas may be obtained upon request to the FAA, Washington, D.C.

116. CONTROLLED FIRING AREAS

Controlled Firing Areas contain activities which, if not conducted in a controlled environment, could be hazardous to nonparticipating aircraft. The distinguishing feature of the Controlled Firing Area, as compared to other special use airspace, is that its activities are suspended immediately when spotter aircraft, radar, or ground lookout positions indicate an aircraft might be approaching the area. There

SPECIAL USE AIRSPACE

is no need to chart Controlled Firing Areas since they do not cause a nonparticipating aircraft to change its flight path.

117—129. RESERVED

Section 5.   OTHER AIRSPACE AREAS

130. AIRPORT TRAFFIC AREAS

a.   Unless otherwise specifically designated (FAR—93), Airport traffic areas consist of the airspace within a horizontal radius of 5 statute miles from the geographical center of any airport at which a control tower is operating, extending from the surface up to, but not including, an altitude of 3,000 feet above the elevation of the airport.

b.   The rules prescribed for airport traffic areas are established in FAR—91.70, FAR—91.85, and FAR—91.87. They require, in effect, that unless a pilot is landing or taking off from an airport within the airport traffic area, *the pilot must avoid the area unless specifically authorized by ATC,* either directly from the ATC facility responsible for the airport traffic area, or from the facility from which the pilot is receiving radar services. When authorized by ATC to operate in an airport traffic area, the pilot may expect traffic advisory service on a workload-permitting basis.

c.   Unless otherwise authorized, a pilot operating to or from an airport served by a control tower must: (1) establish and maintain radio communications with the tower prior to and while operating in the airport traffic area, (2) Maintain radio communications with the tower while operating on the movement areas of the airport. Maximum indicated airspeeds are prescribed. Airport traffic areas are indicated on VFR Navigation Charts by the blue airport symbol, but the actual boundary is not depicted. (See PARA—71 - GENERAL DIMENSIONS OF AIRSPACE SEGMENTS.)

131. AIRPORT ADVISORY AREA

a.   The airport advisory area is the area within 10 statute miles of an airport where a control tower is not operating but where a FSS is located. At such locations, the FSS provides advisory service to arriving and departing aircraft. (See PARA—157 - TRAFFIC AIRPORT ADVISORY PRACTICES AT AIRPORTS WHERE A TOWER IS NOT IN OPERATION.)

b.   It is not mandatory that pilots participate in the Airport Advisory Service program, but it is strongly recommended that they do.

132. MILITARY TRAINING ROUTES (MTR)

a.   National security depends largely on the deterrent effect of our airborne military forces. To be proficient, the military services must train in a wide range of airborne tactics. One phase of this training involves "low level" combat tactics. The required maneuvers and high speeds are such that they may occasionally make the see-and-avoid aspect of VFR flight more difficult without increased vigilance in areas containing such operations. In an effort to ensure the greatest practical level of safety for all flight operations, the MTR program was conceived.

b.   The MTRs program is a joint venture by the FAA and the Department of Defense (DOD). MTR routes are mutually developed for use by the military for the purpose of conducting low-altitude, high-speed training. The routes above 1,500 feet above ground level (AGL) are developed to be flown, to the maximum extent possible, under IFR. The routes at 1,500 feet AGL and below are generally developed to be flown under Visual Flight Rules (VFR).

c.   Generally, MTRs are established below 10,000 feet MSL for operations at speeds in excess of 250 knots. However, route segments may be defined at higher altitudes for purposes of route continuity. For example, route segments may be defined for descent, climbout, and mountainous terrain. There are IFR and VFR routes as follows:

(1)   IFR Military Training Routes — IR: Operations on these routes are conducted in accordance with IFRs regardless of weather conditions.

(2)   VFR Military Training Routes — VR: Operations on these routes are conducted in accordance with VFRs.

d.   Military training routes will be identified and charted as follows:

(1)   Route identification.

(a)   *IR and VR at or below 1,500 feet AGL* (with no segment above 1,500) will be identified by four digit numbers; e.g., IR 1006, VR 1007, etc.

(b)   *IR and VR above 1,500 feet AGL* (segments of these routes may be below 1,500) will be identified by three digit numbers; e.g., IR 008, VR 009, etc.

(c)   Alternate IR/VR routes or route segments are identified by using the basic/principal route designation followed by a letter suffix, e.g., IR008A, VR1007B, etc.

(2)   Route charting.

(a)   IFR Low Altitude En Route Chart — This chart will depict all IR routes and all VR routes that accommodate operations above 1,500 feet AGL.

(b)   VFR Planning Chart — This chart will depict routes (military training activities such as IR and VR regardless of altitude), MOAs, and restricted, warning and alert areas.

(c)   Area Planning (AP/1B) Chart (DOD Flight Information Publication — FLIP). This chart is published by the DOD primarily for military users and contains detailed information on both IR and VR routes. (See PARA—625 - AUXILIARY CHARTS.)

e.   The FLIP contains charts and narrative descriptions of these routes. This publication is available to the general public by single copy or annual subscription from the DIRECTOR, DMACSC, Attention: DOCP, Washington, DC 20315-0020. This DOD FLIP is available for pilot briefings at FSS and many airports.

f.   Nonparticipating aircraft are not prohibited from flying within an MTR; however, extreme vigilance should be exercised when conducting flight through or near these routes. Pilots should contact FSSs within 100 NM of a particular MTR to obtain current information or route usage in their vicinity. Information available includes times of scheduled activity, altitudes in use on each route segment, and actual route width. Route width varies for each MTR and can extend several miles on either side of the charted MTR centerline. Route width information for IR and VR MTR's is also available in the FLIP AP/1B along with additional MTR (SR/AR) information. When requesting MTR information, pilots should give the FSS their position, route of flight, and destination in order to reduce frequency congestion and permit the FSS specialist to identify the MTR routes which could be a factor.

133. TEMPORARY FLIGHT RESTRICTIONS

a. This paragraph describes the types of conditions under which the FAA may impose temporary flight restrictions. It also explains which FAA elements have been delegated authority to issue a temporary flight restrictions NOTAM and lists the types of responsible agencies/offices from which the FAA will accept requests to establish temporary flight restrictions. The FAR is explicit as to what operations are prohibited, restricted, or allowed in a temporary flight restrictions area. Pilots are responsible to comply with FAR 91.91 when planning flight for, or conducting flight in, an area where a temporary flight restrictions area is in effect. (REFERENCES: Part 91 of the FAR and Amendment No. 91-186 which amends FAR Section 91.91, Temporary Flight Restrictions.)

b. The purpose for establishing a temporary flight restrictions area is to:

(1) Protect persons and property in the air or on the surface from an existing or imminent hazard associated with an incident on the surface when the presence of low flying aircraft would magnify, alter, spread, or compound that hazard (FAR 91.91(b));

(2) Provide a safe environment for the operation of disaster relief aircraft (FAR 91.91(c));

(3) Or prevent an unsafe congestion of sightseeing aircraft above an incident or event which may generate a high degree of public interest (FAR 91.91(d)).

c. Except for hijacking situations, when the provisions of FAR 91.91(b) or (c) are necessary, a temporary flight restrictions area will only be established by or through the area manager at the air route traffic control center (ARTCC) having jurisdiction over the area concerned. A temporary flight restrictions NOTAM involving the conditions of FAR 91.91(d) will be issued at the direction of the regional air traffic division manager having oversight of the airspace concerned. When hijacking situations are involved, a temporary flight restrictions area will be implemented through the FAA Washington Headquarters Office of Civil Aviation Security. The appropriate FAA air traffic element, upon receipt of such a request, will establish a temporary flight restrictions area under FAR 91.91(b).

d. The FAA accepts recommendations for the establishment of a temporary flight restrictions area under FAR 91.91(b) from military major command headquarters, regional directors of the Office of Emergency Planning, Civil Defense State Directors, State Governors, or other similar authority. For the situations involving FAR 91.91(c), the FAA accepts recommendations from military commanders serving as regional, subregional, or Search and Rescue (SAR) coordinators; by military commanders directing or coordinating air operations associated with disaster relief; or by civil authorities directing or coordinating organized relief air operations (includes representatives of the Office of Emergency Planning, U.S. Forest Service, and State aeronautical agencies). Appropriate authorities for a temporary flight restrictions establishment under FAR 91.91(d) are any of those listed above or by State, county, or city government entities.

e. The type of restrictions issued will be kept to a minimum by the FAA consistent with achievement of the necessary objective. Situations which warrant the extreme restrictions of FAR 91.91(b) include, but are not limited to: toxic gas leaks or spills, flammable agents, or fumes which if fanned by rotor or propeller wash could endanger persons or property on the surface, or if entered by an aircraft could endanger persons or property in the air; imminent volcano eruptions which could endanger airborne aircraft and occupants; nuclear accident or incident; and hijackings. Situations which warrant the restrictions associated with FAR 91.91(c) include:

forest fires which are being fought by releasing fire retardants from aircraft; and aircraft relief activities following a disaster (earthquake, tidal wave, flood, etc.). FAR 91.91 (d) restrictions are established for events and incidents that would attract an unsafe congestion of sightseeing aircraft.

f. The amount of airspace needed to protect persons and property or provide a safe environment for rescue/relief aircraft operations is normally limited to within 2,000 feet above the surface and within a two nautical mile radius. Incidents occurring within an airport traffic area or terminal control area (TCA) will normally be handled through existing procedures and should not require the issuance of temporary flight restrictions NOTAM.

g. The FSS nearest the incident site is normally the "coordination facility." When FAA communications assistance is required, the designated FSS will function as the primary communications facility for coordination between emergency control authorities and affected aircraft. The ARTCC may act as liaison for the emergency control authorities if adequate communications cannot be established between the designated FSS and the relief organization. For example, the coordination facility may relay authorizations from the on-scene emergency response official in cases where news media aircraft operations are approved at the altitudes used by relief aircraft.

h. ATC may authorize operations in a temporary flight restrictions area under its own authority only when flight restrictions are established under FAR 91.91(c) and (d) and only when such operations are conducted under instrument flight rules (IFR). The appropriate ARTCC/air traffic control tower manager will, however, ensure that such authorized flights do not hamper activities or interfere with the event for which restrictions were implemented. However, ATC will not authorize local IFR flights into the temporary flight restrictions area.

i. To preclude misunderstanding, the implementing NOTAM will contain specific and formatted information. The facility establishing a temporary flight restrictions area will format a NOTAM beginning with the phrase "FLIGHT RESTRICTIONS" followed by: the location of the temporary flight restrictions area; the effective period; the area defined in statute miles; the altitudes affected; the FAA coordination facility and commercial telephone number; the reason for the temporary flight restrictions; the agency directing any relief activities and its commercial telephone number; and other information considered appropriate by the issuing authority.

EXAMPLE FAR 91.91(b):

The following NOTAM prohibits all aircraft operations except those specified in the NOTAM.

FLIGHT RESTRICTIONS MATTHEWS, VIRGINIA, EFFECTIVE IMMEDIATELY UNTIL 1200 GMT JANUARY 20, 1987. PURSUANT TO FAR 91.91(b) TEMPORARY FLIGHT RESTRICTIONS ARE IN EFFECT. RESCUE OPERATIONS IN PROGRESS. ONLY RELIEF AIRCRAFT OPERATIONS UNDER THE DIRECTION OF THE DEPARTMENT OF DEFENSE ARE AUTHORIZED IN THE AIRSPACE AT AND BELOW 5,000 FEET MSL WITHIN A TWO MILE RADIUS OF LASER AFB, MATTHEWS, VIRGINIA. COMMANDER, LASER AFB, IN CHARGE (897) 946-5543. BURNS FSS IS THE FAA COORDINATION FACILITY (792) 555-6141.

EXAMPLE FAR 91.91(c):

The following NOTAM permits the on-site emergency response official to authorize media aircraft operations below the altitudes used by the relief aircraft.

FLIGHT RESTRICTIONS 25 MILES EAST OF BRANSOME, IDAHO, EFFECTIVE IMMEDIATELY UNTIL 2359

JANUARY 20, 1987. PURSUANT TO FAR 91.91(c) TEMPORARY FLIGHT RESTRICTIONS ARE IN EFFECT WITHIN A FOUR MILE RADIUS OF THE INTERSECTION OF COUNTY ROADS 564 and 315 AT AND BELOW 3,500 FEET MSL TO PROVIDE A SAFE ENVIRONMENT FOR FIRE FIGHTING AIRCRAFT OPERATIONS. DAVIS COUNTY SHERIFF'S DEPARTMENT (792) 555-8122 IS IN CHARGE OF ON-SCENE EMERGENCY RESPONSE ACTIVITIES. GLIVINGS FSS (792) 555-1618 IS THE FAA COORDINATION FACILITY.

EXAMPLE FAR 91.91(d):

The following NOTAM prohibits sightseeing aircraft operations.

FLIGHT RESTRICTIONS BROWN, TENNESSEE, DUE TO OLYMPIC ACTIVITY. EFFECTIVE 1100 GMT JUNE 18, 1987, UNTIL 0200 GMT JULY 19, 1987. PURSUANT TO FAR 91.91(d) TEMPORARY FLIGHT RESTRICTIONS ARE IN EFFECT WITHIN A THREE MILE RADIUS OF THE BASSETT SPORTS COMPLEX AT AND BELOW 2,500 FEET MSL. NORTON FSS (423) 555-6742 IS THE FAA COORDINATION FACILITY.

134. FLIGHT LIMITATIONS/PROHIBITIONS

a. Flight Limitations in the proximity of Space Flight Operations are designated in a Notice to Airman (NOTAM). FAR—

91.102 provides protection from potentially hazardous situations for pilots and space flight crews and costly delays of shuttle operations.

b. Flight Restrictions in the proximity of Presidential and Other Parties are put into effect because numerous aircraft and large assemblies of persons may be attracted to areas to be visited or traveled by the President or Vice President, heads of foreign states, and other public figures. Such conditions may create a hazard to aircraft engaged in air commerce and to persons and property on the ground. In addition, responsible agencies of the United States Government may determine that certain regulatory actions should be taken in the interest of providing protection for these public figures. FAR—91.104 provides for the issuance of a regulatory NOTAM to establish flight restrictions where required in such cases.

135. PARACHUTE JUMP AIRCRAFT OPERATIONS

a. Procedures relating to parachute jump areas are contained in FAR—105. Tabulations of parachute jump areas in the U.S. are contained in the Airport/Facility Directory.

b. Pilots of aircraft engaged in parachute jump operations are reminded that all reported altitudes must be with reference to mean sea level, or flight level, as appropriate, to enable ATC to provide meaningful traffic information.

136—149. RESERVED

Chapter 4. AIR TRAFFIC CONTROL

Section 1. SERVICES AVAILABLE TO PILOTS

150. AIR ROUTE TRAFFIC CONTROL CENTERS

Centers are established primarily to provide Air Traffic Service to aircraft operating on IFR flight plans within controlled airspace, and principally during the en route phase of flight.

151. CONTROL TOWERS

Towers have been established to provide for a safe, orderly and expeditious flow of traffic on and in the vicinity of an airport. When the responsibility has been so delegated, towers also provide for the separation of IFR aircraft in the terminal areas (See PARA—362 - APPROACH CONTROL.)

152. FLIGHT SERVICE STATIONS

FSSs are air traffic facilities which provide pilot briefings, en route communications and VFR search and rescue services, assist lost aircraft and aircraft in emergency situations, relay ATC clearances, originate Notices to Airmen, broadcast aviation weather and NAS information, receive and process IFR flight plans, and monitor NAVAIDS. In addition, at selected locations FSSs provide En Route Flight Advisory Service (Flight Watch), take weather observations, issue airport advisories, and advise Customs and Immigration of transborder flights.

153. RECORDING AND MONITORING

a. Calls to air traffic control (ATC) facilities (ARTCCs, Towers, FSSs, Central Flow, and Operations Centers) over radio and ATC operational telephone lines (lines used for operational purposes such as controller instructions, briefings, opening and closing flight plans, issuance of IFR clearances and amendments, counter hijacking activities, etc.) may be monitored and recorded for operational uses such as accident investigations, accident prevention, search and rescue purposes, specialist training and evaluation, and technical evaluation and repair of control and communications systems.

b. Where the public access telephone is recorded, a beeper tone is not required. In place of the "beep" tone the FCC has substituted a mandatory requirement that persons to be recorded be given notice they are to be recorded and give consent. Notice is given by this entry, consent to record is assumed by the individual placing a call to the operational facility.

154. COMMUNICATIONS RELEASE OF IFR AIRCRAFT LANDING AT AN AIRPORT NOT BEING SERVED BY AN OPERATING TOWER

Aircraft operating on an IFR flight plan, landing at an airport not being served by a tower will be advised to change to the airport advisory frequency when direct communications with ATC is no longer required. Towers and centers do not have nontower airport traffic and runway in use information. The instrument approach

may not be aligned with the runway in use; therefore, if the information has not already been obtained, pilots should make an expeditious change to the airport advisory frequency when authorized. (See PARA—363-ADVANCE INFORMATION ON INSTRUMENT APPROACH.)

155. PILOT VISITS TO AIR TRAFFIC FACILITIES

Pilots are encouraged to visit air traffic facilities (Towers, Centers and FSSs) and participate in "Operation Raincheck". Operation Raincheck is a program designed to familiarize pilots with the ATC system, its functions, responsibilities and benefits. On rare occasions, facilities may not be able to approve a visit because of ATC workload or other reasons. It is therefore requested that pilots contact the facility prior to the visit and advise of the number of persons in the group, the time and date of the proposed visit and the primary interest of the group. With this information available, the facility can prepare an itinerary and have someone available to guide the group through the facility.

156. APPROACH CONTROL SERVICE FOR VFR ARRIVING AIRCRAFT

a. Numerous approach control facilities have established programs for arriving VFR aircraft to contact approach control for landing information. This information includes: wind, runway, and altimeter setting at the airport of intended landing. This information may be omitted if contained in the ATIS broadcast and the pilot states the appropriate ATIS code.

NOTE.—Pilot use of "have numbers" does not indicate receipt of the ATIS broadcast. In addition, the controller will provide traffic advisories on a workload permitting basis.

b. Such information will be furnished upon initial contact with concerned approach control facility. The pilot will be requested to change to the *tower* frequency at a predetermined time or point, to receive further landing information.

c. Where available, use of this procedure will not hinder the operation of VFR flights by requiring excessive spacing between aircraft or devious routing.

d. Compliance with this procedure is not mandatory but pilot participation is encouraged. (See PARA—165-TERMINAL RADAR PROGRAMS FOR VFR AIRCRAFT.)

157. TRAFFIC ADVISORY PRACTICES AT AIRPORTS WITHOUT OPERATING CONTROL TOWERS

(See Table 4-1.)

a. Airport Operations Without Operating Control Tower

(1) There is no substitute for alertness while in the vicinity of an airport. It is essential that pilots be alert and look for other traffic and exchange traffic information when approaching or departing an airport without an operating control tower. This is of

particular importance since other aircraft may not have communication capability or, in some cases, pilots may not communicate their presence or intentions when operating into or out of such airports. To achieve the greatest degree of safety, it is essential that all radio-equipped aircraft transmit/receive on a common frequency identified for the purpose of airport advisories.

(2) An airport may have a full or part-time tower or flight service station (FSS) located on the airport, a full or part-time UNICOM station or no aeronautical station at all. There are three ways for pilots to communicate their intention and obtain airport/traffic information when operating at an airport that does not have an operating tower: by communicating with an FSS, a UNICOM operator, or by making a self-announce broadcast.

    b.   **Communicating on a Common Frequency.**

(1) The key to communicating at an airport without an operating control tower is selection of the correct common frequency. The acronym *CTAF* which stands for Common Traffic Advisory Frequency, is synonymous with this program. A CTAF is a frequency designated for the purpose of carrying out airport advisory practices while operating to or from an airport without an operating control tower. The CTAF may be a UNICOM, MULTICOM, FSS, or tower frequency and is identified in appropriate aeronautical publications.

(2) The CTAF frequency for a particular airport is contained in the Airport/Facility Directory (A/FD), Alaska Supplement, Alaska Terminal Publication, Instrument Approach Procedure Charts, and Standard Instrument Departure (SID) charts. Also, the CTAF frequency can be obtained by contacting any FSS. Use of the appropriate CTAF, combined with a visual alertness and application of the following recommended good operating practices, will enhance safety of flight into and out of all uncontrolled airports.

    c.   **Recommended Traffic Advisory Practices.**

All inbound traffic should monitor and communicate as appropriate on the designated CTAF from 10 miles to landing. Departing aircraft should monitor/communicate on the appropriate frequency from start-up, during taxi, and until 10 miles from the airport unless the FARs or local procedures require otherwise.

    d.   **Airport Advisory Service Provided by an FSS.**

(1) Airport Advisory Service (AAS) is a service provided by an FSS physically located on an airport which does not have a control tower or where the tower is operated on a part-time basis. The CTAF for FSSs which provide this service will be disseminated in appropriate aeronautical publications.

(2) In communicating with a CTAF FSS, establish two-way communications before transmitting outbound/inbound intentions or information. An inbound aircraft should report approximately 10 miles from the airport, reporting altitude and aircraft type, location relative to the airport, state whether landing or overflight, and request airport advisory. Departing aircraft should state the aircraft type, full identification number, type of flight planned, i.e., VFR or IFR and the planned destination or direction of flight. Report before taxiing and before taxiing on the runway for departure. If communications with a UNICOM are necessary after initial report to FSS, return to FSS frequency for traffic update.

      (a)   Inbound

EXAMPLE:

VERO BEACH RADIO, CENTURION SIX NINER DELTA DELTA IS TEN MILES SOUTH, TWO THOUSAND, LANDING VERO BEACH. REQUEST AIRPORT ADVISORY.

      (b)   Outbound

EXAMPLE:

VERO BEACH RADIO, CENTURION SIX NINER DELTA DELTA, READY TO TAXI, VFR, DEPARTING TO THE SOUTHWEST. REQUEST AIRPORT ADVISORY.

(3) A CTAF FSS provides wind direction and velocity, favored or designated runway, altimeter setting, known traffic, notices to airmen, airport taxi routes, airport traffic pattern information, and instrument approach procedures. These elements are varied so as to best serve the current traffic situation. Some airport managers have specified that under certain wind or other conditions designated runways be used. Pilots should advise the FSS of the runway they intend to use.

CAUTION: All aircraft in the vicinity of an airport may not be in communication with the FSS.

    e.   **Information Provided by Aeronautical Advisory Stations (UNICOM).**

(1) UNICOM is a nongovernment air/ground radio communication station which may provide airport information at public use airports where there is no tower or FSS.

(2) On pilot request, UNICOM stations may provide pilots with weather information, wind direction, the recommended runway, or other necessary information. If the UNICOM frequency is designated as the CTAF, it will be identified in appropriate aeronautical publications.

(3) Should AAS by an FSS or, Aeronautical Advisory Station (UNICOM) be unavailable, wind and weather information may be obtainable from nearby controlled airports via Automatic Terminal Information Service (ATIS) or Automated Weather Observing System (AWOS) frequency.

    f.   **Self-Announce Position and/or Intentions.**

(1) **General.** *Self-announce* is a procedure whereby pilots broadcast their position or intended flight activity or ground operation on the designated CTAF. This procedure is used primarily at airports which do not have an FSS on the airport. The self-announce procedure should also be used if a pilot is unable to communicate with the FSS on the designated CTAF.

(2) If an airport has a tower and it is temporarily closed, or operated on a part-time basis and there is no FSS on the airport or the FSS is closed, use the CTAF to self-announce your position or intentions.

(3) Where there is no tower, FSS, or UNICOM station on the airport, use MULTICOM frequency 122.9 for self-announce procedures. Such airports will be identified in appropriate aeronautical publications.

(4) **Practice Approaches.** Pilots conducting practice instrument approaches should be particularly alert for other aircraft that may be departing in the opposite direction. When conducting any practice approach, regardless of its direction relative to other airport operations, pilots should make announcements on the CTAF as follows:

      (a) departing the final approach fix, inbound (non precision approach) or departing the outer marker or fix used in lieu of the outer marker, inbound (precision approach);

      (b) established on the final approach segment or immediately upon being released by ATC;

      (c) upon completion or termination of the approach; and

      (d) upon executing the missed approach procedure.

(5) Departing aircraft should always be alert for arrival aircraft coming from the opposite direction.

(6) **Recommended Self—Announce Phraseologies:**It should be noted that aircraft operating to or from another nearby airport may be making self-announce broadcasts on the same UNICOM or MULTICOM frequency. To help identify one airport from another, the airport name should be spoken at the beginning and end of each self-announce transmission.

(a) Inbound

EXAMPLE:

STRAWN TRAFFIC, APACHE TWO TWO FIVE ZULU, (POSITION), (ALTITUDE), (DESCENDING) OR ENTER- ING DOWNWIND/BASE/FINAL (AS APPROPRIATE) RUNWAY ONE SEVEN FULL STOP, TOUCH-AND-GO, STRAWN.

STRAWN TRAFFIC APACHE TWO TWO FIVE ZULU LEAVING RUNWAY ONE SEVEN STRAWN.

(b) Outbound

EXAMPLE:

STRAWN TRAFFIC, QUEEN AIR SEVEN ONE FIVE FIVE BRAVO (LOCATION ON AIRPORT) TAXIING TO RUNWAY TWO SIX STRAWN.

STRAWN TRAFFIC, QUEEN AIR SEVEN ONE FIVE FIVE BRAVO DEPARTING RUNWAY TWO SIX. "DEPARTING THE PATTERN TO THE (DIRECTION), CLIMBING TO (ALTITUDE) STRAWN."

(c) Practice Instrument Approach

EXAMPLE:

STRAWN TRAFFIC, CESSNA TWO ONE FOUR THREE QUEBEC (NAME - FINAL APPROACH FIX) INBOUND DESCENDING THROUGH (ALTITUDE) PRACTICE (TYPE) APPROACH RUNWAY THREE FIVE STRAWN.

STRAWN TRAFFIC, CESSNA TWO ONE FOUR THREE QUEBEC PRACTICE (TYPE) APPROACH COMPLETED OR TERMINATED RUNWAY THREE FIVE STRAWN.

g. UNICOM Communications Procedures.

(1) In communicating with a UNICOM station, the following practices will help reduce frequency congestion, facilitate a better understanding of pilot intentions, help identify the location of air- craft in the traffic pattern, and enhance safety of flight:

(a) Select the correct UNICOM frequency.

(b) State the identification of the UNICOM station you are calling in each transmission.

(c) Speak slowly and distinctly.

(d) Report approximately 10 miles from the airport, re- porting altitude, and state your aircraft type, aircraft identification, location relative to the airport, state whether landing or overflight, and request wind information and runway in use.

(e) Report on downwind, base, and final approach.

(f)Report leaving the runway.

(2) Recommended UNICOM Phraseologies:

(a) Inbound

EXAMPLE:

FREDERICK UNICOM CESSNA EIGHT ZERO ONE TANGO FOXTROT 10 MILES SOUTHEAST DESCENDING THROUGH (ALTITUDE) LANDING FREDERICK, RE- QUEST WIND AND RUNWAY INFORMATION FREDER- ICK.

FREDERICK TRAFFIC CESSNA EIGHT ZERO ONE TANGO FOXTROT ENTERING DOWNWIND/BASE/FINAL (AS APPROPRIATE) FOR RUNWAY ONE NINE FULL STOP, TOUCH-AND-GO FREDERICK.

FREDERICK TRAFFIC CESSNA EIGHT ZERO ONE TANGO FOXTROT LEAVING RUNWAY ONE NINE FREDERICK.

(b) Outbound

EXAMPLE:

FREDERICK UNICOM CESSNA EIGHT ZERO ONE TANGO FOXTROT (LOCATION ON AIRPORT) TAXIING TO RUNWAY ONE NINE, REQUEST WIND AND TRAF- FIC INFORMATION FREDERICK.

FREDERICK TRAFFIC CESSNA EIGHT ZERO ONE TANGO FOXTROT DEPARTING RUNWAY ONE NINE. "REMAINING IN THE PATTERN" OR "DEPARTING THE PATTERN TO THE (DIRECTION) (AS APPROPRI- ATE)" FREDERICK.

158. IFR APPROACHES/GROUND VEHICLE OPERATIONS

a. IFR Approaches.

When operating in accordance with an IFR clearance and ATC approves a change to the advisory frequency, make an expeditious change to the CTAF and employ the recommended traffic advisory procedures.

b. Ground Vehicle Operation.

Airport ground vehicles equipped with radios should monitor the CTAF frequency when operating on the airport movement area and remain clear of runways/taxiways being used by aircraft. Radio transmissions from ground vehicles should be confined to safety- related matters.

c. Radio Control of Airport Lighting Systems.

Whenever possible, the CTAF will be used to control airport lighting systems at airports without operating control towers. This eliminates the need for pilots to change frequencies to turn the lights on and allows a continuous listening watch on a single fre- quency. The CTAF is published on the instrument approach chart and in other appropriate aeronautical information publications. For further details concerning radio controlled lights, see AC 150/ 5340.27.

159. DESIGNATED UNICOM/MULTICOM FREQUENCIES

a. Communications Between Aircraft.

CAUTION—The Federal Communications Commission (FCC) requires an aircraft station license to operate on UNICOM/MULTI- COM frequencies and usage must be in accordance with Part 87 of the FCC Rules (See Section 87.29 regarding license applications). Misuse of these frequencies may result in either the imposition of fines and/or revocation/suspension of FCC aircraft station license.

b. Frequency Use.

The following listing depicts UNICOM and MULTICOM fre- quency uses as designated by the Federal Communications Commission (FCC).

FREQUENCY..USE

122.700	Airports without an operating control tower
122.725	Airports without an operating control tower
122.800	Airports without an operating control tower
123.000	Airports without an operating control tower
122.975	Airports without an operating control tower
122.900	...(MULTICOM frequency) Airports with no tower, FSS, or UNICOM
122.950	Airports with a control tower
122.725	Private airports (not open to public)
122.750	Private airports (not open to public) and air-to-air communications
122.975	High altitude
123.050	Heliports
123.075	Heliports

NOTE—In some areas of the country, frequency interference may be encountered from nearby airports using the same UNICOM frequency. Where this is a problem, UNICOM operators are encouraged to develop a *least interference* frequency assignment plan for airports concerned using the five frequencies designated for airports without operating control towers. UNICOM licensees may then request FCC to assign frequencies in accordance with the plan, which they will review and consider for approval.

160. USE OF UNICOM FOR ATC PURPOSES

UNICOM service may be used for air traffic control purposes, only under the following circumstances:

    (1)   Revision to proposed departure time.

    (2)   Takeoff, arrival, or flight plan cancellation time.

    (3)   ATC clearance, provided arrangements are made between the ATC facility and the UNICOM licensee to handle such messages.

161. AUTOMATIC TERMINAL INFORMATION SERVICE (ATIS)

    a. ATIS is the continuous broadcast of recorded noncontrol information in selected high activity terminal areas. Its purpose is to improve controller effectiveness and to relieve frequency congestion by automating the repetitive transmission of essential but routine information. Pilots are urged to cooperate in the ATIS program as it relieves frequency congestion on approach control, ground control, and local control frequencies. The Airport Facility/Directory indicates airports for which ATIS is provided.

    b. ATIS information includes the time of the latest weather sequence, ceiling, visibility (if the weather is above a ceiling/sky condition of 5,000 feet and the visibility is 5 miles or more, inclusion of the ceiling/sky condition, visibility, and obstructions to vision in the ATIS message is optional), obstructions to visibility, temperature, dew point (if available), wind direction (magnetic) and velocity, altimeter, other pertinent remarks, instrument approach and runways in use is continuously broadcast on the voice feature of a TVOR/VOR/VORTAC located on or near the airport, or in a discrete VHF/UHF frequency. The departure runway will only be given if different from the landing runway except at locations having a separate ATIS for departure. Where VFR arrival aircraft are expected to make initial contact with approach control, this fact and the appropriate frequencies may be broadcast on ATIS. Pilots of aircraft arriving or departing the terminal area can receive the

continuous ATIS broadcasts at times when cockpit duties are least pressing and listen to as many repeats as desired. ATIS broadcasts shall be updated upon the receipt of any official weather, regardless of content change and reported values. A new recording will also be made when there is a change in other pertinent data such as runway change, instrument approach in use, etc.

EXAMPLE:

    DULLES INTERNATIONAL INFORMATION SIERRA. 1300 ZULU WEATHER. MEASURED CEILING THREE THOUSAND OVERCAST. VISIBILITY THREE, SMOKE. TEMPERATURE SIX EIGHT. WIND THREE FIVE ZERO AT EIGHT. ALTIMETER TWO NINER NINER TWO. ILS RUNWAY ONE RIGHT APPROACH IN USE. LANDING RUNWAY ONE RIGHT AND LEFT. DEPARTURE RUNWAY THREE ZERO. ARMEL VORTAC OUT OF SERVICE. ADVISE YOU HAVE SIERRA.

    c. Pilots should listen to ATIS broadcasts whenever ATIS is in operation.

    d. Pilots should notify controllers on initial contact that they have received the ATIS broadcast by repeating the alphabetical code word appended to the broadcast.

EXAMPLE:

    "INFORMATION SIERRA RECEIVED."

    e. When the pilot acknowledges that he has received the ATIS broadcast, controllers may omit those items contained in the broadcast if they are current. Rapidly changing conditions will be issued by ATC and the ATIS will contain words as follows:

EXAMPLE:

    "LATEST CEILING/VISIBILITY/ALTIMETER/WIND/(other conditions) WILL BE ISSUED BY APPROACH CONTROL/ TOWER."

NOTE.—The absence of a sky condition or ceiling and/or visibility on ATIS indicates a sky condition or ceiling of 5,000 feet or above and visibility of 5 miles or more. A remark may be made on the broadcast, "the weather is better than 5000 and 5," or the existing weather may be broadcast.

    f. Controllers will issue pertinent information to pilots who do not acknowledge receipt of a broadcast or who acknowledge receipt of a broadcast which is not current.

    g. To serve frequency limited aircraft, FSSs are equipped to transmit on the omnirange frequency at most en route VORs used as ATIS voice outlets. Such communication interrupts the ATIS broadcast. Pilots of aircraft equipped to receive on other FSS frequencies are encouraged to do so in order that these override transmissions may be kept to an absolute minimum.

    h. While it is a good operating practice for pilots to make use of the ATIS broadcast where it is available, some pilots use the phrase "Have Numbers" in communications with the control tower. Use of this phrase means that the pilot has received wind, runway, and altimeter information ONLY and the tower does not have to repeat this information. It does not indicate receipt of the ATIS broadcast and should never be used for this purpose.

162. RADAR TRAFFIC INFORMATION SERVICE

This is a service provided by radar ATC facilities. Pilots receiving this service are advised of any radar target observed on the radar display which may be in such proximity to the position of their aircraft or its intended route of flight that it warrants their attention. This service is not intended to relieve the pilot of his responsibility for continual vigilance to see and avoid other aircraft.

a. **Purpose of the Service:**

(1) The issuance of traffic information as observed on a radar display is based on the principle of assisting and advising a pilot that a particular radar target's position and track indicates it may intersect or pass in such proximity to his intended flight path that it warrants his attention. This is to alert the pilot to the traffic so that he can be on the lookout for it and thereby be in a better position to take appropriate action should the need arise.

(2) Pilots are reminded that the surveillance radar used by ATC does not provide altitude information unless the aircraft is equipped with MODE C and the Radar Facility is capable of displaying altitude information.

b. **Provisions of the Service:**

(1) Many factors, such as limitations of the radar, volume of traffic, controller workload and communications frequency congestion, could prevent the controller from providing this service. The controller possesses complete discretion for determining whether he is able to provide or continue to provide this service in a specific case. His reason against providing or continuing to provide the service in a particular case is not subject to question nor need it be communicated to the pilot. In other words, the provision of this service is entirely dependent upon whether the controller believes he is in a position to provide it. Traffic information is routinely provided to all aircraft operating on IFR Flight Plans except when the pilot advises he does not desire the service, or the pilot is operating within positive controlled airspace. Traffic information may be provided to flights not operating on IFR Flight Plans when requested by pilots of such flights.

NOTE.—Radar ATC facilities normally display and monitor both primary and secondary radar when it is available, except that secondary radar may be used as the sole display source in Positive Control Airspace (PCA), and under some circumstances outside of PCA (beyond primary coverage and in en route areas where only secondary is available). Secondary radar may also be used outside PCA as the sole display source when the primary radar is temporarily unusable or out of service. Pilots in contact with the affected ATC facility are normally advised when a temporary outage occurs; i.e., "primary radar out of service; traffic advisories available on transponder aircraft only." This means simply that only the aircraft which have transponders installed and in use will be depicted on ATC radar indicators when the primary radar is temporarily out of service.

(2) When receiving VFR radar advisory service, pilots should monitor the assigned frequency at all times. This is to preclude controllers' concern for radio failure or emergency assistance to aircraft under his jurisdiction. VFR radar advisory service does not include vectors away from conflicting traffic unless requested by the pilot. When advisory service is no longer desired, advise the controller before changing frequencies and then change your transponder code to 1200, if applicable. Pilots should also inform the controller when changing VFR cruising altitude. Except in programs where radar service is automatically terminated, the controller will advise the aircraft when radar is terminated.

NOTE.—Participation by VFR pilots in formal programs implemented at certain terminal locations constitutes pilot request. This also applies to participating pilots at those locations where arriving VFR flights are encouraged to make their first contact with the tower on the approach control frequency.

c. **Issuance of Traffic Information**— Traffic information will include the following concerning a target which may constitute traffic for an aircraft that is:

(1) Radar identified:

(a) Azimuth from the aircraft in terms of the 12 hour clock, or

(b) When rapidly maneuvering civil test or military aircraft prevent accurate issuance of traffic as in (a) above, specify the direction from an aircraft's position in terms of the eight cardinal compass points (N, NE, E, SE, S, SW, W, NW). This method shall be terminated at the pilot's request.

(c) Distance from the aircraft in nautical miles;

(d) Direction in which the target is proceeding; and

(e) Type of aircraft and altitude if known.

EXAMPLE:

Traffic 10 o'clock, 3 miles, west-bound (type aircraft and altitude, if known, of the observed traffic). The altitude may be known, by means of MODE C, but not verified with the pilot for accuracy. (To be valid for separation purposes by ATC, the accuracy of MODE C readouts must be verified. This is usually accomplished upon initial entry into the radar system by a comparison of the readout to pilot stated altitude, or the field elevation in the case of continuous readout being received from an aircraft on the airport.) When necessary to issue traffic advisories containing unverified altitude information, the controller will issue the advisory in the same manner as if it were verified due to the accuracy of these readouts. The pilot may upon receipt of traffic information, request a vector (heading) to avoid such traffic. The vector will be provided to the extent possible as determined by the controller provided the aircraft to be vectored is within the airspace under the jurisdiction of the controller.

(2) Not radar identified:

(a) Distance and direction with respect to a fix;

(b) Direction in which the target is proceeding; and

(c) Type of aircraft and altitude if known.

EXAMPLE:

Traffic 8 miles south of the airport northeastbound, (type aircraft and altitude if known).

d. The examples depicted in the following figures point out the possible error in the position of this traffic when it is necessary for a pilot to apply drift correction to maintain this track. This error could also occur in the event a change in course is made at the time radar traffic information is issued.

(1) In *Figure 4-1* traffic information would be issued to the pilot of aircraft "A" as 12 o'clock. The actual position of the traffic as seen by the pilot of aircraft "A" would be 2 o'clock. Traffic information issued to aircraft "B" would also be given as 12 o'clock, but in this case, the pilot of "B" would see his traffic at 10 o'clock.

(2) In *Figure 4-2* traffic information would be issued to the pilot of aircraft "C" as 2 o'clock. The actual position of the traffic as seen by the pilot of aircraft "C" would be 3 o'clock. Traffic information issued to aircraft "D" would be at an 11 o'clock position. Since it is not necessary for the pilot of aircraft "D" to apply wind correction (crab) to make good his track, the actual position of the traffic issued would be correct. Since the radar controller can only observe aircraft track (course) on his radar display, he must issue traffic advisories accordingly, and pilots should give due consideration to this fact when looking for reported traffic.

163. SAFETY ALERT

A safety alert will be issued to pilots of aircraft being controlled by ATC if the controller is aware the aircraft is at an altitude which, in the controller's judgment, places the aircraft in unsafe proximity to terrain, obstructions or other aircraft. The provision of this service is contingent upon the capability of the controller to have an awareness of a situation involving unsafe proximity to terrain, obstructions and uncontrolled aircraft. The issuance of a safety alert cannot be mandated, but it can be expected on a reasonable, though intermittent basis. Once the alert is issued, it is solely the pilot's prerogative to determine what course of action, if any, he will take. This procedure is intended for use in time critical situations where aircraft safety is in question. Noncritical situations should be handled via the normal traffic alert procedures.

a. Terrain or Obstruction Alert:

(1) The controller will immediately issue an alert to the pilot of an aircraft under his control when he recognizes that the aircraft is at an altitude which, in his judgment, may be in unsafe proximity to terrain/obstructions. The primary method of detecting unsafe proximity is through MODE C automatic altitude reports.

EXAMPLE:

LOW ALTITUDE ALERT, CHECK YOUR ALTITUDE IMMEDIATELY. THE, as appropriate, MEA/MVA/MOCA IN YOUR AREA IS (altitude) or, if past the final approach fix (non precision approach) or the outer marker or fix used in lieu of the outer marker (precision approach), THE, as appropriate, MDA/DH (if known) is (altitude).

(2) Terminal ARTS IIA, III, AND IIIA facilities have an automated function which, if operating, alerts the controller when a tracked MODE C equipped aircraft under his control is below or is predicted to be below a predetermined minimum safe altitude. This function, called Minimum Safe Altitude Warning (MSAW), is designed solely as a controller aid in detecting potentially unsafe aircraft proximity to terrain/ obstructions. The ARTS IIA, III, and IIIA facility will, when MSAW is operating, provide MSAW monitoring for all aircraft with an operating MODE C altitude encoding transponder that are tracked by the system and are:

(a) Operating on an IFR flight plan, or

(b) Operating VFR and have requested MSAW monitoring.

(3) Terminal AN/TPX-42A (number beacon decoder system) facilities have an automated function called Low Altitude Alert System (LAAS). Although not as sophisticated as MSAW, LAAS alerts the controller when a MODE C transponder equipped aircraft operating on an IFR flight plan is below a predetermined minimum safe altitude.

NOTE.—Pilots operating VFR may request MSAW or LAAS monitoring if their aircraft are equipped with MODE C transponders.

EXAMPLE:

APACHE THREE THREE PAPA REQUEST MSAW/LAAS.

b. Aircraft Conflict Alert:

(1) The controller will immediately issue an alert to the pilot of an aircraft under his control if he is aware of another aircraft which is not under his control is at an altitude which, in the controller's judgment, places both aircraft in unsafe proximity to each other. With the alert, when feasible, the controller will offer the pilot the position of the traffic if time permits and an alternate course(s) of action. Any alternate course(s) of action the controller may recommend to the pilot will be predicated only on other traffic under his control.

EXAMPLE:

AMERICAN THREE, TRAFFIC ALERT, (position of traffic, if time permits), ADVISE YOU TURN RIGHT/LEFT HEADING (degrees) AND/OR CLIMB/DESCEND TO (altitude) IMMEDIATELY.

164. RADAR ASSISTANCE TO VFR AIRCRAFT

a. Radar equipped FAA ATC facilities provide radar assistance and navigation service (vectors) to VFR aircraft provided the aircraft can communicate with the facility, are within radar coverage, and can be radar identified.

b. Pilots should clearly understand that authorization to proceed in accordance with such radar navigational assistance does not constitute authorization for the pilot to violate FARs. In effect, assistance provided is on the basis that navigational guidance information issued is advisory in nature and the job of flying the aircraft safely, remains with the pilot.

c. In many cases, the controller will be unable to determine if flight into instrument conditions will result from his instructions. To avoid possible hazards resulting from being vectored into IFR conditions, pilots should keep the controller advised of the weather conditions in which he is operating and along the course ahead.

d. Radar navigation assistance (vectors) may be initiated by the controller when one of the following conditions exist:

(1) The controller suggests the vector and the pilot concurs.

(2) A special program has been established and vectoring service has been advertised.

(3) In the controller's judgment the vector is necessary for air safety.

e. Radar navigation assistance (vectors) and other radar derived information may be provided in response to pilot requests. Many factors, such as limitations of radar, volume of traffic, communications frequency, congestion, and controller workload could prevent the controller from providing it. The controller has complete discretion for determining if he is able to provide the service in a particular case. His decision not to provide the service in a particular case is not subject to question.

165. TERMINAL RADAR PROGRAMS FOR VFR AIRCRAFT

a. Basic Radar Service

(1) In addition to the use of radar for the control of IFR aircraft, all commissioned radar facilities provide traffic advisories and limited vectoring (on a workload permitting basis) to VFR aircraft.

NOTE.—When the STAGE services were developed, two basic radar services (traffic advisories and limited vectoring) were identified as STAGE I. This definition became, over the years, unnecessary. Therefore, the term STAGE I has been eliminated from use in the field and the handbooks. These basic services will still be provided by all commissioned terminal radar facilities whether they are STAGE II, III, or neither.

(2) Vectoring service may be provided when requested by the pilot or with pilot concurrence when suggested by ATC.

(3) Pilots of arriving aircraft should contact approach control on the publicized frequency and give their position, altitude, radar beacon code (if transponder equipped), destination, and request traffic information.

(4) Approach control will issue wind and runway, except when the pilot states "HAVE NUMBERS" or this information is contained in the ATIS broadcast and the pilot indicates he has received the ATIS information. Traffic information is provided on a workload permitting basis. Approach control will specify the time or place at which the pilot is to contact the tower on local control frequency for further landing information. Upon being told to contact the tower, radar service is automatically terminated.

b. Stage II Service (Radar Advisory and Sequencing for VFR Aircraft)

(1) This service has been implemented at certain terminal locations (See locations listed in the Airport/Facility Directory). The purpose of the service is to adjust the flow of arriving VFR and IFR aircraft into the traffic pattern in a safe and orderly manner and to provide radar traffic information to departing VFR aircraft. Pilot participation is urged but it is not mandatory.

(2) Pilots of arriving VFR aircraft should initiate radio contact on the publicized frequency with approach control when approximately 25 miles from the airport at which Stage II services are being provided. On initial contact by VFR aircraft, approach control will assume that Stage II service is requested. Approach control will provide the pilot with wind and runway (except when the pilot states "HAVE NUMBERS" or that he has received the ATIS information), routings, etc., as necessary for proper sequencing with other participating VFR and IFR traffic en route to the airport. Traffic information will be provided on a workload permitting basis. If an arriving aircraft does not want the service, the pilot should state "NEGATIVE STAGE II" or make a similar comment, on initial contact with approach control.

(3) After radar contact is established, the pilot may navigate on his own into the traffic pattern or, depending on traffic conditions, may be directed to fly specific headings to position the flight behind a preceding aircraft in the approach sequence. When a flight is positioned behind the preceding aircraft and the pilot reports having that aircraft in sight, he will be directed to follow it. If other "nonparticipating" or "local" aircraft are in the traffic pattern, the tower will issue a landing sequence. Radar service will be continued to the runway.

(4) Standard radar separation will be provided between IFR aircraft until such time as the aircraft is sequenced and the pilot sees the traffic he is to follow. Standard radar separation between VFR or between VFR and IFR aircraft will not be provided.

(5) Pilots of departing VFR aircraft are encouraged to request radar traffic information by notifying ground control on initial contact with their request and proposed direction of flight.

EXAMPLE:

XRAY GROUND CONTROL, NOVEMBER ONE EIGHT SIX, READY TO TAXI, VFR SOUTHBOUND, HAVE INFORMATION BRAVO AND REQUEST RADAR TRAFFIC INFORMATION.

NOTE.—Following takeoff, the tower will advise when to contact departure control.

(6) Pilots of aircraft transiting the area and in radar contact/communication with approach control will receive traffic information on a controller workload permitting basis. Pilots of such aircraft should give their position, altitude, radar beacon code (if transponder equipped), destination, and/or route of flight.

c. Stage III Service (Radar Sequencing and Separation Service for VFR Aircraft).

(1) This service has been implemented at certain terminal locations. The service is advertised in the Airport/Facility Directory. The purpose of this service is to provide separation between all participating VFR aircraft and all IFR aircraft operating within the airspace defined as the Terminal Radar Service Area (TRSA). Pilot participation is urged but it is not mandatory.

(2) If any aircraft does not want the service, the pilot should state "NEGATIVE STAGE III" or make a similar comment, on initial contact with approach control or ground control, as appropriate.

(3) TRSAs are depicted on sectional aeronautical charts and listed in the airport/facility directory.

(4) While operating within a TRSA, pilots are provided Stage III service and separation as prescribed in this paragraph. In the event of a radar outage, separation and sequencing of VFR aircraft will be suspended as this service is dependent on radar. The pilot will be advised that the service is not available and issued wind, runway information, and the time or place to contact the tower. Traffic information will be provided on a workload permitting basis.

(5) Visual separation is used when prevailing conditions permit and it will be applied as follows:

(a) When a VFR flight is positioned behind the preceding aircraft and the pilot reports having that aircraft in sight, he will be directed to follow it. Radar service will be continued to the runway.

(b) When IFR flights are being sequenced with other traffic and the pilot reports the aircraft he is to follow in sight, the pilot may be directed to follow it and will be cleared for a "visual approach."

(c) If other "nonparticipating" or "local" aircraft are in the traffic pattern, the tower will issue a landing sequence.

(d) Departing VFR aircraft may be asked if they can visually follow a preceding departure out of the TRSA. If the pilot concurs, he will be directed to follow it until leaving the TRSA.

(6) Until visual separation is obtained, standard vertical or radar separation will be provided.

(a) 1000 feet vertical separation may be used between IFR aircraft.

(b) 500 feet vertical separation may be used between VFR aircraft, or between a VFR and an IFR aircraft.

(c) Radar separation varies depending on size of aircraft and aircraft distance from the radar antenna. The minimum separation used will be 1 1/2 miles for most VFR aircraft under 12,500 pounds GWT. If being separated from larger aircraft, the minimum is increased appropriately.

(7) Pilots operating VFR under Stage III in a TRSA—

(a) Must maintain an altitude when assigned by ATC unless the altitude assignment is to maintain at or below a specified altitude. ATC may assign altitudes for separation that do not conform to FAR—91.109. When the altitude assignment is no longer needed for separation or when leaving the TRSA, the instruction will be broadcast, "RESUME APPROPRIATE VFR ALTITUDES." Pilots must then return to an altitude that conforms to FAR—91.109 as soon as practicable.

(b) When not assigned an altitude, the pilot should coordinate with ATC prior to any altitude change.

(8) Within the TRSA, traffic information on observed but unidentified targets will, to the extent possible, be provided all IFR and participating VFR aircraft. At the request of the pilot, he will be vectored to avoid the observed traffic, insofar as possible, provided the aircraft to be vectored is within the airspace under the jurisdiction of the controller.

(9) Departing aircraft should inform ATC of their intended destination and/or route of flight and proposed cruising altitude.

(10) ATC will normally advise participating VFR aircraft when leaving the geographical limits of the TRSA. Radar service is not automatically terminated with this advisory unless specifically stated by the controller.

d. PILOT RESPONSIBILITY: THESE PROGRAMS ARE NOT TO BE INTERPRETED AS RELIEVING PILOTS OF THEIR RESPONSIBILITIES TO SEE AND AVOID OTHER

TRAFFIC OPERATING IN BASIC VFR WEATHER CONDITIONS, TO ADJUST THEIR OPERATIONS AND FLIGHT PATH AS NECESSARY TO PRECLUDE SERIOUS WAKE ENCOUNTERS, TO MAINTAIN APPROPRIATE TERRAIN AND OBSTRUCTION CLEARANCE, OR TO REMAIN IN WEATHER CONDITIONS EQUAL TO OR BETTER THAN THE MINIMUMS REQUIRED BY FAR—91.105. WHENEVER COMPLIANCE WITH AN ASSIGNED ROUTE, HEADING AND/OR ALTITUDE IS LIKELY TO COMPROMISE PILOT RESPONSIBILITY RESPECTING TERRAIN AND OBSTRUCTION CLEARANCE, VORTEX EXPOSURE, AND WEATHER MINIMUMS, APPROACH CONTROL SHOULD BE SO ADVISED AND A REVISED CLEARANCE OR INSTRUCTION OBTAINED.

166. RESERVED.

167. TOWER EN ROUTE CONTROL (TEC)

a. TEC is an ATC program to provide a service to aircraft proceeding to and from metropolitan areas. It links designated approach control areas by a network of identified routes made up of the existing airway structure of the National Airspace System. The FAA initiated an expanded TEC program to include as many facilities as possible. The program's intent is to provide an overflow resource in the low altitude system which would enhance ATC services. A few facilities have historically allowed turbojets to proceed between certain city pairs, such as Milwaukee and Chicago, via tower en route and these locations may continue this service. However, the expanded TEC program will be applied, generally, for nonturbojet aircraft operating at and below 10,000 feet. The program is entirely within the approach control airspace of multiple terminal facilities. Essentially, it is for relatively short flights. Participating pilots are encouraged to use TEC for flights of two hours duration or less. If longer flights are planned, extensive coordination may be required within the multiple complex which could result in unanticipated delays.

b. Pilots requesting TEC are subject to the same delay factor at the destination airport as other aircraft in the ATC system. In addition, departure and en route delays may occur depending upon individual facility workload. When a major metropolitan airport is incurring significant delays, pilots in the TEC program may want to consider an alternative airport experiencing no delay.

c. There are no unique requirements upon pilots to use the TEC program. Normal flight plan filing procedures will ensure proper flight plan processing. Pilots should include the acronym "TEC" in the remarks section of the flight plan when requesting tower en route.

d. All approach controls in the system may not operate up to the maximum TEC altitude of 10,000 feet. IFR flight may be planned to any satellite airport in proximity to the major primary airport via the same routing.

168—169. RESERVED

170. TRANSPONDER OPERATION

a. GENERAL

(1) Pilots should be aware that proper application of transponder operating procedures will provide both VFR and IFR aircraft with a higher degree of safety in the environment where high-speed closure rates are possible. Transponders substantially increase the capability of radar to see an aircraft and the MODE C feature enables the controller to quickly determine where potential traffic conflicts may exist. Even VFR pilots who are not in contact with ATC will be afforded greater protection from IFR aircraft and VFR aircraft which are receiving traffic advisories. Nevertheless, pilots should never relax their visual scanning vigilance for other aircraft.

(2) Air Traffic Control Radar Beacon System (ATCRBS) is similar to and compatible with military coded radar beacon equipment. Civil MODE A is identical to military MODE 3.

(3) Civil and military transponders should be adjusted to the "on" or normal operating position as late as practicable prior to takeoff and to "off" or "standby" as soon as practicable after completing landing roll, unless the change to "standby" has been accomplished previously at the request of ATC. IN ALL CASES, WHILE IN CONTROLLED AIRSPACE EACH PILOT OPERATING AN AIRCRAFT EQUIPPED WITH AN OPERABLE ATC TRANSPONDER MAINTAINED IN ACCORDANCE WITH FAR—91.172 SHALL OPERATE THE TRANSPONDER, INCLUDING MODE C IF INSTALLED, ON THE APPROPRIATE CODE OR AS ASSIGNED BY ATC. IN UNCONTROLLED AIRSPACE, THE TRANSPONDER SHOULD BE OPERATING WHILE AIRBORNE UNLESS OTHERWISE REQUESTED BY ATC.

(4) If a pilot on an IFR flight cancels his IFR flight plan prior to reaching his destination, he should adjust his transponder according to VFR operations.

(5) If entering a U.S. domestic control area from outside the U.S., the pilot should advise on first radio contact with a U.S. radar ATC facility that such equipment is available by adding "transponder" to the aircraft identification.

(6) It should be noted by all users of the ATC Transponders that the coverage they can expect is limited to "line of sight." Low altitude or aircraft antenna shielding by the aircraft itself may result in reduced range. Range can be improved by climbing to a higher altitude. It may be possible to minimize antenna shielding by locating the antenna where dead spots are only noticed during abnormal flight attitudes.

b. TRANSPONDER CODE DESIGNATION

(1) For ATC to utilize one or a combination of the 4096 discrete codes FOUR DIGIT CODE DESIGNATION will be used, e.g., code 2100 will be expressed as TWO ONE ZERO ZERO. Due to the operational characteristics of the rapidly expanding automated air traffic control system, THE LAST TWO DIGITS OF THE SELECTED TRANSPONDER CODE SHOULD ALWAYS READ "00" UNLESS SPECIFICALLY REQUESTED BY ATC TO BE OTHERWISE.

c. AUTOMATIC ALTITUDE REPORTING (MODE C)

(1) Some transponders are equipped with a MODE C automatic altitude reporting capability. This system converts aircraft altitude in 100 foot increments to coded digital information which is transmitted together with MODE C framing pulses to the interrogating radar facility. The manner in which transponder panels are designed differs, therefore, a pilot should be thoroughly familiar with the operation of his transponder so that ATC may realize its full capabilities.

(2) Adjust transponder to reply on the MODE A/3 code specified by ATC and, if equipped, to reply on MODE C with altitude reporting *capability activated* unless deactivation is directed by ATC or unless the installed aircraft equipment has not been tested and calibrated as required by FAR—91.36. If deactivation is required by ATC, turn off the altitude reporting feature of your transponder. An instruction by ATC to "STOP ALTITUDE SQUAWK,

ALTITUDE DIFFERS (number of feet) FEET," may be an indication that your transponder is transmitting incorrect altitude information or that you have an incorrect altimeter setting. While an incorrect altimeter setting has no effect on the MODE C altitude information transmitted by your transponder (transponders are preset at 29.92), it would cause you to fly at an actual altitude different from your assigned altitude. When a controller indicates that an altitude readout is invalid, the pilot should initiate a check to verify that the aircraft altimeter is set correctly.

(3) Pilots of aircraft with operating MODE C altitude reporting transponders should report exact altitude or flight level to the nearest hundred foot increment when establishing initial contact with an ATC facility. Exact altitude or flight level reports on initial contact provide ATC with information that is required prior to using MODE C altitude information for separation purposes. This will significantly reduce altitude verification requests.

d. TRANSPONDER IDENT FEATURE

(1) The transponder shall be operated only as specified by ATC. Activate the "IDENT" feature only upon request of the ATC controller.

e. CODE CHANGES

(1) When making routine code changes, pilots should avoid inadvertent selection of codes 7500, 7600 or 7700 thereby causing momentary false alarms at automated ground facilities. For example when switching from code 2700 to code 7200, switch first to 2200 then to 7200, NOT to 7700 and then 7200. This procedure applies to nondiscrete code 7500 and all discrete codes in the 7600 and 7700 series (i.e. 7600-7677, 7700-7777) which will trigger special indicators in automated facilities. Only nondiscrete code 7500 will be decoded as the hijack code.

(2) Under no circumstances should a pilot of a civil aircraft operate the transponder on Code7777. This code is reserved for military interceptor operations.

(3) Military pilots operating VFR or IFR within restricted/warning areas should adjust their transponders to code 4000 unless another code has been assigned by ATC.

f. DEVIATIONS FROM TRANSPONDER REQUIREMENTS

(1) Specific details concerning requirements, exceptions, and ATC authorized deviations for transponder and MODE C operation above 12,500 feet and below 18,000 feet MSL are found in FAR—91.24. In general, the FAR requires aircraft to be equipped with MODE A/3 (4096 codes) and MODE C altitude reporting capability when operating in controlled airspace of the 48 contiguous states, and the District of Columbia above 12,500 feet MSL, excluding airspace at and below 2,500 feet AGL. Pilots shall ensure that their aircraft transponder is operating on an appropriate ATC assigned VFR/IFR code and MODE C when operating in such airspace. If in doubt about the operational status of either feature of your transponder while airborne, contact the nearest ATC facility or FSS and they will advise you what facility you should contact for determining the status of your equipment. In-flight requests for "immediate" deviation may be approved by controllers only when the flight will continue IFR or when weather conditions prevent VFR descent and continued VFR flight in airspace not affected by the FAR. All other requests for deviation should be made by contacting the nearest Flight Service or Air Traffic facility in person or by telephone. The nearest ARTCC will normally be the controlling agency and is responsible for coordinating requests involving deviations in other ARTCC areas.

g. TRANSPONDER OPERATION UNDER VISUAL FLIGHT RULES (VFR)

(1) Unless otherwise instructed by an Air Traffic Control Facility, adjust Transponder to reply on MODE 3/A code 1200 regardless of altitude.

(2) Adjust transponder to reply on MODE C, with altitude reporting *capability activated* if the aircraft is so equipped, unless deactivation is directed by ATC or unless the installed equipment has not been tested and calibrated as required by FAR—91.36. If deactivation is required and your transponder is so designed, turn off the altitude reporting switch and continue to transmit MODE C framing pulses. If this capability does not exist, turn off MODE C.

h. RADAR BEACON PHRASEOLOGY

Air traffic controllers, both civil and military, will use the following phraseology when referring to operation of the Air Traffic Control Radar Beacon System (ATCRBS). Instructions by ATC refer only to MODE A/3 or MODE C operation and do not affect the operation of the transponder on other MODEs.

(1) **SQUAWK (number)**— Operate radar beacon transponder on designated code in MODE A/3.

(2) **IDENT**— Engage the "IDENT" feature (military I/P) of the transponder.

(3) **SQUAWK (number) and IDENT**— Operate transponder on specified code in MODE A/3 and engage the "IDENT" (military I/P) feature.

(4) **SQUAWK STANDBY**— Switch transponder to standby position.

(5) **SQUAWK LOW/NORMAL**— Operate transponder on low or normal sensitivity as specified. Transponder is operated in "NORMAL" position unless ATC specifies "LOW", ("ON" is used instead of "NORMAL" as a master control label on some types of transponders.)

(6) **SQUAWK ALTITUDE**— Activate MODE C with automatic altitude reporting.

(7) **STOP ALTITUDE SQUAWK**— Turn off altitude reporting switch and continue transmitting MODE C framing pulses. If your equipment does not have this capability, turn off MODE C.

(8) **STOP SQUAWK (mode in use)**— Switch off specified mode. (Used for military aircraft when the controller is unaware of military service requirements for the aircraft to continue operation on another MODE.)

(9) **STOP SQUAWK**— Switch off transponder.

(10) **SQUAWK MAYDAY**— Operate transponder in the emergency position (MODE A Code 7700 for civil transponder. MODE 3 Code 7700 and emergency feature for military transponder.)

171. HAZARDOUS AREA REPORTING SERVICE

a. Selected FSSs provide flight monitoring where regularly traveled VFR routes cross large bodies of water, swamps, and mountains. This service is provided for the purpose of expeditiously alerting Search and Rescue facilities when required. *(See Figure 4-3.)*

(1) When requesting the service either in person, by telephone or by radio, pilots should be prepared to give the following information — type of aircraft, altitude, indicated airspeed, present position, route of flight, heading.

(2) Radio contacts are desired at least every 10 minutes. If contact is lost for more than 15 minutes, Search and Rescue will be

alerted. Pilots are responsible for canceling their request for service when they are outside the service area boundary. Pilots experiencing two-way radio failure are expected to land as soon as practicable and cancel their request for the service. The accompanying illustration titled "LAKE, ISLAND, MOUNTAIN AND SWAMP REPORTING SERVICE" depicts the areas and the FSS facilities involved in this program.

b. LONG ISLAND SOUND REPORTING SERVICE

The New York and Bridgeport AFSSs provide Long Island Sound Reporting service on request for aircraft traversing Long Island Sound.

(1) When requesting the service pilots should ask for SOUND REPORTING SERVICE and should be prepared to provide the following appropriate information:

(a) Type and color of aircraft,

(b) The specific route and altitude across the sound including the shore crossing point,

(c) The overwater crossing time,

(d) Number of persons on board,

(e) True air speed.

(2) Radio contacts are desired at least every 10 minutes, however, for flights of shorter duration a midsound report is requested. If contact is lost for more than 15 minutes Search and Rescue will be alerted. Pilots are responsible for canceling their request for the Long Island Sound Reporting Service when outside the service area boundary. Aircraft experiencing radio failure will be expected to land as soon as practicable and cancel their request for the service.

(3) COMMUNICATIONS: Primary communications—pilots are to transmit on 122.1 MHz and listen on one of the following VOR frequencies:

(a) NEW YORK AFSS CONTROLS:

1. Hampton VORTAC (FSS transmits on 113.6 and receives on 122.1 MHz).

2. Calverton VORTAC (FSS transmits on 117.2 and receives on standard FSS frequencies).

3. Kennedy VORTAC (FSS transmits on 115.9 and receives on 122.1 MHz).

(b) BRIDGEPORT AFSS CONTROLS:

1. Madison VORTAC (FSS transmits on 110.4 and receives on 122.1 MHz).

2. Trumbull VOR (FSS transmits on 111.8 and receives on 122.1 MHz).

3. Bridgeport VOR (FSS transmits on 108.8 and receives on 122.1 MHz).

c. BLOCK ISLAND REPORTING SERVICE

Within the Long Island Reporting Service, the New York FSS also provides an additional service for aircraft operating between Montauk Point and Block Island. When requesting this service, pilots should ask for BLOCK ISLAND REPORTING SERVICE and should be prepared to provide the same flight information as required for the Long Island Sound Reporting Service.

(1) A minimum of three position reports are mandatory for this service; these are:

(a) Reporting leaving either Montauk Point or Block Island.

(b) Midway report.

(c) Report when over either Montauk Point or Block Island. At this time, the overwater service is canceled.

(2) COMMUNICATIONS: Pilots are to transmit on 122.1 MHz and listen on the Hampton VORTAC (HTO) frequency 113.6 MHz.

NOTE.—Pilots are advised that 122.1 MHz is a remote receiver located at the Hampton VORTAC site and designed to provide radio coverage between Hampton and Block Island. Flights proceeding beyond Block Island may contact the Bridgeport AFSS by transmitting on 122.1 MHz and listening on Trumbull VOR (TMU) frequency 111.8 MHz.

d. CAPE COD AND ISLANDS RADAR OVERWATER FLIGHT FOLLOWING

In addition to normal VFR radar advisory services, traffic permitting, Otis Approach Control provides a radar overwater flight following service for aircraft traversing the Cape Cod and adjacent Island area. Pilots desiring this service may contact Otis RAPCON on 118.2 MHz.

(1) Pilots requesting this service should be prepared to give the following information:

(a) type and color of aircraft,

(b) altitude,

(c) position and heading,

(d) route of flight, and

(e) true airspeed.

(2) For best radar coverage, pilots are encouraged to fly at 1,500 feet MSL or above.

(3) Pilots are responsible for canceling their request for overwater flight following when they are over the mainland and/or outside the service area boundary.

172—189. RESERVED

Section 2.   RADIO COMMUNICATIONS PHRASEOLOGY AND TECHNIQUES

190. GENERAL

a.   Radio communications are a critical link in the ATC system. The link can be a strong bond between pilot and controller or it can be broken with surprising speed and disastrous results. Discussion herein provides basic procedures for new pilots and also highlights safe operating concepts for all pilots.

b.   The single, most important thought in pilot-controller communications is understanding. It is essential, therefore, that pilots acknowledge each radio communication with ATC by using the appropriate aircraft call sign. Brevity is important, and contacts should be kept as brief as possible, but the controller must know what you want to do before he can properly carry out his control duties. And you, the pilot, must know exactly what he wants you to do. Since concise phraseology may not always be adequate, use whatever words are necessary to get your message across.

c.   All pilots will find the Pilot/Controller Glossary very helpful in learning what certain words or phrases mean. Good phraseology enhances safety and is the mark of a professional pilot. Jargon, chatter and "CB" slang have no place in ATC communications. The Pilot/Controller Glossary is the same glossary used in the ATC controller's handbook. We recommend that it be studied and reviewed from time to time to sharpen your communication skills.

191. RADIO TECHNIQUE

a.   *Listen* before you transmit. Many times you can get the information you want through ATIS or by monitoring the frequency. Except for a few situations where some frequency overlap occurs, if you hear someone else talking, the keying of your transmitter will be futile and you will probably jam their receivers causing them to repeat their call. If you have just changed frequencies, pause, listen and make sure the frequency is clear.

b.   *Think* before keying your transmitter. Know what you want to say and if it is lengthy, e.g., a flight plan or IFR position report, jot it down.

c.   The microphone should be very close to your lips and after pressing the mike button, a slight pause may be necessary to be sure the first word is transmitted. Speak in a normal conversational tone.

d.   When you release the button, wait a few seconds before calling again. The controller or FSS specialist may be jotting down your number, looking for your flight plan, transmitting on a different frequency, or selecting his transmitter to your frequency.

e.   Be alert to the sounds *or lack of sounds* in your receiver. Check your volume, recheck your frequency and *make sure that your microphone is not stuck* in the transmit position. Frequency blockage can, and has, occurred for extended periods of time due to unintentional transmitter operation. This type of interference is commonly referred to as a "stuck mike," and controllers may refer to it in this manner when attempting to assign an alternate frequency. If the assigned frequency is completely blocked by this type of interference, use the procedures described for en route IFR radio frequency outage, to establish or reestablish communications with ATC.

f.   Be sure that you are within the performance range of your radio equipment and the ground station equipment. Remote radio

sites do not always transmit and receive on all of a facilities available frequencies, particularly with regard to VOR sites where you can hear but not reach a ground station's receiver. Remember that higher altitude increases the range of VHF "line of sight" communications.

192. CONTACT PROCEDURES

a.   Initial Contact.

(1)   The term initial contact or initial callup means the first radio call you make to a given facility, or the first call to a different controller or FSS specialist within a facility. *Use the following format:*

(a)   name of facility being called,

(b)   your *full* aircraft identification as filed in the flight plan or as discussed under Aircraft Call Signs below,

(c)   type of message to follow or your request if it is short, and

(d)   the word "Over", if required.

EXAMPLE:

"NEW YORK RADIO, MOONEY THREE ONE ONE ECHO."

EXAMPLE:

"COLUMBIA GROUND, CESSNA THREE ONE SIX ZERO FOXTROT, IFR MEMPHIS."

EXAMPLE:

"MIAMI CENTER BARON FIVE SIX THREE HOTEL, REQUEST VFR TRAFFIC ADVISORIES."

(2)   If radio reception is reasonably assured, inclusion of your request, your position or altitude, the phrase "Have numbers" or "Information Charlie received" (for ATIS) in the initial contact helps decrease radio frequency congestion. Use discretion and do not overload the controller with information he does not need. If you do not get a response from the ground station, recheck your radios or use another transmitter but keep the next contact short.

EXAMPLE:

"ATLANTA CENTER, DUKE FOUR ONE ROMEO, REQUEST VFR TRAFFIC ADVISORIES, TWENTY NORTHWEST ROME, SEVEN THOUSAND FIVE HUNDRED, OVER."

b.   Initial Contact When your Transmitting and Receiving Frequencies are Different.

(1)   If you are attempting to establish contact with a ground station and you are receiving on a different frequency than that transmitted, indicate the VOR name or the frequency on which you expect a reply. Most FSSs and control facilities can transmit on several VOR stations in the area. Use the appropriate FSS call sign as indicated on charts.

EXAMPLE:

New York FSS transmits on the Kennedy, Hampton and Calverton VORTACs. If you are in the Calverton area, your callup should be "NEW YORK RADIO, CESSNA THREE ONE SIX ZERO FOXTROT, RECEIVING CALVERTON VOR, OVER."

(2) If the chart indicates FSS frequencies above the VORTAC or in FSS communications boxes, transmit or receive on those frequencies nearest your location.

(3) When unable to establish contact and you wish to call *any* ground station, use the phrase "ANY RADIO (tower) (station), GIVE CESSNA THREE ONE SIX ZERO FOXTROT A CALL ON (frequency) OR (VOR)." If an emergency exists or you need assistance, so state.

c. Subsequent Contacts and Responses to Callup from a Ground Facility.

Use the same format as used for initial contact except you should state your message or request with the callup in one transmission. The ground station name and the word "Over" may be omitted if the message requires an obvious reply and there is no possibility for misunderstandings. *You should acknowledge all callups or clearances* unless the controller or FSS specialist advises otherwise. There are some occasions when the controller must issue time-critical instructions to other aircraft and he may be in a position to observe your response, either visually or on radar. If the situation demands your response, take appropriate action or immediately advise the facility of any problem. Acknowledge with your aircraft identification and one of the words "Wilco, Roger, Affirmative, Negative" or other appropriate remarks (e.g., "PIPER TWO ONE FOUR LIMA, ROGER"). If you have been receiving services (e.g., VFR traffic advisories and you are leaving the area or changing frequencies), advise the ATC facility and terminate contact.

d. Acknowledgement of Frequency Changes.

(1) When advised by ATC to change frequencies, acknowledge the instruction. If you select the new frequency without an acknowledgement, the controller's workload is increased because he has no way of knowing whether you received the instruction or have had radio communications failure.

(2) At times, a controller/specialist may be working a sector with multiple frequency assignments. In order to eliminate unnecessary verbiage and to free the controller/specialist for higher priority transmissions, the controller/specialist may request the pilot "(Identification), change to my frequency 123.4." This phrase should alert the pilot that he is only changing frequencies, not controller/specialist, and that initial call up phraseology may be abbreviated.

EXAMPLE:
"UNITED 222 ON 123.4."

e. Compliance with Frequency Changes.

When instructed by ATC to change frequencies, select the new frequency as soon as possible unless instructed to make the change at a specific time, fix, or altitude. A delay in making the change could result in an untimely receipt of important information. If you are instructed to make the frequency change at a specific time, fix, or altitude, monitor the frequency you are on until reaching the specified time, fix, or altitudes unless instructed otherwise by ATC. (See PARA—340 - ARTCC COMMUNICATIONS.)

193. AIRCRAFT CALL SIGNS

a. Precautions in the Use of Call Signs.

(1) Improper use of call signs can result in pilots executing a clearance intended for another aircraft. Call signs should *never be abbreviated on an initial contact or at any time when other aircraft call signs have similar numbers/sounds or identical letters/number* (e.g., Cessna 6132F, Cessna 1622F, Baron 123F, Cherokee 7732F, etc.).

EXAMPLE:
Assume that a controller issues an approach clearance to an aircraft at the bottom of a holding stack and an aircraft with a similar call sign (at the top of the stack) acknowledges the clearance with the last two or three numbers of his call sign. If the aircraft at the bottom of the stack did not hear the clearance and intervene, flight safety would be affected, and there would be no reason for either the controller or pilot to suspect that anything is wrong. This kind of "human factors" error can strike swiftly and is extremely difficult to rectify.

(2) Pilots; therefore, must be certain that aircraft identification is complete and clearly identified before taking action on an ATC clearance. ATC specialists will not abbreviate call signs of air carrier or other civil aircraft having authorized call signs. ATC specialists may initiate abbreviated call signs of other aircraft by using the *prefix and the last three digits/letters* of the aircraft identification after communications are established. The pilot may use the abbreviated call sign in subsequent contacts with the ATC specialist. When aware of similar/identical call signs, ATC specialists will take action to minimize errors by emphasizing certain numbers/letters, by repeating the entire call sign, repeating the prefix, or by asking pilots to use a different call sign temporarily. Pilots should use the phrase "VERIFY CLEARANCE FOR (your complete call sign)" if doubt exists concerning proper identity.

(3) Civil aircraft pilots should state the aircraft type, model or manufacturer's name followed by the digits/letters of the registration number. When the aircraft manufacturer's name or model is stated, the prefix "N" is dropped (e.g. Aztec Two Four Six Four Alpha).

EXAMPLE:
BONANZA SIX FIVE FIVE GOLF.

EXAMPLE:
BREEZY SIX ONE THREE ROMEO EXPERIMENTAL (omit "Experimental" after initial contact).

(4) Air Taxi or other commercial operators *not* having FAA authorized call signs should prefix their normal identification with the phonetic word "Tango".

EXAMPLE:
TANGO AZTEC TWO FOUR SIX FOUR ALPHA.

(5) Air carriers and commuter air carriers having FAA authorized call signs should identify themselves by stating the complete call sign, using group form for the numbers and the word "heavy" if appropriate.

EXAMPLE:
UNITED TWENTY-FIVE HEAVY.

EXAMPLE:
MIDWEST COMMUTER SEVEN ELEVEN.

(6) Military aircraft use a variety of systems including serial numbers, word call signs and combinations of letters/numbers. Examples include Army Copter 48931, Air Force 61782, MAC 31792, Pat 157, Air Evac 17652, Navy Golf Alfa Kilo 21, Marine 4 Charlie 36, etc.

b. Air Ambulance Flights.

Because of the priority afforded air ambulance flights in the ATC system, extreme discretion is necessary when using the term "LIFEGUARD." It is only intended for those missions of an urgent medical nature and to be utilized only for that portion of the flight requiring expeditious handling. When requested by the pilot, necessary notification to expedite ground handling of patients, etc., is provided by ATC; however, when possible, this information should be passed in advance through nonATC communications sytems.

(1) Civilian air ambulance flights responding to medical emergencies (first call to an accident scene, carrying patients, organ donors, organs, or other urgently needed lifesaving medical material) will be expedited by ATC when necessary. When expeditious handling is necessary, add the word "LIFEGUARD" in the remarks section of the flight plan. In radio communications, use the call sign "LIFEGUARD" followed by the aircraft type and registration letters/numbers.

(2) Similar provisions have been made for the use of "AIR EVAC" and "MED EVAC" by military air ambulance flights, except that these military flights will receive priority handling only when specifically requested.

EXAMPLE:
LIFEGUARD CESSNA TWO SIX FOUR SIX.

(3) Air carrier and air taxi flights responding to medical emergencies will also be expedited by ATC when necessary. The nature of these medical emergency flights usually concerns the transportation of urgently needed lifesaving medical materials or vital organs. IT IS IMPERATIVE THAT THE COMPANY/PILOT DETERMINE, BY THE NATURE/URGENCY OF THE SPECIFIC MEDICAL CARGO, IF PRIORITY ATC ASSISTANCE IS REQUIRED. Pilots shall ensure that the word "LIFEGUARD" is included in the remarks section of the flight plan and use the call sign "LIFEGUARD" followed by the company name and flight number, for all transmissions when expeditious handling is required. It is important for ATC to be aware of "LIFEGUARD" status, and it is the pilot's responsibility to ensure that this information is provided to ATC.

EXAMPLE:
LIFEGUARD CESSNA TWO SIX FOUR SIX.

EXAMPLE:
LIFEGUARD DELTA THIRTY-SEVEN.

EXAMPLE:
LIFEGUARD TANGO NOVEMBER ONE THREE FOUR FIVE ECHO.

c. Student Pilots Radio Identification.

(1) The FAA desires to help the student pilot in acquiring sufficient practical experience in the environment in which he will be required to operate. To receive additional assistance while operating in areas of concentrated air traffic, a student pilot need only identify himself as a student pilot during his initial call to an FAA radio facility.

EXAMPLE:
DAYTON TOWER, THIS IS FLEETWING 1234, STUDENT PILOT.

(2) This special identification will alert FAA ATC personnel and enable them to provide the student pilot with such extra assistance and consideration as he may need. This procedure is not mandatory.

194. DESCRIPTION OF INTERCHANGE OR LEASED AIRCRAFT

a. Controllers issue traffic information based on familiarity with airline equipment and color/markings. When an air carrier dispatches a flight using another company's equipment and the pilot does not advise the terminal ATC facility, the possible confusion in aircraft identification can compromise safety.

b. Pilots flying an "interchange" or "leased" aircraft not bearing the colors/markings of the company operating the aircraft should inform the terminal ATC facility on first contact the name of the operating company and trip number, followed by the company name as displayed on the aircraft, and aircraft type.

EXAMPLE:
AIR CAL 311, UNITED (INTERCHANGE/LEASE), BOEING 727.

195. GROUND STATION CALL SIGNS

Pilots, when calling a ground station, should begin with the name of the facility being called followed by the type of the facility being called, as indicated in the following examples.

Airport Unicom	"Shannon Unicom"
FAA Flight Service Station	"Chicago Radio"
FAA Flight Service Station (En Route Flight Advisory Service (Weather)	"Seattle Flight Watch"
Airport Traffic Control Tower	"Augusta Tower"
Clearance Delivery Position (IFR)	"Dallas Clearance Delivery"
Ground Control Position in Tower	"Miami Ground"
Radar or Nonradar Approach Control Position	"Oklahoma City Approach"
Radar Departure Control Position	"St. Louis Departure"
FAA Air Route Traffic Control Center	"Washington Center"

196. PHONETIC ALPHABET

The International Civil Aviation Organization (ICAO) phonetic alphabet is used by FAA personnel when communications conditions are such that the information cannot be readily received without their use. ATC facilities may also request pilots to use phonetic letter equivalents when aircraft with similar sounding identifications are receiving communications on the same frequency. Pilots should use the phonetic alphabet when identifying their aircraft during initial contact with air traffic control facilities. Additionally use the phonetic equivalents for single letters and to spell out groups of letters or difficult words during adverse communications conditions. *(See Table 4-2.)*

197—199. RESERVED

200. FIGURES

a. Figures indicating hundred and thousands in round number, as for ceiling heights, and upper wind levels up to 9900 shall be spoken in accordance with the following:

EXAMPLE:
500... FIVE HUNDRED

EXAMPLE:
4500........................FOUR THOUSAND FIVE HUNDRED

b. Numbers above 9900 shall be spoken by separating the digits preceding the word "thousand."

EXAMPLE:
10,000...ONE ZERO THOUSAND

EXAMPLE:
13,500............ONE THREE THOUSAND FIVE HUNDRED

c. Transmit airway or jet route numbers as follows:

EXAMPLE:
V12.. VICTOR TWELVE

EXAMPLE:
J533.. J FIVE THIRTY-THREE

d. All other numbers shall be transmitted by pronouncing each digit.

EXAMPLE:
10...ONE ZERO

e. When a radio frequency contains a decimal point, the decimal point is spoken as "POINT."

EXAMPLE:
122.1....................................ONE TWO TWO POINT ONE

NOTE.—ICAO Procedures require the decimal point be spoken as "DECIMAL" and FAA will honor such usage by military aircraft and all other aircraft required to use ICAO Procedures.

201. ALTITUDES AND FLIGHT LEVELS

a. Up to but not including 18,000 feet MSL — state the separate digits of the thousands, plus the hundreds, if appropriate.

EXAMPLE:
12,000...ONE TWO THOUSAND

EXAMPLE:
12,500...............ONE TWO THOUSAND FIVE HUNDRED

b. At and above, 18,000 feet MSL (FL 180) state the words "flight level" followed by the separate digits of the flight level.

EXAMPLE:
190..............................FLIGHT LEVEL ONE NINER ZERO

202. DIRECTIONS

The three digits of bearing, course, heading or wind direction should always be magnetic. The word "true" must be added when it applies.

EXAMPLE:
(magnetic course) 005...............................ZERO ZERO FIVE

EXAMPLE:
(true course) 050............................ZERO FIVE ZERO TRUE

EXAMPLE:
(magnetic bearing) 360............................ THREE SIX ZERO

EXAMPLE:
(magnetic heading) 100............................ ONE ZERO ZERO

EXAMPLE:
(wind direction) 220....................................TWO TWO ZERO

203. SPEEDS

The separate digits of the speed followed by the word "KNOTS." Except, controllers may omit the word "KNOTS" when using speed adjustment procedures, e.g., "REDUCE/INCREASE SPEED TO TWO FIVE ZERO."

EXAMPLES:
(speed) 250.................................TWO FIVE ZERO KNOTS
(speed) 190............................... ONE NINER ZERO KNOTS

The separate digits of the mach number preceded by "MACH."

EXAMPLES:
(mach number) 1.5.......................MACH ONE POINT FIVE
(mach number) .64.......................MACH POINT SIX FOUR
(mach number) .7............................MACH POINT SEVEN

204. TIME

a. FAA uses Coordinated Universal Time (UTC) for all operations. The term "Zulu" is used when ATC procedures require a reference to UTC.

EXAMPLE:
0920..ZERO NINER TWO ZERO

b. To Convert from Standard Time to Coordinated Universal Time:

Eastern Standard Time...Add 5 hours
Central Standard Time..Add 6 hours
Mountain Standard Time...................................... Add 7 hours
Pacific Standard Time..Add 8 hours
Alaska Standard Time...Add 9 hours
Hawaii Standard Time.. Add 10 hours

NOTE.—For Daylight Time subtract 1 hour.

c. The 24-hour clock system is used in radiotelephone transmissions. The hour is indicated by the first two figures and the minutes by the last two figures.

EXAMPLE:
0000..ZERO ZERO ZERO ZERO

EXAMPLE:
0920..ZERO NINER TWO ZERO

d. Time may be stated in minutes only (two figures) in radio telephone communications when no misunderstanding is likely to occur.

e. Current time in use at a station is stated in the nearest quarter minute in order that pilots may use this information for time checks. Fractions of a quarter minute less than eight seconds are stated as the preceding quarter minute; fractions of a quarter minute of eight seconds or more are stated as the succeeding quarter minute.

EXAMPLE:
0929:05.........................TIME, ZERO NINER TWO NINER

EXAMPLE:
0929:10...TIME, ZERO NINER TWO NINER AND ONE-QUARTER

205. COMMUNICATIONS WITH TOWER WHEN AIRCRAFT TRANSMITTER OR RECEIVER OR BOTH ARE INOPERATIVE

a. Arriving Aircraft

(1) Receiver inoperative — If you have reason to believe your receiver is inoperative, remain outside or above the airport traffic area until the direction and flow of traffic has been determined, then advise the tower of your type aircraft, position, altitude, intention to land and request that you be controlled with light signals. (See PARA—233 - TRAFFIC CONTROL OF LIGHT SIGNALS.) When you are approximately 3 to 5 miles from the airport, advise the tower of your position and join the airport traffic pattern. From this point on, watch the tower for light signals. Thereafter, if

a complete pattern is made, transmit your position downwind and/or turning base leg.

(2) Transmitter inoperative — Remain outside or above the airport traffic area until the direction and flow of traffic has been determined, then join the airport traffic pattern. Monitor the primary local control frequency as depicted on Sectional Charts for landing or traffic information, and look for a light signal which may be addressed to your aircraft. During hours of daylight, acknowledge tower transmissions or light signals by rocking your wings. At night, acknowledge by blinking the landing or navigation lights. To acknowledge tower transmissions during daylight hours, hovering helicopters will turn in the direction of the controlling facility and flash the landing light. While in flight, helicopters should show their acknowledgement of receiving a transmission by making shallow banks in opposite directions. At night, helicopters will acknowledge receipt of transmissions by flashing either the landing or the search light.

(3) Transmitter and receiver inoperative — Remain outside or above the airport traffic area until the direction and flow of traffic has been determined, then join the airport traffic pattern and maintain visual contact with the tower to receive light signals. Acknowledge light signals as noted above.

b. Departing Aircraft

(1) If you experience radio failure prior to leaving the parking area, make every effort to have the equipment repaired. If you are unable to have the malfunction repaired, call the tower by telephone and request authorization to depart without two-way radio communications. If tower authorization is granted, you will be given departure information and requested to monitor the tower frequency or watch for light signals, as appropriate. During daylight hours, acknowledge tower transmissions or light signals by moving the ailerons or rudder. At night, acknowledge by blinking the landing or navigation lights. If radio malfunction occurs after departing the parking area, watch the tower for light signals or monitor tower frequency.

NOTE.—Refer to FAR—91.87 and FAR—91.77.

206. COMMUNICATIONS FOR VFR FLIGHTS

a. FSSs are allocated frequencies for different functions, for example, 122.0 MHz is assigned as the En Route Flight Advisory Service frequency at selected FSSs. In addition, certain FSSs provide Airport Advisory Service on 123.6 MHz. Other FSS frequencies are listed in the Airport/Facility Directory. If you are in doubt as to what frequency to use, 122.2 MHz is assigned to the majority of FSSs as a common en route simplex frequency.

b. Certain VOR voice channels are being utilized for recorded broadcasts, i.e., ATIS, HIWAS, etc. These services and appropriate frequencies are listed in the Airport/Facility Directory. On VFR flights, pilots are urged to monitor these frequencies. When in contact with a control facility, notify the controller if you plan to leave the frequency to monitor these broadcasts.

207—219. RESERVED

Section 3. AIRPORT OPERATIONS

220. GENERAL

Increased traffic congestion, aircraft in climb and descent attitudes, and pilots preoccupation with cockpit duties are some factors that increase the hazardous accident potential near the airport. The situation is further compounded when the weather is marginal — that is, just meeting VFR requirements. Pilots must be particularly alert when operating in the vicinity of an airport. This section defines some rules, practices and procedures that pilots should be familiar with, and adhere to, for safe airport operations.

221. TOWER CONTROLLED AIRPORTS

a. When operating at an airport where traffic control is being exercised by a control tower, pilots are required to maintain two-way radio contact with the tower while operating within the airport traffic area unless the tower authorizes otherwise. Initial call-up should be made about 15 miles from the airport. Unless there is a good reason to leave the tower frequency before exiting the airport traffic area it is a good operating practice to remain on the tower frequency for the purpose of receiving traffic information. In the interest of reducing tower frequency congestion, pilots are reminded that it is not necessary to request permission to leave the tower frequency once outside of the airport traffic area.

b. When necessary, the tower controller will issue clearances or other information for aircraft to generally follow the desired flight path (traffic patterns) when flying in the airport traffic area/control zone, and the proper taxi routes when operating on the ground. If not otherwise authorized or directed by the tower, pilots of fixed-wing aircraft approaching to land must circle the airport to the left. Pilots approaching to land in a helicopter must avoid the flow of fixed-wing traffic. However, in all instances, an appropriate clearance must be received from the tower before landing.

c. The following terminology for the various components of a traffic pattern has been adopted as standard for use by control towers and pilots: *(See Figure 4-4.)*

(1) **Upwind leg** —A flight path parallel to the landing runway in the direction of landing.

(2) **Crosswind leg** —A flight path at right angles to the landing runway off its takeoff end.

(3) **Downwind leg** —A flight path parallel to the landing runway in the opposite direction of landing.

(4) **Base leg** —A flight path at right angles to the landing runway off its approach end and extending from the downwind leg to the intersection of the extended runway centerline.

(5) **Final approach** —A flight path in the direction of landing along the extended runway centerline from the base leg to the runway.

d. Many towers are equipped with a tower radar display. The radar uses are intended to enhance the effectiveness and efficiency of the local control, or tower, position. They are not intended to provide radar services or benefits to pilots except as they may accrue through a more efficient tower operation. The four basic uses are:

(1) **To determine an aircraft's exact location**—This is accomplished by radar identifying the VFR aircraft through any of the techniques available to a radar position; such as having the aircraft ident. Once identified, the aircraft's position and spatial relationship to other aircraft can be quickly determined and standard instructions regarding VFR operation in the airport traffic area will be issued. Once initial radar identification of a VFR aircraft has been established and the appropriate instructions have been issued, radar monitoring may be discontinued. The reason being that the local controller's primary means of surveillance in VFR conditions is visually scanning the airport and local area.

(2) **To provide radar traffic advisories**—Radar traffic advisories may be provided to the extent that the local controller is able to monitor the radar display. Local control has primary control responsibilities to the aircraft operating on the runways which will normally supersede radar monitoring duties.

(3) **To provide a direction or suggested heading**—The local controller may provide pilots flying VFR with generalized instructions which will facilitate operations (e.g.,"PROCEED SOUTHWEST BOUND, ENTER A RIGHT DOWNWIND RUNWAY THREE ZERO"); or provide a suggested heading to establish radar identification or as an advisory aid to navigation (e.g., "SUGGESTED HEADING TWO TWO ZERO, FOR RADAR IDENTIFICATION"). In both cases, the instructions are advisory aids to the pilot flying VFR and are not radar vectors. PILOTS HAVE COMPLETE DISCRETION REGARDING ACCEPTANCE OF THE SUGGESTED HEADING OR DIRECTION AND HAVE SOLE RESPONSIBILITY FOR SEEING AND AVOIDING OTHER AIRCRAFT.

(4) **To provide information and instructions to aircraft operating within the airport traffic area**—In an example of this situation, the local controller would use the radar to advise a pilot on an extended downwind when to turn base leg.

NOTE.—The above tower radar applications are intended to augment the standard functions of the local control position. There is no controller requirement to maintain constant radar identification and, in fact, such a requirement could compromise the local controllers ability to visually scan the airport and local area to meet FAA responsibilities to the aircraft operating on the runways and within the airport traffic area. Normally, pilots will not be advised of being in radar contact since that continued status cannot be guaranteed and since the purpose of the radar identification is not to establish a link for the provision of radar services.

e. A few of the radar equipped towers are authorized to use the radar to ensure separation between aircraft in specific situations, while still others may function as limited radar approach controls. The various radar uses are strictly a function of FAA operational need. The facilities may be indistinguishable to pilots since they are all referred to as tower and no publication lists the degree of radar use. Therefore, WHEN IN COMMUNICATION WITH A TOWER CONTROLLER WHO MAY HAVE RADAR AVAILABLE, DO NOT ASSUME THAT CONSTANT RADAR MONITORING AND COMPLETE ATC RADAR SERVICES ARE BEING PROVIDED.

222. VISUAL INDICATORS AT UNCONTROLLED AIRPORTS

a. At those airports *without an operating control tower*, a segmented circle visual indicator system, if installed, is designed to provide traffic pattern information. (See PARA—157 - TRAFFIC

ADVISORY PRACTICES AT AIRPORTS WHERE A TOWER IS NOT IN OPERATION). The segmented circle system consists of the following components:

(1) **The segmented circle** —Located in a position affording maximum visibility to pilots in the air and on the ground and providing a centralized location for other elements of the system.

(2) **The Wind Direction Indicator** —A wind cone, wind sock, or wind tee installed near the operational runway to indicate wind direction. The large end of the wind cone/wind sock points into the wind as does the large end (cross bar) of the wind tee. In lieu of a tetrahedron and where a wind sock or wind cone is collocated with a wind tee, the wind tee may be manually aligned with the runway in use to indicate landing direction. These signaling devices may be located in the center of the segmented circle and may be lighted for night use. Pilots are cautioned against using a tetrahedron to indicate wind direction.

(3) **The Landing Direction Indicator** —A tetrahedron is installed when conditions at the airport warrant its use. It may be used to indicate the direction of landings and takeoffs. A tetrahedron may be located at the center of a segmented circle and may be lighted for night operations. The small end of the tetrahedron points in the direction of landing. Pilots are cautioned against using a tetrahedron for any purpose other than as an indicator of landing direction. Further, pilots should use extreme caution when making runway selection by use of a tetrahedron in very light or calm wind conditions as the tetrahedron may not be aligned with the designated calm-wind runway. At airports with control towers, the tetrahedron should only be referenced when the control tower is not in operation. Tower instructions supersede tetrahedron indications.

(4) **Landing strip indicators** —Installed in pairs as shown in the segmented circle diagram and used to show the alignment of landing strips.

(5) **Traffic pattern indicators** —Arranged in pairs in conjunction with landing strip indicators and used to indicate the direction of turns when there is a variation from the normal left traffic pattern. (If there is no segmented circle installed at the airport, traffic pattern indicators may be installed on or near the end of the runway.)

b. Preparatory to landing at an airport without a control tower, or when the control tower is not in operation, the pilot should concern himself with the indicator for the approach end of the runway to be used. When approaching for landing, all turns must be made to the left unless a traffic pattern indicator indicates that turns should be made to the right. If the pilot will mentally enlarge the indicator for the runway to be used, the base and final approach legs of the traffic pattern to be flown immediately become apparent. Similar treatment of the indicator at the departure end of the runway will clearly indicate the direction of turn after takeoff.

c. When two or more aircraft are approaching an airport for the purpose of landing, the aircraft at the lower altitude has the right of way, but it shall not take advantage of this rule to cut in front of another which is on final approach to land, or to overtake that aircraft (FAR—91.67(f)).

223. TRAFFIC PATTERNS

At most airports and military air bases, traffic pattern altitudes for propeller driven aircraft generally extend from 600 feet to as high as 1,500 feet above the ground. Also, traffic pattern altitudes for military turbojet aircraft sometimes extend up to 2,500 feet above the ground. Therefore, pilots of en route aircraft should be constantly on the alert for other aircraft in traffic patterns and avoid these areas whenever possible. Traffic pattern altitudes should be

maintained unless otherwise required by the applicable distance from cloud criteria (FAR—91.105). *(See Figure 4-5.)*

224. UNEXPECTED MANEUVERS IN THE AIRPORT TRAFFIC PATTERN

There have been several incidents in the vicinity of controlled airports that were caused primarily by aircraft executing unexpected maneuvers. ATC service is based upon observed or known traffic and airport conditions. Controllers establish the sequence of arriving and departing aircraft by requiring them to adjust flight as necessary to achieve proper spacing. These adjustments can only be based on observed traffic, accurate pilot reports, and anticipated aircraft maneuvers. Pilots are expected to cooperate so as to preclude disruption of traffic flow or creation of conflicting patterns. The pilot in command of an aircraft is directly responsible for and is the final authority as to the operation of his aircraft. On occasion it may be necessary for a pilot to maneuver his aircraft to maintain spacing with the traffic he has been sequenced to follow. The controller can anticipate minor maneuvering such as shallow "S" turns. The controller cannot, however, anticipate a major maneuver such as a 360 degree turn. If a pilot makes a 360 degree turn after he has obtained a landing sequence, the result is usually a gap in the landing interval and more importantly it causes a chain reaction which may result in a conflict with following traffic and interruption of the sequence established by the tower or approach controller. Should a pilot decide he needs to make maneuvering turns to maintain spacing behind a preceding aircraft, he should always advise the controller if at all possible. Except when requested by the controller or in emergency situations, a 360 degree turn should never be executed in the traffic pattern or when receiving radar service without first advising the controller.

225. RESERVED

226. USE OF RUNWAYS

a. Runways are identified by numbers which indicate the nearest 10-degree increment of the azimuth of the runway centerline. For example, where the magnetic azimuth is 183 degrees, the runway designation would be 18, for a magnetic azimuth of 87 degrees, the runway designation would be 9. For a magnetic azimuth ending in the number 5, such as 185, the runway designation could be either 18 or 19. Wind direction issued by the tower is also magnetic and wind velocity is in knots.

b. Airport proprietors are responsible for taking the lead in local aviation noise control. Accordingly, they may propose specific noise abatement plans to the FAA. If approved, these plans are applied in the form of Formal or Informal Runway Use Programs (see Glossary) for noise abatement purposes.

(1) At airports where no runway use program is established, ATC clearances may specify:

(a) the runway most nearly aligned with the wind when it is 5 knots or more,

(b) the "calm wind" runway when wind is less than 5 knots, or

(c) another runway if operationally advantageous.

NOTE.—It is not necessary for a controller to specifically inquire if the pilot will use a specific runway or to offer him a choice of runways. If a pilot prefers to use a different runway than that specified or the one most nearly aligned with the wind, he is expected to inform ATC accordingly.

(2) At airports where a runway use program is established, ATC will assign runways deemed to have the least noise impact. If in the interest of safety a runway different than that specified is preferred, the pilot is expected to advise ATC accordingly. ATC will honor such requests and advise pilots when the requested runway is noise sensitive. When use of a runway other than the one assigned is requested, pilot cooperation is encouraged to preclude disruption of traffic flows or creation of conflicting patterns.

227. LOW LEVEL WIND SHEAR ALERT SYSTEM (LLWAS)

a. This computerized system detects the presence of a possible hazardous low-level wind shear by continuously comparing the winds measured by sensors installed around the periphery of an airport with the wind measured at the center field location. If the difference between the center field wind sensor and a peripheral wind sensor becomes excessive, a thunderstorm or thunderstorm gust front wind shear is probable. When this condition exists, the tower controller will provide arrival and departure aircraft with an advisory of the situation which includes the center field wind plus the remote site location and wind.

b. Since the sensors are not all associated with specific runways, descriptions of the remote sites will be based on an eight point compass system.

EXAMPLE:
DELTA ONE TWENTY FOUR CENTER FIELD WIND TWO SEVEN ZERO AT ONE ZERO. SOUTH BOUNDARY WIND ONE FOUR ZERO AT THREE ZERO.

c. An airport equipped with the Low Level Wind Shear Alert System is so indicated in the Airport/Facility Directory under *Weather Data Sources* for that particular airport.

228. BRAKING ACTION REPORTS

a. ATC furnishes pilots the quality of braking action received from pilots or the airport management. The quality of braking action is described by the terms "good," "fair," "poor," and "nil" or a combination of these terms. Where available from airport management and when airports are covered with compacted snow and/or ice, numerical readings from friction measurement devices including the Mu-Meter, Saab Friction Tester, Runway Friction Tester, Bowmonk, Skiddometer, and Tapley Meter will be issued at pilot's request. These numbers will be below 0.4 and reflect the slipperiness of the pavement surface. This information should be used with other knowledge including previous experience, aircraft type and weight, wind conditions, and tire type to determine the runway suitability.

b. Pilots should describe the quality of braking action by using the terms noted above. In describing braking action for a portion of a runway, pilots should use descriptive terms that are easily understood, such as, "braking action poor the first/last half of the runway." Reports reference to local landmarks, buildings, etc., should be avoided.

229. BRAKING ACTION ADVISORIES

a. When tower controllers have received runway braking action reports which include the terms *poor* or *nil*, or whenever weather conditions are conducive to deteriorating or rapidly changing runway braking conditions, the tower will include on the ATIS broadcast the statement, *"BRAKING ACTION ADVISORIES ARE IN EFFECT."*

b. During the time that Braking Action Advisories are in effect, ATC will issue the latest braking action report for the runway in use to each arriving and departing aircraft. Pilots should be prepared for deteriorating braking conditions and should request current runway condition information if not volunteered by control-

lers. Pilots should also be prepared to provide a descriptive runway condition report to controllers after landing.

230. INTERSECTION TAKEOFFS

a. In order to enhance airport capacities, reduce taxiing distances, minimize departure delays, and provide for more efficient movement of air traffic, controllers may initiate intersection takeoffs as well as approve them when the pilot requests. If for ANY reason a pilot prefers to use a different intersection or the full length of the runway or desires to obtain the distance between the intersection and the runway end, HE IS EXPECTED TO INFORM ATC ACCORDINGLY.

b. An aircraft is expected to taxi to (but not onto) the end of the assigned runway unless prior approval for an intersection departure is received from ground control.

c. Controllers are required to separate small aircraft (12,500 pounds or less, maximum certificated takeoff weight) departing (same or opposite direction) from an intersection behind a large nonheavy aircraft on the same runway, by ensuring that at least a 3-minute interval exists between the time the preceding large aircraft has taken off and the succeeding small aircraft begins takeoff roll. To inform the pilot of the required 3-minute hold, the controller will state, "Hold for wake turbulence." If after considering wake turbulence hazards, the pilot feels that a lesser time interval is appropriate, he may request a waiver to the 3-minute interval. Pilots must initiate such a request by stating, "Request waiver to 3-minute interval," or by making a similar statement. Controllers may then issue a takeoff clearance if other traffic permits, since the pilot has accepted responsibility for his own wake turbulence separation.

d. The 3-minute interval will not be applied when the intersection is 500 feet or less from the threshold and both aircraft are taking off in the same direction. When a small aircraft is departing from an intersection 500 feet or less from the runway threshold behind a large nonheavy aircraft and both aircraft are taking off in the same direction, the 3-minute interval will not be applied. Controllers will issue a clearance to permit the small aircraft to alter course to avoid the flight path of the preceding departure.

e. The 3-minute interval is mandatory behind a heavy aircraft in all cases.

231. SIMULTANEOUS OPERATIONS ON INTERSECTING RUNWAYS

a. Despite the many new and lengthened runways which have been added to the nation's airports in recent years, limited runway availability remains a major contributing factor to operational delays. Many high-density airports have gained operational experience with intersecting runways which clearly indicates that simultaneous operations are safe and feasible. Tower controllers may authorize simultaneous landings or a simultaneous landing and takeoff on intersecting runways when the following conditions are met:

(1) The runways are dry and the controller has received no reports that braking action is less than good.

(2) A simultaneous takeoff and landing operation may be conducted only in VFR conditions between sunrise and sunset.

(3) Instructions are issued to restrict one aircraft from entering the intersecting runway being used by another aircraft.

(4) Traffic information issued is acknowledged by the pilots of both aircraft.

(5) The measured distance from runway threshold to intersection is issued if the pilot requests it.

(6) The conditions specified in 3, 4 and 5 are met at or before issuance of the landing clearance.

(7) The distance from landing threshold to the intersection is adequate for the category of aircraft being held short. Controllers are provided a general table of aircraft category/minimum runway length requirements as a guide. Operators of STOL aircraft should identify their aircraft as such on initial contact with the tower, unless a Letter of Agreement concerning this fact, is in effect. IT IS INCUMBENT ON THE PILOT TO DETERMINE HIS ABILITY TO HOLD SHORT OF AN INTERSECTION AFTER LANDING, WHEN SO INSTRUCTED.

(8) There is no tailwind for the landing aircraft restricted to hold short of the intersection.

b. THE SAFETY AND OPERATION OF AN AIRCRAFT REMAIN THE RESPONSIBILITY OF THE PILOT. IF FOR ANY REASON, (e.g. DIFFICULTY IN DISCERNING LOCATION OF AN INTERSECTION AT NIGHT, INABILITY TO HOLD SHORT OF AN INTERSECTION, WIND FACTORS, ETC.) A PILOT ELECTS TO USE THE FULL LENGTH OF THE RUNWAY, A DIFFERENT RUNWAY OR DESIRES TO OBTAIN THE DISTANCE FROM THE LANDING THRESHOLD TO THE INTERSECTION, HE IS EXPECTED TO PROMPTLY INFORM ATC ACCORDINGLY.

232. LOW APPROACH

a. A low approach (sometimes referred to as a low pass) is the go-around maneuver following approach. Instead of landing or making a touch-and-go, a pilot may wish to go around (low approach) in order to expedite a particular operation — a series of practice instrument approaches is an example of such an operation. Unless otherwise authorized by ATC, the low approach should be made straight ahead, with no turns or climb made until the pilot has made a thorough visual check for other aircraft in the area.

b. When operating within an airport traffic area, a pilot intending to make a low approach should contact the tower for approval. This request should be made prior to starting the final approach.

c. When operating to an airport, not within an airport traffic area, a pilot intending to make a low approach should, prior to leaving the final approach fix inbound (non precision approach) or the outer marker or fix used in lieu of the outer marker inbound (precision approach), so advise the FSS, UNICOM, or make a broadcast, as appropriate (See PARA—157 - TRAFFIC ADVISORY PRACTICES AT AIRPORTS WITHOUT OPERATING CONTROL TOWERS).

233. TRAFFIC CONTROL LIGHT SIGNALS

a. The following procedures are used by ATCTs in the control of aircraft, groundvehicles, equipment, and personnel not equipped with radio. These same procedures will be used to control aircraft, ground vehicles, equipment, and personnel equipped with radio if radio contact cannot be established. ATC personnel use a directive traffic control signal which emits an intense narrow light beam of a selected color (either red, white, or green) when controlling traffic by light signals.

b. Although the traffic signal light offers the advantage that some control may be exercised over nonradio equipped aircraft, pilots should be cognizant of the disadvantages which are:

(1) The pilot may not be looking at the control tower at the time a signal is directed toward him.

(2) The directions transmitted by a light signal are very limited since only approval or disapproval of a pilot's anticipated actions may be transmitted. No supplement or explanatory information may be transmitted except by the use of the "General Warning Signal" which advises the pilot to be on the alert.

c. Between sunset and sunrise, a pilot wishing to attract the attention of the control tower should turn on a landing light and taxi the aircraft into a position, clear of the active runway, so that light is visible to the tower. The landing light should remain on until appropriate signals are received from the tower.

d. Air Traffic Control Tower Light Gun Signals: *(See Table 4-3.)*

e. During daylight hours, acknowledge tower transmissions or light signals by moving the ailerons or rudder. At night, acknowledge by blinking the landing or navigation lights. If radio malfunction occurs after departing the parking area, watch the tower for light signals or monitor tower frequency.

234. RESERVED

235. COMMUNICATIONS

a. Pilots of departing aircraft should communicate with the control tower on the appropriate ground control/clearance delivery frequency prior to starting engines to receive engine start time, taxi and/or clearance information. Unless otherwise advised by the tower, remain on that frequency during taxiing and runup, then change to local control frequency when ready to request takeoff clearance. (See PARA. 161 - AUTOMATIC TERMINAL INFORMATION SERVICE (ATIS) for continuous broadcast of terminal information.)

b. The majority of ground control frequencies are in the 121.6—121.9 MHz bandwidth. Ground control frequencies are provided to eliminate frequency congestion on the tower (local control) frequency and are limited to communications between the tower and aircraft on the ground and between the tower and utility vehicles on the airport, provide a clear VHF channel for arriving and departing aircraft. They are used for issuance of taxi information, clearances, and other necessary contacts between the tower and aircraft or other vehicles operated on the airport. A pilot who has just landed should not change from the tower frequency to the ground control frequency until he is directed to do so by the controller. Normally, only one ground control frequency is assigned at an airport; however, at locations where the amount of traffic so warrants, a second ground control frequency and/or another frequency designated as a clearance delivery frequency, may be assigned.

c. A controller may omit the ground or local control frequency if the controller believes the pilot knows which frequency is in use. If the ground control frequency is in the 121 MHz bandwidth the controller may omit the numbers preceding the decimal point; (e.g., 121.7, "CONTACT GROUND POINT SEVEN.") However, if any doubt exists as to what frequency is in use, the pilot should promptly request the controller to provide that information.

d. Controllers will normally avoid issuing a radio frequency change to helicopters, known to be single-piloted, which are hovering, air taxiing, or flying near the ground. At times, it may be necessary for pilots to alert ATC regarding single pilot operations to minimize delay of essential ATC communications. Whenever possible, ATC instructions will be relayed through the frequency being monitored until a frequency change can be accomplished. You must promptly advise ATC if you are unable to comply with a frequency change. Also, you should advise ATC if you must land to accomplish the frequency change unless it is clear the landing, e.g., on a taxiway or in a helicopter operating area, will have no impact on other air traffic.

236. GATE HOLDING DUE TO DEPARTURE DELAYS

a. Pilots should contact ground control or clearance delivery prior to starting engines as gate hold procedures will be in effect whenever departure delays exceed or are anticipated to exceed 15 minutes. The sequence for departure will be maintained in accordance with initial call up unless modified by flow control restrictions. Pilots should monitor the ground control or clearance delivery frequency for engine startup advisories or new proposed start time if the delay changes.

b. The tower controller will consider that pilots of turbine powered aircraft are ready for takeoff when they reach the runway or warm-up block unless advised otherwise.

237. VFR FLIGHTS IN TERMINAL AREAS

Use reasonable restraint in exercising the prerogative of VFR flight, especially in terminal areas. The weather minimums and distances from clouds are minimums. Giving yourself a greater margin in specific instances is just good judgment.

a. Approach Area.

Conducting a VFR operation in a Control Zone when the official visibility is 3 or 4 miles is not prohibited, but good judgment would dictate that you keep out of the approach area.

b. Reduced Visibility.

It has always been recognized that precipitation reduces forward isibility. Consequently, although again it may be perfectly legal to cancel your IFR flight plan at any time you can proceed VFR, it is good practice, when precipitation is occurring, to continue IFR operation into a terminal area until you are reasonably close to your destination.

c. Simulated Instrument Flights.

In conducting simulated instrument flights, be sure that the weather is good enough to compensate for the restricted visibility of the safety pilot and your greater concentration on your flight instruments. Give yourself a little greater margin when your flight plan lies in or near a busy airway or close to an airport.

238. VFR HELICOPTER OPERATIONS AT CONTROLLED AIRPORTS

a. GENERAL

(1) The following ATC procedures and phraseologies recognize the unique capabilities of helicopters and were developed to improve service to all users. Helicopter design characteristics and user needs often require operations from movement and nonmovement areas within the airport boundary. In order for ATC to properly apply these procedures, it is essential that pilots familiarize themselves with the local operations and make it known to controllers when additional instructions are necessary.

(2) Insofar as possible, helicopter operations will be instructed to avoid the flow of fixed-wing aircraft to minimize overall delays; however, there will be many situations where faster/larger helicopters may be integrated with fixed-wing aircraft for the bene-

fit of all concerned. Examples would include IFR flights, avoidance of noise sensitive areas, or use of runways/taxiways to minimize the hazardous effects of rotor downwash in congested areas.

(3) Because helicopter pilots are intimately familiar with the effects of rotor downwash, they are best qualified to determine if a given operation can be conducted safely. Accordingly, the pilot has the final authority with respect to the specific airspeed/altitude combinations. ATC clearances are in no way intended to place the helicopter in a hazardous position. It is expected that pilots will advise ATC if a specific clearance will cause undue hazards to persons or property.

b. Controllers normally limit ATC ground service and instruction to *movement* areas; therefore, operations from *nonmovement* areas are conducted at pilot discretion and should be based on local policies, procedures, or letters of agreement. In order to maximize the flexibility of helicopter operations, it is necessary to rely heavily on sound pilot judgment. For example, hazards such as debris, obstructions, vehicles, or personnel must be recognized by the pilot, and action should be taken as necessary to avoid such hazards. Taxi, hover taxi, and air taxi operations are considered to be ground movements. Helicopters conducting such operations are expected to adhere to the same conditions, requirements, and practices as apply to other ground taxiing and ATC procedures in the AIM.

(1) The phraseology *taxi* is used when it is intended or expected that the helicopter will taxi on the airport surface, either via taxiways or other prescribed routes. *Taxi* is used primarily for helicopters equipped with wheels or in response to a pilot request. Preference should be given to this procedure whenever it is necessary to minimize effects of rotor downwash.

(2) Pilots may request a *hover taxi* when a slow forward movement is desired, or when it may be appropriate to move very short distances. Pilots should avoid this procedure if rotor downwash is likely to cause damage to parked aircraft, or if blowing dust/snow could obscure visibility. If it is necessary to operate above 25 feet AGL when hover taxiing, the pilot should initiate a request to ATC.

(3) *Air taxi* is the preferred method for helicopter ground movements on airports provided ground operations and conditions permit. Unless otherwise requested or instructed, pilots are expected to remain below 100 feet AGL. However, if a higher than normal airspeed or altitude is desired, the request should be made prior to lift-off. The pilot is solely responsible for selecting a safe airspeed for the altitude/operation being conducted. Use of *air taxi* enables the pilot to proceed at an optimum airspeed/altitude, minimize downwash effect, conserve fuel, and expedite movement from one point to another. Helicopters should avoid overflight of other aircraft, vehicles, and personnel during air-taxi operations. Caution must be exercised concerning active runways and pilots must be certain that air taxi instructions are understood. Special precautions may be necessary at unfamiliar airports or airports with multiple/intersecting active runways. The taxi procedures in PARA 241 thru PARA 243 also apply. (See Pilot/Controller Glossary - Taxi, Hover Taxi, Air Taxi definitions.)

c. Takeoff and Landing Procedures

(1) Helicopter operations may be conducted from a runway, taxiway, portion of a landing strip, or any clear area which could be used as a landing site such as the scene of an accident, a construction site, or the roof of a building. The terms used to describe designated areas from which helicopters operate are: movement area, landing/takeoff area, apron/ramp, heliport and helipad (see Pilot/Controller Glossary). These areas may be improved or unimproved and may be separate from or located on an airport/heliport.

ATC will issue takeoff clearances from *movement* areas other than active runways, or in diverse directions from active runways, with additional instructions as necessary. Whenever possible, take-off clearance will be issued in lieu of extended hover/air taxi operations. Phraseology will be "CLEARED FOR TAKEOFF FROM (taxiway, helipad, runway number, etc.) MAKE RIGHT/LEFT TURN FOR (direction, heading, NAVAID radial) DEPARTURE/ DEPARTURE ROUTE (number, name, etc.)." Unless requested by the pilot, downwind takeoffs will not be issued if the tailwind exceeds 5 knots.

(2) Pilots should be alert to wind information as well as to wind indications in the vicinity of the helicopter. ATC should be advised of the intended method of departing. A pilot request to takeoff in a given direction indicates that the pilot is willing to accept the wind condition and controllers will honor the request if traffic permits. Departure points could be a significant distance from the control tower and it may be difficult or impossible for the controller to determine the helicopter's relative position to the wind.

(3) If takeoff is requested from *nonmovement* areas, the phraseology "PROCEED AS REQUESTED" will be used. Additional instructions will be issued as necessary. The pilot is responsible for operating in a safe manner and should exercise due caution. When other known traffic is not a factor and takeoff is requested from an area not visible from the tower, an area not authorized for helicopter use, an unlighted area at night, or an area not on the airport, the phraseology "DEPARTURE FROM (location) WILL BE AT YOUR OWN RISK (with reason, and additional instructions as necessary)."

(4) Similar phraseology is used for helicopter landing operations. Every effort will be made to permit helicopters to proceed direct and land as near as possible to their final destination on the airport. Traffic density, the need for detailed taxiing instructions, frequency congestion, or other factors may affect the extent to which service can be expedited. As with ground movement operations, a high degree of pilot/controller cooperation and communication is necessary to achieve safe and efficient operations.

239—240. RESERVED

241. TAXIING

a. General: Approval must be obtained prior to moving an aircraft or vehicle onto the movement area during the hours an airport traffic control tower is in operation.

(1) Always state your position on the airport when calling the tower for taxi instructions.

(2) The movement area is normally described in local bulletins issued by the airport manager or control tower. These bulletins may be found in FSSs, fixed base operators offices, air carrier offices and operations offices.

(3) The control tower also issues bulletins describing areas where they cannot provide ATC service due to nonvisibility or other reasons.

(4) A clearance must be obtained prior to taxiing on a runway, taking off, or landing during the hours an airport traffic control tower is in operation.

(5) When ATC clears an aircraft to "taxi to" an assigned takeoff runway, the absence of holding instructions authorizes the aircraft to "cross" all runways which the taxi route intersects except the assigned takeoff runway. It does not include authorization to "taxi onto" or "cross" the assigned takeoff runway at any

point. In order to preclude misunderstandings in radio communications, ATC will not use the word "cleared" in conjunction with authorization for aircraft to taxi.

(6) In the absence of holding instructions, a clearance to "taxi to" any point other than an assigned takeoff runway is a clearance to cross all runways that intersect the taxi route to that point.

(7) When ATC authorizes an aircraft to taxi to an assigned departure runway and hold short instructions will be issued, they will first specify the runway, issue taxi instructions, and then state the hold short instructions. This does not authorize the aircraft to "enter" or "cross" the assigned departure runway at any point.

b. ATC clearances or instructions pertaining to taxiing are predicated on known traffic and known physical airport conditions. Therefore, it is important that pilots clearly understand the clearance or instruction. Although an ATC clearance is issued for taxiing purposes, when operating in accordance with the FARs, it is the responsibility of the pilot to avoid collision with other aircraft. Since "the pilot in command of an aircraft is directly responsible for, and is the final authority as to, the operation of that aircraft" the pilot should obtain clarification of any clearance or instruction which is not understood. (See PARA—540.)

(1) Good operating practice dictates that pilots acknowledge all runway crossing, hold short, or takeoff clearances unless there is some misunderstanding at which time the pilot should query the controller until the clearance is understood. When cleared on to the active runway for departure, pilots operating single pilot airplanes should monitor only assigned ATC communication frequencies until flight from the airport traffic area is completed. After receipt of clearance for landing, they should monitor only assigned ATC communication frequencies until the landing and taxi activities are completed. In all cases, proper effective scanning for other aircraft, surface vehicles, or other objects, should the continuously exercised.

c. At those airports where the U.S. Government operates the control tower and ATC has authorized noncompliance with the requirement for two-way radio communications while operating within the airport traffic area, or at those airports where the U.S. Government does not operate the control tower and radio communications cannot be established, pilots shall obtain a clearance by visual light signal prior to taxiing on a runway and prior to takeoff and landing.

d. The following phraseologies and procedures are used in radio-telephone communications with aeronautical ground stations.

(1) **Request for taxi instructions prior to departure:** State your aircraft identification, location, type of operation planned (VFR or IFR) and the point of first intended landing.

EXAMPLE:

Aircraft: "WASHINGTON GROUND, BEECHCRAFT ONE THREE ONE FIVE NINER AT HANGAR EIGHT, READY TO TAXI, IFR TO CHICAGO."

Tower: "BEECHCRAFT ONE THREE ONE FIVE NINER, TAXI TO RUNWAY THREE SIX, WIND ZERO THREE ZERO AT TWO FIVE, ALTIMETER THREE ZERO ZERO FOUR."

Tower: "BEECHCRAFT ONE THREE ONE FIVE NINER, RUNWAY TWO SEVEN, TAXI VIA TAXIWAYS CHARLIE AND DELTA, HOLD SHORT OF RUNWAY THREE THREE LEFT."

(2) **Receipt of ATC clearance:** ARTCC clearances are relayed to pilots by airport traffic controllers in the following manner:

EXAMPLE:

Tower: BEECHCRAFT ONE THREE ONE FIVE NINER CLEARED TO THE CHICAGO MIDWAY AIRPORT, VIA VICTOR EIGHT, MAINTAIN EIGHT THOUSAND.

Aircraft: "BEECHCRAFT ONE THREE ONE FIVE NINER CLEARED TO THE CHICAGO MIDWAY AIRPORT, VIA VICTOR EIGHT, MAINTAIN EIGHT THOUSAND."

NOTE.—Normally, an ATC IFR clearance is relayed to a pilot by the ground controller. At busy locations, however, pilots may be instructed by the ground controller to "CONTACT CLEARANCE DELIVERY" on a frequency designated for this purpose. No surveillance or control over the movement of traffic is exercised by this position of operation.

(3) Request for taxi instructions after landing: State your aircraft identification, location, and that you request taxi instructions.

EXAMPLE:

Aircraft: "DULLES GROUND BEECHCRAFT ONE FOUR TWO SIX ONE CLEARING RUNWAY ONE RIGHT ON TAXIWAY E3, REQUEST CLEARANCE TO PAGE."

Tower: "BEECHCRAFT ONE FOUR TWO SIX ONE, TAXI TO PAGE VIA TAXIWAYS E3, E1 and E9."

242. TAXI DURING LOW VISIBILITY

a. Pilots and aircraft operators should be constantly aware that during certain low visibility conditions the movement of aircraft and vehicles on airports may not be visible to the tower controller. This may prevent visual confirmation of an aircraft's adherence to taxi instructions. Pilots should, therefore, exercise extreme vigilance and proceed cautiously under such conditions.

b. Of vital importance is the need for pilots to notify the controller when difficulties are encountered or at the first indication of becoming disoriented. Pilots should proceed with extreme caution when taxiing toward the sun. When vision difficulties are encountered pilots should immediately inform the controller.

243. EXITING THE RUNWAY AFTER LANDING

After landing, unless otherwise instructed by the control tower, continue to taxi in the landing direction, proceed to the nearest suitable taxiway and exit the runway without delay. Do not turn on to another runway or make a 180 degree turn to taxi back on an active runway or change to ground control frequency while on the active runway without authorization from the tower.

244. PRACTICE INSTRUMENT APPROACHES

a. Various air traffic incidents have indicated the necessity for adoption of measures to achieve more organized and controlled operations where practice instrument approaches are conducted. Practice instrument approaches are considered to be instrument approaches made by either a VFR aircraft not on an IFR flight plan or an aircraft on an IFR flight plan. To achieve this and thereby enhance air safety, it is Air Traffic Operations Service policy to provide for separation of such operations at locations where approach control facilities are located and, as resources permit, at certain other locations served by ARTCCs or parent approach control facilities. Pilot requests to practice instrument approaches may be approved by ATC subject to traffic and workload conditions. Pilots should anticipate that in some instances the controller may find it necessary to deny approval or withdraw previous approval when traffic conditions warrant. It must be clearly understood, however, that even though the controller may be providing separation, pilots on VFR flight plans are required to comply with basic visual flight rules (FAR—91.105). Application of ATC procedures or any action taken by the controller to avoid traffic conflictions does not relieve IFR and VFR pilots of their responsibility to see and avoid other traffic while operating in VFR conditions. (FAR—91.67) In addition to the normal IFR separation minimums (which includes visual separation) during VFR conditions, 500 feet vertical separation may be applied between VFR aircraft and between a VFR aircraft and the IFR aircraft. Pilots not on IFR flight plans desiring practice instrument approaches should always state 'practice' when making requests to ATC. Controllers will instruct VFR aircraft requesting an instrument approach to maintain VFR. This is to preclude misunderstandings between the pilot and controller as to the status of the aircraft. If the pilot wishes to proceed in accordance with instrument flight rules, he must specifically request and obtain, an IFR clearance.

b. Before practicing an instrument approach, pilots should inform the approach control facility or the tower of the type of practice approach they desire to make and how they intend to terminate it, i.e., full-stop landing, touch-and-go, or missed or low approach maneuver. This information may be furnished progressively when conducting a series of approaches. Pilots on an IFR flight plan, who have made a series of instrument approaches to full stop landings should inform ATC when they make their final landing. The controller will control flights practicing instrument approaches so as to ensure that they do not disrupt the flow of arriving and departing itinerant IFR or VFR aircraft. The priority afforded itinerant aircraft over practice instrument approaches is not intended to be so rigidly applied that it causes grossly inefficient application of services. A minimum delay to itinerant traffic may be appropriate to allow an aircraft practicing an approach to complete that approach.

c. At airports without a tower, pilots wishing to make practice instrument approaches should notify the facility having control jurisdiction of the desired approach as indicated on the approach chart. All approach control facilities and ARTCCs are required to publish a Letter to Airmen depicting those airports where they provide standard separation to both VFR and IFR aircraft conducting practice instrument approaches.

d. The Controller will provide approved separation between both VFR and IFR aircraft when authorization is granted to make practice approaches to airports where an approach control facility is located and to certain other airports served by approach control or an ARTCC. Controller responsibility for separation of VFR aircraft begins at the point where the approach clearance becomes effective, or when the aircraft enters ARSA/TRSA/TCA airspace, whichever comes first.

e. VFR aircraft practicing instrument approaches are not automatically authorized to execute the missed approach procedure. This authorization must be specifically requested by the pilot and approved by the controller. Separation will not be provided unless the missed approach has been approved by ATC.

f. Except in an emergency, aircraft cleared to practice instrument approaches must not deviate from the approved procedure until cleared to do so by the controller.

g. At radar approach control locations when a full approach procedure (procedure turn, etc.) cannot be approved, pilots should expect to be vectored to a final approach course for a practice instrument approach which is compatible with the general direction of traffic at that airport.

h. When granting approval for a practice instrument approach, the controller will usually ask the pilot to report to the tower prior to or over the final approach fix inbound (non precision approaches) or over the outer marker or fix used in lieu of the outer marker inbound (precision approaches).

i. When authorization is granted to conduct practice instrument approaches to an airport with a tower, but where approved standard separation is not provided to aircraft conducting practice instrument approaches, the tower will approve the practice approach, instruct the aircraft to maintain VFR and issue traffic information, as required.

j. When an aircraft notifies a FSS providing Airport Advisory Service to the airport concerned of the intent to conduct a practice instrument approach and whether or not separation is to be provided, the pilot will be instructed to contact the appropriate facility on a specified frequency prior to initiating the approach. At airports where separation is not provided, the FSS will acknowledge the message and issue known traffic information but will neither approve or disapprove the approach.

k. Pilots conducting practice instrument approaches should be particularly alert for other aircraft operating in the local traffic pattern or in proximity to the airport.

245. OPTION APPROACH

The "Cleared for the Option" procedure will permit an instructor, flight examiner or pilot the option to make a touch-and-go, low approach, missed approach, stop-and-go, or full stop landing. This procedure can be very beneficial in a training situation in that neither the student pilot nor examinee would know what maneuver would be accomplished. The pilot should make his request for this procedure passing the final approach fix inbound on an instrument approach or entering downwind for a VFR traffic pattern. The advantages of this procedure as a training aid are that it enables an instructor or examiner to obtain the reaction of a trainee or examinee under changing conditions, the pilot would not have to discontinue an approach in the middle of the procedure due to student error or pilot proficiency requirements, and finally it allows more flexibility and economy in training programs. This procedure will only be used at those locations with an operational control tower and will be subject to ATC approval.

246. USE OF AIRCRAFT LIGHTS

a. Aircraft position and anticollision lights are required to be lighted on aircraft operated from sunset to sunrise. Anticollision lights, however, need not be lighted when the pilot in command determines that, because of operating conditions, it would be in the interest of safety to turn off the lights (FAR—91.73). For example, strobe lights should be turned off on the ground when they adversely affect ground personnel or other pilots, and in flight when there are adverse reflection from clouds.

b. An aircraft anticollision light system can use one or more rotating beacons and/or strobe lights, be colored either red or white, and have different (higher than minimum) intensities when com-

pared to other aircraft. Many aircraft have both a rotating beacon and a strobe light system.

c. The FAA has a voluntary pilot safety program. *Operation Lights On,* to enhance the *see-and-avoid* concept. Pilots are encouraged to turn on their anticollision lights anytime the engine(s) are running day or night. Use of these lights are especially encouraged when operating on airport surfaces during periods of reduced visibility and when snow or ice control vehicles are or may be operating. Pilots are also encouraged to turn on the landings lights during takeoff; i.e., either after takeoff clearance has been received or when beginning takeoff roll. Pilots are further encouraged to turn on their landing lights when operating below 10,000 feet, day or night, especially when operating within 10 miles of any airport or in conditions of reduced visibility and in areas where flocks of birds may be expected, i.e., coastal areas, lake areas, around refuse dumps, etc. Althrouh turning on aircraft lights does enhance the *see-and-avoid* concept, pilots should not become complacement about keeping a sharp lookout for other aircraft. Not all aircraft are equipped with lights and some pilots may not have their lights turned on. Aircraft manufacturer's recommendations for operation of landing lights and electrical systems should be observed.

d. Prop and jet blast forces generated by large aircraft have overturned or damaged several smaller aircraft taxiing behind them. To avoid similar results, and in the interest of preventing upsets and injuries to ground personnel from such forces, the FAA recommends that air carriers and commercial operators turn on their rotating beacons anytime their aircraft engines are in operation. General aviation pilots using rotating beacon equipped aircraft are also encouraged to participate in this program which is designed to alert others to the potential hazard. Since this is a voluntary program, exercise caution and do not rely solely on the rotating beacon as an indication that aircraft engines are in operation.

247. FLIGHT INSPECTION/'FLIGHT CHECK' AIRCRAFT IN TERMINAL AREAS

a. *Flight check* is a call sign used to alert pilots and air traffic controllers when a FAA aircraft is engaged in flight inspection/certification of NAVAIDs and flight procedures. Flight Check aircraft fly preplanned high/low altitude flight patterns such as grids, orbits, DME arcs, and tracks, including low passes along the full length of the runway to verify NAVAID performance. In most instances, these flight checks are being automatically recorded and/or flown in an automated mode.

b. Pilots should be especially watchful and avoid the flight paths of any aircraft using the call sign "Flight Check" or "Flight Check recorded." The latter call sign, e.g. "Flight Check 47 recorded" indicates that automated flight inspections are in progress in terminal areas. These flights will normally receive special handling from ATC. Pilot patience and cooperation in allowing uninterrupted recordings can significantly help expedite flight inspections, minimize costly, repetitive runs, and reduce the burden on the U.S. taxpayer.

248—258 RESERVED.

259. HAND SIGNALS

(See Figure 4-6.)

Section 4. ATC CLEARANCES/SEPARATIONS

260. CLEARANCE

a. A clearance issued by ATC is predicated on known traffic and known physical airport conditions. An ATC clearance means an authorization by ATC, for the purpose of preventing collision between known aircraft, for an aircraft to proceed under specified conditions within controlled airspace. IT IS NOT AUTHORIZATION FOR A PILOT TO DEVIATE FROM ANY RULE REGULATION OR MINIMUM ALTITUDE NOR TO CONDUCT UNSAFE OPERATION OF HIS AIRCRAFT.

b. FAR—91.3(a) states: "The pilot in command of an aircraft is directly responsible for, and is the final authority as to, the operation of that aircraft." If ATC issues a clearance that would cause a pilot to deviate from a rule or regulation, or in the pilot's opinion, would place the aircraft in jeopardy, IT IS THE PILOT'S RESPONSIBILITY TO REQUEST AN AMENDED CLEARANCE. Similarly, if a pilot prefers to follow a different course of action, such as make a 360 degree turn for spacing to follow traffic when established in a landing or approach sequence, land on a different runway, takeoff from a different intersection, takeoff from the threshold instead of an intersection or delay his operation, HE IS EXPECTED TO INFORM ATC ACCORDINGLY. When he requests a different course of action, however, the pilot is expected to cooperate so as to preclude disruption of traffic flow or creation of conflicting patterns. The pilot is also expected to use the appropriate aircraft call sign to acknowledge all ATC clearances, frequency changes, or advisory information.

~. When weather conditions permit, during the time an IFR ht is operating, it is the direct responsibility of the pilot to avoid ∽ner aircraft since VFR flights may be operating in the same area without the knowledge of ATC. Traffic clearances provide standard separation only between IFR flights.

261. CLEARANCE PREFIX

A clearance, control information, or a response to a request for information originated by an ATC facility and relayed to the pilot through an air to ground communication station will be prefixed by "ATC CLEARS," "ATC ADVISES," or "ATC REQUESTS."

262. CLEARANCE ITEMS

ATC clearances normally contain the following:

a.An ATC clearance must be obtained *prior* to operating within a control zone when the weather is less than that required for VFR flight. A VFR pilot may request and be given a clearance to enter, leave or operate within most control zones in special VFR conditions, traffic permitting, and providing such flight will not delay IFR operations. All special VFR flights must remain clear of clouds. The visibility requirements for Special VFR aircraft (other than helicopters) are:

(1) At least one statute mile flight visibility for operations within the control zone.

(2) At least one statute mile ground visibility if taking off or landing. If ground visibility is not reported at that airport, the flight visibility must be at least one statute mile.

(3) The restriction in (1) and (2) do not apply to helicopters. Helicopters must remain clear of clouds and may operate in central zones with less than one statute mile visibility.

(1) Clearances are normally issued for the altitude or flight level and route filed by the pilot. However, due to traffic conditions, it is frequently necessary for ATC to specify an altitude or flight level or route different from that requested by the pilot. In addition, flow patterns have been established in certain congested areas, or between congested areas, whereby traffic capacity is increased by routing all traffic on preferred routes. Information on these flow patterns is available in offices where preflight briefing is furnished or where flight plans are accepted.

(2) When required, air traffic clearances include data to assist pilots in identifying radio reporting points. It is the responsibility of the pilot to notify ATC immediately if his radio equipment cannot receive the type of signals he must utilize to comply with his clearance.

d. Altitude Data.

(1) The altitude or flight level instructions in an ATC clearance normally require that a pilot "MAINTAIN" the altitude or flight level at which the flight will operate when in controlled airspace. Altitude or flight level changes while en route should be requested prior to the time the change is desired.

(2) When possible, if the altitude assigned is different from the altitude requested by the pilot, ATC will inform the pilot when to expect climb or descent clearance or to request altitude change from another facility. If this has not been received prior to crossing the boundary of the ATC facility's area and assignment at a different altitude is still desired, the pilot should reinitiate his request with the next facility.

(3) The term "CRUISE" may be used instead of "MAINTAIN" to assign a block of airspace, to a pilot, from the minimum IFR altitude up to and including the altitude specified in the cruise clearance. The pilot may level off at any intermediate altitude within this block of airspace. Climb/descent within the block is to be made at the discretion of the pilot. However, once the pilot starts descent and verbally reports leaving an altitude in the block, he may not return to that altitude without additional ATC clearance.

NOTE.—See definition of CRUISE in the PILOT CONTROLLER GLOSSARY.

e. Holding Instructions.

(1) Whenever an aircraft has been cleared to a fix other than the destination airport and delay is expected, it is the responsibility of the ATC controller to issue complete holding instructions (unless the pattern is charted), an EFC time, and his best estimate of any additional en route/terminal delay.

(2) If the holding pattern is charted and the controller doesn't issue complete holding instructions, the pilot is expected to hold as depicted on the appropriate chart. When the pattern is charted, the controller may omit all holding instructions except the charted holding direction and the statement *AS PUBLISHED*, e.g., "*HOLD EAST AS PUBLISHED.*" Controllers shall always issue complete holding instructions when pilots request them.

NOTE.— Only those holding patterns depicted on U.S. Government or commercially produced (meeting FAA requirements) *Low/High Altitude En route, and Area or Star charts* should be used.

(3) If no holding pattern is charted and holding instructions have not been issued, the pilot should ask ATC for holding instructions prior to reaching the fix. This procedure will eliminate the

possibility of an aircraft entering a holding pattern other than that desired by ATC. If the pilot is unable to obtain holding instructions prior to reaching the fix (due to frequency congestion, stuck microphone, etc.), he should hold in a standard pattern on the course on which he approached the fix and request further clearance as soon as possible. In this event, the altitude/flight level of the aircraft at the clearance limit will be protected so that separation will be provided as required.

(4) When an aircraft is 3 minutes or less from a clearance limit and a clearance beyond the fix has not been received, the pilot is expected to start a speed reduction so that he will cross the fix, initially, at or below the maximum holding airspeed.

(5) When no delay is expected, the controller should issue a clearance beyond the fix as soon as possible and, whenever possible, at least 5 minutes before the aircraft reaches the clearance limit.

(6) Pilots should report to ATC the time and altitude/flight level at which the aircraft reaches the clearance limit and report leaving the clearance limit.

NOTE.—In the event of two-way communications failure, pilots are required to comply with FAR 91.127.

263. AMENDED CLEARANCES

a. Amendments to the initial clearance will be issued at any time an air traffic controller deems such action necessary to avoid possible conflication between aircraft. Clearances will require that a flight "hold" or change altitude prior to reaching the point where standard separation from other IFR traffic would no longer exist.

NOTE.—Some pilots have questioned this action and requested "traffic information" and were at a loss when the reply indicated "no traffic report." In such cases the controller has taken action to prevent a traffic conflication which would have occurred at a distant point.

b. A pilot may wish an explanation of the handling of his flight at the time of occurrence; however, controllers are not able to take time from their immediate control duties nor can they afford to overload the ATC communications channels to furnish explanations. Pilots may obtain an explanation by directing a letter or telephone call to the chief controller of the facility involved.

c. The pilot has the privilege of requesting a different clearance from that which has been issued by ATC if he feels that he has information which would make another course of action more practicable or if aircraft equipment limitations or company procedures forbid compliance with the clearance issued.

264. SPECIAL VFR CLEARANCES

a. An ATC clearance must be obtained *prior* to operating within a control zone when the weather is less than that required for VFR flight. A VFR pilot may request and be given a clearance to enter, leave or operate within most control zones in special VFR conditions, traffic permitting, and providing such flight will not delay IFR operations. All special VFR flights must remain clear of clouds. The visibility requirements for Special VFR fixed-wing aircraft are:

(1) One mile flight visibility for operations within the control zone.

(2) One mile ground visibility if taking off or landing.

b. When a control tower is located within the control zone, requests for clearances should be to the tower. If no tower is located within the control zone, a clearance may be obtained from the nearest tower, FSS or center.

c. It is not necessary to file a complete flight plan with the ? quest for clearance but the pilot should state his intentions in suf?. cient detail to permit ATC to fit his flight into the traffic flow. The clearance will not contain a specific altitude as the pilot must remain clear of clouds. The controller may require the pilot to fly at or below a certain altitude due to other traffic, but the altitude specified will permit flight at or above the minimum safe altitude. In addition, at radar locations, flights may be vectored if necessary for control purposes or on pilot request.

NOTE.The pilot is responsible for obstacle or terrain clearance (reference FAR—91.79).

d. Special VFR clearances are effective within control zones only. ATC does not provide separation after an aircraft leaves the control zone on a special VFR clearance.

e. Special VFR operations by fixed-wing aircraft are prohibited in some control zones due to the volume of IFR traffic. A list of these control zones is contained in FAR—93.113. They are also depicted on Sectional Aeronautical Charts.

f. ATC provides separation between special VFR flights and between these flights and other IFR flights.

g. Special VFR operations by fixed-wing aircraft are prohibited between sunset and sunrise unless the pilot is instrument rated and the aircraft is equipped for IFR flight.

265. PILOT RESPONSIBILITY UPON CLEARANCE ISSUANCE

a. RECORD ATC CLEARANCE —When conducting an IFR operation, make a written record of your clearance. The specified conditions which are a part of your air traffic clearance may be somewhat different from those included in your flight plan. Additionally, ATC may find it necessary to ADD conditions, such as particular departure route. The very fact that ATC specifies diff? ent or additional conditions means that other aircraft are involv? in the traffic situation.

b. ATC CLEARANCE/INSTRUCTION READBACK — Pilots of airborne aircraft should read back *those parts* of ATC clearances and instructions containing altitude assignments or vectors, as a means of mutual verification. The readback of the "numbers" serves as a double check between pilots and controllers and reduces the kinds of communications errors that occur when a number is either "misheard" or is incorrect.

(1) Precede all readbacks and acknowledgements with the aircraft identification. This aids controllers in determining that the correct aircraft received the clearance or instruction. The requirement to include aircraft identification in all readbacks and acknowledgements becomes more important as frequency congestion increases and when aircraft with similar call signs are on the same frequency.

(2) Read back altitudes, altitude restrictions, and vectors in the same sequence as they are given in the clearance or instruction.

(3) Altitudes contained in charted procedures such as SIDs, instrument approaches, etc., should not be read back unless they are specifically stated by the controller.

c. It is the responsibility of the pilot to accept or refuse the clearance issued.

266. IFR CLEARANCE VFR-ON-TOP

a. A pilot on an IFR flight plan operating in VFR weather conditions, may request VFR ON TOP in lieu of an assigned altitude.

This would permit the pilot to select an altitude or flight level of his choice (subject to any ATC restrictions.)

b. Pilots desiring to climb through a cloud, haze, smoke, or other meteorological formation and then either cancel their IFR flight plan or operate VFR ON TOP may request a climb to VFR ON TOP. The ATC authorization shall contain either a top report or a statement that no top report is available, and a request to report reaching VFR ON TOP. Additionally, the ATC authorization may contain a clearance limit, routing and an alternative clearance if VFR ON TOP is not reached by a specified altitude.

c. A pilot on an IFR flight plan, operating in VFR conditions, may request to climb/descend in VFR conditions.

d. ATC may not authorize VFR ON TOP/VFR CONDITIONS operations unless the pilot requests the VFR operation or a clearance to operate in VFR CONDITIONS will result in noise abatement benefits where part of the IFR departure route does not conform to an FAA approved noise abatement route or altitude.

e. When operating in VFR conditions with an ATC authorization to "MAINTAIN VFR ON TOP/MAINTAIN VFR CONDITIONS" pilots on IFR flight plans must:

(1) Fly at the appropriate VFR altitude as prescribed in FAR—91.109.

(2) Comply with the VFR visibility and distance from cloud criteria in FAR—91.105 (BASIC VFR WEATHER MINIMUMS.)

(3) Comply with instrument flight rules that are applicable to this flight (i.e., *minimum IFR altitudes,* position reporting, radio communications, course to be flown, adherence to ATC clearance, etc.).

NOTE.—Pilots should advise ATC prior to any altitude change to insure the exchange of accurate traffic information.

f. ATC authorization to "MAINTAIN VFR ON TOP" is not tended to restrict pilots so that they must operate only *above* an oscuring meteorological formation (layer). Instead, it permits operation above, below, between layers or in areas where there is no meteorological obscuration. It is imperative, however, that pilots understand that clearance to operate "VFR ON TOP/VFR CONDITIONS" does not imply cancellation of the IFR flight plan.

g. Pilots operating VFR ON TOP/VFR CONDITIONS, may receive traffic information, from ATC, on other pertinent IFR or VFR aircraft. However, aircraft operating in TCAs/TRSAs shall be separated as required by FAA Handbook 7110.65.

NOTE.—When operating in VFR weather conditions, it is the pilot's responsibility to be vigilant so as to see and avoid other aircraft.

h. ATC will not authorize VFR or VFR ON TOP operations in PCAs. (See PARA—93 - POSITIVE CONTROL AREA.)

267—269. RESERVED

270. ADHERENCE TO CLEARANCE

a. When air traffic clearance has been obtained under either Visual or Instrument Flight Rules, the pilot in command of the aircraft shall not deviate from the provisions thereof unless an amended clearance is obtained. When ATC issues a clearance or instruction pilots are expected to execute its provisions upon receipt. ATC, in certain situations, will include the word "IMMEDIATELY" in a clearance or instruction to impress urgency of an imminent situation and expeditious compliance by the pilot is expected and necessary for safety. The addition of a VFR or other restriction (i.e., climb or descent point or time, crossing altitude, etc.) does not

authorize a pilot to deviate from the route of flight or any other provision of the ATC clearance.

b. When a heading is assigned or a turn is requested by ATC, pilots are expected to promptly initiate the turn, to complete the turn, and maintain the new heading unless issued additional instructions.

c. The term "at pilot's discretion" included in the altitude information of an ATC clearance means that ATC has offered the pilot the option to start climb or descent when he wishes. He is authorized to conduct the climb or descent at any rate he wishes, and to temporarily level off at any intermediate altitude he may desire. However, once he has vacated an altitude, he may not return to that altitude.

d. When ATC has not used the term "AT PILOT'S DISCRETION" nor imposed any climb or descent restrictions, pilots should initiate climb or descent promptly on acknowledgement of the clearance. Descend or climb at an optimum rate consistent with the operating characteristics of the aircraft to 1,000 feet above or below the assigned altitude, and then attempt to descend or climb at a rate of 500 feet per minute until the assigned altitude is reached. If at anytime the pilot is unable to climb or descend at a rate of at least 500 feet a minute, advise ATC. If it is necessary to level off at an intermediate altitude during climb or descent, advise ATC, except for level off at 10,000 feet MSL on descent or 3,000 feet above airport elevation (prior to entering an airport traffic area), when required for speed reduction (FAR—91.70).

NOTE.—Leveling off at 10,000 feet MSL on descent, or 3,000 feet above airport elevation (prior to entering in an airport traffic area), to comply with FAR—91.70 airspeed restrictions, is commonplace. Controllers anticipate this action and plan accordingly. Leveling off at any other time, on climb or descent, may seriously affect air traffic handling by ATC. Consequently, it is imperative that pilots make every effort to fulfill the above expected actions to aid ATC in safely handling and expediting traffic.

e. If the altitude information of an ATC DESCENT clearance includes a provision to "CROSS (fix) AT or AT OR ABOVE/BELOW (altitude)," "the manner in which the descent is executed to comply with the crossing altitude is at the pilot's discretion." This authorization to descend at pilot's discretion is only applicable to that portion of the flight to which the crossing altitude restriction applies, and the pilot is expected to comply with the crossing altitude as a provision of the clearance. Any other clearance in which pilot execution is optional will so state: "AT PILOT'S DISCRETION."

EXAMPLE:
"UNITED FOUR SEVENTEEN, DESCEND AND MAINTAIN SIX THOUSAND."

NOTE.—The pilot is expected to commence descent upon receipt of the clearance, and to descend at the suggested rates until reaching the assigned altitude of 6,000 feet.

EXAMPLE:
"UNITED FOUR SEVENTEEN, DESCEND AT PILOT'S DISCRETION, MAINTAIN SIX THOUSAND."

NOTE.—The pilot is authorized to conduct descent within the context of the term AT PILOT'S DISCRETION as described above.

EXAMPLE:
"UNITED FOUR SEVENTEEN, CROSS LAKEVIEW VOR AT OR ABOVE FLIGHT LEVEL TWO ZERO ZERO, DESCEND AND MAINTAIN SIX THOUSAND."

NOTE.—The pilot is authorized to conduct descent AT PILOT'S DISCRETION until reaching Lakeview VOR. He must comply with the clearance provision to cross the Lakeview VOR at or above FL 200. After passing Lakeview VOR, he is expected to descend at the suggested rates until reaching the assigned altitude of 6,000 feet.

EXAMPLE:

"UNITED FOUR SEVENTEEN, CROSS LAKEVIEW VOR AT SIX THOUSAND, MAINTAIN SIX THOUSAND."

NOTE.—The pilot is authorized to conduct descent AT PILOT'S DIS-CRETION, however, he must comply with the clearance provision to cross the Lakeview VOR at 6,000 feet.

EXAMPLE:

"UNITED FOUR SEVENTEEN, DESCEND NOW TO FLIGHT LEVEL TWO SEVEN ZERO, CROSS LAKEVIEW VOR AT OR BELOW ONE ZERO THOUSAND, DESCEND AND MAINTAIN SIX THOUSAND."

NOTE.—The pilot is expected to promptly execute and complete descent to FL 270 upon receipt of the clearance. After reaching FL 270 he is authorized to descend "at pilot's discretion" until reaching Lakeview VOR. He must comply with the clearance provision to cross Lakeview VOR at or below 10,000 feet. After Lakeview VOR he is expected to descend at the suggested rates until reaching 6,000 feet.

f. In case emergency authority is used to deviate from provisions of an ATC clearance, the pilot in command shall notify ATC as soon as possible and obtain an amended clearance. In an emergency situation which does not result in a deviation from the rules prescribed in FAR—91 but which requires ATC to give priority to an aircraft, the pilot of such aircraft shall, when requested by ATC, make a report within 48 hours of such emergency situation to the manager of that ATC facility.

g. The guiding principle is that the last ATC clearance has precedence over the previous ATC clearance. When the route or altitude in a previously issued clearance is amended, the controller will restate applicable altitude restrictions. If altitude to maintain is changed or restated, whether prior to departure or while airborne, and previously issued altitude restrictions are omitted, those altitude restrictions are canceled, including SID altitude restrictions.

EXAMPLE:

A departure flight receives a clearance to destination airport to maintain FL 290. The clearance incorporates a SID which has certain altitude crossing restrictions. Shortly after takeoff, the flight receives a new clearance changing the maintaining FL from 290 to 250. If the altitude restrictions are still applicable, the controller restates them.

EXAMPLE:

A departing aircraft is cleared to cross Fluky intersection at or above 3,000 feet, Gordonville VOR at or above 12,000 feet, maintain FL 200. Shortly after departure, the altitude to be maintained is changed to FL 240. If the altitude restrictions are still applicable, the controller issues an amended clearance as follows: "CROSS FLUKY INTERSECTION AT OR ABOVE THREE THOUSAND, CROSS GORDONVILLE VOR AT OR ABOVE ONE TWO THOUSAND, MAINTAIN FLIGHT LEVEL TWO FOUR ZERO.":

EXAMPLE:

An arriving aircraft is cleared to his destination airport via V45 Delta VOR direct, he is cleared to cross Delta VOR at 10,000 feet and then to, maintain 6,000 feet. Prior to Delta VOR, the controller issues amended clearance as follows: "TURN RIGHT HEADING ONE EIGHT ZERO FOR VECTOR TO RUNWAY THREE SIX ILS APPROACH, MAINTAIN 6,000."

NOTE.—Because the altitude restriction "cross Delta VOR at 10,000 feet" was omitted from the amended clearance, it is no longer in effect.

h. Pilots of turbojet aircraft equipped with afterburner engines should advise ATC prior to takeoff if they intend to use afterburning during their climb to the en route altitude. Often, the controller may be able to plan his traffic to accommodate a high performance climb and allow the pilot to climb to his planned altitude without restriction.

271. IFR SEPARATION STANDARDS

a. ATC effects separation of aircraft vertically by assigning different altitudes; longitudinally by providing an interval expressed in time or distance between aircraft on the same, converging, or crossing courses, and laterally by assigning different flight paths.

b. Separation will be provided between all aircraft operating on IFR flight plans except during that part of the flight (outside of a TCA or TRSA) being conducted on a VFR ON TOP/ VFR CONDITIONS clearance. Under these conditions, ATC may issue traffic advisories but it is the sole responsibility of the pilot to be vigilant so as to see and avoid other aircraft.

c. When radar is employed in the separation of aircraft at the same altitude, a minimum of 3 miles separation is provided between aircraft operating within 40 miles of the radar antenna site, and 5 miles between aircraft operating beyond 40 miles from the antenna site. These minima may be increased or decreased in certain specific situations.

272. SPEED ADJUSTMENTS

a. ATC will issue speed adjustments to pilots of radar controlled aircraft to achieve or maintain required or desire spacing.

b. ATC will express all speed adjustments in terms of knots based on indicated airspeed (IAS) in 10 knot increments except that at or above FL 240 speeds may be expressed in terms of mach numbers in .01 increments. The use of mach numbers is restricted to turbojet aircraft with mach meters.

c. Pilots complying with speed adjustments are expected to maintain a speed within plus or minus 10 knots or .02 mach number of the specified speed.

d. Unless pilot concurrence is obtained, ATC requests for speed adjustments will be in accordance with the following minimums:

(1) To aircraft operating between FL 280 and 10,000 feet, a speed not less than 250 knots or the equivalent mach number.

(2) To turbine powered aircraft operating below 10,000 feet:

(a) A speed not less than 210 knots, except;

(b) Within 20 flying miles of the airport of intended landing, a speed not less than 170 knots.

(3) Reciprocating engine or turboprop aircraft within 20 flying miles of the runway threshold of the airport of intended landing, a speed not less than 150 knots.

(4) To departing aircraft:

(a) Turbine powered aircraft, a speed not less than 230 knots.

(b) Reciprocating engine aircraft, a speed not less than 150 knots.

e. When ATC combines a speed adjustment with a descent clearance, the sequence of delivery, with the word "then" between, indicates the expected order of execution;

EXAMPLE:

DESCEND AND MAINTAIN (altitude) THEN REDUCE SPEED TO (speed).

EXAMPLE:

REDUCE SPEED TO (speed) THEN DESCEND AND MAINTAIN (altitude).

NOTE.—The maximum speeds below 10,000 feet as established in FAR—91.70 still apply. If there is any doubt concerning the manner in which such a clearance is to be executed, request clarification from ATC.

f. If ATC determines (before an approach clearance is issued) that it is no longer necessary to apply speed adjustment procedures, they will inform the pilot to resume normal speed. Approach clearances supersede any prior speed adjustment assignments and pilots are expected to make their own speed adjustments, as necessary, to complete the approach. Under certain circumstances; however, it may be necessary for ATC to issue further speed adjustments after approach clearance is issued to maintain separation between successive arrivals. Under such circumstances previously issued speed adjustments will be restated if that speed is to be maintained or additional speed adjustments are requested. ATC must obtain pilot concurrence for speed adjustments after approach clearances are issued. Speed adjustments should not be assigned inside the final approach fix on final or a point 5 miles from the runway, whichever is closer to the runway.

g. The pilots retain the prerogative of rejecting the application of speed adjustment by ATC if the minimum safe airspeed for any particular operation is greater than the speed adjustment. IN SUCH CASES, PILOTS ARE EXPECTED TO ADVISE ATC OF THE SPEED THAT WILL BE USED.

h. Pilots are reminded that they are responsible for rejecting the application of speed adjustment by ATC if, in their opinion, it will cause them to exceed the maximum indicated airspeed prescribed by FAR—91.70(a). IN SUCH CASES, THE PILOT IS EXPECTED TO SO INFORM ATC. Pilots operating at or above 10,000 feet MSL who are issued speed adjustments which exceed 250 knots IAS and are subsequently cleared below 10,000 feet MSL are expected to comply with FAR—91.70(a).

i. For operations conducted below 10,000 feet MSL when outside the United States and beneath a TCA, airspeed restrictions apply to all U.S. registered aircraft. For operations conducted below 10,000 feet MSL when outside the United States within a TCA, there are no speed restrictions.

j. For operations in an airport traffic area, ATC is authorized to request or approve a speed greater than the maximum indicated airspeeds prescribed for operation within that airspace (FAR—91.70(b)).

k. When in communication with the ARTCC, pilots should, as a good operating practice, state any ATC assigned speed restriction on initial radio contact associated with an ATC communications frequency change.

273. RUNWAY SEPARATION

Tower controllers establish the sequence of arriving and departing aircraft by requiring them to adjust flight or ground operation as necessary to achieve proper spacing. They may "HOLD" an aircraft short of the runway to achieve spacing between it and an arriving aircraft; the controller may instruct a pilot to "EXTEND DOWNWIND" in order to establish spacing from an arriving or departing aircraft. At times a clearance may include the word "IMMEDIATE." For example: "CLEARED FOR IMMEDIATE TAKEOFF." In such cases "IMMEDIATE" is used for purposes of *air traffic separation.* It is up to the pilot to refuse the clearance if, in his opinion, compliance would adversely affect his operation. (See PARA—236 - GATE HOLDING DUE TO DEPARTURE DELAYS.)

274. VISUAL SEPARATION

a. Visual separation is a means employed by ATC to separate aircraft only in terminal areas. There are two methods employed to effect this separation:

(1) The tower controller sees the aircraft involved and issues instructions, as necessary, to ensure that the aircraft avoid each other.

(2) A pilot sees the other aircraft involved and upon instructions from the controller provides his own separation by maneuvering his aircraft to avoid it. This may involve following in-trail behind another aircraft or keeping it in sight until it is no longer a factor.

b. A pilot's acceptance of instructions to follow another aircraft or provide visual separation from it is an acknowledgment that the pilot will maneuver his/her aircraft as necessary to avoid the other aircraft or to maintain in-trail separation. In operations conducted behind heavy jet aircraft, it is also an acknowledgment that the pilot accepts the responsibility for wake turbulence separation.

c. WHEN A PILOT HAS BEEN TOLD TO FOLLOW ANOTHER AIRCRAFT OR TO PROVIDE VISUAL SEPARATION FROM IT HE/SHE SHOULD PROMPTLY NOTIFY THE CONTROLLER IF VISUAL CONTACT WITH THE OTHER AIRCRAFT IS LOST OR CANNOT BE MAINTAINED OR IF THE PILOT CANNOT ACCEPT THE RESPONSIBILITY FOR THE SEPARATION FOR ANY REASON.

d. Pilots should remember, however, that they have a regulatory responsibility (FAR 91.67(a)) to see and avoid other aircraft when weather conditions permit.

275. USE OF VISUAL CLEARING PROCEDURES

a. **Before Takeoff.** Prior to taxiing onto a runway or landing area in preparation for takeoff, pilots should scan the approach areas for possible landing traffic, executing appropriate clearing maneuvers to provide him a clear view of the approach areas.

b. **Climbs and Descents.** During climbs and descents in flight conditions which permit visual detection of other traffic, pilots should execute gentle banks, left and right at a frequency which permits continuous visual scanning of the airspace about them.

c. **Straight and level.** Sustained periods of straight and level flight in conditions which permit visual detection of other traffic should be broken at intervals with appropriate clearing procedures to provide effective visual scanning.

d. **Traffic pattern.** Entries into traffic patterns while descending create specific collision hazards and should be avoided.

e. **Traffic at VOR sites.** All operators should emphasize the need for sustained vigilance in the vicinity of VORs and airway intersections due to the convergence of traffic.

f. **Training operations.** Operators of pilot training programs are urged to adopt the following practices:

(1) Pilots undergoing flight instruction at all levels should be requested to verbalize clearing procedures (call out, "clear" left, right, above or below) to instill and sustain the habit of vigilance during maneuvering.

(2) High-wing airplane, momentarily raise the wing in the direction of the intended turn and look.

(3) Low-wing airplane, momentarily lower the wing in the direction of the intended turn and look.

(4) Appropriate clearing procedures should precede the execution of all turns including chandelles, lazy eights, stalls, slow flight, climbs, straight and level, spins and other combination maneuvers.

276—289. RESERVED

Section 5. PREFLIGHT

290. PREFLIGHT PREPARATION

a. Every pilot is urged to receive a preflight briefing and to file a flight plan. This briefing should consist of weather, airport, and en route NAVAID information. Briefing service may be obtained from a FSS either by telephone or interphone, by radio when airborne, or by a personal visit to the station.

NOTE.—Pilots filing flight plans via "fast file" who desire to have their briefing recorded, should include a statement at the end of the recording as to the source of their weather briefing.

b The information requried by the FAA to process flight plans is contained on FAA Form 7233-1, Flight Plan. (See paragraphs 295-298.) The forms are available at all flight service stations. Additional copies will be provided on request.

c. Consult an FSS or Weather Service Office (WSO) for preflight weather briefing.

d. FSSs are required to advise of pertinent NOTAMs, but if they are overlooked, don't hesitate to remind the specialist that you have not received NOTAM information.

NOTE.—NOTAMS which are known in sufficient time for publication and are of 7 days duration or longer are normally incorporated into the Notices to Airmen (Class II) publication and carried there until cancellation time. FDC NOTAMs, which apply to instrument flight procedures, are also included in the Notices to Airmen publication up to and including the number indicated in the FDC NOTAM legend. Class II NOTAMs are not provided during a briefing unless specifically requested by the pilot since the FSS specialist has no way of knowing whether the pilot has already checked the Notices to Airmen (Class II) publication prior to calling. Remember to *ask* for Class II NOTAMs in the Notices to Airmen publication. This information is not normally furnished during your briefing. (See PARA—294 - NOTICE TO AIRMEN (NOTAM) SYSTEM.)

e. Pilots are urged to use only the latest issue of aeronautical charts in planning and conducting flight operations. Aeronautical charts are revised and reissued on a regular scheduled basis to ensure that depicted data are current and reliable. In the conterminous U.S., Sectional Charts are updated each 6 months, IFR En route Charts each 56 days, and amendments to civil IFR Approach Charts are accomplished on a 56 day cycle with a change notice volume issued on the 28 day midcycle. Charts that have been superseded by those of a more recent date may contain obsolete or incomplete flight information. (See PARA—623 - GENERAL DESCRIPTION OF EACH CHART SERIES.)

f. When requesting a preflight briefing, identify yourself as a pilot and provide the following:

(1) Type of flight planned, e.g., VFR or IFR.

(2) Aircraft number or pilot's name.

(3) Aircraft type.

(4) Departure Airport.

(5) Route of flight.

(6) Destination.

(7) Flight altitude(s).

(8) ETD and ETE.

g. Prior to conducting a briefing, briefers are required to have the background information listed above so that they may tailor the briefing to the needs of the proposed flight. The objective is to communicate a "picture" of meteorological and aeronautical information necessary for the conduct of a safe and efficient flight. Briefers use all available weather and aeronautical information to summarize data applicable to the proposed flight. They do not read weather reports and forecasts verbatim unless specifically requested by the pilot. Refer to PARA—502 for those items of a weather briefing that should be expected or requested.

h. The Federal Aviation Administration (FAA) by Federal Aviation Regulation, Part 93, Subpart K, has designated High Density Traffic Airports (HDTA) and has prescribed air traffic rules and requirements for operating aircraft (excluding helicopter operations) to and from these airports (see details in Airport/Facility Directory, Special Notices Section).

i. In addition to the filing of a flight plan, if the flight will traverse or land in one or more foreign countries, it is particularly important that pilots leave a complete itinerary with someone directly concerned, keep that person advised of the flight's progress and inform him that, if serious doubt arises as to the safety of the flight, he should first contact the FSS. (See PARA—300 - FLIGHTS OUTSIDE THE UNITED STATES AND U.S. TERRITORIES.)

j. Pilots operating under provisions of FAR—135, and not having an FAA assigned 3-letter designator, are urged to prefix the normal registration (N) number with the letter "T" on flight plan filing, (e.g., TN1234B). (See PARA—193 - AIRCRAFT CALL SIGNS.)

291. FOLLOW IFR PROCEDURES EVEN WHEN OPERATING VFR

a. To maintain IFR proficiency, pilots are urged to practice IFR procedures whenever possible, even when operating VFR. Some suggested practices include:

(1) Obtain a complete preflight and weather briefing. Check the NOTAMS.

(2) File a flight plan. This is an excellent low cost insurance policy. The cost is the time it takes to fill it out. The insurance includes the knowledge that someone will be looking for you if you become overdue at your destination.

(3) Use current charts.

(4) Use the navigation aids. Practice maintaining a good course—keep the needle centered.

(5) Maintain a constant altitude which is appropriate for the direction of flight.

(6) Estimate en route position times.

(7) Make accurate and frequent position reports to the FSSs along your route of flight.

b. Simulated IFR flight is recommended (under the hood); however, pilots are cautioned to review and adhere to the requirements specified in FAR—91.21 before and during such flight.

c. When flying VFR at night, in addition to the altitude appropriate for the direction of flight, pilots should maintain an altitude which is at or above the minimum en route altitude as shown on charts. This is especially true in mountainous terrain, where there is usually very little ground reference. Do not depend on your eyes alone to avoid rising unlighted terrain, or even lighted obstructions such as TV towers.

292—293. RESERVED

294. NOTICE TO AIRMEN (NOTAM) SYSTEM

a. Time-critical aeronautical information which is of either a temporary nature or is not sufficiently known in advance to permit publication on aeronautical charts or in other operational publications, receives immediate dissemination via the National Notice to Airmen (NOTAM) System.

NOTE.—NOTAM information is that aeronautical information that could affect a pilot's decision to make a flight. It includes such information as airport or primary runway closures, changes in the status of navigational aids, ILSs, radar service availability, and other information essential to planned enroute, terminal or landing operations.

b. NOTAM information is classified into three categories. These are NOTAM (D) or distant, NOTAM (L) or local, and Flight Data Center (FDC) NOTAMs.

(1) NOTAM (D)

(a) NOTAM (D) information is disseminated for all navigational facilities that are part of the National Airspace System (NAS), all IFR airports with approved IAPs, and for those VFR airports annotated with the NOTAM Service Symbol (§) in the Airport/Facility Directory (A/FD). The complete file of all NOTAM (D) information is maintained in a computer data base at the National Communications Center (NATCOM), located in Kansas City. This category of information is distributed automatically, appended to the hourly weather reports, via the Service A telecommunications system. Air traffic facilities, primarily FSS, with Service A capability, have access to the entire NATCOM data base of NOTAMs. These NOTAMs remain available via Service A for the duration of their validity or until published.

(2) NOTAM (L)

(a) NOTAM (L) information includes such data as taxiway closures, men and equipment near or crossing runways, airport rotating beacon outages, and airport lighting aids that do not affect instrument approach criteria, such as VASI. This category of NOTAM also contains all NOTAM information concerning airports that are not annotated with the NOTAM Service Symbol in the A/FD, including airport and runway closures.

(b) NOTAM (L) information is distributed locally only, and is not attached to the hourly weather reports. A separate file of local NOTAMs is maintained at each FSS, for facilities in their area only. NOTAM (L) information for other FSS areas must be specifically requested directly from the FSS that has responsibility for the airport concerned.

(3) FDC NOTAMS

(a) On those occasions when it becomes necessary to disseminate information which is regulatory in nature, the National Flight Data Center (NFDC), in Washington, D.C., will issue an FDC NOTAM. FDC NOTAMs contain such things as amendments to published IAPs and other current aeronautical charts. They are also used to advertise temporary flight restrictions caused by such things as natural disasters or large scale public events, that may generate a congestion of air traffic over a site.

(b) FDC NOTAMs are transmitted via Service A only once, and are kept on file at the FSS until published or canceled. FSSs are responsible for maintaining a file of current, unpublished FDC NOTAMs concerning conditions within 400 miles of their facilities. FDC information concerning conditions that are more than 400 miles from the FSS, or that is already published, is given to a pilot only on request.

c. An integral part of the NOTAM System is the biweekly Notice to Airmen (Class II) publication. Data is included in this publication to reduce congestion on the telecommunications circuits, and therefore is not available via Service A. This information once published, is not provided during pilot weather briefings unless specifically requested by the pilot.

NOTE.—The term "Class II" refers to the fact that the NOTAMs or notices, appear in printed form for mail distribution as opposed to NOTAMs which are distributed via telecommunications. The latter are considered Class I.

(1) This publication contains two sections:

(a) The first section consists of notices which meet the criteria for NOTAM (D), and are expected to remain in effect for an extended period, and FDC NOTAMs current at the time of publication. Occasionally, some NOTAM (L) and other unique information is included in this section when it will contribute to flight safety.

(b) The second section contains special notices that are too long or concern a wide or unspecified geographic area and are not suitable for inclusion in the first section. The content of these notices vary widely and there are no specific criteria for their inclusion, other than their enhancement of flight safety.

(c) The number of the last FDC NOTAM included in the publication, is noted on the first page to aid the user, in updating the listing contained, with any FDC NOTAMs which may have been issued between the cut-off date and the date the publication is received. All information contained will be carried until the information expires, is canceled, or in the case of permanent conditions, is published in other publications, such as the A/FD.

(d) All new notices entered, excluding FDC NOTAMs, will be published only if the information is expected to remain in effect for at least 7 days after the effective date of the publication.

295. FLIGHT PLAN — VFR FLIGHTS

a. Except for operations in or penetrating a Coastal or Domestic ADIZ or DEWIZ (See PARA—430 - NATIONAL SECURITY), a flight plan is not required for VFR flight. However, it is strongly recommended that one be filed with an FAA FSS. This will ensure that you receive VFR Search and Rescue Protection. (Refer to PARA—456.g. for the proper method of filing.)

b. To obtain maximum benefits from the flight plan program, flight plans should be filed directly with the nearest FSS. For your convenience, FSSs provide aeronautical and meteorological briefings while accepting flight plans. Radio may be used to file if no other means are available.

NOTE.—Some states operate aeronautical communications facilities which will accept and forward flight plans to the FSS for further handling.

c. When a "stopover" flight is anticipated, it is recommended that a separate flight plan be filed for each "leg" when the stop is expected to be more than 1 hour duration.

d. Pilots are encouraged to give their departure times directly to the FSS serving the departure airport or as otherwise indicated by the FSS when the flight plan is filed. This will ensure more efficient flight plan service and permit the FSS to advise you of significant changes in aeronautical facilities or meteorological conditions. When a VFR flight plan is filed, it will be held by the FSS until 1 hour after the proposed departure time unless:

(1) The actual departure time is received.

PREFLIGHT

(2) A revised proposed departure time is received.

(3) At a time of filing, the FSS is informed that the proposed departure time will be met, but actual time cannot be given because of inadequate communications (assumed departures).

e. On pilot's request, at a location having an active tower, the aircraft identification will be forwarded by the FSS to the tower for reporting the actual departure time. This procedure should be avoided at busy airports.

f. Although position reports are not required for VFR flight plans, periodic reports to FAA, FSSs along the route are good practice. Such contacts permit significant information to be passed to the transiting aircraft and also serve to check the progress of the flight should it be necessary for any reason to locate the aircraft.

EXAMPLE:

BONANZA 314K, OVER KINGFISHER AT (Time), VFR FLIGHT PLAN, TULSA TO AMARILLO.

EXAMPLE:

CHEROKEE 5133J, OVER OKLAHOMA CITY AT (Time), SHREVEPORT TO DENVER, NO FLIGHT PLAN.

g. Pilots not operating on an IFR flight plan, and when in level cruising flight, are cautioned to conform with VFR cruising altitudes appropriate to direction of flight.

h. Indicate aircraft equipment capabilities when filing VFR flight plans by appending the appropriate suffix to aircraft type in the same manner as that prescribed for IFR flight (see PARA—298 — FLIGHT PLAN - IFR FLIGHTS). Under some circumstances, ATC computer tapes can be useful in constructing the radar history of a downed or crashed aircraft. In each case, knowledge of the aircraft's transponder equipment is necessary in determining whether or not such computer tapes might prove effective.

i. **FLIGHT PLAN FORM.** *(See Figure 4-7.)*

j. **EXPLANATION OF VFR FLIGHT PLAN ITEMS.**

Block 1. Check the type flight plan. Check both the VFR and IFR blocks if composite VFR/IFR.

Block 2. Enter your complete aircraft identification including the prefix "N" if applicable.

Block 3. Enter the designator for the aircraft or, if unknown, the aircraft manufacturer's name.

Block 4. Enter your true airspeed (TAS).

Block 5. Enter the departure airport identifier code (or the name if identifier is unknown).

Block 6. Enter the proposed departure time in Coordinated Universal Time (UTC). If airborne, specify the actual or proposed departure time as appropriate.

Block 7. Enter the appropriate VFR altitude (to assist the briefer in providing weather and wind information).

Block 8. Define the route of flight by using NAVAID identifier codes and airways.

Block 9. Enter the destination airport identifier code (or name if identifier is unknown).

NOTE.—Include the city name (or even the state name) if needed for clarity.

Block 10. Enter your estimated time en route, in hours and minutes.

Block 11. Enter only those remarks pertinent to ATC or to the clarification of other flight plan information such as the appropriate radiotelephony (call sign) associated with the designator filed in Block 2. Items of a personal nature are not accepted.

Block 12. Specify the fuel on board, in hours and minutes.

Block 13. Specify an alternate airport if desired.

Block 14. Enter your complete name, address, and telephone number. Enter sufficient information to identify home base, airport, or operator.

NOTE.—This information is essential in the event of search and rescue operations.

Block 15. Enter total number of persons on board including crew (POB).

Block 16. Enter the predominant colors.

Block 17. Record the FSS name for closing the flight plan. If the flight plan is closed with a different FSS or facility, state the recorded FSS name that would normally have closed your flight plan.

NOTE.—The information transmitted to the destination FSS will consist only of flight plans blocks 2,3,9, and 10. Estimated time en route (ETE) will be converted to the correct estimated time of arrival (ETA).

296. FLIGHT PLAN — DEFENSE VFR (DVFR) FLIGHTS

VFR flights into a Coastal or Domestic ADIZ/DEWIZ are required to file a VFR flight plan for security purposes. Detailed ADIZ procedures are found in the National Security section of this chapter. (See FAR—99.)

297. COMPOSITE FLIGHT PLAN (VFR/IFR FLIGHTS)

a. Flight plans which specify VFR operation for one portion of a flight, and IFR for another portion, will be accepted by the FSS at the point of departure. If VFR flight is conducted for the first portion of the flight, the pilot should report his departure time to the FSS with which he filed his VFR/IFR flight plan; and, subsequently, close the VFR portion and request ATC clearance from the FSS nearest the point at which change from VFR to IFR is proposed. Regardless of the type facility you are communicating with (FSS, center, or tower), it is the pilot's responsibility to request that facility to "CLOSE VFR FLIGHT PLAN." The pilot must remain in VFR weather conditions until operating in accordance with the IFR clearance.

b. When a flight plan indicates IFR for the first portion of flight and VFR for the latter portion, the pilot will normally be cleared to the point at which the change is proposed. Once the pilot has reported over the clearance limit and does not desire further IFR clearance, he should advise ATC to cancel the IFR portion of his flight plan. Then, he should contact the nearest FSS to activate the VFR portion of his flight plan. If the pilot desires to continue his IFR flight plan beyond the clearance limit, he should contact ATC at least 5 minutes prior to the clearance limit and request further IFR clearance. If the requested clearance is not received prior to reaching the clearance limit fix, the pilot will be expected to established himself in a standard holding pattern on the radial or course to the fix unless a holding pattern for the clearance limit fix is depicted on a U.S. Government or commercially produced (meeting FAA requirements) Low or High Altitude En Route, Area or STAR Chart. In this case the pilot will hold according to the depicted pattern.

298. FLIGHT PLAN — IFR FLIGHTS

a. **GENERAL**

(1) Prior to departure from within, or prior to entering controlled airspace, a pilot must submit a complete flight plan and receive an air traffic clearance, if weather conditions are below VFR minimums. Instrument flight plans may be submitted to the nearest FSSs or ATCT either in person or by telephone (or by radio if no other means are avaialble). Pilots should file IFR flight plans at least 30 minutes prior to estimated time of departure to preclude possible delay in receiving a departure clearance from ATC. To minimize your delay in entering the control zone at destination when IFR weather conditions exist or are forecast at that airport, an IFR flight plan should be filed before departure. Otherwise, a 30 minute delay is not unusual in receiving an ATC clearance because of time spent in processing flight plan data. Traffic saturation frequently prevents control personnel from accepting flight plans by radio. In such cases, the pilot is advised to contact the nearest FSS for the purpose of filing the flight plan.

NOTE.—There are several methods of obtaining IFR clearances at non-tower, non-FSSs, and outlying airports. The procedure may vary due to geographical features, weather conditions, and the complexity of the ATC system. To determine the most effective means of receiving an IFR clearance, pilots should ask the nearest FSS the most appropriate means of obtaining the IFR clearance.

(2) When filing an IFR flight plan for a Heavy aircraft, add the prefix H to the aircraft type.

EXAMPLE:

H/DC10/U

(3) When filing an IFR flight plan for flight in an aircraft equipped with a radar beacon transponder, DME equipment, TACAN only equipment or a combination of both, identify equipment capability by adding a suffix to the AIRCRAFT TYPE preceded by a slant, as follows:

/X — no transponder.

/T — transponder with no altitude encoding capability.

/U — transponder with altitude encoding capability.

/D — DME, but no transponder.

/B — DME and transponder, but no altitude encoding capability.

/A — DME and transponder and with altitude encoding capability.

/M — TACAN only, but no transponder.

/N — TACAN only and transponder, but with no altitude encoding capability.

/P — TACAN only and transponder with altitude encoding capability.

/C — RNAV and transponder, but with no altitude encoding capability.

/R — RNAV and transponder with altitude encoding capability.

/W — RNAV but no transponder.

(4) It is recommended that pilots file the maximum transponder or navigation capability of their aircraft in the equipment suffix. This will provide ATC with the necessary information to utilize all facets of navigational equipment and transponder capabilities available. In the case of area navigation equipped aircraft, pilots should file the /C, /R, or /W capability of the aircraft even though an RNAV route or random RNAV route has not been requested. This will ensure ATC awareness of the pilot's ability to navigate point-to-point and may be utilized to expedite the flight.

NOTE.—The suffix is not to be added to the aircraft identification or be transmitted by radio as part of the aircraft identification.

b. AIRWAYS/JET ROUTES DEPICTION ON FLIGHT PLAN

(1) It is vitally important that the route of flight be accurately and completely described in the flight plan. To simplify defini-

tion of the proposed route, and to facilitate ATC, pilots are requested to file via airways or jet routes established for use at the altitude or flight level planned.

(2) If flight is to be conducted via designated airways or jet routes, describe the route by indicating the type and number designators of the airway(s) or jet route(s) requested. If more than one airway or jet route is to be used, clearly indicate points of transition. If the transition is made at an unnamed intersection, show the next succeeding NAVAID or named intersection on the intended route and the complete route from that point. Reporting points may be identified by using authorized name/code as depicted on appropriate aeronautical charts. The following two examples illustrate the need to specify the transition point when two routes share more than one transition fix.

EXAMPLE:

FL 250 ALB J37 BUMPY J14 BHM

SPELLED OUT: Requesting Flight Level 250 from Albany, New York, via Jet Route 37 transitioning to Jet Route 14 at BUMPY intersection, thence via Jet Route 14 to Birmingham, Alabama.

EXAMPLE:

FL 250 ALB J37 ENO J14 BHM

SPELLED OUT: Requesting Flight Level 250 from Albany, New York, via Jet Route 37 transitioning to Jet Route 14 at Kenton VORTAC (ENO) thence via Jet Route 14 to Birmingham, Alabama.

(a) The route of flight may also be described by naming the reporting points or NAVAIDs over which the flight will pass, provided the points named are established for use at the altitude or flight level planned.

EXAMPLE:

30 BWI V44 SWANN V433 DQO

SPELLED OUT: Requesting 3,000 feet from Baltimore-Washington International, via Victor 44 to Swann Intersection, transitioning to Victor 433 at Swann, thence via V433 to Dupont.

(b) When the route of flight is defined by named reporting points, whether alone or in combination with airways or jet routes, and the navigational aids (VOR, VORTAC, TACAN, NDB) to be used for the flight are a combination of different types of aids, enough information should be included to clearly indicate the route requested.

EXAMPLE:

FL 310 LAX J5 LKV J3 GEG YXC FL 330 HL500 VLR HL515 YWG

SPELLED OUT: Requesting FL 310 from Los Angeles International via Jet Route 5 Lakeview, Jet Route 3 Spokane, direct Kimberly, British Columbia Low Frequency Range, Flight Level 330 High Level Airway 500 to Langruth, Manitoba VOR, High Level Airway 515 to Winnepeg, Manitoba.

(c) When filing IFR, it is to the pilot's advantage to file a preferred route.

NOTE.—Preferred IFR routes are described and tabulated in the Airport/Facility Directory.

(d) ATC may issue a SID or a STAR, as appropriate. (See PARA—325 - INSTRUMENT DEPARTURE and PARA—360 - STANDARD TERMINAL ARRIVAL (STAR).)

NOTE.—Pilots not desiring a SID or STAR should so indicate in the remarks section of the flight plan as "NO SID" or "NO STAR".

c. DIRECT FLIGHTS

(1) All or any portions of the route which will not be flown on the radials or courses of established airways or routes, such as direct route flights, must be defined by indicating the radio fixes over which the flight will pass. Fixes selected to define the route shall be those over which the position of the aircraft can be accurately determined. Such fixes automatically become compulsory reporting points for the flight, unless advised otherwise by ATC. Only those navigational aids established for use in a particular structure, i.e., in the low or high structures, may be used to define the en route phase of a direct flight within that altitude structure.

(2) The azimuth feature of VOR aids and that azimuth and distance (DME) features of VORTAC and TACAN aids are assigned certain frequency protected areas of airspace which are intended for application to established airway and route use, and to provide guidance for planning flights outside of established airways or routes. These areas of airspace are expressed in terms of cylindrical service volumes of specified dimensions called "class limits" or "categories." (See PARA—10 - CLASS OF NAVAIDs.) An operational service volume has been established for each class in which adequate signal coverage and frequency protection can be assured. To facilitate use of VOR, VORTAC or TACAN aids, consistent with their operational service volume limits, pilot use of such aids for defining a direct route of flight in controlled airspace should not exceed the following:

(a) Operations above FL 450 — use aids not more than 200 NM apart. These aids are depicted on En Route High Altitude Charts.

(b) Operation off established routes from 18,000 feet MSL to FL 450 - use aids not more than 260 NM apart. These aids are depicted on En Route High Altitude Charts.

(c) Operation off established airways below 18,000 feet MSL — use aids not more than 80 NM apart. These aids are depicted on En Route Low Altitude Charts.

(d) Operation off established airways between 14,500 feet MSL and 17,999 feet MSL in the conterminous U.S. — (H) facilities not more than 200 NM apart may be used.

(3) Increasing use of self-contained airborne navigational systems which do not rely on the VOR/VORTAC/TACAN system has resulted in pilot requests for direct routes which exceed NAVAID service volume limits. These direct route requests will be approved only in a radar environment, with approval based on pilot responsibility for navigation on the authorized direct route. Radar flight following will be provided by ATC for ATC purposes.

(4) At times, ATC will initiate a direct route in a radar environment which exceeds NAVAID service volume limits. In such cases ATC will provide radar monitoring and navigational assistance as necessary.

(5) Airway or jet route numbers, appropriate to the stratum in which operation will be conducted, may also be included to describe portions of the route to be flown.

EXAMPLE:

140 MDW V262 BDF V10 BRL STJ SLN GCK

SPELLED OUT: Requesting 14,000 feet from Chicago Midway Airport via Victor 262 to Bradford, Victor 10 to Burlington, Iowa, direct St. Joseph, Missouri, direct Salina, Kansas, direct Garden City, Kansas.

NOTE.—When route of flight is described by radio fixes, the pilot will be expected to fly a direct course between the points named.

(6) Pilots are reminded that they are responsible for adhering to obstruction clearance requirements on those segments of direct routes that are outside of controlled airspace. The MEA's and other altitudes shown on Low Altitude IFR En Route Charts pertain to those route segments within controlled airspace, and those altitudes may not meet obstruction clearance criteria when operating off those routes.

d. AREA NAVIGATION (RNAV)

(1) Random RNAV routes can only be approved in a radar environment. Factors that will be considered by ATC in approving random RNAV routes include the capability to provide radar monitoring and compatibility with traffic volume and flow. ATC will radar monitor each flight, however, navigation on the random RNAV route is the responsibility of the pilot.

(2) To be certified for use in the National Airspace System, RNAV equipment must meet the specifications outlined in AC 90-45. The pilot is responsible for variations in equipment capability, and must advise ATC if a RNAV clearance can not be accepted as specified. The controller need only be concerned that the aircraft is RNAV equipped; if the flight plan equipment suffix denotes RNAV capability, the RNAV routing can be applied.

(3) Pilots of aircraft equipped with operational area navigation equipment may file for random RNAV routes throughout the National Airspace System, where radar monitoring by ATC is available, in accordance with the following procedures.

(a) File airport to airport flight plans prior to departure.

(b) File the appropriate RNAV capability certification suffix in the flight plan.

(c) Plan the random route portion of the flight plan to begin and end over appropriate arrival and departure transition fixes or appropriate navigation aids for the altitude stratum within which the flight will be conducted. The use of normal preferred departure and arrival routes (SID/STAR), where established, is recommended.

(d) File route structure transitions to and from the random route portion of the flight.

(e) Define the random route by waypoints. File route description waypoints by using degree-distance fixes based on navigational aids which are appropriate for the altitude stratum.

(f) File a minimum of one route description waypoint for each ARTCC through whose area the random route will be flown. These waypoints must be located within 200 NM of the preceding center's boundary.

(g) File an additional route description waypoint for each turnpoint in the route.

(h) Plan additional route description waypoints as required to ensure accurate navigation via the filed route of flight. Navigation is the pilots's responsibility unless ATC assistance is requested.

(i) Plan the route of flight so as to avoid Prohibited and Restricted Airspace by 3 NM unless permission has been obtained to operate in that airspace and the appropriate ATC facilities are advised.

(4) Pilots of aircraft equipped with latitude/longitude coordinate navigation capability, independent of VOR/TACAN references, may file for random RNAV routes at and above FL 390, within the conterminous United States, using the following procedures.

(a) File airport to airport flight plans prior to departure.

(b) File the appropriate RNAV capability certification suffix in the flight plan.

(c) Plan the random route portion of the flight to begin and end over published departure/arrival transition fixes or appropriate navigation aids for airports without published transition procedures. The use of preferred departure and arrival routes, such as SID and STAR where established, is recommended.

(d) Plan the route of flight so as to avoid prohibited and restricted airspace by 3 NM unless permission has been obtained to operate in that airspace and the appropriate ATC facility is advised.

(e) Define the route of flight after the departure fix, including each intermediate fix (turnpoint) and the arrival fix for the destination airport in terms of latitude/longitude coordinates plotted to the nearest minute. The arrival fix must be identified by both the latitude/longitude coordinates and a fix identifier.

Example:

MIA[1]SRQ[2]3407/10615[3]3407/11546 TNP[4]LAX[5]

1. Departure airport.
2. Departure fix.
3. Intermediate fix (turning point).
4. Arrival fix.
5. Destination airport.

(f) Record latitude/longitude coordinates by four figures describing latitude in degrees and minutes followed by a solidus and five figures describing longitude in degrees and minutes.

(g) File at FL 390 or above for the random RNAV portion of the flight.

(h) Fly all routes/route segments on Great Circle tracks.

(i) Make any inflight requests for random RNAV clearances or route amendments to an en route ATC facility.

e. **FLIGHT PLAN FORM.** *(See Figure 4-7.)*

f. **EXPLANATION OF IFR FLIGHT PLAN ITEMS.**

Block 1. Check the type flight plan. Check both the VFR and IFR blocks if composite VFR/IFR.

Block 2. Enter your complete aircraft identification including the prefix "N" if applicable.

Block 3. Enter the designator for the aircraft or, if unknown, the aircraft manufacturer's name (e.g., Cessna); followed by a slant(/) and the transponder or DME equipment code letter (e.g., C-182/U). Heavy aircraft add prefix "H" to aircraft type: example: H/DC10/U.

Block 4. Enter your computed true airspeed (TAS).

NOTE.—Enter the average TAS changes plus or minus 5 percent or 10 knots, whichever is greater, advise ATC.

Block 5. Enter the departure airport identifier code (or the name if identifier is unknown).

NOTE.—Use of identifier codes will expedite the processing of your flight plan.

Block 6. Enter the proposed departure time in Coordinated Universal Time (UTC) (Z). If airborne, specify the actual or proposed departure time as appropriate.

Block 7. Enter the requested en route altitude or flight level.

NOTE.—Enter only the initial requested altitude in this block. When more than one IFR altitude or flight level is desired along the route of flight, it is best to make a subsequent request direct to the controller.

Block 8. Define the route of flight by using NAVAID identifier codes (or names if the code is unknown), airways, jet routes, and waypoints (for RNAV).

NOTE.—Use NAVAIDs or WAYPOINTs to define direct routes and radials/bearings to define other unpublished routes.

Block 9. Enter the destination airport identifier code (or name if identifier is unknown).

Block 10. Enter your estimated time en route based on latest forecast winds.

Block 11. Enter only those remarks pertinent to ATC or to the clarification of other flight plan information such as the appropriate radiotelephony (call sign) associated with the designator filed in Block 2. Items of a personal nature are not accepted. Do not assume that remarks will be automatically transmitted to every controller. Specific ATC or en route requests should be made directly to the appropriate controller.

Block 12. Specify the fuel on board, computed from the departure point.

Block 13. Specify an alternate airport if desired or required, but do not include routing to the alternate airport.

Block 14. Enter your complete name, address, and telephone number of pilot in command or, in the case of a formation flight, the formation commander. Enter sufficient information to identify home base, airport, or operator.

NOTE.—This information would be essential in the event of search and rescue operation.

Block 15. Enter the total number of persons on board including crew.

Block 16. Enter the predominant colors.

NOTE.—Close IFR flight plans with tower, approach control, or ARTCCs, or if unable, with FSS. When landing at an airport with a functioning control tower, IFR flight plans are automatically canceled.

g. The information transmitted to the ARTCC for IFR Flight Plans will consist of only flight plan blocks 2, 3, 4, 5, 6, 7, 8, 9, 10, and 11.

h. A description of the International Flight Plan Form is contained in the International Flight Information Manual.

299. IFR OPERATIONS TO HIGH ALTITUDE DESTINATIONS

a. Pilots planning IFR flights to airports located in mountainous terrain are cautioned to consider the necessity for an alternate airport even when the forecast weather conditions would technically relieve them from the requirement to file one (Reference: FAR—91.23(b)). The FAA has identified three possible situations where the failure to plan for an alternate airport when flying IFR to such a destination airport could result in a critical situation if the weather is less than forecast and sufficient fuel is not available to proceed to a suitable airport.

(1) An IFR flight to an airport where the MDAs or landing visibility minimums for *ALL INSTRUMENT APPROACHES* are higher than the forecast weather minimums specified in FAR—91.23(b). For example, there are 10 high altitude airports in the United States with approved instrument approach procedures where all of the Minimum Descent Altitudes (MDAs) are greater than 2000 feet and/or the landing visibility minimums are greater than 3 miles (Bishop, California; South Lake Tahoe, California; Ukiah, California; Butte, Montana; Helena, Montana; Missoula, Montana; Chadron, Nebraska; Ely, Nevada; Klamath Falls, Oregon; and Omak, Washington). In the case of these 10 airports, it is possible for a pilot to elect, on the basis of forecasts, not to carry sufficient fuel to get to an alternate when the ceiling and/or visibility is actually lower than that necessary to complete the approach.

(2) A small number of other airports in mountainous terrain have MDAs which are slightly (100 to 300 feet) below 2000 feet AGL. In situations where there is an option as to whether to plan for an alternate, pilots should bear in mind that just a slight worsening of the weather conditions from those forecast could place the airport below the published IFR landing minimums.

PREFLIGHT

Para—304.

(3) An IFR flight to an airport which requires special equipment, i.e., DME, glide slope, etc., in order to make the available approaches to the lowest minimums. Pilots should be aware that all other minimums on the approach charts may require weather conditions better than those specified in FAR—91.23(b). An inflight equipment malfunction could result in the inability to comply with the published approach procedures or, again, in the position of having the airport below the published IFR landing minimums for all remaining instrument approach alternatives.

300. FLIGHTS OUTSIDE THE UNITED STATES AND U.S. TERRITORIES

a. When conducting flights, particularly extended flights, outside the U.S. and its territories, full account should be taken of the amount and quality of air navigation services available in the airspace to be traversed. Every effort should be made to secure information on the location and range of navigational aids, availability of communications and meteorological services, the provision of air traffic services, including alerting service, and the existence of search and rescue services.

b. Pilots should remember that there is a need to continuously guard the VHF emergency frequency 121.5 MHz when on long over-water flights, except when communications on other VHF channels, equipment limitations, or cockpit duties prevent simultaneous guarding of two channels. Guarding of 121.5 MHz is particularly critical when operating in proximity to flight information region (FIR) boundaries, for example, operations on Route R220 between Anchorage and Tokyo, since it serves to facilitate communications with regard to aircraft which may experience in-flight emergencies, communications, or navigational difficulties. (Reference ICAO Annex 10, Vol II Paras 5.2.2.1.1.1 and 5.2.2.1.1.2.)

c. The filing of a flight plan, always good practice, takes on added significance for extended flights outside U.S. airspace and is, in fact, usually required by the laws of the countries being visited or overflown. It is also particularly important in the case of such flights that pilots leave a complete itinerary and schedule of the flight with someone directly concerned, keep that person advised of the flight's progress and inform him that if serious doubt arises as to the safety of the flight he should first contact the appropriate FSS. Round Robin Flight Plans to Mexico are not accepted.

d. All pilots should review the foreign airspace and entry restrictions published in the IFIM during the flight planning process. Foreign airspace penetration without official authorization can involve both danger to the aircraft and the imposition of severe penalties and inconvenience to both passengers and crew. A flight plan on file with ATC authorities does not necessarily constitute the prior permission required by certain other authorities. The possibility of fatal consequences cannot be ignored in some areas of the world.

e. Current NOTAMs for foreign locations must also be reviewed. The publication International Notices to Airmen, published biweekly, contains considerable information pertinent to foreign flight. Current foreign NOTAMs are also available from the U.S. International NOTAM Office in Washington, D.C., through any local FSS.

f. When customs notification is required, it is the responsibility of the pilot to arrange for customs notification in a timely manner. The following guidelines are applicable:

(1) When customs notification is required on flights to Canada and Mexico and a predeparture flight plan cannot be filed or an advise customs message (ADCUS) cannot be included in a predeparture flight plan, call the nearest en route domestic or International FSS as soon as radio communication can be established and file a VFR or DVFR flight plan, as required, and include as the last item the advise customs information. The station with which such a flight plan is filed will forward it to the appropriate FSS who will notify the customs office responsible for the destination airport.

(2) If the pilot fails to include ADCUS in the radioed flight plan, it will be assumed that other arrangements have been made and FAA will not advise customs.

(3) The FAA assumes no responsibility for any delays in advising customs if the flight plan is given too late for delivery to customs before arrival of the aircraft. It is still the pilot's responsibility to give timely notice even though a flight plan is given to FAA.

301. CHANGE IN FLIGHT PLAN

In addition to altitude or flight level, destination and/or route changes, increasing or decreasing the speed of an aircraft constitutes a change in a flight plan. Therefore, at any time the average true airspeed at cruising altitude between reporting points varies or is expected to vary from that given in the flight plan by *plus or minus 5 percent, or 10 knots, whichever is greater*, ATC should be advised.

302. CHANGE IN PROPOSED DEPARTURE TIME

a. To prevent computer saturation in the en route environment, parameters have been established to delete proposed departure flight plans which have not been activated. Most centers have this parameter set so as to delete these flight plans a minimum of 1 hour after the proposed departure time. To ensure that a flight plan remains active, pilots whose actual departure time will be delayed 1 hour or more beyond their filed departure time, are requested to notify ATC of their departure time.

b. Due to traffic saturation, control personnel frequently will be unable to accept these revisions via radio. It is recommended that you forward these revisions to the nearest FSS.

303. CLOSING VFR/DVFR FLIGHT PLANS

A pilot is responsible for ensuring that his VFR or DVFR flight plan is canceled (FAR—91.83). You should close your flight plan with the nearest FSS, or if one is not available, you may request any ATC facility to relay your cancellation to the FSS. *Control towers do not automatically close VFR or DVFR flight plans* since they do not know if a particular VFR aircraft is on a flight plan. If you fail to report or cancel your flight plan within 1/2 hour after your ETA, Search and Rescue procedures are started.

304. CANCELING IFR FLIGHT PLAN

a. FAR—91.83 includes the statement "When a flight plan has been filed, the pilot in command, upon canceling or completing the flight under the flight plan, shall notify the nearest FSS or ATC facility."

b. An IFR flight plan may be canceled at any time the flight is operating in VFR conditions outside positive controlled airspace by the pilot stating "CANCEL MY IFR FLIGHT PLAN" to the controller or air/ground station with which he is communicating. Immediately after canceling an IFR flight plan, a pilot should take necessary action to change to the appropriate air/ground frequency, VFR radar beacon code and VFR altitude or flight level.

c. ATC separation and information services will be discontinued, including radar services (where applicable). Consequently, if the canceling flight desires VFR radar advisory service, the pilot must specifically request it.

NOTE.—Pilots must be aware that other procedures may be applicable to a flight that cancels an IFR flight plan within an area where a special program has been established such as a designated TRSA or TCA.

d. If a DVFR flight plan requirement exists, the pilot is responsible for filing this flight plan to replace the canceled IFR flight plan. If a subsequent IFR operation becomes necessary, a new IFR flight plan must be filed and an ATC clearance obtained before operating in IFR conditions.

e. If operating on an IFR flight plan to an airport with a functioning control tower, the flight plan is automatically closed upon landing.

f. If operating on an IFR flight plan to an airport where there is no functioning control tower, the pilot must initiate cancellation of the IFR flight plan. This can be done after landing if there is a functioning FSS or other means of direct communications with ATC. In the event there is no FSS and air/ground communications with ATC is not possible below a certain altitude, the pilot should, weather conditions permitting, cancel his IFR flight plan while still airborne and able to communicate with ATC by radio. This will not only save the time and expense of canceling the flight plan by telephone but will quickly release the airspace for use by other aircraft.

305—319. RESERVED

Section 6. DEPARTURE PROCEDURES

320. PRE-TAXI CLEARANCE PROCEDURES

a. Certain airports have established Pre-taxi Clearance programs whereby pilots of departing IFR aircraft may elect to receive their IFR clearances before they start taxiing for takeoff. The following provisions are included in such procedures:

(1) Pilot participation is not mandatory.

(2) Participating pilots call clearance delivery or ground control not more than 10 minutes before proposed taxi time.

(3) IFR clearance (or delay information, if clearance cannot be obtained) is issued at the time of this initial call-up.

(4) When the IFR clearance is received on clearance delivery frequency, pilots call ground control when ready to taxi.

(5) Normally, pilots need not inform ground control that they have received IFR clearance on clearance delivery frequency. Certain locations may, however, require that the pilot inform ground control of a portion of his routing or that he has received his IFR clearance.

(6) If a pilot cannot establish contact on clearance delivery frequency or has not received his IFR clearance before he is ready to taxi, he contacts ground control and informs the controller accordingly.

b. Locations where these procedures are in effect are indicated in the Airport/Facility Directory.

321. TAXI CLEARANCE

Pilots on IFR flight plans should communicate with the control tower on the appropriate ground control or clearance delivery frequency, prior to starting engines, to receive engine start time, taxi and/or clearance information.

322. ABBREVIATED IFR DEPARTURE CLEARANCE (CLEARED...AS FILED) PROCEDURES

a. ATC facilities will issue an abbreviated IFR departure clearance based on the ROUTE of flight filed in the IFR flight plan, provided the filed route can be approved with little or no revision. These abbreviated clearance procedures are based on the following conditions:

(1) The aircraft is on the ground or it has departed VFR and the pilot is requesting IFR clearance while airborne.

(2) That a pilot will not accept an abbreviated clearance if the route or destination of a flight plan filed with ATC has been changed by him or the company or the operations officer before departure.

(3) That it is the responsibility of the company or operations office to inform the pilot when they make a change to the filed flight plan.

(4) That it is the responsibility of the pilot to inform ATC in his initial call-up (for clearance) when the filed flight plan has been either:

(a) amended, or

(b) canceled and replaced with a new filed flight plan.

NOTE.—The facility issuing a clearance may not have received the revised route or the revised flight plan by the time a pilot requests clearance.

b. The controller will issue a detailed clearance when he knows that the original filed flight plan has been changed or when the pilot requests a full route clearance.

c. The clearance as issued will include the destination airport filed in the flight plan.

d. ATC procedures now require the controller to state the SID name, the current number and the SID Transition name after the phrase "Cleared to (destination) airport" and prior to the phrase, "then as filed," for ALL departure clearances when the SID or SID Transition is to be flown. The procedures apply whether or not the SID is filed in the flight plan.

e. STARs, when filed in a flight plan, are considered a part of the filed route of flight and will not normally be stated in an initial departure clearance. If the ARTCC's jurisdictional airspace includes both the departure airport and the fix where a STAR or STAR Transition begins, the STAR name, the current number and the STAR Transition name MAY be stated in the initial clearance.

f. "Cleared to (destination) airport as filed" does NOT include the en route altitude filed in a flight plan. An en route altitude will be stated in the clearance or the pilot will be advised to expect an assigned or filed altitude within a given time frame or at a certain point after departure. This may be done verbally in the departure instructions or stated in the SID.

g. In both radar and nonradar environments, the controller will state "Cleared to (destination) airport as filed" or:

(1) If a SID or SID Transition is to be flown, specify the SID name, the current SID number, the SID Transition name, the assigned altitude/flight level, and any additional instructions (departure control frequency, beacon code assignment, etc.) necessary to clear a departing aircraft via the SID or SID Transition and the route filed.

EXAMPLE:

NATIONAL SEVEN TWENTY CLEARED TO MIAMI AIRPORT INTERCONTINENTAL ONE DEPARTURE, LAKE CHARLES TRANSITION THEN AS FILED, MAINTAIN FLIGHT LEVEL TWO SEVEN ZERO.

(2) When there is no SID or when the pilot cannot accept a SID, the controller will specify the assigned altitude or flight level, and any additional instructions necessary to clear a departing aircraft via an appropriate departure routing and the route filed.

NOTE.—A detailed departure route description or a radar vector may be used to achieve the desired departure routing.

(3) If it is necessary to make a minor revision to the filed route, the controller will specify the assigned SID or SID Transition (or departure routing), the revision to the filed route, the assigned altitude or flight level and any additional instructions necessary to clear a departing aircraft.

EXAMPLE:

JET STAR ONE FOUR TWO FOUR CLEARED TO ATLANTA AIRPORT, SOUTH BOSTON TWO DEPARTURE THEN AS FILED EXCEPT CHANGE ROUTE TO READ SOUTH BOSTON VICTOR 20 GREENSBORO, MAINTAIN ONE SEVEN THOUSAND.

(4) Additionally, in a nonradar environment, the controller will specify one or more fixes, as necessary, to identify the initial route of flight.

EXAMPLE:

CESSNA THREE ONE SIX ZERO FOXTROT CLEARED TO CHARLOTTE AIRPORT AS FILED VIA BROOKE, MAINTAIN SEVEN THOUSAND.

h. To ensure success of the program, pilots should:

(1) Avoid making changes to a filed flight plan just prior to departure.

(2) State the following information in the initial call-up to the facility when no change has been made to the filed flight plan: Aircraft call sign, location, type operation (IFR) and the name of the airport (or fix) to which you expect clearance.

EXAMPLE:

"WASHINGTON CLEARANCE DELIVERY (or ground control if appropriate) AMERICAN SEVENTY SIX AT GATE ONE, IFR LOS ANGELES."

(3) If the flight plan has been changed, state the change and request a full route clearance.

EXAMPLE:

"WASHINGTON CLEARANCE DELIVERY, AMERICAN SEVENTY SIX AT GATE ONE. IFR SAN FRANCISCO. MY FLIGHT PLAN ROUTE HAS BEEN AMENDED (or destination changed). REQUEST FULL ROUTE CLEARANCE."

(4) Request verification or clarification from ATC if ANY portion of the clearance is not clearly understood.

(5) When requesting clearance for the IFR portion of a VFR/IFR flight, request such clearance prior to the fix where IFR operation is proposed to commence in sufficient time to avoid delay. Use the following phraseology:

EXAMPLE:

"LOS ANGELES CENTER, APACHE SIX ONE PAPA, VFR ESTIMATING PASO ROBLES VOR AT THREE TWO, ONE THOUSAND FIVE HUNDRED, REQUEST IFR TO BAKERSFIELD."

323. DEPARTURE RESTRICTIONS, CLEARANCE VOID TIMES, HOLD FOR RELEASE, AND RELEASE TIMES

a. ATC may assign departure restrictions, clearance void times, hold for release, and release times, when necessary, to separate departures from other traffic or to restrict or regulate the departure flow.

(1) CLEARANCE VOID TIMES —If operating from an airport not served by a control tower, the pilot may receive a clearance containing a provision that if the flight has not departed by a specific time, the clearance is void. In this situation, the pilot who does not depart prior to the void time must advise ATC as soon as possible, but no later than 30 minutes, of his intentions. Failure to take this action can result in costly delays and reroutes of other IFR traffic because ATC will take action on the assumption that the pilot departed as cleared. Additionally, extensive search and rescue operations may be initiated if nothing is heard from the pilot after he accepts the ATC clearance.

EXAMPLE:

CLEARANCE VOID IF NOT OFF BY (clearance void time) and, if required, IF NOT OFF BY (clearance void time)

ADVISE (facility) NOT LATER THAN (time) OF INTENTIONS.

(2) HOLD FOR RELEASE —ATC may issue "hold for release" instructions in a clearance to delay an aircraft's departure for traffic management reasons (i.e., weather, traffic volume, etc.). When ATC states in the clearance, "hold for release," the pilot may not depart until he receives a release time or is given additional instructions by ATC. In addition, ATC will include departure delay information in conjunction with "hold for release" instructions.

EXAMPLE:

(aircraft identification) CLEARED TO (destination) AIRPORT AS FILED, MAINTAIN (altitude), and, if required (additional instructions or information), HOLD FOR RELEASE, EXPECT (time in hours and/or minutes) DEPARTURE DELAY.

(3) RELEASE TIMES —A "release time" is a departure restriction issued to a pilot by ATC, specifying the earliest time an aircraft may depart. ATC will use "release times" in conjunction with traffic management procedures and/or to separate a departing aircraft from other traffic.

EXAMPLE:

(aircraft identification) RELEASED FOR DEPARTURE AT (time in hours and/or minutes).

324. DEPARTURE CONTROL

a. Departure Control is an approach control function responsible for ensuring separation between departures. So as to expedite the handling of departures, Departure Control may suggest a take off direction other than that which may normally have been used under VFR handling. Many times it is preferred to offer the pilot a runway that will require the fewest turns after take off to place the pilot on his filed course or selected departure route as quickly as possible. At many locations particular attention is paid to the use of preferential runways for local noise abatement programs, and route departures away from congested areas.

b. Departure Control utilizing radar will normally clear aircraft out of the terminal area using SIDs via radio navigation aids. When a departure is to be vectored immediately following take off, the pilot will be advised prior to take off of the initial heading to be flown but may not be advised of the purpose of the heading. Pilots operating in a radar environment are expected to associate departure headings with vectors to their planned route or flight. When given a vector taking his aircraft off a previously assigned nonradar route, the pilot will be advised briefly what the vector is to achieve. Thereafter, radar service will be provided until the aircraft has been reestablished "on-course" using an appropriate navigation aid and the pilot has been advised of his position or a handoff is made to another radar controller with further surveillance capabilities.

c. Controllers will inform pilots of the departure control frequencies and, if appropriate, the transponder code before takeoff. Pilots should not operate their transponder until ready to start the takeoff roll or change to the departure control frequency until requested. Controllers may omit the departure control frequency if a SID has or will be assigned and the departure control frequency is published on the SID.

325. INSTRUMENT DEPARTURES

a. STANDARD INSTRUMENT DEPARTURES (SID)

(1) A SID is an ATC coded departure procedure which has been established at certain airports to simplify clearance delivery procedures.

(2) Pilots of civil aircraft operating from locations where SID procedures are effective may expect ATC clearances containing a SID. Use of a SID requires pilot possession of at least the textual description of the SID procedures. Controllers may omit the departure control frequency if a SID clearance is issued and the departure control frequency is published on the SID. If the pilot does not possess a charted SID or a preprinted SID description or, for any other reason, does not wish to use a SID, he is expected to advise ATC. Notification may be accomplished by filing "NO SID" in the remarks section of the filed flight plan or by the less desirable method of verbally advising ATC.

(3) All effective SIDs are published in textual and graphic form by the National Ocean Service in East and West SID booklets.

(4) SID procedures will be depicted in one of two basic forms.

(a) **Pilot Navigation (Pilot NAV) SIDs:** are established where the pilot is primarily responsible for navigation on the SID route. They are established for airports when terrain and safety related factors indicate the necessity for a pilot NAV SID. Some pilot NAV SIDs may contain vector instructions which pilots are expected to comply with until instruction are received to resume normal navigation on the filed/assigned route or SID procedure.

(b) **Vector SIDs:** are established where ATC will provide radar navigational guidance to a filed/assigned route or to a fix depicted on the SID.

b. OBSTRUCTION CLEARANCE DURING DEPARTURE

(1) Published instrument departure procedures and SIDs assist pilots conducting IFR flight in avoiding obstacles during climbout to minimum en route altitude (MEA). These procedures are established only at locations where instrument approach procedures are published. Standard instrument takeoff minimums and departure procedures are prescribed in FAR 91.116. Airports with takeoff minimums other than standard (one statute mile for aircraft having two engines or less and one-half statute mile for aircraft having more than two engines) are described in airport listings on separate pages titled IFR TAKE-OFF MINIMUMS AND DEPARTURE PROCEDURES, at the front of each U.S. Government published IAP and SID book. The approach chart and SID chart for each airport where takeoff minimums are not standard and/or departure procedures are published is annotated with a special symbol▽. The use of this symbol indicates that the separate listing should be consulted. These minimums also apply to SIDs unless the SIDs specify different minimums.

(2) Obstacle clearance is based on the aircraft climbing at least 200 feet per nautical mile, crossing the end of the runway at least 35 feet AGL, and climbing to 400 feet above airport elevation before turning, unless otherwise specified in the procedure. A slope of 152 feet per nautical mile, starting no higher than 35 feet above the departure end of the runway, is assessed for obstacles. A minimum obstacle clearance of 48 feet per nautical mile is provided in the assumed climb gradient.

(a) If no obstacles penetrate the 152 feet per nautical mile slope, IFR departure procedures are not published.

(b) If obstacles do penetrate the slope, avoidance procedures are specified. These procedures may be: a ceiling and visibility to allow the obstacles to be seen and avoided; a climb gradient greater than 200 feet per nautical mile; detailed flight maneuvers; or a combination of the above. In extreme cases, IFR takeoff may not be authorized for some runways.

EXAMPLE:

Rwy 17, 300-1 or standard with minimum climb of 220 feet per NM to 1100.

(3) Climb gradients are specified when required for obstacle clearance. Crossing restrictions in the SIDs may be established for traffic separation or obstacle clearance. When no gradient is specified, the pilot is expected to climb at least 200 feet per nautical mile to MEA unless required to level off by a crossing restriction.

EXAMPLE:

"CROSS ALPHA INTERSECTION AT OR BELOW 4000; MAINTAIN 6000." The pilot climbs at least 200 feet per nautical mile to 6000. If 4000 is reached before ALPHA, the pilot levels off at 4000 until passing ALPHA; then immediately resumes at least 200 feet per nautical mile climb.

(4) Climb gradients may be specified to an altitude/fix, above which the normal gradient applies.

EXAMPLE:

"MINIMUM CLIMB 340 FEET PER NM TO 2700." The pilot climbs at least 340 feet per nautical mile to 2700, then at least 200 feet per NM to MEA.

(5) Some IFR departure procedures require a climb in visual conditions to cross the airport (or an on-airport NAVAID) in a specified direction, at or above a specified altitude.

EXAMPLE:

"CLIMB IN VISUAL CONDITIONS SO AS TO CROSS THE McELORY AIRPORT SOUTHBOUND, AT OR ABOVE 6000, THEN CLIMB VIA KEEMMLING R-033 TO KEEMMLING VORTAC."

(a) When climbing in visual conditions it is the pilot's responsibility to see and avoid obstacles. Specified ceiling and visibility minimums will allow visual avoidance of obstacles until the pilot enters the standard obstacle protection area. Obstacle avoidance is not guaranteed if the pilot maneuvers farther from the airport than the visibility minimum.

(b) That segment of the procedure which requires the pilot to see and avoid obstacles ends when the aircraft crosses the specified point at the required altitude. Thereafter, standard obstacle protection is provided.

(6) Each pilot, prior to departing an airport on an IFR flight should consider the type of terrain and other obstacles on or in the vicinity of the departure airport and:

(a) Determine whether a departure procedure and/or SID is available for obstacle avoidance.

(b) Determine if obstacle avoidance can be maintained visually or that the departure procedure or SID should be followed.

(c) Determine what action will be necessary and take such action that will assure a safe departure.

Note—The term **Radar Contact,** when used by the controller during departure, should not be interpreted as relieving pilots of their responsibility to maintain appropriate terrain and obstruction clearance.

Terrain/obstruction clearance is not provided by ATC until the controller begins to provide navigational guidance, i.e., Radar Vectors.

326—339. RESERVED

Section 7. EN ROUTE PROCEDURES

340. ARTCC COMMUNICATIONS

a. DIRECT COMMUNICATIONS — CONTROLLERS AND PILOTS

(1) ARTCCs are capable of direct communications with IFR air traffic on certain frequencies. Maximum communications coverage is possible through the use of Remote Center Air/Ground (RCAG) sites comprised of both VHF and UHF transmitters and receivers. These sites are located throughout the U.S.. Although they may be several hundred miles away from the ARTCC, they are remoted to the various ARTCCs by land lines or microwave links. Since IFR operations are expedited through the use of direct communications, pilots are requested to use these frequencies strictly for communications pertinent to the control of IFR aircraft. Flight plan filing, en route weather, weather forecasts and similar data should be requested through FSSs, company radio, or appropriate military facilities capable of performing these services.

(2) An ARTCC is divided into sectors. Each sector is handled by one or a team of controllers and has its own sector discrete frequency. As a flight progresses from one sector to another, the pilot is requested to change to the appropriate sector discrete frequency.

(3) **ATC Frequency Change Procedures:**

(a) The following phraseology will be used by controllers to effect a frequency change:

EXAMPLE:

(Aircraft Identification) CONTACT (facility name or location name and terminal function) (frequency) AT (time, fix or altitude).

NOTE.—Pilots are expected to maintain a listening watch on the transferring controller's frequency until the time, fix or altitude specified. ATC will omit frequency change restrictions whenever pilot compliance is expected upon receipt.

(b) The following phraseology should be utilized by pilots for establishing contact with the designated facility:

1. When a position report will be made:

EXAMPLE:

(Name) CENTER, (aircraft identification), (position).

2. When no position report will be made:

EXAMPLE:

(Name) CENTER, (aircraft identification), ESTIMATING (reporting point and time) AT (altitude or flight level) CLIMBING (or descending) TO MAINTAIN (altitude or flight level).

3. When operating in a radar environment and no position report is required:

EXAMPLE:

(Name) CENTER, (aircraft identification) AT (exact altitude or flight level); or, if appropriate,

EXAMPLE:

LEAVING (exact altitude or flight level) CLIMBING (or descending) TO MAINTAIN (altitude or flight level).

NOTE.—Exact altitude or flight level means to the nearest 100 foot increment. Exact altitude or flight level reports on initial contact provide ATC with information required prior to using MODE C altitude information for separation purposes.

(c) At times controllers will ask pilots to verify that they are at a particular altitude. The phraseology used will be: "VERIFY AT (altitude)." In climbing or descending situations, controllers may ask pilots to "VERIFY ASSIGNED ALTITUDE AS (altitude)." Pilots should confirm that they are at the altitude stated by the controller or that the assigned altitude is correct as stated. If this is not the case, they should inform the controller of the actual altitude being maintained or the different assigned altitude.

CAUTION:Pilots should not take action to change their actual altitude or different assigned altitude to the altitude stated in the controllers verification request unless the controller specifically authorizes a change.

(4) **ARTCC Radio Frequency Outage:**

(a) ARTCCs normally have at least one back up radio receiver and transmitter system for each frequency which can usually be placed into service quickly with little or no disruption of ATC service. Occasionally, technical problems may cause a delay but switchover seldom takes more than 60 seconds. When it appears that the outage will not be quickly remedied, the ARTCC will usually request a nearby aircraft, if there is one, to switch to the affected frequency to broadcast communications instructions. It is important, therefore, that the pilot wait at least 1 minute before deciding that the ARTCC has actually experienced a radio frequency failure. When such an outage does occur, the pilot should, if workload and equipment capability permit, maintain a listening watch on the affected frequency while attempting to comply with the following recommended communications procedures:

1. If two-way communications cannot be established with the ARTCC after changing frequencies, a pilot should attempt to recontact the transferring controller for the assignment of an alternative frequency or other instructions.

2. When an ARTCC radio frequency failure occurs after two-way communications have been established, the pilot should attempt to reestablish contact with the center on any other known ARTCC frequency, preferably that of the next responsible sector when practicable, and ask for instructions. However, when the next normal frequency change along the route is known to involve another ATC facility, the pilot should contact that facility, if feasible, for instructions. If communications cannot be reestablished by either method, the pilot is expected to request communications instructions from the FSS appropriate to the route of flight.

NOTE.—The exchange of information between an aircraft and an ARTCC through an FSS is quicker than relay via company radio because the FSS has direct interphone lines to the responsible ARTCC sector. Accordingly, when circumstances dictate a choice between the two, during an ARTCC frequency outage, relay via FSS radio is recommended.

341. POSITION REPORTING

The safety and effectiveness of traffic control depends to a large extent on accurate position reporting. In order to provide the proper separation and expedite aircraft movements, ATC must be able to make accurate estimates of the progress of every aircraft operating on an IFR flight plan.

a. POSITION IDENTIFICATION

(1) When a position report is to be made passing a VOR radio facility, the time reported should be the time at which the first complete reversal of the "to/from" indicator is accomplished.

(2) When a position report is made passing a facility by means of an airborne ADF, the time reported should be the time at which the indicator makes a complete reversal.

(3) When an aural or a light panel indication is used to determine the time passing a reporting point, such as a fan marker, Z marker, cone of silence or intersection of range courses, the time should be noted when the signal is first received and again when it ceases. The mean of these two times should then be taken as the actual time over the fix.

(4) If a position is given with respect to distance and direction from a reporting point, the distance and direction should be computed as accurately as possible.

(5) Except for terminal area transition purposes, position reports or navigation with reference to aids not established for use in the structure in which flight is being conducted will not normally be required by ATC.

b. POSITION REPORTING POINTS

(1) FARs require pilots to maintain a listening watch on the appropriate frequency and, unless operating under the provisions of (c), to furnish position reports passing certain reporting points. Reporting points are indicated by symbols on en route charts. The designated compulsory reporting point symbol is a solid triangle and the "on request" reporting point symbol is the open triangle. Reports passing an "on request" reporting point are only necessary when requested by ATC.

c. POSITION REPORTING REQUIREMENTS

(1) **Flights along airways or routes** —A position report is required by all flights regardless of altitude, including those operating in accordance with an ATC clearance specifying "VFR ON TOP," over each designated compulsory reporting point along the route being flown.

(2) **Flight Along a Direct Route** —Regardless of the altitude or flight level being flown, including flights operating in accordance with an ATC clearance specifying "VFR ON TOP", pilots shall report over each reporting point used in the flight plan to define the route of flight.

(3) **Flights in a Radar Environment** —When informed by ATC that their aircraft are in "RADAR CONTACT," PILOTS SHOULD DISCONTINUE POSITION REPORTS OVER DESIGNATED REPORTING POINTS. They should resume normal position reporting when ATC advises "RADAR CONTACT LOST" or "RADAR SERVICE TERMINATED."

NOTE.—ATC will inform a pilot that he is in "RADAR CONTACT" (a) when his aircraft is initially identified in the ATC system; and (b) when radar identification is reestablished after radar service has been terminated or radar contact lost. Subsequent to being advised that the controller has established radar contact, this fact will not be repeated to the pilot when handed off to another controller. At times, the aircraft identity will be *confirmed* by the receiving controller; however, this should not be construed to mean that radar contact has been lost. The identity of transponder equipped aircraft will be confirmed by asking the pilot to "IDENT," "SQUAWK STANDBY," or to change codes. Aircraft without transponders will be advised of their position to confirm identity. In this case, *the pilot is expected to advise the controller if he disagrees with the position given*. If the pilot cannot confirm the accuracy of the position given because he is not tuned to the NAVAID referenced by the controller, the pilot should ask for another radar position relative to the NAVAID to which he is tuned.

d. POSITION REPORT ITEMS

(1) Position reports should include the following items:

(a) Identification.

(b) Position.

(c) Time.

(d) Altitude or flight level (include actual altitude or flight level when operating on a clearance specifying VFR ON TOP.)

(e) Type of flight plan (not required in IFR position reports made directly to ARTCCs or approach control),

(f) ETA and name of next reporting point.

(g) The name only of the next succeeding reporting point along the route of flight, and

(h) Pertinent remarks.

342. ADDITIONAL REPORTS

a. The following reports should be made to ATC or FSS facilities without a specific ATC request:

(1) *At all times:*

(a) When vacating any previously assigned altitude or flight level for a newly assigned altitude or flight level.

(b) When an altitude change will be made if operating on a clearance specifying VFR ON TOP.

(c) When *unable* to climb/descend at a rate of at least 500 feet per minute.

(d) When approach has been missed. (Request clearance for specific action; i.e., to alternative airport, another approach, etc.)

(e) Change in the average true airspeed (at cruising altitude) when it varies by 5 percent or 10 knots (whichever is greater) from that filed in the flight plan.

(f) The time and altitude or flight level upon reaching a holding fix or point to which cleared.

(g) When leaving any assigned holding fix or point.

NOTE.—The reports in subparagraphs (f) and (g) may be omitted by pilots of aircraft involved in instrument training at military terminal area facilities when radar service is being provided.

(h) Any loss, in controlled airspace, of VOR, TACAN, ADF, low frequency navigation receiver capability, complete or partial loss of ILS receiver capability or impairment of air/ground communications capability.

(i) Any information relating to the safety of flight.

(2) *When not in radar contact:*

(a) When leaving final approach fix inbound on final approach (non precision approach) or when leaving the outer marker or fix used in lieu of the outer marker inbound on final approach (precision approach).

(b) A corrected estimate at anytime it becomes apparent that an estimate as previously submitted is in error in excess of 3 minutes.

b. Pilots encountering weather conditions which have not been forecast, or hazardous conditions which have been forecast, are expected to forward a report of such weather to ATC. (See PARA—520 - PILOT WEATHER REPORTS (PIREPs) and FAR—91.125(b) and (c).)

343. AIRWAYS AND ROUTE SYSTEMS

a. Two fixed route systems are established for air navigation purposes. They are the VOR and L/MF system, and the jet route system. To the extent possible, these route systems are aligned in an overlying manner to facilitate transition between each.

(1) The VOR and L/MF Airway System consists of airways designated from 1,200 feet above the surface (or in some instances higher) up to but not including 18,000 feet MSL. These airways are depicted on En Route Low Altitude Charts.

(a) Except in Alaska and coastal North Carolina, the VOR AIRWAYS are predicated solely on VOR or VORTAC navigation aids; are depicted in blue on aeronautical charts; and are identified by a "V" (Victor) followed by the airway number (e.g., V12).

NOTE.—Segments of VOR airways in Alaska and North Carolina (V56, V290) are based on L/MF navigation aids and charted in brown instead of blue on en route charts.

1. A segment of an airway which is common to two or more routes carries the numbers of all the airways which coincide for that segment. When such is the case, a pilot filing a flight plan needs to indicate only that airway number of the route which he is using.

2. *Alternate Airways* are identified by their location with respect to the associated main airway. "Victor 9 West" indicates an alternate airway associated with, and lying to the west of Victor 9.

NOTE.—A pilot who intends to make an airway flight, using VOR facilities, will simply specify the appropriate "Victor" airways(s) in his flight plan. For example, if a flight is to be made from Chicago to New Orleans at 8,000 feet, using omniranges only, the route may be indicated as "Departing from Chicago-Midway, cruising 8,000 feet via Victor 9 to Moisant International." If flight is to be conducted in part by means of L/MF navigation aids and in part on omniranges, specifications of the appropriate airways in the flight plan will indicate which types of facilities will be used along the described routes, and, for IFR flight, permit ATC to issue a traffic clearance accordingly. A route may also be described by specifying the station over which the flight will pass, but in this case since many VOR's and L/MF aids have the same name, the pilot must be careful to indicate which aid will be used at a particular location. This will be indicated in the route of flight portion of the flight plan by specifying the type of facility to be used after the location name in the following manner. Newark L/MF, Allentown VOR.

3. With respect to position reporting, reporting points are designated for VOR Airway Systems. Flights using Victor Airways will report over these points unless advised otherwise by ATC.

(b) THE L/MF AIRWAYS (colored airways) are predicated solely on L/MF navigation aids and are depicted in brown on aeronautical charts and are identified by color name and number (e.g., Amber One). Green and Red airways are plotted east and west. Amber and Blue airways are plotted north and south.

NOTE.—Except for G13 in North Carolina, the colored airway system exists only in the State of Alaska. All other such airways formerly so designated in the conterminous U.S. have been rescinded.

(2) THE JET ROUTE SYSTEM consists of jet routes established from 18,000 feet MSL to FL 450 inclusive.

(a) These routes are depicted on En Route High Altitude Charts. Jet routes are depicted in blue on aeronautical charts and are identified by a "J" (Jet) followed by the airway number (e.g., J 12). Jet routes, as VOR airways, are predicated solely on VOR or VORTAC navigation facilities (except in Alaska).

NOTE.—Segments of jet routes in Alaska are based on L/MF navigation aids and are charted in brown color instead of blue on en route charts.

(b) With respect to position reporting, reporting points are designated for Jet Route systems. Flights using Jet Routes will report over these points unless otherwise advised by ATC.

(3) AREA NAVIGATION (RNAV) ROUTES

(a) RNAV is a method of navigation that permits aircraft operations on any desired course within the coverage of station referenced navigation signals or within the limits of a self-contained system capability or combination of these.

(b) Fixed RNAV routes are permanent, published routes which can be flight planned for use by aircraft with RNAV capability. A previously established fixed RNAV route system has been terminated except for a few high altitude routes in Alaska.

(c) Random RNAV routes are direct routes, based on area navigation capability, between waypoints defined in terms of latitude/longitude coordinates, degree-distance fixes, or offsets from established routes/airways at a specified distance and direction. Radar monitoring by ATC is required on all random RNAV routes.

b. OPERATION ABOVE FL 450 may be conducted on a point-to-point basis. Navigational guidance is provided on an area basis utilizing those facilities depicted on the En Route High Altitude Charts.

c. Radar Vectors. Controllers may vector aircraft within controlled airspace for separation purposes, noise abatement considerations, when an operational advantage will be realized by the pilot or the controller, or when requested by the pilot. Vectors outside of controlled airspace will be provided only on pilot request. Pilots will be advised as to what the vector is to achieve when the vector is controller initiated and will take the aircraft off a previously assigned nonradar route. To the extent possible, aircraft operating on RNAV routes will be allowed to remain on their own navigation.

d. Pilots are cautioned when flying in Canadian airspace, to review Canadian Air Regulations.

(1) Special attention should be given to the parts which differ from U.S. FARs.

(a) The Canadian Airways CLASS B airspace restriction is an example. CLASS B airspace is all controlled low level airspace above 12,500 feet MSL or the MEA, whichever is higher, within which only IFR and controlled VFR flights are permitted. (Low level airspace means an airspace designated and defined as such in the *Designated Airspace Handbook.*)

(b) Regardless of the weather conditions or the height of the terrain, no person shall operate an aircraft under VFR conditions within CLASS B airspace except in accordance with a clearance for VFR flight issued by ATC.

(c) Unless otherwise authorized by the Director General, Civil Aeronautics of the Department of Transportation, no person holding a commercial or private pilot license without an instrument rating shall operate an aircraft in VFR flight within CLASS B airspace unless successful completion of a written examination demonstrating knowledge of radio navigation and of ATC procedures applicable to IFR flight including clearances and position reports is accomplished. The pilot license must be endorsed to that effect.

(2) Segments of VOR airways and high level routes in Canada are based on L/MF navigation aids and are charted in brown color instead of blue on en route charts.

344. AIRWAY OR ROUTE COURSE CHANGES

a. Pilots of aircraft are required to adhere to airways or routes being flown. Special attention must be given to this requirement during course changes. Each course change consists of variables that make the technique applicable in each case a matter only the pilot can resolve. Some variables which must be considered are turn radius, wind effect, airspeed, degree of turn, and cockpit instrumentation. An early turn, as illustrated below, is one method of adhering to airways or routes. The use of any available cockpit instrumentation, such as distance measuring equipment, may be used by the pilot to lead his turn when making course changes. This *is consistent* with the intent of FAR—91.123, which requires pilots to operate along the centerline of an airway and along the direct course between navigational aids or fixes.

b. Turns which begin at or after fix passage may exceed airway or route boundaries. The following illustration contains an example flight track depicting this, together with an example of an early turn. *(See Figure 4-8.)*

c. Without such actions as leading a turn, aircraft operating in excess of 290 knots TAS can exceed the normal airway or route boundaries depending on the amount of course change required, wind direction and velocity, the character of the turn fix (DME, overhead navigation aid, or intersection), and the pilot's technique in making a course change. For example, a flight operating at 17,000 feet MSL with a TAS of 400 knots, a 25 degree bank, and a course change of more than 40 degrees would exceed the width of the airway or route; i.e., 4 nautical miles each side of centerline. However, in the airspace below 18,000 feet MSL, operations in excess of 290 knots TAS are not prevalent and the provision of additional IFR separation in all course change situations for the occasional aircraft making a turn in excess of 290 knots TAS creates an unacceptable waste of airspace and imposes a penalty upon the preponderance of traffic which operate at low speeds. Consequently, the FAA expects pilots to lead turns and take other actions they consider necessary during course changes to adhere as closely as possible to the airways or route being flown.

d. Due to the high airspeeds used at 18,000 feet MSL and above, FAA provides additional IFR separation protection for course changes made at such altitude levels.

345. CHANGEOVER POINTS (COP)

a. COPs are prescribed for federal airways, jet routes, area navigation routes, or other direct routes for which an MEA is designated under FAR—95. The COP is a point along the route or airway segment between two adjacent navigation facilities or way points where changeover in navigation guidance should occur. At this point, the pilot should change navigation receiver frequency from the station behind the aircraft to the station ahead.

b. The COP is located midway between the navigation facilities for straight route segments, or at the intersection of radials or courses forming a dogleg in the case of dogleg route segments. When the COP is NOT located at the midway point, aeronautical charts will depict the COP location and give the mileage to the radio aids.

c. COPs are established for the purpose of preventing loss of navigation guidance, to prevent frequency interference from other facilities, and to prevent use of different facilities by different aircraft in the same airspace. Pilots are urged to observe COPs to the fullest extent.

346. RESERVED

347. HOLDING

a. Whenever an aircraft is cleared to a fix other than the destination airport and delay is expected, it is the responsibility of the ATC controller to issue complete holding instructions (unless the pattern is charted), * an EFC time and his best estimate of any additional en route/terminal delay.

b. If the holding pattern is charted and the controller doesn't issue complete holding instructions, the pilot is expected to hold as depicted on the appropriate chart. When the pattern is charted, the controller may omit all holding instructions except the charted holding direction and the statement *AS PUBLISHED*—e.g., *HOLD EAST AS PUBLISHED.* Controllers shall always issue complete holding instructions when pilots request them.

NOTE.—'Only those holding patterns depicted on U.S. Government or commercially produced (meeting FAA requirements) *Low/High Altitude En route, and Area or STAR* charts should be used.

c. If no holding pattern is charted and holding instructions have not been issued, the pilot should ask ATC for holding instructions prior to reaching the fix. This procedure will eliminate the possibility of an aircraft entering a holding pattern other than that desired by ATC. If the pilot is unable to obtain holding instructions prior to reaching the fix (due to frequency congestion, stuck microphone, etc.), he should hold in a standard pattern on the course on which he approached the fix and request further clearance as soon as possible. In this event, the altitude/flight level of the aircraft at the clearance limit will be protected so that separation will be provided as required.

d. When an aircraft is 3 minutes or less from a clearance limit and a clearance beyond the fix has not been received, the pilot is expected to start a speed reduction so that he will cross the fix, initially, at or below the maximum holding airspeed.

e. When no delay is expected, the controller should issue a clearance beyond the fix as soon as possible and, whenever possible, at least 5 minutes before the aircraft reaches the clearance limit.

f. Pilots should report to ATC the time and altitude/flight level at which the aircraft reaches the clearance limit and report leaving the clearance limit.

NOTE.—In the event of two-way communications failure, pilots are required to comply with FAR 91.127.

g. When holding at a VOR station, pilots should begin the turn to the outbound leg at the time of the first complete reversal of the to/from indicator.

h. Patterns at the most generally used holding fixes are depicted (charted) on U.S. Government or commercially produced (meeting FAA requirements) Low or High Altitude En route, Area and STAR Charts. Pilots are expected to hold in the pattern depicted unless specifically advised otherwise by ATC.

i. An ATC clearance requiring an aircraft to hold at a fix where the pattern is not charted will include the following information: *(See Figure 4-9.)*

    (1) Direction of holding from the fix in terms of the eight cardinal compass points (i.e., N, NE, E, SE, etc.).

    (2) Holding fix (the fix may be omitted if included at the beginning of the transmission as the clearance limit).

    (3) Radial, course, bearing, airway or route on which the aircraft is to hold.

    (4) Leg length in miles if DME or RNAV is to be used (leg length will be specified in minutes on pilot request or if the controller considers it necessary).

    (5) Direction of turn if left turns are to be made, the pilot requests, or the controller considers it necessary.

    (6) Time to expect further clearance and any pertinent additional delay information.

j. Holding pattern airspace protection is based on the following procedures. They are the only procedures for entry and holding recommended by FAA.

(1)   Descriptive Terms
  (a)   Standard Pattern : Right turns *(See Figure 4-10.)*
  (b)   Nonstandard Pattern : Left turns
(2)   Airspeeds (maximum)
  (a)   Propeller-driven
      1.   All (including turboprop)................. 175K IAS
  (b)   Civil turbojet
      1.   MHA through 6,000 feet...................200K IAS
      2.   Above 6,000 feet through
14,000 feet...210K IAS
      3.   Above 14,000 feet............................ 230K IAS
  (c)   Military turbojet
      1.   All-except aircraft listed
below.. 230K IAS
      2.   F-84F, F-100, F-102, F-104, F-
106, T-38, F-4, F-8, F-11, F-14,
         F-15, F-16, A-5, A-7
(USAF only), AV-8 .... 265K IAS
      3.   F-4 (USAF only).............................. 280K IAS
      4.   F-100, F/RF-101, F-104, F-105,
F-111, SR-71..310K IAS
      5.   T-37... 175K IAS

NOTE.—Holding speed depends upon weight and drag configuration.

(3)   Entry *(See Figure 4-11.)*
  (a)   Parallel Procedure —Parallel holding course, turn
left, and return to holding fix or intercept holding course.
  (b)   Teardrop Procedure —Proceed on outbound track of
30 degrees (or less) to holding course, turn right to intercept
holding course.
  (c)   Direct Entry Procedure —Turn right and fly the
pattern.
(4)   Timing:
  (a)   Inbound Leg
      1.   At/below 14,000 Ft. MSL - 1 minute.
      2.   Above 14,000 Ft. MSL - 1 and 1/2 minute.

NOTE.—The *initial* outbound leg should be flown for 1 minute or 1 and
1/2 min. (appropriate to altitude). Timing for subsequent outbound legs
should be adjusted as necessary to achieve proper inbound leg time. Pilots
may use any navigational means available (i.e. DME, RNAV, etc.) to insure
the appropriate inbound leg times.

  (b)   Outbound leg timing begins *over / abeam* the fix,
whichever occurs later. If the *abeam* position cannot be determined,
start timing when turn to outbound is completed.
(5)   Distance Measuring Equipment (DME)
  (a)   DME holding is subject to the same entry and holding
procedures except that distances (nautical miles) are used in lieu of
time values. The *outbound course* of a DME holding pattern is
called the outbound leg of the pattern. The length of the outbound
leg will be specified by the controller. The end of the outbound leg
is determined by the odometer reading. *(See Figures 4-12 and 4-13.)*
(6)   Pilot Action
  (a)   Start speed reduction when 3 minutes or less from the
holding fix. Cross the holding fix, initially, at or below the
maximum holding airspeed.
  (b)   Make all turns during entry and while holding at:
      1.   3 degrees per second, or
      2.   30 degree bank angle, or

      3.   25 degree bank provided a flight director system is
used.

NOTE.—Use whichever requires the least bank angle.

  (c)   Compensate for wind effect primarily by drift
correction on the inbound and outbound legs. When outbound,
double the (inbound) drift correction to avoid major turning
adjustments; e.g., if correcting left by 8 degrees when inbound,
correct right by 16 degrees when outbound.
  (d)   Determine entry turn from aircraft heading upon
arrival at the holding fix. Plus/minus 5 degrees in heading is
considered to be within allowable good operating limits for
determining entry.
  (e)   Advise ATC immediately if any increased airspeed is
necessary due to turbulence, icing, etc., or if unable to accomplish
any part of the holding procedures. When such higher speeds
become no longer necessary, operate according to the appropriate
published holding speed and notify ATC.

NOTE.—Airspace protection for turbulent air holding is based on a maximum of 280K IAS/Mach 0.8, whichever is lower. Considerable impact on
traffic flow will result when turbulent air holding patterns are used; thus,
pilot discretion will ensure their use is limited to bona fide conditions or
requirements.

(7)   Nonstandard Holding Pattern —Fix end and outbound
end turns are made to the left. Entry procedures to a nonstandard
pattern are oriented in relation to the 70 degree line on the holding
side just as in the standard pattern.

k.   When holding at a fix and instructions are received specifying the time of departure from the fix, the pilot should adjust his
flight path within the limits of the established holding pattern in
order to leave the fix at the exact time specified. After departing
the holding fix, normal speed is to be resumed with respect to other
governing speed requirements such as terminal area speed limits,
specific ATC requests, etc. Where the fix is associated with an instrument approach, and timed approaches are in effect, a procedure
turn shall not be executed unless the pilot advises ATC, since aircraft holding are expected to proceed inbound on final approach directly from the holding pattern when approach clearance is received.

l.   RADAR SURVEILLANCE OF OUTER FIX HOLDING
PATTERN AIRSPACE AREAS.

(1)   Whenever aircraft are holding at an outer fix, ATC will
usually provide radar surveillance of the outer fix holding pattern
airspace area, or any portion of it, if it is shown on the controller's
radar scope.
(2)   The controller will attempt to detect any holding aircraft
that stray outside the holding pattern airspace area and will assist
any detected aircraft to return to the assigned airspace area.

NOTE.—Many factors could prevent ATC from providing this additional
service, such as workload, number of targets, precipitation, ground clutter,
and radar system capability. These circumstances may make it unfeasible to
maintain radar identification of aircraft to detect aircraft straying from the
holding pattern. The provision of this service depends entirely upon whether
the controller believes he is in a position to provide it and does not relieve
a pilot of his responsibility to adhere to an accepted ATC clearance.

(3)   If an aircraft is established in a published holding pattern
at an assigned altitude above the published minimum holding altitude and subsequently cleared for the approach, the pilot may descend to the published minimum holding altitude. The holding pattern would only be a segment of the IAP *if* it is published on the
instrument procedure chart and is used in lieu of a procedure turn.

m.   For those holding patterns where there are no published
minimum holding altitudes, the pilot, upon receiving an approach

clearance, must maintain his last assigned altitude until leaving the holding pattern and established on the inbound course. Thereafter, the published minimum altitude of the route segment being flown will apply. It is expected that the pilot will be assigned a holding altitude that will permit a normal descent on the inbound course.

348—359. RESERVED

Section 8. ARRIVAL PROCEDURES

360. STANDARD TERMINAL ARRIVAL (STAR)

a. A STAR is an ATC coded IFR arrival route established for application to arriving IFR aircraft destined for certain airports. Its purpose is to simplify clearance delivery procedures.

b. Pilots of IFR civil aircraft destined to locations for which STARs have been published may be issued a clearance containing a STAR whenever ATC deems it appropriate. Until military STAR publications and distribution is accomplished, STARs will be issued to military pilots only when requested in the flight plan or verbally by the pilot.

c. Use of STARs requires pilot possession of at least the approved textual description. As with any ATC clearance or portion thereof, it is the responsibility of each pilot to accept or refuse an issued STAR. A pilot should notify ATC if he does not wish to use a STAR by placing "NO STAR" in the remarks section of the flight plan or by the less desirable method of verbally stating the same to ATC.

d. A bound booklet containing all STAR charts is available on subscription from the National Ocean Service.

361. LOCAL FLOW TRAFFIC MANAGEMENT PROGRAM

a. This program is a continuing effort by the FAA to enhance safety, minimize the impact of aircraft noise and conserve aviation fuel. The enhancement of safety and reduction of noise is achieved ї this program by minimizing low altitude maneuvering of arriving urbojet and turboprop aircraft weighing more than 12,500 pounds and, by permitting departure aircraft to climb to higher altitudes sooner, as arrivals are operating at higher altitudes at the points where their flight paths cross. The application of these procedures also reduces exposure time between controlled aircraft and uncontrolled aircraft at the lower altitudes in and around the terminal environment. Fuel conservation is accomplished by absorbing any necessary arrival delays for aircraft included in this program operating at the higher and more fuel efficient altitudes.

b. A fuel efficient descent is basically an uninterrupted descent (except where level flight is required for speed adjustment) from cruising altitude to the point when level flight is necessary for the pilot to stabilize his final approach. The procedure for a fuel efficient descent is based on an altitude loss which is most efficient for the majority of aircraft being served. This will generally result in a descent gradient window of 250-350 feet per nautical mile.

c. When crossing altitudes and speed restrictions are issued verbally or are depicted on a chart, ATC will expect the pilot to descend first to the crossing altitude and then reduce speed. Verbal clearances for descent will normally permit an uninterrupted descent in accordance with the procedure as described in paragraph b. above. Acceptance of a charted fuel efficient descent (Runway Profile Descent) clearance requires the pilot to adhere to the altitudes, speeds, and headings depicted on the charts unless otherwise instructed by ATC. PILOTS RECEIVING A CLEARANCE FOR A FUEL EFFICIENT DESCENT ARE EXPECTED TO ADVISE ATC IF THEY DO NOT HAVE RUNWAY PROFILE DESCENT CHARTS PUBLISHED FOR THAT AIRPORT OR ARE UNABLE TO COMPLY WITH THE CLEARANCE.

362. APPROACH CONTROL

a. Approach control is responsible for controlling all instrument flight operating within its area of responsibility. Approach control may serve one or more airfields, and control is exercised primarily by direct pilot and controller communications. Prior to arriving at the destination radio facility, instructions will be received from ARTCC to contact approach control on a specified frequency.

b. Radar Approach Control

(1) Where radar is approved for approach control service, it is used not only for radar approaches (ASR and PAR) but is also used to provide vectors in conjunction with published nonradar approaches based on radio NAVAIDs (ILS, MLS, VOR, NDB, TACAN). Radar vectors can provide course guidance and expedite traffic to the final approach course of any established IAP or to the traffic pattern for a visual approach. Approach control facilities that provide this radar service will operate in the following manner:

(a) Arriving aircraft are either cleared to an outer fix most appropriate to the route being flown with vertical separation and, if required, given holding information or, when radar handoffs are effected between the ARTCC and approach control, or between two approach control facilities, aircraft are cleared to the airport or to a fix so located that the handoff will be completed prior to the time the aircraft reaches the fix. When radar handoffs are utilized, successive arriving flights may be handed off to approach control with radar separation in lieu of vertical separation.

(b) After release to approach control, aircraft are vectored to the final approach course (ILS, MLS, VOR, ADF, etc.). Radar vectors and altitude or flight levels will be issued as required for spacing and separating aircraft. *Therefore, pilots must not deviate from the headings issued by approach control.* Aircraft will normally be informed when it is necessary to vector across the final approach course for spacing or other reasons. If approach course crossing is imminent and the pilot has not been informed that he will be vectored across the final approach course, he should query the controller.

(c) The pilot is not expected to turn inbound on the final approach course unless an approach clearance has been issued. This clearance will normally be issued with the final vector for interception of the final approach course, and the vector will be such as to enable the pilot to establish his aircraft on the final approach course prior to reaching the final approach fix.

(d) In the case of aircraft already inbound on the final approach course, approach clearance will be issued prior to the aircraft reaching the final approach fix. When established inbound on the final approach course, radar separation will be maintained and the pilot will be expected to complete the approach utilizing the approach aid designated in the clearance (ILS, MLS, VOR, radio beacons, etc.) as the primary means of navigation. Therefore, once established on the final approach course, pilots must not deviate from it unless a clearance to do so is received from ATC.

(e) After passing the final approach fix on final approach, aircraft are expected to continue inbound on the final approach course and complete the approach or effect the missed approach procedure published for that airport.

(2) Whether aircraft are vectored to the appropriate final approach course or provide their own navigation on published routes to it, radar service is automatically terminated when the landing is completed or when instructed to change to advisory frequency at uncontrolled airports, whichever occurs first.

363. ADVANCE INFORMATION ON INSTRUMENT APPROACH

a. When landing at airports with approach control services and where two or more IAPs are published, pilots will be provided in advance of their arrival with the type of approach to expect or that they may be vectored for a visual approach. This information will be broadcast either by a controller or on ATIS. It will not be furnished when the visibility is three miles or better and the ceiling is at or above the highest initial approach altitude established for any low altitude IAP for the airport.

b. The purpose of this information is to aid the pilot in planning arrival actions; however, it is not an ATC clearance or commitment and is subject to change. Pilots should bear in mind that fluctuating weather, shifting winds, blocked runway, etc., are conditions which may result in changes to approach information previously received. It is important that the pilot advise ATC immediately if he is unable to execute the approach ATC advised will be used, or if he prefers another type of approach.

c. When making an IFR approach to an airport not served by a tower or FSS, after the ATC controller advises "CHANGE TO ADVISORY FREQUENCY APPROVED" you should broadcast your intentions, including the type of approach being executed, your position, and when over the final approach fix inbound (non precision approach) or when over the outer marker or fix used in lieu of the outer marker inbound (precision approach). Continue to monitor the appropriate frequency (UNICOM, etc.) for reports from other pilots.

364. INSTRUMENT APPROACH PROCEDURE CHARTS

a. FAR—91.116a (Instrument Approaches to Civil Airports) requires the use of SIAPs prescribed for the airport in Part 97 unless otherwise authorized by the Administrator (including ATC). FAR—91.116g (Military Airports) requires civil pilots flying into or out of military airports to comply with the IAPs and takeoff and landing minimums prescribed by the authority having jurisdiction at those airports.

(1) All IAPs (standard and special, civil and military) are based on joint civil and military criteria contained in the U.S. Standard for TERPs. The design of IAPs based on criteria contained in TERPs, takes into account the interrelationship between airports, facilities, and the surrounding environment, terrain, obstacles, noise sensitivity, etc. Appropriate altitudes, courses, headings, distances, and other limitations are specified and, once approved, the procedures are published and distributed by government and commercial cartographers as instrument approach charts.

(2) Not all IAPs are published in chart form. Radar IAPs are established where requirements and facilities exist but they are printed in tabular form in appropriate U.S. Government Flight Information Publications.

(3) A pilot adhering to the altitudes, flight paths, and weather minimums depicted on the IAP chart or vectors and altitudes issued by the radar controller, is assured of terrain and obstruction clearance and runway or airport alignment during approach for landing.

(4) IAPs are designed to provide an IFR descent from the route environment to a point where a safe landing can be made. They are prescribed and approved by appropriate civil or military authority to ensure a safe descent during instrument flight conditions at a specific airport. It is important that pilots understand these procedures and their use prior to attempting to fly instrument approaches.

(5) TERPs criteria are provided for the following type of instrument approach procedures:

(a) Precision approaches where an electronic glide slope is provided (PAR and ILS) and,

(b) Nonprecision approaches where glide slope information is not provided (all approaches except PAR and ILS).

b. The method used to depict prescribed altitudes on instrument approach charts differs according to techniques employed by different chart publishers. Prescribed altitudes may be depicted in three different configurations: Minimum, maximum, and mandatory. The U.S. Government distributes charts produced by Defense Mapping Agency (DMA) and NOS. Altitudes are depicted on these charts in the profile view with underscore, overscore, or both to identify them as minimum, maximum, or mandatory.

(1) Minimum Altitude will be depicted with the altitude value underscored. Aircraft are required to maintain altitude at or above the depicted value.

(2) Maximum Altitude will be depicted with the altitude value overscored. Aircraft are required to maintain altitude at or below the depicted value.

(3) Mandatory Altitude will be depicted with the altitude value both underscored and overscored. Aircraft are required to maintain altitude at the depicted value.

NOTE.— The underscore and overscore to identify mandatory altitudes and the overscore to identify maximum altitudes are used almost exclusively by DMA for military charts. With very few exceptions, civil approach charts produced by NOS utilize only the underscore to identify minimum altitudes. Pilots are cautioned to adhere to altitudes as prescribed because, in certain instances, they may be used as the basis for vertical separation of aircraft by ATC. When a depicted altitude is specified in the ATC clearance, that altitude becomes mandatory as defined above.

c. Minimum Safe Altitudes (MSA) are published for emergency use on approach procedure charts utilizing NDB or VOR type facilities. The altitude shown provides at least 1,000 feet of clearance above the highest obstacle in the defined sector to a distance of 25 NM from the facility. As many as four sectors may be depicted with different altitudes for each sector displayed in rectangular boxes in the plan view of the chart. A single altitude for the entire area may be shown in the lower right portion of the plan view. Navigational course guidance is not assured at the MSA within these sectors.

d. Minimum Vectoring Altitudes (MVA) are established for use by ATC when radar ATC is exercised. MVA charts are prepared by air traffic facilities at locations where there are numerous different minimum IFR altitudes. Each MVA chart has sectors large enough to accommodate vectoring of aircraft within the sector at the MVA. Each sector boundary is at least 3 miles from the obstruction determining the MVA. To avoid a large sector with an excessively high MVA due to an isolated prominent obstruction, the obstruction may be enclosed in a buffer area whose boundaries are at least 3 miles from the obstruction. This is done to facilitate vectoring around the obstruction. *(See Figure 4-14.)*

(1) The minimum vectoring altitude in each sector provides 1,000 feet above the highest obstacle in nonmountainous areas and 2,000 feet above the highest obstacle in designated mountainous areas. Where lower MVAs are required in designated mountainous

areas to achieve compatibility with terminal routes or to permit vectoring to an IAP, 1,000 feet of obstacle clearance may be authorized with the use of Airport Surveillance Radar (ASR). The minimum vectoring altitude will provide at least 300 feet above the floor of controlled airspace.

(2) Because of differences in the areas considered for MVA, and those applied to other minimum altitudes, and the ability to isolate specific obstacles, some MVAs may be lower than the nonradar Minimum En route Altitudes (MEA), Minimum Obstruction Clearance Altitudes (MOCA) or other minimum altitudes depicted on charts for a given location. While being radar vectored, IFR altitude assignments by ATC will be at or above MVA.

e. Visual Descent Points (VDP) are incorporated in selected nonprecision approach procedures. The VDP is a defined point on the final approach course of a nonprecision straight-in approach procedure from which normal descent from the MDA to the runway touchdown point may be commenced, provided visual reference required by FAR—91.116(c)(3) is established. The VDP will normally be identified by DME on VOR and LOC procedures. The VDP is identified on the profile view of the approach chart by the symbol: V .

(1) VDPs are intended to provide additional guidance where they are implemented. No special technique is required to fly a procedure with a VDP. The pilot should not descend below the MDA prior to reaching the VDP and acquiring the necessary visual reference in accordance with FAR—91.116(c)(3)(4).

(2) Pilots not equipped to receive the VDP should fly the approach procedure as though no VDP had been provided.

365. APPROACH CLEARANCE

a. An aircraft which has been cleared to a holding fix and subsequently "cleared . . . approach" has not received new routing. Even though clearance for the approach may have been issued prior to the aircraft reaching the holding fix, ATC would expect the pilot to proceed via the holding fix (his last assigned route), and the feeder route associated with that fix (if a feeder route is published on the approach chart) to the initial approach fix (IAF) to commence the approach. *When cleared for the approach, the published off airway (feeder) routes that lead from the en route structure to the IAF are part of the approach clearance.*

b. If a feeder route to an IAF begins at a fix located along the route of flight prior to reaching the holding fix, and clearance for an approach is issued, a pilot should commence his approach via the published feeder route; i.e., the aircraft would not be expected to overfly the feeder route and return to it. The pilot is expected to commence his approach in a similar manner at the IAF, if the IAF for the procedure is located along the route of flight to the holding fix.

c. If a route of flight directly to the initial approach fix is desired, it should be so stated by the controller with phraseology to include the words "direct . . .," "proceed direct" or a similar phrase which the pilot can interpret without question. If the pilot is uncertain of his clearance, he should immediately query ATC as to what route of flight is desired.

366—369. RESERVED

370. INSTRUMENT APPROACH PROCEDURES

a. Minimums are specified for various aircraft approach categories based upon a value 1.3 times the stalling speed of the air-

craft in the landing configuration at maximum certificated gross landing weight. (See FAR 97.3(b)). If it is necessary, while circling to land, to maneuver at speeds in excess of the upper limit of the speed range for each category, due to the possibility of extending the circling maneuver beyond the area for which obstruction clearance is provided, the circling minimum for the next higher approach category should be used. For example, an aircraft which falls in Category C, but is circling to land at a speed of 141 knots or higher should use the approach category "D" minimum when circling to land.

b. When operating on an unpublished route or while being radar vectored, the pilot, when an approach clearance is received, shall, in addition to complying with the minimum altitudes for IFR operations (FAR—91.119), maintain his last assigned altitude unless a different altitude is assigned by ATC, or until the aircraft is established on a segment of a published route or IAP. After the aircraft is so established, published altitudes apply to descent within each succeeding route or approach segment unless a different altitude is assigned by ATC. Notwithstanding this pilot responsibility, for aircraft operating on unpublished routes or while being radar vectored, ATC will, except when conducting a radar approach, issue an IFR approach clearance only after the aircraft is established on a segment of a published route or IAP, or assigned an altitude to maintain until the aircraft is established on a segment of a published route or instrument approach procedure. For this purpose, the procedure turn of a published IAP shall not be considered a segment of that IAP until the aircraft reaches the initial fix or navigation facility upon which the procedure turn is predicated.

EXAMPLE:

CROSS REDDING VOR AT OR ABOVE FIVE THOUSAND, CLEARED FOR VOR RUNWAY THREE FOUR APPROACH. *or*

EXAMPLE:

FIVE MILES FROM OUTER MARKER, TURN RIGHT HEADING THREE THREE ZERO, MAINTAIN TWO THOUSAND UNTIL ESTABLISHED ON THE LOCALIZER, CLEARED FOR ILS RUNWAY THREE SIX APPROACH.

NOTE.— The altitude assigned will assure IFR obstruction clearance from the point at which the approach clearance is issued until established on a segment of a published route or IAP. If a pilot is uncertain of the meaning of his clearance, he shall immediately request clarification from ATC.

c. Several IAPs, using various navigation and approach aids may be authorized for an airport. ATC may advise that a particular approach procedure is being used, primarily to expedite traffic. (See PARA—363 - ADVANCE INFORMATION ON INSTRUMENT APPROACH.) If a pilot is issued a clearance that specifies a particular approach procedure, he is expected to notify ATC immediately if he desires a different one. In this event it may be necessary for ATC to withhold clearance for the different approach until such time as traffic conditions permit. However, if the pilot is involved in an emergency situation he will be given priority. If the pilot is not familiar with the specific approach procedure, ATC should be advised and they will provide detailed information on the execution of the procedure.

d. At times ATC may not specify a particular approach procedure in the clearance, but will state "CLEARED FOR APPROACH." Such clearance indicates that the pilot may execute any one of the authorized IAPs for that airport. This clearance does not constitute approval for the pilot to execute a contact approach or a visual approach.

e. When cleared for a specifically prescribed IAP; i.e., "cleared for ILS runway one niner approach" or when "cleared for approach" i.e., execution of any procedure prescribed for the airport, pilots shall execute the entire procedure as described on the IAP Chart unless an appropriate new or revised ATC clearance is received, or the IFR flight plan is canceled.

f. Pilots planning flights to locations served by special IAPs should obtain advance approval from the owner of the procedure. Approval by the owner is necessary because special procedures are for the exclusive use of the single interest unless otherwise authorized by the owner. Additionally, some special approach procedures require certain crew qualifications training, or other special considerations in order to execute the approach. Also, some of these approach procedures are based on privately owned navigational aids. Owners of aids that are not for public use may elect to turn off the aid for whatever reason they may have; i.e., maintenance, conservation, etc. Air traffic controllers are not required to question pilots to determine if they have permission to use the procedure. Controllers presume a pilot has obtained approval and is aware of any details of the procedure if he files an IFR flight plan to that airport.

g. When executing an instrument approach and in radio contact with an FAA facility, unless in "radar contact," report passing the final approach fix inbound (non precision approach) or the outer marker or fix used in lieu of the outer marker inbound (precision approach).

h. If a missed approach is required, advise ATC and include the reason (unless initiated by ATC). Comply with the missed approach instructions for the instrument approach procedure being executed, unless otherwise directed by ATC. (See PARA—382 - MISSED APPROACH and PARA—404 - MISSED APPROACH.)

371. PROCEDURE TURN

a. A procedure turn is the maneuver prescribed when it is necessary to reverse direction to establish the aircraft inbound on an intermediate or final approach course. It is a required maneuver except when the symbol NoPT is shown, when RADAR VECTORING is provided, when a holding pattern is published in lieu of procedure turn, or when the procedure turn is not authorized. The altitude prescribed for the procedure turn is a *minimum*altitude until the aircraft is established on the inbound course. The maneuver must be completed within the distance specified in the profile view.

(1) On U.S. Government charts, a barbed arrow indicates the direction or side of the outbound course on which the procedure turn is made. Headings are provided for course reversal using the 45 degree type procedure turn. However, the point at which the turn may be commenced and the type and rate of turn is left to the discretion of the pilot. Some of the options are the 45 degree procedure turn, the racetrack pattern, the tear-drop procedure turn, or the 80 degree - 260 degree course reversal. Some procedure turns are specified by procedural track. These turns must be flown exactly as depicted.

(2) When the approach procedure involves a procedure turn, a maximum speed of not greater than 250 knots (IAS) should be observed and the turn should be executed within the distance specified in the profile view. The normal procedure turn distance is 10 miles. This may be reduced to a minimum of 5 miles where only Category A or helicopter aircraft are to be operated or increased to as much as 15 miles to accommodate high performance aircraft.

(3) A teardrop procedure or penetration turn may be specified in some procedures for a required course reversal. The teardrop procedure consists of departure from an initial approach fix on an outbound course followed by a turn toward and intercepting the

inbound course at or prior to the intermediate fix or point. Its purpose is to permit an aircraft to reverse direction and lose considerable altitude within reasonably limited airspace. Where no fix is available to mark the beginning of the intermediate segment, it shall be assumed to commence at a point 10 miles prior to the final approach fix. When the facility is located on the airport, an aircraft is considered to be on final approach upon completion of the penetration turn. However, the final approach segment begins on the final approach course 10 miles from the facility.

(4) A procedure turn need not be established when an approach can be made from a properly aligned holding pattern. In such cases, the holding pattern is established over an intermediate fix or a final approach fix. The holding pattern maneuver is completed when the aircraft is established on the inbound course after executing the appropriate entry. If cleared for the approach prior to returning to the holding fix, and the aircraft is at the prescribed altitude, additional circuits of the holding pattern are not necessary nor expected by ATC. If the pilot elects to make additional circuits to lose excessive altitude or to become better established on course, it is his responsibility to so advise ATC when he receives his approach clearance.

(5) A procedure turn is not required when an approach can be made directly from a specified intermediate fix to the final approach fix. In such cases, the term "NoPT" is used with the appropriate course and altitude to denote that the procedure turn is not required. If a procedure turn is desired, and when cleared to do so by ATC, descent below the procedure turn altitude should not be made until the aircraft is established on the inbound course, since some NoPT altitudes may be lower than the procedure turn altitudes.

b. Limitations on Procedure Turns.

(1) In the case of a radar initial approach to a final approach fix or position, or a timed approach from a holding fix, or where the procedure specifies "NoPT", no pilot may make a procedure turn unless, when he receives his final approach clearance, he so advises ATC and a clearance is received.

(2) When a teardrop procedure turn is depicted and a course reversal is required, this type turn must be executed.

(3) When holding pattern replaces the procedure turn, the standard entry and the holding pattern must be followed except when RADAR VECTORING is provided or when NoPT is shown on the approach course. As in the procedure turn, the descent from the minimum holding pattern altitude to the final approach fix altitude (when lower) may not commence until the aircraft is established on the inbound course.

(4) The absence of the procedure turn barb in the Plan View indicates that a procedure turn is not authorized for that procedure.

372. TIMED APPROACHES FROM A HOLDING FIX

a. TIMED APPROACHES may be conducted when the following conditions are met:

(1) A control tower is in operation at the airport where the approaches are conducted.

(2) Direct communications are maintained between the pilot and the center or approach controller until the pilot is instructed to contact the tower.

(3) If more than one missed approach procedure is available, none require a course reversal.

(4) If only one missed approach procedure is available, the following conditions are met:

(a) Course reversal is not required; and,

(b) Reported ceiling and visibility are equal to or greater than the highest prescribed circling minimums for the IAP.

(5) When cleared for the approach, pilots shall not execute a procedure turn. (FAR—91.116.)

b. Although the controller will not specifically state that "timed approaches are in progress", his assigning a time to depart the final approach fix inbound (non precision approach) or the outer marker or fix used in lieu of the outer marker inbound (precision approach) is indicative that timed approach procedures are being utilized, or in lieu of holding, he may use radar vectors to the final approach course to establish a mileage interval between aircraft that will insure the appropriate time sequence between the final approach fix/outer marker or fix used in lieu of the outer marker and the airport.

c. Each pilot in an approach sequence will be given advance notice as to the time he should leave the holding point on approach to the airport. When a time to leave the holding point has been received, the pilot should adjust his flight path to leave the fix as closely as possible to the designated time. *(See Figure 4-15.)*

373. RADAR APPROACHES

a. The only airborne radio equipment required for radar approaches is a functioning radio transmitter and receiver. The radar controller vectors the aircraft to align it with the runway centerline. The controller continues the vectors to keep the aircraft on course until the pilot can complete the approach and landing by visual reference to the surface. There are two types of radar approaches: Precision (PAR) and Surveillance (ASR).

b. A radar approach may be given to any aircraft upon request and may be offered to pilots of aircraft in distress or to expedite traffic, however, an ASR might not be approved unless there is an ATC operational requirement, or in an unusual or emergency situation. Acceptance of a PAR or ASR by a pilot does not waive the prescribed weather minimums for the airport or for the particular aircraft operator concerned. The decision to make a radar approach when the reported weather is below the established minimums rests with the pilot.

c. PAR and ASR minimums are published on separate pages in the NOS IAP Charts.

(1) A PRECISION APPROACH (PAR) is one in which a controller provides highly accurate navigational guidance in azimuth and elevation to a pilot. Pilots are given headings to fly, to direct them to, and keep their aircraft aligned with the extended centerline of the landing runway. They are told to anticipate glide path interception approximately 10 to 30 seconds before it occurs and when to start descent. The published decision height will be given only if the pilot requests it. If the aircraft is observed to deviate above or below the glide path, the pilot is given the relative amount of deviation by use of terms "slightly" or "well" and is expected to adjust his rate of descent to return to the glide path. Trend information is also issued with respect to the elevation of the aircraft and may be modified by the terms "rapidly" and "slowly"; e.g., "well above glide path, coming down rapidly." Range from touchdown is given at least once each mile. If an aircraft is observed by the controller to proceed outside of specified safety zone limits in azimuth and/or elevation and continue to operate outside these prescribed limits, the pilot will be directed to execute a missed approach or to fly a specified course unless he has the runway environment (runway, approach lights, etc.) in sight. Navigational guidance in azimuth and elevation is provided the pilot until the aircraft reaches the published Decision Height (DH).

Advisory course and glidepath information is furnished by the controller until the aircraft passes over the landing threshold, at which point the pilot is advised of any deviation from the runway centerline. Radar service is automatically terminated upon completion of the approach.

(2) A SURVEILLANCE APPROACH (ASR) is one in which a controller provides navigational guidance in azimuth only. The pilot is furnished headings to fly to align his aircraft with the extended centerline of the landing runway. Since the radar information used for a surveillance approach is considerably less precise than that used for a precision approach, the accuracy of the approach will not be as great and higher minimums will apply. Guidance in elevation is not possible but the pilot will be advised when to commence descent to the minimum descent altitude (MDA) or, if appropriate, to an intermediate step-down fix minimum crossing altitude and subsequently to the prescribed MDA. In addition, the pilot will be advised of the location of the missed approach point (MAP) prescribed for the procedure and his position each mile on final from the runway, airport or heliport or MAP, as appropriate. If requested by the pilot, recommended altitudes will be issued at each mile, based on the descent gradient established for the procedure, down to the last mile that is at or above the MDA. Normally, navigational guidance will be provided until the aircraft reaches the MAP. Controllers will terminate guidance and instruct the pilot to execute a missed approach unless at the MAP the pilot has the runway, airport or heliport in sight or, for a helicopter point-in-space approach, the prescribed visual reference with the surface is established. Also, if, at any time during the approach the controller considers that safe guidance for the remainder of the approach can not be provided, he will terminate guidance and instruct the pilot to execute a missed approach. Similarly, guidance termination and missed approach will be effected upon pilot request and, for civil aircraft only, controllers may terminate guidance when the pilot reports the runway, airport/heliport or visual surface route (point-in-space approach) in sight or otherwise indicates that continued guidance is not required. Radar service is automatically terminated at the completion of a radar approach.

NOTE.— The published MDA for straight-in approaches will be issued to the pilot before beginning descent. When a surveillance approach will terminate in a circle to land maneuver, the pilot must furnish the aircraft approach category to the controller. The controller will then provide the pilot with the appropriate MDA.

(3) A NO-GYRO APPROACH is available to a pilot under radar control who experiences circumstances wherein his directional gyro or other stabilized compass is inoperative or inaccurate. When this occurs, he should so advise ATC and request a No-Gyro vector or approach. Pilots of aircraft not equipped with a directional gyro or other stabilized compass who desire radar handling may also request a No-Gyro vector or approach. The pilot should make all turns at standard rate and should execute the turn immediately upon receipt of instructions. For example, "TURN RIGHT," "STOP TURN." When a surveillance or precision approach is made, the pilot will be advised after his aircraft has been turned onto final approach to make turns at half standard rate.

374. RADAR MONITORING OF INSTRUMENT APPROACHES

a. PAR facilities operated by the FAA and the military services at some joint-use (civil and military) and military installations monitor aircraft on instrument approaches and issue radar advisories to the pilot when weather is below VFR minimums (1,000 and 3), at night, or when requested by a pilot. This service is provided only when the PAR final approach course coincides with the final approach of the navigational aid and only during the operational hours of the PAR. The radar advisories serve only as a secondary aid since the pilot has selected the navigational aid as the primary aid for the approach.

b. Prior to starting final approach, the pilot will be advised of the frequency on which the advisories will be transmitted. If, for any reason, radar advisories cannot be furnished, the pilot will be so advised.

c. Advisory information, derived from radar observations, includes information on:

(1) Passing the final approach fix inbound (non precision approach) or passing the outer marker or fix used in lieu of the outer marker inbound (precision approach).

NOTE.— At this point, the pilot may be requested to report sighting the approach lights or the runway.

(2) Trend advisories with respect to elevation and/or azimuth radar position and movement will be provided.

NOTE.— Whenever the aircraft nears the PAR safety limit, the pilot will be advised that he is well above or below the glidepath or well left or right of course. Glidepath information is given only to those aircraft executing a precision approach, such as ILS or MLS. Altitude information is not transmitted to aircraft executing other than precision approaches because the descent portions of these approaches generally do not coincide with the depicted PAR glidepath. At locations where the MLS glidepath and PAR glidepath are not coincidental, only azimuth monitoring will be provided.

(3) If, after repeated advisories, the aircraft proceeds outside the PAR safety limit or if a radical deviation is observed, the pilot will be advised to execute a missed approach unless the prescribed visual reference with the surface is established.

d. Radar service is automatically terminated upon completion of the approach.

375. SIMULTANEOUS ILS/MLS APPROACHES

(See Figure 4-16.)

a. **System:** An approach system permitting simultaneous ILS/MLS, or ILS and MLS approaches to airports having parallel runways separated by at least 4,300 feet between centerlines. Integral parts of a total system are ILS or MLS, radar, communications, ATC procedures, and appropriate airborne equipment. The Approach Procedure Chart permitting simultaneous approaches will contain the note "simultaneous approach authorized Rwys 14L and 14R" identifying the appropriate runways as the case may be. When advised that simultaneous ILS approaches are in progress, pilots shall advise approach control immediately of malfunctioning or inoperative receivers or if simultaneous approach is not desired.

b. **Radar Monitor Service:** This service is provided for each ILS/MLS to insure prescribed lateral separation during approaches. Pilots will be assigned frequencies to receive advisories and instructions. Aircraft deviating from either final approach course to the point where the no transgression zone (an area at least 2,000 feet wide) may be penetrated will be instructed to take corrective action. If an aircraft fails to respond to such instruction, the aircraft on the adjacent final approach course may be instructed to alter course.

c. **Radar Advisories:** Whenever simultaneous approaches are in progress radar advisories will be provided on the tower frequency.

(1) The monitor controller will have the capability of overriding the tower controller on the tower frequency.

(2) The pilot will be advised to monitor the tower frequency.

(3) The monitor will automatically be terminated no farther than one mile from the runway threshold.

(4) The monitor controller will *not* advise when the monitor is terminated.

376. PARALLEL ILS/MLS APPROACHES

a. Parallel approaches are an ATC procedure permitting parallel ILS, MLS, or ILS and MLS approaches to airports having parallel runways separated by at least 2,500 feet between centerlines. Integral parts of a total system are ILS or MLS, radar, communications, ATC procedures, and appropriate airborne equipment.

b. A parallel approach differs from a simultaneous approach in that the minimum distance between parallel runway centerlines is reduced; there is no requirement for radar monitoring or advisories; and a staggered separation of aircraft on the adjacent localizer course is required.

c. Aircraft are afforded a minimum of two miles radar separation between successive aircraft on the adjacent localizer course and a minimum of three miles radar separation from aircraft on the same final approach course. In addition, a minimum of 1,000 feet vertical or a minimum of three miles radar separation is provided between aircraft during turn on.

d. Whenever parallel approaches are in progress, aircraft are informed that approaches to both runways are in use. In addition, the radar controller will have the interphone capability of communicating directly with the tower controller where the responsibility for radar separation is not performed by the tower controller.

377. SIMULTANEOUS CONVERGING INSTRUMENT APPROACHES

a. ATC may conduct instrument approaches simultaneously to converging runways; i.e., runways having an included angle from 15 to 100 degrees, at airports where a program has been specifically approved to do so.

b. The basic concept requires that dedicated, separate standard instrument approach procedures be developed for each converging runway included. Missed approach points must be as least 3 miles apart and missed approach procedures ensure that missed approach protected airspace does not overlap.

c. Other requirements are: radar availability, nonintersecting final approach courses, precision (ILS/MLS) approach systems on each runway and, if runways intersect, controllers must be able to apply visual separation as well as intersecting runway separation criteria. Intersecting runways also require minimums of at least 700 and 2. Straight in approaches and landings must be made.

d. Whenever simultaneous converging approaches are in progress, aircraft will be informed by the controller as soon as feasible after initial contact or via ATIS. Additionally, the radar controller will have direct communications capability with the tower controller where separation responsibility has not been delegated to the tower.

378—379. RESERVED

380. SIDE-STEP MANEUVER

a. ATC may authorize an approach procedure which serves either one of parallel runways that are separated by 1,200 feet or less followed by a straight-in landing on the adjacent runway.

b. Aircraft that will execute a side-step maneuver will be cleared for a specified approach and landing on the adjacent parallel runway. Example, "cleared for ILS runway 07 left approach, side-step to runway 07 right." Pilots are expected to commence the side-step maneuver as soon as possible after the runway or runway environment is in sight.

c. Landing minimums to the adjacent runway will be higher than the minimums to the primary runway, but will normally be lower than the published circling minimums.

381. APPROACH AND LANDING MINIMUMS

a. **LANDING MINIMUMS.** The rules applicable to landing minimums are contained in FAR—91.116.

b. **Published Approach Minimums** — Approach minimums are published for different aircraft categories and consist of a minimum altitude (DH, MDA) and required visibility. These minimums are determined by applying the appropriate TERPS criteria. When a fix is incorporated in a nonprecision final segment, two sets of minimums may be published: one, for the pilot that is able to identify the fix, and a second for the pilot that cannot. Two sets of minimums may also be published when a second altimeter source is used in the procedure.

c. **Obstacle Clearance** — Final approach obstacle clearance is provided from the start of the final segment to the runway or missed approach point, whichever occurs last. Side-step obstacle protection is provided by increasing the width of the final approach obstacle clearance area. Circling approach protected areas are defined by the tangential connection of arcs drawn from each runway end. The arc radii distance differs by aircraft approach category. Because of obstacles near the airport, a portion of the circling area may be restricted by a procedural note: e.g., "Circling NA E of RWY 17-35." Obstacle clearance is provided at the published minimums for the pilot that makes a straight-in approach, side-steps, circles, or executes the missed approach. Missed approach obstacle clearance requirements may dictate the published minimums for the approach. *(See Figure 4-17.)*

d. **Straight-in Minimums** are shown on the IAP when the final approach course is within 30 degrees of the runway alignment and a normal descent can be made from the IFR altitude shown on the IAP to the runway surface. When either the normal rate of descent or the runway alignment factor of 30 degrees is exceeded, a straight-in minimum is not published and a circling minimum applies. The fact that a straight-in minimum is not published does not preclude pilots from landing straight-in if they have the active runway in sight and have sufficient time to make a normal approach for landing. Under such conditions and when ATC has cleared them for landing on that runway, pilots are not expected to circle even though only circling minimums are published. If they desire to circle, they should advise ATC.

e. **Side-Step Maneuver Minimums** — Landing minimums for a side-step maneuver to the adjacent runway will normally be higher than the minimums to the primary runway.

f. **Circling Minimums** — In some busy terminal areas, ATC may not allow circling and circling minimums will not be published. Published circling minimums provide obstacle clearance when pilots remain within the appropriate area of protection. Pilots

should remain at or above the circling altitude until the aircraft is continuously in a position from which a descent to a landing on the intended runway can be made at a normal rate of descent using normal maneuvers. Circling may require maneuvers at low altitude, at low airspeed, and in marginal weather conditions. Pilots must use sound judgment, have an indepth knowledge of their capabilities, and fully understand the aircraft performance to determine the exact circling maneuver since weather, unique airport design, and the aircraft position, altitude, and airspeed must all be considered. The following basic rules apply:

(1) Maneuver the shortest path to the base or downwind leg, as appropriate, considering existing weather conditions. There is no restriction from passing over the airport or other runways.

(2) It should be recognized that circling maneuvers may be made while VFR or other flying is in progress at the airport. Standard left turns or specific instruction from the controller for maneuvering must be considered when circling to land.

(3) At airports without a control tower, it may be desirable to fly over the airport to observe wind and turn indicators and other traffic which may be on the runway or flying in the vicinity of the airport.

g. **Instrument Approach At a Military Field** — When instrument approaches are conducted by civil aircraft at military airports, they shall be conducted in accordance with the procedures and minimums approved by the military agency having jurisdiction over the airport.

382. MISSED APPROACH

a. When a landing cannot be accomplished, advise ATC and, upon reaching the missed approach point defined on the approach procedure chart, the pilot must comply with the missed approach instructions for the procedure being used or with an alternate missed approach procedure specified by ATC.

b. Protected obstacle clearance areas for missed approach are predicated on the assumption that the abort is initiated at the missed approach point not lower than the MDA or DH. Reasonable buffers are provided for normal maneuvers. However, no consideration is given to an abnormally early turn. Therefore, when an early missed approach is executed, pilots should, unless otherwise cleared by ATC, fly the IAP as specified on the approach plate to the missed approach point at or above the MDA or DH before executing a turning maneuver.

c. If visual reference is lost while circling to land from an instrument approach, the missed approach specified for that particular procedure must be followed (unless an alternate missed approach procedure is specified by ATC). To become established on the prescribed missed approach course, the pilot should make an initial climbing turn toward the landing runway and continue the turn until he is established on the missed approach course. Inasmuch as the circling maneuver may be accomplished in more than one direction, different patterns will be required to become established on the prescribed missed approach course, depending on the aircraft position at the time visual reference is lost. Adherence to the procedure will assure that an aircraft will remain within the circling and missed approach obstruction clearance areas. *(See Figure 4-18.)*

d. At locations where ATC Radar Service is provided, the pilot should conform to radar vectors when provided by ATC in lieu of the published missed approach procedure. *(See Figure 4-19.)*

e. When approach has been missed, request clearance for specific action; i.e., to alternative airport, another approach, etc.

383. VISUAL APPROACH

a. When it will be operationally beneficial, ATC may authorize an aircraft to conduct a visual approach to an airport or to follow another aircraft when flight to, and landing at, the airport can be accomplished in VFR weather. The aircraft must have the airport or the identified preceding aircraft in sight before the clearance is issued. If the pilot has the airport in sight but cannot see the aircraft he is following, ATC may still clear the aircraft for a visual approach; however, ATC retains both separation and wake vortex separation responsibility. When visually following a preceding aircraft, acceptance of the visual approach clearance, constitutes acceptance of pilot responsibility for maintaining a safe approach interval and adequate wake turbulence separation.

b. When operating to an airport with an operating control tower, aircraft may be authorized to conduct a visual approach to one runway while other aircraft are conducting IFR or VFR approaches to another runway. When operating to airports with parallel runways separated by less than 2,500 feet, the succeeding aircraft must report sighting the preceding aircraft unless standard separation is being provided by ATC. When operating to parallel runways separated by at least 2,500 feet but less than 4,300 feet, controllers will clear/vector aircraft to the final at an angle not greater than 30 degrees unless radar, vertical, or visual separation is provided during the turn-on. The purpose of the 30 degree intercept angle is to reduce the potential for overshoots of the final and to preclude side-by-side operations with one or both aircraft in a *belly-up* configuration during the turn-on. Once the aircraft are established within 30 degrees of final, or on the final, these operations may be conducted simultaneously. When the parallel runways are separated by 4,300 feet or more, or intersecting/converging runways are in use, ATC may authorize a visual approach after advising all aircraft involved that other aircraft are conducting operations to the other runway.

c. When operating to an airport without weather reporting service, ATC may initiate a visual approach provided area weather reports indicate that VFR conditions exist at the airport and there is reasonable assurance that descent and flight to the airport can be made in VFR conditions. Pilot acceptance of a visual approach clearance or a pilot's request for a visual approach will indicate to ATC that the pilot can comply with FAR 91.105. ATC will advise the pilot when weather is not available at the destination airport.

d. Authorization to conduct a visual approach is an IFR authorization and does not alter IFR flight plan cancellation responsibility. (See PARA—304 - CANCELING IFR FLIGHT PLAN.)

e. A visual approach is not an IAP and therefore has no missed approach segment. If a go around is necessary for any reason, aircraft operating at controlled airports will be issued an appropriate advisory/clearance/instruction by the tower. At uncontrolled airports, aircraft are expected to remain in VFR conditions and complete a landing as soon as possible. If a landing cannot be accomplished, the aircraft is expected to remain in VFR conditions and contact ATC as soon as possible for further clearance. Separation from other IFR aircraft will be maintained under these circumstances.

f. Visual approaches are initiated by ATC to reduce pilot/controller workload and expedite traffic by shortening flight paths to the airport. It is the pilot's responsibility to advise ATC as soon as possible if a visual approach is not desired.

384. CHARTED VISUAL FLIGHT PROCEDURES (CVFP)

a. CVFPs are charted visual approaches established at locations with jet operations for noise abatement purposes. The approach charts depict prominent landmarks, courses, and recommended altitudes to specific runways.

b. These procedures will be used only in a radar environment at airports with an operating control tower.

c. Most approach charts will depict some NAVID information which is for supplemental navigational guidance only.

d. Unless indicating a TCA floor, all depicted altitudes are for noise abatement purposes and are recommended only. Pilots are not prohibited from flying other than recommended altitudes if operational requirements dictate.

e. When landmarks used for navigation are not visible at night, the approach will be annotated "PROCEDURE NOT AUTHORIZED AT NIGHT."

f. CVFPs usually begin within 15 flying miles from the airport.

g. Published weather minimums for CVFPs are based on minimum vectoring altitudes rather than the recommended altitudes depicted on charts.

h. CVFPs are not instrument approaches and do not have missed approach segments.

i. ATC will not issue clearances for CVFPs when the weather is less than the published minimum.

j. ATC will clear aircraft for a CVFP after the pilot reports siting a charted landmark or a preceding aircraft. If instructed to follow a preceding aircraft, pilots are responsible for maintaining a safe approach interval and wake turbulence separation.

k. Pilots should advise ATC if at any point they are unable to continue an approach or lose site of a preceding aircraft. Missed approaches will be handled as a go-around.

385. CONTACT APPROACH

a. Pilots operating in accordance with an IFR flight plan, provided they are clear of clouds and have at least 1 mile flight visibility and can reasonably expect to continue to the destination airport in those conditions, may request ATC authorization for a contact approach.

b. Controllers may authorize a contact approach provided:

(1) The Contact Approach is specifically requested by the pilot. ATC cannot initiate this approach.

EXAMPLE:
REQUEST CONTACT APPROACH.

(2) The reported ground visibility at the destination airport is at least 1 statute mile.

(3) The contact approach will be made to an airport having a standard or special instrument approach procedure.

(4) Approved separation is applied between aircraft so cleared and between these aircraft and other IFR or special VFR aircraft.

EXAMPLE:
CLEARED FOR CONTACT APPROACH (and, if required) AT OR BELOW (altitude) (Routing) IF NOT POSSIBLE (alternative procedures) AND ADVISE.

c. A Contact Approach is an approach procedure that may be used by a pilot (with prior authorization from ATC) in lieu of contacting a standard or special IAP to an airport. It is not intended for use by a pilot on an IFR flight clearance to operate to an airport not having an authorized IAP. Nor is it intended for an aircraft to conduct an instrument approach to one airport and then, when "in the clear", to discontinue that approach and proceed to another airport. In the execution of a contact approach, the pilot assumes the responsibility for obstruction clearance. If radar service is being received, it will automatically terminate when the pilot is told to contact the tower.

386. LANDING PRIORITY

A clearance for a specific type of approach (ILS, MLS, ADF, VOR or Straight-in Approach) to an aircraft operating on an IFR flight plan does not mean that landing priority will be given over other traffic. ATCTs handle all aircraft, regardless of the type of flight plan, on a "first-come, first-served" basis. Therefore, because of local traffic or runway in use, it may be necessary for the controller in the interest of safety, to provide a different landing sequence. In any case, a landing sequence will be issued to each aircraft as soon as possible to enable the pilot to properly adjust his flight path.

387—399. RESERVED

Section 9. PILOT/CONTROLLER ROLES AND RESPONSIBILITIES

400. GENERAL

a. The roles and responsibilities of the pilot and controller for effective participation in the ATC system are contained in several documents. Pilot responsibilities are in the FARs and the air traffic controller's are in the Air Traffic Control Handbook (7110.65) and supplemental FAA directives. Additional and supplemental information for pilots can be found in the current Airman's Information Manual (AIM), Notices to Airmen, Advisory Circulars and aeronautical charts. Since there are many other excellent publications produced by nongovernment organizations, as well as other government organizations, with various updating cycles, questions concerning the latest or most current material can be resolved by cross-checking with the above mentioned documents.

b. The pilot in command of an aircraft is directly responsible for, and is the final authority as to the safe operation of that aircraft. In an emergency requiring immediate action, the pilot in command may deviate from any rule in the General Subpart A and Flight Rules Subpart B in accordance with FAR—91.3.

c. The air traffic controller is responsible to give first priority to the separation of aircraft and to the issuance of radar safety alerts, second priority to other services that are required, but do not involve separation of aircraft and third priority to additional services to the extent possible.

d. In order to maintain a safe and efficient air traffic system, it is necessary that each party fulfill his responsibilities to the fullest.

e. The responsibilities of the pilot and the controller intentionally overlap in many areas providing a degree of redundancy. Should one or the other fail in any manner, this overlapping responsibility is expected to compensate, in many cases, for failures that may affect safety.

f. The following, while not intended to be all inclusive, is a brief listing of pilot and controller responsibilities for some commonly used procedures or phases of flight. More detailed explanations are contained in other portions of this publication, the appropriate FARs, ACs and similar publications. The information provided is an overview of the principles involved and is not meant as an interpretation of the rules nor is it intended to extend or diminish responsibilities.

401. AIR TRAFFIC CLEARANCE

a. Pilot

(1) Acknowledge receipt and understanding of an ATC clearance.

(2) Request clarification or amendment, as appropriate, any time a clearance is not fully understood, or considered unacceptable from a safety standpoint.

(3) Promptly comply with air traffic clearance upon receipt except as necessary to cope with an emergency. If deviation is necessary, advise ATC as soon as possible and obtain an amended clearance.

b. Controller

(1) Issues appropriate clearances for the operation to be conducted, or being conducted, in accordance with established criteria.

(2) Assigns altitudes in IFR clearances that are at or above the minimum IFR altitudes in controlled airspace.

(3) Ensures acknowledgement by the pilot for issued information, clearance or instructions.

(4) Ensures that readbacks by the pilot of altitude, heading, or other items are correct. If incorrect, distorted, or incomplete, makes corrections as appropriate.

402. CONTACT APPROACH

a. Pilot

(1) This approach must be requested by the pilot, and is made in lieu of a standard or special instrument approach.

(2) By requesting the contact approach, the pilot indicates that the flight is operating clear of clouds, has at least one mile flight visibility, and can reasonably expect to continue to the destination airport in those conditions.

(3) Be aware that while conducting a contact approach, the pilot assumes responsibility for obstruction clearance.

(4) Advise ATC immediately if you are unable to continue the contact approach or if you encounter less than one mile flight visibility.

b. Controller

(1) Issues clearance for contact approach only when requested by the pilot. Does not solicit the use of this procedure.

(2) Before issuing clearance, ascertains that reported ground visibility at destination airport is at least one mile.

(3) Provides approved separation between aircraft cleared for contact approach and other IFR or special VFR aircraft. When using vertical separation, does not assign a fixed altitude but clears the aircraft at or below an altitude which is at least 1,000 feet below any IFR traffic but not below minimum safe altitudes prescribed in FAR—91.79.

(4) Issues alternative instructions if, in his judgment, weather conditions may make completion of the approach impracticable.

403. INSTRUMENT APPROACH

a. Pilot

(1) Be aware that the controller issues clearance for approach based only on known traffic.

(2) Follow the procedure as shown on the IAP, including all restrictive notations, such as:

    (a) Procedure not authorized at night;

    (b) Approach not authorized when local area altimeter not available;

    (c) Procedure not authorized when control tower not in operation;

    (d) Procedure not authorized when glide slope not used;

    (e) Straight-in minimums not authorized at night; etc.

    (f) Radar required; or

    (g) The circling minimums published on the instrument approach chart provide adequate obstruction clearance and the pilot should not descend below the circling altitude until the aircraft is in a position to make final descent for landing. Sound judgment and knowledge of his and the aircraft's capabilities are the criteria for a pilot to determine the exact maneuver in each instance since airport design and the aircraft, position, altitude and airspeed must all be considered. (See PARA—381d, - CIRCLING MINIMUMS)

(3) Upon receipt of an approach clearance while on an unpublished route or being radar vectored:

(a) Comply with the minimum altitude for IFR, and

(b) Maintain last assigned altitude until established on a segment of a published route or IAP, at which time published altitudes apply.

b. Controller

(1) Issues an approach clearance based on known traffic.

(2) Issues an IFR approach clearance only after the aircraft is established on a segment of published route or IAP, or assigns an appropriate altitude for the aircraft to maintain until so established.

404. MISSED APPROACH

a. Pilot

(1) Execute a missed approach when one of the following conditions exist:

(a) Arrival at the Missed Approach Point (MAP) or the Decision Height (DH) and visual reference to the runway environment is insufficient to complete the landing.

(b) Determined that a safe landing is not possible.

(c) Instructed to do so by ATC.

(2) Advise ATC that a missed approach will be made. Include the reason for the missed approach unless the missed approach is initiated by ATC.

(3) Comply with the missed approach instructions for the IAP being executed unless other *missed approach* instructions are specified by ATC.

(4) If executing a missed approach prior to reaching the MAP or DH, fly the instrument procedure to the MAP at an altitude at or above the Minimum Descent Altitude (MDA) or DH before executing a turning maneuver.

(5) Radar vectors issued by ATC when informed that a missed approach is being executed supersedes the previous missed approach procedure.

(6) If making a missed approach from a radar approach, execute the missed approach procedure previously given or climb to the altitude and fly the heading specified by the controller.

(7) Following missed approach, request clearance for specific action; i.e., another approach, hold for improved conditions, proceed to an alternate airport, etc.

b. Controller

(1) Issues an approved alternate missed approach procedure if it is desired that the pilot execute a procedure other than as depicted on the instrument approach chart.

(2) May vector a radar identified aircraft executing a missed approach when operationally advantageous to the pilot or the controller.

(3) In response to the pilot's stated intentions, issues a clearance to an alternate airport, to a holding fix, or for reentry into the approach sequence, as traffic conditions permit.

405. RADAR VECTORS

a. Pilot

(1) Promptly comply with headings and altitudes assigned to you by the controller.

(2) Question any assigned heading or altitude believed to be incorrect.

(3) If operating VFR and compliance with any radar vector or altitude would cause a violation of any FAR, advise ATC and obtain a revised clearance or instruction.

b. Controller

(1) Vectors aircraft in controlled airspace:

(a) For separation.

(b) For noise abatement.

(c) To obtain an operational advantage for the pilot or controller.

(2) Vectors aircraft in controlled and uncontrolled airspace when requested by the pilot.

(3) Vectors IFR aircraft at or above minimum vectoring altitudes.

(4) May vector VFR aircraft, not at an ATC assigned altitude, at any altitude. In these cases, terrain separation is the pilot's responsibility.

406. SAFETY ALERT

a. Pilot

(1) Initiate appropriate action if a safety alert is received from ATC.

(2) Be aware that this service is not always available and that many factors affect the ability of the controller to be aware of a situation in which unsafe proximity to terrain, obstructions or another aircraft may be developing.

b. Controller

(1) Issues a safety alert if he is aware an aircraft under his control is at an altitude which, in the controller's judgment, places the aircraft in unsafe proximity to terrain, obstructions or another aircraft. Types of safety alerts are:

(a) **Terrain or Obstruction Alert:** — Immediately issued to an aircraft under his control if he is aware the aircraft is at an altitude believed to place the aircraft in unsafe proximity to terrain or obstructions.

(b) **Aircraft Conflict Alert:** — Immediately issued to an aircraft under his control if he is aware of an aircraft not under his control at an altitude believed to place the aircraft in unsafe proximity to each other. With the alert, he offers the pilot an alternative, if feasible.

(2) Discontinues further alerts if informed by the pilot that he is taking action to correct the situation or that he has the other aircraft in sight.

407. SEE AND AVOID

a. Pilot

(1) When meteorological conditions permit, regardless of type of flight plan, whether or not under control of a radar facility, the pilot is responsible to see and avoid other traffic, terrain or obstacles.

b. **Controller**

(1) Provides radar traffic information to radar identified aircraft operating outside positive control airspace on a workload permitting basis.

(2) Issues a safety alert to an aircraft under his control if he is aware the aircraft is at an altitude believed to place the aircraft in unsafe proximity to terrain, obstructions or other aircraft.

408. SPEED ADJUSTMENTS

a. **Pilot**

(1) Advise ATC any time cruising airspeed varies plus or minus 5 percent, or 10 knots, whichever is greater, from that given in the flight plan.

(2) Comply with speed adjustments from ATC unless:

(a) The minimum or maximum safe airspeed for any particular operation is greater or less than the requested airspeed. In such cases, advise ATC.

(b) Operating at or above 10,000 feet MSL on an ATC assigned SPEED ADJUSTMENT of more than 250 knots IAS and subsequent clearance is received for descent below 10,000 feet MSL. In such cases, pilots are expected to comply with FAR—91.70(a).

(3) When complying with speed adjustments assignment, maintain an indicated airspeed within plus or minus 10 knots or .02 mach numbers of the specified speed.

b. **Controller**

(1) Assigns speed adjustments to aircraft when necessary but not as a substitute for good vectoring technique.

(2) Adheres to the restrictions published in the Controllers Handbook (7110.65) as to when speed adjustment procedures may be applied.

(3) Avoids speed adjustments requiring alternate decreases and increases.

(4) Assigns speed adjustments to a specified IAS (KNOTS)/mach number or to increase or decrease speed using increments of 10 knots or multiples thereof.

(5) Advises pilots to resume normal speed when speed adjustments are no longer required.

(6) Gives due consideration to aircraft capabilities to reduce speed while descending.

409. TRAFFIC ADVISORIES (Traffic Information)

a. **Pilot**

(1) Acknowledge receipt of traffic advisories.

(2) Inform controller if traffic in sight.

(3) Advise ATC if a vector to avoid traffic is desired.

(4) Do not expect to receive radar traffic advisories on all traffic. Some aircraft may not appear on the radar display. Be aware that the controller may be occupied with higher priority duties and unable to issue traffic information for a variety of reasons.

(5) Advise controller if service not desired.

b. **Controller**

(1) Issues radar traffic to the maximum extent consistent with higher priority duties except in positive controlled airspace.

(2) Provides vectors to assist aircraft to avoid observed traffic when requested by the pilot.

(3) Issues traffic information to aircraft in the airport traffic area for sequencing purposes.

410. VISUAL APPROACH

a. **Pilot**

(1) If a visual approach is not desired, advise ATC.

(2) Comply with controller's instructions for vectors toward the airport of intended landing or to a visual position behind a preceding aircraft.

(3) After being cleared for a visual approach, proceed to the airport in a normal manner or follow designated traffic and/or charted flight procedures, as appropriate remaining in VFR at all times.

(4) Acceptance of a visual approach clearance to visually follow a preceding aircraft is pilot acknowledgement that he will establish a safe landing interval behind the preceding aircraft, if so cleared, and that he accepts responsibility for his own wake turbulence separation.

(5) Advise ATC immediately if you are unable to continue following a designated aircraft or encounter less than basic VFR weather conditions.

(6) Be aware that radar service is automatically terminated, without advising the pilot, when the aircraft is instructed to change to advisory frequency.

(7) Be aware that there may be other traffic in the traffic pattern and the landing sequence may differ from the traffic sequence assigned by the approach control or ARTCC.

b. **Controller**

(1) Does not vector an aircraft for a visual approach to an airport with weather reporting service unless the reported ceiling at the airport is 500 feet or more above the MVA and visibility is three miles or more.

(2) Informs the pilot when weather is not available for the destination airport and does not vector for a visual approach to those airports unless there is reasonable assurance that descent and flight to the airport can be made in VFR conditions.

(3) Does not clear an aircraft for a visual approach unless the aircraft is and can remain in VFR conditions.

(4) Issues visual approach clearance when the pilot reports sighting the airport or a preceding aircraft which is to be followed.

(5) Provides separation except when visual separation is being applied by the pilot of the aircraft executing the visual approach.

(6) Continues flight following and traffic information until the aircraft has landed or has been instructed to change to advisory frequency.

(7) Informs the pilot conducting the visual approach of the aircraft class when pertinent traffic is known to be a heavy aircraft.

411. VISUAL SEPARATION

a. **Pilot**

(1) Acceptance of instructions to follow another aircraft or to provide visual separation from it is an acknowledgment that the pilot will maneuver his/her aircraft as necessary to avoid the other aircraft or to maintain in-trail separation.

(2) If instructed by ATC to follow another aircraft or to provide visual separation from it, promptly notify the controller if you lose sight of that aircraft, are unable to maintain continued visual

contact with it, or cannot accept the responsibility for your own separation for any reason.

(3) The pilot also accepts responsibility for wake turbulence separation under these conditions.

b. Controller

(1) Applies visual separation only within a terminal area when a controller has both aircraft in sight or by instructing a pilot who sees the other aircraft to maintain visual separation from it.

412. VFR-ON-TOP

a. Pilot

(1) This clearance must be requested by the pilot on an IFR flight plan and if approved, permits the pilot to select an altitude or flight level of his choice (subject to any ATC restrictions) in lieu of an assigned altitude.

Note 1.— VFR-ON-TOP is not permitted in certain airspace areas, such as positive control airspace, certain restricted areas, ect. Consequently, IFR flights operating VFR-ON-TOP will avoid such airspace.

Note 2.— See related AIM paragraphs, 98 - IFR Altitudes and Flight Levels, 266 - IFR Clearance VFR-ON-TOP, 271 - IFR Separation Standards, 341 - Position Reporting, and 342 - Additional Reports.

(2) By requesting a VFR-ON-TOP clearance, the pilot indicates that he is assuming the sole responsibility to be vigilant so as to see and avoid other aircraft and that he will:

(a) Fly at the appropriate VFR altitude as prescribed in FAR—91.109.

(b) Comply with the VFR visibility and distance from criteria in FAR—91.105 (Basic VFR Weather Minimums).

(c) Comply with instrument flight rules that are applicable to this flight (i.e., minimum IFR altitudes, position reporting, radio communications, course to be flown, adherence to ATC clearance, etc.).

(3) Should advise ATC prior to any altitude change to ensure the exchange of accurate traffic information.

b. Controller

(1) May clear an aircraft to maintain VFR-ON-TOP if the pilot of an aircraft on an IFR flight plan requests the clearance.

(2) Inform the pilot of an aircraft cleared to climb to VFR-ON-TOP: the reported height of the tops or that no top report is available, issues an alternate clearance if necessary, and once the aircraft reports reaching VFR-ON-TOP, reclears the aircraft to maintain VFR-ON-TOP.

(3) Before issuing clearance, ascertains that the aircraft is not in or will not enter positive control airspace.

413. INSTRUMENT DEPARTURES

a. Pilot

(1) Prior to Departure: Consider the type of terrain and other obstructions on or in the vicinity of the departure airport.

(2) Determine if obstruction avoidance can be maintained visually or that the departure procedure should be followed.

(3) Determine whether a departure procedure and/or SID is available for obstruction avoidance.

(4) At airports where IAPs have not been published, hence no published departure procedure, determine what action will be necessary and take such action that will assure a safe departure.

b. Controller

(1) At locations with airport traffic control service, when necessary, specifies direction of takeoff, turn or initial heading to be flown after takeoff.

(2) At locations without airport traffic control service, but within a control zone when necessary to specify direction of takeoff/turn or initial heading to be flown, obtains pilot's concurrence that the procedure will allow him to comply with local traffic patterns, terrain, and obstruction avoidance.

(3) Includes established departure procedures as part of the ATC clearance when pilot compliance is necessary to ensure separation.

414. MINIMUM FUEL ADVISORY

a. Pilot

(1) Advise ATC of your minimum fuel status when your fuel supply has reached a state where, upon reaching destination, you cannot accept any undue delay.

(2) Be aware this is not an emergency situation but merely an advisory that indicates an emergency situation is possible should any undue delay occur.

(3) Be aware a minimum fuel advisory does not imply a need for traffic priority.

(4) If the remaining usable fuel supply suggests the need for traffic priority to ensure a safe landing you should declare an emergency, account low fuel, and report fuel remaining in minutes.

b. Controller

(1) When an aircraft declares a state of minimum fuel, relay this information to the facility to whom control jurisdiction is transferred.

(2) Be alert for any occurrence which might delay the aircraft.

415—429. RESERVED

Section 10. NATIONAL SECURITY AND INTERCEPTION PROCEDURES

430. NATIONAL SECURITY

a. National security in the control of air traffic is governed by (FAR—99).

b. All aircraft entering domestic U.S. airspace from points outside must provide for identification prior to entry. To facilitate early aircraft identification of all aircraft in the vicinity of U.S. and international airspace boundaries, Air Defense Identification Zones (ADIZ) have been established. (See PARA—433 - ADIZ BOUNDARIES AND DESIGNATED MOUNTAINOUS AREAS.)

c. Operational requirements for aircraft entering an ADIZ are as follows:

(1) Flight Plan — A flight plan must be filed with an appropriate aeronautical facility for flight in an ADIZ. In the Alaskan DEWIZ (Distant Early Warning Identification Zone), the flight plan must be filed before departure, except as otherwise permitted in FAR—99.13.

(2) Two-way Radio — An operative two-way radio must be available for flight in ADIZ/DEWIZ areas. Exceptions are only as provided in FAR—99.1.

(3) Position Reporting — Normal IFR position reports are required in all ADIZ/DEWIZ areas. In the domestic and coastal ADIZ areas, flights under Defense VFR (DVFR) flight plans must give the estimated time of ADIZ penetration at least 15 minutes prior to penetration. In the coastal ADIZ, inbound foreign aircraft must report at least 1 hour prior to ADIZ penetration. In the Alaskan DEWIZ, DVFR flights must report prior to penetration (correlation of ground filed flight plan data may be required).

(4) Aircraft Position Tolerances:

(a) In a domestic ADIZ tolerance is within plus or minus 5 minutes from the estimated time over a reporting point or point of penetration and within 10 NM from the centerline of an intended track over an estimated reporting point or penetration point.

(b) In a Coastal ADIZ/DEWIZ the tolerance is plus or minus 5 minutes from the estimated time over a reporting point or point of penetration and within 20 NM from the centerline of the intended track over an estimated reporting point or point of penetration.

d. Aircraft operating within an ADIZ may be exempted from the National Security requirements of FAR—99 (except as may be applicable under FAR—99.7) if the aircraft is operating:

(1) Within the 48 contiguous states and the District of Columbia, or within the State of Alaska, and remains within 10 miles of departure point.

(2) In a Coastal or Domestic ADIZ north of 30 degrees North latitude or west of 86 degrees West longitude at a true air speed of less than 180 knots.

(3) In Alaskan DEWIZ at TAS of less than 180 knots while pilot maintains listening watch on appropriate frequency.

(4) Over or within three miles of any island in Hawaiian Coastal ADIZ.

e. Exemptions (except for FAR—99.7) may also be granted by the ARTCC, on a local basis, for some operations within an ADIZ.

f. An Airfiled VFR Flight Plan makes an aircraft subject to interception for positive identification when entering an ADIZ.

Pilots are therefore urged to file the required DVFR flight plan either in person or by telephone prior to departure.

g. Special Security Instructions

(1) During defense emergency or air defense emergency conditions, additional special security instructions may be issued in accordance with the Security Control of Air Traffic and Air Navigation Aids (SCATANA) Plan.

(2) Under the provisions of the SCATANA Plan, the military will direct the action to be taken—in regard to landing, grounding, diversion, or dispersal of aircraft and the control of air navigation aids in the defense of the U.S. during emergency conditions.

(3) At the time a portion of all of SCATANA is implemented, ATC facilities will broadcast appropriate instructions received from the military over available ATC frequencies. Depending on instructions received from the military, VFR flights may be directed to land at the nearest available airport, and IFR flights will be expected to proceed as directed by ATC.

(4) Pilots on the ground may be required to file a flight plan and obtain an approval (through FAA) prior to conducting flight operation.

(5) In view of the above, all pilots should guard an ATC or FSS frequency at all times while conducting flight operations.

431. INTERCEPTION PROCEDURES

a. General

(1) Identification intercepts during peacetime operations are vastly different than those conducted under increased states of readiness. Unless otherwise directed by the control agency, intercepted aircraft will be identified by type only. When specific information is required (i.e. markings, serial numbers, etc.) the interceptor aircrew will respond only if the request can be conducted in a safe manner. During hours of darkness or Instrument Meteorological Conditions (IMC), identification of unknown aircraft will be by type only. The interception pattern described below is the typical peacetime method used by air interceptor aircrews. In all situations, the interceptor aircrew will use caution to avoid startling the intercepted aircrew and/or passengers.

b. Intercept phases *(See Figure 4-20.)*

(1) **Phase One — Approach Phase:** During peacetime, intercepted aircraft will be approached from the stern. Generally two interceptor aircraft will be employed to accomplish the identification. The flight leader and his wingman will coordinate their individual positions in conjunction with the ground controlling agency. Their relationship will resemble a line abreast formation. At night or in IMC, a comfortable radar trail tactic will be used. Safe vertical separation between interceptor aircraft and unknown aircraft will be maintained at all times.

(2) **Phase Two — Identification Phase:** The intercepted aircraft should expect to visually acquire the lead interceptor and possibly the wingman during this phase in visual meteorological conditions (VMC). The wingman will assume a surveillance position while the flight leader approaches the unknown aircraft. Intercepted aircraft personnel may observe the use of different drag devices to allow for speed and position stabilization during this phase. The flight leader will then initiate a gentle closure toward the intercept-

ed aircraft, stopping at a distance no closer than absolutely necessary to obtain the information needed. The interceptor aircraft will use every possible precaution to avoid startling intercepted aircrew or passengers. Additionally, the interceptor aircrews will constantly keep in mind that maneuvers considered normal to a fighter aircraft may be considered hazardous to passengers and crews of nonfighter aircraft. When interceptor aircrews know or believe that an unsafe condition exists, the identification phase will be terminated. As previously stated, during darkness or IMC identification of unknown aircraft will be by type only. Positive vertical separation will be maintained by interceptor aircraft throughout this phase.

(3) **Phase Three — Post Intercept Phase:** Upon identification phase completion, the flight leader will turn away from the intercepted aircraft. The wingman will remain well clear and accomplish a rejoin with his leader.

c. Communication interface between interceptor aircrews and the ground controlling agency is essential to ensure successful intercept completion. Flight Safety is paramount. An aircraft which is intercepted by another aircraft shall immediately:

(1) Follow the instructions given by the intercepting aircraft, interpreting and responding to the visual signals.

(2) Notify, if possible, the appropriate air traffic services unit.

(3) Attempt to establish radio communication with the intercepting aircraft or with the appropriate intercept control unit, by making a general call on the emergency frequency 243.0 MHz and repeating this call on the emergency frequency 121.5 MHz, if practicable, giving the identity and position of the aircraft and the nature of the flight.

(4) If equipped with SSR transponder, select MODE 3/A Code 7700, unless otherwise instructed by the appropriate air traffic services unit. If any instructions received by radio from any sources conflict with those given by the intercepting aircraft by visual or radio signals, the intercepted aircraft shall request immediate clarification while continuing to comply with the instructions given by the intercepting aircraft.

432. INTERCEPTION SIGNALS

(See Tables 4-4 and 4-5.)

433. ADIZ BOUNDARIES AND DESIGNATED MOUNTAINOUS AREAS

(See Figure 4-21.)

434—439. RESERVED

Chapter 5. EMERGENCY PROCEDURES

Section 1. GENERAL

440. PILOT RESPONSIBILITY AND AUTHORITY

a. The pilot in command of an aircraft is directly responsible for and is the final authority as to the operation of that aircraft. In an emergency requiring immediate action, the pilot in command may deviate from any rule in the FAR, Subpart A, General, and Subpart B, Flight Rules, to the extent required to meet that emergency. (FAR—91.3(b).)

b. If the emergency authority of FAR 91.3.(b) is used to deviate from the provisions of an ATC clearance, the pilot in command must notify ATC as soon as possible and obtain an amended clearance.

c. Unless deviation is necessary under the emergency authority of FAR—91.3, pilots of IFR flights experiencing two-way radio communications failure are expected to adhere to the procedures prescribed under "IFR operations, two-way radio communications failure." (FAR—91.127)

441. EMERGENCY CONDITION - REQUEST ASSISTANCE IMMEDIATELY

a. An emergency can be either a *distress* or *urgency* condition as defined in the Pilot/Controller Glossary. Pilots do not hesitate to declare an emergency when they are faced with *distress* conditions such as fire, mechanical failure, or structural damage. However, some are reluctant to report an *urgency* condition when they encounter situations which may not be immediately perilous, but are potentially catastrophic. An aircraft is in at least an *urgency* condition the moment the pilot becomes doubtful about position, fuel endurance, weather, or any other condition that could adversely affect flight safety. This is the time to ask for help, not after the situation has developed into a *distress* condition.

b. Pilots who become apprehensive for their safety for *any* reason should *request assistance immediately*. Ready and willing help is available in the form of radio, radar, direction finding stations and other aircraft. Delay has caused accidents and cost lives. *Safety is not a luxury! Take action!*

442—449. RESERVED

Section 2. EMERGENCY SERVICES AVAILABLE TO PILOTS

450. RADAR SERVICE FOR VFR AIRCRAFT IN DIFFICULTY

a. Radar equipped ATC facilities can provide radar assistance and navigation service (vectors) to VFR aircraft in difficulty when the pilot can talk with the controller, and the aircraft is within radar coverage. Pilots should clearly understand that authorization to proceed in accordance with such radar navigational assistance does not constitute authorization for the pilot to violate FARs. In effect, assistance is provided on the basis that navigational guidance information is advisory in nature, and the responsibility for flying the aircraft safely remains with the pilot.

b. Experience has shown that many pilots who are not qualified for instrument flight cannot maintain control of their aircraft when they encounter clouds or other reduced visibility conditions. In many cases, the controller will not know whether flight into instrument conditions will result from his instructions. To avoid possible hazards resulting from being vectored into IFR conditions, a pilot in difficulty should keep the controller advised of the weather conditions in which he is operating and the weather along the course ahead and observe the following:

(1) If a course of action is available which will permit flight and a safe landing in VFR weather conditions, noninstrument rated pilots should choose the VFR condition rather than requesting a vector or approach that will take them into IFR weather conditions; or

(2) If continued flight in VFR conditions is not possible, the noninstrument rated pilot should so advise the controller and indicating the lack of an instrument rating, declare a *distress* condition, or

(3) If the pilot is instrument rated and current, and the aircraft is instrument equipped, the pilot should so indicate by requesting an IFR flight clearance. Assistance will then be provided on the basis that the aircraft can operate safely in IFR weather conditions.

451. TRANSPONDER EMERGENCY OPERATION

a. When a *distress* or *urgency* condition is encountered, the pilot of an aircraft with a coded radar beacon transponder, who desires to alert a ground radar facility, should squawk MODE 3/A, Code 7700/Emergency and MODE C altitude reporting and then immediately establish communications with the ATC facility.

b. Radar facilities are equipped so that Code 7700 normally triggers an alarm or special indicator at all control positions. Pilots should understand that they might not be within a radar coverage area. Therefore, they should continue squawking Code 7700 and establish radio communications as soon as possible.

452. DIRECTION FINDING INSTRUMENT APPROACH PROCEDURE

a. DF equipment has long been used to locate lost aircraft and to guide aircraft to areas of good weather or to airports. Now at most DF equipped airports, DF instrument approaches may be given to aircraft in a *distress* or *urgency* condition.

b. Experience has shown that most emergencies requiring DF assistance involve pilots with little flight experience. With this in mind, DF approach procedures provide maximum flight stability in the approach by using small turns, and wings-level descents. The DF specialist will give the pilot headings to fly and tell the pilot when to begin descent.

c. DF IAPs are for emergency use only and will not be used in IFR weather conditions unless the pilot has declared a *distress* or *urgency* condition.

d. To become familiar with the procedures and other benefits of DF, pilots are urged to request practice DF guidance and approaches in VFR weather conditions. DF specialists welcome the practice and will honor such requests, workload permitting.

453. INTERCEPT AND ESCORT

a. The concept of airborne intercept and escort is based on the Search and Rescue (SAR) aircraft establishing visual and/or electronic contact with an aircraft in difficulty, providing in-flight assistance, and escorting it to a safe landing. If bailout, crash landing or ditching becomes necessary, SAR operations can be conducted without delay. For most incidents, particularly those occurring at night and/or during instrument flight conditions, the availability of intercept and escort services will depend on the proximity of SAR units with suitable aircraft on alert for immediate dispatch. In limited circumstances, other aircraft flying in the vicinity of an aircraft in difficulty can provide these services.

b. If specifically requested by a pilot in difficulty or if a *distress* condition is declared, SAR coordinators *will* take steps to intercept and escort an aircraft. Steps *may* be initiated for intercept and escort if an *urgency* condition is declared and unusual circumstances make such action advisable.

c. It is the pilot's prerogative to refuse intercept and escort services. Escort services will normally be provided to the nearest adequate airport. Should the pilot receiving escort services continue onto another location after reaching a safe airport, or decide not to divert to the nearest safe airport, the escort aircraft is not obligated to continue and further escort is discretionary. The decision will depend on the circumstances of the individual incident.

454. EMERGENCY LOCATOR TRANSMITTERS

a. GENERAL. Emergency Locator Transmitters (ELTS) are required for most general aviation airplanes (FAR—91.52). ELTs of various types have been developed as a means of locating downed aircraft. These electronic, battery operated transmitters emit a distinctive downward swept audio tone on 121.5 MHz and 243.0 MHz. If "armed" and when subject to crash generated forces they are designed to automatically activate and continuously emit these signals. The transmitters will operate continuously for at least 48 hours over a wide temperature range. A properly installed and maintained ELT can expedite search and rescue operations and save lives.

b. TESTING. ELTs should be tested in accordance with the manufacturer's instructions, preferably in a shielded or screened room to prevent the broadcast of signals which could trigger a false alert. When this cannot be done, aircraft operational testing is authorized on 121.5 MHz and 243.0 MHz as follows:

(1) Tests should be conducted only during the first 5 minutes after any hour. If operational tests must be made outside of this time-frame, they should be coordinated with the nearest FAA Control Tower or FSS.

(2) Tests should be no longer than three audible sweeps.

(3) If the antenna is removable, a dummy load should be substituted during test procedures.

(4) Airborne tests are not authorized.

c. FALSE ALARMS. Caution should be exercised to prevent the inadvertent activation of ELTs in the air or while they are being handled on the ground. Accidental or unauthorized activation will generate an emergency signal that cannot be distinguished from the real thing, leading to expensive and frustrating searches. A false ELT signal could also interfere with genuine emergency transmissions and hinder or prevent the timely location of crash sites. Frequent false alarms could also result in complacency and decrease the vigorous reaction that must be attached to all ELT signals. Numerous cases of inadvertent activation have occurred as a result of aerobatics, hard landings, movement by ground crews and aircraft maintenance. These false alarms can be minimized by monitoring 121.5 MHz and/or 243.0 MHz as follows:

(1) In flight when a receiver is available.

(2) Prior to engine shut down at the end of each flight.

(3) When the ELT is handled during installation or maintenance.

(4) When maintenance is being performed in the vicinity of the ELT.

(5) When the aircraft is moved by a ground crew.

(6) If an ELT signal is heard, turn off the ELT to determine if it is transmitting. If it has been activated, maintenance might be required before the unit is returned to the "ARMED" position.

d. IN-FLIGHT MONITORING AND REPORTING. Pilots are encouraged to monitor 121.5 MHz and/or 243.0 MHz while in-flight to assist in identifying possible emergency ELT transmissions. On receiving a signal, report the following information to the nearest air traffic facility:

(1) Your position at the time the signal was first heard.

(2) Your position at the time the signal was last heard.

(3) Your position at maximum signal strength.

(4) Your flight altitudes and frequency on which the emergency signal was heard - 121.5 MHz or 243.0 MHz. If possible, positions should be given relative to a navigation aid. If the aircraft has homing equipment, provide the bearing to the emergency signal with each reported position.

455. FAA SPONSORED EXPLOSIVES DETECTION (DOG/HANDLER TEAM) LOCATIONS

a. At many of our major airports a program has been established by the FAA to make available explosives detection dog/handler teams. The dogs are trained by the Air Force and the overall program is run by FAA's Office of Civil Aviation Security. Local police departments are the caretakers of the dogs and are allowed to use the dogs in their normal police patrol functions. The local airport, however, has first call on the teams' services. The explosives detection teams were established so that no aircraft in flight is more than 1 hour from an airport at which it can be searched if a bomb threat is received. The following list contains those locations that presently have a team in existence. This list will be updated as more teams are established. If you desire this service, notify your company or an FAA facility.

b. Team Locations: *(See Table 5-1.)*

c. If due to weather or other considerations an aircraft with a suspected hidden explosive problem were to land or intended to land at an airport other than those listed in b. above, it is recommended that they call the FAA's Washington Operations Center (telephone 202-426-3333, if appropriate) or have an air traffic facility with which you can communicate contact the above center requesting assistance.

456. SEARCH AND RESCUE

a. GENERAL. SAR is a lifesaving service provided through the combined efforts of the federal agencies signatory to the National SAR Plan, and the agencies responsible for SAR within each state. Operational resources are provided by the U.S. Coast Guard, DOD components, the Civil Air Patrol, the Coast Guard Auxiliary, state, county and local law enforcement and other public safety agencies, and private volunteer organizations. Services include search for missing aircraft, survival aid, rescue, and emergency medical help for the occupants after an accident site is located.

b. NATIONAL SEARCH AND RESCUE PLAN. By federal interagency agreement, the National Search and Rescue Plan provides for the effective use of all available facilities in all types of SAR missions. These facilities include aircraft, vessels, pararescue and ground rescue teams, and emergency radio fixing. Under the Plan, the U.S. Coast Guard is responsible for the coordination of SAR in the Maritime Region, and the USAF is responsible in the Inland Region. To carry out these responsibilities, the Coast Guard and the Air Force have established Rescue Coordination Centers (RCCs) to direct SAR activities within their Regions. For aircraft emergencies, distress and urgency information normally will be passed to the appropriate RCC through an ARTCC or FSS.

c. COAST GUARD RESCUE COORDINATION CENTERS

Boston, MA	Long Beach, CA
617-223-3644	213-590-2225
New York, NY	San Francisco, CA
212-668-7055	415-437-3700
Portsmouth, VA	Seatle, WA
804-398-6231	206-442-5886
Miami, FL	Juneau, AK
305-536-5611	907-586-7340
New Orleans, LA	Honolulu, HI
504-589-6225	808-546-7109
Cleveland, OH	Kodiak, AK
216-522-3984	907-487-5888
St. Louis, MO	San Juan, Puerto Rico
314-425-4614	809-722-2943

d. AIR FORCE RESCUE COORDINATION CENTERS

Air Force Rescue Coordination Center - 48 Contiguous States

Scott AFB, Illinois	PHONE
Commercial	618-256-4815
WATS	800-851-3051
AUTOVON	576-4815
FTS	277-9447

*Alaskan Air Command Rescue Coordination Center -
Alaska*

Elmendorf AFB, Alaska	PHONE
Commercial	907-552-5375
AUTOVON	552-5375 or 2426

e.   JOINT RESCUE COORDINATION CENTERS
Honolulu Joint Rescue Coordination Center - Hawaii

HQ 14ᵗʰCoast Guard District Honolulu	PHONE
Commercial	808-531-1112
AUTOVON	315-421-4845

f.   OVERDUE AIRCRAFT.

(1) ARTCCs and FSSs will alert the SAR system when information is received from any source that an aircraft is in difficulty, overdue, or missing. *A filed flight plan is the most timely and effective indicator that an aircraft is overdue.* Flight plan information is invaluable to SAR forces for search planning and executing search efforts.

(2) Prior to departure on every flight, local or otherwise, someone at the departure point should be advised of your destination and route of flight if other than direct. Search efforts are often wasted and rescue is often delayed because of pilots who thoughtlessly takeoff without telling anyone where they are going. File a flight plan for *your* safety.

(3) According to the National Search and Rescue Plan, "The life expectancy of an injured survivor decreases as much as 80 percent during the first 24 hours, while the chances of survival of uninjured survivors rapidly diminishes after the first 3 days."

(4) An Air Force Review of 325 SAR missions conducted during a 23-month period revealed that "Time works against people who experience a *distress* but are not on a flight plan, since 36 hours normally pass before family concern initiates an (alert)."

g.   VFR SEARCH AND RESCUE PROTECTION.

(1) To receive this valuable protection, *file a VFR Flight Plan* with an FAA FSS. For maximum protection, file only to the point of first intended landing, and refile for each leg to final destination. When a lengthy flight plan is filed, with several stops en route and an ETE to final destination, a mishap could occur on any leg, and unless other information is received, it is probably that no one would start looking for you until 30 minutes after your ETA at your final destination.

(2) If you land at a location other than the intended destination, report the landing to the nearest FAA FSS and advise them of your original destination.

(3) If you land en route and are delayed more than 30 minutes, report this information to the nearest FSS and give them your original destination.

(4) If your ETE changes by 30 minutes or more, report a new ETA to the nearest FSS and give them your original destination. Remember that if you fail to respond within one-half hour after your ETA at final destination, a search will be started to locate you.

(5) It is important that you *close your flight plan IMMEDIATELY AFTER ARRIVAL AT YOUR FINAL DESTINATION WITH THE FSS DESIGNATED WHEN YOUR FLIGHT PLAN WAS FILED. The pilot is responsible for closure of a VFR flight plan; they are not closed automatically.* This will prevent needless search efforts.

(6) The rapidity of rescue on land or water will depend on how accurately your position may be determined. If a flight plan has been followed and your position is on course, rescue will be expedited.

h.   SURVIVAL EQUIPMENT.

(1) For flight over uninhabited land areas, it is wise to take and know how to use survival equipment for the type of climate and terrain.

(2) If a forced landing occurs at sea, chances for survival are governed by the degree of crew proficiency in emergency procedures and by the availability and effectiveness of water survival equipment.

i.   OBSERVANCE OF DOWNED AIRCRAFT.
(See Figures 5-1 and 5-2.)

(1) Determine if crash is marked with a yellow cross; if so, the crash has already been reported and identified.

(2) If possible, determine type and number of aircraft and whether there is evidence of survivors.

(3) Fix the position of the crash as accurately as possible with reference to a navigational aid. If possible provide geographic or physical description of the area to aid ground search parties.

(4) Transmit the information to the nearest FAA or other appropriate radio facility.

(5) If circumstances permit, orbit the scene to guide in other assisting units until their arrival or until you are relieved by another aircraft.

(6) Immediately after landing, make a complete report to the nearest FAA facility, or Air Force or Coast Guard Rescue Coordination Center. The report can be made by long distance collect telephone.

457—459. RESERVED

Section 3. DISTRESS AND URGENCY PROCEDURES

460. DISTRESS AND URGENCY COMMUNICATIONS

a. A pilot who encounters a *distress* or *urgency* condition can obtain assistance simply by contacting the air traffic facility or other agency in whose area of responsibility the aircraft is operating, stating the nature of the difficulty, pilot's intentions and assistance desires. *Distress* and *urgency* communications procedures are prescribed by the International Civil Aviation Organization (ICAO), however, and have decided advantages over the informal procedure described above.

b. *Distress* and *urgency* communications procedures discussed in the following paragraphs relate to the use of air ground voice communications.

c. The initial communication, and if considered necessary, any subsequent transmissions by an aircraft in *distress* should begin with the signal MAYDAY, preferably repeated three times. The signal PAN-PAN should be used in the same manner for an *urgency* condition.

d. *Distress* communications have absolute priority over all other communications, and the word MAYDAY commands radio silence on the frequency in use. *Urgency* communications have priority over all other communications except *distress,* and the word PAN-PAN warns other stations not to interfere with *urgency* transmissions.

e. Normally, the station addressed will be the air traffic facility or other agency providing air traffic services, on the frequency in use at the time. If the pilot is not communicating and receiving services, the station to be called will normally be the air traffic facility or other agency in whose area of responsibility the aircraft is operating, on the appropriate assigned frequency. If the station addressed does not respond, or if time or the situation dictates, the *distress* or *urgency* message may be broadcast, or a collect call may be used, addressing "Any Station (Tower)(Radio)(Radar)."

f. The station addressed should immediately acknowledge a *distress* or *urgency* message, provide assistance, coordinate and direct the activities of assisting facilities, and alert the appropriate search and rescue coordinator if warranted. Responsibility will be transferred to another station only if better handling will result.

g. All other stations, aircraft and ground, will continue to listen until it is evident that assistance is being provided. If any station becomes aware that the station being called either has not received a *distress* or *urgency* message, or cannot communicate with the aircraft in difficulty, it will attempt to contact the aircraft and provide assistance.

h. Although the frequency in use or other frequencies assigned by ATC are preferable, the following emergency frequencies can be used for distress or urgency communications, if necessary or desirable:

(1) 121.5 MHz and 243.0 MHz - Both have a range generally limited to line of sight. 121.5 MHz is guarded by direction finding stations and some military and civil aircraft. 243.0 MHz is guarded by military aircraft. Both 121.5 MHz and 243.0 MHz are guarded by military towers, most civil towers, FSSs, and radar facilities. Normally ARTCC emergency frequency capability does not extend to radar coverage limits. If an ARTCC does not respond when called on 121.5 MHz or 243.0 MHz, call the nearest tower or FSS.

(2) 2182 kHz - The range is generally less than 300 miles for the average aircraft installation. It can be used to request assistance from stations in the maritime service. 2182 kHz is guarded by major radio stations serving Coast Guard Rescue Coordination Centers, and Coast Guard units along the sea coasts of the U.S. and shores of the Great Lakes. The call "Coast Guard" will alert all Coast Guard Radio Stations within range. 2182 kHz is also guarded by most commercial coast stations and some ships and boats.

461. OBTAINING EMERGENCY ASSISTANCE

a. A pilot in any *distress* or *urgency* condition should *immediately* take the following action, not necessarily in the order listed, to obtain assistance:

(1) Climb, if possible, for improved communications, and better radar and direction finding detection. However, it must be understood that unauthorized climb or descent under IFR conditions within controlled airspace is prohibited, except as permitted by FAR—91.3(b).

(2) If equipped with a radar beacon transponder (civil) or IFF/SIF (military):

(a) Continue squawking assigned MODE A/3 discrete code/VFR code and MODE C altitude encoding when in radio contact with an air traffic facility or other agency providing air traffic services, unless instructed to do otherwise.

(b) If unable to immediately establish communications with an air traffic facility/agency, squawk MODE A/3, Code 7700/ Emergency and MODE C.

(3) Transmit a *distress* or *urgency* message consisting of *as many as necessary* of the following elements, preferably in the order listed:

(a) If distress, MAYDAY, MAYDAY, MAYDAY; if *urgency*, PAN-PAN, PAN-PAN, PAN-PAN.

(b) Name of station addressed.

(c) Aircraft identification and type.

(d) Nature of *distress* or *urgency.*

(e) Weather.

(f) Pilots intentions and request.

(g) Present position, and heading, or if *lost,* last known position, time, and heading since that position.

(h) Altitude or flight level.

(i) Fuel remaining in hours and minutes.

(j) Number of people on board.

(k) Any other useful information.

b. After establishing radio contact, comply with advice and instructions received. Cooperate. Do not hesitate to ask questions or clarify instructions when you do not understand or if you cannot comply with clearance. Assist the ground station to control communications on the frequency in use. Silence interfering radio stations. Do not change frequency or change to another ground station unless absolutely necessary. If you do, advise the ground station of the new frequency and station name prior to the change, transmitting in the blind if necessary. If two-way communications cannot be established on the new frequency, return immediately to the frequency or station where two-way communications last existed.

c. When in a distress condition with bailout, crash landing or ditching imminent, take the following additional actions to assist search and rescue units:

(1) Time and circumstances permitting, transmit as many as necessary of the message elements in PARA—461a(3) and any of the following that you think might be helpful

(a) ELT status.

(b) Visible landmarks.

(c) Aircraft color.

(d) Number of persons on board.

(e) Emergency equipment on board.

(2) Actuate your ELT if the installation permits.

(3) For bailout, and for crash landing or ditching if risk of fire is not a consideration, set your radio for continuous transmission.

(4) If it becomes necessary to ditch, make every effort to ditch near a surface vessel. If time permits, an FAA facility should be able to get the position of the nearest commercial or Coast Guard vessel from a Coast Guard Rescue Coordination Center.

(5) After a crash landing unless you have good reason to believe that you will not be located by search aircraft or ground teams, it is best to remain with your aircraft and prepare means for signalling search aircraft.

462. DITCHING PROCEDURES

(See Figure 5-3.)

a. A successful aircraft ditching is dependent on three primary factors. In order of importance they are:

(1) Sea conditions and wind.

(2) Type of aircraft.

(3) Skill and technique of pilot.

b. Common oceanographic terminology:

(1) Sea. The condition of the surface that is the result of both waves and swells.

(2) Wave (or Chop). The condition of the surface caused by the local winds.

(3) Swell. The condition of the surface which has been caused by a distance disturbance.

(4) Swell Face. The side of the swell toward the observer. The backside is the side away from the observer. These definitions apply regardless of the direction of swell movement.

(5) Primary Swell. The swell system having the greatest height from trough to crest.

(6) Secondary Swells. Those swell systems of less height than the primary swell.

(7) Fetch. The distance the waves have been driven by a wind blowing in a constant direction, without obstruction.

(8) Swell Period. The time interval between the passage of two successive crests at the same spot in the water, measured in seconds.

(9) Swell Velocity. The speed and direction of the swell with relation to a fixed reference point, measured in knots. There is little movement of water in the horizontal direction. Swells move primarily in a vertical motion, similar to the motion observed when shaking out a carpet.

(10) Swell Direction. The direction *from* which a swell is moving. This direction is not necessarily the result of the wind present at the scene. The swell may be moving into or across the local wind. Swells, once set in motion, tend to maintain their origi-

nal direction for as long as they continue in deep water, regardless of changes in wind direction.

(11) Swell Height. The height between crest and trough, measured in feet. The vast majority of ocean swells are lower than 12 to 15 feet, and swells over 25 feet are not common at any spot on the oceans. Successive swells may differ considerably in height.

c. In order to select a good heading when ditching an aircraft, a basic evaluation of the sea is required. Selection of a good ditching heading may well minimize damage and could save your life. It can be extremely dangerous to land into the wind without regard to sea conditions; the swell system, or systems, must be taken into consideration. Remember one axiom - AVOID THE FACE OF A SWELL.

(1) In ditching parallel to the swell, it makes little difference whether touchdown is on the top of the crest or in the trough. It is preferable, however, to land on the top or back side of the swell, if possible. After determining which heading (and its reciprocal) will parallel the swell, select the heading with the most into the wind component.

(2) If only one swell system exists, the problem is relatively simple - even with a high, fast system. Unfortunately, most cases involve two or more swell systems running in different directions. With more than one system present, the sea presents a confused appearance. One of the most difficult situations occurs when two swell systems are at right angles. For example, if one system is eight feet high, and the other three feet, plan to land parallel to the primary system, and on the down swell of the secondary system. If both systems are of equal height, a compromise may be advisable - select an intermediate heading at 45 degrees down swell to both systems. When landing down a secondary swell, attempt to touch down on the back side, not on the face of the swell.

(3) *If the swell system is formidable, it is considered advisable, in landplanes, to accept more crosswind in order to avoid landing directly into the swell.*

(4) The secondary swell system is often from the same direction as the wind. Here, the landing may be made parallel to the primary system, with the wind and secondary system at an angle. There is a choice to two directions paralleling the primary system. One direction is downwind and down the secondary swell, and the other is into the wind and into the secondary swell, the choice will depend on the velocity of the wind versus the velocity and height of the secondary swell.

d. The simplest method of estimating the wind direction and velocity is to examine the windstreaks on the water. These appear as long streaks up and down wind. Some persons may have difficulty determining wind direction after seeing the streaks on the water. Whitecaps fall forward with the wind but are overrun by the waves thus producing the illusion that the foam is sliding backward. Knowing this, and by observing the direction of the streaks, the wind direction is easily determined. Wind velocity can be estimated by noting the appearance of the whitecaps, foam and wind streaks.

(1) The behavior of the aircraft on making contact with the water will vary within wide limits according to the state of the sea. If landed parallel to a single swell system, the behavior of the aircraft may approximate that to be expected on a smooth sea. If landed into a heavy swell or into a confused sea, the deceleration forces may be extremely great - resulting in breaking up of the aircraft. Within certain limits, the pilot is able to minimize these forces by proper sea evaluation and selection of ditching heading.

(2) When on final approach the pilot should look ahead and observe the surface of the sea. There may be shadows and whitecaps - signs of large seas. Shadows and whitecaps close together indicate short and rough seas. Touchdown in these areas is to be avoided. Select and touchdown in any area (only about 500 feet is needed) where the shadows and whitecaps are not so numerous.

(3) Touchdown should be at the *lowest* speed and rate of descent which permit safe handling and optimum nose up attitude on impact. Once first impact has been made, there is often little the pilot can do to control a landplane.

e. Once preditching preparations are completed, the pilot should turn to the ditching heading and commence let-down. The aircraft should be flown low over the water, and slowed down until ten knots or so above stall. At this point, additional power should be used to overcome the increased drag caused by the nose up attitude. When a smooth stretch of water appears ahead, cut power, and touchdown at the best recommended speed as fully stalled as possible. By cutting power when approaching a relatively smooth area, the pilot will prevent overshooting and will touchdown with less chance of planing off into a second uncontrolled landing. Most experienced seaplane pilots prefer to make contact with the water in a semi-stalled attitude, cutting power as the tail makes contact. This technique eliminates the chance of misjudging altitude with a resultant heavy drop in a fully stalled condition. Care must be taken not to drop the aircraft from too high altitude or to balloon due to excessive speed. The altitude above water depends on the aircraft. Over glassy smooth water, or at night without sufficient light, it is very easy, for even the most experienced pilots to misjudge altitude 50 feet or more. Under such conditions, carry enough power to maintain nine to twelve degrees nose up attitude, and 10 to 20 percent over stalling speed until contact is made with the water. The proper use of power on the approach is of great importance. If power is available on one side only, a little power should be used to flatten the approach; however, the engine should not be used to such an extent that the aircraft cannot be turned against the good engines right down to the stall with a margin of rudder movement available. When near the stall, sudden application of excessive unbalanced power may result in loss of directional control. If power is available on one side only, a slightly higher than normal glide approach speed should be used. This will insure good control and some margin of speed after leveling off without excessive use of power. The use of power in ditching is so important that when it is certain that the coast cannot be reached, the pilot should, if possible, ditch before fuel is exhausted. The use of power in a night or instrument ditching is far more essential than under daylight contact conditions.

(1) If no power is available, a greater than normal approach speed should be used down to the flare-out. This speed margin will allow the glide to be broken early and more gradually, thereby giving the pilot time and distance to feel for the surface - decreasing the possibility of stalling high or flying into the water. When landing parallel to a swell system, little difference is noted between landing on top of a crest or in the trough. If the wings of aircraft are trimmed to the surface of the sea rather than the horizon, there is little need to worry about a wing hitting a swell crest. The actual slope of a swell is very gradual. If forced to land into a swell, touchdown should be made just after passage of the crest. If contact is made on the face of the swell, the aircraft may be swamped or thrown violently into the air, dropping heavily into the next swell. If control surfaces remain intact, the pilot should attempt to maintain the proper nose above the horizon attitude by rapid and positive use of the controls.

f. After Touchdown: In most cases drift, caused by crosswind can be ignored; the forces acting on the aircraft after touchdown are of such magnitude that drift will be only a secondary consideration. If the aircraft is under good control, the "crab" may be

kicked out with rudder just prior to touchdown. This is more important with high wing aircraft, for they are laterally unstable on the water in a crosswind and may roll to the side in ditching.

NOTE.— This information has been extracted from Appendix II of the "National Search And Rescue Manual."

463. SPECIAL EMERGENCY (AIR PIRACY)

a. A special emergency is a condition of air piracy, or other hostile act by a person(s) aboard an aircraft, which threatens the safety of the aircraft or its passengers.

b. The pilot of an aircraft reporting a special emergency condition should:

(1) If circumstances permit, apply *distress or urgency* radiotelephony procedures (see PARA—460). Include the details of the special emergency.

(2) If circumstances do not permit the use of prescribed *distress* or *urgency* procedures, transmit:

(a) On the air/ground frequency in use at the time.

(b) As many as possible of the following elements spoken distinctly and in the following order:

1. Name of the station addressed (time and circumstances permitting).

2. The identification of the aircraft and present position.

3. The nature of the special emergency condition and pilot intentions (circumstances permitting).

4. If unable to provide this information, use code words and/or transponder as follows: state "TRANSPONDER SEVEN FIVE ZERO ZERO". Meaning: "I am being hijacked/forced to a new destination"; and/or use Transponder Setting MODE 3/A, Code 7500.

NOTE.— Code 7500 will never be assigned by ATC without prior notification from the pilot that his aircraft is being subjected to unlawful interference. The pilot should refuse the assignment of Code 7500 in any other situation and inform the controller accordingly. Code 7500 will trigger the special emergency indicator in all radar ATC facilities.

c. Air traffic controllers will acknowledge and confirm receipt of transponder Code 7500 by asking the pilot to verify it. If the aircraft is not being subjected to unlawful interference, the pilot should respond to the query by broadcasting in the clear that he is not being subjected to unlawful interference. Upon receipt of this information, the controller will request the pilot to verify the code selection depicted in the code selector windows in the transponder control panel and change the code to the appropriate setting. If the pilot replies in the affirmative or does not reply, the controller will not ask further questions but will flight follow, respond to pilot requests and notify appropriate authorities.

d. If it is possible to do so without jeopardizing the safety of the flight, the pilot of a hijacked passenger aircraft, after departing from the cleared routing over which the aircraft was operating, will attempt to do one or more of the following things, insofar as circumstances may permit:

(1) Maintain a true airspeed of no more than 400 knots, and preferably an altitude of between 10,000 and 25,000 feet.

(2) Fly a course toward the destination which the hijacker has announced.

e. If these procedures result in either radio contact or air intercept, the pilot will attempt to comply with any instructions received which may direct him to an appropriate landing field.

464. FUEL DUMPING

a. Should it become necessary to dump fuel, the pilot should immediately advise ATC. Upon receipt of information that an aircraft will dump fuel, ATC will broadcast or cause to be broadcast immediately and every 3 minutes thereafter the following on appropriate ATC and FSS radio frequencies:

EXAMPLE:

ATTENTION ALL AIRCRAFT — FUEL DUMPING IN PROGRESS OVER — (location) AT (altitude) BY (type aircraft) (flight direction).

b. Upon receipt of such a broadcast, pilots of aircraft affected, which are not on IFR flight plans or special VFR clearances, should clear the area specified in the advisory. Aircraft on IFR flight plans or special VFR clearances will be provided specific separation by ATC. At the termination of the fuel dumping operation, pilots should advise ATC. Upon receipt of such information, ATC will issue, on the appropriate frequencies, the following:

EXAMPLE:

ATTENTION ALL AIRCRAFT — FUEL DUMPING BY — (type aircraft) — TERMINATED.

465—469. RESERVED

Section 4. TWO-WAY RADIO COMMUNICATIONS FAILURE

470. TWO-WAY RADIO COMMUNICATIONS FAILURE

a. It is virtually impossible to provide regulations and procedures applicable to all possible situations associated with two-way radio communications failure. During two-way radio communications failure, when confronted by a situation not covered in the regulation, pilots are expected to exercise good judgment in whatever action they elect to take. Should the situation so dictate they should not be reluctant to use the emergency action contained in FAR—91.3(b).

b. Whether two-way communications failure constitutes an emergency depends on the circumstances, and in any event, it is a determination made by the pilot. FAR—91.3(b) authorizes a pilot to deviate from any rule in Subparts A and B to the extent required to meet an emergency.

c. In the event of two-way radio communications failure, ATC service will be provided on the basis that the pilot is operating in accordance with FAR—91.127. A pilot experiencing two-way communications failure should (unless emergency authority is exercised) comply with FAR—91.127 quoted below. Capitalization and examples added for emphasis.

1. "91.127 IFR operations; two-way radio communications failure."

(1) General. Unless otherwise authorized by ATC, each pilot who has two-way radio communications failure when operating under IFR shall comply with the rules of this section.

(2) VFR conditions. If the failure occurs in VFR conditions, or if VFR conditions are encountered after the failure, each pilot shall continue the flight under VFR and land as soon as practicable.

NOTE.— This procedure also applies when two-way radio failure occurs while operating in Positive Control Airspace (PCA). The primary objective of this provision in FAR—91.127 is to preclude extended IFR operation in the ATC system in VFR weather conditions. Pilots should recognize that operation under these conditions may unnecessarily as well as adversely affect other users of the airspace, since ATC may be required to reroute or delay other users in order to protect the failure aircraft. However, it is not intended that the requirement to "land as soon as practicable" be construed to mean "as soon as possible." The pilot retains his prerogative of exercising his best judgment and is not required to land at an unauthorized airport, at an airport unsuitable for the type of aircraft flown, or to land only minutes short of his destination.

(3) IFR conditions. If the failure occurs in IFR conditions, or if paragraph (b) of this section cannot be complied with, each pilot shall continue the flight according to the following:

(a) Route.

1. By the route assigned in the last ATC clearance received;

2. If being radar vectored, by the direct route from the point of radio failure to the fix, route, or airway specified in the vector clearance;

3. In the absence of an assigned route, by the route that ATC has advised may be expected in a further clearance; or

4. In the absence of an assigned route or a route that ATC has advised may be expected in a further clearance by the route filed in the flight plan.

(b) Altitude. At the HIGHEST of the following altitudes or flight levels FOR THE ROUTE SEGMENT BEING FLOWN:

1. The altitude or flight level assigned in the last ATC clearance received;

2. The minimum altitude (converted, if appropriate, to minimum flight level as prescribed in FAR 91.81. (c)) for IFR operations; or

3. The altitude or flight level ATC has advised may be expected in a further clearance.

NOTE.— The intent of the rule is that a pilot who has experienced two-way radio failure should, during any segment of his route, fly at the appropriate altitude specified in the rule for that particular segment. The appropriate altitude is whichever of the three is highest in each given phase of flight: (1) the altitude or flight level last assigned; (2) the MEA or (3) the altitude or flight level the pilot has been advised to expect in a further clearance.

EXAMPLE:

A pilot with two-way radio failure had an assigned altitude of 7,000 feet, and while en route comes to a route segment for which the MEA was 9,000 feet. He would climb to 9,000 feet at the time or place where it became necessary to comply with the 9,000 feet MEA. (See FAR—91.119(b).) If later, while still proceeding to his destination, the MEA dropped from 9,000 feet to 5,000 feet, he would descend to *7,000 feet* (the last assigned altitude), because that altitude is *higher* than the MEA.

EXAMPLE:

The MEA between A and B —5,000 feet. The MEA between B and C —5,000 feet. The MEA between C and D —11,000 feet. The MEA between D and E —7,000 feet. A pilot had been cleared via A, B, C, D, to E. While flying between A and B his assigned altitude was 6,000 feet and he was told to expect a clearance to 8,000 feet at B. Prior to receiving the higher altitude assignment, he experienced two-way failure. The pilot would maintain 6,000 to B, then climb to 8,000 feet (the altitude he was advised to expect.) He would maintain 8,000 feet, then climb to 11,000 at C, or prior to C if necessary to comply with an MCA at C. (FAR—91.119(b)). Upon reaching D, the pilot would descend to *8,000 feet* (even though the MEA was 7,000 feet), as 8,000 was the highest of the altitude situations stated in the rule (FAR—91.127).

(c) Leave clearance limit.

1. When the clearance limit is a fix from which an approach begins, commence descent or descent and approach as close as possible to the expect further clearance time if one has been received, or if one has not been received, as close as possible to the estimated time of arrival as calculated from the filed or amended (with ATC) estimated time en route.

2. If the clearance limit is not a fix from which an approach begins, leave the clearance limit at the expect further clearance time if one has been received, or if none has been received, upon arrival over the clearance limit, and proceed to a fix from which an approach begins and commence descent or descent and approach as close as possible to the estimated time of arrival as calculated from the filed or amended (with ATC) estimated time en route.

471. TRANSPONDER OPERATION DURING TWO-WAY COMMUNICATIONS FAILURE

a. If a pilot of an aircraft with a coded radar beacon transponder experiences a loss of two-way radio capability he should:

(1) Adjust his transponder to reply on MODE A/3, Code 7700 for a period of 1 minute.

(2) Then change to Code 7600 and remain on 7600 for a period of 15 minutes or the remainder of the flight, whichever comes first.

(3) Repeat steps (1) and (2) as practicable.

b. The pilot should understand that he may not be in an area of radar coverage.

472. REESTABLISHING RADIO CONTACT

a. In addition to monitoring the NAVAID voice feature, the pilot should attempt to reestablish communications by attempting contact:

(1) on the previously assigned frequency, or

(2) with an FSS or *ARINC.

b. If communications are established with an FSS or ARINC, the pilot should advise that radio communications on the previously assigned frequency has been lost giving the aircraft's position, altitude, last assigned frequency and then request further clearance from the controlling facility. The preceding does not preclude the use of 121.5 MHz. There is no priority on which action should be attempted first. If the capability exists, do all at the same time.

NOTE.—*AERONAUTICAL RADIO/INCORPORATED (ARINC) - is a commercial communications corporation which designs, constructs, operates, leases or otherwise engages in radio activities serving the aviation community. ARINC has the capability of relaying information to/from ATC facilities throughout the country.

473—499. RESERVED

Chapter 6. SAFETY OF FLIGHT

Section 1. METEOROLOGY

500. NATIONAL WEATHER SERVICE AVIATION PRODUCTS

a. Weather service to aviation is a joint effort of the National Weather Service (NWS), the Federal Aviation Administration (FAA), the military weather services, and other aviation oriented groups and individuals. The NWS maintains an extensive surface, upper air and radar weather observing program; a nationwide aviation weather forecasting service; and also provides pilot briefing service. The majority of pilot weather briefings are provided by FAA personnel at Flight Service Stations (FSSs). Surface weather observations are taken by the NWS and NWS certified FAA, contract and supplemental observers and by automated observing systems. (See paragraph 509)

b. Aviation forecasts are prepared by 52 Weather Service Forecast Offices (WSFOs). These offices prepare and distribute approximately 500 terminal forecasts 3 times daily for specific airports in 50 states and the Caribbean (4 times daily in Alaska and Hawaii). These forecasts, which are amended as required, are valid for 24 hours. The last 6 hours are given in categorical outlook terms as described in PARA—505. WSFOs also prepare a total of over 300 route forecasts and 39 synopses for Pilots Automatic Telephone Weather Answering Service (PATWAS), Transcribed Weather Broadcast (TWEB), and briefing purposes. The route forecasts that are issued during the morning and mid-day are valid for 12 hours while the evening issuance is valid for 18 hours. A new centralized aviation forecast program originating from the National Aviation Weather Advisory Unit (NAWAU) in Kansas City was implemented in November 1982. In the conterminous U.S., all In-flight Advisories (SIGMETs, convective SIGMETs, and AIRMETs) and all Area Forecasts (6 areas) are now issued by NAWAU. The Area Forecasts are prepared 3 times a day in the conterminous states (4 times in Hawaii), and amended as required, while In-flight Advisories are issued only when conditions warrant. (See PARA—504.) Winds aloft forecasts are provided for 176 locations in the 48 contiguous states and 21 in Alaska for flight planning purposes. (Winds aloft forecasts for Hawaii are prepared locally). All of the aviation weather forecasts are given wide distribution through the Weather Message Switching Center in Kansas City (WMSC).

501. FAA WEATHER SERVICES

a. The FAA maintains a nationwide network of Flight Service Stations (FSSs) to serve the weather needs of pilots. In addition, NWS meteorologists are assigned to most Air Route Traffic Control Centers (ARTCCs) as part of the Center Weather Service Unit (CWSU). They provide advisory service and short-term forecasts (nowcasts) to support the needs of the FAA and other users of the system.

b. The primary source of preflight weather briefings is an individual briefing obtained from a briefer at the FSS or NWS. These briefings, which are tailored to your specific flight, are available 24 hours a day through the local FSS or through the use of toll free lines (INWATS). Numbers for these services can be found in the Airport/ Facility Directory under the FAA and NWS Weather and Aeronautical Information Telephone Numbers section and the DOT, Federal Aviation Administration or Department of Commerce, National Weather Service listing under U.S. Government in your local telephone directory. See paragraph-502 for the types of preflight briefings available and the type of information contained in each. NWS pilot briefers do not provide aeronautical information (NOTAMs, flow control advisories, etc.) nor do they accept flight plans.

c. Other sources of weather information are as follows:

(1) The A.M. Weather telecast on the PBS television network is a jointly sponsored 15-minute weather program designed for pilots. It is broadcast Monday through Friday mornings. Check TV listings in your area for station and exact times.

(2) The Transcribed Weather Broadcast (TWEB), telephone access to the TWEB (TEL-TWEB) and Pilots Automatic Telephone Weather Answering Service (PATWAS) provide continuously updated recorded weather information for short or local flights. Separate paragraphs in this section give additional information regarding these services.

(3) The Interim Voice Response System (IVRS) is now available in 24 metropolitan areas. Using this system, a limited weather data base can be accessed through the use of a TOUCH-TONE®telephone. The IVRS provides weather information for the conterminous United States 24 hours a day. Six weather products are provided: Severe Weather Forecast Alerts (AWW), Convective Sigmets (WST), Surface Observations (SA), Terminal Forecasts (FT), Winds Aloft Forecasts (GF), and TWEB Route Forecasts (TR). Pilots should be aware that among the products not provided are non-convective SIGMETS, AIRMETS, and Center Weather Advisories (CWA). These issuances must be obtained from the FSS or other available sources to supplement the IVRS information for flight planning purposes. A 24 hour toll-free number (800-367-4877) is available to answer pilot questions, to explain system operation and to respond to any system problems. Detailed instructions on how to use IVRS are contained in *"A Pilot's Guide to IVRS"*. A copy can be obtained from any FAA Flight Standards District Office or Flight Service Station. Comments, questions and requests for additional information may be directed to: IVRS Project Office, Federal Aviation Administration, APM-230, Washington, D.C. 20591. Telephone numbers for IVRS facilities in individual metropolitan areas are listed in the Airport/Facility Directories under the FAA and NWS weather and Aeronautical Information Telephone Numbers section.

(4) Weather and aeronautical information is also available from numerous private industry sources on an individual or contract pay basis. Information on how to obtain this service should be available from local pilot organizations.

d. In-flight weather information is available from any FSS within radio range. See PARA-506 through PARA—508 for information on broadcasts. En route Flight Advisory Service (EFAS) is provided to serve the nonroutine weather needs of pilots in flight. See PARA—503 for details on this service.

502. PREFLIGHT BRIEFING

a. Flight Service Stations (FSSs) are the primary source for obtaining preflight briefings and in-flight weather information. In some locations, the Weather Service Office (WSO) provides preflight briefings on a limited basis. Flight Service Specialists are qualified and certificated by the NWS as Pilot Weather Briefers. They are not authorized to make original forecasts, but are authorized to translate and interpret available forecasts and reports directly into terms describing the weather conditions which you can expect along your flight route and at your destination. Available aviation weather reports and forecasts are displayed at each FSS and WSO. Some of the larger FSSs provide a separate display for pilot use. Pilots should feel free to use these self briefing displays where available, or to ask for a briefing or assistance from the specialist on duty. Three basic types of preflight briefings are available to serve your specific needs. These are: Standard Briefing, Abbreviated Briefing, and Outlook Briefing. You should specify to the briefer the type of briefing you want, along with appropriate background information. (Refer to PARA—290 for items that are required.) This will enable the briefer to tailor the information to your intended flight. The following paragraphs describe the types of briefings available and the information provided in each.

b. STANDARD BRIEFING—You should request a Standard Briefing any time you are planning a flight and you have not received a previous briefing or have not received preliminary information through mass dissemination media; e.g., TWEB, PATWAS, VRS, etc. The briefer will automatically provide the following information in the sequence listed, except as noted, when it is applicable to your proposed flight.

(1) Adverse Conditions—Significant meteorological and aeronautical information that might influence the pilot to alter the proposed flight, e.g., hazardous weather conditions, runway closures, NAVAID outages, etc.

(2) VFR Flight Not Recommended—When VFR flight is proposed and sky conditions or visibilities are present or forecast, surface or aloft, that in the briefer's judgment would make flight under visual flight rules doubtful, the briefer will describe the conditions, affected locations, and use the phrase *"VFR flight is not recommended."* This recommendation is advisory in nature. The final decision as to whether the flight can be conducted safely rests solely with the pilot.

(3) Synopsis—A brief statement describing the type, location and movement of weather systems and/or air masses which might affect the proposed flight.

NOTE— These first 3 elements of a briefing may be combined in any order when the briefer believes it will help to more clearly describe conditions.

(4) Current Conditions—Reported weather conditions applicable to the flight will be summarized from all available sources; e.g., SAs, PIREPs, RAREPs. This element will be omitted if the proposed time of departure is beyond two hours, unless the information is specifically requested by the pilot.

(5) En Route Forecast—Forecast en route conditions for the proposed route are summarized in logical order; i.e., departure-climbout, en route, and descent.

(6) Destination Forecast—The destination forecast for the planned ETA. Any significant changes within 1 hour before and after the planned arrival are included.

(7) Winds Aloft—Forecast winds aloft will be summarized for the proposed route. The briefer will interpolate wind directions and speeds between levels and stations as necessary to provide expected conditions at planned altitudes.

(8) Notices to Airmen (NOTAMs)—

(a) Available NOTAM(D) information pertinent to the proposed flight.

(b) NOTAM(L) information pertinent to the departure and/or local area, if available, and pertinent FDC NOTAMs within approximately 400 miles of the FSS providing the briefing.

NOTE 1— NOTAM information may be combined with current conditions when the briefer believes it is logical to do so.

NOTE 2— NOTAM(D) information and FDC NOTAMs which have been published in the Notices to Airmen (Class II) Publication are not included in pilot briefings unless a review of this publication is specifically requested by the pilot. For complete flight information you are urged to review Class II NOTAMs and the Airport/Facility Directory in addition to obtaining a briefing.

(9) ATC Delays—Any known ATC delays and flow control advisories which might affect the proposed flight.

(10) Pilots may obtain the following from FSS briefers upon request:

(a) Information on military training routes and MOA activity within 100 NM of facility conducting briefing.

NOTE— For flights beyond 100 miles, pilots are encouraged to request updated information from en route FSSs.

(b) A review of the Notices to Airmen Publication (Class II NOTAMs) for pertinent NOTAMs and Special Notices.

(c) Approximate density altitude data.

(d) Information regarding such items as air traffic services and rules, customs/immigration procedures, ADIZ rules, search and rescue, etc.

(e) LORAN-C NOTAMs.

(f) Other assistance as required.

c. ABBREVIATED BRIEFING— Request an Abbreviated Briefing when you need information to supplement mass disseminated data, update a previous briefing, or when you need only one or two specific items. Provide the briefer with appropriate background information, the time you received the previous information, and/or the specific items needed. You should indicate the source of the information already received so that the briefer can limit the briefing to the information that you have not received, and/or appreciable changes in meteorological conditions since your previous briefing. To the extent possible, the briefer will provide the information in the sequence shown for a Standard Briefing. If you request only one or two specific items, the briefer will advise you if adverse conditions are present or forecast. Details on these conditions will be provided at your request.

d. OUTLOOK BRIEFING— You should request an Outlook Briefing whenever your proposed time of departure is six or more hours from the time of the briefing. The briefer will provide available forecast data applicable to the proposed flight. This type of briefing is provided for planning purposes only. You should obtain a Standard or Abbreviated Briefing prior to departure in order to obtain such items as current conditions, updated forecasts, winds aloft and NOTAMs.

e. INFLIGHT BRIEFING— You are encouraged to obtain your preflight briefing by telephone or in person before departure. In those cases where you need to obtain a preflight briefing or an update to a previous briefing by radio, you should contact the nearest FSS to obtain this information. After communications have been established, advise the specialist of the type briefing you require and provide appropriate background information. You will be provided information as specified in the above paragraphs, depending on the type briefing requested. In addition, the specialist will recommend shifting to the flight watch frequency when conditions along the intended route indicate that it would be advantageous to do so.

f. Following any briefing, feel free to ask for any information that you or the briefer may have missed. It helps to save your questions until the briefing has been completed. This way, the briefer is able to present the information in a logical sequence, and lessens the chance of important items being overlooked.

503. EN ROUTE FLIGHT ADVISORY SERVICE (EFAS)

a. EFAS is a service specifically designed to provide en route aircraft with timely and meaningful weather advisories pertinent to the type of flight intended, route of flight and altitude. In conjunction with this service, EFAS is also a central collection and distribution point for pilot reported weather information. It is normally available throughout the conterminous U.S. and Puerto Rico from 6 a.m. to 10 p.m. EFAS provides communications capabilities for aircraft flying at 5,000 feet above ground level on a common frequency of 122.0 MHz. High altitude EFAS, now in the process of being implemented in some areas of the country, provides a separate discrete frequency within each Air Route Traffic Control Center's area for use only by aircraft flying at an altitude of 18,000 feet MSL and above. EFAS is provided by specially trained specialists in selected FSSs controlling one or more remote communications outlets covering a large geographical area.

NOTE.—When an EFAS outlet is located in a time zone different from the zone in which the control station is located, the availability of service normally provided by the EFAS outlets may be plus or minus 1 hour from the normal operating hours of the flight watch control station.

b. Contact flight watch by using the name of the parent facility, followed by your aircraft identification and append the name of the nearest VOR to your position. The specialist needs to know this approximate location to select the most appropriate outlet for communications coverage.

EXAMPLE:
CLEVELAND FLIGHT WATCH, CESSNA ONE TWO THREE FOUR KILO, MANSFIELD VOR OVER.

c. Charts depicting the location of the flight watch control stations (parent facility) and the outlets they use are contained in the Airport Facility Directories (A/FD). If you do not know in which flight watch area you are flying, initiate contact by using the words "FLIGHT WATCH," your aircraft identification, and the name of the nearest VOR. The facility will respond using the name of the flight watch facility.

EXAMPLE:
FLIGHT WATCH, CESSNA ONE TWO THREE FOUR KILO, MANSFIELD VOR OVER.

d. FSSs which provide En route Flight Advisory Service are listed regionally in the Airport/Facilities Directories.

e. EFAS is not intended to be used for filing or closing flight plans, position reporting, to get a complete preflight briefing, or to obtain random weather reports and forecasts. In such instances, the flight watch specialist will provide the name and radio frequency of the FSS to contact for such services. Pilot participation is essential to the success of EFAS through a continuous exchange of information on winds, turbulence, visibility, icing, etc., between pilots inflight and flight watch specialists on the ground. Pilots are encouraged to report good as well as bad and expected as well as unexpected flight conditions to flight watch facilities.

504. IN-FLIGHT WEATHER ADVISORIES

a. The NWS issues in-flight weather advisories designated as Severe Weather Forecasts Alerts (AWW), Convective SIGMETs (WST), SIGMETs (WS), Center Weather Advisory (CWA), or AIRMETs (WA). These advisories are issued individually, however, the information contained in them is also included in relevant portions of the Area Forecast (FA). When these advisories are issued subsequent to the FA, they automatically amend appropriate portions of the FA until the FA itself has been amended. In-flight advisories serve to notify en route pilots of the possibility of encountering hazardous flying conditions which may not have been forecast at the time of the preflight briefing. Whether or not the condition described is potentially hazardous to a particular flight is for the pilot to evaluate on the basis of experience and the operational limits of the aircraft.

b. Severe Weather Forecast Alerts (AWW) are preliminary messages issued in order to alert users that a Severe Weather Bulletin (WW) is being issued. These messages define areas of possible severe thunderstorms or tornado activity. The messages are unscheduled and issued as required by the National Severe Storm Forecast Center at Kansas City, Missouri.

c. Convective SIGMETs are issued for the following phenomena:

(1) Tornadoes.

(2) Lines of thunderstorms.

(3) Embedded thunderstorms.

(4) Thunderstorm areas greater than or equal to thunderstorm intensity level 4 with an area coverage of 4/10 (40 percent) or more. (See RADAR WEATHER ECHO INTENSITY LEVELS in Pilot/Controller Glossary.)

(5) Hail greater than or equal to 3/4 inch diameter.

NOTE.— Since thunderstorms are the reason for issuing the convective SIGMET, severe or greater turbulence, severe icing, and low-level wind shear (gust fronts, etc) are implied and will not be specified in the advisory.

d. CONVECTIVE SIGMET BULLETINS:

(1) Three Convective SIGMET bulletins, each covering a specified geographic area, are issued. These areas are the Eastern (E), Central (C), and Western (W) U.S. These bulletins are issued on a scheduled basis, hourly at 55 minutes past the hour (H+55), and as special bulletins on an unscheduled basis. The boundaries that separate the Eastern and Central, and the Central and Western U.S. are 87 and 107 degrees West, respectively. (See following figure for VORs and major locations used as reference points for the In-Flight Weather Advisory messages.)

(2) Each of the Convective SIGMET bulletins will be:

(a) Made up of one or more individually numbered Convective SIGMETs,

(b) Valid for 1 hour, and

(c) Removed from system automatically at 40 minutes past the hour (H+40).

(3) On an hourly basis, an outlook is made for each of the three Convective SIGMET regions. The outlook for a particular region is appended to the Convective SIGMET bulletin for the same region. However, it is not appended to special convective SIGMET's. The outlook is reviewed each hour and revised when necessary. The outlook is a forecast and meteorological discussion for thunderstorm systems that are expected to require Convective SIGMET issuances during a time period 2-6 hours into the future. Furthermore, an outlook will always be made for each of the three regions, even if it is a negative statement.

e. SIGMETs within the conterminous U.S. are issued by the National Aviation Weather Advisory Unit (NAWAU) for the following hazardous weather phenomena:

(1) Severe and extreme turbulence.

(2) Severe icing.

(3) Widespread duststorms, sandstorms, or volcanic ash lowering visibilities to below three miles.

f. Center Weather Advisory: The CWA is an unscheduled inflight, flow control, air traffic, and air crew advisory. By nature of its short lead time, the CWA is not a flight planning product. It is generally a Nowcast for conditions beginning within the next 2 hours. CWAs will be issued:

(1) As a supplement to an existing SIGMET, Convective SIGMET, AIRMET, or Area Forecast (FA).

(2) When an In-flight Advisory has not been issued but observed or expected weather conditions meet SIGMET/AIRMET criteria based on current pilot reports and reinforced by other sources of information about existing meteorological conditions.

(3) When observed or developing weather conditions do not meet SIGMET, Convective SIGMET, or AIRMET criteria, e.g., in terms of intensity or area coverage, but current pilot reports or other weather information sources indicate that existing or anticipated meteorological phenomena will adversely affect the safe flow of air traffic within the air route traffic control center (ARTCC) area of responsibility.

g. AIRMETs within the conterminous U.S. are issued by the NAWAU for the following weather phenomena which are potentially hazardous to aircraft:

(1) Moderate icing.

(2) Moderate turbulence.

(3) Sustained winds of 30 knots or more at the surface.

(4) Widespread area of ceilings less than 1,000 feet and/or visibility less than three miles.

(5) Extensive mountain obscurement.

NOTE— If the above phenomena are adequately forecast in the FA, an AIRMET will not be issued.

h. SIGMETs and AIRMETs are identified by an alphanumeric designator which consists of an alphabetic identifier and issuance number. The first time an advisory is issued for a phenomenon associated with a particular weather system, it will be given the next alphabetic designator in the series, and will be numbered as the first for that designator, e.g., BRAVO 1. Subsequent advisories will retain the same alphabetic designator until the phenomenon ends. In the conterminous U.S., this means that a phenomenon that is assigned an alphabetic designator in one area will retain that designator as it moves within the area or into one or more other areas. Issuances for the same phenomenon will be sequentially numbered, using the same alphabetic designator until the phenomenon no longer exist. Alphabetic designators ALFA—NOVEMBER are used only for SIGMETs, while designators OSCAR—ZULU are used for AIRMETs.

i. Each CWA will have a phenomenon number (1-6) immediately following the ARTCC identifier. This number will be assigned to each meteorologically distinct condition or conditions (e.g., jet stream clear air turbulence or low IFR and icing northwest of a low pressure center) meeting CWA issuance criteria. Following the product type (CWA) a two digit issuance number will be entered starting at midnight local each day. In addition those CWAs based on existing nonconvective SIGMETs/AIRMETs will include the associated alphanumeric designator (e.g. ALPHA 4).

EXAMPLE:
ZKC1 CWA01/ALPHA 4

j. Each AWW is numbered sequentially beginning January 1 of each year.

EXAMPLE:

MKC AWW 161755
WW 279 SEVERE TSTM NY PA NJ 161830Z-170000Z.
AXIS..70 STATUTE MILES EITHER SIDE OF LINE..10W MSS TO 20E ABE.
HAIL SURFACE AND ALOFT..2 INCHES. SURFACE WIND GUSTS..65 KNOTS.
MAX TOPS TO 540. MEAN WIND VECTOR 19020.
REPLACES WW 278..OH PA NY

Status reports are issued as needed on Severe Weather Watch Bulletins to show progress of storms and to delineate areas no longer under the threat of severe storm activity. Cancellation bulletins are issued when it becomes evident that no severe weather will develop or that storms have subsided and are no longer severe. *(See Figure 6-1.)*

505. CATEGORICAL OUTLOOKS

a. Categorical outlook terms, describing general ceiling and visibility conditions for advanced planning purposes, are defined as follows:

(1) **LIFR (Low IFR)** — Ceiling less than 500 feet and/or visibility less than 1 mile.

(2) **IFR** — Ceiling 500 to less than 1,000 feet and/or visibility 1 to less than 3 miles.

(3) **MVFR (Marginal VFR)** — Ceiling 1,000 to 3,000 feet and/or visibility 3 to 5 miles inclusive.

(4) **VFR** — Ceiling greater than 3,000 feet and visibility greater than 5 miles.

b. The cause of LIFR, IFR, or MVFR is indicated by either ceiling or visibility restrictions or both. The contraction "CIG" and/or weather and obstruction to vision symbols are used. If winds or gusts of 25 knots or greater are forecast for the outlook period, the word "WIND" is also included for all categories, including VFR.

EXAMPLE:
LIFR CIG — Low IFR due to low ceiling.

EXAMPLE:
IFR F — IFR due to visibility restricted by fog.

EXAMPLE:
MVFR CIG H K — Marginal VFR due both to ceiling and to visibility restricted by haze and smoke.

EXAMPLE:
IFR CIG R WIND — IFR due both to low ceiling and to visibility restricted by rain: wind expected to be 25 knots or greater.

506. PILOTS AUTOMATIC TELEPHONE WEATHER ANSWERING SERVICE (PATWAS) AND TELEPHONE INFORMATION BRIEFING SERVICE (TIBS)

a. PATWAS is provided by non automated flight service stations. PATWAS is a continuous recording of meteorological and aeronautical information which is available at selected locations by telephone. Normally the recording contains a summary of data for an area within 50NM of the parent station; however, at some locations route information similar to that available on the Transcribed Weather Broadcast (TWEB) is included.

b. PATWAS is not intended to substitute for specialist provided preflight briefings except for local flights. It is, however, recommended for use as a preliminary briefing, and often will be valuable in helping you to make a "go or no go" decision.

c. TIBS is provided by Automated Flight Service Stations (AFSS) and provides continuous telephone recordings of meteorological and/or aeronautical information. Specifically, TIBS provides area and/or route briefings, airspace procedures and special announcements (if applicable) concerning aviation interests.

d. Depending on user demand, other items may be provided; i.e., surface observations, terminal forecasts, winds/temperatures aloft forecasts, etc. A touch-tone telephone is necessary to fully utilize the TIBS program.

e. Pilots are encouraged to avail themselves of this service. PATWAS and TIBS locations are found in the Airport/Facility Directory under the FSS and National Weather Service Telephone Numbers section.

507. TRANSCRIBED WEATHER BROADCAST (TWEB)

a. Equipment is provided at selected FSSs by which meteorological and aeronautical data are recorded on tapes and broadcast continuously over selected low-frequency (190-535 kHz) navigational aids (L/MF range or H facility) and/or VORs. Broadcasts are made from a series of individual tape recordings, and changes, as they occur, are transcribed onto the tapes. The information provided varies depending on the type equipment available. Generally the broadcast contains route oriented data with specially prepared NWS forecasts, In-flight Advisories and winds aloft, plus preselected current information such as weather reports, NOTAMs and special notices. In some locations, the information is broadcast over the local VOR and is limited to such items as the hourly weather for the parent station and up to 5 immediately adjacent stations, local NOTAM information, terminal forecast (FT) for the parent station, adverse conditions extracted from In-flight Advisories and other potentially hazardous conditions. At selected locations telephone access to the TWEB has been provided (TEL-TWEB). Telephone numbers for this service are found in the FSS and National Weather Service Telephone Numbers section of the Airport/Facility Directory. These broadcasts are made available primarily for preflight and in-flight planning, and as such, should not be considered as a substitute for specialist provided preflight briefings except for local flights.

508. IN-FLIGHT WEATHER BROADCASTS

a. WEATHER ADVISORY BROADCASTS - FAA FSSs broadcast Severe Weather Forecast Alerts (AWW), Convective SIGMETs, SIGMETs, CWAs, and AIRMETs during their valid period when they pertain to the area within 150 NM of the FSS or a broadcast facility controlled by the FSS as follows:

(1) Severe Weather Forecast Alerts (AWW) and Convective SIGMET - Upon receipt and at 15-minute intervals H+00, H+15, H+30, and H+45 for the first hour after issuance.

EXAMPLE:

AVIATION BROADCAST, WEATHER ADVISORY, SEVERE WEATHER FORECAST ALERT OR CONVECTIVE SIGMET (IDENTIFICATION) (TEXT OF ADVISORY).

(2) SIGMETs, CWAs, and AIRMETs - Upon receipt and at 30-minute intervals at H+15 and H+45 for the first hour after issuance.

EXAMPLE:

AVIATION BROADCAST, WEATHER ADVISORY, (AREA OR ARTCC IDENTIFICATION) SIGMET, CWA, OR AIRMET (IDENTIFICATION) (TEXT OF ADVISORY).

(3) Thereafter, a summarized alert notice will be broadcast at H+15 and H+45 during the valid period of the advisories.

EXAMPLE:

AVIATION BROADCAST, WEATHER ADVISORY, A (SEVERE WEATHER FORECAST ALERT) (CONVECTIVE SIGMET) (SIGMET) (CWA) OR (AIRMET) IS CURRENT FOR (DESCRIPTION OF WEATHER) (AREA AFFECTED).

(4) Pilots, upon hearing the alert notice, if they have not received the advisory or are in doubt, should contact the nearest FSS and ascertain whether the advisory is pertinent to their flights.

b. ARTCCs broadcast a Severe Weather Forecast Alert (AWW), Convective SIGMET, SIGMET, or CWA alert once on all frequencies, except emergency, when any part of the area described is within 150 miles of the airspace under their jurisdiction. These broadcasts contain SIGMET or CWA (Identification) and a brief description of the weather activity and general area affected.

EXAMPLE:

ATTENTION ALL AIRCRAFT, SIGMET DELTA THREE, FROM MYTON TO TUBA CITY TO MILFORD, SEVERE TURBULENCE, AND SEVERE CLEAR ICING BELOW ONE ZERO THOUSAND FEET. EXPECTED TO CONTINUE BEYOND ZERO THREE ZERO ZERO ZULU.

EXAMPLE:

ATTENTION ALL AIRCRAFT, CONVECTIVE SIGMET TWO SEVEN EASTERN. FROM THE VICINITY OF ELMIRA TO PHILLIPSBURG. SCATTERED EMBEDDED THUNDERSTORMS MOVING EAST AT ONE ZERO KNOTS. A FEW INTENSE LEVEL FIVE CELLS, MAXIMUM TOPS FOUR FIVE ZERO.

EXAMPLE:

ATTENTION ALL AIRCRAFT, KANSAS CITY CENTER WEATHER ADVISORY ONE ZERO THREE. NUMEROUS REPORTS OF MODERATE TO SEVERE ICING FROM EIGHT TO NINER THOUSAND FEET IN A THREE ZERO MILE RADIUR OF ST. LOUIS. LIGHT OR NEGATIVE ICING REPORTED FROM FOUR THOUSAND TO ONE TWO THOUSAND FEET REMAINDER OF KANSAS CITY CENTER AREA.

NOTE.— Terminal control facilities have the option to limit the AWW, Convective SIGMET, SIGMET, or CWA broadcast as follows: local control and approach control positions may opt to broadcast SIGMET or CWA alerts only when any part of the area described is within 50 miles of the airspace under their jurisdiction.

c. HAZARDOUS IN-FLIGHT WEATHER ADVISORY SERVICE (HIWAS) - This is a continuous broadcast of in-flight weather advisories including summarized AWW, SIGMETs, Convective SIGMETs, CWAs, AIRMETs and urgent PIREPs. HIWAS has been adopted as a national program and will be implemented throughout the conterminous U.S. as resources permit. In those areas where HIWAS is commissioned, ARTCC, Terminal ATC and

FSS facilities have discontinued the broadcast of in-flight advisories as described in the preceding paragraph. HIWAS is an additional source of hazardous weather information which makes these data available on a continuous basis. It is not, however, a replacement for preflight or in-flight briefings or real-time weather updates from Flight Watch (EFAS). As HIWAS is implemented in individual center areas, the commissioning will be advertised in the Notices to Airmen (Class II) Publication.

(1) Where HIWAS Has Been Implemented - A HIWAS alert will be broadcast on all except emergency frequencies once upon receipt by ARTCC and terminal facilities which will include an alert announcement, frequency instruction, number, and type of advisory updated, e.g., AWW, SIGMET, Convective SIGMET, or CWA.

EXAMPLE:

ATTENTION ALL AIRCRAFT, MONITOR HIWAS OR CONTACT A FLIGHT SERVICE STATION ON FREQUENCY ONE TWO TWO POINT ZERO OR ONE TWO TWO POINT TWO FOR NEW CONVECTIVE SIGMET (IDENTIFICATION) INFORMATION.

(2) In HIWAS ARTCC Areas - FSSs will broadcast a HIWAS update announcement once on all except emergency frequencies upon completion of recording an update to the HIWAS broadcast. Included in the broadcast will be the type of advisory updated, e.g., AWW, SIGMET, convective SIGMET, CWA, ect.

EXAMPLE:

ATTENTION ALL AIRCRAFT, MONITOR HIWAS OR CONTACT FLIGHT WATCH OR FLIGHT SERVICE FOR NEW CONVECTIVE SIGMET INFORMATION.

d. UNSCHEDULED BROADCASTS - These broadcasts are made by FSSs on VOR and selected VHF frequencies upon receipt of special weather reports, PIREPs, NOTAMs and other information considered necessary to enhance safety and efficiency of flight. These broadcasts will be made at random times and will begin with the announcement "Aviation Broadcast" followed by identification of the data.

EXAMPLE:

AVIATION BROADCAST, SPECIAL WEATHER REPORT, (Notice to Airmen, Pilot Report, etc.) (location name twice) THREE SEVEN (past the hour) OBSERVATION...etc.

e. ALASKAN SCHEDULED BROADCASTS - Selected FSSs in Alaska having voice capability on radio ranges (VOR) or radio beacons (NDB) broadcast weather reports and Notice to Airmen information at 15 minutes past each hour from reporting points within approximately 150 miles from the broadcast station.

509. WEATHER OBSERVING PROGRAMS

a. Manual Observations - Surface weather observations are taken at more than 600 locations in the United States. With only a few exceptions, these stations are located at airport sites and most are manned by FAA or NWS personnel who manually observe, perform calculations, and enter the observation into the distribution system. The format and coding of these observations are contained in paragraph 528.

b. Automated Weather Observing System (AWOS)

(1) Automated weather reporting systems are now being installed at several airports. These systems consist of various sensors, a processor, a voice synthesizer, and transmitter to relay local real-time weather data directly to the pilot.

(2) Generically referred to as AWOS (Automated Weather Observing System), these real-time systems are operationally classified into three basic levels: AWOS-1, AWOS-2, and AWOS-3. AWOS-1 reports altimeter setting and wind data, and usually temperature, dewpoint, and density altitude. AWOS-2, when approved for operational use, will provide the information provided by

AWOS-1, plus visibility. AWOS-3, when approved for operational use, will provide the information provided by AWOS-1, plus visibility and cloud/ceiling data.

(3) The information is transmitted over a radio frequency or the voice portion of a local NAVAID. AWOS transmissions are receivable within 25 NM of the AWOS site, at or above 3000 feet AGL. In many cases, AWOS signals are receivable on the surface of the airport. Most devices automatically transmit a 20 to 30 second weather message once each minute. Pilots should monitor the designated frequency for the automated weather message. There is no two-way communication capability. Most AWOS weather data can be accessed via telephone.

(4) Selected individual systems may be incorporated into nationwide data collection and dissemination networks in the future. AWOS information (system level, frequency, phone number, etc.) concerning specific locations, will be published as they become operational, in the Airport/Facility Directory, and where applicable, on published Instrument Approach Procedures.

c. Automatic Meteorological Observing Stations (AMOS)

(1) Full parameter AMOS facilities provide data for the basic weather program at remote, unstaffed, or part-time staffed locations at approximately ninety locations in the United States. They report temperature, dew point, wind, pressure, and precipitation (liquid) amount. At staffed AMOS locations, an observer may manually add visually observed and manually calculated elements to the automatic reports. The elements manually added are sky condition, visibility, weather, obstructions to vision, and sea level pressure. The content and format of AMOS reports is the same as the manually observed reports, except the acronym "AMOS" or "RAMOS" (for Remote Automatic Meteorological Observing Station) will be the first item of the report.

(2) Partial parameter AMOS stations only report some of the elements contained in the full parameter locations, normally wind. These observations are not normally disseminated through aviation weather circuits.

d. Automated Weather Observing System (AWOS)

(1) Automated weather reporting systems are increasingly being installed at airports. These systems consist of various sensors, a processor, a computer-generated voice subsystem, and a transmitter to broadcast local, minute-by-minute weather data directly to the pilot.

(2) Referred to as AWOS (Automated Weather Observing System), these real-time systems are operationally classified into three basic levels: AWOS-1, AWOS-2, and AWOS-3. AWOS-1 usually reports altimeter setting, wind data, temperature, dewpoint, and density altitude. AWOS-2 provides the information provided by AWOS-1, plus visibility. AWOS-3 provides the information provided by AWOS-1, plus visibility. AWOS-3 provides the information provided by AWOS-2, plus cloud ceiling data.

(3) The information is transmitted over a discrete radio frequency or the voice portion of a local NAVAID. AWOS transmissions are receivable within 25 NM of the AWOS site, at or above 3000 feet AGL. In many cases, AWOS signals may be received on the surface of the airport. The system transmits a 20 to 30 second weather message updated each minute. Pilots should monitor the designated frequency for the automated weather broadcast. A description of the broadcast is contained in paragraph. There is no two-way communication capability. Most AWOS sites also have a dial-up capability so that the minute-by-minute weather messages can be accessed via telephone.

(4) AWOS information (system level, frequency, phone number, etc.) concerning specific locations is published as the systems become operational, in the Airport/Facility Directory, and where applicable, on published Instrument Approach Procedures. Selected individual systems may be incorporated into nationwide data collection and dissemination networks in the future.

e. Automated Weather Observing System (AWOS) Broadcasts

Computer-generated voice is used in Automated Weather Observing Systems (AWOS) to automate the broadcast of the minute-by-minute weather observations. In addition, some systems are configured to permit the addition of an operator-generated voice message (e.g., weather remark) following the automated parameters. The phraseology used generally follows that used for other weather broadcasts. Following are explanations and examples of the exceptions.

(1) *Location and Time.* The location/name and the phrase "AUTOMATED WEATHER OBSERVATION" followed by the time are announced.

(a) If the airport's specific location is included in the airport's name, the airport's name is announced.

EXAMPLES:

"BREMERTON NATIONAL AIRPORT AUTOMATED WEATHER-OBSERVATION 1456 ZULU.":

"RAVENSWOOD JACKSON COUNTY AIRPORT AUTOMATED-WEATHEROBSERVATION 1456 ZULU."

(b) If the airport's specific location is *not* included in the airport's name, the location is announced followed by the airport's name.

EXAMPLES:

"SAULT STE MARIE, CHIPPEWA COUNTYINTERNATIONAL AIRPORT AUTOMATED WEATHER OBSERVATION.":

"SANDUSKY COWLEY FIELD AUTOMATED WEATHEROBSERVATION."

The word "TEST" is added following "OBSERVATION" when the system is not in commissioned status.

EXAMPLE:

"BREMERTON NATIONAL AIRPORT AUTOMATED WEATHEROB-SERVATION TEST 1456 ZULU."

The phrase "TEMPORARILY INOPERATIVE" is added when the system is inoperative.

EXAMPLE:

"BREMERTON NATIONAL AIRPORT AUTOMATED WEATHEROB-SERVING SYSTEM TEMPORARILY INOPERATAIVE."

(2) *Ceiling and Sky Cover.*

(a) Ceiling is announced as either "CEILING" or "INDEFINITE CEIL-ING". The phrases "MEASURED CEILING" and "ESTIMATED CEIL-ING" are used only when the ceiling is a manual input in remarks (see example in paragraph e.(4)(b). below). With the exception of in-definite ceilings, all automated ceiling heights are measured.

EXAMPLES:

"BREMERTON NATIONAL AIRPORT AUTOMATED WEATHEROB-SERVATION 1456 ZULU CEILING TWO THOUSAND OVER-CAST.":

"BREMERTON NATIONAL AIRPORT AUTOMATED WEATHER-OBSERVATION 1456 ZULU INDEFINITE CEILING TWO HUN-DRED, SKY OBSCURED."

(b) The word "CLEAR" is not used in AWOS due to limitations in the height ranges of the sensors used. No clouds detected is announced as no clouds below XXX (where XXX is the range limit of the sensor).

EXAMPLE:

"NO CLOUDS BELOW ONE TWO THOUSAND."

(c) A sensor for determining ceiling and sky cover is not in-cluded in some AWOS. In these systems, ceiling and sky cover are not announced. "SKY CONDITION MISSING" is announced only if the system is configured with a ceilometer and the ceiling and sky cover information is not avaialble.

(3) *Visibility.*

(a) The lowest reportable visibility value in AWOS is "less than 1/4". It is announced as "VISIBILITY LESS THAN ONE QUART-ER."

(b) A sensor for determining visibility is not included in some AWOS. In these systems, visibility is not announced. "VISIBILITY MISSING" is announced only if the system is configured with visibility sensor and visibility information is not available.

(4) *Weather.* Some AWOS are configured to determine the oc-currence of precipitation. However, the type and intensity are not always determined. In these systems, the word "PRECIPITATION" is announced if precipitation is occurring but the type and inten-sity are not determined.

(5) *Remarks.* If remarks are included in the observation, the word "REMARKS" is announced following the altimeter setting.

(a) If the remark is a manual input, the word "OBSERVER" pre-cedes the remark.

EXAMPLE:

"REMARKS . . . OBSERVER VISIBILITY TWO.":

(b) If an automated parameter is "missing", and a manual input for that parameter is available and added in "REMARKS", the automated parameter is not announced and the manual input is announced in "REMARKS". For example, a report with the auto-mated temperature and dew point "missing", but determined by an observer, would be announced as follows:

EXAMPLE:

"NO CLOUDS BELOW ONE TWO THOUSAND . . . VISIBILITY FIVE . . . WIND, TWO THREE ZERO AT TWO FIVE, PEAK GUSTS THREE FIVE . . . ALTIMETER, TWO NINER NINER TWO . . . REMARKS . . . OBSERVER TEMPERATURE TWO, DEW POINT MINUS FIVE."

(c) If an automated parameter is "missing" and no manual input for that parameter is available, the parameter is announced as "MISSING." For example, a report with the dew point "missing", and no manual input available, would be announced as follows:

EXAMPLE:

"CEILING ONE THOUSAND OVERCAST . . . VISIBILITY . . . THREE . . . PRECIPITATION . . . TEMPERATURE THREE ZERO, DEW POINT MISSING . . . WIND CALM . . . ALTIMETER THREE ZERO ZERO ONE."

(d) "REMARKS" are announced in the following order of priority:

1. Automated "REMARKS":
   i Density Altitude
   ii Variable Visibility
   iii Variable Wind Direction

2. Manual Input "REMARKS." As a general rule, the remarks are announced in the same order as the parameters appear in the basic text of the observation, i.e., SKY CONDITION, VISI-BILITY, WEATHER AND OBSTRUCTIONS TO VISION, TEM-PERATURE, DEW POINT, WIND, AND ALTIMETER SETTING.

EXAMPLE:

"REMARKS . . . DENSITY ALTITUDE, TWO THOUSAND FIVE-HUNDRED . . . VISIBILITY VARIABLE BETWEEN ONE AND TWO . . . WIND DIRECTION VARIABLE BETWEEN TWO FOUR ZERO AND THREE ONE ZERO . . . OBSERVER CEILING ESTI-MATED TWO THOUSAND BROKEN . . . OBSERVER TEMPERA-TURE TWO, DEW POINT MINUS FIVE."

510. WEATHER RADAR SERVICES

(See Figure 6-2.)

a. The National Weather Service operates a network of 56 radar sites for detecting coverage, intensity, and movement of precipitation. The network is supplemented by FAA and DOD radar sites in the western sections of the country. Another 72 local warning radars augment the network by operating on an as needed basis to support warning and forecast programs.

b. Scheduled radar observations are taken hourly and transmitted in alpha-numeric format on weather telecommunications circuits for flight planning purposes. Under certain conditions special radar reports are issued in addition to the hourly transmittals. Data contained in the reports is also collected by the National Meteorological Center and used to prepare hourly national radar summary charts for dissemination on facsimile circuits.

c. All En Route Flight Advisory Service facilities and many Flight Service Stations have equipment to directly access the radar displays from the individual weather radar sites. Specialists at these locations are trained to interpret the display for pilot briefing and in-fight advisory services. The Center Weather Service Units located in the Air Route Traffic Control Centers also have access to weather radar displays and provide support to all air traffic facilities within their center's area.

d. A clear radar display (no echoes) does not mean that there is no significantweather within the coverage of the radar site. Clouds and fog are not detected by the radar, however, when echoes are present, turbulence can be implied by the intensity of the precipitation and icing is implied by the presence of the precipitation at temperatures at or below zero degrees Celsius. Used in conjunction with other weather products, the radar provides invaluable information for weather avoidance and flight planning.

e. Additional information on weather radar products and services can be found in Advisory Circular 00-45, AVIATION WEATHER SERVICES. Also, see Glossary, Radar Weather Echo Intensity Levels and paragraph 526, Thunderstorms.

511. ATC IN-FLIGHT WEATHER AVOIDANCE ASSISTANCE

a. ATC Radar Weather Display

(1) Areas of radar weather clutter result from rain or moisture. Radars cannot detect turbulence. The determination of the intensity of the weather displayed is based on its precipitation density. Generally, the turbulence associated with a very heavy rate of rainfall will normally be more severe than any associated with a very light rainfall rate.

(2) ARTCCs are phasing in computer generated digitized radar displays to replace broadband radar display. This new system, known as Narrowband Radar, provides the controller with two distinct levels of weather intensity by assigning radar display symbols for specific precipitation densities measured by the narrowband system.

b. Weather Avoidance Assistance

(1) To the extent possible, controllers will issue pertinent information on weather or chaff areas and assist pilots in avoiding such areas when requested. Pilots should respond to a weather advisory by either acknowledging the advisory or by acknowledging the advisory and requesting an alternative course of action as follows:

(a) Request to deviate off course by stating the number of miles and the direction of the requested deviation. In this case, when the requested deviation is approved, the pilot is expected to provide his own navigation, maintain the altitude assigned by ATC and to remain within the specified mileage of his original course.

(b) Request a new route to avoid the affected area.

(c) Request a change of altitude.

(d) Request radar vectors around the affected areas.

(2) For obvious reasons of safety, an IFR pilot must not deviate from the course or altitude or flight level without a proper ATC clearance. When weather conditions encountered are so severe that an immediate deviation is determined to be necessary and time will not permit approval by ATC, the pilot's emergency authority may be exercised.

(3) When the pilot requests clearance for a route deviation or for an ATC radar vector, the controller must evaluate the air traffic picture in the affected area, and coordinate with other controllers (if ATC jurisdictional boundaries may be crossed) before replying to the request.

(4) It should be remembered that the controller's primary function is to provide safe separation between aircraft. Any additional service, such as weather avoidance assistance, can only be provided to the extent that it does not derogate the primary function. It's also worth noting that the separation workload is generally greater than normal when weather disrupts the usual flow of traffic. ATC radar limitations and frequency congestion may also be a factor in limiting the controller's capability to provide additional service.

(5) It is very important, therefore, that the request for deviation or radar vector be forwarded to ATC as far in advance as possible. Delay in submitting it may delay or even preclude ATC approval or require that additional restrictions be placed on the clearance. Insofar as possible the following information should be furnished to ATC when requesting clearance to detour around weather activity:

(a) Proposed point where detour will commence.

(b) Proposed route and extent of detour (direction and distance).

(c) Point where original route will be resumed.

(d) Flight conditions (IFR or VFR).

(e) Any further deviation that may become necessary as the flight progresses.

(f) Advise if the aircraft is equipped with functioning airborne radar.

(6) To a large degree, the assistance that might be rendered by ATC will depend upon the weather information available to controllers. Due to the extremely transitory nature of severe weather situations, the controller's weather information may be of only limited value if based on weather observed on radar only. Frequent updates by pilots giving specific information as to the area affected, altitudes intensity and nature of the severe weather can be of considerable value. Such reports are relayed by radio or phone to other pilots and controllers and also receive widespread teletypewriter dissemination.

(7) Obtaining IFR clearance or an ATC radar vector to circumnavigate severe weather can often be accommodated more readily in the en route areas away from terminals because there is usually less congestion and, therefore, offer greater freedom of action. In terminal areas, the problem is more acute because of traffic density, ATC coordination requirements, complex departure and arrival routes, adjacent airports, etc. As a consequence, controllers are less likely to be able to accommodate all requests for weather detours in a terminal area or be in a position to volunteer such routing to the pilot. Nevertheless, pilots should not hesitate to advise controllers of any observed severe weather and should specifically advise controllers if they desire circumnavigation of observed weather.

512. RUNWAY VISUAL RANGE (RVR)

a. RVR visibility values are measured by transmissometers mounted on towers along the runway. A full RVR system consists of:

(1) Transmissometer projector and related items.

(2) Transmissometer receiver (detector) and related items.

(3) Analogue recorder.

(4) Signal data converter and related items.

(5) Remote digital or remote display programmer.

b. The transmissometer projector and receiver are mounted on towers either 250 or 500 feet apart. A known intensity of light is emitted from the projector and is measured by the receiver. Any obscuring matter such as rain, snow, dust, fog, haze or smoke reduces the light intensity arriving at the receiver. The resultant intensity measurement is then converted to an RVR value by the signal data converter. These values are displayed by readout equipment in the associated air traffic facility and updated approximately once every minute for controller issuance to pilots.

c. The signal data converter receives information on the high intensity runway edge light setting in use (step 3, 4, or 5); transmission values from the transmissometer, and the sensing of day or night conditions. From the three data sources, the system will compute appropriate RVR values. Due to variable conditions, the reported RVR values may deviate somewhat from the true observed visual range due to the slant range consideration, brief time delays between the observed RVR conditions and the time they are transmitted to the pilot, and rapidly changing visibility conditions.

d. An RVR transmissometer established on a 500 foot baseline provides digital readouts to a minimum of 1,000 feet. A system established on a 250 foot baseline provides digital readouts to a minimum of 600 feet, which are displayed in 200 foot increments to 3000 feet and in 500 foot increments from 3,000 feet to a maximum value of 6,000 feet.

e. RVR values for Category IIIa operations extend down to 700 feet RVR; however, only 600 and 800 feet are reportable RVR increments. The 800 RVR reportable value covers a range of 701 feet to 900 feet and is therefore a valid minimum indication of Category IIIa operations.

f. Approach categories with the corresponding minimum RVR values are as follows:

Category	Visibility (RVR)
Nonprecision	2400 feet
Category I	1800 feet
Category II	1200 feet
Category IIIa	700 feet
Category IIIb	150 feet
Category IIIc	0 feet

g. Ten minute maximum and minimum RVR values for the designated RVR runway are reported in the remarks section of the aviation weather report when the prevailing visibility is less than one mile and/or the RVR is 6,000 feet or less. ATCTs report RVR when the prevailing visibility is 1 mile or less and/or the RVR is 6,000 feet or less.

h. Details on the requirements for the operational use of RVR are contained in FAA ADVISORY CIRCULAR—97-1, "RUNWAY VISUAL RANGE." Pilots are responsible for compliance with minimums prescribed for their class of operations in appropriate FARs and/or operations specifications.

513. REPORTING OF CLOUD HEIGHTS

a. Ceiling, by definition in FARs, and as used in Aviation Weather Reports and Forecasts, is the height *above ground (or water) level* of the lowest layer of clouds or obscuring phenomenon that is reported as "broken", "overcast", or "obscuration" and not classified as "thin" or "partial". For example, a forecast which reads "CIGS WILL BE GENLY 1 TO 2 THSD FEET" refers to heights *above ground level* (AGL). A forecast which reads "BRKN TO OVC LYRS AT 8 TO 12 THSD MSL" states that the height is *above mean sea level* (MSL).

b. Pilots usually report height values above MSL, since they determine heights by the altimeter. This is taken in account when disseminating and otherwise applying information received from pilots. ("Ceilings" heights are always above ground level.) In reports disseminated as PIREPs, height references are given the same as received from pilots, that is, above MSL. In the following example of an hourly observation, a pilot report of the heights of the bases and tops of an overcast layer in the terminal area is converted by the reporting station to reflect AGL to report the base of the overcast layer (E12). The pilot's reported top of the overcast layer (23) is not converted to AGL and is shown in the remarks section (last item) of the weather reporting (top ovc 23).

EXAMPLE:

E12 OVC 2FK 132/49/47/0000/002/TOP OVC 23

c. In aviation forecasts (Terminal, Area, or In-flight Advisories) ceilings are denoted by the prefix "C" when used with sky cover symbols as in "LWRG to C5 OVC-1TRW", or by the contraction "CIG" before, or the contraction "AGL" after, the forecast cloud height value. When the cloud base is given in height above MSL, it is so indicated by the contraction "MSL" or "ASL" following the height value. The heights of clouds tops, freezing level. icing and turbulence are always given in heights above ASL or MSL.

514. REPORTING PREVAILING VISIBILITY

a. Surface (horizontal) visibility is reported in weather observations in terms of statute miles and increments thereof (e.g., 1/16, 1/8, 1/4, 1/2, 3/4, 1, 1 1/4, etc.). Visibility is determined through the ability to see and identify preselected and prominent objects at a known distance from the usual point of observation. Visibilities which are determined to be less than 7 miles identify the obscuring atmospheric condition, (e.g., fog, haze, smoke, etc., or combinations thereof).

b. Prevailing visibility is the greatest visibility equalled or exceeded throughout at least half of the horizon circle, which need not be continuous. Segments of the horizon circle which may have a significantly lower visibility may be reported in the remarks section of the weather report (i.e., the southeastern quadrant of the horizon circle may be determined to be 2 miles in fog while the remaining quadrants are determined to be 3 miles in fog).

c. When the prevailing visibility at the usual point of observation, or at the tower level, is less than 4 miles, certificated tower personnel will take visibility observations in addition to those taken at the usual point of observation. The lower of these two values will be used as the prevailing visibility for aircraft operations.

515. ESTIMATING INTENSITY OF PRECIPITATION

a. **LIGHT** — Scattered drops or flakes that do not completely wet or cover an exposed surface, regardless of duration, to 0.10 inch per hour; maximum 0.01 inch in 6 minutes.

b. **MODERATE** — .11 inch to 0.30 inch per hour; more than 0.01 inch to 0.03 inch in 6 minutes.

c. **HEAVY** — More than 0.30 inch per hour; more than 0.03 inch in 6 minutes.

516. ESTIMATING INTENSITY OF DRIZZLE

a. **LIGHT** — Scattered drops that do not completely wet surface, regardless of duration, to 0.01 inch per hour.

b. **MODERATE** — More than 0.01 inch to 0.02 inch per hour.

c. **HEAVY** — More than 0.02 inch per hour.

517. ESTIMATING INTENSITY OF SNOW

a. **LIGHT** — Visibility 5/8 statute mile or more.

b. **MODERATE** — Visibility less than 5/8 statute mile but not less than 5/16 statute mile.

c. **HEAVY** — Visibility less than 5/16 statute mile.

518—519. RESERVED

520. PILOT WEATHER REPORTS (PIREP)

a. FAA air traffic facilities are required to solicit PIREPs when the following conditions are reported or forecast: Ceilings at or below 5,000 feet; Visibility at or below 5 miles; Thunderstorms and related phenomena; Icing of light degree or greater; Turbulence of moderate degree or greater; and Windshear.

b. Pilots are urged to cooperate and promptly volunteer reports of these conditions and other atmospheric data such as: Cloud bases, tops and layers; Flight visibility; Precipitation; Visibility restrictions such as haze, smoke and dust; Wind at altitude; and Temperature aloft.

c. PIREPs should be given to the ground facility with which communications are established, i.e., EFAS, FSS, ARTCC or terminal ATC. One of the primary duties of EFAS facilities, radio call "FLIGHT WATCH", is to serve as a collection point for the exchange of PIREPs with en route aircraft.

d. If pilots are not able to make PIREPs by radio, reporting upon landing of the in-flight conditions encountered to the nearest FSS or Weather Service Office will be helpful. Some of the uses made of the reports are:

(1) The ATCT uses the reports to expedite the flow of air traffic in the vicinity of the field and for hazardous weather avoidance procedures.

(2) The FSS uses the reports to brief other pilots, to provide in-flight advisories, and weather avoidance information to en route aircraft.

(3) The ARTCC uses the reports to expedite the flow of en route traffic, to determine most favorable altitudes, and to issue hazardous weather information within the center's area.

(4) The NWS uses the reports to verify or amend conditions contained in aviation forecast and advisories. In some cases, pilot reports of hazardous conditions are the triggering mechanism for the issuance of advisories. They also use the reports for pilot weather briefings.

(5) The NWS, other government organizations, the military, and private industry groups use PIREPs for research activities in the study of meteorological phenomena.

(6) All air traffic facilities and the NWS forward the reports received from pilots into the weather distribution system to assure the information is made available to all pilots and other interested parties.

e. The FAA, NWS, and other organizations that enter PIREPs into the weather reporting system use the format listed in *Table 6-1*. Items 1 through 6 are included in all transmitted PIREPs along with one or more of items 7 through 13. Although the PIREP should be as complete and concise as possible, pilots should not be overly concerned with strict format or phraseology. The important thing is that the information is relayed so other pilots may benefit from your observation. If a portion of the report needs clarification, the ground station will request the information.

Completed PIREPs will be transmitted to weather circuits as in the following examples:

CMH UA /OV APE 230010/TM 1516/FL085/TP BE80/SK BKN 065/WX FV03 H K/TA 20/TB LGT

Translation: One zero miles southwest of Appleton VOR; Time 1516 UTC; Altitude eight thousand five hundred; Aircraft type BE80; Top of the broken cloud layer is six thousand five hundred; Flight visibility 3 miles with haze and smoke; Air Temperature 20 degrees Celsius; Light turbulence.

CRW UV /OV BKW 360015-CRW/TM 1815/FL120//TP BE99/SK OVC/WX R/TA -08 /WV 290030/TB LGT-MDT/IC LGT RIME/RM MDT MXD ICG DURGC ROA NWBND FL080-100 1750

Translation: From 15 miles north of Beckley VOR to Charleston VOR; Time 1815 UTC; Altitude 12,000 feet; Type aircraft, BE-99; In clouds; Rain; Temperature -08 Celsius; Wind 290 degrees magnetic at 30 knots; Light to moderate turbulence; Light Rime Icing; Encountered moderate mixed icing during climb northwestbound from Roanoke Va between 8000 and 10,000 feet at 1750 UTC.

521. PIREPS RELATING TO AIRFRAME ICING

a. The effects of ice on aircraft are cumulative — Thrust is reduced, Drag increases, Lift lessens, Weight increases. The results are an increase in stall speed and a deterioration of aircraft performance. In extreme cases, 2 to 3 inches of ice can form on the leading edge of the airfoil in less than 5 minutes. It takes but 1/2 inch of ice to reduce the lifting power of some aircraft by 50 percent and increases the frictional drag by an equal percentage.

b. A pilot can expect icing when flying in visible precipitation such as rain or cloud droplets, and the temperature is 0 degrees Celsius or colder. When icing is detected, a pilot should do one of two things (particularly if the aircraft is not equipped with deicing equipment), he should get out of the area of precipitation or go to an altitude where the temperature is above freezing. This "warmer" altitude may not always be a lower altitude. Proper preflight action includes obtaining information on the freezing level and the above-freezing levels in precipitation areas. Report icing to ATC/FSS, and if operating IFR, request new routing or altitude if icing will be a hazard. Be sure to give type of aircraft to ATC when reporting icing. The following describes how to report icing conditions.

(1) **Trace** — Ice becomes perceptible. Rate of accumulation is slightly greater than the rate of sublimation. It is not hazardous

even though deicing/anti-icing equipment is not utilized, unless encountered for an extended period of time (over 1 hour).

(2) **Light** — The rate of accumulation may create a problem if flight is prolonged in this environment (over 1 hour). Occasional use of deicing/anti-icing equipment removes/prevents accumulation. It does not present a problem if the deicing/anti-icing equipment is used.

(3) **Moderate** — The rate of accumulation is such that even short encounters become potentially hazardous and use of deicing/anti-icing equipment or flight diversion is necessary.

(4) **Severe** — The rate of accumulation is such that deicing/anti-icing equipment fails to reduce or control the hazard. Immediate flight diversion is necessary.

EXAMPLE:
Pilot Report: Give Aircraft Identification, Location, Time (UTC), Intensity of Type, Altitude/FL, Aircraft Type, IAS, and Outside Air Temperature.

NOTE 1.—Rime Ice: Rough, milky, opaque ice formed by the instantaneous freezing of small supercooled water droplets

NOTE 2.—Clear Ice: A glossy, clear, or translucent ice formed by the relatively slow freezing of large supercooled water droplets.

NOTE 3.—The Outside Air Temperature should be requested by the FSS/ATC if not included in the PIREP.

522. PIREPS RELATING TO TURBULENCE

a. When encountering turbulence, pilots are urgently requested to report such conditions to ATC as soon as practicable. PIREPs relating to turbulence should state:

(1) Aircraft location.
(2) Time of occurrence in UTC.
(3) Turbulence intensity.
(4) Whether the turbulence occurred in or near clouds.
(5) Aircraft altitude, or Flight Level.
(6) Type of Aircraft.
(7) Duration of turbulence.

EXAMPLE:
OVER OMAHA, 1232Z, MODERATE TURBULENCE IN CLOUDS AT FLIGHT LEVEL THREE ONE ZERO, BOEING 707.

EXAMPLE:
FROM FIVE ZERO MILES SOUTH OF ALBUQUERQUE TO THREE ZERO MILES NORTH OF PHOENIX, 1250Z, OCCASIONAL MODERATE CHOP AT FLIGHT LEVEL THREE THREE ZERO, DC8.

b. Duration and classification of intensity should be made using *Table 6-2:*

523. WIND SHEAR PIREPS

a. Because unexpected changes in wind speed and direction can be hazardous to aircraft operations at low altitudes on approach to and departing from airports, pilots are urged to promptly volunteer reports to controllers of wind shear conditions they encounter. An advance warning of this information will assist other pilots in avoiding or coping with a wind shear on approach or departure.

b. When describing conditions, use of the terms "negative" or "positive" wind shear should be avoided. PIREPs of *"negative wind shear on final,"* intended to describe loss of airspeed and lift, have been interpreted to mean that *no* wind shear was encountered.

The recommended method for wind shear reporting is to state the loss or gain of airspeed and the altitudes at which it was encountered.

EXAMPLE:
DENVER TOWER, CESSNA 1234 ENCOUNTERED WIND SHEAR, LOSS OF 20 KNOTS AT 400 FEET.

EXAMPLE:
TULSA TOWER, AMERICAN 721 ENCOUNTERED WIND SHEAR ON FINAL, GAINED 25 KNOTS BETWEEN 600 AND 400 FEET FOLLOWED BY LOSS OF 40 KNOTS BETWEEN 400 FEET AND SURFACE.

(1) Pilots who are not able to report wind shear in these specific terms are encouraged to make reports in terms of the effect upon their aircraft.

EXAMPLE:
MIAMI TOWER, GULFSTREAM 403 CHARLIE ENCOUNTERED AN ABRUPT WIND SHEAR AT 800 FEET ON FINAL, MAX THRUST REQUIRED.

(2) Pilots using Inertial Navigation Systems should report the wind and altitude both above and below the shear level.

524. CLEAR AIR TURBULENCE (CAT) PIREPS

CAT has become a very serious operational factor to flight operations at all levels and especially to jet traffic flying in excess of 15,000 feet. The best available information on this phenomenon must come from pilots via the PIREP reporting procedures. All pilots encountering CAT conditions are urgently requested to report *time, location* and *intensity* (light, moderate, severe or extreme) of the element to the FAA facility with which they are maintaining radio contact. If time and conditions permit, elements should be reported according to the standards for other PIREPs and position reports. (See PARA—522 - PIREPS RELATING TO TURBULENCE.)

525. MICROBURSTS

(See Figure 6-3.)

a. Relatively recent meteorological studies have confirmed the existence of microburst phenomenon. Microbursts are small-scale intense downdrafts which, on reaching the surface, spread outward in all directions from the downdraft center. This causes the presence of both vertical and horizontal wind shears that can be extremely hazardous to all types and categories of aircraft, especially at low altitudes. Due to their small size, short life-span, and the fact that they can occur over areas without surface precipitation, microbursts are not easily detectable using conventional weather radar or wind shear alert systems.

b. Parent clouds producing microburst activity can be any of the low or middle layer convective cloud types. Note, however, that microbursts commonly occur within the heavy rain portion of thunderstorms, and in much weaker, benign-appearing convective cells that have little or no precipitation reaching the ground.

c. The life cycle of a microburst as it descends in a convective rain shaft is seen in Figure 1. An important consideration for pilots is the fact that the microburst intensifies for about 5 minutes after it strikes the ground.

d. Characteristics of microbursts include:

(1) **Size** — The microburst downdraft is typically less than 1 mile in diameter as it descends from the cloud base to about 1,000 - 3,000 feet above the ground. In the transition zone near the

ground, the downdraft changes to a horizontal outflow that can extend to approximately 2 1/2 miles in diameter.

(2) **Intensity** — The downdrafts can be as strong as 6,000 feet per minute. Horizontal winds near the surface can be as strong as 45 knots resulting in a 90 knot shear (headwind to tailwind change for a traversing aircraft) across the microburst. These strong horizontal winds occur within a few hundred feet of the ground.

(3) **Visual Signs** — Microbursts can be found almost anywhere that there is convective activity. They may be embedded in heavy rain associated with a thunderstorm or in light rain in benign-appearing virga. When there is little or no precipitation at the surface accompanying the microburst, a ring of blowing dust may be the only visual clue of its existence.

(4) **Duration** — An individual microburst will seldom last longer than 15 minutes from the time it strikes the ground until dissipation. The horizontal winds continue to increase during the first 5 minutes with the maximum intensity winds lasting approximately 2- 4- minutes. Sometimes microbursts are concentrated into a line structure and, under these conditions, activity may continue for as long as an hour. Once microburst activity starts, multiple microbursts in the same general area are not uncommon and should be expected.

e. Microburst wind shear may create a severe hazard for aircraft within 1,000 feet of the ground, particularly during the approach to landing and landing and take-off phases. The impact of a microburst on aircraft which have the unfortunate experience of penetrating one is characterized in Figure 2. The aircraft may encounter a headwind (performance increasing), followed by a downdraft and tailwind (both performance decreasing), possibly resulting in terrain impact.

f. Pilots should heed wind shear PIREPS, as a previous pilot's encounter with a microburst may be the only indication received. However, since the wind shear intensifies rapidly in its early stages a PIREP may not indicate the current severity of a microburst. Flight in the vicinity of suspected or reported microburst activity should always be avoided. Should a pilot encounter one, a wind shear PIREP should be made at once.

526. THUNDERSTORMS

a. Turbulence, hail, rain, snow, lightning, sustained updrafts and downdrafts, icing conditions — all are present in thunderstorms. While there is some evidence that maximum turbulence exists at the middle level of a thunderstorm, recent studies show little variation of turbulence intensity with altitude.

b. There is no useful correlation between the external visual appearance of thunderstorms and the severity or amount of turbulence or hail within them. The visible thunderstorm cloud is only a portion of a turbulent system whose updrafts and downdrafts often extend far beyond the visible storm cloud. Severe turbulence can be expected up to 20 miles from severe thunderstorms. This distance decreases to about 10 miles in less severe storms.

c. Weather radar, airborne or ground based, will normally reflect the areas of moderate to heavy precipitation (radar does not detect turbulence). The frequency and severity of turbulence generally increases with the radar reflectivity which is closely associated with the areas of highest liquid water content of the storm. NO FLIGHT PATH THROUGH AN AREA OF STRONG OR VERY STRONG RADAR ECHOS SEPARATED BY 20-30 MILES OR LESS MAY BE CONSIDERED FREE OF SEVERE TURBULENCE.

d. Turbulence beneath a thunderstorm should not be minimized. This is especially true when the relative humidity is low in any layer between the surface and 15,000 feet. Then the lower altitudes may be characterized by strong out-flowing winds and severe turbulence.

e. The probability of lightning strikes occurring to aircraft is greatest when operating at altitudes where temperatures are between minus 5 degrees Celsius and plus 5 degrees Celsius. Lightning can strike aircraft flying in the clear in the vicinity of a thunderstorm.

f. The NWS recognizes only two classes of intensities of thunderstorms as applied to aviation surface weather observations:

(1) Thunderstorm T;

(2) Severe T+

g. NWS radar systems are able to objectively determine radar weather echo intensity levels by use of Video Integrator Processor (VIP) equipment. These thunderstorm intensity levels are on a scale of one to six. (See RADAR WEATHER ECHO INTENSITY LEVELS in the Pilot/Controller Glossary.)

EXAMPLE:

Alert provided by an ATC facility to an aircraft: (aircraft identification) LEVEL FIVE INTENSE WEATHER ECHO BETWEEN TEN O'CLOCK AND TWO O'CLOCK, ONE ZERO MILES MOVING EAST AT TWO ZERO KNOTS, TOP FLIGHT LEVEL THREE NINE ZERO.

EXAMPLE:

Alert provided by a FSS: (aircraft identification) LEVEL FIVE INTENSE WEATHER ECHO TWO ZERO MILES WEST OF ATLANTA VOR TWO FIVE MILES WIDE, MOVING EAST AT TWO ZERO KNOTS, TOPS FLIGHT LEVEL THREE NINE ZERO.

527. THUNDERSTORM FLYING

a. Above all, remember this: never regard any thunderstorm "lightly" even when radar observers report the echoes are of light intensity. Avoiding thunderstorms is the best policy. Following are some Do's and Don'ts of thunderstorm avoidance:

(1) Don't land or takeoff in the face of an approaching thunderstorm. A sudden gust front of low level turbulence could cause loss of control.

(2) Don't attempt to fly under a thunderstorm even if you can see through to the other side. Turbulence and wind shear under the storm could be disastrous.

(3) Don't fly without airborne radar into a cloud mass containing scattered embedded thunderstorms. Scattered thunderstorms not embedded usually can be visually circumnavigated.

(4) Don't trust the visual appearance to be a reliable indicator of the turbulence inside a thunderstorm.

(5) Do avoid by at least 20 miles any thunderstorm identified as severe or giving an intense radar echo. This is especially true under the anvil of a large cumulonimbus.

(6) Do clear the top of a known or suspected severe thunderstorm by at least 1,000 feet altitude for each 10 knots of wind speed at the cloud top. This should exceed the altitude capability of most aircraft.

(7) Do circumnavigate the entire area if the area has 6/10 thunderstorm coverage.

(8) Do remember that vivid and frequent lightning indicates the probability of a severe thunderstorm.

(9) Do regard as extremely hazardous any thunderstorm with tops 35,000 feet or higher whether the top is visually sighted or determined by radar.

b. If you cannot avoid penetrating a thunderstorm, following are some Do's *before* entering the storm:

(1) Tighten your safety belt, put on your shoulder harness if you have one and secure all loose objects.

(2) Plan and hold your course to take you through the storm in a minimum time.

(3) To avoid the most critical icing, establish a penetration altitude below the freezing level or above the level of minus 15 degrees Celsius.

(4) Verify that pitot heat is on and turn on carburetor heat or jet engine anti-ice. Icing can be rapid at any altitude and cause almost instantaneous power failure and/or loss of airspeed indication.

(5) Establish power settings for turbulence penetration airspeed recommended in your aircraft manual.

(6) Turn up cockpit lights to highest intensity to lessen temporary blindness from lightning.

(7) If using automatic pilot, disengage altitude hold mode and speed hold mode. The automatic altitude and speed controls will increase maneuvers of the aircraft thus increasing structural stress.

(8) If using airborne radar, tilt the antenna up and down occasionally. This will permit you to detect other thunderstorm activity at altitudes other than the one being flown.

c. Following are some Do's and Don'ts *during* the thunderstorm penetration:

(1) Do keep your eyes on your instruments. Looking outside the cockpit can increase danger of temporary blindness from lightning.

(2) Don't change power settings; maintain settings for the recommended turbulence penetration airspeed.

(3) Do maintain constant attitude; let the aircraft "ride the waves." Manuevers in trying to maintain constant altitude increases stress on the aircraft.

(4) Don't turn back once you are in the thunderstorm. A straight course through the storm most likely will get you out of the hazards most quickly. In addition, turning maneuvers increase stress on the aircraft.

528. KEY TO AVIATION WEATHER OBSERVATIONS AND FORECASTS

(See Figure 6-4.)

529. AUTOB DECODING KEY

(See Table 6-3.)

Section 2. ALTIMETER SETTING PROCEDURES

530. GENERAL

a. The accuracy of aircraft altimeters is subject to the following factors:

(1) Nonstandard temperatures of the atmosphere.

(2) Aircraft static pressure systems (position error).

(3) Nonstandard atmospheric pressure, and

(4) Instrument error.

b. Pilots should disregard the effect of nonstandard atmospheric temperatures and pressures except that low temperatures and pressures need to be considered for terrain clearance purposes.

NOTE.— Standard temperature at sea level is 15 degrees Celsius (59 degrees Fahrenheit). The temperature gradient from sea level is 2 degrees Celsius (3.6 degrees Fahrenheit) per 1,000 feet. Pilots should apply corrections for static pressure systems and/or instruments, if appreciable errors exist.

c. Experience gained through volume of operations has led to the adoption of a standard altimeter setting for flights operating in the higher altitudes. A standard setting eliminates altitude conflicts caused by altimeter settings derived from different geographical sources. In addition, it eliminates station barometer errors and some of the altimeter instrument errors.

531. PROCEDURES

a. The cruising altitude or flight level of aircraft shall be maintained by reference to an altimeter which shall be set, when operating:

(1) **Below 18,000 feet MSL** — to the current reported altimeter setting of a station along the route and within 100 NM of the aircraft, or if there is no station within this area, the current reported altimeter setting of an appropriate available station. When an aircraft is en route on an instrument flight plan, the ATC controller will furnish this information to the pilot at least once while the aircraft is in his area of jurisdiction. In the case of an aircraft not equipped with a radio, set to the elevation of the departure airport or use an appropriate altimeter setting available prior to departure.

(2) **At or above 18,000 feet MSL** — to 29.92 inches of mercury (standard setting). The lowest usable flight level is determined by the atmospheric pressure in the area of operation as shown in the following table:

Altimeter Setting (Current Reported)	Lowest usable flight level
29.92 or higher	180
29.91 to 29.42	185
29.41 to 28.92	190
28.91 to 28.42	195
28.41 to 27.92	200

(3) Where the minimum altitude, as prescribed in FAR—91.109 and FAR—91.119, is above 18,000 feet MSL, the lowest usable flight level shall be the flight level equivalent of the minimum altitude plus the number of feet specified in the following table:

Altimeter Setting	Correction Factor
29.92 or higher	none
29.91 to 29.42	500 Feet
29.41 to 28.92	1000 Feet
28.91 to 28.42	1500 Feet
28.41 to 27.92	2000 Feet
27.91 to 27.42	2500 Feet

EXAMPLE:

The minimum safe altitude of a route is 19,000 feet MSL and the altimeter setting is reported between 29.92 and 29.42 inches of mercury, the lowest usable flight level will be 195, which is the flight level equivalent of 19,500 feet MSL (minimum altitude plus 500 feet).

532. ALTIMETER ERRORS

a. Most pressure altimeters are subject to mechanical, elastic, temperature, and installation errors. (Detailed information regarding the use of pressure altimeters is found in the Instrument Flying Handbook, Chapter IV.) Although manufacturing and installation specifications, as well as the periodic test and inspections required by regulations (Far 43, Appendix E), act to reduce these errors, any scale error may be observed in the following manner:

(1) Set the current reported altimeter setting on the altimeter setting scale.

(2) Altimeter should now read field elevation if you are located on the same reference level used to establish the altimeter setting.

(3) Note the variation between the known field elevation and the altimeter indication. If this variation is in the order of plus or minus 75 feet, the accuracy of the altimeter is questionable and the problem should be referred to an appropriately rated repair station for evaluation and possible correction.

b. Once in flight, it is very important to frequently obtain current altimeter settings en route. If you do not reset your altimeter when flying *from* an area of high pressure or high temperatures *into* an area of low pressures or low temperature, *your aircraft will be closer to the surface than the altimeter indicates.* An inch error on the altimeter equals 1,000 feet of altitude. To quote an old saying: "GOING FROM A HIGH TO A LOW, LOOK OUT BELOW."

c. A reverse situation, without resetting the altimeter when going from a low temperature or low pressure area into a high temperature or high pressure area, *your aircraft will be higher than the altimeter indicates.*

d. The possible results of the above situations is obvious, particularly if operating at the minimum altitude or when conducting an instrument approach. If the altimeter is in error, you may still be on instruments when reaching the minimum altitude (as indicated on the altimeter), whereas you might have been in the clear and able to complete the approach if the altimeter setting was correct.

ALTIMETER SETTING PROCEDURES

533. HIGH BAROMETRIC PRESSURE

a. Cold, dry air masses may produce barometric pressures in excess of 31.00 inches of Mercury. Most altimeters do not have an accurate means of being adjusted for altimeter settings of these levels.

b. The altimeter setting announced by air traffic controllers will be 31.00 inches of Mercury (Three One Zero Zero) when the barometric pressure equals or exceeds that value. Actual barometric pressure will be provided upon request.

c. The altimeter error caused by the high pressure will be in the opposite direction to the error caused by the cold temperature.

534—539. RESERVED

Section 3. WAKE TURBULENCE

540. GENERAL

a. Every aircraft generates a wake while in flight. Initially, when pilots encountered this wake in flight, the disturbance was attributed to "prop wash." It is known, however, that this disturbance is caused by a pair of counter rotating vortices trailing from the wing tips. The vortices from large aircraft pose problems to encountering aircraft. For instance, the wake of these aircraft can impose rolling movements exceeding the roll control capability of some aircraft. Further, turbulence generated within the vortices can damage aircraft components and equipment if encountered at close range. The pilot must learn to envision the location of the vortex wake generated by large aircraft and adjust his flight path accordingly.

b. During ground operations and during takeoff, jet engine blast (thrust stream turbulence) can cause damage and upsets if encountered at close range. Exhaust velocity versus distance studies at various thrust levels have shown a need for light aircraft to maintain an adequate separation behind large turbojet aircraft. *Table 6-4* contains examples of the distance requirements to avoid exhaust velocities of greater than 25 mph.

c. Operators of light aircraft can minimize their exposure to jet blast by:

(1) Holding well back of the runway edge or taxiway hold line to avoid the drifting turbulence;

(2) Aligning the aircraft to face the possible jet blast; and

(3) Ensuring adequate separation when landing or taking off behind a departing large jet aircraft.

Pilots of large aircraft should be particularly careful to consider the effects of their jet blasts on other aircraft.

541. VORTEX GENERATION

Lift is generated by the creation of a pressure differential over the wing surface. The lowest pressure occurs over the upper wing surface and the highest pressure under the wing. This pressure differential triggers the roll up of the airflow aft of the wing resulting in swirling air masses trailing downstream of the wing tips. After the roll up is completed, the wake consists of two counter rotating cylindrical vortices. *(See Figure 6-5.)*

542. VORTEX STRENGTH

a. The strength of the vortex is governed by the weight, speed, and shape of the wing of the generating aircraft. The vortex characteristics of any given aircraft can also be changed by extension of flaps or other wing configuring devices as well as by change in speed. However, as the basic factor is weight, the vortex strength increases proportionately. During tests, peak vortex tangential velocities were recorded at 224 feet per second, or about 133 knots. The greatest vortex strength occurs when the generating aircraft is HEAVY, CLEAN, and SLOW.

b. INDUCED ROLL

(1) In rare instances a wake encounter could cause in-flight structural damage of catastrophic proportions. However, the usual hazard is associated with induced rolling movements which can

exceed the rolling capability of the encountering aircraft. In flight experiments, aircraft have been intentionally flown directly up trailing vortex cores of large aircraft. It was shown that the capability of an aircraft to counteract the roll imposed by the wake vortex primarily depends on the wing span and counter responsiveness of the encountering aircraft.

(2) Counter control is usually effective and induced roll minimal in cases where the wing span and ailerons of the encountering aircraft extend beyond the rotational flow field of the vortex. It is more difficult for aircraft with short wing span (relative to the generating aircraft) to counter the imposed roll induced by vortex flow. Pilots of short span aircraft, even of the high performance type, must be especially alert to vortex encounters. *(See Figure 6-6.)*

(3) The wake of large aircraft requires the respect of all pilots.

543. VORTEX BEHAVIOR

a. Trailing vortices have certain behavioral characteristics which can help a pilot visualize the wake location and thereby take avoidance precautions.

(1) Vortices are generated from the moment aircraft leave the ground, since trailing vortices are a by-product of wing lift. Prior to takeoff or touchdown pilots should note the rotation or touchdown point of the preceding aircraft. *(See Figure 6-7.)*

(2) The vortex circulation is outward, upward and around the wing tips when viewed from either ahead or behind the aircraft. Tests with large aircraft have shown that the vortex flow field, in a plane cutting through the wake at any point downstream, covers an area about 2 wing spans in width and one wing span in depth. The vortices remain so spaced (about a wing span apart) even drifting with the wind, at altitudes greater than a wing span from the ground. In view of this, if persistent vortex turbulence is encountered, a slight change of altitude and lateral position (preferably upwind) will provide a flight path clear of the turbulence. *(See Figure 6-8.)*

(3) Flight tests have shown that the vortices from large aircraft sink at a rate of about 400 to 500 feet per minute. They tend to level off at a distance about 900 feet below the flight path of the generating aircraft. Vortex strength diminishes with time and distance behind the generating aircraft. Atmospheric turbulence hastens breakup. Pilots should fly at or above the large aircraft's flight path, altering course as necessary to avoid the area behind and below the generating aircraft. *(See Figure 6-9.)*

(4) When the vortices of large aircraft sink close to the ground (within about 200 feet), they tend to move laterally over the ground at a speed of about 5 knots. *(See Figure 6-10.)*

b. A crosswind will decrease the lateral movement of the upwind vortex and increase the movement of the downwind vortex. Thus a light wind of 3 to 7 knots could result in the upwind vortex remaining in the touchdown zone for a period of time and hasten the drift of the downwind vortex toward another runway. Similarly, a tailwind condition can move the vortices of the preceding aircraft forward into the touchdown zone. THE LIGHT QUARTERING TAILWIND REQUIRES MAXIMUM CAUTION. Pilots should be alert to large aircraft upwind from their approach and takeoff flight paths. *(See Figure 6-11)*

544. OPERATIONS PROBLEM AREAS

a. A wake encounter is not necessarily hazardous. It can be one or more jolts with varying severity depending upon the direction of the encounter, distance from the generating aircraft, and point of vortex encounter. The probability of induced roll increases when the encountering aircraft's heading is generally aligned with the vortex trail or flight path of the generating aircraft.

b. AVOID THE AREA BELOW AND BEHIND THE GENERATING AIRCRAFT, ESPECIALLY AT LOW ALTITUDE WHERE EVEN A MOMENTARY WAKE ENCOUNTER COULD BE HAZARDOUS.

c. Pilots should be particularly alert in calm wind conditions and situations where the vortices could:

(1) Remain in the touchdown area.

(2) Drift from aircraft operating on a nearby runway.

(3) Sink into the takeoff or landing path from a crossing runway.

(4) Sink into the traffic patterns from other airport operations.

(5) Sink into the flight path of VFR flights operating at 500 feet AGL and below.

d. Pilots of all aircraft should visualize the location of the vortex trail behind large aircraft and use proper vortex avoidance procedures to achieve safe operation. It is equally important that pilots of large aircraft plan or adjust their flight paths to minimize vortex exposure to other aircraft.

545. VORTEX AVOIDANCE PROCEDURES

a. Under certain conditions, airport traffic controllers apply procedures for separating aircraft from heavy jet aircraft. The controllers will also provide VFR aircraft, with whom they are in communication and, which in the tower's opinion may be adversely affected by wake turbulence from a large aircraft, the position, altitude and direction of flight of the large aircraft followed by the phrase "CAUTION — WAKE TURBULENCE." WHETHER OR NOT A WARNING HAS BEEN GIVEN, HOWEVER, THE PILOT IS EXPECTED TO ADJUST HIS OPERATIONS AND FLIGHT PATH AS NECESSARY TO PRECLUDE SERIOUS WAKE ENCOUNTERS.

b. The following vortex avoidance procedures are recommended for the various situations:

(1) **Landing behind a large aircraft — same runway:** Stay at or above the large aircraft's final approach flight path — note his touchdown point — land beyond it.

(2) **Landing behind a large aircraft — when parallel runway is closer than 2,500 feet:** Consider possible drift to your runway. Stay at or above the large aircraft's final approach flight path — note his touchdown point.

(3) **Landing behind a large aircraft — crossing runway:** Cross above the large aircraft's flight path.

(4) **Landing behind a departing large aircraft — same runway:** Note the large aircraft's rotation point — land well prior to rotation point.

(5) **Landing behind a departing large aircraft — crossing runway:** Note the large aircraft's rotation point — if past the intersection — continue the approach — land prior to the intersection.

If large aircraft rotates prior to the intersection, avoid flight below the large aircraft's flight path. Abandon the approach unless a landing is assured well before reaching the intersection.

(6) **Departing behind a large aircraft:** Note the large aircraft's rotation point — rotate prior to large aircraft's rotation point — continue climb above and stay upwind of the large aircraft's climb path until turning clear of his wake. Avoid subsequent headings which will cross below and behind a large aircraft. Be alert for any critical takeoff situation which could lead to a vortex encounter.

(7) **Intersection takeoffs — same runway:** Be alert to adjacent large aircraft operations particularly upwind of your runway. If intersection takeoff clearance is received, avoid subsequent heading which will cross below a large aircraft's path.

(8) **Departing or landing after a large aircraft executing a low approach, missed approach or touch-and-go landing:** Because vortices settle and move laterally near the ground, the vortex hazard may exist along the runway and in your flight path after a large aircraft has executed a low approach, missed approach or a touch-and-go landing, particular in light quartering wind conditions. You should assure that an interval of at least 2 minutes has elapsed before your takeoff or landing.

(9) **En route VFR (thousand-foot altitude plus 500 feet):** Avoid flight below and behind a large aircraft's path. If a large aircraft is observed above on the same track (meeting or overtaking) adjust your position laterally, preferably upwind.

546—549. RESERVED

550. HELICOPTERS

In a slow hover-taxi or stationary hover near the surface, helicopter main rotor(s) generate downwash producing high velocity outwash vortices to a distance approximately three times the diameter of the rotor. When rotor downwash hits the surface, the resulting outwash vortices have behavioral characteristics similar to wing tip vortices produced by fixed wing aircraft. However, the vortex circulation is outward, upward, around, and away from the main rotor(s) in all directions. Pilots of small aircraft should avoid operating within three rotor diameters of any helicopter in a slow hover taxi or stationary hover. In forward flight, departing or landing helicopters produce a pair of high velocity trailing vortices similar to wing tip vortices of large fixed wing aircraft. Pilots of small aircraft should use caution when operating behind or crossing behind landing and departing helicopters.

551. PILOT RESPONSIBILITY

a. Government and industry groups are making concerted efforts to minimize or eliminate the hazards of trailing vortices. However, the flight disciplines necessary to assure vortex avoidance during VFR operations must be exercised by the pilot. Vortex visualization and avoidance procedures should be exercised by the pilot using the same degree of concern as in collision avoidance.

b. Wake turbulence may be encountered by aircraft in flight as well as when operating on the airport movement area. (See WAKE TURBULENCE in the Pilot/Controller Glossary.)

c. Pilots are reminded that in operations conducted behind all aircraft, acceptance of instructions from ATC in the following situations is an acknowledgment that the pilot will ensure safe takeoff and landing intervals and accepts the responsibility of providing his own wake turbulence separation.

    (1) Traffic information,

    (2) Instructions to follow an aircraft, and

    (3) The acceptance of a visual approach clearance.

    d. For operations conducted behind heavy aircraft, ATC will specify the word "heavy" when this information is known. Pilots of heavy aircraft should always use the word "heavy" in radio communications.

552. AIR TRAFFIC WAKE TURBULENCE SEPARATIONS

    a. Because of the possible effects of wake turbulence, controllers are required to apply no less than specified minimum separation for aircraft operating behind a heavy jet and, in certain instances, behind large nonheavy aircraft.

    (1) Separation is applied to aircraft operating directly behind a heavy jet at the same altitude or less than 1,000 feet below:

        (a) Heavy jet behind heavy jet — 4 miles.

        (b) Small/large aircraft behind heavy jet — 5 miles.

    (2) Also, separation, measured at the time the preceding aircraft is over the landing threshold, is provided to small aircraft:

        (a) Small aircraft landing behind heavy jet — 6 miles.

        (b) Small aircraft landing behind large aircraft - 4 miles.

NOTE.— See Aircraft Classes in Pilot/Controller Glossary.

    (3) Additionally, appropriate time or distance intervals are provided to departing aircraft:

        (a) Two minutes or the appropriate 4 or 5 mile radar separation when takeoff behind a heavy jet will be:

    -from the same threshold

    -on a crossing runway and projected flight paths will cross

    -from the threshold of a parallel runway when staggered ahead of that of the adjacent runway by less than 500 feet and when the runways are separated by less than 2,500 feet.

NOTE.— Pilots, after considering possible wake turbulence effects, may specifically request waiver of the 2-minute interval by stating, "request waiver of 2-minute interval" or a similar statement. Controllers may acknowledge this statement as pilot acceptance of responsibility for wake turbulence separation and, if traffic permits, issue takeoff clearance.

    b. A 3-minute interval will be provided when a small aircraft will takeoff:

    (1) From an intersection on the same runway (same or opposite direction) behind a departing large aircraft,

    (2) In the opposite direction on the same runway behind a large aircraft takeoff or low/missed approach.

NOTE.— This 3-minute interval may be waived upon specific pilot request.

    c. A 3-minute interval will be provided for all aircraft taking off when the operations are as described in b(1) and (2) above, the preceding aircraft is a heavy jet, and the operations are on either the same runway or parallel runways separated by less than 2,500 feet. Controllers may not reduce or waive this interval.

    d. Pilots may request additional separation i.e., 2 minutes instead of 4 or 5 miles for wake turbulence avoidance. This request should be made as soon as practical on ground control and at least before taxiing onto the runway.

NOTE.— FAR 91.3(a) states: "The pilot in command of an aircraft is directly responsible for and is the final authority as to the operation of that aircraft."

553—559. RESERVED

SECTION 4. BIRD HAZARDS, AND FLIGHT OVER NATIONAL REFUGES, PARKS, AND FORESTS

560. MIGRATORY BIRD ACTIVITY

a. Bird strike risk increases because of bird migration during the months of March through April, and August through November.

b. The altitudes of migrating birds vary with winds aloft, weather fronts, terrain elevations, cloud conditions, and other environmental variables. While over 90 percent of the reported bird strikes occur at or below 3,000 feet AGL, strikes at higher altitudes are common during migration. Ducks and geese are frequently observed up to 7,000 feet AGL and pilots are cautioned to minimize en route flying at lower altitudes during migration.

c. Considered the greatest potential hazard to aircraft because of their size, abundance, or habit of flying in dense flocks are gulls, waterfowl, vultures, hawks, owls, egrets, blackbirds, and starlings. Four major migratory flyways exist in the United States. The Atlantic flyway parallels the Atlantic Coast. The Mississippi Flyway stretches from Canada through the Great Lakes and follows the Mississippi River. The Central Flyway represents a broad area east of the Rockies, stretching from Canada through Central America. The Pacific Flyway follows the west coast and overflies major parts of Washington, Oregon, and California. There are also numerous smaller flyways which cross these major north-south migratory routes.

561. REDUCING BIRD STRIKE RISKS

a. The most serious strikes are those involving ingestion into an engine (turboprops and turbine jet engines) or windshield strikes. These strikes can result in emergency situations requiring prompt action by the pilot.

b. Engine ingestions may result in sudden loss of power or engine failure. Review engine out procedures, especially when operating from airports with known bird hazards or when operating near high bird concentrations.

c. Windshield strikes have resulted in pilots experiencing confusion, disorientation, loss of communications, and aircraft control problems. Pilots are encouraged to review their emergency procedures before flying in these areas.

d. When encountering birds en route, climb to avoid collision, because birds in flocks generally distribute themselves downward, with lead birds being at the highest altitude.

e. Avoid overflight of known areas of bird concentration and flying at low altitudes during bird migration. Charted wildlife refuges and other natural areas contain unusually high local concentration of birds which may create a hazard to aircraft.

562. REPORTING BIRD STRIKES

Pilots are urged to report strikes using FAA Form 5200-7, Bird Strike/Incident Report. This form is available at any FSS, General Aviation District Office, Air Carrier District Office, or at an FAA Regional Office. The data derived from these reports is used to develop standards to cope with this extensive hazard to aircraft and for documentation of necessary habitat control on airports.

563. REPORTING BIRD AND OTHER WILDLIFE ACTIVITIES

If you observe birds or other animals on or near the runway, request airport management to disperse the wildlife before taking off. Also contact the nearest FAA ARTCC, FSS, or tower (including non-Federal towers) regarding large flocks of birds and report the:

(1) eographic location

(2) Bird type (geese, ducks, gulls, etc.)

(3) Approximate numbers

(4) Altitude

(5) Direction of bird flight path

564. PILOT ADVISORIES ON BIRD AND OTHER WILDLIFE HAZARDS

Many airports advise pilots of other wildlife hazards caused by large animals on the runway through the Airport/Facility Directory and the NOTAM system. Collisions of landing and departing aircraft and animals on the runway are increasing and are not limited to rural airports. These accidents have also occurred at several major airports. Pilots should exercise extreme caution when warned of the presence of wildlife on and in the vicinity of airports. If you observe deer or other large animals in close proximity to movement areas, advise the FSS, tower, or airport management.

565. FLIGHTS OVER CHARTED U.S. WILDLIFE REFUGES, PARKS, AND FOREST SERVICE AREAS

a. The landing of aircraft is prohibited on lands or waters administered by the National Park Service, U.S. Fish and Wildlife Service, or U.S. Forest Service without authorization from the respective agency. Exceptions, including

(1) when forced to land due to an emergency beyond the control of the operator,

(2) at officially designated landing sites, or

(3) an approved official business of the Federal Government.

b. All aircraft are requested to maintain a minimum altitude of 2,000 feet above the *surface* of the following: National Parks, Monuments, Seashores, Lakeshores, Recreation Areas and Scenic Riverways administered by the National Park Service, National Wildlife Refuges, Big Game Refuges, Game Ranges and Wildlife Ranges administered by the U.S. Fish and Wildlife Service, and Wilderness and Primitive areas administered by the U.S. Forest Service.

NOTE.— FAA Advisory Circular 91-36, Visual Flight Rules (VFR) Flight Near Noise-Sensitive Areas, defines the *surface* of a National Park Area (including Parks, Forests, Primitive Areas, Wilderness Areas, Recreational Areas, National Seashores, National Monuments, National Lakeshores, and National Wildlife Refuge and Range Areas) as: the highest terrain within 2,000 feet laterally of the route of flight, *or* the upper-most rim of a canyon or valley.

c. Federal statutes prohibit certain types of flight activity and/or provide altitude restrictions over *designated* U.S. Wildlife Refuges,

Para—569.   BIRD HAZARDS, AND FLIGHT OVER NATIONAL REFUGES, PARKS, AND FORESTS

Parks, and Forest Service Areas. These designated areas, for example: Boundary Waters Canoe Wilderness Areas, Minnesota; Haleakala National Park, Hawaii; Yosemite National Park, California; are charted on Sectional Charts.

d.   Federal regulations also prohibit airdrops by parachute or other means of persons, cargo, or objects from aircraft on lands ad-

ministered by the three agencies without authorization from the respective agency. Exceptions include:

(1)   emergencies involving the safety of human life, or

(2)   threat of serious property loss.

566-569. RESERVED.

Section 5. POTENTIAL FLIGHT HAZARDS

570. ACCIDENT CAUSE FACTORS

a. The 10 most frequent cause factors for General Aviation Accidents that involve the pilot in command are:

  (1) Inadequate preflight preparation and/or planning.

  (2) Failure to obtain and/or maintain flying speed.

  (3) Failure to maintain direction control.

  (4) Improper level off.

  (5) Failure to see and avoid objects or obstructions.

  (6) Mismanagement of fuel.

  (7) Improper in-flight decisions or planning.

  (8) Misjudgment of distance and speed.

  (9) Selection of unsuitable terrain.

  (10) Improper operation of flight controls.

b. This list remains relatively stable and points out the need for continued refresher training to establish a higher level of flight proficiency for all pilots. A part of the FAA's continuing effort to promote increased aviation safety is the General Aviation Accident Prevention Program. For information on Accident Prevention activities contact your nearest General Aviation or Flight Standards District Office.

c. ALERTNESS — Be alert at all times, especially when the weather is good. Most pilots pay attention to business when they are operating in full IFR weather conditions, but strangely, air collisions almost invariably have occurred under ideal weather conditions. Unlimited visibility appears to encourage a sense of security which is not at all justified. Considerable information of value may be obtained by listening to advisories being issued in the terminal area, even though controller workload may prevent a pilot from obtaining individual service.

d. GIVING WAY — If you think another aircraft is too close to you, give way instead of waiting for the other pilot to respect the right-of-way to which you may be entitled. It is a lot safer to pursue the right-of-way angle after you have completed your flight.

571. VFR IN CONGESTED AREAS

A high percentage of near midair collisions occur below 8,000 feet AGL and within 30 miles of an airport. When operating VFR in these highly congested areas, whether you intend to land at an airport within the area or are just flying through, it is recommended that extra vigilance be maintained and that you monitor an appropriate control frequency. Normally the appropriate frequency is an approach control frequency. By such monitoring action you can "get the picture" of the traffic in your area. When the approach controller has radar, radar traffic advisories may be given to VFR pilots upon request. (See PARA—162 - RADAR TRAFFIC INFORMATION SERVICE.)

572. OBSTRUCTIONS TO FLIGHT

a. Antenna Towers

Extreme caution should be exercised when flying less than 2,100 feet above ground level (AGL) because of the numerous skeletal structures (radio and television antenna towers) exceeding 1,000 feet AGL with some extending higher than 2,000 feet AGL. Most skeletal structures are supported by guy wires. The wires are difficult to see in good weather and can be totally obscured during periods of dusk and reduced visibility. These wires can extend about 1,500 feet horizontally from a structure; therefore, all skeletal structures should be avoided by at least 2,000 feet.

b. Overhead Wires

Overhead transmission and utility lines often span approaches to runways and scenic flyways such as lakes, rivers, and canyons. The supporting structures of these lines may not always be readily visible and the wires may be virtually invisible under certain conditions. Most of these installations do not meet criteria which determine them to be obstructions to air navigation and therefore do not require marking and/or lighting. The supporting structures of some overhead transmission lines are equipped with flashing strobe lights. These lights indicate wires exist between the strobed structures.

573. AVOID FLIGHT BENEATH UNMANNED BALLOONS

a. The majority of unmanned free balloons currently being operated have, extending below them, either a suspension device to which the payload or instrument package is attached, or a trailing wire antenna, or both. In many instances these balloon subsystems may be invisible to the pilot until his aircraft is close to the balloon, thereby creating a potentially dangerous situation. Therefore, good judgment on the part of the pilot dictates that aircraft should remain well clear of all unmanned free balloons and flight below them should be avoided at all times.

b. Pilots are urged to report any unmanned free balloons sighted to the nearest FAA ground facility with which communication is established. Such information will assist FAA ATC facilities to identify and flight follow unmanned free balloons operating in the airspace.

574. MOUNTAIN FLYING

a. Your first experience of flying over mountainous terrain (particularly if most of your flight time has been over the flatlands of the midwest) could be a never-to-be-forgotten nightmare if proper planning is not done and if you are not aware of the potential hazards awaiting. Those familiar section lines are not present in the mountains; those flat, level fields for forced landings are practically nonexistent; abrupt changes in wind direction and velocity occur; severe updrafts and downdrafts are common, particularly near or above abrupt changes of terrain such as cliffs or rugged areas; even the clouds look different and can build up with startling rapidity. Mountain flying need not be hazardous if you follow the recommendations below:

b. File a flight plan. Plan your route to avoid topography which would prevent a safe forced landing. The route should be over populated areas and well known mountain passes. Sufficient altitude should be maintained to permit gliding to a safe landing in the event of engine failure.

c. Don't fly a light aircraft when the winds aloft, at your proposed altitude, exceed 35 miles per hour. Expect the winds to be of much greater velocity over mountain passes than reported a few miles from them. Approach mountain passes with as much altitude as possible. Downdrafts of from 1,500 to 2,000 feet per minute are not uncommon on the leeward side.

d. Don't fly near or above abrupt changes in terrain. Severe turbulence can be expected, especially in high wind conditions.

e. Some canyons run into a dead end. Don't fly so far up a canyon that you get trapped. ALWAYS BE ABLE TO MAKE A 180 DEGREE TURN!

f. Plan your trip for the early morning hours. As a rule, the air starts to get bad at about 10 a.m., and grows steadily worse until around 4 p.m., then gradually improves until dark. Mountain flying at night in a single engine light aircraft is asking for trouble.

g. When landing at a high altitude field, the same indicated airspeed should be used as at low elevation fields. *Remember:* that due to the less dense air at altitude, this same indicated airspeed actually results in higher true airspeed, a faster landing speed, and more important, a longer landing distance. During gusty wind conditions which often prevail at high altitude fields, a power approach and power landing is recommended. Additionally, due to the faster groundspeed, your takeoff distance will increase considerably over that required at low altitudes.

h. Effects of Density Altitude. Performance figures in the aircraft owner's handbook for length of takeoff run, horsepower, rate of climb, etc., are generally based on standard atmosphere conditions (59 degrees Fahrenheit (15 degrees Celsius), pressure 29.92 inches of mercury)at sea level. However, inexperienced pilots, as well as experienced pilots, may run into trouble when they encounter an altogether different set of conditions. This is particularly true in hot weather and at higher elevations. Aircraft operations at altitudes above sea level and at higher than standard temperatures are commonplace in mountainous areas. Such operations quite often result in a drastic reduction of aircraft performance capabilities because of the changing air density. Density altitude is a measure of air density. It is not to be confused with pressure altitude, true altitude or absolute altitude. It is not to be used as a height reference, but as a determining criteria in the performance capability of an aircraft. Air density decreases with altitude. As air density decreases, density altitude increases. The further effects of high temperature and high humidity are cumulative, resulting in an increasing high density altitude condition. High density altitude reduces all aircraft performance parameters. To the pilot, this means that the normal horsepower output is reduced, propeller efficiency is reduced and a higher true airspeed is required to sustain the aircraft throughout its operating parameters. It means an increase in runway length requirements for takeoff and landings, and decreased rate of climb. An average small airplane, for example, requiring 1,000 feet for takeoff at sea level under standard atmospheric conditions will require a takeoff run of approximately 2,000 feet at an operational altitude of 5,000 feet.

NOTE.— A turbo-charged aircraft engine provides some slight advantage in that it provides sea level horsepower up to a specified altitude above sea level.

(1) Density Altitude Advisories — at airports with elevations of 2,000 feet and higher, control towers and FSSs will broadcast the advisory "Check Density Altitude" when the temperature reaches a predetermined level. These advisories will be broadcast on appropriate tower frequencies or, where available, ATIS. FSSs will broadcast these advisories as a part of Airport Advisory Service, and on TWEB.

(2) These advisories are provided by air traffic facilities, as a reminder to pilots that high temperatures and high field elevations will cause significant changes in aircraft characteristics. The pilot retains the responsibility to compute density altitude, when appropriate, as a part of preflight duties.

NOTE.— All FSSs will compute the current density altitude upon request.

i. Mountain Wave. Many pilots go all their lives without understanding what a mountain wave is. Quite a few have lost their lives because of this lack of understanding. One need not be a licensed meteorologist to understand the mountain wave phenomenon.

(1) Mountain waves occur when air is being blown over a mountain range or even the ridge of a sharp bluff area. As the air hits the upwind side of the range, it starts to climb, thus creating what is generally a smooth updraft which turns into a turbulent downdraft as the air passes the crest of the ridge. From this point, for many miles downwind, there will be a series of downdrafts and updrafts. Satellite photos of the Rockies have shown mountain waves extending as far as 700 miles downwind of the range. Along the east coast area, such photos of the Appalachian chain have picked up the mountain wave phenomenon over a hundred miles eastward. All it takes to form a mountain wave is wind blowing across the range at 15 knots or better at an intersection angle of not less than 30 degrees.

(2) Pilots from flatland areas should understand a few things about mountain waves in order to stay out of trouble. When approaching a mountain range from the upwind side (generally the west), there will usually be a smooth updraft; therefore, it is not quite as dangerous an area as the lee of the range. From the leeward side, it is always a good idea to add an extra thousand feet or so of altitude because downdrafts can exceed the climb capability of the aircraft. Never expect an updraft when approaching a mountain chain from the leeward. Always be prepared to cope with a downdraft and turbulence.

(3) When approaching a mountain ridge from the downwind side, it is recommended that the ridge be approached at approximately a 45 degrees angle to the horizontal direction of the ridge. This permits a safer retreat from the ridge with less stress on the aircraft should severe turbulence and downdraft be experienced. If severe turbulence is encountered, simultaneously reduce power and adjust pitch until aircraft approaches maneuvering speed, then adjust power and trim to maintain maneuvering speed and fly away from the turbulent area.

575—579. RESERVED

Section 6. SAFETY, ACCIDENT AND HAZARD REPORTS

580. AVIATION SAFETY REPORTING PROGRAM

a. The FAA has established a voluntary Aviation Safety Reporting Program designed to stimulate the free and unrestricted flow of information concerning deficiencies and discrepancies in the aviation system. This is a positive program intended to ensure the safest possible system by identifying and correcting unsafe conditions before they lead to accidents. The primary objective of the program is to obtain information to evaluate and enhance the safety and efficiency of the present system.

b. This program applies primarily to that part of the system involving the safety of aircraft operations, including departure, en route, approach and landing operations and procedures, ATC procedures, pilot/controller communications, the aircraft movement area of the airport, and near midair collisions. Pilots, air traffic controllers, and all other members of the aviation community and the general public are asked to file written reports of any discrepancy or deficiency noted in these areas.

c. The report should give the date, time, location, persons and aircraft involved (if applicable), nature of the event, and all pertinent details.

d. To ensure receipt of this information, the program provides for the waiver of certain disciplinary actions against persons, including pilots and air traffic controllers, who file timely written reports concerning potentially unsafe incidents. To be considered timely, reports must be delivered or postmarked within 10 days of the incident unless that period is extended for good cause. Reporting forms are available at FAA facilities.

e. The FAA utilizes the National Aeronautics and Space Administration (NASA) to act as an independent third party to receive and analyze reports submitted under the program. This program is described in ADVISORY CIRCULAR—00-46.

581. AIRCRAFT ACCIDENT AND INCIDENT REPORTING

a. OCCURRENCES REQUIRING NOTIFICATION — The operator of an aircraft shall immediately, and by the most expeditious means available, notify the nearest National Transportation Safety Board (NTSB) Field Office when:

(1) An aircraft accident or any of the following listed incidents occur:

(a) Flight control system malfunction or failure;

(b) Inability of any required flight crew member to perform his normal flight duties as a result of injury or illness;

(c) Failure of structural components of a turbine engine excluding compressor and turbine blades and vanes.

(d) In-flight fire;

(e) Aircraft collide in flight.

(2) An aircraft is overdue and is believed to have been involved in an accident.

b. MANNER OF NOTIFICATION:

(1) The most expeditious method of notification to the NTSB by the operator will be determined by the circumstances existing at that time. The NTSB has advised that any of the following would

be considered examples of the type of notification that would be acceptable:

(a) Direct telephone notification.

(b) Telegraphic notification.

(c) Notification to the FAA who would in turn notify the NTSB by direct communication; i.e., dispatch or telephone.

c. ITEMS TO BE NOTIFIED — The notification required above shall contain the following information, if available:

(1) Type, nationality, and registration marks of the aircraft;

(2) Name of owner and operator of the aircraft;

(3) Name of the pilot-in-command;

(4) Date and time of the accident, or incident;

(5) Last point of departure and point of intended landing of the aircraft;

(6) Position of the aircraft with reference to some easily defined geographical point;

(7) Number of persons aboard, number killed, and number seriously injured;

(8) Nature of the accident, or incident, the weather, and the extent of damage to the aircraft, so far as is known; and

(9) A description of any explosives, radioactive materials, or other dangerous articles carried.

d. FOLLOW UP REPORTS:

(1) The operator shall file a report on NTSB Form 6120.1 or 6120.2, available from NTSB Field Offices, or from the NTSB, Washington, D.C., 20594.

(a) Within 10 days after an accident;

(b) When, after 7 days, an overdue aircraft is still missing;

(c) A report on an incident for which notification is required as described in subparagraph a(1) shall be filed only as requested by an authorized representative of the NTSB.

(2) Each crewmember, if physically able at the time the report is submitted, shall attach a statement setting forth the facts, conditions and circumstances relating to the accident or incident as they appear to him. If the crewmember is incapacitated, he shall submit the statement as soon as he is physically able.

e. WHERE TO FILE THE REPORTS

(1) The operator of an aircraft shall file with the NTSB Field Office nearest the accident or incident any report required by this section.

(2) The NTSB Field Offices are listed under U.S. Government in the telephone directories in the following cities: Anchorage, AK; Atlanta, GA; Chicago, IL; Denver, CO; Forth Worth, TX; Kansas City, MO; Los Angeles, CA; Miami, FL; New York, NY; Seattle, WA.

582. NEAR MIDAIR COLLISION REPORTING

a. PURPOSE AND DATA USES — The primary purpose of the Near Midair Collision (NMAC) Reporting Program is to provide information for use in enhancing the safety and efficiency of the National Airspace System. Data obtained from NMAC reports are used by the FAA to improve the quality of FAA services to users and to develop programs, policies, and procedures aimed at the reduction of NMAC occurrences. All NMAC reports are thoroughly investigated by Flight Standards Facilities in coordination with Air Traffic Facilities. Data from these investigations are transmitted to FAA Headquarters in Washington, D.C. where they are compiled and analyzed, and where safety programs and recommendations are developed.

b. DEFINITION — A near midair collision is defined as an incident associated with the operation of an aircraft in which a possibility of collision occurs as a result of proximity of less than 500 feet to another aircraft, or a report is received from a pilot or a flight crew member stating that a collision hazard existed between two or more aircraft.

c. REPORTING RESPONSIBILITY — It is the responsibility of the pilot and/or flight crew to determine whether a near midair collision did actually occur and, if so, to initiate a NMAC report. Be specific, as ATC will not interpret a casual remark to mean that a NMAC is being reported.

d. WHERE TO FILE REPORTS — Pilots and/or flight crew members involved in NMAC occurrences are urged to report each incident immediately:

(1) By radio or telephone to the nearest FAA ATC facility or FSS.

(2) In writing, in lieu of the above, to the nearest Air Carrier District Office (ACDO), General Aviation District Office (GADO), or Flight Standards District Office (FSDO).

e. ITEMS TO BE REPORTED —

(1) Date and Time (UTC) of incident.

(2) Location of incident and altitude.

(3) Identification and type of reporting aircraft, aircrew destination, name and home base of pilot.

(4) Identification and type of other aircraft, aircrew destination, name and home base of pilot.

(5) Type of flight plans; station altimeter setting used.

(6) Detailed weather conditions at altitude or flight level.

(7) Approximate courses of both aircraft: indicate if one or both aircraft were climbing or descending.

(8) Reported separation in distance at first sighting, proximity at closest point horizontally and vertically, length of time in sight prior to evasive action.

(9) Degree of evasive action taken, if any (from both aircraft, if possible).

(10) Injuries, if any.

f. INVESTIGATION — The district office responsible for the investigation and reporting of NMAC's will be:

(1) The Air Carrier or Flight Standards District Office in whose area the incident occurred when an air carrier aircraft is involved.

(2) The General Aviation or Flight Standards District Office in whose area the incident occurred in all other cases.

Existing radar, communication, and weather data will be examined in the conduct of the investigation. When possible, all cockpit crew members will be interviewed regarding factors involving the NMAC incident. Air Traffic controllers will be interviewed in cases where one or more of the involved aircraft was provided ATC service. Both flight and ATC procedures will be evaluated. When the investigation reveals a violation of an FAA regulation, enforcement action will be pursued.

583—599. RESERVED

Chapter 7.   MEDICAL FACTS FOR PILOTS

Section 1.   FITNESS FOR FLIGHT

600. FITNESS FOR FLIGHT

a. Medical Certification

(1) All pilots except those flying gliders and free air balloons must possess valid medical certificates in order to exercise the privileges of their airman certificates. The periodic medical examinations required for medical certification are conducted by designated Aviation Medical Examiners, who are physicians with a special interest in aviation safety and training in aviation medicine.

(2) The standards for medical certification are contained in FAR—67. Pilots who have a history of certain medical conditions described in these standards are mandatorily disqualified from flying. These medical conditions include a personality disorder manifested by overt acts, a psychosis, alcoholism, drug dependence, epilepsy, an unexplained disturbance of consciousness, myocardial infarction, angina pectoris and diabetes requiring medication for its control. Other medical conditions may be temporarily disqualifying, such as acute infections, anemia, and peptic ulcer. Pilots who do not meet medical standards may still be qualified under special issuance provisions or the exemption process. This may require that either additional medical information be provided or practical flight tests be conducted.

(3) Student pilots should visit an Aviation Medical Examiner as soon as possible in their flight training in order to avoid unnecessary training expenses should they not meet the medical standards. For the same reason, the student pilot who plans to enter commercial aviation should apply for the highest class of medical certificate that might be necessary in the pilot's career.

> *Caution:* The FARs prohibit a pilot who possesses a current medical certificate from performing crewmember duties while the pilot has a known medical condition or increase of a known medical condition that would make the pilot unable to meet the standards for the medical certificate.

b. Illness

(1) Even a minor illness suffered in day-to-day living can seriously degrade performance of many piloting tasks vital to safe flight. Illness can produce fever and distracting symptoms that can impair judgment, memory, alertness, and the ability to make calculations. Although symptoms from an illness may be under adequate control with a medication, the medication itself may decrease pilot performance.

(2) The safest rule is not to fly while suffering from any illness. If this rule is considered too stringent for a particular illness, the pilot should contact an Aviation Medical Examiner for advice.

c. Medication

(1) Pilot performance can be seriously degraded by both prescribed and over-the-counter medications, as well as by the medical conditions for which they are taken. Many medications, such as tranquilizers, sedatives, strong pain relievers, and cough-suppressant preparations, have primary effects that may impair judgment, memory, alertness, coordination, vision, and the ability to make calculations. Others, such as antihistamines, blood pressure drugs, muscle relaxants, and agents to control diarrhea and motion sickness, have side effects that may impair the same critical functions.

Any medication that depresses the nervous system, such as a sedative, tranquilizer or antihistamine, can make a pilot much more susceptible to hypoxia.

(2) The FARs prohibit pilots from performing crewmember duties while using any medication that affects the faculties in any way contrary to safety. The safest rule is not to fly as a crewmember while taking any medication, unless approved to do so by the FAA.

d. Alcohol

(1) Extensive research has provided a number of facts about the hazards of alcohol consumption and flying. As little as one ounce of liquor, one bottle of beer or four ounces of wine can impair flying skills, with the alcohol consumed in these drinks being detectable in the breath and blood for at least 3 hours. Even after the body completely destroys a moderate amount of alcohol, a pilot can still be severely impaired for many hours by hangover. There is simply no way of increasing the destruction of alcohol or alleviating a hangover. Alcohol also renders a pilot much more susceptible to disorientation and hypoxia.

(2) A consistently high alcohol related fatal aircraft accident rate serves to emphasize that alcohol and flying are a potentially lethal combination. The FARs prohibit pilots from performing crewmember duties within 8 hours after drinking any alcoholic beverage or while under the influence of alcohol. However, due to the slow destruction of alcohol, a pilot may still be under influence 8 hours after drinking a moderate amount of alcohol. Therefore, an excellent rule is to allow at least 12 to 24 hours between "bottle and throttle," depending on the amount of alcoholic beverage consumed.

e. Fatigue

(1) Fatigue continues to be one of the most treacherous hazards to flight safety, as it may not be apparent to a pilot until serious errors are made. Fatigue is best described as either acute (short-term) or chronic (long-term).

(2) A normal occurrence of everyday living, acute fatigue is the tiredness felt after long periods of physical and mental strain, including strenuous muscular effort, immobility, heavy mental workload, strong emotional pressure, monotony and lack of sleep. Consequently, coordination and alertness, so vital to safe pilot performance, can be reduced. Acute fatigue is prevented by adequate rest and sleep, as well as regular exercise and proper nutrition.

(3) Chronic fatigue occurs when there is not enough time for full recovery between episodes of acute fatigue. Performance continues to fall off, and judgment becomes impaired so that unwarranted risks may be taken. Recovery from chronic fatigue requires a prolonged period of rest.

f. Stress

(1) Stress from the pressures of everyday living can impair pilot performance, often in very subtle ways. Difficulties, particularly at work, can occupy thought processes enough to markedly decrease alertness. Distraction can so interfere with judgment that unwarranted risks are taken, such as flying into deteriorating weath-

er conditions to keep on schedule. Stress and fatigue (see above) can be an extremely hazardous combination.

(2) Most pilots do not leave stress "on the ground." Therefore, when more than usual difficulties are being experienced, a pilot should consider delaying flight until these difficulties are satisfactorily resolved.

g. Emotion

(1) Certain emotionally upsetting events, including a serious argument, death of a family member, separation or divorce, loss of job and financial catastrophe, can render a pilot unable to fly an aircraft safely. The emotions of anger, depression, and anxiety from such events not only decrease alertness but also may lead to taking risks that border on self-destruction. Any pilot who experiences an emotionally upsetting event should not fly until satisfactorily recovered from it.

h. Personal Checklist

(1) Aircraft accident statistics show that pilots should be conducting preflight checklists on themselves as well as their aircraft, for pilot impairment contributes to many more accidents than failures of aircraft systems. A personal checklist that can be easily committed to memory, which includes all of the categories of pilot impairment as discussed in this section, is being distributed by the FAA in the form of a wallet-sized card.

PERSONAL CHECKLIST

I'm physically and mentally safe to fly — not being impaired by:

I llness,

M edication,

S tress,

A lcohol,

F atigue,

E motion.

601. EFFECTS OF ALTITUDE

a. Hypoxia

(1) Hypoxia is a state of oxygen deficiency in the body sufficient to impair functions of the brain and other organs. Hypoxia from exposure to altitude is due only to the reduced barometric pressures encountered at altitude, for the concentration of oxygen in the atmosphere remains about 21 percent from the ground out to space.

(2) Although a deterioration in night vision occurs at a cabin pressure altitude as low as 5,000 feet, other significant effects of altitude hypoxia usually do not occur in the normal healthy pilot below 12,000 feet. From 12,000 to 15,000 feet of altitude, judgment, memory, alertness, coordination and ability to make calculations are impaired, and headache, drowsiness, dizziness and either a sense of well-being (euphoria) or belligerence occur. The effects appear following increasingly shorter periods of exposure to increasing altitude. In fact, pilot performance can seriously deteriorate within 15 minutes at 15,000 feet.

(3) At cabin pressure altitudes above 15,000 feet, the periphery of the visual field grays out to a point where only central vision remains (tunnel vision). A blue coloration (cyanosis) of the fingernails and lips develops. The ability to take corrective and protective action is lost in 20 to 30 minutes at 18,000 feet and 5 to 12 minutes at 20,000 feet, followed soon thereafter by unconsciousness.

(4) The altitude at which significant effects of hypoxia occur can be lowered by a number of factors. Carbon monoxide inhaled in smoking or from exhaust fumes, lowered hemoglobin (anemia), and certain medications can reduce the oxygen-carrying capacity of the blood to the degree that the amount of oxygen provided to body tissues will already be equivalent to the oxygen provided to the tissues when exposed to a cabin pressure altitude of several thousand feet. Small amounts of alcohol and low doses of certain drugs, such as antihistamines, tranquilizers, sedatives and analgesics can, through their depressant action, render the brain much more susceptible to hypoxia. Extreme heat and cold, fever, and anxiety increase the body's demand for oxygen, and hence its susceptibility to hypoxia.

(5) The effects of hypoxia are usually quite difficult to recognize, especially when they occur gradually. Since symptoms of hypoxia do not vary in an individual, the ability to recognize hypoxia can be greatly improved by experiencing and witnessing the effects of hypoxia during an altitude chamber "flight." The FAA provides this opportunity through aviation physiology training, which is conducted at the FAA Civil Aeromedical Institute and at many military facilities across the United States. Pilots can apply for this training by contacting the Airman Education Section, AAM-142, FAA Civil Aeromedical Institute, P.O. Box 25082, Oklahoma City, Oklahoma 73125.

(6) Hypoxia is prevented by heeding factors that reduce tolerance to altitude, by enriching the inspired air with oxygen from an appropriate oxygen system and by maintaining a comfortable, safe cabin pressure altitude. For optimum protection, pilots are encouraged to use supplemental oxygen above 10,000 feet during the day, and above 5,000 feet at night. The FARs require that the minimum flight crew be provided with and use supplemental oxygen after 30 minutes of exposure to cabin pressure altitudes between 12,500 and 14,000 feet, and immediately on exposure to cabin pressure altitudes above 14,000 feet. Every occupant of the aircraft must be provided with supplemental oxygen at cabin pressure altitudes above 15,000 feet.

b. Ear Block

(1) As the aircraft cabin pressure decreases during ascent, the expanding air in the middle ear pushes the eustachian tube open and, by escaping down it to the nasal passages, equalizes in pressure with the cabin pressure. But during descent, the pilot must periodically open the eustachian tube to equalize pressure. This can be accomplished by swallowing, yawning, tensing muscles in the throat or, if these do not work, by the combination of closing the mouth, pinching the nose closed and attempting to blow through the nostrils (Valsalva maneuver).

(2) Either an upper respiratory infection, such as a cold or sore throat, or a nasal allergic condition can produce enough congestion around the eustachian tube to make equalization difficult. Consequently, the difference in pressure between the middle ear and aircraft cabin can build up to a level that will hold the eustachian tube closed, making equalization difficult if not impossible. The problem is commonly referred to as an "ear block."

(3) An ear block produces severe ear pain and loss of hearing that can last from several hours to several days. Rupture of the ear drum can occur in flight or after landing. Fluid can accumulate in the middle ear and become infected.

(4) An ear block is prevented by not flying with an upper respiratory infection or nasal allergic condition. Adequate protection is usually not provided by decongestant sprays or drops to reduce congestion around the eustachian tubes. Oral decongestants have side effects that can significantly impair pilot performance.

(5) If an ear block does not clear shortly after landing, a physician should be consulted.

c. Sinus Block

(1) During ascent and descent, air pressure in the sinuses equalizes with the aircraft cabin pressure through small openings that connect the sinuses to the nasal passages. Either an upper respiratory infection, such as a cold or sinusitis, or a nasal allergic condition can produce enough congestion around an opening to slow equalization and, as the difference in pressure between the sinus and cabin mounts, eventually plug the opening. This "sinus block" occurs most frequently during descent.

(2) A sinus block can occur in the frontal sinuses, located above each eyebrow, or in the maxillary sinuses, located in each upper cheek. It will usually produce excruciating pain over the sinus area. A maxillary sinus block can also make the upper teeth ache. Bloody muscus may discharge from the nasal passages.

(3) A sinus block is prevented by not flying with an upper respiratory infection or nasal allergic condition. Adequate protection is usually not provided by decongestant sprays or drops to reduce congestion around the sinus openings. Oral decongestants have side effects that can impair pilot performance.

(4) If a sinus block does not clear shortly after landing, a physician should be consulted.

d. Decompression Sickness After Scuba Diving

(1) A pilot or passenger who intends to fly after scuba diving should allow the body sufficient time to rid itself of excess nitrogen absorbed during diving. If not, decompression sickness due to evolved gas can occur during exposure to low altitude and create a serious in-flight emergency.

(2) The recommended waiting time before flight to cabin pressure altitudes of 8,000 feet or less is at least 4 hours after diving which has not required controlled ascent (nondecompression diving), and at least 24 hours after diving which has required controlled ascent (decompression diving). The waiting time before flight to cabin pressure altitudes above 8,000 feet should be at least 24 hours after any scuba diving.

602. HYPERVENTILATION IN FLIGHT

a. Hyperventilation, or an abnormal increase in the volume of air breathed in and out of the lungs, can occur subconsciously when a stressful situation is encountered in flight. As hyperventilation "blows off" excessive carbon dioxide from the body, a pilot can experience symptoms of lightheadedness, suffocation, drowsiness, tingling in the extremities, and coolness—and react to them with even greater hyperventilation. Incapacitation can eventually result from incoordination, disorientation, and painful muscle spasms. Finally, unconsciousness can occur.

b. The symptoms of hyperventilation subside within a few minutes after the rate and depth of breathing are consciously brought back under control. The buildup of carbon dioxide in the body can be hastened by controlled breathing in and out of a paper bag held over the nose and mouth.

c. Early symptoms of hyperventilation and hypoxia are similar. Moreover, hyperventilation and hypoxia can occur at the same time. Therefore, if a pilot is using an oxygen system when symptoms are experienced, the oxygen regulator should immediately be set to deliver 100 percent oxygen, and then the system checked to assure that it has been functioning effectively before giving attention to rate and depth of breathing.

603. CARBON MONOXIDE POISONING IN FLIGHT

a. Carbon monoxide is a colorless, odorless and tasteless gas contained in exhaust fumes. When breathed even in minute quantities over a period of time, it can significantly reduce the ability of the blood to carry oxygen. Consequently, effects of hypoxia occur.

b. Most heaters in light aircraft work by air flowing over the manifold. Use of these heaters while exhaust fumes are escaping through manifold cracks and seals is responsible every year for several nonfatal and fatal aircraft accidents from carbon monoxide poisoning.

c. A pilot who detects the odor of exhaust or experiences symptoms of headache, drowsiness, or dizziness while using the heater should suspect carbon monoxide poisoning, and immediately shut off the heater and open air vents. If symptoms are severe, or continue after landing, medical treatment should be sought.

604. ILLUSIONS IN FLIGHT

a. Introduction

(1) Many different illusions can be experienced in flight. Some can lead to spatial disorientation. Others can lead to landing errors. Illusions rank among the most common factors cited as contributing to fatal aircraft accidents.

b. Illusions Leading to Spatial Disorientation

(1) Various complex motions and forces and certain visual scenes encountered in flight can create illusions of motion and position. Spatial disorientation from these illusions can be prevented only by visual reference to reliable, fixed points on the ground or to flight instruments.

(2) The leans — An abrupt correction of a banked attitude, which has been entered too slowly to stimulate the motion sensing system in the inner ear, can create the illusion of banking in the opposite direction. The disoriented pilot will roll the aircraft back into its original dangerous attitude or, if level flight is maintained, will feel compelled to lean in the perceived vertical plane until this illusion subsides.

(a) Coriolis illusion — An abrupt head movement in a prolonged constant-rate turn that has ceased stimulating the motion sensing system can create the illusion of rotation or movement in an entirely different axis. The disoriented pilot will maneuver the aircraft into a dangerous attitude in an attempt to stop rotation. This most overwhelming of all illusions in flight may be prevented by not making sudden, extreme head movements, particularly while making prolonged constant-rate turns under IFR conditions.

(b) Graveyard spin — A proper recovery from a spin that has ceased stimulating the motion sensing system can create the illusion of spinning in the opposite direction. The disoriented pilot will return the aircraft to its original spin.

(c) Graveyard spiral— An observed loss of altitude during a coordinated constant-rate turn that has ceased stimulating the motion sensing system can create the illusion of being in a descent with the wings level. The disoriented pilot will pull back on the controls, tightening the spiral and increasing the loss of altitude.

(d) Somatogravic illusion — A rapid acceleration during takeoff can create the illusion of being in a nose up attitude. The disoriented pilot will push the aircraft into a nose low, or dive attitude. A rapid deceleration by a quick reduction of the throttles can have the opposite effect, with the disoriented pilot pulling the aircraft into a nose up, or stall attitude.

(e) Inversion illusion — An abrupt change from climb to straight and level flight can create the illusion of tumbling backwards. The disoriented pilot will push the aircraft abruptly into a nose low attitude, possibly intensifying this illusion.

(f) Elevator illusion — An abrupt upward vertical acceleration, usually by an updraft, can create the illusion of being in a climb. The disoriented pilot will push the aircraft into a nose low attitude. An abrupt downward vertical acceleration, usually by a downdraft, has the opposite effect, with the disoriented pilot pulling the aircraft into a nose up attitude.

(g) False horizon — Sloping cloud formations, an obscured horizon, a dark scene spread with ground lights and stars, and certain geometric patterns of ground light can create illusions of not being aligned correctly with the actual horizon. The disoriented pilot will place the aircraft in a dangerous attitude.

(h) Autokinesis — In the dark, a static light will appear to move about when stared at for many seconds. The disoriented pilot will lose control of the aircraft in attempting to align it with the light.

(3) Illusions Leading to Landing Errors

(a) Various surface features and atmospheric conditions encountered in landing can create illusions of incorrect height above and distance from the runway threshold. Landing errors from these illusions can be prevented by anticipating them during approaches, aerial visual inspection of unfamiliar airports before landing, using electronic glide slope or VASI systems when available, and maintaining optimum proficiency in landing procedures.

(b) Runway width illusion — a narrower-than-usual runway can create the illusion that the aircraft is at a higher altitude than it actually is. The pilot who does not recognize this illusion will fly a lower approach, with the risk of striking objects along the approach path or landing short. A wider-than-usual runway can have the opposite effect, with the risk of leveling out high and landing hard or overshooting the runway.

(c) Runway and terrain slopes illusion — An upsloping runway, upsloping terrain, or both, can create the illusion that the aircraft is at a higher altitude than it actually is. The pilot who does not recognize this illusion will fly a lower approach. A downsloping runway, downsloping approach terrain, or both, can have the opposite effect.

(d) Featureless terrain illusion — An absence of ground features, as when landing over water, darkened areas and terrain made featureless by snow, can create the illusion that the aircraft is at a higher altitude than it actually is. The pilot who does not recognize this illusion will fly a lower approach

(e) Atmospheric illusions — Rain on the windscreen can create the illusion of greater height, and atmospheric haze the illusion of being at a greater distance from the runway. The pilot who does not recognize these illusions will fly a lower approach. Penetration of fog can create the illusion of pitching up. The pilot who does not recognize this illusion will steepen the approach, often quite abruptly.

(f) Ground lighting illusions — Lights along a straight path, such as a road, and even lights on moving trains can be mistaken for runway and approach lights. Bright runway and approach lighting systems, especially where few lights illuminate the surrounding terrain, may create the illusion of less distance to the runway. The pilot who does not recognize this illusion will fly a higher approach. Conversely, the pilot overflying terrain which has few lights to provide height cues may make a lower than normal approach.

605. VISION IN FLIGHT

a. Introduction

(1) Of the body senses, vision is the most important for safe flight. Major factors that determine how effectively vision can be used are the level of illumination and the technique of scanning the sky for other aircraft.

b. Vision Under Dim and Bright Illumination

(1) Under conditions of dim illumination, small print and colors on aeronautical charts and aircraft instruments become unreadable unless adequate cockpit lighting is available. Moreover, another aircraft must be much closer to be seen unless its navigation lights are on.

(2) In darkness, vision becomes more sensitive to light, a process called dark adaptation. Although exposure to total darkness for at least 30 minutes is required for complete dark adaptation, the pilot can achieve a moderate degree of dark adaptation within 20 minutes under dim red cockpit lighting. Since red light severely distorts colors, especially on aeronautical charts, and can cause serious difficulty in focusing the eyes on objects inside the aircraft, its use is advisable only where optimum outside night vision capability is necessary. Even so, white cockpit lighting must be available when needed for map and instrument reading, especially under IFR conditions. Dark adaptation is impaired by exposure to cabin pressure altitudes above 5,000 feet, carbon monoxide inhaled in smoking and from exhaust fumes, deficiency of Vitamin A in the diet, and by prolonged exposure to bright sunlight. Since any degree of dark adaptation is lost within a few seconds of viewing a bright light, the pilot should close one eye when using a light to preserve some degree of night vision.

(3) Excessive illumination, especially from light reflected off the canopy, surfaces inside the aircraft, clouds, water, snow, and desert terrain, can produce glare, with uncomfortable squinting, watering of the eyes, and even temporary blindness. Sunglasses for protection from glare should absorb at least 85 percent of visible light (15 percent transmittance) and all colors equally (neutral transmittance), with negligible image distortion from refractive and prismatic errors.

c. Scanning for Other Aircraft

(1) Scanning the sky for other aircraft is a key factor in collision avoidance. It should be used continuously by the pilot and copilot (or right seat passenger) to cover all areas of the sky visible from the cockpit. Although pilots must meet specific visual acuity requirements, the ability to read an eye chart does not ensure that one will be able to efficiently spot other aircraft. Pilots must develop an effective scanning technique which maximizes one's visual capabilities. The probability of spotting a potential collision threat obviously increases with the time spent looking outside the cockpit. Thus, one must use timesharing techniques to efficiently scan the surrounding airspace while monitoring instruments as well.

(2) While the eyes can observe an approximate 200 degree arc of the horizon at one glance, only a very small center area called the fovea, in the rear of the eye, has the ability to send clear, sharply focused messages to the brain. All other visual information that is not processed directly through the fovea will be of less detail. An aircraft at a distance of 7 miles which appears in sharp focus within the foveal center of vision would have to be as close as 7/10 of a mile in order to be recognized if it were outside of foveal vision. Because the eyes can focus only on this narrow viewing area, effective scanning is accomplished with a series of short, regularly spaced eye movements that bring successive areas of the sky into the central visual field. Each movement should not exceed 10 degrees, and each area should be observed for at least one second to enable detection. Although horizontal back-and-forth eye movements seem preferred by most pilots, each pilot should develop a scanning pattern that is most comfortable and then adhere to it to assure optimum scanning.

(3) Studies show that the time a pilot spends on visual tasks inside the cabin should represent no more that 1/4 to 1/3 of the scan time outside, or no more than 4 to 5 seconds on the instrument panel for every 16 seconds outside. Since the brain is already trained to process sight information that is presented from left to right, one may find it easier to start scanning over the left shoulder and proceed across the windshield to the right.

(4) Pilots should realize that their eyes may require several seconds to refocus when switching views between items in the cockpit and distant objects. The eyes will also tire more quickly when forced to adjust to distances immediately after close-up focus, as required for scanning the instrument panel. Eye fatigue can be reduced by looking from the instrument panel to the left wing past the wing tip to the center of the first scan quadrant when beginning the exterior scan. After having scanned from left to right, allow the eyes to return to the cabin along the right wing from its tip inward. Once back inside, one should automatically commence the panel scan.

(5) Effective scanning also helps avoid "empty-field myopia." This condition usually occurs when flying above the clouds or in a haze layer that provides nothing specific to focus on outside the aircraft. This causes the eyes to relax and seek a comfortable focal distance which may range from 10 to 30 feet. For the pilot, this means looking without seeing, which is dangerous.

606. AEROBATIC FLIGHT

a. Airmen planning to engage in aerobatics should be aware of the physiological stresses associated with accelerative forces during aerobatic maneuvers. Many prospective aerobatic trainees enthusiastically enter aerobatic instruction but find their first experiences with G forces to be unanticipated and very uncomfortable. To minimize or avoid potential adverse effects, the aerobatic instructor and trainee must have a basic understanding of the physiology of G force adaptation.

b. Forces experienced with a rapid push-over maneuver result in the blood and body organs being displaced toward the head. Depending on forces involved and individual tolerance, the airman may experience discomfort, headache, "red-out," and even unconsciousness.

c. Forces experienced with a rapid pull-up maneuver result in the blood and body organ displacement toward the lower part of the body away from the head. Since the brain requires continuous blood circulation for an adequate oxygen supply, there is a physiologic limit to the time the pilot can tolerate higher forces before losing consciousness. As the blood circulation to the brain decreases as a result of forces involved, the airman will experience "narrowing" of visual fields, "gray-out," "black-out," and unconsciousness. Even a brief loss of consciousness in a maneuver can lead to improper control movement causing structural failure of the aircraft or collision with another object or terrain.

d. In steep turns, the centrifugal forces tend to push the pilot into the seat, thereby resulting in blood and body organ displacement toward the lower part of the body as in the case of rapid pull-up maneuvers and with the same physiologic effects and symptoms.

e. Physiologically, humans progressively adapt to imposed strains and stress, and with practice, any maneuver will have decreasing effect. Tolerance to G forces is dependent on human phys-

iology and the individual pilot. These factors include the skeletal anatomy, the cardiovascular architecture, the nervous system, the quality of the blood, the general physical state, and experience and recency of exposure. The airman should consult an Aviation Medical Examiner prior to aerobatic training and be aware that poor physical condition can reduce tolerance to accelerative forces.

f. The above information provides the airman a brief summary of the physiologic effects of G forces. It does not address methods of "counteracting" these effects. There are numerous references on the subject of G forces during aerobatics available to the airman. Among these are "G Effects on the Pilot During Aerobatics," (FAA-AM-72-28), "G Incapacitation in Aerobatic Pilots: A Flight Hazard" (FAA-AM-82-13). These are available from the National Technical Information Service, Springfield, Virginia 22161. See also FAA Advisory Circular — 91-61, "A HAZARD IN AEROBATICS: EFFECTS OF G-FORCES ON PILOTS."

607. JUDGMENT ASPECTS OF COLLISION AVOIDANCE

a. Introduction

(1) The most important aspects of vision and the techniques to scan for other aircraft are described in Paragraph 605 above. Pilots should also be familiar with the following information to reduce the possibility of mid-air collisions.

b. Determining Relative Altitude

(1) Use the horizon as a reference point. If the other aircraft is above the horizon, it is probably on a higher flight path. If the aircraft appears to be below the horizon, it is probably flying at a lower altitude.

c. Taking Appropriate Action

(1) Pilots should be familiar with rules on right-of-way, so if an aircraft is on an obvious collision course, one can take immediately evasive action, preferably in compliance with applicable Federal Aviation Regulations.

d. Consider Multiple Threats

(1) The decision to climb, descend, or turn is a matter of personal judgment, but one should anticipate that the other pilot may also be making a quick maneuver. Watch the other aircraft during the maneuver and begin your scanning again immediately since there may be other aircraft in the area.

e. Collision Course Targets

(1) Any aircraft that appears to have no relative motion and stays in one scan quadrant is likely to be on a collision course. Also, if a target shows no lateral or vertical motion, but increases in size, *take evasive action.*

f. Recognize High Hazard Areas

(1) Airways and especially VORs and airport traffic areas are places where aircraft tend to cluster.

(2) Remember, most collisions occur during days when the weather is good. Being in a "radar environment" still requires vigilance to avoid collisions.

g. Cockpit Management

(1) Studying maps, checklists, and manuals before flight, with other proper preflight planning (e.g., noting necessary radio frequencies) and organizing cockpit materials, can reduce the amount of time required to look at these items during flight, permitting more scan time.

h. Windshield Conditions

(1) Dirty or bug-smeared windshields can greatly reduce the ability of pilots to see other aircraft. Keep a clean windshield.

i. Visibility Conditions

(1) Smoke, haze, dust, rain, and flying towards the sun can also greatly reduce the ability to detect targets.

j. Visual Obstructions in the Cockpit

(1) Pilots need to move their heads to see around blind spots caused by fixed aircraft structures, such as door posts, wings, etc. It will be necessary at times to maneuver the aircraft (e.g., lift a wing) to facilitate seeing.

(2) Pilots must insure curtains and other cockpit objects (e.g., maps on glare shield) are removed and stowed during flight.

k. Lights On

(1) Day or night, use of exterior lights can greatly increase the conspicuity of any aircraft.

(2) Keep interior lights low at night.

l. ATC support

(1) ATC facilities often provide radar traffic advisories on a workload-permitting basis. Flight through the new Airport Radar Service Areas (ARSAs) requires communication with ATC. Use this support whenever possible or when required.

608—619. RESERVED

Chapter 8. AERONAUTICAL CHARTS AND RELATED PUBLICATIONS

Section 1. TYPES OF CHARTS AVAILABLE

620. GENERAL

Aeronautical charts for the U.S. and its territories and possessions are produced by the National Ocean Service (NOS), a part of the Department of Commerce, from information furnished by the FAA.

621. OBTAINING CIVIL AERONAUTICAL CHARTS

En route Aeronautical Charts, En route Supplements, Approach Procedure Charts, Regional Airport/Facility Directories and other publications described in this Chapter are available upon subscription from the

National Ocean Service
NOAA Distribution Branch (N/CG33)
Riverdale, Maryland 20737
Phone: (301) 436-6990

622. TYPES OF CHARTS AVAILABLE

Sectional and VFR Terminal Area Charts
World Aeronautical Charts (U.S.)
En route Low Altitude Charts
En route High Altitude Charts
Alaska En route Charts (Low and High)
Planning Charts
Instrument Approach Procedure Charts
Standard Instrument Departure (SID) Charts
Standard Terminal Arrival (STAR) Charts
Alaska Terminal Publication
Helicopter Route Charts

623. GENERAL DESCRIPTION OF EACH CHART SERIES

a. Sectional and VFR Terminal Area Charts

(1) These charts are designed for visual navigation of slow and medium speed aircraft. They are produced to the following scales:

Sectional Charts — 1:500,000 (1 in=6.86 NM)
VFR Terminal Area Charts — 1:250,000
(1 in=3.43 NM)

(2) Topographic information features the portrayal of relief and a judicious selection of visual check points for VFR flight (Terminal Area Charts include populated places, drainage, roads, railroads, and other distinctive landmarks). Aeronautical information includes visual and radio aids to navigation, airports, controlled airspace, restricted areas, obstructions, and related data. The VFR Terminal Area Charts also depict the airspace designated as "terminal control area" which provides for the control or segrega-

tion of all aircraft within the terminal control area. The Puerto Rico-Virgin Islands Terminal Area Chart contains basically the same information as that shown on Sectional and Terminal Area Charts. It includes the Gulf of Mexico and Caribbean Planning Chart on the reverse side (See PLANNING CHARTS). Charts are revised semiannually except for several Alaskan Sectionals and the Puerto Rico-Virgin Islands Terminal Area which are revised annually.

b. World Aeronautical Charts

(1) These charts are designed to provide a standard series of aeronautical charts, covering land areas of the world, at a size and scale convenient for navigation by moderate speed aircraft. They are produced at a scale of 1:1,000,000 (1 in=13.7 NM). Topographic information includes cities and towns, principal roads, railroads, distinctive landmarks, drainage and relief. The latter is shown by spot elevations, contours, and gradient tints. Aeronautical information includes visual and radio aids to navigation, airports, airways, restricted areas, obstructions and other pertinent data. These charts are revised annually except several Alaskan charts and the Mexican/Caribbean charts which are revised every 2 years.

c. En route Low Altitude Charts

(1) These charts are designed to provide aeronautical information for en route navigation under Instrument Flight Rules (IFR) in the low altitude stratum. The series also includes En route Area Charts which furnish terminal data at a large scale in congested areas, and is included with the subscription to the series. Information includes the portrayal of L/MF and VHF airways, limits of controlled airspace, position, identification and frequencies of radio aids, selected airports, minimum en route and obstruction clearance altitudes, airway distances, reporting points, special use airspace areas, military training routes and related information. Charts are printed back to back. Charts are revised every 56 days effective with the date of airspace changes. An En route Change Notice may be issued as required.

d. En route High Altitude Charts

(1) These charts are designed to provide aeronautical information for en route navigation under IFR in the high altitude stratum. Information includes the portrayal of jet routes, position, identification and frequencies of radio aids, selected airports, distances, time zones, special use airspace areas and related information. Charts are revised every 56 days effective with the date of airspace changes. An En route Change Notice may be issued as required.

e. Alaska En route Charts (Low and High)

(1) These charts are produced in a low altitude and high altitude series with purpose and makeup identical to Low and High Altitude Charts described above. Charts are revised every 56 days effective with the date of airspace changes. An En route Change Notice may be issued as required.

f. Charted VFR Flyway Planning Chart

(1) These charts are designed to identify flight paths clear of the major controlled traffic flows. The program is intended to provide charts showing multiple VFR routings through high density traffic areas which may be used as an alternative to flight within

TCAs. Ground references are provided as guides for improved visual navigation. These charts are not intended to discourage VFR operations within the TCAs, but are designed for information and planning purposes. They are produced at a scale of 1:250,000 (1 in = 3.43 NM). These charts are revised semi-annually and are published on the back of the existing VFR Terminal Area Charts.

g. Planning Charts

(1) *VFR/IFR Planning Chart*

(a) These charts are designed to fulfill the requirements of preflight planning for flights under VFR/IFR. They are produced at a scale of 1:2,333,232 (1 in=32 NM). The chart is printed in two parts in such a manner that, when assembled, it forms a composite VFR Planning Chart on one side and IFR Planning Chart on the other. Information on the IFR chart depicts low altitude airways and mileages, navigational facilities, special use airspace areas, time zones, airports, isogonic lines, and related data. Information on the VFR chart includes selected populated places, large bodies of water, major drainage, shaded relief, navigational facilities, airports, special use airspace areas, military training routes and related data.

(2) *Flight Case Planning Chart*

(a) This chart is designed for preflight and en route flight planning for VFR flights. It is produced at a scale of 1:4,374,803 (1 in=60 NM). This chart contains basically the same information as the VFR/IFR Planning Chart with the addition of selected FSS and Weather Service Offices located at airport sites, parachute jumping areas, a tabulation of special use airspace areas, a mileage table listing distances between 174 major airports and a city/aerodrome location index.

(3) *Gulf of Mexico and Caribbean Planning Chart*

(a) This chart is designated for preflight planning for VFR flights. It is produced at a scale of 1:6,270,551 (1 in=86 NM). This chart is on the reverse of the Puerto Rico-Virgin Islands Terminal Area Chart. Information includes mileage between Airports of Entry, a selection of special use airspace areas and a Directory of Airports with their available facilities and servicing.

(4) *North Atlantic Route Chart*

(a) This five-color chart is designed for use of Air Traffic Controllers in monitoring transatlantic flights and for FAA planners. Oceanic control areas, coastal navigation aids, major coastal airports, and oceanic reporting points are depicted. Geographic coordinates for NAVIDS and reporting points are included. The chart may be used for pre- and in-flight planning. This chart is revised each 24 weeks. Chart available in two sizes, scale: full size 1:5,500,000, 58 by 41 inches/half size 1:11,000,000, 29 by 20-1/2 inches.

(5) *North Pacific Oceanic Route Chart*

(a) This chart series, like the North Atlantic Route Chart series, is designed for FAA Air Traffic Controllers' use in monitoring transoceanic air traffic. Charts are available in two scales: 1:12,000,000 composite small scale planning chart, which covers the entire North Pacific and four 1:7,000,000 Area Charts. They are revised every 24 weeks. The charts are available unfolded, flat only and contain established intercontinental air routes including all reporting points with geographic positions.

(6) *Enroute High Altitude Planning Chart*

(a) This chart is designed specifically for IFR enroute planning at or above 18,000 ft. MSL. It may be used for pre- and in-flight planning and is equivalent in scale to the Flight Case Planning Chart. The chart contains published jet routes, restricted areas, a navigation aid location index, and a special use airspace index. It is a four-color chart using a green vignette for water areas, blue for

special use airspace, black for high frequency jet routes, and brown for low frequency routes. It is revised every 56 days.

h. Instrument Approach Procedure (IAP) Charts

(1) IAP charts portray the aeronautical data which is required to execute instrument approaches to airports. These charts are published in 15 bound volumes covering the conterminous U.S. and the Puerto Rico-Virgin Islands. Each new volume is superseded by a new volume each 56 days. Changes to procedures occurring between the 56 day publication cycle is reflected in a change notice volume issued on the 28 day midcycle. These changes are in the form of a new chart. The publication of a new 56 day volume incorporates all the changes and replaces the preceding volume and the change notice. The bound volumes are 5 3/8 x 8 1/4 inches and bound on the top edge. Each chart contained depicts the IAP, all related navigation data, communications information and an airport sketch. Each procedure is designated for use with a specific electronic navigational aid, such as ILS, VOR, NDB, RNAV, etc. Airport Diagram Charts where published, are included.

i. Standard Instrument Departure (SID) Charts

(1) These charts are designed to expedite clearance delivery and to facilitate transition between takeoff and en route operations. They are published in a bound book, 5 3/8 inches by 8 1/4 inches, and furnish pilots departure routing clearance information in graphic and textual form. These are two bound volumes which are issued every 56 days.

j. Standard Terminal Arrival (STAR) Charts

(1) These charts are designed to expedite ATC arrival route procedures and to facilitate transition between en route and instrument approach operations. These charts, published in a bound book, 5 3/8 inches by 8 1/4 inches, present to the pilot preplanned IFR ATC arrival route procedures in graphic and textual form. Each STAR procedure is presented as a separate chart and may serve a single airport or more than one airport in a given geographic location. One bound volume of STAR charts for the U.S., excluding Alaska, is issued every 56 days.

k. Alaska Terminal Publication

(1) This publication contains charts depicting all terminal flight procedures in the State of Alaska for civil and military aviation. They are

Instrument Approach Procedure (IAP) Charts.

Standard Instrument Departure (SID) Charts.

Standard Terminal Arrival (STAR) Charts.

Airport Diagram Charts.

Radar Minimums.

(2) All supplementary supporting data, i.e.: IFR Takeoff and Departure Procedures, IFR Alternate Minimums, Rate of Descent Table, Inoperative Components Table, etc., is also included.

(3) The Alaska Terminal is published in a bound book 5 3/8 inches by 8 1/4 inches, and is arranged alphabetically by airport name with all procedures appropriate to the airport following the airport name: STAR, IAP, DIAGRAM, SID. The publication is issued every 56 days with provisions for an as required "Terminal Change" on the 28 day midpoint.

l. Helicopter Route Charts

(1) These are a standardized series of charts for major metropolitan areas that have high concentrations of helicopter activity. The scale is 1:125,000, some may include insets. The colors are blue, brown, and black. Topographic information includes urban tint, principal roads, railroads, pictorial symbols and spot elevations. Aeronautical information includes routes, four classes of heliports, NAVIDS, special use airspace, obstacles, control tower frequency tabulation, TCA surface area tint, etc. These charts are revised on an as needed basis.

624. RELATED PUBLICATIONS

a. The Airport Facility Directory

(1) This directory is issued in seven volumes with each volume covering a specific geographic area of the conterminous U.S., including Puerto Rico and the U.S. Virgin Islands. The directory is 5 3/8 X 8 1/4 inches and is bound on the side. Each volume is reissued in its entirety each 56 days. Each volume is indexed alphabetically by state, airport, navigational aid, and ATC facility for the area of coverage. All pertinent information concerning each entry is included.

b. Alaska Supplement

(1) This supplement is a joint Civil and Military Flight Information Publication (FLIP), published and distributed every 56 days by the NOS. It is designed for use with the Flight Information Publication En route Charts, Alaska Terminal, WAC and Sectional Aeronautical Charts. This Supplement contains an Airport/Facility Directory of all airports shown on En route Charts, and those requested by appropriate agencies, communications data, navigational facilities, special notices and procedures applicable to the area of chart coverage.

c. Pacific Supplement

(1) This Chart Supplement is a Civil Flight Information Publication, published and distributed every 56 days by the NOS. It is designed for use with the Flight Information En route Publication Charts and the Sectional Aeronautical Chart covering the State of Hawaii and that area of the Pacific served by U.S. facilities. An Amendment Notice is published 4 weeks after each issue of the Supplement. This chart Supplement contains an Airport/Facility Directory of all airports open to the public, and those requested by appropriate agencies, communications data, navigational facilities, special notices and procedures applicable to the Pacific area.

d. Digital Aeronautical Chart Supplement (DACS)

(1) DACS is a subset of the data NOAA provides to FAA controllers every 56 days. The DACS is designed to assist with flight planning and should not be considered a substitute for a chart. The supplement is divided into eight individual sections. They are

Section 1 — High Altitude Airways — Conterminous U.S.

Section 2 — Low Altitude Airways — Conterminous U.S.

Section 3 — (not yet available)

Section 4 — Military Training Routes

Section 5 — Alaska, Hawaii, Puerto Rico, Bahama and Selected Oceanic Routes

Section 6 — STARs - Standard Terminal Arrivals and Profile Descent Procedures

Section 7 — SIDs - Standard Instrument Departures

Section 8 — Preferred IFR Routes (Low and High Altitudes)

Section 9 — Air Route and Airport Surveillance Radar Facilities (updated yearly)

Sections 8 and 9 are not digital products, but contain pertinent air route data associated with the other sections.

e. NOAA Aeronautical Chart User's Guide

(1) This guide is designed to be used as a teaching aid, reference document, and an introduction to the wealth of information provided on NOAA's aeronautical charts and publications. The guide includes the complete contents of the VFR Chart User's Guide, and a new discussion of IFR chart terms and symbols. This guide also includes a comprehensive index of symbols used on NOAA's VFR, IFR, and Planning charts.

f. Defense Mapping Agency Aerospace Center (DMAAC) Publications

Defense Mapping Agency Aeronautical Charts and Products are available prepaid from

DIRECTOR

DMA Combat Support Center

Attention: DDCP

Washington, DC 20315-0010

Phone: CONUS Toll free telephone number

1-800-826-0342

(1) **Pilotage Charts (PC/TPC)** — Scale 1:500,000 used for detail preflight planning and mission analysis. Emphasis in design is on ground features significant in visual and radar, low-level high speed navigation.

(2) **Jet Navigation Charts (JNC-A)** — Scale 1:3,000,000. Designed to provide greater coverage than the 1:2,000,000 scale Jet Navigation Charts described below. Uses include preflight planning and en route navigation by long-range jet aircraft with dead reckoning, radar, celestial and grid navigation capabilities.

(3) **LORAN Navigation & Consol LORAN Navigation Charts (LJC/CJC)** — Scale 1:2,000,000. Used for preflight planning and in-flight navigation on long-range flights in the Polar areas and adjacent regions utilizing LORAN and CONSOL navigation aids.

(4) **Continental Entry Chart (CEC)** — Scale 1:2,000,000. Used for CONSOLAN and LORAN navigation for entry into the U.S. when a high degree of accuracy is required to comply with Air Defense identification and reporting procedures. Also suitable as a basic dead reckoning sheet and for celestial navigation.

(5) **Aerospace Planning Chart (ASC)** — Scale 1:9,000,000 and 1:18,000,000. Six charts at each scale and with various projections, cover the world. Charts are useful for general planning, briefings, and studies.

(6) **Air Distance/Geography Chart (GH-2, 2a)** — Scales 1:25,000,000 and 1:50,000,000. This chart shows great circle distances between major airports. It also shows major cities, international boundaries, shaded relief and gradient tints.

(7) **LORAN C Navigation Chart (LCC)** — Scale 1:3,000,000. Primarily designed for preflight and in-flight long-range navigation where LORAN C is used as the basic navigation aid.

(8) **DOD Weather Plotting Chart (WPC)** — Various scales. Designed as nonnavigational outline charts which depict locations and identifications of meteorological observing stations. Primarily used to forecast and monitor weather and atmospheric conditions throughout the world.

(9) **Flight Information Publications (FLIP)** — These include En route Low Altitude and High Altitude Charts, En route Supplements, Terminal (Instrument Approach Charts), and other informational publications for various areas of the world.

NOTE.— FLIP. Terminal publications do not necessarily include all instrument approach procedures for all airports. They include only those required for military operations.

(10) **World Aeronautical (WAC) and Operational Navigation Charts (ONC)** — The Operational Navigation Charts (ONC) have the same purpose and contain essentially the same information as the WAC series except the terrain is portrayed by shaded relief as well as contours. The ONC series is replacing the WAC series

and the WAC's will be available only where the ONC's have not been issued. ONC's are 42 X 57 1/2 inches, WAC's are 22 X 30 inches. These charts are revised on a regular schedule.

(11) **Jet Navigation Charts** — These charts are designed to fulfill the requirements for long-range high altitude, high speed navigation. They are produced at a scale of 1:2,000,000 (1 in=27.4 NM). Topographic features include large cities, roads, railroads, drainage and relief. The latter is indicated by contours, spot elevations and gradient tints. All aeronautical information necessary to conform to the purpose of the chart is shown. This includes restricted areas, L/MF and VOR ranges, radio beacons and a selection of standard broadcasting stations and airports. The runway patterns of the airports are shown to exaggerated scale in order that they may be readily identified as visual landmarks. Universal Jet Navigation Charts are used as plotting charts in the training and practice of celestial and dead reckoning navigation. They may also be used for grid navigational training.

(12) **Global Navigational Charts** — These charts are designed to fulfill the requirements for aeronautical planning, operations over long distances, and en route navigation in long-range, high altitude, high speed aircraft. They are produced at a scale of 1:5,000,000 (1 in=68.58 NM). Global Navigation Charts (GNC) are 42 by 57 1/2 inches. They show principal cities, towns and drainage, primary roads and railroads, prominent culture and shadient relief augmented with tints and spot elevations. Aeronautical data includes radio aids to navigation, aerodrome and restricted areas. Charts 1 and 26 have a polar navigation grid and charts 2 and 6 have sub-polar navigation grids. Global LORAN Navigation Charts (GLC) are the same size and scale and cover the same area as the GNC charts. They contain major cities only, coast lines, major

lakes and rivers, and land tint. No relief or vegetation. Aeronautical data includes radio aids to navigation and LORAN lines of position.

625. AUXILIARY CHARTS

a. **Airport Obstruction Charts (OC):**

(1) The Airport Obstruction Chart is a 1:12,000 scale graphic depicting Federal Aviation Regulations Part 77 (FAR—77) surfaces, a representation of objects that penetrate these surfaces, aircraft movement and apron areas, navigational aids, prominent airport buildings, and a selection of roads and other planimetric detail in the airport vicinity. Also included are tabulations of runway and other operational data.

b. **Military Training Routes:**

(1) Charts and Booklet: The Defense Mapping Agency Aerospace Center (DMAAC) publishes a narrative description in booklet form and charts depicting the IFR and VFR Training Routes.

(2) The charts and booklet are published every 56 days. Both the charts and narrative route description booklet are available to the general public as a brochure by single copy or annual subscription.

(3) Subscription and single-copy requests should be for the "DOD Area Planning AP/1B, Military Training Routes". (See PARA—132 - MILITARY TRAINING ROUTES (MTR).)

NOTE.— The DOD provides these booklets and charts to each FSS for use in preflight pilot briefings. Pilots should review this information to acquaint themselves with those routes that are located along their route of flight and in the vicinity of the airports from which they operate.

626—999. RESERVED

APPENDIX 1

Figures

(Figure 1-1)

STANDARD HIGH
ALTITUDE SERVICE VOLUME
(refer to FIGURE 5 for altitudes
below 1000 feet)

(Figure 1-2)

STANDARD LOW
ALTITUDE SERVICE VOLUME
(refer to FIGURE 5 for altitudes
below 1000 feet)

NOTE: All elevations shown are with respect
to the station's site elevation (AGL).
Coverage is not available in a cone of
airspace directly above the facility.

(Figure 1-3)

STANDARD TERMINAL
SERVICE VOLUME
(refer to FIGURE 4 for altitudes
below 1000 feet)

(Figure 1-4)

DEFINITION OF THE LOWER EDGE OF THE STANDARD T
(TERMINAL) SERVICE VOLUME

(Figure 1-5)

DEFINITION OF THE LOWER EDGE OF THE STANDARD H
(HIGH) AND L (LOW) SERVICE VOLUMES

(Figure 1-6)

(Figure 1-7)

ILS

[FAA INSTRUMENT LANDING SYSTEM]

STANDARD CHARACTERISTICS AND TERMINOLOGY

ILS approach charts should be consulted to obtain variations of individuals systems.

VHF LOCALIZER
Provides Horizontal Guidance.

108.10 to 111.95 MHz. Radiates about 100 watts. Horizontal polarization. Modulation frequencies 90 and 150 Hz. Modulation depth on course 20% for each frequency. Code identification (1020 Hz, 5%) and voice communication (modulated 50%) provided on same channel.

1000 ft typical. Localizer transmitter building is offset 250 ft minimum from center of antenna array and within 90° ± 30° from approach end. Antenna is on centerline and normally is under 50:1 clearance plane.

Point of intersection runway and glide slope extended

Runway length 7000 ft (typical)

250 to 600 ft from centerline of runway

3000' to 6000' from threshold

+ 200'

Sited to provide 55 ft (± 5 ft) runway threshold crossing height

UHF GLIDE SLOPE TRANSMITTER
Provides Vertical Guidance

329.3 to 335.0 MHz. Radiates about 5 watts. Horizontal polarization, modulation on path 40% for 90 Hz and 150 Hz. The glide slope is established nominally at an angle of 2.5 degrees, or higher, depending on local terrain.

MIDDLE MARKER Decision Height. Indicates Approximate Height Point. Modulation 1300 Hz, 95% Keying 95 Alternate Dot & Dash Combinations/Minute

Amber Light

Localizer modulation frequency
90 Hz   150 Hz

Glide slope 150 Hz modulation frequency
90 Hz

Outer marker located 4 to 7 miles from end of runway, where glide slope intersects the procedure turn (minimum holding) altitude, ± 50 ft vertically.

OUTER MARKER
Provides Final Approach Fix For Non-Precision Approach

Modulation 400 Hz, 95%
Keying: Two dashes/second

Blue light

Flag indicates if facility not on the air or receiver malfunctioning

Approximately 1.4° width (full scale limits)

0.7° (approx.)

3° above horizontal (optimum)

Course width varies: between 3°-6°— tailored to provide 700 ft at threshold (full scale limits)

All marker transmitters approximately 2 watts of power modulated about 95%.

* Figures marked with asterisk are typical. Actual figures vary with deviations in distances to markers, glide angles and localizer widths.

NOTE:
Compass locators, rated at 25 watts output 190 to 535 KHz, are installed at many outer and some middle markers. A 400 Hz or a 1020 Hz tone modulating the carrier about 95%, is keyed with the first two letters of the ILS identification on the outer locator and the last two letters on the middle locator. At some locators, simultaneous voice transmissions from the control tower are provided, with appropriate reduction in identification percentage.

RATE OF DESCENT CHART
(feet per minute)

Speed (Knots)	2 1/2 °	2 3/4 °	3 °
90	400	440	475
110	485	535	585
130	575	630	690
150	665	730	795
160	707	778	849

Angle

(Figure 1-8)

(Figure 1-9)

The nearby target absorbs and scatters so much of the out-going and returning
energy that the radar does not detect the distant target.

(Figure 1-10)

ARTS III Radar Scope with Alphanumeric Data. Note: A number of radar terminals do not have ARTS equipment. Those facilities and certain ARTCC's outside the contiguous US would have radar displays similar to the lower right hand subset. ARTS facilities and NAS Stage A ARTCC's, when operating in the non-automation mode would also have similar displays and certain services based on automation may not be available.

(Figure 1-11)

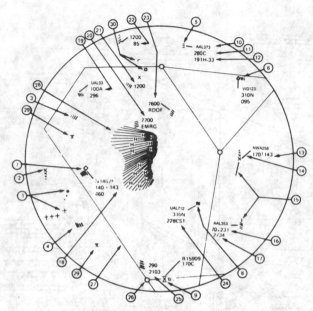

Target Symbols

1 Uncorrelated primary radar target   + ●
2 *Correlated primary radar target   X
3 Uncorrelated beacon target   /
4 Correlated beacon target   \
5 Identing beacon target   ☰
   (*Correlated means the association
   of radar data with the computer projected track of an identified aircraft)

Position Symbols

6 Free track (No flight plan tracking) △
7 Flat track (flight plan tracking)   ◇
8 Coast (Beacon target lost)   ⚮
9 Present Position Hold   X̄

Data Block Information

10 *Aircraft Identification
11 *Assigned Altitude FL 280, mode C altitude
   same or within ±200' of asgnd altitude

12 *Computer ID #191, Handoff is to Sector 33
   (0-33 would mean handoff accepted)
   (*Nr's 10, 11, 12 constitute a "full data
   block")
13 Assigned altitude 17,000', aircraft is
   climbing, mode C readout was 14,300
   when last beacon interrogation was
   received
14 Leader line connecting target symbol
   and data block
15 Track velocity and direction vector
   line (Projected ahead of target)
16 Assigned altitude 7000, aircraft is
   descending, last mode C readout (or
   last reported altitude was 100'
   above FL230
17 Transponder code shows in full data block
   only when different than assigned code
18 Aircraft is 300' above assigned
   altitude
19 Reported altitude (No mode C readout)
   same as assigned. An "N" would indicate no reported altitude)
20 Transponder set on emergency code 7700
   (EMRG flashes to attract attention)

21 Transponder code 1200 (VFR) with no
   mode C
22 Code 1200 (VFR) with mode C and last
   altitude readout
23 Transponder set on Radio Failure code
   7600, (RDOF flashes)
24 Computer ID #228, CST indicates target is
   in Coast status
25 Assigned altitude FL290, transponder
   code (These two items constitute a
   "limited data block")

Other symbols

26 Navigational Aid
27 Airway or jet route
28 Outline of weather returns based on
   primary radar (See Chapter 4, ARTCC
   Radar Weather Display. H's represent
   areas of high density precipitation
   which might be thunderstorms. Radial
   lines indicate lower density precipitation)
29 Obstruction
30 Airports Major: □ , Small: Γ

NAS Stage A Controllers View Plan Display. This figure illustrates the controller's radar scope (PVD) when operating in the full
automation (RDP) mode, which is normally 20 hours per day. (Note: When not in automation mode, the display is similar to the broadband mode
shown in the ARTS III Radar Scope figure. Certain ARTCC's outside the contiguous U.S. also operate in "broadband" mode.)

(Figure 2-1)

Precision Instrument Configurations

NOTE: Civil ALSF-2 may be operated as SSALR during favorable weather conditions.

ALSF 2   ALSF 1   SSALR / MALSR

▲ Flashing Light
● Steady Burning Light

Nonprecision Instrument Configurations

▲ Flashing Light
● Steady Burning Light

MALSF   ODALS

Omnidirectional Flashing Light

(Figure 2-2)

Far Bar
Near Bar

Below Glide Path   On Glide Path   Above Glide Path

■ = Red
□ = White

(Figure 2-3)

Far Bar
Middle Bar
Near Bar

Below Both Glide Paths   On Lower Glide Path   On Upper Glide Path   Above Both Glide Paths

(Figure 2-4)

2 Bar
2 Light Units
On Glide Path

2 Bar
12 Light Units
on Glide Path

3 Bar
16 Light Units
on Lower Glide Path

(Figure 2-5)

High
(More Than
3.5 Degrees)

Slightly High
(3.2 Degrees)

O White
● Red

On Glide Path
(3 Degrees)

Slightly Low
(2.8 Degrees)

Low
(Less Than
2.5 Degrees)

(Figure 2-6)

Amber

Above Glide Path

Green
Amber

On Glide Path

Red

Below Glide Path

Caution: When the aircraft descends from green to red, the pilot may see a dark amber color during the transition from green to red.

(Figure 2-7)

Pulsating White
Steady White or
Alternating Red/White
Pulsating Red

Above Glide Path
On Glide Path
Below Glide Path

Threshold

Caution: When viewing the pulsating visual approach slope indicators in the pulsating white or pulsating red sectors, it is possible to mistake this lighting aid for another aircraft or a ground vehicle. Pilots should exercise caution when using this type of system.

(Figure 2-8)

Above Glide Path   On Glide Path   Below Glide Path

(Figure 2-9)

VISUAL RUNWAY

(Figure 2-10)

NON-PRECISION INSTRUMENT RUNWAY

(Figure 2-11)

THRESHOLD MARKER TOUCHDOWN ZONE MARKER FIXED DISTANCE MARKER

PRECISION INSTRUMENT RUNWAY

(Figure 2-12)

NON-LANDING PORTION OF RUNWAY DISPLACED THRESHOLD LANDING PORTION OF RUNWAY THRESHOLD

(Figure 2-13)

STOPWAY AND BLAST
PAD AREA

(Figure 2-14)

CLOSED RUNWAY OR TAXIWAY

(Figure 2-15)

STOL RUNWAY

(Figure 2-16)

HELICOPTER LANDING AREA

Recommended Marking for
Civil Heliports

Some Civil and Military Heliports May
Be Marked With This Symbol

Recommended Marking for
Closed Heliports

Recommended Marking for
Hospital Heliports

(Figure 3-1)

Airport Radar Service Area (ARSA)

(Figure 3-2)

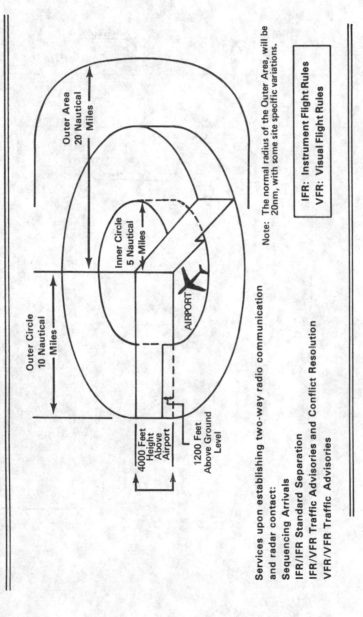

Outer Area
20 Nautical
Miles

Inner Circle
5 Nautical
Miles

Outer Circle
10 Nautical
Miles

AIRPORT

4000 Feet
Height
Above
Airport

1200 Feet
Above Ground
Level

Note: The normal radius of the Outer Area, will be
20nm, with some site specific variations.

IFR: Instrument Flight Rules
VFR: Visual Flight Rules

Services upon establishing two-way radio communication
and radar contact:
Sequencing Arrivals
IFR/IFR Standard Separation
IFR/VFR Traffic Advisories and Conflict Resolution
VFR/VFR Traffic Advisories

(Figure 4-1)

(Figure 4-2)

(Figure 4-3)

LAKE/ISLAND, MOUNTAIN AND SWAMP REPORTING SERVICE
Flight Service Station (FSS)

(Figure 4-4)

NOTE.—This diagram is intended only to illustrate terminology used in identifying various components of a traffic pattern. It should not be used as a reference or guide on how to enter a traffic pattern.

(Figure 4-5)

Key:

① Enter pattern in level flight, abeam the midpoint of the runway, at pattern altitude. (1000' AGL is recommended pattern altitude unless established otherwise).

② Maintain pattern altitude until abeam approach end of the landing runway, or downwind leg.

③ Complete turn to final at least ¼ mile from the runway.

④ Continue straight ahead until beyond departure end of runway.

⑤ If remaining in the traffic pattern, commence turn to crosswind leg beyond the departure end of the runway, within 300 feet of pattern altitude.

⑥ If departing the traffic pattern, continue straight out, or exit with a 45° left turn beyond the departure end of the runway, after reaching pattern altitude.

⑦ Do not overshoot final or continue on a track which will penetrate the final approach of the parallel runway.

⑧ Do not continue on a track which will penetrate the departure path of the parallel runway.

(Figure 4-6)

SIGNALMAN DIRECTS TOWING

SIGNALMAN'S POSITION

FLAGMAN DIRECTS PILOT TO SIGNALMAN IF TRAFFIC CONDITIONS REQUIRE

ALL CLEAR (O.K.)

START ENGINE

POINT TO ENGINE TO BE STARTED

PULL CHOCKS

COME AHEAD

LEFT TURN

RIGHT TURN

SLOW DOWN

STOP

INSERT CHOCKS

CUT ENGINES

NIGHT OPERATION (Uses same hand movements as day operation)

EMERGENCY STOP

(Figure 4-7)

Form Approved: OMB No. 2120-0026

U.S. DEPARTMENT OF TRANSPORTATION FEDERAL AVIATION ADMINISTRATION **FLIGHT PLAN**	(FAA USE ONLY) ☐ PILOT BRIEFING ☐ VNR ☐ STOPOVER	TIME STARTED	SPECIALIST INITIALS

1. TYPE	2. AIRCRAFT IDENTIFICATION	3. AIRCRAFT TYPE/ SPECIAL EQUIPMENT	4. TRUE AIRSPEED	5. DEPARTURE POINT	6. DEPARTURE TIME		7. CRUISING ALTITUDE
VFR					PROPOSED (Z)	ACTUAL (Z)	
IFR							
DVFR			KTS				

8. ROUTE OF FLIGHT

9. DESTINATION (Name of airport and city)	10. EST. TIME ENROUTE		11. REMARKS
	HOURS	MINUTES	

12. FUEL ON BOARD		13. ALTERNATE AIRPORT(S)	14. PILOT'S NAME, ADDRESS & TELEPHONE NUMBER & AIRCRAFT HOME BASE	15. NUMBER ABOARD
HOURS	MINUTES			
			17. DESTINATION CONTACT/TELEPHONE (OPTIONAL)	

16. COLOR OF AIRCRAFT	CIVIL AIRCRAFT PILOTS. FAR Part 91 requires you file an IFR flight plan to operate under instrument flight rules in controlled airspace. Failure to file could result in a civil penalty not to exceed $1,000 for each violation (Section 901 of the Federal Aviation Act of 1958, as amended). Filing of a VFR flight plan is recommended as a good operating practice. See also Part 99 for requirements concerning DVFR flight plans.

FAA Form 7233-1 (8-82)   CLOSE VFR FLIGHT PLAN WITH_____ FSS ON ARRIVAL

(Figure 4-8)

EARLY TURN

TURN AT OR AFTER FIX PASSAGE

Airway/Route

Boundary

Turning Fix

Airway/Route Boundary

(Figure 4-9)

EXAMPLES OF HOLDING

TYPICAL PROCEDURE ON AN ILS OUTER MARKER

**TYPICAL PROCEDURE AT INTERSECTION
OF VOR RADIALS**

HOLDING COURSE AWAY FROM NAVAID   HOLDING COURSE TOWARD NAVAID

VORTAC

15 NM DME FIX   10 NM DME FIX

TYPICAL PROCEDURE AT DME FIX

(Figure 4-10)

(Figure 4-11)

STANDARD PATTERN

(Figure 4-12)

When the inbound course is *toward* the NAVAID and the fix distance is 10 NM, and the leg length is 5NM, then the end of the outbound leg will be reached when the DME reads 15 NM.

(Figure 4-13)

When the inbound course is *away* from the NAVAID and the fix distance is 28 NM and the leg length is 8 NM, then the end of the outbound leg will be reached when the DME reads 20 NM.

(Figure 4-14)

(Figure 4-15)

Time Approach Example — a final approach procedure from a holding pattern at a final approach fix (FAF).

At 12:03 local time, in the example shown, a pilot holding, receives instructions to leave the fix inbound at 12:07. These instructions are received just as the pilot has completed turn at the outbound end of the holding pattern and is proceeding inbound towards the fix. Arriving back over the fix, the pilot notes that the time is 12:04 and that he has 3 minutes to lose in order to leave the fix at the assigned time. Since the time remaining is more than 2 minutes, the pilot plans to fly a race track pattern rather than a 360 degrees turn, which would use up 2 minutes. The turns at the ends of the race track pattern will consume approximately 2 minutes. Three minutes to go, minus 2 minutes required for turns, leaves 1 minute for level flight. Since two portions of level flight will be required to get back to the fix inbound, the pilot halves the 1 minute remaining and plans to fly level for 30 seconds outbound before starting his turn back toward the fix on final approach. If the winds were negligible at flight altitude, this procedure would bring the pilot inbound across the fix precisely at the specified time of 12:07. However, if the pilot expected a headwind on final approach, he should shorten his 30 seconds outbound course somewhat, knowing that the wind will carry him away from the fix faster while outbound and decrease his ground speed while returning to the fix. On the other hand, if the pilot knew he would have a tailwind on final approach, he should lengthen his calculated 30-second outbound heading somewhat, knowing that the wind would tend to hold him closer to the fix while outbound and increase his ground speed while returning to the fix.

(Figure 4-16)

(Figure 4-18)

(Figure 4-17)

CIRCLING APPROACH AREA RADII

Approach Category	Radius (Miles)
A	1.3
B	1.5
C	1.7
D	2.3
E	4.5

CONSTRUCTION OF CIRCLING APPROACH AREA.

(Figure 4-19)

MISSED APPROACH-EXAMPLE

Portion of a Published Procedure

(Figure 4-20)

INTERCEPTION PATTERNS
FOR IDENTIFICATION OF
INTERCEPTED AIRCRAFT
(TYPICAL)

APPROACH
PHASE (DAY)

IDENTIFICATION PHASE

POST INTERCEPT PHASE

TRANSPORT

INTERCEPTORS

WINGMAN

FLIGHT LEAD

Note: During Night/IMC,
approach will be from
below flight path.

(Figure 4-21)

(Figure 5-1)

GROUND-AIR VISUAL CODE FOR USE BY SURVIVORS

NO.	MESSAGE	CODE SYMBOL
1	Require assistance	V
2	Require medical assistance	X
3	No or Negative	N
4	Yes or Affirmative	Y
5	Proceeding in this direction	↑

IF IN DOUBT, USE INTERNATIONAL SYMBOL   **S O S**

INSTRUCTIONS

1. Lay out symbols by using strips of fabric or parachutes, pieces of wood, stones, or any available material.
2. Provide as much color contrast as possible between material used for symbols and background against which symbols are exposed.
3. Symbols should be at least 10 feet high or larger. Care should be taken to lay out symbols exactly as shown.
4. In addition to using symbols, every effort is to be made to attract attention by means of radio, flares, smoke, or other available means.
5. On snow covered ground, signals can be made by dragging, shoveling or tramping. Depressed areas forming symbols will appear black from the air.
6. Pilot should acknowledge message by rocking wings from side to side.

GROUND-AIR VISUAL CODE FOR USE BY GROUND SEARCH PARTIES

NO.	MESSAGE	CODE SYMBOL
1	Operation completed.	L L L
2	We have found all personnel.	L L
3	We have found only some personnel.	⊬
4	We are not able to continue. Returning to base.	X X
5	Have divided into two groups. Each proceeding in direction indicated.	⚡
6	Information received that aircraft is in this direction.	⇢
7	Nothing found. Will continue search.	N N

"Note: These visual signals have been accepted for international use and appear in Annex 12 to the Convention on International Civil Aviation."

(Figure 5-2)

VISUAL EMERGENCY SIGNALS

**NEED MEDICAL
ASSISTANCE—URGENT**
Used only when life is at stake

ALL OK—DO NOT WAIT
Wave one arm overhead

**CAN PROCEED SHORTLY—
WAIT IF PRACTICABLE**
One arm horizontal

**NEED MECHANICAL HELP
OR PARTS—LONG DELAY**
Both arms horizontal

USE DROP MESSAGE

Make throwing motion

**OUR RECEIVER IS
OPERATING**
Cup hands over ears

**DO NOT ATTEMPT
TO LAND HERE**
Both arms waved across face

LAND HERE
Both arms forward horizontally,
squatting and point in direction of landing—Repeat

NEGATIVE (NO)

White cloth waved horizontally

AFFIRMATIVE (YES)

White cloth waved vertically

**PICK US UP—
PLANE ABANDONED**
Both arms vertical

AFFIRMATIVE (YES)

Dip nose of plane several times

NEGATIVE (NO)

Fishtail plane

HOW TO USE THEM

If you are forced down and are able to attract the attention of the pilot of
a rescue airplane, the body signals illustrated on this page can be used to
transmit messages to him as he circles over your location. Stand in the open
when you make the signals. Be sure that the background, as seen from the air,
is not confusing. Go through the motions slowly and repeat each signal until
you are positive that the pilot understands you.

(Figure 5-3)

WIND-SWELL-DITCH HEADING SITUATIONS

DIRECTION OF
SWELL MOVEMENT

BEST

GOOD   FAIR
          GOOD

Landing parallel to the major swell

GOOD!!   POOR!!!

BACK SIDE   FACE

Landing on the face and back of swell

Single Swell System - Wind 15 knots

Double Swell System - Wind 15 knots

Double Swell System - Wind 30 knots

Wind - 50 knots
Aircraft with low landing speeds - land into the wind.
Aircraft with high landing speeds - choose compromise
       heading between wind and swell.
Both - Land on back side of swell.

(Figure 6-1)

(Figure 6-1)

(Figure 6-2)

(Figure 6-3)

Figure 1. Vertical cross section of the evolution of a microburst wind field. T is the time of initial divergence at the surface. The shading refers to the vector wind speeds. Figure adapted from Wilson et al., 1984, Microburst Wind Structure and Evaluation of Doppler Radar for Wind Shear Detection, DOT/FAA Report No. DOT/FAA/PM-84/29, National Technical Information Service, Springfield, VA 37 pp.

Figure 2. A microburst encounter during takeoff. The airplane first encounters a headwind and experiences increasing performance (1), this is followed in short succession by a decreasing headwind component (2), a downdraft (3), and finally a strong tailwind (4), where 2 through 5 all result in decreasing performance of the airplane. Position (5) represents an extreme situation just prior to impact. Figure courtesy of Walter Frost, FWG Associates, Inc., Tullahoma, Tennessee.

(Figure 6-4)

KEY TO AVIATION WEATHER OBSERVATIONS

LOCATION IDENTIFIER TYPE AND TIME OF REPORT *	SKY AND CEILING	VISIBILITY WEATHER AND OBSTRUCTION TO VISION	SEA-LEVEL PRESSURE	TEMPERATURE AND DEW POINT	WIND	ALTIMETER SETTING	REMARKS AND CODED DATA
MCI SA 0758	15 SCT M25 OVC	1R−F	132	/58/56	/1807	/993/	R01VR20V40

SKY AND CEILING

Sky cover contractions are for each layer in ascending order. Figures preceding contractions are base heights in hundreds of feet above station elevation. Sky cover contractions used are

CLR = Clear. Less than Ø.1 sky cover.
SCT = Scattered. Ø.1 to Ø.5 sky cover.
BKN = Broken. Ø.6 to Ø.9 sky cover.
OVC = Overcast. More than Ø.9 sky cover.

— = Thin (When prefixed to SCT, BKN, OVC).
−X = Partly obscured. Ø.9 or less of sky hidden by precipitation or obstruction to vision (bases at surface).
X = Obscured. 1.Ø sky hidden by precipitation or obstruction to vision (bases at surface).

A letter preceding the height of a base identifies a ceiling layer and indicates how ceiling height was determined. Thus

E = Estimated
M = Measured
W = Vertical visibility into obscured sky

V = Immediately following the height of a base indicates a variable ceiling

VISIBILITY

Reported in statute miles and fractions
(V = Variable)

WEATHER AND OBSTRUCTION TO VISION SYMBOLS

A	Hail	IC	Ice crystals	S	Snow
BD	Blowing dust	IF	Ice fog	SG	Snow grains
BN	Blowing sand	IP	Ice pellets	SP	Snow pellets
BS	Blowing snow	IPW	Ice pellet showers	SW	Snow showers
D	Dust	K	Smoke	T	Thunderstorms
F	Fog	L	Drizzle	T+	Severe thunderstorm
GF	Ground fog	R	Rain	ZL	Freezing drizzle
H	Haze	RW	Rain showers	ZR	Freezing rain

Precipitation intensities are indicated thus: − Light, (no sign) Moderate, + Heavy

WIND Direction in tens of degrees from true north, speed in knots. ØØØØ indicates calm. G indicates gusty. Q indicates Squalls. Peak wind speed in the past 1Ø minutes follows G or Q when gusts or squalls are reported. The contraction WSHFT, followed by GMT time group in remarks, indicates windshift and its time of occurrence. (Knots x 1.15 = statute mi/hr.)

EXAMPLES: 3627 = wind from 360 Degrees at 27 knots.
3627G4Ø = wind from 360 Degrees at 27 knots, peak speed in gusts 40 knots

ALTIMETER SETTING
The first figure of the actual altimeter setting is always omitted from the report.

RUNWAY VISUAL RANGE (RVR)

RVR is reported from some stations. For planning purposes, the value range during 10 minutes prior to observations and based on runway light setting 5 are reported in hundreds of feet. Runway identification precedes RVR report.

PILOT REPORTS (PIREPs)

When available, PIREPs in fixed-format may be appended to weather observations. PIREPs are designated by UA or UUA for urgent PIREPs.

DECODED REPORT

Kansas City International: Record observation completed at Ø758 UTC. 15ØØ feet scattered clouds, measured ceiling 25ØØ feet overcast, visibility 1 mile, light rain, fog, sea-level pressure 1Ø13.2 millibars, temperature 58ºF, dewpoint 56ºF, wind from 18Øº at 7 knots, altimeter setting 29.93 inches. Runway Ø1, visual range 2ØØØ feet lowest 4ØØØ feet highest in past 1Ø minutes.

• TYPE OF REPORT

SA = a scheduled record observation
SP = an unscheduled special observation indicating a significant change in one or more elements
RS = a scheduled record observation that also qualifies as a special observation

The designator for all three types of observations (SA, SP, RS) is followed by a 24-hour-clock-time-group in Coordinated Universal Time (UTC or Z).

U.S. DEPARTMENT OF COMMERCE—NATIONAL OCEANIC AND ATMOSPHERIC ADMINISTRATION—NATIONAL WEATHER SERVICE

KEY TO AVIATION WEATHER FORECASTS

TERMINAL FORECASTS contain information for specific airports on expected ceiling, cloud heights, cloud amounts, visibility, weather and obstructions to vision, and surface wind. They are issued 3 times/day, amended as needed, and are valid for up to 24 hours. The last six hours of each forecast period are covered by a categorical statement indicating whether VFR, MVFR, IFR or LIFR conditions are expected (L in LIFR and M in MVFR indicate "low" and "marginal"). Terminal forecasts are written in the following form:

CEILING Identified by the letter "C" (for lowest layer with cumulative sky cover greater than 5/1Ø)
CLOUD HEIGHTS in hundreds of feet above the station (ground)
SKY COVER AMOUNT (including any obscuration)
CLOUD LAYERS Stated in ascending order of height
VISIBILITY In statute miles (omitted if over 6 miles)
WEATHER AND OBSTRUCTION TO VISION Standard weather and obstruction to vision symbols are used
SURFACE WIND In tens of degrees and knots (omitted when less than 6 knots)

EXAMPLE OF TERMINAL FORECAST
DCA 221010: DCA Forecast 22nd day of month - valid time 1ØZ-1ØZ.
1ØSCT C18 BKN 5SW−3415G25 OCNL C8 X 1/2SW: Scattered clouds at 1ØØØ feet, ceiling 18ØØ feet broken, visibility 5 miles, light snow showers, surface wind from 34Ø degrees at 15 knots. Gusts to 25 knots, occasional ceiling 8 hundred feet sky totally obscured, visibility 1/2 mile in moderate snow showers.
12Z C5Ø BKN 3312G22: By 12Z becoming ceiling 5ØØØ feet broken, surface wind 33Ø degrees at 12 knots. Gusts to 22.
Ø4Z MVFR CIG: Last 6 hours of FT after Ø4Z marginal VFR due to ceiling

AREA FORECASTS are 12-hour aviation forecasts plus a 6-hour categorical outlook prepared 3 times/day, with each section amended as needed, giving general descriptions of potential hazards, airmass and frontal conditions, icing and freezing level, turbulence and low-level windshear and significant clouds and weather for an area the size of several states. Heights of cloud bases and tops, turbulence and icing are referenced ABOVE MEAN SEA LEVEL (MSL); unless indicated by Ceiling (CIG) or ABOVE GROUND LEVEL (AGL). Each SIGMET OR AIRMET affecting an FA area will also serve to amend the Area Forecast.

SIGMET, AIRMET and CWA messages (In-flight advisories) broadcast by FAA on NAVAID voice channels warn pilots of potentially hazardous weather. SIGMET's concern severe and extreme conditions of importance to all aircraft (i.e. icing, turbulence and dust storms/sandstorms or volcanic ash). Convective SIGMET's are issued for thunderstorms if they are sufficiently strong, wide spread or embedded. AIRMET's concern less severe conditions which may be hazardous to aircraft particularly smaller aircraft and less experienced or VFR only pilots. CWA's (Center Weather Advisories) concern both SIGMET and AIRMET type conditions described in greater detail and relating to a specific ARTCC area.

WINDS AND TEMPERATURES ALOFT (FD) FORECASTS are 6, 12, and 24-hour forecasts of wind direction (nearest 1Øº true N) and speed (knots) for selected flight levels. Forecast Temperatures Aloft (ºC) are included for all but the 3ØØØ-foot level.

EXAMPLES OF WINDS AND TEMPERATURES ALOFT (FD) FORECASTS
FD WBC 121645
BASED ON 1212ØØZ DATA
VALID 13ØØØØZ FOR USE 21ØØ-Ø6ØØZ TEMPS NEG ABV 24000 FT

	3000	6000	9000	12000	18000	24000	30000	34000	39000
BOS	3127	3425 07	3420 11	3421 16	3516 27	3512 38	311649	292451	283451
JFK	1026	3327 08	3324 12	3322 16	3123 27	2923 38	284248	285150	285749

At 6ØØØ feet MSL over JFK wind from 33Øº at 27 knots and temperature minus 8ºC

TWEB (CONTINUOUS TRANSCRIBED WEATHER BROADCAST) Individual route forecasts covering a 25-nautical-mile zone either side of the route. By requesting a specific route number, detailed en route weather for a 15-hour period plus a synopsis can be obtained.

PILOTS. . . . report in-flight weather to nearest FSS. The latest surface weather reports are available by phone at the nearest pilot weather briefing office by calling at H + 10.

U.S. DEPARTMENT OF COMMERCE—NATIONAL OCEANIC AND ATMOSPHERIC ADMINISTRATION—NATIONAL WEATHER SERVICE — REVISED JANUARY 1987

(Figure 6-5)

VORTEX
FLOW

VORTEX
CORE

(Figure 6-6)

(Figure 6-7)

(Figure 6-8)

Vortex Flow Field in Aircraft Wake

(Figure 6-9)

(Figure 6-10)

Vortex Movement in Ground Effect - No Wind

(Figure 6-11)

APPENDIX 2

Tables

(Table 1-1)

SSV CLASS DESIGNATOR	ALTITUDE AND RANGE BOUNDARIES
T (Terminal)	From 1000 feet above ground level (AGL) up to and including 12,000 feet AGL at radial distances out to 25 NM. See Figures 1-3 and 1-4.
L (Low Altitude)	From 1000 feet AGL up to and including 18,000 feet AGL at radial distances out to 40 NM. See Figures 1-2 and 1-5.
H (High Altitude)	From 1000 feet AGL up to and including 14,500 feet AGL at radial distances out to 40 NM. From 14,500 feet AGL up to and including 60,000 feet at radial distances out to 100 NM. From 18,000 feet AGL up to and including 45,000 feet AGL at radial distances out to 130 NM. See Figures 1-1 and 1-5.

(Table 1-2)

CLASS	DISTANCE (RADIUS)
Compass Locator	15 NM
MH	25 NM
H	50 NM*
HH	75 NM

* Service ranges of individual facilities may be less than 50 nautical miles (NM). Restrictions to service volumes are first published in the Notice to Airmen and then with the alphabetical listing of the NAVAID in the Airport/Facility Directory.

(Table 1-3)

Localizer MHz	Glide Slope
108.10	334.70
108.15	334.55
108.3	334.10
108.35	333.95
108.5	329.90
108.55	329.75
108.7	330.50
108.75	330.35
108.9	329.30
108.95	329.15
109.1	331.40
109.15	331.25
109.3	332.00
109.35	331.85
109.50	332.60
109.55	332.45
109.70	333.20
109.75	333.05
109.90	333.80
109.95	333.65

(Table 1-3)

Localizer MHz	Glide Slope
110.1	334.40
110.15	334.25
110.3	335.00
110.35	334.85
110.5	329.60
110.55	329.45
110.70	330.20
110.75	330.05
110.90	330.80
110.95	330.65
111.10	331.70
111.15	331.55
111.30	332.30
111.35	332.15
111.50	332.9
111.55	332.75
111.70	333.5
111.75	333.35
111.90	331.1
111.95	330.95

(Table 1-4)

CHAN-NEL NUM-BER	FRE-QUENCY (MHz)	CHAN-NEL NUM-BER	FRE-QUENCY (MHz)	CHAN-NEL NUM-BER	FRE-QUENCY (MHz)	CHAN-NEL NUM-BER	FRE-QUENCY (MHz)	CHAN-NEL NUM-BER	FRE-QUENCY (MHz)
5000	5031.0	540	5043.0	580	5055.0	620	5067.0	660	5079.0
501	5031.3	-	-	-	-	-	-	-	-
502	5031.6	-	-	-	-	-	-	-	-
503	5031.9	-	-	-	-	-	-	-	-
504	5032.2	-	-	-	-	-	-	-	-
505	5032.5	545	5044.5	585	5056.5	625	5068.5	665	5080.5
-	-	-	-	-	-	-	-	-	-
-	-	-	-	-	-	-	-	-	-
510	5034.0	550	5046.0	590	5058.0	630	5070.0	670	5982.0
-	-	-	-	-	-	-	-	-	-
-	-	-	-	-	-	-	-	-	-
515	5035.5	555	5047.5	595	5059.5	635	5071.5	675	5083.5
-	-	-	-	-	-	-	-	-	-
-	-	-	-	-	-	-	-	-	-
520	5037.0	560	5049.0	600	5061.0	640	5073.0	680	5085.0
-	-	-	-	-	-	-	-	-	-
-	-	-	-	-	-	-	-	-	-
525	5038.5	565	5050.5	605	5062.5	645	5074.5	685	5086.5
-	-	-	-	-	-	-	-	-	-
-	-	-	-	-	-	-	-	-	-
530	5040.0	570	5052.0	610	5064.0	650	5076.0	690	5088.0
-	-	-	-	-	-	-	-	-	-
-	-	-	-	-	-	-	-	-	-
535	5041.5	575	5053.5	615	5065.5	655	5077.5	695	5089.5
-	-	-	-	-	-	-	-	696	5089.8
-	-	-	-	-	-	-	-	697	5090.1
-	-	-	-	-	-	-	-	698	5090.4
-	-	-	-	-	-	-	-	699	5090.7

(Table 1-5)

DME CHANNEL (NUMBER)	VHF CHANNEL (MHz)	C-BAND CHANNEL (MHz)	ANGLE CHANNEL (NUMBER)	INTERROGA-TOR FREQUENCY (MHz)	NON-PRECI-SION INTERRO-GATOR PULSE CODE (USEC)	PRECI-SION INTERRO-GATOR PULSE CODE (USEC)	TRANS-PONDER FREQUEN-CY (MHz)	TRANS-PONDER PULSE CODE (USEC)
1X				1025	12		962	12
1Y				1025	36		1088	30
2X				1026	12		963	12
2Y				1026	36		1089	30
3X				1027	12		964	12
3Y				1027	36		1090	30
4X				1028	12		965	12
4Y				1028	36		1091	30
5X				1029	12		966	12
5Y				1029	36		1092	30
6X				1030	12		967	12
6Y				1030	36		1093	30
7X				1031	12		968	12
7Y				1031	36		1094	30
8X				1032	12		969	12
8Y				1032	36		1095	30
9X				1033	12		970	12
9Y				1033	36		1096	30
10X				1034	12		971	12
10Y				1034	36		1097	30
11X				1035	12		972	12
11Y				1035	36		1098	30
12X				1036	12		973	12
12Y				1036	36		1099	30
13X				1037	12		974	12
13Y				1037	36		1100	30
14X				1038	12		975	12
14Y				1038	36		1101	30
15X				1039	12		976	12
15Y				1039	36		1102	30
16X				1040	12		977	12
16Y				1040	36		1103	30
17X	108.00	—	—	1041	12		978	12
17Y	108.05	5043.00	540	1041	36	42	1104	30
17Z	—	5043.30	541	1041	21	27	1104	15
18X	108.10	5031.00	500	1042	12	18	979	12
18W	—	5031.30	501	1042	24	33	979	24

(Table 1-5)

DME CHANNEL (NUMBER)	VHF CHANNEL (MHz)	C-BAND CHANNEL (MHz)	ANGLE CHANNEL (NUMBER)	INTERROGATOR FREQUENCY (MHz)	NON-PRECISION INTERROGATOR PULSE CODE (USEC)	PRECISION INTERROGATOR PULSE CODE (USEC)	TRANSPONDER FREQUENCY (MHz)	TRANSPONDER PULSE CODE (USEC)
18Y	108.15	5043.60	542	1042	36	42	1105	30
18Z	—	5043.90	543	1042	21	27	1105	15
19X	108.20	—	—	1043	12	—	980	12

(Table 1-6)

RATE	CHAIN	TELEPHONE
5930	Canadian East Coast	709-454-3261*
7980	Southeast U.S.	904-569-5241
8970	Great Lakes	607-869-5395
9960	Northeast U.S.	607-869-5395

*St. Anthony, Newfoundland, Canada
Information can also be obtained directly from the office of the Coordinator of Chain Operations (COCO) for each chain. The following telephone numbers are for each COCO office:

(Table 1-7)

RATE	CHAIN	TELEPHONE	LOCATION
4990	Central Pacific	808-247-5591	Kaneohe, HI
5930	Canadian East Coast	709-454-2392	St. Anthony, NF
5990	Canadian West Coast	707-987-2911	Middletown, CA
7930	North Atlantic	011-44-1-409-4758	London, UK
7960	Gulf of Alaska	907-487-5583	Kodiak, AK
7970	Norwegian Sea	011-44-1-409-4758	London, UK
7980	Southeast U.S.	904-569-2223	Malone, FL
7990	Mediterranean Sea	011-44-1-409-4758	London, UK
8970	Great Lakes	607-869-5393	Seneca, NY
9940	West Coast U.S.	707-987-2911	Middletown, CA
9960	Northeast U.S.	607-869-5393	Seneca, NY
9970	Northwest Pacific	415-437-3224	San Francisco, CA
9990	North Pacific	907-487-5583	Kodiak, AK

RUNWAYS WITH APPROACH LIGHTS

(Table 2-1)

Lighting System	No. of Int. Steps	Status During Nonuse Period	Intensity Step Selected Per No. of Mike Clicks		
			3 Clicks	5 Clicks	7 Clicks
Approach Lights (Med. Int.)	2	Off	Low	Low	High
Approach Lights (Med. Int.)	3	Off	Low	Med	High
MIRL	3	Off or Low	◊	◊	◊
HIRL	5	Off or Low	◊	◊	◊
VASI	2	Off	◊	◊	◊

NOTES:
◊ Predetermined intensity step.
◊ Low intensity for night use. High intensity for day use as determined by photocell control.

RUNWAYS WITHOUT APPROACH LIGHTS

(Table 2-2)

Lighting System	No. of Int. Steps	Status During Nonuse Period	Intensity Step Selected Per No. of Mike Clicks		
			3 Clicks	5 Clicks	7 Clicks
MIRL	3	Off or Low	Low	Med.	High
HIRL	5	Off or Low	Step 1 or 2	Step 3	Step 5
LIRL	1	Off	On	On	On
VASI♥	2	Off	◊	◊	◊
REIL♥	1	Off	Off	On / Off	On
REIL♥	3	Off	Low	Med.	High

NOTES:
◊ Low intensity for night use. High intensity for day use as determined by photocell control.
♥ The control of VASI and/or REIL may be independent of other lighting systems.

VFR Visibility and Distance from Clouds

(Table 3-1)

ALTITUDE	UNCONTROLLED AIRSPACE		CONTROLLED AIRSPACE	
	Flight Visibility	Distance From Clouds	**Flight Visibility	**Distance From Clouds
1200′or less above the surface, regardless of MSL Altitude.	*1 statute mile	Clear of clouds	3 statute miles	500′ below 1000′ above 2000′ horizontal
More than 1200′above the surface, but less than 10,000′MSL.	1 statute mile	500′ below 1000′ above 2000′ horizontal	3 statute miles	500′ below 1000′ above 2000′ horizontal
More than 1200′above the surface and at or above 10,000′MSL.	5 statute miles	1000′ below 1000′ above 1 statute mile horizontal	5 statute miles	1000′ below 1000′ above 1 statute mile horizontal

*Helicopters may operate with less than 1 mile visibility, outside controlled airspace at 1200 feet or less above the surface, provided they are operated at a speed that allows the pilot adequate opportunity to see any air traffic or obstructions in time to avoid collisions.

**In addition, when operating within a control zone beneath a ceiling, the ceiling must not be less than 1000′. If the pilot intends to land or takeoff or enter a traffic pattern within a control zone, the ground visibility must be at least 3 miles at that airport. If ground visibility is not reported at the airport, 3 miles flight visibility is required. (FAR 91.105)

(Table 3-2)

CONTROLLED AND UNCONTROLLED AIRSPACE VFR ALTITUDES AND FLIGHT LEVELS			
If your magnetic course (ground track) is	More than 3000′above the surface but below 18,000′MSL fly	Above 18,000′MSL to FL 290 (except within Positive Control Area, FAR 71.193) fly	Above FL 290 (except within Positive Control Area, FAR 71.193) fly 4000′intervals
0° to 179°	Odd thousands, MSL, plus 500′(3500, 5500, 7500, etc.).	Odd Flight Levels plus 500′(FL 195, FL 215, FL 235, etc.).	Beginning at FL 300 (FL 300, 340, 380, etc.)
180° to 359°	Even thousands, MSL, plus 500′(4500, 6500, 8500, etc.).	Even Flight Levels plus 500′(FL 185, FL 205, FL 225, etc.).	Beginning at FL 320 (FL 320, 360, 400, etc.)

(Table 3-3)

UNCONTROLLED AIRSPACE - IFR ALTITUDES AND FLIGHT LEVELS

If your magnetic course (ground track) is	Below 18,000'MSL fly	At or above 18,000'MSL but below FL 290, fly	At or above FL 290, fly 4000'intervals
0° to 179°	Odd thousands, MSL, (3000, 5000, 7000, etc.).	Odd Flight Levels, FL 190, 210, 230, etc.).	Beginning at FL 290, (FL 290, 330, 370, etc.)
180° to 359°	Even thousands, MSL, (2000, 4000, 6000, etc.).	Even Flight Levels (FL 180, 200, 220, etc.).	Beginning at FL 310, (FL 310, 350, 390, etc.)

(Table 3-4)

These areas are currently designated as Group I TCAs and are depicted on VFR Terminal Area Charts.

Atlanta	Miami
Boston	New York
Chicago	San Francisco
Dallas	Washington, D.C.
Los Angeles	

(Table 3-5)

These areas are currently designated as Group II TCAs and are depicted on VFR Terminal Area Charts.

Cleveland	Kansas City	Pittsburgh
Denver	Las Vegas	Seattle
Detroit	Minneapolis	St. Louis
Honolulu	New Orleans	San Diego
Houston	Philadelphia	

(Table 3-6)

These areas are currently designated as ARSAs and are depicted on Sectional Charts. They will be updated as additional ARSAs are implemented. Pilots should consult current sectional charts and NOTAMs for the latest information on services available. Pilots should be aware that some ARSAs underlie or are adjacent to TCAs.

STATE	CITY
ALABAMA	Birmingham
	Huntsville
	Mobile
ALASKA	Anchorage
ARIZONA	Davis-Monthan AFB
	Phoenix
	Tuscon
ARKANSAS	Little Rock
CALIFORNIA	Beale AFB
	Burbank
	Castle AFB (Merced)
	El Toro MCAS
	March AFB
	Mather AFB
	McClellan AFB
	Norton AFB
	Oakland
	Ontario
	Sacramento
CONNECTICUT	Windsor Locks (Bradley)
DISTRICT OF COLUMBIA	Washington (Dulles)
FLORIDA	Pensacola
	Whiting NAS
	Pensacola NAS
	Daytona Beach
	Ft. Lauderdale
	Ft. Myers (Southwest Florida Regional)
	Jacksonville
	Orlando
	West Palm Beach
	Sarasota
	Tallahassee (Muni)
	Tampa
GEORGIA	Columbus
	Savannah
HAWAII	Kahului
IDAHO	Boise
ILLINOIS	Champaign
	Chicago (Midway)
	Springfield
INDIANA	Evansville
	Fort Wayne
	Indianapolis
	South Bend
IOWA	Cedar Rapids
	Des Moines
KANSAS	Wichita
KENTUCKY	Lexington
	Louisville

(Table 3-6)

These areas are currently designated as ARSAs and are depicted on Sectional Charts. They will be updated as additional ARSAs are implemented. Pilots should consult current sectional charts and NOTAMs for the latest information on services available. Pilots should be aware that some ARSAs underlie or are adjacent to TCAs.

STATE	CITY
LOUISIANA	Barksdale AFB
	Lafayette
	Shreveport
MAINE	Portland
MARYLAND	Baltimore
MICHIGAN	Flint
	Grand Rapids
	Lansing
MISSISSIPPI	Columbus AFB
	Jackson
NEBRASKA	Omaha
	Offutt AFB
NEVADA	Reno
NEW JERSEY	Atlantic City (Intl)
NEW MEXICO	Albuquerque
NEW YORK	Albany
	Buffalo
	Islip
	Rochester
	Syracuse
NORTH CAROLINA	Charlotte
	Fayetteville
	Greensboro
	Pope AFB (Fayetteville)
	Raleigh/Durham
OKLAHOMA	Oklahoma City
	Tinker AFB
	Tulsa
OHIO	Columbus
	Cincinnati (Covington, KY)
	Dayton
	Toledo
OREGON	Portland
PENNSYLVANIA	Allentown
PUERTO RICO	San Juan
RHODE ISLAND	Providence
SOUTH CAROLINA	Charleston (AFB/Intl)
	Columbia
	Greer
	Shaw AFB
TENNESSEE	Chattanooga
	Knoxville
	Memphis
	Nashville
TEXAS	Abilene
	Amarillo
	Austin
	Corpus Christi
	Dallas (Love)

(Table 3-6)

These areas are currently designated as ARSAs and are depicted on Sectional Charts. They will be updated as additional ARSAs are implemented. Pilots should consult current sectional charts and NOTAMs for the latest information on services available. Pilots should be aware that some ARSAs underlie or are adjacent to TCAs.

STATE	CITY
	Dyess AFB (Abilene)
	El Paso
	Houston (William P. Hobby)
	Laughlin AFB
	Lubbock
	Midland
	San Antonio
UTAH	Salt Lake City
VERMONT	Burlington
VIRGINIA	Norfolk
	Richmond
	Roanoke
WASHINGTON	Spokane (Intl)
	Spokane (Fairchild AFB)
	Whidbey Island (NAS)
WISCONSIN	Green Bay
	Madison
	Milwaukee

SUMMARY OF RECOMMENDED COMMUNICATION PROCEDURES

(Table 4-1)

	FACILITY AT AIRPORT	FREQUENCY USE	COMMUNICATION/BROADCAST PROCEDURES		
			OUTBOUND	*INBOUND*	*PRACTICE INSTRU-MENT APPROACH*
1.	UNICOM (No Tower or FSS)	Communicate with UNICOM station on published CTAF frequency (122.7, 122.8, 122.725, 122.975, or 123.0). If unable to contact UNICOM station, use self-announce procedures on CTAF.	Before taxiing and before taxiing on the runway for departure.	10 miles out. Entering downwind, base, and final. Leaving the runway.	
2.	No Tower, FSS, or UNICOM	Self-announce on MULTICOM frequency 122.9.	Before taxiing and before taxiing on the runway for departure.	10 miles out. Entering downwind, base, and final. Leaving the runway.	Departing final approach fix (name) or on final approach segment inbound.
3.	No Tower in operation, FSS open	Communicate with FSS on CTAF frequency.	Before taxiing and before taxiing on the runway for departure.	10 miles out. Entering downwind, base, and final. Leaving the runway.	Approach completed/ terminated.
4.	FSS closed (No Tower)	Self-announce on CTAF.	Before taxiing and before taxiing on the runway for departure.	10 miles out. Entering downwind, base, and final. Leaving the runway.	
5.	Tower or FSS not in operation	Self-announce on CTAF.	Before taxiing and before taxiing on the runway for departure.	10 miles out. Entering downwind, base, and final. Leaving the runway.	

(Table 4-2)

CHARACTER	MORSE CODE	TELEPHONY	PHONIC (PRONUNCIATION)
A	● ▬	Alfa	(AL-FAH)
B	▬ ● ● ●	Bravo	(BRAH-VOH)
C	▬ ● ▬ ●	Charlie	(CHAR-LEE) or (SHAR-LEE)
D	▬ ● ●	Delta	(DELL-TAH)
E	●	Echo	(ECK-OH)
F	● ● ▬ ●	Foxtrot	(FOKS-TROT)
G	▬ ▬ ●	Golf	(GOLF)
H	● ● ● ●	Hotel	(HOH-TEL)
I	● ●	India	IN-DEE-AH)
J	● ▬ ▬ ▬	Juliett	(JEW-LEE-ETT)
K	▬ ● ▬	Kilo	(KEY-LOH)
L	● ▬ ● ●	Lima	(LEE-MAH)
M	▬ ▬	Mike	(MIKE)
N	▬ ●	November	(NO-VEM-BER)
O	▬ ▬ ▬	Oscar	(OSS-CAH)
P	● ▬ ▬ ●	Papa	(PAH-PAH)
Q	▬ ▬ ● ▬	Quebec	(KEH-BECK)
R	● ▬ ●	Romeo	(ROW-ME-OH)
S	● ● ●	Sierra	(SEE-AIR-RAH)
T	▬	Tango	(TANG-GO)
U	● ● ▬	Uniform	(YOU-NEE-FORM) or (OO-NEE-FORM)
V	● ● ● ▬	Victor	(VIK-TAH)
W	● ▬ ▬	Whiskey	(WISS-KEY)
X	▬ ● ● ▬	Xray	(ECKS-RAY)
Y	▬ ● ▬ ▬	Yankee	(YANG-KEY)
Z	▬ ▬ ● ●	Zulu	(ZOO-LOO)
1	● ▬ ▬ ▬ ▬	One	(WUN)
2	● ● ▬ ▬ ▬	Two	(TOO)
3	● ● ● ▬ ▬	Three	(TREE)
4	● ● ● ● ▬	Four	(FOW-ER)
5	● ● ● ● ●	Five	(FIFE)
6	▬ ● ● ● ●	Six	(SIX)
7	▬ ▬ ● ● ●	Seven	(SEV-EN)
8	▬ ▬ ▬ ● ●	Eight	(AIT)
9	▬ ▬ ▬ ▬ ●	Nine	(NIN-ER)
0	▬ ▬ ▬ ▬ ▬	Zero	(ZEE-RO)

ATCT Light Gun Signals

(Table 4-3)

	MEANING		
COLOR AND TYPE OF SIGNAL	MOVEMENT OF VEHICLES EQUIPMENT AND PERSONNEL	AIRCRAFT ON THE GROUND	AIRCRAFT IN FLIGHT
Steady green	Cleared to cross, proceed or go	Cleared for takeoff	Cleared to land
Flashing green	Not applicable	Cleared for taxi	Return for landing (to be followed by steady green at the proper time)
Steady red	STOP	STOP	Give way to other aircraft and continue circling
Flashing red	Clear the taxiway/runway	Taxi clear of the runway in use	Airport unsafe, do not land
Flashing white	Return to starting point on airport	Return to starting point on airport	Not applicable
Alternating red and green	Exercise extreme caution	Exercise extreme caution	Exercise extreme caution

INTERCEPTION SIGNALS

(Table 4-4)

Signals initiated by intercepting aircraft and responses by intercepted aircraft

(as set forth in ICAO Annex 2 — Appendix A, 2.1)

Series	INTERCEPTING Aircraft Signals	Meaning	INTERCEPTED Aircraft Responds	Meaning
1	DAY — Rocking wings from a position in front and, normally, to the left of intercepted aircraft and, after acknowledgement, a slow level turn, normally to the left, on to the desired heading. NIGHT — Same and, in addition, flashing navigational lights at irregular intervals. *Note 1. — Meteorological conditions or terrain may require the intercepting aircraft to take up a position in front and to the right of the intercepted aircraft and to make the subsequent turn to the right.* *Note 2. — If the intercepted aircraft is not able to keep pace with the intercepting aircraft, the latter is expected to fly a series of race-track patterns and to rock its wings each time it passes the intercepted aircraft.*	You have been intercepted. Follow me.	AEROPLANES: DAY — Rocking wings and following. NIGHT — Same and, in addition, flashing navigational lights at irregular intervals. HELICOPTERS: DAY or NIGHT — Rocking aircraft, flashing navigational lights at irregular intervals and following.	Understood, will comply.
2	DAY or NIGHT — An abrupt break-away maneuver from the intercepted aircraft consisting of a climbing turn of 90 degrees or more without crossing the line of flight of the intercepted aircraft.	You may proceed.	AEROPLANES: DAY or NIGHT — Rocking wings. HELICOPTERS: DAY or NIGHT — Rocking aircraft.	Understood, will comply.
3	DAY — Circling aerodrome, lowering landing gear and overflying runway in direction of landing or, if the intercepted aircraft is a helicopter, overflying the helicopter landing area. NIGHT — Same and, in addition, showing steady landing lights.	Land at this aerodrome.	AEROPLANES: DAY — Lowering landing gear, following the intercepting aircraft and, if after overflying the runway landing is considered safe, proceeding to land. NIGHT — Same and, in addition, showing steady landing lights (if carried). HELICOPTERS: DAY or NIGHT — Following the intercepting aircraft and proceeding to land, showing a steady landing light (if carried).	Understood, will comply.

INTERCEPTION SIGNALS

(Table 4-5)

Signals and Responses During Aircraft Intercept

Signals initiated by intercepted aircraft and responses by intercepting aircraft

(as set forth in ICAO Annex 2 — Appendix A, 2.2)

Series	INTERCEPTED Aircraft Signals	Meaning	INTERCEPTING Aircraft Responds	Meaning
4	AEROPLANES: DAY — Raising landing gear while passing over landing runway at a height exceeding 300m (1,000 ft) but not exceeding 600m (2,000 ft) above the aerodrome level, and continuing to circle the aerodrome. NIGHT — Flashing landing lights while passing over landing runway at a height exceeding 300m (1,000 ft) but not exceeding 600m (2,000 ft) above the aerodrome level, and continuing to circle the aerodrome. If unable to flash landing lights, flash any other lights available.	Aerodrome you have designated is inadequate.	DAY or NIGHT — If it is desired that the intercepted aircraft follow the intercepting aircraft to an alternate aerodrome, the intercepting aircraft raises its landing gear and uses the Series 1 signals prescribed for intercepting aircraft. If it is decided to release the intercepted aircraft, the intercepting aircraft uses the Series 2 signals prescribed for intercepting aircraft.	Understood, follow me. Understood, you may proceed.
5	AEROPLANES: DAY or NIGHT — Regular switching on and off of all available lights but in such a manner as to be distinct from flashing lights.	Cannot comply.	DAY or NIGHT — Use Series 2 signals prescribed for intercepting aircraft.	Understood.
6	AEROPLANES: DAY or NIGHT — Irregular flashing of all available lights. HELICOPTERS: DAY or NIGHT — Irregular flashing of all available lights.	In distress.	DAY or NIGHT — Use Series 2 signals prescribed for intercepting aircraft.	Understood.

(Table 5-1)

Airport Symbol	Location
ATL	Atlanta, Georgia
BWI	Baltimore, Maryland
BHM	Birmingham, Alabama
BIS	Bismarck, North Dakota
BOS	Boston, Massachusetts
BUF	Buffalo, New York
ORD	Chicago, Illinois
CLE	Cleveland, Ohio
DFW	Dallas, Texas
IAH	Houston, Texas
JAX	Jacksonville, Florida
MCI	Kansas City, Missouri
LAX	Los Angeles, California
MEM	Memphis, Tennessee
MIA	Miami, Florida
MSY	New Orleans, Louisiana
PHX	Phoenix, Arizona
PIT	Pittsburgh, Pennsylvania
PDX	Portland, Oregon
SLC	Salt Lake City, Utah
SAN	San Diego, California
SFO	San Francisco, California
SJU	San Juan, Puerto Rico
SEA	Seattle, Washington
GEG	Spokane, Washington
STL	St. Louis, Missouri
TUS	Tucson, Arizona
TUL	Tulsa, Oklahoma

(Table 6-1)

	PIREP ELEMENTS	PIREP CODE	CONTENTS
1.	3-letter station identifier	XXX	Nearest weather reporting location to the reported phenomenon
2.	Report type	UA or UUA	Routine or Urgent PIREP
3.	Location	/OV	In relation to a VOR
4.	Time	/TM	Coordinated Universal Time
5.	Altitude	/FL	Essential for turbulence and icing reports
6.	Type Aircraft	/TP	Essential for turbulence and icing reports
7.	Sky cover	/SK	Cloud height and coverage (scattered, broken, or overcast)
8.	Weather	/WX	Flight visibility, precipitation, restrictions to visibility, etc.
9.	Temperature	/TA	Degrees Celsius
10.	Wind	/WV	Direction in degrees magnetic and speed in knots
11.	Turbulence	/TB	See paragraph 522
12.	Icing	/IC	See paragraph 521
13.	Remarks	/RM	For reporting elements not included or to clarify previously reported items

(Table 6-2)

TURBULENCE REPORTING CRITERIA TABLE			
INTENSITY	AIRCRAFT REACTION	REACTION INSIDE AIRCRAFT	REPORTING TERM-DEFINITION
Light	Turbulence that momentarily causes slight, erratic changes in altitude and/or attitude (pitch, roll, yaw). Report as **Light Turbulence**;* or Turbulence that causes slight, rapid and somewhat rhythmic bumpiness without appreciable changes in altitude or attitude. Report as **Light Chop**.	Occupants may feel a slight strain against seat belts or shoulder straps. Unsecured objects may be displaced slightly. Food service may be conducted and little or no difficulty is encountered in walking.	Occasional – Less than 1/3 of the time. Intermittent – 1/3 to 2/3. Continuous – More than 2/3.
Moderate	Turbulence that is similar to Light Turbulence but of greater intensity. Changes in altitude and/or attitude occur but the aircraft remains in positive control at all times. It usually causes variations in indicated airspeed. Report as **Moderate Turbulence**;* or Turbulence that is similar to Light Chop but of greater intensity. It causes rapid bumps or jolts without appreciable changes in aircraft altitude or attitude. Report as **Moderate Chop**.	Occupants feel definite strains against seat belts or shoulder straps. Unsecured objects are dislodged. Food service and walking are difficult.	**NOTE** 1. Pilots should report location(s), time (UTC), intensity, whether in or near clouds, altitude, type of aircraft and, when applicable, duration of turbulence. 2. Duration may be based on time between two locations or over a single location. All locations should be readily identifiable. EXAMPLES: a. Over Omaha, 1232Z, Moderate Turbulence, in cloud, Flight Level 310, B707.
Severe	Turbulence that causes large, abrupt changes in altitude and/or attitude. It usually causes large variations in indicated airspeed. Aircraft may be momentarily out of control. Report as **Severe Turbulence**. *	Occupants are forced violently against seat belts or shoulder straps. Unsecured objects are tossed about. Food service and walking are impossible.	b. From 50 miles south of Albuquerque to 30 miles north of Phoenix, 1210Z to 1250Z, occasional Moderate Chop, Flight Level 330, DC8.
Extreme	Turbulence in which the aircraft is violently tossed about and is practically impossible to control. It may cause structural damage. Report as **Extreme Turbulence**.*		

* High level turbulence (normally above 15,000 feet ASL) not associated with cumuliform cloudiness, including thunderstorms, should be reported as CAT (clear air turbulence) preceded by the appropriate intensity, or light or moderate chop.

DECODING OBSERVATIONS FROM AUTOB STATIONS

(Table 6-3)

EXAMPLE: **ENV AUTOB E25 BKN BV7 P 33/29/3606/975 PK WND 08 001**

ENCODE	DECODE	EXPLANATION
ENV AUTOB	STATION IDENTIFICATION: AUTOMATIC STATION IDENTIFIER	(Wendover, UT) Identifies report using FAA identifiers.
E25 BKN	SKY & CEILING:	(Estimated 2500 ft. broken) Figures are height in 100s of feet above ground. Contraction after height is amount of sky cover. Letter preceding height indicates ceiling. WX reported if visibility is less than 2 miles and no clouds are detected. *NO CLOUDS REPORTED ABOVE 6000 FEET.*
BV7	BACKSCATTER VISIBILITY AVERAGED IN PAST MINUTE:	Reported in whole miles from 1 to 7.
P	PRECIPITATION OCCURRENCE:	(P=precipitation in past 10 minutes).
33	TEMPERATURE:	(33 degrees F.) Minus sign indicates sub-zero temperatures.
/29	DEW POINT:	(29 degrees F.) Minus sign indicates sub-zero temperatures.
/3606	WIND:	(360 degrees true at 6 knots) Direction is first two digits and is reported in tens of degrees. To decode, add a zero to first two digits. The last digits are speed; e.g., 2524 = 250 degrees at 24 knots.
/975	ALTIMETER SETTING:	(29.75 inches) The tens digit and decimal are omitted from report. To decode, prefix a 2 to code if it begins with 8 or 9. Otherwise, prefix a 3; e.g., 982 = 29.82, 017 = 30.17.
PK WND 08	PEAK WIND SPEED:	(8 knots) Reported speed is highest detected since last hourly observation.
001	PRECIPITATION ACCUMULATION:	(0.01 inches) Amount of precipitation since last synoptic time (00, 06, 12, 1800 UTC).

NOTE: If no clouds are detected below 6,000 feet and the visibility is greater than 2 miles, the reported sky condition will be *CLR BLO 60*.

(Table 6-4)

25 MPH VELOCITY	B-727	DC-8	DC-10 / L-1011	B-747, B-767, B-757, A-300, and all re-engined B-707 / DC-8 aircraft
Takeoff Thrust	550 Ft.	700 Ft.	2,100 Ft.	1,752 Ft.
Breakaway Thrust	200 Ft.	400Ft.	850 Ft.	1,250 Ft.
Idle Thrust	150 Ft.	100 Ft.	350 Ft.	620 Ft.

APPENDIX 3

Aeronautical Charts

INSTRUMENT APPROACH PROCEDURE CHARTS

AIRPORT/FACILITY DIRECTORY

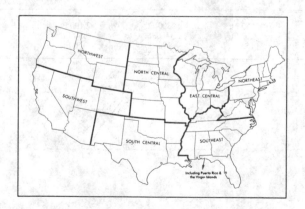

ENROUTE LOW ALTITUDE CHARTS

ENROUTE HIGH ALTITUDE CHARTS

ALASKA ENROUTE CHARTS

FLIGHT INFORMATION PUBLICATIONS
CARIBBEAN AND SOUTH AMERICA ENROUTE

PLANNING CHARTS

SECTIONAL AND VFR TERMINAL AREA CHARTS
CONTERMINOUS U.S. AND HAWAIIAN ISLANDS

ALASKA

VFR Terminal Area Charts are indicated thus: ●

*Indicates annual revision

WORLD AERONAUTICAL CHARTS
CONTERMINOUS U.S., MEXICO, AND CARIBBEAN

ALASKA

PILOT/CONTROLLER GLOSSARY

U.S. Department of Transportation
Federal Aviation Administration

ASA / 1989

PILOT/CONTROLLER GLOSSARY

JUNE 23, 1988

This Glossary was compiled to promote a common understanding of the terms used in the Air Traffic Control system. It includes those terms which are intended for pilot/controller communications. Those terms most frequently used in pilot/controller communications are printed in **bold italics**. The definitions are primarily defined in an operational sense applicable to both users and operators of the National Airspace System. Use of the Glossary will preclude any misunderstandings concerning the system's design, function, and purpose.

Because of the international nature of flying, terms used in the *Lexicon,* published by the International Civil Aviation Organization (ICAO), are included when they differ from FAA definitions. These terms are *italicized.* For the reader's convenience, there are also cross references to related terms in other parts of the Glossary and to other documents, such as the Federal Aviation Regulations (FAR's) and the Airman's Information Manual (AIM).

This Glossary will be revised, as necessary, to maintain a common understanding of the system.

ABBREVIATED IFR FLIGHT PLANS — An authorization by ATC requiring pilots to submit only that information needed for the purpose of ATC. It includes only a small portion of the usual IFR flight plan information. In certain instances, this may be only aircraft identification, location, and pilot request. Other information may be requested if needed by ATC for separation/control purposes. It is frequently used by aircraft which are airborne and desire an instrument approach or by aircraft which are on the ground and desire a climb to VFR-on-top. (See VFR-ON-TOP) (Refer to AIM)

ABEAM — An aircraft is "abeam" a fix, point, or object when that fix, point, or object is approximately 90 degrees to the right or left of the aircraft track. Abeam indicates a general position rather than a precise point.

ABORT — To terminate a preplanned aircraft maneuver; e.g., an aborted takeoff.

ACKNOWLEDGE — Let me know that you have received my message.

ICAO—ACKNOWLEDGE — Let me know that you have received and understood this message.

ACROBATIC FLIGHT — An intentional maneuver involving an abrupt change in an aircraft's attitude, an abnormal attitude, or abnormal acceleration not necessary for normal flight. (Refer to FAR Part 91)

ICAO—ACROBATIC FLIGHT — Manoeuvres intentionally performed by an aircraft involving an abrupt change in its attitude, an abnormal attitude, or an abnormal variation in speed.

ADDITIONAL SERVICES — Advisory information provided by ATC which includes but is not limited to the following:

1. Traffic advisories.

2. Vectors, when requested by the pilot, to assist aircraft receiving traffic advisories to avoid observed traffic.

3. Altitude deviation information of 300 feet or more from an assigned altitude as observed on a verified (reading correctly) automatic altitude readout (Mode C).

4. Advisories that traffic is no longer a factor.

5. Weather and chaff information.

6. Weather assistance.

7. Bird activity information.

8. Holding pattern surveillance.

Additional services are provided to the extent possible contingent only upon the controller's capability to fit them into the performance of higher priority duties and on the basis of limitations of the radar, volume of traffic, frequency congestion, and controller workload. The controller has complete discretion for determining if he is able to provide or continue to provide a service in a particular case. The controller's reason not to provide or continue to provide a service in a particular case is not subject to question by the pilot and need not be made known to him. (See Traffic Advisories) (Refer to AIM)

ADMINISTRATOR — The Federal Aviation Administrator or any person to whom he has delegated his authority in the matter concerned.

ADVISE INTENTIONS — Tell me what you plan to do.

ADVISORY — Advice and information provided to assist pilots in the safe conduct of flight and aircraft movement. (See Advisory Service)

ADVISORY FREQUENCY — The appropriate frequency to be used for Airport Advisory Service. (See Airport Advisory Service and UNICOM) (Refer to Advisory Circular No. 90-42 and AIM)

ADVISORY SERVICE — Advice and information provided by a facility to assist pilots in the safe conduct of flight and aircraft movement. (See Airport Advisory Service, Traffic Advisories, Safety Alerts, Additional Services, Radar Advisory, En Route Flight Advisory Service) (Refer to AIM)

AERIAL REFUELING/IN-FLIGHT REFUELING — A procedure used by the military to transfer fuel from one aircraft to another during flight. (Refer to VFR/IFR Wall Planning Charts).

AERODROME — A defined area on land or water (including any buildings, installations and equipment) intended to be used either wholly or in part for the arrival, departure, and movement of aircraft.

AERONAUTICAL BEACON — A visual NAVAID displaying flashes of white and/or colored light to indicate the location of an airport, a heliport, a landmark, a certain point of a Federal airway in mountainous terrain, or an obstruction. (See Airport Rotating Beacon) (Refer to AIM)

AERONAUTICAL CHART — A map used in air navigation containing all or part of the following: Topographic features, hazards and obstructions, navigation aids, navigation routes, designated airspace, and airports. Commonly used aeronautical charts are:

1. Sectional Charts (1:500,000) — Designed for visual navigation of slow or medium speed aircraft. Topographic information on these charts features the portrayal of relief and a judicious selection of visual check points for VFR flight. Aeronautical information includes visual and radio aids to navigation, airports, controlled airspace, restricted areas, obstructions, and related data.

2. VFR Terminal Area Charts (1:250,000) — Depict Terminal Control Area (TCA) airspace which provides for the control or segregation of all the aircraft within the TCA. The chart depicts topographic information and aeronautical information which includes visual and radio aids to navigation, airports, controlled airspace, restricted areas, obstructions, and related data.

3. World Aeronautical Charts (WAC) (1:1,000,000) — Provide a standard series of aeronautical charts covering land areas of the world at a size and scale convenient for navigation by moderate speed aircraft. Topographic information includes cities and towns, principal roads, railroads, distinctive landmarks, drainage, and relief. Aeronautical information includes visual and radio aids to navigation, airports, airways, restricted areas, obstructions, and other pertinent data.

4. En Route Low Altitude Charts — Provide aeronautical information for en route instrument navigation (IFR) in the low altitude stratum. Information includes the portrayal of airways, limits of controlled airspace, position identification and frequencies of radio aids, selected airports, minimum en route and minimum obstruction clearance altitudes, airway distances, reporting points, restricted areas, and related data. Area charts, which are a part of this series, furnish terminal data at a larger scale in congested areas.

5. En Route High Altitude Charts — Provide aeronautical information for en route instrument navigation (IFR) in the high altitude stratum. Information includes the portrayal of jet routes, identification and frequencies of radio aids, selected airports, distances, time zones, special use airspace, and related information.

6. Instrument Approach Procedures (IAP) Charts — Portray the aeronautical data which is required to execute an instrument approach to an airport. These charts depict the procedures, including all related data, and the airport diagram. Each procedure is designated for use with a specific type of electronic navigation system including NDB, TACAN, VOR, ILS/MLS, and RNAV. These charts are identified by the type of navigational aid(s) which provide final approach guidance.

7. Standard Instrument Departure (SID) Charts — Designed to expedite clearance delivery and to facilitate transition between takeoff and en route operations. Each SID procedure is presented as a separate chart and may serve a single airport or more than one airport in a given geographical location.

8. Standard Terminal Arrival (STAR) Charts — Designed to expedite air traffic control arrival procedures and to facilitate transition between en route and instrument approach operations. Each STAR procedure is presented as a separate chart and may serve a single airport or more than one airport in a given geographical location.

9. Airport Taxi Charts — Designed to expedite the efficient and safe flow of ground traffic at an airport. These charts are identified by the official airport name; e.g., Washington National Airport.

ICAO—AERONAUTICAL CHART — A representation of a portion of the earth, its culture and relief, specifically designated to meet the requirements of air navigation.

AFFIRMATIVE — Yes.

AIR CARRIER DISTRICT OFFICE/ACDO — An FAA field office serving an assigned geographical area, staffed with Flight Standards personnel serving the aviation industry and the general public on matters related to the certification and operation of scheduled air carriers and other large aircraft operations.

AIRCRAFT — Device/s that are used or intended to be used for flight in the air, and when used in air traffic control terminology, may include the flight crew.

ICAO—AIRCRAFT — Any machine that can derive support in the atmosphere from the reactions of the air other than the reactions of the air against the earth's surface.

AIRCRAFT APPROACH CATEGORY — A grouping of aircraft based on a speed of 1.3 times the stall speed in the landing configuration at maximum gross landing weight. An aircraft shall fit in only one category. If it is necessary to maneuver at speeds in excess of the upper limit of a speed range for a category, the minimums for the next higher category should be used. For example, an aircraft which falls in Category A, but is circling to land at a speed in excess of 91 knots, should use the approach Category B minimums when circling to land. The categories are as follows:

1. Category A—Speed less than 91 knots.

2. Category B—Speed 91 knots or more but less than 121 knots.

3. Category C—Speed 121 knots or more but less than 141 knots.

4. Category D—Speed 141 knots or more but less than 166 knots.

5. Category E—Speed 166 knots or more.

(Refer to FAR Parts 1 and 97)

AIRCRAFT CLASSES — For the purposes of Wake Turbulence Separation Minima, ATC classifies aircraft as Heavy, Large, and Small as follows:

1. Heavy—Aircraft capable of takeoff weights of 300,000 pounds or more whether or not they are operating at this weight during a particular phase of flight.

2. Large—Aircraft of more than 12,500 pounds, maximum certificated takeoff weight, up to 300,000 pounds.

3. Small—Aircraft of 12,500 pounds or less maximum certificated takeoff weight. (Refer to AIM)

AIR DEFENSE EMERGENCY — A military emergency condition declared by a designated authority. This condition exists when an attack upon the continental U.S., Alaska, Canada, or U.S. installations in Greenland by hostile aircraft or missiles is considered probable, is imminent, or is taking place. (Refer to AIM)

AIR DEFENSE IDENTIFICATION ZONE/ADIZ — The area of airspace over land or water, extending upward from the surface, within which the ready identification, the location, and the control of aircraft are required in the interest of national security.

1. Domestic Air Defense Identification Zone—An ADIZ within the United States along an international boundary of the United States.

2. Coastal Air Defense Identification Zone—An ADIZ over the coastal waters of the United States.

3. Distant Early Warning Identification Zone (DEWIZ)— An ADIZ over the coastal waters of the State of Alaska.

ADIZ locations and operating and flight plan requirements for civil aircraft operations are specified in FAR Part 99. (Refer to AIM)

AIRMAN'S INFORMATION MANUAL/AIM — A primary FAA publication whose purpose is to instruct airmen about operating in the National Airspace System of the U.S. It provides basic flight information, ATC Procedures and general instructional information concerning health, medical facts, factors affecting flight safety, accident and hazard reporting, and types of aeronautical charts and their use.

ICAO—AERONAUTICAL INFORMATION PUBLICATION — A publication issued by or with the authority of a State and containing aeronautical information of a lasting character essential to air navigation.

AIRMET/WA/AIRMAN'S METEOROLOGICAL INFORMATION — In-flight weather advisories issued only to amend the area forecast concerning weather phenomena which are of operational interest to all aircraft and potentially hazardous to aircraft having limited capability because of lack of equipment, instrumentation, or pilot qualifications. AIRMET's concern weather of less severity than that covered by SIGMET's or Convective SIGMET's. AIRMET's cover moderate icing, moderate turbulence, sustained winds of 30 knots or more at the surface, widespread areas of ceilings less than 1,000 feet and/or visibility less than 3 miles, and extensive mountain obscurement. (See AWW, SIGMET, Convective SIGMET, and CWA) (Refer to AIM)

AIR NAVIGATION FACILITY — Any facility used in, available for use in, or designed for use in, aid of air navigation, including landing areas, lights, any apparatus or equipment for disseminating weather information, for signaling, for radio-directional finding, or for radio or other electrical communication, and any other structure or mechanism having a similar purpose for guiding or controlling flight in the air or the landing and take-off of aircraft. (See Navigational Aid)

AIRPORT — An area on land or water that is used or intended to be used for the landing and takeoff of aircraft and includes its buildings and facilities, if any.

AIRPORT ADVISORY AREA — The area within ten miles of an airport without a control tower or where the tower is not in operation, and on which a Flight Service Station is located. (See Airport Advisory Service) (Refer to AIM)

AIRPORT ADVISORY SERVICE/AAS — A service provided by flight service stations or the military at airports not serviced by an operating control tower. This service consists of providing information to arriving and departing aircraft concerning wind direction and speed, favored runway, altimeter setting, pertinent known traffic, pertinent known field conditions, airport taxi routes and traffic patterns, and authorized instrument approach procedures. This information is advisory in nature and does not constitute an ATC clearance. (See Airport Advisory Area)

AIRPORT ELEVATION/FIELD ELEVATION — The highest point of an airport's usable runways measured in feet from mean sea level. (See Touchdown Zone Elevation)

ICAO—AERODROME ELEVATION — The elevation of the highest point of the landing area.

AIRPORT/FACILITY DIRECTORY — A publication designed primarily as a pilot's operational manual containing all airports, seaplane bases, and heliports open to the public including communications data, navigational facilities, and certain special notices and procedures. This publication is issued in seven volumes according to geographical area.

AIRPORT INFORMATION DESK/AID — An airport unmanned facility designed for pilot self-service briefing, flight planning, and filing of flight plans. (Refer to AIM)

AIRPORT LIGHTING — Various lighting aids that may be installed on an airport. Types of airport lighting include:

1. Approach Light System/ALS—An airport lighting facility which provides visual guidance to landing aircraft by radiating light beams in a directional pattern by which the pilot aligns the aircraft with the extended centerline of the runway on his final approach for landing. Condenser-Discharge Sequential Flashing Lights/Sequenced Flashing Lights may be installed in conjunction with the ALS at some airports. Types of Approach Light Systems are:

    a. ALSF-1—Approach Light System with Sequenced Flashing Lights in ILS Cat-I configuration.

    b. ALSF-2—Approach Light System with Sequenced Flashing Lights in ILS Cat-II configuration. The ALSF-2 may operate as an SSALR when weather conditions permit.

    c. SSALF—Simplified Short Approach Light System with Sequenced Flashing Lights.

    d. SSALR—Simplified Short Approach Light System with Runway Alignment Indicator Lights.

e. MALSF—Medium Intensity Approach Light System with Sequenced Flashing Lights.

f. MALSR—Medium Intensity Approach Light System with Runway Alignment Indicator Lights.

g. LDIN—Sequenced Flashing Lead-in Lights.

h. RAIL—Runway Alignment Indicator Lights (Sequenced Flashing Lights which are installed only in combination with other light systems).

i. ODALS—Omnidirectional Approach Lighting System consists of seven omnidirectional flashing lights located in the approach area of a nonprecision runway. Five lights are located on the runway centerline extended with the first light located 300 feet from the threshold and extending at equal intervals up to 1,500 feet from the threshold. The other two lights are located, one on each side of the runway threshold, at a lateral distance of 40 feet from the runway edge, or 75 feet from the runway edge when installed on a runway equipped with a VASI. (Refer to Order 6850.2A)

2. Runway Lights/Runway Edge Lights—Lights having a prescribed angle of emission used to define the lateral limits of a runway. Runway lights are uniformly spaced at intervals of approximately 200 feet, and the intensity may be controlled or preset.

3. Touchdown Zone Lighting—Two rows of transverse light bars located symmetrically about the runway centerline normally at 100 foot intervals. The basic system extends 3,000 feet along the runway.

4. Runway Centerline Lighting—Flush centerline lights spaced at 50-foot intervals beginning 75 feet from the landing threshold and extending to within 75 feet of the opposite end of the runway.

5. Threshold Lights—Fixed green lights arranged symmetrically left and right of the runway centerline, identifying the runway threshold.

6. Runway End Identifier Lights/REIL—Two synchronized flashing lights, one on each side of the runway threshold, which provide rapid and positive identification of the approach end of a particular runway.

7. Visual Approach Slope Indicator/VASI—An airport lighting facility providing vertical visual approach slope guidance to aircraft during approach to landing by radiating a directional pattern of high intensity red and white focused light beams which indicate to the pilot that he is ''on path'' if he sees red/white, ''above path'' if white/white, and ''below path'' if red/red. Some airports serving large aircraft have three-bar VASIs which provide two visual glide paths to the same runway.

8. Boundary Lights—Lights defining the perimeter of an airport or landing area. (Refer to AIM)

AIRPORT MARKING AIDS — Markings used on runway and taxiway surfaces to identify a specific runway, a runway threshold, a centerline, a hold line, etc. A runway should be marked in accordance with its present usage such as:

1. Visual.

2. Nonprecision instrument.

3. Precision instrument. (Refer to AIM)

AIRPORT RADAR SERVICE AREA/ARSA — (See Controlled Airspace)

AIRPORT ROTATING BEACON — A visual NAVAID operated at many airports. At civil airports, alternating white and green flashes indicate the location of the airport. At military airports, the beacons flash alternately white and green, but are differentiated from civil beacons by dualpeaked (two quick) white flashes between the green flashes. (See Special VFR Operations, Instrument Flight Rules) (Refer to AIM, Rotating Beacons)

ICAO—AERODROME BEACON — Aeronautical beacon used to indicate the location of an aerodrome from the air.

AIRPORT SURFACE DETECTION EQUIPMENT/ASDE — Radar equipment specifically designed to detect all principal features on the surface of an airport, including aircraft and vehicular traffic, and to present the entire image on a radar indicator console in the control tower. Used to augment visual observation by tower personnel of aircraft and/or vehicular movements on runways and taxiways.

AIRPORT SURVEILLANCE RADAR/ASR — Approach control radar used to detect and display an aircraft's position in the terminal area. ASR provides range and azimuth information but does not provide elevation data. Coverage of the ASR can extend up to 60 miles.

AIRPORT TRAFFIC AREA — Unless otherwise specifically designated in FAR Part 93, that airspace within a horizontal radius of 5 statute miles from the geographical center of any airport at which a control tower is operating, extending from the surface up to, but not including, an altitude of 3,000 feet above the elevation of an airport. Unless otherwise authorized or required by ATC, no person may operate an aircraft within an airport traffic area except for the purpose of landing at or taking off from an airport within that area. ATC authorizations may be given as individual approval of specific operations or may be contained in written agreements between airport users and the tower concerned. (Refer to FAR, Parts 1 and 91).

AIRPORT TRAFFIC CONTROL SERVICE — A service provided by a control tower for aircraft operating on the movement area and in the vicinity of an airport. (See Movement Area, Tower)

ICAO-AERODROME CONTROL SERVICE — Air traffic control service for aerodrome traffic.

AIR ROUTE SURVEILLANCE RADAR/ARSR — Air route traffic control center (ARTCC) radar used primarily to detect and display an aircraft's position while en route between terminal areas. The ARSR enables controllers to provide radar air traffic control service when aircraft are within the ARSR coverage. In some instances, ARSR may enable an ARTCC to provide terminal radar services similar to but usually more limited than those provided by a radar approach control.

AIR ROUTE TRAFFIC CONTROL CENTER/ARTCC — A facility established to provide air traffic control service to aircraft operating on IFR flight plans within controlled airspace and principally during the en route phase of flight. When equipment capabilities and controller workload permit, certain advisory/assistance services may be provided to VFR aircraft. (See NAS Stage A, En Route Air Traffic Control Service) (Refer to AIM)

AIRSPEED — The speed of an aircraft relative to its surrounding air mass. The unqualified term "airspeed" means one of the following:

1. Indicated Airspeed—The speed shown on the aircraft airspeed indicator. This is the speed used in pilot/controller communications under the general term "airspeed." (Refer to FAR Part 1)

2. True Airspeed—The airspeed of an aircraft relative to undisturbed air. Used primarily in flight planning and en route portion of flight. When used in pilot/controller communications, it is referred to as "true airspeed" and not shortened to "airspeed."

AIRSTART — The starting of an aircraft engine while the aircraft is airborne, preceded by engine shutdown during training flights or by actual engine failure.

AIR TAXI — Used to describe a helicopter/VTOL aircraft movement conducted above the surface but normally not above 100 feet AGL. The aircraft may proceed either via hover taxi or flight at speeds more than 20 knots. The pilot is solely responsible for selecting a safe airspeed/altitude for the operation being conducted. (See Hover Taxi) (Refer to AIM)

AIR TRAFFIC — Aircraft operating in the air or on an airport surface, exclusive of loading ramps and parking areas.

ICAO—AIR TRAFFIC — All aircraft in flight or operating on the manoeuvring area of an aerodrome.

AIR TRAFFIC CLEARANCE/ATC CLEARANCE — An authorization by air traffic control, for the purpose of preventing collision between known aircraft, for an aircraft to proceed under specified traffic conditions within controlled airspace. (See ATC Instructions)

ICAO—AIR TRAFFIC CONTROL CLEARANCE — Authorization for an aircraft to proceed under conditions specified by an air traffic control unit.

Note 1. — For conveniece, the term *air traffic control clearance* is frequently abbreviated to *clearance* when used in appropriate contexts.

Note 2. — The abbreviated term *clearance* may be prefixed by the words *taxi, takeoff, departure, en route, approach* or *landing* to indicate the particular portion of flight to which the air traffic control clearance relates.

AIR TRAFFIC CONTROL/ATC — A service operated by appropriate authority to promote the safe, orderly and expeditious flow of air traffic.

ICAO—AIR TRAFFIC CONTROL SERVICE — A service provided for the purpose of:

1) Preventing collisions:

a) Between aircraft; and

b) On the maneuvering area between aircraft and obstructions; and

2) Expediting and maintaining an orderly flow of air traffic.

AIR TRAFFIC CONTROL COMMAND CENTER/ ATCCC — An Air Traffic Operations Service facility consisting of four operational units.

1. Central Flow Control Function/CFCF—Responsible for coordination and approval of all major intercenter flow control restrictions on a system basis in order to obtain maximum utilization of the airspace. (See Quota Flow Control)

2. Central Altitude Reservation Function/CARF—Responsible for coordinating, planning, and approving special user requirements under the Altitude Reservation (ALTRV) concept. (See Altitude Reservation)

3. Airport Reservation Office/ARO—Responsible for approving IFR flights at designated high density traffic airports (John F. Kennedy, LaGuardia, O'Hare, and Washington National) during specified hours. (Refer to FAR Part 93 and Airport/Facility Directory)

4. ATC Contingency Command Post—A facility which enables the FAA to manage the ATC system when significant portions of the system's capabilities have been lost or are threatened.

AIR TRAFFIC CONTROL SERVICE — (See Air Traffic Control)

AIR TRAFFIC CONTROL SPECIALIST/CONTROLLER — A person authorized to provide air traffic control service. (See Air Traffic Control, Flight Service Station)

ICAO—CONTROLLER — A person authorized to provide air traffic control services.

AIRWAY BEACON — Used to mark airway segments in remote mountain areas. The light flashes Morse Code to identify the beacon site. (Refer to AIM)

AIRWAY/FEDERAL AIRWAY — A control area or portion thereof established in the form of a corridor, the centerline of which is defined by radio navigational aids. (Refer to FAR Part 71, AIM)

ICAO—AIRWAY — A control area or portion thereof established in the form of corridor equipped with radio navigational aids.

ALERT AREA — (See Special Use Airspace)

ALERT NOTICE/ALNOT — A request originated by a flight service station (FSS) or an air route traffic control center (ARTCC) for an extensive communication search for overdue, unreported, or missing aircraft.

ALPHANUMERIC DISPLAY/DATA BLOCK — Letters and numerals used to show identification, altitude, beacon code, and other information concerning a target on a radar display. (See Automated Radar Terminal Systems, NAS Stage A)

ALTERNATE AIRPORT — An airport at which an aircraft may land if a landing at the intended airport becomes inadvisable.

ICAO—ALTERNATE AERODROME — An aerodrome specified in the flight plan to which a flight may proceed when it becomes inadvisable to land at the aerodrome of intended landing.

Note. — An alternate aerdrome may be the aerodrome of departure.

ALTIMETER SETTING — The barometric pressure reading used to adjust a pressure altimeter for variations in existing atmospheric pressure or to the standard altimeter setting (29.92). (Refer to FAR Part 91, AIM)

ALTITUDE — The height of a level, point, or object measured in feet Above Ground Level (AGL) or from Mean Sea Level (MSL). (See Flight Level)

1. MSL Altitude—Altitude expressed in feet measured from mean sea level.

2. AGL Altitude—Altitude expressed in feet measured above ground level.

3. Indicated Altitude—The altitude as shown by an altimeter. On a pressure or barometric altimeter it is altitude as shown uncorrected for instrument error and uncompensated for variation from standard atmospheric conditions.

ICAO—ALTITUDE — The vertical distance of a level, a point or an object considered as a point, measured from mean sea level (MSL).

ALTITUDE READOUT/AUTOMATIC ALTITUDE REPORT — An aircraft's altitude, transmitted via the Mode C transponder feature, that is visually displayed in 100-foot increments on a radar scope having readout capability. (See Automated Radar Terminal Systems, NAS Stage A, Alphanumeric Display) (Refer to AIM)

ALTITUDE RESERVATION/ALTRV — Airspace utilization under prescribed conditions normally employed for the mass movement of aircraft or other special user requirements which cannot otherwise be accomplished. ALTRVs are approved by the appropriate FAA facility. (See Air Traffic Control Command Center)

ALTITUDE RESTRICTION — An altitude or altitudes, stated in the order flown, which are to be maintained until reaching a specific point or time. Altitude restrictions may be issued by ATC due to traffic, terrain, or other airspace considerations.

ALTITUDE RESTRICTIONS ARE CANCELED — Adherence to previously imposed altitude restrictions is no longer required during a climb or descent.

APPROACH CLEARANCE — Authorization by ATC for a pilot to conduct an instrument approach. The type of instrument approach for which a clearance and other pertinent information is provided in the approach clearance when required. (See Instrument Approach Procedure, Cleared for Approach) (Refer to AIM and FAR Part 91)

APPROACH CONTROL FACILITY — A terminal ATC facility that provides approach control service in a terminal area. (See Approach Control Service, Radar Approach Control Facility.

APPROACH CONTROL SERVICE — Air traffic control service provided by an approach control facility for arriving and departing VFR/IFR aircraft and, on occasion, en route aircraft. At some airports not served by an approach control facility, the ARTCC provides limited approach control service. (Refer to AIM)

ICAO—APPROACH CONTROL SERVICE — Air traffic control service for arriving or departing controlled flights.

APPROACH GATE — An imaginary point used within ATC as a basis for vectoring aircraft to the final approach course. The gate will be established along the final approach course 1 mile from the outer marker (or the fix used in lieu of the outer marker) on the side away from the airport for precision approaches and 1 mile from the final approach fix on the side away from the airport for nonprecision approach-

es. In either case when measured along the final approach course, the gate will be no closer than 5 miles from the landing threshold.

APPROACH LIGHT SYSTEM — (See Airport Lighting)

APPROACH SEQUENCE — The order in which aircraft are positioned while on approach or awaiting approach clearance. (See Landing Sequence)

ICAO—APPROACH SEQUENCE — The order in which two or more aircraft are cleared to approach to land at the aerodrome.

APPROACH SPEED — The recommended speed contained in aircraft manuals used by pilots when making an approach to landing. This speed will vary for different segments of an approach as well as for aircraft weight and configuration.

APRON/RAMP — A defined area on an airport or heliport intended to accommodate aircraft for purposes of loading or unloading passengers or cargo, refueling, parking, or maintenance. With regard to seaplanes, a ramp is used for access to the apron from the water.

ICAO—APRON — A defined area, on a land aerodrome, intended to accommodate aircraft for purposes of loading or unloading passengers, mail or cargo, refuelling, parking or maintenance.

ARC — The track over the ground of an aircraft flying at a constant distance from a navigational aid by reference to distance measuring equipment (DME).

AREA NAVIGATION/RNAV — A method of navigation that permits aircraft operation on any desired course within the coverage of station-referenced navigation signals or within the limits of a self-contained system capability. Random area navigation routes are direct routes, based on area navigation capability, between waypoints defined in terms of latitude/longitude coordinates, degree/distance fixes, or offsets from published or established routes/airways at a specified distance and direction. The major types of equipment are:

1. VORTAC referenced or Course Line Computer (CLC) systems, which account for the greatest number of RNAV units in use. To function, the CLC must be within the service range of a VORTAC.

2. OMEGA/VLF, although two separate systems, can be considered as one operationally. A long-range navigation system based upon Very Low Frequency radio signals transmitted from a total of 17 stations worldwide.

3. Inertial (INS) systems, which are totally self-contained and require no information from external references. They provide aircraft position and navigation information in response to signals resulting from inertial effects on components within the system.

4. MLS Area Navigation (MLS/RNAV), which provides area navigation with reference to an MLS ground facility.

5. LORAN-C is a long-range radio navigation system that uses ground waves transmitted at low frequency to provide user position information at ranges of up to 600 to 1,200 nautical miles at both en route and approach altitudes. The useable signal coverage areas are determined by the signal-to-noise ratio, the envelope-to -cycle difference, and the geometric relationship between the positions of the user and the transmitting stations.

ICAO—AREA NAVIGATION/RNAV — A method of navigation which permits aircraft operation on any desired flight path within the coverage of station-referenced navigation aids or within the limits of the capability of self-contained aids, or a combination of these.

ARMY AVIATION FLIGHT INFORMATION BULLETIN/USAFIB — A bulletin that provides air operation data covering Army, National Guard, and Army Reserve aviation activities.

ARRESTING SYSTEM — A safety device consisting of two major components, namely, engaging or catching devices and energy absorption devices for the purpose of arresting both tailhook and/or nontailhook-equipped aircraft. It is used to prevent aircraft from overrunning runways when the aircraft cannot be stopped after landing or during aborted takeoff. Arresting systems have various names; e.g., arresting gear, hook device, wire barrier cable. (See Abort) (Refer to AIM)

ARRIVAL TIME — The time an aircraft touches down on arrival.

ARTCC — (See Air Route Traffic Control Center)

ASR APPROACH — (See Surveillance Approach)

ATC ADVISES — Used to prefix a message of noncontrol information when it is relayed to an aircraft by other than an air traffic controller. (See Advisory)

ATC ASSIGNED AIRSPACE/ATCAA — Airspace of defined vertical/lateral limits, assigned by ATC, for the purpose of providing air traffic segregation between the specified activities being conducted within the assigned airspace and other IFR air traffic. (See Special Use Airspace)

ATC CLEARANCE — (See Air Traffic Clearance)

ATC CLEARS — Used to prefix an ATC clearance when it is relayed to an aircraft by other than an air traffic controller.

ATC INSTRUCTIONS — Directives issued by air traffic control for the purpose of requiring a pilot to take specific actions; e.g., "Turn left heading two five zero," "Go around," "Clear the runway." (Refer to FAR Part 91)

ATCRBS — (See Radar)

ATC REQUESTS — Used to prefix an ATC request when it is relayed to an aircraft by other than an air traffic controller.

AUTOMATED RADAR TERMINAL SYSTEMS/ARTS — The generic term for the ultimate in functional capability afforded by several automation systems. Each differs in functional capabilities and equipment. ARTS plus a suffix roman numeral denotes a specific system. A following letter indicates a major modification to that system. In general, an ARTS displays for the terminal controller aircraft identification, flight plan data, other flight associated information; e.g., altitude, speed, and aircraft position symbols in conjunction with his radar presentation. Normal radar co-exists with the alphanumeric display. In addition to enhancing visualization of the air traffic situation, ARTS facilitate intra/inter-facility transfer and coordination of flight information. These capabilities are enabled by specially designed computers and subsystems tailored to the radar and communications equipments and operational requirements of each automated facility. Modular design permits adoption of improvements in computer software and electronic technologies as they become available while retaining the characteristics unique to each system.

1. ARTS II—A programmable nontracking, computer-aided display subsystem capable of modular expansion. ARTS II systems provide a level of automated air traffic control capability at terminals having low to medium activity. Flight identification and altitude may be associated with the display of secondary radar targets. The system has the capability of communicating with ARTCC's and other ATRS II, IIA, III, and IIIA facilities.

2. ARTS IIA—A programmable radar-tracking computer subsystem capable of modular expansion. The ARTS IIA detects, tracks, and predicts secondary radar targets. The targets are displayed by means of computer- generated symbols, ground speed, and flight plan data. Although it does not track primary radar targets, they are displayed coincident with the secondary radar as well as the symbols and alphanumerics. The system has the capability of communicating with ARTCC's and other ARTS II, IIA, III, and IIIA facilities.

3. ARTS III—The Beacon Tracking Level (BTL) of the modular programmable automated radar terminal system in use at medium to high activity terminals. ARTS III detects, tracks, and predicts secondary radar-derived aircraft targets. These are displayed by means of computer-generated symbols and alphanumeric characters depicting flight identification, aircraft altitude, ground speed, and flight plan data. Although it does not track primary targets, they are displayed coincident with the secondary radar as well as the symbols and alphanumerics. The system has the capability of communicating with ARTCC's and other ARTS III facilities.

4. ARTS IIIA—The Radar Tracking and Beacon Tracking Level (RT&BTL) of the modular, programmable automated radar terminal system. ARTS IIIA detects, tracks, and predicts primary as well as secondary radar-derived aircraft targets. This more sophisticated computer-driven system upgrades the existing ARTS III system by providing improved tracking, continuous data recording, and fail-soft capabilities.

AUTOMATIC ALTITUDE REPORTING — That function of a transponder which responds to Mode C interrogations by transmitting the aircraft's altitude in 100-foot increments.

AUTOMATIC CARRIER LANDING SYSTEM/ACLS — U.S. Navy final approach equipment consisting of precision tracking radar coupled to a computer data link to provide continuous information to the aircraft, monitoring capability to the pilot, and a backup approach system.

AUTOMATIC DIRECTION FINDER/ADF — An aircraft radio navigation system which senses and indicates the direction to a L/MF nondirectional radio beacon (NDB) ground transmitter. Direction is indicated to the pilot as a magnetic bearing or as a relative bearing to the longitudinal axis of the aircraft depending on the type of indicator installed in the aircraft. In certain applications, such as military, ADF operations may be based on airborne and ground transmitters in the VHF/UHF frequency spectrum. (See Bearing, Nondirectional Beacon)

AUTOMATIC TERMINAL INFORMATION SERVICE/ATIS — The continuous broadcast of recorded noncontrol information in selected terminal areas. Its purpose is to improve controller effectiveness and to relieve frequency congestion by automating the repetitive transmission of essential but routine information; e.g.,"Los Angeles information Alfa. One three zero zero Coordinated Universal Time. Weather, measured ceiling two thousand overcast, visibility three, haze, smoke, temperature seven one, dew point five seven, wind two five zero at five, altimeter two niner niner six. I-L-S Runway Two Five Left approach in use, Runway Two Five Right closed, advise you have Alfa.'' (Refer to AIM)

ICAO—AUTOMATIC TERMINAL INFORMATION SERVICE — The provision of current, routine information to arriving and departing aircraft by means of continuous and repetitive broadcasts throughout the day or a specified portion of the day.

AUTOROTATION — A rotorcraft flight condition in which the lifting rotor is driven entirely by action of the air when the rotorcraft is in motion.

1. Autorotative Landing/Touchdown Autorotation—Used by a pilot to indicate that he will be landing without applying power to the rotor.

2. Low Level Autorotation—Commences at an altitude well below the traffic pattern, usually below 100 feet AGL and is used primarily for tactical military training.

3. 180 degrees Autorotation—Initiated from a downwind heading and is commenced well inside the normal traffic pattern. "Go around" may not be possible during the latter part of this maneuver.

AVIATION WEATHER SERVICE — A service provided by the National Weather Service (NWS) and FAA which collects and disseminates pertinent weather information for pilots, aircraft operators, and ATC. Available aviation weather reports and forecasts are displayed at each NWS office and FAA FSS. (See En Route Flight Advisory Service, Transcribed Weather Broadcast, Weather Advisory, Pilots Automatic Telephone Weather Answering Service) (Refer to AIM)

AZIMUTH, MLS — A magnetic bearing extending from an MLS navigation facility. Note: azimuth bearings are described as magnetic and are referred to as "azimuth" in radio telephone communications.

BASE LEG — (See Traffic Pattern)

BEACON — (See Radar, Nondirectional Beacon, Marker Beacon, Airport Rotating Beacon, Aeronautical Beacon, Airway Beacon))

BEARING — The horizontal direction to or from any point, usually measured clockwise from true north, magnetic north, or some other reference point through 360 degrees. (See Nondirectional Beacon)

BELOW MINIMUMS — Weather conditions below the minimums prescribed by regulation for the particular action involved; e.g., landing minimums, takeoff minimums.

BLAST FENCE — A barrier that is used to divert or dissipate jet or propeller blast.

BLIND SPEED — The rate of departure or closing of a target relative to the radar antenna at which cancellation of the primary radar target by moving target indicator (MTI) circuits in the radar equipment causes a reduction or complete loss of signal.

ICAO—BLIND VELOCITY — The radial velocity of a moving target such that the target is not seen on primary radars fitted with certain forms of fixed echo suppression.

BLIND SPOT/BLIND ZONE — An area from which radio transmissions and/or radar echoes cannot be received. The term is also used to describe portions of the airport not visible from the control tower.

BOUNDARY LIGHTS — (See Airport Lighting)

BRAKING ACTION (GOOD, FAIR, POOR, OR NIL) — A report of conditions on the airport movement area providing a pilot with a degree/quality of braking that he might expect. Braking action is reported in terms of good, fair, poor, or nil. (See Runway Condition Reading)

BRAKING ACTION ADVISORIES — When tower controllers have received runway braking action reports which include the terms "poor" or "nil," or whenever weather conditions are conducive to deteriorating or rapidly changing runway braking conditions, the tower will include on the ATIS broadcast the statement, "BRAKING ACTION ADVISORIES ARE IN EFFECT." During the time Braking Action Advisories are in effect, ATC will issue the latest braking action report for the runway in use to each arriving and departing aircraft. Pilots should be prepared for deteriorating braking conditions and should request current runway condition information if not volunteered by controllers. Pilots should also be prepared to provide a descriptive runway condition report to controllers after landing.

BROADCAST — Transmission of information for which an acknowledgement is not expected.

ICAO—BROADCAST — A transmission of information relating to air navigation that is not addressed to a specific station or stations.

CALL UP — Initial voice contact between a facility and an aircraft, using the identification of the unit being called and the unit initiating the call. (Refer to AIM)

CARDINAL ALTITUDES OR FLIGHT LEVELS — "Odd" or "Even" thousand-foot altitudes or flight levels; e.g., 5,000, 6,000, 7,000, FL 250, FL 260, FL 270. (See Altitude, Flight Levels)

CEILING — The heights above the earth's surface of the lowest layer of clouds or obscuring phenomena that is reported as "broken," "overcast," or "obscuration," and not classified as "thin" or "partial".

ICAO—CEILING — The height above the ground or water of the base of the lowest layer of cloud below 6 000 metres (20 000 feet) covering more than half the sky.

DELAY INDEFINITE (REASON IF KNOWN) EXPECT FURTHER CLEARANCE (TIME) — Used by ATC to inform a pilot when an accurate estimate of the delay time and the reason for the delay cannot immediately be determined; e.g., a disabled aircraft on the runway, terminal or center area saturation, weather below landing minimums, etc. (See Expect Further Clearance)

CENTER — (See Air Route Traffic Control Center)

CENTER'S AREA — The specified airspace within which an air route traffic control center (ARTCC) provides air traffic control and advisory service. (See Air Route Traffic Control Center) (Refer to AIM)

CENTER WEATHER ADVISORY/CWA — An unscheduled weather advisory issued by Center Weather Service Unit meteorologists for ATC use to alert pilots of existing or anticipated adverse weather conditions within the next 2 hours.

A CWA may modify or redefine a SIGMET. (See AWW, SIGMET, Convective SIGMET, and AIRMET) (Refer to AIM)

CHAFF — Thin, narrow metallic reflectors of various lengths and frequency responses, used to reflect radar energy. These reflectors when dropped from aircraft and allowed to drift downward result in large targets on the radar display.

CHARTED VFR FLYWAYS — Charted VFR Flyways are flight paths recommended for use to bypass areas heavily traversed by large turbine-powered aircraft. Pilot compliance with recommended flyways and associated altitudes is strictly voluntary. VFR Flyway Planning charts are published on the back of existing VFR Terminal Area charts.

CHARTED VISUAL FLIGHT PROCEDURE (CVFP) APPROACH — An approach wherein a radar-controlled aircraft on an IFR flight plan, operating in VFR conditions and having an ATC authorization, may proceed to the airport of intended landing via visual landmarks and altitudes depicted on a charted visual flight procedure.

CHASE/CHASE AIRCRAFT — An aircraft flown in proximity to another aircraft normally to observe its performance during training or testing.

CIRCLE-TO-LAND MANEUVER/CIRCLING MANEUVER — A maneuver initiated by the pilot to align the aircraft with a runway for landing when a straight-in landing from an instrument approach is not possible or is not desirable. This maneuver is made only after ATC authorization has been obtained and the pilot has established required visual reference to the airport (See Circle to Runway, Landing Minimums) (Refer to AIM)

CIRCLE TO RUNWAY (RUNWAY NUMBERED) — Used by ATC to inform the pilot that he must circle to land because the runway in use is other than the runway aligned with the instrument approach procedure. When the direction of the circling maneuver in relation to the airport/runway is required, the controller will state the direction (eight cardinal compass points) and specify a left or right downwind or base leg as appropriate; e.g., "Cleared VOR Runway Three Six Approach circle to Runway Two Two," or "Circle northwest of the airport for a right downwind to Runway Two Two." (See Circle-to-Land Maneuver, Landing Minimums) (Refer to AIM)

CIRCLING APPROACH — (See Circle-to-Land Maneuver)

CIRCLING MINIMA — (See Landing Minimums)

CLEAR-AIR TURBULENCE/CAT — Turbulence encountered in air where no clouds are present. This term is commonly applied to high-level turbulence associated with wind shear. CAT is often encountered in the vicinity of the jet stream. (See Wind Shear, Jet Stream)

CLEARANCE — (See Air Traffic Clearance)

CLEARANCE LIMIT — The fix, point, or location to which an aircraft is cleared when issued an air traffic clearance.

ICAO—CLEARANCE LIMIT — The point of which an aircraft is granted an air traffic control clearance.

CLEARANCE VOID IF NOT OFF BY (TIME) — Used by ATC to advise an aircraft that the departure clearance is automatically cancelled if takeoff is not made prior to a specified time. The pilot must obtain a new clearance or cancel his IFR flight plan if not off by the specified time.

ICAO—CLEARANCE VOID TIME — A time specified by an air traffic control unit at which a clearance ceases to be valid unless the aircraft concerned has already taken action to comply therewith.

CLEARED AS FILED — Means the aircraft is cleared to proceed in accordance with the route of flight filed in the flight plan. This clearance does not include the altitude, SID, or SID Transition. (See Request Full Route Clearance) (Refer to AIM)

CLEARED FOR (Type Of) APPROACH — ATC authorization for an aircraft to execute a specific instrument approach procedure to an airport; e.g., "Cleared for ILS Runway Three Six Approach." (See Instrument Approach Procedure, Approach Clearance) (Refer to AIM, FAR Part 91)

CLEARED FOR APPROACH — ATC authorization for an aircraft to execute any standard or special instrument approach procedure for that airport. Normally, an aircraft will be cleared for a specific instrument approach procedure. (See Instrument Approach Procedure, Cleared for (Type of) Approach) (Refer to AIM, FAR Part 91)

CLEARED FOR TAKEOFF — ATC authorization for an aircraft to depart. It is predicated on known traffic and known physical airport conditions.

CLEARED FOR THE OPTION — ATC authorization for an aircraft to make a touch-and-go, low approach, missed approach, stop and go, or full stop landing at the discretion of the pilot. It is normally used in training so that an instructor can evaluate a student's performance under changing situations. (See Option Approach) (Refer to AIM)

CLEARED THROUGH — ATC authorization for an aircraft to make intermediate stops at specified airports without refiling a flight plan while en route to the clearance limit.

CLEARED TO LAND — ATC authorization for an aircraft to land. It is predicated on known traffic and known physical airport conditions.

CLEARWAY — An area beyond the takeoff runway under the control of airport authorities within which terrain or fixed obstacles may not extend above specified limits. These areas may be required for certain turbine-powered operations and the size and upward slope of the clearway will differ depending on when the aircraft was certificated. (Refer to FAR Part 1)

CLIMBOUT — That portion of flight operation between takeoff and the initial cruising altitude. in the event of two-way communication failure. It also provides altitude

CLIMB TO VFR — ATC authorization for an aircraft to climb to VFR conditions within a control zone when the only weather limitation is restricted visibility. The aircraft must remain clear of clouds while climbing to VFR. (See Special VFR) (Refer to AIM)

CLOSED RUNWAY — A runway that is unusable for aircraft operations. Only the airport management/military operations office can close a runway.

CLOSED TRAFFIC — Successive operations involving takeoffs and landings or low approaches where the aircraft does not exit the traffic pattern.

CLUTTER — In radar operations, clutter refers to the reception and visual display of radar returns caused by precipitation, chaff, terrain, numerous aircraft targets, or other phenomena. Such returns may limit or preclude ATC from providing services based on radar. (See Ground Clutter, Chaff, Precipitation, Target)

ICAO—Radar Clutter — The visual indication on a radar display of unwanted signals.

COASTAL FIX — A navigation aid or intersection where an aircraft transitions between the domestic route structure and the oceanic route structure.

CODES/TRANSPONDER CODES — The number assigned to a particular multiple pulse reply signal transmitted by a transponder. (See Discrete Code)

COMBINED CENTER-RAPCON/CERAP — An air traffic facility which combines the functions of an ARTCC and a radar approach control facility. (See Air Route Traffic Control Center/ARTCC, Radar Approach Control Facility)

COMMON ROUTE/COMMON PORTION — That segment of a North American Route between the inland navigation facility and the coastal fix.

COMMON TRAFFIC ADVISORY FREQUENCY/CTAF — A frequency designed for the purpose of carrying out airport advisory practices while operating to or from an uncontrolled airport. The CTAF may be a UNICOM, Multicom, FSS, or tower frequency and is identified in appropriate aeronautical publications. (Refer to AC—90-42C)

COMPASS LOCATOR — A low power, low or medium frequency (L/MF) radio beacon installed at the site of the outer or middle marker of an instrument landing system (ILS). It can be used for navigation at distances of approximately 15 miles or as authorized in the approach procedure.

1. Outer Compass Locator/LOM—A compass locator installed at the site of the outer marker of an instrument landing system. (See Outer Marker)

2. Middle Compass Locator/LMM—A compass locator installed at the site of the middle marker of an instrument landing system. (See Middle Marker)

ICAO—LOCATOR — An LM/MF NDB used as an aid to final approach.

> *Note.* — A locator usually has an average radius of rated coverage of between 18.5 and 46.3 km (10 and 25 NM).

COMPASS ROSE — A circle, graduated in degrees, printed on some charts or marked on the ground at an airport. It is used as a reference to either true or magnetic direction.

COMPOSITE FLIGHT PLAN — A flight plan which specifies VFR operation for one portion of flight and IFR for another portion. It is used primarily in military operations. (Refer to AIM)

COMPOSITE ROUTE SYSTEM — An organized oceanic route structure, incorporating reduced lateral spacing between routes, in which composite separation is authorized.

COMPOSITE SEPARATION — A method of separating aircraft in a composite route system where, by management of route and altitude assignments, a combination of half the lateral minimum specified for the area concerned and half the vertical minimum is applied.

COMPULSORY REPORTING POINTS — Reporting points which must be reported to ATC. They are designated on aeronautical charts by solid triangles or filed in a flight plan as fixes selected to define direct routes. These points are geographical locations which are defined by navigation aids/fixes. Pilots should discontinue position reporting over compulsory reporting points when informed by ATC that their aircraft is in "radar contact."

CONFLICT ALERT — A function of certain air traffic control automated systems designed to alert radar controllers to existing or pending situations recognized by the program parameters that require his immediate attention/action.

CONFLICT RESOLUTION — The resolution of potential conflictions between IFR aircraft and VFR aircraft that are radar identified and in communication with ATC by ensuring that radar targets do not touch. Pertinent traffic advisories shall be issued when this procedure is applied. Note: This separation procedure will not be provided utilizing fully digitized radar systems. (See Controlled Airspace: Airport Radar Service Area/ARSA; Outer Area)

CONSOLAN — A low frequency, long-distance NAVAID used principally for transoceanic navigations.

CONTACT —

1. Establish communication with (followed by the name of the facility and, if appropriate, the frequency to be used).

2. A flight condition wherein the pilot ascertains the attitude of his aircraft and navigates by visual reference to the surface. (See Contact Approach, Radar Contact)

CONTACT APPROACH — An approach wherein an aircraft on an IFR flight plan, having an air traffic control authorization, operating clear of clouds with at least 1 mile flight visibility and a reasonable expectation of continuing to the destination airport in those conditions, may deviate from the instrument approach procedure and proceed to the destination airport by visual reference to the surface. This approach will only be authorized when requested by the pilot and the reported ground visibility at the destination airport is at least 1 statute mile. (Refer to AIM)

CONTERMINOUS U.S. — The 48 adjoining States and the District of Columbia.

CONTINENTAL CONTROL AREA — (See Controlled Airspace)

CONTINENTAL UNITED STATES — The 49 States located on the continent of North America and the District of Columbia.

CONTROL AREA — (See Controlled Airspace)

CONTROLLED AIRSPACE — Airspace designated as a control zone, airport radar service area, terminal control area, transition area, control area, continental control area, and positive control area within which some or all aircraft may be subject to air traffic control. (Refer to AIM, FAR Part 71)

ICAO—CONTROLLED AIRSPACE — Airspace of defined dimensions within which air traffic control service is provided to controlled flights.

Types of U.S. Controlled Airspace:

1. Control Zone—Controlled airspace which extends upward from the surface of the earth and terminates at the base of the continental control area. Control zones that do not underlie the continental control area have no upper limit. A control zone may include one or more

airports and is normally a circular area with a radius of 5 statute miles and any extensions necessary to include instrument approach and departure paths.

*ICAO—Control Zone—*A controlled airspace extending upwards from the surface of the earth to a specified upper limit.

2. Airport Radar Service Area/ARSA—Regulatory airspace surrounding designated airports wherein ATC provides radar vectoring and sequencing on a full-time basis for all IFR and VFR aircraft. The service provided in an ARSA is called ARSA service which includes: IFR/IFR—standard IFR separation; IFR/VFR—traffic advisories and conflict resolution; and VFR/VFR—traffic advisories and, as appropriate, safety alerts. The AIM contains an explanation of ARSA. The ARSA's are depicted on VFR aeronautical charts. (See Conflict Resolution, Outer Area) (Refer to AIM, Airport/Facility Directory, FAR Part 91)

3. Terminal Control Area/TCA—Controlled airspace extending upward from the surface or higher to specified altitudes, within which all aircraft are subject to operating rules and pilot and equipment requirements specified in FAR Part 91. TCA's are depicted on Sectional, World Aeronautical, En Route Low Altitude, DOD FLIP, and TCA charts. (Refer to FAR Part 91, AIM)

*ICAO—Terminal Control Area—*A control area normally established at the confluence of ATS routes in the vicinity of one or more major aerodromes.

4. Transition Area—Controlled airspace extending upward from 700 feet or more above the surface of the earth when designated in conjunction with an airport for which an approved instrument approach procedure has been prescribed; or from 1,200 feet or more above the surface of the earth when designated in conjunction with airway route structures or segments. Unless otherwise specified, transition areas terminate at the base of the overlying controlled airspace. Transition areas are designed to contain IFR operations in controlled airspace during portions of the terminal operation and while transiting between the terminal and en route environment.

5. Control Area—Airspace designated as Colored Federal airways, VOR Federal airways, control areas associated with jet routes outside the continental control area (FAR 71.161), additional control areas (FAR 71.163), control area extensions (FAR 71.165), and area low routes. Control areas do not include the continental control area, but unless otherwise designated, they do include the airspace between a segment of a main VOR Federal airway and its associated alternate segments with the vertical extent of the area corresponding to the vertical extent of the related segment of the main airway. The vertical extent of the various categories of airspace contained in control areas is defined in FAR Part 71.

*ICAO—Control Area—*A controlled airspace extending upward from a specified limit above the earth.

6. Continental Control Area—The airspace of the 48 contiguous States, the District of Columbia and Alaska, excluding the Alaska peninsula west of Long. 160° 00' 00''W, at and above 14,500 feet MSL, but does not include:

a. The airspace less than 1,500 feet above the surface of the earth; or

b. Prohibited and restricted areas, other than the restricted areas listed in FAR Part 71.

7. Positive Control Area/PCA—Airspace designated in FAR, Part 71 within which there is positive control of aircraft. Flight in PCA is normally conducted under instrument flight rules. PCA is designated throughout most of the conterminous United States and its vertical extent is from 18,000 feet MSL to and including flight level 600. In Alaska PCA does not include the airspace less than 1,500 feet above the surface of the earth nor the airspace over the Alaska Peninsula west of longitude 160 degrees West. Rules for operating in PCA are found in FARs 91.97 and 91.24.

CONTROLLED DEPARTURE TIME (CDT) PROGRAMS — These programs are the flow control process whereby aircraft are held on the ground at the departure airport when delays are projected to occur in either the en route system or the terminal of intended landing. The purpose of these programs is to reduce congestion in the air traffic system or to limit the duration of airborne holding in the arrival center or terminal area. A CDT is a specific departure slot shown on the flight plan as an expected departure clearance time (EDCT).

CONTROLLER — (See Air Traffic Control Specialist)

CONTROL SECTOR — An airspace area of defined horizontal and vertical dimensions for which a controller or group of controllers has air traffic control responsibility, normally within an air route traffic control center or an approach control facility. Sectors are established based on predominant traffic flows, altitude strata, and controller workload. Pilot-communications during operations within a sector are normally maintained on discrete frequencies assigned to the sector. (See Discrete Frequency)

CONTROL SLASH — A radar beacon slash representing the actual position of the associated aircraft. Normally, the control slash is the one closest to the interrogating radar beacon site. When ARTCC radar is operating in narrowband (digitized) mode, the control slash is converted to a target symbol.

CONTROL ZONE — (See Controlled Airspace)

CONVECTIVE SIGMET /WST/CONVECTIVE SIGNIFICANT METEOROLOGICAL INFORMATION — A weather advisory concerning convective weather significant to the safety of all aircraft. Convective SIGMET's are issued for tornadoes, lines of thunderstorms, embedded thunderstorms of any intensity level, areas of thunderstorms greater than or equal to VIP level 4 with an areal coverage of 4/10 (40%) or more, and hail 3/4 inch or greater. (See AWW, SIGMET, CWA, and AIRMET) (Refer to AIM)

COORDINATES — The intersection of lines of reference, usually expressed in degrees/minutes/seconds of latitude and longitude, used to determine position or location.

COORDINATION FIX — The fix in relation to which facilities will handoff, transfer control of an aircraft, or coordinate flight progress data. For terminal facilities, it may also serve as a clearance for arriving aircraft.

CORRECTION — An error has been made in the transmission and the correct version follows.

COURSE —

1. The intended direction of flight in the horizontal plane measured in degrees from north.

2. The ILS localizer signal pattern usually specified as the front course or the back course.

3. The intended track along a straight, curved, or segmented MLS path.

(See Bearing, Radial, Instrument Landing System, Microwave Landing System)

CRITICAL ENGINE — The engine which, upon failure, would most adversely affect the performance or handling qualities of an aircraft.

CROSS (FIX) AT (ALTITUDE) — Used by ATC when a specific altitude restriction at a specified fix is required.

CROSS (FIX) AT OR ABOVE (ALTITUDE) — Used by ATC when an altitude restriction at a specified fix is required. It does not prohibit the aircraft from crossing the fix at a higher altitude than specified; however, the higher altitude may not be one that will violate a succeeding altitude restriction or altitude assignment. (See Altitude Assignment, Altitude Restriction.) (Refer to AIM)

CROSS (FIX) AT OR BELOW (ALTITUDE) — Used by ATC when a maximum crossing altitude at a specific fix is required. It does not prohibit the aircraft from crossing the fix at a lower altitude; however, it must be at or above the minimum IFR altitude. (See Minimum IFR Altitude, Altitude Restriction) (Refer to FAR Part 91)

CROSSWIND —

1. When used concerning the traffic pattern, the word means "crosswind leg." (See Traffic Pattern)

2. When used concerning wind conditions, the word means a wind not parallel to the runway or the path of an aircraft. (See Crosswind Component)

CROSSWIND COMPONENT — The wind component measured in knots at 90 degrees to the longitudinal axis of the runway.

CRUISE — Used in an ATC clearance to authorize a pilot to conduct flight at any altitude from the minimum IFR altitude up to and including the altitude specified in the clearance. The pilot may level off at any intermediate altitude within this block of airspace. Climb/descent within the block is to be made at the discretion of the pilot. However, once the pilot starts descent and verbally reports leaving an altitude in the block, he may not return to that altitude without additional ATC clearance. Further, it is approval for the pilot to proceed to and make an approach at destination airport and can be used in conjunction with:

1. An airport clearance limit at locations with a standard/special instrument approach procedure. The FAR's require that if an instrument letdown to an airport is necessary, the pilot shall make the letdown in accordance with a standard/special instrument approach procedure for that airport, or

2. An airport clearance limit at locations that are within/below/outside controlled airspace and without a standard/special instrument approach procedure. Such a clearance is NOT AUTHORIZATION for the pilot to descend under IFR conditions below the applicable minimum IFR altitude nor does it imply that ATC is exercising control over aircraft in uncontrolled airspace; however, it provides a means for the aircraft to proceed to destination airport, descend, and land in accordance with applicable FAR's governing VFR flight operations. Also, this provides search and rescue protection until such time as the IFR flight plan is closed. (See Instrument Approach Procedure)

CRUISING ALTITUDE/LEVEL — An altitude or flight level maintained during en route level flight. This is a constant altitude and should not be confused with a cruise clearance. (See Altitude)

ICAO—CRUISING LEVEL — A level maintained during a significant portion of a flight.

DECISION HEIGHT/DH — With respect to the operation of aircraft, means the height at which a decision is made during an ILS, MLS, or PAR instrument approach to either continue the approach or to execute a missed approach.

ICAO—DECISION ALTITUDE/HEIGHT (DA/DH) — A specified altitude or height (A/H) in the precision approach at which a missed approach must be initiated if the required visual reference to continue the approach has not been established.

> *Note 1.* — Decision altitude (DA) is referenced to mean sea level (MSL) and decision height (DH) is referenced to the threshold elevation.

> *Note 2.* — The required visual reference means that section of the visual aids or of the approach area which should have been in view for sufficient time for the pilot to have made an assessment of the aircraft position and rate of change of position, in relation to the desired flight path.

DECODER — The device used to decipher signals received from ATCRBS transponders to effect their display as select codes. (See Codes, Radar)

DEFENSE VISUAL FLIGHT RULES/DVFR — Rules applicable to flights within an ADIZ conducted under the visual flight rules in FAR, Part 91. (See Air Defense Identification Zone) (Refer to FAR, Part 99)

DEPARTURE CONTROL — A function of an approach control facility providing air traffic control service for departing IFR and, under certain conditions, VFR aircraft. (See Approach Control) (Refer to AIM)

DEPARTURE TIME — The time an aircraft becomes airborne.

DEVIATIONS —

1. A departure from a current clearance, such as an off course maneuver to avoid weather or turbulence.

2. Where specifically authorized in the FAR's and requested by the pilot, ATC may permit pilots to deviate from certain regulations. (Refer to AIM)

DF APPROACH PROCEDURE — Used under emergency conditions where another instrument approach procedure cannot be executed. DF guidance for an instrument approach is given by ATC facilities with DF capability. (See DF Guidance, Direction Finder) (Refer to AIM)

DF FIX — The geographical location of an aircraft obtained by one or more direction finders. (See Direction Finder)

DF GUIDANCE/DF STEER — Headings provided to aircraft by facilities equipped with direction finding equipment. These headings, if followed, will lead the aircraft to a predetermined point such as the DF station or an airport. DF guidance is given to aircraft in distress or to other aircraft which request the service. Practice DF guidance is provided when workload permits. (See Direction Finder, DF Fix) (Refer to AIM)

DIRECT — Straight line flight between two navigational aids, fixes, points, or any combination thereof. When used by pilots in describing off-airway routes, points defining direct route segments become compulsory reporting points unless the aircraft is under radar contact.

DIRECT ALTITUDE AND IDENTITY READOUT/DAIR — The DAIR System is a modification to the AN/TPX-42 Interrogator System. The Navy has two adaptations of the DAIR System — Carrier Air Traffic Control Direct Altitude and Identification Readout System for Aircraft Carriers and Radar Air Traffic Control Facility Direct Altitude and Identity Readout System for land-based terminal operations. The DAIR detects, tracks, and predicts secondary radar aircraft targets. Targets are displayed by means of computer-generated symbols and alphanumeric characters depicting flight identification, altitude, ground speed, and flight plan data. The DAIR System is capable of interfacing with ARTCC's.

DIRECTION FINDER/DF/UDF/VDF/UVDF — A radio receiver equipped with a directional sensing antenna used to take bearings on a radio transmitter. Specialized radio direction finders are used in aircraft as air navigation aids. Others are ground-based, primarily to obtain a "fix" on a pilot requesting orientation assistance or to locate downed aircraft. A location "fix" is established by the intersection of two or more bearing lines plotted on a navigational chart using either two separately located Direction Finders to obtain a fix on an aircraft or by a pilot plotting the bearing indications of his DF on two separately located ground-based transmitters, both of which can be identified on his chart. UDF's receive signals in the ultra high frequency radio broadcast band; VDF's in the very high frequency band; and UVDF's in both bands. ATC provides DF service at those air traffic control towers and flight service stations listed in the Airport/Facility Directory and the DOD FLIP IFR En Route Supplement. (See DF Guidance, DF Fix)

DISCRETE CODE/DISCRETE BEACON CODE — As used in the Air Traffic Control Radar Beacon System (ATCRBS), any one of the 4096 selectable Mode 3/A aircraft transponder codes except those ending in zero zero; e.g., discrete codes: 0010, 1201, 2317, 7777; non-discrete codes: 0100, 1200, 7700. Non-discrete codes are normally reserved for radar facilities that are not equipped with discrete decoding capability and for other purposes such as emergencies (7700), VFR aircraft (1200), etc. (See Radar) (Refer to AIM)

DISCRETE FREQUENCY — A separate radio frequency for use in direct pilot-controller communications in air traffic control which reduces frequency congestion by controlling the number of aircraft operating on a particular frequency at one time. Discrete frequencies are normally designated for each control sector in en route/terminal ATC facilities. Discrete frequencies are listed in the Airport/Facility Directory and the DOD FLIP IFR En Route Supplement. (See Control Sector)

DISPLACED THRESHOLD — A threshold that is located at a point on the runway other than the designated beginning of the runway. (See Threshold) (Refer to AIM)

DISTANCE MEASURING EQUIPMENT/DME — Equipment (airborne and ground) used to measure, in nautical miles, the slant range distance of an aircraft from the DME navigational aid. (See TACAN, VORTAC, Microwave Landing System)

DISTRESS — A condition of being threatened by serious and/or imminent danger and of requiring immediate assistance.

DIVERSE VECTOR AREA/DVA — In a radar environment, that area in which a prescribed departure route is not required as the only suitable route to avoid obstacles. The area in which random radar vectors below the MVA/MIA, established in accordance with the TERPS criteria for diverse departures obstacles and terrain avoidance, may be issued to departing aircraft.

DME FIX — A geographical position determined by reference to a navigational aid which provides distance and azimuth information. It is defined by a specific distance in nautical miles and a radial, azimuth, or course (i.e., localizer) in degrees magnetic from that aid. (See Distance Measuring Equipment/DME, Fix, Microwave Landing System)

DME SEPARATION — Spacing of aircraft in terms of distances (nautical miles) determined by reference to distance measuring equipment (DME). (See Distance Measuring Equipment)

DOD FLIP — Department of Defense Flight Information Publications used for flight planning, en route, and terminal operations. FLIP is produced by the Defense Mapping Agency for world-wide use. United States Government Flight Information Publications (en route charts and instrument approach procedure charts) are incorporated in DOD FLIP for use in the National Airspace System (NAS).

DOWNWIND LEG — (See Traffic Pattern)

DRAG CHUTE — A parachute device installed on certain aircraft which is deployed on landing roll to assist in deceleration of the aircraft.

EMERGENCY — A *distress* or an *urgency* condition.

EMERGENCY LOCATOR TRANSMITTER/ELT — A radio transmitter attached to the aircraft structure which operates from its own power source on 121.5 MHz and 243.0 MHz. It aids in locating downed aircraft by radiating a downward sweeping audio tone, 2-4 times per second. It is designed to function without human action after an accident. (Refer to FAR, Part 91, AIM)

EMERGENCY SAFE ALTITUDE — (See Minimum Safe Altitude)

E-MSAW — (See En Route Minimum Safe Altitude Warning)

EN ROUTE AIR TRAFFIC CONTROL SERVICES — Air traffic control service provided aircraft on IFR flight plans, generally by centers, when these aircraft are operating between departure and destination terminal areas. When equipment, capabilities, and controller workload permit, certain advisory/assistance services may be provided to VFR aircraft. (See NAS Stage A, Air Route Traffic Control Center) (Refer to AIM)

EN ROUTE AUTOMATED RADAR TRACKING SYSTEM/EARTS — An automated radar and radar beacon tracking system. Its functional capabilities and design are essentially the same as the terminal ARTS IIIA system except for the EARTS capability of employing both short-range (ASR) and long-range (ARSR) radars, use of full digital radar displays, and fail-safe design. (See Automated Radar Terminal Systems/ARTS)

EN ROUTE CHARTS — (See Aeronautical Charts)

EN ROUTE DESCENT — Descent from the en route cruising altitude which takes place along the route of flight.

EN ROUTE FLIGHT ADVISORY SERVICE/FLIGHT WATCH — A service specifically designed to provide, upon pilot request, timely weather information pertinent to his type of flight, intended route of flight, and altitude. The FSS's providing this service are listed in the Airport/Facility Directory. (Refer to AIM)

EN ROUTE MINIMUM SAFE ALTITUDE WARNING/E-MSAW — A function of the NAS Stage A en route computer that aids the controller by alerting him when a tracked aircraft is below or predicted by the computer to go below a predetermined minimum IFR altitude (MIA).

ICAO—ESTIMATED ELAPSED TIME — The estimated time required to proceed from one significant point to another. (See Total Estimated Elapsed Time)

ICAO—ESTIMATED OFF-BLOCK TIME — The estimated time at which the aircraft will commence movement associated with departure.

EXECUTE MISSED APPROACH — Instructions issued to a pilot making an instrument approach which means continue inbound to the missed approach point and execute the missed approach procedure as described on the Instrument Approach Procedure Chart or as previously assigned by ATC. The pilot may climb immediately to the altitude specified in the missed approach procedure upon making a missed approach. No turns should be initiated prior to reaching the missed approach point. When conducting an ASR or PAR approach, execute the assigned missed approach procedure immediately upon receiving instructions to "execute missed approach." (Refer to AIM)

EXPECT (ALTITUDE) AT (TIME) or (FIX) — Used under certain conditions to provide a pilot with an altitude to be used in the event of two-way communications failure. It also provides altitude information to assist the pilot in planning. (Refer to AIM)

EXPECTED DEPARTURE CLEARANCE TIME/EDCT — The runway release time assigned to an aircraft in a controlled departure time program and shown on the flight progress strip as an EDCT.

EXPECT FURTHER CLEARANCE (TIME)/EFC — The time a pilot can expect to receive clearance beyond a clearance limit.

EXPECT FURTHER CLEARANCE VIA (AIRWAYS, ROUTES OR FIXES) — Used to inform a pilot of the routing he can expect if any part of the route beyond a short range clearance limit differs from that filed.

EXPEDITE — Used by ATC when prompt compliance is required to avoid the development of an imminent situation.

FAST FILE — A system whereby a pilot files a flight plan via telephone that is tape recorded and then transcribed for transmission to the appropriate air traffic facility. Locations having a fast file capability are contained in the Airport/Facility Directory. (Refer to AIM)

FEATHERED PROPELLER — A propeller whose blades have been rotated so that the leading and trailing edges are nearly parallel with the aircraft flight path to stop or minimize drag and engine rotation. Normally used to indicate shutdown of a reciprocating or turboprop engine due to malfunction.

FEEDER FIX — The fix depicted on Instrument Approach Procedure Charts which establishes the starting point of the feeder route.

FEEDER ROUTE — A route depicted on instrument approach procedure charts to designate routes for aircraft to proceed from the en route structure to the initial approach fix (IAF). (See Instrument Approach Procedure)

FERRY FLIGHT — A flight for the purpose of:

1. Returning an aircraft to base.

2. Delivering an aircraft from one location to another.

3. Moving an aircraft to and from a maintenance base.

Ferry flights, under certain conditions, may be conducted under terms of a special flight permit.

FILED — Normally used in conjunction with flight plans, meaning a flight plan has been submitted to ATC.

FILED EN ROUTE DELAY — Any of the following preplanned delays at points/areas along the route of flight which require special flight plan filing and handling techniques.

1. Terminal Area Delay—A delay within a terminal area for touch-and-go, low approach, or other terminal area activity.

2. Special Use Airspace Delay—A delay within a Military Operating Area, Restricted Area, Warning Area, or ATC Assigned Airspace.

3. Aerial Refueling Delay—A delay within an Aerial Refueling Track or Anchor.

FINAL — Commonly used to mean that an aircraft is on the final approach course or is aligned with a landing area. (See Final Approach Course, Final Approach—IFR, Traffic Pattern, Segments of an Instrument Approach Procedure)

FINAL APPROACH COURSE — A published MLS course, a straight line extension of a localizer, a final approach radial/bearing, or a runway centerline all without regard to distance. (See Final Approach-IFR, Traffic Pattern)

FINAL APPROACH FIX/FAF — The fix from which the final approach (IFR) to an airport is executed and which identifies the beginning of the final approach segment. It is designated on Government charts by the Maltese Cross symbol for nonprecision approaches and the lightning bolt symbol for precision approaches; or when ATC directs a lower-than-published Glideslope/path Intercept Altitude, it is the resultant actual point of the glideslope/path intercept. (See Final Approach Point, Glideslope/path Intercept Altitude, Segments of an Instrument Approach Procedure)

FINAL APPROACH-IFR — The flight path of an aircraft which is inbound to an airport on a final instrument approach course, beginning at the final approach fix or point and extending to the airport or the point where a circle-to-land maneuver or a missed approach is executed. (See Segments of an Instrument Approach Procedure, Final Approach Fix, Final Approach Course, Final Approach Point)

ICAO—FINAL APPROACH — That part of an instrument approach procedure which commences at the specified final approach fix or point, or where such a fix or point is not specified,

  a) At the end of the last procedure turn, base turn or inbound turn of a racetrack procedure, if specified; or

  b) At the point of interception of the last track specified in the approach procedure; and ends at a point in the vicinity of an aerodrome from which:

    1) A landing can be made; or

    2) A missed approach procedure is initiated.

FINAL APPROACH POINT/FAP — The point, applicable only to a nonprecision approach with no depicted FAF (such as an on-airport VOR), where the aircraft is established inbound on the final approach course from the procedure turn and where the final approach descent may be commenced. The FAP serves as the FAF and identifies the beginning of the final approach segment. (See Final Approach Fix, Segments of an Instrument Approach Procedure)

FINAL APPROACH SEGMENT — (See Segments of an Instrument Approach Procedure)

FINAL APPROACH-VFR — (See Traffic Pattern)

FINAL CONTROLLER — The controller providing information and final approach guidance during PAR and ASR approaches utilizing radar equipment. (See Radar Approach)

FIX — A geographical position determined by visual reference to the surface, by reference to one or more radio NAVAIDs, by celestial plotting, or by another navigational device.

FLAG/FLAG ALARM — A warning device incorporated in certain airborne navigation and flight instruments indicating that:

  1. Instruments are inoperative or otherwise not operating satisfactorily, or

  2. Signal strength or quality of the received signal falls below acceptable values.

FLAMEOUT — Unintended loss of combustion in turbine engines resulting in the loss of engine power.

FLIGHT CHECK — A call-sign prefix used by FAA aircraft engaged in flight inspection/certification of navigational aids and flight procedures. The word "recorded" may be added as a suffix; e.g., "Flight Check 320 recorded" to indicate that an automated flight inspection is in progress in terminal areas. (See Flight Inspection/Flight Check) (Refer to AIM).

FLIGHT INFORMATION REGION/FIR — An airspace of defined dimensions within which Flight Information Service and Alerting Service are provided.

  1. Flight Information Service—A service provided for the purpose of giving advice and information useful for the safe and efficient conduct of flights.

  2. Alerting Service—A service provided to notify appropriate organizations regarding aircraft in need of search and rescue aid and to assist such organizations as required.

FLIGHT INSPECTION/FLIGHT CHECK — Inflight investigation and evaluation of a navigational aid to determine whether it meets established tolerances. (See Navigational Aid)

FLIGHT LEVEL — A level of constant atmospheric pressure related to a reference datum of 29.92 inches of mercury. Each is stated in three digits that represent hundreds of feet. For example, flight level 250 represents a barometric altimeter indication of 25,000 feet; flight level 255, an indication of 25,500 feet.

ICAO—FLIGHT LEVEL — A surface of constant atmospheric pressure which is related to a specific pressure datum, 1013.2 hPa (1013.2 mb), and is separated from other such surfaces by specific pressure intervals.

  Note 1. — A pressure type altimeter calibrated in accordance with the standard atmosphere:

    a) When set to a QNH altimeter setting, will indicate altitude;

    b) When set to a QFE altimeter setting, will indicate height above the QFE reference datum; and

    c) When set to a pressure of 1013.2 hPa (1013.2 mb), may be used to indicate flight levels.

  Note 2. — The terms *height* and *altitude,* used in *Note 1* above, indicate altimetric rather than geometric heights and altitudes.

FLIGHT LINE — A term used to describe the precise movement of a civil photogrammetric aircraft along a predetermined course(s) at a predetermined altitude during the actual photographic run.

FLIGHT PATH — A line, course, or track along which an aircraft is flying or intended to be flown. (See Track, Course)

FLIGHT PLAN — Specified information relating to the intended flight of an aircraft that is filed orally or in writing with an FSS or an ATC facility. (See Fast File, Filed) (Refer to AIM)

FLIGHT RECORDER — A general term applied to any instrument or device that records information about the performance of an aircraft in flight or about conditions encountered in flight. Flight recorders may make records of airspeed, outside air temperature, vertical acceleration, engine RPM, manifold pressure, and other pertinent variables for a given flight.

ICAO—FLIGHT RECORDER — Any type of recorder installed in the aircraft for the purpose of complementing accident/incident investigation.

  Note. — See Annex 6, Part I, for specifications relating to flight recorders.

FLIGHT SERVICE STATION/FSS — Air traffic facilities which provide pilot briefing, en route communications and VFR search and rescue services, assist lost aircraft and aircraft in emergency situations, relay ATC clearances, originate Notices to Airmen, broadcast aviation weather and NAS information, receive and process IFR flight plans, and monitor NAVAID's. In addition, at selected locations, FSS's provide Enroute Flight Advisory Service (Flight Watch), take weather observations, issue airport advisories, and advise Customs and Immigration of transborder flights. (Refer to AIM)

FLIGHT STANDARDS DISTRICT OFFICE/FSDO — An FAA field office serving an assigned geographical area and staffed with Flight Standards personnel who serve the aviation industry and the general public on matters relating to the certification and operation of air carrier and general aviation aircraft. Activities include general surveillance of operational safety, certification of airmen and aircraft, accident prevention, investigation, enforcement, etc.

FLIGHT TEST — A flight for the purpose of:

1. Investigating the operation/flight characteristics of an aircraft or aircraft component.

2. Evaluating an applicant for a pilot certificate or rating.

FLIGHT VISIBILITY — (See Visibility)

FLIGHT WATCH — A shortened term for use in air-ground contacts to identify the flight service station providing En Route Flight Advisory Service; e.g., "Oakland Flight Watch." (See En Route Flight Advisory Service)

FLIP — (See DOD FLIP)

FLOW CONTROL — Measures designed to adjust the flow of traffic into a given airspace, along a given route, or bound for a given aerodrome (airport) so as to ensure the most effective utilization of the airspace. (See Quota Flow Control) (Refer to Airport/Facility Directory

FLY HEADING (DEGREES) — Informs the pilot of the heading he should fly. The pilot may have to turn to, or continue on, a specific compass direction in order to comply with the instructions. The pilot is expected to turn in the shorter direction to the heading unless otherwise instructed by ATC.

FORMATION FLIGHT — More than one aircraft which, by prior arrangement between the pilots, operate as a single aircraft with regard to navigation and position reporting. Separation between aircraft within the formation is the responsibility of the flight leader and the pilots of the other aircraft in the flight. This includes transition periods when aircraft within the formation are maneuvering to attain separation from each other to effect individual control and during join-up and breakaway.

1. A standard formation is one in which a proximity of no more than 1 mile laterally or longitudinally and within 100 feet vertically from the flight leader is maintained by each wingman.

2. Nonstandard formations are those operating under any of the following conditions:

   a. When the flight leader has requested and ATC has approved other than standard formation dimensions.

   b. When operating within an authorized altitude reservation (ALTRV) or under the provisions of a letter of agreement.

   c. When the operations are conducted in airspace specifically designed for a special activity. (See Altitude Reservation) (Refer to FAR Part 91)

FSS — (See Flight Service Station)

FUEL DUMPING — Airborne release of usable fuel. This does not include the dropping of fuel tanks. (See Jettisoning of External Stores)

FUEL SIPHONING/FUEL VENTING — Unintentional release of fuel caused by overflow, puncture, loose cap, etc.

GATE HOLD PROCEDURES — Procedures at selected airports to hold aircraft at the gate or other ground location whenever departure delays exceed or are anticipated to exceed

15 minutes. The sequence for departure will be maintained in accordance with initial call-up unless modified by flow control restrictions. Pilots should monitor the ground control/clearance delivery frequency for engine startup advisories or new proposed start time if the delay changes. (See Flow Control)

GENERAL AVIATION — That portion of civil aviation which encompasses all facets of aviation except air carriers holding a certificate of public convenience and necessity from the Civil Aeronautics Board and large aircraft commercial operators.

ICAO—GENERAL AVIATION — All civil aviation operations other than scheduled air services and non-scheduled air transport operations for remuneration or hire.

GENERAL AVIATION DISTRICT OFFICE/GADO — An FAA field office serving a designated geographical area and staffed with Flight Standards personnel who have the responsibility for serving the aviation industry and the general public on all matters relating to the certification and operation of general aviation aircraft.

GLIDESLOPE/GLIDEPATH — Provides vertical guidance for aircraft during approach and landing. The glideslope/glidepath is based on the following:

1. Electronic components emitting signals which provide vertical guidance by reference to airborne instruments during instrument approaches such as ILS/MLS, or

2. Visual ground aids, such as VASI, which provide vertical guidance for a VFR approach or for the visual portion of an instrument approach and landing.

3. PAR. Used by ATC to inform an aircraft making a PAR approach of its vertical position (elevation) relative to the descent profile.

ICAO—GLIDEPATH — A descent profile determined for vertical guidance during a final approach.

GLIDESLOPE/GLIDEPATH INTERCEPT ALTITUDE — The minimum altitude to intercept the glideslope/path on a precision approach. The intersection of the published intercept altitude with the glideslope/path, designated on Government charts by the lightning bolt symbol, is the precision FAF; however, when ATC directs a lower altitude, the resultant lower intercept position is then the FAF. (See Final Approach Fix, Segments of an Instrument Approach Procedure)

GO AHEAD — Proceed with your message. Not to be used for any other purpose.

GO AROUND — Instructions for a pilot to abandon his approach to landing. Additional instructions may follow. Unless otherwise advised by ATC, a VFR aircraft or an aircraft conducting visual approach should overfly the runway while climbing to traffic pattern altitude and enter the traffic pattern via the crosswind leg. A pilot on an IFR flight plan making an instrument approach should execute the published missed approach procedure or proceed as instructed by ATC; e.g., "Go around" (additional instructions if required). (See Low Approach, Missed Approach)

GROUND CLUTTER — A pattern produced on the radar scope by ground returns which may degrade other radar returns in the affected area. The effect of ground clutter is minimized by the use of moving target indicator (MTI) circuits in the radar equipment resulting in a radar presentation which displays only targets which are in motion. (See Clutter)

GROUND CONTROLLED APPROACH/GCA — A radar approach system operated from the ground by air traffic control personnel transmitting instructions to the pilot by radio. The approach may be conducted with surveillance radar (ASR) only or with both surveillance and precision approach radar (PAR). Usage of the term "GCA" by pilots is discouraged except when referring to a GCA facility. Pilots should specifically request a "PAR" approach when a precision radar approach is desired or request an "ASR" or "surveillance" approach when a nonprecision radar approach is desired. (See Radar Approach)

GROUND DELAY — The amount of delay attributed to ATC, encountered prior to departure, usually associated with a CDT program.

GROUND SPEED — The speed of an aircraft relative to the surface of the earth.

GROUND VISIBILITY — (See Visibility)

HANDOFF — An action taken to transfer the radar identification of an aircraft from one controller to another if the aircraft will enter the receiving controller's airspace and radio communications with the aircraft will be transferred.

HAVE NUMBERS — Used by pilots to inform ATC that they have received runway, wind, and altimeter information only.

HAZARDOUS INFLIGHT WEATHER ADVISORY SERVICE/HIWAS — A program for broadcasting hazardous weather information (AWW's, SIGMET's, Convective SIGMET's, CWA's, AIRMET's, and Urgent PIREP's) on a continuous basis over selected VOR's. (Refer to AIM)

HEAVY (AIRCRAFT) — (See Aircraft Classes)

HEIGHT ABOVE AIRPORT/HAA — The height of the Minimum Descent Altitude above the published airport elevation. This is published in conjunction with circling minimums. (See Minimum Descent Altitude)

HEIGHT ABOVE LANDING/HAL — The height above a designated helicopter landing area used for helicopter instrument approach procedures. (Refer to FAR Part 97)

HEIGHT ABOVE TOUCHDOWN/HAT — The height of the Decision Height or Minimum Descent Altitude above the highest runway elevation in the touchdown zone (first 3,000 feet of the runway). HAT is published on instrument approach charts in conjunction with all straight-in minimums. (See Decision Height, Minimum Descent Altitude)

HELICOPTER/COPTER — Rotorcraft that, for its horizontal motion, depends principally on its engine-driven rotors.

ICAO—HELICOPTER — A heavier-than-air aircraft supported in flight chiefly by the reactions of the air on one or more power-driven rotors on substantially vertical axes.

HELIPAD — A small, designated area, usually with a prepared surface, on a heliport, airport, landing/takeoff area, apron/ramp, or movement area used for takeoff, landing, or parking of helicopters.

HELIPORT — An area of land, water, or structure used or intended to be used for the landing and takeoff of helicopters and includes its buildings and facilities if any.

HERTZ/HZ — The standard radio equivalent of frequency in cycles per second of an electromagnetic wave. Kilohertz (kHz) is a frequency of one thousand cycles per second. Megahertz (MHz) is a frequency of one million cycles per second.

HIGH FREQUENCY/HF — The frequency band between 3 and 30 MHz. (See High Frequency Communications)

HIGH FREQUENCY COMMUNICATIONS/HF COMMUNICATIONS — High radio frequencies (HF) between 3 and 30 MHz used for air-to-ground voice communication in overseas operations.

HIGH SPEED TAXIWAY/EXIT/TURNOFF — A long radius taxiway designed and provided with lighting or marking to define the path of aircraft, traveling at high speed (up to 60 knots), from the runway center to a point on the center of a taxiway. Also referred to as long radius exit or turn-off taxiway. The high speed taxiway is designed to expedite aircraft turning off the runway after landing, thus reducing runway occupancy time.

HOLD/HOLDING PROCEDURE — A predetermined maneuver which keeps aircraft within a specified airspace while awaiting further clearance from air traffic control. Also used during ground operations to keep aircraft within a specified area or at a specified point while awaiting further clearance from air traffic control. (See Holding Fix) (Refer to AIM)

HOLDING FIX — A specified fix identifiable to a pilot by NAVAID's or visual reference to the ground used as a reference point in establishing and maintaining the position of an aircraft while holding. (See Fix, Hold, Visual Holding) (Refer to AIM)

HOLD FOR RELEASE — Used by ATC to delay an aircraft for traffic management reasons; i.e., weather, traffic volume, etc. Hold for release instructions (including departure delay information) are used to inform a pilot or a controller (either directly or through an authorized relay) that a departure clearance is not valid until a release time or additional instructions have been received.

ICAO—HOLDING POINT — A specified location, identified by visual or other means, in the vicinity of which the position of an aircraft in flight is maintained in accordance with air traffic control clearances.

HOMING — Flight toward a NAVAID, without correcting for wind, by adjusting the aircraft heading to maintain a relative bearing of zero degrees. (See Bearing)

ICAO—HOMING — The procedure of using the direction-finding equipment of one radio station with the emission of another radio station, where at least one of the stations is mobile, and whereby the mobile station proceeds continuously towards the other station.

HOVER CHECK — Used to describe when a helicopter/VTOL aircraft requires a stabilized hover to conduct a performance/power check prior to hover taxi, air taxi, or takeoff. Altitude of the hover will vary based on the purpose of the check.

HOVER TAXI — Used to describe a helicopter/VTOL aircraft movement conducted above the surface and in ground effect at airspeeds less than approximately 20 knots. The actual height may vary, and some helicopters may require hover taxi above 25 feet AGL to reduce ground effect turbulence or provide clearance for cargo slingloads. (See Air Taxi, Hover Check) (Refer to AIM)

HOW DO YOU HEAR ME? — A question relating to the quality of the transmission or to determine how well the transmission is being received.

IDENT — A request for a pilot to activate the aircraft transponder identification feature. This will help the controller to confirm an aircraft identity or to identify an aircraft. (Refer to AIM)

IDENT FEATURE — The special feature in the Air Traffic Control Radar Beacon System (ATCRBS) equipment. It is used to immediately distinguish one displayed beacon target from other beacon targets. (See Ident)

IF FEASIBLE, REDUCE SPEED TO (SPEED) — (See Speed Adjustment)

IF NO TRANSMISSION RECEIVED FOR (TIME) — Used by ATC in radar approaches to prefix procedures which should be followed by the pilot in event of lost communications. (See Lost Communications)

IFR AIRCRAFT/IFR FLIGHT — An aircraft conducting flight in accordance with instrument flight rules.

IFR CONDITIONS — Weather conditions below the minimum for flight under visual flight rules. (See Instrument Meteorological Conditions)

IFR DEPARTURE PROCEDURE — (See IFR Takeoff Minimums and Departure Procedures) (Refer to AIM)

IFR MILITARY TRAINING ROUTES (IR) — Routes used by the Department of Defense and associated Reserve and Air Guard units for the purpose of conducting low-altitude navigation and tactical training in both IFR and VFR weather conditions below 10,000 feet MSL at airspeeds in excess of 250 knots IAS.

IFR TAKEOFF MINIMUMS AND DEPARTURE PROCEDURES — FAR, Part 91, prescribes standard takeoff rules for certain civil users. At some airports, obstructions or other factors require the establishment of nonstandard takeoff minimums, departure procedures, or both to assist pilots in avoiding obstacles during climb to the minimum en route altitude. Those airports are listed in NOS/DOD Instrument Approach Charts (IAP's) under a section entitled "IFR Takeoff Minimums and Departure Procedures." The NOS/DOD IAP chart legend illustrates the symbol used to alert the pilot to nonstandard takeoff minimums and departure procedures. When departing IFR from such airports or from any airports where there are no departure procedures, SID's, or ATC facilities available, pilots should advise ATC of any departure limitations. Controllers may query a pilot to determine acceptable departure directions, turns, or headings after takeoff. Pilots should be familiar with the departure procedures and must assure that their aircraft can meet or exceed any specified climb gradients.

ILS CATEGORIES —

1. ILS Category I—An ILS approach procedure which provides for approach to a height above touchdown of not less than 200 feet and with runway visual range of not less than 1,800 feet.

2. ILS Category II—An ILS approach procedure which provides for approach to a height above touchdown of

not less than 100 feet and with runway visual range of not less than 1,200 feet.

3. ILS Category III.

   a. IIIA—An ILS approach procedure which provides for approach without a decision height minimum and with runway visual range of not less than 700 feet.

   b. IIIB—An ILS approach procedure which provides for approach without a decision height minimum and with runway visual range of not less than 150 feet.

   c. IIIC—An ILS approach procedure which provides for approach without a decision height minimum and without runway visual range minimum.

IMMEDIATELY — Used by ATC when such action compliance is required to avoid an imminent situation.

INCREASE SPEED TO (SPEED) — (See Speed Adjustment)

INFORMATION REQUEST/INREQ — A request originated by an FSS for information concerning an overdue VFR aircraft.

INITIAL APPROACH FIX/IAF — The fixes depicted on instrument approach procedure charts that identify the beginning of the initial approach segment(s). (See Fix, Segments of an Instrument Approach Procedure)

INITIAL APPROACH SEGMENT — (See Segments of an Instrument Approach Procedure)

INNER MARKER/IM/INNER MARKER BEACON — A marker beacon used with an ILS (CAT II) precision approach located between the middle marker and the end of the ILS runway, transmitting a radiation pattern keyed at six dots per second and indicating to the pilot, both aurally and visually, that he is at the designated decision height (DH), normally 100 feet above the touchdown zone elevation, on the ILS CAT II approach. It also marks progress during a CAT III approach. (See Instrument Landing System) (Refer to AIM)

INSTRUMENT APPROACH PROCEDURE/IAP/INSTRUMENT APPROACH — A series of predetermined maneuvers for the orderly transfer of an aircraft under instrument flight conditions from the beginning of the initial approach to a landing or to a point from which a landing may be made visually. It is prescribed and approved for a specific airport by competent authority. (See Segments of an Instrument Approach Procedure) (Refer to FAR, Part 91, AIM)

1. U. S. civil standard instrument approach procedures are approved by the FAA as prescribed under FAR, Part 97 and are available for public use.

2. U.S. military standard instrument approach procedures are approved and published by the Department of Defense.

3. Special instrument approach procedures are approved by the FAA for individual operators but are not published in FAR, Part 97 for public use.

ICAO—INSTRUMENT APPROACH PROCEDURE — A series of predetermined manoeuvres by reference to flight instruments with specified protection from obstacles from the intial approach fix, or where applicable, from the beginning of a defined arrival route to a point from which a landing can be completed and thereafter, if a landing is not completed, to a position at which holding or en route obstacle clearance criteria apply.

INSTRUMENT FLIGHT RULES/IFR — Rules governing the procedures for conducting instrument flight. Also a term used by pilots and controllers to indicate type of flight plan. (See Visual Flight Rules, Instrument Meteorological Conditions, Visual Meteorological Conditions) (Refer to AIM)

ICAO—INSTRUMENT FLIGHT RULES — A set of rules governing the conduct of flight under instrument meteorological conditions.

INSTRUMENT LANDING SYSTEM/ILS — A precision instrument approach system which normally consists of the following electronic components and visual aids:

1. Localizer. (See Localizer)

2. Glideslope. (See Glideslope)

3. Outer Marker. (See Outer Marker)

4. Middle Marker. (See Middle Marker)

5. Approach Lights. (See Airport Lighting)

(Refer to FAR Part 91, AIM)

INSTRUMENT METEOROLOGICAL CONDITIONS/ IMC — Meteorological conditions expressed in terms of visibility, distance from cloud, and ceiling less than the minima specified for visual meteorological conditions. (See Visual Meteorological Conditions, Instrument Flight Rules, Visual Flight Rules)

INSTRUMENT RUNWAY — A runway equipped with electronic and visual navigation aids for which a precision or nonprecision approach procedure having straight-in landing minimums has been approved.

ICAO—INSTRUMENT RUNWAY — One of the following types of runways intended for the operation of aircraft using instrument approach procedures:

   a) *Non-precision Approach Runway.* An instrument runway served by visual aids and a nonvisual aid providing at least directional guidance adequate for a straight-in approach.

   b) *Precision Approach Runway, Category I.* An instrument runway served by ILS and visual aids intended for operations down to 60 m (200 feet) decision height and down to an RVR of the order of 800 m.

   c) *Precision Approach Runway, Category II.* An instrument runway served by ILS and visual aids intended for operations down to 30 m (100 feet) decision height and down to an RVR of the order of 400 m.

   d) *Precision Approach Runway, Category III.* An instrument runway served by ILS to and along the surface of the runway and:

     A — Intended for operations down to an RVR of the order of 200 m (no decision height being applicable) using visual aids during the final phase of landing;

     B — Intended for operations down to an RVR of the order of 50 m (no decision height being applicable) using visual aids for taxiing;

     C — Intended for operations without reliance on visual reference for landing or taxiing.

Note 1. — See Annex 10, Volume I, Part I Chapter 3, for related ILS specifications.

Note 2. — Visual aids need not necessarily be matched to the scale of non-visual aids provided. The criterion for the selection of visual aids is the conditions in which operations are intended to be conducted.

INTERMEDIATE APPROACH SEGMENT — (See Segments of an Instrument Approach Procedure)

INTERMEDIATE FIX/IF — The fix that identifies the beginning of the intermediate approach segment of an instrument approach procedure. The fix is not normally identified on the instrument approach chart as an intermediate fix (IF). (See Segments of an Instrument Approach Procedure)

INTERNATIONAL AIRPORT — Relating to international flight, it means:

1. An airport of entry which has been designated by the Secretary of Treasury or Commissioner of Customs as an international airport for customs service.

2. A landing rights airport at which specific permission to land must be obtained from customs authorities in advance of contemplated use.

3. Airports designated under the Convention on International Civil Aviation as an airport for use by international commercial air transport and/or international general aviation. (Refer to Airport/Facility Directory and IFIM)

ICAO—INTERNATIONAL AIRPORT — Any airport designated by the Contracting State in whose territory it is situated as an airport of entry and departure for international air traffic, where the formalities incident to customs, immigration, public health, animal and plant quarantine and similar procedures are carried out.

INTERNATIONAL CIVIL AVIATION ORGANIZATION/ ICAO — A specialized agency of the United Nations whose objective is to develop the principles and techniques of international air navigation and to foster planning and development of international civil air transport.

INTERNATIONAL FLIGHT INFORMATION MANUAL/ IFIM — A publication designed primarily as a pilot's preflight planning guide for flights into foreign airspace and for flights returning to the U.S. from foreign locations.

INTERROGATOR — The ground-based surveillance radar beacon transmitter-receiver, which normally scans in synchronism with a primary radar, transmitting discrete radio signals which repetitiously request all transponders on the mode being used to reply. The replies received are mixed with the primary radar returns and displayed on the same plan position indicator (radar scope). Also, applied to the airborne element of the TACAN/DME system. (See Transponder) (Refer to AIM)

INTERSECTING RUNWAYS — Two or more runways which cross or meet within their lengths. (See Intersection)

INTERSECTION —

1. A point defined by any combination of courses, radials, or bearings of two or more navigational aids.

2. Used to describe the point where two runways, a runway and a taxiway, or two taxiways cross or meet.

INTERSECTION DEPARTURE/INTERSECTION TAKE-OFF — A takeoff or proposed takeoff on a runway from an intersection. (See Intersection)

I SAY AGAIN — The message will be repeated.

JAMMING — Electronic or mechanical interference which may disrupt the display of aircraft on radar or the transmission/reception of radio communications/navigation.

JET BLAST — Jet engine exhaust (thrust stream turbulence). (See Wake Turbulence)

JET ROUTE — A route designed to serve aircraft operations from 18,000 feet MSL up to and including flight level 450. The routes are referred to as "J" routes with numbering to identify the designated route; e.g., J105. (See Route) (Refer to FAR Part 71)

JET STREAM — A migrating stream of high-speed winds present at high altitudes.

JETTISONING OF EXTERNAL STORES — Airborne release of external stores; e.g., tiptanks, ordnance. (See Fuel Dumping) (Refer to FAR Part 91)

JOINT USE RESTRICTED AREA — (See Restricted Area)

KNOWN TRAFFIC — With respect to ATC clearances, means aircraft whose altitude, position, and intentions are known to ATC.

LANDING/TAKEOFF AREA — Any locality either on land, water, or structures, including airports/heliports and intermediate landing fields, which is used, or intended to be used, for the landing and takeoff of aircraft whether or not facilities are provided for the shelter, servicing, or for receiving or discharging passengers or cargo.

ICAO—LANDING AREA — That part of a movement area intended for the landing or takeoff of aircraft.

LANDING DIRECTION INDICATOR — A device which visually indicates the direction in which landings and takeoffs should be made. (See Tetrahedron) (Refer to AIM)

LANDING MINIMUMS/IFR LANDING MINIMUMS — The minimum visibility prescribed for landing a civil aircraft while using an instrument approach procedure. The minimum applies with other limitations set forth in FAR Part 91 with respect to the Minimum Descent Altitude (MDA) or Decision Height (DH) prescribed in the instrument approach procedures as follows:

1. Straight-in landing minimums—A statement of MDA and visibility, or DH and visibility, required for a straight-in landing on a specified runway, or

2. Circling minimums—A statement of MDA and visibility required for the circle-to-land maneuver.

Descent below the established MDA or DH is not authorized during an approach unless the aircraft is in a position from which a normal approach to the runway of intended landing can be made and adequate visual reference to required visual cues is maintained. (See Straight-in Landing, Circle-to-Land Maneuver, Decision Height, Minimum Descent Altitude, Visibility, Instrument Approach Procedure) (Refer to FAR Part 91)

LANDING ROLL — The distance from the point of touchdown to the point where the aircraft can be brought to a stop or exit the runway.

LANDING SEQUENCE — The order in which aircraft are positioned for landing. (See Approach Sequence)

LAST ASSIGNED ALTITUDE — The last altitude/flight level assigned by ATC and acknowledged by the pilot. (See Maintain) (Refer to FAR Part 91)

LATERAL SEPARATION — The lateral spacing of aircraft at the same altitude by requiring operation on different routes or in different geographical locations. (See Separation)

LIGHTED AIRPORT — An airport where runway and obstruction lighting is available. (See Airport Lighting) (Refer to AIM)

LIGHT GUN — A handheld directional light signaling device which emits a brilliant narrow beam of white, green, or red light as selected by the tower controller. The color and type of light transmitted can be used to approve or disapprove anticipated pilot actions where radio communication is not available. The light gun is used for controlling traffic operating in the vicinity of the airport and on the airport movement area. (Refer to AIM)

LOCALIZER — The component of an ILS which provides course guidance to the runway. (See Instrument Landing System) (Refer to AIM)

ICAO—LOCALIZER COURSE (ILS) — The locus of points, in any given horizontal plane, at which the DDM (difference in depth of modulation) is zero.

LOCALIZER TYPE DIRECTIONAL AID/LDA — A NAVAID used for nonprecision instrument approaches with utility and accuracy comparable to a localizer but which is not a part of a complete ILS and is not aligned with the runway. (Refer to AIM)

LOCALIZER USABLE DISTANCE — The maximum distance from the localizer transmitter at a specified altitude, as verified by flight inspection, at which reliable course information is continuously received. (Refer to AIM)

LOCAL TRAFFIC — Aircraft operating in the traffic pattern or within sight of the tower, or aircraft known to be departing or arriving from flight in local practice areas, or aircraft executing practice instrument approaches at the airport. (See Traffic Pattern)

LONGITUDINAL SEPARATION — The longitudinal spacing of aircraft at the same altitude by a minimum distance expressed in units of time or miles. (See Separation) (Refer to AIM)

LORAN/LONG RANGE NAVIGATION — An electronic navigational system by which hyperbolic lines of position are determined by measuring the difference in the time of reception of synchronized pulse signals from two fixed transmitters. Loran A operates in the 1750-1950 kHz frequency band. Loran C and D operate in the 100-110 kHz frequency band. (Refer to AIM)

LOST COMMUNICATIONS/TWO-WAY RADIO COMMUNICATIONS FAILURE — Loss of the ability to communicate by radio. Aircraft are sometimes referred to as NORDO (No Radio). Standard pilot procedures are specified in FAR Part 91. Radar controllers issue procedures for pilots to follow in the event of lost communications during a radar approach when weather reports indicate that an aircraft will likely encounter IFR weather conditions during the approach. (Refer to FAR Part 91, AIM)

LOW ALTITUDE AIRWAY STRUCTURE/FEDERAL AIRWAYS — The network of airways serving aircraft operations up to but not including 18,000 feet MSL. (See Airway) (Refer to AIM)

LOW ALTITUDE ALERT, CHECK YOUR ALTITUDE IMMEDIATELY — (See Safety Alert)

LOW ALTITUDE ALERT SYSTEM/LAAS — An automated function of the TPX-42 that alerts the controller when a Mode C transponder-equipped aircraft on an IFR flight plan is below a predetermined minimum safe altitude. If requested by the pilot, LAAS monitoring is also available to VFR Mode C transponder-equipped aircraft.

LOW APPROACH — An approach over an airport or runway following an instrument approach or a VFR approach including the go-around maneuver where the pilot intentionally does not make contact with the runway. (Refer to AIM)

LOW FREQUENCY/LF — The frequency band between 30 and 300 kHz. (Refer to AIM)

MACH NUMBER — The ratio of true airspeed to the speed of sound; e.g., MACH .82, MACH 1.6. (See Airspeed)

MAINTAIN —

1. Concerning altitude/flight level, the term means to remain at the altitude/flight level specified. The phrase "climb and" or "descend and" normally precedes "maintain" and the altitude assignment; e.g., "descend and maintain 5,000."

2. Concerning other ATC instructions, the term is used in its literal sense; e.g., maintain VFR.

MAKE SHORT APPROACH — Used by ATC to inform a pilot to alter his traffic pattern so as to make a short final approach. (See Traffic Pattern)

MANDATORY ALTITUDE — An altitude depicted on an instrument Approach Procedure Chart requiring the aircraft to maintain altitude at the depicted value.

MARKER BEACON — An electronic navigation facility transmitting a 75 MHz vertical fan or boneshaped radiation pattern. Marker beacons are identified by their modulation frequency and keying code, and when received by compatible airborne equipment, indicate to the pilot, both aurally and visually, that he is passing over the facility. (See Outer Marker, Middle Marker, Inner Marker) (Refer to AIM)

MAXIMUM AUTHORIZED ALTITUDE/MAA — A published altitude representing the maximum usable altitude or flight level for an airspace structure or route segment. It is the highest altitude on a Federal airway, jet route, area navigation low or high route, or other direct route for which an MEA is designated in FAR Part 95 at which adequate reception of navigation aid signals is assured.

MAYDAY — The international radiotelephony distress signal. When repeated three times, it indicates imminent and grave danger and that immediate assistance is requested. (See Pan-Pan) (Refer to AIM)

METEOROLOGICAL IMPACT STATEMENT/MIS — An unscheduled planning forecast describing conditions expected to begin within 4 to 12 hours which may impact the flow of air traffic in a specific center's (ARTCC) area.

METERING — A method of time-regulating arrival traffic flow into a terminal area so as not to exceed a predetermined terminal acceptance rate.

METERING FIX — A fix along an established route from over which aircraft will be metered prior to entering terminal airspace. Normally, this fix should be established at a distance from the airport which will facilitate a profile descent 10,000 feet above airport elevation (AAE) or above.

MIA — (See Minimum IFR Altitudes)

MICROWAVE LANDING SYSTEM/MLS — A precision instrument approach system operating in the microwave spectrum which normally consists of the following components:

1. Azimuth Station.

2. Elevation Station.

3. Precision Distance Measuring Equipment. (See MLS Categories)

MIDDLE COMPASS LOCATOR — (See Compass Locator)

MIDDLE MARKER/MM — A marker beacon that defines a point along the glide slope of an ILS normally located at or near the point of decision height (ILS Category I). It is keyed to transmit alternate dots and dashes, with the alternate dots and dashes keyed at the rate of 95 dot/dash combinations per minute on a 1300 Hz tone, which is received aurally and visually by compatible airborne equipment. (See Marker Beacon, Instrument Landing System) (Refer to AIM)

MID RVR — (See Visibility)

MILITARY AUTHORITY ASSUMES RESPONSIBILITY FOR SEPARATION OF AIRCRAFT/MARSA — A condition whereby the military services involved assume responsibility for separation between participating military aircraft in the ATC system. It is used only for required IFR operations which are specified in letters of agreement or other appropriate FAA or military documents.

MILITARY OPERATIONS AREA/MOA — (See Special Use Airspace)

MILITARY TRAINING ROUTES/MTR — Airspace of defined vertical and lateral dimensions established for the conduct of military flight training at airspeeds in excess of 250 knots IAS. (See IFR (IR) and VFR (VR) Military Training Routes)

MINIMUM CROSSING ALTITUDE/MCA — The lowest altitude at certain fixes at which an aircraft must cross when proceeding in the direction of a higher minimum en route IFR altitude (MEA). (See Minimum En Route IFR Altitude)

MINIMUM DESCENT ALTITUDE/MDA — The lowest altitude, expressed in feet above mean sea level, to which descent is authorized on final approach or during circle-to-land maneuvering in execution of a standard instrument approach procedure where no electronic glide slope is provided. (See Nonprecision Approach Procedure)

MINIMUM EN ROUTE IFR ALTITUDE/MEA — The lowest published altitude between radio fixes which assures acceptable navigational signal coverage and meets obstacle clearance requirements between those fixes. The MEA prescribed for a Federal airway or segment thereof, area navigation low or high route, or other direct route applies to the entire width of the airway, segment, or route between the radio fixes defining the airway, segment, or route. (Refer to FAR Parts 91 and 95; AIM)

MINIMUM FUEL — Indicates that an aircraft's fuel supply has reached a state where, upon reaching the destination, it can accept little or no delay. This is not an emergency situation but merely indicates an emergency situation is possible should any undue delay occur. (Refer to AIM)

MINIMUM HOLDING ALTITUDE/MHA — The lowest altitude prescribed for a holding pattern which assures navigational signal coverage, communications, and meets obstacle clearance requirements.

MINIMUM IFR ALTITUDES/MIA — Minimum altitudes for IFR operations as prescribed in FAR Part 91. These altitudes are published on aeronautical charts and prescribed in FAR Part 95 for airways and routes, and in FAR Part 97 for standard instrument approach procedures. If no applicable minimum altitude is prescribed in FAR Parts 95 or 97, the following minimum IFR altitude applies:

1. In designated mountainous areas, 2,000 feet above the highest obstacle within a horizontal distance of 5 statute miles from the course to be flown; or

2. Other than mountainous areas, 1,000 feet above the highest obstacle within a horizontal distance of 5 statute miles from the course to be flown; or

3. As otherwise authorized by the Administrator or assigned by ATC. (See Minimum En Route IFR Altitude, Minimum Obstruction Clearance Altitude, Minimum Crossing Altitude, Minimum Safe Altitude, Minimum Vectoring Altitude) (Refer to FAR Part 91)

MINIMUM OBSTRUCTION CLEARANCE ALTITUDE/ MOCA — The lowest published altitude in effect between radio fixes on VOR airways, off-airway routes, or route segments which meets obstacle clearance requirements for the entire route segment and which assures acceptable navigational signal coverage only within 25 statute (22 nautical) miles of a VOR. (Refer to FAR Part 91 and 95)

MINIMUM RECEPTION ALTITUDE/MRA — The lowest altitude at which an intersection can be determined. (Refer to FAR Part 95)

MINIMUM SAFE ALTITUDE/MSA —

1. The minimum altitude specified in FAR Part 91 for various aircraft operations.

2. Altitudes depicted on approach charts which provide at least 1,000 feet of obstacle clearance for emergency use within a specified distance from the navigation facility upon which a procedure is predicated. These altitudes will be identified as Minimum Sector Altitudes or Emergency Safe Altitudes and are established as follows:

   a. Minimum Sector Altitudes—Altitudes depicted on approach charts which provide at least 1,000 feet of obstacle clearance within a 25-mile radius of the navigation facility upon which the procedure is predicated. Sectors depicted on approach charts must be at least 90 degrees in scope. These altitudes are for emergency use only and do not necessarily assure acceptable navigational signal coverage.

ICAO—Minimum Sector Altitude—The lowest altitude which may be used under emergency conditions which will provide

a minimum clearance of 300 m (1 000 feet) above all obstacles located in an area contained within a sector of a circle of 46 km (25 NM) radius centered on a radio aid to navigation.

   b. Emergency Safe Altitudes—Altitudes depicted on approach charts which provide at least 1,000 feet of obstacle clearance in nonmountainous areas and 2,000 feet of obstacle clearance in designated mountainous areas within a 100-mile radius of the navigation facility upon which the procedure is predicated and normally used only in military procedures. These altitudes are identified on published procedures as "Emergency Safe Altitudes."

MINIMUM SAFE ALTITUDE WARNING/MSAW — A function of the ARTS III computer that aids the controller by alerting him when a tracked Mode C- equipped aircraft is below or is predicted by the computer to go below a predetermined minimum safe altitude. (Refer to AIM)

MINIMUMS/MINIMA— Weather condition requirements established for a particular operation or type of operation; e.g., IFR takeoff or landing, alternate airport for IFR flight plans, VFR flight, etc. (See Landing Minimums, IFR Takeoff Minimums, VFR Conditions, IFR Conditions) (Refer to FAR Part 91, AIM)

MINIMUM VECTORING ALTITUDE/MVA — The lowest MSL altitude at which an IFR aircraft will be vectored by a radar controller, except as otherwise authorized for radar approaches, departures, and missed approaches. The altitude meets IFR obstacle clearance criteria. It may be lower than the published MEA along an airway or J-route segment. It may be utilized for radar vectoring only upon the controller's determination that an adequate radar return is being received from the aircraft being controlled. Charts depicting minimum vectoring altitudes are normally available only to the controllers and not to pilots. (Refer to AIM)

MISSED APPROACH —

1. A maneuver conducted by a pilot when an instrument approach cannot be completed to a landing. The route of flight and altitude are shown on instrument approach procedure charts. A pilot executing a missed approach prior to the Missed Approach Point (MAP) must continue along the final approach to the MAP. The pilot may climb immediately to the altitude specified in the missed approach procedure.

2. A term used by the pilot to inform ATC that he is executing the missed approach.

3. At locations where ATC radar service is provided, the pilot should conform to radar vectors when provided by ATC in lieu of the published missed approach procedure. (See Missed Approach Point) (Refer to AIM)

ICAO—MISSED APPROACH PROCEDURE — The procedure to be followed if the approach cannot be continued.

MISSED APPROACH POINT/MAP — A point prescribed in each instrument approach procedure at which a missed approach procedure shall be executed if the required visual reference does not exist. (See Missed Approach, Segments of an Instrument Approach Procedure)

MISSED APPROACH SEGMENT — (See Segments of an Instrument Approach Procedure)

MLS — (See Microwave Landing System)

MLS CATEGORIES —

1. MLS Category I—An MLS approach procedure which provides for an approach to a height above touchdown of not less than 200 feet and a runway visual range of not less than 1,800 feet.

2. MLS Category II—Undefined until data gathering/analysis completion.

3. MLS Category III—Undefined until data gathering/analysis completion.

MODE — The letter or number assigned to a specific pulse spacing of radio signals transmitted or received by ground interrogator or airborne transponder components of the Air Traffic Control Radar Beacon System (ATCRBS). Mode A (military Mode 3) and Mode C (altitude reporting) are used in air traffic control. (See Transponder, Interrogator, Radar) (Refer to AIM)

ICAO—MODE (SSR MODE) — The letter or number assigned to a specific pulse spacing of the interrogation signals transmitted by an interrogator. There are 4 modes, A, B, C and D specified in Annex 10, corresponding to four different interrogation pulse spacings.

MOVEMENT AREA — The runways, taxiways, and other areas of an airport/heliport which are utilized for taxiing/hover taxiing, air taxiing, takeoff, and landing of aircraft, exclusive of loading ramps and parking areas. At those airports/heliports with a tower, specific approval for entry onto the movement area must be obtained from ATC.

ICAO—MOVEMENT AREA — That part of an aerodrome to be used for the takeoff, landing and taxiing of aircraft, consisting of the manoeuvring area and the apron(s).

MOVING TARGET INDICATOR/MTI — An electronic device which will permit radar scope presentation only from targets which are in motion. A partial remedy for ground clutter.

MSAW — (See Minimum Safe Altitude Warning)

MULTICOM — A mobile service not open to public correspondence used to provide communications essential to conduct the activities being performed by or directed from private aircraft (FAR 87.277).

NAS STAGE A — The en route ATC system's radar, computers and computer programs, controller plan view displays (PVDs/Radar Scopes), input/output devices, and the related communications equipment which are integrated to form the heart of the automated IFR air traffic control system. This equipment performs Flight Data Processing (FDP) and Radar Data Processing (RDP). It interfaces with automated terminal systems and is used in the control of en route IFR aircraft. (Refer to AIM)

NATIONAL AIRSPACE SYSTEM/NAS — The common network of U.S. airspace; air navigation facilities, equipment and services, airports or landing areas; aeronautical charts, information and services; rules, regulations and procedures, technical information, and manpower and material. Included are system components shared jointly with the military.

NATIONAL BEACON CODE ALLOCATION PLAN AIRSPACE/NBCAP AIRSPACE — Airspace over United States territory located within the North American continent between Canada and Mexico, including adjacent territorial waters outward to about boundaries of oceanic control areas (CTA)/

Flight Information Regions (FIR). (See Flight Information Region)

NATIONAL FLIGHT DATA CENTER/NFDC — A facility in Washington D.C., established by FAA to operate a central aeronautical information service for the collection, validation, and dissemination of aeronautical data in support of the activities of government, industry, and the aviation community. The information is published in the National Flight Data Digest. (See National Flight Data Digest)

NATIONAL FLIGHT DATA DIGEST/NFDD — A daily (except weekends and Federal holidays) publication of flight information appropriate to aeronautical charts, aeronautical publications, Notices to Airmen, or other media serving the purpose of providing operational flight data essential to safe and efficient aircraft operations.

NATIONAL SEARCH AND RESCUE PLAN — An interagency agreement which provides for the effective utilization of all available facilities in all types of search and rescue missions.

NAVAID CLASSES — VOR, VORTAC, and TACAN aids are classed according to their operational use. The three classes of NAVAID's are:

T—Terminal.

L—Low altitude.

H—High altitude.

The normal service range for T, L, and H class aids is found in the AIM. Certain operational requirements make it necessary to use some of these aids at greater service ranges than specified. Extended range is made possible through flight inspection determinations. Some aids also have lesser service range due to location, terrain, frequency protection, etc. Restrictions to service range are listed in Airport/Facility Directory.

NAVIGABLE AIRSPACE — Airspace at and above the minimum flight altitudes prescribed in the FAR's including airspace needed for safe takeoff and landing. (Refer to FAR Part 91)

NAVIGATIONAL AID/NAVAID — Any visual or electronic device airborne or on the surface which provides point-to-point guidance information or position data to aircraft in flight. (See Air Navigation Facility)

NDB — (See Nondirectional Beacon)

NEGATIVE — "No," or "permission not granted," or "that is not correct."

NEGATIVE CONTACT — Used by pilots to inform ATC that:

1. Previously issued traffic is not in sight. It may be followed by the pilot's request for the controller to provide assistance in avoiding the traffic.

2. They were unable to contact ATC on a particular frequency.

NIGHT — The time between the end of evening civil twilight and the beginning of morning civil twilight, as published in the American Air Almanac, converted to local time.

ICAO—NIGHT — The hours between the end of evening civil twilight and the beginning of morning civil twilight or such other period between sunset and sunrise as may be specified by the appropriate authority.

> *Note.* — Civil twilight ends in the evening when the centre of the sun's disk is 6 degrees below the horizon and begins in the morning when the centre of the sun's disk is 6 degrees below the horizon.

NO GYRO APPROACH/VECTOR — A radar approach/ vector provided in case of a malfunctioning gyro-compass or directional gyro. Instead of providing the pilot with headings to be flown, the controller observes the radar track and issues control instructions "turn right/left" or "stop turn" as appropriate. (Refer to AIM)

NONAPPROACH CONTROL TOWER — Authorizes aircraft to land or takeoff at the airport controlled by the tower or to transit the airport traffic area. The primary function of a nonapproach control tower is the sequencing of aircraft in the traffic pattern and on the landing area. Nonapproach control towers also separate aircraft operating under instrument flight rules clearances from approach controls and centers. They provide ground control services to aircraft, vehicles, personnel, and equipment on the airport movement area.

NONCOMPOSITE SEPARATION — Separation in accordance with minima other than the composite separation minimum specified for the area concerned.

NONDIRECTIONAL BEACON/RADIO BEACON/ NDB — An L/MF or UHF radio beacon transmitting nondirectional signals whereby the pilot of an aircraft equipped with direction finding equipment can determine his bearing to or from the radio beacon and "home" on or track to or from the station. When the radio beacon is installed in conjunction with the Instrument Landing System marker, it is normally called a Compass Locator. (See Compass Locator, Automatic Direction Finder)

NONPRECISION APPROACH PROCEDURE/NONPRECISION APPROACH — A standard instrument approach procedure in which no electronic glide slope is provided; e.g., VOR, TACAN, NDB, LOC, ASR, LDA, or SDF approaches.

NONRADAR — Precedes other terms and generally means without the use of radar, such as:

1. Nonradar Approach—Used to describe instrument approaches for which course guidance on final approach is not provided by ground- based precision or surveillance radar. Radar vectors to the final approach course may or may not be provided by ATC. Examples of nonradar approaches are VOR, NDB, TACAN, and ILS/MLS approaches. (See Final Approach—IFR, Final Approach Course, Radar Approach, Instrument Approach Procedure)

2. Nonradar Approach Control—An ATC facility providing approach control service without the use of radar. (See Approach Control, Approach Control Service)

3. Nonradar Arrival—An aircraft arriving at an airport without radar service, or at an airport served by a radar facility but without radar services being provided. (See Radar Arrival, Radar Service)

4. Nonradar Route—A flight path or route over which the pilot is performing his own navigation. The pilot may be receiving radar separation, radar monitoring, or other ATC services while on a nonradar route. (See Radar Route)

5. Nonradar Separation—The spacing of aircraft in accordance with established minima without the use of radar; e.g., vertical, lateral, or longitudinal separation. (See Radar Separation)

ICAO—Nonradar Separation—The separation used when aircraft position information is derived from sources other than radar.

NORDO — (See Lost Communications)

NORTH AMERICAN ROUTE — A numerically coded route preplanned over existing airway and route systems to and from specific coastal fixes serving the North Atlantic. North American Routes consist of the following:

1. Common Route/Portion—That segment of a North American Route between the inland navigation facility and the coastal fix.

2. Non-Common Route/Portion—That segment of a North American Route between the inland navigation facility and a designated North American terminal.

3. Inland Navigation Facility—A navigation aid on a North American Route at which the common route and/or the non-common route begins or ends.

4. Coastal Fix—A navigation aid or intersection where an aircraft transitions between the domestic route structure and the oceanic route structure.

NOTICES TO AIRMEN PUBLICATION — A publication designed primarily as a pilot's operational manual containing current NOTAM information considered essential to the safety of flight as well as supplemental data to other aeronautical publications. (See Notice to Airmen/NOTAM)

NOTICE TO AIRMEN/NOTAM — A notice containing information (not known sufficiently in advance to publicize by other means) concerning the establishment, condition, or change in any component (facility, service, or procedure of, or hazard in the National Airspace System) the timely knowledge of which is essential to personnel concerned with flight operations.

1. NOTAM(D)—A NOTAM given (in addition to local dissemination) distant dissemination beyond the area of responsibility of the Flight Service Station. These NOTAM's will be stored and available until canceled.

2. NOTAM(L)—A NOTAM given local dissemination by voice and other means, such as telautograph and telephone, to satisfy local user requirements.

3. FDC NOTAM—A NOTAM regulatory in nature, transmitted by USNOF and given system wide dissemination.

ICAO—NOTAM — A notice containing information concerning the establishment, condition or change in any aeronautical facility, service, procedure or hazard, the timely knowledge of which is essential to personnel concerned with flight operations.

> *Class I Distribution.* Distribution by means of telecommunication.

> *Class II Distribution.* Distribution by means other than telecommunications.

NUMEROUS TARGETS VICINITY (LOCATION) — A traffic advisory issued by ATC to advise pilots that targets on the radar scope are too numerous to issue individually. (See Traffic Advisories)

OBSTACLE — An existing object, object of natural growth, or terrain at a fixed geographical location or which may be expected at a fixed location within a prescribed area with reference to which vertical clearance is or must be provided during flight operation.

OBSTRUCTION — Any object/obstacle exceeding the obstruction standards specified by FAR Part 77, Subpart C.

OBSTRUCTION LIGHT — A light or one of a group of lights, usually red or white, frequently mounted on a surface structure or natural terrain to warn pilots of the presence of an obstruction.

OFF-ROUTE VECTOR — A vector by ATC which takes an aircraft off a previously assigned route. Altitudes assigned by ATC during such vectors provide required obstacle clearance.

OFFSET PARALLEL RUNWAYS — Staggered runways having centerlines which are parallel.

ON COURSE —

1. Used to indicate that an aircraft is established on the route centerline.

2. Used by ATC to advise a pilot making a radar approach that his aircraft is lined up on the final approach course. (See On-Course Indication)

ON-COURSE INDICATION — An indication on an instrument, which provides the pilot a visual means of determining that the aircraft is located on the centerline of a given navigational track, or an indication on a radar scope that an aircraft is on a given track.

OPTION APPROACH — An approach requested and conducted by a pilot which will result in either a touch-and-go, missed approach, low approach, stop-and-go, or full stop landing. (See Cleared for the Option) (Refer to AIM)

ORGANIZED TRACK SYSTEM — A moveable system of oceanic tracks that traverses the North Atlantic between Europe and North America the physical position of which is determined twice daily taking the best advantage of the winds aloft.

OUT — The conversation is ended and no response is expected.

OUTER AREA (associated with ARSA) — Nonregulatory airspace surrounding designated ARSA airports wherein ATC provides radar vectoring and sequencing on a full-time basis for all IFR and participating VFR aircraft. The service provided in the outer area is called ARSA service which includes: IFR/IFR—standard IFR separation; IFR/VFR—traffic advisories and conflict resolution; and VFR/VFR—traffic advisories and, as appropriate, safety alerts. The normal radius will be 20 nautical miles with some variations based on site-specific requirements. The outer area extends outward from the primary ARSA airport and extends from the lower limits of radar/radio coverage up to the ceiling of the approach control's delegated airspace excluding the ARSA and other airspace as appropriate. (See Controlled Airspace—Airport Radar Service Area / ARSA, Conflict Resolution)

OUTER COMPASS LOCATOR — (See Compass Locator)

OUTER FIX — A general term used within ATC to describe fixes in the terminal area, other than the final approach fix. Aircraft are normally cleared to these fixes by an Air Route Traffic Control Center or an Approach Control Facility. Aircraft are normally cleared from these fixes to the final approach fix or final approach course.

OUTER MARKER/OM — A marker beacon at or near the glide slope intercept altitude of an ILS approach. It is keyed to transmit two dashes per second on a 400 Hz tone, which is received aurally and visually by compatible airborne equipment. The OM is normally located four to seven miles from the runway threshold on the extended centerline of the runway. (See Marker Beacon, Instrument Landing System) (Refer to AIM)

OVER — My transmission is ended; I expect a response.

OVERHEAD APPROACH/360 OVERHEAD — A series of predetermined maneuvers prescribed for VFR arrival of military aircraft (often in formation) for entry into the VFR traffic pattern and to proceed to a landing. The pattern usually specifies the following:

1. The radio contact required of the pilot.

2. The speed to be maintained.

3. An initial approach 3 to 5 miles in length.

4. An elliptical pattern consisting of two 180 degree turns.

5. A break point at which the first 180 degree turn is started.

6. The direction of turns.

7. Altitude (at least 500 feet above the conventional pattern).

8. A "Roll-out" on final approach not less than 1/4 mile from the landing threshold and not less than 300 feet above the ground.

PAN-PAN — The international radio-telephony urgency signal. When repeated three times, indicates uncertainty or alert followed by the nature of the urgency. (See MAYDAY) (Refer to AIM)

PARALLEL ILS/MLS APPROACHES — Approaches to parallel runways by IFR aircraft which, when established inbound toward the airport on the adjacent final approach courses, are radar-separated by at least 2 miles. (See Final Approach Course, Simultaneous ILS/MLS Approaches).

PARALLEL OFFSET ROUTE — A parallel track to the left or right of the designated or established airway/route. Normally associated with Area Navigation (RNAV) operations. (See Area Navigation)

PARALLEL RUNWAYS — Two or more runways at the same airport whose centerlines are parallel. In addition to runway number, parallel runways are designated as L (left) and R (right) or, if three parallel runways exist, L (left), C (center), and R (right).

PERMANENT ECHO — Radar signals reflected from fixed objects on the earth's surface; e.g., buildings, towers, terrain. Permanent echoes are distinguished from "ground clutter' by being definable locations rather than large areas. Under certain conditions they may be used to check radar alignment.

PHOTO RECONNAISSANCE (PR) — Military activity that requires locating individual photo targets and navigating to the targets at a preplanned angle and altitude. The activity normally requires a lateral route width of 16NM and altitude range of 1,500 feet to 10,000 feet AGL.

PILOT BRIEFING/PRE-FLIGHT PILOT BRIEFING — A service provided by the FSS to assist pilots in flight planning. Briefing items may include weather information, NOTAMS, military activities, flow control information, and other items as requested. (Refer to AIM)

PILOT IN COMMAND — The pilot responsible for the operation and safety of an aircraft during flight time. (Refer to FAR Part 91)

PILOTS AUTOMATIC TELEPHONE WEATHER ANSWERING SERVICE/PATWAS — A continuous telephone recording containing current and forecast weather information for pilots. (See Flight Service Station) (Refer to AIM)

PILOT'S DISCRETION — When used in conjunction with altitude assignments, means that ATC has offered the pilot the option of starting climb or descent whenever he wishes and conducting the climb or descent at any rate he wishes. He may temporarily level off at any intermediate altitude. However, once he has vacated an altitude, he may not return to that altitude.

PILOT WEATHER REPORT/PIREP — A report of meteorological phenomena encountered by aircraft in flight. (Refer to AIM)

POSITION REPORT/PROGRESS REPORT — A report over a known location as transmitted by an aircraft to ATC. (Refer to AIM)

POSITION SYMBOL — A computer-generated indication shown on a radar display to indicate the mode of tracking.

POSITIVE CONTROL — The separation of all air traffic within designated airspace by air traffic control. (See Positive Control Area)

POSITIVE CONTROL AREA/PCA — (See Controlled Airspace)

PRACTICE INSTRUMENT APPROACH — An instrument approach procedure conducted by a VFR or an IFR aircraft for the purpose of pilot training or proficiency demonstrations.

PRECIPITATION — Any or all forms of water particles (rain, sleet, hail, or snow) that fall from the atmosphere and reach the surface.

PRECISION APPROACH PROCEDURE/PRECISION APPROACH — A standard instrument approach procedure in which an electronic glideslope/glidepath is provided; e.g., ILS/MLS and PAR. (See Instrument Landing System, Microwave Landing System, Precision Approach Radar)

PRECISION APPROACH RADAR/PAR — Radar equipment in some ATC facilities operated by the FAA and/or the military services at joint-use civil/military locations and separate military installations to detect and display azimuth, elevation, and range of aircraft on the final approach course to a runway. This equipment may be used to monitor certain non-radar approaches, but is primarily used to conduct a precision instrument approach (PAR) wherein the controller issues guidance instructions to the pilot based on the aircraft's position in relation to the final approach course (azimuth), the glidepath (elevation), and the distance (range) from the touch-

down point on the runway as displayed on the radar scope. (See Glidepath, PAR) (Refer to AIM)

The abbreviation "PAR" is also used to denote preferential arrival routes in ARTCC computers. (See Preferential Routes)

ICAO—PRECISION APPROACH RADAR (PAR) — Primary radar equipment used to determine the position of an aircraft during final approach, in terms of lateral and vertical deviations relative to a nominal approach path, and in range relative to touchdown.

> *Note.* — Precision approach radars are designed to enable pilots of aircraft to be given guidance by radiocommunication during the final stages of the approach to land.

PREFERENTIAL ROUTES — Preferential routes (PDR's, PAR's, and PDAR's) are adapted in ARTCC computers to accomplish inter/intrafacility controller coordination and to assure that flight data is posted at the proper control positions. Locations having a need for these specific inbound and outbound routes normally publish such routes in local facility bulletins, and their use by pilots minimizes flight plan route amendments. When the workload or traffic situation permits, controllers normally provide radar vectors or assign requested routes to minimize circuitous routing. Preferential routes are usually confined to one ARTCC's area and are referred to by the following names or acronyms:

1. Preferential Departure Route/PDR—A specific departure route from an airport or terminal area to an en route point where there is no further need for flow control. It may be included in a Standard Instrument Departure (SID) or a Preferred IFR Route.

2. Preferential Arrival Route/PAR—A specific arrival route from an appropriate en route point to an airport or terminal area. It may be included in a Standard Terminal Arrival (STAR) or a Preferred IFR Route. The abbreviation "PAR" is used primarily within the ARTCC and should not be confused with the abbreviation for Precision Approach Radar.

3. Preferential Departure and Arrival Route/PDAR—A route between two terminals which are within or immediately adjacent to one ARTCC's area. PDAR's are not synonomous with Preferred IFR Routes but may be listed as such as they do accomplish essentially the same purpose. (See Preferred IFR Routes, NAS Stage A)

PREFERRED IFR ROUTES — Routes established between busier airports to increase system efficiency and capacity. They normally extend through one or more ARTCC areas and are designed to achieve balanced traffic flows among high density terminals. IFR clearances are issued on the basis of these routes except when severe weather avoidance procedures or other factors dictate otherwise. Preferred IFR Routes are listed in the Airport/Facility Directory. If a flight is planned to or from an area having such routes but the departure or arrival point is not listed in the Airport/Facility Directory, pilots may use that part of a Preferred IFR Route which is appropriate for the departure or arrival point that is listed. Preferred IFR Routes are correlated with SID's and STAR's and may be defined by airways, jet routes, direct routes between NAVAID's, Waypoints, NAVAID radials/DME, or any combinations thereof. (See Standard Instrument Departure, Standard Terminal Arrival, Preferential Routes, Center's craft operating in the vicinity of one or more civil and/ or military airports in a terminal area. The facility may provide services of a ground controlled approach (GCA); i.e., ASR and PAR approaches. A radar approach control facility may be operated by FAA, USAF, US Army, USN, USMC, or jointly by FAA and a military service. Specific facility nomenclatures are used for administrative purposes only and are related to the physical location of the facility and the operating service generally as follows:

Army Radar Approach Control/ARAC (Army).

Radar Air Traffic Control Facility/ RATCF (Navy/FAA).

Radar Approach Control/RAPCON (Air Force/FAA).

Terminal Radar Approach Control/TRACON (FAA).

Tower/Airport Traffic Control Tower/ATCT (FAA). (Only those towers delegated approach control authority.)

RADAR ARRIVAL — An aircraft arriving at an airport served by a radar facility, in radar contact with the facility, and receiving radar srvice. (See Nonradar Arrival, Radar Service)

RADAR BEACON — (See Radar)

RADAR CONTACT —

1. Used by ATC to inform an aircraft that it is identified on the radar display and radar flight following will be provided until radar identification is terminated. Radar service may also be provided within the limits of necessity and capability. When a pilot is informed of "radar contact," he automatically discontinues reporting over compulsory reporting points. (See Radar Flight Following, Radar Contact Lost, Radar Service, Radar Service Terminated). (Refer to AIM)

2. The term used to inform the controller that the aircraft is identified and approval is granted for the aircraft to enter the receiving controllers airspace.

ICAO—RADAR CONTACT — The situation which exists when the radar blip or radar position symbol of a particular aircraft is seen and identified on a radar display.

RADAR CONTACT LOST — Used by ATC to inform a pilot that radar identification of his aircraft has been lost. The loss may be attributed to several things including the aircraft's merging with weather or ground clutter, the aircraft's flying below radar line of sight, the aircraft's entering an area of poor radar return, or a failure of the aircraft transponder or the ground radar equipment. (See Clutter, Radar Contact)

RADAR ENVIRONMENT — An area in which radar service may be provided. (See Radar Contact, Radar Service, Additional Services, Traffic Advisories)

RADAR FLIGHT FOLLOWING — The observation of the progress of radar identified aircraft, whose primary navigation is being provided by the pilot, wherein the controller retains and correlates the aircraft identity with the appropriate target or target symbol displayed on the radar scope. (See Radar Contact, Radar Service) (Refer to AIM)

RADAR IDENTIFICATION — The process of ascertaining that an observed radar target is the radar return from a particular aircraft. (See Radar Contact, Radar Service)

ICAO—RADAR IDENTIFICATION — The process of correlating a particular radar blip or radar position symbol with a specific aircraft.

RADAR IDENTIFIED AIRCRAFT — An aircraft, the position of which has been correlated with an observed target or symbol on the radar display. (See Radar Contract, Radar Contact Lost)

RADAR MONITORING — (See Radar Service)

RADAR NAVIGATIONAL GUIDANCE — (See Radar Service)

RADAR POINT OUT/POINT OUT — Used between controllers to indicate radar handoff action where the initiating controller plans to retain communications with an aircraft penetrating the other controller's airspace and additional coordination is required.

RADAR ROUTE — A flight path or route over which an aircraft is vectored. Navigational guidance and altitude assignments are provided by ATC. (See Flight Path, Route)

RADAR SEPARATION — (See Radar Service)

RADAR SERVICE — A term which encompasses one or more of the following services based on the use of radar which can be provided by a controller to a pilot of a radar identified aircraft.

ICAO—RADAR SERVICE — Term used to indicate a service provided directly by means of radar.

1. Radar Monitoring—The radar flight-following of aircraft, whose primary navigation is being performed by the pilot, to observe and note deviations from its authorized flight path, airway, or route. When being applied specifically to radar monitoring of instrument approaches; i.e., with precision approach radar (PAR) or radar monitoring of simultaneous ILS/MLS approaches, it includes advice and instructions whenever an aircraft nears or exceeds the prescribed PAR safety limit or simultaneous ILS/MLS no transgression zone. (See Additional Services, Traffic Advisories)

ICAO—Radar Monitoring—The use of radar for the purpose of providing aircraft with information and advice relative to significant deviations from nominal flight path.

2. Radar Navigational Guidance—Vectoring aircraft to provide course guidance.

3. Radar Separation—Radar spacing of aircraft in accordance with established minima.

ICAO—Radar Separation—The separation used when aircraft position information is derived from radar sources.

RADAR SERVICE TERMINATED — Used by ATC to inform a pilot that he will no longer be provided any of the services that could be received while in radar contact. Radar service is automatically terminated, and the pilot is not advised in the following cases:

1. An aircraft cancels its IFR flight plan, except within a TCA, TRSA, ARSA, or where Stage II service is provided.

2. An aircraft conducting an instrument, visual, or contact approach has landed or has been instructed to change to advisory frequency.

Area) (Refer to Airport/Facility Directory and Notices to Airmen Publication)

PREVAILING VISIBILITY — (See Visibility)

PROCEDURE TURN INBOUND — That point of a procedure turn maneuver where course reversal has been completed and an aircraft is established inbound on the intermediate approach segment or final approach course. A report of "procedure turn inbound" is normally used by ATC as a position report for separation purposes. (See Final Approach Course, Procedure Turn, Segments of an Instrument Approach Procedure)

PROCEDURE TURN/PT — The maneuver prescribed when it is necessary to reverse direction to establish an aircraft on the intermediate approach segment or final approach course. The outbound course, direction of turn, distance within which the turn must be completed, and minimum altitude are specified in the procedure. However, unless otherwise restricted, the point at which the turn may be commenced and the type and rate of turn are left to the discretion of the pilot.

ICAO—PROCEDURE TURN — A manoeuvre in which a turn is made away from a designated track followed by a turn in the opposite direction to permit the aircraft to intercept and proceed along the reciprocal of the designated track.

> *Note 1.* — Procedure turns are designated "left" or "right" according to the direction of the initial turn.

> *Note 2.* — Procedure turns may be designated as being made either in level flight or while descending, according to the circumstances of each individual approach procedure.

PROFILE DESCENT — An uninterrupted descent (except where level flight is required for speed adjustment; e.g., 250 knots at 10,000 feet MSL) from cruising altitude/level to interception of a glide slope or to a minimum altitude specified for the initial or intermediate approach segment of a nonprecision instrument approach. The profile descent normally terminates at the approach gate or where the glide slope or other appropriate minimum altitude is intercepted.

PROGRAMMABLE INDICATOR DATA PROCESSOR/PIDP — The PIDP is a modification to the AN/TPX-42 interrogator system currently installed in fixed RAPCON's. The PIDP detects, tracks, and predicts secondary radar aircraft targets. These are displayed by means of computer-generated symbols and alphanumeric characters depicting flight identification, aircraft altitude, ground speed, and flight plan data. Although primary radar targets are not tracked, they are displayed coincident with the secondary radar targets as well as with the other symbols and alphanumerics. The system has the capability of interfacing with ARTCC's.

PROHIBITED AREA — (See Special Use Airspace).

ICAO—PROHIBITED AREA — An airspace of defined dimensions, above the land areas or territorial waters of a State, within which the flight of aircraft is prohibited.

PROPOSED BOUNDARY CROSSING TIME/PBCT — Each center has a PBCT parameter for each internal airport. Proposed internal flight plans are transmitted to the adjacent center if the flight time along the proposed route from the departure airport to the center boundary is less than or equal to the value of PBCT or if airport adaptation specifies transmission regardless of PBCT.

PUBLISHED ROUTE — A route for which an IFR altitude has been established and published; e.g., Federal Airways, Jet Routes, Area Navigation Routes, Specified Direct Routes.

QUADRANT — A quarter part of a circle, centered on a NAVAID, oriented clockwise from magnetic north as follows: NE quadrant 000-089, SE quadrant 090-179, SW quadrant 180-269, NW quadrant 270-359.

QUICK LOOK — A feature of NAS Stage A and ARTS which provides the controller the capability to display full data blocks of tracked aircraft from other control positions.

QUOTA FLOW CONTROL/QFLOW — A flow control procedure by which the Central Flow Control Function (CFCF) restricts traffic to the ARTC Center area having an impacted airport, thereby avoiding sector/area saturation. (See Air Traffic Control Systems Command Center) (Refer to Airport/Facility Directory)

RADAR/RADIO DETECTION AND RANGING — A device which, by measuring the time interval between transmission and reception of radio pulses and correlating the angular orientation of the radiated antenna beam or beams in azimuth and/or elevation, provides information on range, azimuth, and/or elevation of objects in the path of the transmitted pulses.

ICAO—RADAR — A radio detection device which provides information on range, azimuth and/or elevation of objects.

1. Primary Radar—A radar system in which a minute portion of a radio pulse transmitted from a site is reflected by an object and then received back at that site for processing and display at an air traffic control facility.

ICAO—Primary Radar—A radar system which uses reflected radio signals.

2. Secondary Radar/Radar Beacon/ATCRBS—A radar system in which the object to be detected is fitted with cooperative equipment in the form of a radio receiver/transmitter (transponder). Radar pulses transmitted from the searching transmitter/receiver (interrogator) site are received in the cooperative equipment and used to trigger a distinctive transmission from the transponder. This reply transmission, rather than a reflected signal, is then received back at the transmitter/receiver site for processing and display at an air traffic control facility. (See Transponder, Interrogator) (Refer to AIM)

ICAO—Secondary Radar—A radar system wherein a radio signal transmitted from a radar station initiates the transmission of a radio signal from another station.

RADAR ADVISORY — The provision of advice and information based on radar observations. (See Advisory Service)

RADAR APPROACH — An instrument approach procedure which utilizes Precision Approach Radar (PAR) or Airport Surveillance Radar (ASR). (See PAR Approach, Surveillance Approach, Airport Surveillance Radar, Precision Approach Radar, Instrument Approach Procedure) (Refer to AIM)

ICAO—RADAR APPROACH — An approach, executed by an aircraft, under the direction of a radar controller.

RADAR APPROACH CONTROL FACILITY — A terminal ATC facility that uses radar and nonradar capabilities to provide approach control services to aircraft arriving, departing, or transiting airspace controlled by the facility (see Approach Control Service). Provides radar ATC services to air-

ICAO—RESCUE CO-ORDINATION CENTRE — A unit responsible for promoting efficient organization of search and rescue service and for co-ordinating the conduct of search and rescue operations within a search and rescue region.

RESTRICTED AREA — (See Special Use Airspace).

ICAO—RESTRICTED AREA — An airspace of defined dimensions, above the land areas or territorial waters of a State, within which the flight of aircraft is restricted in accordance with certain specified conditions.

RESUME OWN NAVIGATION — Used by ATC to advise a pilot to resume his own navigational responsibility. It is issued after completion of a radar vector or when radar contact is lost while the aircraft is being radar vectored. (See Radar Contact Lost, Radar Service Terminated)

RNAV — (See Area Navigation)

RNAV APPROACH — An instrument approach procedure which relies on aircraft area navigation equipment for navigational guidance. (See Instrument Approach Procedure, Area Navigation)

ROAD RECONNAISSANCE (RC) — Military activity requiring navigation along roads, railroads, and rivers. Reconnaissance route/route segments are seldom along a straight line and normally require a lateral route width of 10NM to 30NM and an altitude range of 500 feet to 10,000 feet AGL.

ROGER — I have received all of your last transmission. It should not be used to answer a question requiring a yes or a no answer. (See Affirmative, Negative)

ROLLOUT RVR — (See Visibility)

ROUTE — A defined path, consisting of one or more courses in a horizontal plane, which aircraft traverse over the surface of the earth. (See Airway, Jet Route, Published Route, Unpublished Route)

ROUTE SEGMENT — As used in Air Traffic Control, a part of a route that can be defined by two navigational fixes, two NAVAID's, or a fix and a NAVAID. (See Fix, Route)

ICAO—ROUTE SEGMENT — A portion of a route to be flown, as defined by two consecutive significant points specified in a flight plan.

RUNWAY — A defined rectangular area on a land airport prepared for the landing and takeoff run of aircraft along its length. Runways are normally numbered in relation to their magnetic direction rounded off to the nearest 10 degrees; e.g., Runway 01, Runway 25. (See Parallel Runways)

ICAO—RUNWAY — A defined rectangular area on a land aerodrome prepared for the landing and takeoff of aircraft.

RUNWAY CENTERLINE LIGHTING — (See Airport Lighting)

RUNWAY CONDITION READING/RCR — Numerical decelerometer readings relayed by air traffic controllers at USAF and certain civil bases for use by the pilot in determining runway braking action. These readings are routinely relayed only to USAF and Air National Guard Aircraft. (See Braking Action)

RUNWAY END IDENTIFIER LIGHTS — (See Airport Lighting)

RUNWAY GRADIENT — The average slope, measured in percent, between two ends or points on a runway. Runway gradient is depicted on Government aerodrome sketches when total runway gradient exceeds 0.3%.

RUNWAY HEADING — The magnetic direction indicated by the runway number. When cleared to "fly/maintain runway heading," pilots are expected to comply with the ATC clearance by flying the heading indicated by the runway number without applying any drift correction; e.g., Runway 4, 040° magnetic heading; Runway 20, 200° magnetic heading.

RUNWAY IN USE/ACTIVE RUNWAY/DUTY RUNWAY — Any runway or runways currently being used for takeoff or landing. When multiple runways are used, they are all considered active runways.

RUNWAY LIGHTS — (See Airport Lighting)

RUNWAY MARKINGS — (See Airport Marking Aids.)

RUNWAY PROFILE DESCENT — An instrument flight rules (IFR) air traffic control arrival procedure to a runway published for pilot use in graphic and/or textual form and may be associated with a STAR. Runway Profile Descents provide routing and may depict crossing altitudes, speed restrictions, and headings to be flown from the en route structure to the point where the pilot will receive clearance for and execute an instrument approach procedure. A Runway Profile Descent may apply to more than one runway if so stated on the chart. (Refer to AIM)

RUNWAY USE PROGRAM — A noise abatement runway selection plan designed to enhance noise abatement efforts with regard to airport communities for arriving and departing aircraft. These plans are developed into runway use programs and apply to all turbojet aircraft 12,500 pounds or heavier; turbojet aircraft less than 12,500 pounds are included only if the airport proprietor determines that the aircraft creates a noise problem. Runway use programs are coordinated with FAA offices, and safety criteria used in these programs are developed by the Office of Flight Operations. Runway use programs are administered by the Air Traffic Service as "Formal" or "Informal" programs.

1. Formal Runway Use Program—An approved noise abatement program which is defined and acknowledged in a Letter of Understanding between Flight Operations, Air Traffic Service, the airport proprietor, and the users. Once established, participation in the program is mandatory for aircraft operators and pilots as provided for in FAR 91.87.

2. Informal Runway Use Program—An approved noise abatement program which does not require a Letter of Understanding, and participation in the program is voluntary for aircraft operators/pilots.

RUNWAY VISIBILITY VALUE — (See Visibility)

RUNWAY VISUAL RANGE — (See Visibility)

SAFETY ALERT — A safety alert issued by ATC to aircraft under their control if ATC is aware the aircraft is at an altitude which, in the controller's judgment, places the aircraft in unsafe proximity to terrain, obstructions, or other aircraft. The controller may discontinue the issuance of further alerts if the pilot advises he is taking action to correct the situation or has the other aircraft in sight.

1. Terrain/Obstruction Alert—A safety alert issued by ATC to aircraft under their control if ATC is aware the aircraft is at an altitude which, in the controller's judg-

3. An arriving VFR aircraft, receiving radar service to a tower-controlled airport within a TCA, TRSA, ARSA, or where Stage II service is provided, has landed; or to all other airports, is instructed to change to tower or advisory frequency.

4. An aircraft completes a radar approach.

RADAR SURVEILLANCE — The radar observation of a given geographical area for the purpose of performing some radar function.

RADAR TRAFFIC ADVISORIES — (See Traffic Advisories)

RADAR TRAFFIC INFORMATION SERVICE — (See Traffic Advisories)

RADAR WEATHER ECHO INTENSITY LEVELS — Existing radar systems cannot detect turbulence. However, there is a direct correlation between the degree of turbulence and other weather features associated with thunderstorms and the radar weather echo intensity. The National Weather Service has categorized six levels of radar weather echo intensity. The levels are sometimes expressed during communications as "VIP LEVEL" 1 through 6 (derived from the component of the weather radar that produces the information—Video Integrator and Processor). The following list gives the weather features likely to be associated with these levels during thunderstorm weather situations:

1. Level 1 (WEAK) and Level 2 (MODERATE). Light to moderate turbulence is possible with lightning.

2. Level 3 (STRONG). Severe turbulence possible, lightning.

3. Level 4 (VERY STRONG). Severe turbulence likely, lightning.

4. Level 5 (INTENSE). Severe turbulence, lightning, organized wind gusts, hail likely.

5. Level 6 (EXTREME). Severe turbulence, large hail, lightning, extensive wind gusts, and turbulence.

RADIAL — A magnetic bearing extending from a VOR/VORTAC/TACAN navigation facility.

RADIO —

1. A device used for communication.

2. Used to refer to a flight service station; e.g., "Seattle Radio" is used to call Seattle FSS.

RADIO ALTIMETER/RADAR ALTIMETER — Aircraft equipment which makes use of the reflection of radio waves from the ground to determine the height of the aircraft above the surface.

RADIO BEACON — (See Nondirectional Beacon)

RADIO MAGNETIC INDICATOR/RMI — An aircraft navigational instrument coupled with a gyro compass or similar compass that indicates the direction of a selected NAVAID and indicates bearing with respect to the heading of the aircraft.

RAMP — (See Apron)

READ BACK — Repeat my message back to me.

RECEIVING CONTROLLER/FACILITY — A controller/facility receiving control of an aircraft from another controller/facility.

REDUCE SPEED TO (SPEED) — (See Speed Adjustment)

RELEASE TIME — A departure time restriction issued to a pilot by ATC (either directly or through an authorized relay) when necessary to separate a departing aircraft from other traffic.

ICAO—RELEASE TIME — Time prior to which an aircraft should be given further clearance or prior to which it should not proceed in case of radio failure.

REMOTE COMMUNICATIONS AIR/GROUND FACILITY/RCAG — An unmanned VHF/UHF transmitter/receiver facility which is used to expand ARTCC air/ground communications coverage and to facilitate direct contact between pilots and controllers. RCAG facilities are sometimes not equipped with emergency frequencies 121.5 MHz and 243.0 MHz. (Refer to AIM)

REMOTE COMMUNICATIONS OUTLET/RCO AND REMOTE TRANSMITTER/RECEIVER/RTR — An unmanned communications facility remotely controlled by air traffic personnel. RCO's serve FSS's. RTR's serve terminal ATC facilities. An RCO or RTR may be UHF or VHF and will extend the communication range of the air traffic facility. There are several classes of RCO's and RTR's. The class is determined by the number of transmitters or receivers. Classes A through G are used primarily for air/ground purposes. RCO and RTR class O facilities are nonprotected outlets subject to undetected and prolonged outages. RCO (O's) and RTR (O's) were established for the express purpose of providing ground-to-ground communications between air traffic control specialists and pilots located at a satellite airport for delivering en route clearances, issuing departure authorizations, and acknowledging instrument flight rules cancellations or departure/landing times. As a secondary function, they may be used for advisory purposes whenever the aircraft is below the coverage of the primary air/ground frequency.

REMOTE TRANSMITTER/RECEIVER/RTR — (See Remote Communications Outlet)

REPORT — Used to instruct pilots to advise ATC of specified information; e.g., "Report passing Hamilton VOR."

REPORTING POINT — A geographical location in relation to which the position of an aircraft is reported. (See Compulsory Reporting Point) (Refer to AIM)

ICAO—REPORTING POINT — A specified geographical location in relation to which the position of an aircraft can be reported.

REQUEST FULL ROUTE CLEARANCE/FRC — Used by pilots to request that the entire route of flight be read verbatim in an ATC clearance. Such request should be made to preclude receiving an ATC clearance based on the original filed flight plan when a filed IFR flight plan has been revised by the pilot, company, or operations prior to departure.

RESCUE COORDINATION CENTER/RCC — A search and rescue (SAR) facility equipped and manned to coordinate and control SAR operations in an area designated by the SAR plan. The U.S. Coast Guard and the U.S. Air Force have responsibility for the operation of RCC's.

ment, places the aircraft in unsafe proximity to terrain/obstructions; e.g., "Low Altitude Alert, check your altitude immediately."

2. Aircraft Conflict Alert—A safety alert issued by ATC to aircraft under their control if ATC is aware of an aircraft that is not under their control at an altitude which, in the controller's judgment, places both aircraft in unsafe proximity to each other. With the alert, ATC will offer the pilot an alternate course of action when feasible; e.g., "Traffic Alert, advise you turn right heading zero niner zero or climb to eight thousand immediately."

The issuance of a safety alert is contingent upon the capability of the controller to have an awareness of an unsafe condition. The course of action provided will be predicated on other traffic under ATC control. Once the alert is issued, it is solely the pilot's prerogative to determine what course of action, if any, he will take.

SAIL BACK — A maneuver during high wind conditions (usually with power off) where float plane movement is controlled by water rudders/opening and closing cabin doors.

SAY AGAIN — Used to request a repeat of the last transmission. Usually specifies transmission or portion thereof not understood or received; e.g., "Say again all after ABRAM VOR."

SAY ALTITUDE — Used by ATC to ascertain an aircraft's specific altitude/flight level. When the aircraft is climbing or descending, the pilot should state the indicated altitude rounded to the nearest 100 feet.

SAY HEADING — Used by ATC to request an aircraft heading. The pilot should state the actual heading of the aircraft.

SEA LANE — A designated portion of water outlined by visual surface markers for and intended to be used by aircraft designed to operate on water.

SEARCH AND RESCUE FACILITY — A facility responsible for maintaining and operating a search and rescue (SAR) service to render aid to persons and property in distress. It is any SAR unit, station, NET, or other operational activity which can be usefully employed during an SAR Mission; e.g., a Civil Air Patrol Wing, or a Coast Guard Station. (See Search and Rescue)

SEARCH AND RESCUE/SAR — A service which seeks missing aircraft and assists those found to be in need of assistance. It is a cooperative effort using the facilities and services of available Federal, state and local agencies. The U.S. Coast Guard is responsible for coordination of search and rescue for the Maritime Region, and the U.S. Air Force is responsible for search and rescue for the Inland Region. Information pertinent to search and rescue should be passed through any air traffic facility or be transmitted directly to the Rescue Coordination Center by telephone. (See Flight Service Station, Rescue Coordination Center) (Refer to AIM)

SEE AND AVOID — A visual procedure wherein pilots of aircraft flying in visual meteorological conditions (VMC), regardless of type of flight plan, are charged with the responsibility to observe the presence of other aircraft and to maneuver their aircraft as required to avoid the other aircraft. Right-of-way rules are contained in FAR, Part 91. (See Instrument Flight Rules, Visual Flight Rules, Visual Meteorological Conditions, Instrument Meteorological Conditions)

SEGMENTED CIRCLE — A system of visual indicators designed to provide traffic pattern information at airports without operating control towers. (Refer to AIM)

SEGMENTS OF AN INSTRUMENT APPROACH PROCEDURE — An instrument approach procedure may have as many as four separate segments depending on how the approach procedure is structured.

1. Initial Approach—The segment between the initial approach fix and the intermediate fix or the point where the aircraft is established on the intermediate course or final approach course.

ICAO—Initial Approach Segment—That segment of an instrument approach procedure between the initial approach fix and the intermediate approach fix or, where applicable, the final approach fix or point.

2. Intermediate Approach—The segment between the intermediate fix or point and the final approach fix.

ICAO—Intermediate Approach Segment—That segment of an instrument approach procedure between either the intermediate approach fix and the final approach fix or point, or between the end of a reversal, race track or dead reckoning track procedure and the final approach fix or point, as appropriate.

3. Final Approach—The segment between the final approach fix or point and the runway, airport, or missed approach point.

ICAO—Final Approach Segment—That segment of an instrument approach procedure in which alignment and descent for landing are accomplished.

4. Missed Approach—The segment between the missed approach point or the point of arrival at decision height and the missed approach fix at the prescribed altitude. (Refer to FAR, Part 97)

ICAO—Missed Approach Procedure—The procedure to be followed if the approach cannot be continued.

SEPARATION — In air traffic control, the spacing of aircraft to achieve their safe and orderly movement in flight and while landing and taking off. (See Separation Minima)

ICAO—SEPARATION — Spacing between aircraft, levels or tracks.

SEPARATION MINIMA — The minimum longitudinal, lateral, or vertical distances by which aircraft are spaced through the application of air traffic control procedures. (See Separation)

SEVERE WEATHER AVOIDANCE PLAN/SWAP — An approved plan to minimize the affect of severe weather on traffic flows in impacted terminal and/or ARTCC areas. SWAP is normally implemented to provide the least disruption to the ATC system when flight through portions of airspace is difficult or impossible due to severe weather.

SEVERE WEATHER FORECAST ALERTS/AWW — Preliminary messages issued in order to alert users that a Severe Weather Watch Bulletin (WW) is being issued. These messages define areas of possible severe thunderstorms or tornado activity. The messages are unscheduled and issued as required by the National Severe Storm Forecast Center at Kansas City, Missouri. (See SIGMET, Convective SIGMET, CWA, and AIRMET)

SHORT RANGE CLEARANCE — A clearance issued to a departing IFR flight which authorizes IFR flight to a specific fix short of the destination while air traffic control facilities are coordinating and obtaining the complete clearance.

SHORT TAKEOFF AND LANDING AIRCRAFT/STOL AIRCRAFT — An aircraft which, at some weight within its approved operating weight, is capable of operating from a STOL runway in compliance with the applicable STOL characteristics, airworthiness, operations, noise, and pollution standards. (See Vertical Takeoff and Landing Aircraft)

SIDESTEP MANEUVER — A visual maneuver accomplished by a pilot at the completion of an instrument approach to permit a straight-in landing on a parallel runway not more than 1,200 feet to either side of the runway to which the instrument approach was conducted. (Refer to AIM)

SIGMET/WS/**SIGNIFICANT METEOROLOGICAL INFORMATION** — A weather advisory issued concerning weather significant to the safety of all aircraft. SIGMET advisories cover severe and extreme turbulence, severe icing, and widespread dust or sandstorms that reduce visibility to less than 3 miles. (See AWW, Convective SIGMET, CWA, and AIRMET) (Refer to AIM)

ICAO—SIGMET INFORMATION — Information issued by a meteorological watch office concerning the occurrence or expected occurrence of specified en-route weather phenomena which may affect the safety of aircraft operations.

SIMPLIFIED DIRECTIONAL FACILITY/SDF — A NAVAID used for nonprecision instrument approaches. The final approach course is similar to that of an ILS localizer except that the SDF course may be offset from the runway, generally not more than 3 degrees, and the course may be wider than the localizer, resulting in a lower degree of accuracy. (Refer to AIM)

SIMULATED FLAMEOUT/SFO — A practice approach by a jet aircraft (normally military) at idle thrust to a runway. The approach may start at a relatively high altitude over a runway (high key) and may continue on a relatively high and wide downwind leg with a high rate of descent and a continuous turn to final. It terminates in a landing or low approach. The purpose of this approach is to simulate a flameout. (See Flameout)

SIMULTANEOUS ILS/MLS APPROACHES — An approach system permitting simultaneous ILS/MLS approaches to airports having parallel runways separated by at least 4,300 feet between centerlines. Integral parts of a total system are ILS/MLS, radar, communications, ATC procedures, and appropriate airborne equipment. (See Parallel Runways) (Refer to AIM)

SINGLE DIRECTION ROUTES — Preferred IFR Routes which are sometimes depicted on high altitude en route charts and which are normally flown in one direction only. (See Preferred IFR Route) (Refer to Airport/Facility Directory)

SINGLE FREQUENCY APPROACH/SFA — A service provided under a letter of agreement to military single-piloted turbojet aircraft which permits use of a single UHF frequency during approach for landing. Pilots will not normally be required to change frequency from the beginning of the approach to touchdown except that pilots conducting an en route descent are required to change frequency when control is transferred from the air route traffic control center to the terminal facility. The abbreviation "SFA" in the DOD FLIP

IFR Supplement under "Communications" indicates this service is available at an aerodrome.

SINGLE-PILOTED AIRCRAFT — A military turbojet aircraft possessing one set of flight controls, tandem cockpits, or two sets of flight controls but operated by one pilot is considered single-piloted by ATC when determining the appropriate air traffic service to be applied. (See Single Frequency Approach)

SLASH — A radar beacon reply displayed as an elongated target.

SLOW TAXI — To taxi a float plane at low power or low RPM.

SPEAK SLOWER — Used in verbal communications as a request to reduce speech rate.

SPECIAL EMERGENCY — A condition of air piracy or other hostile act by a person(s) aboard an aircraft which threatens the safety of the aircraft or its passengers.

SPECIAL INSTRUMENT APPROACH PROCEDURE — (See Instrument Approach Procedure)

SPECIAL USE AIRSPACE — Airspace of defined dimensions identified by an area on the surface of the earth wherein activities must be confined because of their nature and/or wherein limitations may be imposed upon aircraft operations that are not a part of those activities. Types of special use airspace are:

1. Alert Area—Airspace which may contain a high volume of pilot training activities or an unusual type of aerial activity, neither of which is hazardous to aircraft. Alert Areas are depicted on aeronautical charts for the information of nonparticipating pilots. All activities within an Alert Area are conducted in accordance with Federal Aviation Regulations, and pilots of participating aircraft as well as pilots transiting the area are equally responsible for collision avoidance.

2. Controlled Firing Area—Airspace wherein activities are conducted under conditions so controlled as to eliminate hazards to nonparticipating aircraft and to ensure the safety of persons and property on the ground.

3. Military Operations Area (MOA)—An MOA is an airspace assignment of defined vertical and lateral dimensions established outside positive control areas to separate/segregate certain military activities from IFR traffic and to identify for VFR traffic where these activities are conducted. (Refer to AIM).

4. Prohibited Area—Designated airspace within which the flight of aircraft is prohibited. (Refer to En Route Charts, AIM).

5. Restricted Area—Airspace designated under FAR, Part 73, within which the flight of aircraft, while not wholly prohibited, is subject to restriction. Most restricted areas are designated joint use and IFR/VFR operations in the area may be authorized by the controlling ATC facility when it is not being utilized by the using agency. Restricted areas are depicted on en route charts. Where joint use is authorized, the name of the ATC controlling facility is also shown. (Refer to FAR, Part 73 and AIM)

6. Warning Area—Airspace which may contain hazards to nonparticipating aircraft in international airspace.

SPECIAL VFR CONDITIONS — Weather conditions in a control zone which are less than basic VFR and in which some aircraft are permitted flight under Visual Flight Rules. (See Special VFR Operations) (Refer to FAR, Part 91)

SPECIAL VFR OPERATIONS — Aircraft operating in accordance with clearances within control zones in weather conditions less than the basic VFR weather minima. Such operations must be requested by the pilot and approved by ATC. (See Special VFR Conditions)

ICAO—SPECIAL VFR FLIGHT — A controlled VFR flight authorized by air traffic control to operate within a control zone under meteorological conditions below the visual meteorological conditions.

SPEED — (See Airspeed, Groundspeed)

SPEED ADJUSTMENT — An ATC procedure used to request pilots to adjust aircraft speed to a specific value for the purpose of providing desired spacing. Pilots are expected to maintain a speed of plus or minus 10 knots or 0.02 mach number of the specified speed.

Examples of speed adjustments are:

1. "Increase/reduce speed to mach point (number)."
2. "Increase/reduce speed to (speed in knots)" or "Increase/reduce speed (number of knots) knots."
3. "If practical, reduce speed to (speed);" or "If practical, reduce speed (number of) knots."

SPEED BRAKES/DIVE BRAKES — Moveable aerodynamic devices on aircraft that reduce airspeed during descent and landing.

SQUAWK (Mode, Code, Function) — Activate specific modes/codes/functions on the aircraft transponder; e.g., "Squawk three/alpha, two one zero five, low." (See Transponder)

STAGE I/II/III SERVICE — (See Terminal Radar Program)

STANDARD INSTRUMENT APPROACH PROCEDURE/ SIAP — (See Instrument Approach Procedure)

STANDARD INSTRUMENT DEPARTURE/SID — A preplanned instrument flight rule (IFR) air traffic control departure procedure printed for pilot use in graphic and/or textual form. SID's provide transition from the terminal to the appropriate en route structure. (See IFR Takeoff Minima and Departure Procedures) (Refer to AIM)

STANDARD RATE TURN — A turn of three degrees per second.

STANDARD TERMINAL ARRIVAL/STAR — A preplanned instrument flight rule (IFR) air traffic control arrival procedure published for pilot use in graphic and/or textual form. STAR's provide transition from the en route structure to an outer fix or an instrument approach fix/arrival waypoint in the terminal area.

STAND BY — Means the controller or pilot must pause for a few seconds, usually to attend to other duties of a higher priority. Also means to wait as in "stand by for clearance." If a delay is lengthy, the caller should reestablish contact.

STATIONARY RESERVATIONS — Altitude reservations which encompass activities in a fixed area. Stationary reservations may include activities, such as special tests of weapons systems or equipment, certain U.S. Navy carrier, fleet, and anti-submarine operations, rocket, missile and drone operations, and certain aerial refueling or similar operations.

STEPDOWN FIX — A fix permitting additional descent within a segment of an instrument approach procedure by identifying a point at which a controlling obstacle has been safely overflown.

STEP TAXI — To taxi a float plane at full power or high RPM.

STEP TURN — A maneuver used to put a float plane in a planing configuration prior to entering an active sea lane for takeoff. The STEP TURN maneuver should only be used upon pilot request.

STEREO ROUTE — A routinely used route of flight established by users and ARTCC's identified by a coded name; e.g., ALPHA 2. These routes minimize flight plan handling and communications.

STOP ALTITUDE SQUAWK — Used by ATC to inform an aircraft to turn-off the automatic altitude reporting feature of its transponder. It is issued when the verbally reported altitude varies 300 feet or more from the automatic altitude report. (See Altitude Readout, Transponder)

STOP AND GO — A procedure wherein an aircraft will land, make a complete stop on the runway, and then commence a takeoff from that point. (See Low Approach, Option Approach)

STOPOVER FLIGHT PLAN — A flight plan format which permits in a single submission the filing of a sequence of flight plans through interim full-stop destinations to a final destination.

STOP SQUAWK (Mode or Code) — Used by ATC to tell the pilot to turn specified functions of the aircraft transponder off. (See Stop Altitude Squawk, Transponder)

STOP STREAM/BURST/BUZZER — Used by ATC to request a pilot to suspend electronic countermeasure activity. (See Jamming)

STOPWAY — An area beyond the takeoff runway designated by the airport authorities as able to support an airplane during an aborted takeoff. (Refer to FAR, Part 1)

STRAIGHT-IN APPROACH—IFR — An instrument approach wherein final approach is begun without first having executed a procedure turn, not necessarily completed with a straight-in landing or made to straight-in landing minimums. (See Straight-in Landing, Landing Minimums, Straight-in Approach-VFR)

STRAIGHT-IN APPROACH—VFR — Entry into the traffic pattern by interception of the extended runway centerline (final approach course) without executing any other portion of the traffic pattern. (See Traffic Pattern)

STRAIGHT-IN LANDING — A landing made on a runway aligned within 30° of the final approach course following completion of an instrument approach. (See Straight-in Approach-IFR)

STRAIGHT-IN LANDING MINIMUMS/STRAIGHT-IN MINIMUMS — (See Landing Minimums)

SUBSTITUTE ROUTE — A route assigned to pilots when any part of an airway or route is unusable because of NAVAID status. These routes consist of:

1. Substitute routes which are shown on U.S. Government charts.

2. Routes defined by ATC as specific NAVAID radials or courses.

3. Routes defined by ATC as direct to or between NAVAID's.

SUNSET AND SUNRISE — The mean solar times of sunset and sunrise as published in the Nautical Almanac, converted to local standard time for the locality concerned. Within Alaska, the end of evening civil twilight and the beginning of morning civil twilight, as defined for each locality.

SUPER HIGH FREQUENCY/SHF — The frequency band between 3 and 30 gigahertz (gHz). The elevation and azimuth stations of the microwave landing system operate from 5031MHz to 5091MHz in this spectrum.

SURVEILLANCE APPROACH — An instrument approach wherein the air traffic controller issues instructions, for pilot compliance, based on aircraft position in relation to the final approach course (azimuth), and the distance (range) from the end of the runway as displayed on the controller's radar scope. The controller will provide recommended altitudes on final approach if requested by the pilot. (See PAR Approach) (Refer to AIM)

SYSTEM STRATEGIC NAVIGATION/SN — Military activity accomplished by navigating along a preplanned route using internal aircraft systems to maintain a desired track. This activity normally requires a lateral route width of 10NM and altitude range of 1,000 feet to 6,000 feet AGL with some route segments that permit terrain following.

TACAN-ONLY AIRCRAFT — An aircraft, normally military, possessing TACAN with DME but no VOR navigational system capability. Clearances must specify TACAN or VORTAC fixes and approaches.

TACTICAL AIR NAVIGATION/TACAN — An ultra-high frequency electronic rho-theta air navigation aid which provides suitably equipped aircraft a continuous indication of bearing and distance to the TACAN station. (See VORTAC) (Refer to AIM)

TARGET — The indication shown on a radar display resulting from a primary radar return or a radar beacon reply. (See Radar, Target Symbol)

ICAO—TARGET — In radar:

1. Generally, any discrete object which reflects or retransmits energy back to the radar equipment.

2. Specifically, an object of radar search or surveillance.

TARGET SYMBOL — A computer-generated indication shown on a radar display resulting from a primary radar return or a radar beacon reply.

TAXI — The movement of an airplane under its own power on the surface of an airport (FAR Part 135.100-Note). Also, it describes the surface movement of helicopters equipped with wheels. (See Air Taxi, Hover Taxi) (Refer to AIM)

TAXI INTO POSITION AND HOLD — Used by ATC to inform a pilot to taxi onto the departure runway in takeoff position and hold. It is not authorization for takeoff. It is used when takeoff clearance cannot immediately be issued because of traffic or other reasons. (See Hold, Cleared for Takeoff)

TAXI PATTERNS — Patterns established to illustrate the desired flow of ground traffic for the different runways or airport areas available for use.

TELEPHONE INFORMATION BRIEFING SERVICE (TIBS) — A continuous telephone recording of meteorological and/or aeronautical information. (refer to AIM)

TERMINAL AREA — A general term used to describe airspace in which approach control service or airport traffic control service is provided.

TERMINAL AREA FACILITY — A facility providing air traffic control service for arriving and departing IFR, VFR, Special VFR, and on occasion en route aircraft. (See Approach Control, Tower)

TERMINAL CONTROL AREA — (See Controlled Airspace)

TERMINAL RADAR PROGRAM — A national program instituted to extend the terminal radar services provided IFR aircraft to VFR aircraft. Pilot participation in the program is urged but is not mandatory. The program is divided into two parts and referred to as Stage II and Stage III. The Stage service provided at a particular location is contained in the Airport/Facility Directory.

1. Stage I originally comprised two basic radar services (traffic advisories and limited vectoring to VFR aircraft). These services are provided by all commissioned terminal radar facilities, but the term "Stage I" has been deleted from use.

2. Stage II/Radar Advisory and Sequencing for VFR Aircraft—Provides, in addition to the basic radar services, vectoring and sequencing on a full-time basis to arriving VFR aircraft. The purpose is to adjust the flow of arriving IFR and VFR aircraft into the traffic pattern in a safe and orderly manner and to provide traffic advisories to departing VFR aircraft.

3. Stage III/Radar Sequencing and Separation Service for VFR Aircraft—Provides, in addition to the basic radar services and Stage II, separation between all participating VFR aircraft. The purpose is to provide separation between all participating VFR aircraft and all IFR aircraft operating within the airspace defined as a Terminal Radar Service Area (TRSA) or Terminal Control Area (TCA). (See Controlled Airspace, Terminal Radar Service Area) (Refer to AIM, Airport/Facility Directory)

TERMINAL RADAR SERVICE AREA/TRSA — Airspace surrounding designated airports wherein ATC provides radar vectoring, sequencing, and separation on a full-time basis for all IFR and participating VFR aircraft. Service provided in a TRSA is called Stage III Service. The AIM contains an explanation of TRSA. TRSA's are depicted on VFR aeronautical charts. Pilot participation is urged but is not mandatory. (See Terminal Radar Program) (Refer to AIM, Airport/Facility Directory)

TERRAIN FOLLOWING/TF — The flight of a military aircraft maintaining a constant AGL altitude above the terrain or the highest obstruction. The altitude of the aircraft will constantly change with the varying terrain and/or obstruction.

TETRAHEDRON — A device normally located on uncontrolled airports and used as a landing direction indicator. The small end of a tetrahedron points in the direction of landing. At controlled airports, the tetrahedron, if installed, should be disregarded because tower instructions supersede the indicator. (See Segmented Circle) (Refer to AIM)

THAT IS CORRECT — The understanding you have is right.

THRESHOLD — The beginning of that portion of the runway usable for landing. (See Airport Lighting, Displaced Threshold)

THRESHOLD CROSSING HEIGHT/TCH — The theoretical height above the runway threshold at which the aircraft's glideslope antenna would be if the aircraft maintains the trajectory established by the mean ILS glideslope or MLS glidepath. (See Glide Slope, Threshold)

THRESHOLD LIGHTS — (See Airport Lighting)

TIME GROUP — Four digits representing the hour and minutes from the 24-hour clock. Time groups without time zone indicators are understood to be UTC (Coordinated Universal Time); e.g., "0205." The term "Zulu" is used when ATC procedures require a reference to UTC. A time zone designator is used to indicate local time; e.g., "0205M." The end and the beginning of the day are shown by "2400" and "0000," respectively.

TORCHING — The burning of fuel at the end of an exhaust pipe or stack of a reciprocating aircraft engine, the result of an excessive richness in the fuel air mixture.

ICAO—TOTAL ESTIMATED ELAPSED TIME — For IFR flights, the estimated time required from take-off to arrive over that designated point, defined by reference to navigation aids, from which it is intended that an instrument approach procedure will be commenced, or, if no navigation aid is associated with the destination aerodrome, to arrive over the destination aerodrome. For VFR flights, the estimated time required from takeoff to arrive over the destination aerodrome. (See Estimated Elapsed Time)

TOUCH-AND-GO/TOUCH-AND-GO LANDING — An operation by an aircraft that lands and departs on a runway without stopping or exiting the runway.

TOUCHDOWN —

1. The point at which an aircraft first makes contact with the landing surface.

2. Concerning a precision radar approach (PAR), it is the point where the glide path intercepts the landing surface.

ICAO—TOUCHDOWN — The point where the nominal glide path intercepts the runway.

Note. — Touchdown as defined above is only a datum and is not necessarily the actual point at which the aircraft will touch the runway.

TOUCHDOWN RVR — (See Visibility)

TOUCHDOWN ZONE — The first 3,000 feet of the runway beginning at the threshold. The area is used for determination of Touchdown Zone Elevation in the development of straight-in landing minimums for instrument approaches.

ICAO—TOUCHDOWN ZONE — The portion of a runway, beyond the threshold, where it is intended landing aircraft first contact the runway.

TOUCHDOWN ZONE ELEVATION/TDZE — The highest elevation in the first 3,000 feet of the landing surface. TDZE is indicated on the instrument approach procedure

chart when straight-in landing minimums are authorized. (See Touchdown Zone)

TOUCHDOWN ZONE LIGHTING — (See Airport Lighting)

TOWER/AIRPORT TRAFFIC CONTROL TOWER/ ATCT — A terminal facility that uses air/ground communications, visual signaling, and other devices to provide ATC services to aircraft operating in the vicinity of an airport or on the movement area. Authorizes aircraft to land or takeoff at the airport controlled by the tower or to transit the airport traffic area regardless of flight plan or weather conditions (IFR or VFR). A tower may also provide approach control services (radar or nonradar). (See Airport Traffic Area, Airport Traffic Control Service, Approach Control/Approach Control Facility, Approach Control Service, Movement Area, Tower En Route Control Service/Tower to Tower) (Refer to AIM)

ICAO—AERODROME CONTROL TOWER — A unit established to provide air traffc control service to aerodrome traffic.

TOWER EN ROUTE CONTROL SERVICE/TOWER TO TOWER — The control of IFR en route traffic within delegated airspace between two or more adjacent approach control facilities. This service is designed to expedite traffic and reduce control and pilot communication requirements.

TPX-42 — A numeric beacon decoder equipment/system. It is designed to be added to terminal radar systems for beacon decoding. It provides rapid target identification, reinforcement of the primary radar target, and altitude information from Mode C. (See Automated Radar Terminal Systems, Transponder)

TRACK — The actual flight path of an aircraft over the surface of the earth. (See Course, Route, Flight Path)

ICAO—TRACK — The projection on the earth's surface of the path of an aircraft, the direction of which path at any point is usually expressed in degrees from North (True, Magnetic, or Grid).

TRAFFIC —

1. A term used by a controller to transfer radar identification of an aircraft to another controller for the purpose of coordinating separation action. Traffic is normally issued (a) in response to a handoff or point out, (b) in anticipation of a handoff or point out, or (c) in conjunction with a request for control of an aircraft.

2. A term used by ATC to refer to one or more aircraft.

TRAFFIC ADVISORIES — Advisories issued to alert pilots to other known or observed air traffic which may be in such proximity to the position or intended route of flight of their aircraft to warrant their attention. Such advisories may be based on:

1. Visual observation.

2. Observation of radar identified and nonidentified aircraft targets on an ATC radar display, or

3. Verbal reports from pilots or other facilities.

The word "traffic" followed by additional information, if known, is used to provide such advisories; e.g., "Traffic, 2 o'clock, one zero miles, southbound, eight thousand."

Traffic advisory service will be provided to the extent possible depending on higher priority duties of the controller or other limitations; e.g., radar limitations, volume of traffic, frequency congestion, or controller workload. Radar/nonradar traffic advisories do not relieve the pilot of his responsibility to see and avoid other aircraft. Pilots are cautioned that there are many times when the controller is not able to give traffic advisories concerning all traffic in the aircraft's proximity; in other words, when a pilot requests or is receiving traffic advisories, he should not assume that all traffic will be issued. (Refer to AIM, Radar Traffic Information Service)

TRAFFIC ALERT AND COLLISION AVOIDANCE SYSTEM/TCAS — An airborne collision avoidance system based on radar beacon signals which operates independent of ground-based equipment. TCAS-I generates traffic advisories only. TCAS-II generates traffic advisories, and resolution (collision avoidance) advisories in the vertical plane.

(Identification), TRAFFIC ALERT. ADVISE YOU TURN LEFT/RIGHT (specific heading if appropriate), AND/OR CLIMB/DESCEND (specific altitude if appropriate) IMMEDIATELY. (See Safety Alert)

TRAFFIC INFORMATION — (See Traffic Advisories)

TRAFFIC IN SIGHT — Used by pilots to inform a controller that previously issued traffic is in sight. (See Negative Contact, Traffic Advisories)

TRAFFIC NO LONGER A FACTOR — Indicates that the traffic described in a previously issued traffic advisory is no longer a factor.

TRAFFIC PATTERN — The traffic flow that is prescribed for aircraft landing at, taxiing on, or taking off from an airport. The components of a typical traffic pattern are upwind leg, crosswind leg, downwind leg, base leg, and final approach.

1. Upwind Leg—A flight path parallel to the landing runway in the direction of landing.

2. Crosswind Leg—A flight path at right angles to the landing runway off its upwind end.

3. Downwind Leg—A flight path parallel to the landing runway in the direction opposite to landing. The downwind leg normally extends between the crosswind and the base leg.

4. Base Leg—A flight path at right angles to the landing runway off its downwind end. The base leg normally extends from the downwind leg to the intersection of the extended runway centerline.

5. Final Approach—A flight path in the direction of landing along the extended runway centerline. The final approach normally extends from the base leg to the runway. An aircraft making a straight-in approach VFR is also considered to be on final approach.

(See Straight-In Approach--VFR, Taxi Patterns) (Refer to AIM, FAR Part 91)

ICAO—AERODROME TRAFFIC CIRCUIT — The specified path to be flown by aircraft operating in the vicinity of an aerodrome.

TRANSCRIBED WEATHER BROADCAST/TWEB — A continuous recording of meteorological and aeronautical information that is broadcast on L/MF and VOR facilities for pilots. (Refer to AIM)

TRANSFER OF CONTROL — That action whereby the responsibility for the separation of an aircraft is transferred from one controller to another.

ICAO—TRANSFER OF CONTROL — Transfer of responsibility for providing air traffic control service.

TRANSFERRING CONTROLLER/FACILITY — A controller/facility transferring control of an aircraft to another controller/facility.

ICAO—TRANSFERRING UNIT/CONTROLLER — Air traffic control unit/air traffic controller in the process of transferring the responsibility for providing air traffic control service to an aircraft to the next air traffic control unit/air traffic controller along the route of flight.

Note. — See definition of *accepting unit/controller*.

TRANSITION —

1. The general term that describes the change from one phase of flight or flight condition to another; e.g., transition from en route flight to the approach or transition from instrument flight to visual flight.

2. A published procedure (SID Transition) used to connect the basic SID to one of several en route airways/jet routes, or a published procedure (STAR Transition) used to connect one of several en route airways/jet routes to the basic STAR. (Refer to SID/STAR Charts)

TRANSITION AREA — (See Controlled Airspace)

TRANSMISSOMETER — An apparatus used to determine visibility by measuring the transmission of light through the atmosphere. It is the measurement source for determining runway visual range (RVR) and runway visibility value (RVV). (See Visibility)

TRANSMITTING IN THE BLIND/BLIND TRANSMISSION — A transmission from one station to other stations in circumstances where two-way communication cannot be established, but where it is believed that the called stations may be able to receive the transmission.

TRANSPONDER — The airborne radar beacon receiver/transmitter portion of the Air Traffic Control Radar Beacon System (ATCRBS) which automatically receives radio signals from interrogators on the ground, and selectively replies with a specific reply pulse or pulse group only to those interrogations being received on the mode to which it is set to respond. (See Interrogator) (Refer to AIM)

ICAO—TRANSPONDER — A receiver/transmitter which will generate a reply signal upon proper interrogation; the interrogation and reply being on different frequencies.

TURBOJET AIRCRAFT — An aircraft having a jet engine in which the energy of the jet operates a turbine which in turn operates the air compressor.

TURBOPROP AIRCRAFT — An aircraft having a jet engine in which the energy of the jet operates a turbine which drives the propeller.

T-VOR/TERMINAL-VERY HIGH FREQUENCY OMNIDIRECTIONAL RANGE STATION — A very high frequency terminal omnirange station located on or near an airport and used as an approach aid. (See Navigational Aid, VOR)

TWO WAY RADIO COMMUNICATIONS FAILURE — (See Lost Communications)

ULTRAHIGH FREQUENCY/UHF — The frequency band between 300 and 3,000 MHz. The bank of radio frequencies used for military air/ground voice communications. In some instances this may go as low as 225 MHz and still be referred to as UHF.

ULTRALIGHT VEHICLE — An aeronautical vehicle operated for sport or recreational purposes which does not require FAA registration, an airworthiness certificate, nor pilot certification. They are primarily single occupant vehicles, although some two-place vehicles are authorized for training purposes. Operation of an ultralight vehicle in certain airspace requires authorization from ATC. (See FAR 103)

UNABLE — Indicates inability to comply with a specific instruction, request, or clearance.

UNCONTROLLED AIRSPACE — Uncontrolled airspace is that portion of the airspace that has not been designated as continental control area, control area, control zone, terminal control area, or transition area and within which ATC has neither the authority nor the responsibility for exercising control over air traffic. (See Controlled Airspace)

UNDER THE HOOD — Indicates that the pilot is using a hood to restrict visibility outside the cockpit while simulating instrument flight. An appropriately rated pilot is required in the other control seat while this operation is being conducted. (Refer to FAR, Part 91)

UNICOM — A nongovernment communication facility which may provide airport information at certain airports. Locations and frequencies of UNICOMs are shown on aeronautical charts and publications. (Refer to AIM, Airport/Facility Directory)

UNPUBLISHED ROUTE — A route for which no minimum altitude is published or charted for pilot use. It may include a direct route between NAVAIDS, a radial, a radar vector, or a final approach course beyond the segments of an instrument approach procedure. (See Published Route, Route)

UPWIND LEG — (See Traffic Pattern)

URGENCY — A condition of being concerned about safety and of requiring timely but not immediate assistance; a potential *distress* condition.

ICAO—URGENCY — A condition concerning the safety of an aircraft or other vehicle, or of person on board or in sight, but which does not require immediate assistance.

VECTOR — A heading issued to an aircraft to provide navigational guidance by radar.

ICAO—RADAR VECTORING — Provision of navigational guidance to aircraft in the form of specific headings, based on the use of radar.

VERIFY — Request confirmation of information; e.g., "verify assigned altitude."

VERIFY SPECIFIC DIRECTION OF TAKEOFF (OR TURNS AFTER TAKEOFF) — Used by ATC to ascertain an aircraft's direction of takeoff and/or direction of turn after takeoff. It is normally used for IFR departures from an airport not having a control tower. When direct communication with the pilot is not possible, the request and information may be relayed through an FSS, dispatcher, or by other means. (See IFR Takeoff Minimums and Departure Procedures)

VERTICAL SEPARATION — Separation established by assignment of different altitudes or flight levels. (See Separation)

ICAO—VERTICAL SEPARATION — Separation between aircraft expressed in units of vertical distance.

VERTICAL TAKEOFF AND LANDING AIRCRAFT/ VTOL AIRCRAFT — Aircraft capable of vertical climbs and/or descents and of using very short runways or small areas for takeoff and landings. These aircraft include, but are not limited to, helicopters. (See Short Takeoff and Landing Aircraft)

VERY HIGH FREQUENCY/VHF — The frequency band between 30 and 300 MHz. Portions of this band, 108 to 118 MHz, are used for certain NAVAIDS; 118 to 136 MHz are used for civil air/ground voice communications. Other frequencies in this band are used for purposes not related to air traffic control.

VERY LOW FREQUENCY/VLF — The frequency band between 3 and 30 kHz.

VFR AIRCRAFT/VFR FLIGHT — An aircraft conducting flight in accordance with visual flight rules. (See Visual Flight Rules)

VFR CONDITIONS — Weather conditions equal to or better than the minimum for flight under visual flight rules. The term may be used as an ATC clearance/instruction only when:

1. An IFR aircraft requests a climb/descent in VFR conditions.

2. The clearance will result in noise abatement benefits where part of the IFR departure route does not conform to an FAA approved noise abatement route or altitude.

3. A pilot has requested a practice instrument approach and is not on an IFR flight plan.

All pilots receiving this authorization must comply with the VFR visibility and distance from cloud criteria in FAR Part 91. Use of the term does not relieve controllers of their responsibility to separate aircraft in TCAs/TRSAs as required by FAA Handbook 7110.65. When used as an ATC clearance/ instruction, the term may be abbreviated "VFR;" e.g., "MAINTAIN VFR," "CLIMB/DESCEND VFR," etc.

VFR-ON-TOP — ATC authorization for an IFR aircraft to operate in VFR conditions at any appropriate VFR altitude (as specified in FAR and as restricted by ATC). A pilot receiving this authorization must comply with the VFR visibility, distance from cloud criteria, and the minimum IFR altitudes specified in FAR Part 91. The use of this term does not relieve controllers of their responsibility to separate aircraft in TCA's/TRSA's as required by FAA Handbook 7110.65.

VFR MILITARY TRAINING ROUTES/VR — Routes used by the Department of Defense and associated Reserve and Air Guard units for the purpose of conducting low-altitude navigation and tactical training under VFR below 10,000 feet MSL at airspeeds in excess of 250 knots IAS.

VFR NOT RECOMMENDED — An advisory provided by a flight service station to a pilot during a preflight or inflight weather briefing that flight under visual flight rules is not recommended. To be given when the current and/or forecast weather conditions are at or below VFR minimums. It does not abrogate the pilot's authority to make his own decision.

VIDEO MAP — An electronically displayed map on the radar display that may depict data such as airports, heliports, runway centerline extensions, hospital emergency landing areas, NAVAID's and fixes, reporting points, airway/route centerlines, boundaries, handoff points, special use tracks, obstructions, prominent geographic features, map alignment indicators, range accuracy marks, minimum vectoring altitudes.

VISIBILITY — The ability, as determined by atmospheric conditions and expressed in units of distance, to see and identify prominent unlighted objects by day and prominent lighted objects by night. Visibility is reported as statute miles, hundreds of feet or meters. (Refer to FAR Part 91, AIM)

ICAO—VISIBILITY — The ability, as determined by atmospheric conditions and expressed in units of distance, to see and identify prominent unlighted objects by day and prominent lighted objects by night.

1. Flight Visibility—The average forward horizontal distance, from the cockpit of an aircraft in flight, at which prominent unlighted objects may be seen and identified by day and prominent lighted objects may be seen and identified by night.

ICAO—Flight Visibility—The visibility forward from the cockpit of an aircraft in flight.

2. Ground Visibility—Prevailing horizontal visibility near the earth's surface as reported by the United States National Weather Service or an accredited observer.

ICAO—Ground Visibility—The visibility at an aerodrome as reported by an accredited observer.

3. Prevailing Visibility—The greatest horizontal visibility equaled or exceeded throughout at least half the horizon circle which need not necessarily be continuous.

4. Runway Visibility Value/RVV—The visibility determined for a particular runway by a transmissometer. A meter provides a continuous indication of the visibility (reported in miles or fractions of miles) for the runway. RVV is used in lieu of prevailing visibility in determining minimums for a particular runway.

5. Runway Visual Range/RVR—An instrumentally derived value, based on standard calibrations, that represents the horizontal distance a pilot will see down the runway from the approach end. It is based on the sighting of either high intensity runway lights or on the visual contrast of other targets whichever yields the greater visual range. RVR, in contrast to prevailing or runway visibility, is based on what a pilot in a moving aircraft should see looking down the runway. RVR is horizontal visual range, not slant visual range. It is based on the measurement of a transmissometer made near the touchdown point of the instrument runway and is reported in hundreds of feet. RVR is used in lieu of RVV and/or prevailing visibility in determining minimums for a particular runway.

a. Touchdown RVR—The RVR visibility readout values obtained from RVR equipment serving the runway touchdown zone.

b. Mid-RVR—The RVR readout values obtained from RVR equipment located midfield of the runway.

c. Rollout RVR—The RVR readout values obtained from RVR equipment located nearest the rollout end of the runway.

ICAO—Runway Visual Range (RVR)—The range over which the pilot of an aircraft on the centre line of a runway can see the runway surface markings or the lights delineating the runway or identifying its centre line.

VISUAL APPROACH — An approach wherein an aircraft on an IFR flight plan, operating in VFR conditions under the control of an air traffic control facility and having an air traffic control authorization, may proceed to the airport of destination in VFR conditions.

ICAO—VISUAL APPROACH — An approach by an IFR flight when either part or all of an instrument approach procedure is not completed and the approach is executed in visual reference to terrain.

VISUAL APPROACH SLOPE INDICATOR — (See Airport Lighting)

VISUAL DESCENT POINT/VDP — A defined point on the final approach course of a nonprecision straight-in approach procedure from which normal descent from the MDA to the runway touchdown point may be commenced, provided the approach threshold of that runway, or approach lights, or other markings identifiable with the approach end of that runway are clearly visible to the pilot.

VISUAL FLIGHT RULES/VFR — Rules that govern the procedures for conducting flight under visual conditions. The term "VFR" is also used in the United States to indicate weather conditions that are equal to or greater than minimum VFR requirements. In addition, it is used by pilots and controllers to indicate type of flight plan. (See Instrument Flight Rules, Instrument Meteorological Conditions, Visual Meteorological Conditions) (Refer to FAR, Part 91 and AIM)

VISUAL HOLDING — The holding of aircraft at selected, prominent geographical fixes which can be easily recognized from the air. (See Hold, Holding Fixes)

VISUAL METEOROLOGICAL CONDITIONS/VMC — Meteorological conditions expressed in terms of visibility, distance from cloud, and ceiling equal to or better than specified minima. (See Instrument Flight Rules, Instrument Meteorological Conditions, Visual Flight Rules)

VISUAL SEPARATION — A means employed by ATC to separate aircraft in terminal areas. There are two ways to effect this separation:

1. The tower controller sees the aircraft involved and issues instructions, as necessary, to ensure that the aircraft avoid each other.

2. A pilot sees the other aircraft involved and upon instructions from the controller provides his own separation by maneuvering his aircraft as necessary to avoid it. This may involve following another aircraft or keeping it in sight until it is no longer a factor. (See See and Avoid) (Refer to FAR, Part 91)

VORTAC/VHF OMNIDIRECTIONAL RANGE/TACTICAL AIR NAVIGATION — A navigation aid providing VOR azimuth, TACAN azimuth, and TACAN distance measuring equipment (DME) at one site. (See Distance Measuring Equipment, Navigational Aid TACAN, VOR) (Refer to AIM)

VORTICES/WING TIP VORTICES — Circular patterns of air created by the movement of an airfoil through the air when generating lift. As an airfoil moves through the atmosphere in sustained flight, an area of area of low pressure is created above it. The air flowing from the high pressure area to the low pressure area around and about the tips of the airfoil tends to roll up into two rapidly rotating vortices, cylindrical in shape. These vortices are the most predominant parts of aircraft wake turbulence and their rotational force is dependent upon the wing loading, gross weight, and speed of the generating aircraft. The vortices from medium to heavy aircraft can be of extremely high velocity and hazardous to smaller aircraft. (See Aircraft Classes Wake Turbulence) (Refer to AIM)

VOR/VERY HIGH FREQUENCY OMNIDIRECTIONAL RANGE STATION — A ground-based electronic navigation aid transmitting very high frequency navigation signals, 360 degrees in azimuth, oriented from magnetic north. Used as the basis for navigation in the National Airspace System. The VOR periodically identifies itself by Morse Code and may have an additional voice identification feature. Voice features may be used by ATC or FSS for transmitting instructions/information to pilots. (See Navigational Aid) (Refer to AIM)

VOT/VOR TEST SIGNAL — A ground facility which emits a test signal to check VOR receiver accuracy. Some VOT's are available to the user while airborne, and others are limited to ground use only. (Refer to FAR, Part 91, AIM, Airport/Facility Directory)

WAKE TURBULENCE — Phenomena resulting from the passage of an aircraft through the atmosphere. The term includes vortices, thrust stream turbulence, jet blast, jet wash, propeller wash, and rotor wash both on the ground and in the air. (See Aircraft Classes, Jet Blast, Vortices) (Refer to AIM)

WARNING AREA — (See Special Use Airspace)

WAYPOINT — A predetermined geographical position used for route/instrument approach definition, or progress reporting purposes, that is defined relative to a VORTAC station or in terms of latitude/longitude coordinates.

WEATHER ADVISORY/INFLIGHT WEATHER ADVISORY — (See SIGMET, AIRMET)

WEATHER ADVISORY/WS/WST/WA/CWA — In aviation weather forecast practice, an expression of hazardous weather conditions not predicted in the area forecast, as they affect the operation of air traffic and as prepared by the NWS.

WHEN ABLE — When used in conjunction with ATC instructions, gives the pilot the latitude to delay compliance until a condition or event has been reconciled. Unlike "pilot discretion," when instructions are prefaced "when able," the pilot is expected to seek the first opportunity to comply. Once a maneuver has been initiated, the pilot is expected to continue until the specifications of the instructions have been met. "When able," should not be used when expeditious compliance is required.

WILCO — I have received your message, understand it, and will comply with it.

WIND SHEAR — A change in wind speed and/or wind direction in a short distance resulting in a tearing or shearing effect. It can exist in a horizontal or vertical direction and occasionally in both.

WORDS TWICE —

1. As a request: "Communication is difficult. Please say every phrase twice."

2. As information: "Since communications are difficult, every phrase in this message will be spoken twice."

INDEX

[References are to Paragraph numbers]

A

ABBREVIATED DEPARTURE CLEARANCE [322]
Abbreviated IFR Flight Plans [Glossary]
Abeam [Glossary]
Abort [Glossary]
ACCIDENT   *see*   Accident Cause Factors
ACCIDENT   *see*   Accident Prevention Program
ACCIDENT   *see*   Aircraft Accident Reporting
ACCIDENT CAUSE FACTORS [570]
ACCIDENT PREVENTION PROGRAM [570]
Acknowledge [Glossary]
ACROBATIC FLIGHT [606]
Acrobatic Flight [Glossary]
Additional Services [Glossary]
ADHERENCE TO CLEARANCE [270] [401] [511]
Administrator [Glossary]
Advise Intentions [Glossary]
ADVISORY   *see*   Aeronautical Advisory Stations (UNICOM)
ADVISORY   *see*   Aircraft Conflict Advisory
ADVISORY   *see*   Airport Advisory Area
ADVISORY   *see*   Airport Advisory Service/AAS
ADVISORY   *see*   Braking Action Advisories
ADVISORY   *see*   Common Traffic Advisory Frequency (CTAF)
ADVISORY   *see*   Conflict Advisory
ADVISORY   *see*   En Route Flight Advisory Service/Flight Watch
ADVISORY   *see*   Fuel Advisory Departure Procedures
ADVISORY   *see*   Fuel Advisory Departure/FAD
ADVISORY   *see*   Minimum Fuel Advisory
ADVISORY   *see*   Obstruction Advisory
ADVISORY   *see*   Pilot Traffic Advisory Practices
ADVISORY   *see*   RADAR Advisory Service
ADVISORY   *see*   RADAR Traffic Advisory
ADVISORY   *see*   Safety Advisory
ADVISORY   *see*   Terrain Advisory
ADVISORY   *see*   Traffic Advisory
ADVISORY   *see*   Weather Advisory/WS/WA
Advisory Frequency [Glossary]
Advisory [Glossary]
Advisory Service [Glossary]
Aerial Refueling/Inflight Refueling [Glossary]
AEROBATICS [606]
Aerodrome [Glossary]
AERONAUTICAL ADVISORY STATIONS (UNICOM) [157] [159]
   [160]
Aeronautical Beacon [Glossary]
AERONAUTICAL CHART [290] [620] [621] [622] [623] [624]
   [625]
Aeronautical Chart [Glossary]
AERONAUTICAL LIGHT BEACON [48] [50] [51] [53]
AERONAUTICAL MULTICOM SERVICE [157] [159]
Affirmative [Glossary]
AIR AMBULANCE FLIGHTS [193]
Air Carrier District Office/ACDO [Glossary]
AIR DEFENSE EMERGENCY [430]
Air Defense Emergency [Glossary]

AIR DEFENSE IDENTIFICATION ZONE/ADIZ [430]
Air Defense Identification Zone/ADIZ [Glossary]
Air Navigation Facility [Glossary]
AIR ROUTE SURVEILLANCE RADAR/ARSR [32]
Air Route Surveillance RADAR/ARSR [Glossary]
AIR ROUTE TRAFFIC CONTROL CENTER/ARTCC [150] [340]
Air Route Traffic Control Center/ARTCC [Glossary]
AIR TAXI [238]
Air Taxi [Glossary]
Air Traffic Clearance/ATC Clearance [Glossary]
Air Traffic Control Command Center/ATCCC [Glossary]
AIR TRAFFIC CONTROL RADAR BEACON SYSTEM [31]
Air Traffic Control Service [Glossary]
Air Traffic Control Specialist/Controller [Glossary]
Air Traffic Control/ATC [Glossary]
AIR TRAFFIC FACILITIES [150] [151] [152] [155]
Air Traffic [Glossary]
AIRBORNE VOR CHECK POINTS [4]
AIRCRAFT   *see*   Aircraft Accident Reporting
AIRCRAFT   *see*   Aircraft Approach Category
AIRCRAFT   *see*   Aircraft Arresting Device
AIRCRAFT   *see*   Aircraft Checklist
AIRCRAFT   *see*   Aircraft Conflict Advisory
AIRCRAFT   *see*   Aircraft Identification
AIRCRAFT   *see*   Aircraft Incident Reporting
AIRCRAFT   *see*   Aircraft Interception
AIRCRAFT   *see*   Aircraft Lights
AIRCRAFT   *see*   Aircraft Operations Manual
AIRCRAFT   *see*   Aircraft Traffic Control Light Signals
AIRCRAFT   *see*   Aircraft Transponder Equipment
AIRCRAFT   *see*   Downed Aircraft
AIRCRAFT   *see*   Flight Check Aircraft
AIRCRAFT   *see*   Interchange Aircraft
AIRCRAFT   *see*   Leased Aircraft
AIRCRAFT   *see*   Overdue Aircraft
AIRCRAFT ACCIDENT REPORTING [581]
AIRCRAFT APPROACH CATEGORY [12] [512]
Aircraft Approach Category [Glossary]
AIRCRAFT ARRESTING DEVICE [61]
Aircraft Classes [Glossary]
AIRCRAFT CONFLICT ADVISORY [409]
AIRCRAFT CONFLICT ALERT [406]
Aircraft [Glossary]
AIRCRAFT IDENTIFICATION [193] [260] [290]
AIRCRAFT INCIDENT REPORTING [581]
AIRCRAFT INTERCEPTION [431] [432]
AIRCRAFT LIGHTS [233]
AIRCRAFT TRAFFIC CONTROL LIGHT SIGNALS [233]
AIRCRAFT TRANSPONDER EQUIPMENT [298]
AIRFRAME ICING [521]
AIRFRAME ICING REPORTING CRITERIA [521]
Airman's Information Manual/AIM [Glossary]
AIRMET [504]
AIRMET/Airman's Meteorological Information [Glossary]
AIRPORT   *see*   Airport (Rotating) Beacon

INDEX—Continued

[References are to Paragraph numbers]

APPROACH *see* Precision Approach RADAR Procedures
APPROACH *see* Pulsating Visual Approach Slope Indicator
APPROACH *see* RADAR Approach Monitoring
APPROACH *see* Simultaneous ILS Approach
APPROACH *see* Surveillance Approach
APPROACH *see* Terminal Instrument Approach Procedures
APPROACH *see* Timed Approach
APPROACH *see* Tricolor Visual Approach Slope Indicator
APPROACH *see* Visual Approach
APPROACH *see* Visual Approach Light System
APPROACH *see* Visual Approach Restrictions
APPROACH *see* Visual Approach Slope Indicator/VASI
APPROACH AZIMUTH GUIDANCE [14]
APPROACH CLEARANCE [272] [362] [370]
Approach Clearance [Glossary]
APPROACH CONTROL [156] [167] [362]
Approach Control Facility [Glossary]
Approach Control Service [Glossary]
Approach Gate [Glossary]
APPROACH AND LANDING MINIMUMS [381]
Approach Light System [Glossary]
APPROACH LIGHT SYSTEM/ALS [40]
APPROACH MINIMUMS [381]
APPROACH PROCEDURES CHART [157] [364]
APPROACH SEQUENCE [165] [372] [404]
Approach Sequence [Glossary]
Approach Speed [Glossary]
Apron/Ramp [Glossary]
Arc [Glossary]
AREA NAVIGATION ROUTE [298] [343]
AREA NAVIGATION/RNAV [298] [343]
Area Navigation/RNAV [Glossary]
Army Aviation Flight Information Bulletin/USAFIB [Glossary]
Arresting System [Glossary]
ARRIVAL *see* Arrival Minimums
ARRIVAL *see* Arrival Procedures
ARRIVAL *see* Standard Terminal Arrival/STAR
ARRIVAL PROCEDURES [221] [222] [360] [361] [362] [363] [364]
[365] [370] [371] [372] [373] [374] [375] [376] [380] [381] [382]
[383] [384] [385] [386] [402] [403] [404] [405] [409] [410] [470]
Arrival Time [Glossary]
ARSA DESCRIPTION [100]
ARSA [Glossary]
ARSA OPERATION [101]
ARTCC [Glossary]
ASR Approach [Glossary]
ATC Advises [Glossary]
ATC Assigned Airspace/ATCAA [Glossary]
ATC CLEARANCE [238] [260] [261] [262] [263] [264] [265] [266]
[401]
ATC Clearance [Glossary]
ATC Clears [Glossary]
ATC Instructions [Glossary]
ATC Requests [Glossary]
ATC SERVICES [101]
ATCRBS [Glossary]
AUTOB [509] [529]
AUTOMATED OBSERVING SYSTEMS [500]
AUTOMATED RADAR TERMINAL SYSTEMS/ARTS [163]
Automated RADAR Terminal Systems/ARTS [Glossary]
AUTOMATED WEATHER OBSERVING SYSTEM (AWOS) [509]
AUTOMATIC ALTITUDE REPORTING [97] [162] [170]

Automatic Altitude Reporting [Glossary]
Automatic Carrier Landing System/ACLS [Glossary]
Automatic Direction Finder/ADF [Glossary]
AUTOMATIC METEOROLOGICAL OBSERVING STATIONS
(AMOS) [509]
AUTOMATIC TERMINAL INFORMATION SERVICE/ATIS [156]
[161] [165] [191] [206] [235] [363] [574]
Automatic Terminal Information Service/ATIS [Glossary]
Autorotation [Glossary]
AVIATION SAFETY REPORTING PROGRAM [580]
AVIATION WEATHER FORECAST [500] [528]
Aviation Weather Service [Glossary]
Azimuth, MLS [Glossary]

B

BACK AZIMUTH GUIDANCE [14]
BACK COURSE MARKER/BCM [12]
BALLOONS *see* Unmanned Balloons
BASE LEG [221]
Base Leg [Glossary]
BEACON *see* Aeronautical Light Beacon
BEACON *see* Air Traffic Control RADAR Beacon System
BEACON *see* Airport (Rotating) Beacon
BEACON *see* Airway Beacon
BEACON *see* Code Beacons
BEACON *see* Inner Marker/IM/Inner Marker Beacon
BEACON *see* Marker Beacon/MB
BEACON *see* Military Airport (Rotating) Beacon
BEACON *see* Nondirectional Beacon/Radio Beacon/NDB
BEACON *see* RADAR Beacon
BEACON *see* RADAR Beacon Phraseology
BEACON *see* Rotating Beacon
Beacon [Glossary]
Bearing [Glossary]
Below Minimums [Glossary]
BIRD HAZARDS [561]
BIRD INCIDENTS [562]
BIRD MIGRATION [560]
BIRD STRIKES [562]
Blast Fence [Glossary]
Blind Speed [Glossary]
Blind Spot/Blind Zone [Glossary]
Boundary Lights [Glossary]
BRAKING *see* Braking Action
BRAKING *see* Braking Action Advisories
BRAKING *see* Braking Action Reports
BRAKING ACTION [228]
Braking Action (Good, Fair, Poor, Nil) [Glossary]
BRAKING ACTION ADVISORIES [229]
Braking Action Advisories [Glossary]
BRAKING ACTION REPORTS [228]
BRIEFING *see* Pilot Briefing
BRIEFING *see* Preflight Briefing
BRIEFING *see* Telephone Aviation Briefing System (TABS)
BRIEFING *see* Weather Briefing
BROADCAST *see* Fuel Dumping Broadcast
BROADCAST *see* Pilot Broadcast
BROADCAST *see* Scheduled Broadcast
BROADCAST *see* Transcribed Weather Broadcast/TWEB
BROADCAST *see* Unscheduled Weather Broadcast
BROADCAST *see* Weather Broadcast

[References are to Paragraph numbers]

FREE UPDATE SERVICE

This book will be updated with information current on September 5, 1989. The update will be mailed in mid to late September.

If you wish to have a copy of this update, clip out the form on this page, fill out completely, put in an envelope and mail to:

asa PUBLICATIONS
6001 - 6th Avenue So.
Seattle, WA 98108-3307

BELOW IS YOUR SHIPPING LABEL; PLEASE PRINT CLEARLY.

_____

Please send an update of asa's 1989 FAR/AIM to:

Name:_____

Street: _____

City: _____State _____ Zip _____

☐ **Please send me information on other asa Products.**

_____

ASA has more to offer . . .

For 45 years ASA has been concerned with students. Our goal has always been and continues to be, providing the most current, comprehensive, and effective training materials possible. Here is part of the '88/'89 line up of ASA training material —what we believe to be the best available in learning programs, test preparation books, and pilot supplies for students, whether beginning or advanced.

VIDEO COURSES

ASA introduces two of the finest home video courses ever, for the private and instrument pilot. ASA videos are produced by a professional TV production team, using striking graphics, and narrated by a meteorologist/news commentator. These state-of-the-art video cassettes are what you have come to expect from ASA . . . the finest.

CASSETTE COURSES

Each course contains six 90-minutes cassettes and 200-plus pages of text material, all in an attractive binder. Courses featured are Private, Commercial, Instrument, Airline Transport Pilot Part 135, Flight Instructor, and Flight Engineer. Learn at your own pace in the car or at home with ASA Cassette Courses.

TEXT BOOKS

ASA's textbooks are all written by highly qualified instructors and experts in the aviation industry. These books provide students with up-to-date information as well as thorough, conceptual and practical understanding, assuring exam preparedness.

THE COMPLETE STUDENT KITS

New from ASA, these kits offer student pilots the best in aviation courses with a choice of products and prices.

THE COMPLETE PRIVATE PILOT DE-LUXE ELECTRONIC COMPUTER KIT
For Part 141, includes Textbook, Workbook, Syllabus, Stage and Final Exam. Graduation Certificate, Standard Plotter, Student Flight Record, Maneuvers Manual, Logbook, Flight Case, plus . . the CX-1a Pathfinder Flight Computer.
#ASA-PPT-DL-E.

THE COMPLETE PRIVATE PILOT DE-LUXE PAPER MANUAL COMPUTER KIT
Contains all that the Electronic Computer Kit does but replaces the CX-1a with a high quality fiber board E6B.
#ASA-PPT-DL-P.

THE COMPLETE PRIVATE PILOT BASIC KIT
For Part 61, includes Textbook, Workbook, Final Exam, and Graduation Certificate.
#ASA-PPT-BAS.

THE COMPLETE INSTRUMENT PILOT BASIC KIT
For Part 61, this kit has the Textbook, Workbook, Final Exam and Graduation Certificate.
#ASA-IPT-BAS.

THE COMPLETE PRIVATE PILOT DE-LUXE METAL MANUAL COMPUTER KIT
Has all that the Electronic Computer Kit does, but replaces the CX-1a with a high quality E6B Metal Flight Computer
#ASA-PPT-DL-M.

THE COMPLETE PRIVATE PILOT STANDARD KIT
For Part 141, this kit contains Textbook, Workbook, Syllabus, Stage and Final Exams, Graduation Certificate, and Maneuvers Manual.
#ASA-PPT-STD.

THE COMPLETE INSTRUMENT PILOT STANDARD KITS
For Part 141, contains Flight Case, Textbook, Workbook, Syllabus, Stage and Final Exams, Graduation Certificate, and Student Flight Record Folder.
#ASA-IPT-STD.

TEST GUIDES

ASA Test Guides feature exact duplicates of the current FAA written test questions for every rating as well as answers, explanations, and references. ASA Test Guides, with time proven, accurate answers and comprehensive explanations have been favorites of pilots for years.

TEST PREP SERIES

ASA's new Test Prep Series provides airplane students with exact FAA questions, answers and explanations, references, and ASA's expert textbook material. Arranged by subject category, textbook material precedes each set of questions in a subject. The left hand column of the page contains the test questions. The right hand column of the page has an answer, explanation and reference for corresponding questions. ASA features the Private, Commercial, and Instrument ratings in the Test Prep Series.

FAA REPRINTS: QUESTION BOOKS

These handy reprints are exact duplicates of current FAA written tests. ASA inserts an answer sheet into the back of each book. These are excellent quiz books and we have one for virtually every rating.

CX-1a PATHFINDER
Now with a sleek corporate look . . . the Cx-1a

Designed to keep pace with the demands of pilots worldwide, the CX-1a is equipped to remain state-of-the-art for years to come.

An extensive MENU and the unique Information Guidance System are the meat of the CX-1a, but ASA didn't stop there. The CX-1 features 8K ROM, making it faster than any other hand-held flight computer. It is sized conveniently to slip into an attractive simulated leather case, which fits easily into your pocket.

Once again, ASA gives you a top-of-the-line aviation product. See your dealer today and make sure you ask for the ASA CX-1a (patented).
#ASA-CX-1a
ASA-CX-1a Battery Pack, two per pack.
#ASA-CX-1/B.

COMPUTERS - PLOTTERS

Now ASA has a computer/plotter series featuring the Fixed Plotter and the Rotating Azimuth Plotter. Both are made of sturdy plastic material with easy-to-read scales.

Also featured are the Aluminum E6B Flight Computer, and the E6B Paper Flight computer. Both are made of very durable material. They have easy reference charts, eye saving reversed color scales, and accurate tracking.

MECHANICS SERIES

ASA's new Mechanics Series goes a long way toward providing a Mechanic applicant with the materials to become the best.

GENERAL:

AVIATION MECHANIC: GENERAL HANDBOOK
Text material helps the student prepare for the General Rating. FAA Reprint.
#ASA-AC65-9A

AVIATION MECHANIC: GENERAL HANDBOOK STUDY GUIDE:
A comprehensive study guide to accompany the general handbook.
#ASA-AC65-9A SG

AVIATION MECHANIC: GENERAL WORKBOOK:
Companion to the General Handbook and Study Guide.
#ASA-AC65-9A WK

AVIATION MECHANIC: GENERAL QUESTION BOOK
Exact FAA Reprint of test T-8080-10B. Includes answers.
#ASA-8080-10B

AVIATION MECHANIC GENERAL TEST GUIDE:
For FAA test T-8080-10B. Includes FAST TRACK learning method and Practical & Oral test.
#ASA-AMG-C